RED BOOK

3RD EDITION

RED BOOK

American State, County, and Town Sources

Edited by Alice Eichholz, Ph.D., CG

Ancestry

Library of Congress Cataloging-in-Publication Data

Red book : American state, county & town sources / [edited by Alice Eichholz].—3rd
    ed.

    p. cm.

  Rev. ed. of: Ancestry's red book. Rev. ed. c1992.

  ISBN 1-59331-166-4 (hardcover : alk. paper)

  1. United States—Genealogy—Handbooks, manuals, etc. I. Eichholz, Alice.
    II. Ancestry Publishing. III. Ancestry's red book.

CS49.R44 2004

929'.1'072073—dc22

                                                                    2004015926

The following are service marks for the Board for Certification of Genealogists: Certified Genealogist, CG, Certified Lineage
Specialist, CLS, Certified Genealogical Records Specialist, CGRS, Certified Genealogical Lecturer, CGL, and Certified
Genealogical Instructor, CGI. These service marks are used under license by associates who meet prescribed genealogical
competency standards. FASG identifies elected fellows of the American Society of Genealogists. FNGS signifies genealogists who
have been named fellows of the National Genealogical Society. FUGA designates fellows of the Utah Genealogical Association.
FGBS designates fellows of the New York Genealogical and Biographical Society

Published 1989. Revised Edition 1992. Third Edition 2004

10 9 8 7 6 5 4 3

Printed in the United States of America.

To our quest for connection

TABLE OF CONTENTS

TABLE OF CONTENTS

ACKNOWLEDGMENTS

The decade following the earlier editions of *Ancestry's Red Book* has brought enormous change to the field of family history research. Thankfully, many of the same people who were involved in the earlier editions are still active in the field and returned to update and revise their original state chapters. Others were not available to work on the third edition, but I am grateful for their original important contributions, still evident in their respective state chapters: Sharon Sholars Brown, CG; Carol L. Maki; Gareth Mark, AG; Brian E. Michaels; Mary Bess Kirksey Paluzzi; Marsha Hoffman Rising, CG, FUGA, FASG; Thelma Berkey Walsmith; Margaret Windham; and Nell Sachse Woodard.

This third edition of *Red Book* could not have been completed without the assistance of many genealogists, librarians, archivists, and government employees throughout the states. In addition to those who assisted in the original editions, the following individuals generously shared both information and expertise for this work:

Jane Gardner Aprill, CGRS
Hon. John D. Austin, Jr., FASG
Robert E. Bailey
Robert Barnes
Debra A. Blake
Jeffery Brown
Starr Hailey Campbell
Noel Carmack
Paul Carnahan
James C. Cooper
Donn Devine, CG, CGI
Cindy Steinhoff Drake
Janice Duffy
Conley L. Edwards
Jeanette Fiskum
James D. Folts, Ph.D.
Kay H. Freilich, CG, CGL
Edwin S. Gleaves, Ph.D.
Myra Vanderpool Gormley, CG
Linda Grieve
Robert D. Griffin
James L. Hansen, FASG

Mark Harvey
James H. Henderson
Sandra M. Hewlett, CGRS
Henry B. Hoff, CG, FASG
James K. Jeffrey
Heather C. Jones
Walter Jones
Angela Kasek
Joseph R. Klett
Susan S. Koelble, CGRS
Chad Leinaweaver
J. Mark Lowe, CG
Joan M. Lowry
Cynthia A. Luckie
Harry Macy, Jr., FGBS, FASG
Shaner Magalhaesz
Frank C. Mevers, Ph.D.
Betsy Michaels
Molly L. Miller
Catherine J. Morris
Jean O. Morris
Suzanne Nurnberg

Cindy Refuse
Richard C. Roberts
Donna Valley Russell, CG, FASG
Melinde L. Sanborn, FASG
D. Greg Sanford
Arlene Schmuland
Janet Seegmiller
Michael Sherman, Ph.D.
John Sillito
Jonathan R. Stayer
Melanie Sturgeon
Frazine Taylor
Maureen A. Taylor
Linda Thatcher
Steven D. Tuttle
Delores Vyzralek
Betty L. Warren
Paula Stuart Warren, CGRS
Annie Lipscomb Webster
Nelson A. Weller, Ph.D.
Brad Westwood
Kenneth Williams

ACKNOWLEDGMENTS

Maps, originally prepared by William Dollarhide with drafting assistance from Robert Lindquist and Linda Lawless, have been updated and rescanned. The new format, cover design, and layout was created by Robert Davis.

In every phase of this third edition, Loretto Dennis Szucs, Vice President of Publications at MyFamily.com, provided welcome insight and suggestions. I was also ably assisted by people in her division, notably Jennifer Browning, Matt Wright, Julie Duncan, and Mark Mugleston who proofed, entered changes, and assisted in numerous ways.

The project would never have been completed without the good humor and "can-do" work ethic of two essential people at Ancestry.com—Jennifer Utley, who managed the project (and had a baby at the same time); and Valerie Holladay whose editing and good sense provided steady persistence and editorial guidance. It was a pleasure to work with the whole Ancestry publishing team.

Each of the new and returning contributors demonstrated, through their work, the increase in professional standards and quality of research sources available in family history research today. I am grateful for their attentive participation in the project:

Scott Andrew Bartley

Beth Bauman

Johni Cerny

Pamela J. Cooper and the Florida Pioneer Descendants Certification Program of the Florida State Genealogical Society

Robert S. Davis, M.A., M.Ed.

Karen Stein Daniel, CG

Mary Clement Douglass, CGRS

Wendy Bebout Elliott, Ph.D., FUGA

Arleigh P. Helfer, Jr.

Laura Hall Heuermann

Birdie Monk Holsclaw, CG

Kathleen Stanton Hutchinson

Roger D. Joslyn, CG, FUGA, FGBS, FASG

Dawn M. Knauft

Pamela Boyer Porter, CGRS, CGL

Michael John Neill

Dwight A. Radford

George F. Sanborn, Jr.

Patricia Lyn Scott

Beth A. Starr, CGRS

Gary Topping, Ph.D.

When working on such a large project, it is important to have people around you who are grounded in what is going on in the rest of the world. In that regard, my daughter Cady Eddy, my sister Carol Baron, Ph.D., the rest of my family, and my colleagues and students at Union Institute & University have all played a critical role.

With the assistance and input of so many people and institutions, the editor, contributors, and publisher sincerely hope the book presents the most useful information coherently and accurately. The intent has been to produce a quality resource guide that assists in improving both the quality of family history research in the field and continued growth of interest in family history among a broader audience. We are extremely grateful for the efforts of everyone involved in that process.

Alice Eichholz, Ph.D., CG
Montpelier, Vermont

CONTRIBUTORS

Scott Andrew Bartley is a professional genealogist specializing in Vermont, French-Canadian, and colonial American problems. He was the archivist for the New England Historic Genealogical Society where he worked for fifteen years. Currently, he takes private clients, lectures, teaches online genealogy courses, and edits two journals (*Mayflower Descendant* and *Vermont Genealogy*).

Beth H. Bauman is a charter member and past president of Bismarck Mandan Historical and Genealogical Society, and member of North Dakota State Genealogical Society. As past director for the Bismarck Family History Center, she continues to act as consultant and librarian. She is co-editor of two Burleigh county and two Morton county resource books.

Johni Cerny, president and founder of Lineages, Inc., is a nationally known lecturer and researcher specializing in slave, colonial Virginia, and immigrant ancestry. She has been an editor of many major genealogical resource publications, including co-editor of Ancestry's *The Library: A Guide to the LDS Family History Library*, which won the Reference Book of the Year Award from the American Library Association in 1989.

Pamela J. Cooper has been the Supervisor of the Florida History and Genealogy Department for the Indian River County Main Library, Vero Beach, Florida, since 1986. She has served as Director of the Federation of Genealogical Societies (FGS), Director of the Florida Historical Society, President of the Florida State Genealogical Society (FSGS), and Co-Chair of the FGS/FSGS 2003 National Conference in Orlando. She is the recipient of the 2000 National Genealogical Society Filby Prize for Genealogical Librarianship.

Robert S. Davis, M.A., M.Ed., is director of the Family & Regional History Program of Wallace State College, Hanceville, Alabama. A nationally recognized author and speaker on American genealogy, history, and records, he has written more than 1,000 publications, including thirty books.

Karen Stein Daniel, CG, resides in Albuquerque, New Mexico and is editor of the *New Mexico Genealogist* for the New Mexico Genealogical Society. She has been actively involved in genealogical research for over thirty years, and is the author of six books and numerous articles. She is a past recipient of the National Genealogical Society Award of Merit.

Mary Clement Douglass, CGRS, has an undergraduate degree in social science education and is a director of the Association of Professional Genealogists and past director of the Genealogical Speakers Guild. Owner of Historical Matters—Historical and Genealogical Research in Kansas, she specializes in land records, oral histories, and preservation of historical collections. Mary lectures nationally on Kansas resources and genealogical methodology and is compiling a publication on WPA Kansas pioneer interviews. Her article, "Genealogical Research in Kansas" appears in the *National Genealogical Society Quarterly* 92 (June 2004): 119–142.

Alice Eichholz, Ph.D., CG, is Director of Lifelong Learning and Professor of Liberal Studies at Union Institute and University, located on the Vermont College campus in Montpelier, Vermont. With thirty-five years of genealogical research experience, she is a nationally known researcher and writer focusing on New England and multigenerational patterns in families. She serves as a consultant for the Multigenerational research project at the Bowen Center for the Study of the Family; and mentor to undergraduate, master's, and doctoral studies in family history.

Wendy Bebout Elliott, Ph.D., FUGA, is a professor of history at California State University, Fullerton, where she teaches a variety of courses in U.S., California, oral, and public history. She is past president of the Southwest Oral History Association (SOHA). An internationally known genealogy teacher and speaker, she is Federation of Genealogical Societies' First Vice President for Administration. She has been a contributing author to Ancestry's *Printed Sources* (1998) and co-editor of *The Library: A Guide to the LDS Family History Library*, which won the

CONTRIBUTORS

Reference Book of the Year Award from the American Library Association in 1989.

Arleigh P. Helfer Jr. is a retired automotive executive, living in the Detroit suburb of Bloomfield Hills, with an avid interest in genealogical research. In addition to his ancestral research activities, he pursues bridge, playing the French horn in community bands, Stanford alumni event planning, and golf. His interests in family also extend to enjoying his three grandchildren.

Laura Hall Heuermann, J.D., is a practicing attorney with a long-term interest in genealogical problem solving in South Dakota.

Birdie Monk Holsclaw, CG, FUGA, is a genealogical researcher, writer, lecturer, editor, and winner of 2003 NGS Family History Writing Contest. She has served as a board or committee chair for the Association of Professional Genealogists and the Federation of Genealogical Societies, an indexer of the *National Genealogical Society Quarterly*, and member of GENTECH's Lexicon Working Group (1996–1999). She lectures at numerous national and regional conferences. Her current major research project is compiling family histories for earliest students at the Colorado School for the Deaf and the Blind, all children of Colorado pioneer families.

Kathleen Stanton Hutchison is currently Systems Librarian at Mississippi College where she works towards keeping stride with technological changes affecting information retrieval. She co-authored with Anne Lipscombe Webster, *Tracing Your Mississippi Ancestors* (University Press of Mississippi, 1994). She received a B.S. degree from Mississippi University for Women and a master's degree from Louisiana State University.

Roger D. Joslyn, CG, FUGA, FGBS, FASG, has been a full-time professional genealogist for a quarter of a century, providing full-service research, due diligence, expert witness testimony, and coordination of national and international research for private clients, attorneys, Native American tribes, and others. He is a frequent contributor to scholarly journals and other publications, a popular lecturer, a past president of the Association of Professional Genealogists, and the current president of the American Society of Genealogists.

Dawn M. Knauft is a professional genealogist specializing in Wisconsin research after 1848. She is a native of Wisconsin and lives near Madison.

Michael John Neill writes a weekly genealogy column for the *Ancestry Daily News* and lectures nationally on a wide variety of genealogical topics. A faculty member at Carl Sandburg College in Galesburg, Illinois, he also coordinates the college's annual weeklong series of genealogical computing workshops. Michael also writes for a variety of genealogical publications and is involved in many professional genealogical organizations. He has a master's degree from Western Illinois University.

Pamela Boyer Porter, CGRS, CGL, is a researcher, author, lecturer, and teacher specializing in Southeast Missouri migration paths into and out of Missouri, and computer resources for genealogists. Pam is co-author of *Online Roots: How to Discover Your Family's History and Heritage with the Power of the Internet* (Nashville: Rutledge Hill Press, 2003) and "Genealogical Research in Missouri," *National Genealogical Society Quarterly* 87 (June 1999): 85–116, a past board member of the Federation of Genealogical Societies, past editor of the *Association of Professional Genealogists Quarterly*, and an honorary life member of St. Louis Genealogical Society.

Dwight A. Radford is a professional genealogist residing in Salt Lake City, Utah. He specializes in Irish and Irish immigrant research and is co-author of the book *A Genealogist's Guide to Discovering Your Irish Ancestor* (Cincinnati: Betterway Books, 2001).

George F. Sanborn, Jr., FASG, is a Fellow of the Society of Antiquaries of Scotland, and is a long-time reference librarian at the New England Historic Genealogical Society in Boston, Massachusetts. He is a native of Moultonborough, New Hampshire, and past president of the New Hampshire Society of Genealogists as well as the first editor of the revived quarterly, *The New Hampshire Genealogical Record*.

Patricia Lyn Scott is a Certified Archivist and has been with the Utah State Archives since 1984, serving as a local government records archivist, and since January 2004 also Records Analysis Section Manager. She has an M.L.S. from Wayne State University specializing in Archival Management (1977) and an M.A. in History of the American West from the University of Utah (1983). She is also the author of various articles on local history and women's history.

Beth A. Stahr, MLS, CGRS, is an academic librarian in Louisiana and a professional genealogical researcher. She is the First Vice President of the Louisiana Genealogical and Historical Society, a past trustee of the Association of Professional Genealogists and a current trustee of the Board for Certification of Genealogists.

Gary Topping, Ph.D., teaches American history at Salt Lake Community College and serves as archivist-historian of the Roman Catholic Diocese of Salt Lake City.

How to Use This Book

ALICE EICHHOLZ, Ph.D., CG

Family history research is easier than it has ever been. Today, with the increased awareness of the necessity for preserving local records and with the burgeoning use of the Internet and computer technology for organizing and indexing records, we can discover a great deal regarding the specifics of our family's past in the United States—no matter what the locality.

Designed to help you recover the multigenerational facts of your ancestry, this book is an expansive guide to the most useful resources in each of the fifty United States and the District of Columbia. Conducting research at a distance from the places one's ancestors lived can be quite a challenge for any genealogist, and there still is no substitute for on-site research because not *everything* is, or probably ever will be, on the Internet, microfilm, in print, or available through interlibrary loan. But the information in this book will assist the research process by describing some original, printed, microfilmed, and online sources for every state and the District of Columbia.

The book is arranged alphabetically by state. Within this chapter and each state's chapter, topics are arranged consistently to suggest *one* methodological strategy for research. While research in different locations may require different strategies, the format of this book was designed to provide a consistent and detailed guide within limited space for each state. Background Sources in each state's chapter suggests other excellent guides to help you modify your research strategy in a specific state.

Every state's chapter begins with a brief historical background discussion, since records used in genealogical research are best understood within their historical context. Your own genealogical research will benefit from knowing about the history, settlement patterns, and context in which the records were kept.

Vital Records

Far too often family historians neglect to procure vital records for those family members and relatives within recent or living memory. Collecting *all* vital records available for every generation is essential because small details on any one of the records may provide important clues. The process of gathering all available vital records for each generation of an entire family encourages consideration of collateral lines in problem solving.

Every state government has a department charged with the responsibility of maintaining and dispersing information from its vital record holdings. The vital records section for each state in *Red Book* indicates the availability of birth, death, marriage, and divorce records, and the agencies responsible for maintaining them, including ways of obtaining records through the Internet. Information about obtaining vital records from those agencies in all states and, in many cases, ordering those records, can be found at the following two important websites:

VitalChek Network, Inc. <www.vitalchek.com>

Vital Records Information <www.vitalrec.com>

Another option for locating updated information about vital records and where to obtain them is the Center for Disease Control, National Center for Health Statistics, which offers information links or a downloadable file of *Where to Write for Vital Records* from its website at <www.cdc.gov/nchs/howto/w2w/w2welcom.htm>.

A collection of vital records application forms for all states can be found in Thomas J. Kemp, *International Vital Records Handbook*, 4th ed. (Baltimore: Genealogical Publishing Co., 2000).

One major index to birth and marriage records in all states, although far from comprehensive, is the International Genealogical Index (IGI), amended regularly by the Genealogical Society of Utah and accessible through its Family History Library (FHL) and branch centers (see Archives, Libraries, and Societies). The IGI, arranged alphabetically by state and therein by surname, includes *some,* but not all, primary and secondary sources for birth and marriage records. It provides a reference for each entry, making it possible to verify the information with the original source. Since the material in the IGI comes from either a program of extracting primary source material in state vital records, or from information submitted by members of The Church of Jesus Christ of Latter-day Saints (LDS, or Mormon church), it is essential to verify the source of the information and its accuracy. The "extracted" records are considerably more accurate than the "submitted" ones.

The searchable, constantly updated Social Security Death Index is available on the Internet (see <www.familysearch. org>, <http://ssdi.rootsweb.com>, or <www.ancestry.com>). Included in the index are deaths of those U.S. citizens who filed claims with the Social Security Administration (except minors and some government workers) and died from 1962 through the present.

Many sources for information about birth, death, and marriage events are not found in a state's vital records office. Cemeteries, church records, newspapers, military records, immigration and naturalization records, as well as family records in letters and Bibles are all places where evidence of vital events might be found. Suggestions for locating these alternate sources are described in later sections of each chapter.

Divorce records are handled differently depending on states. Some have centralized indexes. Some are considered court records instead of vital records. The discussion on each state will clarify this distinction as well as the location of these records.

Once vital records have been researched—and especially if none are available for the location and time period required—a good procedure would be to try to locate ancestors using census records.

Census Records

There are numerous ways to determine the location in which to concentrate research for an ancestor. One of the most popular and productive is the nationwide census. In the United States, the federal census has been taken every ten years since 1790. Federal population schedules through the 1930 census exist and are available to the general public online; and through many libraries and research facilities, such as the U.S. National Archives and Records Administration (NARA) and its Regional Centers, and the Family History Library and its centers. Only fragments of the 1890 population schedules remain since they were badly damaged by fire in 1921. Some states have incomplete or no schedules for other years because of the loss of census records.

Each census offers slightly different information depending on what Congress was interested in enumerating for that decade. The earlier federal census schedules name only the head of household in each locality and number of males and females in different age categories. Except for the earliest censuses that were sometimes alphabetical, the order of households listed is usually the result of door-to-door visits by the census takers. Later census returns include the name of every member of the household, becoming progressively more detailed and including such information as relationship to the head of household, the address (and consequently neighbors), month and year of birth, location of parents' births, number of years married, date of immigration, occupation, and value of personal and real estate. For a detailed listing of what information was collected for each census, see "Factfinder for the Nation: Availability of Census Records for Individuals," downloadable from <www.census. gov>.

Along with the population schedules, supplemental federal schedules were taken with the 1850 through 1880 census returns. Not all schedules exist for each state, but where they are known to exist, they are described in the state's chapter. These include:

Mortality Schedules. Names, dates, and causes of death for those who died in the twelve-month period preceding the 1850, 1860, 1870, and 1880 census enumerations are listed in this schedule. There is no central location for all of them. NARA has many available on microfilm (see <www.archives.gov> for its holdings), while others are in state archives (AL, DE, ME, MS, NY, RI, WV), state libraries (AR, CA, CT, IN, MD, NH, OR, VT), or historical societies (ID, MN, MO, NV, WI). Others are available at the DAR library (see Archives, Libraries, and Societies). The FHL has some microfilm copies for some states.

Industry Schedules. Goods and services provided and quantities furnished by listed businesses were added in separate volumes to the 1850, 1860, 1870, and 1880 federal enumerations. The 1880 schedules are labeled "Manufacturers."

Agriculture Schedules. Acreage farmed with different commodities, and extent and type of animal husbandry listed by farmer's name, are among those items listed in this separate schedule for 1850, 1860, 1870, and 1880.

Union Veterans and Widows of Union Veterans of the Civil War (hereafter Union Veterans Schedules). Those who qualified, including pensioners, widows, and minors, and who were receiving pensions in 1890, were enumerated in a separate schedule. Returns for Alabama to Kansas appear to have been lost before 1943.

HOW TO USE THIS BOOK

Slave Schedules. While free African Americans are named and slaves are counted (but not named) in federal returns beginning in 1790, separate Slave Schedules were generated for slave-owning states in 1850 and 1860. These tally the number of males and females in specific age groupings listed by slave owner's name. All are available on NARA microfilm.

Many mortality and Union veterans' schedules have been indexed and published while other supplemental schedules—slave, industry, and agriculture—have been microfilmed. The census section under each state indicates what federal supplemental schedules have survived and where they can be found.

Census information is to be used as a *guide* to the facts about a family and is not always accurate. When using census records for research keep the following in mind:

- Census information forwarded to the federal government was hand-copied and consequently subject to human error; microfilm copies reproduce the same errors. Some original copies of specific censuses are extant in some state repositories. If they are known to exist, the discussion in the state's chapter will so specify.
- Some handwriting is difficult to read. Try to compare the way the writer patterned letters in other names that are easier to read.
- The type of information on each census varies. For example, the 1840 census specified Revolutionary War veterans receiving a pension; the 1870 census, which was taken after African Americans were granted citizenship, is the first one that lists all African Americans by name; and the 1900 census reports the number of children born to a woman and the number still living.
- County lines changed very quickly during the nineteenth century. You will want to refer to William Thorndale and William Dollarhide, *Map Guide to the U.S. Federal Censuses, 1790–1920* (1987; reprint. Baltimore: Genealogical Publishing Co., 2003), to determine how the county lines changed between ten-year periods. In some cases, ward maps of municipalities may be necessary to pinpoint a location in metropolitan areas.

An index coding system for surnames, the Soundex was used by the Works Project Administration (WPA) in the preparation of three-by-five-inch index cards. These were eventually microfilmed and used for locating a particular person on the actual census. Available for the 1880, 1900, 1920, and some 1910 and 1930 census records, the Soundex coding system drops all vowels and a few consonants in a surname and produces a number code to be used in locating families with similarly sounding surnames in any given state. Such an index is particularly useful given the wide variations in spelling of many surnames. The Soundex for 1880 was used only for households in which there was a child under age ten. However, more recent indexes make it possible to locate any person, not just by head of household (see discussion below of census records on the Internet).

Census records for a few states in the 1910 census have a different finding aid called Miracode. This system uses the same coding as Soundex, but Miracode cards reference the full census returns with a number given in order of visitation by the census taker instead of the page and line number reference on the Soundex cards.

Online Access

All of the federal population schedules available for every state are indexed and available online through subscription databases. The most extensive online access can be obtained with a subscription membership to Ancestry.com <www.ancestry.com> (see Internet Sources). Subscribers can find and view images of census pages using every-name indexes for many census years. HeritageQuest also offers an alternative for some census years through online access to its member libraries (see Internet Sources and <www.heritagequest.com>). All of the online census records are indexed (either through one site or the other), and in the case of 1850, 1860, 1870, and 1930 every name is indexed at Ancestry.com, not just the head of household. Other every-name indexes are being developed.

The Family History Library (see Archives, Libraries, and Societies) developed an every-name index for the 1880 U.S. Federal Census, available online for no charge at <www.familysearch.org> with direct links to the images of census pages offered to subscribing members of <www.ancestry.com>. The original thirty-six CD-ROM set of the 1880 *Federal Census and National Index* from which this online index is drawn may be available in some libraries where Internet access is not available. It offers an easily used state and national index that can be searched using a number of fields. Most FHL centers provide online access to Ancestry.com's indexes and online images of the census records.

A limited, but growing, number of census records are available for free on the Internet through Access Genealogy <www.accessgenealogy.com>.

Microfilm Access

For those without Internet access, full sets of microfilmed federal census records and the published indexes (see below) can be viewed for free at the National Archives and its regional centers as well as the FHL in Salt Lake City (see Archives, Libraries, and Societies for both). Additionally, through the FHL's loan program in its centers, it is possible to order microfilm reels of the federal census records to view in centers for a small fee.

Most published indexes to the microfilmed population schedules were originally created by Accelerated Indexing Systems International, Inc. (AISI), or Ancestral Genealogical Endexing Schedules (AGES), now both owned by Genealogical

Services, P.O. Box 1227, West Jordan, UT 84084-1227 <www.genealogicalservices.com>. An online catalog of its printed indexes is available at its website. Microfiche versions of many of these indexes may still be available at the FHL and its centers.

Precision Indexing has also published a wide variety of microform, printed, and loose-leaf-bound indexes, not limited to census records. These, along with the AISI and AGES indexes, are the source for many of the indexed census indexes available through <www.ancestry.com>; however, Ancestry.com is in the process of re-indexing all the federal census records.

Library Access

If you do not have Internet access and if the National Archives, one of its regional centers, or the FHL are not near you, you can order films from the FHL to use at local Family History Centers or use the interlibrary loan program at your local library, which makes census microfilms available for your use.

Libraries or individuals (with access to a microfilm machine) can borrow the necessary microfilm reels through interlibrary loan from the National Archives Census Microfilm Rental Program, P.O. Box 30, 9050 Junction Dr., Annapolis Junction, MD 20701. (See links to this service at <www.archives.gov>). The program uses the National Archives numbering system to identify the reels of either Soundex or censuses. Guides for ordering films are also available from the above address. A nominal fee is charged for the loan of the reels. Microfilm guides identifying the ordering number for reels are also available on the National Archives website under "Publications" at <www.archives.gov>.

Most states hold microfilm copies of their own federal census records in various public and university libraries. The narrative in this section indicates places in the state where they are available.

In census research, it is appropriate to start with the most recent census for a geographic area and work backwards in time to develop a census history for a family. Available federal census schedules—population, mortality, agriculture and industry, slave, veterans—are listed first in each state's Census Records section. If more important printed indexes exist besides the online, AISI, or AGES indexes described above, they are described in the narrative portion of each state's chapter following the federal listings.

In addition to federal censuses, some states conducted their own enumerations at various times, including territorial or colonial censuses before statehood. These are outlined following federal listings for each state.

For more detailed discussion of census records, see the following:

Szucs, Loretto Dennis. "Research in Census Records" in *The Source: A Guidebook of American Genealogy*. Loretto Dennis Szucs and Sandra Hargreaves Luebking, eds. Rev. ed. Salt Lake City: Ancestry, Inc., 1997.

Val D. Greenwood, *The Researcher's Guide to American Genealogy*, 3d ed. Baltimore: Genealogical Publishing Co., 2000.

Anne Bruner Eales and Robert M. Kvasnicka, *Guide to Genealogical Research in the National Archives of the United States*. 3d ed. Washington, D.C.: National Archives Trust Fund Board, 2001.

Census records provide a way to determine the presence of an ancestor in a particular location. Tracing a family through the census provides a history of migration and indicates the locations in which research should be centered. Once a family is located in the census records, the next step is to determine *everything* that locality has to offer in providing clues or direct proof of ancestors.

Background Sources

Targeting an area for research requires an awareness of three groups of background sources. The first two readings in local history and guides to appropriate methodology and resources are covered in Background Sources for each state. Maps are covered in the following section. There is a wide variety of helpful resources. Individual contributors have included their reference material, used to develop their chapters, and their personal suggestions based on their professional experience.

Three resources should be used to augment these individual state discussions:

Filby, P. William. A *Bibliography of American County Histories*. Baltimore: Genealogical Publishing Co., 1985. Very incomplete, but it contains bibliographic surveys of some printed county histories for every state.

Genealogical Publishing Company. *Genealogical & Local History Books in Print: U.S. Sources and Resources*. 2 vols. 5th ed. Baltimore: the author, 1997. A handy reference to a large number of books and microforms in print, organized by state and county and therein by topic, it is revised in updated editions.

Kaminkow, Marion J. *United States Local Histories in the Library of Congress—A Bibliography*. 5 vols. Baltimore: Magna Carta, 1975. With a supplement dated 1986, this resource lists the large number of local histories available in the Library of Congress. Although they cannot be obtained on interlibrary loan through this library, other local or regional libraries may allow some volumes of their accessions to circulate.

Two libraries with extensive genealogical collections, the National Genealogical Society Library collection, now housed at the St. Louis Public Library in Missouri, and the New England Historic Genealogical Society in Boston (see Archives, Libraries, and Societies for both) offer book-loan services by mail for their members. The FHL's huge research facility in Salt Lake City has microfilmed or microfiched nearly all printed material

in its collection, which can be ordered for viewing at any of its local branch center libraries. Search the online catalog <www.familysearch.org> by locality for publications that can be ordered for rental at local branch centers.

Most major libraries have online access to the indispensable OCLC's FirstSearch, a world access library catalog that indicates which libraries in its system hold any particular book.

Maps

The third group of materials used in targeting an area for research is maps, an often-overlooked research tool. People often lived on political boundaries, across state lines, or rivers, and traveled the path of least geographic resistance. Maps can therefore provide important clues for where to look next when an ancestor disappears from a locality. This section provides ideas for obtaining helpful maps for genealogical research purposes. Maps without present-day political boundaries can be helpful in understanding migration trails and the geographic features that may have influenced settlements. When political divisions became established, maps help determine what jurisdictions to consider in looking for genealogical evidence such as land, probate, and court records.

County atlases, detailing roads, physical features, and often structures' or owners' names, are found in abundance throughout the country. Political boundaries (wards, school districts, townships, etc.) are often standard in many atlases, aiding considerably in pinpointing the location of people in the context of their surroundings. Plat maps indicate how specific counties and towns were divided and identified, providing a visual reference to use with descriptions of land in deeds and divisions of estates. Many state highway departments print present-day maps with more helpful and detailed information than standard road maps.

AniMap Plus (3.0) is a software program available on CD-ROM that includes the historical boundaries of U.S. counties and SiteFinder, a database that will mark the spot of over 190,000 places in the continental U.S., such as towns, cities, railroad stations, trading posts, farms and ranches, plantations, Native American villages, mining camps, and more. It is distributed by The Gold Bug, P.O. Box 588, Alamo, CA 94507 <www.goldbug.com>.

For several states, the maps suggested are the Sanborn Fire Insurance maps, which were extensively used to map structures in towns in the late nineteenth century and early twentieth century. Now officially in the custody of the Library of Congress <www.loc.gov>, access to the 700,000 maps in the collection is available at libraries in many states, with either printed or digitized copies of these maps. In addition, online access for all states is available to authorized users at subscribing institutions through ProQuest Information and Learning Company <http://sanborn.umi.com>

or by ordering online at Environmental Data Resources, at <www.edrnet.com>.

U.S. Geological Survey (USGS) maps are another often overlooked source. They exist for all states, illustrating geographical features of an area including the location of structures and cemeteries. Local USGS maps are often available in stationery and office supply stores or at sporting outfitters for hiking, fishing, and hunting. An index to identify the map sections needed for an area is available from the U.S. Geological Survey Office, Reston, VA 22092 <www.usgs.gov> but all map sales are handled through the USGS Information Services (Map and Book Sales), Box 25286, Denver Federal Center, Denver, CO 80225, or online through the Earth Science Information Center <http://ask.usgs.gov>.

Many map sources are now pervasively available on the Internet. Three examples are TopoZone <www.topozone.com>, Old Maps of New York & New England <www.oldmapsne.com>, and Cyndi's List <www.cyndislist.com>, the last having links to an extensive number of individual maps and collections on the Internet.

Once vital records and census histories have been collected on ancestral lines, and an understanding of the area from background sources and maps has been achieved, it is time to turn to the genealogical source materials available in the county, town, or parish records. While the order of topics discussed is consistent throughout the book, beginning with this next topic, a research strategy may need to be specially tailored depending on a specific problem or location. For example, in some situations, using probate records is more productive first because of their specificity in indicating family relationships, but by far, more people owned land than appear in probate records. Consequently using land records may prove more successful.

Land Records

The Land Records section of each state's chapter focuses on what types of land records are available, and whether they are indexed, abstracted, or published in book form, on microfilm, or in some cases, online. This section indicates the officials or repositories in charge of the original records.

The following is a very brief discussion of general types of land records. For an excellent, comprehensive discussion of the history and use of land records in the United States, see E. Wade Hone, *Land & Property Research in the United States* (Salt Lake City: Ancestry, 1997). All essential aspects of land acquisitions and sales from prior to U.S. possession through individual sales today are covered with strategies for using the records in research. Other good discussions can be found in Sandra Hargreaves Luebking, "Research in Land and Tax Records," in *The Source:*

A *Guidebook of American Genealogy*, edited by Loretto D. Szucs and Sandra H. Luebking, rev. ed. (Salt Lake City: Ancestry, Inc., 1997); Val D. Greenwood, *The Researcher's Guide to American Genealogy*, 3d ed. (Baltimore: Genealogical Publishing Co., 2000); and E. K. Kirkham, *The Land Records of America and Their Genealogical Value* (Salt Lake City: Deseret, 1964).

Land records begin when the government claiming the land (be it crown, colonial, territorial, and, later, federal or state) conveys it to others, including private individuals, groups and corporate entities for, among other reasons, political favors, a fee, military service, or homesteading. These first-grant records are generally kept by the government that issued them.

After the Revolution, land or property was transferred to private individuals either by the federal government in public-domain (federal-land) states or by the state in state-land states. Public-domain states include Alabama, Alaska, Arizona, Arkansas, California, Colorado, Florida, Idaho, Illinois, Indiana, Iowa, Kansas, Louisiana, Michigan, Minnesota, Mississippi, Missouri, Montana, Nebraska, Nevada, New Mexico, North Dakota, Ohio, Oklahoma, Oregon, South Dakota, Utah, Washington, Wisconsin, and Wyoming.

Federal land was divided into townships emanating from one or more principal meridians and a base line (rectangular survey). Both Hone's book and Thorndale's discussion (cited above) include illustrations of the rectangular survey system of identifying land in addition to a comprehensive explanation of the types of records generated.

See also James Truslow Adams and Roy V. Coleman, *Atlas of American History*, rev. ed. (New York: Charles Scribner's Sons, 1978).

Essential references for dealing with federal land in addition to Howe, cited above, are:

McMullin, Phillip W., ed. *Grassroots of America: A Computerized Index to the American State Papers: Land Grants and Claims, 1789–1837.* Reprint. Greenville, S.C.: Southern Historical Press, 1994. This indexes *American State Papers, Public Lands* (Washington, S.C.: Gales and Seaton, 1832–61).

Smith, Clifford Neal. *Federal Land Series.* 4 vols. (Vol. 4 in 2 pts.) Reprint. Baltimore: Clearfield Publishing, 1999—.

Yoshpe, Harry P., and Philip P. Brower. *Preliminary Inventory of Land-Entry Papers of the General Land Office.* Reprint. San Jose, Calif.: Rose Family Association, 1996.

Land records in public-domain states east of the Mississippi River and those on the west bank of the river are served by the Bureau of Land Management, Eastern States Land Office, 7450 Boston Blvd., Springfield, VA 22153-3121 <www.glorecords.blm.gov>. Titles for land records in that area from 1820 to 1908 can be searched on the website.

Western public-domain states are served by General Land Offices within each state or an adjacent state, but copies of tractbooks for western states are also in the National Archives. Both sets—those held by the Eastern States Land Office and those by the National Archives—are available on microfilm at those locations. The National Archives holdings on land records are outlined in Anne Bruner Eales and Robert M. Kvasnicka, *Guide to Genealogical Research in the National Archives of the United States*, 3d ed. (Washington, D.C.: National Archives Trust Fund Board, 2001).

Regional centers of the National Archives (see Archives, Libraries, and Societies) often have copies of microfilms dealing with transactions in that region. In some cases the claims for donation or homestead land have been abstracted and published.

State-land states include Connecticut, Delaware, Georgia, Hawaii, Kentucky, Maine, Maryland, Massachusetts, New Hampshire, New Jersey, New York, North Carolina, Pennsylvania, Rhode Island, South Carolina, Tennessee, Texas, Vermont, Virginia, and West Virginia. Legal descriptions for land in these states do not use the rectangular survey, but several other means of surveying—metes and bounds, or range and lot numbers among them. In addition to Hone's strategies (cited above) for using land records to solve family history research problems, an explanation of metes and bounds and mapping terms can be found in, Julian G. Hoffman and B. Ransom McBride, "Mapping," in Helen F. M. Leary, *North Carolina Research: Genealogy and Local History* (2d ed., Raleigh, N.C.: North Carolina Genealogical Society, 1996). Software programs, such as DeedMapper, sold by Direct Line Software, 71 Neshobe Rd., Newton, MA 02468 <http://users.rcn.com/deeds/index.shtml> make it possible to analyze and draw metes and bounds descriptions to assist in land research.

Once land has been conveyed by the government, a second group of land records documents transactions between individuals. Each state's discussion indicates where government conveyances and individual conveyances are found. In the large majority of states, the county exercises jurisdiction over land transactions. But in others, deeds were recorded with towns, parishes, and judicial districts. Each state's section clarifies this. States may have used different terms in deeds to describe the property, and those differences are reported in this section.

Probate Records

Depending on the state, various courts or districts were responsible for recording the disposition of property after the death of its owner, whether by will (testate) or without one (intestate). Probate records might show not only dispositions of estates but also guardianships, adoptions, name changes, and other functions that they served as well. This section will provide an understanding of peculiarities in probate for that state, the title and location of the governmental agency responsible in the area, and an understanding of the changing boundaries of jurisdiction.

While probate records produce some of the most definitive information for genealogical research, not everyone had the disposition of his or her property documented in probate records. When an estate is probated, there are usually two kinds of materials generated by the proceedings. The clerk enters specific documents in the probate record book or volume. However, many of the original "loose" papers pertaining to the proceedings are not entered into the probate book. Some are only kept in an estate file or packet, separate from the record books. Included in estate files might be the original will with the signatures of the testator and witnesses, creditors and legatee receipts for payments from the estate, and petitions from guardians. Availability of both probate record books and packet files or "loose" papers is reported in this section when they are applicable for a state.

Understanding probate terminology is an important aspect of using probate material. A testate estate is any estate with a valid will; in general, valid wills conform to current estate law, name one or more executors, and are properly witnessed. An intestate estate is an estate without a valid will; a technically invalid will may be used as a guide to property division in an intestate estate. Executors conduct testate estates, and administrators are appointed by the probate court for intestate estates.

Common law rules of descent still generally apply today, although each state (and colony) modified them by their own laws. Two important principles during the colonial period were primogeniture and the right of dower. Primogeniture, although only applied in certain colonies, was a procedure by which an estate was given to the eldest son, by right of birth. The right of dower provided a woman a portion of her deceased husband's real estate for the remainder of her natural life; the dower was generally one-third. Widows also had a dower right to their late husbands' personal property; once again, the dower was generally one-third, but sometimes there was an equal division with all of the surviving children. Most states provide somewhat differently for widows today. Two publications that discuss the legal process of probate are Val D. Greenwood, ed., *The Researcher's Guide to American Genealogy*, 3d ed. (Baltimore: Genealogical Publishing Co., 2000); and Arlene H. Eakle, "Research in Court Records," in Szucs and Luebking, *The Source: A Guidebook of American Genealogy*, rev. ed. (Salt Lake City: Ancestry, Inc., 1997).

Court Records

Court systems and the records they produce are outlined next for each of the states. Although naturalization and divorce records are matters for courts as well, they may be discussed in other sections. In this section the concentration is on civil and criminal court records. Although each of the state's County (or Town or Parish) Resources section indicates the first dates when *some*

court proceedings are extant in that location, the exact court from which those records emanate is not necessarily indicated.

The value of civil and criminal cases found in court records is in the portrait they paint of the lives involved. Civil cases regarding debt are historically the most common concerns coming before a local court. Inability to pay a debt may have provided a reason for leaving an area as well. But there are numerous other types of disputes gracing the pages of court records, including divorces.

Criminal court records, or at least the results of them, are often detailed in the pages of newspapers if not through the court records themselves. The proceedings are likely to be much more detailed than civil court cases and allow a glimpse of the strains of life experienced by our ancestors.

Nearly all states have too large an array of court records to be discussed in total here. Instead, referring to the discussion in this section will provide a background understanding with which to guide your research. For a more comprehensive discussion of records generated by court proceedings, see:

Arlene H. Eakle, "Research in Court Records," in Szucs and Luebking, eds. *The Source: A Guidebook of American Genealogy*, rev. ed. (Salt Lake City: Ancestry, Inc., 1997).

Tax Records

Taxes serve a variety of purposes in genealogical research. Tax records can indicate age (or at least majority status), wealth, and presence in an area, even for those who were not landowners.

There are numerous examples of interesting tax lists and the information they convey. Few are published. Most exist in original form in a state or local repository. This section discusses availability of those tax records. See also:

Sandra Hargreaves Luebking, "Research in Land and Tax Records," in Szucs and Luebking, eds. *The Source: A Guidebook of American Genealogy*, rev. ed. (Salt Lake City: Ancestry, Inc., 1997).

Cemetery Records

Cemetery records usually refer to information collected from grave markers. Inscriptions on gravestones and the location of a grave in relation to those of others in the same cemetery provide good evidence for genealogical research. The major problem with using cemetery records is trying to locate the cemetery in which a person was buried.

If the cemetery records for a targeted area have not been transcribed and published, which is likely to be the case then on-site work may be the solution. Although more and more local

historical groups have been transcribing gravestones found in their local cemeteries, many stones are illegible or missing and there may not be cemetery sexton's records to consult. For years, local and state chapters of the National Society of the Daughters of the American Revolution (DAR) have been making yearly contributions to this source material. They combine cemetery records with family, Bible, and church records in local areas to document vital events and family relationships. Three typescript copies are made for each volume produced. One copy stays with the chapter, and one is deposited in one of the state's repositories. Some states have not identified a single repository to be the recipient of the volumes, and they are spread out among several sites. The third copy is held by the DAR Library in Washington, D.C. Many volumes have been microfilmed and are additionally available through the FHL. Some states have active associations that are cataloging the locations and conditions of cemeteries. These associations are listed in the appropriate state chapter.

There is a growing collection of gravestone transcriptions on the Internet. Two important sites for these are <www.interment. net> and the many projects offered through the USGenWeb <www.usgenweb.org>. Another alternative is to try entering "cemeteries in _____ location" in an online search engine, like Google, to locate online records or sources.

To locate a funeral home, the best book is *The National Yellow Book of Funeral Directors* (Youngstown, Ohio: Norris Publications, annually). Two websites for locating funeral home addresses are <www.funeralnet.com> and <www.usafuneralhomes.com>.

Church Records

Church records of baptisms, marriages, and burials can be a valuable major source of vital record documentation. In addition, membership lists can indicate migration by noting movement from one church to another. Minutes of meetings may describe values held and community concerns—providing a richer understanding of the tensions and relationships in a community. Many publications on microfilm, in print and, most recently, on CD-ROM or the Internet have increased the accessibility of church records for research. Some states, such as Pennsylvania, have extensive collections of this material. Others have little to none. Denominational newspapers should not be overlooked for vital records information. As an example of what can be found, David C. Young and Robert L. Taylor, *Death Notices from Freewill Baptist Publications, 1811–1851* (Bowie, Md: Heritage Books, 1985) and a comparable 1994 volume on marriage and divorce records from the same publication are available in individual printed volumes or combined in CD-ROM format. Both cover the denomination's newspaper and publications for all geographical areas, not just one location.

Each state's section will next outline a sample of church records known to be available in published volumes, in CD-ROM form or online, and what guides and sources exist for locating the original records. A search online for the locality through <www. usgenweb.com> or the subscription databases (see Internet Sources) would be a good place to check.

The national headquarters for a particular denomination, described in the appropriate state sections where they are located, may be able to supply the information regarding availability of records. The search for church records will encourage your best detective work.

For an excellent discussion on church records, see Richard W. Dougherty, "Research in Church Records," in Szucs and Luebking, eds., *The Source: A Guidebook of American Genealogy*, rev. ed. (Salt Lake City: Ancestry, Inc., 1997).

Military Records

War has been a frequent occurrence in United States history, and with it comes a monumental number of records. Besides chronicles of campaigns in various forms, both service records and pension records play a role in discovering ancestors.

There are military records for all the wars, although the most popularly used for genealogical purposes are undoubtedly those of the Revolutionary War (including Loyalists), War of 1812, and Civil War, principally because they can provide the most genealogical information for the most people through pension records.

Surviving records of military service during the colonial period are often in print. Service records for most states in the three principal wars of genealogical research interest listed above may also be found in print. Those that are available are outlined in each state's section.

NARA has extensive holdings, not all in microform, of both military service and pension records beginning with the Revolutionary War, many of which are also available through its regional centers, the FHL, and online through subscription databases (see Internet Sources). James Neagles, *U.S. Military Records: A Guide to Federal and State Sources, Colonial America to the Present* (Salt Lake City: Ancestry, Inc., 1994), is the most comprehensive description of what records are available, where to find them and how to use them, although its publication pre-dates many of the online sources. Anne Bruner Eales and Robert M. Kvasnicka, *Guide to Genealogical Research in the National Archives*, 3d ed. (Washington, D.C.: National Archives and Records Administration, 2001), has an important section on use of military records in its holdings.

Major publications or online service provide access to the follow important service or pension records:

Revolutionary War

National Genealogical Society, *Index of Revolutionary War Pension Applications in the National Archives*. Washington, D.C.: National Genealogical Society, 1976.

White, Virgil D., comp., *Genealogical Abstracts of Revolutionary War Pension Files*. 4 vols. Waynesboro, Tenn.: National Historical Publishing Co., 1990–92.

_____. *Index to Revolutionary War Service Records*. 4 vols. Waynesboro, Tenn.: National Historical Publishing Co., 1995.

War of 1812

National Archives and Records Service. *Index to Compiled Service Records of Volunteer Soldiers Who Served During the War of 1812*. 5 vols. Washington, D.C.: the compiler, 1966.

White, Virgil D., comp. *Index to War of 1812 Pension Files*. 2 vols. Waynesboro, Tenn.: National Historical Publishing Co., 1987.

Indian Wars

White, Virgil D., comp. *Index to Soldiers in the Indian Wars and Disturbances, 1815–1858*. 2 vols. Waynesboro, Tenn.: National Historical Publishing Co., 1994

_____. *Index to Indian Wars Pension Files, 1892–1926*. 2 vols. Waynesboro, Tenn.: National Historical Publishing Co., 1987.

Mexican War

National Archives and Records Service. *Index to Compiled Service Records of Volunteer Soldiers Who Served During the Mexican War*. 4 vols. Washington, D.C.: the compiler, 1964.

White, Virgil D., comp. *Index to Mexican War Pension Files* Waynesboro, Tenn.: National Historical Publishing Co., 1989.

Wolfe, Barbara Schull. *Index to Mexican War Pension Applications*. Indianapolis: Heritage House, 1985.

Civil War

Civil War service records for both Union and Confederate soldiers are included in the NARA microfilm collection and are available through its Regional Centers and the FHL. Online subscription databases at <www.ancestry.com> provide an index to, and views of, Union Civil War original application cards for Civil War pensions, not the files themselves. A massive project of abstracting the pension files is presently being developed. They are not on microfilm and can only be accessed at the National Archives in Washington, D.C. in person, or by mail. Appropriate application forms are downloadable from the National Archives website <www.archives.gov>.

Some individual and state projects for abstracting pension records can be found at <www.usgenweb.com>.

Spanish-American War

The Spanish-American War Compiled Military Service Records are located at the National Archives, Washington, D.C., with some its regional research centers also holding microfilm copies. See the NARA website for updated information <www.archives.gov>.

Twentieth-Century Wars

Many states have published volumes or memorials to those who served in twentieth-century conflicts. Records for those serving in later wars are located at NARA's National Personnel Records Center, 9700 Page Ave., St. Louis, MO 63132-5100 <www.archives.gov/facilities/mo/st_louis.html>. Restriction to access varies. It is best to consult the Records Center for specific details.

Selective Service Draft Registration Cards (1917–18) images are being added to the online subscription database at <www.ancestry.com> (see Internet Resources).

An excellent discussion of military records and their use in research can be found in Johni Cerny, Lloyd DeWitt Bockstruck, and David T. Thackery, "Military Records," in Szucs and Luebking, eds., *The Source: A Guidebook of American Genealogy*, rev. ed. (Salt Lake City: Ancestry, Inc., 1997).

Periodicals, Newspapers, and Manuscript Collections

Periodicals

Every year the list of genealogical and historical periodicals grows. There are hundreds that are distributed to subscribers that often do not make it to a local library for research purposes. They vary even more as to their quality. Any of them might include records of value that have been transcribed or show useful methodology.

The major currently published periodicals of high professional quality that generally cover more than one state or region and offer superb examples of problem-solving approaches in determining relationships or record sources are:

The American Genealogist (TAG), P.O. Box 398, Demorest, GA 30535-0398 <www.americangenealogist.com>.

National Genealogical Society Quarterly (NGSQ) <www.ngsgenealogy.org> (see Archives, Libraries, and Societies below.

The New England Historical and Genealogical Register (*The Register*) <www.newenglandancestors.org> (see Archives, Libraries, and Societies below; and Massachusetts—Periodicals).

The New York Genealogical and Biographical Record (The Record) <www.newyorkancestors.org> (see New York—Periodicals).

Detroit Society for Genealogical Research Magazine <www.dsgr.org> (see Michigan—Periodicals).

The first three focus principally on publishing well-documented, compiled, multigenerational accounts of individuals and families in addition to illustrating use of resources and methodology. The fourth one focuses in more recent volumes on local Michigan material and families. All have individual indexes, but many are also indexed in combined indexes (see below).

Most states have periodicals as well, either published by state or local historical or genealogical societies. Each state's section will outline a few. In some states many local genealogical societies publish periodicals. In fact, their number is too extensive to report each here. Local state libraries and genealogical organizations, the Federation of Genealogical Societies (see Archives, Libraries, and Societies) and Juliana Szucs Smith, comp. *Ancestry Family Historian's Address Book,* 2d rev. ed. (Provo, Utah: Ancestry Publishing, 2003) can direct a researcher to those periodicals that are currently being published.

There are combined periodical indexes as well. Each periodical generally indexes its own issues annually, but some indexes are available for several periodicals. Donald Lines Jacobus, *Index to Genealogical Periodicals* (reprint; Baltimore: Genealogical Publishing Co., 1963–65), indexes those prominent in the first part of the twentieth century. The annually published *Genealogical Periodical Annual Index* (Bowie, Md.: Heritage Books, 1974-present) indexes 277 periodicals currently being published. *PERiodical Source Index (PERSI),* produced by the Allen County Public Library (see Archives, Libraries, and Societies), covers over 6,000 periodicals and is divided into five sections: Surnames, U.S. Locality, Canadian Locality, Foreign Locality, and Methodology.

There are several useful subscription magazines with excellent articles on research approaches, record sources, and generally helpful hints on doing family history research. They include *Ancestry Magazine* and *Genealogical Computing,* published by MyFamily.com, Inc. (see Internet Sources); *Family Tree Magazine,* published by F&W Publishers, P.O. Box 420235, Palm Coast, FL 32142-0235 <www.familytreemagazine.com>; *Family Chronicle,* published by Moorshead Magazines Ltd., U.S. Mailing Address: P.O. Box 1111, Niagara Falls, NY 14304-1111 <www.familychronicle.com>; and *Heritage Quest Magazine,* published by HeritageQuest (see Internet Sources).

Newspapers

Death (including cause) and marriage (occasionally with parents of couple indicated) notices might appear in a newspaper, although birth notices rarely do before the twentieth century. Obituaries for non-prominent persons begin to appear more regularly at the end of the nineteenth century. However, extensive social notices (including travels and visitors), court decisions, accidents, military engagements and those serving in them, weather conditions and events, business events, letters unclaimed at the post office, and ships' arrivals give a more detailed description of the press' perception of life in the community of readers. See James L. Hansen, "Research in Newspapers," in Szucs and Luebking, *The Source: A Guidebook of American Genealogy,* rev. ed. (Salt Lake City: Ancestry, Inc., 1997) for a broader discussion.

The U.S. Newspaper Program, sponsored by the National Endowment for the Humanities, "is a cooperative national effort among the states and the federal government to locate, catalog, and preserve on microfilm newspapers published in the United States from the eighteenth century to the present" (see <www.neh.gov/projects/usnp.html>). This information is made available at Online Computer Library Center (OCLC). Contributing libraries are able to borrow microfilm copies of holdings from other libraries.

A national union list is also available in print, which indexes newspapers by name, place of publication, language, and date of publication. Each entry indicates extant issues of each newspaper and repositories holding those issues. Larger libraries and archives should have the publication in either book of microform: *United States Newspaper Program National Union List, Microfilm: June 1987,* 4th ed. (Dublin, Ohio: OCLC, 1993). Most state libraries develop their own "Union List" for newspaper holdings in their state.

Since the vast majority of older newspapers are on microfilm, it is possible to borrow many on interlibrary loan through a local library. Titles and dates of publication are listed for some newspapers in this section for each state, although most major libraries have the *Union List* or OCLC access or know how to request microfilmed newspapers through interlibrary loan. The following sources can help in locating specific newspapers:

Brigham, Clarence Saunders. *History and Bibliography of American Newspapers, 1690–1820.* 2 vols. 1947. Reprint. Westport, Conn.: Greenwood Press, 1976.

Gregory, Winifred, ed. *American Newspapers 1821–1936: A Union List of Files Available in the United States and Canada.* New York: H.W. Wilson Co., 1937. This is continued by the work of Brigham (above).

Library of Congress. Catalog Publication Division. *Newspapers in Microforms: United States, 1948–1972.* Washington, D.C.: Library of Congress, 1984.

Both present and historic newspapers are available in electronic format, including those searchable online through library or individual subscriptions. Full-text, indexed online access to the *New York Times, 1851–1923,* is available through subscription databases (see Internet Sources) and on microfiche at many libraries. Many other historical newspapers have also been digitized and included in the same searchable

subscription databases. More recent editions of newspapers generally have online access to indexes and digitized pages for the late twentieth century to the present time frame. Individual state chapters describe other newspaper sources specific to that state.

Manuscripts

The extent of any library's manuscript collection may vary considerably. Manuscripts of note are included for each state in this section. However, there are thousands more available.

The Library of Congress publishes the *National Union Catalog of Manuscript Collections (NUCMC),* which is continuously updated. Each repository is listed with details about the holdings of its manuscript collection including diaries and personal papers. "Finding Manuscript Collections: NUCMC, NIDS, and RLIN," by Mary McCampbell Bell, Clifford Dwyer, and William Abbot Henderson, in *National Genealogical Society Quarterly* 77 (September 1989): 208–18, can be helpful in learning how to locate specific manuscript material. The NUCMC cataloging in print covers 1962–94 material, and includes annual indexes. More recent cataloged material can be found online at the Library of Congress website <http://lcweb.loc.gov/coll/nucmu>.

A source for diaries is Laura Arksey, Nancy Pries, and Marcia Reed, *An Annotated Bibliography of Published American Diaries and Journals,* 2 vols. (Detroit: Gale Research, 1983–87).

Archives, Libraries, and Societies

This section indicates the major genealogically significant repositories and organizations for each state. Those that have collections or memberships that are national in scope are included below, but often referred to in individual state chapters.

Archives

National Archives and Records Administration
Eighth and Pennsylvania Ave.
Washington, DC 20408
www.archives.gov

NARA has extensive holdings, often referred to throughout *Red Book*. The indispensable guide, Anne Bruner Eales and Robert M. Kvasnicka, *Guide to Genealogical Research in the National Archives of the United States,* 3d ed. (Washington, D.C.: National Archives Trust Fund Board, 2001) indicates some of the extent of the records for genealogical research. Additional guides are available for purchase from NARA and, also downloadable from its website, are outlined in other sections of "How to Use This Book." Many of the records available in Washington, D.C. (census, war, pension, immigration, etc.) are also available on microfilm at the NARA Research and Records Centers (see below). The NARA website provides Access to

Archival Databases (AAD), which makes some of the more popular electronic records, primarily covering the last part of the twentieth century, available through the Internet (see <www.archives.gov/aad>).

National Archives at College Park
University of Maryland
8601 Adelphi Rd.
College Park, MD 10740
www.archives.gov/facilities/md/archives_2.html

The National Archives at College Park was established in 1994 to house U.S. maps, architectural, presidential, post-World War II, photographic materials, and records of civilian agencies.

NARA's regional centers have been established throughout the United States. These centers hold duplicate microfilms of the major holdings in Washington, D.C., making the records considerably more accessible. The regional centers also have considerable original source material that is endemic only to that region, such as naturalizations, court records, and land records. In addition to individual published guides available for each regional center, *The Archives: A Guide to the National Archives Field Branches,* compiled by Loretto Dennis Szucs and Sandra Hargreaves Luebking (Salt Lake City: Ancestry, 1988), is an important reference to the records in each of the centers.

National Archives—Northeast Region (Boston)
380 Trapelo Rd.
Waltham, MA 02154
www.archives.gov/facilities/ma/boston.html

Serves Connecticut, Maine, Massachusetts, New Hampshire, Rhode Island, and Vermont.

National Archives—Northeast Region (Pittsfield)
10 Conte Dr.
Pittsfield, MA 01201
www.archives.gov/facilities/ma/pittsfield.html

A microfilm reading facility for major National Archives collections.

National Archives—Northeast Region (New York City)
201 Varick St.
New York, NY 10014
www.archives.gov/facilities/ny/new_york_city.html

Serves New York, New Jersey, Puerto Rico, and U.S. Virgin Islands.

National Archives—Mid-Atlantic Region
900 Market St.
Philadelphia, PA 19107
www.archives.gov/midatlantic/public_services/public_services.html

Serves Pennsylvania, Delaware, Maryland, Virginia, and West Virginia.

National Archives—Southeast Region
1557 St. Joseph Ave.
East Point, GA 30344 (new facility in Morrow, GA after 2004)
www.archives.gov/facilities/ga/atlanta.html
Serves Alabama, Georgia, Florida, Kentucky, Mississippi, North Carolina, South Carolina, and Tennessee.

National Archives—Great Lakes Region (Dayton)
3150 Springboro Rd.
Dayton, OH 45439-1883
www.archives.gov/facilities/oh/dayton.html
Provides access to retired federal records from Indiana, Michigan, and Ohio and selected Internal Revenue sites.

National Archives—Great Lakes Region (Chicago)
7358 South Pulaski Rd.
Chicago, IL 60629
www.archives.gov/facilities/il/chicago.html
Serves Illinois, Indiana, Michigan, Minnesota, Ohio, and Wisconsin.

National Archives—Central Plains Region (Lee's Summit)
200 Space Center Dr.
Lee's Summit, MO 64064-1182
www.archives.gov/facilities/mo/lees_summit.html
Provides access to retired records from most Department of Veterans Affairs offices nationwide.

National Archives—Central Plains Region (Kansas City)
2312 East Bannister Rd.
Kansas City, MO 64131
www.archives.gov/facilities/mo/kansas_city.html
Serves Iowa, Kansas, Missouri, and Nebraska.

National Archives—Southwest Region
501 West Felix St.
P.O. Box 6216
Fort Worth, TX 76115
www.archives.gov/facilities/tx/fort_worth.html
Serves Arkansas, Louisiana, Oklahoma, and Texas.

National Archives—Rocky Mountain Region
Bldg. 48, Denver Federal Center
Denver, CO 80225
www.archives.gov/facilities/co/denver.html
Serves Colorado, Montana, New Mexico, North Dakota, South Dakota, Utah, and Wyoming.

National Archives—Pacific Region (San Francisco)
1000 Commodore Dr.
San Bruno, CA 94066
www.archives.gov/facilities/ca/san_francisco.html

Serves northern California, Hawaii, Nevada (except Clark County), Pacific Trust Territories, and American Samoa.

National Archives—Pacific Region (Laguna Niguel)
24000 Avila Rd./P.O. Box 6719
Laguna Niguel, CA 92677
www.archives.gov/facilities/ca/laguna_niguel.html
Serves southern California, Arizona, and Nevada (Clark County).

National Archives—Pacific Alaska Region (Seattle)
6125 Sand Point Way N.E.
Seattle, WA 98115
www.archives.gov/facilities/wa/seattle.html
Serves Idaho, Oregon, and Washington.

National Archives—Pacific Alaska Region (Anchorage)
Federal Office Bldg.
654 W. Third Ave., Rm. 012
Anchorage, AK 99501
www.archives.gov/facilities/ak/anchorage.html
Serves Alaska.

Washington National Records Center
4205 Suitland Rd.
Suitland, MD 20746
www.archives.gov/facilities/md/suitland.html
Mailing address: National Archives
Civil Archives Division
Washington, DC 20409
This branch holds records for the District of Columbia, field offices of Federal agencies located in the District of Columbia, Maryland, Virginia, and West Virginia. It also serves Federal Courts located in the District of Columbia and Armed Forces worldwide.

Libraries

Bibliographic information for every book cataloged in numerous libraries is entered into a national online computer database called the Online Computer Library Center (OCLC). Most libraries (public, private, and university) have access to this extremely important resource. OCLC makes it possible to determine what printed material is available at specific locations in the country and whether it is accessible by interlibrary loan.

Family History Library of The Church of Jesus Christ of Latter-day Saints (the Mormons)
35 N. West Temple
Salt Lake City, UT 84150
www.familysearch.org
The FHL has the largest international collection of family history research materials. Although physically located at the above address and open for research to the general public, nearly all of the FHL's materials that are on microfilm can be borrowed

through any of the local Family History Centers, most of which are attached to local meetinghouses of the church. Some materials are restricted and must be used at the FHL. There is usually a waiting period for receiving films, but the cost is nominal. For a listing of all currently operating FHL centers, write to the above address or visit the website to find one of the centers near you and learn how to access their Internet sources, and the microfilm and microfiche materials in the library. Online access to the federal census records and indexes otherwise offered by subscription through <www.ancestry.com> is available at most FHL centers.

A number of important materials are available on its website. These include the updated catalog of extensive holdings; the IGI (see Vital Records above); the 1880 Federal Census every-person index linked to transcribed household entries and to the actual census view for a fee through <www.ancestry.com>; the Ancestral File of submitted family information; and the Social Security Death Index, in addition to other international sources. See also Johni Cerny and Wendy Elliott, eds., *The Library: A Guide to the LDS Family History Library* (Salt Lake City: Ancestry, 1988); and Paula Stewart Warren and James W. Warren, *Your Guide to the Family History Library* (Cincinnati: Betterway Publications, 2001).

Library of Congress and Annex
1st-2nd Streets, SE
Washington, DC 20504
www.loc.gov

The Library of Congress has extensive holdings on local and family history. James C. Neagles, *The Library of Congress: A Guide to Genealogical and Historical Research* (Salt Lake City: Ancestry, 1990), provides an explanation of the library's resources and how they can be used.

Societies with Libraries

National Genealogical Society
4527 Seventeenth St. North
Arlington, VA 22207
www.ngsgenealogy.org

A membership society currently operating in Virginia, it has an excellent library of books, magazines, pamphlets, and manuscripts open to the public at the St. Louis Public Library in Missouri <www.slpl.lib.mo.us>. The publisher of the *National Genealogical Society Quarterly,* the society offers an extensive educational program, computer interest group, and annual national conferences covering research methods and sources.

National Society,
Daughters of the American Revolution Library
1776 D St., NW
Washington, DC 20006
www.dar.org

A membership society with an extensive library including original source material and collection of family and cemetery records gathered by local chapters. The library is open to the general public for a small fee.

New England Historic Genealogical Society
101 Newbury St.
Boston, MA 02116
www.newenglandancestors.org

Not limited to research material on New England, the extensive collection here is described in the Massachusetts chapter. Members have access to its growing collection of online New England sources. New material is added regularly to the master database.

Other Libraries

The Newberry Library in Chicago (see Illinois), the New York Public Library in New York City (see New York), the Allen County Public Library in Fort Wayne (see Indiana), and the Wisconsin Historical Society (see Wisconsin) all have extensive collections not limited to the state in which they are located, and include printed and microform materials from many regions of the country.

Societies

Federation of Genealogical Societies (FGS)
P.O. Box 200940
Austin, TX 78720-0940
www.fgs.org

This federation of a large number of state and local genealogical societies is an excellent source for locating genealogical and historical societies not covered in each state's section. FGS produces the quarterly FGS *Forum,* which is available by subscription and at a discount to all members of genealogical societies belonging to the FGS, which also sponsors annual national conferences where attendees can learn about research sources and methodology.

A current list of some genealogical and historical societies is included in Juliana Szucs Smith, comp. *Ancestry Family Historian's Address Book,* rev. ed. (Orem, Utah: Ancestry, 2003). In addition there are many libraries, public and private, throughout the country that have significant collections of genealogical material. Some of these are listed in *Directory of American Libraries with Genealogy or Local History Collections,* compiled by P. William Filby (Wilmington, Del.: Scholarly Resources, 1988).

Professional Associations

The following organizations establish standards of practice in the profession and serve the general public with information about the genealogical profession and its practitioners.

Board for Certification of Genealogists
P.O. Box 14291
Washington, DC 20044
www.bcgcertification.org

International Commission for the Accreditation of Professional Genealogists
P.O. Box 970204
Orem, UT 97097-0204
www.icapgen.org

The Association for Professional Genealogists
P.O. Box 350998
Westminster, CO 80035-0998
www.apgen.org

Special Focus Categories

This section discusses topics that, for each state, require a special emphasis. Although not every state includes discussion of all categories, African-American research, Native-American research, immigration and naturalization, and research on particular ethnic groups are the most commonly discussed. Some resources for these categories that apply to all states are:

Immigration

We are, with the exception of Native American residents, all descendants of immigrants, although not all immigrants came to America by choice. Nearly all of twentieth-century immigration records from ships' arrivals on the eastern and southern coasts of the United States have been indexed or Soundexed (as with census records) and can be viewed on microfilm in collections at the National Archives. Its publication, *Immigrant and Passenger Arrivals: A Select Catalog of National Archives Microfilm Publications*, available online under "Publications" on its website <www.archives.com> lists these records.

Federal immigration records from before the twentieth century are on microfilm, and although not completely indexed, are becoming more available online. When indexes do not exist, the passenger lists may still exist, but the port of entry, name of ship, and date of arrival need to be known. Even when aided by the 1900 or 1930 census information as to year of immigration (if accurately given), it still means searching through several reels of microfilm.

The most comprehensive index to all immigrant arrivals is published in the multi-volume set edited initially by P. William Filby and Mary K. Meyer and updated annually by Filby and others: *Passenger and Immigration Lists Index, 1500s–1900s* (Farmington Hills, Mich.: Gale Research, 2003) lists millions of names in both the original volumes and the annual supplements. These and a growing number of lists from the National Archives indexes are now available online through subscription membership at <www.ancestry.com>. The original and secondary source material used in the compilation may still need to be located to verify accuracy.

The American Family Immigration Family History Center (<www.EllisIsland.org>) provides online access to ships manifest records for the 22 million who entered through Ellis Island in the Port of New York from 1892–1924. Registration is required to access some of its holdings. Access to Ellis Island immigration records is made easier through <www.stevemorse.org>.

Naturalization

Many naturalization records (mostly federal) are now held by the regional centers of the National Archives, but an immigrant's naturalization might have been initiated in nearly any court in any state. Since locating the correct court is not always easy, it is essential to be familiar with the naturalization process. The first step for a new immigrant was to go to court to declare the intent to become a citizen. After this, a court record was initiated. Once the requirements of citizenship had been met, the person applying for naturalization reappeared in a court, though not necessarily the same court where they initially applied. Finally, the court would award citizenship. At all three stops, records were produced.

After 1906 the naturalization process was carried out in U.S. district courts, with records generally available through the appropriate court for each state. For an excellent discussion of the process and the records it created, see John J. Newman, *American Naturalization Processes and Procedures, 1790–1985: What They Are and How to Use Them* (Indianapolis, Ind.: Indiana Historical Society, 1996); and Loretto Dennis Szucs, *They Became Americans: Finding Naturalization Records and Ethnic Origins* (Salt Lake City: Ancestry Publishing, 1998). For some states, naturalization is discussed under Court Records. Some naturalization records are included in <www.ancestry.com> databases.

African American

Research on families with African-American ancestry generally follows the same techniques as those with European-American ancestry. Records chronicling the lives of Americans of African descent exist in abundance in the Western world and Africa. All the record sources discussed here (vital, land, probate, court, etc.) include evidence for research on African-American families, particularly "free blacks," although not always specifically identifying an individual with any ethnic or racial description.

The historical past of those with African ancestry is likely to include ancestors who were slaves as well as free, African American as well as white. The institution of slavery generated a voluminous number of documents about slaves. Unfortunately, most of them have not been published or microfilmed and remain

difficult to locate for genealogical purposes. The major exceptions to this are the enumerations of free African Americans and slaves on the federal census (see Census Records) and other record groups, such as the Freedmen's Bureau records, held by the National Archives. National Archives Trust Fund Board's *Black Studies: A Select Catalog of NARA Microfilm Publications* (Washington, D.C.: National Archives, 1984, 1996) catalogs and describes the extent of these holdings. Information about the records and access to a growing number of them is available at <www.freedmensbureau.com>. Marriage records in several states documented in the bureau's holdings are among those available online, for example.

During the 1930s, the WPA collected oral histories from many elderly ex-slaves. A superb collection, it has been reproduced in a multi-volume set, organized by state. See the multi-volume series, George P. Rawick, ed., *The American Slave: A Composite Autobiography* (Westport, Conn.: Greenwood Publishing Co., 1972–79). Several projects are underway to digitize the over 2000 narratives for Internet access. See the Library of Congress, "Born in Slavery" <http://memory.loc.gov>; University of North Carolina at Chapel Hills, "North American Slave Narratives," a National Endowment for the Humanities project <http://docsouth.unc.edu/neh/neh.html> among others. The slave narratives are also available via CD-ROM and online from Ancestry.com.

Websites, organizations, and books focused on African-American genealogy include <www.afrigeneas.com> and <www.accessgenealogy.com/african>.

The Afro-American Historical and Genealogical Society, P.O. Box 73086, Washington, DC 20056 <www.aahgs.org>.

African American Genealogy Group, P.O. Box 27356, Philadelphia, PA 19118 <www.aagg.org>.

Blockson, Charles L. with Ron Fry. *Black Genealogy*. Rev. Baltimore: Black Classic Press, 1991.

Burroughs, Tony. *Black Roots: A Beginner's Guide to Tracing the African American Family Tree*. New York: Simon and Schuster, 2001. Topics include oral history, family records, social security, census, and a discussion of electronic genealogy.

Fears, Mary L. Jackson. *Slave Ancestral Research: It's Something Else*. Bowie, Md.: Heritage Books, 1995. Follows the author's research in her own family with hints for research in other families.

Rose, James M. and Alice Eichholz. *Black Genesis: A Resource Guide for African American Genealogy*. 2d ed. Baltimore: Genealogical Publishing Co., 2003. A state-by-state comprehensive guide to the use of the extensive genealogical records involving African Americans.

Smith, Franklin Carter and Emily Anne Croom. *A Genealogist's Guide to Discovering Your African-American Ancestors.* Cincinnati: Betterway, 2002. Comprehensive guide with focus on pre-Civil War case studies.

Thackery, David T. *Finding Your African American Ancestors: A Beginner's Guide*. Provo, UT: Ancestry, 2000.

_____ . "Tracking African American Family History" in Szucs and Luebking, *The Source: A Guidebook of American Genealogy*. rev. ed. Salt Lake City: Ancestry, Inc., 1997.

_____ and Dee Parmer Woodtor. *Case Studies in Afro-American Genealogy*. Chicago: Newberry Library, 1989. Four case studies using different methodological approaches as examples for guiding research in other cases.

Woodtor, Dee Parmer. *Finding a Place Called Home: A Guide to African American Genealogy and Historical Identity*. New York: Random House, 1999. An essential handbook and guide.

Native American

Research in Native American ancestry produces another challenge and, unlike research for African Americans and other groups, such research relies heavily on federal records and not the county or state material.

The last decades of the twentieth century brought considerable attention to sources for Native Americans, making more of them readily available. Some require a knowledge of Native American beliefs and customs, which makes it important to do background historical and cultural reading. In addition to the sources listed under the states where Native American research requires a special focus, Native American records are cited in the National Archives and Records Service, *American Indians: A Select Catalog of National Archives Microfilm Publications* (Washington, D.C.: National Archives Trust Fund Board, 1998), available online at <www.archives.gov> under "Publications."

Edward E. Hill, *Preliminary Inventory of the Records of the Bureau of Indian Affairs*, 2 vols. (Washington, D.C.: National Archives and Records Service, 1965), explains the administrative structure of the Bureau of Indian Affairs and helps locate appropriate records for genealogical purposes. Like his *Guide to Records in the National Archives of the United States Relating to American Indians* (Washington, D.C.: National Archives and Records Service, 1981), Hill's inventory is an essential reference.

Other important sources include Curt B. Witcher and George J. Nixon, "Tracking Native American Family History," in Szucs and Luebking, *The Source: A Guidebook of American Genealogy*, rev. ed. (Salt Lake City: Ancestry, Inc., 1997), which proves a significant reference tool and provides explanations and descriptions of many available records; and Stewart Rafert, "American-Indian Genealogical Research in the Midwest:

Resources and Perspectives," in *National Genealogical Society Quarterly* 76 (September 1988): 212–24. See also:

Byers, Paula K., ed. *Native American Genealogical Sourcebook.* New York: Gale Research, 1995. Details records and research sources.

Federal and State Indian Reservations and Indian Trust Areas. (Washington, D.C.: U.S. Department of Commerce, Government Printing Office, stock number 0311-00076). Provides addresses of reservations and other useful resources.

Kirkham, E. Kay. *Our Native Americans and Their Records of Genealogical Value.* 2 vols. (Logan, Utah: Everton Publishers, 1980–84) lists a number of helpful resources.

The Native North American Almanac: A Reference Work on Native North Americans in the United States and Canada. Detroit: Gale Research, 1994. Overview on history, culture, language, law, religion, and other topics.

Websites that provide assistance in locating resources for Native American research include the Bureau of Indian Affairs at <www.doi.gov/bureau-indian-affairs.html>, <www.accessgenealogy.com/native>, <www.500nations.com>, <www.indianscoutbooks.com>, and the National Park Service's Historic Preservation Service <www2.cr.nps.gov>, which lists tribal offices.

Other Ethnic Groups

Some other ethnic groups have more prominence in individual states and consequently have more detailed discussions under Special Focus Categories. For the most comprehensive listing of resources for any ethnic, religious group or nationality, see Cyndi's List <www.cyndislist.com> (see also Internet Resources).

Jewish genealogical sources have become increasingly available through publications, such as Arthur Kurzweil and Miriam Weiner, eds., *The Encyclopedia of Jewish Genealogy: Sources in the United States and Canada (The Encyclopedia of Jewish Genealogy)*, vol. 1 (Northvale, N.J.: Jason Aronson, Inc., 1991); it is also available in a 1997 paperback edition. One leading publisher of works on Jewish genealogy is Avotaynu <www.avotaynu.com>. Online sources and research information can be found on the Internet at <www.jewishgen.org>.

Hispanics are one of the faster growing ethnic groups in the United States in the twenty-first century, with roots in Mexico, Central and South America, and the West Indies. Some general references for Hispanic research in addition to those located on <www.cyndislist.com> under that topic, include:

Platt, Lyman D. *Hispanic Surnames and Family History.* Baltimore: Genealogical Publishing Co., 1996.

Ryskamp, George R. *Finding Your Hispanic Roots.* Baltimore: Genealogical Publishing Co., Inc., 1997.

Internet Resources

Resources for tracing family history on the Internet are abundant, and some are integrated into this section of each state chapter. A full discussion of all online sources is the subject of other publications (see below), but some general websites have tremendous use to researchers. They may either have free access or require a subscription membership. Each requires some explanation.

Free Access

Cyndi's List <www.cyndislist.com> is a comprehensive listing of, and links to, genealogical websites. It is organized alphabetically by such wide-ranging topics as ethnic groups, publishers, educational opportunities, and research subject topics as well as individual states and countries. Each alphabetical entry is then subdivided into other topics, all with links to the website related to that information. A published guide is also available, Cyndi Howells, *Cyndi's List: A Comprehensive List of 40,000 Genealogy Sites on the Internet,* 2d ed. (Baltimore: Genealogical Publishing Company, 2001).

Family Search <www.familysearch.org> is the family history website for The Church of Jesus Christ of Latter-day Saints. The site has three major categories of information: Search, which offers several online searchable databases with millions of names; Share, which is a way to add information to the Pedigree Resource File; and Library, which gives information on the Family History Library, its branch centers, and a complete catalog of its extensive research materials (see also FHL listing in the Archives, Libraries, and Societies section above for more complete descriptions).

USGenWeb Project <www.usgenweb.net> consists of a group of volunteers who take responsibility for managing either individual state sites or the gateways to county sites, all providing Internet access to resources in each area. State sites include information on general topics (such as histories, maps, queries, reunions), although some have ongoing projects to index and make available actual records. County sites are generally more specific (vital records, land records, probates, church records, and cemetery records, as examples). Because of the volunteer nature of the projects, information for each location varies.

RootsWeb <www.rootsweb.com> describes itself as the "oldest and largest free genealogy site." Currently supported by Ancestry.com (see below), RootsWeb was originally organized to support research and share queries on message boards related to surnames. Today its reach extends far beyond their surname "bulletin boards" to provide links, information, and a wide array of research tools (such as free search engines, databases, and mailing lists). RootsWeb also provides shared data, such as WorldConnect Family Trees, message boards, and hosted

volunteer projects to digitize a wide variety of records from all locations in cooperation with USGenWeb (described above). Subscription to a free genealogical newsletter, *RootsWeb Review*, is available from the website.

Subscription Access

Ancestry.com <www.ancestry.com> is the largest collection of family history material on the Internet. In addition to all extant U.S. Census Records, 1790 to 1930 for all states with growing indexes linked to actual census images, subscribers can have access to the U.S. Immigration Collection (millions of ships passenger arrivals from the 1500s to the 1900s, including New York Passenger arrivals [1851-1991], and numerous other databases); birth, death and marriage records from many (but not all) U.S. locations; Historical Newspaper Collection (1786–2001); military, court, land, and probate records; biographical references books, directories of various kinds; Social Security Death Index; and links to RootsWeb message boards, or Ancestry World Trees (submitted by subscribers). Many of these are referred to in individual sections of this book. New database entries are added daily. All are searchable by name with some ability to develop advanced searches. Ancestry.com is owned by MyFamily.com, 360 W. 4800 N., Provo, UT 84604, which also owns Genealogy.com, RootsWeb.com, MyFamily.com, and Ancestry.co.uk.

Through its acquisition of Genealogy.com, Ancestry.com has added to its collection the extensive resources of World Family Tree and local and family history books and also the Family Tree Maker™ software program. Fourteen-day free trials are usually available to try out the power of the subscription. Ancestry.com also publishes a number of important, comprehensive research guides and references, as well as the extensive collection of CD-ROMs originally produced by Genealogy.com and Family Tree Maker™. An Ancestry Library Edition version of the subscription is available to libraries with Internet access to make the rich source of databases available to patrons in that library.

HeritageQuest™ <www.heritagequest.com> provides online access in subscribing libraries to U.S. census records, with slightly different search capabilities from those offered by <www.ancestry.com>. Included are complete indexes to the 1790, 1800, 1810, 1820, 1860, 1870, 1900, and 1910 censuses, although subscription is through participating libraries and not individual membership. The online database also contains a large number of local and family histories, searchable by both basic and advanced query, by people, places or publications. In addition, it publishes a large number of microfilm and microfiche collections, as well as producing CD-ROMs. HeritageQuest is owned by ProQuest Information and Learning, 300 North Zeeb Rd., P.O. Box 1346, Ann Arbor, MI 48106-1346 <www.proquest.com>, which also hosts the ProQuest Historical Newspapers™ Project, described under Newspapers, above. Some libraries hosted by

societies, such as New York Genealogical and Biographical Society, offer access to HeritageQuest's online services off-site to library members, as well as in the library.

Books

Books on the topic of online genealogical research abound and, by their very nature, require frequent updating. Some useful, recent editions are:

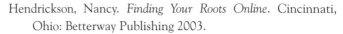

Clifford, Karen. *The Complete Beginner's Guide to Genealogy, the Internet, and Your Genealogy Computer Program.* Baltimore: Genealogical Publishing Co., 2001.

Hendrickson, Nancy. *Finding Your Roots Online.* Cincinnati, Ohio: Betterway Publishing 2003.

Porter, Pamela Boyer et al. *Online Roots: How to Discover Your Family's History and Heritage with the Power of the Internet.* Nashville: Rutledge Hill Press, 2003.

Search Engines

In the always-changing world of the Internet, a search engine may provide the most up-to-date access to any website, record source, or book. The easiest one to use for genealogical research is Google <www.google.com>. Throughout this reference book, a number of URLs are listed for access to specific records, information or organizations. While we are certain that these Internet addresses were accurate at the time of publication, webmasters are often changing the navigation and location of web information, particularly as new material is added or reorganized. For that reason, the twenty-first century family history researcher is advised to get used to using a search engine, such as Google. Once at the Google site, enter in the search window any phrase from a title, type of record, or name, and click Search. Google will search the web to provide you with the most updated links.

County Resources

Finally, each state's chapter outlines, in chart form, the county (or town or parish) resources that can be found either on microfilm or in the local holding agencies. Addresses are given for those agencies, with the date that the county or town was formed, parent counties, other names, and (where possible or available) the first year that primary sources remain extant in that location. Beginning dates for vital records, land, probate, and court records held in the counties, towns, or parishes are included. Inquiries to these counties should be addressed to the county courthouse or town clerk's office at that address. The column labeled "Map" gives coordinates that correspond to the state map giving the location of the county or town within that state. Accompanying each state's chart is a map detailing the political divisions and some geographic features.

Information for each state's county resources section was gathered in a number of ways. State archives, county officials, the FHL, and local repository catalogs were all used. Not all sources agree, and numerous discrepancies were found. An annotated edition would have produced a volume three times this size. The listing of beginning dates for primary sources is a *guide* only and not to be considered a definitive statement of every extant record in every location. A question mark (?) indicates that records exist, but the starting date is uncertain. Dashes (—) indicate that there are no known records in that category. Many states are thoroughly organized with centralized records. However, many states are not. Several have not had many of their records microfilmed, and others are in progress. What is given in the county chart here is the best information that could be gathered.

Sources for county formation used in this section, in addition to the personal knowledge of the contributors and sources listed under each state, included:

Thorndale, William, and William Dollarhide. *Map Guide to the U.S. Federal Censuses, 1790–1920.* rev. ed. Baltimore: Genealogical Publishing Co., 2000.

Long, John H., ed. *Historical Atlas and Chronology of County Boundaries, 1788–1980.* 5 vols. Boston: G.K. Hall, 1984.

National Association of Counties, 440 First Street, NW, Washington, DC 20001 <www.naco.org>.

Abbreviations

The following abbreviations are used throughout the text:

AISI: Accelerated Indexing Systems International of Bountiful, Utah.

BLM: Bureau of Land Management (see GLO).

DAR: Daughters of the American Revolution.

FHL: Family History Library in Salt Lake City, Utah.

GLO: General Land Office (became the BLM in 1946).

IGI: International Genealogical Index.

M### (also T###): A capital *T* or *M* followed by a number is the reference for a National Archives microfilm.

NARA: National Archives and Records Administration.

OCLC: On-line Computer Library Center.

USGS: United States Geological Survey.

WPA: Works Progress Administration (also Work Projects Administration).

Conclusion

The challenge in genealogical research is the complexity and depth of the problem. It is somewhat like piecing together a multi-layered jigsaw puzzle. One's own resistance to finding out about the past can impede progress, but this resistance can be overcome.

Somehow we feel that others must have known more than we do, and consequently, all that has been found is all that can be found. People who have spent years researching a family line will often tell stories about how they "happened" upon information. It probably was just as much skill as accident. We all are capable of acquiring some of that skill. It is like trying to understand your car. Maybe you never will be a mechanic who is expert in fixing a car or an engineer who can design one, but everyone can be capable of having a meaningful discussion about one.

Genealogical research is like that. Even if you never become a professional genealogist, you can acquire many skills in order to construct a good research strategy, solve many problems, and have a good working relationship with any professional with whom you consult in problem solving.

There are numerous guides to help overcome the concern about not knowing enough. Among the most valuable are the following:

Szucs, Loretto Dennis and Sandra Hargreaves Luebking, eds. *The Source: A Guidebook of American Genealogy.* rev. ed. Salt Lake City: Ancestry, Inc., 1997.

Greenwood, Val D. *The Researcher's Guide to American Genealogy.* 3d ed. Baltimore: Genealogical Publishing Co., 2000.

Jacobus, Donald Lines. *Genealogy as Pastime and Profession.* Baltimore: Genealogical Publishing Co., 1978.

Mills, Elizabeth S. *Professional Genealogy: A Manual for Researchers, Writers, Editors, Lecturers, and Librarians.* Baltimore: Genealogical Publishing Co., 2001.

Stratton, Eugene A. *Applied Genealogy.* Salt Lake City: Ancestry, 1988.

Stevenson, Noel. *Genealogical Evidence: A Guide to Standards of Proof Relating to Pedigrees, Ancestry, Heirship and Family History.* Rev. ed. Laguna Hills, Calif.: Aegean Park Press, 1989.

The process of research requires documentation of sources. A standard format used for documenting family relationships is presented in Elizabeth S. Mills, *Evidence! Citation & Analysis for the Family Historian* (Baltimore: Genealogical Publishing Co., 2000).

Another type of resistance we may feel in approaching our genealogy has to do with concern about what will be discovered—those "skeletons in the closet." We all have them.

We all descend from a very diverse group of people. No one has a "perfect" ancestry any more than we have "perfect" parents. Each of our ancestors probably did the best that he or she could, frequently under extremely difficult circumstances. We all have divorces, illegitimacies, felons, adulterers, dissenters, persecutors, rich, poor, Democrats, Republicans, religious zealots, and dissenters, and people from diverse ethnic or racial groups in our backgrounds. We all have ancestors who perished in or survived unfavorable odds—slavery, crossing the ocean, leaving the "known" and journeying into the "unknown," loss of income, childbirth, successive deaths, disease, plagues, droughts, disasters. We are all both ordinary and special.

One of the most pleasurable rewards of genealogy is sharing and celebrating what you have done and learned with others—whether it is at a national or local conference, with a professional, or with other family members. Searching for roots can establish a clear understanding of the past in order to provide tethers as we approach an even more rapid-paced future.

Alabama

ROBERT S. DAVIS AND MARY BESS PALUZZI

Alabama shares the rich cultural history of the Southeastern region. From 1519, when the first Spanish explorer, Alonso Alvarez de Pineda, navigated Mobile Bay, the state was claimed, explored, and then settled by the Spanish, French, and British.

The first permanent European settlers in Alabama were French. The LeMoyne brothers, Pierre LeMoyne, Sieur d'Iberville, and Jean Baptiste LeMoyne, Sieur de Bienville, sailed into Mobile Bay in 1699. By 1702, Fort Louis (on the present site of Mobile) had been settled as the capital of the French colony known as Louisiana.

With the Treaty of Paris in 1763, the French ceded most of Louisiana to Great Britain. When Spain declared war on Great Britain in 1779, the American Revolution came to Alabama. In 1780, Bernardo Galvez captured Mobile from the British. The Treaty of Paris in 1783 ceded to Spain the British holdings in the Mobile region.

In 1795, the Treaty of San Lorenzo more specifically stated that all Alabama lands below the 31st parallel belonged to Spain, and lands above the 31st parallel belonged to the United States and in turn to the Native Americans living there. At the same time the Ellicott Line was being surveyed, "squatters" (those having no legal claim to the lands they settled) began to move into Alabama, forcing the various tribes off their lands. The area below the 31st parallel was added to Mississippi Territory in 1812. Later counties were created as more white settlers moved into ceded native lands until Alabama Territory was created on 3 March 1817. Alabama became a state on 14 December 1819 and, in 1835, the last native lands were ceded. Massive waves of settlement from both Europeans and African Americans came with the opening of this territory as federal lands.

During the early years of statehood the most significant genealogical event was the opening of lands formerly held by Native Americans to white settlers between 1802 and 1838. These developments are detailed in Mary Elizabeth Young, *Redskins, Ruffleshirts and Rednecks: Indian Allotments in Alabama and Mississippi, 1830–1860* (Norman, Okla.: University of Oklahoma Press, 1961). By 1840, all but a few scattered remnants of tribes had been moved west beyond the Mississippi River.

Alabama suffered economic and agricultural problems in the 1840s and 1850s. The financial panic and depression that swept across the United States in 1837 resulted in banking problems that caused many Alabamians to lose their savings. Crops were ruined by drought, and several epidemics of yellow fever brought added suffering.

Economic rivalry between the industrial North and the agricultural South raised conflicts concerning states' rights and slavery. The unresolved conflict deepened until, on 11 January 1861, Alabama seceded from the Union and joined the Confederate States of America, created in Montgomery on 6 February 1861.

When compared with other Confederate states, Alabama, with the exception of the Mobile area, experienced relatively little military action. However, the conflict devastated the economic, political, and social life of the state. The state was readmitted to the Union on 25 June 1868, though the Reconstruction period led to deepening poverty and mass migration. In the 1860s and 1870s, 10 to 15 percent of the entire white population of Alabama migrated, with a third of these migrants going to Texas.

Railroads were built across the state in the 1870s, expanding the industry of mining of Alabama's rich mineral deposits of coal, iron ore, and limestone. By 1880, steel, iron, lumber, and textile industries were rapidly expanding, creating the cities of Anniston, Birmingham, and Cullman.

Alabama's industry and commerce grew with the United States' entry into World War I. Agricultural production increased, and a significant growth in Mobile's shipbuilding industry led to increased foreign trade. During the Great Depression, Alabamians suffered new financial hardships. The Tennessee Valley Authority, established in 1933 by the federal government, developed dams and power plants on the Tennessee River for inexpensive electricity, boosting Alabama's industrial growth.

World War II led to expansion of the state's agricultural and industrial production, and the installation of several military training sites, including Redstone Arsenal in Huntsville—which launched the United States into the space age. During the 1950s and 1960s, agriculture and industry became more diversified, requiring fewer agricultural workers who were forced to seek employment in urban areas outside the state. Alabama faced serious racial questions during the time period. The Montgomery Bus Boycott, which lasted from 1955 to 1956, the Birmingham demonstrations in 1963, and the Selma March in 1965 attracted much media attention. With the passage of the U.S. Voting Rights Act in August 1965, African Americans played an increasing role in local and state politics and commerce.

Vital Records

A limited amount of information concerning births and deaths of a few individuals before 1881 is available indirectly from probate court records. Such records include guardianships, apprenticeships, recorded wills, and the various other records maintained in the settlement and division of an estate.

An act of 1881 provided that all births and deaths were to be registered with a county health officer. Later legislation required that these registrations be made within the first five days after the birth or death and required that the county health officer's registry books be deposited with the county probate judge. Such records, when they survive at all, are found today in the individual county probate courts. The date for the beginning of mandatory state-level registration of births and deaths in Alabama is 1 January 1908.

All original birth and death records are now filed with the Alabama Department of Public Health. A fee of $12 is charged for a record search and one certified copy of a certificate. A $4 charge is made for each additional copy requested at the same time. A fee of $15 is required to amend an omission or to amend information that was incorrectly given. Allow six to eight weeks for each request. Certified copies of birth and death certificates may be requested from Alabama Vital Records, P.O. Box 5625, Montgomery, AL 36103-5625.

Birth, death, marriage (1936–), and divorce (1950–) records can be obtained at the appropriate Alabama county health department or through the Alabama Center for Health Statistics website at <http://ph.state.al.us/chs/VitalRecords/VRECORDS.HTML>.

Indexes to Alabama death certificates (1908–59), birth certificates (1917–19), deaths of convicts (1884–1952), and divorce records (1818–64, 1908–37, 1950–59) are widely available on microfilm. They can be ordered through local Family History Centers, which work with the Family History Library (FHL) in Salt Lake City. Researchers can access Alabama death certificates (1908–74), marriage records (1936–92), and divorce decrees (1818–64, 1908–92) on microfilm. The index to death certificates is available through <www.ancestry.com>.

A marriage license has been required since the territorial period in 1799. Marriage licenses were issued by the clerk of the county Orphans' Courts in which the bride resided. After 1850 the orphans' court was superseded by the probate court, which is still charged with the issuance of marriage licenses.

To enter into a marriage contract a man had to be at least seventeen years of age and a woman had to be at least fourteen years of age. If the man was under twenty-one or the woman under eighteen and as yet unmarried, the consent of the parent or guardian of the minor was required before a license could be issued. The marriage of these licensed parties could then be solemnized by a territorial, state, or county judge, an ordained minister, or a justice of the peace. The officiant was then required to file a marriage certificate with the probate judge of the county in which the marriage took place.

Before 1888, a marriage certificate indicated the names of the bride, groom, bondsmen, and officiant along with the license bond and marriage date. Starting in 1910 records may also include the names of parents, physical descriptions, ages and occupations of the parties, the number of previous marriages for each, and the blood relationship, if any, between the parties.

A certified copy of a marriage certificate may be obtained from the probate judge of the county in which the certificate was filed and recorded. A fee is required, and six to eight weeks should be allowed for response to a request.

Though divorce decrees were tried in county chancery court until 1865, the state legislature had the exclusive right to finalize all divorce decrees. These early decrees are thus a part of the legislative record and are published in the *Senate and House Journals*.

After 1865 the county chancery court was authorized to issue final divorce decrees. In 1917 the chancery court was merged with the circuit court of the county. Thus, divorce records from 1819 are maintained among the equity records of the circuit court of the county in which the suit was filed.

Though not required by law, several county clerks maintained divorce records separate from other equity files. A certified copy of a divorce certificate may be obtained from the circuit court clerk in the county in which the divorce suit was tried. A fee is required, and six to eight weeks should be allowed for response.

Census Records

Federal

Population Schedules
- Indexed—1830, 1840, 1850, 1860, 1870, 1880, 1890 (fragment), 1900, 1910, 1920, 1930
- Soundex—1880, 1900, 1910, 1920, 1930

Industry and Agriculture Schedules
- 1850, 1860, 1870, 1880

Mortality Schedules
- 1850, 1860, 1870, 1880

Slave Schedules
- 1850, 1860

The only extant records for Alabama of the almost-destroyed 1890 census are portions of Perryville (Beat No. 11) and Severe (Beat No. 8) of Perry County.

Territorial and State

A state census was taken in 1820, although records exist for only eight counties. These counties are Baldwin, Conecuh, Dallas, Franklin, Limestone, St. Clair, Shelby, and Wilcox. These records have been published and indexed.

Alabama's early census records are scant when compared with other states of the same age. Elizabeth Shown Mills cites twelve groups of census or census substitute materials for 1706 through 1816–19, all with enumerations compiled before statehood, in her essay "Alabama" in *Genealogical Research: Methods and Sources*, vol. 2, rev. ed. (Washington, D.C.: American Society of Genealogists, 1983). Sources for locating the census and substitutes are cited as well.

State censuses were taken sporadically. A sizable but incomplete collection exists for 1855, which is indexed. The 1850 and 1866 censuses survive and are widely available on microfilm, but are not indexed. Information on them includes only the head of household and demographic enumeration for the household. The 1866 census adds information about household members killed, wounded or missing in the Civil War. The originals are housed in the Alabama Department of Archives and History. Microfilmed copies may be purchased from them (see Archives, Libraries, and Societies for address). Enumerations of Native American Alabama inhabitants were made before cession of

their lands. Other significant sources for Alabama's Native Americans are cited in National Archives and Records Service, *American Indians: A Select Catalog of National Archives Microfilm Publications* (Washington, D.C.: NARA, 1984) (see page 15). The enumerations include these works:

Crumpton, Barbara J. *1884 Hester Roll of the Eastern Cherokee.* Duncan, Okla.: Creative Copies, 1986 (NARA M685, reel 12).

Felldin, Jeanne Roby, and Charlotte Magee Tucker. *1832 Census of Creek Indians Taken By Parsons and Abbott (With an Added Full Names Index of "White" Names).* Tomball, Tex.: Genealogical Publications, 1978 (NARA T275, 1 reel).

———. *Index to the Cherokee Indians East of the Mississippi River.* Tomball, Tex.: Genealogical Publications, 1978 (Henderson Roll, 1835, NARA T496, 1 reel).

Jordan, Jerry Wright. *Cherokee By Blood: Records of Eastern Cherokee Ancestry in the U.S. Court of Claims, 1906–1910.* Bowie, Md.: Heritage Books, 1987-present (Guion Miller Roll, NARA M685, 12 reels).

Siler, David W. *The Eastern Cherokees: A Census of the Cherokee Nation in North Carolina, Tennessee, Alabama and Georgia in 1851.* Cottonport, La.: Polyanthos, 1972.

U.S. Congress. *American State Papers. Documents of the Congress of the United States in Relation to Public Land....* Vol. 7. Washington, D.C.: Gales and Seaton, 1860 (Armstrong Roll of Choctaws, 1831).

In 1907 a census was taken of Alabama's Confederate veterans. County tax assessors canvassed all persons who were receiving a pension for Confederate service. Information enumerated includes name, place of residence, date and place of birth, enlistment and discharge or parole, rank, and name of military unit. Originals are housed in the Alabama Department of Archives and History and are now available from them on microfilm. From 1958 through 1982, the *Alabama Genealogical Society, Inc., Magazine* published Alabama Confederate pensioners lists from several counties.

Another census was taken in 1921 of Confederate pensioners in Alabama. This census was taken by mail with each pensioner being asked to complete and return the form to the state. The original forms may be examined at the Alabama Department of Archives and History and are widely available on microfilm, as is the 1927 census of widow pensioners.

Background Sources

A statewide guide to Alabama research is Robert S. Davis, *Tracing Your Alabama Past* (Jackson, Miss.: University Press of Mississippi, 2002). Additional excellent guides to local sources include Marcia

K. Smith Collier, *Alabama County Data and Resources* (Titus, Ala.: the author, 1999), and Marilyn Davis Barefield, *Researching in Alabama: A Genealogical Guide* (Birmingham: Birmingham Public Library, 1998). Ralph N. Brannen's *Alabama Bibliography* (Oxford, Ala.: the author, 1996) provides bibliographic sources for Alabama history.

The WPA project, "Index to Alabama Biography: An Index to Biographical Sketches of Individual Alabamians in State, Local, and to Some Extent National Collections" (Birmingham: WPA Project sponsored by the Birmingham Public Library, 1956) can assist the researcher looking for persons in Alabama in the late nineteenth and early twentieth centuries. The project indexed over 100 biographical and historical works. Some of the titles included are:

DuBose, Joel C. *Notable Men of Alabama.* 2 vols. Atlanta: Southern Historical Association, 1904.

Memorial Record of Alabama. 2 vols. Madison, Wis.: Brant & Fuller, 1893.

Moore, Albert Burton. *History of Alabama and Her People.* 3 vols. Chicago: American Historical Society, 1927.

Owen, Thomas McAdory. *History of Alabama and Dictionary of Alabama Biography.* 4 vols. Chicago: S. J. Clark, 1921.

Saunders, James Edwards. *Early Settlers of Alabama.* New Orleans: L. Graham & Sons, 1899.

The index is available in the Tutwiler Collection of the Birmingham Public Library (see Archives, Libraries, and Societies).

Maps

Several books of Alabama locations, place-names, boundaries, and maps exist. The most important are discussed in Robert S. Davis, *Tracing Your Alabama Past* (see Background Sources). Changes in county boundaries are shown in detail on modern county maps in Peggy Tuck Sinko, *Alabama: Atlas of Historical County Boundaries* (New York: Simon & Schuster, Inc., 1996). Volume 1 of W. Craig Remington and Thomas J. Kallsen, *Historical Atlas of Alabama* (Tuscaloosa: University of Alabama, Department of Geography, 1997) locates historical sites on modern maps.

All of Alabama has been mapped in cooperation with the U.S. Geological Survey and the Geological Survey of Alabama (see page 5). These topographic quadrangle maps show selected man-made and natural features as well as the shape and elevation of features. Features include state, county, and municipal boundary lines; townships, ranges, roads, railroads, and buildings; and mountains, valleys, streams, and rivers. The earliest survey maps for Alabama are dated from 1901. Modern maps are indexed in volume 4 of *Omni Gazetteer of the United States of America* (Detroit: Omnigraphics, 1991) and at the USGS website (see page 5).

The Alabama Highway Department has prepared a series of county road maps. These maps contain more detailed information about man-made features than the geological survey maps. In addition to roads and boundaries, these maps include rural communities, churches, and cemeteries. The maps are available for a nominal fee from the Alabama Highway Department, Bureau of Planning and Programming, Montgomery, AL 36130.

Another important series of maps for incorporated municipalities is the Sanborn Fire Insurance maps (see page 5). These maps, dating from 1884 to 1950, include 110 Alabama communities. The maps indicate street names, property boundaries, building use, and, in some cases, property owners. Originals are available in the Library of Congress and in the University of Alabama Library (see Archives, Libraries, and Societies). They were microfilmed (twelve reels) in 1982 by Chadwyck-Healy of Alexandria, Virginia.

Sara Elizabeth Mason's bibliography, *A List of Nineteenth Century Maps of the State of Alabama* (Birmingham: Birmingham Public Library, 1973) is very helpful in identifying and locating early Alabama maps. The list includes the holdings of the library of the Alabama Department of Archives and History, Auburn University in Auburn, the University of Alabama, Samford University, Mobile Public Library, and Birmingham Public Library (see Archives, Libraries, and Societies). Descriptive annotations as well as detailed physical descriptions add to the usefulness of the list.

The Rucker Agee Map Collection, a privately acquired donation at the Birmingham Public Library, is an incomparable collection of maps documenting the cartographic history of the southeast and in particular Alabama.

Land Records

Public-Domain State

Colonial settlers acquired title to Alabama lands from the French, the Spanish, the British, and the Native Americans. Original copies of these grants from the first three groups may be found, respectively, in the Archives Nationales in Paris, the Archivo General de Indias in Seville, and the Public Record Office in London. When land title was transferred from Great Britain to the United States in 1783, following the American Revolution, preemptive landowners were required to file proof of their land title with the U.S. General Land Office (GLO). Abstracts of the files are found in the *American States Papers: Documents, Legislative and Executive of the Congress, Class VIII, Public Lands* (Washington, D.C.: Gales and Seaton, 1832–61). These volumes are indexed in *C.I.S. U.S. Serial Set Index, Part I,*

American States Papers and the 15th–34th Congresses, 1789–1857 (Washington, D.C.: Congressional Information Services, 1977).

Title to previously ungranted lands was vested in the federal government, and titles were conveyed to individuals either by sale, by bounty-land warrant, or homestead. The Land Act of 1800, as amended in 1803, simplified the claiming of land titles by authorizing local public land offices to survey and auction lands within their charge. Sales were sanctioned through thirteen land offices including St. Stephens (established December 1806, transferred to Mobile, 1867); Huntsville (established at Nashville in March 1807, transferred to Huntsville, 1811, transferred to Montgomery, May 1866); Cahaba (established at Milledgeville, Georgia, August 1817, transferred to Cahaba, October 1818, transferred to Greenville, 1856); Tuscaloosa (established May 1820, transferred to Montgomery, 1832); Sparta-Conecuh Courthouse (established May 1820, transferred to Montgomery, 1854); Montgomery (established July 1832, closed 1927); Mardisville-Montevallo (established July 1832, transferred to Lebanon, 1842); Demopolis (established March 1833, transferred to Montgomery, March 1866); Lebanon (established April 1842, transferred to Centre 1858); Elba (established April 1854, transferred to Montgomery, April 1867); Greenville (established 1856, transferred to Montgomery 1866); Centre (established 1858, transferred to Huntsville 1866); and Mobile (established 1867, transferred to Montgomery June 1879).

Indexes to Alabama land grants originating with the BLM are widely available. These indexes do not include pre-1820 land grants on credit, military bounty warrants (1842–58), and homestead applications that were not completed. The National Archives has an index to all of these grants and other federal land states, which should also be consulted for the otherwise omitted land grant records. These may contain significant genealogical information. Researchers should note that persons who gave aid to the Confederate cause were barred from receiving homestead land grants from 1866 to 1876.

When the land offices were closed, their original records were sent to the Washington, D.C., office. Photocopies of the original records may be requested from the Washington National Reference Center at Suitland, Md. (see page []). Presidential patents are available and can be searched and copied for free from the Bureau of Land Management website: <www.glorecords.blm.gov>. The BLM Eastern States (750 Boston Blvd., Springfield, VA 22153-3121 <www.es.blm.gov/lands/index.asp>) has additional files and materials relating to Alabama lands. Duplicate copies of some of these records are located in the Alabama Department of Archives and History, the office of the Alabama Secretary of State, and the University of Alabama library's special collections. Plat maps and field notes for these original land grants are also available at these repositories. The Southern Historical Press has published Marilyn Davis Hahn Barefield's incomplete abstracts of several of the land offices' records including those of Centre,

Demopolis, Elba, Huntsville, Lebanon, Mardisville, Sparta, St. Stephens, and Tuscaloosa counties; Southern University Press has published her abstracts from the Cahaba Land Office. Abstracts for north Alabama counties published by Margaret M. Cowart abstracts are for Colbert, Franklin, Jackson, Limestone, Madison, and Morgan counties.

Tract books indicating the original sale of property from the federal government, or the state of Alabama in case of a sixteenth section, are housed in the county probate judge's office. The books, arranged by legal description, include the name of the purchaser, the number of acres purchased, the price, date of purchase, certificate number, and whether or not the land was obtained under a military act. These records do not include lands cut away to form new counties or subsequent sales of original tracts.

All subsequent title transactions following the original title transfer from the federal government are recorded in the probate judge's records of the county in which the property lies. These records include conveyance records, which detail the transfer of property either by sale or donation.

In some counties, mortgages were recorded in the same volumes as outright conveyance of real property, while in others, liens and deeds of trust are recorded separately as "Mortgages."

Probate Records

The office of the probate judge, designated as the "orphans court" before 1850, is the county office where the most significant genealogical records are created and maintained in Alabama. A variety of records are housed in this office.

These records may be labeled wills, estates, inventories, administrations or guardian's bonds, and orphans' court records. Within each category there may or may not be separate volumes labeled "record" or "minutes." The "record" volumes contain relatively full accounts of probate proceedings, while the "minutes" volumes normally contain only brief abstracts of the proceedings. Early adoption records and records for the binding-out of poor orphans are recorded here. Until the 1900s, adoption records were not filed separately. Record books and files created especially for adoption proceedings are now closed to the public by law. Sometimes bastardy cases and naturalization records are here. In all cases these records are merely copies of the original and contain only such data as the clerk thought legally important. More significant than the clerk's ledger, the "loose papers" contain the documents submitted to prove a will, such as the petition to probate, which listed all heirs of the deceased. Generally, these files are not housed in the record room. The researcher should request these files from the probate clerk. The office of the probate judge in Alabama also recorded other documents intermittently in

probate, deed, or commissioner's court records. Particularly useful are proofs of freedom filed by free African Americans or Native Americans (often with white deponents), indenture papers, contracts for hiring military substitutes during the Civil War, and lists of slaves brought into the state or loaned to the Confederacy. The Genealogical Society of Utah has begun microfilming these "loose papers" in Alabama counties.

Court Records

The records of the office of the court clerk or the circuit court records are the most poorly organized and most frequently missing court records. In smaller counties both chancery and circuit court records are maintained by the same clerk. In larger counties the records may be separated. The state administrative office of the court oversees the maintenance of the circuit court records.

The state-level office of the supreme court clerk has authority over the records of the state supreme court.

Alabama Digest, 1820 to Date.... (St. Paul, Minn.: West Publishing Co., 1950-present) indexes the decisions and opinions of the Alabama Supreme Court, court of criminal appeals, and court of civil appeals as well as the federal courts from the district level to the supreme court. The final volume is a defendant-plaintiff name index to cases cited.

Tax Records

County tax records are arranged by legal description and are not indexed. There are few counties with tax records before 1860. The National Archives has a microfilm publication titled *Internal Revenue Assessment Lists for Alabama, 1865–1866* (NARA M754, 6 reels). The Alabama Department of Archives and History has 1867–68 Voter Lists ("Returns for Qualified Voters") that are rich in naturalization information. Returns for Walker and Winston counties include county and date of birth for those registered. These returns, and those for Marion and Mobile counties, have been published.

Cemetery Records

Locations of major cemeteries and identification of large families buried in them can be found in volume two of W. Craig Remington's *Historical Atlas of Alabama* (Tuscaloosa: University of Alabama, Department of Geography, 1999). Scattered volumes have been published by various patriotic, historical, and genealogical societies. Many individual cemetery transcriptions have been published in periodicals.

Church Records

Samford University Library, Birmingham, Alabama, microfilms church records of all denominations in Alabama and makes these records available for public use. The Baptists (Southern Convention) form the largest denomination in Alabama. The first Baptist Church was founded 2 October 1808 on Flint River near Huntsville. The Baptists are the only denomination having some form of centralized state and congregational historic records. Their records are housed in the Samford University Library. Included are not only microfilmed minutes of defunct and active congregations, but also the personal papers of many churchmen and a run of the denomination's state newspaper, the *Alabama Baptist* (1835-present).

The state's oldest denomination, Roman Catholic, has records dating from the coming of Iberville's colony near Mobile in 1699. Most parish records are maintained by the local church. Publication of the early records of Mobile parish is in process.

The first ordained Episcopal minister in the state was licensed in 1764 to minister to British settlers. The WPA Historical Records Survey in 1939 compiled a volume surveying the records of the Protestant Episcopal Church in Alabama. The inventory contains a brief history of each parish, a statement on extant parish records, and an index by location and by parish names. Parish records are maintained by the parish. Unfortunately, the survey did not inventory any other denominational records. A copy of Alabama Historical Records Survey, *Inventory of the Church Archives of Alabama, Protestant Episcopal Church* (Birmingham: Historical Records Survey Project, 1939) is at the Birmingham Public Library.

In 1803 Lorenzo Dow, a Methodist, did his first preaching in Alabama. Methodist missionaries were sent by the South Carolina Conference into the Tombigbee area in 1809. Today, some Methodist records for north Alabama churches are housed at Birmingham Southern College, and south Alabama church records are housed at Huntingdon College, Montgomery. Birmingham Southern College has a run of the state denominational newspaper, the *Christian Advocate* (1880-present).

The first Presbyterian Church was organized in 1818 at Huntsville. Historical records for active Presbyterian churches are usually maintained by the local congregation. Some records of defunct churches are held by Samford University and the Alabama Department of Archives and History.

Military Records

Alabamians have seen military service in all wars of the United States. Military records are found at both the state and federal levels. The most voluminous and readily available military records for Alabama are those of the National Archives (see pages 8-9).

Roster of Revolutionary Soldiers and Patriots Alabama (Montgomery: Alabama Society DAR, 1979) lists those soldiers who lived and died in Alabama as well as some who died in other states. Data from scattered published and unpublished sources was edited and compiled. The volume includes a statement on the soldier's military service; a brief biographical sketch including the names of his parents, wife, and children; and bibliographic citations to sources.

The Alabama Department of Archives and History has made their military service surname files available on microfilm. These files include a series for Revolutionary War veterans residing in Alabama; service in the Indian Wars of 1812, 1813, and 1814; territorial service in 1818; the Indian War of 1836; the Mexican War in 1846; the Civil War (1861–1865); the Spanish-American War in 1898; and World War I (1917–18). The series contains a card for each soldier indicating name, military unit, rank, and the source of the information. Most of the sources cited are unofficial as there are limited records for state military service.

Several lists of Alabama Civil War soldiers exist although records do not survive for every veteran. The most complete lists have been published by the Broadfoot Company and are accessible through <www.ancestry.com>. The Alabama Department of Archives and History's index to Confederate records, including pensions and pensioner censuses of 1907, 1921, and 1927 is widely available on microfilm, while the files on individual regiments, histories of units are published in a number of sources: Willis Brewer, *Brief Historical Sketches of Military Organizations Raised in Alabama during the Civil War* (Montgomery: Alabama Department of Archives and History, 1966); Joseph H. Crute, *Units of the Confederate States Army* (Midlothian, Va.: Derwent Books, 1987); and Stewart Sifakis, *Compendium of Confederate Armies* (New York: Facts on File, 1992). Histories on the First Alabama Infantry, USA have been published. The Family and Regional History Program at Wallace State College, Hanceville, Alabama, is an important center for Civil War research.

The state of Alabama offered pensions to its indigent resident Confederate veterans, and to widows of veterans. The files contain the usual military pension application information: name, rank, unit, dates of service, places of enlistment and discharge, if wounded, and qualifications for pension. If the widow was making the application in 1920, she stated when and where she was born, her father's name, date, and place of his death, and the date and place of her marriage. To qualify, a pensioner's annual income could not exceed $300 and his real property could not be valued at more than $400. The original files are housed in the Alabama Department of Archives and History. The applications have been microfilmed by the Genealogical Society of Utah and are available on loan through the FHL.

Periodicals, Newspapers, and Manuscript Collections

Periodicals

Most organizations listed below have websites. For a current list, see Alabama Department of Archives and History at <www.archives.state.al.us/referenc/hsglist.html>. There are more than thirty-five periodicals published in Alabama by local and state historical and genealogical organizations. The *Genealogical Periodical Annual Index* and the *Periodical Source Index, 1847–1985* (see page 10) survey some of these publications as well as articles on Alabama from periodicals done outside the state.

The following are useful genealogical and historical publications:

Alabama Family History and Genealogy News (1980-present). Publication of North Central Alabama Genealogical Society, P.O. Box 13, Cullman, AL 35056-0013.

Alabama Genealogical Register (1959–69).

Alabama Genealogical Society, Inc. Magazine (1967-present). Publication of the Alabama Genealogical Society, 800 Lakeshore Dr., Birmingham, AL 35229.

Alabama Historical Quarterly, vols. 1–44 (1930–82). Publication of Alabama Department of Archives and History.

Alabama Review (1942-present). Publication of Alabama Historical Association.

Central Alabama Genealogical Society Quarterly (1976-present). Publication of the Central Alabama Genealogical Society, P.O. Box 125, Selma, AL 36701.

Deep South Genealogical Quarterly (1963-present). Publication of Mobile Genealogical Society, P.O. Box 6224, Mobile, AL 36606.

Natchez Trace Traveler (1981-present). Publication of the Natchez Trace Genealogical Society, P.O. Box 420, Florence, AL 35631.

Pea River Trails (1975-present). Publication of the Pea River Historical Society, P.O. 107 Main St., Enterprise, AL 36330.

Pioneer Trails (1959-present). Publication of the Birmingham Genealogical Society, P.O. Box 2432, Birmingham, AL 35201.

Settlers of Northeast Alabama (1962-present). Publication of the Northeast Alabama Genealogical Society, P.O. Box 674, Gadsden, AL 35902.

Tap Roots (1963-present). Publication of the Genealogical Society of East Alabama, P.O. Drawer 1351, Auburn, AL 36831-1351.

Valley Leaves (1966-present). Publication of the Tennessee Valley Genealogical Society, P.O. Box 1568, Huntsville, AL 35807-0568.

Wiregrass Roots (1995–). Publication of Southeast Alabama Genealogical Society, P.O. Box 246, Dothan, AL 36302-0246.

Newspapers

The earliest newspapers in the state were located in the Tombigbee-Mobile area and included the *Mobile Sentinel*, Fort Stoddert (1811); *Mobile Gazette*, Mobile (1812); *Halcyon*, St. Stephens (1815); and *Blakeley Sun* and *Alabama Advertiser*, Blakeley (1819). Early newspapers from the Tennessee Valley included the *Madison Gazette*, Huntsville (1812); *Florence Gazette*, Florence (1820); and *Tuscumbia Advertiser*, Tuscumbia (1821). Other pre-statehood papers included the *Cahawba Press* and *Alabama Intelligencer*, Cahawba (1819); *Alabama Courier*, Claiborne (1819); and *Tuscaloosa Republican*, Tuscaloosa (1819). Books of abstracts from Alabama newspapers compiled and published by Pauline Jones Gandrud, and others by Michael Kelsey, Nancy Graff Floyd, and Ginny Guinn Parsons, are available in print.

Alabama law requires all county newspapers that carry legal notices to be maintained by that county's probate judge. Few of the county collections are complete.

The Alabama Department of Archives and History has participated in a National Endowment for the Humanities project to preserve old newspapers. A statewide inventory of all repositories was followed by a project to microfilm newspapers of historic significance.

Through the Alabama Newspaper Project, the Alabama Department of Archives and History has microfilmed newspapers from every county in the state. A list of those on microfilm both at the archives and through FHL can be found on its website <www.archives.state.al.us/newsmicro/search.cfm>. These are available for purchase or through interlibrary loan from the department. A list of other original newspapers, not microfilmed, and a statewide alphabetical collection of funeral notices and anniversary announcement in newspapers 1950 to 1978 is also available.

Manuscripts

Several important genealogical manuscript collections concerning Alabama should be considered. The *National Union Catalog of Manuscript Collections* (see page 11) is the first source to check for major collections in Alabama, although many minor collections will not be cited. The Alabama Department of Archives and History is the official repository for records of all state agencies and for the personal papers of many important public figures. Of significance to the genealogist, in the University of Alabama's William Stanley Hoole Library is the professional correspondence of Pauline Jones Gandrud, a professional genealogical researcher for over forty-five years. Gandrud also compiled 245 volumes of abstracted records from forty Alabama counties. These have been published under the title *Alabama Records* and are available from Southern Historical Press (1980–). The Hoole Library also maintains various pre-statehood records for Madison County.

Archives, Libraries, and Societies

Alabama Department of Archives and History (ADAH)
624 Washington St.
Montgomery, AL 36130
www.archives.state.al.us

Military and state census records are housed at this repository in addition to most copies of county materials on microfilm. The library's reference room provides family histories and papers, the state's most inclusive collection of Alabama newspapers and books, and a card index to the part of their collection that is cataloged. The website has an excellent group of databases for online researching.

Alabama Historical Association
C/O Alabama Department of History and Archives (see above)

Founded in 1947, the association is composed of both lay and professional historians.

Birmingham Public Library
2100 Park Pl.
Birmingham, AL 35203

The Tutwiler Collection located here is the South's most comprehensive genealogical collection for southern research. Included are extensive microfilm holdings of U.S. Bureau of Indian Affairs records for Alabama, state and U.S. census records, military service and pension records, Jefferson county newspapers, and Alabama county records. The BPL also has WPA compilations of Alabama source material found nowhere else. Book and map collections are among the largest for southeastern United States. The library also maintains the Birmingham Archives.

University of Alabama Libraries
William Stanley Hoole Special Collections
P.O. Box 870266
Tuscaloosa, AL 35487-0266
www.lib.ua.edu/libraries/hoole

The special collections include published and unpublished records documenting the history of the state. Of particular importance is the comprehensive manuscript collection, which contains business and personal papers. The map holdings cover the Sanborn insurance maps (see page 5) and copies of many original surveyor's plat maps and field notes.

Mobile Public Library

701 Government St.

Mobile, AL 36602

www.mplonline.org/lhg.htm

The genealogical department is the starting place for research in the state's colonial Gulf Coast history. The collection has holdings of Mobile newspapers and the WPA transcripts of pre-statehood land records. (Mobile and nearby Pensacola also have other libraries and archives of interest to the Alabama genealogist.)

Samford University Library

800 Lakeshore Dr.

Birmingham, AL 35229

http://library.samford.edu/about/special.html

In addition to housing the Alabama Baptist Historical Society records, the library's Special Collections also includes extensive family history vertical files and the Albert E. Casey Collection, one of the largest accumulations of research materials on Ireland in the country. A bibliography of the materials is available from the Samford University Library for $10. The Bledsoe-Kelly Collection, gathered by Maude McLure Kelly, contains abstracted local and state records as well as church, family, and correspondence files. See <http://davisweb.samford.edu>.

The Samford University Institute of Genealogy and Historical Research was begun in 1965. The institute is cosponsored by the Samford University Library and History Department and the National Board for Certification of Genealogists. The training format includes courses in beginning and intermediate research as well as advanced research in southern states. In recent years, the program has expanded to include a course for research in the British Isles held at Samford's London Study Center. See <www.samford.edu/schools/ighr/ighr.html>.

Wallace State College

Family and Regional History Program

P.O. Box 2000

Hanceville, AL 35077-2000

http://wallacestate.edu/genealogy.html

With an extensive genealogical library with public access, the center offers resources for southern and general family history studies, research courses and field trips. It has one of the nation's most extensive collections for research on individual Civil War soldiers.

There are numerous other genealogical and historical societies scattered across Alabama. For current information, check ADAH's website at <www.archives.state.al.us/referenc/hsglist.html>.

Special Focus Categories

Immigration

Mobile served as a port of entry and is included in the National Archives microfilm of *Copies of Lists of Passengers arriving at Miscellaneous Ports on the Atlantic and Gulf Coasts and at Ports on the Great Lakes, 1820–1873* (NARA Microfilm Publication M575). An index is available entitled *Index to Passenger Lists of Vessels Arriving at Ports in Alabama, Florida, Georgia, and South Carolina, 1890–1924* (T517). Most foreign-born immigrants to Alabama arrived through the port of New York.

African American

Several distinct sources for researching African-American families in Alabama are available. As previously stated, separate slave censuses, listing slave owners only with demographic information on slaves were taken in 1850 and 1860, in addition to enumerations of slaves on earlier censuses. The records of the Bureau of Refugees, Freedmen, and Abandoned Lands (see page []) detail this bureau's work to ease the problems faced by freedmen after the Civil War. Three microfilmed series are available from the National Archives: *Records of the Alabama Field Offices, Bureau of Refugees, Abandoned Lands, and Freedmen, 1865–1870* (M1900, 34 reels); *Records of the Assistant Commissioner for the State of Alabama, 1867–70* (M809, 23 reels); and *Records of the Superintendent of Education for the State of Alabama, 1865–70* (M810, 8 reels). The genealogically rich surviving records of the Huntsville and Mobile branches of the Freedman's Savings and Trust Company, 1865–74, have been abstracted by the Genealogical Society of Utah and have been placed on CD-ROM computer disks.

A resource published by the Alabama Center for Higher Education, Collection and Evaluation Materials about Black Americans Program entitled *Catalogue of the Records of Black Organizations in Alabama* (Birmingham: Alabama Center for Higher Education, 1979) should be particularly helpful to researchers seeking access to records of African-American business, religious, civic, political, social, and educational organizations. Entries for 239 different organizations indicate briefly when the organization was founded, what records are available, and whom to contact for access to the records.

See also the brief discussion of free African Americans in Probate Records.

Native American

Census records have already been cited as resources. A sizable group of materials on native inhabitants who occupied Alabama's land has been microfilmed through the National Archives (see page 11-12). Topics included are documents relating to the

negotiation of ratified and unratified treaties (T494); Cherokee Indian Agency in Tennessee (M208), which concerns Alabama residents; and trading house rolls for the Creek and Choctaw (M4 and T500 respectively). The Family and Regional History Program, Wallace State College (see Archives, Libraries, and Societies) and the Anniston Public Library have extensive collections of materials for Native American research in the southeast.

County Resources

County level records have been microfilmed and are available at the Alabama Department of Archives and History and the FHL. County records vary widely from county to county in both quality and quantity. Some have been carefully preserved while others have been much abused and neglected. Some records have simply disappeared. Other scattered records are now preserved by the Alabama Department of Archives and History, the University of Alabama Library, and the Samford University Library.

North Alabama counties of Blount, Cullman, Lawrence, Madison, Morgan, and St. Clair have local archives. See Marcia K. Smith Collier's *Alabama County Data and Resources* (see Background Sources). The Genealogical Society of Utah is now microfilming "loose papers" in Alabama counties for researching through the FHL.

Ten Alabama counties have had significant destruction of records by fire. These "burned" counties and counties that have had less destructive fires are indicated on the chart. However, not all records were lost.

Between 1935 and 1945 the Historical Records Survey conducted a preliminary inventory of fifteen county archives; see Alabama Historical Records Survey, *Inventory of the County Archives of Alabama* (Birmingham: Alabama Historical Records Survey, 1838–1942). Each county's volume contains a historical sketch of the county followed by a description and history of each county office as well as an inventory of each office's records. The counties that were surveyed include Clay, Colbert, Conecuh, Cullman, Greene, Hale, Lauderdale, Lowndes, Madison, Marengo, Sumter, Talladega, Wilcox, and Winston. Unfortunately, the inventory has never been updated, revised, or expanded to include counties not originally surveyed. The University of Alabama Library's special collections department also has inventories of the DeKalb and Cherokee county courthouse holdings compiled in 1979.

In the chart that follows, former names of counties are indicated and the addresses listed are for county courthouses. Court records are at the circuit court at the county seat, although no survey has been completed for all counties. Land and probate records come in a variety of forms for each county. Many are on microfilm (see discussion in those sections above). Three counties have two county seats. Record availability on the chart is drawn from the Alabama Archives and History's information on county records. To keep current with county record changes and holdings, check <www.archives.state.al.us/referenc/procount.html>.

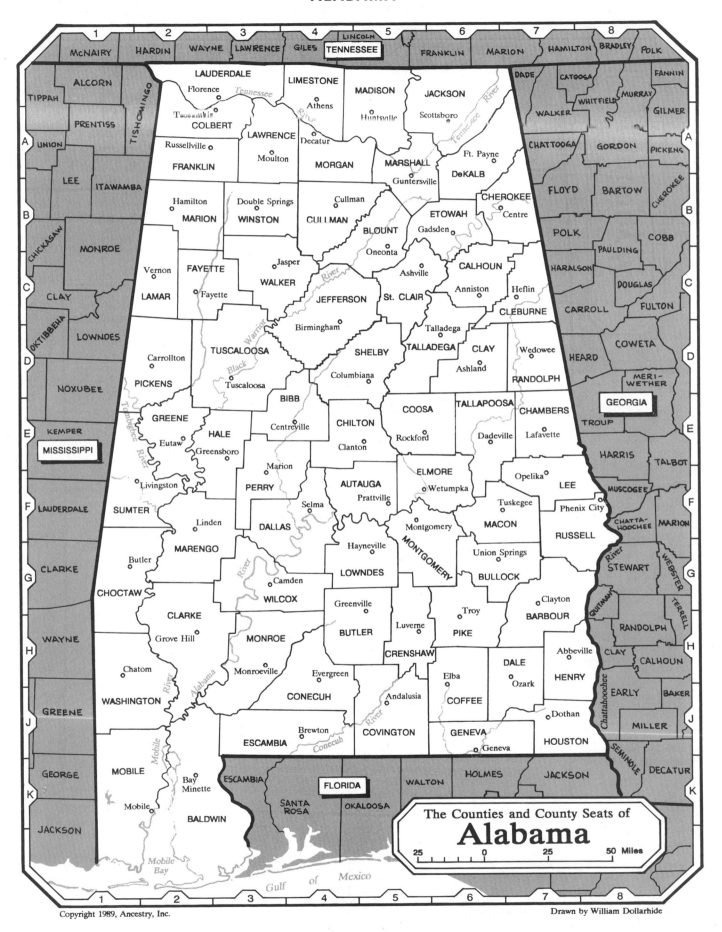

The Counties and County Seats of

Alabama

25   0   25   50 Miles

Drawn by William Dollarhide

Map	County Address	Date Formed Parent County/ies	Birth Marriage Death	Land Probate Court
F4	Autauga 176 W. Fifth St. Prattville 36067	1818 Montgomery	1908 1839 1908	1819 1824 ?
	Baine	1866 (abolished 1867) Blount/Calhoun/Cherokee/ DeKalb/Marshall/St. Clair		
	Baker	1868 (renamed Chilton, 1874)		
K2	Baldwin P.O. Box 459 Bay Minette 36507	1809 Washington/	1886 1810 1886	1809 1809 ?
H7	Barbour/Clayton Division 1 Court Sq. Clayton 36016 and Barbour/Eufaula Division Broad St. Eufaula 36027	1832 Creek cession/Pike Bullock/Russell	1881 1838 1881	1833 1820 ?
	Benton	1832 (renamed Calhoun, 1858)		
E4	Bibb 8 Courthouse Sq. West, Ste. A Centreville 35042	1818 Monroe/Montgomery (Cahawba)	1900 1818 1900	1818 1818 ?
	Blaine	1868 (renamed Etowah)		
B5	Blount 220 Second Ave., Rm 106 Oneonta 35121	1818 Creek cession	—— 1820 ——	1818 1829 ?
G6	Bullock 217 N. Prairie St. Union Springs 36089	1866 Barbour/Macon/ Montgomery/Pike	—— 1867 ——	1867 1867 ?
H4	Butler 700 Court Sq. Greenville 36037 Record loss, 1853.	1819 Conecuh/Monroe	1894 1853 1894	1853 1853 ?
	Cahawba	1818 (renamed Bibb, 1820)		
C6	Calhoun 1702 Noble St., Ste. 102 Anniston 36201 Record loss, 1861 and 1865.	1832 Creek cession (Benton, 1858)	1919 1834 1919	1832 1891 1835
E7	Chambers Court Sq. Lafayette 36862	1832 Creek cession	—— 1853 ——	1833 1833 ?
B7	Cherokee 100 Main St. Centre 35960 Record loss, 1882 and 1895.	1836 Cherokee cession	1899 1882 ——	1882 1882 ?
E4	Chilton 2nd Ave./P.O. Box 501 Clanton 35045 Record loss, 1870.	1868 Autauga/Bibb/Perry/ Shelby (Baker)	1908–19 1870 1908–19	1868 1887 ?
G1	Choctaw 117 S. Mulberry Butler 36904 Record loss, 1859 and 1871.	1847 Sumter/Washington	1881–93 1871 1881–93	1871 1871 ?
H2	Clarke P.O. Box 548 Grove Hill 36451	1812 Washington	1908 1814 1908	1812 1813 ?
D6	Clay Courthouse Sq./P.O. Box 1120 Ashland 36251 Record loss, 1875.	1866 Randolph/Talladega	1920 1872 1920	1875 1876 1876
C7	Cleburne 406 Vickery St. Heflin 36264	1866 Calhoun/Randolph/ Talladega	—— —— ——	1867 1867 ?
J6	Coffee/Elba Division 230 N. Court St. Elba 36232 Record loss, 1851 and 1863 and Coffee/Enterprise Division N. Edward St. Enterprise 36330	1841 Dale	1908 1866 1920 1907 1907 1907	1851 1862 ?
A2	Colbert 201 N. Main Tuscumbia 35674	1867 reorganized 1869 (Franklin)	1881 1867 1881	1867 1861 1867
J4	Conecuh Court Sq./P.O. Box 149 Evergreen 36401 Record loss, 1868, 1875, 1885, 1895.	1818 Monroe	1881 1866 1881	1866 1866 1881
E5	Coosa P.O. Box 218 Rockford 35136 Record loss, 1900.	1832 Creek cession	1878 1834 1920	1832 1834 ?
	Cotaco	1818 (renamed Morgan, 1821)		
J5	Covington 1 Court Sq./P.O. Drawer 789 Andalusia 36420	1821 Henry	1889 1895 1909	1881 1882 ?
H5	Crenshaw Glenwood Ave. Luverne 36049 Record loss, 1898.	1865 Butler/Coffee/Pike/ Covington/Lowndes	—— 1882 ——	1868 1871 ?
B4	Cullman 500 2nd Ave. S.W./P.O. Box 237 Cullman 35055	1877 Blount/Morgan/ Winston	1877 1877 1887	1877 1877 ?
H7	Dale P.O. Box 580 Ozark 36361 Record loss, 1869, 1884.	1824 Covington/Henry	1919 1884 1920	1895 1895 ?

Map	County Address	Date Formed Parent County/ies	Birth Marriage Death	Land Probate Court
F4	Dallas / 105 Lauderdale St. / Selma 36701	1818 / Montgomery	1922 / 1818 / 1922	1818 / 1821 / ?
A6	DeKalb / 301 Grand Ave. S.W., Ste. 200 / Fort Payne 35967	1836 / Cherokee cession	1885 / 1836 / 1885	1835 / 1848 / ?
F5	Elmore / P.O. Box 280 / Wetumpka 36092	1866 / Autauga/Coosa/ Montgomery/Tallapoosa	1884 / 1867 / 1927	1867 / 1867 / ?
J3	Escambia / Belleville Ave./P.O. Box 557 / Brewton 36427 / *Record loss, 1868.*	1868 / Baldwin/Conecuh	1909 / 1879 / 1909	1868 / 1868 / ?
B6	Etowah / 800 Forrest Ave. / Gadsden 35901	1868 (as Baine; renamed 1868 / Blount/Calhoun/Dekalb/ Marshall/St. Clair	1894 / 1867 / 1898	1867 / 1867 / ?
C2	Fayette / 113 Temple Ave./P.O. Box 509 / Fayette 35555 / *Record loss, 1866 and 1916.*	1824 / Marion/Pickens/ Tuscaloosa	1884 / 1866 / 1899	1824 / 1851 / ?
A2	Franklin / 410 Jackson St./P.O. Box 70 / Russellville 35653 / *Record loss, 1890.*	1818 / Cherokee and Chickasaw cession	1916 / 1897 / 1890–1930	1890 / 1890 / ?
J6	Geneva / P.O. Box 430 / Geneva 36340 / *Record loss, 1898.*	1868 / Dale/Henry/Coffee	1912 / 1898 / 1912	1898 / 1883 / ?
E2	Greene / Main and Prairie/P.O. Box 790 / Eutaw 35462 / *Record loss, 1868.*	1819 / Marengo/Tuscaloosa	1912 / 1823 / 1909	1819 / 1820 / 1867
E2	Hale / 1001 Main St. / Greensboro 36744	1867 / Greene/Marengo/Perry	1881 / 1867 / 1881	1867 / 1867 / 1865
	Hancock	1850 (renamed Winston, 1858)		
H7	Henry / P.O. Box 457 / Abbeville 36310	1819 / Conecuh	1931 / 1823 / 1930	1819 / 1822 / ?
J7	Houston / 100 North Oates St. / Dothan 36302	1903 / Dale/Geneva/Henry	1908 / 1903 / 1908	1903 / 1903 / ?
A6	Jackson / Courthouse Sq./P.O. Box 128 / Scottsboro 35768 / *Record loss, 1864, 1920.*	1819 / Cherokee cession	—— / 1851 / ——	1819 / 1866 / ?
C4	Jefferson / 716 N. 21st St. / Birmingham 35203 / *Also for Bessemer station in 1918, record loss, 1870* / and / 1801 Third Ave. N. / Bessemer 35020	1819 / Blount	1881 / 1823* / 1881	1819 / 1819 / ?
	Jones	1867 (renamed Sanford, 1868; renamed Lamar, 1877)		
C2	Lamar / Pond St./P.O. Box 338 / Vernon 35592	1867 / Marion/Fayette/Pickens (Jones) (Sanford)	—— / 1867 / ——	1867 / 1867 / ?
A3	Lauderdale / South Court St./P.O. Box 1059 / Florence 35631	1818 / Cherokee and Chickasaw cession	1880 / 1820 / 1890	1818 / 1818 / 1858
A3	Lawrence / 14330 Court St. / Moulton 35650	1818 / Cherokee and Chickasaw cession	------ / 1818 / ------	1818 / 1818 / ?
F7	Lee / 215 Ninth St./P.O. Box 2266 / Opelika 36803	1866 / Chambers/Macon Russell/Tallapoosa	1916 / 1867 / 1916	1863 / 1861 / ?
A4	Limestone / Courthouse Sq./P.O. Box 1145 / Athens 35611 / *Record loss, 1862.*	1818 / Cherokee and Chickasaw cession	1881 / 1832 / 1881	1818 / 1818 / ?
G4	Lowndes / P.O. Box 5 / Hayneville 36040	1830 / Butler/Dallas/ Montgomery	1881 / 1830 / 1881	1830 / 1830 / 1830
F6	Macon / Courthouse Sq. / Tuskegee 36083	1832 / Creek cession	1928 / 1834 / 1928	1837 / 1834 / ?
A5	Madison / 100 Northside Sq. / Huntsville 35801	1808 / Cherokee and Chickasaw cession	1881 / 1809 / 1881	1810 / 1818 / 1820
G2	Marengo / 101 E. Coats Ave. P.O. 48066 / Linden 36748 / *Record loss, 1848, 1965.*	1818 / Choctaw cession	1881 / 1819 / 1906	1820 / 1818 / 1917
B2	Marion / Military St. / Hamilton 35570 / *Record loss, 1887.*	1818 / Tuscaloosa	1902 / 1887 / 1902	1887 / 1887 / ?
A5	Marshall / 425 Gunter Ave. / Guntersville 35976	1836 / Blount/Jackson/ Cherokee cession	—— / 1836 / ——	1836 / 1836 / ?
K2	Mobile / 109 Government St./P.O. Box 7 / Mobile 36601 / *Record loss, 1823, 1840, 1872.*	1812 / Mississippi Territory	1871 / 1813 / 1820	1812 / 1814 / ?

Map	County Address	Date Formed Parent County/ies	Birth Marriage Death	Land Probate Court
H3	Monroe P.O. Box 665 Monroeville 36460 *Record loss, 1833.*	1815 Creek cession/ Washington	1881 1833 1908	1833 1833 ?
G5	Montgomery 251 S. Lawrence St./P.O. Box 223 Montgomery 36104	1816 Monroe	1908 1817 1908	1816 1819 ?
A4	Morgan 302 Lee St. N.E./P.O. Box 848 Decatur 35602	1818 (as Cotaco; renamed, 1821) Cherokee cession	1983 1821 1893	1818 1818 ?
F3	Perry P.O. Box 478 Marion 36756	1819 Montgomery	1908 1820 1908	1819 1821 ?
D2	Pickens 100 Phoenix Ave./Box 370 Carrollton 35447 *Record loss, 1864 and 1876.*	1820 Tuscaloosa	1903 1876 1903	1876 1876 ?
H6	Pike Church Street Troy 36081 *Record loss, 1828.*	1821 Henry/Montgomery	1881 1833 1881	1830 1830 ?
D7	Randolph Main Street/P.O. Box 249 Wedowee 36278 *Record loss, 1896.*	1832 Creek cession	1886 1896 1886	1897 1897 ?
F7	Russell P.O. Box 700 Phenix City 36868 **Also births, marriages, and death for Seale—1913, 1934, 1913 respectively.*	1832 Creek cession	1934* 1834* 1934*	1832 1837 ?
C5	St. Clair 129 Fifth Ave. Ashville 35953 *and* Cogswell Ave. Pell City 35125 *Births, marriages, and deaths for Pell City-1916, 1903, 1896 respectively.*	1818 Shelby	1893 1819 ——	1818 1819 ?
	Sanford	1867 (as Jones; renamed Sanford, 1868; renamed Lamar, 1877)		
D5	Shelby Main St. Columbiana 35051	1818 Montgomery	—— —— ——	1819 1819 ?
F2	Sumter Marshall St. Livingston 35470 *Record loss, 1901.*	1832 Choctaw Cession	1888 1833 1881	1825 1828 1876
D5	Talladega P.O. Drawer 755 Talladega 35160	1832 Creek Cession	1897 1834 1897	1833 1833 1833
E6	Tallapoosa 125 N. Broadnax St. Dadeville 36853	1832 Creek Cession	—— 1834 ------	1832 1838 ?
D3	Tuscaloosa 714 Greensboro Ave./P.O. Box 67 Tuscaloosa 35402	1823 Cherokee and Choctaw Cession	1880 1823 1880	1823 1821 ?
C3	Walker 19th St./P.O. Box 502 Jasper 35502 *Record loss, 1865, 1877, 1896, 1932.*	1823–77 Marion/Tuscaloosa	1929 1877 1890	1877 1877 ?
J1	Washington P.O. Box 549 Chatom 36518	1800 Mississippi Territory/ Baldwin	1908 1826 1908	1786 1820 ?
G3	Wilcox P.O. Box 688 Camden 36726	1819 Monroe/Dallas	1905 1820 1905	1820 1820 ?
B3	Winston P.O. Box 27 Double Springs 35553 **Also Haleyville 1920.*	1850 Walker	1889 1891 1912*	1891 1891 1892

Alaska

DWIGHT A. RADFORD

Vitus Bering, a Dane in the service of Russia, made the first European sighting of the Alaskan coast in 1741. It was not until the end of the eighteenth century, however, that the Russians gained control of the area.

The Russian-American Company was chartered in 1799 for twenty years, to monopolize Russian activities in America. The company did little more than develop the fur trading along the coast and among the island chains. Russians explored the Yukon and Kuskokwim region to a limited extent. Although Russian settlements had been founded, their populations were small and scattered.

The Crimean War had depleted the Russian treasury, and their American colony's expenses were mounting. It was decided that the sale of Russian America would replenish the treasury and unload an indefensible and unprofitable colony, since the fur industry had collapsed. The Russians knew of the existence of gold in the colony, and they thought that the United States might eventually annex the area just as they did California. Russia preferred that the United States gain control of the region rather than Great Britain, Russia's principal foe. Thus, Alaska would provide a buffer between Russian Siberia and British North America.

Many Americans and Russians did not welcome the American purchase of Alaska from Russia, which, in 1867, was bought for $7.2 million, although the United States was not totally unaware of the economic potential of Alaska. American trading ships and whalers knew Alaskan waters well, and the Western Union Telegraph Company had made a survey from Canada to the Bering Strait.

The Alaska Gold Rush was not a single strike; rather, it was a combination of strikes. Gold was mined at Stewart River, Forty Mile, Circle, Nome, Valdez, Fairbanks, and Dawson. Gold was found and mined in neighboring Yukon Territory, Canada, by Americans. The Alaskan Gold Rush of 1897/98 brought some 50,000 persons into the region before it began to subside in 1920. At that time, the population of Alaska dropped from 64,000 to 55,000.

Nome was founded in 1899 and Fairbanks in 1902 by gold miners. Anchorage was founded in 1915 as the headquarters of the Alaska Railroad, and Alaska became a U.S. territory in 1912.

In 1943, 140,000 U.S. military personnel were stationed in Alaska. Many remained after the close of the war. However, a substantial increase in the settlement of Alaska did not begin until after World War II. Alaska became a state on 3 January 1959. Although Alaska is America's largest state geographically, its permanent population is estimated at 640,000.

A summary of the governmental jurisdictions of Alaska is as follows: Russian American Company (1799–1861); Russian Imperial Administration (1861–67); U.S. War Department (1867–77); U.S. Treasury Department Administration for Customs (1868–77); U.S. Treasury Department Administration (1877–84); U.S. District status (1884–1912); U.S. Territorial status (1912–59); and statehood (1959-present).

Vital Records

Alaska began recording births, deaths, and marriages in 1913. Copies of certificates can be obtained by writing the Department of Health and Social Services, Bureau of Vital Statistics, 5441 Commercial Blvd., Juneau, AK 99801 <www.hss.state.ak.us/dph/bvs/default.htm>. They require a photo ID to order vital records. Since the department does not accept personal checks from individuals, money orders should be used and made payable to Bureau of Vital Records.

The Bureau of Vital Statistics has an extensive collection of Alaska church records, in order to create delayed birth certificates for people who did not have an official record at their birth. The department borrows the original church registers, microfilms them, and returns them to the congregation of origin. The Bureau of Vital Statistics will conduct searches of these "delayed" birth records, but requests will be denied if the information is needed for genealogical purposes. For a listing of some of the church records collected and microfilmed by the Bureau of Vital Statistics, see Church Records.

Alaska has divorce records beginning in 1950, which can be obtained from the Bureau of Vital Statistics. Earlier divorce records are at the clerk of superior court in the judicial district where the divorce was granted. This includes Juneau and Ketchikan (First District), Nome (Second District), Anchorage (Third District), and Fairbanks (Fourth District).

Another important source for vital records is the periodical *Anchorage Genealogical Society Quarterly*, which has serialized the society's extraction of early vitals.

Census Records

Federal

Population Schedules
- Indexed—1900, 1910, 1920, 1930
- Soundex—1900, 1920

Although Alaska was purchased in 1867, the U.S. government did not record an 1870 census. The U.S. censuses for 1880 and 1890 for accessible villages have not survived.

In the absence of Alaskan counties, the census takers created enumeration areas for 1900 and used judicial divisions for 1910. The Act of 1912, which made Alaska a territory, prohibited the creation of counties without the approval of Congress; therefore, no counties were ever created. The 1910 federal census was enumerated in four judicial divisions.

Alaska censuses were enumerated for Sitka in 1879 and 1881; the Aleutian Islands (villages of Belkovsky, Nicholayevsk, and Protossoff, which is also called Morzovog) in 1878; St. Paul and St. George Islands in 1904, 1905, 1906–07, 1914, and 1917; Cape Smyth, Point Barrow in 1885; and the Pribiloff Islands in 1890–95. Early Alaskan censuses are indexed in several different publications as well as the volume entitled *Alaska Census Records, 1870–1907*, by Ronald Vern Jackson (Bountiful, Utah: Accelerated Indexing Systems, 1976).

Background Sources

Antonson, Joan M., and William S. Hanable. *Alaska's Heritage.* 2 vols. Anchorage: Alaska Historical Society, 1992. Volume 1 contains information on the natural history and human presence in Alaska to 1867 and volume 2 covers its history since 1867. This important work has been approved as a textbook for teaching Alaska history in the secondary school system.

Balcom, Mary G. *Ghost Towns of Alaska.* Chicago: Adams Press, 1965. A short guide to the ghost towns of Alaska and other sites such as mines, canneries, hatcheries, military forts, and cemeteries.

Bradbury, Connie, David A. Hales, and Nancy Lesh. *Alaska People Index.* 2 vols. Anchorage: Alaska Historical Commission, 1986. Volume 1 of this work indexes over 20,000 names, primarily from obituaries listed in the "End of the Trail" column in the *Alaska Sportsman* (1935–69) and *Alaska* magazine (1970–85). Volume 2 is an index to individuals who appear in twenty-three other unique sources that a genealogist would use.

Bradbury, Connie Malcolm, and David Albert Hales. *Alaska Sources: A Guide to Historical Records and Information Resources.* North Salt Lake: HeritageQuest, 2001. This is the encyclopedia for understanding Alaska records and how to use them. All Alaska research should begin with this book.

Frederick, Robert A. "Caches of Alaskana: Library and Archival Sources of Alaskan History," *Alaska Review* 2 (Fall and Winter 1966–67). This excellent reference provides a bibliography of Alaskan newspapers, manuscript collections, maps, and photograph collections not only in Alaska libraries and archives, but nationwide.

Gibson, James R. *Imperial Russia in Frontier America: The Changing Geography of Russian America, 1784–1867.* New York: Oxford University Press, 1976. This volume covers topics such as the Russian occupation of Alaska, overseas transport (from Siberia and Russia), agriculture, and foreign trade. A well-written volume with numerous graphs, drawings, and a bibliography at the end of each chapter.

Lada-Mocarski, Valerian. *Bibliography of Books on Alaska Published Before 1868.* New Haven and London: Yale University

Press, 1969. Twenty-five percent of the works listed in this bibliography are in Russian. Topics listed include the settlement of Alaska, religious books, geographical atlases, and single maps.

Orth, Donald J. *Dictionary of Alaska Place Names*. Washington, D.C.: Government Printing Office, 1967. This book is an alphabetical list of the geographic names that are now applied and have been applied to places and features of Alaska.

Pierce, Richard A. *Russian America: A Biographical Dictionary*. Kingston, Ont and Fairbanks, Ak: Limestone Press, 1990. This work contains 675 biographies of the early people who influenced Alaskan history. It is not just limited to Russians, but includes people from many countries.

Ulibarri, George S. *Documenting Alaskan History: Guide to Federal Archives Relating to Alaska*. Fairbanks: University of Alaska Press, 1982. This guide is an aid to locating federal records in the National Archives and Records Administration.

Woodman, Lyman L. *Duty Station Northwest: The U.S. Army in Alaska and Western Canada, 1867–1987*. 3 vols. Anchorage: Alaska Historical Society, 1999. Few institutions have been more important to Alaska's history than the U.S. Army. These three volumes provide an encyclopedic scope of this relationship between Alaska and the U.S. Army.

Maps

The United States Geological Survey publishes a catalog of topographical maps that cover the entire state of Alaska. Ask for the publications entitled "Alaska Catalog of Topographical and Other Published Maps" and "Alaska Index to Topographic and Map Coverage." The catalog lists the over-the-counter dealers of U.S. Geological maps in Alaska (see page 5). Residents of Alaska may order Alaska maps from the Alaska Distribution Section, U.S. Geological Survey, New Federal Bldg., Box 12, 101 Twelfth Ave., Fairbanks, AK 99701.

Many libraries maintain reference files of the published maps of the U.S. Geological Survey. In Alaska, maps are deposited in the libraries of the Alaska Division of Geological and Geophysical Surveys in Anchorage; Alaska Division of Geological and Geophysical Surveys at College, the University of Alaska at Fairbanks; the Alaska Department of Fish and Game and the Alaska Division of Geological and Geophysical Surveys, both in Juneau; the Alaska Division of Geological and Geophysical Surveys and the public library in Ketchikan; and the Matanuska-Susitna Community College in Palmer.

The National Archives—Pacific Alaska Region (see page 12) has a large collection of Alaskan maps indexed in the "Guide to Cartographic Records in the National Archives" (Special List

#13). They include railroad maps, federal lands, various historical maps, mining areas, judicial district maps, mineral claims, steamship routes, early Eskimo and Russian settlements, and topographical maps. One map of special interest in conducting native research is an 1875 map showing the distribution of native tribes in Alaska and the adjoining territories. The Massachusetts Historical Society in Boston (see Massachusetts—Archives, Libraries, and Societies) has an unusual collection of Alaska historical maps (1865–88) that should not be overlooked.

Land Records
Public-Domain State

The First Organic Act of 1884 extended the laws of Oregon to Alaska only "so far as [they] may be applicable." Alaska became public domain, and unclaimed land was surveyed by the federal government and sold. Land offices were established at Sitka in 1885, Juneau in 1902, and Nome in 1907.

A person could obtain a title to a tract of public land only after it had been surveyed. After an individual obtained a certificate of title, a patent was issued. Copies of these are in patent books in the Bureau of Land Management (BLM) in Washington, D.C. (see page 6).

Records for the land offices of Juneau, Nome, and Sitka include cash entries, homestead final certificates, canceled homestead entries, and canceled Indian allotments. The BLM in Washington, D.C., has these records as well as an index to the cash entry files for Alaska.

Patents, tract books, and township plats are on file at the BLM, 222 W. 7th Ave. #13, Anchorage, AK 99513-7599 <www. ak.blm.gov/blmaso.html>.

The National Archives—Pacific Alaska Region (see page 12) has records of the surveyor general of the territory of Alaska. These records generally include correspondence and applications from settlers for land or mineral surveys (Fairbanks, Copper River, and Seward Meridians). Copies of the tract books, township plats, and other records of the U.S. General Land Office (GLO, forerunner to the BLM) can be found here.

Land records outside the BLM are available at the Division of Lands, Department of Natural Resources, 550 W. 7th Ave., Ste. 1260, Anchorage, AK 99501-3551. The DNR also has land records online by locality <www.dnr.state.ak.us/>. The Alaska State Archives has descriptions and maps of mining claims.

Land transferred by sale or grant to private ownership could be sold again, inherited, or lost. These records are filed at the office of the district recorder in each judicial district (see County Resources), which is similar to a county recorder in other states. Some land records are also available in the Territorial Era District Court records.

ALASKA

Probate Records

Probate records in Alaska were kept by the district courts prior to statehood in 1959. After 1959, Alaska created the superior court, which has probate jurisdiction. Probate records are available at the Alaska State Archives.

Court Records

Alaska court records are one of the best sources of genealogical information in the Alaska State Archives. These records relate to ethnic groups, particularly the naturalization records.

From the Alaska purchase in 1867 until 1884, there was no formal government in Alaska. An act of Congress in 1884 provided for a government at Sitka and conferred district status on Alaska. An act of 1912 designated Alaska a U.S. territory. Its capital was established at Juneau.

Prior to 1959 when Alaska became a state, the U.S. District Court of the Territory of Alaska administered its judicial affairs. The U.S. commissioner's courts administered the justices of the peace.

The pre-1959 district courts were districtwide courts and had jurisdiction over civil and criminal affairs. Federal judges were appointed as early as 1884. The whole of Alaska Territory at that time had only one district that was administered by a judge in Sitka until 1903. Prior to 1884, cases were tried in a district court of California, Oregon, or Washington. The general laws of Oregon were made applicable to the territory and appeals were to be taken to the circuit court in Oregon.

In 1903 three judicial divisions were established with judges in Juneau, Saint Michaels, and Eagle City. A fourth district was created in 1909, and the four seats were placed in Juneau, Nome, Valdez, and Fairbanks. The Valdez district seat was moved to Anchorage in 1948. These districts, for all practical purposes, can be compared to counties in other American states.

District 1 (Juneau) covers the southeastern Alexander Archipelago, including the cities of Juneau, Ketchikan, Sitka, and Wrangell.

District 2 (Nome) covers the northern portion of Alaska, including the cities of Barrow and Nome.

District 3 (Valdez and later Anchorage) covers the southern portion of Alaska, including the Aleutian Islands and the cities of Anchorage and Kodiak.

District 4 (Fairbanks) covers the central portion of Alaska, including Bethel, Fairbanks, and Toksook Bay.

Since statehood, district court records, which are similar to the circuit and district courts of other states, have been limited to minor civil and criminal matters. The post-1959 district court duties include the issuing of marriage licenses, arrest warrants, misdemeanor cases, and acting as the temporary custodian of a deceased person's property.

The Alaska State Archives has the territorial court records in Record Groups 505-509, which include Record Group (RG) 505, District of Alaska (1884–1900); RG 506, First Judicial District (1900–1960); RG 507, Second Judicial District (1900–60); RG 508, Third Judicial District (1900–60); and RG 509, Fourth Judicial District (1900–60). Many of these records are also on file at the National Archives—Pacific Alaska Region. An inventory of Alaskan territorial court records is available through the state archives in the booklet entitled *Record Group Inventory: District and Territorial Court System* (Juneau: Alaska State Archives, Department of Administration, 1987).

Alaskan territorial courts were endowed with authorities commonly assumed by county governments and school districts in other portions of the United States. Thus, Alaskan territorial district court records provide a valuable tool in studying Alaskan frontier life.

The post-1959 Alaska state court system was extended to include the supreme court, superior court, and the magistrate's court. The supreme court is a statewide appellate court that issues injunctions and other writs. The superior court is also a statewide court with jurisdiction over all civil and criminal matters, including probate and juvenile matters, as well as appeals from the magistrate's court. Magistrate's courts are districtwide courts with jurisdiction over misdemeanors and violations of municipal ordinances. There is one supreme court in Juneau, four superior courts, four district courts, and sixty-two magistrate courts.

Tax Records

The Department of Taxation was an agency of the Territory of Alaska, and the Department of Revenue was an agency of the State of Alaska. When Alaska became a state, the Department of Revenue absorbed many of the functions of the seven territorial agencies.

The Alaska State Archives has published both the Record Group Inventory and the unpublished Series Inventories and Container List that cover the Department of Revenue records, including territorial records. The state archives also has records created by the following territorial agencies having revenue or taxation functions:

RG 103 Territorial Department of Taxation, 1949–52.

RG 105 Office of the Territorial Treasurer, 1913–57 (Series Inventories and Container Lists).

RG 106 Territorial Department of Audit, Series 102, Fox Brand Program, 1923–43 (Series Inventory and Container Lists).

RG 321 Territorial Banking Board, 1914–58 (unpublished Series Inventories and Container Lists).

Cemetery Records

There is no major statewide collection or inventory of cemetery records for Alaska. See pages 7–8 for suggestions.

Church Records

Alaska is home to many different faiths. Because of the lack of early Alaska vital records, church records should not be overlooked as a major record source. Before the twentieth century the Russian Orthodox Church was the largest religious organization in Alaska. Other large denominations include the Episcopal, Methodist, Moravian, Presbyterian, Roman Catholic, and The Church of Jesus Christ of Latter-day Saints (Mormons).

Many church registers have been collected by the Alaska Bureau of Vital Statistics and used to compile delayed birth certificates. Once the certificate has been generated, the use of the information is stipulated by the Bureau of Vital Statistics just like any other birth record.

The Russian Orthodox Church, Diocese of Alaska, gave their record archives to the Library of Congress in 1927. These valuable records were in turn translated from Russian, indexed, and microfilmed. This vast collection of 401 rolls of microfilm is inventoried in the volume entitled *Inventory: The Alaskan Russian Church Archives* (Washington, D.C.: Manuscript Division, Library of Congress, 1984). Microfilm copies of the Russian Orthodox Church Archives are available at the National Archives—Pacific Alaska Region; the University of Alaska, Rasmuson Library, Fairbanks, Alaska; the Alaska State Library, Juneau; University of Alaska Library in Anchorage; and the Family History Library (FHL) in Salt Lake City. An index of early Russian Orthodox parish registers is found in John Dorosh, *Index to Baptisms, Marriages and Deaths in the Archives of the Russian Orthodox Greek Catholic Church in Alaska, 1816–1886* (Washington, D.C.: Library of Congress, 1973).

The Roman Catholic Church officially arrived in the Alaska territory in 1902 through efforts of the Sisters of Providence. They were responsible for establishing hospitals in Anchorage, Fairbanks, and Nome. The Sisters of Providence Archives is located at 4800 37th Ave. S.W., Seattle, WA 90126-2793 <www.providence.org/home/default.htm>. This archives houses the hospital records of Providence Hospital of Anchorage (1938-present); St. Joseph Hospital in Fairbanks (1910–68), and Holy Cross Hospital in Nome (1902–14).

There is no central repository for Alaskan Catholic parish registers and most are still in the custody of the local parish. There are three dioceses in Alaska: Diocese of Juneau, 415 Sixth St., Ste. 300, Juneau, AK 99801-1091 <www.dioceseofjuneau.org>; Catholic Diocese of Fairbanks, 1316 Peger Rd., Fairbanks, AK 99709-5199 <www.cbna.info> and the Archdiocese of Anchorage, 225 Cordova St., Anchorage, AK 99501 <www.archdioceseofanchorage.org>.

Moravian Church records have mainly been deposited in Bethel, Alaska. Contact Alaska Moravian Church, P.O. Box 312, Bethel, AK 99559 <www.alaskamoravian.org>. The records for the Moravian Church at Aleknagik and Dillingham are at the Dillingham Moravian Church, P.O. Box 203, Dillingham, AK 99576. Recent church records are held by the pastor in charge of a district within the church.

Presbyterian ministers arrived in Alaska during the 1870s. Mission work was conducted at Fort Wrangel and Sitka. The Presbyterian Church records through 1965 are deposited at the Presbyterian Historical Society, 425 Lombard St., Philadelphia, PA 19147 <www.history.pcusa.org>.

The Alaska Friends Church is largely Native American. Alaska Quaker records are included in the "Alaska Quaker Documents Collection" on file at the Alaska and Polar Regions Collection at the University of Alaska, Fairbanks. See also:

Roberts, Arthur O. *Tomorrow Is Growing Old: Stories of the Quakers in Alaska*. Newberg, Ore.: The Barclay Press, 1978.

Military Records

United States servicemen have been in Alaska since 1867. At that time Alaska was placed under the jurisdiction of the War Department. Most of the resident soldiers were from the lower forty-eight states. For information on the Sitka National Cemetery, see Cemetery Records.

The National Archives—Pacific Alaska Region has U.S. Military Post returns for Fort Davis, Dyea, Fort Egbert, Fort Gibbon, Fort Kodiak, Fort Liscum, Fort St. Michael, Sitka, Skagway, Fort Tongass, Valdez, Fort Wm. H. Seward, Fort Wrangall, Circle City, Council City, Dutch Harbor, New Archangel, Camp Rampart, St. Paul Island, and Greadwell. These records are part of M617, Alaska Post Returns (1867–1916). Post returns generally show the units that were stationed at a particular post, officers present and absent, record of events, and official communications.

Periodicals, Newspapers, and Manuscript Collections

Periodicals
Several periodicals of historical and genealogical value concerning Alaska have been published. These include the *Alaska Journal*, published quarterly by the Alaska Northwest Publishing Company, which contains many articles on Alaska culture and history; the semi-annual *Alaska History*, the official journal of the Alaska Historical Society; and the *Anchorage Genealogical Society Quarterly*.

Newspapers

The Alaska State Library has compiled a 301-page guide *Alaska Newspapers on Microfilm, 1866–1998*, which is available for download on the Alaska State Library website. The films to all the newspapers are available from the Alaska State Library through interlibrary loan. An index to vital records extracted from various Fairbanks newspapers is *Index of Births, Deaths, Marriages and Divorces in Fairbanks, Alaska Newspapers, 1903–1930* (Anchorage: Alaska Historical Commission Studies in History, 1986). The index was compiled by members of the Fairbanks Genealogical Society who utilized the following newspapers: *Fairbanks News; Fairbanks Evening News; Fairbanks Daily News;* and the *Fairbanks Daily News Miner.*

The Alaskan, a newspaper published in Sitka, has been indexed in Robert N. DeArmond, *Subject Index to The Alaskan, 1885–1907, A Sitka Newspaper* (Juneau: Alaska Division of State Libraries, 1974).

An index to the *Anchorage Daily Times* obituaries (1915–80) and an index to the newspapers in Petersburg are on file at the Rasmuson Library in Fairbanks.

Several newspapers were published by the Alaskan native population, some of which are on file at the Oregon Historical Society in Portland (see Oregon—Archives, Libraries, and Societies). For additional information on these newspapers, see Daniel F. Littlefield, Jr., and James W. Parins, *American Indian and Alaska Native Newspapers and Periodicals, 1826–1924* (Westport, Conn.: Greenwood Press, 1984).

Manuscripts

The microfilm collection of the Russian Orthodox Church Archives provides historical materials as well as the church's parish registers. These Alaska diocesan records are divided into eight basic series (see Church Records). Because of the lack of early Alaska record sources, this is a major collection.

Although the Russians left Alaska in 1867, they had a small consulate in Nome. Their records are filed with the Seattle Russian Consulate (for additional details on these records, see Hawaii—Periodicals, Newspapers, and Manuscript Collections).

The Alaska and Polar Regions Department of the Rasmuson Library, University of Alaska, Fairbanks, is a major repository in Alaska. The library attempts to collect at least one copy of everything ever printed on Alaska.

Manuscript collections outside of Alaska include the Governor Brady Collection at Yale University, New Haven, Connecticut. This collection consists of the early records of the unofficial town government of Sitka. The Yale library also has most of the early maps showing the exploration of the Alaskan coast. The Library of Congress (see page 13) has the Russian-American Company Papers (1786–1830), which relate to the exploration and colonization of Alaska (MS 63-410).

Sheldon Jackson was the U.S. General Agent for education in Alaska. His papers, known as the Sheldon Jackson Collection, mainly consist of correspondence and cover the period from 1885 to 1907. This collection provides historical accounts of education in Alaska and its teachers and is deposited at the Presbyterian Historical Society in Philadelphia with microfilm copies at the FHL.

Archives, Libraries, and Societies

Alaska Historical Society
P.O. Box 100299
Anchorage, AK 99510
www.alaskahistoricalsociety.org

Alaska State Archives and Record Management Services
141 Willoughby Ave.
Juneau, AK 99801-1720
www.archives.state.ak.us

Consortium Library, University of Alaska, Anchorage
3211 Providence Dr.
Anchorage, AK 99508
www.lib.uaa.alaska.edu/archives

E.E. Rasmuson Library
Alaska and Polar Region Collection
310 Tanana Dr.
University of Alaska, Fairbanks
Fairbanks, AK 99775-6800
www.uaf.edu/library

Alaska State Library—Historical Collections
P.O. Box 110571
Juneau, AK 99811
www.library.state.ak.us/hist/hist.html

Fairbanks Genealogical Society
P.O. Box 60534
Fairbanks, AK 99706

The Alaska GenWeb Project <www.akgenweb.org> has links to the major repositories and genealogical societies in the state. As it is constantly being updated, it is a major resource for Alaska research to stay current.

Special Focus Categories

Immigration

Alaska had six major ports of immigration: Anchorage, Juneau, Ketchikan, Kodiak, Nome, and Sitka. No passenger arrival

records have currently been located. The 1898 gold rush to the Yukon, along with the impending Yukon-Alaska boundary disputes, prompted the Canadian government to send two divisions of the mounted police to the Yukon. These divisions, headquartered at Dawson and Whitehorse, maintained registrations of persons and boats entering and leaving the Yukon at various ports. Many of those registered came to Alaska. These records are held at the Public Archives of Canada in Ottawa, Ontario, and the Glenbow-Alberta Institute of Archives, Calgary, Alberta. These have been indexed on various databases including on the Yukon GenWeb Project at <www.rootsweb.com/~canyk/index.html>.

Many people who came during the Alaska Gold Rush in 1898 were never heard from again. Often families were left behind with no knowledge of a husband's or father's whereabouts. One valuable source for locating missing immigrants to Alaska is the Pioneers' Home. Many of these people lived and died in the various Alaska Pioneers' Homes, the Sitka Home being the oldest institution. Other homes were located in Anchorage, Fairbanks, Juneau, Ketchikan, Palmer, and Sitka. The Alaska Pioneers' Homes were state agencies and thus transferred permanent records to the state archives. Many of these records are currently on file at the state archives. A listing of the residents as well as the deaths at each home up to 1 October 1920 has been published in Joe H. Ashby, "Alaska's Greatest Institution, The Pioneers' Home," *Illinois State Genealogical Society Quarterly* 13 (Winter 1981): 221–24.

One historical migration from the lower forty-eight took place in 1935. This migration, known as the Matanuska colony, was a government-sponsored relocation of 200 farming families from Michigan, Minnesota, and Wisconsin to the Matanuska Valley near Anchorage. Orlando W. Miller, *The Frontier in Alaska and the Matanuska Colony* (New Haven and London: Yale University Press, 1975), provides an excellent account of this colonization experiment. The National Archives—Pacific Alaska Region has many documents relating to the Matanuska colony. A list of the colonists and their origins in the lower forty-eight can be found on the Internet website "Explore North" <http://explorenorth.com/library/yafeatures/bl-matanuska.htm>.

Naturalization

Residents of Alaska became U.S. citizens when the area was purchased from Russia in 1867. Naturalization and citizenship records for those arriving after that time were filed in the judicial districts. These are also on file at the Alaska State Archives and the FHL, and they include old territorial records of Fairbanks, Juneau, and Nome that have been transferred to the superior court. The National Archives—Pacific Alaska Region has many citizenship records for Alaska. These include declaration of intention (1900–29) and special court orders (1914–32) for Juneau; declaration of intention (1901–17) for Skagway; petition case files (1910–14) for Fairbanks; and petition case files (1910–20) for Iditarod.

Native Alaskan

There are three separate groups of native Alaskans who make up the population. These three tribes are the Athabascan, the Tlingit, and the Haida. The Athabascan tribal area originally covered most of the Alaskan interior, the Tlingit tribe occupied the southeastern and some coastal areas of Alaska, and the Haida tribe was largely confined to the island of Prince of Wales in southeastern Alaska. The major groups of Alaskan Native Americans and their numerous offshoots now number about 22,000 persons.

The native population also consists of those inappropriately called "Eskimos." These groups differ in origin from what could be called the Indians. The Eskimos call themselves Inuit (or Inupiat) and Yupik, all of which mean "people," and number about 50,000. About 8,000 Inuits are Aleuts. The Dawes Act (1924) extended United States citizenship to all Native Americans, including Alaska natives. The Russian Orthodox Church is the predominant religion of the Aleuts, and many other Inuits still practice native religions. A valued collection of Barrow "Eskimo" genealogy is *Genealogical Records of Barrow Eskimo Families*, compiled by Edna MacLean (Barrow, Alaska: Naval Arctic Research Laboratory, 1971), which is on microfiche at the Rasmuson Library (see Archives, Libraries, and Societies) and the FHL. Many Native Alaskan records are available, including the Juneau Area Agency records (1905–64), which are at the National Archives—Pacific Alaska Region and on microfilm at the FHL. These records include such things as student case files, welfare case files, and individual accounts. Juneau Agency School records (1927–52) include school censuses, applications, village histories, age lists of village children, and village censuses.

Another valuable collection that should be examined when conducting Native Alaskan research is the Oregon Province Archives of the Society of Jesus Alaska Mission Collection. This massive collection of records covers twenty-four Jesuit mission stations in Alaska between 1886 and 1955. The mission records typically generated by these Jesuit missions include diaries, censuses, and church records for the native population.

Mission stations included in this massive collection are Akularak, Andreafsky, Bethel District, Chaniliut, Dillingham, Douglas, Eagle, Fairbanks, Holy Cross, Hooper Bay, Juneau, Kashunuk, Ketchikan, King Island and Little Diomede, Kokrines, Kotzebue, Mountain Village, Nome, Nulato, Pilgrim Springs, Pilot Station, St. Michael, Southeast Alaska (Cordova, Seward, Sitka, Skagway, Valdez, and Wrangell), and Tanana.

This collection is on file at the Oregon Province Archives, Crosby Library, Gonzaga University, in Spokane, Washington, with microfilm copies available. For a guide to the microfilm

version of these collections, refer to Robert C. Carriker, Jennifer Ann Boharski, Eleanor R. Carriker, and Clifford A. Carroll, *Guide to the Microfilm Edition of the Oregon Province Archives of the Society of Jesus Alaska Mission Collection* (Spokane, Wash.: Gonzaga University, 1980).

A valuable book in the study of the native Alaskans is June Helms, *The Indians of the Subarctic: A Critical Bibliography* (Bloomington: Indiana University Press, n.d.). This bibliography provides many sources concerning culture, individual tribes, and historical and contemporary issues.

In researching Native Alaskan dispersals, the following major sources should not be overlooked: Indian Agency records of British Columbia, the Yukon, and Washington State; the Chemawa Indian School (see Oregon Chapter under "Native American Records"); and early Catholic parish records of Washington State.

The search for Native dispersals should also stretch as far east as Manitoba, Canada. A Manitoba source that should not be overlooked is D.N. Sprague and R.P. Frye's work, *The Genealogy of the First Metis Nation: The Development and Dispersal of the Red River Settlement, 1820–1900* (Winnipeg, Manitoba: Pemmican Publications, 1983).

District Resources

Alaska does not have counties; instead there are fourteen divisions called municipalities and boroughs, and another thirteen Alaska Native Claims Settlement Act Corporations (ANCSA). These twenty-seven divisions were created after statehood. Many of the original district records are deposited at the State Archives or the National Archives—Pacific Alaska Region (see page 12).

The State of Alaska website has an "Alaska Division of Elections" with contact information to cities and boroughs that is updated regularly <www.gov.state.ak.us/ltgov/elections/munis.htm>. The Alaska local government municipalities and boroughs are as follows:

Municipalities and Boroughs

Aleutians East Borough
P.O. Box 349
Sand Point, AK 99661
Incorporation Date: 1987
www.aleutianseast.org

Municipality of Anchorage
P.O. Box 196650
Anchorage, AK 99519–6650
Incorporation Date: 1975
www.muni.org

Bristol Bay Borough
P.O. Box 189
Naknek, AK 99633
Incorporation Date: 1962
www.theborough.com

Denali Borough
P.O. Box 480
Healy, AK 99743
www.denaliborough.govoffice.com

Fairbanks North Star Borough
P.O. Box 71267
Fairbanks, AK 99707
Incorporation Date: 1964
www.co.fairbanks.ak.us

Haines Borough
P.O. Box 1049
Haines, AK 99827
Incorporation Date: 1968
www.cityofhaines.org

City and Borough of Juneau
155 S. Seward St.
Juneau, AK 99801
Incorporation Date: 1970
www.juneau.org

Kenai Peninsula Borough
144 N. Binkley St.
Soldotna, AK 99669
Incorporation Date: 1964
www.borough.kenai.ak.us

Ketchikan Gateway Borough
344 Front St.
Ketchikan, AK 99901
Incorporation Date: 1963
www.borough.ketchikan.ak.us

Kodiak Island Borough
710 Mill Bay Rd.
Kodiak, AK 99615
Incorporation Date: 1963
www.kib.co.kodiak.ak.us

Lake and Peninsula Borough
P.O. Box 495
King Salmon, AK 99613
Incorporation Date: 1989
http://www.lakeandpen.com/

Matanuska-Susitna Borough
350 E. Dahlia Ave.
Palmer, AK 99645
Incorporation Date: 1964
www.co.mat-su.ak.us

North Slope Borough
P.O. Box 69
Barrow, AK 99723
Incorporation Date: 1972
www.co.north-slope.ak.us

Northwest Arctic Borough
P.O. Box 1110
Kotzebue, AK 99752
Incorporation Date: 1986
www.northwestarcticborough.org

City and Borough of Sitka
100 Lincoln St.
Sitka, AK 99835
Incorporation Date: 1971
www.cityofsitka.com

City and Borough of Yakutat
P.O. Box 160
Yakutat, AK 99689

Alaska Native Claims Settlement Act Corporations

ANCSA Regional Corporations
Ahtna, Inc.
P.O. Box 649
Glennallen, AK 99588

Aleut Corporation
One Aleut Plaza, Ste. 300
4000 Old Seward Hwy, Ste. 300
Anchorage, AK 99503
www.aleutcorp.com

Arctic Slope Regional Corporation
P.O. Box 129
Barrow, AK 99723
www.asrc.com/intro.html

Bering Straits Native Corporation
P.O. Box 1008
Nome, AK 99762
www.beringstraits.com

Bristol Bay Native Corporation
800 Cordova St,. Ste. 200
Anchorage, AK 99501-6299
www.bbnc.net

Calista Corporation
301 Calista Court, Ste. A
Anchorage, AK 99518-3028
www.calistacorp.com

Chugach Alaska Corporation
560 E. 34th Ave.
Anchorage, AK 99503
www.chugach-ak.com

Cook Inlet Region, Inc.
2525 "C" St., Ste. 500
Anchorage, AK 99509-3330
www.ciri.com

Doyon, Ltd.
1 Doyon Pl., Ste. 300
Fairbanks, AK 99701
www.doyon.com

Koniag, Inc.
4300 B. St., Ste. 407
Anchorage, AK 99503
www.koniag.com/koniag/index.cfm

NANA Corporation
P.O. Box 49
Kotzebue, AK 99752
www.nana.com

Sealaska Corporation
One Sealaska Plaza, Ste. 400
Juneau, AK 99801
www.sealaska.com

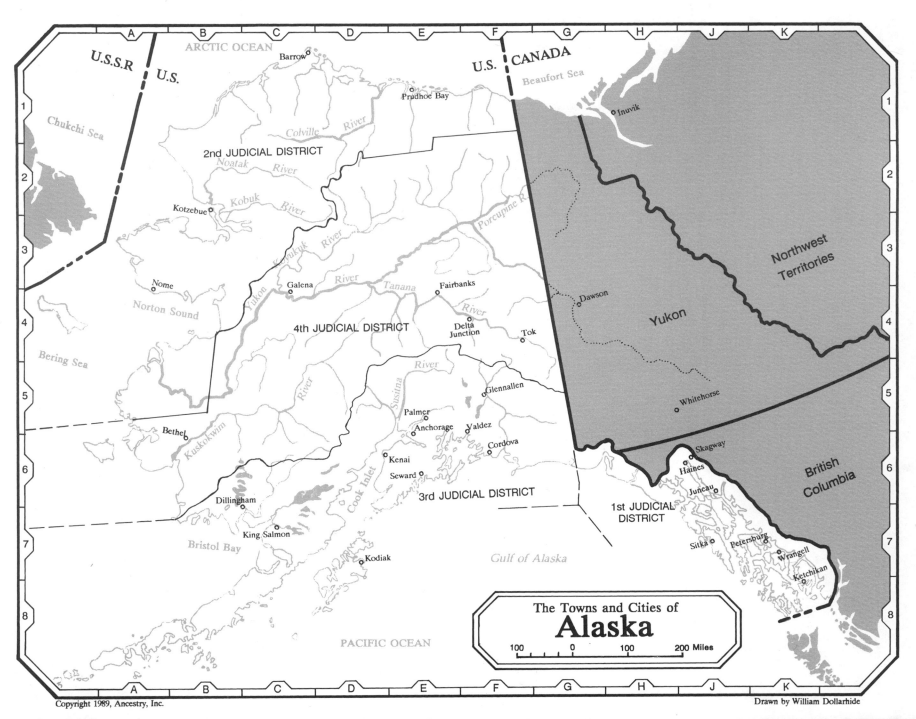

The Towns and Cities of
Alaska

100 0 100 200 Miles

Drawn by William Dollarhide

44

ALASKA

U.S.S.R.

U.S.

ARCTIC OCEAN

Chukchi Sea

U.S. CANADA

Beaufort Sea

Barrow

Prudhoe Bay

Inuvik

Colville River

2nd JUDICIAL DISTRICT

Noatak River

Kobuk River

Kotzebue

Porcupine R.

Northwest
Territories

Nome

Norton Sound

Galena

Koyukuk River

Yukon River

River

Tanana River

Fairbanks

Delta Junction

Tok

Dawson

Yukon

Bering Sea

4th JUDICIAL DISTRICT

Kuskokwim River

Susitna River

River

Glennallen

Whitehorse

Bethel

Palmer

Anchorage

Valdez

Cordova

Northwest
Territories

Kenai

Seward

Cook Inlet

3rd JUDICIAL DISTRICT

Skagway

Haines

Juneau

British
Columbia

Dillingham

1st JUDICIAL
DISTRICT

King Salmon

Bristol Bay

Kodiak

Gulf of Alaska

Sitka

Petersburg

Wrangell

Ketchikan

PACIFIC OCEAN

Arizona

DWIGHT A. RADFORD AND NELL SACHSE WOODARD

Although early Spanish explorers came into what is present-day Arizona in the middle 1500s, it was considerably later before settlement began. Under the Spanish crown, an area extending south from the Gila River (corresponding to that portion which became part of the Gadsden Purchase) was part of the Primeria Alta (land of the Upper Pima), which included the northern part of Sonora in Mexico.

In their search for the fabled cities of gold, Spanish expeditions encountered the Hopi and Zuni, sandstone villages of centuries-old, cliff-dwelling civilizations, and the more recently arrived nomadic Apache and Navajo. Governor Diego Ortiz Parilla established a fort at Tubac in 1753, and Tucson was founded in 1775. Marauding Apaches later forced the Spanish out of the region, although Tucson remained under a Mexican flag until the 1840s. Garrisons occupied the presidios at Tucson, Tubac, and Santa Cruz beginning in 1826, with their surrounding settlements precarious because the Apache had not conceded the frontier to Mexico.

Mexico's independence from Spain in 1821, and the Mexican War (1846–48), provided the opportunity for the United States to acquire the region north of the Gila River. The Gadsden Purchase in 1853 added the area south of the river. Both were part of the New Mexico Territory until the Arizona Territory was separated from it in 1863.

Treks to the west for California's gold, primarily along Cooke's Wagon Route in the south, brought some settlement to the territory, principally along the Gila and Santa Cruz rivers. The Civil War produced only minor skirmishes, while the intensity of conflict between the Apache and the newly forming mining, cattle ranching, and trading establishments heated up in the two decades following the war. Railroad lines between Albuquerque, New Mexico, and San Bernardino, California, included a stop at Flagstaff in the northern part of the territory. As part of the network of transportation from east to west, more people entered the territory.

The history of Arizona's frontier days has been often chronicled on television and in the movies, not always accurately. Tombstone, Cochise and Geronimo, the O.K. Corral, and the Earp brothers, among others, have left their indelible marks on many, providing a striking contrast to life today in Arizona's suburban developments.

A more populous settlement, and statehood, had to wait until the twentieth century. Arizona became a state in 1912, after a long struggle for that status. The ethnic composition of its population reflects its history. Mexican, Native American (Navajo, Hopi, Havasupai, Yuma, Cocopah, Mohave, Apache, Pima, and Maricopa among them), and those with frontier heritage all comprise a prominent portion of the political and economic life of the state, alongside the more recently arrived health-seekers and retirees from other parts of the United States.

In the recent past, attention has been directed toward preserving, making accessible, and microfilming early Spanish and Mexican records, along with those developed during the territorial and statehood periods.

Vital Records

Arizona began statewide recording of births and deaths in July 1909, though marriage records are still recorded only in the county

clerk of the superior court's office where the marriage occurred. The Office of Vital Records, Arizona Department of Health Services (1818 W. Adams, Phoenix, AZ 85007, mailing address: P.O. Box 3887, Phoenix, AZ 85030-3887) has the originals and can provide certified copies of births and death records. Images of birth certificates (1887–1928) and death certificates (1878–1953) are now online at the Arizona Department of Health Services <http://genealogy.az.gov>. The Arizona State Archives has microfilm of the original births over seventy-five years old and deaths over fifty years old. The Family History Library (FHL) in Salt Lake City has microfilm of Arizona births (1855–1924, 1926). This collection includes state registration from 1909, which made delayed certificates as well as county registration of births prior to 1909. The FHL also has death records (ca. 1870–1949, 1951), which include state registrations from 1909 and earlier county registers.

Divorces may be found in civil court records in the county although responsibility for divorce records in Arizona has varied. Originally part of the Territorial Legislature (1863), it moved to the district courts (see Court Records) during the 1870s. The specific court with the responsibility for divorce records within the superior court has changed over time.

Census Records

Federal

Population Schedules
- Indexed—1860 (Arizona County only), 1870, 1880, 1900, 1910, 1920, 1930
- Soundex—1880, 1900, 1920

Mortality Schedules
- 1870 (Mohave through Yuma counties only), 1880 (index available)

The 1860 federal census contains only that portion of the state below the Gila River (as Arizona County) that was enumerated as part of the New Mexico Territory. People who resided in Pah-Ute County in 1870 were enumerated as part of Pah-Ute County, Nevada, and possibly part of Washington County, Utah.

Territorial and State

Both the 1864 and 1866 territorial censuses are available as well. Original and duplicates of the 1864 territorial census, in addition to being on microfilm, are housed in the Arizona State Archives, which also holds microfilm copies of the 1882 state census available for Cochise, Gila, Graham, Maricopa, Mohave, Pima, Yavapai, and Yuma counties.

Several territorial censuses are indexed at <www.ancestry.com>. These include the 1831 census of Santa Cruz County,

1862, 1866, and 1867 censuses. These are also on microfilm through the FHL. The 1801 Mexican census of Pimeria Alta (the southern pre-territorial portion of Arizona) has been transcribed and published by the Arizona State Genealogical Society (1986). The Mexican census of 1852 of Pimeria Alta in the District of Altar, Sonora has also been transcribed and published by the Arizona State Genealogical Society (1986).

Although not a census, a source that can be used to document people in a similar fashion as a census or tax list would be the "great registers" of voters. These can be used to place a person at a particular place at a particular time and are at the Arizona State Archives, with many on microfilm at the FHL. The following counties are represented: Apache (1884–1910); Cochise (1882–1910); Coconino (1894–1910); Gila (1882–1910); Graham (1882–1911); Maricopa (1876–1938); Mohave (1866–82); Navajo (1895–1932); Pima (1876–1913); Pinal (1894–1911); Santa Cruz (1902–35); Yuma (1882–1910); and Yavapai (1882–1906). The Great Registers allowed people to vote who were white, male, and over twenty-one years of age. In 1913, females and African Americans were allowed to vote, and in 1948, Native Americans were allowed. The 1890 Great Register for the entire Arizona Territory has been indexed and published by the Arizona Genealogical Advisory Board, which provides a viable substitute for the lost 1890 federal enumeration.

Background Sources

Bancroft, Hubert Howe. *The History of Arizona and New Mexico 1530–1888*. Vol.17. San Francisco: History Publishing Co., 1889.

Beers, Henry Putney. *Spanish and Mexican Records of the American Southwest: A Bibliographical Guide to Archive and Manuscript Sources*. Tucson: University of Arizona Press, 1979.

Faulk, Odie B. *Arizona: A Short History*. Norman, Okla.: University of Oklahoma Press, 1970.

Granger, Byrd H. *Will C. Barnes' Arizona Place Names*. Tucson: University of Arizona Press, 1960.

Luckingham, Bradford. *Phoenix: The History of a Southwestern Metropolis* (Tucson: University of Arizona Press, 1989). This is the first comprehensive history of the southwest's largest city.

_____. *Minorities in Phoenix: A Profile of Mexican American, Chinese American, and African American Communities, 1860–1992*. Tucson: University of Arizona Press, 1994. This second work of Luckingham's deals with Phoenix minority studies. It traces the struggles against segregation and discrimination encountered by minorities to their rise and contributions to the Phoenix community. The author draws from newspaper files, statistical data, and oral accounts.

Officer, James E. *Hispanic Arizona, 1536–1856*. Tucson: University of Arizona Press, 1988. This encyclopedic work covers Native American relations, the Mexican War, boundary problems, politics, and the Gadsden Purchase. An important work for background to the subject of Hispanic Arizona.

Powell, Lawrence Clark. *Arizona: A Bicentennial History*. New York: W. W. Norton and Co.; and Nashville: American Association for State and Local History, 1976.

Sheridan, Thomas E. *Arizona: A History*. Tucson: University of Arizona Press, 1995. A modern survey of the state's history including Native Americans, Hispanics, and Anglos.

Wagoner, Jay J. *Early Arizona: Prehistory to Civil War*. Tucson: University of Arizona Press, 1975.

_____. *Arizona Territory, 1863–1912: A Political History*. Tucson: University of Arizona Press, 1970.

Maps

All of the Sanborn maps of Arizona are on microfilm at the Arizona State Archives. County and city maps in various sizes may be purchased from the Arizona Department of Transportation, Highways Division, 1651 W. Jackson St., Phoenix, AZ 85007 <www.dot.state.az.us>.

Map collections are also found at Arizona State University in Tempe and the University of Arizona at Tucson, Arizona 85721. The Arizona Historical Society (see Archives, Libraries, and Societies) lists several thousand maps from the Spanish era to the present.

There are two works that are important for this area of Arizona research. The first is Will C. Barnes's *Arizona Place Names* (Tucson: University of Arizona Press, 1988), which is a reprint of the classic 1935 edition. This work intersperses facts with the state's folklore to help understand place-names in the state. The second resource is Henry P. Walker and Don Bufkin's *Historical Atlas of Arizona*, 2d ed. (Norman: University of Oklahoma Press, 1989), which provides details on the development of the state.

The United States Geological Survey (USGS) has topographical maps of Arizona for sale, which can be found at <www.usgs.gov>. The USGS also has a large map library in Flagstaff that is open for research and is located at the USGS Library, 225 N. Gemini Dr., Flagstaff, AZ 86001. USGS state information can be accessed from the main USGS website (see page 5).

Land Records

Public-Domain State

On 24 February 1863, Arizona became a territory. From 1850 until that date, it was part of New Mexico Territory. In 1866,
what was then Pah-Ute County was ceded to Nevada. Long after its early explorers came in the 1500s, the state had very little settlement, and then only in the area of Tucson.

The wars with Native Americans did not end until 1886 and were a continuing impediment to frontier expansion. For lands granted to the United States in 1848 and for private land claims, write to the National Archives—Southwest Region. In the late 1800s, by the time U.S. authorities authenticated private land claims, fraudulent claims were relatively frequent. In 1960 these private land registers were transferred to the National Archives—Southwest Region. The Pima County Recorder's Office at Tucson should be researched for Gadsden Purchase land records, which also include mission claims.

Arizona is a public-domain state, meaning that land could be acquired directly from the federal government. Arizona was admitted as a territory in 1863, and it was in that year that the U.S. Federal District Land Office opened. Land offices opened in Prescott (1863), Florence and Gila (1873) that moved to Tucson (1881), and Phoenix (1905). The land office in Phoenix replaced all earlier offices. Many of these early land claims were for mining enterprises. Patents, copies of tract books, and plat maps are at the BLM Arizona State Office, 222 N. Central, Phoenix, AZ 85044 <http://azwww.az.blm.gov>. When searching for early land records in Arizona, one needs to include the U.S. Land Office entries at the National Archives—Southwest Region (see page 12), which has mining and homestead surveys, land claims, grazing service records, and rights-of-way claims and settlements for Gila, Salt River, and Navajo Meridians; or the National Archives—Rocky Mountain Region (see page 12), which has land entry case files. When inquiring, indicate the person's name, state of Arizona, and whether it was before 1908. Arizona records prior to 1908 have been alphabetically indexed.

The county recorder for each county has jurisdiction over land records within their respective counties. Before good use can be made of land records in Arizona, the researcher must bear in mind how ownership was acquired. Since Arizona entered the jurisdiction of the United States as part of the New Mexico Territory, where pueblos had already been established, most of the previous claims were recognized by the federal government. In examining land records, it will be normal to find Spanish phrases such as "leagues" and "varas" as units of measurement for surveys. The FHL has microfilm copies of most county land records in Arizona.

Probate Records

Probate records, generated by the legal aspects surrounding a person's death, adoption, or guardianship, are valuable sources

in Arizona for solving numerous problems relating to individuals, families, and family relationships. Probate-related records are located in the offices of the clerk of the superior court.

If a person died testate, meaning that a proper last will and testament was prepared, the estate was heard in the county of residence or where property was held. Intestates (without a will) are filed in the same way. If minor heirs are involved, additional records will be forthcoming, and, depending on the ages of these minors, their names may appear in court records for as long as they remained minors. A search of probate records should include a careful examination of all indexes and cases involving all of the pertinent court records in order to uncover all of the information in these materials. Probate records also handle adoptions. The FHL has microfilm copies of probate records for many counties.

Court Records

Arizona's judicial system is similar to that of other states in this region. Courts start close to their people and progress by steps to more complicated and further removed cases and jurisdiction. The justice of the peace hears civil and small claims, while municipal courts hear town and city violations. Each county has a clerk of the superior courts whose function is to maintain the court calendar and records. The superior courts hear both civil and criminal cases of their own, including divorces, as well as appeals from justices of the peace and municipal (or city magistrate or police) courts in their counties. The supreme court functions statewide and hears extraordinary writs and appeals from the court of appeals, which sits at Phoenix and Tucson, and also hears both writs and appeals from the county superior courts. The FHL has microfilm copies of many court records for many counties.

Tax Records

The Arizona State Archives has county tax, license, and assessment rolls for many counties. Some are for a single year, and others are for consecutive years. For specifics on lists available, refer to the archives' printed *Guide,* cited under its listing in Archives, Libraries, and Societies.

Cemetery Records

Three volumes of books published by the Arizona Genealogical Society on cemeteries in the state are located at the Department of Library, Archives, and Public Records, Research Division. The archives also holds more than three hundred sheets of microfiche alphabetically listing people who lived in the state thirty years or

more prior to their death. It is derived from an index to obituaries recorded mainly in Phoenix newspapers, but covering deaths from all over the state between 1865 and 1986.

The US GenWeb Project has a growing transcription database from cemeteries throughout the state. It can be accessed by county <www.rootsweb.com~cemetery/arizona.html>. Another growing database of Arizona cemetery transcriptions is the website <www.interment.net>.

Church Records

The oldest denomination in the state is the Roman Catholic Church, and it remains the largest today. Spanish efforts to plant missions in Pimeria Alta (Arizona) were abortive well into the 1800s. The Jesuits fell out of favor and were followed by the Franciscans, who fared no better. In 1833 the missions yielded to the Mexican Act of Secularization and succumbed to decay. Only a tiny fraction of vital and historical records are extant. In modern times, the state is served by two dioceses. The Diocese of Phoenix is located at 400 E. Monroe St., Phoenix, AZ 85004-2336 <www.diocesephoenix.org>; and the Diocese of Tucson: 111 S. Church Ave., P.O. Box 31, Tucson, AZ 85702-0031 <www.diocesetucson.org>, Archives: 880 E. 22nd St., Tucson, AZ 85710. The websites for both dioceses have links to individual parishes.

The second largest denomination in the state is The Church of Jesus Christ of Latter-day Saints, or Mormons, who came to the state originally as missionaries from Utah to the Native Americans. However, permanent Mormon colonies were not established until 1877, when settlers arrived and founded towns throughout the state with a major center growing up in Mesa (a modern suburb of Phoenix). These colonies provided the bases from which a predominant Mormon population in parts of the state developed and remain today. All congregation records, mission reports, and genealogical sketches for church members are on microfilm at the FHL. The Church also operates the huge Mesa Family History Center, which has its own building adjoining the Mesa temple grounds and is open to the public. This has developed into a major genealogical library in the state.

The Episcopal Church in the state is served through the Episcopal Diocese of Arizona, 114 W. Roosevelt St., Phoenix, AZ 85003-1406 <www.episcopal-az.org>. The Episcopal presence in the state dates from 1865 when Arizona and Nevada were constructed as a missionary jurisdiction. In 1874 Arizona was separated out. The diocese website has contact information and links to parishes throughout the state.

The United Methodist Church is served through the Desert Southwest District, 1550 E. Meadow Brook Ave., Ste. 200, Phoenix, AZ 85014-4040 <www.desertsw.org>. This district office should be contacted as a starting place for Methodist records.

The Jewish presence in the state has also been strong. The Arizona Jewish Historical Society, 4710 N. Sixteenth St., Ste. 201, Phoenix, AZ 85066 <http://aspin.asu.edu/azjhs> seeks to record the Jewish contribution to the state in areas of politics, economics, social, and cultural history. There are also several major collections that should be considered in Jewish research. The Leona G. and David A. Bloom Southwest Jewish Archives at the University of Arizona Library in Tucson holds a wealth of information on the Jewish experience in West Texas, New Mexico, Arizona, and Southern California. The University of Arizona Library also holds the Rochlia Collection of Arizona Jewish History, which has oral interviews and historical material. Arizona State University holds the Shema Arizona: The Arizona Jewish Historical Society Oral History Project.

Military Records

The Arizona Historical Society has a good collection of government records, including the records of each of the frontier military posts in Arizona, and quartermaster records relating to supply, construction, and equipment of Arizona military posts. The collection has been microfilmed and cross-filed in their card catalog. Members of the society will consult the catalog and supply copies of their materials for a small fee.

State military records are housed at the Arizona State Adjutant General's Office, 5636 E. McDowell Rd., Phoenix, AZ 85008.

There is one roll of NARA microfilm (M532) of the Union Army Volunteers of the Civil War and one roll for Confederate service (M318). These are available on microfilm at the FHL, along with the WWI Draft Registration Cards (1917–18). See also: Melton, Brad and Dan Smith, eds., *Arizona Goes to War: The Home Front and the Front Lines During World War II* (Tucson: University of Arizona, 1995). This work documents the growth of military installations all over the state as thousands of airmen trained and soldiers bound for North Africa came to train in the desert. Also documented is the story of the Native Americans who registered for the draft in record numbers and the unjust incarceration of Japanese Americans in desert detention centers. The war transformed Arizona probably more than any other state.

Periodicals, Newspapers, and Manuscript Collections

Periodicals
Arizona Highways (published by Arizona Department of Transportation) and *Journal of Arizona History* (published by Arizona Historical Society) are located in numerous libraries

around the country. The major genealogical publication in the state is *Copper State Journal*, a publication of the Arizona State Genealogical Society.

Newspapers
The Arizona Historical Society has newspapers on microfilm for Arizona and surrounding states. The Arizona State Archives has a large microfilm collection of newspapers. The Arizona Newspaper Project is a cooperative effort with national organizations to locate, catalog, and microfilm newspapers. The Project is based at the Arizona State Library, Archives, and Public Records. Of the 1,520 newspapers identified, no issues for 136 of them have ever been found. A list of the newspapers that make up the Arizona Newspaper Project is on the Arizona State Library, Archives and Public Records website. See <www.lib.az.us/anp>.

Manuscripts
The most extensive collection of manuscript materials is at the Arizona State Archives and the Arizona State Historical Society.

In the recent past, much attention has been directed toward preserving, making accessible, and microfilming early Spanish and Mexican records. Manuscript collections of much of the material can be found at both repositories.

The Arizona State University Arizona Collection includes papers of politicians, family papers, labor and mining business papers, and collections for the American Indians. They have digitized some of their collections. One such collection being digitized and online is the Hayden Arizona Pioneer Biographies Collection. These can be found at <www.asu.edu/lib/archives>.

Archives, Libraries, and Societies

Arizona State Archives
Department of Library, Archives, and Public Records
State Capitol
1700 W. Washington St.
Phoenix, AZ 85007
www.lib.az.us
A *Guide to Public Records in the Arizona State Archives* is available. Researchers are encouraged to call or write before using the archives to make sure the material they want can be available from off-site storage.

Arizona Historical Society
949 E. Second St.
Tucson, AZ 85719
www.ahs.state.az.us

The society holds a fine collection of 60,000 books and pamphlets, letters, diaries, maps, and newspapers on microfilm. The holdings date from the earliest Spanish colonial period to the present. Their photographic department boasts 250,000 separate items. Each item is cross-referenced in the card catalog.

Arizona State Genealogical Society
P.O. Box 42075
Tucson, AZ 85733
www.rootsweb.com/~asgs/

The Arizona State Genealogical Society website offers an Arizona Research Sources page indicating where records are located statewide. The Special Libraries Association—Arizona Chapter website <www.sla.org/chapter/caz/library.html> has links to library associations statewide.

Mesa Family History Center
41 S. Hobson St.
Mesa, AZ 85204-1021

For researching while in the state, this is a noteworthy repository owned and operated by The Church of Jesus Christ of Latter-day Saints. One of the largest family history centers in the country, it is housed in its own building. Collections include material not found at the FHL.

The Arizona Genealogical Advisory Board website has links to genealogical and historical societies statewide <www.azgab. org>.

Special Focus Categories

Native American

Arizona is home to a large population of Native Americans. These include the Apache, Chemehuevis, Cocopah, Havasupai, Hualapai, Hopi, Kaibab-Paiute, Maricopa, Mojave, Navajo, Pascua Yaqui, Pima, Quechan, Southern Paiute, Tohono O'odham (Papago), and Yavapai. Many tribes belong to the Inter Tribal Council of Arizona: 2214 N. Central Ave., Ste. 100, Phoenix, AZ 85004 <www.itcaonline.com/>. The website has links to the various tribes, historical sketches, current status, and contact information. They are not, however, a research facility.

Scores of records were generated through governmental agencies that had jurisdiction over these tribes. However, records about Arizona Native Americans may be found in agencies outside of the state. For example, the Navajo are a very large tribe and the Navajo Nation covers parts of Arizona, New Mexico, and Utah. Therefore, Navajo-related records may be found in agencies based in these three states. Continuing with the Navajo example, records are deposited at the National Archives regional branches in Denver, Los Angeles, and Washington, D.C. (see pages 11-12). The Navajo records are also scattered between the Western Navajo, Eastern Navajo, and Northern Navajo. Sometimes records will be found in more than one of these offices for the same family; thus, it is important to consider them all. As there is so much crossover between the Arizona and New Mexico Navajos, some New Mexico records are also being listed such as those for Shiprock, New Mexico. Other Navajo records will be found in the records of the Santa Fe Agency (1890–1935) and the Leupp Training School (1915–35), both at the NARA Denver; the Albuquerque School (1890–1960) at the NARA in Denver and Fort Worth; and the Pueblo Bonito (1909–26) at the National Archives in Washington, D.C.

In addition to records under the auspices of the NARA, a large collection of the National Archives Indian agency records is on microfilm at the FHL.

County Resources

Researchers should be aware that many Arizona records pre-date the county formation due to mining claims, grants, territorial court cases, etc.

Current contact information for each county can be found through the State of Arizona website <www.az.gov/webapp/ portal>. The Arizona State Library, Archives, and Public Records website has links to "Accessing Arizona Public Records" with public record and county information.

ARIZONA

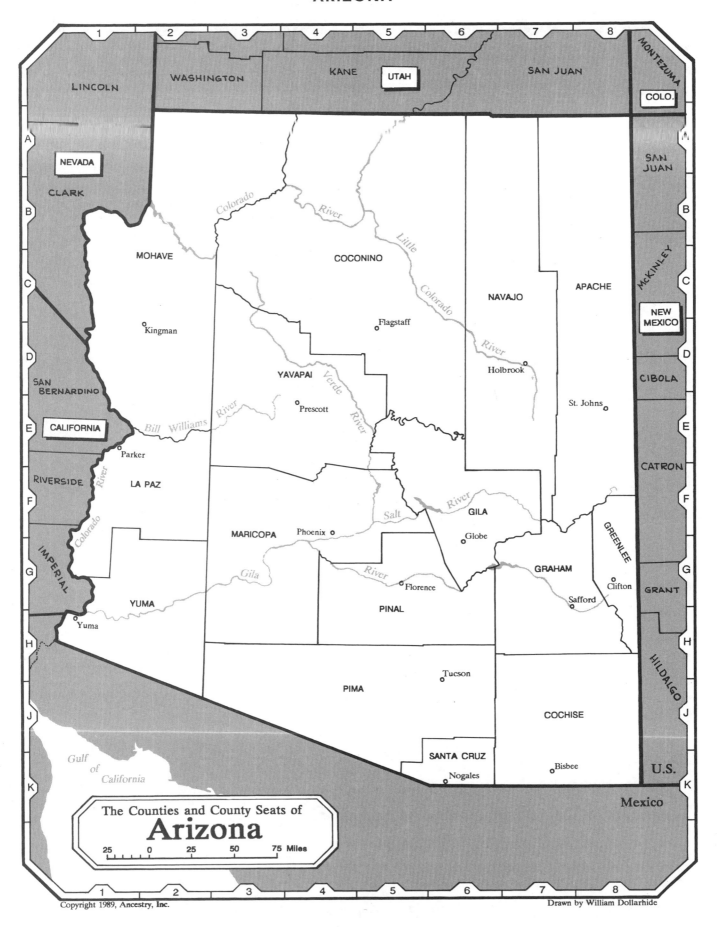

The Counties and County Seats of
Arizona

25 0 25 50 75 Miles

Drawn by William Dollarhide

Map	County Address	Date Formed Parent County/ies	Birth Marriage Death	Land Probate Court
C8	Apache 70 W. 3rd S. St. Johns 85936-0667	1879 Yavapai	1887 1879 1887	1880 1879 1880
	Arizona	1859 (as part of New Mexico Territory; see New Mexico)		
J7	Cochise 1415 W. Melody Lane Bisbee 85603	1881	1887 1881 1887	1866 1880 1881
B4	Coconino 200 N. San Francisco Flagstaff 86001	1891 Yavapai	1892 1891 1892	1891 1892 1891
F6	Gila 1400 E. Ash St. Globe 85501-1483	1881 Maricopa/Pinal	1887 1889 1887	1881 1881 1881
G7	Graham 921 Thatcher Blvd. Safford 85546	1881 Pima/Apache	1889 1881 1889	1881 1881 1881
G8	Greenlee 5th St. & Leonard Clifton 85533	1909 Graham	—— 1911 ——	1881 1911 1911
F1	La Paz 1108 Joshua Ave. Parker 85344-5735	1983 Yuma	—— 1983 ——	1983 1983 1983
F4	Maricopa 301 W. Jefferson Phoenix 85003-2143	1871 Yavapai/Yuma/Pima	1881 1871 1881	1871 1871 1878
C2	Mohave 401 Spring St. Kingman 86401	1864 original	1887 1887 1887	1863 1865 1880
C7	Navajo 100 E. Carter Dr. Holbrook 86025	1895 Apache	1895 1895 1895	1895 1895 1895
	Pah-ute	1865 (abolished; became part of Mohave, 1871) Mohave *See also Pah-ute County in Nevada.*		
J5	Pima 130 W. Congress St. Tucson 85701-1332	1864 original *Territorial capital 1867–77, including all of Gadsden Purchase of 1854 in Arizona.*	1889 1872 1889	1866 1864 1864
G5	Pinal 31 N. Pinal St. Florence 85232	1875 Pima/Yavapai	1887 1875 1887	1875 1875 1883
K6	Santa Cruz 2150 N. Congress Dr. Nogales 85621-1090	1899 Pima	1903 1899 1903	1864 1899 1912
D3	Yavapai 120 S. Cortez Prescott 86301	1864 original	1887 1865 1887	1864 1864 1865
G1	Yuma 168 S. Second Ave. Yuma 85364-2363	1864 original	1888 1864 1888	1864 1864 1864

Arkansas

WENDY BEBOUT ELLIOTT, Ph.D., FUGA

Geographically located north of Louisiana and flanked on the east by the Mississippi River's west bank, the development of the state of Arkansas spanned three centuries. Long before frontiersmen from the newly formed United States crossed the Blue Ridge Mountains and attempted settlement along the Ohio and Mississippi rivers, Spanish and French explorers came upon the native peoples living in what is now Arkansas. In 1541 Hernando de Soto's Spanish expedition crossed the Mississippi River to Arkansas, spending several months in the area.

During the seventeenth century, French explorers made their way through today's Arkansas. A small French expedition of two canoes from Canada voyaged down the Mississippi River to Arkansas in 1673, led by Jacques Marquette, a Catholic priest, and Louis Joliet, a fur trader. LaSalle's expedition followed nearly ten years later, claiming the land for France. In 1686, Henri de Tonti founded Arkansas Post, the first settlement in the lower Mississippi River Valley. It served as a trading post, a way station for Mississippi River travel, and the home of a Jesuit mission for a few years. The French later established several settlements south of the Arkansas Post in 1699, including Natchez and Orleans.

Prior to France's decisive defeat by Britain in the Seven Years War (or French and Indian War), in 1762 France ceded to Spain both New Orleans and land west of the Mississippi River, which eventually became the Louisiana Purchase. The Spanish began governing the area in 1766, but their authority was not firmly established for several years. Arkansas Post remained the center of administration for the District of Arkansas, a huge, undefined region, including all of present-day Arkansas and

Oklahoma. The area was supervised by a lieutenant governor at St. Louis.

Settlers from the British colonies, preoccupied with severing their ties from the Crown, had not yet broken through the Blue Ridge Mountains to the east. Once independence was won, however, the land formerly held by Native Americans became "fair game" for grants to those who had served their new country well in battle. Because of this, settlers—the majority from Kentucky and Tennessee—began to increase in number, making their homes along the rivers of eastern and southern Arkansas. By 1792, early settlements had cropped up at Big Prairie, near the mouth of the St. Francis River, and present-day Helena, though inhabitants were few.

Following the Louisiana Purchase in 1803, Arkansas settlements officially came under United States jurisdiction as part of Louisiana Territory. In June 1812, Arkansas became part of Missouri Territory as a result of Louisiana's admittance to the union.

The northern quarter of Arkansas was established as part of the New Madrid District in Louisiana Territory. Directly to the south and running to the Arkansas River, an area shaped like a mirror image of Virginia formed the District of Arkansas. Both districts became counties when Missouri Territory was created. The remaining half of Arkansas, located on the southern side of the Arkansas River, was claimed by Native Americans.

The Osage and Quapaw had resided in the area from a much earlier time, while the Cherokee and Choctaw received land grants from the federal government for land in Arkansas, having been forced out of their homelands in the east. Delaware,

Shawnee, Caddo, and other native tribes made Arkansas their home. The Quapaw claimed the land south of the Arkansas River for approximately 100 miles and indefinitely to the west. The Osage had claimed a large region north of the Arkansas River, and in 1808 ceded land that became part of the District of Arkansas, then still part of Louisiana Territory. Treaties with the Osage chiefs were made again in 1816, 1818, and 1825, resulting in the loss of their Arkansas land and their removal to today's Oklahoma.

Two million acres, situated between the Arkansas and St. Francis rivers, were offered as bounty land for military service in the War of 1812. Each veteran was given a warrant for 160 acres, allocated by a lottery process.

An 1818 conference between the Osage and Cherokee met with Major William Lovely, Cherokee agent in Missouri Territory, resulting in the Osage ceding lands they had held in the northeastern section of present-day Oklahoma and a northwestern portion of today's Arkansas, at the time still part of Missouri Territory.

Arkansas Territory was organized from Missouri Territory in 1819 with a little over 14,000 inhabitants, exclusive of native peoples. All of present-day Oklahoma except the panhandle was included. Arkansas Post was designated as the capital. Lands formerly belonging to the Cherokee nation were organized as Crawford County. Little Rock became the capital in 1821. As the territory continued to develop between 1819 and 1836, more cession agreements between native tribes in Arkansas and the United States government opened the land to further settlement and eventual statehood.

Arkansas became the twenty-fifth state in 1836. Following the Panic of 1837, many people moved into Arkansas from both southern and eastern states. Men from Arkansas served in the U.S. Army during the Mexican War, some receiving bounty lands prior to 1855. The Gold Rush in California attracted people from Arkansas; most began the trek from Fort Smith.

During the Civil War, Arkansas men served in both the Union and Confederate armies, although the greater majority served for the Confederate cause. In May 1861, after Arkansas seceded from the United States, the Provisional Congress of the Confederate States of America divided Arkansas into eastern and western districts, with governmental seats at Little Rock and Van Buren, respectively. Federal forces occupied Van Buren in late 1862 and took control of Little Rock on 10 September 1863, forcing the state government to relocate to Washington in Hempstead County during the occupation. By late 1863, Confederates were forced into southwestern Arkansas, leaving most of Arkansas under Union control with subsequent raiding and plundering by Union troops.

One of the many campaigns and skirmishes fought on Arkansas soil was at Pea Ridge in Benton County in 1862.

Among later ones were those at Fort Smith, Little Rock, Prairie Grove, and Pine Bluff.

During the strife, some families moved and others sent their sons to Texas to avoid the difficulties. Some families from northwestern Arkansas migrated north into Missouri and Illinois to escape the conflict. Others moved west to Kansas and as far north as Minnesota. After the close of the war, Arkansas tried to attract European immigrants. Some settled on the rich land located between the Arkansas and White rivers. The development of railroads in the last quarter of the nineteenth century encouraged more foreign-born immigration. Immigration continued into the twentieth century, but the population remained predominantly rural, with an economy reliant on cotton, until after World War II. African Americans, many with ancestors who have been part of Arkansas history from the territorial period, make up about one-fifth of the population.

Vital Records

Statewide registration of births and deaths in Arkansas did not begin until February 1914. Compliance was not complete for approximately three decades. The Division of Vital Records, Arkansas Department of Health, 4815 W. Markham St., Little Rock, AR 72201, has records from that date. Some local vital records for Little Rock and Fort Smith are maintained by the Arkansas History Commission (see Archives, Libraries, and Societies). When requesting copies, include a statement of purpose and your relationship. Delayed birth certificates are also available.

In addition to death records noted in newspapers (see Manuscripts, Newspapers, and Periodicals), Arkansas Genealogical Society's *Masonic Deaths in Arkansas, 1838–1916* (Hot Springs: Arkansas Genealogical Society, 1999) contains abstracts and supplemented data compiled from annual proceedings of the Grand Lodge. See also vital record resources published by Desmond Walls Allen through Arkansas Research, Inc. <www.arkansasresearch.com>.

Statewide registration of marriage did not begin until 1917, but once counties were organized, most of them began recording marriages. The Division of Vital Records maintains marriage records only since 1917. Earlier records must be obtained from the respective county clerk where the license was issued, which is frequently the county of the bride's residence. Many early marriage records include names of bride and groom, ages, and residence. Later records contain more information. The Arkansas History Commission has indexes to marriage records on microfiche for the years 1933–39. These are marriages reported to the Arkansas Health Department, alphabetically arranged by groom's names and referenced by the county in which the marriage was recorded.

Full certified copies of divorce records may be obtained from the circuit or chancery clerk in the respective county in which the divorce was granted. Records of divorces granted beginning in 1923 are also available from the Division of Vital Records. The Arkansas History Commission has an index to some Arkansas divorce records reported to the Arkansas Health Department on microfiche (1923–27 and 1934–39).

Many county vital records have been microfilmed by the Family History Library (FHL) in Salt Lake City; copies are held by the Arkansas History Commission. To access the microfilm number and determine which records have been microfilmed, see the FHL catalog or <www.ark-ives.com/selected_materials/index.php>.

Census Records

Federal

Population Schedules
- Indexed—1830, 1840, 1850, 1860, 1870, 1880, 1900, 1910, 1920, 1930
- Soundex—1880, 1900, 1910 (Miracode), 1920, 1930

Industry and Agriculture Schedules
- 1850, 1860, 1870, 1880

Mortality Schedules
- 1850, 1860, 1870, 1880

Slave Schedules
- 1850, 1860

The Arkansas History Commission has an excellent collection of compiled and/or published federal censuses and census indexes for most of the state's counties in addition to microfilm copies of all federal censuses for the state. The original agriculture, industry, and mortality schedules are maintained by the Special Collections Library of the University of Arkansas (see Archives, Libraries, and Societies). Microfilm copies of the agriculture, industry, mortality, and slave schedules are housed at the Arkansas History Commission. Originals of the slave schedules are at the National Archives. Arkansas mortality schedules have been indexed and published (1850–80) in Bobbi Jones McLane, *Mortality Schedules for Arkansas*, 4 vols. (Hot Springs, Ark.: Arkansas Ancestors, 1968–75).

The Arkansas Genealogical Society (see Archives, Libraries, and Societies) sponsored a statewide program to reconstruct the missing 1890 federal census with compilations of tax and other local records for that period. Many of these have been published by the individual counties. The Arkansas Genealogical Society should be contacted for the current status of the project. An

example of one of the better compilations is Nancy L. Matthews, *1890 Tax Receipts, Real Estate Tax, Personal Property Tax and Poll Tax, Craighead County, Arkansas* (Jonesboro, Ark.: the author, 2002).

Recent publications as a result of this project include Margaret Hubbard, *Pulaski County, Arkansas 1890 After Reconstruction: A Sesquicentennial Project* (Hot Springs, Ark.: the author, 1987). This compilation includes both northern and southern districts of the county and was compiled from tax assessment records. Additionally, the 1893 tax assessment rolls for the southern district are included in this volume. Some reconstructions of the 1890 census have been published by others, such as Billie W. New's *Bradley County, Arkansas, 1890* (Jacksonville, Ark.: the author, 1988).

A source developed from 1850 federal population census information was originally published in 1958–60 in *Genealogical Newsletter* (Washington, D.C.: Waldenmaier, 1956–60). Inez Waldenmaier, *Arkansas Travelers* (Washington, D.C.: the author, n.d.) contains the names of each man in every Arkansas county in 1850 who was sixty years old or older.

Territorial and State

A collection of French and Spanish records that lists early Europeans in Arkansas (1686–1804) is Morris S. Arnold and Dorothy Jones Core, comps. and eds., *Arkansas Colonials* (Gillett, Ark.: Grand Prairie Historical Society, 1986).

Federal territorial census records for 1810 included those settlements in the Arkansas District of Hopefield (West Memphis), St. Francis, and settlements along the Arkansas River, but these enumerations were lost. The 1820 federal territorial census included Miller County, which was organized that year by the Arkansas territorial government but actually was partially in Texas under Spanish control. This census was also lost.

Arkansas Territory sheriffs were directed to enumerate the citizens biennially beginning in 1823. Although these censuses were recorded in 1823, 1825, and 1827, only the 1823 schedule for Arkansas County remains of the three early enumerations. The 1829 sheriff's census includes the name of the head of household, but only fragments remain. Those counties for which complete returns are available are Arkansas, Chicot, Clark, Conway, Crawford, Crittenden, Independence, Lawrence, Miller (old), St. Francis, and Washington. None are available for Pope or Sevier counties, and only the total number of inhabitants was submitted by the sheriffs of Hempstead, Izard, Lafayette, Phillips, and Pulaski counties. The extant 1823 and 1829 records have been published as Ronald Vern Jackson and Gary Ronald Teeples, eds., *Arkansas Sheriff's Censuses: 1823 & 1829* (Salt Lake City: Accelerated Indexing Systems, n.d.).

Background Sources

Excellent, comprehensive discussions of Arkansas history are available and were used in developing the material in this chapter. John L. Ferguson and J. H. Atkinson, *Historic Arkansas* (Little Rock: Arkansas History Commission, 1966) and John Gould Fletcher, *Arkansas* (Chapel Hill: University of North Carolina Press, 1947) are two excellent single-volume treatments of all periods of Arkansas history.

Probably the best reference for genealogists is Rhonda S. Norris, *Arkansas Links: A Comprehensive Guide to Genealogical Research in the Natural State* (Russellville, Ark.: Arkansas Genealogical Research, 1999). Arranged by counties, it provides reference information for maps, city directories, county histories, land patents, and newspapers, as well as census, county, land, church, cemetery, marriage, military, vital records, and an invaluable bibliography.

Other helpful reference works include the Arkansas Genealogical Society's *Original Resource Directory*, 5th ed., updated and revised (Hot Springs, Ark.: Arkansas Genealogical Society, 2000), and *The WPA Guide to 1930s Arkansas: Compiled by Workers of the Writers' Program of the Work Projects Administration in the State of Arkansas*, with a new introduction by Elliott West (Lawrence, Kans.: University of Kansas, 1987).

Several regionally based volumes of biographical and historical information on Arkansas and its people were published by Goodspeed Publishing Company in the late 1880s. These volumes, reprinted in 1978 by Southern Historical Press, are divided into the following regions: East, West, Northeast, Northwest (which included the Ozark region), and South. The counties of Baxter, Boone, Cleburne, Marion, Newton, Searcy, Stone, and Van Buren in the Ozark region of the state are only briefly covered in the Northwest volume.

Originally published in 1864 and recently released is William Baxter, *Pea Ridge and Prairie Grove*, with an introduction by William L. Shea (Fayetteville: University of Arkansas Press, 2000). This invaluable primary source provides background information concerning civilians in Arkansas during the Civil War.

Many histories have been published for Arkansas counties. Copies of these are in the Arkansas History Commission, which maintains two alphabetical card files—one biographical and the other on subject/place—abstracted from primary sources and published volumes. These cards note names, dates, places, and sources in various works pertaining to Arkansas and its people.

Numerous works are helpful in developing an understanding of Arkansas, including:

Carter, Clarence Edwin, comp. and ed. *The Territorial Papers of the United States: The Territory of Arkansas, 1819–1825.* Vol. 19. Washington, D.C.: Government Printing Office, 1953.

———. *The Territorial Papers of the United States: The Territory of Arkansas, 1825–1829.* Vol. 20. Washington, D.C.: Government Printing Office, 1953.

———. *The Territorial Papers of the United States: The Territory of Arkansas, 1829–1836.* Vol. 21. Washington, D.C.: Government Printing Office, 1953.

Dillard, Tom W., and Michael B. Dougan, comps. *Arkansas History: A Selected Research Bibliography.* Little Rock: Rose Publishers, 1979. A valuable list of publications pertaining to the state.

Hallum, John. *Biographical and Pictorial History of Arkansas, 1887.* Reprint. Easley, S.C.: Southern Historical Press, n.d. Early history of the state and its pioneers.

Hempstead, Fay. *Historical Review of Arkansas, 1911.* Reprint. Easley, S.C.: Southern Historical Press, 1977.

Herndon, Dallas Tabor. *Centennial History of Arkansas, 1922.* 3 vols. Reprint. Easley, S.C.: Southern Historical Press, 1977. Volume 1 is general history; volumes 2 and 3 are biographical sketches.

———. *Annals of Arkansas, 1947: A Narrative....* 4 vols. Hopkinsville, Ark.: Historical Records Association, 1947. A continuation of the above three volumes by Herndon.

Shinn, Josiah Hazen. *Pioneers and Makers of Arkansas.* 1908. Reprint. Baltimore: Genealogical Publishing Co., 1967. Basic reference for Arkansas researchers.

Thomas, David Yancey, ed. *Arkansas and Its People, A History, 1541–1930.* 4 vols. New York: American Historical Society, 1930. A detailed historical work with biographical information.

Writers' Program, WPA, Arkansas. *Arkansas: A Guide to the State.* New York: n.p., 1941. Contains historical data and an excellent bibliography.

Maps

The Arkansas State Highway Commission, in cooperation with the U.S. Department of Agriculture, prepared a complete set of Arkansas county maps entitled *General Highway and Transportation Maps of Counties of Arkansas* (n.p., n.d.). These detailed maps show such landmarks as roads, cemeteries, towns, railroads, watercourses, dwellings, farms, churches, schools, businesses, factory or industrial plants, and sawmills for each county in the state. Copies of this softbound compilation, no longer available for purchase, are available for research at the Arkansas History Commission, which also houses a fine collection of maps pertaining to Arkansas. Copies of a few of these are included in Norris' *Arkansas Links* (see Background Sources).

Copies of individual county maps and reproductions of old Arkansas maps may be obtained from the Arkansas State

Highway and Transportation Department, Map Sales, P.O. Box 2261, Little Rock, Arkansas 72203. A large collection of maps, atlases, and gazetteers for Arkansas and other states is maintained by the University of Arkansas at Fayetteville (see Archives, Libraries, and Societies).

Other helpful map sources include:

Arkansas Encyclopedia. 4 vols. Little Rock: Arkansas Industrial Development Commission, 1968. An industrial history and economic atlas.

Baker, Russell Pierce. *From Memdag to Norsk: A Historical Directory of Arkansas Post Offices, 1832–1971.* Hot Springs, Ark.: Arkansas Genealogical Society, 1988.

————. *Township Atlas of Arkansas, 1819–1930.* Revised. Hot Springs, Ark.: Arkansas Genealogical Society, 2003. Data taken from federal census, "Civil Appointment" in the secretary of state's office, and county court records. Includes township location, date of formation and changes in name, and area covered.

————. *Arkansas Township Atlas: A History of the Minor Civil Divisions in Each Arkansas County.* Hot Springs, Ark.: Arkansas Genealogical Society, 1989.

Land Records

Public-Domain State

When Missouri Territory, encompassing the present state of Arkansas, was established in 1812, the United States government agreed to acknowledge private land previously granted by Spain and Mexico. Two grants were also awarded to previous French claims.

The largest percentage of Spanish and Mexican grants were located in the present-day counties of Arkansas and Desha. Preemption rights were acknowledged in 1814, and private land claims were heard by land commissions. Spanish control of land was loose, and many officials and landowners failed to comply with regulations, resulting in continuous claim problems, some extending for forty years after statehood. At times, no surveys were conducted for these grants. Frequently forgeries were made of the governor's signature on land grants, resulting in a high percentage of fraudulent claims. Early Spanish land claims and the original tract book are available at the National Archives and the FHL (see *Territorial Papers* references in Background Sources).

A French measurement term used in some Spanish grants is "arpents"; one arpent is a little more than four-fifths of an acre. Most early land grants to heads of household were for parcels of 800 arpents, or approximately sixty-eight acres. An additional parcel of fifty arpents or about forty-two acres was awarded for each child.

Between 1803 and 1836, Native Americans were forced to cede their lands in Arkansas and move west. As the federal government acquired land, it was made available for settlement. Territorial land transactions began in 1803 for the Arkansas District (which was part of Louisiana Territory until 1812 when the district became part of Missouri Territory) and again in 1819, when the district became Arkansas Territory. *First Settlers of the Missouri Territory,* 2 vols. (Nacogdoches, Tex.: Ericson Books, 1983), lists early land grants in Arkansas. An index, arranged by county in several volumes, is available for those who acquired land through the Bureau of Land Management (BLM): Sherida K. Eddlemon, *Index to the Arkansas General Land Office, 1820–1907* (Bowie, Md.: Heritage Publishers, various dates). Originally negotiated by William Lovely as cession land, Lovely purchase donation claims generated from the private sale of land for the present-day area of northwest Arkansas are grouped and microfilmed along with disputed Spanish land claims and the original tract book. A recent compilation provides a complete transcript of the depositions made at the federal land offices at Batesville, Fayetteville, Helena, and Little Rock: Melinda Blanchard Crawford and Don L. Crawford, *The Settlers of Lovely and Miller County, Arkansas Territory, 1820–1830* (Rockport, Me: Picton Press, 2002). This work is a must for those researching any one of the over 1800 individuals who were displaced when this region was ceded to the Choctaw and Cherokee nations.

Bounty land for War of 1812 service was distributed by lottery. See Katherine Christensen, *Arkansas Military Bounty Grants, War of 1812* (Hot Springs, Ark.: Arkansas Ancestors, 1971). Limited information is available through a commercial site <www.digisources.com/military.ctm>. The master index for the War of 1812 Bounty Land Warrants can be accessed by name. This extremely limited but helpful search can be conducted by Soundex, warrant number, or regiment, and lists the General Land Office patent accession number. Other possibilities are <www.state.ar.us> and NARA (see pages 11-12).

The rectangular survey system (see page 6) of land measurement was incorporated in 1815 with one principal meridian located at the eastern border of present-day Monroe and at the western border of Lee and Phillips counties. The first land office was established in 1818 with the U.S. General Land Office (GLO) ordering a survey of sixty townships. The first survey was finished in 1819, but no land was actually sold until 1821. Land offices opened at Arkansas Post and Davidsonville in 1820 were soon moved to Little Rock and Batesville, respectively.

In 1832 Congress divided the territory into four land districts. Two additional land offices were then opened at Fayetteville and Washington. Increased demand for land led to additional offices at Helena and Clarksville before 1840,

followed by Champagnole before 1850 and Huntsville in the next decade. New land offices appeared by 1870 at Camden, Dardanelle, and Harrison. But between 1880 and 1900 the only land offices open in all of Arkansas were those located in Camden, Dardanelle, Harrison, and Little Rock. The latter remained open until 1933. The federal government records for 1820 to 1908 are accessible via the Internet at <www.glorecords.blm.gov>. These show the initial transfer of land from the federal government to an individual. The data included on the website includes name of individual, legal description of the land, county, and date of issue. Images of these documents are also available.

The original case files, claims, applications, and records for initial acquisition of Arkansas' public-domain land are in the National Archives (see pages 11-12). Land patents granted for successful claims are housed at the BLM, Eastern States Land Office (see page 6). Copies of tract books, plat maps, and field notes of land offices are kept at the Arkansas State Land Commissioner's Office, State Capitol, Little Rock, AR 72206. These records are organized by legal description or claim number only, and there is no comprehensive index yet. Microfilm copies of the tract books are in the Arkansas History Commission. Arkansas land records from the federal government's Bureau of Land Management are available online at <www.glorecords.blm.gov>.

Land patents of federally owned land in Arkansas have been published by county with all seventy-five counties included in the fifty-seven volumes. Under a general title of *Arkansas Land Patents* (Conway, Ark.: Arkansas Research, 1991), these records were prepared for publication by Desmond Walls Allen and Bobbie Jones McLane. Most counties are separate, but those combined with others include: Arkansas, Chicot, and Desha counties; Clay, Craighead, Crittenden, Cross, Greene, Lee, Mississippi, Monroe, Phillips, Poinsett, and St. Francis; Conway, Faulkner, and Perry; Grant and Saline; Jackson, Lawrence, and Woodruff; and Lonoke and Prairie.

In 1862 Congress passed the Homestead Act; Arkansas was included since it was a federal-land state. Original and entry case files and application papers for homestead land are in the National Archives. The Arkansas History Commission has some homestead records, although not case files, generated by the state.

After the initial acquisition, all subsequent land transfers are recorded at the county seat through the county clerk's office. Many Arkansas county land records have been microfilmed by the FHL, and copies are held at the Arkansas History Commission. To access the microfilm number and determine which records have been microfilmed, see <www.ark-ives.com/selected_materials/index.php>.

Probate Records

Generally, probate court records in Arkansas are generated by the chancery court and maintained by the county clerk. Wills and records created from probate proceedings for both testate and intestate estates are among the most valuable county records. Bound volumes of probate records include the recorded will, appointments of administrators, court orders for the inventory of an estate, the inventory, estate sale records, guardianship appointments and accounts, administrator/executor accounts, list of heirs, and final accounts.

Probate records and/or wills for the period prior to 1920 for most of the counties in Arkansas are available on microfilm through the FHL and the Arkansas History Commission. Volumes of published wills or probate records are available for some Arkansas counties.

Most county clerks also maintain bundles of loose probate records. These packets contain documents, not always in the record books themselves, filed in probate court in connection with estate settlements, guardianships, and insanity cases. Some are arranged in chronological order. Others are organized in semi-alphabetical order regardless of date. Original Pulaski County loose probate packets are at the Arkansas History Commission. To access the microfilm number and determine which records have been microfilmed, see <www.ark-ives.com/selected_materials/index.php>. Desmond Walls Allen, Henryetta Walls Vanaman, and Connie Olds Trent, *Guide to Faulkner County, Arkansas, Loose Probate Packets 1873–1917* (Conway, Ark.: Arkansas Research, 1987) was compiled in an attempt to save information from loose probate packets before the records deteriorate.

Corinne Cox Stevenson and Mrs. Edward Lynn Westbrooke, *Index to Wills and Administrations of Arkansas from the Earliest to 1900* (Jonesboro, Ark.: Vowels Printing Co., 1986) is arranged by county, with alphabetical lists within each county, but not statewide.

Court Records

Courts with countywide jurisdiction are circuit, chancery, county, and justice of peace. Jurisdiction varies from county to county, but generally circuit courts hear criminal, naturalization, and major civil cases. Chancery courts have jurisdiction over equity, divorce, probate, and adoption cases. County courts have jurisdiction over juvenile, tax, and claim cases, as well as county financial matters. Justice of peace courts hear preliminary criminal and minor contract cases. These records are generally available from the time of the county's organization except in those counties where records were destroyed by fire or other causes. Courts of common pleas existed during the territorial period, but no records remain. The county clerk's office maintains records for

all courts functioning in the county. Because jurisdiction varies, check each county for its procedures. Many county court records have been microfilmed by the FHL, and copies are held at the Arkansas History Commission. To access the microfilm number and determine which records have been microfilmed, see <www.ark-ives.com/selected_materials/index.php>.

The state supreme court has appellate jurisdiction from lower courts, and its records can be valuable for those counties with record losses. This particular group of records was indexed in Joan Thurman Taunton's *Abstracts of Arkansas Reports: January 1837 through January 1861* (Hot Springs, Ark.: Arkansas Genealogical Society, 1988). Jack Damon Ruple, *Genealogist's Guide to Arkansas Courthouse Research* (n.p., 1989), is also useful.

Tax Records

Tax records are available at the respective county courthouses and in the Arkansas History Commission. Nearly 600 tax books, original or microfilmed, for Arkansas counties are included in the collection at the Commission or available through the FHL. To access the microfilm number and determine which records have been microfilmed, see <www.ark-ives.com/selected_materials/index.php>.

Where county records were lost, the state auditor's copies are especially valuable. A complete list of these extant early tax records is included in Russell Pierce Baker, *Guide to Microfilmed County Records at the Arkansas History Commission* (Conway, Ark.: Professional Genealogists of Arkansas, 1989).

Personal property tax records have been published for a few counties. Tax lists, along with other sources, are being used to reconstruct the lost 1890 federal population census (see Census Records).

Cemetery Records

Local county genealogical and historical organizations have copied, cataloged, and published records of local cemeteries. Most of these are in the collection at the Arkansas History Commission; many are in the Daughters of the American Revolution Library (DAR; see page 13). Most of those in the DAR collection have been microfilmed by the FHL.

The Arkansas Family Historian, a publication of the Arkansas Genealogical Society (see Periodicals), publishes transcriptions of gravestones from cemeteries, as do many local and regional periodicals. No statewide index to cemetery records exists, but notable publications include the following:

Andreas, Leonardo, comp. *Graveyards in Arkansas.* Salt Lake City: filmed by the Genealogical Society of Utah, 1974.

Cemetery Records of Arkansas. 8 vols. Salt Lake City: Genealogical Society of Utah, 1957.

Daughters of the American Revolution, Prudence Hall Chapter. *Index to Sources for Arkansas Cemetery Inscriptions.* North Little Rock: Daughters of the American Revolution, ca. 1976. An excellent guide to compiled cemetery records for the state.

Knight, Rena Marie. *Civil War Soldiers Buried in Arkansas National Cemeteries.* Jacksonville, Ark.: the author, 1996. Alphabetical arrangement of primarily Union soldiers; it includes name, unit, death, cemetery, and grave number.

_____. *Confederate Soldiers Buried in Arkansas: A Compilation Representative of All Confederate States.* Jacksonville, Ark.: the author, 1999. Contains an alphabetical list of soldiers with rank, service unit, cemetery where buried, and county. Some birth and death details are included.

Roberts, Lewis E. *Cemetery Inscriptions Published in Thirty Years of The Arkansas Family Historian.* Reprint. Hot Springs, Ark.: Arkansas Genealogical Society, 1992.

Church Records

Some church records for Arkansas churches are available at the Arkansas History Commission. These include published church histories, church records, newspapers, and manuscript collections.

The following are repositories for Arkansas church records:

Baptist. Arkansas Baptist State Convention Collection, Ouachita Baptist University, Riley Library, 410 Ouachita, Arkadelphia, AR 71923.

Episcopal. The Bishop's Office, 509 Scott St., Little Rock, AR 72201.

Lutheran. Missouri Synod of the Lutheran Church, 3558 S. Jefferson St., St. Louis, MO 63103.

Methodist. North Arkansas Conference Depository, Hendrix College, Olin C. Bailey Library, Washington and Front Streets, Conway, AR 72032; and Little Rock Conference Depository, Methodist Headquarters Building, 1723 Broadway, Little Rock, AR 72204.

Presbyterian. Arkansas College Library, Batesville, AR 72501.

Roman Catholic. Chancery Office, St. John's Seminary, North Tyler and I St., Little Rock, AR 72201.

Other helpful sources include the following:

WPA. *A Directory of Churches and Religious Organizations in the State of Arkansas.* Little Rock, Ark.: Historical Records Survey, 1942.

_____. *Guide to Vital Statistics Records in Arkansas.* Vol. 2, Church Archives. Little Rock, Ark.: Historical Records Survey, 1942.

Military Records

The Arkansas History Commission maintains the finest collection of records pertaining to Arkansas military men and service. Included are microfilmed indexes to many of the National Archives-compiled service records, such as those for the Revolutionary War, War of 1812, and various Indian wars. The commission also has compiled service records for Arkansas men for the Mexican War, Civil War (both Union and Confederate), and Spanish-American War; returns from United States Military Posts (1800–1916), including reports, rosters, and related papers; Confederate States Army Casualties: Lists and Narrative Reports (1861–65); Register of Confederate Soldiers, Sailors, and Citizens Who Died in Federal Prisons and Military Hospitals in the North (1861–65); and Registers of Confederate Prisoners Held in the Military Prison at Little Rock, Arkansas (1863–65). The commission's pamphlet "Historical and Genealogical Source Materials," available upon request with a self-addressed stamped envelope, describes these holdings.

In addition, the commission has the state's Confederate veteran or widow's pension applications and indexes to Confederate pension records for Arkansas, Oklahoma, Tennessee, and Texas. In 1911 the Public Acts of Arkansas, Number 353, provided that an enumeration of Confederate veterans residing in the state be made by each county's tax assessor. Records are available for forty-four of the counties, but there are no extant records for thirty-one counties. There are 1,751 questionnaires, which usually include the following information: full name of veteran; his address; date and place of birth; date, state, and county of enlistment; full name and place of birth of veteran's parents, grandparents; maiden name of wife, with date and place of marriage; names of her parents; and full list of children with spouses. These applications are published in Bobbie Jones McLane and Capitola Glazner's *Arkansas 1911 Census of Confederate Veterans*, 3 vols. (n.p., 1977–81). An *Index to the Three Volumes: Arkansas 1911 Census of Confederate Veterans* (Hot Springs, Ark.: Arkansas Ancestors, 1899), compiled by Bobbie Jones McLane, is an every-name index. The Arkansas History Commission has the actual 1911 Confederate veterans census for Arkansas and copies of *Confederate Veteran* magazine (1893–1932).

Confederate veteran or widow pension applications, not just those for veterans living in 1911, contain valuable information such as name, rank, unit, length of time of service, veteran's wife's name, widow's birth date, veteran's death date, veteran or widow's residence at time of application, and the amount of the approved pension. Frances Ingmire, *Arkansas Confederate Veterans and Widows Pension Applications* (St. Louis, Mo.: the author, 1985) serves as an alphabetically arranged guide to soldiers' and widows' pension applications, listing name, unit, residence, and date of application.

Several indexes to military records have been compiled by Desmond Walls Allen and are available from the publisher, Arkansas Research, P.O. Box 303, Conway, AR 72032-0303. They include *Arkansas' Mexican War Soldiers* (1988); *Index to Arkansas Confederate Soldiers* (3 vols., 1990); *Arkansas' Damned Yankees: An Index to Union Soldiers in Arkansas Regiments* (1987); *Arkansas Union Soldiers Pension Application Index* (1987); and *Arkansas' Spanish American War Soldiers* (1988).

In addition to Christensen's volume on military bounty grants (see Land Records) for the War of 1812, the following are helpful printed sources for military related data:

Payne, Dorothy. *Arkansas Pensioners, 1818–1900: Records of Some Arkansas Residents Who Applied to the Federal Government for Benefits….* Easley, S. C.: Southern Historical Press, 1985.

Pompey, Sherman Lee. *Muster Lists of the Arkansas Confederate Troops….* Independence, Calif.: Historical and Genealogical Publishing Co., 1965. A guide to names of men who served under the Confederate flag.

War of 1812 Pensioners Living in Arkansas During the 1880's: Abstracted from the Executive Documents. Cullman, Ala.: Gregath Co., 1980.

Watkins, Raymond Wesley. *Confederate Burials in Arkansas Cemeteries.* Little Rock, Ark.: n.p., 1981. Typescript available at the Arkansas History Commission.

Periodicals, Newspapers, and Manuscript Collections

Periodicals

The Arkansas Genealogical Society's publication *Arkansas Family Historian* serves the entire state. An index is available for a few years; see John Sanders, *Consolidated Index of* The Arkansas Family Historian, *1981–1988.* (Hot Springs: Arkansas Genealogical Society, n.d.). *The Arkansas Historical Quarterly*, published for over fifty years by the Arkansas Historical Association, University of Arkansas, Fayetteville, Arkansas 72701, contains relevant background information for both genealogists and historians. Many other county and regional genealogical and/or historical societies publish periodicals that contain valuable records pertaining to the region or locality they serve. Often these publications carry articles concerning records that are not available elsewhere. The Arkansas History Commission maintains copies of most of the state's published periodicals.

Newspapers

Two important early newspapers were the *Arkansas Advocate* and the *Arkansas Gazette*. Abstracts of articles and data from both newspapers have been published. These volumes are available

at the Arkansas History Commission. A valuable source is the *Union List of Arkansas Newspapers, 1819–1942: Partial Inventory of Arkansas Newspaper Files Available in Offices of Publishers, Libraries, and Private Collections in Arkansas*, prepared by the Historical Records Survey, Division of Community Service Programs, WPA (Little Rock, Ark.: Historical Records Survey, 1942). Although current publications are not included, it is an excellent guide to those newspapers published during the territorial period through the beginning of World War I.

The Arkansas History Commission maintains files of approximately 700 Arkansas newspapers published at about 200 different places for the period 1819 to date. It also has an index to the *Arkansas Gazette* for 1819 through 1881 and 1964 through 1983. See also:

Allsopp, Fred W. *History of the Arkansas Press for a Hundred Years and More.* 1922. Reprint. Easley, S.C.: Southern Historical Press, 1978.

Several recent compilations cover vital records abstracts from Arkansas newspapers. Examples include:

Morgan, James Logan. *Arkansas Newspaper Abstracts, 1819–1845.* Vol 1. *Obituaries and Biographical Notes from Arkansas Newspapers.* Newport, Ark.: Morgan Books, 1981.

Russell, Oscar G. *Index to Death Notices Appearing in the* Arkansas Democrat-Gazette. North Little Rock, Ark.: the author, various years. Each compilation is alphabetically arranged, and includes approximately 10,000-plus deaths reported to Little Rock's only daily newspaper.

Manuscripts

Copies of the DAR (see page 13) collection of vital records, which includes family records, marriages, and Bible records for Arkansas, are available at the Downtown Branch, Central Arkansas Library System, 700 S. Louisiana, Little Rock, AR 72203 and on microfilm both at the Arkansas History Commission and through the FHL.

The Arkansas History Commission in Little Rock has a card index to its extensive manuscript collection. A second major source of manuscript material is located at the Special Collections Library, University of Arkansas at Fayetteville.

Archives, Libraries, and Societies

Arkansas History Commission
One Capitol Mall
Little Rock, AR 72201
www.ark-ives.com

Indubitably the finest in Arkansas and one of the oldest state agencies, this excellent repository maintains territorial, state, and county records for each county and region. It is

the state's official repository for legislative records, acts of Arkansas, senate and house journals, journals of constitutional conventions, and various special studies and reports, all from 1819 to date. It is a public research facility that makes an extensive array of material available. Research materials are not limited to those examples described in the various sections of this chapter.

The commission maintains selected copies of records for seventy-five counties from 1797 to 1920, including records of marriage, estates, deeds, county courts, inventories, and some indexes. A valuable guide to the collection is available (see County Resources). Some sources and lists are available online through its website <www.ark-ives.com/selected_materials/index.php>. An example is its list of 3,000 newspapers from 250 places within the state from 1819 to the present.

Arkansas Genealogical Society
P.O. Box 17653
Little Rock, AR 72212
www.rootsweb.com/~args

Publishes *Arkansas Family Historian*. Send requests to <AskAGS@comcast.net>.

Downtown Branch Central Arkansas Library System
700 S. Louisiana
Little Rock, AR 72203
www.cals.lib.ar.us

This branch holds an extensive genealogy section.

Orphan Train Heritage Society of America
P.O. Box 322
Concordia, KS 66901
www.orphantrainriders.com

A national organization, previously based in Arkansas, publishes *The Orphan Train Heritage Society of America Newsletter.*

Professional Genealogists of Arkansas, Inc.
P.O. Box 1807
Conway, AR 72032

As a statewide society of professionals, it publishes *PGA Newsletter.*

Southwest Arkansas Regional Archives
Old Washington Historic State Park
Washington, AR 71862

A few records for counties in this region are located here.

University of Arkansas
Special Collections Library
Fayetteville, AR 72701
http://libinfo.uark.edu/

Maps, manuscripts, and census records can be found here.

There are approximately forty county genealogical/historical societies in Arkansas. An excellent guide to these is *Genealogists' Arkansas Address Book* (Conway, Ark.: Professional Genealogists of Arkansas, 1989). It also has information concerning statewide sources, courthouse addresses, funeral homes, libraries, chambers of commerce, and newspapers.

Special Focus Categories

Naturalization

Naturalization records for Arkansas are maintained by the federal district courts in Little Rock, Helena, Batesville, Fort Smith, and Texarkana. Naturalization records for 1809 to 1906 were indexed in 1942 by the Works Projects Administration (WPA; originally called the Works Progress Administration). Some World War I soldiers from throughout the Midwest who were stationed at Camp Pike during the war were naturalized in Pulaski County Circuit Court. See Desmond Walls Allen, *1918 Camp Pike, Arkansas, Index to Soldiers' Naturalizations* (Conway, Ark.: Arkansas Research, 1988).

Native American

The Arkansas History Commission maintains an excellent collection of Native American records. Included in the collection are agency records, correspondence, and census of Creek Indians, 1832; census of Cherokees east of the Mississippi, 1835 and index; Cherokee census, 1890; Old Settler Cherokee census roll, 1895; index to payment roll, Old Settler Cherokees, 1896; compilation of Choctaw Nation records, 1896; Choctaw Nation census index for 1896 and final rolls of citizens and freedmen of the Cherokee, Choctaw, and Chickasaw tribes, and the Creek and Seminole tribes in Indian Territory, 1906; enrollment cards for the Five Civilized Tribes (in Oklahoma), 1896–1914; and the U.S. census Indian Territory, 1900. Some of the Commission's information for Native Americans is online at <www.ark-ives.com/selected_materials/index.php>. *The WPA Guide to 1930s Arkansas* (see Background Sources) contains a succinct overview.

Other references include:

Baker, Jack D. *Cherokee Emigration Rolls, 1817–1835.* Oklahoma City: Baker Publishing, 1977. Transcription of records maintained by the Bureau of Indian Affairs.

Edgington, Billy Dubois, and Carol Anne Buswell, eds. *Vital Information from the Guion Miller Roll (Eastern Cherokee Court of Claims), 1906–1909.* Mill Creek, Wash.: Indian Scout Publications, 1998. Over 1,000 pages of information, alphabetically arranged. Data includes given and surnames; Miller Roll application number; gender; birth year; birth state; city, county, and state of residence; and Soundex codes of surname.

Foreman, Grant. *Indian Removal: The Emigration of the Five Civilized Tribes of Indians.* Norman, Okla.: University of Oklahoma Press, 1986. A history of the Trail of Tears.

African American

A few African-American slaves were in Arkansas before the Louisiana Purchase; however, after statehood, many moved into Arkansas with migrating white families coming from Alabama, Mississippi, and Tennessee. Their lives were primarily tied to the delta region in the southeastern part of the state where a plantation economy existed. In addition to copies of the slave enumerations associated with the federal census (see page 3) located at the Arkansas History Commission, Freedmen's Bureau records (see page[]) in the National Archives are a valuable source for research on African-American families in Arkansas.

The Butler Center for Arkansas Studies includes African-American history online sites through <www.cals.lib.ar.us>. Among other data, one can access a "Selected Arkansas Black Bibliography," a list of African-American Arkansas newspapers from 1869 to date, and a list of African-American Arkansas schools. The Arkansas History Commission maintains a list of African-American newspapers on its website <www.ark-ives.com/selected_materials/index.php>.

A succinct history and background of African Americans in Arkansas is provided through <www.afrigeneas.com/states/ar/>. This site also links with several others with record lists, including a few Civil War units, state and local resources, and other Arkansas history links. Of special interest is the Arkansas Freedman's Bureau marriage records at <www.freedmensbureau.com/arkansas/arkansasmarriages.htm>.

A recently re-released work deals with slavery issues in the state. Orville W. Taylor, *Negro Slavery in Arkansas* (Fayetteville: University of Arkansas Press, 2000), with an introduction by Carl Moneyhan, is based on previously unpublished sources such as diaries, plantation records, letters, family papers, church, city, and county records.

The Afro-American Historical and Genealogical Society maintains a chapter for the state. The address is AAHGS, P.O. Box 4294, Little Rock, AR 72214. Someone from the group can be reached by e-mail contact at <TRTL0793@aol.com>.

The Arkansas Black History Advisory Committee collects African-American historical materials for the Arkansas History Commission (see Archives), encourages research, and cooperates with the Arkansas Department of Education to develop historical materials for use in public schools. The historical materials collected by the committee include letters, diaries, journals, business records, photographs, church and lodge records, personal memoirs, and other related documents.

County Resources

Arkansas county vital, land, and probate records are held by the county clerk, with some counties having two courthouses. This is indicated by "and" followed by a second address. Either one might have been used for recording purposes. Some county clerks also maintain court records, but most are at the office of the clerk of the circuit court. Addresses for county courthouses are given at <www.accessarkansas.org/government_local.php>. Most Arkansas counties do not provide online services; however, postings on this site include current telephone numbers for each county judge's office. Calls can be transferred to the county clerk and/or clerk of the circuit court's offices. A random check indicates most telephone listings are current, but some listings show 501 prefixes, which have now changed to 479.

Dates given are for the first known records in the category in that county; these dates do not imply that all records are extant from that date. For data concerning county record losses, creation dates, boundary changes, and additional information, see Russell Pierce Baker, *Guide to the Microfilmed County Records at the Arkansas History Commission* (Conway, Ark.: Professional Genealogists of Arkansas, 1989), and James Logan Morgan, *A Survey of the County Records of Arkansas* (Newport, Ark.: Arkansas Records Association, 1972). Both were used in compiling the chart that follows.

Although 1914 was the date of initial registration of births and deaths, compliance was extremely limited; therefore, only a small percentage of actual births and deaths were recorded during the first decades after the law was enacted. For that reason, beginning dates of births and deaths are not given in the chart.

Parent counties are those defined here as those in session laws. Later boundary changes between counties also occurred, but these are not included. See the Baker and Morgan sources cited above for this information.

ARKANSAS

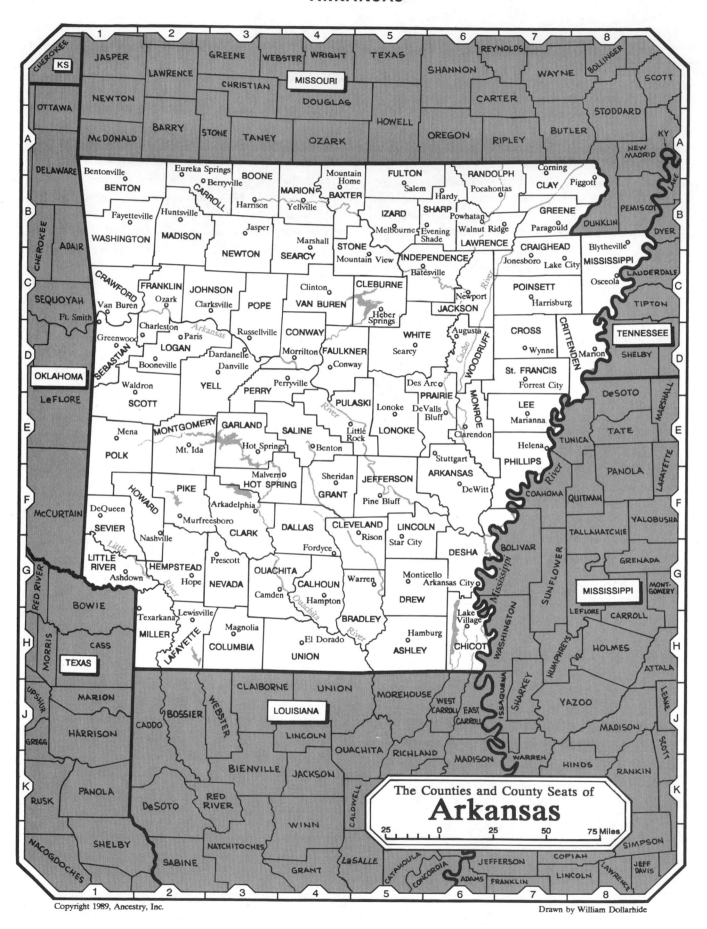

The Counties and County Seats of
Arkansas

25   0   25   50   75 Miles

Drawn by William Dollarhide

ARKANSAS

Map	County Address	Date Formed Parent County/ies	Birth Marriage Death	Land Probate Court
F6	Arkansas 101 Court Sq. Do Witt 72042	1813 original	—— 1839 ——	1808 1809 1819
H5	Ashley 215 E. Jefferson St. Hamburg 71646	1848 Chicot/Union/Drew	—— 1848 ——	1849 1849 1849
B4	Baxter 1 E. 7th St. Mountain Home 72653	1873 Fulton/Izard/Marion/Searcy	—— 1873 ——	1876 1874 1874
B1	Benton 215 E. Central Bentonville 72712	1836 Washington	—— 1861 ——	1837 1866 1837
B3	Boone 100 N. Main St. Harrison 72601	1869 Carroll/Marion	—— 1869 ——	1869 1869 1869
G5	Bradley 101 E. Cedar St. Warren 71671	1840 Union	—— 1846 ——	1841 1850 1841
G4	Calhoun Main Street/P.O. Box 566 Hampton 71744	1850 Dallas/Ouachita/Union	—— 1851 ——	1851 1880 1880
B2	Carroll 210 W. Church St. Berryville 72616 and 44 S. Main St. Eureka Springs 72632	1833 Izard	—— 1870 ——	1870 1870 1870
H6	Chicot 108 N. Main St. Lake Village 71653	1823 Arkansas	—— 1840 ——	1823 1839 1824
F3	Clark 401 Clay St. Arkadelphia 71923	1818 Arkansas	—— 1821 ——	1819 1840 1838
B7	Clay 151 S. 2nd Ave. Piggott 72454 and 800 W. 2nd St. Corning 72422	1873 Randolph/Greene	—— 1893 ——	1893 1893 1893
C5	Cleburne 301 W. Main St. Heber Springs 72543	1883 White/Van Buren/Independence	—— 1883 ——	1883 1883 1883
G5	Cleveland 20 Magnolia St./P.O. Box 348 Rison 71665 *Created as Dorsey County; name changed to Cleveland in 1888.*	1873 (as Dorsey; renamed, 1885) Bradley/Dallas/Jefferson/Lincoln	—— 1880 ——	1873 1873 1873
H3	Columbia 1 Court Sq. Magnolia 71753	1852 Layfayette/Hempstead/ Ouachita/Union	—— 1853 ——	1853 1853 1860
D4	Conway 117 S. Moose St. Morrilton 72110	1825 Pulaski	—— 1858 ——	1825 1837 1842
C7	Craighead 511 S. Main St. Jonesboro 72401 and 107 Cobean St. Lake City 72437	1859 Mississippi/Greene/Poinsett	—— 1878 ——	1900 1878 1878
C1	Crawford 300 Main St. Van Buren 72956	1820 Pulaski	—— 1877 ——	1877 1877 1877
D8	Crittenden 100 Court Sq. Marion 72364	1825 Phillips	—— 1837 ——	1826 1839 1826
D7	Cross 705 E. Union St. Wynne 72396	1862 Crittenden/Poinsett/ St. Francis	1863 1863 ——	1865 1863 1865
F4	Dallas 202 3rd St. West Fordyce 71742	1845 Clark/Bradley	—— 1855 ——	1845 1845 1845
G6	Desha Robert S. Moore St./P.O. Box 188 Arkansas City 71630 *During courthouse renovation, records will be held at 604 President St., Arkansas City, AR 71630.*	1838 Arkansas	—— 1865 ——	1839 1852 1840
	Dorsey	1873 (renamed Cleveland, 1885)		
G5	Drew 210 S. Main Monticello 71655	1846 Arkansas/Bradley	—— 1847 ——	1847 1847 1847
D4	Faulkner 801 Locust St. Conway 72034	1873 Pulaski/Conway	—— 1873 ——	1873 1873 1873
C2	Franklin 211 W. Commercial St. Ozark 72949 and 606 E. Main St. Charleston 72933	1837 Crawford	—— 1850 ——	1837 1838 1852
B5	Fulton 123 S. Main Salem 72576	1842 Izard	—— 1887 ——	1870 1870 1870
E3	Garland 501 Ouachita Ave. Hot Springs 71901	1873 Montgomery/Hot Spring/Saline	—— 1874 ——	1873 1877 1874
F4	Grant 101 W. Center Sheridan 72150	1869 Jefferson/Hot Spring/Saline	—— 1877 ——	1877 1877 1877

65

Map County Address	Date Formed Parent County/ies	Birth Marriage Death	Land Probate Court
B7 Greene 320 W. Court St. Paragould 72451	1833 Lawrence	—— 1876 ——	1858 1876 1871
G2 Hempstead 400 S. Washington St. Hope 71802	1818 Arkansas	—— 1823 ——	1900 1826 1819
F3 Hot Spring 210 Locust St. Malvern 72104	1829 Clark	—— 1825 ——	1831 1834 1843
F2 Howard 421 N. Main St. Nashville 71852	1873 Pike/Hempstead/Polk/Sevier	—— 1873 1873	1873 1873 1873
C6 Independence 192 E. Main St. Batesville 72501	1820 Arkansas/Lawrence	—— 1826 ——	1820 1839 1821
B5 Izard Main and Lunen St. Melbourne 72556	1825 Independence/Fulton	—— 1889 1889	1889 1889 1889
C6 Jackson 208 Main St. Newport 72112	1829 Independence	—— 1843 ——	1845 1845 1845
F5 Jefferson 101 W. Barraque St. Pine Bluff 71601	1829 Arkansas/Pulaski	—— 1830 ——	1830 1829 1837
C3 Johnson 215 W. Main/P.O. Box 57 Clarksville 72830	1833 Pope	—— 1855 ——	1836 1844 1841
H2 Lafayette 2 Courthouse Sq. Lewisville 71845	1827 Hempstead	—— 1828 ——	1828 1828 1828
B6 Lawrence 315 W. Main Walnut Ridge 72476	1815 New Madrid, Mo.	—— 1821 ——	1815 1817 1816
E7 Lee 15 E. Chestnut St. Marianna 72360	1873 Phillips/Monroe/ Crittenden/Saint Francis	—— 1873 ——	1873 1873 1873
F5 Lincoln 300 S. Drew St. Star City 71667	1871 Arkansas/Bradley/ Desha/Drew/Jefferson	—— 1871 ——	1871 1871 1871
G1 Little River 351 N. 2nd St. Ashdown 71822	1867 Hempstead/Sevier	—— 1880 ——	1867 1880 1868
D2 Logan 25 W. Walnut St. Paris 72855 *and* 366 N. Broadway Booneville 72927 *Created as Sarber County in 1871; name changed to Logan in 1875.*	1875 Franklin/Scott/ Yell/Johnson	—— 1877 ——	1878 1873 1877

Map County Address	Date Formed Parent County/ies	Birth Marriage Death	Land Probate Court
E5 Lonoke 3rd & Center St. Lonoke 72086	1873 Pulaski/Prairie	—— 1873 ——	1873 1873 1873
Lovely	1827 (abolished, 1828) Crawford/Lovely Purchase		
B2 Madison 1 Main St. Huntsville 72740	1836 Washington/Carroll	—— 1896 ——	1843 1901 1866
B4 Marion Hwy. 62 Yellville 72687 *Formerly Searcy County; changed name to Marion County, 1836*	1835 Izard	—— 1887 ——	1887 1887 1887
Miller (old) *In 1828 a boundary change left old Miller County entirely in Texas. In 1838, it was abolished to create Red River County, Texas. Extant records at Arkansas History Commission include probate (1830–38); circuit court (1830–35); and tax records (1832,1837).*	1820 (abolished, 1838; see also Texas) Hempstead		
H2 Miller (present) 400 Laurel St. Texarkana 71854	1874 Lafayette	—— 1875 ——	1874 1874 1874
C8 Mississippi 200 W. Walnut Blytheville 72315 *and* Osceola 72370	1833 Crittenden	—— 1850 ——	1865 1865 1865
E6 Monroe 123 Madison St. Clarendon 72029	1829 Phillips/Arkansas	—— 1850 ——	1829 1839 1830
E2 Montgomery 105 Hwy. 270 East Mount Ida 71957	1842 Hot Spring	—— 1845 ——	1845 1845 1845
G3 Nevada 215 E. 2nd St. South Prescott 71857	1871 Hempstead/Columbia/Ouachita	—— 1871 ——	1871 1871 1871
New Madrid	(now in Missouri)		
B3 Newton 100 E. Court St. Jasper 72641	1842 Carroll	—— 1866 ——	1866 1880 1880
G3 Ouachita 145 Jefferson St. SW Camden 71711	1842 Union	—— 1875 ——	1869 1876 1875
D4 Perry Main Street/P.O. Box 358 Perryville 72126	1840 Conway	—— 1882 ——	1882 1882 1882
E7 Phillips 600 Cherry St. Helena 72342	1820 Arkansas	—— 1831 ——	1820 1850 1820

Map County Address	Date Formed Parent County/ies	Birth Marriage Death	Land Probate Court
F2 **Pike** 225 S. Washington Murfreesboro 71958	1833 Clark/Hempstead	—— 1895 ——	1895 1895 1895
C7 **Poinsett** 401 Market St. Harrisburg 72432	1838 Greene/St. Francis	—— 1873 ——	1873 1873 1871
E1 **Polk** 507 Church St. Mena 71953	1844 Sevier	—— 1881 ——	1885 1900 1885
C3 **Pope** 100 W. Main St. Russellville 72801	1829 Crawford	—— 1830 1965	1828 1844 1857
E6 **Prairie** 200 Court Sq./P.O. Box 1101 Des Arc 72040 *and* 1 Magnolia St. (So. District) De Valls Bluff 72041	1846 Pulaski	—— 1854 ——	1854 1854 1854
E4 **Pulaski** 201 S. Broadway Little Rock 72201	1818 Arkansas	—— 1839 ——	1819 1820 1839
B6 **Randolph** 107 W. Broadway Pocahontas 72455	1835 Lawrence	—— 1837 ——	1836 1837 1836
D7 **St. Francis** 313 S. Izard St. Forrest City 72335	1827 Phillips	—— 1875 ——	1860 1910 1872
E4 **Saline** 200 N. Main St. Benton 72015	1835 Pulaski	—— 1836 ——	1871 1836 1836
Sarber	(see Logan)		
E1 **Scott** 100 W. First St. Waldron 72958	1833 Crawford/Pope	—— 1882 ——	1882 1882 1882
B4 **Searcy** U.S. Hwy. 65 Marshall 72650	1838 Marion	—— 1881 ——	1866 1881 1881
D1 **Sebastian** 35 S. Sixth Fort Smith 72901 *and* 312 E. Center (So. District) Greenwood 72936	1851 Scott/Polk/Crawford	—— 1865 ——	1861 1865 1851
F1 **Sevier** 115 N. Third De Queen 71832	1828 Hempstead/Miller (old)	—— 1829 ——	1830 1829 1830
B6 **Sharp** U.S. Hwy. 167 North Ash Flat 72513	1868 Lawrence	—— 1880 ——	1880 1880 1880
C5 **Stone** Main Street/P.O. Box 1437 Mountain View 72560	1873 Izard/Independence/ Searcy/Van Buren	—— 1873 ——	1873 1873 1873
H4 **Union** 101 N. Washington El Dorado 71730	1829 Hempstead/Clark	—— 1847 ——	1830 1839 1830
C4 **Van Buren** 106 E. Main St./P.O. Box 180 Clinton 72031	1833 Independence/Conway/Izard	—— 1859 ——	1855 1859 1859
B1 **Washington** 280 N. College Ave. Fayetteville 72701	1828 Crawford/Lovely	—— 1845 ——	1834 1830 1835
Whashita	(alternate spelling of Ouachita)		
D5 **White** 300 N. Spruce Searcy 72143	1835 Pulaski/Jackson/Independence	—— 1836 ——	1837 1848 1836
D6 **Woodruff** 500 N. Third St. Augusta 72006	1862 Jackson/St. Francis	—— 1865 ——	1851 1865 1865
D3 **Yell** Main Street Danville 72833 *and* Dardanelle 72834	1840 Pope/Scott	—— 1865 ——	1849 1858 1865

California

DWIGHT A. RADFORD, THELMA BERKEY WALSMITH, AND NELL SACHSE WOODARD

In 1769 a small group of military men and missionaries, sent by the Spanish crown, arrived at what was to become San Diego. Alta (Upper) California, as it was known during the Spanish and Mexican eras, was inhabited at that time by various indigenous tribes. It was Spain's goal to conquer the natives and settle the area. They built missions a day's journey apart on El Camino Real (the King's Highway) in fertile valleys beside permanent streams. Inhabitants raised crops and livestock. Several missions were destroyed when a severe earthquake struck in 1812. However, construction continued until the Mexican government secularized the mission holdings in 1833 and the land passed into private ownership. Citizens of Spain and Mexico occupied the coastal area between San Diego and the San Francisco Bay.

The first considerable gold discovery in California was made thirty-five miles north of Los Angeles in 1842 by a Mexican rancher named Francisco Lopez. This was followed by a larger discovery at Sutter's Mill in Coloma in 1848. But California is not only known for its yellow ore. California's reputation as the "Golden State" came from the early sea otter and cattle-hide trade, the black gold of oil, the fruit-growing industry in Southern California, and the large development of agriculture statewide beginning in the nineteenth century.

In 1800 the Russian American Fur Company of Alaska had loaned twenty Aleut natives to a New England ship captain to engage in the illegal but highly successful hunting of sea otters off the California coast. The Russians followed and built Fort Ross about eighty miles north of San Francisco Bay. Some of their descendants are living in the area today.

On 31 July 1846, over 200 Mormons from New York landed in San Francisco after sailing around Cape Horn. These Mormons decided to stay on the Coast and work in lumber camps on the Marin Peninsula across the Golden Gate from San Francisco.

Following the discovery of gold and the Mexican War in 1848, the United States acquired all of the southwestern Mexican possessions. A large number of immigrants, including a substantial influx of Italians, began arriving in California after the declaration of statehood on 9 September 1850. The acquisition of the southwestern lands resulted in many land claims, and much litigation was required both in the courts and in the regulatory agencies before these cases were adjudicated. Not until March 1851 did Congress send land commissioners west to review all grant titles.

The Central Railroad (later Southern Pacific), after its completion in May 1869, brought thousands of new migrants and goods westward. Numerous towns grew up along the transcontinental route. Thousands of Chinese migrated to California, providing cheap labor in the mines as well as on the railroads. The most severe earthquake in California's recorded history occurred on 18 April 1906 in San Francisco. The quake and subsequent fire destroyed much of the city and caused the loss of many important records.

The depression of the 1920s and drought of the 1930s were followed, with the advent of World War II, by an ever-growing demand for labor and military and naval personnel. Since 1945 the growth of the state has been phenomenal. The census bureau counted almost thirty-four million residents in 2000, ten million more than 1980. While early settlers may have been drawn to

California for fishing, hunting otters, raising livestock, searching for gold, and engaging in grain agriculture, others later came to the "Golden State" attracted by the entertainment, aerospace, and technological (computer) industries.

Vital Records

Vital records in California have been kept by the state registrar of vital statistics since 1 July 1905. Earlier vital records are entered in the county where the event took place. Pre-1905 records in the counties may be quite slim. In Sacramento County, for example, only three births were entered for the period between 1858 and 1874, and only forty-three deaths between 1858 and 1864. Marriages, on the other hand, seem to have been recorded more regularly. Some court-ordered delayed birth certificates have been registered by the state registrar. For all vital records, contact the California Department of Health Services, Office of Vital Records, 304 "S" St., Sacramento, CA 95819 (Mailing address: P.O. Box 730241, Sacramento, CA 94244-0241) <www.dhs.ca.gov/hisp/default.htm>. There is no statewide index that includes the pre-1905 records held by counties; however, the Family History Library (FHL) in Salt Lake City has microfilm copies of many pre-1905 California county vital records.

The early California births kept by the state are indexed and online for selected years at <www.ancestry.com>, which also has the California Death Index online (1940–97). The California Department of Health Services has a CD-ROM index of births (1905–95) and deaths (1905–90), which is currently available at many libraries. However, because of changing California laws regarding the state's vital records, the availability of these may change in the future. The website <www.vitalsearch-ca.com> has indexes to California state vital records.

The FHL has microfilm copies of most California marriages kept by the counties. There is an ongoing project to provide a statewide index to these records on the Internet through the BYU-Idaho Family History Center in Rexburg, Idaho, as part of its Western States Historical Marriage Records database. It can be searched at <http://abish.byui.edu/specialCollections/fhc/gbsearch.htm>.

Divorce records are available in the office of the clerk of the superior court in the county in which the proceedings were conducted.

Census Records

Federal

Population Schedules
- Indexed—1850, 1860, 1870, 1880, 1900, 1910, 1920, 1930
- Soundex—1880, 1900, 1910 (Miracode), 1920

Industry and Agriculture Schedules
- 1850, 1860, 1870, 1880

Mortality Schedules
- 1850, 1860, 1870, 1880

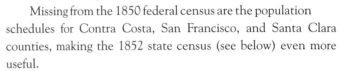

The California State Library is a repository for the microfilm of California original federal censuses. The California State Archives (see Archives, Libraries, and Societies) holds the original state copies for the federal 1860 and 1880 population schedules. Both repositories and the California Genealogical Society have microfilm copies of the state's federal censuses.

Missing from the 1850 federal census are the population schedules for Contra Costa, San Francisco, and Santa Clara counties, making the 1852 state census (see below) even more useful.

Mission and State
Censuses were taken for the following missions: San Carlos (1796), San Luis Obispo (1797, 1798), San Antonio (1798), and Soledad (1798). They are all in original form at the California State Archives. They have been reprinted in *Historical Society of Southern California Quarterly*, volumes 41–43.

The California Constitution of 1849 provided for a census of the state population in the years 1852 and 1855 and each succeeding ten years thereafter. The census of 1852, similar to the 1850 federal census but using an additional column showing the prior residence of each person, was the only one actually taken. The original returns for 1852 are in the California State Archives with microfilm at the California State Library and the FHL. The constitution was altered in 1879 to provide for the use of the federal census in the matter of apportioning the state for legislative representation.

A few cities and towns have special censuses for California through the twentieth century. The California State Archives has a listing of its holdings in this category.

Background Sources

Bancroft, Hubert Howe. *The History of California: 1542–1880.* San Francisco: A. L. Bancroft and Co., 1884–90. These classic volumes in California history have been republished several times by several publishers. The companion volume, *California Pioneer Register and Index, 1542–1848, Including Inhabitants of California, 1769–1800 and List of Pioneers,* extracted from Hubert Howe Bancroft's *History of California* (1884–90; reprint, Baltimore, Maryland: Genealogical Publishing Co., 1964) is a handy reference to history and early settlers.

Beals, Kathleen C. *A Useful Guide to Researching San Francisco Ancestry.* Oakland: California Genealogical Society, 1994.

This guide helps to circumvent the record loss in San Francisco County due to the 1906 earthquake and fire.

Close, Barbara Ross, comp. *California Surname Index: Biographies From Selected Histories.* Oakland: California Genealogical Society, 2000. This work indexes 18,000 biographical sketches of early Californians found in forty-two works in the California Genealogical Society's George R. Dorman Genealogical Collection.

Fusaolnada, Lawson, ed. *Only What We Could Carry: The Japanese American Internment Experience.* San Francisco: California Historical Society and Heyday Books, 2000. This work documents the history of Japanese Americans after the attack on Pearl Harbor when 100,000 West Coast residents were uprooted from their homes and banished to internment camps.

Harlow, Neal. *California Conquered: The Annexation of a Mexican Province, 1846–1850.* Berkeley: University of California Press, 1989. The author documents the end of Mexican rule in California and the beginnings of American rule.

Northrop, Marie E. *Spanish-Mexican Families of Early California: 1769–1850.* Vol. 1. Burbank, Calif.: Southern California Genealogical Society, 1986.

_____. *Spanish-Mexican Families of Early California, 1769–1850.* Vol. 2. Burbank, Calif.: Southern California Genealogical Society, 1984. These are two excellent genealogical volumes to the early Hispanic families in Spanish California.

Parker, J. Carlyle. *Index to Biographees [sic] in 19th Century California County Histories.* Detroit: Gale Research, 1979. An excellent cross index to a large number of California's county histories.

Ryskamp, George R. *Tracing Your Hispanic Heritage.* Riverside, Calif.: Hispanic Family History Research, 1984. An excellent text for tracing Hispanic ancestry including insights on early California residents.

Strobridge, William F. *Regulars in the Redwoods: The U.S. Army in Northern California, 1852–1861.* Spokane, Wash.: Arthur H. Clark, 1994. A history of the U.S. Army in Northern California between the Gold Rush and the Civil War.

Stein, Walter J. *California and the Dust Bowl Migrations: Contributions in American History.* No. 21. Westport, Conn.: Greenwood Press, 1973.

Maps

Several books are helpful in researching the evolution of California. Warren A. Beck's *Historical Atlas of California* (Norman: University of Oklahoma Press, 1975), available in many libraries, provides a basic map reference at different points in California's history. William O. Bright's classic work, *1500 California Place Names: Their Origins and Meaning* (Berkeley: University of California Press, 1998), is an excellent resource for place-names and the history behind them.

The United States Geological Survey (USGS) website offers topographical maps of California for sale at <www.usgs.gov>. The California USGS office is at Placer Hall, 6000 J St., Sacramento, CA 95819-6129.

Land Records

Public-Domain State

The earliest land records relate to the Spanish (1769–1822) and Mexican (1822–48) eras and are mostly in Spanish. During the Spanish period, California was divided into four districts for purposes of administration: San Diego in 1769, Monterey in 1770, San Francisco in 1776, and finally the district of Santa Barbara in 1782. The bulk of the surviving records are in the county recorders' offices. The most notable collection of this period is undoubtedly the recorder's collection (1781–1850) in Monterey County. It covers a multitude of proceedings as Monterey was the seat of government for Alta California. Santa Cruz has a similar set of documents (1797–1845), and the San Jose clerk's archives hold various records from 1792.

For the period of Mexican jurisdiction, there are two major collections, one in Los Angeles and one in San Francisco, with the larger group of land records in San Francisco.

Under both the Spanish and Mexican regimes, land in California was allocated first to pueblos for the use of its towns and its inhabitants, second to presidios for use of the military in defending the citizenry and in keeping the peace, and third to the Catholic missions for the purpose of extending the church's theology to the native population.

Almost as soon as the last of the edifices in the chain of missions was completed in 1833, the Mexican government secularized all mission lands (about one-sixth of Alta California) and allowed these lands to be bought for private use. By 1846 some 500 ranches were parceled out, generating numerous records and documents.

Spain had begun the practice of allowing concessions of private ranchos when, in 1784, Governor Pedro Fages bestowed ranchos upon three of his soldados de cuero (leather jacket troops) that he had led into California in 1769. These ranchos were San Rafael, San Pedro, and Los Nietos. By 1851, when the U.S. Board of Land Commissioners and the courts of record began hearing land claims cases, there were over 900 private land claims of named ranchos and an additional twenty-six unnamed grants. From 1851 through 1856, the Commission heard 813 cases in which title to over twelve million acres was decided. Of these, the board approved 520 claims and refused to recognize 273. Only a fraction of these decisions

were overturned by the courts. Since the land commission met in San Francisco, a great hardship was created for the Southern California claimants. The California State Archives has a database of these records on its website (see Archives, Libraries, and Societies).

Records pertaining to Spanish and Mexican land claims were bound into seven volumes by the U.S. Surveyor General's office, a part of the Department of the Interior. For details, write to the U.S. Geological Survey Office, 119 National Center, Reston, VA 22092. The records of the Bureau of Land Management (BLM; Record Group 49), Private Land Claims No. 183, are located in the National Archives in Washington, D.C.

Robert Cowan writes in *Ranchos of California: A List of Spanish Concessions, 1775–1822 and Mexican Grants, 1822–1846* (Los Angeles: Historical Society of Southern California, 1977) that there were 3,500 people in Alta California, and by the end of the Mexican administration in 1846, the population had increased to almost 7,000. The Alta California records for the period of the Mexican-American war (1846–48) may be found in the archives in Los Angeles, Monterey, San Francisco, and Sonoma counties.

During the Spanish and Mexican occupations, a government agent called the *alcalde* was the equivalent of our present-day mayor; however, his powers were greatly enhanced and his jurisdictions were singular in that he performed many functions not commonly associated with that office today. Several counties have preserved their *alcades'* records for the period when California statehood became official. Counties with such records include Contra Costa, El Dorado, Marin, Monterey, Napa, Sacramento, San Francisco, San Luis Obispo, Santa Clara, Santa Cruz, Sonoma, Sutter, and Yuba.

California is a public-domain land state (see pages []); consequently, land acquired by the U.S. Government in 1848 was disposed of by means of patents. The first of ten land offices opened in Benicia and Los Angeles in 1853. Those properties that continued to the final patent are indexed and on the Bureau of Land Management website <www.glorecords.blm.gov>. Patents and copies of tract books and maps are located at the BLM California State Office, 2800 Cottage Way, Ste. W-1834, Sacramento, CA 95825-1886 <www.ca.blm.gov>.

After the patent process the lands went into private hands and became a record of the county. These are filed with the county recorder for each county, with many on microfilm at the FHL.

Land records for sales between private individuals throughout the state begin with the formation of the county, with the possible exception of those counties where there have been unusual circumstances, such as the San Francisco earthquake and fire of 1906. Contact the county recorder for the county in which the land is situated. In some instances the parent county must be searched as well.

The county recorder is usually in charge of land documents, except where the records are so old that they have been placed in an archive within the county or in the state archives in Sacramento. Ultimately, the county board of supervisors is responsible for the records and repositories. In order to chart the ownership of land in California, the records are executed with a "chain of title." This record begins with the oldest entry of the land down to the most recent.

A compilation of indexes to real property owners was begun in the 1980s. In the alphabetical lists (for 1984, 1988, and 1989, available at the California State Library), a researcher can find the names and mailing addresses of all property owners. Because the state no longer allows open access to all driver's license applications, and city and county directories are not available for all locations, the Property Owners Index is quite useful for tracing living persons.

Land Definitions

The following definitions will be useful for anyone conducting research in California.

Haciendas: Not widely used in California, it is the Mexican equivalent of *rancho*.

Ranchos: Land grants made by the government. The first one made in California was for 140 varas near Carmel. Of some 800 *ranchos* that were in existence when the U.S. government took possession of California, just over 500 were later confirmed by American courts.

Pueblos: Towns for civilian settlers, a tract four square leagues or 17,500 acres.

Presidios: Land granted for the use of the military to carry out its duties to defend the province against foreign invasion and to keep civil order. Title was actually passed in fee simple. Presidios were established in Santa Barbara, Monterey, San Diego, and San Francisco.

Missions: Land set aside for the use of the Roman Catholic Church in its work with the Indians native to the area. Title was not passed to the mission, nor to an individual. After the Act of Secularization, the missions were broken up and the lands were mostly granted to those making a petition to the government.

Districts: There were originally four districts set up for the administration of each province of Alta California, as mentioned earlier. Later, Los Angeles was added to the list. Each district had a presidio and a mission, although there might have been more than one mission in each.

Probate Records

The court that has jurisdiction over an estate is the superior court in the county in which the person resided at the time of

his or her death. When a probate case is opened, the clerk of the court keeps a journal for that particular numbered file and maintains that file when the case is closed. Files can be searched at the office of the clerk of the superior court in which the probate occurred. Check for the file and then request the entire journal. The "Petition for Final Distribution" is ordered when all of the legal requirements have been met and the estate is to be distributed to the heirs. Many counties have had their probate materials microfilmed, especially for the nineteenth century, with copies available at the FHL.

Court Records

The California court system has four levels of jurisdiction: the municipal court, which largely took the place of the earlier justice of the peace court at the local level; the superior court, a countywide court that handles both civil and criminal cases and cases involving minors; the six district courts of appeal, which review all cases coming from the superior courts except those involving the death penalty; and the state supreme court, which takes extraordinary writs, all appeals in death penalty cases, and may review all other appeals.

Each of these courts has a clerk of the court, and correspondence regarding a particular case should be directed to the clerk of the court having jurisdiction over the litigation. If there is doubt as to which court to seek information from, the State Attorney General's Office, 1515 K St., Sacramento, CA 95814, can provide this information <www.caag.state.ca.us>.

The California State Archives has many state and county court records. The archives' website (see Archives) has inventories of records listed by county.

Tax Records

The U.S. Internal Revenue Service Assessment List for California (1862–66) is available on microfilm at the California State Library in Sacramento and the FHL. The lists include names, location, and description of business, and tax rate for individuals taxed.

Similar to tax records in their yearly listing of residents are the "Great Registers" of California, which are miscellaneous county voting registers that exist from the mid-nineteenth century. The registers were compiled and printed about every two years. Before 1900, they show name, address, and age (although sometimes that age may remain the same after a man's first entry). From about the mid-1800s, physical descriptions are included, but after the 1898 register, only the name, address, party affiliation, and sometimes occupation are listed. The FHL also has a large collection of the Great Registers especially for the nineteenth century.

Before 1892, the lists are countywide, but usually alphabetical only by first letter or surname. They are particularly valuable for foreign-born voters, as the date and court of naturalization are listed. Copies of the Great Registers (1866–1944) are at the California State Library. Records from 1946 are with the individual county registrars of voters.

The Great Registers provide a viable substitute for the destroyed 1890 federal census and have been transcribed and indexed by the California State Genealogical Alliance in Janice G. Cloud's (ed.) three-volume work, *The California 1890 Great Register of Voters Index* (North Salt Lake: Heritage Quest, 2001).

Cemetery Records

Printed secondary sources of transcribed cemeteries exist for most California counties. The California State Society of the Daughters of the American Revolution (DAR) has collected hundreds of such records. Transcripts are housed both at the national DAR (see page 13) and with some local chapters and libraries. They are also available on microfilm through the FHL and the Sutro Library in San Francisco (see Archives, Libraries, and Societies). A complete set of the DAR records (more than 180 volumes) is also in the California Room of the California State Library. Included in this collection are census, newspaper, cemetery, court, Bible, and family records.

Most cemeteries previously located in San Francisco were "moved" out of the city in the 1930s to South San Francisco and Coloma in San Mateo County, for example.

Church Records

California has always been a place where East met West in religious and philosophical areas. Its beginnings as a Spanish colony and its annexation to the United States all had religious overtones. It was founded by the Roman Catholics who established the early Spanish missions, and it was occupied by the Mormon Battalion after the Mexican-American War. California has become the home of all forms of Catholicism (Roman and Eastern Rite), Protestantism, Orthodoxy, Mormonism, Judaism, Buddhism, Shintoism, Hinduism, Sikism, and Islam. The mix of beliefs also gives rise to new forms of religion, uniquely blending both East and West.

Spanish missions have played a central role in California's religious history. Father Junipero Serra, a Franciscan, raised the standard to his sovereign on 2 June 1769 and began the trek that led him the length of the state of California. He founded a string of missions that would lead the state in the settlement of the vast uncharted land and the conversion of its natives. About a third of the total missions built were founded by Father Serra. Microfiche of some vital records from the missions is available at the FHL.

CALIFORNIA

Today the Roman Catholic Church is served through twelve dioceses. The policy of record preservation is different within each diocese, as some have archives where records are deposited and others have individual parishes that retain their own records. Each diocese has a website with links to individual parishes, making the search for parish registers easier than previously.

Archdiocese of Los Angeles (covers Los Angeles, Santa Barbara, and Ventura counties): 3424 Wilshire Blvd., Los Angeles, CA 90010-2210 <www.la-archdiocese.org/english>.

Archiocese of San Francisco (covers Marin, San Francisco, and San Mateo counties): One Peter Yorke Way, San Francisco, CA 94109 <www.sfarchdiocese.org/archdiocese.html>.

Diocese of Fresno Archives (covers Fresno, Inyo, Kern, Kings, Madera, Merced, Mariposa, and Tulare counties): 1550 N. Fresno St., Fresno, CA 93703-3788 <www.dioceseoffresno.org>.

Diocese of Monterey Archives (covers Monterey, San Benito, San Luis Obispo, and Santa Cruz counties): P.O. Box 2048, Monterey, CA 93942 <www.dioceseofmonterey.org>.

Diocese of Oakland (covers Alameda and Contra Costa counties): 2900 Lake Shore Ave., Oakland, CA 94610-3697 <www.oakdiocese.org>.

Diocese of Orange (covers Orange County): P.O. Box 14195, Orange, CA 92863-1595; 2811 E. Villa Real Dr., Orange, CA 92867-1999 <www.rcbo.org>.

Diocese of Sacramento (covers the twenty Northern California counties of Amador, Butte, Colusa, El Dorado, Glenn, Lassen, Modoc, Nevada, Placer, Plumas, Sacramento, Shasta, Sierra, Siskiyou, Solano, Sutter, Tehama, Trinity, Yolo, and Yuba): Pastoral Center, 2110 Broadway, Sacramento, CA 95818 <www.diocese-sacramento.org/index.htm>.

Diocese of San Bernardino (covers Riverside and San Bernardino counties): 1201 E. Highland Ave., San Bernardino, CA 92404-4641 <www.sbdiocese.org>.

Diocese of San Diego (covers Imperial and San Diego counties): P.O. Box 85728, San Diego, CA 92186-5728 <www.diocese-sdiego.org>.

Diocese of San Jose (covers Santa Clara County): 900 Lafayette St., Ste. 301, Santa Clara, CA 95050-4966 <www.dsj.org>.

Diocese of Santa Rosa (covers Del Norte, Humboldt, Lake, Mendocino, Napa, and Sonoma counties): 320 Tenth St., Santa Rosa, CA 95401 <www.santarosacatholic.org>.

Diocese of Stockton (covers Alpine, Calaveras, Mono, San Joaquin, Stanislaus, and Tuolumne counties): 1105 N. Lincoln St., Stockton, CA 95203 <www.stocktondiocese.org/english/index.html>.

The Episcopal Church arrived in California from its earliest days as a U.S. possession, and all current dioceses were carved from the original Episcopal Diocese of California. Today the state is served by six dioceses whose websites have links to parishes:

Diocese of El Camino Real (covers Monterey, San Benito, San Luis Obispo, Santa Clara, and Santa Cruz counties): Trinity Cathedral, 81 N. 2nd St., San Jose, CA 95113 <www.ecrweb.org>.

Diocese of Los Angeles (covers Los Angeles, Orange, Riverside, San Bernardino, Santa Barbara, and Ventura counties): The Cathedral Center of St. Paul, 840 Echo Park Ave., Los Angeles, CA 90026 <www.ladiocese.org>.

Diocese of Northern California (covers south of Sacramento north to the Oregon border): P.O. Box 161268, Sacramento, CA 95816-1268 <www.dncweb.org>.

Diocese of San Diego (covers Imperial, Riverside, and San Diego counties and some of Yuma County, Arizona): 2728 Sixth Ave., San Diego, CA 92103 <www.edsd.org>.

Diocese of San Joaquin (Northern boundary south of Sacramento; Southern boundary south of Bakersfield; Eastern boundary Nevada border; Western boundary west of Interstate 5): 4159 E. Dakota Ave., Fresno, CA 93726-5227 <www.sjoaquin.net>.

Episcopal Diocese of California (covers Alameda, Contra Costa, Marin, San Francisco, and Southern Alameda counties): 1055 Taylor St., San Francisco, CA 94108 <www.diocal.org>.

The United Methodist Church is served through the two conferences in California which manage its affairs. The conference can be contacted for information on records and for contact information on local congregations. The two conferences are: California-Nevada Conference, P.O. Box 980250, West Sacramento, CA 95798-0250 <www.cnumc.org>, and the California Pacific Conference, P.O. Box 6006, Pasadena, CA 91108-6006 <www.cal-pac.org>.

The Presbyterian denomination in California is served by two synods, each of which is comprised of several presbyteries, and within each presbytery are several congregations. These synods include:

Pacific Synod (presbyteries in Berkeley, Petaluma, Sacramento, San Jose, Stockton, and Visalia counties): 8 Fourth St., Petaluma, CA 94952-3004 <www.synodpacific.org>.

Southern California and Hawaii Synod (has presbyteries in Los Ranchos, Pacific, Riverside, San Diego, San Fernando, San Gabriel, and Santa Barbara counties): 1501 Wilshire Blvd., Los Angeles, CA 90017-2205 <www.synod.org>.

There is a large collection of Presbyterian registers on microfilm at the FHL. These collections include congregations

from all branches of Presbyterianism; however, not all Presbyterian records for California are deposited at the Presbyterian Historical Society in Philadelphia or on microfilm at the FHL. For older records, contact the synods for additional assistance.

Another large denomination for California, The Church of Jesus Christ of Latter-day Saints (the Mormons), has played a pivotal role in the state since its earliest days. Mormons came to California ports as a migratory approach to Utah and served the early U.S. Army in the Mormon Battalion. Mormon colonies such as San Bernardino were meant, initially, to be an extension of the Mormon Zion webbing out from Salt Lake City. Some could not resist the appeal of the gold rush and found themselves separated from the main body in Utah. Others came to California as settlers and "gold missionaries" to earn money to take back to Utah to help buy necessities. Mission, congregation, and family genealogies for all California activities of the Church are at the FHL.

The Seventh-Day Adventist Church has had a presence in the state since 1859. From its early days it formed church-related schools and health facilities. Records are kept with one of four local conferences or with the local congregations themselves. Information on the church, its history, and its records can be found in the Del E. Webb Memorial Library, Loma Linda University, Loma Linda, CA 92350 <www.llu.edu/llu/library/>.

Jews have been in California, migrating from elsewhere in the United States as well as from Europe, since the gold rush days. The legacy of their presence can be seen in the number of Jewish record collections as well as historical and genealogical societies. A good place to begin the search into California Jewish ancestry is Jewish GenWeb <www.jewishgen.org>. The website has links to all of California's Jewish Genealogical Society branches including societies in Los Angeles, Orange County, Palm Springs, Sacramento, San Diego, and the San Francisco Bay Area society.

The San Francisco Bay Area society has links to websites and repositories for Northern California with Jewish interest <www.jewishgen.org/sfbajgs>. The Los Angeles society website has links to Southern California synagogues, cemeteries, and mortuaries <www.jgsla.org>. The society members also publish the journal *RootsKey*. Historical and genealogical collections of the Los Angeles society are housed at the Los Angeles Family History Center of the LDS Church (see Archives, Libraries, and Societies).

There are no centralized repositories dealing with church records in California. Scattered records can be found in genealogical publications, the DAR compilations (see page 13), and on microfilm. Three comprehensive articles about church records can be found in the Summer, Fall, and Winter 1990 issues of *Southern California Historical Quarterly*, published by the Historical Society of Southern California, 200 E. Ave. 43, Los Angeles, CA 90031. Entitled "Archival Sources for the History of Religion in California," Part 1 is subtitled "Catholic Sources" and was compiled by Monsignor Francis J. Weber; Part 2, "Jewish Religious Sources," is by William M. Kramer and Norton B. Stern; and Part 3, "Protestant Sources," is by Eldon G. Ernst.

The Spanish missions have played a central role in California's religious history. Father Junipero Serra, a Franciscan, raised the standard to his sovereign on 2 June 1769 and began the trek that led him the length of the state of California. He founded a string of missions that would lead the state in the settlement of the vast uncharted land and the conversion of its natives. About a third of the total missions built were founded by Father Serra.

Military Records

The California State Archives has become the state's official repository for service records of Californians from the Indian Wars through the World Wars, including National Guard records. Among the archives collections are organizational papers, correspondence, election of officers, muster rolls, loyalty oaths, and material relating to independent militia units. Some of these collections are on microfilm at the National Archives. Some are also on microfilm at the FHL.

Another collection of California military records is housed at the California State Military Museum, 1119 Second St., Sacramento, CA 95814 <www.militarymuseum.org>. Its collection housed at the Major General Walter P. Story Memorial Library and Research Center is among the best archives of Western Americana military history in the nation, including original unit rosters of early California militia units. The website has links to various websites on California military history.

Richard H. Orton, ed., *Records of California Men in the War of Rebellion, 1861–1867* (Sacramento: State Printing Office, 1890) and J. Carlyle Parker, comp., *A Personal Name Index to Orton's...*, vol. 5 of Gale Genealogy and Local History Series (Detroit: Gale Research, 1978) provide printed sources for those serving in the Civil War. The National Archives' seven-roll microfilm index to compiled service records for California's Union Army Volunteers is available for research at the California State Library and through the FHL.

The California State Library also has the National Archives' seventeen-roll microfilm series of the California War History Committee's "World War I Records of California Service Men." The information in this collection was submitted voluntarily and therefore does not cover all California veterans, but includes birth date, parents, service records, and sometimes material such as educational background and newspaper clippings. The World War I Draft Registration Cards for California are available on microfilm from the National Archives with copies at the FHL.

Periodicals, Newspapers, and Manuscript Collection

Periodicals

Nearly every local genealogical society in the state has some form of publication. These journals and newsletters will be at the major California repositories with genealogical collections, especially the Sutro Branch of the California State Library (see Archives, Libraries, and Societies). Large collections will also be found at the FHL and at the Allen County Public Library in Fort Wayne, Indiana (see page 204).

The official periodical of the California Historical Society is *California History*, which began in 1922. This quality publication is available at some 500 libraries in the United States. The society's website (see Archives, Libraries, and Societies) has an index to the journal and listing of libraries holding its journal.

Newspapers

The California Newspaper Project, managed by the University of California, is a major effort to identify and microfilm all the state's newspapers. The project has thus far identified 12,500 titles of an estimated 16,000 California newspapers. The project's online database of newspapers can be searched by title, place, subject, and institution at <http://cbsr26.ucr.edu/cnp>.

Some major indexes exist for newspapers. The California State Library in Sacramento's "California Information File," also on microfilm at the FHL, covers more than just newspapers. The library also holds an index of about 922,000 cards with more than 1.8 million citations of San Francisco newspaper items from 1904 to the present. A published index to the *San Francisco Call* covers that newspaper back to 1894.

Manuscripts

Probably the largest manuscript collection in the state is at the Bancroft Library, University of California at Berkeley. The library's collection on the West is strong and includes many diaries, collections of personal papers, and letters. A guide to the manuscript collection is available. Both the Bancroft Library and the California State Library have excellent websites that make accessing information in their collections easy (see Archives, Libraries, and Societies).

Archives, Libraries, and Societies

California State Archives, Office of Secretary of State
1020 O St., Rm. 130
Sacramento, CA 95814
www.ss.ca.gov/archives/archives.htm

The collections in the California State Archives are indicated in various sections in the preceding pages and in the County Resources section (see page 79). The website has a link for family history resources.

California State Library
Library and Courts Bldg. 1
914 Capitol Mall
Sacramento, CA 95814
www.library.ca.gov/index.cfm

The library's website provides access to its catalog and electronic databases and a "California Library Directory" that draws from academic, special, state, state agencies, public, and county law libraries. In addition to the materials already described above, its genealogy collections include:

Pioneer Record File: biographical material on Californians who came before 1860—information submitted by the actual pioneers or by their descendants.

Biographical files: California artists, authors, actors, and musicians along with material on California political leaders.

Directories: a large collection of city, county (from the 1850s) and telephone directories (from 1897).

Sutro Library
California State Library (Sutro Branch)
480 Winston Dr.
San Francisco, CA 94132

This branch of the California State Library differs from the main library in Sacramento in its major focus on genealogical research, including material beyond California. See the main website above.

California Historical Society
678 Mission St.
San Francisco, CA 94105
www.californiahistoricalsociety.org

Some of the extensive collections on California history are described above, including the quarterly publication *California History*.

California Genealogical Society and Library
1611 Telegraph Ave., Ste. 100
Oakland, CA 94612-2154
www.calgensoc.org

The society's library resources are extensive for California as well as for other states. The website has current links to genealogy societies and research libraries throughout the state.

University of California
Bancroft Library
Berkeley, CA 94720
http://bancroft.berkeley.edu

The vast manuscript collection includes considerable material on California's history.

Los Angeles Public Library
History and Genealogy Department
630 W. 5th St.
Los Angeles, California 90071
www.lapl.org/central/history.html

With more than 40,000 volumes, including 10,000 genealogies, the library's website includes a family name index to the History and Genealogy collection.

Chinese Historical Society
965 Clay St.
San Francisco, CA 94108
www.chsa.org

Dedicated to the study and preservation of Chinese American history, the society offers a learning center, programs for children, and an extensive calendar of activities related to cultural history.

Two additional sources are the Family History Centers, branches of the main Family History Library in Salt Lake City. Centers in Los Angeles (10741 Santa Monica Blvd., West Los Angeles, CA 90025 <www.lafhc.org>) and in Oakland (Temple Hill Family History Center, 4766 Lincoln Ave., Oakland, CA 94602 <www.templehill.com>) are among the largest libraries within the FHL system. Collections include material not at the FHL in Salt Lake City.

Special Focus Categories

Immigration

California provided several ports and points of entry for immigrants. San Francisco, in the north, is the largest. In the south, at the mouth of the Los Angeles Harbor are the ports of San Pedro, Wilmington, and Los Angeles; however, these are considered one port of entry in passenger arrivals by sea. Southern land points of entry include San Ysidro, Campo, and Tecate in San Diego County, and Andrade in Imperial County from Mexico.

The California State Library has microfilms of the National Archives arrivals lists, and these are also available on microfilm at the FHL. Many immigrants in this period were from China and Japan, but a good number were from Europe, Australia, India, Chile, Peru, and elsewhere. Below is a list of NARA resources and some compilations.

Other record types can serve to document immigrants from outside the United States and emigrants from within the United States, such as records for the Russian Consular in San Francisco (1862–1928), which document Jews, Poles, Ukranians, Lithuanians, and Finns, among others.

NARA Resources

Port/Point of Entry	Records	Source
Miscellaneous	1906–35	"Pioneer Card File" at State Library
San Pedro/ Wilmington/LA	1907–48	Passengers List, NARA (M1763, M1764)
San Francisco	1850–53	Published in four volumes: Louis J. Rasmussen's *San Francisco Ship Passenger Lists, 1850–1984* (Colma, Calif.: San Francisco Historic Records, 1965–70; vol. 1. 1965; reprint, Baltimore: Genealogical Publishing Co., 1978)
San Francisco from Honolulu	1902–07	NARA (M1440)
San Francisco	1903–18	Customs Lists, NARA (M1412)
San Francisco from U.S. islands	1907–11	Passenger List, NARA (M1438)
San Francisco	1850–53	Published in six volumes: Peter E. Carr's *San Francisco Passenger Departure Lists, 1850–53* (n.p.: TCI Genealogical Resources, 1993–2000)
San Francisco	1854–92	Crew lists, 1854–56, 1861–62, 1883, 1886, 1892, U.S. Custom House, San Francisco
San Francisco	1896–1921	Admitted alien crew lists, NARA (M1436)
San Francisco	1905–21	Crew lists, NARA (M1416)
San Francisco	1882–88	Chinese laborers, NARA (M1413)
San Francisco	1882–1914	Chinese passengers, NARA (M1414)
San Francisco	1903–21	Chinese applying for admission, NARA (M1476)
San Francisco	before 1854	Hamburg citizens arriving in California published in Renate Hauschild-Thiessen's German work *Die Ersten Hamburger in Goldland Kalifornien* (n.p.: n.d.)
San Francisco	1840–1954	List of ships arriving, NARA (M1437)
San Ysidro, San Diego Co	1908–52	Arrivals across the border from Tijuana, Mexico, NARA (M1767)
Andrade, Imperial Co. & Campo, San Diego Co.	1910–52	Arrivals from Mexico, NARA (M2030)

Naturalization

As with other states, prior to 1906 a person might have filed for naturalization in any court in the state; for this time period, there are no guides for locating a naturalization in the state other than for those records that were entered at federal district court. Many of those naturalization records have been gathered and are located at either of the National Archives regional branches: Pacific (San Bruno) or Pacific (Laguna Niguel) (see page 12). These collections include the Northern U.S. Circuit Court (1855–1905) in San Francisco; U.S. District—Northern District (1846–1989) at San Francisco and San Jose; and the U.S. District Eastern Court (1917–58). The FHL also has a large microfilm collection of the NARA microfilm as well as a large collection of citizenship records filed in California counties.

Native American

California's Native American population was unique in that there were many small tribes living a pastoral life when the Spaniards arrived, founding missions and presidios. The missions fell into decay, and the natives dispersed after the Mexican revolution.

For research on Native Americans in California, there are several websites that provide links to the tribes themselves: "Tribes and Villages of California" <www.

Native American Agency Records

Tribe	Agency	DC/NARA	Census
Chemehuevi	Colorado River Agency, 1867–55	Los Angeles	no
Concow	Round Valley Agency, 1893–1920	San Franciso	yes
Digger	Digger Agency, 1916–20	San Francisco	no
Digger	Greenville School and Agency, 1897–1921	San Francisco	no
Grande Ronde	Roseburg Agency, 1912–18	San Francisco	no
Hoopa	Hoopa Valley Agency and School, 1891–1929	San Francisco	no
Hoopa	California Superintendency	DC	yes
Hupa	California Superintendency, 1849–80	DC	yes
Klamath	Hoopa Valley Agency, 1891–1929	San Francisco	yes
Klamath, Lower	Greenville School and Agency, 1897–1921	San Francisco	no
Klamath, Lower	Roseburg Agency, 1913–18	San Francisco	yes
Little Lake Valley	Round Valley Agency	San Francisco	yes
Mission	Million Tule River Agency, 1920–53	Los Angeles	yes
Mission	Pala Subagency, 1905–07, 1916–20	Los Angeles	yes
Modoc	Digger Agency, 1916–20	San Francisco	yes
Paiute	Fort Bidwell Agency, 1910–31	San Francisco	yes
Pit River	Fort Bidwell Agency, 1910–31	San Francisco	yes
Pit River	Round Valley Agency, 1893–1917	San Francisco	yes
Redwood	Round Valley Agency	San Francisco	yes
Shasta	Roseburg Agency, 1912–18	San Francisco	yes
Tule	Tule River Agency	San Francisco	yes
Tule	Sacramento Agency	San Francisco	yes
Tule	Pala Superintendency, 1903–21	Los Angeles	no
Wailaki	Round Valley Agency	San Francisco	yes
Washo	Walker River Agency	San Francisco	yes
Whikut	California Superintendency, 1849–80	DC	no
Wikchamni	California Superintendency	DC	no
Yuma	California Superintendency	DC	no
Yuma	Colorado River Agency, 1867–1955	Los Angeles	yes
Yuma	Fort Yuma Agency, 1901–51	Los Angeles	yes
Yuma	San Carlos Agency, 1900–52	Los Angeles	no
Yuki	Round Valley Agency	San Francisco	yes

hanksville.org/sand/contacts/tribal/CA.php> and "California Tribes Contact Information by Rancheria (Reservation) Name" <www.kstrom.net/isk/maps/ca/sacramento.html> has valuable maps showing location of tribes in the state and contact information for the Sacramento Area Office of the Bureau of Indian Affairs and the Central, Northern, Southern, and Palm Springs agencies.

A large collection of the National Archives Indian agency records on microfilm is at the FHL. This includes a group of various censuses in one collection. Miscellaneous California Census (1907–15) is part of the NARA microfilms with copies at the FHL. The list "Native American Agency Records" refers to the tribe, Indian agency and years of collection, and the NARA location of records. Some tribes are additionally mentioned in the agency records for the border states of Arizona, Nevada, and Oregon. This includes the Colorado River Agency, Fort Yuma Agency, and the San Carlos Agency, which take in tribes in both Arizona and California.

Ethnic Groups

By the time of the first census in 1850, California's nonnative population swelled to 92,600. Of this population, 70,000 were Americans living mostly in Northern California.

Migrants, from every ethnic group in the country, continued to arrive at roughly the rate of 300,000 annually until 1900. Many were farmers from the southern tier of the United States including Texas, Missouri, Arkansas, and Oklahoma. The population increased at an even higher rate for the next four decades.

The Golden Promised Land, as California has been thought of, has not always been a paradise for minority groups. Chinese, Japanese, Hindus, and other Asians from many eastern lands came to work on the railroad projects and were subject to the prejudices of the resident population. The Okies, from the drought-stricken dust bowl, tried to find work in southern California and the San Joaquin Valley in the 1930s. The demand for workers rose abruptly during World War II, bringing many African Americans, Mexicans, and more recently Latin Americans, and Southeast Asians. The public records of California include all ethnic groups, and most libraries can be helpful in focusing research on any particular group. In addition to Ryskamp's resource guide (see Background Sources) and Beers' guide (see Manuscripts), the following are sources or contain background information for some California ethnic groups:

Beasely, Delilah Leontium. *The Negro Trail Blazers of California.* New York: Negro University Press, 1969.

Burchell, R. A. *The San Francisco Irish, 1848–1880.* Berkeley: University of California Press, 1980.

Goode, Kenneth G. *California's Black Pioneers: A Brief Historical Survey.* Santa Barbara: McNally & Loftin, 1974.

Nicosia, Francesco M. *Italian Pioneers of California.* Italian American Chamber of Commerce of the Pacific Coast, 1960.

Northrop, Marie E. *Spanish-Mexican Families of Early California: 1769–1850.* Vol. 1. Burbank: Southern California Genealogical Society, 1986. *Spanish-Mexican Families of Early California: 1769–1850.* Vol. 2. Burbank: Southern California Genealogical Society, 1984.

Gold Rush

For anyone seeking an ancestor who left for the California gold fields between 1848 and 1850, it would be wise to examine the emigrant companies from Massachusetts and the available lists of Argonauts. Northern California pioneers were called Argonauts in reference to those in ancient Greek mythology who sailed with Jason on the ship *Argo.* Octavius Thorndike Howe's *Argonauts of '49: History and Adventures of the Emigrant Companies from Massachusetts, 1849–1850* (Cambridge, Mass.: Harvard University Press, 1923) includes a list of the mining companies sailing from Massachusetts to California in 1849. The list gives the name of the company, the ship's name, the ship's master, and the date of sailing. It catalogs 124 sailings and the number of persons in the company.

In 1890 Charles Warren Haskins published his personal memoirs, *The Argonauts of California: Being the Reminiscences of Scenes and Incidents That Occurred in California in Early Mining Days; by a Pioneer* (New York: Fords, Howard and Hulbert, 1890). In his narrative, Haskins included the names of a number of persons who arrived in California from both land and sea routes. Original sources are not indicated for entries because many sources that might have been used were lost in the San Francisco earthquake and fire. J. Carlyle Parker's preface in the Society of California Pioneers' *Index to the Argonauts of California* (New Orleans: Polyanthos Press, 1975) is a discussion of the problems with Argonaut lists and has an index.

The Libera Martina Spinazze index cards were deposited in the California State Library and, in time, the Sequoia Chapter, DAR, acquired four incomplete copies of these files. The files were finally completed and bound into four sets, copies of which were given by the DAR to the DAR Library in Washington, D.C., the Bancroft Library at the University of California at Berkeley, the California Historical Society, the California State Library in Sacramento, and the Los Angeles Public Library.

The 1852 census, the catalog, and manuscript and published material in the California State Library are other useful sources regarding the gold rush era. The Bancroft collection of diaries at the University of California at Berkeley is also useful. The San Joaquin Genealogical Society published five volumes of probate records, newspapers, and vital records covering the period of 1850 to 1866 for its county in *Gold Rush Days,* which is available from the Western Reserve Historical Society, 10825 E. Blvd., Cleveland, OH 44106.

County Resources

The following is a listing of the extant vital, land, probate, and court records for each county. Some counties encompass land settled in the eighteenth century; their records pre-date county formation. Land transactions and vital records recorded in the county are at the county recorder's office. The county clerk generally has probate books and files from the county's superior court, civil court records, and naturalizations. Divorces may be in either place, depending on how they were filed.

The California State Archives and the FHL both have microfilms of selected county records. Current information for county offices can be found at <www.state.ca.us/state/portal/myca_hompage.jsp> and the California Association of Counties website at <www.csac.counties.org>.

California's records are fairly complex, due in part to the nature of how counties were formed. Land was often added to the different counties several times for years after a county was formed. It is therefore an extremely subjective process to determine a beginning date for California's early records, a process that is complicated by the changes in jurisdiction during the territorial period, Mexican period, and the Spanish period,

which all generated records. The result is that any inventory of beginning dates for county records will vary depending on how a county record is defined. To address this problem, several published sources and Internet sites were consulted and compared to verify the county list that follows, including the following references:

Coy, Owen C. *California County Boundaries: A Study of the Division of the State into Counties and the Subsequent Changes in Their Boundaries.* Berkeley: California Historical Survey Commission, 1923.

———. *Guide to the County Archives of California.* Sacramento: California State Printing Office, 1919.

"The Birth of Each County and Later Significant Boundary Changes," found at <www.csac.counties.org>.

Sperling, Muriel. *Sources of Genealogical Help in California.* Burbank, Calif.: The Southern California Genealogical Society, 1990. Reprinted 2000.

Nicklas, Laurie. *The California Locator: A Directory of Public Records for Locating People Dead or Alive in California.* Modesto, Calif.: Nicklas Publishing Co., 1996.

CALIFORNIA

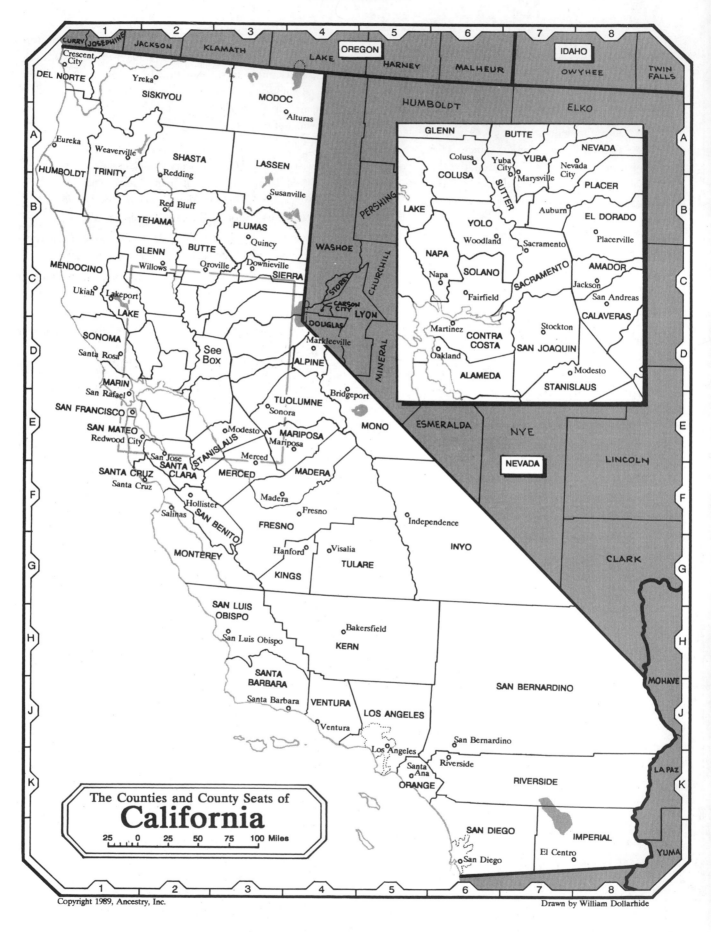

The Counties and County Seats of
California

25 0 25 50 75 100 Miles

Copyright 1989, Ancestry, Inc.

Drawn by William Dollarhide

CALIFORNIA

Map	County / Address	Date Formed / Parent County/ies	Birth Marriage Death	Land Probate Court
D6	Alameda 1221 Oak St., Ste. 536 Oakland 94612-4224	1853 Contra Costa/Santa Clara	1873 1853 1869	1853 1853 1853
D4	Alpine 99 Water St./ P.O. Box 158 Markleeville 91620-0158	1864 El Dorado/Amador/ Calaveras/Tuolumne	1873 1864 1864	1864 1864 1864
C8	Amador 500 Argonaut Lane Jackson 95642-6470	1854 Calaveras/El Dorado	1873 1854 1873	1854 1854 1854
		Land from El Dorado County was added in 1855 and again in 1857 and 1863.		
	Branciforte	(renamed Santa Cruz in 1850) original		
C2	Butte 25 County Center Dr. Oroville 95965-3316	1850 original	1859 1851 1859	1846 1850 1850
C8	Calaveras 891 Mountain Ranch Road San Andreas 95249-9713	1850 original	1858 1854 1858	1850 1866 1850
A6	Colusa 546 Jay St. Colusa 95932-2400	1850 original	1873 1853 1873	1844 1851 1851
		Attached to Butte County for administration until it was organized in 1851. Land was later added from counties Yolo (1851), Butte (1856), and Sutter (1856).		
D6	Contra Costa 651 Pine St. Rm 106 Martinez 94553-1229	1850 original	1850 1850 1850	1850 1850 1850
A1	Del Norte 555 H St. Crescent City 95531	1857 Klamath	1873 1857 1873	1853 1848 1848
		Land was later added from counties Siskiyou (1887) and Humboldt (1901).		
B8	El Dorado 330 Fair Lane Placerville 95667-4103	1850 original	1878 1851 1907	1851 1850 1850
		Land from Placer County was added in 1863.		
G3	Fresno 2281 Tulare St. Fresno 93721	1856 Mariposa/Merced/Tulare	1873 1856 1873	1856 1880 1856
		Land was later added from counties Merced (1856) and Tulare (1856).		
C2	Glenn 526 W. Sycamore St. Willows 95988-2746	1891 Colusa	1895 1891 1891	1891 1891 1891
		Land from Mendocino County was added in 1907.		
A1	Humboldt 825 Fifth St. Eureka 95501-1153	1853 Trinity	1873 1864 1873	1874 1853 1853
		Land was later added from counties Mendocino (1860), Klamath (1875), and Del Norte (1901).		
K8	Imperial 940 W. Main St. El Centro 92243-2869	1907 San Diego	1900 1903 1900	1851 1907 1907
G6	Inyo 168 N. Edwards St. Independence 93526	1866 Tulare/Mono	1905 1873 1905	1866 1866 1866
		Land was later added from counties Mono (1870), San Bernardino (1872), and Kern (1872).		
H5	Kern 1115 Truxton Ave. Bakersfield 93301-4617	1866 Tulare/Los Angeles	1850 1850 1850	1850 1866 1866
		Land from San Luis Obispo County was added in 1866.		
G4	Kings 1400 W. Lacy Blvd. Hanford 93230-5905	1893 Tulare	1893 1893 1893	1893 1893 1893
		Land from Fresno County was added in 1909.		
	Klamath	1851 Trinity		
		Abolished 1874; parts annexed to Humboldt and Siskiyou.		
C1	Lake 255 N. Forbes St. Lakeport 95453-4759	1861 Napa	1867 1867 1867	1867 1867 1867
		Land was later added from counties Mendocino (1864) and Colusa (1868).		
A3	Lassen 221 S. Roop St. Susanville 96130	1864 Plumas/Shasta	1864 1864 1874	1857 1864 1863
		Land from Plumas County was added in 1872.		
J5	Los Angeles 500 W. Temple St. Los Angeles 90012-2713	1850 original	1849 1850 1874	1850 1850 1850
		Land was later added from counties Mariposa (1851) and Santa Barbara (1851).		
F4	Madera 209 W. Yosemite Ave. Madera 93637-3534	1893 Fresno	1883 1893 1892	1893 1893 1893
D1	Marin Civic Center, Rm. 329 San Raphael 94903	1850 original	1868 1857 1873	1834 1850 1850
E4	Mariposa 5100 Bullion St. Mariposa 95338	1850 original	1873 1851 1873	1850 1850 1850
C1	Mendocino 501 Low Gap Rd. Ukiah 95482-3734	1850 original	1859 1859 1859	1852 1854 1858
		Attached to Sonoma County for administrative purposes until 1859.		
F3	Merced 2222 M St. Merced 95340-3729	1855 Mariposa	1873 1855 1889	1856 1855 1855
A4	Modoc 204 Court St. Alturas 96101	1874 Siskiyou	1894 1874 1882	1874 1874 1874
E5	Mono P.O. Box 715 Bridgeport 93517	1861 Calaveras/Fresno/Mariposa	1873 1862 1877	1861 1864 1864
		Land from Amador County was added in 1866.		

Map	County / Address	Date Formed / Parent County/ies	Birth Marriage Death	Land Probate Court
G2	**Monterey** 240 Church St. Salinas 93901-2695	1850 original	1824 1887 1887	1850* 1850 1850

*Alcalde records from 1781. See Land Records.
Land from San Luis Obispo County was added in 1863 and 1872.

Map	County / Address	Date Formed / Parent County/ies	Birth Marriage Death	Land Probate Court
C6	**Napa** 1195 Third St., Rm. 310 Napa 94559-3035	1850 original	1868 1850 1873	1848 1851 1849

Land was later added from counties Lake (1872) and Solano (1855).

| A8 | **Nevada** 950 Maidu Ave. Nevada City 95959-8617 | 1851 Yuba | 1873 1856 1873 | 1856 1856 1886 |

Land was added from counties Yuba (1852) and Sierra (1856).

| K5 | **Orange** 10 Civic Center Plaza Santa Ana 92701-4017 | 1889 Los Angeles | 1887 1889 1889 | 1889 1889 1889 |

| B8 | **Placer** 175 Fulweiler Ave. Auburn 95603-4543 | 1851 Yuba/Sutter | 1873 1851 1873 | 1851 1850 1852 |

Land was added from El Dorado County in 1913.

| B3 | **Plumas** 520 W. Main St. Quincy 95971-9115 | 1854 Butte | 1873 1854 1873 | 1854 1854 1854 |

Land was added from Sierra County in 1866.

| K7 | **Riverside** 4080 Lemon St., 14th Floor Riverside 92501-3679 | 1893 San Diego/ San Bernardino | 1893 1893 1893 | 1893 1893 1893 |

| C7 | **Sacramento** 700 H St. Sacramento 95814-1216 | 1850 original | 1858 1850 1850 | 1848 1849 1849 |

| F2 | **San Benito** 481 Fourth St. Hollister 95023-3840 | 1874 Monterey | 1850 1874 1874 | 1850 1874 1874 |

Land was later added from counties Fresno (1887) and Merced (1887).

| J7 | **San Bernardino** 385 N. Arrowhead Ave. San Bernardino 92415-0110 | 1853 Los Angeles | 1854 1854 1873 | 1854 1856 1853 |

Land was added from Los Angeles County in 1878.

| K6 | **San Diego** 1600 Pacific Hwy. San Diego 92101-2429 | 1850 original | 1860 1850 1851 | 1850 1848 1855 |

| F1 | **San Francisco** 1 Dr. Carlton B. Goodlet Place San Francisco 94102-4603 | 1850 original | 1906 1860 1865 | 1838 1850 1850 |

Extensive record loss caused by the 1906 earthquake; some records re-registered.

| D7 | **San Joaquin** 222 E. Weber Ave., Rm. 701 Stockton 95202-2709 | 1850 original | 1850 1850 1858 | 1850 1850 1851 |

Land was later added from Sacramento County in 1878.

Map	County / Address	Date Formed / Parent County/ies	Birth Marriage Death	Land Probate Court
H3	**San Luis Obispo** 1050 Monterey, Rm 370 San Luis Obispo 93408-2040	1850 original	1857 1850 1873	1881 1854 1854

Land was later added from counties Santa Barbara (1854 and 1872), Monterey (1861), and Kern (1885).

| E1 | **San Mateo** 400 County Center Redwood City 94063-1668 | 1856 San Francisco/ Santa Cruz | 1865 1853 1865 | 1856 1856 1871 |

Land from Santa Cruz County was added in 1868.

| J3 | **Santa Barbara** 105 E. Anapamu St. Santa Barbara 93101-6054 | 1850 original | 1859 1850 1873 | 1844* 1854 1850 |

*Alcalde records included from 1779. See Land Records.
Land was added from San Louis Obispo County in 1852 and 1872.

| F2 | **Santa Clara** 70 W. Hedding St. San Jose 95110 | 1850 original | 1873 1846 1873 | 1850 1850 1850 |

| F2 | **Santa Cruz** 701 Ocean St. Santa Cruz 95060-4003 | 1850 (as Branciforte; renamed, 1850) original | 1873 1851 1873 | 1847* 1850 1850 |

*Alcalde records included from 1779. See Land Records.

| A2 | **Shasta** 1815 Yuba St., Ste. 1 Redding 96001 | 1850 original | 1873 1852 1873 | 1852 1850 1850 |

Land was added from Plumas County in 1872.

| C3 | **Sierra** P.O. Box D Downieville 95936 | 1852 Yuba | 1857 1853 1873 | 1852 1852 1852 |

Land was later added from counties Yuba (1866) and Plumas (1863 and 1866).

| A2 | **Siskiyou** P.O. Box 338 Yreka 96097 | 1852 Shasta/Klamath | 1850 1852 1873 | 1852 1852 1852 |

Land was later added from counties Klamath (1875) and Del Norte (1887).

| C6 | **Solano** 580 Texas St. Fairfield 94533 | 1850 original | 1873 1850 1873 | 1848 1850 1850 |

Land was added from Mare Island in Solano County in 1853.

| D1 | **Sonoma** 575 Administration Dr. Santa Rosa 95401 | 1850 original | 1858 1846 1873 | 1841 1850 1848 |

Land was added from Mendocino County in 1855 and again in 1859.

| E3, D7 | **Stanislaus** 1010 Tenth St., Ste. 6500 Modesto 95354 | 1854 Tuolumne/San Joaquin | 1873 1854 1873 | 1854 1854 1854 |

Land was added from counties San Joaquin (1860) and Merced (1868).

| B7 | **Sutter** 1160 Civic Center Blvd. Yuba City 95993 | 1850 original | 1873 1850 1873 | 1849 1872 1854 |

Land was later added from counties Placer (1866) and Butte (1852, 1854, and 1866).

Map	County Address	Date Formed Parent County/ies	Birth Marriage Death	Land Probate Court
B2	Tehama 332 Pine St./P.O. Box 250 Red Bluff 96080	1856 Colusa/Butte/Shasta	1889 1856 1889	1856 1856 1856
	Land later added from Shasta (1857) and Butte (1859).			
B1	Trinity 101 Court St./P.O.Box 1613 Weaverville 96093	1850 original	1873 1857 1873	1855 1860 1854
	For the first year of organization, Trinity County was attached to Shasta County. *Land was later added from counties Klamath (1855) and Mendocino (1860, 1872).*			
G4	Tulare 2800 W. Burrel Visalia 93291	1852 Mariposa	1852 1852 1873	1854 1854 1854
E4	Tuolumne 2 S. Green St. Sonora 95370	1850 original	1858 1850 1859	1850 1852 1852
J4	Ventura 800 S. Victoria Ave. Ventura 93009	1872 San Luis Obispo/Santa Barbara	1873 1873 1872	1871* 1873 1873
	Probate records from 1850 county level records begin 1873. *Land was later added from Los Angeles County in 1881.*			
B6	Yolo 625 Court St. Woodland 95695	1850 original	1878 1873 1863	1849 1850 1850
	Land was later added from Solano County in 1857.			
A7	Yuba 215 Fifth St. Marysville 95901	1850 original	1853 1851 1858	1850 1850 1851

Colorado

**BIRDIE MONK HOLSCLAW, CG
AND MARSHA HOFFMAN RISING, CG, FUGA, FASG**

olorado fell under several governmental jurisdictions during its developmental history, being for a time part of the territories of Spain, Missouri, Mexico, Utah, the United States, New Mexico, unorganized Native American land, and finally Nebraska and Kansas. Non-federal records, however, exist only for the domains of Utah, New Mexico, Kansas, and Nebraska territories. The territory of Colorado, with its seventeen counties, was formed in 1861. Sixteen years later, on 1 August 1876, it was admitted as the thirty-eighth state in the Union.

Bent's Fort, built in 1833 and now a national historic site near La Junta, established an extensive trading system between Native Americans and fur trappers, but the San Luis Valley was the site of the first permanent nonnative settlement in what became Colorado, with the town of San Luis being founded in 1851. One year later, Fort Massachusetts, later replaced by Fort Garland, was erected on the Ute Creek to protect travelers on the Santa Fe Trail. At that time most pioneers were not settling in Colorado but rather moving through to California and Oregon.

Mining accounted for the first extensive settlement around what is now Denver. Reports of gold began in the spring of 1858 and brought many newcomers to the area. Later that year the "Pike's Peak or Bust" gold rush began, and in 1859 a "Second Stampede" brought additional thousands searching for gold, including both settlers and speculators. Within only a few years, however, the population began to shift from speculator to settler. The 1860 territorial census of Colorado counted 32,654 white males and 1,577 white females, but by May 1861 the census

taken by Territorial Governor William Gilpin counted 20,798 males and 4,484 females. Clearly, as the men were moving on to other ventures, the type of people coming to Colorado began to change.

Early native tribes in Colorado included the Ute, the Apache, and "the wandering tribes" of Cheyenne, Arapaho, and Sioux. On 18 February 1861, the Cheyenne and Arapaho negotiated a treaty at Fort Wise, Kansas, in which they ceded all lands in the Pike's Peak region to the United States. A treaty with the Ute followed in 1864, ceding all Ute land east of the Continental Divide. Despite the treaties, the period from 1861 to 1864 was a time of enormous tension between natives and the settlers. Before the Sand Creek massacre in November 1864 there were numerous raids and killings. By 1881 the Ute Indians completed moving from the western part of the state into Utah, and large sections of Colorado became open for settlement.

During the Civil War, over 8,000 men served in Colorado units. Many Northerners living in Colorado returned to their prior residences in other states to help fight for the Union cause, while some settlers remained in their new domicile. Colorado participated in a major battle in the Civil War that occurred in March 1862 when Governor Gilpin organized one of three Colorado companies to stop the Confederate attempt to block the western supply of gold to the eastern states. Forces clashed at Glorieta Pass, New Mexico, and the Confederates retreated.

After the Civil War, the population of Colorado began to expand primarily through the development of railroads. The first "Iron Horse" arrived in Denver on 24 June 1870. The researcher with early Colorado ancestors should therefore watch

for migration during the 1870s and follow the growth of the railroads. A promotional organization, the Colorado Board of Immigration, was created in 1872, and the population of Colorado tripled between 1870 and 1875. Unfortunately, this decade also brought grasshoppers and economic depression, forcing many settlers to return to the East or go farther west. Throughout these difficult times, mining and agriculture remained the two important industries.

Most migration to Colorado came from a block of states extending from New York and Pennsylvania on the east to Kansas and Nebraska on the west. In 1860 the greatest number of immigrants to Colorado came from Ohio, followed by Illinois, New York, Missouri, and Indiana. The population explosion after the Civil War brought native-born Americans primarily from the states of Missouri, Kansas, Nebraska, and Iowa. The population of Colorado also included a large number of foreign-born immigrants including Czechs, Slovaks, Irish, Germans, Russians, Canadians, Swedish, Scots, Italians, and Chinese. By 1880, one-fifth of the population of Colorado was foreign-born and the state had three official languages: English, Spanish, and German. In the 1890s more Germans arrived, an ethnic group that continues to dominate in eastern Colorado today.

Vital Records

A law enacted in 1875 provided for registration of births and deaths, but compliance was sporadic and minimal. Some early vital records may be located in the county courthouses or the county health departments, but their location is not consistent. The *Guide to Vital Statistics of Colorado*, prepared by Colorado Historical Records Survey, Division of Community Service Programs of the Works Progress Administration (WPA), is out of date but remains the only comprehensive state guide. Volume 1 of the publication describes the records held by public archives, and volume 2 discusses those held in church archives. This guide is located in the Colorado Historical Society Library (see Archives, Libraries, and Societies) as well as other major libraries and repositories.

Statewide registration of births began in 1910; registration for deaths began earlier, in 1900. Although the county health departments existed in one form or another from 1900, Colorado did not join the national death registration system until 1906. Birth registration was even later, beginning in 1928. Birth and death records are available from the Colorado Department of Public Health and Environment, Vital Records Section, 4300 Cherry Creek Drive South, Denver, CO 80246-1530. Some restrictions determine who may gain access to these records, with death records more available than birth. A list of persons eligible to apply for the records is printed on the back of the application form. Some relatives of a deceased individual

who are pursuing genealogical research may be issued a death certificate. Application forms, rules, and current prices are all available on the office's website <www.cdphe.state.co.us/hs/certs.asp>.

Some county health departments do have incomplete birth records from earlier dates that are not available at the state level. Unless they have been turned over to the Colorado State Archives, they are still held by the county health department.

The county's clerk and recorder maintains marriage records (generally available from the early days of the county), and the clerk of the district court holds divorce records. A statewide list of marriages and divorces indexed by name of the groom exists for the years 1900 through 1939 (with one quarter of entries pre-1900) and is located at the Colorado State Archives and Denver Public Library—Western History and Genealogy Department (see Archives, Libraries, and Societies) and the Family History Library (FHL) in Salt Lake City. Denver Public Library has an online version of the marriage index (1975-present) that will include brides as well as grooms at <www.denverlibrary.org/research/genealogy/index.html>.

The divorces are indexed online at <www.sctc.state.co.us/marriages/divorces.aspx>. Both agencies have a microfiche marriage index, by bride and groom (1975-present) and a divorce index (1968-present). An up-to-date version of these indexes for this later time period is being made available online at <www.cdphe.state.co.us/hs/marriage.html>.

The Colorado Historical Society has a small card catalog index for early vital records (births, deaths, marriages) that appeared in Colorado newspapers between 1860 and 1940. The general index in the Denver Public Library—Western History and Genealogy Department also includes many births, marriages, and deaths, mostly taken from newspaper references.

The Colorado Genealogical Society (see Archives, Libraries, and Societies) publication *Marriages of Arapahoe County, Colorado, 1859–1901* (Denver: the society, 1986) includes marriages from the area of Colorado that later evolved into the counties of Adams, Arapahoe, Denver, Clear Creek, Jefferson, Elbert, Lincoln, Washington, and the others located in east central Colorado. The certificates themselves are located at the Colorado State Archives.

Census Records

Federal

Population Schedules
- Indexed—1860 (as various territories, see below), 1870, 1880, 1900, 1910, 1920, 1930

- Soundex—1880, 1900, 1920

Mortality Schedules
- 1870, 1880

Industry and Agriculture Schedules
- 1870, 1880

The Colorado Historical Society has microfilmed copies of the Colorado decennial census with indexes for 1860, 1870, and 1880. Although it does not currently own the Soundex to the 1900 census, one is located at the National Archives—Rocky Mountain Region in Denver and the Norlin Library, University of Colorado. The Denver Public Library—Western History and Genealogy Department holds copies of almost all microfilm of Colorado population schedules (including 1860 Kansas and Nebraska territorial schedules, which include parts of Colorado), as well as printed indexes and microfilmed Soundex. The Colorado State Archives has the 1860 censuses on microfilm for Utah, New Mexico, Nebraska, and Kansas that cover the present geographic boundaries of Colorado. No survey of available state copies of the federal censuses exists; however, Clear Creek County holds their census records for 1880, and other copies may exist. Norlin Library at University of Colorado at Boulder (see Archives, Libraries, and Societies) maintains microfilm copies of Colorado population schedules (including Kansas, Nebraska, and Utah territorial schedules), as well as most related Soundexes.

Microfilmed copies of the 1870 and 1880 mortality schedules are located at the National Archives—Rocky Mountain Region (see page 12) and the Denver Public Library. A printed index has been compiled. The original schedules are housed with the Daughters of the American Revolution (DAR) in Washington, D.C. (see page 13). A printed index has been compiled, and is also available online at <www.ancestry.com>.

Territorial and State

The first census in what would become Colorado was taken in 1860 as part of several territorial censuses. Arapahoe County, which covered the central eastern section, was included in the Kansas territorial census for that year. The areas of Boulder City, Altoona City, Boulder Creek Settlement, Gold Hill Settlement, Miraville City, and the Platte River Settlement were enumerated with Nebraska Territory, and are transcribed online by Ted and Carol Miller at <www.rootsweb.com/~usgenweb/ne/state/1860cens.htm#colorado60>. Denver City was enumerated partly with Nebraska and partly with the Kansas territorial census. The southeast portion of Colorado was enumerated in parts of Taos and Mora counties of New Mexico Territory. Leadville, although a booming mining town at the time and located in what is now Lake County, was in Utah Territory and not enumerated.

The Colorado Territory was organized in 1861, and voters residing in the territory were listed at that time. The original poll books (which list only males) remain in the Colorado State Archives and have been microfilmed. An index by the Colorado Genealogical Society (see Archives, Libraries, and Societies for address) Computer Interest Group has been printed, and is also available online at <www.denver.lib.co.us/research/genealogy/election.html>.

An 1866 enumeration was taken, but the only extant returns are for the northeastern section which included the counties of Logan, Morgan, Phillips, Sedgwick, Weld, and parts of Washington and Yuma. Heads of household with number of males over and under twenty-one and females over and under eighteen are included in a document available at the Colorado State Archives.

The microfilmed copy of the 1885 special federal census, encompassing population, agricultural, manufacturing, and mortality returns is located at the Colorado State Archives, the National Archives—Rocky Mountain Region in Denver, Colorado Historical Society, the Denver Public Library, and FHL. Most of this census is indexed at <www.ancestry.com>. An excellent index to the large Arapahoe County portion (now Arapahoe, Denver and parts of Adams, Washington, and Yuma counties) has been compiled by the Colorado Genealogical Society. Several other counties have been indexed by various local societies. Some counties have abridged copies that arranged residents alphabetically, so that they appear to be indexes. However, researchers should be aware this "index" does not refer the reader to the page number of the original census and is an incomplete extraction with only partial data from the census. For complete information, the researcher will need to use the original and not the county copy.

Background Sources

Abbott, Carl, et al. *Colorado: History of the Centennial State.* Boulder: Colorado Associated University Press, 1982.

Atheran, Robert G. *The Coloradans.* Albuquerque: University of New Mexico Press, 1976.

Baker, James H., and LeRoy R. Hafen. *History of Colorado.* 3 vols. Denver: Linderman Co., 1927. Two of these volumes are biographies.

Colorado Genealogical Society, comp. *Colorado Families: A Territorial Heritage.* Denver: Colorado Genealogical Society, 1981. These family pedigrees and histories of families in Colorado by or before 1876 include maps and an every-name index.

Gannett, Henry. *A Gazetteer of Colorado.* Washington, D.C.: Government Printing Office, 1906. Helps in locating Colorado towns, villages, and sites.

Hafen, LeRoy R. *Colorado and Its People: A Narrative and Topical History of the Centennial State.* 4 vols. New York: Lewis Historical Publishing Co., 1948.

Hinckley, Kathleen W. "Genealogical Research in Colorado," *National Genealogical Society Quarterly* 77 (June 1989), 107-27. Provides a current survey of resources in the state.

Joy, Carol M., and Terry Ann Mood, comps. *Colorado Local History: A Directory.* Denver: Colorado Historical Society, 1986. Contains descriptions of over 100 smaller repository collections.

Ubbelohde, Carl, et. al. *A Colorado History.* 6th ed. Boulder: Pruett Publishing Co., 1988.

Wynar, Bohdan S., and Roberta J. Depp, eds. *Colorado Bibliography.* Littleton: Libraries Unlimited, Inc., for the National Society of Colonial Dames of America in the State of Colorado, 1980.

The Colorado Historical Society has a card index of some names that have been extracted from Colorado published histories. The staff will check the index by mail for specific names.

References for early Colorado records include these:

Blodgett, Ralph E. "Colorado Territorial Board of Immigration," *Colorado Magazine* 46 (Summer 1969): 345-56.

Noel, Thomas J, ed. *The W.P.A. Guide to 1930s Colorado.* Reprint. Lawrence: University of Kansas Press, 1987.

Maps

Colorado Geological Survey Maps are available from the Rocky Mountain Mapping Center, Building 810, Denver Federal Center, 6th and Kipling, Denver, CO; Mailing address, P.O. Box 25286, Denver, CO 80225 <www.usgs.gov>. Map dealers also offer these maps; Map Express (1708 13th Street, Boulder, CO 80302) is one commercial service that provides same-day shipping for all USGS maps.

The Western History and Genealogy Department at the Denver Public Library has an extensive collection of over 2,000 maps, which includes explorations, surveys, railroad maps, trails, mining expeditions, and land grants. Included in their collection is George R. Erchler's *Colorado Place Names* (Boulder, Colo.: Johnson Publishing, 1980).

Good map collections are also located at the University of Colorado map library in the Benson Earth Sciences building, Boulder, 80224; Colorado State Archives (see Archives, Libraries, and Societies); and the School of Mines' Arthur Lakes Library.

Guide to the Colorado Ghost Towns and Mining Camps, 4th ed. rev. (Athens, Ohio: Shallow Press, 1974), compiled by Perry Eberhart, discusses an important aspect of Colorado's political geography.

Two fine sources for place-names in Colorado are:

Blecha, Arvid D. (Donald R. Elliott, comp.) *Blecha's Colorado Place Names: A Genealogical & Historical Guide to Colorado Sites.* Denver: Colorado Genealogical Society, 2001.

Elliott, Donald R. and Doris J. Salmen Elliott, *Place Names in Colorado: Reference Guide to Place Names and Pointers to Publications with Additional Information.* Denver: Colorado Council of Genealogical Societies, 1999.

Land Records

Public-Domain State

Records of the Spanish and Mexican land grants are located in the Denver Public Library Western History and Genealogy Department (see Archives, Libraries, and Societies). Once the area fell under U.S. jurisdiction, land was transferred from the federal government to individuals. The Homestead Act of 1862, along with other federal statutes, provided for the disposal of most of Colorado's land.

Land offices existed in Central City, Del Norte, Denver/Golden City, Durango, Glenwood Springs, Gunnison, Hugo, Lamar, Leadville/Fairplay, Montrose/Lake City, Pueblo, Akron, and Sterling. Some early land records of Denver were lost to floods, while others have survived. The Homestead Tract Books and Register of Homestead Entries are found at the National Archives—Rocky Mountain Region in Denver (see page 12). While some early land records of Denver were lost in the Cherry Creek flood of 1864, others have survived. The patent case files are located at the National Archives, Washington, D.C. The researcher must know the legal description of the land of interest.

Once granted, transactions of land are recorded at the county level in deed books. These land records, including mortgages and land plats, are the responsibility of the county clerk and recorder's office. In some cases, indexes are found in a different location from the files.

Probate Records

The county court, created by the 1876 state constitution, retains jurisdiction of all matters of probate. Researchers can expect to find indexes to probate records, case files of probate records, administration of estates including record of wills, letters of testamentary and administration, appraisements, inventories, sales records, and guardianships. These records are held at the county level, although some early records have been deposited with the Colorado State Archives.

Court Records

The district court holds original jurisdiction in all equity cases, probate, divorce proceedings, naturalizations granted by the county court, coroner's inquests, civil cases, criminal cases, adoptions, juvenile cases, and paternity suits. Denver is the only district in Colorado that has separate probate and juvenile courts.

County courts handle civil cases involving no more than $15,000, misdemeanors, bonds, preliminary hearings, and traffic cases. County judges also issue search warrants and restraining orders.

Tax Records

Tax records in Colorado may be found in a variety of locations. Some are located in the treasurer's office at the county level, while others have been moved to libraries, historical societies, or the state archives. Others have been lost or, with permission of the state of Colorado, destroyed. A few dating to the 1870s or earlier have survived. The researcher may wish to check for an extant WPA Historical Records Survey (see County Resources) for the county of interest. Otherwise, a search on an individual basis will be required.

Cemetery Records

Kay R. Merrill, ed., *The Colorado Cemetery Directory* (Colorado Council of Genealogical Societies, 1985) attempts to identify, locate, and publish information from every known cemetery in the state of Colorado. The book is divided by county and then by alphabetical name of the cemetery. Location, type of cemetery, history, status, and existence of published records are included in this comprehensive publication. Contact the staff at Denver Public Library—Western History and Genealogy (see Archives, Libraries, and Societies), for update information.

A number of Colorado cemeteries have been indexed or abstracted on various websites, particularly those associated with the USGenWeb project. See <www.rootsweb.com/usgenweb/co/cofiles.htm> for links to many of these cemetery records.

The Colorado National Guard maintains an incomplete registration for military graves that covers military burials (1862–1949). These restricted records are located at the Colorado State Archives, but an unrestricted index is available at its website <http://www.colorado.gov/dpa/doit/archives/military/graves/>. If a copy of the original or cause of death is desired, the researcher will need authorization from the Office of the Adjutant General, Colorado Department of Military Affairs, Administration, 6848 S. Revere Pkwy., Englewood, CO 80112.

There are two national cemeteries in Colorado: Fort Logan National Cemetery, 3698 S. Sheridan Blvd., Denver, CO 80235, and Fort Lyon National Cemetery, VA Medical Center, Fort Lyon, CO 81038. An index to each of these is available at <www.interment.net/data/us/co/denver/logan/index.htm> and <www.interment.net/data/us/co/bent/ftlyonnat> respectively.

Church Records

Guide to Vital Statistics Records in Colorado—Church Records, published under the auspices of the WPA of the U.S. government, is housed at the Colorado State Historical Society. It is also available at the FHL and several other major repositories. The best collection of Roman Catholic records for northern Colorado is located in the Archdiocese of Denver, for east-central Colorado at the Archdiocese of Colorado Springs, and for the southern section at the Archdiocese of Pueblo. These records may be used by genealogical researchers. Contact Archdiocese of Denver, 1300 S. Steele, Denver, CO 80210; Archdiocese of Pueblo, 1001 Grand Ave., Pueblo, CO 81003; or Archdiocese of Colorado Springs, 228 N. Cascade Avenue, Colorado Springs, CO 80903 (for records beginning in 1984; prior records are in the Archdiocese of Denver).

Mary Troudt Mills has published numerous volumes of Colorado church records for the American Historical Society of Germans from Russia. An updated listing can be found at the University of Northern Colorado Library's website at <www.unco.edu/library/gov/hist480/weld/religion.htm>.

A few Colorado church records have been microfilmed and are available for loan through the FHL. A more detailed discussion of church records can be found in Hinckley's article "Genealogical Research in Colorado" (see Background Sources).

Military Records

The Colorado State Archives holds the National Guard muster rolls (1861–1919) and the Colorado National Guard service records (1861–1945). The Adjutant General (see Cemetery Records for address) has a microfilmed copy of the "Index to Compiled Service Records of the Union Army for Colorado." This can also be found at National Archives—Rocky Mountain Branch, Denver Public Library, and FHL.

The researcher may also wish to search Sherman Lee Pompey's *Confederate Soldiers Buried in Colorado* (Independence, Calif.: Historical and Genealogical Publishing Co., 1965) and John H. Nankivel's *History of the Military Organizations of the State of Colorado, 1860–1935* (Denver: W. H. Kistler Stationary Co., ca. 1935).

Soldiers' discharge papers for post World War II and later conflicts are located at the county level in the clerk and recorder's office; however, many counties are closing the veterans' discharge papers.

Periodicals, Newspapers, and Manuscript Collections

Periodicals

The Colorado Magazine, published by the State Historical Society of Colorado from 1923, and called *Heritage* after 1979, contains excellent background material for understanding Colorado family history in the context of local history.

The Colorado Genealogical Society has published *The Colorado Genealogist* since 1939. The subject index for volumes 1–42 was compiled in 1982 by Kay R. Merrill and is very helpful in locating published county records. Every-name indexes to the journal are also available.

Other periodicals include quarterlies from the Boulder Genealogical Society, P.O. Box 3246, Boulder, CO 80307-3246 <www.rootsweb.com/~bgs/index.html>; Weld County Genealogical Society, P.O. Box 278, Greeley, CO 80632 <www.rootsweb.com/~cowcgs>; Southeastern Colorado Genealogical Society, P.O. Box 4207, Pueblo, CO 81003-4207>; and *The Foothills Inquirer,* published by the Foothills Genealogical Society, P.O. Box 15382, Lakewood, CO 80215.

Newspapers

One of the first serious indications of settlement is the formation of a newspaper, and the first issue of *The Rocky Mountain News* was printed on 23 April 1859. The most extensive newspaper collections are housed at the Colorado Historical Society, the Denver Public Library, and Norlin Library of University of Colorado, Boulder, CO 80309. There is an unpublished card index to *The Rocky Mountain News* (1865–85) at the Western History and Genealogy Collection at Denver Public Library. This library also holds an obituary file for *The Denver Post* and *The Rocky Mountain News* beginning in 1939 and includes a few earlier records. These will be searched by library staff for a fee; some years are covered in an online index at <www.denver.lib.co.us/research/genealogy/obituaries.html>. Microfilm of the newspaper collection at the Colorado Historical Society is available for purchase. The most recent price was $22 per roll.

Colorado's part of the National Newspaper Program has been completed, with 3,400 newspaper titles cataloged and 1.7 million pages microfilmed. Cataloging information is available on OCLC's FirstSearch (see page 10).

Two helpful aids to the researcher are Donald E. Oehlerts, comp., *Guide to Colorado Newspapers, 1859–1963* (Denver:

Bibliographic Center for Research, 1964), and Walter R. Griffin and Jay L. Rasmussen, "A Comprehensive Guide to the Location of Published and Unpublished Newspaper Indexes in Colorado Repositories," *The Colorado Magazine* 72 (Fall 1972): 328–39.

Manuscripts

The Western History and Genealogy Department at the Denver Public Library has a good variety of diaries, journals, letters, membership lists of organizations, and other unpublished sources. It has diaries of Central City and Black Hawk covering years 1859, 1860, and 1861. Other records include the Spanish land grants, Mexican land grants, and mining manuscripts. A catalog of holdings is available online (see Archives, Libraries, and Societies).

The Colorado Portrait and Biographical Index, developed by Henrietta Bromwell, is housed at the Colorado Historical Society Library and Western History and Genealogy Department at Denver Public Library. It is a pre-1900, four-volume index to the biographical works of Colorado, with an appendix of two volumes. The developer attempted to include all names mentioned in published works including some magazines and newspapers. A planned index will be available online at the Denver Public Library website.

The Dawson Scrapbooks, with an unpublished index, is an eighty-volume collection of names and biographies housed at the Colorado Historical Society.

The 1876 Colorado Business Directory and Denver city directories (beginning 1873) are located at the Colorado Historical Society. The Denver Public Library also holds many of these early directories.

Archives, Libraries, and Societies

Colorado State Archives
1313 Sherman St., Rm 1B-20
Denver, CO 80203
www.colorado.gov/dpa/doit/archives

Many of the holdings of the state archives have been described in various sections above. All out-of-state requests are charged a search fee of $25 per name, payable in advance. This fee is then applied to the copies of information up to three pages. Additional pages are $1.25 per page. There is an additional fee of $10 if certified copies are needed.

Colorado Historical Society
The Stephen H. Hart Library
Colorado Heritage Center
1300 Broadway
Denver, CO 80203
www.coloradohistory.org

There is an admission fee to the state museum but no fee to use the library, which has extensive holdings as described above. No material is circulated.

Denver Public Library
Western History and Genealogy
10 W. Fourteenth Ave. Pkwy
Denver, CO 80204-2731
www.denver.lib.co.us

In addition to being a superb collection of genealogical research materials and having a microfilm collection of newspapers and census records, the Western history collection is a rich source for regional history and manuscripts.

Norlin Library
University of Colorado
1157 18th St. (18th and Colorado), Box 184
Boulder, CO 80309-0184
http://ucblibraries.colorado.edu/

Their Government Publications Department is a federal regional depository as well as a Colorado state publications depository. It holds nearly complete microfilmed census population schedules and Soundexes, in addition to many other publications of interest to Colorado and other researchers. The Archives Department has many printed and manuscript materials relating to Colorado and Western history.

Colorado Genealogical Society
P.O. Box 9218
Denver, CO 80209-0218
www.rootsweb.com/~cocgs

Colorado Council of Genealogical Societies
P.O. Box 24379
Denver, CO 80224
www.rootsweb.com/~coccgs

The council will provide an electronic copy of all genealogical societies in the state on its website if requested by e-mail, or a hard copy of the list by regular mail when a self-addressed stamped envelope is included with the request.

County Resources

The WPA published a number of county inventories for Colorado. These have been reprinted and placed on microfiche by the Colorado Genealogical Society. The unpublished manuscripts for these have been deposited at the Colorado State Archives. A survey was *not*, however, completed for every county. With the exceptions listed in the chart below, it is presumed that county records exist from the date of county formation, but this has not been verified for all counties. The individual researcher will need to check the specific county of interest. Many of Colorado's early county records have been deposited at the Colorado State Archives <www.colorado.gov/dpa/doit/archives>. Unless otherwise noted, in the chart below, marriage records are located at the clerk and recorder's office in the county seat along with land records. Other vital records created before state recording began (see Vital Records) are located in the various County Vital Records offices. A list of telephone numbers is available at <www.cdphe.state.co.us/hs/vroffices.htm>.

Court records are found in county and district courts, with probate records in the district courts (unless moved to the Colorado State Archives).

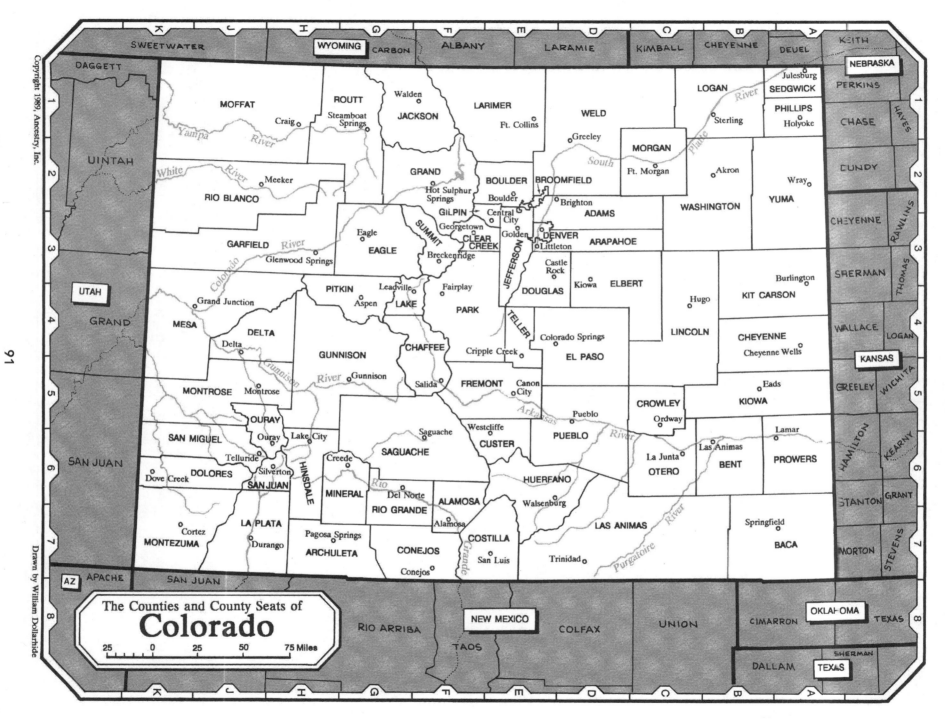

The Counties and County Seats of
Colorado

25   0   25   50   75 Miles

COLORADO

91

Map	County Address	Date Formed Parent County/ies	Birth Marriage Death	Land Probate Court
G3	Adams 450 S. 4th Ave. Brighton 80601	1901 Arapahoe	1902–06 1902 1902–08	1902 1902 1902

Part of Denver County; annexed, 1909.

E7	Alamosa P.O. Box 178 Alamosa 81101	1913 Costilla/Conejos	—— 1913 1913*	1913 1913 1913

*At Lorton and Miracle Mortuaries in Alamosa.

G3	Arapahoe 5334 S. Prince St. Littleton 80166	1861 original	1872–1902* 1861 1860–1903* 1902** 1887–1902* 1902**	

*At Colorado Department of Health, Vital Records Section.
**Most records for Denver prior to 1902 have been deposited with the Colorado State Archives. Early land records, surveys, post offices, and territorial government papers are extant for Arapahoe County, and some are located in both the Colorado and Kansas historical societies. However, typical county records such as probate or county court minutes do not exist for the early territorial period of the county before state formation.

C7	Archuleta P.O. Box 1507 Pagosa Springs 81147	1885 Conejos	1892–1907 1886 1886 1900–07	1886 1886 1886

K7	Baca 741 Main St. Springfield 81073	1889 Las Animas	—— 1889 ——	1889 1889 1889

J6	Bent P.O. Box 350 Las Animas 81054	1870 Indian Reserves Lands/ Las Animas/Greenwood	—— 1888 ——	1874? 1874? 1874?

Greenwood dissolved in 1874 to Bent and Elbert counties.

F2	Boulder P.O. Box 471 Boulder 80301	1861 original	1880–1909* 1864 1864 1880–1903* 1864	

Boulder was called Jackson County when it was part of Jefferson Territory.
*City Hall in Boulder. Estate files from 1862 are housed at the Colorado State Archives.

E2	Broomfield 1 DesCombes Dr. Broomfield 80020	2001 Adam/Boulder/Jefferson/ Weld	2001 2001 2001	2001 2001 2001

	Carbonate	1861 (renamed Lake, 1879)		

E4	Chaffee P.O. Box 699 Salida 81201	1861 (as Lake; renamed, 1879) original	1884–1907 1879? 1866 1884–1907 1879?	

Formerly Lake County until 1879.

K4	Cheyenne P.O. Box 567 Cheyenne Wells 80810-0567	1889 Bent/Elbert	1893–1907 1889? 1889 1893–1904 1889?	

E3	Clear Creek 405 Argentine St. Georgetown 80444	1861 original	1905–07* 1859 1864* 1902–07* 1861	1861

*County Archives in Georgetown.

E7	Conejos P.O. Box 157 Conejos 81129	1861 (as Guadalupe; renamed, 1869) original	1877–1907 1871 1871 1875 1877–1907 1877	

Some loss of records occurred by fire.

F7	Costilla P.O. Box 100 San Luis 81152	1861 original	—— 1863 1902–07*	1861 1876 1876

*Alamosa County, Lorton, and Miracle Mortuary.

H5	Crowley 110 E. 6th St. Ordway 81063	1911 Bent/Otero	—— 1911 ——	1911 1911 1911

F6	Custer P.O. Box 150 Westcliffe 81252	1877 Fremont	1905–07 1877 1877* 1877 1902–07 1877	

*Some earlier in Fremont County miscellaneous file.

B4	Delta 501 Palmer St., Ste. 227 Delta 81416	1883 Gunnison	1895–1909 1883 1883 1883 1895–1909 1883	

F3	Denver 1437 Bannock St. Denver 80202	1901 Arapahoe	1872–1907 1902 1860 1865–1959 1887–1907 1902	

In 1911, Denver City and Denver County merged. Births and Deaths, 1964-present, are at Vital Statistics Room, Denver General Hospital.
*Many early Denver records have been deposited at the Colorado State Archives.

B6	Dolores P.O. Box 608 Dove Creek 81324	1881 Ouray	1894 1881 1881 1881 1894–1907 1881	

F3	Douglas 100 Third St. Castle Rock 80104	1861 original	1894–1908 1863 1864 1861? 1894– 1861?	

Original county seat at Franktown.
Small part of Cheyenne and Arapahoe Reservations added in 1870.
Courthouse burned in 1978 but minimal loss of records.

D3	Eagle P.O. Box 850 Eagle 81631	1883 Summit	1894–1901 1883 1879 1883 1894–1901 1883	

G3	Elbert P.O. Box 597 Kiowa 80117	1874 Douglas	1894–1907 1874 1874* 1874 1876–96 1874	

G4	El Paso 27 E. Vermijo Ave. Colorado Springs 80903	1861 original	1890–1906* 1861 1861 1861? 1893–1907* 1861?	

*City Health Department.

E5	Fremont 615 Macon Ave., Ste. 102 Canon City 81212	1861 original	1884–1907 1862 1865 1874 1884–1907 1868	

B3	Garfield 108 8th St. Glenwood Springs 81601	1883 Summit	1893–1909 1883 1884 1883 1883–89* 1883	

*Rio Blanco County marriages 1883–89.

E22	Gilpin P.O. Box 366 Central City 80427	1861 original	—— 1865 ——	1861? 1861? 1861?

Map	County / Address	Date Formed / Parent County/ies	Birth / Marriage / Death	Land / Probate Court
E2	**Grand** P.O. Box 264 Hot Sulphur Springs 80451	1874 Summit	1895–1908 1881 1894–1907	1874? 1874? 1874?
	Greenwood	1870 (abolished 1874; parts annexed to Elbert and Bent)		
	Guadalup	1861 (renamed Conejos, 1869) original		
C4	**Gunnison** 200 E Virginia Ave. Gunnison 81230	1877 Lake	1895–1908 1877 1894–97	1877? 1877? 1877?
C6	**Hinsdale** P.O. Box 277 Lake City 81235	1874 Conejos	1899–1907 1876 1899–1907	1874 1876 1876
F6	**Huerfano** 401 Main St. Walsenburg 81089 *Courthouse basement.*	1861 original	—— 1875 1902–06*	1861? 1861? 1861?
D1	**Jackson** P.O. Box 337 Walden 80480	1909 Grand	—— 1909 ——	1909? 1909? 1909?
F3	**Jefferson** 100 Jefferson County Pkwy. Golden 80409 *A small part was annexed to Park, 1903*	1861 original	1893–1906 1874–76; 1881 1893–1906	1861? 1861? 1861?
J5	**Kiowa** P.O. Box 100 Eads 81036	1889 Cheyenne/Bent	—— 1889 ——	1889? 1889? 1889?
K3	**Kit Carson** P.O. Box 160 Burlington 80807 *Courthouse basement; other deaths (1876–1907) at clerk and recorder's office.*	1889 Elbert	1893–1907* 1889 1892–1907*	1889? 1889? 1889?
	Lake (old)	1861 (renamed Chaffee, 1879) original		
E4	**Lake (present)** P.O. Box 964 Leadville 80461 *City clerk, Leadville.*	1861 (as Carbonate; renamed Chaffee, 1879) original	1891–1906* 1869 1881–1903*	1861? 1861? 1861?
B7	**La Plata** 1060 E. Second Ave. Durango 81301 *Vital statistics registrar, City Hall, Durango; also clerk and recorder's office 1900–12; early marriages in San Juan County clerk and recorder's office.*	1874 Conejos/Lake	1895–1918* 1880* 1895–1918	1874? 1874? 1874?
F1	**Larimer** P.O. Box 1190 Fort Collins 80522	1861 original	1902–08 1862 1902–08	1862 1862 1862
G7	**Las Animas** 200 E. First St., Trinidad 81082 *Also, city of Trinidad 1893–1907.*	1866 Huerfano	1893–96* 1868 1893–1904	1866? 1866? 1866?
J4	**Lincoln** P.O. Box 39 Hugo 80821 *Courthouse basement.*	1889 Elbert/Bent	1889–1920* 1887 1889–1907*	1889? 1889? 1889?
J1	**Logan** 315 Main St. Sterling 80751	1887 Weld	—— 1887 ——	1866 1887 1887
B4	**Mesa** P.O. Box 20, 000-5010 Grand Junction 81502-5006 *Courthouse storage.*	1883 Gunnison	1893–1909* 1883 1893 1901*	1883? 1883? 1883?
D6	**Mineral** P.O. Box 70 Creede 81130	1892 Hinsdale/Rio Grande/ Saguache	1896–1909 1891 1896–1907	1893? 1893? 1893?
B1	**Moffat** 221 W. Victory Way Craig 81625	1911 Routt	—— 1911 ——	1911? 1911? 1911?
A7	**Montezuma** 109 W. Main St. Cortez 81321	1889 La Plata	—— 1889 ——	1889? 1889? 1889?
B5	**Montrose** P.O. Box 1289 Montrose 81402 *Courthouse basement vault, births, 1900–07.*	1883 Gunnison	1900–07* 1883 1883–1907*	1883? 1883? 1883?
H2	**Morgan** P.O. Box 596 Fort Morgan 80701 *Vital statistics registrar, Fort Morgan births.*	1889 Weld	1894–1908* 1889 1894–1908*	1873 1889 1889
H6	**Otero** P.O. Box 511 La Junta 81050 *Vital statistics registrar, La Junta.*	1889 Bent	1889* 1889 1887–1907	1889? 1889? 1889?
C5	**Ouray** P.O. Box C Ouray 81427 *Vital statistics registrar, Ouray; also clerk and recorder's office deaths, 1880–1907.*	1877 (as Uncompahgre; Renamed, 1883) Hinsdale/San Juan	1880–1907* 1881 1894*	1877? 1877? 1873
E4	**Park** P.O Box 1373 Fairplay 80440 *A small part of Jefferson was annexed in 1903.*	1861 original	1892–1908 1876 1899–1907	1861? 1861? 1861?
K1	**Phillips** 221 S Interocean Ave. Holyoke 80734	1889 Logan	1903–05 1889 1902–05	1889? 1889? 1889?
D4	**Pitkin** 530 E. Main St., 3rd Fl. Aspen 81611	1881 Gunnison	1890–1907 1881 1890–1907	1881? 1881? 1881?
K6	**Prowers** 301 S. Main St., Ste. 215 Lamar 81052	1889 Bent	1891–1907 1889 1891–1907	1889 1889 1889

Map	County Address	Date Formed Parent County/ies	Birth Marriage Death	Land Probate Court
G6	Pueblo 215 W. 10th St. Pueblo 81003	1861 original	1887–1901 1860 1887–1907	1861 1861 1861

Pueblo City-County Health Department, 1511 Central Mail, Pueblo, CO 81003, has early vital records not found at Colorado Department of Health.

Map	County Address	Date Formed Parent County/ies	Birth Marriage Death	Land Probate Court
B2	Rio Blanco P.O. Box 1 Meeker 81641	1889 Summit	1889–1907 1883 1892–1903*	1889 1889 1889

* Also 1905–07.

Map	County Address	Date Formed Parent County/ies	Birth Marriage Death	Land Probate Court
D6	Rio Grande 925 6th St. Del Norte 81132	1874 Conejos/Costilla	1898–1907 1874 1902–07	1874? 1874? 1874?
D1	Routt P.O. Box 773598 Steamboat Springs 80477	1877 Grand	1903–08 1877 1903–08	1877? 1877? 1877?
D6	Saguache P.O. Box 655 Saguache 81149	1866 Costilla/Lake	1894–1908 1869 1872–1907	1866? 1866? 1866?
C6	San Juan P.O. Box 466 Silverton 81433	1876 La Plata	1901–07* 1871 1902–07*	1876 1876? 1876?

*City clerk, Silverton.

Map	County Address	Date Formed Parent County/ies	Birth Marriage Death	Land Probate Court
B6	San Miguel P.O. Box 1170 Telluride 81435	1861 Ouray	1900–07* 1883 1907–20*	1883? 1883? 1883?

*Vital statistics registrar, Telluride.

Map	County Address	Date Formed Parent County/ies	Birth Marriage Death	Land Probate Court
K1	Sedgwick P.O. Box 50 Julesburg 80737	1889 Logan	1897–1906 1889 1897–1906	1889? 1889? 1889?
E3	Summit P.O. Box 68 Breckenridge 80424	1861 original	1892–96 1862 1892–1905	1861? 1861? 1861?
F4	Teller P.O. Box 959 Cripple Creek 80813	1899 El Paso/Fremont	1904 1899 1902–08*	1899? 1899? 1899?

*Incomplete. County death records are separate and extant from those kept by the city of Cripple Creek, which were lost by fire.

Map	County Address	Date Formed Parent County/ies	Birth Marriage Death	Land Probate Court
	Uncompahgre	1887 (renamed Ouray, 1883)		
J2	Washington 150 Ash Ave. Akron 80720	1887 Weld/Arapahoe	1894–1911* 1887 1894–1907*	1872 1887 1887

*Vital statistics registrar.

Map	County Address	Date Formed Parent County/ies	Birth Marriage Death	Land Probate Court
G1	Weld P.O. Box 758 Greeley 80632	1861 original	1872–1909 1864 1872–1908	1865 1861? 1861?
K2	Yuma 310 Ash St., Ste. A Wray 80758	1889 Arapahoe/Weld/Adams	1893–1907 1889 1893–1907	1889? 1889? 1889?

Connecticut

ALICE EICHHOLZ, Ph.D., CG

The first colonies that would become Connecticut flanked the shores of Long Island Sound and the banks of the Housatonic and Connecticut rivers. Influenced by Rev. Thomas Hooker's principle of authority growing out of the free expression of its people, the utopian experiment of Connecticut Colony began between 1633 and 1635. It produced little class distinction, a change from the heavy-handed authoritarian expectations of the Massachusetts colonies. The Congregational Church would not only be thoroughly integrated into town life, but interpretation of its theology seemed to create less social stratification.

Similar to Rhode Island in its political organization, Connecticut differed from the new settlements in Rhode Island and Providence plantations in that it possessed a rich agricultural terrain. The first settlements along the Connecticut River near Windsor coexisted with Native American villages and a Dutch trading post near what is now Hartford. Settlers from Massachusetts reached these settlements primarily by foot. Concurrently, John Winthrop, Jr., sailed a group from England to establish Saybrook along the coast. By 1638, with other settlements already harvesting their crops and increasing their number of clapboard houses, New Haven Colony, under the theological leadership of John Davenport, entrenched itself along the coast and began building the more elaborate houses they had become accustomed to in England.

New Haven Colony merged with Connecticut Colony in 1662, while new settlements moved farther north on the Connecticut River to settle western Massachusetts towns; one group founded Newark, New Jersey. More and more of the rich agricultural land was purchased from the Native Americans. From the time of their initial settlement through the middle of the eighteenth century, Connecticut's relationship with the original inhabitants, like that of the rest of New England's, continued to deteriorate, culminating in the French and Indian Wars.

Connecticut's homogeneous population and community-centered form of government existed away from the mainstream of royal imperial affairs and remained focused on the town and its people. With events of the impending Revolution espousing the principles of freedom of expression, Connecticut began to move away from a solely town focus and look out toward the broader community of colonies opposing royal authority. Connecticut people fought on both sides of the conflict, with many loyalists migrating north and east to Canada and its eastern provinces.

By the end of the Revolution, family farms were unable to support the large number of young people in the area. The population boom made it necessary for more and more descendants of original settlers to leave for the north, west, and south to provide for themselves and their families. Cheaper, available land elsewhere provided much of the motivation. Farms gave way to the newly burgeoning Industrial Revolution, with growing ethnic populations—Italians, Poles, French-Canadians, and African Americans in the nineteenth century; Puerto Ricans and Asians in the twentieth—wending their way along the Long Island Shoreline of Connecticut's growing metropolitan areas.

Today, Connecticut enjoys the distinction of being the New England state with the most centrally located resources for genealogical research. Its 169 towns function without county government, and the size and shape of Connecticut's land

affords easy, fairly quick access to its centrally located capitol in Hartford.

Vital Records

Marriages were recorded in Connecticut as early as 1640. By 1650, registration of births, marriages, and deaths had become the town clerk's responsibility. Since a fine was assessed for not recording an event, some industrious town clerks have excellent, fairly complete records; however, others do not. Following the Revolution to the mid-nineteenth century, the recording is not as thorough, but by 1870, when the State Board of Health was established, recording in all towns improved.

Recording of vital events has always been the town clerk's responsibility. After 1 July 1897, copies of vital records from every town were sent to the Department of Public Health, Vital Records Section, 410 Capitol Ave., First Floor, P.O. Box 340308, Hartford, CT 06134-0308 <www.dph.state.ct.us/oppe/hpvital. htm>.

There is no statewide index to Connecticut vital records between about 1850 and 1897. It is therefore necessary to know the town in which the event occurred to locate a record for those years. Census records and city directories may be helpful in determining the town. Original Connecticut vital records from the beginning of each town to about 1900 have been microfilmed by the Genealogical Society of Utah and are available for use at the Connecticut State Library or through local Family History Centers.

Although some statewide indexes to vital records after 1897 are available through the Vital Records Section, many of the state's copies of vital records from 1897 to the present are closed for an indefinite period as part of a microfilming and indexing project. Until the section reopens, information will need to be obtained from the town. Subscription Internet database <www.ancestry.com> includes statewide Connecticut deaths (1949–) and marriages (before1850 and after 1959–).

"An Act Concerning Access to Genealogical Records and the Validation of Certain Marriages" (Public Act No. 96-258) provides that birth records less than one hundred years old are only open to certain parties, including the individual in question, her/his guardian or legal representative, or a member of a genealogical society incorporated or authorized to do business or conduct affairs in Connecticut. A list of genealogical societies encompassed by this law can be found at <www.cslib.org/genesoc.htm>.

The Lucius Barnes Barbour Collection, well known to the Connecticut researcher, serves as an index to and an abstract of most pre-1850 Connecticut vital records. It is housed in the Connecticut State Library (see Archives, Libraries, and Societies), but microfilm copies of it are widely available. Begun after establishment of the State Department of Health, Barbour's project was to abstract and collect all town vital records up to

about 1850. There are two formats to the material. The first is a statewide paper slip alphabetical index containing a complete abstract of each vital record taken from the books in each town. The card file holding this index takes up an entire wall at the Connecticut State Library. The second format is the group of separately bound volumes of abstracts of vital records for most towns, prepared from the slips.

Since not all vital events were recorded in the town office before mandatory recording, church and cemetery records need to be consulted as well as other genealogical alternatives to official records.

Divorces are presently granted by the superior court, although this was not always the case. Most of the early records for Connecticut divorces to the mid-twentieth century are at the Connecticut State Library, including the packets of original documents and the superior court records books. Recent divorce packets remain in the court. Grace L. Knox and Barbara Ferris published a two-volume index to early Connecticut divorce packets through Heritage Books. Volume 1 covers New London, Tolland, and Windham counties; volume 2 covers Litchfield and Hartford counties. For details on changes of jurisdiction for divorces in Connecticut, see Henry S. Cohn's "Connecticut's Divorce Mechanism, 1636–1969," *The American Journal of Legal History* 14 (January 1970): 35-54, which is summarized in an information leaflet on divorce records available from the Connecticut State Library and on its website (see Archives, Libraries, and Societies below).

Census Records

Federal

Population Schedules
- Indexed—1790, 1800, 1810, 1820, 1830, 1840, 1850, 1860, 1870, 1880, 1900, 1910, 1920, 1930
- Soundex—1880, 1900, 1920

Industry and Agriculture Schedules
- 1850, 1860, 1870, 1880

Mortality Schedules
- 1850, 1860, 1870, 1880 (not indexed)

Except for 1890, Connecticut has a complete set of federal census records. Either originals or microfilm copies and book indexes to all of the above are at the Connecticut State Library, in addition to those available through online subscription databases (see page 17). A special index for a duplicate set of schedules housed at the Connecticut State Archives (1790–1850) is also at the Connecticut State Library. It is not collated in the same way as the "official" set at the National Archives and consequently cannot be used for locating a particular individual on that set of

returns. However, the Connecticut version of the index includes *all* names in the 1850 census and not just heads of households.

Colonial

A number of inventories and enumerations of population or census substitutes exist (with and without names). The most complete compilation is Jay Mack Holbrook's *Connecticut 1670 Census* (Oxford, Mass.: Holbrook Research Institute, 1977), which combines a number of sources (tax, land, church, freeman, probate) in an attempt to count the heads of household by name for the entire colony in the time period 1667 to 1673. As with all such compilations, it is particularly important to check the original sources the compiler used.

The 1669/1670 Grain Inventory for Hartford, Wethersfield, and Windsor inventories heads of household by name and number of family members as well as bushels of wheat and corn held by the family. Published in volume 21 of *Collections of the Connecticut Historical Society* (Hartford: the society, 1924), 190-99, the inventory is not a complete listing of inhabitants for that year but provides an interesting perspective on the settlements.

Enumerations existed for 1756, 1762, and 1774, but they do not list names, only numbers of people in town in the categories of race, sex, and age groups. Details on the first and last can be found in volume 14, *Public Records of the Colony of Connecticut, 1636–1776* (see Court Records). The 1762 returns are published in Christopher P. Bickford's "The Lost Connecticut Census of 1762 Found," *Connecticut Historical Society Bulletin* 44 (April 1979): 33-43.

State

No state population censuses were taken for Connecticut, but a unique census was taken by the state in the twentieth century. The Military Census of 1917 listed all males between at least twenty to thirty years of age, although most towns reported those sixteen through sixty. It also includes females in key occupations, such as nursing. Given along with the name and age were place of birth and number of dependents, ability to perform certain tasks, and occupation. Both the originally completed sheets and index cards have been microfilmed in a separate series available at the Connecticut State Library and the Family History Library (FHL) in Salt Lake City. The microfilm for the index cards is arranged by town and then alphabetically by surname. The form number on index cards is needed to locate the original sheets on microfilm (Record Group 29).

Background Sources

Connecticut's wealth and centralization of genealogical sources is matched by its compilations of genealogies, guidebooks, place-name directories, and local historical materials.

Perhaps the grandparent of genealogical compilations for an entire community is Donald Lines Jacobus, *Families of Ancient New Haven* (1922–32; reprint, 9 vols. in 3, Baltimore: Genealogical Publishing Co., 1981), which covers the families settled in New Haven before 1800. It comprises the families in the towns of New Haven, East Haven, North Haven, Hamden, Bethany, Woodbridge, and West Haven and incorporates vital, church, cemetery, probate, court, and town records.

Similar compilations were done by others for Guilford, Hartford, Milford, and Wallingford. *The New England Historical and Genealogical Register* has included a succession of articles on Connecticut families that has been reprinted in three volumes as *Genealogies of Connecticut Families* (Baltimore: Genealogical Publishing Co., 1983).

A comprehensive bibliography to local history can be found in Roger Parks, ed., *Connecticut: A Bibliography of its History* (Hanover, N.H.: University Press of New England, 1986).

Although not limited to Connecticut people only, Fremont Rider's *American Genealogical-Biographical Index* (Middletown, Conn.: Godfrey Memorial Library, 1952-present) has its roots in this state. Updated in alphabetical volumes, this unusual index crosses many census records, genealogies, tax lists, and other sources to provide the researcher with a thumbnail indication of different surnames at different times and places. In the days before indexing became the norm for genealogical work, this publication provided one of the first comprehensive indexes not specifically focused on periodicals. A CD-ROM version is now available. See also:

Abbe, Elizabeth. "Connecticut Genealogical Research: Sources and Suggestions," *The New England Historical and Genealogical Register* 134 (January 1980): 3-26.

Bushman, Richard L. *From Puritan to Yankee: Character and the Social Order in Connecticut, 1690–1765*. Cambridge, Mass.: Harvard University Press, 1967. This excellent study encourages a broad overview of understanding the individual in relationship to the community. Studying the psychological and economic underpinnings of a community increases awareness of motivation of our ancestors.

Hughes, Arthur H., and Morse S. Allen. *Connecticut Place Names*. Hartford: Connecticut Historical Society, 1976. This thick, excellent place-name directory lists rivers, topographical features, names of Native American origin, towns and sections of towns, and geological points. It has an excellent cross-index. This is important because early churches, post offices, and industrial sections often had different names from the incorporated town in which they were located.

Kemp, Thomas Jay. *Connecticut Researcher's Handbook*. Detroit: Gale Research Co., 1981. Although most addresses and telephone numbers listed are now obsolete, this guidebook

still provides a solid bibliography by subject and a town-by-town description of resources available.

Morrison, Betty Jane. *Connecting to Connecticut.* East Hartford: Connecticut Society of Genealogists, 1995. As a researcher's perspective on the sources in Connecticut and how to use them, this makes an important contribution.

Secretary of State. *Connecticut State Register and Manual.* Hartford, Conn.: Secretary of State, annually. Known as the Blue Book, this reference guide to state and town information with addresses, phone numbers, and hours of operation is essential in pursing records in person in town offices.

Sperry, Kip. *Connecticut Sources for Family Historians and Genealogists.* Logan, Utah: Everton Publishers, 1980. The itemization of resources indicates availability on the local level, including an excellent listing and description of the archives available at the Connecticut State Library. Those materials on microfilm through the FHL are indicated as well.

Maps

Essential companions to place-name directories in Connecticut are the fine series of Beers atlases produced in the 1860s and 70s detailing structures, property owners, places of business, schools, cemeteries, and churches in each town. Bound in folio-sized books by county, many Connecticut libraries, in addition to the Connecticut State Library, have these excellent resources. The earlier 1852 Clark's county maps are equally available at the same locations.

Present-day street maps by county are readily available in most large stationery stores.

Land Records

State-Land State

England had what it considered legal right to the land in Connecticut, like the rest of New England. It was not until 1662, nearly thirty years after British subjects established the settlements of Connecticut, that a royal charter affirmed the settlements' legal right to land. New Haven Colony and Connecticut Colony formed a united commonwealth of Connecticut as a result of that charter. Previous to 1662, land was generally recognized by settlers as belonging to Native Americans and, consequently, acquired or purchased from them.

The Fundamental Orders of Connecticut, adopted in 1639, provided for the recording of land transactions in town records. The Connecticut General Assembly (originally the Connecticut General Court) had first jurisdiction over the colony and established town proprietors to dispose of land in

their control. Land was divided and sold in lots; registration of deed transactions was the responsibility of the town clerk.

While few land records in Connecticut have been published, the exception is volume 14 of *Collections of The Connecticut Historical Society* (Hartford: the society, 1912), which includes all the Hartford land records from 1639 to the 1680s. A supplement, although only an index, is the *General Index of the Land Records of the Town of Hartford, 1639–1879* (Hartford: Connecticut Historical Society, 1873–83).

Deed books are generally indexed individually. Town clerks usually have comprehensive indexes to grantors and grantees. The deed books to about 1900 have now been microfilmed and can be consulted either in the central location at the Connecticut State Library or through the FHL and its branches. There is no statewide index to all deeds, however.

Probate Records

Connecticut can boast centralization of many research sources and clear jurisdiction on land and vital records. Probate records and finding the correct jurisdiction for a particular time period is more complicated. For the 169 towns, there are currently about 130 probate districts. Jurisdictional lines have changed considerably over the three centuries, but their function has been consistent in probating wills, distributing estates, and appointing guardians.

Before 1698, probates were handled by the General Court (General Assembly) or the secretary of the colony, the particular courts, and then the county courts. When the probate courts were created in 1698, the probate jurisdiction paralleled that of the county, but by 1719 the four original districts started to divide. Each present probate district has a genealogy of its own. Space restrictions in the Town Resources section below necessitate an abbreviated lineage indicating only one parent probate district. A *Checklist of Probate Records in the Connecticut State Library* delineates the lines of descent for each present district. A new revised edition to this publication, originally done in the mid-twentieth century, has been posted on the Connecticut State Library's website at <www.cslib.org/probate/index.htm>. Kemp's research guide (see Background Sources) also indicates which probate district a town belonged to at different times.

As with all probate records, not only the court record books themselves (clerk's transcripts of probate proceedings), but the estate papers or files (original wills, receipts, affidavits, etc.) contain essential genealogical information. Most record books remain in the probate clerk's office with microfilm copies to about 1915 in the Connecticut State Library and the FHL. The exception is New Haven, whose original record books to about 1922 are at the Connecticut State Library instead of the probate clerk's office. Many of the district estate papers or files

to 1900 (some later) have been deposited in the Connecticut State Library. Packets of these original documents have been microfilmed to 1880 (and some to about 1915) and are available on microfilm at both the Connecticut State Library and the FHL. Photocopies of original files are no longer permitted because of their fragile condition. There is a statewide index of these probate packets at the Connecticut State Library.

A printed source for one district is Charles W. Manwaring, *A Digest of the Early Connecticut Probate Records*, 3 vols. (Hartford: R. S. Peck & Co., 1904–06), which covers the early Hartford probate district records (1635–1750).

Court Records

With court records, the researcher finds Connecticut's centralization welcome, with many held at the Connecticut State Library. Despite this centralization, the array of courts whose records might include such things as debts, apprenticeships, warrants, and misdemeanors presents a somewhat complicated research challenge.

Justices of the peace, having been appointed by the General Assembly, represented the law closest to the people up to the early nineteenth century. What remains of many of these records are at the Connecticut State Library.

Before the creation of counties, the particular court was a court of first instance. "Records of the Particular Court of Connecticut, 1639–1663," *Collections of The Connecticut Historical Society*, vol. 22 (Hartford: the society, 1928) conveys these proceedings before county courts took over. Original court records are in the Connecticut State Library.

In the next phase, between 1665 and 1711, the court of assistants became the trial court, and county courts were added. All criminal activities were the purview of the courts of assistants, as well as appeals from lower courts regarding disputes, including divorces. In 1711, the court of assistants was succeeded by the superior court, which remains part of Connecticut's judicial system today. Records of the court of assistants (1665–1771) are generally available at the Connecticut State Library.

Superior court districts are defined by county designation. In the Town Resources section, the county is listed; however, in trying to determine jurisdiction for earlier records, listings of parent counties will be helpful. Records of superior courts operating in each county through the mid-twentieth century are generally available at the Connecticut State Library.

Those matters not in the realm of the superior court were heard by the county courts (initially called prerogative or common pleas courts). The county court, begun in 1666, was abolished in 1855, and its functions were divided between justice courts and superior courts. Most of the county court records, to its abolition date, are at the Connecticut State Library.

Courts of common pleas were authorized in the late nineteenth century to assume work that could not be handled by either the justice or superior courts. In 1961 the court system reorganized, abolishing justice courts, creating district courts, and retaining the county superior court and the statewide supreme court.

Two publications contain court records for the seventeenth century. J. Hammond Trumbull, comp., *The Public Records of the Colony of Connecticut*, 3 vols. (Hartford: State Printers, 1850–59) covers the years 1636–89 for the older colony. The equivalent records for New Haven are in Charles J. Hoadly, ed., *Records of the Colony ... of New Haven*, 2 vols. (Hartford: State Printers, 1857–58). Volume 1 covers 1638–49; volume 2 covers 1653–64.

Tax Records

Taxes were levied for personal property and land through most of Connecticut's history. The town assessor (or lister) made annual lists or rates of all taxables. This generated a considerable number of tax lists across time. The Connecticut State Library has a list of various tax records still at the town clerks' offices. The Connecticut Historical Society and the genealogical collections throughout the state have some records. See Frederick Robertson Jones, *History of Taxation in Connecticut, 1636–1766* (Baltimore: Johns Hopkins Press, 1896).

A highly valuable tax record for Connecticut is the U.S. Direct Tax for 1798. The records are extant for nearly half of the towns, with some also having rate lists for 1813, 1814, 1815, and 1816. The original booklets indicate rate based on land, dwellings, and personal property, the latter of which is usually itemized. Later years indicate out-of-state owners. The records have not been microfilmed as a group, but the originals can be researched at the Connecticut Historical Society.

Cemetery Records

Centralization is the norm for Connecticut's cemetery records. The Connecticut State Library holds the Hale Collection containing over one million gravestone inscriptions. The project to collect these began in 1916 by Charles R. Hale but was continued by act of the General Assembly and the Works Progress Administration (WPA) through the 1930s. While clearly many gravestones had been lost or destroyed by that time, over 2,000 cemeteries were located statewide and included in the collection. Each town's inscriptions are bound in separate volumes, but an alphabetical index across towns is available. Volumes for both the town and statewide indexes have been microfilmed and are available through the FHL.

Cemeteries might have been church, family, town, or private ones. Only twentieth-century death records have place of burial indicated, but most administrators operating cemeteries in the state have records of their own, and many historical societies in the state have collections of town cemeteries not included in the Hale Collection. The DAR's volumes of Bible, cemetery, and family records are deposited at the Connecticut State Library and the DAR Library in Washington, D.C.

Town clerks usually keep "Burial Books," generally beginning in the late nineteenth century, which indicate place of burial in that town for those who died outside of town.

Church Records

Early Connecticut settlers established the Congregational Church as the tax-supported state church until 1818 when the state constitution was accepted, abolishing the connection between church and state. Sometimes, if one parish was getting too large, a second was formed that became a precursor to a new town with the permission of the general assembly. Other denominations followed eventually, particularly the Baptists from Rhode Island on the eastern border with Connecticut, Episcopalians, and Quakers. Information in Connecticut's church records has often been found to be more informative, complete, or accurate than the town vital records.

Among the printed sources of Connecticut church records is Frederick W. Bailey, *Early Connecticut Marriages as Found on Ancient Church Records Prior to 1800* (1896–1906; reprint, 7 vols. in 1, Baltimore: Genealogical Publishing Co., 1982), which covers mainly Congregational and Episcopal records.

Approximately one-quarter of those records housed at the Connecticut State Library have been indexed in a format similar to that of the Barbour (see Vital Records) and Hale (see Cemetery Records) collections with individual index slips and bound compilations of individual churches. This Church Record Index File is statewide, goes beyond 1850, but does not include all church records. Even in a town with more than one Congregational Church, generally only the first is included in this index. Notably, many church records in incorporated cities have not been indexed.

As with all other record categories discussed above, guides are available. *A Guide to Vital Statistics in the Church Records of Connecticut*, prepared by the Connecticut Historical Records Survey (New Haven: Historical Records Survey, 1942), assists in locating what categories of records remain in each town and for each time period. It was incomplete when it was taken and has not been updated. Many town churches have deposited their older records for safekeeping with the Connecticut State Library.

A List of Church Records in the Connecticut State Library (available at the cost of photocopy and postage), the library's Manuscripts and Archives catalogs, and the Church Records Survey conducted by the WPA (State Archives Record Group 33) are additional sources that can be used to locate church records not in the Church Records Index.

As a supplement to vital records, indications of migration are found in listings of church membership, which frequently include dates of admission to the local church or dismissal to a new church.

Military Records

Connecticut's military records, starting with the Pequot War, have been published and are widely available. In addition to the sources available at the National Archives (see pages 11-12) and archival sources at the Connecticut State Library, the following can be consulted:

Shepard, James. *Connecticut Soldiers in the Pequot War of 1637.* Meridan, Conn.: Journal Publishing Co., 1913.

Collections of the Connecticut Historical Society. *Rolls of Connecticut Men in the French and Indian War, 1755–1762.* Vol. 9 and 10. Hartford: Connecticut Historical Society, 1903–05.

Connecticut Adjutant-General. *Record of Service of Connecticut Men in the War of the Revolution, War of 1812, Mexican War.* Hartford: Connecticut General Assembly, 1889. Transcripts of original papers with a cross-index to all records. Connecticut provided large numbers in the ranks of patriots and the largest number of African-American soldiers from all the colonies (see African Americans).

Many Connecticut men were Loyalists as well, although a comprehensive listing of them is not available. Many sought refuge in Canada. See Angus Baxter, *In Search of Your Canadian Roots* (Baltimore: Genealogical Publishing Co., 1989) for a discussion of United Empire Loyalists.

Connecticut Adjutant-General. *Record of Service of Connecticut Men in the Army and Navy of the United States During the War of Rebellion.* Hartford: Case, Lockwood, and Brainard Co., 1889.

Record of Service of Connecticut Men in the Army, Navy and Marine Corps of the United States in the Spanish-American War. Hartford: Case, Lockwood, and Brainard Co., 1919.

Service Records: Connecticut Men and Women in the Armed Forces of the United States During World War I 1917–1920. Hartford: Office of the Adjutant General, [1941?].

The Connecticut Historical Society has a large collection of military documents and manuscripts. The Connecticut State Library maintains a card file on veteran's deaths with place of burial.

Periodicals, Newspapers, and Manuscript Collections

Periodicals

New Haven Genealogical Magazine (formerly *The Families of Ancient New Haven* and now *The American Genealogist*) was begun by Donald Lines Jacobus and still sets a standard for its depth and documentation (see page 10).

Connecticut Nutmegger (1968-present) is a current publication of the Connecticut Society of Genealogists. (See Archives, Libraries, and Societies).

Connecticut Ancestry (1957-present) is the publication of the Connecticut Ancestry Society.

Newspapers

Newspapers are an important source for early marriages and deaths. The Connecticut State Library holds the largest collection of Connecticut newspapers in the United States (approximately 2,050 titles spanning almost 250 years) and makes its newspaper microfilm holdings available on interlibrary loan. The completeness of holdings for titles ranges from a full run of the *Hartford Courant* and its predecessor, the *Connecticut Courant* (1764-present), to the solitary copies of several one-issue-only newspapers. An informative research guide to Connecticut newspapers is included on the Connecticut State Library's website. Most newspapers in the library are included in its online catalog.

The *Connecticut Courant* served not only Connecticut, but the burgeoning frontier to its north, in Massachusetts and Vermont, and west in New York. Reports from the frontier are quite common including land advertisements, letters from former residents, and social items. An index (1754–1820) by Doris Cook is available at the Connecticut Historical Society, and another index (1764–99) at the Connecticut State Library.

The Hale Collection of Newspaper Marriage and Death Notices (ca. 1750–1865) is available at the Connecticut State Library and on microfilm through FHL Family History Centers, and abstracts notices from ninety of the earliest Connecticut newspapers. These notices generally end with the close of the Civil War (ca. 1865–66).

Newspapers in Connecticut Institutions, Updated through June 1997 (Hartford: Connecticut State Library, 1997) identifies and shows the holdings of newspapers in 280 participating Connecticut institutions. Newspapers are listed alphabetically by title, and under each title the names of the institution(s) having copies are given, along with dates of the issues held. Copies are available for consultation at many Connecticut libraries.

Between 1910 and 1967, the *Hartford Times* ran a genealogical query column similar to that of the *Boston Evening Transcript* (see Massachusetts—Newspapers), which has been indexed and microfilmed by the Godfrey Memorial Library in Middletown and distributed to many major research libraries.

Manuscripts

As with all record categories, the manuscript collections in Connecticut are excellent. The major repositories—Connecticut State Library, Connecticut Historical Society, Godfrey Memorial Library in Middletown, Greenwich Library, Ferguson Library in Stamford, and Otis Library in Norwich—all have extensive collections. Family papers abound in these collections, but other items such as school records, church records, and original copies of wills and deeds can sometimes be found. There are no every-name indexes, but the collections are well cataloged.

Archives, Libraries, and Societies

Connecticut State Library
History and Genealogy Unit
231 Capitol Ave.
Hartford, CT 06106
www.cslib.org/handg.htm

This major research repository includes the State Archives and the History and Genealogy Unit. The unit provides the researcher with access in person and by mail to the archival material, genealogical indexes, and published materials described in various sections above. The staff is not available for research, however. Guides to their original source materials are available at the cost of photocopying and postage and on their website. They are extremely helpful in focusing research.

Connecticut Historical Society
1 Elizabeth St.
Hartford, CT 06105
www.chs.org

A major genealogical reference library with excellent holdings in family genealogies, town histories, census records, and a book loan program for members.

Connecticut Society of Genealogists
P.O. Box 435
Glastonbury, CT 06033
www.csginc.org

Their publication, *Connecticut Nutmegger*, is available by subscription or with membership. The society meets often during the year with an educational program for genealogists.

Connecticut Ancestry Society
P.O. Box 249
Stamford, CT 06904

Formerly called the Stamford Genealogical Society, the society holds monthly meetings and produces a publication called *Connecticut Ancestry*, previously *Bulletin of the Stamford Genealogical Society (1971)*.

Godfrey Memorial Library
134 Newfield St.
Middletown, CT 06457
www.godfrey.org

Links to current addresses of all Connecticut libraries, historical societies, and municipal historians are available from the Connecticut State Library's website (see above).

Special Focus Categories

Immigration
Connecticut's immigration lists are included in the NARA microfilm publication, M575, *Copies of Lists of Passengers Arriving at Miscellaneous Ports on the Atlantic and Gulf Coasts, 1820–1873* (see page 11, for earlier sources).

Naturalization
As with other states, naturalizations might have been granted in any Connecticut court up to the twentieth century. Some are still in the county courthouses, but all that were held at the Connecticut State Library were transferred to the National Archives—Northeast Region (see pages 11-12) in 1984 and have been microfilmed with a copy of the film returned for research at the state library. Those filed and granted after 1906 are in the federal district court in Bridgeport, Hartford, or New Haven. See <www.cslib.org/natural.htm> for a full description and explanation.

African American
From colonial times, African Americans have been a major ethnic group in Connecticut, providing a large number of Revolutionary soldiers.

White, David Oliver. *Connecticut's Black Soldiers, 1775–1783*. Connecticut Bicentennial Series, no. 4. Chester, Conn.: Pequot Press, 1973.

Rose, James M., and Barbara W. Brown. *Black Roots in Southeastern Connecticut, 1650–1900*. Reprint. Baltimore: Genealogical Publishing Co., 2001.

Rose, James M. *Tapestry: A Living History of the Black Family in Southeastern Connecticut*. New London, Conn.: New London Historical Society, 1979.

Weed, Ralph Foster. *Slavery in Connecticut*. New Haven: Yale University Press, 1935.

A research guide is available on the Connecticut State Library website <www.cslib.org/blagen.htm>.

Native American
A research guide is available on the Connecticut State Library website <www.cslib.org/indians.htm>. See also Massachusetts—Special Focus Categories for sources on historical background.

County Resources

Counties were abolished officially in 1959, as their purpose had been chiefly to define county court districts. For genealogical research purposes, counties become necessary when using the federal census returns, since census returns are all cataloged by county. Connecticut's original four counties had become eight counties by the time of the first federal census in 1790. Although some towns on the borders crossed county jurisdictions for different census enumerations, the most accurate indication of these changes can be found in William Thorndale and William Dollarhide, *Map Guide to the U.S. Federal Censuses, 1790–1920* (Baltimore: Genealogical Publishing Co., 1987). This guide should be consulted when using census records. Each town's present county is given in the Town Resources section.

Map	County	Date Formed	Parent County/ies
B6	Fairfield	1666	original
E2	Hartford	1666	original
B2	Litchfield	1751	Fairfield/Hartford
F5	Middlesex	1785	Hartford/New Haven
D5	New Haven	1666	original
J5	New London	1666	original
G2	Tolland	1785	Windham
J2	Windham	1726	New London

Drawn by William Dollarhide

CONNECTICUT

BERKSHIRE — Sheffield, New Marlborough, Sandisfield, Tolland, Granville

MASSACHUSETTS — Agawam, Hampden, Monson, Wales, Holland, Sturbridge, Southbridge

HAMPDEN — Suffield, Enfield, Somers, Stafford, Union

WORCESTER — Woodstock, Thompson, Dudley, Webster, Douglas, Uxbridge, Burrillville

PROVIDENCE — Glocester, Killingly, Foster, Scituate

COLUMBIA — Copake, Gallatin, Ancram, Pine Plains, North East

DUTCHESS — Stanford, Amenia, Washington, Union Vale, Dover, Beekman, Pawling

NEW YORK

PUTNAM — Kent, Patterson, Carmel, Southeast, North Salem, Somers

WESTCHESTER — Lewisboro, Bedford, Pound Ridge, North Castle, Harrison, Rye

RHODE ISLAND — Coventry, West Greenwich, Exeter, Richmond, Hopkinton, Charlestown, Westerly

KENT — Coventry, West Greenwich

WASHINGTON

Litchfield area: Salisbury, North Canaan, Canaan, Norfolk, Colebrook, Hartland, Sharon, Cornwall, Goshen, Winchester, Barkhamsted, Kent, Warren, Litchfield, Torrington, New Hartford, Harwinton, Washington, Morris, Bethlehem, Plymouth, Thomaston, Watertown, New Milford, Bridgewater, Roxbury, Woodbury, Sherman, Brookfield, New Fairfield, Southbury, Middlebury, Danbury, Newtown, Bethel, Ridgefield, Redding, Monroe, Oxford, Beacon Falls, Naugatuck, Prospect, Wolcott

Hartford area: Granby, East Granby, Windsor Locks, Windsor, East Windsor, South Windsor, Simsbury, Bloomfield, Canton, Avon, West Hartford, Hartford, East Hartford, Manchester, Farmington, Burlington, Bristol, Plainville, New Britain, Newington, Wethersfield, Glastonbury, Berlin, Rocky Hill, Cromwell, Southington, Cheshire

Tolland area: Ellington, Vernon, Tolland, Willington, Ashford, Eastford, Coventry, Bolton, Andover, Columbia, Mansfield, Hebron, Marlborough, Chaplin, Hampton, Pomfret, Putnam, Brooklyn, Killingly

Windham area: Windham, Scotland, Canterbury, Sprague, Lisbon, Plainfield, Sterling, Griswold, Voluntown

New Haven area: Waterbury, Middlebury, Meriden, Wallingford, Hamden, North Haven, Seymour, Ansonia, Derby, Woodbridge, New Haven, Orange, Shelton, Milford, West Haven, East Haven, Branford, North Branford, Guilford, Madison, Trumbull, Bridgeport, Stratford, Easton, Weston, Wilton, Fairfield, Norwalk, Westport, New Canaan, Stamford, Darien, Greenwich

Middlesex area: Middletown, Durham, Haddam, East Hampton, Portland, Middlefield, Killingworth, Chester, Deep River, Essex, Clinton, Westbrook, Old Saybrook, Old Lyme, Lyme

New London area: Colchester, Salem, East Haddam, Lebanon, Franklin, Bozrah, Norwich, Preston, Montville, Ledyard, Waterford, Groton, Stonington, North Stonington, New London, East Lyme

NOTE:

The state of Connecticut abolished county government in 1960. The county boundaries shown on the map now relate to various state administrative divisions. Counties boundaries are still used for U.S. census statistics. All other functions of the previous county governments are administered either at the town level or at the state level of government.

The Counties and Towns of
Connecticut

5   0   10   20 Miles

Long Island Sound

Atlantic Ocean

CONNECTICUT

Town Resources

In the list of town offices that follows, the first column indicates the address supplied by the secretary of state for the town clerk where town meeting, vital records, and land records are found. If the address specifies "city" or "municipal," the official in charge of the records is the city or municipal clerk. The second column indicates the date the town was incorporated and the parent town or towns; dashes (—) indicate that the town was not original but was formed from unorganized land rather than another town. Some seventeenth-century towns were settled or organized a year or two before incorporation. The third column lists the present county, which can be used for census identification and superior court records (see County Resources). The final column indicates the present probate district, the date the town became part of that district, and the previous chronological parent district or districts. For earlier probate divisions, see the Probate Records section above. If a town was formed *after* its probate district, only that district is listed.

All deeds, vital records, and probate records for all Connecticut towns are available to 1900 on microfilm at the Connecticut State Library or through the FHL. Town meeting records, with their rich material describing various aspects of the town, are not automatically included in the microfilms and may need to be searched in the town office itself.

Information on the town resources is partially based on a chart produced by Ann P. Barry, "Connecticut Towns and Their Establishment" distributed by the Connecticut State Library at <www.cslib.org/cttowns.htm>. Additional sources include informational publications printed by the History and Genealogy Unit of the Library and Marcia D. Melnyk, *Genealogist's Handbook for New England*, 4th. ed. (Boston: New England Historic Genealogical Society, 1999). Recently revised probate resource information can be found at <www.cslib.org/probate.htm>.

See the Connecticut Register and Manual for updated addresses, phone and fax numbers, and town websites at <www.sots.state.ct.us/RegisterManual/TNCLK.htm>. If a town has a P.O. Box listed, use that as the mailing address.

Map	Town Address	Date Formed Parent Towns	County	Probate Parent
G3	Andover 17 School Rd. Andover 06232-0328	1848 Coventry/Hebron	Tolland	Andover 1851 Hebron
C6	Ansonia City Hall 253 Main St. Ansonia 06401-1866	1889 Derby	New Haven	Derby
H2	Ashford 25 Pompey Hollow Road Ashford 06278-1552	1714 ——	Windham	Ashford 1830 Pomfret
D3	Avon 60 W. Main St. Avon 06001-3743	1830 Farmington	Hartford	Avon 1844 Farmington
D2	Barkhamsted 67 Ripley Hill Rd. Barkhamsted 06063	1779 ——	Litchfield	Barkhamsted 1834 New Hartford
C5	Beacon Falls 10 Maple Ave. Beacon Falls 06403-1198	1871 Bethany/Oxford/ Seymour/Naugatuck	New Haven	Naugatuck
E4	Berlin 240 Kensington Rd. Berlin 06037-2647	1785 Farmington/ Middletown/ Wethersfield	Hartford	Berlin 1824 Hartford/ Middletown/ Farmington
D5	Bethany 40 Peck Rd. Bethany 06525-3338	1832 Woodbridge	New Haven	Bethany 1854 New Haven
A5	Bethel 1 School St. Bethel 06801-0003	1855 Danbury	Fairfield	Bethel 1859 Danbury
B4	Bethlehem 36 Main St. South Bethlehem 06751-0160	1787 Woodbury	Litchfield	Woodbury 1719 Fairfield/Hartford New Haven
E2	Bloomfield 800 Bloomfield Ave. P.O. Box 337 Bloomfield 06002-0337	1835 Windsor/Farmington/ Simsbury/Hartford	Hartford	Hartford 1666 original
G3	Bolton 222 Bolton Center Rd. Bolton 06040-7695	1720 ——	Tolland	Andover 1851 Hebron
H4	Bozrah 1 River Rd. Bozrah 06334-0158	1786 Norwich	New London	Bozrah 1843 Norwich
E6	Branford 1019 Main St./P.O. Box 150 Branford 06405-0150	1685 New Haven	New Haven	Branford 1850 Guilford
B7	Bridgeport City Hall 45 Lyon Terrace Bridgeport 06604-4062	1821 Stratford/Fairfield	Fairfield	Bridgeport 1840 Stratford

Map	Town Address	Date Formed Parent Towns	County	Probate Parent
B5	Bridgewater 44 Main St. S. P.O. Box 216 Bridgewater 06752	1856 New Milford	Litchfield	New Milford 1787 Woodbury
D3	Bristol City Hall 111 N. Main St. P.O. Box 114 Bristol 06010-0114	1785 Farmington	Hartford	Bristol 1830 Farmington
A5	Brookfield 100 Poncono Rd. P.O. Box 5106 Brookfield Ctr. 06805-5106	1788 Danbury/New Milford/ Newton	Fairfield	Brookfield 1850 Newton
J2	Brooklyn 4 Wolf Den Rd. P.O. Box 356 Brooklyn 06234-0356	1786 Pomfret/Canterbury	Windham	Brooklyn 1833 Pomfret/ Plainfield
D3	Burlington 200 Spielman Hwy. Burlington 06013-1701	1806 Bristol	Hartford	Burlington 1834 Farmington
B1	Canaan 107 Main St. P.O. Box 47 Falls Village 06031-0047	1739 ——	Litchfield	Canaan 1846 Sharon
J3	Canterbury 1 Municipal Dr. P.O. Box 27 Canterbury 06331-0027	1703 Plainfield	Windham	Canterbury 1835 Plainfield
D2	Canton 4 Market St. P.O. Box 168 Collinsville 06022-0168	1806 Simsbury	Hartford	Canton 1841 Simsbury
H2	Chaplin 495 Phoenixville Rd. P.O. Box 286 Chaplin 06235	1822 Windham/Hampton/ Mansfield	Windham	Chaplin 1850 Windham
D4	Cheshire 84 S. Main St. Cheshire 06410-3108	1780 Wallingford	New Haven	Cheshire 1829 Wallingford
F5	Chester 65 Main St./P.O. Box 218 Chester 06412-0218	1836 Saybrook	Middlesex	Saybrook 1780 Guilford
F6	Clinton 54 E. Main St. Clinton 06413-2035	1838 Killingworth	Middlesex	Clinton 1862 Killingworth
G4	Colchester 127 Norwich Ave. Colchester 06415-1290	1698 ——	New London	Colchester 1832 East Haddam
C1	Colebrook 558 Colebrook Rd./P.O. Box 5 Colebrook Ctr. 06021-0005	1779	Litchfield	Winchester 1838 Norfolk
G3	Columbia Yeomans Hall 323 Jonathan Trumball Hwy. Columbia 06237-1116	1804 Lebanon	Tolland	Andover 1851 Hebron
B2	Cornwall 26 Pine St./P.O. Box 97 Cornwall 06753-0097	1740 ——	Litchfield	Cornwall 1847 Litchfield
G2	Coventry 1712 Main St. Coventry 06238-3615	1712 ——	Tolland	Coventry 1849 Hebron
B2	Cromwell 41 West St. Cromwell 06416-2142	1851 Middletown	Middlesex	Middletown
A5	Danbury City Hall 155 Deer Hill Ave. Danbury 06810-7726	1687 ——	Fairfield	Danbury 1744 Fairfield
A8	Darien 2 Renshaw Road Darien 06820-5344	1820 Stamford	Fairfield	Darien 1921 Stamford
F5	Deep River 174 Main St. Deep River 06417-2008	1635 (as Saybrook; renamed, 1947)	Middlesex	Deep River 1949 Saybrook
C6	Derby City Hall 35 Fifth St. Derby 06418-1897	1675 ——	New Haven	Derby 1858 New Haven
E5	Durham 30 Town House Rd. P.O. Box 428 Durham 06422-0428	1708 ——	Middlesex	Middletown 1752 Hartford/ Guilford/ East Haddam
E1	East Granby 9 Center St. East Granby 06026-0459	1858 Granby/Windsor Locks	Hartford	East Granby 1865 Granby
G5	East Haddam 7 Main St., Box K East Haddam 06423-0295	1734 Haddam	Middlesex	East Haddam 1741 Hartford
F4	East Hampton 20 E. High St. East Hampton 06424-1091	1767 (as Chatham; renamed, 1915) Middletown	Middlesex	East Hampton 1824 Middletown
E3	East Hartford 740 Main St. East Hartford 06108-3114	1783 Hartford	Hartford	East Hartford 1887 Hartford
D6	East Haven 250 Main St. East Haven 06512-3004	1785 New Haven	New Haven	East Haven 1955 New Haven
H5	East Lyme 108 Pennsylvania Ave. Box 519 Niantic 06357-0519	1839 Lyme/Waterford	New London	East Lyme 1843 New London

Map	Town Address	Date Formed Parent Towns	County	Probate Parent
F2	East Windsor 11 Rye St. Box 213 Broad Brook 06016-0213	1768 Windsor	Hartford	East Windsor 1782 Hartford/ Stafford
J2	Eastford 16 Westford Rd. P.O. Box 273 Eastford 06242-0273	1847 Ashford	Windham	Eastford 1849 Ashford
B5	Easton 225 Center Rd. Easton 06612-1398	1845 Weston	Fairfield	Trumbull 1959 Bridgeport
F2	Ellington 55 Main St. P.O. Box 137 Ellington 06029-0137	1786 East Windsor	Tolland	Ellington 1826 East Windsor/ Stafford
F1	Enfield 820 Enfield St. Enfield 06082-2997	1683 (part of Massachusetts until 1749)	Hartford	Enfield 1831 E. Windsor
G6	Essex 29 West Ave. P.O. Box 98 Essex 06426-0098	1852 Saybrook	Middlesex	Essex 1853 Saybrook

Name of town was Old Saybrook from 1852–54, when a new town of Old Saybrook was separated from this one. The town created in 1852 changed its name to Essex. The probate district called Old Saybrook was created and the old one changed its name to Essex.

Map	Town Address	Date Formed Parent Towns	County	Probate Parent
B7	Fairfield 611 Old Post Rd. Fairfield 06430-6690	1639 original	Fairfield	Fairfield 16666 original
D3	Farmington 1 Monteith Dr. Farmington 06034-1053	1645 original	Hartford	Farmington 1769 Hartford
H4	Franklin 7 Meeting House Hill Rd. Franklin 06254-9775	1786 Norwich	New London	Norwich
F3	Glastonbury 2155 Main St. Glastonbury 06033-6523	1690 Wethersfield	Hartford	Glastonbury 1975 Hartford
B2	Goshen 42 North St. P.O. Box 54 Goshen 06756-0054	1739	Litchfield	Torrington 1847 Litchfield
D1	Granby 15 N. Granby Rd. Granby 06035	1786 Simsbury	Hartford	Granby 1807 Simsbury/ Hartford
A8	Greenwich 101 Field Point Rd. P.O. Box 2540 Greenwich 06830-2540	1665 Stamford (part of New Amsterdam, 1642–56)	Fairfield	Greenwich 1853 Stamford

Map	Town Address	Date Formed Parent Towns	County	Probate Parent
J4	Griswold 28 Main St. P.O. Box 369 Jewett City 06351-0369	1815 Preston	New London	Griswold 1979 Norwich
J6	Groton 45 Fort Hill Rd. Groton 06340-4394	1705 New London	New London	Groton 1839 Stonington
E6	Guilford 31 Park St. Guilford 06437-2629	1643	New Haven	Guilford 1719 New Haven/ New London
F5	Haddam 30 Field Park Dr. P.O. Box 87 Haddam 06438-0087	1668	Middlesex	Haddam 1830 Middletown/ Chatham
D5	Hamden Memorial Town Hall 2372 Whitney Ave. Hamden 06518-3207	1786 New Haven	New Haven	Hamden 1945 New Haven
J3	Hampton 164 Main St. P.O. Box 143 Hampton 06247-0143	1786 Windham/Pomfret/ Brooklyn/Canterbury/ Mansfield	Windham	Hampton 1836 Windham
E3	Hartford 550 Main St. Hartford 06103	1635	Hartford	Hartford 1666 original
D1	Hartland 22 South Rd. P.O. Box 297 East Hartland 06027-0297	1761 ———	Hartford	Hartland 1836 Granby
C3	Harwinton 100 Bentley Dr. Harwinton 06791-2200	1737	Litchfield	Harwinton 1835 Litchfield
G3	Hebron 15 Gilead St. P.O. Box 156 Hebron 06248-0156	1708 ———	Tolland	Hebron 1789 Windham/ East Windsor/ East Haddam
	Huntington	1789 (renamed Shelton, 1919)		
A3	Kent 41 Kent Green Blvd. Box 678 Kent 06757-0678	1739 ———	Litchfield	Kent 1831 New Milford
K2	Killingly 172 Main St. P.O. Box 6000 Killingly 06239-6000	1708 ———	Windham	Killingly 1830 Pomfret/ Plainfield
F5	Killingworth 323 Rte. 81 Killingworth 06417-1298	1667	Middlesex	Killingworth 1834 Saybrook

Map	Town Address	Date Formed Parent Towns	County	Probate Parent
H4	Lebanon 579 Exeter Rd. Lebanon 06249-1506	1700 ———	New London	Lebanon 1826 Windham
J5	Ledyard 741 Colonel Ledyard Hwy Ledyard 06339-1541	1836 Groton	New London	Ledyard 1837 Stonington
J4	Lisbon 1 Newent Rd. Lisbon 06351 9802	1786 Norwich	New London	Norwich
B3	Litchfield 74 West St. P.O. Box 488 Litchfield 06759-0488	1719 ———	Litchfield	Litchfield 1742 Hartford/Woodbury New Haven
G5	Lyme 480 Hamburg Rd. Old Lyme 06371-3110	1667 Saybrook	New London	Lyme 1869 Old Lyme
E6	Madison 8 Campus Dr. Madison 06443-2563	1826 Guilford	New Haven	Madison 1834 Guilford
F3	Manchester 41 Center St. P.O. Box 191 Manchester 06040-0191	1823 East Hartford	Hartford	Manchester 1850 East Hartford
H3	Mansfield 4 S. Eagleville Rd. Storrs 06268-2574	1702 Windham	Tolland	Mansfield 1831 Windham
F4	Marlborough 26 N. Main St./P.O. Box 29 Marlborough 06447	1803 Colchester/Glastonbury/ Hebron	Hartford	Marlborough 1846 Colchester
E4	Meriden City Hall, Rm. 124 142 E. Main St. Meriden 06450-5667	1806 Wallingford	New Haven	Meriden 1836 Wallingford
C4	Middlebury 1212 Whittemore Rd. Box 392 Middlebury 06762-0392	1807 Waterbury/Woodbury/ Southbury	New Haven	Waterbury
E4	Middlefield 383 Jackson Hill Rd. Box 179 Middlefield 06455-0179	1866 Middletown	Middlesex	Middletown
F4	Middletown 245 Dekoven Dr. Box 1300 Middletown 06457	1651 ———	Middlesex	Middletown 1752 Hartford/Guilford/ East Haddam
C6	Milford 70 W. River St. Milford 06460	1639 ———	New Haven	Milford 1832 New Haven

Map	Town Address	Date Formed Parent Towns	County	Probate Parent
B6	Monroe 7 Fan Hill Rd. Monroe 06468-1800	1823 Huntington	Fairfield	Trumbull 1959 Bridgeport
H5	Montville 310 Norwich-New London Tnpk Uncasville 06382	1786 New London	New London	Montville 1851 New London
B3	Morris 3 East St./P.O. Box 66 Morris 06763-0066	1859 Litchfield	Litchfield	Litchfield 1742 Hartford/Woodbury/ New Haven
C5	Naugatuck 229 Church St. Naugatuck 06770	1844 Waterbury/Bethany/ Oxford	New Haven	Naugatuck 1863 Waterbury
E3	New Britain City Hall 27 W. Main St. New Britain 06051-2298	1850 Berlin	Hartford	Berlin
A7	New Canaan 77 Main St. P.O. Box 447 New Canaan 06840-0447	1801 Norwalk/Stamford	Fairfield	New Canaan 1937 Norwalk
A5	New Fairfield 4 Brush Hill Rd. New Fairfield 06812-2619	1740 ———	Fairfield	New Fairfield 1975 Danbury
D2	New Hartford 530 Main St./P.O. Box 426 New Hartford 06057-0426	1738 ———	Litchfield	New Hartford 1825 Simsbury
D6	New Haven Kennedy Mitchell Hall of Records 200 Orange St., Rm. 202 New Haven 06510-2067	1638	New Haven	New Haven 1666 original
H6	New London City Hall 181 State St. New London 06320-6346	1648 ———	New London	New London 1666 original
A4	New Milford 10 Main St. New Milford 06776-2831	1712 ———	Litchfield	New Milford 1787 Woodbury/Sharon/ Danbury
E3	Newington 131 Cedar St. Newington 06111-2644	1871 Wethersfield	Hartford	Newington 1975 Hartford
B5	Newtown 45 Main St. Newtown 06470-2185	1711 ———	Fairfield	Newtown 1820 Danbury
B1	Norfolk 19 Maple Ave./P.O. Box 552 Norfolk 06058-0552	1758 ———	Litchfield	Norfolk 1779 Simsbury/Litchfield
E6	North Branford 1599 Foxon Rd. P.O. Box 287 North Branford 06471-0287	1831 Branford	New Haven	North Branford 1937 Guilford/Wallingford

Map	Town Address	Date Formed Parent Towns	County	Probate Parent
B1	North Canaan 100 Pease St. P.O. Box 338 Canaan 06018-0338	1858 Canaan	Litchfield	Canaan
D5	North Haven 18 Church St. North Haven 06473-2503	1786 New Haven	New Haven	North Haven 1955 New Haven
K5	North Stonington 40 Main St. North Stonington 06359-1612	1807 Stonington	New London	N. Stonington 1835 Stonington
A7	Norwalk 125 E. Ave. P.O. Box 5125 Norwalk 06854-5125	1651 ——	Fairfield	Norwalk 1802 Fairfield/Stamford
J4	Norwich City Hall, Rm 215 100 Broadway Norwich 06360-4431	1662 ——	New London	Norwich 1748 New London
G6	Old Lyme 52 Lyme St. Old Lyme 06371-2331	1855 (as South Lyme; renamed, 1857) Lyme	New London	Old Lyme
G6	Old Saybrook 302 Main St. Old Saybrook 06475-2304	1854 (see Essex for explanation of the town's formation) Old Saybrook (now named Essex)	Middlesex	Old Saybrook 1859 Essex
C6	Orange 617 Orange Center Rd. Orange 06477-2423	1822 Milford/New Haven	New Haven	Orange 1975 New Haven
C5	Oxford 486 Oxford Rd. Oxford 06483-1298	1798 Derby/Southbury	New Haven	Oxford 1846 New Haven
J3	Plainfield 8 Community Ave. Plainfield 06374-1238	1699 ——	Windham	Plainfield 1747 Windham
J3	Plainville Municipal Center 1 Central Sq. Plainville 06062-1900	1869 Farmington	Hartford	Plainville 1909 Farmington
C3	Plymouth 80 Main St. Terryville 06786-1295	1795 Watertown	Litchfield	Plymouth 1833 Waterbury
J2	Pomfret 5 Haven Rd. Pomfret Center 06259-1743	1713 ——	Windham	Pomfret 1752 Windham/Plainfield
F4	Portland 33 E. Main St. P.O. Box 71 Portland 06480-0071	1841 Chatham	Middlesex	Portland 1913 Chatham
J4	Preston 389 Rte. 2 Preston 06365-8830	1687 ——	New London	Norwich 1748 New London
D5	Prospect 36 Center St. Prospect 06712-1699	1827 Cheshire/Waterbury	New Haven	Cheshire 1829 Wallingford
K2	Putnam 126 Church St. Putnam 06260-1831	1855 Thompson/Pomfret/ Killingly	Windham	Putnam 1856 Thompson
A6	Redding 100 Hill Rd. P.O. Box 1028 Redding Center 06875-1028	1767 Fairfield	Fairfield	Redding 1839 Danbury
D7	Ridgefield 400 Main St. Ridgefield 06877-4699	1709 ——	Fairfield	Ridgefield 1841 Danbury
E3	Rocky Hill 761 Old Main St. Box 657 Rocky Hill 06067-0657	1843 Wethersfield	Hartford	Newington 1975 Hartford
B4	Roxbury 25 North St. Roxbury 06783-1405	1796 Woodbury	Litchfield	Roxbury 1842 Woodbury
H5	Salem 270 Hartford Rd. Salem 06420-3809	1819 Colchester/Lyme/ Montville	New London	Salem 1841 Colchester/ New London
A1	Salisbury 27 Main St. P.O. Box 548 Salisbury 06068-0548	1741 ——	Litchfield	Salisbury 1847 Sharon
	Saybrook	(renamed Deep River, 1947)		
J3	Scotland 9 Devotion Rd. P.O. Box 122 Scotland 06264-0122	1857 Windham	Windham	Windham 1719 Hartford/ New London
C5	Seymour 1 First St. Seymour 06483-2817	1850 Derby	New Haven	Derby 1858 New Haven
A2	Sharon 63 Main St. P.O. Box 224 Sharon 06069-0224	1739 ——	Litchfield	Sharon 1755 Litchfield
C6	Shelton 54 Hill St. P.O. Box 364 Shelton 06484-0364	1789 Stratford	Fairfield	Shelton 1889 Bridgeport

Both the town and district of Shelton were called Huntington until 1919.

Map	Town Address	Date Formed Parent Towns	County	Probate Parent
A4	Sherman Mallory Town Hall 9 Rte. 39, Box 39 Sherman 06784-0364	1802 New Fairfield	Fairfield	Sherman 1846 New Milford

CONNECTICUT

Map	Town Address	Date Formed Parent Towns	County	Probate Parent
E2	Simsbury 933 Hopmeadow St. Box 495 Simsbury 06070	1670	Hartford	Simsbury 1769 Hartford
G1	Somers 600 Main St. P.O. Box 308 Somers 06071-0308	1734 Enfield (part of Massachusetts until 1749)	Tolland	Somers 1834 Ellington
	South Lyme	1855 (renamed Old Lyme, 1857)		
	South Windsor 1540 Sullivan Ave. South Windsor 06074-2786	1845 East Windsor	Hartford	East Windsor
B5	Southbury 501 Main St. South Southbury 06488-2295	1787 Woodbury	New Haven	Southbury 1967 Woodbury
D4	Southington 75 Main St. Southington 06489-2504	1779 Farmington	Hartford	Southington 1825 Farmington
J4	Sprague 1 Main St. P.O. Box 162 Baltic 06330	1861 Lisbon/Franklin	New London	Norwich
G1	Stafford Warren Memorial Town Hall 1 Main St./ P.O. Box 11 Stafford Springs 06076-0011	1719	Tolland	Stafford 1759 Hartford/Pomfret
A7	Stamford Government Center 888 Washington Blvd. Stamford 06904-2902	1641	Fairfield	Stamford 1728 Fairfield
K3	Sterling 1114 Plainfield Pike Box 157 Oneco 06373-0157	1794 Voluntown	Windham	Sterling 1852 Plainfield
K5	Stonington 152 Elm St./ P.O. Box 352 Stonington 06378-0352 *Was originally part of Rhode Island from 1649 and was called Mistic.*	1662	New London	Stonington 1766 New London
C7	Stratford 2725 Main St., Rm 101 Stratford 06497-5892	1639	Fairfield	Stratford 1782 Fairfield
E1	Suffield 83 Mountain Rd. Suffield 06078-2041	1674 (part of Massachusetts until 1749)	Hartford	Suffield 1821 Hartford/Granby
C3	Thomaston 158 Main St. Thomaston 06787-1744	1875 Plymouth	Litchfield	Thomaston 1882 Litchfield
K1	Thompson 815 Riverside Dr. Box 899 North Grosvenor Dale 06255-0899	1785 Killingly	Windham	Thompson 1832 Pomfret
G2	Tolland Hicks Mem. Municipal Office 21 Tolland Green Tolland 06084-9445	1715	Tolland	Tolland 1830 Stafford
C2	Torrington Municipal Building 140 Main St. Torrington 06790-5201	1740	Litchfield	Torrington 1847 Litchfield
B6	Trumbull 5866 Main St. Trumbull 06611-3193	1797 Stratford	Fairfield	Trumbull 1959 Bridgeport
H1	Union 1043 Buckley Hwy., Rt. 71 Union 06076-9520	1734	Tolland	Stafford 1759 Hartford/Pomfret
G2	Vernon Memorial Building 14 Park Pl. Rockville 06066-3291	1808 Bolton	Tolland	Ellington 1826 East Windsor/ Stafford
K4	Voluntown 115 Main St./P.O. Box 96 Voluntown 06384-0096	1721	New London	Norwich 1830 Plainfield
E5	Wallingford 45 S. Main St. P.O. Box 427 Wallingford 06492-0427	1670 New Haven	New Haven	Wallingford 1776 New Haven/ Guilford
B3	Warren 7 Sackett Hill Rd. Warren 06754-1713	1786 Kent	Litchfield	Litchfield 1742 Woodbury/ New Haven
D4	Washington 2 Bryan Plaza/P.O. Box 383 Washington 06794-0383	1779 Woodbury/Litchfield/ Kent/New Milford	Litchfield	Washington 1832 Litchfield/Woodbury
D5	Waterbury City Hall 235 Grand St. Waterbury 06702-1983	1686	New Haven	Waterbury 1779 Woodbury
H5	Waterford 15 Rope Ferry Rd. Waterford 06385-2806	1801 New London	New London	New London
C4	Watertown 37 Deforest St. Watertown 06795-2200	1780 Waterbury	Litchfield	Watertown 1834 Waterbury
E3	West Hartford 50 S. Main St., Rm 313 West Hartford 06107	1854 Hartford	Hartford	Hartford
D6	West Haven City Hall 355 Main St. P.O. Box 526 West Haven 06516-0526	1921 Orange	New Haven	West Haven 1941 New Haven

109

CONNECTICUT

Map	Town Address	Date Formed Parent Towns	County	Probate Parent
G6	Westbrook 1163 Boston Post Rd. P.O. Box 676 Westbrook 06498	1840 Saybrook	Middlesex	Westbrook 1854 Old Saybrook
A6	Weston 56 Norfield Rd. P.O. Box 1007 Weston 06883-1007	1787 Fairfield	Fairfield	Westport 1835 Weston/Fairfield/ Norwalk
B7	Westport 110 Myrtle Ave. Westport 06881-3514	1835 Fairfield/Norwalk/ Weston	Fairfield	Westport 1835 Fairfield/Norwalk/ Weston
E3	Wethersfield 505 Silas Deane Hwy. Wethersfield 06109-2216	1634 ——	Hartford	Newington 1975 Hartford
H1	Willington 40 Old Farms Rd. West Willington 06279-1720	1727 ——	Tolland	Tolland 1830 Stafford
A7	Wilton 238 Danbury Rd. Wilton 06897-4008	1802 Norwalk	Fairfield	Norwalk 1802 Fairfield/Stamford
C2	Winchester 338 Main St. Winsted 06098-1697	1771 ——	Litchfield	Winchester 1838 Norfolk
H3	Windham 979 Main St. P.O. Box 94 Willimantic 06226-0094	1692 ——	Windham	Windham 1719 Hartford/New London
E2	Windsor 275 Broad St./P.O. Box 472 Windsor 06095-0472	1633 ——	Hartford	Windsor 1855 Hartford
E1	Windsor Locks 50 Church St. Windsor Locks 06096-2331	1854 Windsor	Hartford	Windsor Locks 1961 Hartford
D4	Wolcott 10 Kenea Ave. Wolcott 06716-2114	1796 Waterbury/Southington	New Haven	Waterbury 1779 Woodbury
D6	Woodbridge 11 Meetinghouse Lane Woodbridge 06525-1519	1784 New Haven/Milford	New Haven	New Haven
B4	Woodbury 275 Main St. P.O. Box 369 Woodbury 06798-0369	1673 ——	Litchfield	Woodbury 1719 Hartford/Fairfield/ New Haven
J1	Woodstock 415 Route 169 P.O. Box 123 Woodstock 06281-3039	1690 —— (called New Roxbury at first as a part of Massachusetts until 1749)	Windsor	Woodstock 1831 Pomfret

Delaware

ROGER D. JOSLYN, CG, FUGA, FGBS, FASG

For such a small state (only Rhode Island is smaller), Delaware has an involved history. Henry Hudson discovered Delaware Bay in 1609, but the first attempted settlement was in 1631 by the Dutch, who were driven out by Native Americans. From 1638 to 1655 Delaware was controlled by the Swedes as part of New Sweden. The Dutch regained control for the next nine years, during which time some Finns settled there, as did more Dutch and some Mennonites. When New Netherland was taken over by the English, Delaware fell under the control of the Duke of York from 1664 to 1682, with the Dutch regaining control briefly in 1673 to 1674. By deeds executed in 1682, Delaware became the "Three Lower Counties" of Pennsylvania under a proprietary system. William Penn introduced the English tradition of "hundreds" as subdivisions of counties, and Delaware is the only place in the U.S. where the term is still used today, mostly as a geographical description in wills, deeds, and assessment records. Delaware remained a part of Pennsylvania until the Revolutionary War but had its own assembly from 1704.

While many English came directly to Delaware, others, including English Quakers, migrated from Pennsylvania and Maryland. For a long time a dispute existed between Delaware and Maryland over who controlled the areas of western Kent and western and southern Sussex counties. Consequently, very few Delaware records exist for this area before 1775.

Delaware experienced no major battles during the Revolutionary War, but the British did come through on their way to Philadelphia. It has been estimated that about half the population was Loyalist, although there was not as great an exodus from the colony as there was from New York and New Jersey. After the war, many soldiers headed south to Georgia, where they took advantage of attractive land grants.

The Dutch had imported some slaves to the area from Africa, but Maryland planters were responsible for bringing the largest number of African Americans to Delaware. By the time of the Civil War, however, the number of slaves had decreased substantially, mostly through manumission.

Delaware was also the destination of some French who arrived from the West Indies after the American Revolution, and others who came directly from France, including the famous du Pont family. The mid-nineteenth century saw further immigration of large numbers of Irish Catholics and Germans, and by the end of the century, Jews, Poles, and Italians had arrived, with smaller numbers of eastern Europeans and Scandinavians. Most of these people settled in the Wilmington area.

Calling itself the "First State," Delaware was the first of the former thirteen colonies to ratify the Constitution on 7 December 1787. From that time the state's development has been characterized as stable, conservative, and placid, except during the Civil War. Economically, Delaware was allied with the North, especially with its river trade and the coming of the railroads; but there was also strong sympathy with the South, particularly after the war.

Delaware was originally created as part of Pennsylvania and has long been associated with that state, mostly because it shares the commerce and transportation of the Delaware River. This has also caused major growth in the northern part of the state, with much industry developing in and around Wilmington. By

DELAWARE

the early twentieth century, over half the population and wealth of the state were concentrated in the north, where it remains today. Until recently, the southern part of the state has been more agriculturally oriented. Delaware is one of the most densely populated states.

Vital Records

State copies of vital records for Delaware are available from the Office of Vital Statistics, Division of Public Health, Department of Health and Social Services, Jesse S. Cooper Bldg., Federal and Water Streets, P.O. Box 637, Dover, DE 19901-0637. The vital statistics office holds birth records from 1931 and marriages and deaths from 1963. The current fee is $10 for each record requested. Delaware vital records become public records with no restrictions after seventy-two years for births and forty years for marriages and deaths, at which time they are transferred to the Delaware Public Archives. Printable order forms are online at <www.state.de.us/dhss/dpn/ss/vitalstats.html>.

Earlier records at the Delaware Public Archives (see Archives, Libraries, and Societies) include those formerly at the Office of Vital Statistics, currently covering births and deaths (1861–63), births (1881–1930), deaths (1881–1962), and marriages (1847–1962). Each January, another year of records is transferred from the vital statistics office to the archives. For more information, see the Delaware Public Archives website at <www.state.de.us/sos/dpa>.

After 1881, the city of Wilmington had a registrar of vital statistics with fairly complete records; the earlier Wilmington records are at the Delaware Public Archives. Elsewhere, recording of vital events was the responsibility of the county recorders of deeds, and recording practices were quite poor until the creation of the vital statistics office in 1913. The archives has recorders of deeds' records for a very few births and deaths (1861–63, 1881–1913) and for marriages (1847–1913). Also at the archives are county clerks of the peace marriage bonds from 1744 (but more complete after 1793) to 1913, when bonds were no longer required.

For the period 1680 to the present, the Delaware Public Archives also has cards that index births, baptisms, marriages, and deaths from a variety of sources, such as marriage bonds, church and Bible records, and newspaper notices. There is a supplementary index for some deaths (1888–1910). Some Kent County vital records for the late 1600s were recorded in deed books and published in *Publications of The Genealogical Society of Pennsylvania* 7 (1920): 158-62, and reprinted in *The Maryland and Delaware Genealogist* 10 (1969) and 11 (1970). Some Kent and Sussex County vital records for the late 1600s to the 1750s were published in the *Delaware Genealogical Society Journal* 1 (1982): 92-96. A private doctor's records of births for Sussex County (1835–69) were published in volumes 6–8 of *The Maryland and*

Delaware Genealogist (1965–67). Also, "New Castle County... Court Records ... of Illegitimate Births" was published in *The Pennsylvania Genealogical Magazine* 33 (1984): 353-58.

For the period before 1975, divorces should be sought in the county superior courts, of which the prothonotary is the clerk. Some of these records are at the Delaware Public Archives, but permission to see them must first be obtained from the court. After 1975 the records are in the county family court where the divorce was granted. The earliest divorces in Delaware, to 1773, were a matter for the governor and council. The legislature had jurisdiction until 1897, and the superior court has had concurrent jurisdiction from 1832.

Legislative divorces are indexed as private acts in the published *Laws of Delaware*, 2–20 (1777–1897). Since 1913, courts have been required to register divorces and annulments with the state registrar.

Census Records

Federal

Population Schedules
- Indexed—1800, 1810, 1820, 1830, 1840, 1850, 1860, 1870, 1880, 1900, 1910, 1920, 1930
- Soundex—1880, 1900, 1920

Industry and Agriculture Schedules
- 1850, 1860, 1870, 1880

Mortality Schedules
- 1850, 1860, 1870, 1880 (all published)

Slave Schedules
- 1850, 1860 (both published)

From the second federal census of 1800, the records for Delaware are complete, indexed, and widely available (see pages 2-3). Printed indexes through 1870 are also available, with two each for 1850 and 1870, and three for 1860.

The first census for 1790 was lost or destroyed. The claim that it was found in the Cornell University Library is unfounded, but a reconstruction from tax and assessment records was compiled by former state archivist Leon de Valinger, Jr., and published by the National Genealogical Society as *Reconstructed 1790 Census of Delaware*, NGS Special Publication No. 10, 2d printing (Washington, D.C.: NGS, 1962).

The original mortality schedules, which are at the Delaware Public Archives, have been published, as have the 1850 and 1860 slave schedules. Other non-population schedules for 1850 through 1880 are at the archives, as are the original state copies of the federal population censuses for these years.

Colonial

Some earlier Delaware "censuses" have been published from tax and other records. These include Ralph D. Nelson, Jr., and others, *Delaware 1782 Tax Assessment and Census List* (Wilmington: Delaware Genealogical Society, 1994), and Ronald Vern Jackson, *Early Delaware Census Records, 1665–1697* (Bountiful, Utah: Accelerated Indexing Systems, 1977). A 1688 census for Kent County was published in volume 37 of *The Pennsylvania Genealogical Magazine* in 1991, which corrects the incomplete "Kent County Census" in *Delaware Genealogical Journal* 3 (1986): 49-51. Two works by Peter Stebbins Craig present other early censuses: *The 1671 Census of Delaware* (Philadelphia: Genealogical Society of Pennsylvania, 1999), and *The 1693 Census of the Swedes on the Delaware: Family Histories of the Swedish Lutheran Church Members Residing in Pennsylvania, Delaware, West New Jersey and Cecil County, Maryland, 1638–1693* (Winter Park, Fla.: SAG Publications, 1993).

Background Sources

The earliest state history is *Original Settlements on the Delaware*, by Benjamin Ferris (1846; reprint with index, Wilmington: Delaware Genealogical Society, 1987). The standard for the state, however, is J. Thomas Scharf, *History of Delaware 1609–1888*, 2 vols. (1888; reprint, Washington, N.Y.: Kennikat Press, 1972, and Westminster, Md.: Family Line Publications, 1990), indexed by Gladys M. Coghlan and Dale Fields, 3 vols. (Wilmington: Historical Society of Delaware, 1976). It has errors but is useful for its many lists of names from tax records, petitions, road lists, and other sources. Henry C. Conrad's *History of the State of Delaware*, 3 vols. (Wilmington: the author, 1908) is also helpful for pinpointing individuals through its state and county civil lists.

More modern works are Carol E. Hoffecker, comp., *Readings in Delaware History* (Newark: University of Delaware Press, 1973), and John A. Munroe, *A History of Delaware*, 2d ed. (Newark: University of Delaware Press, 1984).

H. Clay Reed, ed., *Delaware: History of the First State*, 3 vols. (New York: Lewis Historical Publishing Co., 1947) is also good; however, volume three is a "mug book." (The term "mug book" refers to those printed sources that present pictures and biographies of those who subscribed to the publication.) Similar works, which must be used with care, are Wilson Lloyd Bevan, ed., *History of Delaware Past and Present*, 4 vols. (New York: Lewis Historical Publishing Co., 1929), with mug books for the last two volumes; *Biographical and Genealogical History of the State of Delaware*, 2 vols. (Chambersburg, Pa.: J. M. Runk & Co., 1899); and James M. McCarter and B. F. Jackson, *Historical and Biographical Encyclopedia of Delaware* (Wilmington: Aldine Publishing and Engraving Co., 1882).

There are many useful histories with a narrower focus, particularly concerning the Dutch, English, and Swedes. Clinton A. Weslager has written four works: *Dutch Explorers, Traders and Settlers in the Delaware Valley, 1609–1664* (Philadelphia: University of Pennsylvania Press, 1961); *The English on the Delaware, 1610–1682* (New Brunswick: Rutgers University Press, 1967); *The Swedes and Dutch at New Castle*; and *New Sweden on the Delaware, 1638–1655*, the latter two published by Middle Atlantic Press, 1987 and 1988, respectively. Weslager also abstracted Dutch notarial records relating to the colony on the Delaware, 1656–76, published in *Delaware History* 20 (1982): 1-26, 73-97.

Amandus Johnson's *The Swedish Settlements on the Delaware, 1638–1664*, 2 vols. (1911; reprint, Baltimore: Genealogical Publishing Co., 1969) is the standard work on the subject, but Israel Acrelius's *A History of New Sweden* (1874; reprint, New York: Arno Press, 1972) is also one of the basics, as is Rev. Jehu Curtis Clay's *Annals of the Swedes on the Delaware*, 4th ed. (Chicago: John Ericsson Memorial Committee, 1938), although the earlier editions are better. Two excellent newer works are Stellan Dahlgren and Hans Norman, *The Rise and Fall of New Sweden* (Stockholm: Alurqvist and Wiksell, 1988) and Alf Åberg, *The People of New Sweden* (Stockholm: Naturochkultur, 1988). These histories should be used with *New York Historical Manuscripts: Dutch Volumes XVIII–XIX Delaware Papers (Dutch Period)…, 1648–1664* and *New York Historical Manuscripts: Dutch Volumes XX–XXI Delaware Papers (English Period)…, 1664–1682*, both edited by Charles T. Gehring (Baltimore: Genealogical Publishing Co., 1981, 1977). Unfortunately, Evert Alexander Louhi's *The Delaware Finns* (New York: Humanity Press, 1925) is far too imaginative to be considered accurate.

For a later period, see Charles H. B. Turner, comp., *Rodney's Diary and Other Delaware Records* (Philadelphia: Allen, Lane and Scott, 1911), which includes records for 1813 up to 1829 from public and private sources of Delaware as well as Maryland, Pennsylvania, New Jersey, and New York. Bruce A. Bendler's *Colonial Delaware Assemblymen, 1682–1776* (Westminster, Md.: Family Line Publications, 1989), is a biographical dictionary covering over 300 Delaware officials. See the review essays of this work in *The Pennsylvania Genealogical Magazine* 36 (1990): 251-56 and the *Pennsylvania Magazine of History and Biography* 115 (1991): 262-64.

Guides

For a fine general background of history and genealogical sources, consult the chapter on Delaware by Milton Rubincam, FASG, in *Genealogical Research: Methods and Sources*, vol. 1, rev. ed., ed. by Milton Rubincam (Washington, D.C.: American Society of Genealogists, 1980), 261-70. Excellent and more up-to-date is Thomas P. Doherty, *Delaware Genealogical Research Guide*, 3d ed. (Wilmington: Delaware Genealogical Society, 2002), with

updates posted at the genealogical society's website <www.delgensoc.org/dgsguide.html>.

Delaware Place Names, by L. W. Heck and others, Geological Survey Bulletin No. 1245 (Washington, D.C.: Government Printing Office, 1966) is very good and should be supplemented with Henry Gannett's *A Gazetteer of Maryland and Delaware*, 2 vols. (1904; reprint in one volume, Baltimore: Genealogical Publishing Co., 1976).

Henry Clay and Marion B. Reed, *A Bibliography of Delaware Through 1960* (Newark: University of Delaware Press, 1966) lists biographies and family histories and is supplemented by *Bibliography of Delaware 1960–1974* (Newark: University of Delaware Press, 1976) and by updates in *Delaware History*, beginning in volume 17.

Maps

Although somewhat dated, a good collection of maps is the *Atlas of the State of Delaware* by Daniel G. Beers (1868; reprint, Georgetown, Del.: Sussex Prints, 1978). For quick reference, maps of Delaware hundreds are on the inside back cover of the *Delaware Genealogical Society Journal* and in Hancock's *The Reconstructed Delaware State Census of 1782* (see Census Records). One of the best collections of Delaware maps is at the Delaware Public Archives.

Land Records

State-Land State

From 1680 the original deed and mortgage volumes, microfilms of them, or both, are at the Delaware Public Archives, with corresponding indexes. Kent County holdings at the archives extend to 1970, New Castle to 1962, and Sussex to 1968. The archives also has a card index of original land patents, warrants, and surveys, arranged by county, as well as a list of some of the Maryland grants now located in Delaware. Information on related Maryland land should also be sought in the published *Archives of Maryland*. Warrants and surveys made during the proprietorship of the Penn family (1682–1776) are at the archives; those for 1759 to 1761 are included in *Warrants and Surveys of the Province of Pennsylvania including the Three Lower Counties 1759* (see Pennsylvania—Land Records). Some land purchases are chronicled in the *Pennsylvania Archives*, 2d series, vols. 7 and 19. Other published land records are *Original Land Titles in Delaware Commonly Known as The Duke of York Records … 1646–1679* (1899; reprint, Westminster, Md.: Family Line Publications, 1989), and A. R. Dunlap, "Dutch and Swedish Land Records Relating to Delaware: Some New Documents and a Checklist," *Delaware History* 6 (1954): 25-52. The archives has microfilm of official grants of land in present-day Delaware from

New York and Pennsylvania sources, which are listed in Edward E. Heite, *Delaware's Fugitive Records* (Dover, Del.: Delaware Division of Historical and Cultural Affairs, 1980).

In addition to county taxes, colonial Delaware landowners had to pay annual quitrents to the proprietor. The quitrents between 1665 and 1671 (the period Delaware was controlled by New York) were published in B. Fernow, ed., *Documents Relative to the History of Dutch and Swedish Settlements on the Delaware River*, vol. 12 of *Documents Relative to the Colonial History of New York* (Albany, N.Y.: Argus Co., 1877), 490-92. This volume contains other lists of Delaware residents during the 1670s. Some quitrent information is also found in private proprietors' records such as the Logan Papers at the Historical Society of Pennsylvania in Philadelphia.

In each of Delaware's three counties, the recorder of deeds has the primary land records, with deeds and mortgages kept separately. Only the most recent deeds are in the counties, however. Most have been transferred to the Delaware Public Archives. Ten volumes of *Kent County, Delaware, Land Records* have been published covering 1680–1775, the first eight by Mary Marshall Brewer, the last two by Irma Harper. *New Castle County, Delaware, Land Records* for 1673–1765, with some gaps, was compiled in seven volumes by Carol Bryant and Carol J. Garrett. Nine volumes cover *Land Records of Sussex County, Delaware*, for the period from 1681 to 1805, with some gaps, compiled by F. Edward Wright, Elaine Hastings Mason, Judith K. Ardine, Mary Marshall Brewer, and Johnita P. Malone. All were published between 1990 and 2002 by Heritage Books, Inc., Family Line Publications, Delmarva Roots, and Willow Bend Books.

Probate Records

The early probate records for Delaware, from 1676 into the twentieth century, are at the Delaware Public Archives, either in their original form of books and files, or on microfilm, or both. Orphans' Court records dating from the early 1700s and including useful partitions of land of intestates are found through consolidated card file indexes by county covering estates to 1850. Earlier probate information should be sought in records of Maryland, Pennsylvania, and New York. It should also be pointed out that many early wills pertaining to Delaware residents, while proved, were never recorded. Later records are filed with the appropriate county register of wills. Calendars have been published for the wills of all three counties: *Calendar of Kent County Delaware Probate Records, 1680–1800*, and *Calendar of Sussex County Delaware Probate Records, 1680–1800*, both compiled by state archivist Leon de Valinger, Jr. (Dover, Del.: Public Archives Commission, 1944, 1964), and *A Calendar of Delaware Wills New Castle County, 1682–1800*, by the Historic Research Committee of the Delaware Society of the Colonial

Dames of America (1911; reprint, Baltimore: Genealogical Publishing Co., 1977, and Baltimore: Clearfield Co., 1989). The former two include the volume and page numbers not only for the county record volumes but also for those volumes at the archives into which the early original documents were mounted. The latter work on New Castle County does not include intestate records. Indexes for Kent County probate records (1801–33) appear in three volumes by Mary Marshall Brewer (Lewes, Del.: Delmarva Roots, 2002). Marguerite R. Moore prepared indexes for Sussex County wills (1800–69) in three volumes (Westminster, Md.: Family Line Publications, 1995 97). Orphans' Court records for New Castle County (1742–61) and for Sussex County (1708–09 and 1728–77) are also available in print. The Delaware Public Archives has an online probate database with records up to 1925 at <www.state.de.us/sos/dpa/collections/probate.shtml>. This database includes some early probates not included in the published calendars listed above.

Court Records

Many of the early court records of Delaware have been published, such as *Records of the Court of New Castle on Delaware, 1676–1681*, with a second volume for the years 1681–99, *Land and Probate Abstract Only* (Lancaster and Meadville, Pa.: Colonial Society of Pennsylvania, 1904, 1935). Other examples are *Court Records of Kent County, Delaware, 1680–1705*, edited by Leon de Valinger, Jr. (Washington, D.C.: American Historical Association, 1959), and Craig W. Horle's *Sussex County Court Records 1677–1710* (Philadelphia: University of Pennsylvania Press, 1991). *The Inventory of the County Archives of Delaware: No. 1, New Castle County*, by the Delaware Historical Records Survey (Dover, Del.: Public Archives Commission, 1941), while dated and published for only one county, still provides good detail about the court system and records. Charles H. B. Turner's *Some Records of Sussex County Delaware* (1909; reprint, Bowie, Md.: Heritage Books, 1989) includes not only court, but civil, ecclesiastical, vestry, Bible, and other records.

The Delaware Public Archives has state and county-level court records back to the colonial period covering civil and criminal records, naturalizations, and indentures. Some earlier records are in Maryland, New York, and Pennsylvania. At the county level, the court of common pleas and superior court handle civil and criminal matters, depending on the offense. Cases involving equity and trust estates are heard in the chancery court. The office of the county prothonotary has custody of divorces until 1975 as well as civil and criminal court records, and naturalizations, although the latter are now in the archives. Land records are with the recorder of deeds, and the register of wills and Orphans' Court handles estate matters. The Orphans' Court was consolidated in 1975 with the court of chancery to

handle estate disputes and other partitions, with records kept by the register in chancery in each county.

Tax Records

Early tax or assessment lists for the three Delaware counties are found at the Delaware Public Archives and start in 1726 for Kent, 1738 for New Castle, and 1769 for Sussex. Some earlier records are at the Historical Society of Pennsylvania in Philadelphia: from 1693 for all three counties and an incomplete list for 1696 for New Castle County. For the former, see "Provincial Tax List of the Three Lower Counties 1693" in *The Pennsylvania Genealogical Magazine* 37 (1991): 1-32. Bruce A. Bendler's *Colonial Delaware Records: 1681–1713* (Westminster, Md.: Family Line Publications, 1990) includes tax lists as well as rent rolls and quitrents for all three counties.

It has sometimes been stated that the 1798 U.S. direct tax records for Delaware are at the Historical Society of Delaware. They are not extant, however, having perhaps been destroyed in a fire in Philadelphia. Some tax records have been published as "censuses" (see Census Records), and others have been printed, such as Karen M. Ackerman, *Tax Assessments of New Castle County, Delaware, 1816–1817* (Silver Spring, Md.: Family Line Publications, 1986). An 1861 national tax and its corresponding refund records of 1901 are at the Delaware Public Archives. Internal Revenue assessments for Delaware (1862–66) are on microfilm at the National Archives—Mid-Atlantic Region (see page 11). Modern tax information should be sought in county courthouses.

Cemetery Records

The largest central file of gravemarker transcriptions and abstracts is in the Walter G. Tatnall Tombstone Collection at the Delaware Public Archives, compiled in the 1920s by the Historical Records Survey; these are supplemented and to some extent duplicated by transcriptions made by the Works Progress Administration (WPA) Historic Records Survey in the 1930s. Also at the archives is the Hudson Collection of Sussex County tombstones, which is more thorough than the Tatnall. For Kent County, see also Raymond Walter Dill and others, *Souls in Heaven, Names in Stone: Kent County, Delaware Cemetery Records*, 2 vols. (Baltimore: Gateway Press, 1989). Some cemetery records are at the Historical Society of Delaware (see Archives, Libraries, and Societies), and some have been printed in the *Delaware Genealogical Society Journal* and in other publications. Julian H. Priesler covered *Jewish Cemeteries of the Delmarva Peninsula: A Burial Index for Delaware & Maryland's Eastern Shore* (Westminster, Md.: Family Line Publications, 1995).

Church Records

While somewhat dated, the *Directory of Churches and Religious Organizations in Delaware*, compiled and published by the Public Archives Commission of the State of Delaware (Dover, Del., 1942), is good for determining what records existed at that time. It is supplemented by Elizabeth Waterston's *Churches in Delaware During the Revolution* (Wilmington: Historical Society of Delaware, 1925), which also lists available records. Frank P. Zebley's *The Churches of Delaware* (Wilmington: the author, 1947) identifies almost 900 existing and defunct churches in the state, although it does not discuss their records.

The records of one of the oldest and most noted churches were published as *The Records of Holy Trinity (Old Swedes) Church, Wilmington, Del., From 1697 to 1773, with Abstracts of English Records from 1773–1810*, with a supplemental *Catalogue and Errata*, translated and edited by Horace Burr, in Papers of the Historical Society of Delaware, 9 and 9-A (Wilmington: Historical Society of Delaware, 1890, 1919). Because of the erroneous translations, this work should be used with material by Courtland B. Springer and Ruth L. Springer in *Delaware History*, vols. 5 and 6 (1954, 1957); the *Delaware Genealogical Society Journal*; and in manuscript at the Historical Society of Delaware. Other major publications of church records include *Records of the Welsh Tract Baptist Meeting, Pencader Hundred, New Castle County, Delaware, 1701 to 1828*, Papers of the Historical Society of Delaware, 42 (Wilmington: Historical Society of Delaware, 1904); *Friends in Wilmington, 1738–1938* (n.p., n.d.), which includes marriages, burials, and genealogies; and Christopher M. Agnew, ed., *God with Us: A Continuing Presence* (New Castle, Del.: Immanuel Church, 1986), with an alphabetical list of baptisms, marriages, and burials (1714–1985) of New Castle's historic Immanuel Church (Episcopal). Some Delaware church records have been printed in the *Delaware Genealogical Society Journal*, *Delaware History*, in other publications, and in separate volumes. The latter include F. Edward Wright's *Vital Records of Kent and Sussex Counties, Delaware, 1686–1800* (Silver Spring, Md.: Family Line Publications, 1986), a collection of birth, marriage, and death records from church and Quaker records, and his two-volume *Early Church Records of New Castle County*, covering 1701–1800 (Westminster, Md.: Family Line Publications, 1994). Original and WPA-transcribed records of many Delaware churches are at the Delaware Public Archives, and some are at the Historical Society of Delaware. At the historical society, the Kelso Collection contains a large amount of nineteenth- and twentieth-century Methodist records, mostly from rural circuits and charges, for Delaware and Maryland's eastern shore. An index to this valuable collection is in progress. Some Quaker records are at the Delaware Public Archives and the Historical Society of Delaware; others are at the Friends Historical Library in Swarthmore, Pennsylvania.

Parish registers of the Catholic Diocese of Wilmington (which includes Delaware and the nine eastern shore counties of Maryland) have been microfilmed through 1960, with baptisms available through 1930 only, and are available at the archives and historical societies in both states. Every-name extracts from many pre-1900 registers are online at <www.lalley.com>.

Military Records

The *Delaware Archives*, 5 vols. (1911–16; reprint, New York: A.M.S. Press, 1974), contains military rolls, pensions, and other records from colonial soldiers of 1744 through militia lists of 1815. Material for an unfinished sixth volume at the Delaware Public Archives covers nonmilitary records of the Revolutionary War era. Background information on the early period is well covered in *Colonial Military Organization in Delaware, 1638–1776*, by Leon de Valinger, Jr. (Wilmington: Delaware Tercentenary Commission, 1938). *Colonial Delaware Soldiers and Sailors, 1638–1776*, by Henry C. Peden, Jr. (Westminster, Md.: Family Line Publications, 1995) was compiled from various sources. William Gustavus Whiteley compiled *The Revolutionary Soldiers of Delaware*, Papers of the Historical Society of Delaware, 14 (Wilmington: Historical Society of Delaware, 1896). Christopher L. Ward, *The Delaware Continentals, 1776–1783* (Wilmington: Historical Society of Delaware, 1941) should be read for proper historical background, and Harold Bell Hancock, *The Delaware Loyalists* (1940; reprint, Boston: Gregg, 1973) should be consulted for information about those on the other side of the conflict. *Revolutionary Patriots of Delaware ..., 1775–1783* (Westminster, Md.: Family Line Publications, 1996) has a genealogical focus. Scharf included a list of Delaware Civil War soldiers in an appendix in volume one of his *History of Delaware* (see Background Sources). The National Archives—Mid-Atlantic Region (see page 11) has a microfilm index of names of Delaware Civil War soldiers.

Lists of Confederate prisoners at Fort Delaware are in the Delaware Public Archives. The archives has a detailed guide to its Civil War collection on its website. At the archives are several card indexes of those called or who volunteered for federal service in the Civil War, the Spanish-American War, and the Mexican Border Campaign (1916–17). The archives also has a card file of World War I service medal applications, giving service information and often the date of death and place of burial. *Delaware's Role in World War II, 1940–1946*, by William H. Conner and Leon de Valinger, Jr. (Dover, Del.: Public Archives Commission, 1955) does not list all military personnel, although thousands of names are mentioned. De Valinger's collection of World War II photographs, letters, and lists of deceased soldiers should also be consulted at the archives. Much military material is also found at the Historical Society of Delaware.

Periodicals, Newspapers, and Manuscript Collections

Periodicals

Delaware History has been published by the Historical Society of Delaware semi-annually since 1946; volumes 1-7 were reprinted in 1968 by Kraus Reprint of Millwood, N.Y. The society has also published papers in sixty-seven volumes from 1879 to 1922 and in three volumes in a later series from 1927 to 1940.

The *Delaware Genealogical Society Journal* has published, since 1980, the usual fare of source record material, including Bible records, births of African Americans, Orphans' Court indexes (for Sussex County), and Maryland records. For *The Maryland and Delaware Genealogist,* see Maryland—Periodicals.

Two short-lived periodicals with useful source record material are *Delaware Historical and Genealogical Recall* (1933; reprint, Wilmington: Delaware Genealogical Society, 1984) and *Del-Gen-Data Bank,* edited by Mary Fallon Richards (Wilmington: editor, 1986).

Newspapers

For a good list of Delaware papers, see *Union List of Newspapers in Microform* (Newark: Delaware University Press, 1964). The Historical Society of Delaware has an extensive collection of early northern Delaware newspapers, but papers in the adjoining states of Maryland, Pennsylvania, and New Jersey should also be consulted. Southern Delaware newspapers are at the Delaware Public Archives. F. Edward Wright, *Delaware Newspaper Abstracts, 1786-95* (Silver Spring, Md.: Family Line Publications, 1984), covers two Wilmington papers. Mary Fallon Richards and John C. Richards edited five volumes of *Delaware Genealogical Abstracts from Newspapers,* covering 1729-1879 (Wilmington: Delaware Genealogical Society, 1995-2000).

Manuscripts

By far the largest single collection of private, unpublished genealogical material on Delaware families is that of the Rev. Joseph Brown Turner at the Delaware Public Archives, compiled over a forty-year period and arranged by family name. Reverend Turner's interest in families of the Del-Mar-Va peninsula extended to the origins of some in the British Isles. The papers of Harold B. Hancock, also at the archives, likewise contain English material on Delaware families. The collections of the Rev. Charles Henry Black Turner (mostly southern Delaware) and Matilda Spicer Hart are at the Historical Society of Pennsylvania in Philadelphia (see Pennsylvania).

The Delaware Historical Records Survey, *Inventory of the County Archives of Delaware No. 1 New Castle County* (Dover, Del.: Public Archives Commission, 1941), which was published for only one county, is very useful for its historical background and for identifying records.

H. Clay Reed, "Manuscript Books in the Historical Society of Delaware," *Delaware History* 11 (1965): 65-82, is a finding aid to part of that society's collection.

Archives, Libraries, and Societies

Delaware Public Archives
121 Duke of York St.
Dover, DE 19901
www.state.de.us/sos/dpa

The Delaware Public Archives is the central repository for noncurrent state as well as county and municipal records. It also has a large collection of private records, including family Bible records and papers, church and cemetery records, and federal censuses. Its holdings are enhanced by maps, still and motion pictures, and sound recordings, as well as a growing collection of online images of records, such as Civil War records, coroner's inquests, genealogical collections, maps, naturalizations, Orphans' Court files, photographs, and slavery papers. Microfilms of early New York and Pennsylvania material pertaining to what is now Delaware have also been acquired. The *Preliminary Inventory of the Holdings of the Delaware State Archives,* compiled by Joanne Mattern (Dover, Del.: Delaware State Archives, 1978), evolved into the "Guide to Collections" on the archives' website.

The Historical Society of Delaware
505 Market St.
Wilmington, DE 19801
www.hsd.org

Founded in 1864, the Historical Society of Delaware has much manuscript material including church, military, and family Bible records; transcribed gravemarker inscriptions; business and medical records; diaries and journals; and microfilms (with published indexes) of Delaware censuses and many Delaware Public Archives records. The society has a name file for items in newspapers and books, and the Delaware DAR's collection of Bible records. See Dale Fields, "Genealogical Source Material in the Historical Society of Delaware," *The Pennsylvania Genealogical Magazine* 28 (1973): 86-93. Some of the society's material has been published in their journal, *Delaware History.* For a small fee, a search of basic materials can be requested by mail.

Delaware Genealogical Society
505 Market St. Mall
Wilmington, DE 19801-3091
www.delgensoc.org

While it does not maintain a library, the Delaware Genealogical Society publishes the very useful *Delaware Genealogical Society Journal* and books of Delaware interest.

Special Focus Categories

Immigration

Ship passenger arrival lists for Wilmington, 1820–49, are on microfilm at the National Archives—Mid-Atlantic Region (see page 11). See also Carl Boyer, ed., *Ship Passenger Lists: Pennsylvania and Delaware, 1641–1825* (Newhall, Calif.: the author, 1980). Priscilla Thompson's *Arriving in Delaware: The Italian-American Experience* (Wilmington: History Store, 1989) provides a study of one immigrant group, from about 1870.

Naturalization

Federal court naturalizations for 1845–1910 are at the National Archives—Mid-Atlantic Region. An index to federal court naturalization for 1802–1929 is in *Del-Gen-Data Bank* (see Periodicals, Newspapers, and Manuscript Collections). Naturalizations recorded in the county courts of common pleas and supreme courts and, after 1831, the superior court, originally with the prothonotary, are at the Delaware Public Archives, where there is a card index to some for 1788–1905 that also gives brief abstracts of the records. The archives also has an online index to "selected" naturalizations from the county courts, arranged by name and place of origin, at <www.state.de.us/sos/dpa/collections/natrlzndb/nat-index.shtml>. Naturalizations for New Castle County, 1826–58, were published in *The Maryland and Delaware Genealogist* 18 (1977): 2-4 and 19 (1978): 1.

African American

Chapters 29 and 30 of Reed's *History* (see Background Sources) provide an overview on Delaware African Americans, and articles of interest have been published in *Delaware History*. See also two articles by Mary Fallon Richards: "Black Birth Records, New Castle County, Delaware, 1810–1853," *National Genealogical Society Quarterly* 67 (1979): 264-66, which lists the name of the African-American child and date of birth, names of parents (usually mother), of master or mistress, and date of registration; and also "Licenses to Import and Export Slaves," *Delaware Genealogical Society Journal* 1 (1980–81): 8-12, 30-37.

Native American

Information about Delaware's Native Americans is found in at least six works. Frank Gouldsmith Speck wrote *The Nanticoke and Conoy Indians* (Wilmington: Historical Society of Delaware, 1927). The other five, by Clinton A. Weslager, are entitled *Delaware's Forgotten Folk: The Story of the Moors and Nanticokes* (Washington, D.C.: Library of Congress, 1970); *Delaware Indians: A History* (New Brunswick, N.J.: Rutgers University Press, 1972); *The Delaware Indian Westward Migration* (Wallingford, Pa.: Middle Atlantic Press, 1978); *Red Men on the Brandywine* (1953; reprint, Wilmington, Del.: Delmar News Agency, 1976);

and *The Delaware: A Critical Bibliography* (Bloomington: Indiana University Press, 1978).

Special Interest

John Martin Hammond's *Colonial Mansions of Maryland and Delaware* (Philadelphia: J. B. Lippincott Co., 1914) offers an interesting illustrated source for this aspect of family history research.

County Resources

Delaware has only three counties, the smallest number of any state. Most of the earlier records and many into the twentieth century have been transferred to the Delaware Public Archives, although some counties have microfilms of transferred material. Records of land conveyance are found in the county recorder of deeds' offices. Estates are in the office of the register of wills where files are maintained from 1925. The first column below indicates the map coordinate. The second column gives the name of the county and the mailing address of the recorder of deeds. The third column shows the date the county was created and from what county or district. The earliest date of recording of a county deed is listed in the fourth column. The fifth column shows the date the first estate was recorded, followed by the year the Orphans' Court records begin, and then the mailing address of the register of wills, if different from that of the recorder. The prothonotary is the clerk with custody of such records as divorces (to 1975) and civil and criminal court matters. For births, marriages, and deaths recorded by the counties, see Vital Records.

Map	County Recorder of Deeds	Date Formed Parent County	Deeds	Orphans' Court Register of Wills
	Deale	1670 (as Whorekill; renamed Deale, 1680; renamed Sussex, 1682)		
E6	Kent 414 Federal St. Dover 19901-3605	1680 (as St. Jones; renamed, 1682) Whorekill	1680	1681/1766
A6	New Castle 800 French St., 4th Floor Wilmington 19801-3590	1664 (named New Amstel, 1672–73) original	1676	1682/1742 800 French St., 2d Floor
	St. Jones	1680 (renamed Kent, 1682)		
G7	Sussex Courthouse on Cir. Rm 213/P.O. Box 505 Georgetown 19947-0505	1670 (as Whorekill; renamed Deale, 1680; renamed Sussex, 1682) New Castle	1693	1683/1728 P.O. Box 111 Georgetown 19947-0111
	Whorekill (Horekill)	1670 (renamed Deale, 1680; renamed Sussex, 1682)		

DELAWARE

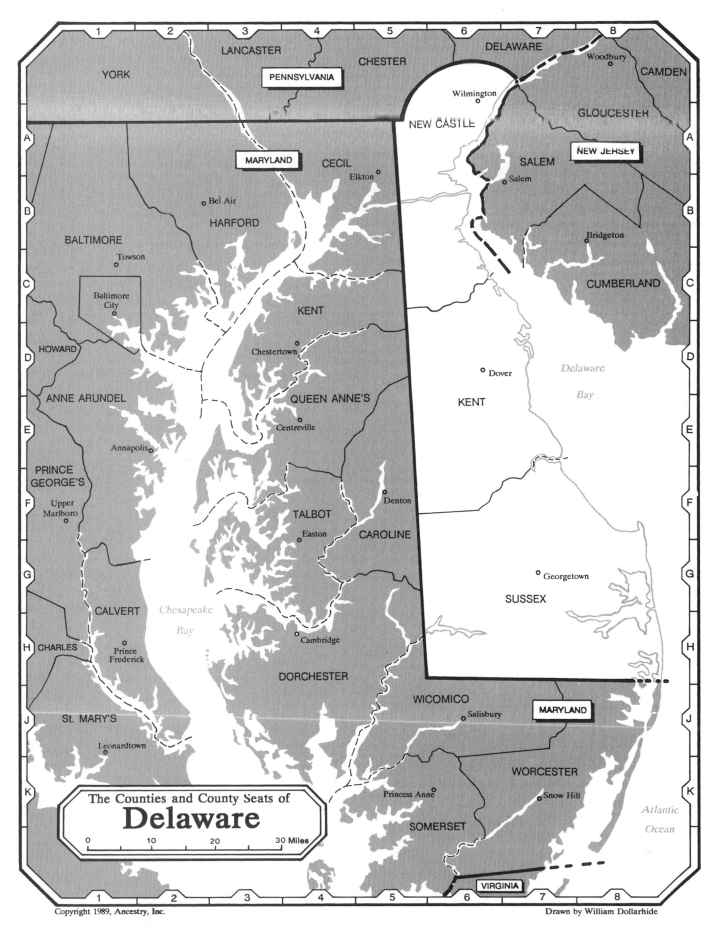

The Counties and County Seats of
Delaware

0   10   20   30 Miles

Drawn by William Dollarhide

District of Columbia

JOHNI CERNY

Congress created the District of Columbia as the seat of the federal government on 16 July 1790. On 9 September 1791 George Washington appointed three commissioners to lay out the city, although the federal government did not relocate to the District of Columbia until 1801. The area chosen as the seat of government was carved from Fairfax County, Virginia (created in 1742) and from part of Prince George's (created 1695) and Montgomery (created 1776) counties, Maryland. The area taken from Virginia was returned to that state in 1846.

By 1800 the District's population was about 14,000, but the federal government was still operating in Philadelphia. In the interim before the government relocated, residents of the District used record-keeping services in Fairfax County, Virginia, and Montgomery County, Maryland, until local government offices were established. By 1820, the population had grown to about 33,000 as more government jobs were made available and retail businesses grew to accommodate the populace. Those moving into the area came mainly from surrounding states, but some merchants arrived from Europe. African Americans have always been a major element of the District's population, and their number increased dramatically during the Civil War and Reconstruction era. Nearly twenty percent of the total population in 1860 was made up of free African Americans; slightly more than four percent were slaves.

Tracing families in the District of Columbia requires a complete understanding of the record periods and jurisdictions and the tenacity to track them down in one of the many repositories.

Records for those living in the area created for the District of Columbia before 1801 have to be sought either in Maryland's or Virginia's records. When the portion of Virginia originally taken to create the District of Columbia was returned in 1846, the pre-1846 records were returned as well.

Vital Records

Birth and death records for the District of Columbia date from 1 August 1874, and can be obtained for a fee from the Department of Human Services, Vital Records Division, 825 N. Capitol Street, NE, 1st Floor, Rm. 1312, Washington, DC 20002. Credit card orders can be made by calling (202) 783-1809. The public may not examine vital records in person; however, District of Columbia law states that when 100 years have elapsed after the date of birth or fifty years after the date of death, those documents become public records and anyone may obtain a copy upon submitting a proper application. Anyone who can prove a relationship to a person of record can obtain a copy of that individual's record for research purposes. Vital records for the District of Columbia at the Family History Library (FHL) in Salt Lake City include microfilm copies of births (1874–97), deaths (1855–1965), and death indexes (1855–1949 and 1855–1965). Death records do not exist for the Civil War years (1861–65).

Marriage records date from December 1811 and continue to the present. Indexes are available through 1921; after that, records are filed chronologically. When fifty years have elapsed after the date of the marriage, a record becomes public and anyone may obtain a copy upon application. Copies of records

may be obtained from the Clerk of the Superior Court of the District of Columbia, Marriage Bureau & Special Services, 500 Indiana Ave., N.W., Rm. 4335, Washington, DC 20001.

The FHL has microfilm copies of marriages (1811–54, 1870–1921, and 1907–50), and a marriage index (1811–1986) for the District of Columbia.

Divorce records in the nation's capitol date from 1803. Early proceedings are logged in the divorce docket (1803–48), consist of four volumes, and are located at the Washington National Records Center in Suitland, Maryland (see page 12). Full divorce records (1803–September 1956) can be obtained from the Clerk of the U.S. District Court, Constitution Ave. and John Marshall Pl., N.W., Washington, DC 20001. Records after that (September 1956-present) are available from the Clerk of the Superior Court, Family Division, 500 Indiana Ave., N.W., Washington, DC 20001.

Census Records

Federal

Population Schedules
- Indexed—1800, 1820, 1830, 1840, 1850, 1860, 1870, 1880, 1890 (fragment), 1900, 1910, 1920, 1930
- Soundex—1880, 1900, 1910 (Miracode), 1920

Industry and Agriculture
- 1850, 1860, 1870, 1880

Mortality Schedules
- 1850, 1860, 1870, 1880

Union Veterans
- 1890

Slave Schedules
- 1850, 1860

When the first federal census was taken in 1790, residents of the nation's capital living north of the Potomac River were enumerated with Prince George's and Montgomery counties in Maryland. Those living south of the river were counted as Virginians; however, the 1790 census for Virginia has been lost. There is no 1810 census for the District of Columbia.

Collections of microfilmed census records can be searched at the National Archives and its regional branches (see pages 11-12); the Washingtoniana Division of the Martin Luther King Jr. Memorial Library (see Archives, Libraries, and Societies); and the Family History Library. Published abstracts of census records can also be found in those repositories.

Background Sources

The following publications provide excellent background on social and cultural history and include comprehensive bibliographies.

Bryan, Wilhelmus Borgart. A History of the National Capital. 2 vols. New York: Macmillan Co., 1914–16.

Green, Constance McLaughlin. Washington, Capital City, 1800–1950. 2 vols. Princeton, N.J.: Princeton University Press, 1962.

The following are excellent references to District of Columbia research and records:

A Guide to Genealogical Research in the Nation's Capitol. 7th ed. N.p.: Annandale Stake, The Church of Jesus Christ of Latter-day Saints, 1989.

Angevine, Erma Miller. "Genealogical Research on Families of the District of Columbia," National Genealogical Society Quarterly 78 (March 1990): 15-32.

Cook, Eleanor M. V. Guide to the Records of Your District of Columbia Ancestors. Silver Spring, Md.: Family Line Publications, 1987.

Pippenger, Wesley E. District of Columbia Ancestors: A Guide to Records of the District of Columbia. Westminster, Md.: Family Line Publications, 1997.

Provine, Dorothy S. Preliminary Inventory of the Records of the Government of the District of Columbia. Record Group 351. Washington, D.C.: National Archives and Records Service, 1976.

Schaefer, Christina K. The Center: A Guide to Genealogical Research in the National Capitol Area. Baltimore: Genealogical Publishing Co., Inc., 1996.

Maps

The largest collections of District of Columbia maps can be found at the National Archives and Library of Congress. The following publications are excellent gazetteers, atlases, and maps for genealogists:

Long. John H. Atlas of Historical Boundaries: Delaware, Maryland, District of Columbia. A Project of the Dr. William M. Scholl Center for Family and Community History, Newberry Library. New York: Charles Scribner's Sons, 1996.

Martin, Joseph. A New and Comprehensive Gazetteer of Virginia and the District of Columbia. Charlottesville, Va.: the author, 1835. Available at the Library of Congress, the FHL in Salt Lake City, and the University of Virginia Library in Charlottesville, Virginia.

National Geographic Society (U.S.) Cartographic Division. *Round About the Nation's Capitol.* Washington, D.C.: National Geographic Society, 1956.

Passonneau, Joseph and Partners. *Washington through Two Centuries in Maps and Images.* New York: Monacelli Press, 2003.

The Library of Congress houses the Sanborn Fire Insurance Maps for Washington, D.C., 1888–1950, with microfilm copies available at the District of Columbia Archives (see Archives, Libraries, and Societies).

The Washingtoniana Division of the Martin Luther King Jr. Memorial Library (see Archives, Libraries, and Societies) has a complete microfilmed set of Baist's Real Estate Atlases for the years 1887–1965 and more than 8,000 maps on microfiche. The Washingtoniana Division and the District of Columbia Historical Society have complete sets of city directories dating from 1822.

The FHL has a series of Washington, DC, ward maps dating from 1829 to 1868. Some Maryland and Virginia gazetteers, maps, and atlases include sections for the District of Columbia.

Land Records

Federal District

Land transactions for the District of Columbia that date prior to 1792 are found among the records for Maryland or Virginia. Microfilm copies of Alexandria County, Virginia, deeds (1783–1865) are available at the FHL, along with Maryland Circuit Court deeds for Prince George's County (1696–1884) and Montgomery County (1777–1863).

Bessie Wilmarth Gahn's *Original Patentees of Land at Washington Prior to 1700* (1836; 1836; reprint, Baltimore: Genealogical Publishing Co., 1969), lists earlier landowners a century before the District of Columbia was created.

Deeds (or an index to them) from 1792 to the present are located at the Recorder of Deeds, 515 D St., N.W., Washington, DC 20001. Earliest deeds are at the National Archives, but a search first of the index at the recorder's office will be helpful.

The FHL has a microfilm collection of original land records (1792–1886) for the District of Columbia (a general index covers 1792–1919). Deeds from 1792 to 1869 (not indexed) are at the National Archives.

Manumission records for slave ancestors will be found among the deeds.

Probate Records

Probate Records for the District of Columbia (see Court Records) include proceedings, indexes to wills and administration of estates case files, transcripts of wills, administration case dockets, accounts, inventories and sales of estates, guardianship records, and apprenticeships.

Original wills from 1801 to the present and related probate records may be obtained by writing to the Register of Wills, Rm. 5006, 500 Indiana Ave., N.W., Washington, DC 20001.

Transcripts of wills dated 1810 to 1888, accompanying name indexes, and related probate case records for 1801 to 1878 are located in Record Group 21, National Archives and Records Administration, General Archives Division (NNFG), Washington National Records Center, Suitland, MD 20409. See Homer A. Walker's *Historical Court Records of Washington, D.C.: Death Records, 1801–78* (Washington, D.C.: the author, n.d.) for a name index to the Administrative Case Files, Old Series, 1801–78, also in the General Archives Division. Also useful are Mrs. Alexander H. Bell, *Abstracts of Wills in the District of Columbia, 1776–1815,* 2 vols. (Washington, D.C., 1945–46); Daughters of the American Revolution, E Pluribus Unum Chapter, *Transcripts of Probate Records, 1799–1837* (Salt Lake City: Genealogical Society of Utah, 1972); and *Record, Abstract of Wills,* 4 vols., 1828–37 (Washington, D.C.: Municipal Court, n.d.).

Court Records

Prior to 1801, land ceded by Maryland, which later became the district's Washington County, was under Prince George's and Montgomery county jurisdiction. The land originally belonging to Virginia consisted of Fairfax County and later Alexandria County. People living in those areas came under those counties' jurisdiction until the district was created.

The District of Columbia's court system began in 1801 with the creation of the U.S. Circuit Court and the U.S. District Court of Potomac and the District of Columbia. A criminal court was added in 1838.

The U.S. Circuit Court, which had jurisdiction in civil and criminal matters, took over the functions previously performed by the Virginia and Maryland county courts. It also had appellate jurisdiction over the Orphans' Courts in the District counties of Washington and Alexandria. This court's records, dating 1801 to 1863, pertaining to law, appellate, and criminal cases (to 1838) include docket books, case papers, bonds to secure release of debtors, and grand jury lists. Chancery or equity functions of this court include divorce and other dockets, case files, and divorce records. Other records dealing with bankruptcy, manumissions and emancipations, fugitive slave case records, habeas corpus papers, and marriage licenses for 1837 to 1862 were also created here.

The U.S. District Court of the District of Potomac and the District of Columbia's records for the pre-1863 period consist of minutes, the docket of admiralty cases, admiralty case files, and title pages of copyright works. This court's records are housed in Record Group 21 at the Washington National Records Center, Suitland, Maryland (see page 12). Circuit court minutes (1801–63) are also on microfilm (NARA M1021).

DISTRICT OF COLUMBIA

The U.S. Criminal Court for the District of Columbia was established in 1838, and it replaced the circuit and district courts' jurisdiction over criminal cases. Records produced by this court between 1838 and 1963 include dockets, minutes, proceedings, and case papers.

The U.S. Supreme Court of the District of Columbia was established in 1863 to replace all the circuit, district, and criminal courts of the District of Columbia. In 1936, its name was changed to the District Court of the United States for the District of Columbia. Records created by this court include minutes, dockets, and case papers in equity cases including adoptions, criminal, and bankruptcy, to name a few.

Records of naturalizations in the courts of the District of Columbia include indexes, naturalization records, copies of declarations of intention, and military naturalization records.

Tax Records

Tax assessments for the District of Columbia, covering 1814 to 1940, are in NARA Record Group 351, Records of the Government of the District of Columbia, National Archives and Records Administration, Washington, DC 20408.

The Washingtoniana Division of the Martin Luther King Jr. Memorial Library has property assessments for 1886 to 1968.

The FHL has these titles in its collection of tax records for the District of Columbia:

Federal Assessments, 1790 to 1805 for the District of Columbia (filmed at the Maryland Hall of Records in 1965).

Georgetown, Maryland. *Records, 1791–1878*, including tax records for the city of Georgetown, which Congress consolidated with Washington, D.C., in 1895.

Property Tax Records, 1800–1820, 1862–1879. National Archives Microfilm Publication: M605. Washington, D.C.: The National Archives, 1965.

Typed copies of Georgetown real property assessments for 1783, 1793, and 1798 are at the Peabody Room of the Georgetown Regional Library, Wisconsin Ave. and R St., N.W., Washington, D.C. The Maryland Historical Society in Baltimore (see Maryland—Archives, Libraries, and Societies) has the original U.S. District Tax of 1798 for the District of Columbia with microfilm copies available at the Georgetown Regional Library of the District of Columbia Archives (see Archives, Libraries, and Societies) and at the Maryland Archives in Annapolis.

Cemetery Records

The DAR has compiled an extensive collection of tombstone inscriptions for the District of Columbia, including the original registers of burials in District of Columbia cemeteries. The six-volume work, covering burials from 1847 to 1938, can be used at the DAR Library in the District of Columbia and the microfilm collection of the FHL.

The Washingtoniana Division of Martin Luther King Jr. Memorial Library (also called the District of Columbia Public Library) has a large collection of published tombstone inscriptions published by the Columbian Harmony Society with the following representative of that collection: Paul E. Sluby, Sr., and Stanton L. Wormley, Sr., *Civil War Cemeteries of the District of Columbia Metropolitan Area; Register of Burials of the Joseph F. Birch Funeral Home* (4 vols., covers the period 1847–1938). The FHL also has an extensive collection of these and other cemetery records for the District of Columbia.

Church Records

A congregation of nearly every major religion practiced in the United States between 1800 and 2000 existed in the District of Columbia. The records of some of the churches have been microfilmed and can be used at the FHL, covering these churches and time periods:

Records of the First Baptist Church, 1805–85
Records of Dumbarton United Methodist Church (compilation), 1813–1991
Concordia Lutheran Evangelical Church, 1833–1944
Western Presbyterian Church, 1854–66
Union Methodist Episcopal Church, 1860–83
Georgetown Presbyterian Church, 1863–1932
Metropolitan Presbyterian Church, 1864–1954
Eastern Presbyterian Church, 1875–1955
Eckington Presbyterian Church, 1896–1900
The Church of Jesus Christ of Latter-day Saints (Mormons), 1907–51

Local historical and archival information for Episcopalians can be found at Episcopal Church Historian, Washington Cathedral, Mount Saint Alban, Washington, DC 29260. See also *Inventory of Church Archives in the District of Columbia: The Protestant Episcopal Church, Diocese of Washington*. Vol. 1: District of Columbia, Montgomery, Prince George's, Chares, St. Mary's counties, Maryland (Washington, D.C.: Historical Records Survey, 1940); and vol. 2: Washington Cathedral (Washington, D.C.: Historical Records Survey, n.d.).

See also Maryland and Virginia—Church Records.

Military Records

Military records for soldiers who served from the District of Columbia are included with other NARA microfilm publications (see page 11). See also:

123

District of Columbia, World War I Selective Service System Draft Cards, 1917–18. Available at the National Archives and FHL.

Pierce, Alycon Trubey. *Selected Final Pension Payment Vouchers, 1818–1864, District of Columbia*. Leesburg, Va.: Willow Bend and Family Line Publications, 1998.

Todd, Frederick P. "Militia and Volunteers of the District of Columbia, 1783–1820," *Records of the Columbia Historical Society*, 1948, 50:387-88, Washington, D.C.: published by the society.

Periodicals, Newspapers, and Manuscript Collections

Periodicals
Washington History, formerly the *Records of the Columbia Historical Society* (first published in 1897 and changed titles in 1989) is the journal of the local historical society of the District of Columbia. See pages 9-10 for periodicals of a national scope that are published in the District of Columbia area.

Newspapers
The Washingtoniana Division of the Martin Luther King Jr. Memorial Library (see Archives, Libraries, and Societies) has a microfilm collection of all major daily newspapers for the District of Columbia dating from 1800 to the present. They have indexes for the *Washington Post* (1971-present) and the *Washington Star* (1906–70).

Manuscripts
See page 11 for discussion of manuscript sources of national interest located in the District of Columbia.

Archives, Libraries, and Societies

Washington National Records Center
4505 Suitland Rd.
Suitland, MD
Mailing address:
General Branch, Civil Archives Division
National Archives and Records Administration
Washington, DC 20409

District of Columbia Archives
1300 Naylor Ct., N.W.
Washington, DC 20001-4255

Historical Society of Washington, D.C.
1307 New Hampshire Ave., N.W.
Washington, DC 20036
Publishes *Washington History*.

District of Columbia Public Library
Martin Luther King Jr. Memorial Library
Washingtoniana Division
901 G St., N.W.
Washington, DC 20001

Maryland State Archives
361 Rowe St.
Annapolis, MD 21401

The National Archives (see pages 11-12) and the following organizations are located in the District of Columbia area. They are of national significance, however, in their holdings for researchers.

Library of Congress and Annex
1st and 2nd Streets, S.E.
Washington, DC 20504

National Genealogical Society
4527 Seventeenth St. North
Arlington, VA 22207

National Society, Daughters of the American Revolution Library
1776 D St., N.W.
Washington, DC 20006

Special Focus Categories

Immigration
Most immigrants to the District of Columbia arrived at ports in Maryland and Pennsylvania. See Maryland—Immigration and Pennsylvania—Immigration.

African American
Large numbers of freedmen and their families began settling in the District of Columbia before the Civil War, and they were joined by thousands of others after the war ended. Most records in the district consist of census schedules, military records, and Freedmen's Bureau and related records compiled by the federal government.

Until about 1821, slave manumissions usually were recorded in deed books. After that time, many appear in the Freedom Registration Books that are Record Group 21 in the General Archives Division of the National Archives.

See also Letitia Woods Brown, *Free Negroes in the District of Columbia, 1790–1846*, The Urban Life in America Series (New York: Oxford University Press, 1972), and Paul E. Sluby, Sr., and Stanton L. Wormley, Sr., *Blacks in the Marriage Records of the District of Columbia, December 23, 1811–June 16, 1870*. 2 vols. (Washington, D.C.: Columbian Harmony Society, n.d.).

County Resources

County Address	Date Formed Parent Count/ies	Birth Marriage Death	Land Probate Court
District of Columbia 1350 Pennsylvania Ave. N.W., Washington, DC 20004-3001	1790 Montgomery, Md./ Prince George's, Md./ Alexandria, Va.	1874* 1811* 1874*	1792 1801 1801

*See Vital Records above for location of records.

Only one courthouse exists for the District of Columbia since its jurisdiction encompasses a single county. Land records are at the recorder of deeds, probate records are at the register of wills, and court records before 1863 are at Washington National Records Center. Later court records are in the appropriate court's office.

Florida

FLORIDA PIONEER DESCENDANTS CERTIFICATION PROGRAM COMMITTEE, FLORIDA STATE GENEALOGICAL SOCIETY, INC.

No man would immigrate into Florida—no, not from Hell itself," declared the Honorable John Randolph of Roanoke, Virginia, in the 1821 United States House of Representatives. The newly annexed territory was, he declared, "a land of swamps, of quagmires, of frogs and alligators and mosquitoes." Nonetheless, Florida's 2000 census would show it to be the nation's fourth most populous state at that time.

The Spanish colonial presence began with the landing of Juan Ponce de Leon at Eastertide in 1513, ninety-four years before the British settlement in Jamestown, Virginia. Spanish Florida ultimately embraced all of the present state and much of the Gulf Coast, including large parts of Alabama, Mississippi, and Louisiana.

In 1564 French Huguenots settled Fort Caroline on the St. Johns River near present-day Jacksonville. The Spanish reacted immediately, by establishing St. Augustine in 1565 as the first permanent European settlement in America, immediately destroying Fort Caroline. After further hostilities, France soon abandoned designs on peninsular Florida. Elizabethan England, however, was not to be so easily intimidated.

Spain was to spend much of the seventeenth century attempting to dissuade the English by scattering its own colonists across Florida. By the 1680s, San Marcos de Apalache (now St. Marks) on the Gulf coast had grown to noteworthy proportions. In the final third of the century, pressure from the French to the west and the English and their Native American allies to the north prompted Spain to fortify St. Augustine and to re-establish a former settlement at Pensacola in 1698. In 1702 and 1703, there were numerous British raids. Seventeen years later,

the French took and briefly held Pensacola before relinquishing the town, joining with Spain against England, and finally retiring further westward along the Gulf Coast.

Following an indecisive treaty in 1748 and a decade of peace with Spain, England was again at war with France. By 1761, Spain, fearful that a French defeat could damage its own colonial interests, finally took sides with France, but it was too late. The Treaty of Paris, ending the Seven Years War in 1763, saw Spain cede Florida to England in exchange for the captured city of Havana, Cuba.

British East Florida reached from the Atlantic to the Apalachicola River; British West Florida ran from the Apalachicola to the Mississippi. In 1765, England sent Surveyor General William Gerard de Brahm and Royal Botanist John Bartram to the new possession and offered bounties, land grants, and other inducements to settlers. Thus, East and West Florida remained loyal to Britain during the American Revolution, and St. Augustine became crowded with Tory refugees from Georgia and the Carolinas.

In 1781, Spain captured Pensacola from Britain, which two years later exchanged both Floridas for the Bahama Islands. For a decade after the American Revolution there were sporadic Spanish-American border disputes until the Pinckney Treaty of 1795 fixed the 31st parallel as the northern boundary of West Florida and gave the United States undisputed control of an area that now comprises nearly a third of Alabama and Mississippi.

Spain supported the British in the War of 1812 but never declared war on the United States. Nonetheless, Andrew Jackson seized and then abandoned Spanish Pensacola in 1814 and helped

convince Spain of the folly of trying to hold an overseas colony contiguous to a large and unfriendly nation already coveting its lands. Under the terms of the Adams-Onis Treaty, which took effect in 1821, Spain gave up East and West Florida in exchange for claims by U.S. citizens, of up to five million dollars against Spain.

In 1821 Congress provided for a territorial governor, territorial courts, and a thirteen-member legislative council. Florida's first two counties were established on 21 July 1821. By its first territorial census in 1830, three years before the skeptical Honorable John Randolph of Roanoke died, Florida boasted 34,730 inhabitants. By statehood fifteen years later, its population had surpassed 66,500.

The massacre of Army Major Francis Langhorne Dade and two companies of soldiers in December 1835 marked the opening hostilities of the Second Seminole War, which would end seven years later after an expenditure of more than $20 million and the loss of 1,500 soldiers. By the end of the third Seminole War (1855–58), over 3,800 Native Americans, free African Americans, and runaway slaves were relocated to the Indian Territory, which is now Oklahoma.

In 1842, a wave of immigrants was enticed by the Armed Occupation Act to bear arms and protect their land against the Indians. After five years, the land became theirs as long as they cultivated and built a home on it. Florida attained statehood on 3 March 1845, the first among the Atlantic coast colonies settled, but the last admitted to the Union. By then, Florida's people had lived under the flags of four sovereign nations: Spain, France, Great Britain, and the United States.

Researchers should be aware that county boundaries changed frequently during three time periods: after the change of ownership from Spain to the U.S. in 1821; after 1900, when the railroad was completed on the East Coast of Florida; and during the "Land Boom," which began right after World War I. The last four counties were created in 1925, followed by five years in which Florida suffered a series of financial disasters caused by the weather—extreme cold in the winter of 1925, extreme heat in the summer, and several major hurricane disasters. Florida experienced its own depression from which it took many years to recover. However, Florida did recover, and by 2000 its "swamps and quagmires" were inhabited by more than 15.9 million Americans—making it the fourth most populated state in the nation.

Vital Records

The Department of Health, Office of Vital Statistics, P.O. Box 210, Jacksonville, FL 32231-0042 <www.doh.state.fl.us> has custody of birth and death records filed from January 1917 to the present date, and marriage records from June 1927 to the present date. However, birth records that are within the last one hundred years are not available to the general public. Applications should be submitted on standard forms available at the above address or online at its website.

As an alternative, birth or death certificates can also be ordered from the local county health departments. Contact information for each county is available at <www.doh.state.fl.us/chdsitelist.htm>. Marriage, divorce, or annulment records are kept at the local county courthouse; contact information for county courthouses can be found at <http://myfloridacounty.com> (see also County Resources).

Indexes to vital records (excluding birth) are available on microfiche and can be found at various libraries throughout Florida and the U.S. For a listing of holdings, visit the Florida State Genealogical Society website (see Archives, Libraries, and Societies). In addition <www.ancestry.com> has some marriage indexes and most of the death indexes.

Birth registration began in 1917, and scattered records from 1865 through 1916 are at the Office of Vital Statistics. Some county health departments have additional records not recorded with the state. For example, Pensacola birth and death records, between 1891 and 1910, are available through the Family History Library (FHL) in Salt Lake City. To obtain a copy of the record, one of the following criteria must be met: 1) be the child named on the certificate and over eighteen years old; 2) be the parent, guardian, or legal representative of the person named on the certificate; or 3) have a court order.

Delayed birth records are filed many years after the event by the people who did not have an original birth record or certificate. Copies of these delayed birth certificates are available at the Florida State Archives for fourteen counties. Most are available at local county health departments. Generally, the first year of delayed registration began in approximately 1942.

Death records begin about 1877, but the first state law mandating registration of deaths was passed in 1899. Records before 1917 are spotty. It is always best to check with city or county health departments. Some years ago, for example, the St. Augustine Health Department deposited with the local historical society library a number of "death certificates and burial permits" written on scraps of paper, prescription blanks, etc., for the late 1870s and early 1880s. Death records are still issued to anyone paying the required fee, but the cause-of-death section of the original certificate is deemed confidential and will not become public information until fifty years after the death date.

Marriage, divorce, and annulment records filed after 6 June 1927 are available at the Office of Vital Statistics. For records prior to that date, query the clerk of courts in the county where the license or decree was issued. Numerous county marriage records began as early as the 1820s. Copies of marriage license applications are available only from the clerk of courts in the

county courthouse. Standard request forms for copies of state-held records are necessary and available as indicated above.

Numerous divorces and resulting name-changes are to be found in currently out-of-print, *Names and Abstracts from the Acts of the Legislative Council of the Territory of Florida, 1822–1845* (Pass-A-Grille Beach, Fla.: William A. and Janet B. Wolfe, 1985).

Florida adoption records are sealed. The original papers are filed with the clerk of the circuit court in the county where the adoption took place. Medical background on the birth family is given to the adoptive family at adoption. It can be obtained by the adoptee at age eighteen from the Florida Department of Children and Families, Florida's Adoption Information Center, 4203 Southpoint Boulevard, Jacksonville, Florida 32216 <www.adoptflorida.com/information-center.htm>.

Since 1982, the Florida Adoption Reunion Registry was established to reunite people affected by adoption. Applications may be obtained from Florida Reunion Registry, 1317 Winewood Boulevard Tallahassee, Florida 32399-0700, or Florida's Adoption Information Center above. There is a one-time fee.

Census Records

Federal

Population Schedules
- Indexed—1830, 1840, 1850, 1860, 1870, 1880, 1885 (see below), 1900, 1910, 1920, 1930
- Soundex—1880, 1900, 1910 (Miracode)

Industry and Agriculture Schedules
- 1850, 1860, 1870, 1880, 1885

Mortality Schedules
- 1850, 1860, 1870, 1880, 1885

Slave Schedules
- 1850, 1860

All of Florida's federal population census records are available at the Florida State Archives (see Archives, Libraries, and Societies) and more widely available through online database services (see pages 16-17), the NARA, and FHL. See also Donna Rachal Mills, *Florida's Unfortunates: The 1880 Federal Census: Defective, Dependent, and Delinquent Classes*, Tuscaloosa, Ala: Mills Historical Press, 1993.

1885 Census

In 1879, Congress passed an act that provided some funding for any state or territory to conduct a census in 1885. Florida was one of five states or territories that took advantage of this opportunity, and it includes the special schedules: mortality, agriculture, and manufacturing. Arrangement within the

schedules is by enumeration district, precinct, or city. An every-name index with 312,551 names is given in William T. Martin and Patricia Martin, *1885 Florida State Census Index* (Miami: W.T. & P. Martin, 1991). Four Florida counties are missing: Alachua, Clay, Columbia, and Nassau.

Spanish Period

The Spanish took a number of censuses during their periods of colonial control (1565–1763 and 1783–1821). Most have been published, though some may be hard to find. "The 1783 Spanish Census of Florida" was translated and published in four consecutive issues of the *Georgia Genealogical Magazine*, beginning with no. 39 (Winter 1971). Approximately one-quarter of the census is available online. (Search for "Florida Census 1783.")

The most significant source for these censuses is located in the "East Florida Papers." These papers, microfilmed on 175 rolls, consist of the Spanish administration (1783–1821) and are therefore completely in Spanish. Roll #148 contains census returns for the following years: 1784–86, 1793, 1813, 1814, and 1815. The early censuses contain considerable information on the Minorcan residents of St. Augustine. The P. K. Yonge Library of Florida History holds typescript translations and transcriptions as well as the complete set of the "East Florida Papers."

Other Spanish census resources include the following:

Coker, William S. and G. Douglas Inglis. *The Spanish Census of Pensacola, 1784–1820: A Genealogical Guide to Spanish Pensacola*. Pensacola, Fla.: Perdido Bay Press, 1980. Reproduces ten valuable censuses and population lists, one or another taken roughly every four years.

Coker, William S. "Religious Censuses of Pensacola, 1796–1801," *Florida Historical Quarterly* 61 (July 1982): 54-63.

Lockey, Joseph B. "The 1786 St. Augustine Census," *Florida Historical Quarterly* 18 (July 1939): 11-31. This important article has been complemented by Phillip D. Rasico in "The Minorcan Population of St. Augustine in the Spanish Census of 1786," *Florida Historical Quarterly* 65 (October 1987): 160-84.

Mills, Donna Rachal. *Florida's First Families: Translated Abstracts of Pre-1821 Spanish Censuses*. Tuscaloosa, Ala.: Mills Historical Press, 1992. Abstracted from microfilm housed in the library of Florida State University and available through interlibrary loan.

"The 1814 East Florida Spanish Census," *Jacksonville Genealogical Society Quarterly* 4 (December 1976): 197-218.

Territorial

The Legislative Council met in 1824 and approved an act to take a census in each of the counties of the Territory. Only a fragment of Leon County exists today. The information listed includes the name of the head of the family, the number of white

males over and under twenty-one years, the number of white females over and under twenty-one years, and the number of slaves. The census fragment was printed in *The Florida Historical Quarterly* 22 (1943): 34-40 by Dorothy Dodd, as "The Florida Census of 1825" and is also available online at <www.rootsweb.com/~flleon/1825cens.htm>.

State Census

The state of Florida conducted its own censuses in 1845, 1855, 1867, 1875, 1885, 1935, and 1945. The state census was abolished in 1949. Only the following fragments of the early one remain at the Florida State Archives.

1845—Alachua, Benton, Columbia, Duval, Gadsden, Hamilton, Hillsborough, Jackson, Jefferson, Leon, Madison, Marion, Orange, St. Johns, Walton, Wakulla, and Washington counties. The enumeration lists the county, the name of the census taker, the number of white males over and under twenty-one, the number of white females over and under eighteen, the number of male and female slaves, and the number of male and female "free coloreds." The enumeration does not list the names of the inhabitants of the Florida counties.

1855—Marion County only. The information recorded in the book includes the name of the head of the family, the number of white males over and under twenty-one, the number of white females over and under eighteen, the number of children between five and eighteen, the number of children in schools, the number of male and female slaves, the value of the slaves, the number of male and female free persons of color, the number of acres and value of land, and the value of buildings, furniture, and plantation livestock.

1867—Franklin, Hernando, Madison, Orange, and Santa Rosa counties only. The books of enumeration have separate listings for "colored" and white inhabitants. Both include the name of the head of the family, the number of males over and under twenty-one, the number of females over and under eighteen, the total number of inhabitants, and the number of males between eighteen and forty-five.

1875—Alachua County only. The information recorded in the returns includes the name, age, sex, and race of all those persons listed. For some entries, other information is provided, including occupation, the value of real estate, the value of personal property, the number of acres planted in cotton, the number of acres planted in cane, and the number of orange trees.

1885—Leon County only. The information recorded includes the name, age, sex, and race of those persons enumerated. The enumeration is segregated by race.

1895—Nassau County only. (Published by Jacksonville Genealogical Society)

1935—complete state
1945—complete state

The original 1935 and 1945 state censuses are located at the Florida State Archives and on microfilm at many public libraries in Florida. It is accessible alphabetically by county and then by numbered election precincts. The schedules give name, address (and whether inside or outside city limits), age, sex, race, relationship to head of family, place of birth, degree of education, and occupation. Several counties have been indexed such as Bay (1935-partial), Gilchrist (1935), Hillsborough (1935-partial), Indian River (1935, 1945), Monroe (1935-Upper Keys only) and Walton (1945). The researcher should check the Internet often for new additions.

Special Census

1855 and 1866—Franklin County only. This is a census of children ages five to eighteen.

1896–1929—Census of youth of school age.

Background Sources

Many of Florida's early records exist at archives and university libraries. Each year new records are discovered, such as those in the Spanish archives in Seville, Spain. Local histories such as county, town, church, and business are available; however, their scarcity means that much of the material can only be found in special collections of archives, historical societies, or libraries at the geographic locations. The largest collection of Florida history can be found at the P. K. Yonge Library in Gainesville and the Florida Room of the State Library of Florida in Tallahassee (see Archives, Libraries, and Societies). A bibliography of county histories, some of which may be acquired by interlibrary loan at public libraries, was published in 1988 by Beverly Pittman Byrd; a copy can be found at the state library or online at its website <http://dlis.dos.state.fl.us> under "Florida Collection."

Florida's history is constantly changing. Michael Gannon, Distinguished Service Professor of History at the University of Florida in Gainesville is the editor of the latest reference, *The New History of Florida* (Gainesville: University Press of Florida, 1996). This book includes some changes, such as the controversial discussion on the initial landing site of Ponce de Leon, and provides an overview from pre-history to the present, including well-known Florida historians who are authorities in their field.

An indispensable source for articles, references, and book reviews is the *Florida Historical Quarterly* publication of the Florida Historical Society (see Archives, Libraries, and Societies). The quarterly and other historical and archaeological collections are fully searchable online at PALMM (Publication of

---

Archival, Library & Museum Materials), a cooperative initiative of the public universities of Florida to provide digital access to important source materials for research and scholarship. See <http://palmm.fcla.edu/collection.html>.

A comprehensive bibliography of excellent resource materials in places beyond the libraries is the James Albert Servies bibliographies: *A Bibliography of Florida* (Pensacola, Fla.: the compiler, 1993–2002), vol. 1, 1507–1845; vol. 2, 1846–80; vol. 3, 1881–99; vol. 4, 1900–15; and *A Bibliography of West Florida* (Pensacola, Fla.: the compiler, 1982, 1978), vol.1, 1535–1915; vol. 2, 1916–71; vol. 3, Index; vol. 4, 1981 supplement.

A worthwhile online project is the Florida migration project, whose purpose is to track groups or individuals into or out of Florida. In some cases, the information is very extensive and well documented (see <www.rootsweb.com/~flgenweb/projects/flmig.html>).

Other publications to help researching and understanding the background history of Florida:

Chapin, George M. *Florida, 1513–1913*. 2 vols. Chicago: S.J. Clarke Publishing Co., 1914.

Cutler, Harry Gardner. *History of Florida, Past and Present: Historical and Biographical*. 3 vols. Chicago and New York: Lewis Publishing Co., 1923.

Fairbanks, George R. *History of Florida: From its Discovery by Ponce de Leon, in 1512, to the Close of the Florida War, in 1842*. Philadelphia: J. B. Lippincott & Co.; Jacksonville, Fla.: Columbus Drew, 1871.

Tebeau, Charlton. *A History of Florida*. Coral Gables, Fla.: University of Miami Press, 1999.

Maps

The P. K. Yonge Library of Florida History, University of Florida Libraries in Gainesville (see Archives, Libraries, and Societies) owns one of the largest collections of Florida and Caribbean maps, and many of them are original prints or drawings. An online search is available of over 2,300 images from 1564 to 1926, which includes the Sanborn maps of Florida. See <http://web.uflib.ufl.edu/spec/pkyonge/fhmaps.html>. The Florida Historical Society Library in Cocoa has many original maps from early-to-modern Florida, although they do not have an online catalog at this time. Some universities outside of Florida have excellent resources for maps on the Internet, such as University of Alabama, Cartographic Research Laboratory, at <http://alabamamaps.ua.edu/historicalmaps/florida/index.html>; and University of Texas at Austin—Perry-Castañeda Library at <www.lib.utexas.edu/maps/florida.html>.

The PALMM (see Background Sources above) World Map Collection at <http://palmm.fcla.edu/map> includes maps from the following contributors: Florida Department of Environmental Protection, Florida International University, Florida State University, University of Florida, University of Miami, University of North Florida, and the University of South Florida.

Sanborn maps (see page 5), which date late 1800s to early 1900s, and other fire insurance maps should not be overlooked for urban areas. The Map Department, University of Florida Libraries (see above) has an excellent set of Sanborn original duplicate copies transferred from the Library of Congress. Many public and academic libraries now own the microfilm collection. Check the online catalogs or the reference department at local libraries.

Bradbury, Alford G. *A Chronology of Florida Post Offices*. Sewall's Point, Fla.: Florida Classics Library, 1993.

Cline, Howard F. *Provisional Historical Gazetteer with Locational Notes on Florida Colonial Communities*. New York: Garland Pub., Co., 1974.

Long, John H., ed. *Atlas of Historical County Boundaries: Florida*. New York: Simon & Schuster, 1996.

McMullen, Edwin Wallace. *English Topographic Terms in Florida, 1563–1874*. Gainesville: University of Florida Press, 1953.

Morris, Allen. *Florida Place Names: Alachua to Zolfo Springs*. Sarasota, Fla.: Pineapple Press, 1995.

Land Records

Public-Domain State

Spanish Land Grants. The Florida State Archives holds the records created from 1763–1821 for the use of the federal government in affirming or denying earlier Spanish grants of land. In many cases, these are the only surviving references to some of the pre-territorial residents of the area. The indexed documents are filed by claimant, and the amount of information they contain varies greatly, but the affidavits often tell when an individual arrived in Florida and how many were in his family, including names and ages. The acreage granted often depended on the number of "heads" in the family. The Florida State Archives is digitizing the land grants at <www.floridamemory.com/Collections/SpanishLandGrants>.

The original fragile records, largely in Spanish, are extant, but the Works Project Administration (WPA) published a five-volume transcript, *Spanish Land Grants in Florida*, which includes Spanish Grants, British Grants, and Private Land Claims. This set can be found at a number of libraries, as well as in an inexpensive microfiche edition from the state archives.

Armed Occupation Act records. The Second Seminole War officially ended on 14 August 1842. The federal government on 4 August 1842 approved a bill that was proposed by Senator Thomas Hart that granted lands to men able to bear arms. They were entitled to apply for 160 acres of land in certain unsettled

areas of East Florida, as long as they built a dwelling, cultivated the land, and lived on it continuously for five years, protecting it from the Native Americans.

A permit to settle shows the name of the applicant, his marital status, the month and year he became a resident of Florida, and a description of the land. The actual scanned images of the permit can be found at the Division of State Lands website (see below).

The final application, after the five years had elapsed, can be found in the donation files at the National Archives. Items such as proof of residency, land and dwelling descriptions, family members, affidavits by neighbors and friends, and sometimes proof of marriage, naturalization, and other documents were included for final approval.

Division of State Lands Records. Florida uses the rectangular survey system. The original surveyors' field notes and plats have been transferred to the state, along with the original tract books and records of all grants of land from the state to the initial grantee, whether by purchase or otherwise. The Florida Department of Environmental Protection (DEP), Division of State Lands, Board of Trustees of the Internal Improvement Trust Fund Land Document System has placed millions of historical land transactions online at <www.dep.state.fl.us/lands>. The search engine is easy to use, and searches can be made by specific type of document, individual, land description (township, range, and section), and county.

"The Seven States Index," a name index to the pre-July 1908 general land entry case files, includes Florida and shows the entryman's name, state, and land office where the entry was made, type of entry, and final certificate or file number. For further detailed information of the Florida land records beginning in 1825, see National Archives publication *Preliminary Inventory of the Land-Entry Papers of the General Land Office.*

Homestead files. The homestead applications filed by Florida settlers, between 1881–1905, have been transferred to the Florida State Archives. Information contained includes name of applicant, place of residence at time of application, tract description, and number of acres granted. There is a surname index. Other homestead records included in this record group include tax receipts required to prove that claimants were paying taxes on their claims, unindexed miscellaneous and legal records concerning homesteads, and correspondence of the State Land Office (1858–1913).

A number of land records can be found indexed in *Florida Land: Records of the Tallahassee and Newnansville General Land Office[s], 1825–1892* compiled by Alvie Davidson (Bowie, Md.: Heritage Books, 1989), which lists lands transferred from the federal government by grant and sale.

Probate Records

Florida probate records include wills, intestacy administrations, bonds, inventories and appraisements, guardianships, and property divisions, families in most states. The records formerly held by probate courts have been transferred to the counties' clerks of courts and are readily accessible in most jurisdictions. Many of the probate records were microfilmed in the 1970s and made available through the FHL. In addition, many Florida counties are adding indexes and original documents online at <www.myfloridacounty.com>.

Court Records

A large percentage of the Florida court records have been microfilmed and are available through the FHL and the Florida State Archives. These records include land, vital, probate, soldiers and sailors discharge papers, naturalizations, guardianship, and more (see County Resources).

Tax Records

Early tax rolls, especially between census years, can be a gold mine for the researcher in Florida. Most existing rolls can be found in the counties of origin, but the Florida State Archives also has some bound volumes sent to the state comptroller for the period between 1829 and 1881. Normal information includes the taxpayer's name, landownership, number of white males (above the taxable age of twenty-one), slaves, horses, wagons, and other taxable items of personal property such as jewelry, watches, musical instruments, and carriages.

A very valuable resource that can document an individual's migration is the *Tax Rolls, 1829–1898,* located at the Florida State Archives and on microfilm at some libraries throughout Florida. However, the series, annually prepared by the county tax assessor, is incomplete for most counties and varies greatly from year to year in the details recorded.

The Internal Revenue Act of July 1, 1862, was intended to provide Internal Revenue "to support the Government and to pay Interest on the Public Debt" (12 Stat. 432). At the Florida State Archives are the Internal Revenue Assessment Lists for the years 1865 and 1866, also available on National Archives microfilm. Almost any item became taxable—carriages, gold watches, pianos, and cattle are listed, which makes the tax list a valuable source of insight into the net worth and personal interests of the taxpayer.

FLORIDA

Cemetery Records

Florida House Bill 3763, *Cemetery Preservation and Consumer Protection Act,* "provides duty of care and maintenance of licenses cemeteries...creates Task Force on Abandoned and Neglected Cemeteries." In 1998, the Task Force was assigned to review and report on the status of neglected and abandoned cemeteries in Florida and, if necessary, to propose legislation to counter this problem.

Florida libraries, historical societies, and archives hold many of the published and unpublished cemetery records. In addition, the Daughters of the American Revolution (DAR) has abstracted a large percentage of the cemeteries in Florida, microfilmed and available through the FHL. E. H. Hayes and The Church of Jesus Christ of Latter-day Saints published *Cemetery Records of Florida* in 1946, nine volumes also available on microfilm.

One important compiled source is the WPA *Register of Deceased Veterans Buried in Florida,* which covers fifty-one of the sixty-seven counties (St. Augustine, Fla.: Veterans' Graves Registration Project, 1940–41). The complete index to this microfilm is being published by the Florida State Genealogical Society in its quarterly *The Florida Genealogist,* starting with volume 22, issue 3, Fall 1999 (86). Information includes veteran's name, military service, birth and death dates, burial locations, next of kin, and other personal information. See also:

Thompson, Sharyn. *Florida's Historic Cemeteries: A Preservation Handbook.* Tallahassee: Historic Tallahassee Preservation Board, 1989.

Florida Cemetery Records Directory. Compiled by volunteers of the Genealogical Society of Utah from sources in the FHL.

Of the general cemetery records sources for all states (see pages 7-8), the following are particularly helpful for Florida:

Florida Tombstone Transcription Project <www.rootsweb.com/~cemetery/florida/florida.htm>

American History and Genealogy Project—Florida Cemetery Transcription and Photo Project <www.usgennet.org/usa/topic/cemetery/florida>.

Florida Cemetery Records online with links to maps at <www.accessgenealogy.com/cemetery/florida.htm>.

Florida funeral records are available at the funeral homes, with a few exceptions. Some of them require proof of relationship. Some funeral home records have been deposited at the Florida State Archives; and the FHL has microfilmed some records from major cities in Florida (see pages 7-8).

Church Records

As in most former frontier societies, early Florida church records are sporadic, but they can be valuable when located. An incomplete but voluminous list of Florida churches that existed in the 1930s is the WPA volume *Preliminary List of Religious Bodies in Florida* (Jacksonville, Fla.: Historical Records Survey, 1939). The original survey forms from which the volume was compiled are now in the State Library of Florida's Florida Room. Another complete WPA set is available at the library of the Florida Historical Society. Church records can also be found at holdings of most libraries and archival depositories throughout the state; denominational representatives should be consulted for locations of their repositories. The most noted repository is the P. K. Yonge Library at the University of Florida in Gainesville. Other good sources include:

Guide to the Supplementary Vital Statistics from Church Records in Florida. 3 vols. Jacksonville: Historical Records Survey, 1942.

The Pioneer Churches of Florida. Chuluota, Fla.: The Mickler House Publishers, 1977.

Roman Catholic. The Roman Catholic faith accompanied the earliest Spanish settlers to Florida. Records for Saint Augustine's Roman Catholic Cathedral Parish include marriages, baptism, and burials and begin in 1594, and are maintained by the parish's current archivist at St. Augustine Catholic Diocese, 11625 St. Augustine Rd., Jacksonville, FL 32241-4000. The P. K. Yonge Library owns copies of the St. Augustine diocese records, in addition to the Diocese of Louisiana and the Floridas (1576–1803) records. In 1941, the Historical Records Survey (WPA) published a two-volume set of the *Roman Catholic Records, St. Augustine Parish, White Baptisms, 1784–1791 and 1792–1799.* See also:

Catholic Church History, 1539–1989, West Coast of Florida. Brandon, Fla.: St. Petersburg Diocesan Council of Catholic Women, 1989.

Gannon, Michael. *The Cross in the Sand: The Early Catholic Church in Florida, 1513–1870.* Gainesville: University of Florida Press, 1983.

Baptists. For information and an excellent bibliography, see Edward Earl Joiner, *A History of Florida Baptists* (Jacksonville, Fla.: Convention Press, 1972). Many of the Baptist associations and their records are described in *Inventory of the Church Archives of Florida: Baptist Bodies* (Jacksonville, Fla.: Historical Records Survey, 1939-40). Most of the Florida Baptist records have been sent to Southern Baptist Historical Library and Archives, 901 Commerce St., Ste. 400, Nashville, TN 37203-3630.

Methodists. Two churches existed in Fernandina as early as 1822 (under the South Carolina Conference) and more than 10,000 members by statehood. See:

Temple, Robert M. Jr. *Florida Flame: A History of the Florida Conference of the United Methodist Church.* Nashville: Parthenon Press, 1987.

Brooks, William Erle. *From Saddlebags to Satellites: A History of Florida Methodism.* Fort Lauderdale: Tropical Press, 1965.

Lazenby, Marion Elias. *History of Methodism in Alabama and West Florida: Being An Account of the Amazing March of Methodism Through Alabama and West Florida.* Nashville: Parthenon, 1960.

Thrift, Charles Tinsley. *The Trail of the Florida Circuit Rider: An Introduction to the Rise of Methodism in Middle and East Florida.* Lakeland, Fla.: The Florida Southern College Press, 1944.

Episcopalians. By 1845 there were parishes at Apalachicola, Jacksonville, Key West, Pensacola, and Tallahassee, in addition to others in several smaller towns. The P. K. Yonge Library has the publications of the Protestant Episcopal Church: *Diocese of Florida: Journal, 1838–1984,* and *Diocese of Central Florida: Diocese, 1894–1984.* See also:

Bentley, George R. *The Episcopal Diocese of Florida, 1892–1975.* Gainesville: University of Florida Press, 1989.

Cushman, Joseph D. *A Goodly Heritage: The Episcopal Church in Florida, 1821–1892.* Gainesville: University of Florida Press, 1965. Includes a bibliography.

Presbyterians. In 1840 Florida Presbyterian churches were divided among the Florida, Georgia, and Alabama Presbyteries. See James R. Bullock, *Heritage and Hope: A Story of Presbyterians in Florida.* Orlando, FL: Synod of Florida, Presybterians Church, 1987.

Military Records

The Florida Department of Military Affairs, St. Francis Barracks, 82 Marine Street, St. Augustine, FL 32084 <www.dma.state.fl.us> has produced an ongoing series of approximately 150 "Special Archives Publications" distributed to a limited number of depositories in Florida and elsewhere. Selected volumes will be noted in the discussions below, but researchers are encouraged to query the director at the above address regarding a list of pertinent titles or see a list online by Anne Futch through the "Archives FTP site" at <www.rootsweb.com/~flgenweb>.

The Revolutionary War. Since Florida remained loyal to the Crown during the war, there are few Revolutionary War military records in Florida repositories. In fact, Florida served as a haven for southern loyalists when its English settlers invited loyalists from other states (especially South Carolina and Georgia) to move to Florida. Several skirmishes took place along the Georgia-Florida border and at Pensacola; later, many soldiers moved to Florida with their families, applied for pensions, and were buried here.

Fritot, Jessie Robinson. *Pension Records of Soldiers of the Revolution Who Removed to Florida.* Jacksonville, Fla.: Jacksonville Chapter, Daughters of the American Revolution, 1946.

Wright, J. Leitch. *Florida in the American Revolution.* Gainesville: University Presses of Florida, 1975.

More current information on soldiers buried or ever living in Florida can be found in:

Cooper, Pamela J. "Revolutionary Soldiers in Florida," *The Florida Genealogist* 24 (Jul/Sept 2001): 94.

Patriots Who Died and/or Are Buried in Florida. Sons of the American Revolution, Florida Chapter <www.sar.org/pat_idx/FL-Patriots/index.htm>.

Excellent resources for identifying many of the Loyalist men who went to Florida for asylum and filed claims are:

Siebert, Wilbur Henry. *Loyalists in East Florida, 1774 to 1785: The most important documents pertaining thereto.* Reprint. Boston: Gregg Press, 1972.

Dwyer, Clifford S. *Index to Series 1 of American Loyalist Claims.* Athens, Ga.: Iberian, 1990.

_____ and J. R. Jones. *Index to Series 2 of American Loyalist Claims.* DeFuniak Springs, Fla.: Ram Pub., 1986.

The actual records associated with the above two indexes are on microfilm.

War of 1812. The War of 1812 occurred before the U.S. acquired Florida. *The East Florida Papers, 1737–1858,* include references to military activities during this period. See Florida War of 1812 Pension Project at <www.rootsweb.com/~usgenweb/pensions/1812/flindex.htm> and James G. Cusick's, *The Other War of 1812: The Patriot War and the American Invasion of Spanish East Florida* (Gainesville: University of Florida Press, 2003).

Indian Wars (1817–18, 1835–42, 1855–58). Many of the following records can be found at major libraries throughout Florida and at the Florida State Archives. There is no state index, but participants are included in the master *Index to Compiled Service Records of Volunteer Soldiers Who Served During Indian Wars and Disturbances, 1815–1858.* See also:

Compiled Service Records of Volunteers Who Served in Organizations from the State of Florida During the Florida Indian Wars, 1835–1858.

Original Florida Territorial Muster Rolls, 1826–1849. Includes a few original muster rolls from the Second Seminole War.

Seminole War Muster Rolls of Florida Militia, 1836–1841, 1856–1858.

Florida Militia Muster Rolls; Seminole Indian Wars. 10 vols. Florida Department of Military Affairs, Historical Services Division. Indexed online by Aurie Morrison (search by title).

In 1903 the Florida Board of State Institutions published an unindexed and somewhat flawed volume entitled *Soldiers of Florida in the Seminole Indian, Civil, and Spanish-American Wars.*

(1903; reprinted, Macclenny, Fla.: Richard J. Ferry, 1983) and digitized at Florida State Library website under Florida History and Materials <http://diglib.lib.fsu.edu>. The P. K. Yonge Library has an index to the Civil War section compiled by the WPA, but the volume's chief usefulness is as a lead to original source materials.

The Mexican War (1846–48). Florida had recently been through the Second Seminole War and had been a state just over a year when the war with Mexico began, yet the five-company quota assigned to Florida was quickly filled. Very little attention has thus far been paid to the new state's part in the Mexican War, but one excellent account, including rosters of the five companies, is T. Frederick Davis, "Florida's Part in the War with Mexico," *Florida Historical Quarterly* 20 (1942): 235-59. The full article can be found online at <http://palmm.fcla.edu/fh/>. In addition to general sources for all states (see pages 8-9), see *Mexican War Muster Rolls of Florida Independent Companies, 1847–1848*, at the Florida State Archives.

Civil War. Florida seceded from the Union on 10 January 1861, remained an independent nation until 22 April 1865, and ended the Civil War with the only Confederate capital east of the Mississippi not captured and occupied by federal forces. More than 16,000 Floridians served in the Civil War (15,000 Confederate and 1,290 Union).

Several volumes of the special publications of the Florida Department of Military Affairs pertain to Union and Confederate soldiers from Florida. The Florida State Archives and many other libraries in Florida have the National Archives microfilm indexes to the Union and Confederate soldiers Service and Pension indexes. See also:

Biographical Rosters of Florida's Confederate and Union Soldiers, 1861–65. 6 vols. Compiled by David W. Hartman & David Coles. Wilmington, N.C.: Broadfoot Publishing Co., 1995.

Confederate Records. Florida granted pensions to Confederate veterans and their widows under laws passed in 1885, 1887, and 1889. The Florida State Archives has a collection of some 14,000 approved and denied pension applications from 1885 to 1954, also available at the FHL. They are now available online at <http://dlis.dos.state.fl.us/barm/PensionFiles.html>. The files are indexed by both veterans' and widows' names.

The Florida Confederate Soldiers and Sailors Home records are kept at the Jacksonville Public Library in three binders and are completely indexed. Microfilmed records and index to Confederate Soldiers in Florida are available at both the National Archives and FHL.

See also Virgil D. White, *Register of Florida CSA Pension Applications* (Waynesboro, Tenn: National Historical Publishing Co., 1989).

Union Records. Union sources also include microfilmed service records and an index for those who served from Florida, which is available at both the National Archives and the FHL. See also:

The Roster of Union Soldiers, 1861–1865. (Florida, vol. 19) Wilmington, N.C.: Broadfoot Publishing. Co., 1997. Bibliographical sources that may be helpful include:

Davis, William Watson. *The Civil War and Reconstruction in Florida.* Reprint. Gainesville: University of Florida Press, 1964.

Florida State Genealogical Society. *Census Department of the South, November 1864: For Jacksonville, Fernandina, and St. Augustine, Florida. Ordered by the Department of the South, Hilton Head, South Carolina.* Bowie, Md.: Heritage Books, 2002.

Schmidt, Lewis G. *The Civil War in Florida: A Military History.* 4 vols. Allentown, Penn.: L.G. Schmidt, 1989–92.

Taylor, Paul. *Discovering the Civil War in Florida: A Reader and Guide.* Sarasota, Fla.: Pineapple Press, 2001.

The Spanish-American War. Most of the Florida volunteers in the infantry units of what John Hay called this "splendid little war" moved smartly about the state, into and out of training camps and guard detachments, but never left it. Several hundred of them are listed, with capsule unit histories, in part 3 of *Soldiers of Florida* (see section on Indian Wars above). The section is unindexed but can serve to alert researchers to further resources. A thirteen-reel National Archives and Records Administration microfilm publication (M1087), *Compiled Service Records of Volunteer Soldiers Who Served in the Florida Infantry During the War with Spain*, is generally more reliable, and access to the records is facilitated by a 126-roll index (M871). The Florida Department of Military Affairs Special Publication No. 3 is *Mobilization Lists, Florida State Troops and Naval Militia, Spanish-American War, 1898–1899.* The Florida Historical Society has an extensive collection. See also:

Soldiers of Florida in the Seminole Indian, Civil, and Spanish-American Wars. Macclenny, Fla.: R.J. Ferry, 1983.

World War I. Sources at the Florida State Archives include:

Summary of Florida Veterans of World War I, 1925. This series contains a summary of the citizens of Florida who served in the armed forces of the United States during World War I from 1916 to 1920. It lists the name, race, period served, the branch served in, ranks attained, those killed or wounded, and any awards or citations earned.

Soldiers and Sailors Discharge Records. These records contain the individual's name, race, rank, serial number, reason for discharge, birthplace, age at time of enlistment, occupation, and physical description. The enlistment record, usually included with the discharge record, gives the length of service, prior service, marital status, arms and horsemanship qualifications, advancement, battles, decorations and honors, leaves of absence, physical condition, and character evaluation. The Florida State Archives has these papers on microfilm for twenty-eight

counties, with microfilm copies at the FHL. Search by the individual county. See also:

The Florida State Archives, Florida Memory Project has the *World War I Service Cards* online at <www.floridamemory. com/Collections/WWI>.

World War I Navy card roster of Floridians, 1925 are at Florida State Archives and FHL.

Florida Department of Military Affairs. *Florida Veterans of the First World War All Services, 1917–1919.* Special Archives Publication Nos. 21-29.

World War II.

The Florida World War II Memorial <www.floridawwii.com/ sites.asp> lists historic sites and research collections if they are available.

World War II Casualty Card Files, 1950. This Florida State Archives series contains cards that were assembled by the Military Department and used as a central file to track the military casualties from Florida during World War II.

Florida Department of Military Affairs. Special Archives Publication Nos. 15, 19, 59-62, 119, 133, 135-137.

Later Conflicts. Names of military personnel who died or are missing in action in the Korean War and Vietnam are available online through the USGenWeb archives (see page 16) for Florida.

Militia. Florida has had a militia since its earliest territorial days. When voters lined up to register for the young state's first election, every able-bodied man over twenty and under forty-five was enrolled in the militia before being allowed to vote; only age and infirmity excused the prospective voter from his military obligation.

Home guard (state militia) units were under state command during the Civil War, and their personnel and other records were never provided to Confederate officials. Most of the records that survived the war were placed in the State Arsenal, which has recently transferred them and other treasures to the Florida State Archives. Including records as early as the 1820s, as well as muster rolls from the Second Seminole, Mexican, and Civil Wars, this new acquisition constitutes a major source for Florida researchers. Later records include documents of the Florida Militia, Florida State Troops, and Florida National Guard (1870–1917). See Robert Hawk, *Florida's Army: Militia/State Troops/National Guard, 1565–1985* (Englewood, Fla.: Pineapple Press, 1986).

Periodicals, Newspapers, and Manuscript Collections

Periodicals

In addition to *The Florida Genealogist,* published by the Florida State Genealogical Society, researchers can turn to *The Southern Genealogists Exchange Quarterly,* published by the Southern Genealogist's Exchange Society in Jacksonville since 1957. The *Florida Historical Quarterly,* published by the Florida Historical Society, has been in publication since 1908, and *Tequesta,* from the Historical Association of Southern Florida, since 1941. A number of local societies also publish useful periodicals. For a listing, see the Florida State Genealogical Society below.

Newspapers

The first newspaper published in Florida was in 1783 by a Tory who wanted to announce the end of the American Revolution. However, it was discontinued when Florida again came under Spanish rule. After Spain relinquished Florida back to the United States, the *Florida Gazette* began publication in St. Augustine in July 1821.

Newspaper collections are found in most large libraries, but local societies and libraries in the area of geographical interest should also be queried. The most comprehensive collection is located at the University of Florida, P. K. Yonge Library of Florida History, and the George A. Smathers Library in Gainesville. According to their website, "a collection and preservation effort begun in 1944 called for acquisition of at least one newspaper from each of Florida's sixty-seven counties on an ongoing basis. The library began to produce in-house microfilm copies of its Florida newspapers in 1947 and films sixty-four current Florida newspapers on a regular basis today." The Florida Newspaper Project website is <www.uflib.ufl.edu/flnews>.

Other major collections can be found at the State Library of Florida in Tallahassee, the Robert Manning Strozier Library at Florida State University in Tallahassee, the John C. Pace Library at the University of West Florida in Pensacola, the University of Miami's Otto G. Richter Library, and the University of South Florida's Tampa Campus Library.

Manuscripts

Not only are manuscript collections found in university and historical libraries throughout the South, but also in several larger public collections as well the Florida State Archives and the state's larger historical societies. The *National Union Catalog of Manuscripts* (see page 11) lists numerous Florida holdings. Specific and limited queries to individual collections can also be productive.

Archives, Libraries, and Societies

Florida State Archives
Division of Library & Information Services
Bureau of Archives & Records Management
500 S. Bronough St., First Floor
Tallahassee, FL 32399-0250
http://dlis.dos.state.fl.us/barm/fsa.html

The state archives is the official repository for the public records of Florida and is located in the same building as the State Library of Florida. Its book collection includes over 10,000 family and county histories. See the Florida Memory Project at <www.floridamemory.com>.

State Library of Florida
Division of Library & Information Services
Bureau of Archives & Records Management
500 S. Bronough St., Second Floor
Tallahassee, FL 32399-0250
http://dlis.dos.state.fl.us/stlib/index.html

The state library maintains the "Florida Collection," which contains printed and secondary source material for the state, such as city directories, histories, biographies, church surveys, and manuscripts.

P. K. Yonge Library of Florida History
University of Florida
Dept. of Special Collections
P.O. Box 117007
Gainesville, FL 32611-7001
http://web.uflib.ufl.edu/spec/pkyonge

This is the largest collection of Spanish colonial documents in the United States and the largest microfilm collection of Florida newspapers. The Florida Historical Map Collection at the P. K. Yonge Library of Florida History contains more than 2,300 images of Florida dating between 1564 and 1926. Other cartographic images of the state include the Sanborn Insurance maps and U.S.G.S. topographic maps.

The Alma Clyde Field Library of Florida History
Florida Historical Society
435 Brevard Ave.
Cocoa, FL 32922-7901
www.florida-historical-soc.org

The Florida Historical Society, founded in 1856, is one of the oldest historical societies in the country with records dating back to the 1500s. Manuscripts, rare books, photographs, postcards, maps, ephemera, and a special collection of WPA records are now housed in the historic WPA Post Office building in downtown Cocoa village, where the Florida State Genealogical Society also houses its collection.

Florida State Genealogical Society, Inc.
P.O. Box 10249
Tallahassee, FL 32302
www.rootsweb.com/~flsgs/

The society, whose permanent collection is at the Florida Historical Society, publishes the *Florida Genealogist* and through its website provides a current list of genealogical societies in the state. The Florida Pioneer Descendants Certificate Program is sponsored by the society.

Since 1977, descendants have been providing documented proof of their lineage to individuals who resided in Florida prior to statehood on 3 March 1845. All records submitted to 1995 have been microfilmed and are available at the society's library, Florida State Archives, and the FHL. Records from 1996 to the present are available for viewing at the Florida State Archives. For detailed information on the program and the index of pioneers, see the society's website.

John C. Pace Library
University of West Florida
11000 University Pkwy.
Pensacola, FL 32514-5750
http://library.uwf.edu/index.shtml

The Special Collections maintains the Panton, Leslie Papers (1783–1821) a significant block of material on British and Spanish West Florida trade with Native Americans. In addition, the collections' focus is on the history and development of Pensacola and the West Florida region (ten counties of the Florida Panhandle, between the Perdido and Apalachicola rivers) from earliest settlement to the present time. It is the largest West Florida research collection in existence and a major repository dealing with Florida and the Gulf Coast region.

Otto G. Richter Library
University of Miami
1300 Memorial Dr., P.O. Box 248214
Coral Gables, FL 33124-0320
www.library.miami.edu/library/archives.html

The Florida Collection here includes material on the historical, political, social, cultural, literary, ethnic development of Florida from the sixteenth century to the present day, with information on the growth and development of South Florida, particularly Miami, and Florida literature.

University of South Florida
Special Collections
4202 E. Fowler Ave., LIB122
Tampa, FL 33620
www.lib.usf.edu/usflibraries/collections.html

The website for Special Collections provides access to their digital collections, which includes indexes and finding aids. About 2,000 marriage records (1878–93) can be found here. Also available online is the Burgert Brothers photograph collection, which records Tampa's development from a small town to a major city. Other marriage records, such as Hillsborough County Marriage Records (1846–1988), are also available.

John F. Germany Public Library
Hillsborough County Public Library Cooperative
900 N. Ashley Dr.
Tampa, FL 33602-3788
www.hcplc.org/hcplc/liblocales/jfg

The History & Genealogy Department is home to both a genealogy and a Florida history collection. A great resource is its online catalogs, which include an index to obituaries (since 1895) and an index to D. B. McKay's *Pioneer Florida* column (1946–60). Additional local history data are added to this database on a regular basis.

Miami-Dade Public Library System

Main Library
101 W. Flagler St.
Miami, FL 33130-1523
www.mdpls.org/default.asp

The comprehensive collection of Floridiana dates from 1578 and includes books, maps, newspapers, periodicals, pictorial images, government documents, and some manuscript material. See the Miami-Dade Public Library System's Online Catalog at its website. The library has an extensive genealogy collection that includes all census records from 1790 to 1930. Other major collections are the Dawes rolls (1898–1914), the Draper Manuscripts, and the Freedman Savings and Trust Registers.

Orlando Public Library

101 E. Central Blvd.
Orlando, FL 32801-2429
www.ocls.lib.fl.us/Locations/locations_genealogy.asp

The Florida Collection at the Orlando Public Library consists mostly of nonfiction materials including a strong collection of state and local histories as well as appropriate government documents. Other items include Orange County maps (1900–80); and vertical file cabinets of clippings, brochures, and images pertaining to Florida history, culture, and civilizations.

The Genealogy Department is generally considered to have the largest genealogy collection in Florida. The core collection was a gift of avid genealogist, Captain Charles Albertson. The library is the official repository of the Florida State Society of the Daughters of the American Revolution.

Jacksonville Public Library

122 N. Ocean St.
Jacksonville, FL 32202
http://jpl.coj.net/DLC/Florida/FloridaCollection.html

The library's Florida Collection is a reference collection with an emphasis on Northeast Florida and Jacksonville. It is one of the largest collections of its type in a public library in Florida.

The Genealogy Collection covers northeast Florida. Indexed microfiche of vital records are available for Florida and Georgia. Books, CDs, and microfilm include census/Soundex rolls, Confederate Pension Records for Florida soldiers, Duval County deeds, marriages and probate records, numerous genealogy periodicals, the *Florida Times-Union* newspaper index back to 1895, and Jacksonville City Directories beginning with 1870.

Indian River County Main Library

Florida History & Genealogy Department
1600 21st St.
Vero Beach, FL 32960
www.rootsweb.com/~flindian/ircl

This is the only library outside of the Florida State Archives that is acquiring all county courthouse records in Florida. In addition, it has all microfilmed Florida records from the National Archives, collections on Florida history and maps, and an extensive genealogy collection of books and microfiche.

St. Augustine Historical Society

271 Charlotte St.
St. Augustine, FL 32084
www.oldcity.com/sites/oldhouse/historical.html

The society has preserved and restored historical buildings from the 1600s. It offers students and researchers access to an exceptional library containing documents, published works, microfilm, maps, and illustrative material.

Pensacola Historical Society

117 E. Government St.
Pensacola, FL 32501
www.pensacolahistory.org

The library and archives is an invaluable resource for local genealogy or the study of Pensacola's rich history, which spans over 400 years, and includes an extensive collection of photographs.

Other libraries with a focus on genealogy and Florida history include:

Elmer's Genealogy Library

203 S. Range St.
Madison, FL 32340-2437
www.elmerslibrary.com

Largo Library

351 East Bay Dr.
Largo, FL 33770
www.largo.com

Polk County Historical and Genealogical Library

100 E. Main St.
Bartow, FL 33830

The Southern Genealogist's Exchange Society

6215 Sauterne Dr.
Jacksonville, Florida
mailing address:
P.O. Box 2801
Jacksonville, FL 32203-2801
www.sgesjax.tripod.com

University of Central Florida
P.O. Box 162666
Orlando, FL 32816
http://library.ucf.edu/Special

Special Focus Categories

Immigration

Florida immigration records, as such, are rare. Most of the early settlers came overland from the neighboring states to the north but below the Mason-Dixon Line, and the majority of them were from Georgia; however, see Frank M. Hawes, "New Englanders in the Florida Census of 1850," *New England Historical and Genealogical Register* 76 (1922): 44-54. There were some seaports through which immigrants came into the territory and state, but most of the recorded activity was in the nineteenth and early twentieth century. Known passenger ship records have been microfilmed by NARA. For a complete listing of microfilm available for research from the National Archives, see pages 11-12.

Naturalizations

These records can be found in county and U.S. district courts in Florida. Not all of the records have been microfilmed at the local level. Query the local courthouse to find out what records they own and the year they start. The Florida State Archives has naturalization records for ten counties: Brevard, Dade, DeSoto, Franklin, Hillsborough, Manatee, Monroe, Orange, Pasco, and Volusia. Dated but potentially still useful is the WPA volume *Naturalization Records in Florida* (Tallahassee, 1940). The National Archives—Southeast Region (see page 12) has petitions for *Naturalization Records of U.S. District Courts in the Southeast, 1790–1958*, and records for the following. The first three are also available from FHL:

U.S. District Court, Florida Southern District. 1847–1941. Key West, Monroe County.

U.S. District Court, Florida Middle District, 1913–32. Miami, Dade County.

U.S. District Court, Florida Southern District, 1909–35. Tampa, Hillsborough County.

U.S. District Court, Florida Northern District, Pensacola, Escambia County and Tallahassee, Leon County. These last records have not been microfilmed.

African American

Voluminous records of various aspects of black life in Florida have been surveyed for *The Black Experience: A Guide to Afro-American Resources in the Florida State Archives* (revised; Tallahassee: Florida State Archives, 2002), which is now available online on its website (see Archives, Libraries, and Societies). Compiled by Debra D. McGriff, former curator of the Florida State Archives' genealogy collection, this invaluable resource gives record groups and series titles, coverage dates, and descriptions for a vast array of primary sources for research on the African Americans of Florida.

The archives' public record and manuscript holdings include slave books, African-American church membership lists, the governors' administrative correspondence, Black Teacher Association papers, and the papers of Judge Joseph Lee, a prominent African-American Republican of Duval County. African-American marriage records, deeds documenting African-American ownership of land, and probate files containing wills and appraisement inventories including lists of slaves are interspersed throughout the archives' county records microfilm collection. A few counties (Gadsden, Leon, and Gulf) provide indexes for "Negro" or "Colored" marriages, but there are no separate indexes for deeds or probates involving African Americans. Chancery case files, marks and brands, mortgages, guardianships, and court-order books can also be useful to the researcher of African-American genealogy.

There are currently two African-American societies in Florida: Afro-American Historical and Genealogical Society-Central Florida Chapter, 6013 Wedgewood Dr., Orlando, FL 32808 (mailing address: P.O. Box 1347, Orlando, FL 32802-1347) <www.rootsweb.com/~flcfaahg/>; and South Jacksonville African American Historical & Genealogical Society, P.O. Box 10693, Jacksonville, FL 32247 <www.jacksonvillestory.com>.

Some research centers available for African-American research are:

Florida Agricultural and Mechanical University, Tallahassee, FL 32307 <www.famu.edu/acad/coleman/index.html> the state's "historically black university," maintains an African American Collection, including a microform reproduction of the New York Public Library's Schomburg Collection of Negro Literature and History, an important resource for the study of African American people.

The African-American Research Library and Cultural Center, 2650 Sistrunk Blvd., Ft. Lauderdale, FL 33311 <www.broward.org/aarlcc.htm> contains more than 75,000 books, documents, artifacts, and related materials that focus on the experiences of people of African descent. Local history is a cornerstone of the available resources.

The Black Archives Collection, History and Research Foundation of South Florida, Inc., The Joseph Caleb Community Center, 5400 NW 22nd Ave., Miami, FL 33142 constitutes another resource for researchers.

In addition to websites of national interest for African-American research (see pages 14-15), Internet sites for Florida include:

Florida African-American Roots <www.rootsweb.com/~flafram/home.html>

Florida Slave Data <www.rootsweb.com/~flafram/Slavedata. htm>

The following is a select group of important or unusual sources:

Brown, Carter, Jr. *Florida's Black Public Officials, 1867–1924*. Tuscaloosa, Ala.: University of Alabama Press, 1998.

Jones, Maxine D. and Kevin M. McCarthy. *African Americans in Florida*. Sarasota, Fla.: Pineapple Press, Inc., 1993.

Midwifery Program Files, 1924–75, at the Florida State Archives, contains a few applications for licensing of black midwives under the state midwifery program.

Rivers, Larry E. *Slavery in Florida: Territorial Days to Emancipation*. Gainesville: University Press of Florida, 2000.

Smith, Julia Floyd. *Slavery and Plantation Growth in Antebellum Florida, 1821–1860*. Gainesville: University of Florida Press, 1973.

Voter registration rolls for 1868, at the Florida State Archives, lists each registrant's name, race, length of residence in the county and state, nativity (by state), naturalization (where, when, how), and the date of registration.

Native American

Today's true "Florida Indians" constitute three separate but historically related groups: the Seminole, the Miccosukee, and the Creek tribes. Thousands of them were transported during the mid-1800s to Oklahoma, where they formed one of the "Five Civilized Tribes." Many still live on federal and state reservations in or near the Everglades. The most common starting place for Native American research on the pertinent tribes is the index to *Final Rolls of the Five Civilized Tribes in Indian Territory: Choctaw, Chickasaw, Cherokee, Creek, Seminole* (Baltimore: Genealogical Publishing Co., 2003).

The Seminole tribe, 6300 Stirling Rd., Hollywood, FL 33024 <www.seminoletribe.com> has more than 3,000 members on six reservations: Big Cypress, Brighton, Fort Pierce, Hollywood, Immokalee, and Tampa. Extensive information about their resources is provided on the website.

The Miccosukee have a reservation forty miles west of Miami on the Tamiami Trail <www.miccosukee.com/tribe.html>.

The Seminole provide community libraries on five of their six reservations:

Billy Osceola Memorial Library
Rt. 6, Box 668
Okeechobee, FL 34974

Dorothy Scott Osceola Memorial Library (Broward County)
3100 NW 63rd Ave.
Hollywood, FL 33024

Willie Frank Library (Hendry County)
HC 61 Box 46A, Big Cypress Reservation
Clewiston, FL 33440

Tampa Reservation Library
5219 Orient Rd., #K
Tampa, FL 33610

Immokalee Reservation Library
303 Lena Frank Dr., Ste. 3
Immokalee, FL 33934

Two research guides assist with Seminole family research:

Lennon, Donna Rachal. *Tracing Ancestors Among the Five Civilized Tribes: Southeastern Indians Prior to Removal*. Baltimore: Genealogical Pub. Co., 2002.

Wickman, Patricia R., Ph.D. *So You Think There's a Seminole in Your Family Tree?* Hollywood, Fla.: Seminole Publications; Seminole Tribe of Florida, 1997.

Some published materials available on researching Florida Native Americans are:

Bowen, Jeff. *Seminole of Florida: Indian Census 1930–1940, with Birth and Death Records 1930–1938*. Signal Mountain, Tenn.: Mountain Press, 1997.

Kersey, Harry A. *The Seminole and Miccosukee Tribes: A Critical Bibliography*. Bloomington: Indiana University Press, 1987.

Lantz, Raymond C. *Seminole Indians of Florida, 1850–1874*. Bowie, Md.: Heritage Books, 1994.

_____. *Seminole Indians of Florida, 1875–1879*. Bowie, Md.: Heritage Books, 1995.

Hispanic

Many Floridians who have Cuban or Spanish ancestry will benefit from the files in the *David Masnata Y De Quesada Collection* at the University of Miami, Otto G. Richter Library, Archives & Special Collection Department (see Archives, Libraries, and Societies). Masnata became a Cuban exile and moved to New York in 1961. When he left Cuba, he left behind records covering many years of researching family and local history. However, he compiled a new collection of documents on Cuban and Spanish families. A complete description of this collection can be found at <www.library.miami.edu/archives/papers/MASNATA.html>.

Other helpful sources, especially for tracing Spanish or Cuban ancestry.

Cuban Genealogy Club of Miami, FL, Inc., 5521 SW 163 Ave., Southwest Ranches, FL 33331 <www.cgcmiami.org/cuba>

Cuban Genealogical Society, P.O. Box 2650, Salt Lake City, UT 84110 <www.rootsweb.com/~utcubangs>

Los Floridanos Society, Inc., P.O. Box 4043, St. Augustine, FL 32085 <www.losfloridanos.org>. Los Floridanos Society

represents descendants of the early Spanish settlers of St. Augustine, Florida, who arrived during the "First Spanish Period, 1565–1763." Currently, the society represents the Solana and Sanchez families.

Cuban Heritage Collection, Otto G. Richter Library, University of Miami, Florida (see Archives, Libraries, and Societies).

Cuba GenWeb <www.cubagen.org> includes church records on the website.

Other resources include:

Caribbean Historical & Genealogical Journal. Published four times a year by TCI Genealogical Resources, P.O. Box 15839, San Luis Obispo, Calif. 93406.

Carr, Peter E. Genealogical resources of Hispanic Central & South America. San Luis Obispo, Calif.: TCI Genealogical Resources, 1996.

Carr, Peter E. Guide to Cuban Genealogical Research—Records and Sources. Chicago: Adams Press, 1991.

Feldman, Lawrence H. Anglo-Americans in Spanish Archives: Lists of Anglo-American Settlers in the Spanish Colonies of America: A Finding Aid. Baltimore: Genealogical Publishing Co., 1991.

Platt, Lyman. D. Cuba General Research Guide. Salt Lake City: Institute of Genealogy and History for Latin-America, 1991.

Other Ethnic Groups

Florida is a melting pot of people from different backgrounds, beyond the historical presence of Native Americans and African Americans. Hispanic migration did not occur until the last half of the twentieth century, except for the Spanish colonial period.

Among the earliest colonies still traceable are the Minorcans, who came from the Mediterranean, Greek, Spanish, and Italian isles with Dr. Andrew Turnbull to settle his ill-fated New Smyrna plantation on the coast south of St. Augustine in 1768. See:

Griffin, Patricia C. Mullet on the Beach: The Minorcans of Florida, 1768–1788. St. Augustine, Fla.: St. Augustine Historical Society, 1990.

Rasico, Philip D. The Minorcans of Florida: Their History, Language, and Culture. New Smyrna Beach, Fla.: Luthers, 1990.

Quinn, Jane. Minorcans in Florida: Their History and Heritage. St. Augustine, Fla.: Mission Press, 1975.

Immigration to southern Florida in the 1920s by Jewish U.S. northeasterners of European heritage boosted today's Jewish population. As a result, there are many Jewish genealogical societies and Holocaust Museums located in Florida, including Jacksonville, Broward County, Greater Miami, Orlando, Palm Beach, Southwest Florida, Tallahassee, and Tampa Bay. Most can be located online through standard search engines (see page 17).

Territorial Records

Volumes 22 to 26 of The Territorial Papers of the United States (Washington, D.C.: Government Printing Office, 1956–65) list the names of thousands of Florida residents between 1821 and 1845 in hundreds of letters, reports, and petitions ("memorials") of the territorial period. Information varies, but the wide coverage and excellent index make the volumes essential to a full understanding of the people and their era. Most large libraries in the United States have these, as do college and university collections.

Not all territorial papers are included in the above volumes, however. The following NARA microfilm publications are also potential sources: Territorial Papers of the United States Senate, 1789–1873: Florida, 1806–1845; State Department Territorial Papers, Florida, 1777–1824; and Territorial Papers of the United States: The Territory of Florida, 1821–1845. Many of the territorial papers generated, however, have never been filmed.

Early Election Records

The Florida State Archives has 2,000 folders of important early election records. Land records can be misleading on absentee owners, but election records were sworn documents requiring proof of residence, usually six months in the county, two years in the state. The files are arranged by year, and then by county, but they must be used in person. These voter rolls and returns list the names of candidates, clerks, and inspectors in local, state, congressional, referendum, and militia elections from 1824. Until 1865 each voter's name and precinct of residence is listed.

Among the most useful records for those tracing ancestors at the time of statehood are the returns of the first statewide election, held on 26 May 1845, in Brian E. Michaels, Florida Voters in Their First Statewide Election (Tallahassee: Florida State Genealogical Society, 1987).

Another voter record of genealogical significance, located at the Florida State Archives, is the 1868 Florida Voter Registration, which required an oath of allegiance to the U.S. government. It was also the first voter enrollment open to African Americans. While it is neither indexed nor complete for all counties, this important re-registration for the post-war constitutional convention election includes name, qualifying date, race, length of residence, nativity by state, and naturalization. The rolls are arranged by county and then by the date of individual registration.

County Resources

In the majority of counties, the original marriage records are retained in the office of the clerk of courts located in the county seat. Queries and requests for information from Florida

FLORIDA

counties should be addressed to: "Clerk of Courts, _____ County Courthouse," at the address given in the following county chart. Names in parentheses are former names of the county. The original birth and death records are available at the county health departments with few exceptions (see Vital Records). Many of the courthouse records have been microfilmed by the LDS church and can be ordered through the FHL.

By 2006, every county will make available indexes to "official records" beginning no later than January 1, 1990, at <www.myfloridacounty.com>. Examples include deeds, marriage certificates, judgments, liens, probate, and other types of documents. Currently, many counties have indexes to earlier dates such as 1900. Once the record is found, records can be ordered and paid for online.

See <www.myfloridacounty.com> or <www.rootsweb.com/~flsgs/flcounties.htm> for current county information.

FLORIDA

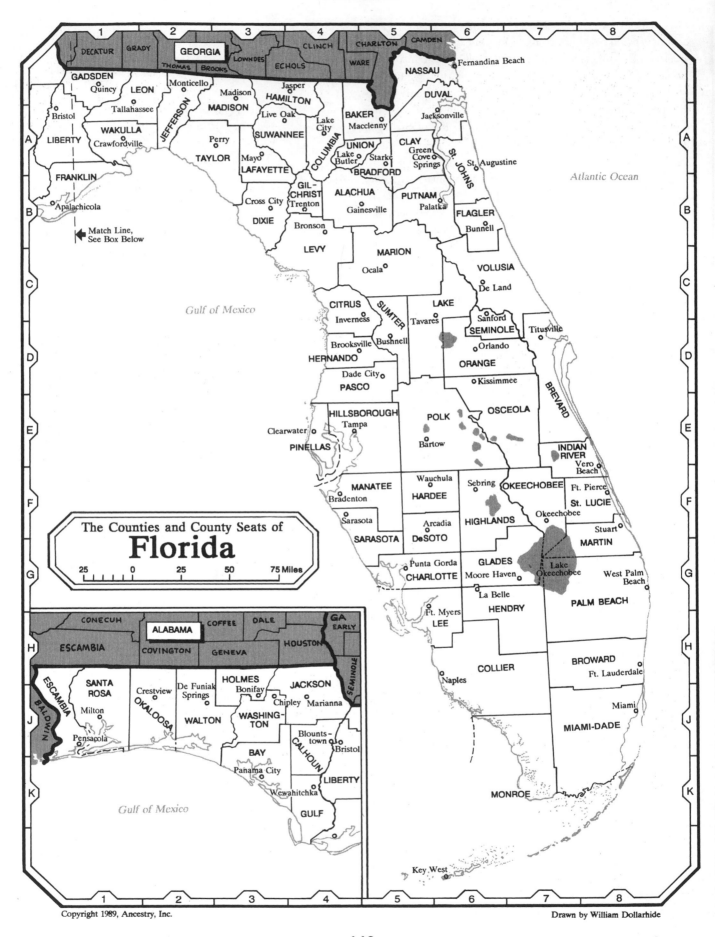

The Counties and County Seats of

Florida

25   0   25   50   75 Miles

Drawn by William Dollarhide

FLORIDA

Map	County Address	Date Formed Parent County/ies	Birth Marriage Death	Land Probate Court
B4	Alachua 201 E. University Ave. P.O. Box 600 Gainesville 32602-0600	1824 Duval/St. Johns	——— 1837	1826 1840 1850
A5	Baker 339 E. Macclenny Ave. Macclenny 32063-2231	1861 New River	——— 1877	1877 1877 1880
K3	Bay 300 E. 4th St. Panama City 32401-3056 *Washington County land records transferred here.*	1913 Calhoun/Washington	——— 1913	1885 1913 1913
	Benton	(see Hernando)		
A5	Bradford P.O. Drawer B Starke 32091	1858 Columbia (New River)	——— 1875 ———	1875 1868 1875
D7	Brevard P.O. Box 999 Titusville 32781-0999	1844 Mosquito (St. Lucie)	1930 1868	1871 1877 1879
H7	Broward 201 S.E. 6th St. Ft. Lauderdale 33301-3303	1915 Dade/Palm Beach	——— 1915 1917	1915 1917 1915
J4	Calhoun 20859 S. E. Central Ave., Rm 130 Blountstown 32424-2263	1838 Franklin	1880 1862 ———	1862 1877 ?
G7	Charlotte 350 E. Marion Ave. P.O. Box 511687 Punta Gorda 33951-1687	1921 DeSoto	1922 1921 1917	1921 1921 1921
C4	Citrus 110 N. Apopka Ave. Inverness 34450-4231	1887 Hernando	——— 1887 ———	1887 1887 1887
A5	Clay 825 N. Orange Ave./P.O. Box 698 Green Cove Springs 32043-0698	1858 Duval	——— 1872 ———	1871 1859 1859
H6	Collier 3301 Tamiami Trail East P.O. Box 413044 Naples 33941-3044	1923 Lee	——— 1923 ———	1923 1923 1923
A4	Columbia 173 N.E. Hernando P.O. Box 2069 Lake City 32056-2069	1832 Alachua	——— 1876 ———	1871 1868 1895
	Dade (See Miami-Dade)			
F5	DeSoto 115 E. Oak St., Rm. 101 Arcadia 34266-2401	1887 Manatee	——— 1887 ———	1887 1887 1887
B3	Dixie P.O. Box 1206 Cross City 32628-1206	1921 Lafayette	——— 1924	1921 1871
A6	Duval 330 E. Bay St., Rm 103 Jacksonville 32202-2921	1822 St. Johns	1893 1822 1901	1901 1905 1901
J1	Escambia 190 Governmental Center Pensacola 32501-5773	1821 original	1891 1821 1919	1821 1821 1821
	Fayette	1832 (abolished, 1834; territory annexed to Jackson)		
B6	Flagler P.O. Box 787 Bunnell 32110-0787	1917 St. Johns/Volusia	——— 1917	? 1917 ?
B1	Franklin 33 Market St., Ste. 203 Apalachicola 32320	1832 Jackson	——— 1887	1874 1832 ?
A1	Gadsden P.O. Box 1649 Quincy 32351-1649	1823 Jackson	——— 1849	1849 1837 ?
B4	Gilchrist 112 S. Main St./P.O. Box 37 Trenton 32693-0037	1925 Alachua	——— 1926	1926 1926 1926
G6	Glades 500 Ave. J, P.O. Box 10 Moore Haven 33471-0010	1921 DeSoto	——— 1921 ———	1921 1921 1921
K4	Gulf 1000 Cecil G. Costin, Sr. Blvd. Rm 148 Port St. Joe 32456	1925 Calhoun	——— 1925 ———	1925 1925 1925
A3	Hamilton 207 First St., N.E., Rm 106 Jasper 32052-6693	1827 Jefferson	——— 1824 ———	1836 1830 1881
F5	Hardee P.O. Drawer 1749 Wauchula 33873-1749	1921 DeSoto	——— 1921 ———	1921 1921 1921
H6	Hendry 25 E. Hickpoochee Ave. P.O. Box 1760 LaBelle 33975-1760	1923 Lee	——— 1923 ———	1923 1923 1923
D4	Hernando 20 N. Main St., Rm 130 Brooksville 34601-2800	1843 Alachua (Benton)	——— 1900 ———	1878 1900 1877
F6	Highlands 590 S. Commerce Ave. Sebring 33870-3867	1921 DeSoto	——— 1921 ———	1921 1921 1921
E4	Hillsborough P.O. Box 1110 Tampa 33601-1110	1834 Alachua	1875 1846 1900	1837 1845 1846
J3	Holmes P.O. Box 397 Bonifay 32425-0397	1848 Jackson/Walton	——— 1902 ———	1900 1902 1900

Map	County Address	Date Formed Parent County/ies	Birth Marriage Death	Land Probate Court
E7	Indian River P.O. Box 1028 Vero Beach 32961-1028	1925 St. Lucie	1925 1925 1925	1925 1925 1925
J4	Jackson P.O. Drawer 510 Marianna 32447-0510	1822 Escambia	—— 1848 ——	1848 1848 1848
A2	Jefferson County Courthouse, Rm 10 Monticello 32344-9539	1827 Leon	—— 1827 ——	1827 1900 1900
A3	Lafayette P.O. Box 88 Mayo 32066-0088	1856 Madison	1857	1873 1838
D5	Lake 550 W. Main St. P.O. Box 7800 Tavares 32778-7800	1887 Orange/Sumter	—— 1887 ——	1887 1887 ?
H5	Lee P.O. Box 2469 Ft. Myers 33902-2469	1887 Monroe	—— 188? ——	? ? ?
A2	Leon P.O. Box 726 Tallahassee 32302-0726	1824 Gadsden/Duval	—— 1825 ——	1825 1824 1825
C4	Levy P.O. Drawer 610 Bronson 32621-0610	1845 Alachua/Hillsborough	1854	1850 1847 1850
A1, K4	Liberty P.O. Box 399 Bristol 32321-0399	1855 Gadsden	—— 1857 ——	1857 1859 1884
A3	Madison P.O. Box 237 Madison 32341-0237	1827 Jefferson	—— 1831 ——	1831 1846 1838
F5	Manatee P.O. Box 25400 Bradenton 34206-5400	1855 Hillsborough	1901 1856 1915	1843 1857 1858
C5	Marion 110 NW 1st Ave. Ocala 34475	1844 Alachua/Mosquito	1844	1844 1846 1849
G8	Martin 100 E. Ocean Blvd., Rm 200 Stuart 34994	1925 Palm Beach/St. Lucie	—— 1925 ——	1925 1925 1925
J8	Miami-Dade 73 W. Flagler St., Ste 242 Miami 33130-1731	1836 Monroe (Dade)	1914 1840 ——	? ? 1888
K7	Monroe 500 Whitehead St. Key West 33040-6581	1823 St. Johns	—— 1826 ——	1826 1888 ?
	Mosquito	(see Orange)		
A5	Nassau P.O. Box 456 Fernandina Beach 32035-0456	1824 Duval	—— 1867 ——	1840 1873 1873
	New River	(see Bradford)		
J2	Okaloosa 101 E. James Lee Blvd. Crestview 32536	1915 Santa Rosa/Walton	—— 1915 ——	1915 1915 1915
F7	Okeechobee 304 N.W. Second St., Rm 101 Okeechobee 34972-4146	1917 Osceola/Palm Beach/ St. Lucie	1915 1925 1915	1887 1917 1917
D6	Orange 425 N. Orange Ave. P.O. Box 4994 Orlando 32801-4627	1824 St. Johns (Mosquito)	—— 1869 ——	1847 1871 1847
E6	Osceola 2 Courthouse Sq., Ste. 2000 Kissimmee 34741-5487	1887 Brevard/Orange	—— 1887 ——	1887 1887 1887
G7	Palm Beach 301 N. Olive Ave. West Palm Beach 33401	1909 Dade	—— 1909 ——	1909 1909 1909
D4	Pasco 38053 Live Oak Ave. Dade City 33523-3894	1887 Hernando	—— 1887 ——	1876 1882 1887
E4	Pinellas 315 Court St. Clearwater 33756-5165	1911 Hillsborough	1912	1911 ? 1911
E5	Polk P.O. Box 9000, Drw. CC-1 Bartow 33831-9000	1861 Brevard/Hillsborough	1892 1862 ——	1862 1861 1867
B5	Putnam P.O. Box 758 Palatka 32178-0758	1849 Alachua/Marion/St. Johns		1849 1849 1849
A6	St. Johns P.O. Box 300 St. Augustine 32085-0300	1821 original	1823	1821 1844 1821
	St. Lucie (I)	1844 (renamed Brevard, 1855)		
F8	St. Lucie (II) 221 S. Indian River Dr. Ft. Pierce 34950-4350	1905 Brevard	—— 1905 ——	? 1905 ?
J1	Santa Rosa P.O. Box 472 Milton 32572-0472	1842 Escambia	—— 1869 ——	1869 1878 1869
G5	Sarasota 2000 Main St. Sarasota 34237-6022	1921 Manatee	—— 1921 ——	1921 1921 1921
D6	Seminole 301 N. Park Ave./P.O. Box 8099 Sanford 32772-1243	1913 Orange	—— 1913 ——	1913 1913 1913

Map	County Address	Date Formed Parent County/ies	Birth Marriage Death	Land Probate Court
D5	Sumter 209 N. Florida St. Bushnell 33513-0141	1853 Marion	——— 1853 ———	1854 1856 1853
A3	Suwannee 200 S. Ohio Ave. Live Oak 32064-3200	1858 Columbia	——— 1859 1859	1859 1860 1859
A2	Taylor P.O. Box 620 Perry 32347-0620	1856 Madison	——— 1857 ———	1857 1870 1857
A4	Union 55 W. Main St., Rm. 103 Lake Butler 32054-1600	1921 Bradford	——— 1921 1921	1921 1921 1921

Map	County Address	Date Formed Parent County/ies	Birth Marriage Death	Land Probate Court
C6	Volusia 101 N. Alabama Ave. DeLand 32724-4316	1854 Orange	——— 1856 ———	1869 1855 1855
A1	Wakulla 3056 Crawfordville Hwy. P.O. Box 6048 Crawfordville 32327-3136	1843 Leon	——— 1892 ———	1843 1892 1843
J2	Walton 571 Hwy 90 East DeFuniak Springs 32433	1824 Escambia/Jackson	——— 1885 ——	1886 1882 1886
J3	Washington 1293 W. Jackson Ave. P.O. Box 647 Chipley 32428-0647	1825 Jackson/Walton	——— 1877 ———	1880 1880 1890

Georgia

JOHNI CERNY AND ROBERT S. DAVIS

Georgia was founded in 1733 to give new lives to deserving non-Roman Catholics in the New World. Despite involvements of Georgia's founder, James Oglethorpe, with debtors' prisons, no debtors or criminals were allowed to be sent to Georgia. Nevertheless, the myth that Georgia was a debtors' colony or a type of Botany Bay seems impossible to lay to rest with the truth.

Trustees of the colony sent about 5,000 persons from Great Britain to Georgia, and information about most of those colonists is published in E. Merton Coulter and Albert B. Saye, *A List of the Early Settlers of Georgia* (Athens, Ga.: University of Georgia Press, 1949). Each colonist received fifty acres of land, while those who paid their own passage might have received up to 500 acres.

The Salzburgers, central European Protestants, became the first non-British group to settle in Georgia beginning in 1734. They established themselves at Ebenezer in what is now Effingham County. After Georgia became a royal province in 1753, settlers began to move in from Virginia and the Carolinas in large numbers. Other immigrants included Scots-Irish, Scots-Highlanders, and Portuguese Jews.

When the Revolutionary War began, Georgia consisted of twelve parishes (which did not function as governments, however) and a large area of ceded lands that the Cherokee and Creek Indians had yielded to the colony in 1773. Georgia's first constitution, dated 1777, provided for the creation of Wilkes, Richmond, Burke, Effingham, Chatham, Liberty, Glynn, and Camden counties. In 1784 Washington and Franklin counties were organized. Eventually Georgia had as many as 161 counties. (Campbell and Milton counties were merged with Fulton County

in 1932.) Many Georgia counties have the same names as towns not in those respective counties, causing endless confusion for researchers. For example, the city of Macon is in Bibb County and not in nearby Macon County. Other counties in Georgia, such as Houston, Randolph and Walton, have the same names as other counties no longer in existence.

The Civil War left Georgia devastated with enormous strains upon the state's few factories and fragile railroad system. Factories and foundries of Atlanta, Griswaldville, Rome, and Roswell were completely destroyed. Millions of dollars in capital were lost by the emancipation of slaves. The soil was worn out and farm animals were gone.

The end of the war did not bring immediate recovery. Federal direct taxes added to the burden. Thousands of people, African American and white, were displaced or missed in the 1870 federal census. Economic and social pressures led to racial conflict.

The decades following the war brought Georgia its last wave of nineteenth-century migration. North Carolinians came south to take advantage of the pine forests for turpentine and naval stores. Lumber, marble, granite, coal, and kaoline became major businesses, although cotton remained "king" through the first half of the twentieth century.

Unlike the state as a whole, Atlanta itself recovered almost immediately after the Civil War as a transportation center. Today, it is still the hub of the South, with interstate roads, railways, and air travel. The growth of Atlanta has been explosive, producing two distinct parts of Georgia—Atlanta and its suburbs, as a modern, industrial, urban complex with many people born

outside the state; and the rest of the state, which remains rural with declining population and wealth.

Vital Records

Georgia attempted to require registration of births, marriages, and deaths on a county level in 1875, but the law was repealed in 1876. Some vital records for fourteen Georgia counties for 1875 have been microfilmed and are available at the Georgia Archives (see Archives, Libraries, and Societies).

In 1919 Georgia law required the registration of all births and deaths in the state. As in many other states, Georgia's county governments were slow to respond to the new law and most did not comply until 1928. See Georgia Historical Records Survey, *Guide to Public Vital Statistics in Georgia* (Atlanta: the author, 1941) for the records kept by individual counties. A few major cities required birth and death registration early on:

- Atlanta—births, 1896; deaths, 1887. Fulton County Health Department, 99 Butler St. S.E., Atlanta, GA 30303.
- Augusta—births, 1823–1896. See Georgia Genealogical Society Quarterly (1968): 1988-93
- Savannah—births, 1890; deaths, 1803. Chatham County Health Department, P.O. Box 14257, Savannah, GA 31406. Early death records have been published by the Georgia Historical Society.
- Macon—births, 1891; deaths, 1882. Bibb County Health Department, 171 Emery Hwy., Macon, GA 31201.
- Columbus—births, 1869; deaths, 1890. Muscogee County Health Department, 2100 Comer Ave., Columbus, GA 31902.
- Gainesville—births, 1865; deaths, 1909. Available on microfilm at the Georgia Archives.

Birth and death records in Georgia can be requested from the Georgia Department of Human Resources, Vital Records Unit, Atlanta, Georgia 30334. For urgent requests, certificates can be ordered and paid for by phone with a Visa or MasterCard. There is an additional fee for this service.

As in most other states, marriage records in Georgia are created at the county level. Some Georgia counties kept some marriage bonds before 1805, although Georgia law did not require marriage licenses to be recorded until 1805. Officials were careless in adhering to the law and consequently some marriages were not recorded at all. Some records were also lost in various courthouse fires. All recorded Georgia marriages to 1900 are available on microfilm at the Georgia Archives and the Family History Library (FHL) in Salt Lake City. The former also has some loose, original county marriage records. Heritage Papers' periodical *Georgia Genealogist* contains civil marriages to 1810. Marriages after that date can be found in Mary B. Warren,

Georgia Marriages 1811 Through 1820 (Danielsville, Ga.: Heritage Papers, 1988).

From 1793 to 1832, divorces in Georgia were subject to legislative approval after being approved by the county superior court. The divorce files remain in the custody of the county superior courts. Divorces, name changes, and decrees of *femme sole* (also called *feme sole*) granted by the Georgia legislature are abstracted in Robert S. Davis Jr., *The Georgia Black Book II* (Easley, S.C.: Southern Historical Press, 1987).

Census Records

Federal

Population Schedules
- Indexed—1820 (partial), 1830, 1840, 1850, 1860, 1870, 1880, 1890 (fragment), 1900, 1910, 1920, 1930
- Soundex—1880, 1900, 1910, 1920, 1930

Industry and Agriculture Schedules
- Industry—1820, 1880
- Agriculture—1850, 1860, 1870, 1880

Mortality Schedules
- 1850, 1860, 1870, 1880

Slave Schedules
- 1850, 1860

Unfortunately, the 1820 census is the earliest enumeration of Georgia's population to have survived, making it necessary to substitute other lists for the missing censuses. More than forty percent of Georgia's population (and likely seventy percent of the frontier migration families) lived in Wilkes County in 1790, making the numerous publications of that one county's extensive surviving records an especially valuable census substitute. The 1820 census of Georgia is also lost for Franklin, Rabun, and Twiggs counties; for many other counties, names were often omitted or unreadable. Land lottery, military, tax lists, and other records, discussed under other headings, are available as census substitutes and supplements for the 1820 and earlier censuses.

Both the Georgia Archives and the FHL have a complete set of Georgia census records and mortality schedules.

State
Georgia conducted state censuses for various years from 1787 to 1866. Only a relatively few of these returns survive, and they are only lists of heads of households with some minor statistical information. The returns prior to 1852 have been published in various sources. Later census returns, when they survive, are almost all on microfilm at the Georgia Archives. To see what has

survived of Georgia state and federal census records, see Robert S. Davis, *Research in Georgia* (see Background Sources), 27-41, 44, 147-68.

Background Sources

Georgia records and research are discussed in detail in Robert S. Davis Jr., *Research in Georgia* (Easley, S.C.: Southern Historical Press, 1980), and Ted O. Brooke and Robert S. Davis, *Georgia Research* (Atlanta: Georgia Genealogical Society, 2002). James E. Dorsey's *Georgia Genealogy and Local History* (Spartanburg, S.C.: Reprint Co., 1983) offers articles and abstracts of Georgia records. It was updated annually in the *Georgia Historical Quarterly* until 1989 when the *Georgia Genealogical Society Quarterly* began publishing the updates.

Sources for the state's history include:

Coleman, Kenneth, ed. *A History of Georgia.* 2d ed. Athens, Ga.: University of Georgia Press, 1991.

Coulter, E. Merton. *Georgia: A Short History.* Chapel Hill: University of North Carolina Press, 1964.

Maps

Early Georgia maps are crucial for tracing colonial families. See Marion R. Hemperley, *Map of Colonial Georgia, 1773–1777* (Atlanta: Georgia Surveyor General Department, 1979), which shows parish boundaries before 1777, and his *Georgia Early Roads and Trails, Circa 1730–1850* (Atlanta: Georgia Surveyor General Department, 1979), which shows migration trails in the state. The Georgia Archives also has maps of Georgia for sale showing the land lottery and the militia districts.

For changes in Georgia county boundaries, see William Thorndale and William Dollarhide, *Map Guide to the U.S. Federal Censuses, 1790–1920* (Baltimore: Genealogical Publishing Co., 1987), and Pat Bryant and Ingrid Shields, *Georgia Counties: Their Changing Boundaries* (Atlanta: Georgia Surveyor General Department, 1983).

The largest collection of historical Georgia maps includes some 30,000 items, with many county maps, and large, detailed state maps can be found at the Georgia Archives. Modern maps of Georgia counties and some cities can be ordered for a fee from Map Room, Georgia Department of Transportation, 2 Capitol Sq., Atlanta, Georgia 30334.

Land Records

State-Land State

Land and property records, combined with tax digests, can be important keys to successful research in Georgia. Surviving colonial and state land grant records of Georgia, including loose, original records not available on microfilm, are in the Georgia Archives. See also Farris Cadle, *Georgia Land Surveying and Law* (Athens, Ga.: University of Georgia Press, 1991); Marion R. Hemperley, *The Georgia Surveyor General Department* (Atlanta: Georgia Surveyor General Department, 1982); and Pat Bryant, *Entry of Claims for Georgia Landholders, 1733–1755* (Atlanta: State Printing Office, 1975). The latter is a book of titles given to Georgians in 1755 for their lands under the trustees between 1733 and 1755.

Three quarters of the pre-1776 surveys (plats) and the last few of the colonial grants have not survived. The most complete record of colonial Georgia land grants between 1758 and 1776 is Mary B. Warren's multi-volume *Georgia Land Owners' Memorials, 1758–1776* (Danielsville, Ga.: Heritage Papers, 1988). The most extensive information on colonial Georgia land grantees is in Mary B. Warren, *Georgia Governor and Council Journals* (4 vols., Athens, Ga.: Heritage Papers, 1991-2003).

The first effective legislation, dated 17 February 1783, concerning land grants after Georgia became a state provided for headrights and bounty-land grants. The law allowed each head of household 200 acres free as his own headright and fifty additional acres for each member of his family and each slave at a cost of one to four shillings per acre. Grants were limited to 1,000 acres, and the grantee was responsible for paying survey and grant fees. Those who had received grants under colonial jurisdiction were entitled to the lands they occupied when the law went into effect.

The 1783 act also provided for establishing a land court in each county; however, except for Wilkes County, almost none of the county land court minutes survive. A land grant applicant would appear before five justices to swear under oath concerning the size of his family and the number of slaves he owned to obtain a warrant of survey. Once the county surveyor completed his layout of the applicant's land, a copy of the plat of survey was forwarded to the surveyor general, and the original was filed in the county. The applicant was then required to live on the land for a year and cultivate three percent of the total acreage. After meeting those requirements, the applicant could apply to the governor's office for his grant and pay all fees. At that point the grant would be issued and recorded. Headright grants were made in Bryan, Bullock, Burke, Camden, Chatham, Clarke, Columbia, Effingham, Elbert, Emanuel, Franklin, Glascock, Glynn, Greene, Hancock, Hart, Jackson, Jefferson, Johnson, Laurens, Liberty, Lincoln, Madison, McDuffie, McIntosh, Montgomery, Oconee, Oglethorpe, Richmond, Screven, Taliaferro, Tattnall, Warren, Washington, and Wilkes counties.

Bounty-land grants were made to soldiers who served in the Georgia military, civilian residents of 1781 and 1782, and Georgia citizens who went to other states during the Revolution to continue the war ("refugees"). Most of the surviving Georgia

Revolutionary War bounty certificates (except for civilian residents) are abstracted (see Hemperley, *Military Certificates* under Military Records).

A second act of 25 February 1784 created new counties and designated some of the area as bounty lands for Georgia veterans who had served in the Continental Line or Navy. Most of the area that later became Greene County was reserved for bounty-land grants. See Silas Emmett Lucas, Jr., *Index to the Headright and Bounty Grants of Georgia, 1756–1909* (Vidalia, Ga.: Georgia Genealogical Reprints, 1970). The Georgia Archives and the FHL have microfilm copies of original land grants and plats.

Georgia has the unique distinction of distributing lands by lottery. Lands given to Georgia citizens by lotteries from 1805 to 1833 are in the present western and northern three-quarters of Georgia. Lotteries took place in 1805, 1807, 1820, 1821, 1827, 1833, and two in 1832. All Georgia citizens were eligible to qualify for a lottery, although the 1820, 1827, and 1832 lotteries also gave special consideration to war veterans. Published lottery books are excellent sources for pinpointing where a Georgia family lived when a lottery was held. For more information on the Georgia land lotteries, consult the following works:

Davis, Robert. *The 1833 Land Lottery of Georgia and Other Missing Names of Winners in the Georgia Land Lotteries.* Greenville, S.C.: Southern Historical Press, 1991.

Davis, Robert S., and Silas E. Lucas. *The Georgia Land Lottery Papers, 1805–1914.* Easley, S.C.: Southern Historical Press, 1979.

Houstun, Martha Lou. *Reprint of Official Register of the Land Lottery of Georgia, 1827.* Baltimore: Genealogical Publishing Co., 1967.

Lucas, Silas E. *The 1807 Land Lottery of Georgia.* Easley, S.C.: Southern Historical Press, 1973.

———. *The 1821 Land Lottery of Georgia.* Easley, S.C.: Southern Historical Press, 1986.

———. *The 1832 Gold Lottery of Georgia: Containing a List of the Fortunate Drawers in Said Lottery.* Easley, S.C.: Southern Historical Press, 1986.

Smith, James F. *The Cherokee Land Lottery..., 1838.* Reprint. Vidalia, Ga.: Georgia Genealogical Reprints, 1968.

Wood, Virginia S. and Ralph V. Wood. *1805 Land Lottery of Georgia.* Cambridge, Mass.: Greenwood Press, 1964. Contains the names of all registrants; the other lottery lists give only the names of winners.

In cases where Georgians sold lots won in the lotteries, researchers will find that deeds may be valuable sources of genealogical information. Those deeds should have been recorded in the counties where the land was located. Land transactions between private individuals are recorded with the clerk of superior court in the appropriate county.

Most surviving pre-1900 county land records, including deeds and land court minutes, are on microfilm at the Georgia Archives and the FHL. Many of the mortgage and county plat books in the individual courthouse have never been microfilmed.

Probate Records

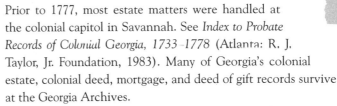

Prior to 1777, most estate matters were handled at the colonial capitol in Savannah. See *Index to Probate Records of Colonial Georgia, 1733–1778* (Atlanta: R. J. Taylor, Jr. Foundation, 1983). Many of Georgia's colonial estate, colonial deed, mortgage, and deed of gift records survive at the Georgia Archives.

County ordinary courts kept probate records from 1777 to 1798 and began keeping them again in 1852. County inferior courts were responsible for probate matters from 1798 to 1868. Almost all pre-1900 county probate records are on microfilm at the Georgia Archives and the FHL. The archives also has many loose, original Georgia county records. Ted O. Brooke, *In the Name of God, Amen, Georgia Wills, 1733–1860: An Index to Testator Wills* (Atlanta: Pilgrim Press, 1976) is an index to Georgia wills.

Court Records

Unfortunately, few colonial Georgia court records survive. Georgia's state constitution provided for two county level courts to be created in 1777. Superior courts were established at the county level to hear cases dealing with divorce, civil, and criminal charges, naturalization, military discharges, homesteads, prisons, and slaves. Simultaneously, courts of ordinary were created to hear and record cases involving probate matters. It also dealt with indentures, minor debt, paupers, licenses, voting, and marriage. Each court kept minutes, which are useful in genealogical research.

Inferior courts were created in 1798 and were responsible for probate matters (until 1852), civil matters, and misdemeanor type civil and criminal cases. Georgia's state supreme court began in 1846, and the case files and records of this court are in the Georgia Archives. The decisions of that court are published annually in the *Georgia Reports*. With the exception of only the most recent records, the federal district and circuit court records for Georgia are at the National Archives—Southeast Region (see page 12).

Georgia's state prison and asylum records are housed at the Georgia Archives. These records are open to researchers when over seventy-five years have passed from the date of their creation. The earliest Georgia prison and asylum records are used in Robert S. Davis Jr.'s two-volume *Georgia Black Book* (Easley, S.C.: Southern Historical Press, 1982).

The FHL has a broad collection of records of Georgia's courts at the county level, as well as the U.S. Circuit Court, District of Georgia.

Tax Records

None of Georgia's colonial tax records have survived. Surviving Georgia tax records begin on a county basis in the late 1780s. By 1783 Georgia tax laws provided for taxing land according to its quality and quantity, and male polls were white males over twenty-one. Other taxes were imposed on town lots, slaves, and free persons of color, buildings and improvements, merchandise, lawyers, and doctors. The poll tax on all adult males has resulted in tax digests, which serve as census substitutes and supplements.

The R. J. Taylor Jr. Foundation in Atlanta has selected and indexed some tax digests for the years 1789–1819. Tax records no longer exist for every county, and others were omitted from the foundation's publications, which makes the title misleading. See *An Index to Georgia Tax Digests, 1789–1819*, 5 vols. (Spartanburg, S.C.: Reprint Co., 1986) and Ruth Blair, *Some Early Tax Digests of Georgia* (1926; reprint, Easley, S.C.: Southern Historical Press, 1971).

Federal direct tax records for Georgia and the southeastern United States for 1865 to 1873 are at the National Archives—Southeast Region (see page 12). The years 1865 to 1866 are on microfilm.

Cemetery Records

The Daughters of the American Revolution (DAR) and others have compiled and published volumes of cemetery records, but no statewide collection has been prepared to date. Publications from the DAR include Bible, court, and probate records in addition to cemetery inscriptions. Consult holdings of the Georgia Archives, DAR Library (see page 13), and the FHL for major collections of published tombstone inscriptions. Other public and private libraries may have smaller collections.

A statewide bibliography of Georgia cemetery records through 1985 is Ted O. Brooke, *Georgia Cemetery Directory and Bibliography* (Marietta, Ga.: the author, 1985) and Davis and Brooke, *Georgia Research* (see Background Sources).

Church Records

Few of Georgia's major religious groups maintained records rich in genealogical information. However, their historical records can provide a deeper understanding of religious life in earlier times and when listed on church membership rolls will document someone's residence.

Georgia's major religious denominations include the following: Baptists (Georgia Baptist Historical Collection, Jack Tarver Library, Mercer University, Macon, GA 31207); Methodists (United Methodist Museum, P.O. Box 408, St. Simons Island, GA 31522); and Roman Catholics (Savannah and Diocesan Archives, 302 E. Liberty St., P.O. Box 8789, Savannah, GA 31402). Other early denominations present in Georgia in fewer numbers include Lutherans, Presbyterians, Episcopalians, and Congregationalists. While their respective repositories house historical records, the Georgia Archives has a good collection of church records on microfilm. Surviving records of Georgia's Wrightsborough Quaker community (located in present-day McDuffie County) for 1767 to 1805 are in the Friends Historical Collection, Guilford College Library, Guilford, North Carolina, and have been published verbatim in Robert S. Davis Jr., *Quaker Records in Georgia* (Augusta, Ga.: Augusta Genealogical Society, 1986). Consult the holdings of other major genealogical libraries with southern collections for additional church sources, including the FHL.

Military Records

Colonial. Georgia was founded to serve as a bulwark against the Spanish and French in the lands beyond the Carolinas, and as such, its men were called into service frequently during the colonial period. Unfortunately, few informative records remain to tell who was involved in what conflict. Murtie June Clark, *Colonial Soldiers of the South, 1732–1774* (Baltimore: Genealogical Publishing Co., 1983), lists soldiers who served prior to the Revolutionary War.

Revolutionary War. Georgia's total population in 1776 numbered less than 20,000 people, of whom perhaps 3,500 men were eligible for military service when the Revolution began. Many of Georgia's soldiers were recruited from the Carolinas and Virginia; many were neutral or fought for the king. With some of the original service records for the Revolutionary War having been destroyed, it is doubtful that a comprehensive list of Georgia veterans of this war exists. Georgia Revolutionary War rolls at the National Archives are published with other records in Robert S. Davis Jr., *Georgia Citizens and Soldiers of the Revolution* (Easley, S.C.: Southern Historical Press, 1979). See also Allen D. Candler, *The Revolutionary Records of the State of Georgia*, 3 vols. (Atlanta: State Printer, 1906) and Mary B. Warren, *Revolutionary Memoirs and Muster Rolls* (Athens, Ga.: Heritage Papers, 1994). Abstracts of lost Revolutionary War pension records are included, along with some files from wars as late as 1848, in National Archives microfilm M1746 Final Revolutionary War Pension Vouchers: Georgia, and in related National Archives records.

Bounty-land warrants were issued to soldiers who served in the Georgia military, civilian residents of 1781 and 1782, and Georgia citizens who went to other states during the Revolution

to continue the war. After the war, soldiers who served in the Continental Line and others applied for a warrant and, when approved, received a certificate to be exchanged for a warrant. The land to be issued was in Georgia. See Marion R. Hemperley, *Military Certificates of Georgia, 1776–1800* (Atlanta: Georgia Surveyor General Department, 1983) and Mary B. Warren, *Georgia's Revolutionary War Bounty Land Records* (Athens, Ga.: Heritage Papers, 1992). The original records are in the Georgia Archives.

Indian Wars (1784–1811, 1815–38); Mexican War (1845–48). Georgia supplied thousands of soldiers for various federal campaigns. The tens of thousands of genealogically significant bounty and pension files are in the National Archives (see page 11). Louise F. Hays, comp., *Georgia Military Affairs, 1775–1842*, 9 vols. (n.p., 1940), includes indexed, unpublished typescripts from the Georgia Archives that cover the broader period beyond the Revolution. This collection is an excellent people-finder and census substitute and supplement. Gordon B. Smith has begun the publication of an ongoing series of histories of the Georgia militia that includes biographical information on thousands of Georgians associated with the state's early military.

War of 1812. Information included in service records for the War of 1812 is similar to that in the same records of soldiers in the colonial wars and Revolutionary War. See also Judy Kratovil, *An Index to War of 1812 Service Records for Volunteer Soldiers of Georgia* (Atlanta: the author, 1986). The National Archives records (see page 11) from which Kratovil's book is taken represents roughly one-fifth of the males of military age in Georgia during the War of 1812.

Civil War. While the original Georgia pension records for resident Confederate veterans and widows of veterans are at the Georgia Archives, microfilm copies are at the FHL. See also *The Georgia Commissary General's Record of Families Supplied with Salt 1862–1864* (CD-ROM computer disk; Atlanta: Georgia Genealogical Society, 2002) and Lillian Henderson, *Roster of the Confederate Soldiers of Georgia, 1861–1865*, 7 vols. (Hapeville, Ga.: Longino and Porter, 1960–64), which does not include Georgia's cavalry, artillery, legions, militia, state troops, and confederate non-state units. Georgians also served in the Union Army, principally in Tennessee units.

The Georgia Archives has extensive state records relating to the Civil War including militia rolls, salt lists, and veterans censuses, to name only a few sources. The most valuable to researchers is an "Alphabetical Index" to Georgia Confederate records on microfilm at the Georgia Archives. See Nancy Cornell, *1864 Census for Re-Organizing the Georgia Militia* (Baltimore: Genealogical Publishing Co., 2000).

Later Wars. Some military records for Georgia after the Civil War are in the Georgia Archives as original records or as microfilm copies. Included are rosters of the Spanish American War, the Philippine Insurrection, and the Poncho Villa Campaign.

The state archives also has microfilm of many county copies of service records for World War I, World War II, the Korean War, and the Vietnam War. The National Archives—Southeast Branch (see page 12) has World War I draft registration records. Service records and photographs of Georgians who died in World War I were published in Bert E. Boss, *Georgia Memorial Book* (Macon: Georgia Memorial Association, 1921).

Periodicals, Newspapers, and Manuscript Collections

Periodicals

Two historical periodicals include *Georgia Historical Quarterly*, published by the Georgia Historical Society, and *Atlanta History: A Journal of Georgia and the South*, published by the Atlanta Historical Society, which has also published general indexes.

A host of periodicals regarding Georgia genealogy is currently being published, including *Georgia Genealogical Society Quarterly* (Atlanta: Georgia Genealogical Society, 1964-present). The Georgia Genealogical Society will soon issue the past issues of its quarterly in a word-searchable CD-ROM disk. The Georgia Archives and the FHL have copies of these periodicals and others.

Newspapers

The Georgia Archives and the University of Georgia Libraries in Athens have the largest newspaper collections. Other university, public, and genealogical libraries have smaller collections. Consult holdings for titles.

The *Georgia Newspaper Project* of the University of Georgia Libraries has to date microfilmed over 8,000 reels of Georgia newspapers. This collection is not available on interlibrary loan, but copies can be purchased. The FHL, Georgia Historical Society in Savannah, the Georgia Archives, and the University of Georgia Libraries in Athens have extensive indexes to the Savannah newspapers (1763–1845). Savannah newspapers (1850–98) are abstracted and indexed in a Works Projects Administration (WPA) publication called *Annals of Savannah*. Indexes have also been published for early Augusta and Milledgeville newspapers. Many other Georgia newspapers have published and indexed abstracts to marriage and death notices. A statewide reference is Mary B. Warren, *Marriages and Deaths from Extant Georgia Newspapers*, 2 vols. (Danielsville, Ga.: Heritage Papers, 1968 and 1972), covering 1763 to 1829. Tad Evans and Elizabeth Evans Kilbourne have published more than 100 volumes of abstracts of Georgia newspapers.

Manuscripts

Georgia has more than 100 manuscript repositories, many of which have excellent local sources. See Robert H. Warnock,

Georgia Sources for Family History (Atlanta: Georgia Genealogical Society, 1995).

The Hargrett Rare Book and Manuscripts Library of the University of Georgia Libraries in Athens and the Georgia Historical Society in Savannah have Georgia's most extensive manuscript collections.

Leon S. Hollingsworth's genealogical card file was microfilmed by the R. J. Taylor Jr. Foundation in 1978. Recently refilmed, the 45,000 three-by-five cards in this collection reference people from thousands of original source records in Georgia. Notations include an abstract of the information and citation of the original source. The collection is both a name file and place-name index. The collection is available at the FHL and for purchase from Reprint Co., Box 4501, Spartanburg, SC 29304. Hollingsworth's research files are only available for use by researchers at the Georgia Archives. The Hargrett Rare Book and Manuscripts Library of the University of Georgia has the similar, but much earlier, James A. LeConte Genealogical Collection on microfilm.

Archives, Libraries, and Societies

The Georgia State Division of Archives and History (The Georgia Archives)
5800 Jonesboro Rd.
Morrow, GA 30260
www.georgiaarchives.org

Official repository for permanent records created as a function of state government, the archives operates a Central Research Room that makes its holdings available to the public. Extremely limited and specific mail requests are answered by mail for a fee.

Georgia Genealogical Society
P.O. Box 38066
Atlanta, GA 30334
www.gagensociety.org

The society publishes *Georgia Genealogical Society Quarterly*.

Georgia Historical Society and Library
501 Whittaker St.
Savannah, GA 31499
www.georgiahistory.com

The oldest collection of private manuscripts is a feature of its library. It publishes the *Georgia Historical Quarterly*.

Atlanta History Center
James G. Kenan Research Ctr.
130 West Paces Ferry Rd. NW
Atlanta, GA 30305-1366
www.atlhist.org

The society maintains a library on Atlanta history and publishes a periodical entitled *Atlanta History* (see Periodicals). It and the Georgia Archives have copies of the selective records for tens of thousands of deceased white Atlantans (1840s–1920) compiled by the late Franklin Garrett. Mail requests are answered.

Atlanta Public Library
1 Margaret Mitchell Sq.
Atlanta, GA 30303
www.atlantic.lib.ia.us

Its Special Collections has separate card catalogs to biographical sketches of Georgians and to biographical sketches of prominent African Americans.

Georgia Salzburger Society
2980 Ebenezer Rd.
Rincon, GA 31326
www.georgiasalzburgers.com

The society publishes *Georgia Salzburger Society Newsletter*.

Special Focus Categories

Immigration

Savannah, Georgia, served as one of the nation's southern immigration ports. Passenger lists of immigrants arriving at Savannah are available (however, they are sketchy during early years) on federal microfilm M575, *Passengers Arriving at Miscellaneous Ports on the Atlantic and Gulf Coasts*, at the National Archives and the FHL.

British merchant claims, published over many years in *Virginia Genealogist* and *The North Carolina Genealogical Society Journal*, respectively, document the migration of thousands of families to Georgia before 1810. Georgia governors issued passports of good character for families passing through the Indian lands for the West prior to 1820. These passports are abstracted in Dorothy Williams Potter, *Passports of Southeastern Pioneers, 1770–1823* (Baltimore: Gateway Press, 1982). See also Marion R. Hemperley, "Savannah Federal Naturalization Oaths, 1790–1860," *Georgia Historical Quarterly* 51 (1967): 454-87; and Linda Woodward Geiger and Meyer L. Frankel, *Index to Georgia's Federal Naturalization Records to 1950, Excluding Military Petitions* (Atlanta: Georgia Genealogical Society, 1996).

Native American

The majority of Georgia's Native American population consisted of Cherokees and Creeks, both of whom were removed from the area to the west onto land that would become the Indian and Oklahoma territories before Oklahoma statehood. Some remaining Creeks removed themselves to land in Alabama. While the history of Georgia's native population differs from that

GEORGIA

of North Carolina, the records in which they are documented are similar. See the Native American section under North Carolina for a complete discussion of available records and their whereabouts. Early federal records of Cherokees are more extensive for Georgia than any other eastern state. These records are in the National Archives in Washington, D.C. The Georgia Archives has indexed unpublished typescripts of state records concerning the Creeks and Cherokees, including information on their white relations.

See Robert S. Davis Jr., *A Guide to Native American (Indian) Research Sources at the Georgia Department of Archives and History* (Jasper, Ga.: the author, 1985).

African American

The Georgia Archives has lists of free persons of color, marriages, slave lists, imported slave lists, apprenticeship bonds, trial dockets, lists of slave owners, cemetery records, church records, bills of sale, deeds transferring slaves, plantation records, and other miscellaneous records. Not every Georgia county created or preserved each type of record listed above. In fact, the number of local records attesting to a specific slave is minuscule when compared to those available for free persons. Many such sources are described in Davis and Brooke, *Georgia Research*, 84-86 (see Background Sources).

In 1940 the Federal Writers' Project produced *Drums and Shadows: Surviving Studies Among the Georgia Coastal Negroes* (Westport, Conn.: Greenwood Press, 1973), which covers the social history of a specific group of African Americans in Georgia's history. For statewide information on narratives of former slaves, see Howard E. Potts, *A Comprehensive Name Index for the American Slave* (Westport, Conn.: Greenwood Press, 1997).

The National Archives has federal census schedules, military records, Freedmen's Bureau, and related records (see pages 14-15). The National Archives will soon have available on microfilm records of the post Civil War Georgia offices of the Freedman's Bureau. The FHL has some federal records pertaining to former slaves and sells a CD-ROM of the extensive personal information on depositors in the Freedman's bank, which had offices in Atlanta, Augusta, and Savannah. Each of the guidebooks noted in Background Sources discusses federal records as they pertain to African American research.

County Resources

Counties were not formed in Georgia until 1777, covering at that time only a portion of Georgia's present jurisdiction. Eventually, as Native American land was acquired, new counties were created. Land records were then recorded with the clerk of the superior court in each county. Probate records were recorded with the clerk of the ordinary court, as were marriages. Most civil court cases were handled completely by the superior court.

Each county office was contacted in order to verify record dates and county addresses. This information can also be found in Davis's *Research in Georgia* (see Background Sources).

The Georgia Archives has nearly all of the state's pre-1900, bound, county records on microfilm and has several collections of loose, original records.

GEORGIA

The Counties and County Seats of
Georgia
25   0   25   50   75 Miles

Map	County Address	Date Formed Parent County/ies	Birth Marriage Death	Land Probate Court
G6	Appling 83 S. Oak St., Ste. A Baxley 31513-0076	1818 Creek lands	——— 1869 ———	1828 1879 1879
H5	Atkinson P.O. Box 518 Pearson 31642	1917 Coffee/Clinch	1929 1919 1929	1919 1919 1919
G6	Bacon P.O. Box 356 Alma 31510	1914 Appling/Ware/Pearce	1915 1919 1915	1919 1919 1919
H2	Baker P.O. Box 607 Newton 31770	1825 Early	——— 1820 ———	1850 1868 1879
D4	Baldwin 121 N. Wilkinson St. Milledgeville 31061	1803 Creek lands/Hancock	——— 1806 ———	1861 1808 1861
B4	Banks P.O. Box 130 Homer 30547	1858 Franklin/Habersham	——— 1859 ———	1859 1859 1859
B4	Barrow 233 E. Broad St. Winder 30680	1914 Jackson/Walton/Gwinnett	1915 1915 1915	1915 1915 1915
B2	Bartow 135 W. Cherokee Ave. Cartersville 30120	1832 (as Cass; renamed 1861) Cherokee	——— 1836 ———	1837 1853 1853
G4	Ben Hill 402-A East Pine St. Fitzgerald 31750	1906 Irwin/Wilcox	——— 1906 ———	1906 1906 1906
H5	Berrien P.O. Box 446 Nashville 31639	1856 Lowndes/Irwin/Coffee	1919 1856 1919	1850 1855 1856
E4	Bibb 601 Mulberry St. Macon 31201	1822 Jones/Monroe/ Twiggs/Houston	——— 1823 ———	1823 1823 1823
F4	Bleckley 306 Second St., SE Cochran 31014	1912 Pulaski	1919 1912 1919	1912 1912 1912
H7	Brantley P.O. Box 398 Nahunta 31553	1920 Charlton/Pierce/Wayne	1921 1921 1921	1921 1921 1921
J4	Brooks P.O. Box 272 Quitman 31643	1858 Lowndes/Thomas	——— 1859 ———	1857 1859 1859
F7	Bryan P.O. Box 430 Pembroke 31321 *Fragmented records.*	1793 Chatham (enlarged with part of Effingham, 1794)	——— 1865 ———	1793 1790s 1794
F7	Bulloch P.O. Box 347 Statesboro 30459	1796 Bryan/Screven	——— 1796 ———	1796 1816 1806
D7	Burke P.O. Box 89 Waynesboro 30830	1777 St. George Parish	1927 1855 1927	1843 1856 1056
D3	Butts 25 Third St. Jackson 30233	1825 Henry/Monroe	——— 1826 ———	1825 1826 1826
H2	Calhoun 111 School St./P.O. Box 111 Morgan 31766	1854 Baker/Early	1928 1854 1928	1854 1854 1854
J7	Camden P.O. Box 599 Woodbine 31569	1777 St. Mary/ St. Thomas parishes	——— 1819 ———	1773 1795 1790
	Campbell	1828 (became part of Fulton, 1932) Carroll/Coweta/ DeKalb/Fayette	1919 1829 1919	1829 1829 1829
F7	Candler 705 N. Lewis St. Metter 30439	1914 Bulloch/Emanuel/Tattnall	1919 1915 1919	1915 1915 1915
C1	Carroll P.O. Box 338 Carrollton 30112	1826 Indian lands	1919 1827 1919	1827 1827 1827
	Cass	1832 (renamed Bartow, 1861)		
A1	Catoosa 7694 Nashville St. Ringgold 30736	1853 Walker/Whitfield	1853 1853 ———	1853 1853 1853
J7	Charlton 100 3rd St. Folkston 31537	1854 Camden/Ware	——— 1854 ———	1878 1878 1879
F8	Chatham P.O. Box 8161 Savannah 31401	1777 Christ Church Parish	——— 1806 ———	1785 1777 1783
F2	Chattahoochee P.O. Box 299 Cusseta 31805	1854 Muscogee/Marion	——— 1854 ———	1854 1854 1854
A1	Chattooga P.O. Box 211 Summerville 30747	1838 Floyd/Walker	——— 1839 ———	1839 1839 1839
B2	Cherokee 90 North St. Canton 30114	1831 Cherokee lands	——— 1841 ———	1833 1833 1832
B4	Clarke 300 E. Washington St. Athens 30601	1801 Jackson	——— 1801 ———	1801 1801 1801
H1	Clay 105 N. Washington St. Fort Gaines 31751	1854 Early/Randolph	——— 1854 ———	1854 1854 1854

Map	County Address	Date Formed Parent County/ies	Birth Marriage Death	Land Probate Court
C3	Clayton 9151 Tara Blvd. Jonesboro 30236	1858 Fayette/Henry	—— 1859 ——	1859 1859 1859
J6	Clinch 100 Court Sq. Homerville 31634	1850 Ware/Lowndes	1919 1867 1919	1868 1867 1868
C2	Cobb 100 Cherokee St. Marietta 30060 *Some earlier records survive.*	1832 Cherokee	—— 1865 ——	1865 1865 1865
H5	Coffee 101 S. Peterson Ave. Douglas 31533	1854 Clinch/Irwin/ Ware/Telfair	—— 1854 ——	1854 1854 1854
H4	Colquitt P.O. Box 517 Moultrie 31776	1856 Lowndes/Thomas	—— 1881 ——	1881 1881 1881
C6	Columbia P.O Box 498 Martinez 30909	1790 Richmond	—— 1787 ——	1790 1790 1790
H4	Cook 209 N. Parrish Ave. Adel 31620	1918 Berrien	1919 1919 1919	1919 1919 1919
D2	Coweta 22 E. Broad St. Newnan 30264	1826 Indian lands	1919 1828 1919	1827 1828 1828
E3	Crawford P.O. Box 1059 Roberts 31078	1822 Houston	—— 1823 ——	1830 1830 1830
G4	Crisp 210 Seventh St. South Cordele 31015	1905 Dooly	—— —— ——	1905 1905 1905
A1	Dade P.O. Box 613 Trenton 30752 *Fragmented records.*	1837 Walker	—— 1866 ——	1849 1853 1854
A3	Dawson 86 Hwy. 53 West Dawsonville 30534	1857 Lumpkin/Gilmer	1858 1858 1858	1858 1858 1858
J2	Decatur P.O. Box 735 Bainbridge 31717	1823 Early	—— 1824 ——	1823 1823 1823
C3	DeKalb 1300 Commerce Dr. Decatur 30030	1822 Henry/Fayette/Gwinnett	—— 1842 ——	1842 1842 1842
F5	Dodge P.O. Box 818 Eastman 31023	1870 Montgomery/Telfair/ Pulaski	—— 1871 ——	1871 1871 1871
F4	Dooly P.O. Box 348 Vienna 31092	1821 Indian lands	—— 1846 ——	1847 1847 1847
H3	Dougherty 225 Pine Ave./P.O. Box 1827 Albany 31702	1852 Baker	—— 1854 ——	1854 1849 1854
C2	Douglas 8700 Hospital Dr. Douglasville 30134	1870 Carroll/Campbell	—— 1871 ——	1871 1871 1871
H2	Early P.O. Box 693 Blakely 31723	1818 Creek lands	—— 1820 ——	1821 1824 1820
J5	Echols P.O. Box 190 Statenville 31648 *Fragmented records.*	1858 Clinch/Lowndes	—— 1898 ——	1897 1897 1898
F8	Effingham P.O. Box 307 Springfield 31329 *Fragmented records.*	1777 St. Mathews/ St. Phillips parishes	1927 1791 1927	1786 1796 1791
B5	Elbert 10 W. Church St. Elberton 30635	1790 Wilkes	—— 1791 ——	1791 1791 1791
E6	Emanuel P.O. Box 787 Swainsboro 30401	1812 Montgomery/Bulloch	—— 1812 ——	1812 1812 1810
F7	Evans 3 Freeman St. Claxton 30417	1914 Bulloch/Tattnall	1915 1915 1915	1915 1915 1915
A2	Fannin 420 W. Main St. Blue Ridge 30513	1854 Gilmer/Union	—— 1854 ——	1854 1854 1854
D2	Fayette 140 Stonewall Ave. West Fayetteville 30214	1812 Indian lands/Henry	—— 1823 ——	1823 1823 1823
B1	Floyd 201 5th Ave. Rome 30161	1832 Cherokee	—— 1834 ——	1840 1837 1840
B3	Forsyth 110 E. Main St. Cumming 30130	1832 Cherokee	—— 1833 ——	1832 1832 1832
A4	Franklin P.O. Box 159 Carnesville 30521	1784 Cherokee lands	—— 1806 ——	1786 1786 1798
C2	Fulton 141 Pryon St., SW, 10th Floor Atlanta 30301	1853 Dekalb	—— 1854 ——	1854 1854 1854
A2	Gilmer 27 Dalton St. Ellijay 30540	1832 Cherokee	—— 1836 ——	1833 1833 1833
D6	Glascock P.O. Box 66 Gibson 30810	1857 Warren	—— 1858 ——	1858 1858 1858

Map	County Address	Date Formed Parent County/ies	Birth Marriage Death	Land Probate Court
H8	**Glynn** 1803 Gloucester St., Rm 114 Brunswick 31520 *Fragment, damaged records.*	1777 St. David Parish/ St. Patrick Parish	—— 1818	1787 1792 1810
A2	**Gordon** P.O. Box 580 Calhoun 30713	1850 Bartow/Floyd	—— 1864 ——	1850 1856 1850
J3	**Grady** 250 N. Broad St. Cairo 31728	1905 Decatur/Thomas	—— 1906 ——	1906 1906 1906
C5	**Greene** 113 N. Main St. Greensboro 30642	1786 Washington	—— 1805 ——	1785 1785 1785
B3	**Gwinnett** 75 Langley Dr. Lawrenceville 30245 *Fragmented records.*	1818 Cherokee lands/ Jackson	—— 1871 ——	1871 1818 1858
A4	**Habersham** 555 Monroe St. Clarkesville 30523	1818 Cherokee lands/Franklin	—— 1824 ——	1819 1819 1819
B3	**Hall** 711 Green St. Gainesville 30503 *Fragmented records.*	1818 Cherokee lands/ Jackson/Franklin	—— 1819 ——	1819 1819 1819
D5	**Hancock** Sparta 31087	1793 Greene/Washington	—— 1806 ——	1794 1794 1794
C1	**Haralson** P.O. Box 489 Buchanan 30113 *Fragmented records.*	1856 Carroll/Polk	—— 1865 ——	1856 1856 1856
E2	**Harris** P.O. Box 365 Hamilton 31811	1827 Muscogee/Troup	—— 1828 ——	1828 1828 1828
B5	**Hart** P.O. Box 279 Hartwell 30643	1853 Elbert/Franklin	—— 1854 ——	1856 1854 1854
D1	**Heard** P.O. Box 40 Franklin 30217	1830 Carroll/Coweta/Troup	1927 1886 1927	1894 1894 1894
D3	**Henry** 140 Henry Pkwy McDonough 30253	1821 Indian lands	—— 1822 ——	1822 1822 1822
F4	**Houston** 201 Perry Pkwy Perry 31069	1821 Indian lands	—— 1822 ——	1822 1822 1822
G5	**Irwin** 207 S. Irwin Ave., Ste. 1 Ocilla 31774	1818 Indian lands	—— 1838 ——	1821 1821 1820

Map	County Address	Date Formed Parent County/ies	Birth Marriage Death	Land Probate Court
B4	**Jackson** 67 Athens St. Jefferson 30549	1796 Franklin	—— 1805 ——	1796 1796 1796
D4	**Jasper** Monticello 31064	1808 (as Randolph (old); renamed 1812) Baldwin	—— 1808 ——	1808 1809 1808
G6	**Jeff Davis** P.O. Box 602 Hazlehurst 31539	1905 Appling/Coffee	—— 1905 ——	1905 1905 1905
D6	**Jefferson** P.O. Box 658 Louisville 30434	1796 Burke/Warren	—— 1803 ——	1865 1796 1796
E7	**Jenkins** P.O. Box 797 Millen 30442	1905 Bullock/Burke/ Emanuel/Screven	—— 1905 ——	1905 1905 1905
E5	**Johnson** P.O. Box 269 Wrightsville 31096	1858 Emanuel/Laurens/ Washington	—— 1859 ——	1859 1859 1859
D4	**Jones** P.O. Box 1359 Gray 31032	1807 Baldwin	—— 1811 ——	1808 1808 1808
D3	**Lamar** 326 Thomaston St. Barnesville 30204	1920 Monroe/Pike	1921 1921 1921	1921 1921 1921
J5	**Lanier** 100 Main St. Lakeland 31635	1919 Berrien/Lowndes/ Clinch	1921 1921 1921	1921 1921 1921
F5	**Laurens** P.O. Box 2011 Dublin 31040 *Fragmented records.*	1807 Montgomery/ Washington/ Wilkinson	—— 1809 ——	1807 1808 1808
G3	**Lee** P.O. Box 889 Leesburg 31763	1826 Indian lands	—— 1867 ——	1858 1858 1858
G8	**Liberty** P.O. Box 829 Hinesville 31310 *Fragmented records.*	1777 St. Andrew Parish/ St. James Parish/ St. Johns Parish	—— ? ——	1784 1786 1784
C6	**Lincoln** P.O. Box 340 Lincolnton 30817	1796 Wilkes	—— 1796 ——	1796 1796 1796
G7	**Long** P.O. Box 476 Ludowici 31316	1920 Liberty	1920 1920 1920	1920 1920 1920
J5	**Lowndes** P.O. Box 1349 Valdosta 31603	1825 Irwin	—— 1870 ——	1858 1862 1862
A3	**Lumpkin** 99 Courthouse Hill Dahlonega 30533	1832 Cherokee/Habersham/Hall	—— 1833 ——	1833 1833 1833

Map	County Address	Date Formed Parent County/ies	Birth Marriage Death	Land Probate Court
F3	Macon, P.O. Box 297, Oglethorpe 31068	1837 Houston/Marion	—, 1858, —	1857, 1857, 1856
B4	Madison, P.O. Box 147, Danielsville 30633	1811 Clarke/Elbert/Franklin/Jackson/Oglethorpe	—, 1812, —	1812, 1811, 1812
F2	Marion, P.O. Box 481, Buena Vista 31803	1827 Lee/Muscogee/Stewart	—, 1846, —	1846, 1842, 1846
C6	McDuffie, P.O. Box 28, Thomson 30824	1870 Columbia/Warren	—, 1871, —	1871, 1871, 1871
H8	McIntosh, P.O. Box 584, Darien 31305	1793 Liberty	—, 1873, —	1873, 1873, 1873
E2	Meriwether, P.O. Box 428, Greenville 30222	1827 Troup	—, 1828, —	1827, 1825, 1828
H2	Miller, 155 S. 1st St., Colquitt 31737	1856 Baker/Early	—, 1893, —	1873, 1873, 1873
	Milton	1857 (became part of Fulton, 1932) Cobb/Cherokee/Forsyth	—, 1867, —	1858, 1868, 1858
H3	Mitchell, P.O. Box 187, Camilla 31730	1857 Baker	—, 1867, —	1858, 1868, 1858
D3	Monroe, P.O. Box 189, Forsyth 31029	1821 Indian lands	—, 1824, —	1822, 1824, 1824
F6	Montgomery, P.O. Box 295, Mount Vernon 30445	1793 Telfair/Washington	1918, 1807, 1918	1793, 1794, 1794
C4	Morgan, P.O. Box 168, Madison 30650	1807 Baldwin	—, 1808, —	1807, 1808, 1808
A2	Murray, P.O. Box 1129, Chatsworth 30705	1832 Cherokee	1924, 1842, 1924	1833, 1840, 1833
F2	Muscogee, 1000 10th St., Columbus 31901	1826 Creek lands	—, 1838, —	1838, 1838, 1838
C3	Newton, 1113 Usher St., Covington 30209	1821 Henry/Jasper/Walton	—, 1822, —	1822, 1822, 1822
C4	Oconee, P.O. Box 145, Watkinsville 30677	1875 Clarke	—, 1875, —	1875, 1875, 1875
C5	Oglethorpe, P.O. Box 261, Lexington 30648	1793 Wilkes	—, 1795, —	1794, 1794, 1794
B2	Paulding, 120 E. Memorial Dr., Dallas 30132	1832 Cherokee	—, 1833, —	1848, 1850, 1859
F4	Peach, P.O. Box 468, Fort Valley 31030	1924 Houston/Macon	1925, 1925, 1925	1925, 1925, 1925
A2	Pickens, 52 N. Main St., Jasper 30143	1853 Cherokee/Gilmer	1924, 1854, 1854	1854, 1854, 1854
H6	Pierce, P.O. Box 679, Blackshear 31516	1857 Appling/Ware	1926, 1875, 1924	1875, 1875, 1875
D3	Pike, P.O. Box 377, Zebulon 30295	1822 Monroe	—, 1822, —	1823, 1823, 1824
B1	Polk, P.O. Box 268, Cedartown 30125	1851 Paulding/Floyd	—, 1852, —	1852, 1852, 1852
F4	Pulaski, P.O. Box 29, Hawkinsville 31036	1808 Laurens/Wilkinson	1935, 1810, 1810	1807, 1810, 1809
D4	Putnam, 100 Jefferson St., Eatonton 31024	1807 Baldwin	1927, 1919, 1923	1806, 1808, 1807
G1	Quitman, P.O. Box 114, Georgetown 31754	1858 Randolph/Stewart	1927, 1879, 1923	1879, 1879, 1879
A4	Rabun, 25 Courthouse Sq./Box 8, Clayton 30525	1819 Cherokee lands/Habersham	—, 1820, —	1821, 1826, 1829
	Randolph (old)	1807 (renamed Jasper, 1812)		
G2	Randolph (present), P.O. Box 221, Cuthbert 31740	1828 Baker/Lee	—, 1835, —	1830, 1835, 1838
D7	Richmond, 530 Green St., Augusta 30911	1777 St. Paul Parish	—, 1785, —	1789, 1782, 1782
C3	Rockdale, 922 Court St., Conyers 30207	1870 Henry/Newton	—, 1871, —	1871, 1871, 1871
F3	Schley, P.O. Box 352, Ellaville 31806	1857 Marion/Sumter	1927, 1858, 1927	1857, 1857, 1857
E7	Screven, P.O. Box 159, Sylvania 30467	1793 Burke/Effingham	1927, 1817, 1927	1794, 1790, 1811

Map	County Address	Date Formed Parent County/ies	Birth Marriage Death	Land Probate Court
J2	Seminole P.O. Box 458 Donalsonville 31745	1920 Decatur/Early	1921 1921 1921	1921 1921 1921
D3	Spalding P.O. Box 1087 Griffin 30223	1851 Fayette/Henry/Pike	— 1852 —	1852 1852 1852
A4	Stephens P.O. Box 386 Toccoa 30577	1905 Franklin/Habersham	— 1906 —	1906 1906 1906
G2	Stewart P.O. Box 157 Lumpkin 31815	1830 Randolph	1927 1828 1927	1830 1830 1830
G3	Sumter P.O. Box 295 Americus 31709	1831 Lee	— 1831 —	1831 1831 1831
E2	Talbot P.O. Box 155 Talbotton 31827	1827 Macon/Muscogee	— 1828 —	1828 1828 1828
C5	Taliaferro P.O. Box 114 Crawfordville 30631	1825 Green/Hancock/Oglethorpe/ Warren/Wilkes	1927 1826 1920	1826 1826 1826
G7	Tattnall P.O. Box 25 Reidsville 30453	1801 Montgomery/Liberty	— 1806 —	1802 1802 1805
F3	Taylor P.O. Box 2044 Butler 31006	1852 Marion/Talbot/Macon	— 1832 —	1852 1852 1852
G5	Telfair 713 Telfair Ave. McRae 31055	1807 Wilkinson	— 1810 —	1809 1831 1810
G2	Terrell P.O. Box 525 Dawson 31742	1856 Lee/Randolph	— 1856 —	1856 1856 1856
J3	Thomas P.O. Box 920 Thomasville 31799	1825 Decatur/Irwin	— 1826 —	1826 1826 1826
H4	Tift P.O. Box 826 Tifton 31793	1905 Berrien/Irwin/Worth	1905 1905 1905	1905 1905 1905
F6	Toombs P.O. Box 112 Lyons 30436	1905 Emanuel/Tattnall Montgomery	1905 1905 1905	1905 1905 1905
A4	Towns 48 River St. Hiawassee 30546	1856 Rabun/Union	— 1856 —	1856 1856 1856
F6	Treutlen P.O. Box 88 Soperton 30457	1917 Emanuel/Montgomery	1919 1919 1919	1919 1919 1919
D1	Troup P.O. Box 1149 La Grange 30241	1826 Indian lands	— 1828 —	1827 1827 1827
G4	Turner P.O. Box 191 Ashburn 31714	1905 Dooly/Irwin/Wilcox/Worth	1906 1906 1906	1906 1906 1906
E4	Twiggs P.O. Box 202 Jeffersonville 31044	1809 Wilkinson	— 1901 —	1901 1901 1901
A3	Union 114 Courthouse St./Box 1 Blairsville 30512	1832 Cherokee	— 1833 —	1860 1851 1854
E3	Upson P.O. Box 889 Thomaston 30286	1824 Crawford/Pike	— 1825 —	1825 1825 1825
A1	Walker P.O. Box 445 LaFayette 30728	1833 Murray	— 1883 —	1883 1883 1883
	Walton (old)	1803 (abolished 1812; in North Carolina) *The area of the original Walton County in Georgia is in what is now Transylvania County, North Carolina. When the boundary between Georgia and North Carolina was fixed, Walton was abolished. At that time, the settlement was adjacent to Buncombe County, North Carolina.*		
C4	Walton (present) P.O. Box 585 Monroe 30655	1818 Cherokee lands	— 1825 —	1819 1820 1819
H6	Ware P.O. Box 1069 Waycross 31502	1824 Appling	— 1874 —	1874 1879 1874
D6	Warren P.O. Box 46 Warrenton 30828	1793 Columbia/Wilkes/ Richmond/Burke	— 1794 —	1796 1794 1794
E5	Washington P.O. Box 308 Sandersville 31082	1784 Indian lands	— 1865 —	1865 1865 1865
H7	Wayne P.O. Box 270 Jesup 31545	1803 Indian lands/Appling/ Glynn/Camden	— 1809 —	1809 1809 1809
G2	Webster P.O. Box 29 Preston 31824	1853 Stewart	— 1878 —	1860 1854 1854
H6	Wheeler 209 W. Forest Ave. Alamo 30411	1912 Montgomery	1927 1913 1927	1913 1913 1913
A4	White 59 S. Main St., Ste. A Cleveland 30528	1857 Habersham	— 1858 —	1858 1858 1858

GEORGIA

Map	County Address	Date Formed Parent County/ies	Birth Marriage Death	Land Probate Court
A2	Whitfield P.O. Box 248 Dalton 30722	1851 Murray	1927 1852 1852	1852 1852 1852
G4	Wilcox 103 N. Broad St. Abbeville 31001	1857 Dooly/Irwin/Pulaski	1919 1858 1919	1858 1858 1858
C5	Wilkes 23 E. Court St. Washington 30673	1777 Indian lands	—— 1790 ——	1777 1777 1778

Map	County Address	Date Formed Parent County/ies	Birth Marriage Death	Land Probate Court
E5	Wilkinson P.O. Box 161 Irwinton 31042 *Fragmented records.*	1803 Creek cession	—— 1854 ——	1855 1854 1855
H3	Worth 201 N. Main St. Sylvester 31791	1852 Dooly/ Irwin	—— 1854 ——	1892 1879 1879

Hawaii

DWIGHT A. RADFORD

The Hawaiian Islands were originally settled by Polynesians a thousand years before any European contact. Captain James Cook visited the Hawaiian Islands in 1778. He named the islands the Sandwich Islands after the Earl of Sandwich, then the first Lord of the British Admiralty. The native Hawaiians identified Captain Cook with their god Lono. Although most of Captain Cook's encounter with the Hawaiians was positive and friendly, his return voyage in 1779 resulted in his death at Kealakekua Bay at the hands of the natives. Cook's discovery awakened international interest in the islands.

Between 1790 and 1810, King Kamehameha I, the first Hawaiian monarch, united the islands and established political and social control. The Hawaiian monarchy ended when Queen Liliuokalanai was overthrown in 1893. During the first part of the monarchy, most of the Europeans and Americans who visited the islands were mainly crews of trading ships and whalers who stopped off for supplies on their voyages to the Orient. The primary sources of information during this time period come from the reports of the voyages. Outside the ruling class, or *alii*, very few Hawaiian names are mentioned.

Next came the Protestant missionaries who arrived from New England in 1820 and converted many native Hawaiians to Protestant Christianity. The missionaries developed a written Hawaiian language and used the printing press to create a fairly literate and educated society by the 1850s. King Kamehameha III agreed to a Western-style constitution in 1839. Roman Catholic missionaries arrived seven years later but were expelled from Hawaii by the Protestant leaders in 1831. Roman Catholics were allowed religious freedom in 1839 after a blockade of Honolulu by

the French. Mormon missionaries arrived from California in 1850 and were successful among the native Hawaiians as well as the white population. They were opposed by both the Catholics and Protestants. It was not until the arrival of Japanese immigrants in 1885 that the written history of Buddhism in Hawaii can be traced.

The huge sugar and pineapple plantations of Hawaii account for the majority of the immigration. Chinese contract laborers came as early as 1852 to work on the plantations. The Reciprocity Treaty of 1876 allowed for Hawaiian sugar to be exported to the United States duty-free. The Reciprocity Treaty led to closer ties between the Kingdom of Hawaii and the United States and eventually to annexation in 1900.

The sugar plantations recruited from many countries, due in part to local pressure against further importation of Chinese. The sugar companies recruited Portuguese in 1878, Japanese in 1884, Puerto Ricans in 1900/01, Koreans in 1903, and Filipinos in 1906.

While Hawaii was annexed to the United States in 1898, it was not formally organized as a territory until June 1900. America entered World War II as a result of the infamous bombing of Pearl Harbor on 7 December 1941. Prior to the war, Japanese-Americans had become part of the larger Hawaiian community demonstrating their patriotism. Hawaii became the fiftieth state on 21 August 1959. New immigrants arrived from Korea, the Philippines, Samoa, and Tonga. Hawaii continues to be the crossroads of the Pacific.

Of all the states in America, Hawaii is probably the most diverse. Hawaii's population is a mixture of Asian, Polynesian,

native Hawaiian, European, American, and Puerto Rican. This poses challenging problems in researching family history in Hawaii. For this reason, this chapter will include many different and diverse record sources. Although not exhaustive, it will provide the basic knowledge necessary to begin research in Hawaii.

Vital Records

Hawaii has birth and death records beginning in 1853. Prior to 1896, however, the records are incomplete. Early vital records were kept by local government authorities and clergymen. There are a few missionary reports that date back as early as 1826. They are on file at the Hawaii State Archives, the Department of Health, and the Daughters of the American Revolution Library in Honolulu at 194 Makiki Heights Dr., Honolulu, HI 96822. Many are also at the Family History Library (FHL) in Salt Lake City.

Since 1911, delayed birth certificates can be applied for in Hawaii. They often contain valuable genealogical information. The FHL has seventy microfilm rolls of delayed birth records for Hawaii. This collection contains 50,000 delayed birth records (1859–1903, with indexes for 1859–1938).

The Hawaii State Health Department has birth, marriage, and death records from 1896 to the present, although some records date back to 1853. These are located at the Office of Health Status Monitoring, Vital Records Section, P.O. Box 3378, Honolulu, HI 96801 <www.cdc.gov/nchs/howto/w2w/hawaii. htm>. Microfilm copies of birth, marriage and death records (1909–25; indexes, 1909–49) are available at the FHL.

The Hawaii State Archives collection contains records of early Hawaii marriages (1826–1929; index for 1826–1910). The FHL in Salt Lake City also has many of these records, as well as the index.

Divorce records were not registered by the State Department of Health until July 1951. Copies of these can be obtained by writing this office. Earlier divorce records were recorded by the circuit court in the county where the divorce was granted. A collection of divorce records from 1849 to circa 1899 is on file at the Hawaii State Archives. These are records from the five circuit courts that have been microfilmed by the Genealogical Society of Utah and are available through the FHL.

For a summary of vital records in Hawaii, see Charles G. Bennett's article "Vital Records in Hawaii," *Hawaii Medical Journal* 15 (November/December 1955).

Census Records

Federal

Population Schedules
- Indexed—1910, 1900, 1920, 1930
- Soundex—1900, 1920

The Hawaiian Islands were annexed to the United States in 1898. The 1900 U.S. census was being taken of the island population when they became a U.S. territory on 14 June 1900. The 1900 U.S. census is arranged by island since there were no counties at the time. The island of Niihau was enumerated as E.D. 84 of Kauai; the island of Kahoolawe as E.D. 107, and Lanai as E.D. 100 of Maui.

Counties were established beginning in 1905. By 1910 these included Kauai County with Niihau as E.D. 16; Maui County with Kahoolawe as E.D. 91, Lanai as E.D. 95, Molokai as E.D. 72, and Honolulu County with the Midway Islands as E.D. 135. The 1910 U.S. census of Hawaii is indexed and has been published. In 1910 Kalawao County on the island of Molokai was comprised of a leper colony.

Territorial and State
Censuses for portions of the Hawaiian Islands were enumerated in 1866, 1878, 1890, and 1896. The 1878 census covers the islands of Hawaii, Maui, and Oahu, and the 1896 census covers Honolulu only. Copies of these early census records are on file at the Hawaii State Archives and the FHL.

The Hawaii State Archives has two "census files" (1840–66 and 1847–96) that contain miscellaneous records such as school censuses, population lists, and vital record summaries. These are also on microfilm at the FHL.

The 1847 "Foreigners in Honolulu" census has been indexed in volume 2, #1-2 (April–July 1993) issue of *Ke Ku'auhau* magazine.

Background Sources

Beechert, Edward D. *Working in Hawaii: A Labor History.* Honolulu: University of Hawaii Press, 1985. This is a comprehensive overview of the working conditions of Hawaii with an emphasis on the last 200 years.

Forbes, David W. *Hawaiian National Bibliography.* 4 vols. Honolulu: University of Hawaii Press, 1999–2003. These volumes are encyclopedic in scope, listing printed material on the development and history of Hawaii. Each volume is divided by time frame: vol. 1: 1780–1830; vol. 2: 1831–1850; vol. 3: 1851–1880; vol. 4: 1881–1900.

Handy, E. S. Craighill, and Mary Kawena Pukui. *The Polynesian Family System in Ka-'u, Hawaii.* Rutland, Vt.: Charles E. Tuttle Co., n.d. This book is valuable for the study of native Hawaiians. It provides an account of old-style Hawaiian life based on the recollections of living informants.

Kuykendall, Ralph S. *The Hawaiian Kingdom, 1778–1854: Foundation and Transformation.* Honolulu: University of Hawaii Press, 1966. Volume 1 of a three-volume definitive history of the Hawaiian Kingdom covers the beginning

of Hawaii and the European discovery of the Islands. *The Hawaiian Kingdom, 1854–1874: Twenty Critical Years*. Volume 2 of this definitive history of the Hawaiian Kingdom covers the middle period of the kingdom's history, between the close of the reign of Kamehamcha III and the accession of Kalakaua. *The Hawaiian Kingdom, 1874–1893: The Kalakaua Dynasty*. Volume 3 of the definitive history of the Hawaiian Kingdom deals with the reigns of Kalakaua and Liliuokalani, the expansive reciprocity era, and the downfall of the monarchy.

Lind, Andrew W. *Hawaii's People*. Honolulu: University Press of Hawaii, 1971. This volume focuses on the life and immigration of ethnic groups in Hawaii and the native Hawaiians. Education and assimilation of the diverse Hawaiian communities is also featured in this work. The first two chapters recount the history and facts of several groups.

Osorino, Jonathan K. K. *Dismembering Lahui: A History of the Hawaiian Nation to 1887*. Honolulu: University of Hawaii Press, 2002. Taken from legislative texts, contemporary newspapers and from historians' research, this volume documents the period that took Hawaii from a traditional subsistence economy to a modern nation.

Norkyke, Eleanor C. *The Peopling of Hawaii*. Honolulu: University of Hawaii Press, 1989. This work includes statistical tables demonstrating the rise of the various ethnic groups within the state and their history.

Pukui, Mary Kawena, Samuel H. Elbert, and Esther T. Mookini. *Place Names of Hawaii*. Honolulu: The University of Hawaii Press, 1974. This excellent work is a glossary of important place-names in Hawaii. These include 4,000 names of valleys, streams, mountains, land sections, towns, villages, and Honolulu streets and buildings.

Maps

The United States Geological Survey (USGS) publishes a catalog of topographical maps covering the state of Hawaii (also American Samoa and Guam). Ask for the publications entitled "Hawaii Catalog of Topographical and Other Published Maps" and "Hawaii Index to Topographical and Other Map Coverage." The catalog lists over-the-counter dealers of U.S. geological maps in Hawaii. Many libraries maintain reference files of the published maps of the Geological Survey. In Hawaii the maps are deposited in the library at the University of Hawaii at Hilo, the Hamilton Library at the University of Hawaii, Manoa, and at the Joseph F. Smith Library on the Brigham Young University–Hawaii Campus.

The Hawaii State Archives has detailed "fire maps" of Honolulu dating back to 1879. Urban areas on other islands also begin as early as 1912. These maps were made for fire insurance purposes and show the placement of buildings on lots and the type of construction.

Many historical maps of Hawaii are online at the Hawaii GenWeb Project website (see page 16). The USGS has excellent maps for the geology and environment of the islands. Its office for Hawaii is at 677 Alamoana Blvd., Ste. 415, Honolulu, HI 96813 <http://geology.wr.usgs.gov/stateinfo/HI.html>.

Land Records

State-Land State

Prior to 1840 there were no land titles in Hawaii. The society was feudalistic and all land belonged to the king. King Kamehameha I had conquered the entire Hawaiian Islands and partitioned the lands among his chiefs. The king received revenue from the chiefs. The chiefs in turn did the same to persons under them by dividing out arable land among the common people. Under this system land allotments could be taken away at any time.

The advent of foreigners and foreign business methods created a change in the land system in Hawaii. This transitional period called the "Great Mahele" of 1848 provided the way to acquire real estate. The Board of Commissioners to Quiet Land Titles was established in 1845. By decision of the king and the chiefs, the king was given his own property, and the remainder was divided equally between the government, the chiefs, and the tenants.

This land commission went to the various islands to meet the people and to prepare them for awarding their claims. This involved the hearing and taking of testimony in connection with nearly 12,000 individual claims. An index to these claims and the Hawaiian terms used in the claims is found in the volume entitled *Indices of Award Made by the Board of Commissioners to Quiet Land Titles in the Hawaiian Islands* by the Office of the Commissioner of Public Lands of the Territory of Hawaii (Honolulu: Territorial Office Building, 1929). These claims cover the period of 1848 to 1852 and are valuable to native Hawaiians for the genealogical material contained in the actual records. A more recent work is Dorothy B. Barrere's *The King's Mahele: The Awardees and Their Lands* (Hawaii: D.B. Barrere, 1994). Another excellent reference tool on the subject is Jon J. Chinen's *The Great Mahele: Hawaii's Land Division of 1848* (Honolulu: University of Hawaii Press, 1958). The Hawaiian Historical Society has an extensive reading list on the topics of Hawaiian lands on its website (see Archives, Libraries, and Societies).

If the claim was approved by the land commission, the claimant received an award, which was then presented to the minister of the interior, who issued a royal patent. The royal patent gave the individual sole ownership of the land once he paid an assessment of cash or land to the government.

The Bureau of Conveyances is part of the Department of Land and Natural Resources, Kalanlmoku Bldg., 1151 Punchbowl St., Honolulu, HI 96813. At <www.hawaii.gov/dlnr/bc/bc.html> are records of the original royal patents and the records of the "Great Mahele" (division of lands) of 1848. These records are for all islands, and since transfers were often made between parents and children or grandparents, statements of relationship are often in these records.

Records in this office begin in the 1840s and include the following record types: grantors index books (1845–1961), with subsequent records on card file or in the daily entries book; recorded deeds in Libers (1845–1961), with subsequent records on card file or in the daily entries book; land court transfer certificates of title; document and land court maps, which are called the "file plan"; liens; and private abstractors. This office is open to the public. Many of these records have been microfilmed and are on file at the FHL in Salt Lake City and the Hawaii State Archives.

The state archives has a "land file" of letters and documents dating from the 1830s, regardless of the office concerned. The "land file" (1830–1900) is filed chronologically, and is one of the most completely translated and indexed group of records in the archives. This collection consists of letters addressed to the Commission to Quiet Land Titles, award books, testimony, and registers of the land documents.

Other records from the Department of Land and Natural Resources include award books (1836–55), patents (1847–1961), foreign testimonies (1846–62), native testimonies (1844–54), native registers (1846–48), and patents upon confirmation of land commission (1847–1961). These are also on microfilm at the FHL.

Probate Records

Probates were filed with the circuit court, and the records begin during the 1840s. There are no earlier probates except for royal families. Many probates (1845–1900) are on file at the Hawaii State Archives and on microfilm at the FHL in Salt Lake City. Indexes (1814–1917) are also available. Additional records are available at the various county courthouses.

Probate records on file at the state archives and the FHL are as follows: first circuit court (Oahu), beginning in 1845; second circuit court (Maui, including Molokai), beginning in 1849; third and fourth circuit courts (Hawaii), beginning in 1849; and fifth circuit court (Kauai), beginning in 1851 (see Court Records below).

Court Records

The "Act to Organize the Judiciary" of 1847 set up four levels of courts in Hawaii: the state supreme court, the superior courts, circuit courts, and district courts. Each of these courts have records of genealogical value. Many of these court records are on file at the Hawaii State Archives and on microfilm at the FHL.

The state supreme court in Hawaii has final appellate jurisdiction in all cases from inferior courts and original jurisdiction to issue all writs over its appellate jurisdiction. Supreme court cases prior to October 1904 are filed with the first circuit court records. If it was an appeal from the first circuit, the records were filed with the original case; if the appeal was from another circuit, the case was given a first circuit number according to the type of case. For example, if a probate was appealed from the second, third, fourth, or fifth circuit, the appeal record will be filed and indexed as though it were a first circuit case. Supreme court cases after October 1904 are filed with the state supreme court clerk's office.

The superior court of law and equity is an appellate court for most cases and a court of origin primarily for cases involving the government, admiralty affairs, bankruptcy, and foreign officials. In 1852 the original state supreme court was abolished and the superior court became the state supreme court.

On 1 January 1893 the circuit court was organized into five districts as follows: first circuit (Oahu); second circuit (Maui, Molokai, and Lanai); third circuit (Kau, Kohala, and Kona on Hawaii); fourth circuit (Hamakua, Hilo, and Puna on Hawaii); fifth circuit (Kauai and Niihau). This division continued until 1943 when the third and fourth circuits were combined, the fourth circuit was abolished and the Island of Hawaii once again became the third circuit court. These courts are over criminal cases, probate cases, and divorce cases. Juvenile cases are under the circuit courts in a family court division.

Family court cases usually involve paternity, guardianship, adoption, FC (misdemeanors and felonies), UCCJ (Uniform Child Custody Jurisdiction), miscellaneous, and domestic abuse. The only type of family court records that are restricted and not open to the public are cases involving adoption, paternity, and guardianship. Others can be viewed at the courthouses as long as they are not marked confidential.

There are four district courts (or justice courts) in Hawaii with divisions the same as the circuit courts. There are smaller districts on each island. Their jurisdiction involves minor criminal and civil cases.

Tax Records

The Hawaii State Archives has both personal and property tax records for Hawaii (1855–93), Kauai (1855–92), Lanai (1855–92), Maui (1887–92), Molokai (1855–92), and Oahu (1855–1929). These tax records are incomplete and are unindexed. The early tax records are a poll tax only. The tax records were taken on a division basis with each island divided into many divisions.

It is necessary to know the correct division in order to search these records.

Property tax records and tax maps were moved from state to county control about 1980. Tax maps dating as early as the 1920s are on microfilm in the Real Property Assessment Office. The address for the City and County of Honolulu is 842 Bethel St., Honolulu, HI 96813.

The Hawaii State Tax Office has a map room with tax maps beginning in 1932. These tax maps give the names of owners, estate heirs, and field books. The field books give the title history and its book and page numbers, which are found in the Bureau of Conveyances.

Cemetery Records

Hawaii's unique mixture of ethnic groups has produced many fascinating and historic cemeteries. A few unique practices need to be understood in order to fully appreciate the various types of tombstones to be found on the islands. For example, when men were "lost at sea" or "buried at sea," tombstones were often raised as a memorial to them in Hawaii's cemeteries. Another example is the Buddhist tombstones, which are found very close together due to the cremation practice of the culture. Chinese immigrants were often returned to China for burial. This practice and the practice of removal of the remains to be shipped to China are reflected in the sexton's records. Many of the Chinese and Japanese tombstones follow Confucian or Buddhist customs for memorializing ancestors. The use of posthumous names and lunar death dates is very common.

The Hawaiian Historical Society (see Archives, Libraries, and Societies for address) publishes a guide to cemetery research on the island of Oahu. Many Hawaiian cemeteries are currently being cataloged and indexed in a computer bank by the Cemetery Research Project. Some cemeteries have been transcribed in the past by members of The Church of Jesus Christ of Latter-day Saints (Mormons) in Hawaii. Transcripts are available through the FHL. The Hawaii GenWeb Project (see page 16) is also a resource for a growing number of tombstone transcripts.

Church Records

Hawaii's blend of cultures has led to a diverse religious community. New England Congregationalists first brought Protestant Christianity to the islands in 1820. Roman Catholic missionaries came to Hawaii in 1827 but were forced to leave by Protestant missionary leaders in 1831. Catholicism was allowed back into Hawaii. Quakers came in 1835 and Mormons in 1850. Methodists came in 1855, and members of the Church of England arrived in 1862.

The history of Buddhism in Hawaii, as a matter of written record, can be traced to the arrival of Soryu Kagahi, a priest of the True Pure Land Sect and a native of Oita Prefecture. He arrived at Honolulu Harbor in March 1889. Japanese Buddhist and Shinto ideas have been in Hawaii since laborers arrived in 1887. For a more detailed account of the development of the various religions and sects in the state, see John F. Mulholland's *Hawaii's Religions* (Rutland, Vt.: Charles E. Tuttle Co., 1970). Today, Hawaii's religious population is generally thirty-three percent Catholic, thirty percent Protestant, twenty percent Buddhist, and seventeen percent other faiths. Other religious groups, Christian and non-Christian, have been active in Hawaii in recent years. Among these are Jehovah's Witnesses, Baha'i, various Pentecostal faiths, Seventh-day Adventists, Lutherans, Baptists, Quakers, and many new religious sects exported from Japan.

The Roman Catholic Church in Hawaii is served by the Diocese of Honolulu, 1184 Bishop St., Honolulu, HI 96813-2858 <www.pono.net>. The diocese website has links and contact information to the various parishes in the diocese, thus making requests to obtain records and information relatively easy. The Catholic Church today is the largest Christian denomination in Hawaii.

The Church of Jesus Christ of Latter-day Saints (Mormons or LDS) has grown rapidly in Hawaii since 1850 when missionaries were sent to the islands. The first Mormon colony was established at Lanai. When the LDS Temple at Laie was completed in 1919, a group of native Hawaiians returned after spending a decade or two at Iosepa in Utah. For additional history on Mormonism in Hawaii, see R. Lanier Britsch, *Mormon: The Mormons in Hawaii* (Laie, Hawaii: Institute for Polynesian Studies, 1989); and Joseph H. Spurrier, *Sandwich Island Saints* (Laie, Hawaii: Joseph H. Spurrier, 1989). Today the LDS Church comprises one of the largest denominations in the state and LDS records are on microfilm at the FHL.

The Episcopal Church arrived in Hawaii in 1866. Prior to that time, in 1862, the Church of England had established itself on the islands. The Episcopal Church in Hawaii, 229 Queen Emma Sq., Honolulu, HI 96813-2304 <www.episcopalhawaii.org/> has records and photos of church ministry beginning in 1862. The diocese website has links to all parish websites.

The first Japanese immigrants to Hawaii probably brought Shinto ideas with them. The first Shinto temple was built in Hilo in 1898. Two recognized Shinto sects that came to Hawaii are Shinto (Honkyoku) and Taishakyo. Other Shinto sects are active in Hawaii and several temples have been built. For information on various sects, contact the individual temples.

Guides such as *A Brief History of Buddhist Temples* (Hilo, Hawaii: Big Island Buddhist Federation, 1979) can be helpful in locating the temples of various sects and their addresses. Several

articles on Buddhism are filed with the Hawaiian and Pacific Collection, Sinclaire Library, University of Hawaii.

Military Records

The Hawaii State Archives has a card list for deceased veterans of the Spanish-American War, Civil War, and World War I. Also in its collection is a list of Hawaiians who served in World War I and members of the Guard of the Republic of Hawaii. Before Hawaii became a U.S. territory, its army consisted of a royal household guard and militia units. A report and rosters of these groups are at the Hawaii State Archives along with records of the Hawaiian navy and the treason trials held after the 1895 counter-revolution.

Periodicals, Newspapers, and Manuscript Collections

Periodicals

An excellent periodical published on Hawaii's history is *The Hawaiian Journal of History*, a scholarly journal published by the Hawaiian Historical Society in Honolulu. Between 1892 and 1940 the Hawaiian Historical Society published the *Hawaiian Historical Society Papers*, which are devoted to scholarly articles, genealogy, and early record sources. The Australian National University, Canberra, Australia, publishes *The Journal of Pacific History*, which has printed many articles on Hawaii. The Institute for Polynesian Studies at Brigham Young University–Hawaii publishes *Pacific Studies*, which also contains articles and book reviews on Hawaii.

Newspapers

The Hawaiian Historical Society publishes *Guide to Newspapers in Hawaii, 1834-2000* (Honolulu: Hawaiian Historical Society, 2000) which can be read online at its website (see Archives, Libraries, and Societies). The Hawaii State Archives has an index to many newspapers published in Hawaii from 1836 to 1950. This index includes the following: *Advertiser, Star Bulletin, Polynesian, Hawaiian Gazette,* and *Friend*. An index to marriages and deaths from English language newspapers in Hawaii (1836–1929) is also available at the archives.

During the history of Hawaii, many Hawaiian language newspapers were published. These newspapers were not only reflections of politics and culture but were primary instruments of movements and individuals. An indispensable guide to Hawaiian language newspapers is Esther K. Mookini's *The Hawaiian Newspapers* (Honolulu: Topgallant Publishing Co., 1974). This work will help in locating Hawaiian language newspapers and the dates they were published.

Native Hawaiian genealogies were published in Hawaiian language newspapers between 1834 and 1900 and are published in *Hawaiian Genealogies: Extracted from Hawaiian Language Newspapers* (Laie, Hawaii: Institute for Polynesian Studies, vol. 1, 1983; vol. 2, 1985) by Edith Kowelohea McKinzie with Ishmael W. Stagner II, editor.

Chinese newspapers can be helpful in reconstructing the Chinese experience in Hawaii. Unfortunately, many Chinese newspapers have not survived, and those that have were often organs for political groups, although vital material can be obtained from these newspapers. Chinese newspapers have been gathered and microfilmed by the University of Hawaii, Hamilton Library. The University of Hawaii–Sinclair Library also has several Chinese newspapers. Among these are the *United Chinese Press, Hawaiian Chinese Journal,* and the *Hawaii Chinese Weekly.*

The FHL has microfilm copies of many older Japanese newspapers in Hawaii. These include the *Nippon Jiji* (1896–1942) and *Hawaii Hochi* (also *Times,* 1912–42). These papers frequently published items on the arrival of immigrants as well as community affairs. The Bishop Museum and Hamilton Library at the University of Hawaii at Manoa have a good collection of early Japanese newspapers. The Hamilton Library also has various early Korean and Filipino newspapers.

Manuscripts

The Hawaiian Mission Children's Society Library has records of the nineteenth-century missionary families sent to Hawaii by the American Mission Board of Commissioners for Foreign Missions. This collection also has information on the early Hawaiian converts. The library is not open to the general public but will accommodate descendants. Fortunately, many of its records have been utilized in various publications over the years. One such publication is *Descendants of New England Protestant Missionaries to the Sandwich Islands (Hawaiian Islands), 1820–1900: An Alphabetically Arranged Copy of Births, Marriages, and Deaths from the Records of the Hawaiian Mission Children's Society Library, Honolulu, Hawaii* (Honolulu: Privately printed, Hawaiian State Regent, National Society of Daughters of the American Revolution, 1984). For a more detailed listing of the holdings of this library, see "The Hawaiian Mission Children's Society Library," *The Journal of Pacific History* 16 (1981): 1-2.

The Hawaii State Archives has supplemented many sources for early Hawaiian research. Some collections have been gathered from outside Hawaii. Sources include the records for the British Consulate in Hawaii (1824–94); Admiralty and Foreign Office records in the Public Record Office, London (1824–75); and the portions of journals concerning Hawaii from Captain Cook's voyage. Other sources include a "Biographical File," which indexes the names of individuals whose names appear in both published and unpublished sources.

Several hundred Hawaiian and "haole" genealogies have been compiled by Bruce Cartwright in the Cartwright Collection at the Hawaii State Archives. Voters records are also available at the state archives. These include the "Great Register of Voters" (1887–88), which gives the name, age, place of birth, and occupation of the voter. This register is arranged by island and precinct. The "Oath and Certificates" of persons registering as voters in 1894, arranged by island, is also available. In some cases they list age and birthplace. Registers from 1900 to about 1960 are presently being organized and microfilmed for availability through the FHL.

The Russian presence has been in Hawaii since the 1800s. Czarist Russian Consulates were in the U.S. port cities of Chicago, Honolulu, New York, Philadelphia, Portland, San Francisco, and Seattle, as well as the office in Nome, Alaska. The Russian Consular Records, deposited at the National Archives in Suitland, Maryland, have been microfilmed by the Genealogical Society of Utah. This collection has been indexed by the Jewish Genealogical Society of Greater Washington in Sallyann Amdur Sack and Susan Fishl Wynne's *The Russian Consular Records Index and Catalog* (New York and London: Garland Publishing, 1987). This valuable collection covers the period of 1849 to 1926, with the majority of documents dating from 1917 to 1926, and is on microfilm at the FHL and the National Archives.

The Hawaii Historical Society in Honolulu has a collection of telephone books from 1909 to 1973 and city directories from 1880 to 1973.

Archives, Libraries, and Societies

Hawaii State Archives
Iolani Palace Grounds
478 S. King St.
Honolulu, HI 96813
www.hawaii.gov/dags/archives/welcome.html

An excellent research repository for Hawaii, with many of its holdings already described above.

Hawaiian Historical Society
560 Kawaiahao St.
Honolulu, HI 96813
www.hawaiianhistory.org

The society has an extensive collection of nineteenth-century materials on Hawaii including manuscripts, maps, and photos.

University of Hawaii, Manoa Campus
Hamilton Library
2550 McCarthy Mall
Honolulu, HI 96822
http://libweb.hawaii.edu/uhmlib/index.htm

This is a government document repository. The library has strong Hawaii and Pacific collections, serials, maps, and the largest genealogical book collection in the state.

Bishop Museum Library
1525 Bernice St.
Honolulu, HI 96817-0916
www.bishopmuseum.org/contact.html

This repository has material on the Hawaiian Royal families and nobility, records of major sugar companies, and a large photographic collection.

Hawaii Chinese History Center
111 N. King St., Rm. 410
Honolulu, HI 96817

Materials relating to the Chinese in Hawaii which include maps, genealogies, histories, photos, and rare documents.

Hawaii State Library
478 S. King St.
Honolulu, HI 96813-2901
www.hcc.hawaii.edu/hspls/hslov.html

The library has large collections and materials on ethnic groups in Hawaii as well as guides on genealogical research.

Hawaiian Mission Children's Society Library
553 S. King St.
Honolulu, HI 96813-3002
www.lava.net/~mhm/lib.htm

Not open to the public, but accessible by mail or phone. Record holdings include journals and photos of early nineteenth-century Congregational missionaries in Hawaii, and the archives of the Congregational Church in Hawaii and the Pacific.

Kona Historical Society
P.O. Box 398
Kona, HI 96704
www.konahistorical.org

Holds materials on the Kona section of the Island of Hawaii.

Maui Historical Society and Museum
2375-A Main St.
P.O. Box 1018
Wailuku, HI 96793
www.mauimuseum.org

This organization has publications, newspaper clippings, and photos of historical value to the island of Maui.

Kauai Historical Society
4428 Rui St.
P.O. Box 1778
Lihue, Hawaii 96766
www.kauaihistoricalsociety.org

Holdings include newspapers, manuscripts, photos, oral histories, and various writings on Kauai Island. Some records for now defunct sugar plantations are also available.

University of Hawaii at Hilo Library
200 W. Kawili St.
Hilo, HI 96720-4091
http://library.uhh.hawaii.edu/

Brigham Young University–Hawaii
Joseph F. Smith Library
55-220 Kulanui St.
Laie, HI 96762
www.byuh.edu/library

The Hawaii State Public Library System has an online catalog to libraries in the state <www.librarieshawaii.org>. This is an excellent tool for gaining quick access to records and learning where they may be deposited. The Hawaii GenWeb Project provides links and addresses to genealogical and historical societies and repositories, and current information on genealogy for the state <www.rootsweb.com/~higenweb/hawaii. htm>. Another good resource is the encyclopedic *Directory of Historical Records Repositories in Hawaii* (Honolulu: Association of Hawaiian Archivist and the Hawaiian Historical Society, 1999), which is updated every few years.

Special Focus Categories

Immigration

The population of Hawaii is a blend of many ethnic groups. Immigrants came to Hawaii to work. The Chinese arrived in 1852, the Portuguese in 1878, the Japanese in 1884, Koreans in 1903, and Filipinos in 1906. The Japanese currently make up about thirty percent of the population and represent Hawaii's largest ethnic group.

Records concerning arrival prior to 1860 have been compiled in the valuable volume entitled *Voyages to Hawaii before 1860* by Bernice Judd (Honolulu: University of Hawaii, ca. 1974). This book is a compilation of narratives in the libraries of the Hawaiian Mission Children's Society and the Hawaii Historical Society.

Passenger lists for persons arriving in Hawaii have been microfilmed from 1843 to 1900. These include a separate index for Chinese arrivals (1854–1900), Japanese arrivals (1888–1900), Portuguese arrivals (1878–1900), and a general index for all others (early to 1900). These ship manifests and the index are on microfilm at the Hawaii State Archives and the FHL. For the time period after 1900, contact the state archives

Although the Chinese arrivals in Hawaii are listed in the passenger lists (1854–1900), many arrivals were not recorded.

The Board of Immigration in Hawaii recorded additional Chinese arrivals. This collection of records (1847–80) is on file at the Hawaii State Archives with microfilm copies at the FHL.

The Chinese Bureau of Hawaii has records of Chinese entry permits (1888–98); card index to Chinese Passports (1884–98); Chinese work permits (1895–97); departures of Chinese from Hawaii (1852–1900); index to entry permits of Chinese minors (1891–98); labor permits of persons who died in Hawaii (1895–97); and special resident permits (1891). Many of these records provide the entry date of the immigrant as well as the vessel. The originals are at the Hawaii State Archives. They have been microfilmed and are also on file at the FHL.

Many passport registrations for Portuguese citizens have been published in the volume entitled *Passport Registrations: Portuguese Immigrants from Azores to Sandwich Isles, 1879–1883* (Honolulu: De Mello Publishing Co., n.d.).

The Japanese Consulate General, 1742 Nuuanu Ave., Honolulu, HI 96817, has records of Japanese nationals who came to Hawaii between 1885 and 1910.

The Hawaiian Sugar Planters' Association Archives has been donated to the University of Hawaii at Manoa, Special Collections (see Archives, Libraries, and Societies). These records consist of the various plantations on the islands and include personnel and payroll records, which will cover the various ethnic workers brought in to work in the sugar fields.

Native Hawaiian

The ethnic group known as Hawaiian is generally reserved for descendants of the original Polynesian inhabitants of the Hawaiian Islands. The present interracial mixture of ethnic groups in the state of Hawaii makes the term "Hawaiian" ambiguous to the point that it is unclear who is a Hawaiian in the modern society of Hawaii.

Many native Hawaiian historical, genealogical, and cultural collections have been gathered and preserved in libraries in Hawaii. In Hawaiian families, the firstborn child (*hoiapo*), whether male or female, became the inheritor of the family name. This means that in conducting Hawaiian genealogical research, it is often not possible to know the sex of the child. To complicate matters, it was often a common practice to name a child after an event, circumstance, or wish, without respect to sex. For additional information on native Hawaiian records and record repositories, see David Kittleson's book, *The Hawaiians: An Annotated Bibliography* (Honolulu: University of Hawaii Press, 1985).

Other Ethnic Groups

Hawaii is a unique state because all racial groups are minorities, and the majority of the population has ancestry in the Pacific Islands or Asia rather than Europe or Africa. Ethnic groups to be examined in this section include the Chinese, Caucasian,

Japanese, African American, Filipino, and Korean. For additional information on the ethnic groups of Hawaii, see Eleanor C. Nordyke's *The Peopling of Hawaii* (Honolulu: University Press of Hawaii, ca. 1977) and Andrew W. Lind's work *Hawaii's People* (Honolulu: University Press of Hawaii, 1971). Information on Asian research and repositories can be found in Greg Gubler's article, "Asian American Records and Research," in Jessie Carney Smith, *Ethnic Genealogy* (Westport, Conn.: Greenwood Press, 1983), 239-308.

For Chinese research in Hawaii, see the following reference works: Clarence E. Glick, *Sojourners and Settlers: Chinese Migrants in Hawaii* (Honolulu: University of Hawaii Press, 1980); Kum Pai Lai and Violet Lai, *Researching One's Chinese Roots* (Honolulu: Hawaii Chinese History Center, 1988); and Nancy Foon Young, *The Chinese in Hawaii: An Annotated Bibliography* (Honolulu: University Press of Hawaii, 1973).

For the Japanese, see the following references: Ronald Kotani, *The Japanese in Hawaii: A Century of Struggle* (Honolulu: Hawaii Hochi, 1985); *Mitsugu Matsuda, The Japanese in Hawaii* (Honolulu: University of Hawaii, 1975), revised by Dennis M. Ogawa, and Jerry Y. Fujioka; and Franklin Odo and Kazuko Shinoto, *A Pictorial History of the Japanese in Hawaii, 1885–1924*, (Honolulu: Bishop Museum, 1985). Patsy Sumie Saiki's *Early Japanese Immigrants in Hawaii* (Honolulu: University of Hawaii Press, 1993) provides details on the hardships and sacrifice of the earliest Japanese immigrants. James H. Okahata's *A History of Japanese in Hawaii* (Honolulu: The United Japanese Society of Hawaii, 1971) covers such topics as the different immigrations of Japanese to Hawaii, disputes between the Kingdom of Hawaii and Japan, the sugar industry and plantation life, the struggle for equality, the 1920 plantation strike, and anti-Japanese feelings in America and Hawaii during World War II.

Filipino resources include Ruben R. Alcantara's work *The Filipinos in Hawaii: An Annotated Bibliography* (Honolulu: Social Research Institute, University of Hawaii, 1972).

The study of the Korean experience in Hawaii continues to be documented in a series of well-written works. For the early period of Korean immigration, Wayne Patterson's *The Korean Frontier in America: Immigration to Hawaii, 1896–1910* (Honolulu: University Press of Hawaii, 1988) provides important background. Patterson also wrote *The Ilse: First Generation Korean Immigrants in Hawaii, 1903–1973* (Honolulu: University of Hawaii Press, 2000), which documents the first generation of Koreans who were known as *Ilse*. This comprehensive work weaves their social history together with the Korean experience. A recent and highly acclaimed work is Jenny Ryun Foster, Heinz Insu Fenkl, and Frank Stewart, *Century of the Tiger: One Hundred Years of Korean Culture in America* (Honolulu: University of Hawaii Press, 2003). This work details the dramatic story of Korean culture in the United States with special emphasis on Hawaii.

County Resources

Many of the pre-1900 Hawaiian records are held at the state archives. Since territorial days, Hawaii has consisted of five counties: Hawaii, Honolulu, Kalawao, Kauai, and Maui. These were created on 1 July 1905, but their purpose does not include administration of land, probate, or court records. After 1900 probate records and court records are accessed through the Hawaii State Judiciary Court, 797 Punchbowl St., Honolulu, HI 96813. For land records, contact the Bureau of Conveyances, 403 Queen St., Honolulu, HI 96813. The addresses that follow are for the individual counties, but in Hawaii, the counties do not hold the records. For a more complete discussion as to the location of county record sources, see preceding sections.

Map	County Address	Date Formed Parent County/ies	Birth Marriage Death	Land Probate Court
J7	Hawaii 25 Aupuni St. Hilo 96720-4245	1905 original	1859 1846 1841	1848 1854 1854
D4	Honolulu County 530 S. Kings St. #202 Honolulu 96813-3006	1905 original	1852 1837 1852	1848 1842 1842
B3	Kauai 4444 Rice St. Lihue 96766-1328	1905 original	1851 1846 1851	1848 1851 1851
F6	Maui 200 S. High St. Wailuku 96793-2155	1905 original	1853 1842 1853	1848 1849 1849

HAWAII

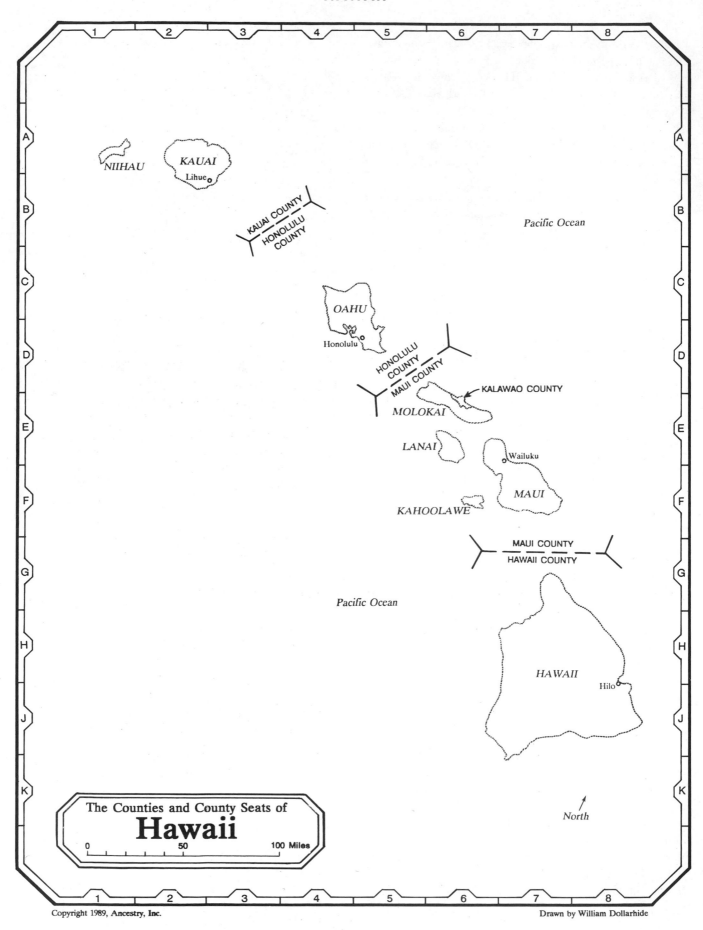

NIIHAU

KAUAI

Lihue ○

Pacific Ocean

KAUAI COUNTY
HONOLULU COUNTY

OAHU

Honolulu ○

HONOLULU COUNTY
MAUI COUNTY

← KALAWAO COUNTY

MOLOKAI

LANAI

Wailuku ○

MAUI

KAHOOLAWE

MAUI COUNTY
HAWAII COUNTY

Pacific Ocean

HAWAII

Hilo ○

North

The Counties and County Seats of
Hawaii

0   50   100 Miles

Drawn by William Dollarhide

Idaho

DWIGHT A. RADFORD

The first permanent settlement of whites in Idaho country was the Mormon colony at Franklin in Cache Valley. But the first major wave of settlers was drawn by the lure of gold. Just three years after gold was discovered, the territory of Idaho was created, in 1863, consisting of ten counties. The new territory included what is now all of Montana and most of present-day Wyoming. At the peak of the mining boom, as many as 70,000 whites may have been in Idaho Territory. By 1870, however, this number had dwindled to 15,000. Mining was Idaho's chief producer of wealth until the beginning of the twentieth century when agriculture became the number one industry.

In 1866 the first district land office in Idaho opened in Boise. Other district offices included Lewiston in 1866, Oxford in 1879, Hailey in 1883, Coeur d'Alene in 1884, and Blackfoot in 1886. After the Civil War, Confederate refugees settled in Idaho. Others came to Idaho during a renewed mining boom during the 1880s and 1890s and with the coming of the railroads to the farmland of southern Idaho.

Idaho's transition from a territory to a state was long and difficult. When the new Idaho Constitution was drafted in 1889, territory officials sought to resolve disagreements about whether to keep northern Idaho from becoming part of Washington territory. Many compromises were reached to set the boundaries before Idaho became a new state on 3 July 1890.

Idaho was never a "melting pot," but it did have its share of ethnic groups, such as the Scandinavian converts to the Mormon faith who colonized in eastern Idaho and the Finns who settled in the high mountain valleys near Payette Lakes. Coeur d'Alene mines attracted miners from Wales and immigrants from the Balkans. Likewise, hundreds of Chinese came to Idaho in the 1860s and 1870s to work in the mines. The Basque migration from the Spanish Pyrenees came primarily to Idaho, northern Nevada, western Oregon, and California as sheepherders. Japanese immigrants began settling in southwestern Idaho prior to World War II. Other Japanese settled near Idaho Falls and Pocatello. Between 1900 and 1910, reclamation projects opened desert lands for farming. This brought a new wave of settlement from nearby states, especially Utah.

Idaho's Native American population lives on four reservations: Nez Perce Reservation, Coeur d'Alene Reservation in northern Idaho, Fort Hall Reservation south of Pocatello, and Duck Valley Reservation in Owyhee County. Many Kootenai Native Americans reside in an enclave near Bonners Ferry, and some Kalispell Native Americans live in an enclave at Cusick on the Idaho-Montana border.

Idaho's development was often turbulent and yet tolerant and just at times as well. The Mormon east, non-Mormon west, and the northern mining part of the state developed three distinct cultures that eventually grew and bonded into the state of Idaho.

Vital Records

The registration of births and deaths on the county level in Idaho was not required until 1907. Prior to that time, the only birth and death records were kept by churches, midwives, mortuaries, and physicians. These records are fragmentary at best. The

County Resources section below lists those vital records that were available on the county level before mandatory recording.

Beginning in 1907 the state of Idaho required that professional midwives and physicians record births. The registration of deaths was the responsibility of any clergyman, coroner, physician, or undertaker who had cared for the deceased during the last sickness or made arrangements for the burial. This information was reported to the county recorder. The law governing the registration of births and deaths was changed in 1911, at which time the county recorder was relieved of this responsibility. After 1911 all births and deaths were registered directly with the state. The Family History Library (FHL) has most Idaho births and deaths on microfilm from 1907 to 1911.

The first laws in Idaho Territory concerning marriages and divorces were enacted in 1864. The first Territorial Legislative Assembly made provisions for books in which to record certificates issued by the person performing the marriage ceremony as well as contracts made by individuals. Under the law, the marriage contract did not have to be a written contract. If it was a written contract, there was no compulsion about making a public record of it. Although some early Idaho Territorial marriage contracts were recorded, most were not. Pre-1895 records are located in the county courthouses. The FHL has most early and later county marriages on microfilm. An essential research tool for Idaho marriages is the "Western States Historical Marriage Record Index," which is online at the Brigham Young University–Idaho website <http://abish.byui.edu/specialCollections/fhc/gbsearch.htm>. This index covers marriages from the territorial days primarily through the 1930s, although some counties have marriages up through the 1950s represented.

District courts in Idaho were given jurisdiction in divorce cases by an act passed by the first Territorial Legislative Assembly in 1864. Divorce and annulment actions were filed in the district court in the same manner as other civil cases.

Statewide records of Idaho's birth and death certificates begin in 1911, and marriage and divorce records begin in 1947. These certificates can be obtained by contacting the Vital Statistics Unit, Idaho Department of Health and Welfare, 450 W. State St., 1st Floor, Boise, ID 83720-9990 <www2.state.id.us/dhw/vital_stats/appmenu.htm>. The FHL has death indexes (1911–50) and certificates (1911–37) on microfilm. There is also an online index to all Idaho deaths (1911–50) on the website of the Idaho GenWeb <www.rootsweb.com/~idgenweb>.

Census Records

Federal

Population Schedules
- Indexed—1870, 1880, 1910, 1920, 1930
- Soundex—1900, 1920

Mortality Schedules
- 1870, 1880 (both indexed)

In 1860, Idaho north of 46 degrees north latitude was part of Spokane County, Washington Territory. The 1860 federal census appears to reflect no white population, and the 1860 federal census of Cache County, Utah Territory, included some persons living in what is now the southeastern corner of the Bear Lake area. The 1870 Idaho territorial census is extant for all counties and has been indexed, although the unorganized area of Kootenai was enumerated with Nez Perce County. A portion of Bear Lake and the Franklin County area was enumerated with Cache County, Utah. An index has been compiled by the Idaho State Historical Society (see Archives, Libraries, and Societies) entitled "Missing 1870 Census of Franklin and Bear Lake Counties Idaho Found in 1870 Census of Utah" (Boise, Idaho: Williams Printing, Co., 1982). Any population in the Yellowstone National Park area of Idaho for 1880 was enumerated in the Wyoming census. An index to the 1910 federal population schedule was published by the Idaho Genealogical Society (see Archives, Libraries, and Societies).

Background Sources

An Illustrated History of the State of Idaho: Containing a History of the State of Idaho from the Earliest Period of Its Discovery to the Present Time, Together With Glimpses of Its Auspicious Futures; Illustrations…and Biographical Mention of Many Pioneers and Prominent Citizens of Today. 4 vols. in 2. Chicago: Lewis Publishing Co., 1899. This two-volume set covers the history of Idaho and contains biographical sketches.

Arrington, Leonard J. *History of Idaho.* 2 vols. Moscow, Idaho: University of Idaho Press, 1994. This excellent work provides a scholarly history of the state. Volume 1 covers the natural setting of the state and the state's history up through WWI. Volume 2 covers the state's history from WWI to the present.

Beal, Merrill. *A History of Southeastern Idaho: An Intimate Narrative of Peaceful Conquest by Empire Builders.* Caldwell, Idaho: Caxton Printers, 1942. This book outlines the history of an area that was influenced by Mormon Utah to the south, mining Montana to the north, and pioneer Oregon to the west.

———, and Merle W. Wells. *History of Idaho.* 3 vols. New York: Lewis Historical Publishing Co., 1959. Volumes 1 and 2 cover the history of the state. Volume 3 is especially noteworthy as it contains personal and family histories.

Bieter, Pat. "Reluctant Shepherds: The Basque of Idaho," *Idaho Yesterdays* 1 (Summer 1957): 10-15. A discussion of the characteristics of the Basque people and why they migrated and settled in Idaho is presented.

Bilbao, Julio B. "Basque of Early Idaho," *Idaho Yesterdays* 15 (Summer 1971): 26. Accounts are given of some of Idaho's earliest settlers who were Basque.

Defenbach, Byron. *Idaho: the Place and Its People: A History of the Gem State from Prehistoric to Present Days*. 3 vols. Chicago. American Historical Society, Inc., 1933. Volume 1 covers the history of the state, and volumes 2 and 3 contain biographical sketches.

Derig, Betty Belle. "Celestials in the Digging," *Idaho Yesterdays* 16 (Fall 1972): 2. A century ago, the typical Idaho miner was Chinese. By 1870, more than 4,000 Chinese had moved into Idaho. This article tells the story of the Chinese miners.

French, Hiram Taylor. *History of Idaho: A Narrative Account of Its Historical Progress, Its People, and Its Principle Interest*. 3 vols. Chicago: Lewis Publishing Co., 1914. This three-volume set is very useful because volumes 2 and 3 are biographical sketches. Volume 1 is a history of the state.

Gazetteer of Cities, Villages, Unincorporated Communities and Landmark Sites in the State of Idaho. Idaho Department of Highways, 1966. A useful book that lists 1,900 places in Idaho. It is especially useful to the researcher because each place is broken down into county, quadrants within the county, township, section, range, post office, highway, railroad, airport, stream, lake or reservoir, principle industry, and notes.

Hawley, James H., ed. *History of Idaho: The Gem of the Mountains*. 4 vols. Chicago: S. J. Clarke Publishing Co., 1920. Volume 1 is a standard history of the state, while the other volumes consist of biographical sketches.

History of Idaho Territory: Showing Its Resources and Advantages; with Illustrations … From Original Drawings. San Francisco: W. W. Elliott, 1884. Valuable because the compilers used the territorial newspapers for many of their sources.

Mercer, Laurie and Carol Simon-Smolinski, eds. *Idaho's Ethnic Heritage: Resource Guide*. 3 vols. Boise, Idaho: Idaho Centennial Commission and Idaho State Historical Society, 1990. These volumes provide guides to the various ethnic cultures historically present in the state. Also included is an extensive bibliography.

Wunder, John. "The Courts and the Chinese in Frontier Idaho." *Idaho Yesterdays* 25 (Spring 1981): 23. Idaho's Supreme Court did not succumb to the anti-Chinese pressures present throughout the West. It upheld a tradition of fundamental fairness.

Maps

Maps are essential in conducting on-site research, locating towns and cemeteries, and plotting mining claims. Several maps are available for Idaho that are helpful in conducting on-site or historical research.

The United States Geological Survey (see page 5) maps are available for Idaho. Major libraries in Idaho have been designated by the U.S. Geological Survey as map depository libraries. They include Boise State University in Boise, Albertsons Library <www.library.boisestate.edu>; University of Idaho in Moscow <www.lib.uidaho.edu>; and Idaho State University in Pocatello <www.isu.edu>.

Ralph N. Preston's *Maps of Early Idaho* (Corvallis, Ore.: Western Guide Publishers, 1972) is an excellent collection of early Idaho maps beginning with the 1804 Lewis and Clark trail map to a present-day map of the state. The various maps detailing the history of Idaho are valuable for genealogical research as they show overland stage routes, old military roads, Indian battlegrounds, old forts, old mining areas, and early towns. Another set of historical maps that has been published by the Idaho State Historical Society and annotated by Meryl W. Wells is *An Atlas of Idaho Territory, 1863–1890* (Boise, Idaho: Idaho State Historical Society, 1978).

Land Records
Public-Domain State

Idaho was a public land state, created from land that was public domain. The federal government administered most of the land that was settled through the Government Land Office, which became the Bureau of Land Management (BLM). These land offices kept records of each land entry, including tract books and township plats. Tract books are records of transactions for each section of land. Township plat books are maps of land entries for each township.

Records for the BLM are on file at the National Archives—Pacific-Alaska (Seattle), and the BLM Office, Idaho State Office, 1387 S. Vinnell Way, Boise, ID 83706 <www.id.blm.gov/index.htm>. BLM lands that went through the patent process are online at the BLM website (see page 6).

BLM land records cover the years 1868 to 1910. The following land office records are on microfiche in Seattle: Boise Land Office (1868–1910); Oxford Land Office (1879–1908); Oxford-Blackfoot Land Office (1879–1901); Blackfoot Land Office (1884–1940); Coeur d'Alene Land Office (1885–1908), Hailey Land Office (1883–1940), Lewiston (1874–1908); and Unidentified Land Office Records (1878–1917). Also on file, are records for the Office of Surveyor General of Idaho (1913–50). There were two types of land entries in Idaho: cash entries and homesteads. For a more detailed discussion of these two land entries, see Washington State—Land Records.

The above land office records include letters sent and received by state offices and sub offices, case files, township tract

books, survey plats, registers, indexes of declaratory statements, entries, receipts, certificates for homesteads, mineral, and timber culture lands.

The custodian of land records on the county level in Idaho is the county recorder. The originals of these county records are on file at the local county courthouses. Many records in Idaho's county courthouses are microfilmed and available through the FHL.

Probate Records

Probate courts were established after Idaho became a state. For a more detailed account of probate courts, see the Court Records section below. Idaho probate records include appraisals, claims, estate cases, fee books, final accounts, guardianships, inheritance tax records, inventories, letters, and wills. These records are available at the various county courthouses.

Those microfilmed are available through the FHL and the Library and Archives of the Idaho State Historical Society.

Court Records

The various Idaho courts that kept records of genealogical value were the district courts, probate courts, justice of the peace courts, and the magistrate divisions of district courts.

District courts have countywide civil and criminal jurisdiction, including naturalization, with some appellate jurisdiction.

Probate courts had jurisdiction over probates, adoptions, and minor civil matters until they were abolished in 1971, and their records and functions were assigned to the district courts of magistrates division of district courts.

Justice of the peace courts had jurisdiction over minor petty cases until 1971, when they were abolished, and their jurisdiction was assigned to the district courts.

Magistrate divisions of district courts are citywide courts assigned court cases by the various district courts. These cases generally include minor civil and criminal cases, probates, and juvenile matters.

Idaho court records are at the local county courthouses although many are microfilmed and available through the FHL.

The Idaho State Historical Society has 1,200 boxes of Idaho Supreme Court case files from the territorial and state court covering 1863 to 1970.

Tax Records

Most of Idaho's county tax records are still located at the county courthouses with some on microfilm at the FHL. Many

early territorial and pre-territorial tax rolls are on file at the Idaho State Historical Society with microfilm copies at the FHL (1865–74).

Cemetery Records

Members of The Church of Jesus Christ of Latter-day Saints transcribed many Idaho cemetery records between 1952 and 1968. These records were published in a twelve-volume set that includes many of the cemeteries in the following counties: Ada, Adams, Bannock, Bear Lake, Bingham, Blaine, Bonneville, Boise, Bonner, Camas, Cassia, Canyon, Clark, Clearwater, Elmore, Franklin, Gem, Gooding, Idaho, Jefferson, Jerome, Kootenai, Lemhi, Madison, Minidoka, Nez Perce, Owyhee, Payette, Power, Twin Falls, Shoshone, Valley, and Washington.

The Idaho State Historical Society also has some transcribed cemetery records. A comprehensive listing of these holdings is online at the society's website. The cemetery inventory is by county, cemetery name, and physical location of the graveyard. The society will then need to be contacted to obtain within the transcript itself. Some county genealogical societies and individuals have also transcribed tombstone inscriptions. The published inscriptions are easily accessible.

Church Records

Idaho has a rich and diverse religious culture. The Mormons settled along the Snake River in eastern Idaho and established farming communities. Among these farming communities was Franklin, the first permanent white settlement in Idaho. Catholic priests founded missions among the Coeur d'Alene Native Americans in 1853. Protestants, such as the Methodists and Episcopalians, arrived during the gold mining era.

The largest religious organization in Idaho is The Church of Jesus Christ of Latter-day Saints (Mormons). Mormons colonized the eastern portion of Idaho by 1860. Due to friction caused by of the practice of plural marriage by Mormons, many Mormon families who had originally moved from Utah to Idaho Territory continued their migration northward into Alberta, Canada, where the Mormon presence remains strong today. Mormon ward/branch and mission records are available at the FHL. Brigham Young University–Idaho is a Mormon institution in Rexburg, Idaho. Their Archives and Special Collections department has manuscripts, photographs, and oral histories concerning the Mormon settlement in the Upper Snake River Valley.

Unlike the Mormons, early Protestant and Catholic efforts in Idaho were focused on converting the Native Americans to Christianity rather than settling the land. Methodists and Presbyterians arrived in the region before the Catholic fathers.

Episcopalians soon followed. These efforts concentrated on northern Idaho with the Nez Perce and Flathead tribes. The Methodist mission board in 1834 took action to establish a mission among the Flathead Tribe.

The first Episcopal clergy arrived in Boise and established St. Michael's Church (at the time, the only Episcopal Church in Idaho, Montana, and Utah) a year after Idaho became a territory. The Episcopal faith spread across southern Idaho, and priests evangelized the Shoshoni-Bannock tribes at Fort Hall with success. Episcopal Church records in Idaho covering 110 years are microfilmed and deposited with the Idaho State Historical Society. Among the items filmed are church registers from Delamar, Fort Hall, and Silver City, as well as district and diocesan records between 1896 and 1924.

The emigration of Swedes and Norwegians to northern Idaho brought the Lutheran faith to the area. Other Scandinavians came from the Midwest in the early 1900s to work on irrigation canals in southern Idaho. Many remained to settle the land. Many Lutheran Finns settled in the Long Valley near Cascade and McCall.

The Catholic mission to Idaho began in 1840 when Father Pierre Desmet was appointed to minister to the Native Americans. The Cataldo Mission near Kellogg was established in 1846; the mission church still stands and is the oldest building in Idaho. When miners came in the 1860s, priests were assigned to pioneer white congregations. Currently, the Catholic Church has the second largest membership in the state. The state is served through the Diocese of Boise and the parish registers have been transcribed for the diocese and published as *Roman Catholic Diocese of Idaho, Catholic Chancery Records of Idaho, Master Index (1872–1964)*. The Diocese of Boise can be contacted at 303 Federal Way, Boise, ID 83705 <www.catholicidaho.org/index.cfm>.

It is uncertain how many Quakers lived in Idaho before the turn of the twentieth century, but by 1918 there were 763. A meeting was opened in Boise in 1898 but was briefly discontinued. At the turn of the century, a few Quakers resided in the Star area, a community about twenty miles from Boise. The promise of irrigation water brought many Quaker families to the Boise Valley. By 1906 the meetings in Fairview and Mountain View were organized into the Mountain View Monthly Meeting. The first Quarterly Meeting in Idaho (Boise Valley) was established in 1906 under the auspices of the Oregon Yearly Meeting. It consisted of New Hope (Star), Boise, and Mountain View Monthly Meeting.

In the last quarter of the nineteenth century, members of the Church of the Brethren began to settle in Idaho, attracted to the farmland of the Snake River Valley in southern Idaho and the Clearwater Plateau in northern Idaho. Railroad agents encouraged Brethren to settle in groups in Idaho. So many congregations were established between 1895 and 1910 that

the Idaho and Western Montana District was organized. Early congregations were established in Moscow, Grafton-Clearwater, Nez Perce, Winchester, Nampa, Boise Valley, Boise, Bowmont, Payette, Weiser, Idaho Falls, Lost River, and Twin Falls. An excellent history of these early congregations is found in Roger E. Sappington, *The Brethren along the Snake River: A History of the Brethren in Idaho and Western Montana* (Elgin, Ill.: The Brethren Press, 1966). Brethren congregations in the southwest part of the state can be contacted through the general website at <www.idahochristiansource.com>.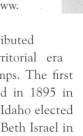

Jewish settlers in Idaho have contributed substantially to the society. During the territorial era Jews became merchants serving the mining camps. The first synagogue, Temple Beth Israel, was constructed in 1895 in Boise. The only other synagogue is in Pocatello. Idaho elected the first Jewish governor in U.S. history. Temple Beth Israel in Boise is the oldest continuous synagogue in existence west of the Mississippi. The historic Congregation Ahavath Beth Israel in Boise can be contacted at 2620 W. Bannock St., Boise, ID 83702. A worthwhile history of the Jewish community in Idaho is Juanita Brooks, *History of the Jews in Utah and Idaho* (Salt Lake City: Western Epics, 1973).

Military Records

Two military collections on file at the Idaho State Historical Society are of interest to the researcher. The first, "Soldier's Home" (AR 19) records, are applications for admission to the Idaho Soldier's Home from 1894 to 1983. Information contained in these applications includes record number, date of admission, name, age, nativity, company, regiment, rank, time served, pension, disabilities, county, occupation, social condition, and literacy. These applications are indexed.

The second collection is entitled "The Adjutant General—State of Idaho: Collection of Official Correspondence, Records, and Documents, 1877–1927" (AR 11). This collection is composed of the following: requests to Governor Brayman for arms and ammunition from worried Idahoans during the Indian Wars of 1877/78, requests for discharge and/or pension benefits from said wars, the actual discharges for at least some Idaho volunteers from the Nez Perce and Bannock Wars, some muster rolls of the Idaho Volunteer Regiments, and other miscellaneous material. Material in this collection also includes various aspects of the draft during World War I and company rosters for the Idaho National Guard units who served during the Mexican Border campaign of 1916.

The Idaho GenWeb Project has transcriptions of all WWI Draft Registrations (1917–18). These are indexed by county.

Periodicals, Newspapers, and Manuscript Collections

Periodicals

Two major periodicals are published in Idaho. The first is the *Idaho Genealogical Society Quarterly,* published by the Idaho Genealogical Society. This publication contains many articles of historical and genealogical value. The second publication is *Idaho Yesterdays: The Quarterly Journal of the Idaho State Historical Society,* an excellent source for a wide range of historical articles, including many concerning ethnic Idaho.

Newspapers

The Idaho State Historical Society has all available newspapers published in the state on microfilm. The society's website has an extensive inventory of newspapers in its collections. The inventory is by city, newspaper title, county, and dates available. Most of the society's newspaper collection is available through interlibrary loan.

Manuscripts

The Idaho State Historical Society has large record collections that are open to the public. Because of limited time and staff, there are limitations on mail requests. The staff is willing to search card indexes for particular names and will make photocopies of material for which a specific citation has been provided. However, they are not capable of extensive research in their archive or manuscript collections.

From 1935 to 1939, the Works Projects Administration (WPA) assembled material on biographies, reminiscences, narrative accounts, diaries, and documents pertinent to the history of Idaho. This WPA collection, MS 70, is indexed and available at the Idaho State Historical Society.

Another indexed collection at the Idaho State Historical Society is a Daughters of the American Revolution (DAR) collection of pioneer reminiscences, biographies, brief histories of Boise Basin towns, and other subjects relating to Idaho's territorial history. This collection is accessed under MS 455. The Pioneer chapter of the DAR compiled this collection between 1908 and 1934.

The remainder of the manuscripts at the Idaho State Historical Society consists of over 2,000 collections, including 150 state and local governmental agencies, 600 large and 800 minor manuscript collections. Many collections relate primarily to Idaho and its history. Files of attorneys, defunct banks, labor organizations, lumber companies, ranches, merchants, church councils, mining companies, and newspapers comprise most of the non-government materials. These are indexed by individual or company name and to some extent by subject in the society's manuscript guide.

The Joyce Dice Owen Collection is on file at the FHL. This collection consists of Idaho genealogies extracted from the *Idaho Daily Statesman,* Boise, Idaho.

Archives, Libraries, and Societies

Idaho State Historical Society
The Library and Archives
1109 Main St., Ste. 250
Boise, ID 83702
http://idahohistory.net/

Idaho State Library
325 W. State St.
Boise, ID 83702
www.lili.org.isl

Idaho Genealogical Society
P.O. Box 1854
Boise, ID 83701-1854
www.lili.org/idahogenealogy

Brigham Young University–Idaho
224 D MacKay Library
525 S. Center St.
Rexburg, ID 83460
http://abish.byui.edu/specialCollections/fhc/FamilyHistory.htm

Two excellent resources for southeastern Idaho research are the Genealogical Library in the David O. McKay Resource Library at Ricks College in Rexford, Idaho; and the Idaho Falls Family History Center in Idaho Falls, Idaho. The latter has all the area mortuary records, cemetery records, and the "Post Register" obituary index (to 1955).

The Idaho Library Directory <www.lili.org/directory/index.php> is an extensive website to the libraries in the state. This includes current information on public, academic, and private libraries and links to these library websites.

Special Focus Categories

Immigration

No common port of entry existed for overseas immigrants who settled in Idaho, nor were there any railroads or emigration trails. Those who arrived and remained in Idaho developed their society in relative isolation. Idaho did have one port of entry at the Canadian border through which immigrants could migrate. By 1924 Idaho was under the jurisdiction of the Spokane, Washington, Office of the Bureau of Immigration. Port of entry was at Eastport, Idaho. Eastport records are filed with the Seattle

passenger lists (1890–1957) at the National Archives. These have been microfilmed but are not indexed. Additional information on people entering through Eastport, Idaho, may be obtained from a search of the (so-called) St. Albans, Vermont District records (see Vermont—Immigration), which are indexed.

Native American

According to the 1900 U.S. census, the following tribal members were residing in Idaho: Bannocks, Cayuse, Coeur d'Alene, Colville, Cree, Crow, Flathead, Kalispell, Kootenai, Omaha, Seletze, Sheepeater, Snake, Spokane, and Umatilla.

Several agencies were set up by the federal government to administer to the affairs of Idaho's Native American population. These records are available at the National Archives—Pacific Alaska (Seattle) and the Idaho State Historical Society. Northern Idaho Agency records are also available at the FHL.

Fort Hall Agency, Fort Hall, Idaho (1889–1952), records include school surveys and censuses, mining permits, grazing leases, ledgers and cards for accounts of individual Indians, records concerning owners of ceded land, irrigation, forestry, loans, and law suits. The Fort Hall Agency administered the affairs of the Boise and Bruneau band of the Shoshone and Bannock tribes. Bannock tribal members from Wyoming came under the jurisdiction of the Fort Hall Agency in 1872.

Northern Idaho Agency, Lapai, Idaho (1875–1964) records include general correspondence and a decimal file, historical files, correspondence concerning Kutenai educational contracts, grazing and timber leases, ledgers for accounts of individual Indians, annuity payrolls, vital statistics, census records, Nez Perce tribal minutes, records concerning forestry, roads, and economic and social surveys. This agency administered the affairs of the Coeur d'Alene, Kootenai, and Nez Perce Reservations.

In researching tribal records in Idaho, two school records and one other major collection should not be overlooked. The Chemawa Indian School in Chemawa, Oregon, and the Fort Shaw School in Cascade County, Montana, enrolled students from the whole of the northwestern United States. For more details, see the Native American Records sections for Montana and Oregon.

Two major Native American collections are the Major James McLaughlin Papers and the Pacific Northwest Tribes Missions Collection of the Oregon Province Archives of the Society of Jesus (1853–1960). For more details on these collections, see Montana—Native American section.

For further explanation of Native American landownership, see Oregon—Native American section.

Other Ethnic Groups

Idaho has its share of ethnic minorities. Because Idaho was a frontier society, many ethnic groups did not readily blend into the society at large. Eastern Idaho was overwhelmingly part of the Mormon intermountain empire, made up mostly of Mormon converts from England and Scandinavia. The fact that the Mormons were distinctive in their religion and culture separated them from the mainstream frontier society. Their court system was administered by the Mormon theocracy; therefore, their dependence on Idaho territorial law was minimal.

The first Chinese came to Idaho in 1864 to mine the Oro Fino gold fields. They were brought from California to alleviate a shortage of labor, and soon every mining town in the territory had an ethnic Chinese community. By 1870 there were 4,274 Chinese in Idaho, which constituted 28.5 percent of Idaho's entire population. At one time, Boise had the largest Chinatown outside of San Francisco.

Idaho's ethnic Chinese originally came from the city of Canton and province of Kuang-Tuang, which at the time was experiencing a great deal of political unrest, as well as severe weather conditions, which affected the economy and made migration to America attractive.

The Chinese paid taxes in Idaho, including miners' tax, property tax, poll tax, and hospital tax. The Masonic lodge was very popular among the Chinese as both a social and a fraternal organization. Very few Chinese became Christians. No regionally organized anti-Chinese groups emerged in Idaho, unlike neighboring states.

In 1880 there were 3,379 Chinese in Idaho. By 1890 the number had declined to 2,007, and in 1900, to 1,467. In the latter part of the nineteenth century, the bulk of the Chinese population could be found in Boise County.

In the early 1970s the building belonging to the Hip Sing Association, a Chinese fraternity, was torn down in Boise, and a large collection of materials from the building was donated to the Idaho State Historical Society. The collection included both items and papers, and these papers, written in Chinese, are currently being inventoried.

The Japanese first came to Idaho in the decade following statehood in 1890, from which time they have constituted the state's largest ethnic group. By the end of the 1890s, Japanese settlements were common features along the length of the Oregon Short Line Railroad, especially in Nampa and Pocatello. By 1920 the number of Japanese in Idaho had reached 1,569.

World War II put the Japanese-American community's loyalty in question in the minds of some Americans. With the relocation of Japanese-Americans to camps set up by the U.S. government, the history of this ethnic group entered a new period. One of the ten camps was in Idaho. This camp, located in Hunt, Idaho, opened in August 1942 and became known as Camp Minidoka. Most of the residents in the camp were from Portland and Seattle. The effect of relocation on Idaho continued to be felt after the war as many Japanese-Americans chose to remain in Idaho rather than return to their former homes.

Another group in Idaho, the Basques, came from the Spanish provinces of Guipuzcoa, Viscaya, Alava, and Navarre in the Pyrenees Mountains. Boise was the center of Basque immigration and probably has the largest Basque-American community in the American West.

Young Basque left their homelands for California in 1876 because of Spanish suppression. As the Basque people moved into southern Idaho, they sent word back to their homeland that jobs were available in the area. Basques came to the Boise Valley in their greatest numbers between 1900 and 1920. As their population grew, a serious religious problem surfaced. The Basques were Catholics who had found their homes in a predominantly Protestant society. However, the Catholic parishes in the Boise Valley were unable to minister to the immigrants as the Basques spoke very little, if any, English. In 1911, the Bishop of the Boise diocese arranged for a Basque-speaking priest to be sent to Idaho. This was the beginning of a viable Basque community in Boise, which centered around a few boarding houses in the southeastern portion of the city. Boise is still home to several Basque organizations (see <http://www.basqueclubs.com/Pages/boise_basque_cover.htm>).

County Resources

Idaho's county resources can be found in the county seat. Land records are filed at the county recorder's office, probate records with the probate clerk, and court records with the district clerk of the court. A survey of the counties indicates that some hold vital records before the date of mandatory recording, and land records and court records, including judgments, minutes, and miscellaneous records, are available previous to county formation. In the list that follows, the year of the earliest known record is indicated. Current addresses are from <www.naco.org>. Naturalizations generally begin at the year of formation and are held by the clerk of the district court. The website "Access Idaho" at <www.accessidaho.org/aboutidaho/county/index.html> provides links to Idaho's county websites.

The Idaho State Historical Society library also holds microfilms of most of these records. Other large collections on microfilm are at the FHL.

IDAHO

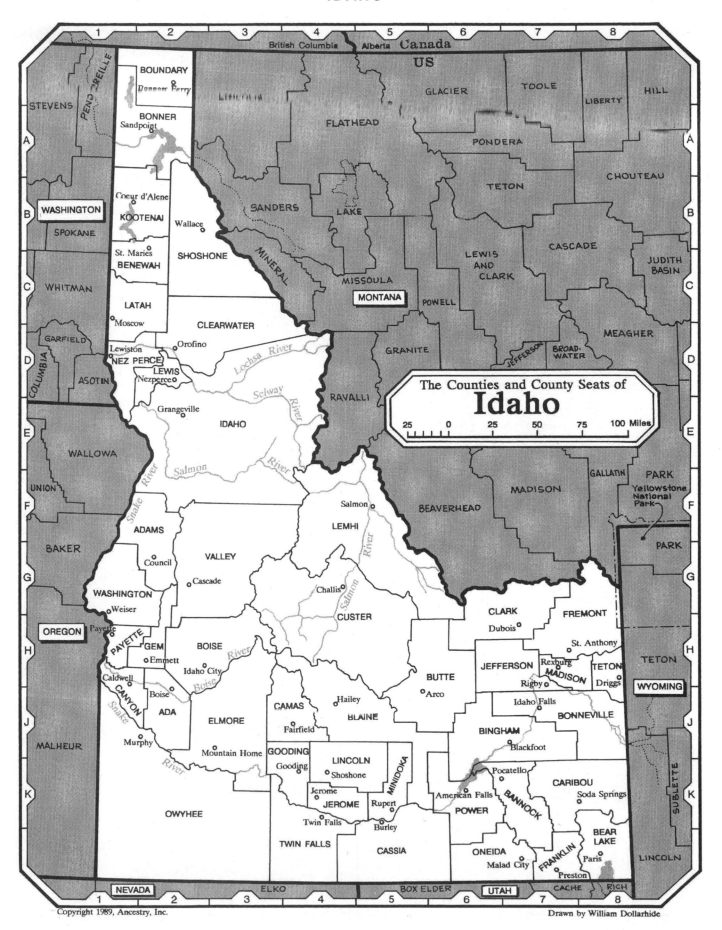

The Counties and County Seats of
Idaho

25   0   25   50   75   100 Miles

Drawn by William Dollarhide

Map	County Address	Date Formed Parent County/ies	Birth Marriage Death	Land Probate Court
J2	Ada 200 W. Front St. Boise 83702	1864 Boise	1907 1864 1907	1865 1869 1865
G2	Adams 201 Industrial Ave. Council 83612-0048	1911 Washington	—— 1911 ——	1876 1886 1911
	Alturas *Records available in Blaine County.*	1864 (abolished 1895 to create Blaine and Lincoln)	—— 1864 ——	1864 1883 1865
K7	Bannock 624 E. Center Pocatello 83201-6274	1893 Bear Lake/Oneida	1905 1895 1905	1880 1888 1866
K8	Bear Lake Box 190 Paris 83261-0190	1875 Oneida	1907 1875 1907	1875 1875 1875
C2	Benewah 701 College Ave. St. Maries 83861-1852	1915 Kootenai	—— 1915 ——	1890 1915 1885
J7	Bingham 501 N. Maple Blackfoot 83221	1885 Oneida	1907 1865 1907	1865 1885 1866
J5	Blaine 206 1st Ave. South Hailey 83333-8429	1895 Alturas/Logan	1907 1864 1908	1863 1883 1865
H3	Boise 420 Main St. Idaho City 83631-0000	1864 original	1907 1867 1907	1863 1863 1863
A2	Bonner 215 S. First Ave. Sandpoint 83864-1305	1907 Kootenai	1907 1907 1907	1885 1891 1885
J7	Bonneville 605 N. Capital Ave. Idaho Falls 83402-3582	1911 Bingham	1911 1911 1911	1911 1888 1911
A2	Boundary P.O. Box 419 Bonners Ferry 83805	1915 Kootenai/Bonner	1907 1915 1907	1886 1883 1883
H6	Butte 248 W. Corand Arco 83213-0737	1917 Bingham/Blaine/ Jefferson	—— 1917 ——	1917 1886 1881
J4	Camas 501 Soldier Rd. Fairfield 83327-9700	1917 Blaine	—— 1917 ——	1885 1897 1870
J2	Canyon 1115 Albany St. Caldwell 83605-3522	1892 Ada/Owyhee	1906 1892 1907	1865 1885 1865
K8	Caribou 159 S. Main St. Soda Springs 82376-1427	1919 Bannock/Oneida	—— 1919 ——	1889 1898 1891
K5	Cassia 1459 Overland Ave. Burley 83318-1862	1879 Oneida	1907 1874 1907	1875 1879 1879
G6	Clark 320 W. Main St. Dubois 83423-0205	1919 Fremont	—— 1919 ——	1866 1909 1890
D3	Clearwater 150 Michigan Ave. Orofino 83544	1911 Nez Perce	—— 1911 ——	1871 1911 1883
H4	Custer 801 Main St. Challis 83226-2360	1881 Alturas	1907 1879 1907	1872 1879 1879
J3	Elmore 150 S. Fourth St. Mountain Home 83647-3060	1889 Ada/Alturas	1907 1889 1907	1889 1892 1889
K7	Franklin 39 W. Oneida St. Preston 83263-1232	1913 Oneida	—— 1913 ——	1874 1910 1878
G8	Fremont 151 W. First St. North St. Anthony 83445-1413	1893 Bingham/Lemhi	1907 1893 1907	1878 1889 1889
H2	Gem 415 E. Main Emmett 83617-3059	1915 Boise/Canyon	—— 1915 ——	1870 1896 1865
K4	Gooding 624 Main St. Gooding 83330-1300	1913 Lincoln	—— 1913 ——	1913 1913 1913
E3	Idaho 320 W. Main St. Grangeville 83530-1948	1864 original	1907 1862 1907	1862 1865 1870
H7	Jefferson 135 N. Clark St. Rigby 83442-1462	1913 Fremont	—— 1914 ——	1913 1901 1891
K4	Jerome 300 N. Lincoln Ave. Jerome 83338-2344	1919 Gooding/Lincoln/ Minidoka	—— 1919 ——	1919 1918 1884
B2	Kootenai 451 Government Way Coeur d'Alene 83814-2988	1864 Nez Perce	1907 1881 1907	1881 1884 1881
C2	Latah 522 S. Adams Moscow 83843-2971	1888 Nez Perce	1907 1888 1907	1881 1881 1879
F5	Lemhi 206 Courthouse Dr. Salmon 83467-3900	1869 Idaho	1907 1869 1907	1867 1880 1868

IDAHO

Map	County Address	Date Formed Parent County/ies	Birth Marriage Death	Land Probate Court
D2	Lewis 510 Oak St. Nezperce 83543	1911 Nez Perce	——— 1911 ———	1868 1911 1883
K4	Lincoln 111 West B St. Shoshone 83352-5364	1895 Alturas/Logan	1907 1895 1907	1863 1883 1882
	Logan *Records available in Blaine County.*	1889 (abolished 1895 to create Blaine and Lincoln)	——— ——— ———	——— ——— ———
H7	Madison 134 E. Main St. Rexburg 83440-0389	1913 Fremont	——— 1915 ———	1913 1913 1893
K5	Minidoka 715 G St. Rupert 83350	1913 Lincoln	——— 1913 ———	1913 1908 1908
D2	Nez Perce 1230 Main St. Lewiston 83501-1975	1864 original	1880 1863 1907	1862 1864 1864
K6	Oneida 10 Court St. Malad City 83252	1864 original	1907 1865 1907	1865 1871 1865
K2	Owyhee HC 79 Mile Marker 29-5 Hwy 78 Murphy 83650-9803	1863 original	1907 1876 1907	1865 1864 1873
H1	Payette 1120 Third North Ave. Payette 83661-2400	1917 Canyon	——— 1917 ———	1917 1896 1917
K6	Power 543 Bannock Ave. American Falls 83211-1200	1913 Bingham/Blaine/Oneida	——— 1913 ———	1913 1913 1913
B3	Shoshone 700 Bank St. Wallace 83873-2355	1864 original	1907 1875 1907	1871 1871 1866
H8	Teton 89 N. Main St. Driggs 83422-5164	1915 Bingham/Fremont/ Madison	——— 1915 ———	1893 1900 1903
K4	Twin Falls 425 Shoshone St. N. Twin Falls 83301-6153	1907 Cassia	1907 1907 1907	1880 1907 1907
G3	Valley 219 N. Main St. Cascade 83611	1917 Boise/Idaho	——— 1917 ———	1876 1917 1879
G1	Washington 256 E. Court St. Weiser 83672-2278	1879 Boise	1907 1879 1907	1873 1878 1880

Illinois

CAROL L. MAKI AND MICHAEL JOHN NEILL

When Louis Jolliet and Father Jacques Marquette arrived in Illinois country in 1673, they found a settler's paradise: fertile soil, sweeping prairies, forests, and water. A traversable network of rivers, easy low-land portages, and the accessibility of Lake Michigan combined to make the future state of Illinois easy to explore. In 1680 Robert Cavelier, sieur de La Salle, with a vision of the economic promise of the area, erected Fort Crevecoeur at the site of Peoria. Henri de Tonti, an Italian, accompanied La Salle. Two years later the two explorers built Fort St. Louis. By 1691, Tonti, who had taken over the settlement when La Salle left in 1685, moved Fort St. Louis eighty miles downstream. The new fort, known as Fort Pimitoui, included several buildings, Father Marquette's mission, and a village of fur traders' European-native families. Cahokia was settled by Seminarian priests in 1699, Kaskaskia by Jesuits four years later. Settlement followed at Fort de Chartres, Prairie du Rocher, St. Phillipe, and St. Genevieve.

In 1717 Illinois country was placed under the French government of Louisiana. France had ceded all possessions east of the Mississippi in 1763, although the British did not take possession, at Fort de Chartres, until two years later. From 1778 to 1782 the present state of Illinois was a territory of Virginia and known as the county of Illinois. The American Revolution and the Treaty of Paris in 1783 extended the American boundary to the Mississippi, thus making the present Illinois part of the United States.

The establishment of the Northwest Territory in 1787 included Illinois land, but the area became part of the Indiana Territory in 1800. Nine years later the Illinois Territory was established, followed by statehood in 1818.

By 1800 the population of 2,000 included Americans from Virginia, Kentucky, Maryland, Tennessee, New York, New Jersey, Pennsylvania, and New England. In the spring of 1817 a group of English immigrants settled in Edwards County. Rhode Island farmers established a colony at Delavan, Tazewell County, in 1837. The states served as a conduit for the Underground Railroad before the Civil War.

Migration *from* Illinois was also significant and should not be overlooked by the genealogist as many Illinois settlers eventually migrated to Kansas and Nebraska. In addition, the gold rush to California, the wagon trains of the Oregon Trail, and the open prairies of Iowa all tempted the populace of Illinois to venture farther west.

From the late nineteenth century to the present, Chicago's accessibility and employment possibilities attracted a cross-section of all the nationalities. Many ethnic groups either settled in or passed through the state, leaving a great diversity of nationalities that have or are populating the city and state.

Vital Records

Marriage records were the first vital records kept by Illinois counties, typically commencing with the formation of the county and continuing through the present. Births and deaths were not generally recorded at the county level until 1877, and

the practice was not universal until 1916. A scattering of records before 1877 may exist. The Works Projects Administration (WPA) *Guide to Public Vital Statistics Records in Illinois* was published in 1941 and outlines available records by county. The Illinois State Archives (see Archives, Libraries, and Societies) makes available the statewide index to all Illinois marriages (1763–1900) at <www.sos.state.il.us/departments/archives/archives.html>. Copies of all marriage records for Illinois can be obtained through the county recorder in the county where the event occurred.

Births and deaths that were recorded prior to 1 January 1916 were only recorded at the county recorder's office. For births and deaths prior to 1916, contact the County Recorder's office in the county where the event took place or Illinois Regional Archives Depository (IRAD; see Archives, Libraries, and Societies). Check the IRAD holdings to determine whether the desired county records are in its collection at <www.cyberdriveillinois.com/departments/archives/irad/iradholdings.html>.

After 1 January 1916, it became mandatory to record births and deaths at both the county recorder's office and the Illinois Department of Public Health. Copies of both births and deaths after 1916 may be ordered from the County Recorder where the event occurred or the Illinois Department of Public Health, Division of Vital Records, 605 W. Jefferson St., Springfield, IL 62702-5097. There is an online statewide index for deaths that took place after 1 January 1916 up to at least fifty years ago (presently 1950) through the Illinois Death Certificate Index at the Illinois State Archives website <www.cyberdriveillinois.com/departments/archives/idphdeathindex.html>. Pre-1916 death records are being indexed at this writing by the state archives with index data being posted on the website. Keep in mind that varying privacy concerns may impact access to both birth and death records, particularly recent ones.

Divorce records are kept by the county clerk of court. It is interesting to note that in 1868, shortly after the end of the Civil War, the city of Chicago granted 400 divorces.

Indexes for marriage and divorce records are kept by the Illinois Department of Public Health from 1962 through the present, but only verification will be made. Copies of the actual record must be requested from the appropriate county. Individuals may not search the state records. The Illinois State Archives has microfilm copies of records found in some Illinois county courthouses, mostly for southern Illinois. Researchers may use these microfilms at the archives and IRAD Centers. Staff will perform a limited amount of research in these county records in response to written requests. Inquiries may be addressed to the IRAD Coordinator, Illinois State Archives.

Census Records

Federal

Population Schedules
- Indexed—1810 (only Randolph County), 1820, 1830, 1840, 1850 (Edgar County lists county of birth), 1860, 1870, 1880, 1890 (only Mound Township of McDonough County survives), 1900, 1910, 1920, 1930
- Soundex—1880, 1900, 1910 (Miracode), 1920

Industry and Agriculture Schedules
- 1850, 1860, 1870, 1880 (agricultural)

Mortality Schedules
- 1850, 1860, 1870 (only counties Ke–Z), 1880

Edgar County lists county of births on the 1850 census. In addition to the generally available indexes in print and online (see page 3), a card index for Cook County developed by Bernice C. Richard is at the Illinois State Archives with microfilm copies at Newberry Library (see Archives, Libraries, and Societies) and National Archives—Great Lakes Region (see page 12). Printed indexes for the same census year have been published by local county organizations. Over 1,000 cards in the "O" section for the Soundex for the 1880 federal population schedules were omitted. All of the aforementioned are at the Illinois State Historical Library (see Archives, Libraries, and Societies). Only Mound Township of McDonough County survives from the 1890 census. Many larger genealogical libraries have print indexes to Illinois federal state censuses through 1870. See pages 16-17 for a full discussion of online sources.

Territorial

Two territorial censuses were taken for the Illinois populace in 1810 (as Indiana Territory) and 1818 (as Illinois Territory). The 1810 extant returns only include Randolph County in the southern portion of the state. What remains of both censuses have been indexed by AISI (see page 3). Originals are at the Illinois State Archives.

State

The state censuses will list only the head of family by name, followed by numerical totals in age categories for the balance of the household. The following enumerations were taken by the state and remain extant.

    1820—Eighteen counties, which included all of Illinois except Edwards County

    1825—Edwards, Fulton, and Randolph counties only

    1830—Morgan County only (includes present counties of Cass, Morgan, and Scott)

1835—Fayette, Fulton, Jasper, and Morgan counties (includes present counties of Cass, Morgan, and Scott)

1840—Thirty-five counties included. Consult *Descriptive Inventory of the Archives of the State of Illinois* (see Archives, Libraries, and Societies) for list of counties.

1845—Cass, Madison, Putnam, and Tazewell counties only

1855—For all counties except Carroll, Champaign, Franklin, Gallatin, Henry, Jefferson, Lake, Stark, Will, and Woodford

1865—For all counties except Gallatin, Mason, Monroe, and Tazewell (Elm Township in Tazewell County has survived)

The "Name Index to Early Illinois Records" (index to state and federal census records 1810–55 and other government documents) is available on interlibrary loan, by surname, from the Illinois State Library (see Archives, Libraries, and Societies) and through the Family History Library (FHL) in Salt Lake City.

Some city census enumerations were made in Illinois in the 1930s. There is also a microfilmed military census, enumerated in 1862, by county, which lists men eighteen to forty-five years of age. It can be borrowed on interlibrary loan from the Illinois State Archives.

Background Sources

A good general history for the state is Robert P. Howard, *Illinois: A History of the Prairie State* (Grand Rapids, Mich.: W.B. Eerdman Publishing, 1972).

For several years the local and family history section of the Newberry Library in Chicago (see Archives, Libraries, and Societies) has been compiling a biography and industry card index. This index, part of an ongoing project, includes references to biographical sketches found in over twenty-five local histories and biographical compendia published in the nineteenth and early twentieth centuries. Most of the indexed works concentrate on Chicago and Cook County, although a few statewide biographical compendia containing a large number of Chicagoans have also been indexed as part of this project. Written requests for no more than three subjects per letter will be answered by the Newberry staff. For more detailed and original local sources, contact the local historical and genealogical groups and city and county libraries that may have regional history collections. The September 1988 *Illinois Libraries* (vol. 70, no. 7) is devoted to Illinois public libraries with genealogical collections, with emphasis on the unique features of each collection. An April 1986 issue (vol. 68, no. 4) of this same publication describes private genealogical collections, university libraries, governmental agencies, and the Shawnee library system.

The scope of historical and genealogical research for the city of Chicago, founded in 1833, is extensive. The Chicago fire of 1871 complicates the search for accurate records prior to that year. Chicago research and resources, however, are thoroughly and expertly covered by Loretto Dennis Szucs in *Chicago and Cook County: A Guide to Research* (Salt Lake City: Ancestry, Inc., 1996). This reference is highly recommended for anyone researching at any level in Chicago.

The bicentennial project sponsored by the Illinois State Genealogical Society (see Archives, Libraries, and Societies) endeavored to index at least one history for each of the 102 Illinois counties. It was completed in 1976 by the Genealogy Projects Committee of the Winnetka Public Library. This index can be used at the Winnetka Public Library or at the Illinois State Archives, where a search request can be made for no more than two specific individuals. If found, copies of the biographical sketches will be sent. A bibliography of county histories at that library can be found in *Illinois Libraries* 82 (2000): 92-141, published by the Illinois State Library. It is also available online at <www.lib.niu.edu/ipo/il0002tc.html>.

Maps

County atlases and plat books at the Illinois State Historical Library (ca. 1870–1930) give details of each township and indicate ownership. Plat books, however, may not be photocopied or loaned. Excellent map collections can also be found at Illinois State Library, Chicago Historical Society, and the map library of the University of Illinois, Champaign–Urbana. A *Checklist of Illinois State Library's Complete Holding of Illinois County Land Ownership Maps and Atlases* (Springfield, Ill.: The Library, n.d.) is available from the Illinois State Library (see Archives, Libraries, and Societies).

Illinois highway maps are available free through either of the following offices: Illinois Secretary of State, Communications Department, Springfield, IL 62756; or Department of Commerce and Community Affairs, 620 E. Adams, Springfield, IL 62701.

The earliest Sanborn map (see page 5) for Illinois in this collection is 1884. Suggested references are:

Adams, James N. *Illinois Place Names.* Springfield, Ill.: Illinois State Historical Society, 1968. Addendum by Lowell M. Volkel. Springfield, Ill.: Illinois State Historical Library, 1989.

Mitchell, S. Augustus. *County and Township Map of the State of Illinois.* N.p., 1979.

Newberry Library. *Checklist of Printed Maps of the Middle West to 1900.* Boston: G. K. Hall, 1980. The eleven volumes list all known pre-1900 plat maps and plat books for the state of Illinois.

Land Records

Public domain State

In 1791 a special act of Congress gave 400 acres to those who were heads of families in the year 1783 at Vincennes or in the Illinois country. This included the region west of Vincennes, Indiana, across the Wabash River. A later act in 1813 provided preemption rights to land occupied in the state.

But the major land disbursements in Illinois occurred based on its status as a public-domain state. The first General Land Office opened at Kaskaskia in 1804 and began selling land ten years later. There were a total of ten land districts. The Bureau of Land Management (BLM) Eastern States Office (see page 6) has patents, tract books, and township plats. Land-entry case files are at the National Archives, Washington, D.C.

Sale of public land was first conducted under a credit system, which proved to be unmanageable. Many purchasers overextended their ability to pay. In April of 1820 the credit system was abolished, requiring full payment for land at time of purchase. The same legislation reduced the minimum purchase from 160 acres to 80 acres and increased the minimum price per acre from $1.25 to $2. Several acts of Congress provided for further credit and extensions on the previously unpaid accounts. For further information on this aspect of land sales in Illinois, see Victoria Irons and Patricia C. Brennan, *Descriptive Inventory of the Archives of the State of Illinois* (Springfield, Ill.: Illinois State Archives, Office of the Secretary of State), Record Group 952. These files, listed as "U.S. General Land Office Records for Illinois" are extensive and include a wide variety of material from "Circulars Received from General Land Office" to lists of names of persons eligible for militia grants and ancient French and British grants affirmed by the Board of Commissioners.

An index created by the Illinois State Archives to the Illinois public domain land sale records is in three parts: 1) a statewide alphabetical listing by name of purchaser; 2) a county-by-county listing arranged alphabetically by purchaser; and 3) a geographic listing arranged by section, township, and range. Over a half million names appear in these records, including lands sold by the ten federal land district offices; lands sold by the Illinois Central Railroad; and certain school, canal, and internal improvement lands sold by the state. The alphabetical listing by purchaser is available for sale as a set of microfiche from the Illinois State Archives. Copies of the entire microfiche are found at the Newberry Library, the National Archives—Great Lakes Region, and other research facilities. This index is also available online at the Illinois State Archives website <www.cyberdriveillinois.com/departments/archives/data_lan.html>.

For information on the War of 1812 bounty land warrants in the military reserves of Illinois, see Lowell M. Volkel, *War of 1812 Bounty Lands in Illinois* (Thomson, Ill.: Heritage House, 1977) and Theodore L. Carlson, *Illinois Military Tract: A Study of Land Occupation, Utilization and Tenure* (Urbana: University of Illinois Press, 1951).

In some counties there are county recorders to register all property transactions. Smaller counties give this responsibility to the county clerk. Land records usually have grantor and grantee indexes, with property records beginning with the creation of the county. Some Illinois counties have a tract or parcel index in addition to the name indexes. This index lists parcels geographically, typically by quarter section in rural areas. More information on using land records can be obtained in Michael John Neill's article "Using a Tract Index for Land and Other Records" (*Illinois State Genealogical Quarterly* 29 [1997]: 195).

Illinois Central Railroad land records are in the appropriate county courthouses.

Probate Records

Probate jurisdiction was initially granted in 1819 to the clerk of a county's commissioner's court, a court that served as administrators for the county. The duties included all matters involving estates and the guardianships of minors. The circuit court for that county had jurisdiction in probate cases when actions of the commissioners were appealed. In 1821 probate functions were moved from commissioner's courts to the county's probate court.

When county courts (see Court Records) were established in 1848, jurisdiction of probate matters was transferred to them. Beginning in 1870, counties with a population of over 50,000 had probate courts separate from county courts. However, the minimum population number changed several times after that. Effective 1 January 1964, probate functions were turned over to circuit courts.

Illinois Regional Archives Depositories has an unusually large collection of probate records and continues to acquire these genealogically valuable resources. Their collection includes files beginning in 1813. Some very early estate records are included in the Kaskaskia manuscripts and in the Perrin collection (see Manuscripts) in the Springfield depository.

Where extant, records not accessioned by the Illinois State Archives and the regional depositories presumably are at the office of the circuit court clerk serving that county. The FHL catalog should also be searched to determine what microfilms of county records are in its collection as well.

Court Records

As the first nation to colonize Illinois, France was also the first to organize its judiciary system. The commandant of Illinois,

under the control of the governor of Louisiana, had jurisdiction for major criminal and civil cases, but appointed town judges for each settlement to handle lesser cases. The first court of which there is any record in Illinois is the Provincial Council, established in 1722 for the primary jurisdiction of civil and criminal cases.

Before statehood, the county court for all of what is now the state of Illinois was established in 1779 by Virginia for its "Illinois County." The court functioned within a revised version of the French law but with the influence of the English common law. Being in debt would have resulted in a jury trial and imprisonment. Although Virginia relinquished their "Illinois County" to the United States in 1784, no legal form of government replaced Virginia's for what became Illinois until the Northwest Ordinance of 1787. The courts of quarter sessions existed from 1788 to 1805 and from 1809 to 1811. From 1788 to 1809 and from 1811 to 1818, the courts of common pleas were in effect. Orphans' Courts existed from 1795 to 1805. Justice's courts survived for only 1818, and circuit courts existed from 1795 to 1812 and from 1814 to 1818.

A system of circuit courts was established by the Illinois state constitution in 1818. These courts were held by circuit-riding justices of the Illinois Supreme Court, each circuit court covering one or more counties. Jurisdiction for these courts included criminal cases, civil suits for more than $20, appeals from the justices of the peace, and some naturalizations. Additional responsibilities have been added through the years, including local, county, and state judicial elections.

Today the clerk of each circuit court is responsible for a wide variety of activities, among them selection of juries, maintaining court records, recording probate actions, and filing reports. Twenty-one circuit courts presently serve the state. Records of the circuit courts remain with their respective clerks except for those that have been archived or otherwise stored.

County courts were established in 1845 for only Cook and Jo Daviess counties. Three years later a statewide county court system was created. At that time county courts handled only probate cases (see Probate Records) and misdemeanors. Between 1848 and 1870 in counties not yet organized, the county judge also headed county commissioner's court, which served the administrative functions of running daily county operations.

The constitution change in 1870 provided for uniformity in all Illinois county courts, with the exception of Cook County, which continues to have a uniquely functioning circuit court. Jurisdiction for county courts was restricted to probate, apprenticeship, and tax delinquency. Two years later, the county courts received responsibility for misdemeanors and for hearing appeals from justices of the peace. Additional responsibilities were added frequently, including divorces and adoptions. However, in 1964 the county courts of Illinois were technically absorbed

by the circuit court serving that county, with the county judge acting as an associate justice of the circuit court.

Some of the county court records before absorption have been transferred to the Illinois Regional Archives Depository (IRAD) collections. Records there for St. Clair County, for example, date back to the eighteenth century. A survey of some of these files indicates that the following types of cases may be included in county court records: criminal and common law proceedings, "feeble-minded" petitions and warrants of commitment, insanity proceedings and case files, bankruptcy inventories, and condemnation of property for railroad use. The depository's collections include *limited* files from these courts, some predating 1800.

The highest level of judicial power in Illinois is the state supreme court. It exercises appellate jurisdiction except in those cases in which it exercises original jurisdiction. Beginning in 1818, the supreme court convened at the seat of the state government. From 1848 to 1897 it met at one of the state's three grand divisions, and since 1897 it has held its sessions at Springfield. The Illinois State Archives holds numerous records from the state supreme court.

Tax Records

The first known tax authorization in Illinois fell under the jurisdiction of the Territory of the United States North West of the River Ohio. The tax was based on every hundred acres of unimproved uncleared prairie or woodland, divided into three classes based on quality of earth surface and soil. The rates were thirty, twenty, and ten cents, to be paid annually. Property with delinquent taxes was sold at public auction. There do not appear to be any surviving tax records from this territorial period.

Beginning with statehood, tax records form a large part of county archival material. The 1819 laws provided the first taxation process, imposing taxes on land, bank stock owned, slaves and indentured negroes or mulattoes, plus a poor tax. The tax was collected by the county, with income divided between the county and state. Taxpayers' lists were eliminated in 1824, and in 1825 a county road tax and school taxes were enacted.

Original and microfilmed tax records at Illinois Regional Archives Depositories include taxable land lists, assessors' books, railroad tax books, road tax records, and collectors' books, the earliest record dated 1817. Other county tax records are located in county seats.

Cemetery Records

The Genealogical Society of Utah and the Daughters of the American Revolution have compiled cemetery records for the state of Illinois. *Soldiers' Burial Places in State of Illinois for Wars,*

1774–1898, is available on thirty-one reels of microfilm from the FHL. Local genealogical societies may have information and possible printed records of cemeteries in their locale.

The Illinois State Genealogical Society is currently coordinating a project statewide to create a directory of cemetery names and locations. The cemetery committee of that society can be contacted for additional information. Information can also be obtained on the society's website.

Church Records

Despite the early Catholic missionaries in Illinois, their church had almost totally disappeared from the state by the time of the American Revolution. Later migration of English-speaking Catholics reestablished the church in the state. In 1850 the largest religious denomination in Illinois was the Methodists. Baptists, Presbyterians, Roman Catholics, Lutherans, and Congregationalists followed. Episcopalians had organized in the state in 1835, the Disciples of Christ were in Illinois prior to 1830, and the Lutherans grew in numbers with the German and Scandinavian emigration of the 1840s.

In the spring of 1839 a group of five thousand Latter-day Saints, following their expulsion from Ohio and Missouri, were led into Illinois by Joseph Smith. At Nauvoo, originally called Venus and Commerce, they established their Mormon community. The population increased, prosperity increased, and opposition against the Mormons increased. This opposition and dissension within their church ended in the murder of Joseph Smith. In September of 1845 the Mormons were told they were being expelled from the state, an expulsion that led to their migration west.

The Bishop Hill colony of Henry County was founded by a group of Swedish immigrants. Fifteen hundred of them, led by Eric Janson, established a communal existence of a "Bible only" sect in 1846. The murder of Janson in 1853 led to the 1860 dissolution of this religious community. Most of the Jansonists eventually became Methodists.

The Primitive Baptist Library (416 Main St., Carthage, IL 62321 <www.carthage.lib.il.us/community/churches/primbap/pbl.html>) has a collection of records and materials for this denomination in Illinois and surrounding states.

Some local genealogical societies have published regional church records in their respective quarterlies.

Original forms for the inventory *Guide to Church Vital Statistics Records in Illinois; Historical Records Survey* (Chicago, 1942) are at the Illinois State Archives. Included in the published inventory are name of county and city/town; church name and address; denomination; date organized; date of lapse, if now defunct; description (by years, volumes, file boxes) of minute book, register book of baptisms, confirmations, marriages, members, and deaths, record book of Sunday school or other organization, and financial record; location and condition of records; general condition of all records; bibliographical information on any published or unpublished historical sketches of the church; and other information, particularly as to origins, history, and previous names of church. Files also include descriptions of records of orphanages, schools, and rest homes affiliated with the respective churches.

A search at the FHL website for the specific city or town where the church was located may reveal records of the church in its collection.

Military Records

The "Index to Compiled Service Records of Volunteer Union Soldiers who Served in Organizations from the State of Illinois," an index to the National Archives records, is located at the Newberry Library (NARA microfilm publication M539) and Allen County Public Library (see Indiana).

A recent addition at the Illinois State Archives is an 898-reel set of microfilmed Revolutionary War records based on the participation of American military, naval and marine, and enlisted men in the war. Most records date between 1800 and 1900 and come from files in National Archives Record Group 15, "Selected Records from Revolutionary War Pension and Bounty-Land Warrant Application Files," M805. This may be used at the Illinois State Archives and may be borrowed through the interlibrary loan service from the Illinois State Library. Arrangement is alphabetical by surname of the veteran.

The Illinois State Archives has indexes to men serving in Illinois units during the Indian Wars, Black Hawk War, Mexican War, Civil War, and Spanish-American War, including the *Honor Roll of Veterans Buried in Illinois*, a multi-volume set organized by county including veteran's name, cemetery, war service, and grave location within cemeteries. Multiple military record databases of cemeteries' state archives sources are available at the archives' website <www.cyberdriveillinois.com/departments/archives/databases.html>.

A National Home for Disabled Volunteer Soldiers (Veterans Administration Center) was created at Danville, Illinois, in 1898. Records are located in National Archives in Record Groups 15 and 231.

The World War I Selective Service Draft Registration Cards for Illinois are on microfilm, available at the Illinois State Archives. The *Records of the Selective Service Board...Illinois, Indiana, Michigan, Minnesota, Ohio and Wisconsin, 1917–1919* (Record Group 163) are at the National Archives—Great Lakes Region; the collection includes an Index to Delinquent and Deserter Forms (incomplete for some states).

The World War II Selective Service Draft Registration cards for Illinois are available in manuscript form at the National Archives—Great Lakes Region (National Archives Record Group 147, Records of the Selective Service System, Illinois State

Office Registration Cards, World War II, 4th Draft Registration). These cards are only available for those men who were born between 28 April 1877 and 16 February 1897.

Periodicals, Newspapers, and Manuscript Collections

Periodicals

Illinois State Genealogical Society Quarterly has been published quarterly since 1969 by the society, surveying Illinois original source material, family genealogies, and research questions.

Illinois Libraries, published by the Illinois State Library, often contains information on genealogical collections within the state.

The Journal of the Illinois State Historical Society, published four times a year since 1908, has excellent articles on local and state history as well as book reviews.

Illinois Heritage, also published by the Illinois State Historical Society, is a bimonthly magazine aimed at a broader audience.

Newspapers

The *Illinois Herald*, published at Kaskaskia in 1814, was the first Illinois newspaper. Numerous indexes of genealogically important data have been compiled from local and county newspapers, not all in print. Researchers wishing to locate these indexes should contact local genealogical and historical societies in addition to searching online library card catalogs. As an example, the Newspaper Research Committee of the Chicago Genealogical Society has published *Vital Records from Chicago Newspapers, 1833–1839* (Chicago: the society, 1971); *Vital Records from Chicago Newspapers, 1845* (Chicago: the society, 1975); and *Vital Records from Chicago Newspapers, 1843–1844* (Chicago: the society, 1974). Some suggested sources for more information on Illinois newspapers follow:

James, Edmund J. *A Bibliography of Newspapers Published in Illinois Prior to 1860*. Illinois State Historical Library Publications, Number 1. Springfield, Ill.: Phillips Brothers, 1899.

Stark, Sandra M. "Newspapers in the Illinois State Library," *Illinois Libraries* 70 (March–April 1988): 3-4. Updated publication in *Illinois Libraries* every three years.

University of Chicago. *Newspapers in the Libraries of Chicago.* Chicago: University of Chicago Library, 1936.

Manuscripts

Some of the very earliest records of Illinois are included in the J. Nick Perrin collection at the Illinois State Archives in Springfield. The Perrin collection is comprised of over 5,000 documents relating to the French, British, and American regimes at Cahokia and to early St. Clair County at Belleville, dating from 1737 to 1850. A 1737 marriage contract is one of the earliest items in this collection. Births and deaths (1840–58) are also included. Land claims, tax records, road petitions, registers of slaves and free negroes, and probate records are only a few of the multitude of historically important documents in the Perrin collection.

Also housed at the Illinois State Archives are the Kaskaskia Manuscripts, another significant collection for Illinois research. The records, which begin in 1708, are almost entirely notarial transactions. They include, among other agreements, acknowledgments of debt, marriage contracts, and land sales. Some clerk of court registers have been included in the notary's files. If a notary was unavailable, a priest might draft documents to be filed with the notary's records.

See also Draper Manuscripts in Wisconsin—Manuscripts.

Archives, Libraries, and Societies

Illinois State Archives
Margaret Cross Norton Bldg.
Capitol Complex
Springfield, IL 62756
www.sos.state.il.us/departments/archives/archives.html

Included in their extensive holdings are federal and state censuses, military records, land records, and other materials as described in the earlier sections of this chapter. Consult the *Descriptive Inventory of the Archives of the State of Illinois* (Springfield, Illinois, 1991, second edition) or request the Genealogical Records and Mail Research Policy brochure from the archives.

Illinois Regional Archives Depository (IRAD)
IRAD Coordinator
Illinois State Archives
Margaret Cross Norton Bldg.
Capitol Complex
Springfield, IL 62756
www.sos.state.il.us/departments/archives/irad/iradhome.html

As part of the state archives system, seven regional depositories at state universities include archival material from 102 counties. The records include original local government records turned over to IRAD and microfilmed local government records as well. The amount of material in IRAD's collection varies from county to county. A printed version of the IRAD holdings and more information on IRAD is available in print form in *A Summary Guide to Local Governmental Records in the Illinois Regional Archives*, 2d ed. (1999) and also on the Illinois State Archives website. The archives also has on their website a variety of research guides discussing county records in Illinois.

Illinois State Library

Gwendolyn Brooks Bldg
300 S. 2nd St.
Springfield, IL 62701-1796
www.cyberdriveillinois.com/departments/library/home.html

As the head of the public library system in the state, the library publishes *Illinois Libraries,* which frequently includes articles of genealogical interest. The Illinois State Library's five million items include more than 150,000 maps, Illinois Sanborn fire insurance atlases, nineteenth and twentieth century county atlases, aerial photos, and census maps.

Illinois State Historical Library (ISHL)

Old State Capitol
Springfield, IL 62701
www.state.il.us/hpa/lib/

The ISHL is scheduled to move to the Abraham Lincoln Library; check the website for updated information. County histories, plat books, census indexes, cemetery indexes, city material, family and association files, microfilmed newspapers, manuscripts, and photographs are included in its collections, much only available on-site. However, microfilmed newspapers from the library's extensive collection can be obtained via interlibrary loan.

Illinois State Genealogical Society

P.O. Box 10195
Springfield, IL 62791
www.rootsweb.com/~ilsgs

The organization publishes a newsletter and a quarterly, and is also involved in a variety of genealogical projects throughout the state. The society also sponsors the annual Genealogical Institute of Mid America, held annually each July on the campus of the University of Illinois–Springfield. Indexes to the quarterly have been created, and an online topical index to articles from the *Quarterly* is available through the society's website.

Newberry Library

60 W. Walton St.
Chicago, IL 60610
www.newberry.org

Peggy Tuck Sinko's *Guide to Local and Family History at the Newberry Library* (Salt Lake City: Ancestry, 1987) gives a comprehensive description of the Illinois sources available at this excellent repository. The library has an especially strong Chicago area collection.

Special Focus Categories

Naturalization

Although not a direct "port of entry" for American immigrants, many individuals regarded Illinois as their destination. County circuit courts in Illinois typically hold naturalization records prior to 1906; some of these are held by the Family History Library and the Illinois Regional Archives System. Early Cook County naturalization files were destroyed in the Chicago Fire of 1871. Numerous Illinois naturalization records are located at the National Archives—Great Lakes Region, 7358 S. Pulaski Rd., Chicago IL 60629; contact the Great Lakes Region for full particulars. Held by this repository is a Soundex index (Records of Immigration and Naturalization Service, Record Group 85) for naturalizations (1871–1950). The index includes several northern Illinois counties (Cook County for 1871–1906), which has been microfilmed by the Genealogical Society of Utah. For any naturalizations that took place in this District Court after 1959, see the United States District Court—Chicago, Naturalization, Rm. 2062, 219 S. Dearborn, Chicago, IL 60604. This court also maintains an index of all naturalizations in the court from 1871 to the present. Szucs' work, listed in Background Sources above, contains information on specific naturalization records from Calumet City and Chicago Heights.

African American

Most African Americans migrating to Illinois during the early years either came from or through the South. As a result, many slaves arrived in Illinois with their white owners. In September 1807 the indenture law allowed slaves aged fifteen and older to be brought into the state by their white owners. The law stated that they must be registered with the clerk of common pleas. Beginning on 8 December 1812, "free blacks" and "mulattoes" were required to register six months after they arrived in Illinois. These records are extant. Many slaves were leased from slave owners in Kentucky and Tennessee to work the salt wells near Shawneetown.

In 1817 Governor Edwards agreed that the indenture law was illegal. The resulting constitutional compromise of 1818 put a one-year limit on new indenture contracts. The free African Americans may have been issued freedom certificates after 17 January 1829, possibly recorded in the common pleas court files. Records of African Americans in Illinois frequently gave places of origin in the slave state from which they came.

The parish records of the Immaculate Conception Church at Kaskaskia, St. Anne's at St. Charles, and St. Joseph's at Prairie du Rocher have records of pre-1916 baptisms, marriages, and deaths of African Americans. The Illinois State Library has a few slave record books from various counties. These include indentured French and freedmen before 1860. See W. Wesley Johnston, "Illinois Free Black Records," in *Illinois State Genealogical Quarterly* 14 (Summer 1982):72-73, for a discussion of extant records. For further study of African-American history in Illinois, see the following:

Carlson, Shirley J. "Black Migration to Pulaski County, Illinois: 1860–1900," *Illinois Historical Journal* 80 (1987). Its focus is southern African Americans who settled in rural areas of the North.

Harris, Norman Dwight. *The History of Negro Servitude in Illinois and of Slavery Agitation in that State, 1719–1864.* 1904. Reprint. New York: Haskell House, 1969. Also available on microfiche (LAC 12841): *Microbook Library of American Civilization.* Chicago: Library Resources, 1970.

Hodges, Carl G. *Illinois Negro Historymakers.* Chicago: Illinois Emancipation Centennial Commission, 1964.

Johnston, W. Wesley. "Illinois Free Black Records," *Illinois State Genealogical Society Quarterly* 14 (Summer 1982): 72-73.

Perrin, J. Nick, Collection. See Manuscripts above.

Tregillis, Helen Cox. *River Roads to Freedom: Fugitive Slave Notices and Sheriff Notices Found in Illinois Sources.* Bowie, Md.: Heritage Books, Inc., 1988.

Native American

When Europeans arrived in the Illinois country, the Illinewek or Illinois Native Americans were being dominated by the Iroquois of New York and were anxious to have the protection of a nearby fort or mission. In the Illinois valley region, they had once been the largest tribe, a loosely organized alliance of the Kaskaskia, Cahokia, Tamroa, Peoria, Michigamea, and Moingwena bands. Warfare and disease took their tolls, and by 1832 there were slightly more than two hundred of the tribe left in Illinois. The last land cession treaty in that year resulted in those few Native Americans being transferred to a Kansas reservation.

Included in the Illinois State Archives are the following: Record Group 103.62, "Executive Section, Executive File" (ca. 1824–32), concerns Native Americans in Illinois (copies of treaties and speeches made by Native Americans and government representatives at peace conferences, and depositions of Illinois citizens taken by state agents dealing with Indian depredations); and Record Group 100, "Records of the Illinois Territory," has material pertaining to speeches of, trade with, and treaties with Indians, and mention of the Cherokee, Delaware, Fox, Kickapoo, Osage, Ottawa, Potawatomi, Sauk, and Shawnee tribes.

In regard to native lands, see Record Group 952.19, "Board of Commissioners, Ancient Grants Rejected," which lists names of original and present (ca. 1809) owners, including Indian claims. See also Record Group 953.14, "Terrier of Grants Made to Potawatomi Indians," describing land grants made under the Treaty of Camp Tippecanoe on 20 October 1832; and Record Group 953.18, "Abstract of Conditions of Surveys of Indian Grants and Reservations," 1850. Other sources include:

Stewart Rafert, "American-Indian Genealogical Research in the Midwest: Resources and Perspectives," *National Genealogical Society Quarterly* 76 (September 1988): 212-24.

Tregillis, Helen Cox. *The Indians of Illinois.* Decorah, Iowa: Amundsen Publishing Co., 1983.

See also Wisconsin—Native Americans.

Other Ethnic Groups

Illinois has been the home of immigrants from many countries. Settlement patterns within the state frequently varied by nationality. One third of the foreign-born population in Illinois in 1850 was German. Religious, political, and economic factors caused the massive migration. Some of the earliest German settlements were in Dutch Hollow and Darmstadt, St. Clair County. One interesting perspective of early German settlers' lives is "Ferdinand Ernst and the Germany Colony at Vandalia" in *Illinois Historical Journal* 80 (Summer 1987), depicting this 1820 settlement in Fayette County.

Many German immigrants came to Illinois as affluent farmers, professionals, and artisans, and were able to continue as such in America. There were also those who came with little or no money to spare. Immigrants came via the Great Lakes to Chicago. Working in the industries of the city, they could make good wages to buy their "American" farm. Unfortunately, living costs were high, savings grew slowly, and land values rose rapidly. The "farmer" often became a city dweller.

The Irish immigrant may have stayed in the cities, employed as a day laborer or factory worker. They moved from place to place within the state, but by 1860 the nucleus of the Irish immigrant community was in Chicago. Many Irish worked on the construction of the Illinois and Michigan canal system. When this project was temporarily abandoned in the early 1840s, large numbers of Irish became farmers.

There was considerable immigration from England, some of it prompted by the London Roman Catholic Emigration Society and the Mormon missionaries sent from Nauvoo by Joseph Smith. Kane County had a considerable Welsh population, and the lead mines brought the Cornish. In 1834 the Scottish began migrating to Illinois, their numbers in 1850 totaling 4,660.

The first Norwegian settlement in the Midwest was founded by a group from New York, in 1834, along the Fox River near Ottawa. Five hundred Swedes established themselves at Bishop Hill in Henry County, and the Mormons settled at Nauvoo. (See Church Records for further information on both of these religious immigrant groups.)

Although there were scattered French-Canadians in Illinois country very early, there were few immigrants from France before 1830. Metamora in Woodford County was the first important French section, established in 1831, followed by several other French settlements. Bourbonnais, in Kankakee County, with a population of 1,719 in 1850, was a French-Canadian village that maintained Canadian customs for many years.

Colonies of religiously exiled Portuguese immigrants were located at Springfield and Jacksonville in 1849. There was

a cluster of Bavarian Jews in Chicago. Although few Swiss immigrated to Illinois, there were settlements in St. Clair County, in Galena, and in Madison County, the most important center of Swiss population in Illinois.

Szucs's publication, listed under Background Sources above, provides bibliographies of information on the following ethnic groups in Chicago: African Americans, Bohemians, Chinese, Czechoslovakian, Dutch, German, Greeks, Irish, Italian, Japanese, Lithuanian, Mexican, Norwegian, Polish, Russian, Swedish, and Ukrainian. According to Szucs, "At different times in its history, Chicago has been the largest Lithuanian city, the second largest Ukranian city, and the third largest Swedish, Irish, Polish, and Jewish city in the world."

Augustana College (Swenson Swedish Immigration Research, Rock Island, IL 61201 <www.augustana.edu/administration/SWENSON>) has immigrant letters and immigration indexes, church papers, a large collection of Swedish-American newspapers, and a significant amount of microfilmed church records from Swedish-American congregations in the Midwest. The *Swedish Pioneer Historical Quarterly* is published by the Swedish-American Historical Society, 5125 N. Spaulding Ave., Chicago, IL 60625 <www.swedishamericanhist.org>, which is an excellent research center for Swedish-American genealogy, particularly in Chicago. Their collections include letters, family histories, organization records, newspapers, diaries, books, oral histories, reference files, and photographs.

The University of Illinois, Slavic Reference Service, 225 Library Bldg., Urbana, IL 61801 <www.reec.uiuc.edu> holds a Czech-American collection of over 31,000 volumes of history, periodicals, original documents, and Czech-American newspapers. A collection of Czech family Bibles and 10,000 Czech history volumes are located at Illinois Benedictine College Library, 5700 College Rd., Lisle, IL 60532.

The Newberry Library has an extensive collection of Irish and English materials. For Irish, contact the Irish American Heritage Center, 4626 N. Knox Ave., Chicago, IL 60630 <www.irishamhc.com> and DePaul University, Lincoln Park Campus Library, 2323 N. Seminary, Chicago, IL 60614 <www.lib.depaul.edu/speccoll/guides/irish.htm>, which has an Irish studies collection.

When researching German ancestry in this state, contact the Palatines to America—Illinois Chapter, P.O. Box 3884, Quincy, IL 62305. Szucs (see Background Sources) states that the detailed church records of German-American churches must be utilized for that nationality in Cook County. Those with Polish ancestry should use the resources of the Polish Genealogical Society, 984 N. Milwaukee Ave., Chicago, IL 60622 <www.pgsa.org> and the Polish collection at the Portage-Cragin Branch Library, 5108 W. Belmont Ave., Chicago, IL, 60641.

Other suggested sources include the Ukrainian National Museum of Chicago, 721 N. Oakley, Chicago, IL 60612 <www.ukrntlmuseum.org>; Chicago Public Library, Chinatown Branch, 2353 S. Wentworth, Chicago, IL 60616 <http://cpl.lib.uic.edu/002branches/chinatown/chinatown.html>; and the Balzekas Museum of Lithuanian Culture, 6500 S. Pulaski, Chicago, IL 60629 <www.lithaz.org/museums/balzekas>.

See also Melvin G. Holli and Peter d'A. Jones, eds., *Ethnic Chicago* (Grand Rapids, Mich.: William B. Eerdmans, ca. 1984); Melvin G. Holli and Peter d'A. Jones, eds., *The Ethnic Frontier: Essays in the History of Group Survival in Chicago and the Midwest* (Grand Rapids, Mich.: Eerdmans, ca. 1977); Ellen M. Whitney's *Illinois History: An Annotated Bibliography* (Westport, Conn.: Greenwood Press, 1995); and Mark Wyman, *Immigration History and Ethnicity in Illinois: A Guide* (Springfield, Ill.: Illinois State Historical Society, 1989).

County Resources

Wills, administrations, and probate matters are at the office of the circuit court. Deeds, mortgages, and leases are the responsibility of the recorder of deeds. In mailing requests to any Illinois county office, use the title of the appropriate county officer and "County Courthouse," with the address listed in the chart below.

For some counties there are two years for "Date Formed." The first is the year the county was created. The second is the year it was fully organized if it differs from the creation year. Under the heading "Parent County/ies," the name/s listed may be the county or counties from which the respective county was formed, or it may be the name by which the county was formerly known. "Unorganized" denotes that some formerly non-county area was included. A county name in parentheses is the county to which the unorganized land may have been attached at that time. Counties listed with an asterisk (*) are those in which you may also find records for the respective county since it may have been "attached" to that county for some period of time.

The date listed for each category of record is the earliest record known to exist in that county. It does not indicate that there are numerous records for that year and certainly does not indicate that all such events that year were actually registered.

The information on earliest dates of Illinois county births, marriages, deaths, land records, probate files, and county court records has been obtained through the courtesy of the Illinois Regional Archives. Karl R. Moore, supervisor of this repository, has been exceedingly kind in providing material for use in this publication. He was assisted in this project by Illinois Regional Archives Division staff members John Reinhardt and David Curtin. The basic sources of information used were the *Historical Records Survey* inventories, published and unpublished, which Moore feels are both thorough and accurate. The IRAD team used more recent data when available, comparing that with the Historical Records Survey findings, stating, "The sources

cited in our report are always the most recent and authoritative that could be established without actually visiting the county courthouses and taking an inventory." Moore also explains, "We also gave especially close scrutiny to records whose beginning date fell after the date of county organization. Since recording of births and deaths did not become mandatory in Illinois until 1877, these records would seldom appear before that date, but marriage, probate, land sale, and court records should have been created from the beginning of a county." Many date discrepancies are explained, according to this report, by the loss of records in fires, floods, or other disasters. When this did not appear to be the explanation, the IRAD team again verified the accuracy of the beginning dates.

In regard to land records Moore states, "Deed records usually coincide with the beginning of a county, so earlier dates in the land sales column usually indicate transcribed records from a parent county, or land patent records that contain information on original land sales from the public domain." He explains, in regard to court records, "The earliest court records for Illinois counties created after 1818 are invariably records of the circuit court. Chancery, civil, and criminal cases are usually filed together at first." For counties created during the territorial period, the following gives the type of their earliest court: St. Clair: Court of the District of Cahokia; Randolph: French Provincial Council; Madison, Gallatin, and Johnson: court of common pleas; Edwards, White, Jackson, Pope, Monroe, Crawford, and Bond: county court; Franklin, Union and Washington: justices' court. Jackson, Cook and Franklin counties lost early court records in fires.

Ernest E. East's "Records Lost in Illinois Court House Fires," *Illinois Libraries* (October 1951): 376-79, provides an interesting history of courthouse fires in the state, plus an informative chart listing the counties, dates, and extent of record loss.

Addresses in the following chart were based on Illinois County courthouse addresses from the Illinois Secretary of State website <www.sos.state.il.us/departments/archives/cntyaddr.html>.

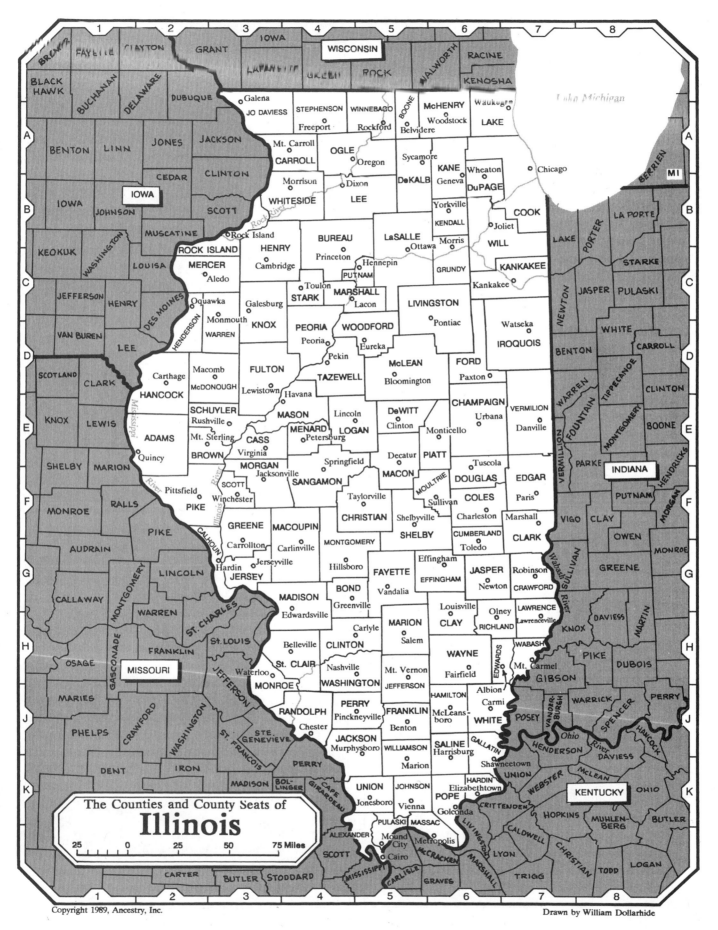

The Counties and County Seats of
Illinois

25   0   25   50   75 Miles

Drawn by William Dollarhide

Map County Address	Date Formed Parent County/ies	Birth Marriage Death	Land Probate Court
E2 Adams 507 Vermont Box 1169 Quincy 62306	1825 Pike/ unorganized	1877 1825 1877	1817 1826 1825
K5 Alexander 2000 Washington Ave. Cairo 62914	1819 unorganized (Union)	1877 1819 1878	1818 1819 1821
G4 Bond County Office Bldg. 200 West College, Rm. 203 Greenville 62246	1817 Madison/Crawford/ Edwards	1877 1817 1877	1817 1821 1817
A5 Boone 601 N. Main St. Belvidere 61008	1837 (1837) Winnebago/ *Jo Daviess	1877 1838 1877	1838 1840 1838
E2 Brown Mt. Sterling 62353	1839 Schuyler	1878 1839 1878	1817 1839 1837
C4 Bureau 700 S. Main St. Princeton 61356	1837 Putnam	1878 1837 1878	1817 1837 1837
G3 Calhoun P.O. Box 187 Hardin 62047	1825 Pike	1878 1825 1878	1825 1833 1825
A3 Carroll 301 N. Main St. Mt. Carroll 61053	1839 Jo Daviess	1877 1839 1877	1837 1839 1837
E3 Cass Virginia 62691	1837 Morgan	1878 1837 1874	1826 1837 1837
E6 Champaign 1776 E. Washington Urbana 61802	1833 Vermilion	1878 1833 1878	1833 1833 1836
F5 Christian P.O. Box 190 Taylorville 62568	1839 Montgomery/ Sangamon/Dane	1877 1839 1877	1828 1839 1839
F7 Clark Marshall 62441	1819 Crawford	1865 1819 1865	1816 1820 1821
H6 Clay P.O. Box 160 Louisville 62858	1824 Fayette/Crawford/ Wayne/Lawrence	1877 1825 1877	1825 1827 1825
H4 Clinton Courthouse Sq. Carlyle 62231	1824 Washington/Fayette/ Bond	1877 1825 1877	1818 1825 1825
F6 Coles P.O. Box 227 Charleston 61920	1830 Clark/ Edgar	1878 1831 1877	1830 1830 1831
B7 Cook 118 North Clark St. Room 402 Chicago 60602	1831 Putnam	1871 1856 1871	* * 1871

* Illinois Regional Archives Depositor states, "Most of the major records for the county (Cook) were destroyed in the Chicago Fire of 1871.... The Cook County Recorder's Office has land records from 1871 onward. Prior to 1871, the Chicago Title Insurance Company has pre-fire tract and copy books as abstracted from the original documents filed in the Cook County Recorder's Office and from the issuance of the first government land patents. The Illinois State Archives has the original documents related to the government land patents. Federal land sale began from the various land offices in Illinois in 1814..." According to Szucs (see Background Sources), a will index survives that begins in the year 1850. The Illinois Historical Records Survey lists a record series titled "Documented Record of Wills," which begins in 1851 and a series titled "Abstract of Probate Proceedings" beginning in 1861. All other probate records begin in 1871.

Map County Address	Date Formed Parent County/ies	Birth Marriage Death	Land Probate Court
G7 Crawford P.O. Box 602 Robinson 62454	1816 Edwards	1877 1817 1877	1816 1818 1817
G6 Cumberland P.O. Box 146 Toledo 62468	1843 Coles	1885 1880 1844	1885 1884 1885
Dane	(see Christian)		
B6 DeKalb 110 E. Sycamore St. Sycamore 60178	1837 Kane	1877 1837 1878	1838 1837 1838
E5 DeWitt 201 W. Washington St. P.O. Box 439 Clinton 61727	1839 McLean/ Macon	1877 1839 1878	1828 1839 1839
F6 Douglas 401 S. Center P.O. Box 467 Tuscola 61953	1859 Coles	1877 1859 1877	1830 1859 1859
B6 DuPage 421 N. County Farm Rd. Wheaton 60189	1839 Cook	1877 1839 1877	1835 1839 1839
F7 Edgar 115 W. Court St. Paris 61944	1823 Clark	1877 1823 1877	1823 1823 1823
H7 Edwards Edwards County Courthouse Albion 62806	1814 Gallatin/Madison	1877 1815 1877	1815 1815 1815
G6 Effingham 101 North 4th P.O. Box 628 Effingham 62401	1831 (1833) Fayette/ Crawford	1877 1833 1877	1833 1838 1833
G5 Fayette 221 S. Seventh St. Vandalia 62471	1821 Bond/Jefferson/ Wayne/Crawford/Clark	1860 1821 1877	1816 1821 1821
D6 Ford 200 W. State St. Paxton 60957	1859 unorganized (Vermilion)	1878 1859 1878	1834 1850 1859

Map	County Address	Date Formed Parent County/ies	Birth Marriage Death	Land Probate Court
J5	Franklin Benton 62812	1818 White/Gallatin/Johnson	1877 1836 1877	1837 1837 1836
D3	Fulton 100 N. Main Lewistown 61542	1823 unorganized (Pike)	1878 1824 1878	1817 1827 1824
J6	Gallatin P.O. Box K Shawneetown 62984	1812 Randolph	1878 1813 1878	1813 1814 1813
F3	Greene 519 N. Main St. Carrollton 62016-1033	1821 Madison	1877 1821 1877	1821 1821 1821
C6	Grundy 111 E. Washington St. Morris 60450	1841 LaSalle	1876 1841 1878	1832 1841 1837
J6	Hamilton Hamilton County Courthouse McLeansboro 62859	1821 White	1878 1821 1878	1823 1821 1821
D2	Hancock P.O. Box 39 Carthage 62321	1825 unorganized (Pike)/ *Adams	1844 1829 1878	1817 1830 1829
K6	Hardin P.O. Box 187 Elizabethtown 62931	1839 Pope	1844 1884 1884	1814 1884 1878
D2	Henderson P.O. Box 308 Oquawka 61469	1841 Warren	1877 1841 1878	1818 1839 1841
C3	Henry 100 S. Main Cambridge 61238	1825 (1837) unorganized (Fulton)/ *Peoria/*Knox	1877 1837 1877	1836 1839 1837
	Highland	1847 (eliminated 1848) Adams/Marquette		
D7	Iroquois 1001 E. Grant St. Watseka 60970	1833 (1834) unorganized (Vermilion)	1878 1866 1878	1834 1834 1834
J5	Jackson Murphysboro 62966	1816 Randolph/Johnson	1877 1843 1877	1814 1840 1843
G6	Jasper 100 W. Jourdan St. Newton 62448	1831 (1835) Crawford/ Clay	1877 1835 1877	1835 1835 1835
J5	Jefferson 100 S. 10th St. Mt. Vernon 62864	1819 Edwards/ White	1877 1819 1877	1816 1820 1819
G3	Jersey 201 W. Pearl St. Jerseyville 62052	1839 Greene	1878 1839 1877	1822 1839 1839
A3	Jo Daviess 330 N. Bench St., Galena 61036	1827 Mercer/Henry/Putnam	1877 1830 1877	1828 1828 1827
K5	Johnson P.O. Box 96 Vienna 62995	1812 Randolph	1878 1835 1878	1809 1821 1812
A6	Kane 719 S. Batavia P.O. Box 70 Geneva 60134	1836 (1836) unorganized (LaSalle)/ Cook	1877 1836 1877	1836 1836 1836
C7	Kankakee 189 E. Court St. Kankakee 60901	1853 Iroquois/Will	1877 1853 1877	1832 1853 1853
B6	Kendall 111 W. Fox St. Yorkville 60560	1841 LaSalle/Kane	1877 1835 1877	1839 1847 1841
D3	Knox 200 S. Cherry St. Galesburg 61401	1825 Fulton/unorganized/ *Peoria	1877 1830 1877	1818 1830 1836
A6	Lake 18 N. County St. Waukegan 60085	1839 McHenry	1877 1839 1877	1839 1839 1840
C5	LaSalle 707 Etna Rd. Ottawa 61350	1831 Putnam/ unorganized	1868 1831 1870	1831 1831 1831
H7	Lawrence Lawrenceville 62439	1821 Crawford/Edwards	1878 1821 1878	1818 1821 1820
B4	Lee P.O. Box 385 Dixon 61021	1839 Ogle	1877 1839 1877	1838 1839 1840
C6	Livingston 112 W. Madison St. Pontiac 61764	1837 LaSalle/McLean/ unorganized (Vermilion)	1877 1837 1878	1835 1837 1839
E4	Logan P.O. Box 278 Lincoln 62656	1839 Sangamon	1878 1857 1878	1829 1855 1857
E5	Macon 141 S. Main St. Decatur 62523	1829 unorganized (Shelby)	1877 1829 1877	1827 1831 1829
G4	Macoupin Carlinville 62626	1829 unorganized (Madison) unorganized (Greene)	1877 1829 1877	1829 1829 1829
G4	Madison 157 N. Main St., Ste. 109 Edwardsville 62025	1812 St. Clair/Randolph	1858 1813 1877	1802 1813 1803
H5	Marion P.O. Box 637 Salem 62881	1823 Fayette/Jefferson	1877 1823 1877	1819 1823 1823

Map County Address	Date Formed Parent County/ies	Birth Marriage Death	Land Probate Court
Marquette	1843 (eliminated 1847) Adams		
C4 Marshall 122 N. Prairie Lacon 61540	1839 Putnam	1870 1830 1877	1839 1830 1840
E4 Mason P.O. Box 90 Havana 62644	1841 Tazewell/Menard	1878 1841 1877	1827 1841 1841
K6 Massac P.O. Box 429 Metropolis 62960	1843 Pope/Johnson	1877 1843 1877	1843 1843 1843
D2 McDonough Macomb 61455	1826 unorganized (Schulyer)	1870 1830 1870	1817 1833 1830
A6 McHenry 2200 N. Seminary Ave. Woodstock 60098	1836 (1837) Cook unorganized (LaSalle)	1877 1837 1877	1839 1840 1838
D5 McLean 104 W. Front Bloomington 61701	1830 Tazewell/ unorganized	1877 1831 1877	1831 1831 1831
E4 Menard P.O. Box 456 Petersburg 62675	1839 Sangamon	1877 1839 1877	1821 1839 1839
C3 Mercer 604 NE 5th Ave./P.O. Box 66 Aledo 61231	1825 (1835) unorganized (Pike)/ *Schulyer/*Peoria/*Warren	1877 1835 1877	1834 1837 1836
J3 Monroe 100 S. Main St. Waterloo 62298	1816 St. Clair/Randolph	1877 1816 1878	1816 1820 1816
G4 Montgomery Hillsboro 62049	1821 Bond/Madison	1862 1821 1877	1819 1821 1821
F3 Morgan 300 W. State St. Jacksonville 62650	1823 Sangamon/ unorganized (Greene)	1851 1827 1851	1824 1824 1827
F6 Moultrie Sullivan 61951	1843 Shelby/Macon	1877 1843 1877	1831 1845 1840
A4 Ogle Washington and S. 4th St. P.O. Box 357 Oregon 61061	1836 (1839) Jo Daviess unorganized (LaSalle)	1878 1837 1878	1836 1836 1837
D4 Peoria 324 Main St. Peoria 61602	1825 Fulton/ unorganized	1878 1825 1877	1818 1825 1825
J4 Perry 612 Virginia Ct. P.O. Box 438 Pinckneyville 62274	1827 Randolph/Jackson	1845 1827 1878	1817 1828 1827
E6 Piatt 101 W. Washington St. P.O. Box 558 Monticello 61856	1841 DeWitt/Macon	1877 1841 1877	1840 1843 1841
F2 Pike Pittsfield 62363	1821 Madison/Bond/Clark	1876 1827 1877	1818 1821 1819
K6 Pope Golconda 62938	1816 Johnson/Gallatin	1877 1813 1877	1816 1816 1817
K5 Pulaski P.O. Box 109 Mound City 62963	1843 Johnson/Alexander	1882 1861 1882	1843 1862 1857
C5 Putnam Hennepin 61327	1825 (1831) unorganized (Fulton)/ *Peoria	1877 1831 1877	1831 1831 1831
J4 Randolph #1 Taylor St. Chester 62263	1795 (territorial; became Illinois county 1809) Clair	1877 1724 1877	1724 1722 1722
H6 Richland 103 W. Main St. Olney 62450	1841 Clay/Lawrence 1877	1877 1841 1842	1836 1841
C2 Rock Island 1504 Third Ave. Rock Island 61201	1831 (1833) Jo Daviess	1861 1833 1877	1835 1835 1834
H4 St. Clair 10 Public Sq. Belleville 62220	1790 (territorial; became Illinois county 1809) unorganized	1830 1763 1832	1786 1772 1778
J6 Saline Harrisburg 62946	1847 (1852) Gallatin	1877 1845 1878	1817 1847 1848
F4 Sangamon 200 S.9th St. Springfield 62701-1629	1821 Madison/ Bond	1877 1821 1877	1822 1821 1821
E3 Schuyler P.O. Box 200 Rushville 62681	1825 unorganized (Pike)/ Fulton	1877 1825 1877	1817 1825 1825
F3 Scott Winchester 62694	1839 Morgan	1877 1839 1877	1823 1839 1839
F5 Shelby Shelbyville 62565	1827 Fayette	1877 1827 1877	1827 1831 1827
C4 Stark 130 W. Main/Box 97 Toulon 61483	1839 Knox/Putnam	1877 1839 1877	1817 1839 1839
A4 Stephenson 15 N. Galena Ave. Freeport 61032	1837 (1837) Winnebago/ Jo Daviess	1878 1837 1878	1837 1837 1837

196

Map	County Address	Date Formed Parent County/ies	Birth Marriage Death	Land Probate Court
D4	Tazewell McKenzie Bldg., 2nd Floor 4th and Court St. Pekin 61554	1827 unorganized (Peoria)	1870 1827 1878	1825 1827 1827
K5	Union P.O. Box H Jonesboro 62952	1818 Johnson	1867 1818 1877	1818 1818 1817
E7	Vermillion 6 N. Vermillion Danville 61832	1826 unorganized (Clark)/ unorganized (Edgar)	1877 1826 1877	1826 1826 1826
H7	Wabash 401 Market St. P.O. Box 277 Mt. Carmel 62863	1824 Edwards	1877 1857 1877	1857 1851 1857
D3	Warren 100 W. Broadway Monmouth 61462	1825 (1831) unorganized (Pike)/ *Schulyer/*Peoria	1877 1831 1875	1800 1830 1832
H4	Washington 101 E. St. Louis St. Nashville 62263	1818 St. Clair	1877 1831 1877	1815 1818 1818
	Wayne, Indiana Territory	1803 (eliminated 1803) Knox/St. Clair		
H6	Wayne P.O. Box 187 Fairfield 62837	1819 Edwards	1870 1850 1866	1865 1886 1819
J6	White P.O. Box 339 Carmi 62821	1815 Gallatin	1877 1816 1877	1816 1816 1816
B4	Whiteside 200 E. Knox St. Morrison 61270	1836 (1840) Jo Daviess/ *Ogle	1877 1857 1877	1838 1839 1838
B6	Will 302 N. Chicago St. Joliet 60431	1836 Cook/Iroquois/ unorganized (Vermilion)	1877 1836 1877	1835 1837 1836
K5	Williamson 200 W. Jefferson Marion 62959	1839 Franklin	1877 1839 1877	1818 1839 1840
A5	Winnebago 404 Elm St. Rockford 61101	1836 (1836) Jo Daviess/ unorganized (LaSalle)	1877 1836 1877	1836 1837 1836
D5	Woodford 115 N. Main, Ste. 202 Eureka 61530	1841 McLean/Tazewell	1877 1841 1877	1831 1841 1841

Indiana

CAROL L. MAKI AND MICHAEL JOHN NEILL

The settlement of Indiana was largely influenced by the area's great variance in terrain and soil. While most of the southern third of the state is hilly and rough, with very poor soil, the central portion has generally level terrain and deep, fertile soil perfectly suited to productive farming. The northern area is paradoxically both flat and heavily glaciated, with considerable marshland.

French explorers engaged in the trapping and transporting of furs in the early 1700s had the first contact with the major Native American tribes of this area, the Miami and Potawatomi. The French policy of mutual economic advantage and cooperation did not challenge the occupation and/or use of the land of the native inhabitants. The French learned native ways and often married native women.

The French and Indian War in the mid-eighteenth century removed France as a serious threat to the British colonial expansion to the Mississippi. However, the resulting Proclamation of 1763 prohibited American colonists from settling west of the Appalachian Mountains since that land had been reserved for Native Americans and licensed fur traders. Great Britain took control of what would become Indiana, but during the Revolution, George Rogers Clark's expedition guaranteed the area for the United States, with Virginia, Connecticut, and Massachusetts all making claims to the area.

At the close of the Revolution, some native tribes in the region chose to continue trade with the French and relocated west of the Mississippi, resulting in land speculators and settlers totally disregarding the earlier proclamation and heading west past the Appalachians. Indiana was first included in Northwest

Territory in 1787 with all of the present state (and part of Illinois) established, in 1790, as Knox County in Northwest Territory. Over the next twenty years, territorial jurisdiction went through several changes at the same time as natives, disillusioned with the incursion of settlers, mounted resistance.

Indiana Territory was established in 1800 out of the Northwest Territory. Michigan and Illinois territories separated from Indiana Territory in 1805 and 1809, respectively. Statehood became a reality for Indiana on 11 December 1816.

Settlers from western Virginia, North Carolina, eastern portions of Tennessee and Kentucky arrived in the southern part of Indiana in increasing numbers after the War of 1812. The majority of these settlers were farm families accustomed to frontier living, and included many Scotch-Irish and Germans who had, in earlier generations, migrated south from Pennsylvania in the 1700s.

In the early nineteenth century, migration to Indiana included upland southerners traveling across the Appalachians and emigrants from the Mid-Atlantic regions coming by land and the Ohio River. Most of the first farms and settlements in Indiana were necessarily located on the Ohio, Wabash, Whitewater, or White rivers, or near the streams and creeks from which they originated.

Northern Indiana was settled last because it was a final refuge for Native Americans and because of its more inaccessible terrain. Migration northward in the state was made difficult by the lack of land routes. Early roads traced native and animal trails or military expedition routes. The Michigan Road, from Michigan City in the north to Madison in the south, was opened

in 1836, providing a vastly improved north-south land route. The National Road, a United States government endeavor to link the East and West, moved across Indiana in the 1830s. Three major canal projects, improved road systems, and a railroad line—all begun by the state government in 1836—immediately ceased with the financial panic and depression of 1837. However, the Wabash and Erie Canal, covering a distance of 468 miles, was completed with assistance from the federal government. Railroads were developed from 1847 through the late 1850s, providing faster and more dependable transportation for people and agricultural products.

From the second half of the nineteenth century to the present, manufacturing began to take a firm position in the state's economy. One key component of this position was the steel industry along the state's northern tier. African Americans from the South and Europeans have significantly added to the state's ethnic composition of today.

Vital Records

The first law regulating marriages in Indiana occurred in 1788, but marriage licenses became mandatory in 1800. The statutes of the Northwest Territory required that 1) the banns be read fifteen days before the marriage, 2) the male be seventeen years of age, and 3) the female be fourteen years of age.

Marriage licenses and certificates have been issued by and kept at the county clerk's office, generally beginning with the formation of each respective county to the present. Marriage applications, beginning in 1906 (with additional family information) and marriage transcripts (1882) may have both been used in various counties. Prior to 1940 it was necessary for a couple to obtain a license from the county in which the female resided. If an Indiana ancestor's marriage record cannot be located in that state, check the Cincinnati marriage records; this area was a "Gretna Green" (no-questions-asked marriage locale) for Ohio, Kentucky, and Indiana.

Statewide collection of marriages from the counties did not begin until 1958. The *Indiana Marriage Index,* compiled by the State Board of Health, Division of Vital Records, 1330 W. Michigan St., Indianapolis, IN 46207 <www.in.gov/isdh> begins in 1958. Marriages are indexed by bride and groom, indicating county of license, marriage, and date. Annual indexes for 1958 to 1965 are in book form; indexes from 1966 to 1981 are on microfilm, available at the Indiana State Archives, Indiana Commission on Public Records (see Archives, Libraries, and Societies).

Birth and death records were recorded by the county health office beginning in 1882, where they remained before mandatory recording with the state board of health began in October 1907 for births and in January 1900 for deaths. There are no indexes to the state death certificates from 1900 to 1918. Certified copies may be obtained from either the county health department or the Division of Vital Records (address above). Some cities have earlier birth registration: Ft. Wayne (1870), Indianapolis (1872), Kokomo (1875), and Logansport (1879). Those with births before the 1882 registration deadline may wish to reference Dawne Slater-Putt, *Pre-1882 Indiana Births from Secondary Sources,* volumes 1 and 2 (Fort Wayne, Ind.: Heritage Pathways, Inc., 1999).

The Works Projects Administration (WPA) began to index vital records, county-by-county, for the entire state, but the agency was abolished before the project was completed. Only sixty-eight of the ninety-two counties had their birth and death records (1882–1920) and marriages (generally 1850–1920) collected. The completed county indexes are available in print at the Indiana State Library and Allen County Public Library (see Archives, Libraries, and Societies) among others.

Several more recent projects have involved indexing marriage records for the state before 1955. *Indiana Marriages Thru 1820: In the Counties of Washington, Jefferson, Clark, Scott, Jackson, Jennings, Switzerland, Ripley* (Indianapolis: Researchers of Indianapolis, 1981) and *The Hoosier Genealogist,* which frequently publishes marriage abstracts, are two such projects. An index for pre-1850 Indiana marriages is available at the Indiana State Library's website <www.statelib.lib.in.us/www/isl/indiana/genealogy/mirr.html> via the Indiana State Library.

Divorce records are kept in the office of the circuit court. Since Indiana had no residency requirements until 1859, it is very possible to find divorce records for numerous individuals from other states in the Indiana files. In 1991, Heritage Quest (see page 17) published the CD-ROM version of Indiana Vital Records Collection, which contains over 5.4 million vital records registrations compiled by the Indiana Works Progress Administration in 1942.

Census Records

Federal

Population Schedules
- Indexed—1820 (Daviess County missing), 1830, 1840, 1850, 1860, 1870, 1880, 1900, 1910, 1920, 1930
- Soundex—1880, 1900, 1920

Industry and Agriculture Schedules
- 1850, 1860, 1870, 1880

Mortality Schedules
- 1850, 1860, 1870, 1880

All of Indiana's federal census schedules through 1930 are available on microfilm at the Indiana State Library and Allen County Public Library (see Archives, Libraries, and Societies). Many rural families were missed during the enumeration of the 1850 U.S. census in Indiana because of poor weather and impassable trails. However, the agriculture schedule of that year was taken at a different time of the year, and most of the rural residents were included in that enumeration.

In addition to the indexes widely available for every state (see page 3), the Indiana Historical Society (see Archives, Libraries, and Societies) has completed a computerized index searchable on every category or variable for the 1860 census. For example, it would be possible, through the historical society's computer printout, to locate by name all the ministers (searching by occupation) born in North Carolina (place of birth). The index is available on microfiche for purchase from the society.

Territorial and State

Census for Indiana Territory for 1807, compiled by Rebah Fraustein, was published by the Indiana Historical Society in 1980. No other state censuses exist, although state enumerations of males (without names) above age twenty-one were taken at various intervals beginning in 1820.

Background Sources

Sources for an overview of the state include:

Beatty, John D. *Research In Indiana.* Arlington, Va.: National Genealogical Society, 1992.

Buley, R. Carlye. *The Old Northwest: Pioneer Period, 1815–1840.* 2 vols. Bloomington: Indiana University Press, 1951.

Carty, Mickey Dimon. *Searching in Indiana: A Reference Guide to Public and Private Records.* Costa Mesa, Calif.: ISC Publications, 1985.

Cockrum, Col. William M. *Pioneer History of Indiana; Including Stories, Incidents and Customs of the Early Settlers.* Oakland City, Ind.: Press of the Oakland City Journal, 1907.

Dorrell, Ruth. *Pioneer Ancestors of Members of the Society of Indiana Pioneers.* Indianapolis: Family History Section, Indiana Historical Society, 1983.

Madison, James H. *The Indiana Way: A State History.* Indiana University Press and Indiana Historical Society, 1986.

Taylor, Robert M. Jr. et al. *Indiana: A New Historical Guide.* Indianapolis: Indiana Historical Society, 1989.

An important indexing project, Indexes of Persons and Firms, was begun by the WPA and resumed in 1979 by the Indiana Historical Society. This typescript index includes every name mentioned in biographical entries of each county's published histories, and copies of the index are available at Indiana State Library, Indiana Historical Society Library, Allen County Public Library, and the Family History Library (FHL) in Salt Lake City as well as through local Family History Centers. A later project on microfiche, *Indiana Biographical Index* (West Bountiful, Utah: Genealogical Indexing Associates, 1983), is a single alphabetical statewide index based on much of the same material as the Indexes of Persons and Firms, but with some additions.

Maps

County maps can be found in the surveyor's office of most courthouses and may sometimes be purchased or photocopied. They include historical county maps and contemporary county, township, and city maps. The *Atlas of Historical County Boundaries: Indiana* (New York: Charles Scribner's Sons, 1996) may also be helpful.

A. T. Andreas, *Maps of Indiana Counties in 1876 …* (Indianapolis: Indiana Historical Society, 1968), a reprint of the *1876 Illustrated Historical Atlas of the State of Indiana* (Chicago: Baskin, Forster, 1876), has been published by and is available from the Indiana Historical Society.

Indiana topographical and geological survey maps are available through the Indiana Department of Conservation, State Office Bldg., Indianapolis, IN 46204.

The earliest Sanborn fire insurance map (see page 5) available for the state of Indiana is 1883. The Indiana State Library has a few Sanborn fire insurance maps on microfilm; the Indiana University Geography and Map Library in Bloomington, however, has an almost complete collection of these maps. Atlas and plat maps for each county and township dating 1875 to present are at the Indiana State Library. County maps show roads, railroads, churches, cemeteries, and schools.

Land Records

Public-Domain State

Following a 1795 treaty with the native residents, the first strip of land was surveyed in southeastern Indiana. In 1801 the Cincinnati Land Office was opened, the first such office to serve Indiana. Vincennes opened in 1807. *Indiana Land Entries,* 2 volumes, by Margaret R. Waters (1948; reprint, Knightstown, Ind.: Bookmark, 1977), includes registers for the Cincinnati (1801–40) and Vincennes (1807–77) land districts. Five additional land offices opened as demand increased, principally following the conclusion of the War of 1812: Jeffersonville (1807), Brookville (1819; moved to Indianapolis in 1825), Terre Haute (1820; moved to Crawfordsville before 1828), Fort Wayne (1823), and LaPorte (1833; moved to Winamac in 1839). Registers are available on microfilm at Indiana State Archives, Allen County Public Library, and through the FHL. Although not all registers

are indexed, some have been published. Land was usually sold for under $2 per acre, frequently at public auction, and it could be purchased on an installment basis. Land patents were issued by the United States government when the total purchase price had been paid. Frequently, the documents recorded at the land offices included the purchaser's "outside of Indiana" residence. Original land records (1805–76), plus microfilmed copies, are at the Indiana State Library, Archives Division.

Private land claims, which are first-title deeds surveyed outside the regular federal system of townships and ranges, also existed in Indiana. The legal description of these lands are in lot numbers assigned by the governor. The parcels of land are frequently long and narrow, giving each owner access to an adjacent river or road. Patents, copies of tract books, and township plats are available through the Bureau of Land Management (BLM) Eastern States Office (see page 6). Land-entry case files are at the National Archives. The BLM offers a searchable database of patents at <www.glorecords.blm.gov>.

National Archives—Great Lakes Region (see page 12) has records of the General Land Office for Indiana (1808–76), which include the cash certificate books denoting completion of purchase of land from the federal government. They are arranged chronologically by land office.

A grant of land was provided for George Rogers Clark and his men for their service in the Revolutionary War. The property was situated in what is now Scott, Floyd, and Clark counties. Clarksville, established in 1784 on the northern bank of the Ohio River and within the grant, was the first American town to be laid out in the northwest. Most land owned by individuals prior to 1800 was either in Clark's Grant or at Vincennes. At Vincennes, between 1779 and 1783, the court would grant land, usually 400 acres, to every American immigrant who wanted property.

The recorder's office of the county courthouses has grantor and grantee indexes, land transfers, deeds, titles, mortgages (and releases and assignments of mortgages), and tract books of original land purchases from the U.S. government. The tract books include name of purchaser, purchase date, location (section number, township, and range), and number of acres.

Probate Records

The court jurisdiction responsible for probate changed a half dozen times in Indiana's history before finally settling in the county's circuit court. The records have remained with the clerk of the circuit court, although they are often stored in the county clerk's office. The records include wills, probate records, administration of estates, letters of administration, inventories of decedent's personal property, final record books, adoption papers, guardianship records, civil court records, records of

minors, records of the insane, and naturalization records and proceedings. A statewide index to wills, *Indiana Wills Index through 1880*, 2 vols. (Indianapolis: Ye Olde Genealogie Shoppe, 1983) is available.

Court Records

Indiana settlers wanted a government that was simple, democratic, and located close to the people. The county courthouse became the axis of politics and government that included a sheriff, coroner, circuit court clerk, recorder, and three county commissioners. The legal system was made up of a state supreme court, numerous circuit courts, and township justices of the peace who had jurisdiction for petty crimes and civil cases involving less than $50.

For additional information on local courts and the types of material they hold, see "Courthouse Research in Indiana" in *Genealogy* (July 1974): 1-13; "Using County Records in Writing Your Community's History" by John Newman, in *Local History Today...* (Indianapolis: Indiana Historical Society, 1979); and "Managing Your Research in Indiana Court Records" by John Newman, in *Genealogy* 62 (July 1981): 1-9. An important genealogical tool pertaining to immigrants in Indiana is *An Index to Indiana Naturalization Records Found in Various Order Books of the Ninety-Two Local Courts Prior to 1907*, published in Indianapolis by the Indiana Historical Society in 1981.

Tax Records

Records of county taxes were kept as early as 1842, although most were discarded. Remaining ones would be at the county courthouse.

National Archives—Great Lakes Region (see page 12) has records of the Internal Revenue Service for Indiana for 1867 to 1873. These are tax assessment records, arranged by district and then chronologically.

Cemetery Records

The commissioner's office of each Indiana county may have burial records for soldiers, sailors, and marines. If available, the records should include name, age, date of enlistment, discharge date, and death date. Records begin about 1862.

The Indiana State Library holds records of inscriptions from some Indiana cemeteries. The "Indiana Cemetery Locator File," compiled by the Genealogy Division, is an alphabetical listing of cemeteries, indicating the location in the state and the designation in the Genealogy Division of the Indiana State Library where inscriptions may be found. *Cemeteries of Indiana,*

by Virgil A. Jewell (typescript, 1970), and *Indiana Cemetery Directory* (Cemetery Association of Indiana, 1961) may also be helpful.

In the 1940s, the American Legion and the Indiana Adjutant General's Office were responsible for the "Veteran's Grave Registration File." The Indiana State Archives holds the original card file; it has been duplicated on thirteen microfilm reels. Included are soldiers buried in Indiana who fought in wars prior to and including World War I. The file includes fifty-one of the ninety-two counties.

Church Records

Although there was a Jesuit priest in Vincennes by 1749, the Catholic religion in Indiana declined in the late 1700s. Catholics in Vincennes and Fort Wayne were reorganized in the 1830s, and Irish and German immigrants added to the religion's numbers in the mid-1800s.

It was Protestantism, however, that conformed to and enhanced the frontier existence of Indiana. The predominant denominations were Methodists, Baptists, and Presbyterians. A large group of Quakers migrated to the Whitewater Valley from North Carolina. German settlement areas were often Lutheran, but German-Americans established the United Brethren Churches in Indiana. The Christian Church (Disciples of Christ) was created in the state in the early 1800s. By the mid-1800s, there were also significant numbers of Jewish families in Indiana, most of them in the larger cities.

Of the predominant Protestant body, the Methodist denomination was the largest. The circuit rider, bringing religion to the scattered pioneers in their log cabins, and the camp meeting, with its religious fervor and social aspect, were precisely appropriate to that time and place.

Baptist records are found at Franklin College (in Franklin); Methodist at DePauw University (in Greencastle); Mennonite at Goshen College (in Goshen); Presbyterian at Hanover College (in Hanover); Disciples of Christ at their historical society in Nashville, Tennessee; and French Catholic at Vincennes University in the Byron R. Lewis Collection. There are also Catholic Church histories and records at the Catholic Archives, University of Notre Dame, South Bend, Indiana. Quaker records are at Earlham College (at Richmond), but an excellent printed source for them exists: Willard Heiss's *Abstracts of the Records of the Society of Friends in Indiana*, 6 vols. with index (Indianapolis: Indiana Historical Society, 1962–77). It is also available on microfiche from the society.

L. C. Rudolph and Judith E. Endelman's *Religion in Indiana: A Guide to Historical Resources* (Bloomington: Indiana University Press, 1986) is organized in three sections: 1) published books, articles, theses, and dissertations; 2) primarily unpublished materials, listed by repository, which do not include individual congregations; and 3) congregational histories listed by county.

The story of Harmony, an intentional religious community of Pennsylvanian Germans that spawned the town by the same name, is covered in Karl J. R. Arndt, A *Documentary History of the Indiana Decade of the Harmony Society, 1814–1824*, 2 vols. (Indianapolis: Indiana Historical Society, 1975, 1978).

A general finding aid is a *Directory of Churches and Religious Organizations in Indiana* (Indianapolis: Indiana Historical Records Survey, 1941).

Military Records

The Indiana State Archives holds the following military records of interest to the genealogist:

Indiana State Militia, 1812–51. Alphabetical index of officers commissioned, giving name, rank, and unit.

Card file of Indiana Civil War Volunteers. This may include name, rank, company, regiment, period of original enlistment, place and date of enrollment and muster, age, physical description, nativity, occupation, date, place and manner of leaving the service, information on promotions, and wounds.

Card file of Indiana Legion, which was the Civil War State Militia. This may include name, company, dates of active duty, age, and county and town where organized.

Card file of Civil War Substitutes. This includes the names of citizens who hired substitutes, the names of the substitutes, and the unit to which that person was assigned.

Veterans' Grave Registration. Card file of veterans; includes fifty-one counties.

Veterans' Enrollments of 1886, 1890, and 1894. The books are arranged by county and township. They include name, company and regiment, state from which the veteran served, number of children under sixteen, medical problems, and current physical condition.

The archives also has card files on Indiana Militia (1877–96), Mexican War Volunteer Index, Black Hawk War Militia Index, Gold Star Roll of Honor for 1914–18, Indiana Spanish-American War Volunteers microfilmed registration cards, and Registers of Visitors to the National Encampment of the Grand Army of the Republic at Indianapolis (4-9 September 1893). This repository has service records for all veterans who applied for the Indiana State Bonus for World War II and Korea; these records are restricted.

In addition to the Civil War material in the state archives, W. H.H. Terrell, comp., *Report of the Adjutant General of the State of Indiana*, 8 vols. (Indianapolis: Indiana Adjutant General's Office, 1869) is a printed source of service records.

The National Archives—Great Lakes Region holds Records of the Selective Service Board (1917–19) for Indiana. Included is

an Index to Delinquent and Deserter Forms (incomplete for some areas) as well as docket books of registrants, arranged within state by county and division. Family historians with earlier settlers to Indiana may wish to reference Estella A. O'Byrne, *Roster of Soldiers and Patriots of the American Revolution Buried in Indiana*, vols. 1-3 (Brookville, Ind.: Indiana Daughters of the American Revolution, 1938–82).

Periodicals, Newspapers, and Manuscript Collections

Periodicals

The Hoosier Genealogist (Indianapolis: Genealogical Section of the Indiana Historical Society) began printing Indiana genealogical information and extractions in January 1961; it is published bimonthly. County, cemetery, church, and family records from this periodical have been published by Willard Heiss in several volumes of *Indiana Source Book, Genealogical Material from the Hoosier Genealogist*, 3 vols. and index (Indianapolis: Indiana Historical Society, 1877–83).

Indiana Magazine of History (Bloomington: Dept. of History, Indiana University in cooperation with Indiana Historical Society), published quarterly, includes well-written and documented state history articles, listings of recent pertinent publications, and reviews of books relevant to Indiana historical research. Elfreda Lang's *Indiana Magazine of History General Index* (vols. 51–75, 1955–79), available from the Indiana Historical Society, serves as an excellent printed index to the magazine. Also see Dorothy L. Riker's *Genealogical Sources Reprinted from the Genealogical Section, Indiana Magazine of History* (1979), which includes marriages, will records, various county records, family Bible records, cemetery and church records, complete with a surname index.

Several genealogical societies publish periodicals as well. The Allen County Public Library is the headquarters for the extensive *Periodical Source Index* (see Archives, Libraries, and Societies and pages 10 and 13), which covers several thousand periodicals, not limited to Indiana's.

Newspapers

Indiana's first newspaper, the *Indiana Gazette*, was published in Vincennes in 1804. The largest newspaper collections in the state are located in the Archives Division of the Indiana State Library and the Indiana University Library (see Archives, Libraries, and Societies). For an excellent Indiana newspaper history and finding guide, see John Miller's *Indiana Newspaper Bibliography* (Indianapolis: Indiana Historical Society, 1982). This is alphabetically arranged within counties by name of town or city where published. It is indexed and includes listings of approximately 8,000 newspapers published between 1804 and 1980, with locations of all known original and/or microform copies.

Indiana has the unusual requirement of having its county recorders maintain, for public use, bound volumes of all newspapers published in their jurisdiction. These may begin as early as 1852. See also Margaret R. Waters, Dorothy Riker, and Doris Leistner, *Abstracts of Obituaries in the Western Christian Advocate, 1834–1850* (Indianapolis: Indiana Historical Society, 1988), which includes all genealogical data found in more than 8,000 obituaries in this Methodist Church newspaper. The entries are not, however, limited to Methodists; they basically cover the states of Kentucky, Ohio, Indiana, and Illinois. There are surname and geographic indexes.

Manuscripts

The major manuscript collections include those at the Indiana Historical Society and the Indiana State Library, with a combined printed guide to both collections (Eric Pumroy and Paul Brockman, comp., *A Guide to Manuscript Collections of the Indiana Historical Society and the Indiana State Library* [Indianapolis: Indiana Historical Society, 1986]). Included in the manuscript collections of the Indiana State Historical Society Library, which may be of interest to genealogists, are the following: Francis Vigo (fur trader) Collection; William H. English Collection (1741–1928); and Society of Friends Records (meetings minutes include records of marriages, births, deaths, removals, and new members).

Betty Jarboe and Katyrn Rumsey's *Studies on Indiana: A Bibliography of Theses and Dissertations Submitted to Indiana Institutions of Higher Education for Advanced Degrees, 1902-1977* (Indiana Historical Bureau, 1980) lists such examples as "The Fur Trade Around Fort Wayne," "The History and Development of the Showers Brothers Furniture Company," "History of the French Lick Springs Hotel," and "Internal Migration in Indiana."

Local history collections exist in other libraries throughout the state. Many can be accessed through the National Union Catalog of Manuscript Collections (see page 11).

See also Wisconsin—Manuscripts—Draper Manuscripts.

Archives, Libraries, and Societies

Indiana State Library
Genealogy Division
140 North Senate Ave.
Indianapolis, IN 46204
www.statelib.lib.in.us

The largest collection of research material in the state is centrally located at the state's capitol. The library's facility includes three major divisions of records: Indiana, Genealogy, and Newspaper. The Indiana State Archives is located in the library;

the Indiana Historical Society is located adjacent to the library. The Indiana Division of the library provides the researcher with printed sources: county histories and indexes, church records, city directories, and newspapers. The Genealogy Division holds the sizable microfilm collection of records: vital, deed, probate, court, church, and cemetery and spearheads the County Records of Indiana Microfilming Project. The Genealogy Division also holds an Indiana Marriage Index, 1958–97, an Indiana Mortality Records Index (index to mortality census schedules from 1850–80), and some online indexes to newspapers for limited periods on their website. Carolynne L. Miller's *Indiana Sources for Genealogical Research in the Indiana State Library* (Indianapolis: The Family History Section, Indiana Historical Society, 1984) provides an excellent guide to both of these divisions. In the Newspaper Division an attempt has been made to preserve all dailies and weeklies in the state. A published guide is available from the Indiana Historical Society.

Indiana State Archives
Commission on Public Records
140 N. Senate Ave.
Indianapolis, IN 46204
www.in.gov/icpr/archives

The keystone to this collection is its focus on military and federal land records, described earlier. Other holdings are described elsewhere in this chapter.

Indiana Historical Society
450 W. Ohio St.
Indianapolis, IN 46202
www.indianahistory.org

Founded in 1830 and adjacent to the Indiana State Library, the society's collections include rare books, manuscripts (see Manuscripts), over 100,000 images of people and scenes, early mid-western and Indiana maps pertaining to the history of Native Americans and the Old Northwest. The society has published or developed numerous materials and guides to records throughout the state, including the 1860 census project (see Census Records).

Allen County Public Library
Genealogy Department
900 Webster St.
Fort Wayne, IN 46802
www.acpl.lib.in.us
Mailing address:
P.O. Box 2270
Fort Wayne, Indiana 46801

This department has thousands of family genealogies; research guides; state, county, and local histories; indexes to births, deaths, marriages, cemetery inscriptions, and wills; census microfilms; passenger lists; and city directories. The collection

is particularly strong for all of mid-western local history, but has other excellent regional collections as well. PERiodical Source Index (PERSI; see page 10) is compiled from its extensive periodical collection. The library is a non-circulating facility, but the staff will do limited research. Response to a written query for information is usually answered promptly and very thoroughly.

Indiana Genealogical Society
P.O. Box 10507
Fort Wayne, IN 46852
www.indgensoc.org

Southern Indiana Genealogical Society
P.O. Box 665
New Albany, IN 47150
www.ka.net/spcarpenter/SIGserve.htm

The Newberry Library
60 W. Walton St.
Chicago, IL 60610
www.newberry.org

This repository, although in Illinois, should be considered a source for Indiana research as Indiana holdings are among the library's strongest state collections. Records include indexes and transcripts of vital records, probates, deeds, cemetery records, naturalizations, church records, and extensive land records.

Special Focus Categories

Naturalization

Records, except bankruptcy cases, of the federal district courts of the United States for the state of Indiana have been transferred to the National Archives—Great Lakes Region. These include the Northern District (1879–1959), encompassing the divisions of Hammond, Ft. Wayne, South Bend, and the Southern District (1819–1959), with the divisions of Indianapolis, Terre Haute, Evansville, and New Albany.

African American

Slavery was prohibited in the future state of Indiana by the Northwest Ordinance of 1787. However, slavery existed in the French households at Vincennes from the mid-1700s and continued despite the ordinance. In 1802 the territory requested a repeal from Congress, stating that a "slave state" would encourage more settlement. Although the petition was denied, in 1805 the territorial government allowed slaves to be brought into the area and held for "longer-than-life" indentures.

The sentiments concerning slavery changed as the government passed from a governor to the pre-state, forty-three delegate convention. An 1816 ruling prohibited slavery, but a "hereafter" clause in the state constitution provided

justification for owners holding the 190 slaves reported in the 1820 census in western counties to keep their slaves. In the anti-slavery southeast area of Indiana, it was determined that slavery of any kind was illegal. Early in the 1820s the Indiana Supreme Court made slavery illegal, including that created in pre-1816 indentures. However, by the 1830s, a few slaves still remained in the state. Despite the anti-slavery sentiments of the Indiana people, African Americans were not allowed to vote, testify in court, or marry whites; their intermarriage with Native Americans, however, was fairly common in Indiana, particularly in the areas of the western frontier.

It is important, in researching African Americans in Indiana, to make note of the commonality of intermarriage, the required registration of African Americans in 1831, and the fact that many free African Americans purchased land. Several Underground Railroad routes through Indiana helped many slaves escape to the North, though many remained in the state. The Emigrant Aid Society helped thousands of North Carolina African Americans migrate to Indianapolis in the 1870s. Additional information can be found in:

McDougald, Lois. *Negro Migration into Indiana, 1800–1860.* Bloomington: the author, 1945.

Lyda, John W. *The Negro History of Indiana.* Terre Haute, Ind.: the author, 1953.

Thornbrough, Emma Lou. *The Negro in Indiana: A Study of a Minority.* Indiana Historical Collections. Vol. 37. Indianapolis: Indiana Historical Bureau, 1957.

Witcher, Curt Bryan. *Bibliography of Sources for Black Family History in the Allen County Public Library Genealogy Department.* Fort Wayne: Allen County Public Library, 1986.

Native American

In the 1818 St. Mary's Treaty, the Delaware and other tribes ceded territory in the central portion of the state known as "The New Purchase." The Delaware agreed to removal west of the Mississippi. The Miami and Potawatomi were the two major tribes remaining in Indiana after 1820. In 1826 they "traded" land needed for the construction of the Michigan Road and the Wabash and Erie Canal. The federal Indian Removal Act of 1830 allowed the Indiana General Assembly to remove the remaining native inhabitants from the state. In 1838 the plans for removing the Potawatomi were in effect, but some of the tribe objected. Eight hundred were "escorted" to Kansas under an armed militia company in a disorganized and tragic march known as the "Trail of Death."

The Treaty of 1840 required that the Miami, the last Indian tribe in Indiana, be removed to Kansas. The migration did not actually occur until 1846, although several chiefs and their families were given individual land near Fort Wayne. Other suggested sources are:

Dillion, J.B. *National Decline of the Miami Indians.* Indianapolis: Indiana State Historical Society, 1897.

Rafert, Stewart. "American-Indian Genealogical Research in the Midwest: Resources and Perspectives," *National Genealogical Society Quarterly* 76 (September 1988). 212–224. See more detail in Wisconsin—Native American.

———. *The Hidden Community: The Miami Indians of Indiana, 1846–1940.* N.p.: the author, 1982.

Witcher, Curt Bryan. *Bibliography of Sources for Native American Family History in the Allen County Public Library Genealogy Department.* Fort Wayne: Allen County Public Library, 1988.

Other Ethnic Groups

Beginning in 1850 and through 1920 the foreign-born were never more than 10 percent of Indiana's population, the largest percentage coming from Germany. Schools, churches, and social clubs of that nationality helped maintain the German culture in the state.

The Irish were the second largest immigrant group in Indiana, although their numbers were not large. Later immigrants, in the twentieth century, came from southern and eastern Europe.

County Resources

During the Great Depression, Indiana pioneered the microfilming of records. A WPA project filmed vital records, court records, naturalizations, wills, slave registers, some Revolutionary War pension files, etc., for at least sixteen counties in the state.

In the 1950s and 1960s the Indiana State Library microfilmed many vital and court records. They receive positive microfilm copies of Indiana county records via a joint effort with the Commission on Public Records, Indiana Historical Bureau, Indiana Historical Society, and the Genealogical Society of Utah. Twenty-eight of the ninety-two Indiana courthouses suffered courthouse fires; many of them were rebuilt only to be destroyed again by fire or natural disaster. The original county of Knox lost all records in a fire of 1814. *Hoosier Genealogist* 4 (1964) includes a listing of courthouse fires in Indiana.

Land records are located at the county recorder's office; probates are at the clerk of the circuit court, along with other court records. County commissioner's records in Indiana courthouses are quite frequently the earliest official records of the organized governments in counties formed directly from Native American purchases. Records may include the names of road supervisors, payments made to individuals, appointments for tax collectors, business licenses, naturalization applications, and early justice of the peace dockets.

For some of the following counties two years are listed for "Date Formed." The first is the year the county was created,

the second is the year it was fully organized if it differs from the creation year. Under the heading "Parent County/ies," the name(s) listed may be the county or counties from which the respective county was formed, or they may be names by which the county was originally known. "Unorganized" denotes that it was formed from non-county lands. A county name in parentheses is the county to which the unorganized land may have been attached at that time. Counties listed with an asterisk (*) are those in which records may exist for the county in question. It may have been "attached" to that county for some period of time.

The date listed for each category of record is the earliest record known to exist in that county. It does not indicate that there are numerous records for that year and certainly does not indicate that all such events that year were actually registered.

Information for this section was obtained from Carolynne L. Miller's *Indiana Sources for Genealogical Research in the Indiana State Library* (cited under Indiana State Library's listing); Willard Heiss, "Indiana," in Kenn Stryker-Rodda, ed., *Genealogical Research: Methods and Sources,* vol. 2 (Washington, D.C.: American Society of Genealogists, 1983); and from those materials available through the County Records of Indiana Microfilm Project (CRIMP) at the Indiana State Library (see Archives, Libraries, and Societies).

Addresses in the following county list were taken from the Family History—Clerks of the Circuit Court address list on the Indiana State Archives website at <www.in.gov/icpr/archives/family/maillist.html>.

INDIANA

The Counties and County Seats of
Indiana

25   0   25   50 Miles

Drawn by William Dollarhide

Map County Address	Date Formed Parent County/ies	Birth Marriage Death	Land Probate Court
Adams New Purchase	1827 (eliminated 1844) Delaware New Purchase		
C7 **Adams** 313 S. Jefferson Decatur 46733	1835 (1836) Adams New Purchase (Allen/Delaware/ Randolph)	1882 1836 1882	1837 1838 ———
B7 **Allen** 715 S. Calhoun St. Fort Wayne 46802	1824 Delaware New Purchase/ unorganized	1882 1824 1870	1824 1825 1824
G5 **Bartholomew** P.O. Box 924 Columbus 47202	1821 Delaware New Purchase	1883 1821 1882	1822 1821 1821
D2 **Benton** 706 E. 5th Ste. 23 Fowler 47944	1840 Jasper	1882 1840 1882	1840 1840 1840
D6 **Blackford** 110 W. Washington St. Hartford City 47348	1838 (1839) Jay	1882 1839 1882	1836 1839 1839
E4 **Boone** 1 Courthouse Sq. Room 212 Lebanon 46052	1830 Wabash New Purchase (Hendricks)/ Adams New Purchase (Hendricks/Marion)	1882 1831 1882	1856 1846 1846
G4 **Brown** Courthouse Annex Nashville 47448 Record loss 1873.	1836 Bartholomew/Jackson/ Monroe	1882 1836 1882	1873 1837 1837
D3 **Carroll** Courthouse 101 W. Main St. Delphi 46923	1828 Adams New Purchase/ (Hamilton) Wabash New Purchase (Fountain)/unorganized	1882 1828 1882	1829 1829 1829
C4 **Cass** 200 Court Park, Rm. 203 Logansport 46947	1829 unorganized (Carroll)	1882 1829 1882	1830 1829 1829
J5 **Clark** City-County Bldg., Rm. 137 Jeffersonville 47130	1801 Knox	1882 1807 1882	1801 1801 1801
G2 **Clay** 609 E. National Ave. Brazil 47834 Record loss 1851.	1825 Owen/Putnam/Vigo/ Sullivan	1881 1851 1882	1825 1873 ———
D4 **Clinton** 265 Courthouse Sq. Frankfort 46041	1830 Adams New Purchase (Tippecanoe)	1882 1830 1882	1829 1830 1832
K4 **Crawford** P.O. Box 375 English 47118	1818 Harrison/Orange/Perry	1882 1818 1882	1818 1818 1818
H3 **Daviess** 200 E. Walnut Washington 47501	1817 Knox	1882 1817 1882	1817 1817 1817
A7 **De Kalb** P.O. Box 230 Auburn 46706	1835 (1837) unorganized (Allen/LaGrange)	1882 1837 1882	1837 1847 1839
G7 **Dearborn** 215-B W. High St. Lawrenceburg 47025 Record loss 1826.	1803 Clark	1882 1806 1882	1821 1824 1824
G6 **Decatur** 150 Courthouse St., Ste 1 Greensburg 47240	1822 unorganized	1882 1822 1882	1822 1822 1822
Delaware New Purchase	1820 (name changed to Adams New Purchase, 1827) unorganized/ *Fayette/*Franklin/ *Jackson/*Jennings/ *Randolph/*Ripley/ *Wayne/*Bartholomew		
E6 **Delaware** 100 W. Main Muncie 47305	1827 Delaware New Purchase/ *Randolph	1882 1827 1882	1829 1830 1828
J3 **Dubois** 1 Courthouse Sq. Jasper 47546 Record loss 1839.	1818 Pike	1882 1839 1882	1839 1840 1840
A5 **Elkhart** 101 N. Main St., Rm. 204 Goshen 46526	1830 unorganized (Cass/Allen)	1882 1830 1882	1831 1830 1830
F6 **Fayette** 401 Central Ave. Connersville 47331	1819 Franklin/Wayne /unorganized	1883 1819 1829	1816 1819 1819
J5 **Floyd** 311 W. 1st St., Rm. 235 New Albany 47150	1819 Clark/ Harrison	1882 1819 1882	1818 1819 ———
E2 **Fountain** P.O. Box 183 Covington 47932	1826 Montgomery/ Wabash New Purchase/ *Parke	1887 1826 1882	1827 1827 ———
G7 **Franklin** 459 Main St. Brookville 47012	1811 Clark/Dearborn	1882 1811 1882	1811 1811 1811
B4 **Fulton** P.O. Box 524 Rochester 46975	1835 (1836) unorganized (Cass/Elkhart/ St. Joseph)	1882 1836 1882	1836 1837 1836
J1 **Gibson** Courthouse Sq./P.O. Box 630 Princeton 47670	1813 Knox	1882 1813 1880	1836 1813 1813

Map	County Address	Date Formed Parent County/ies	Birth Marriage Death	Land Probate Court
D5	Grant 101 E. 4th St. Marion 46953	1831 Adams New Purchase (Randolph/Delaware/ Madison) unorganized (Cass)	—— 1831 ——	1831 1831
H3	Greene P.O. Box 229 Bloomfield 47424	1821 Sullivan/ unorganized (Daviess)	1885 1821 1893	1822 1823 1831
E5	Hamilton 1 Hamilton County Sq., Ste. 106 Noblesville 46060	1823 Delaware New Purchase	1882 1833 1882	1825 1823
	Hamilton County, NW Territory, was formed in 1798 from territorial Knox County and included parts of Ohio and Indiana.			
F5	Hancock 9 E. Main St., Rm. 202 Greenfield 46140	1827 (1828) Madison	1882 1828 1882	1827 1828 ——
K5	Harrison 300 N. Capital Ave., Rm. 203 Corydon 47112	1808 Clark/Knox	1882 1809 1882	1807 1809 1809
F4	Hendricks P.O. Box 599 Danville 46122	1824 Delaware New Purchase/ Wabash New Purchase	1882 1824 1882	1823 1822 1824
E6	Henry P.O. Box B New Castle 47362	1822 Delaware New Purchase	1882 1823 1882	1824 1822 1825
D4	Howard P.O. Box 9004 Kokomo 46901	(see Richardville)	1875 1844 1875	1846 1844 ——
C6	Huntington P.O. Box 228 Huntington 46750	1832 (1834) Adams New Purchase (Allen/Grant)	1875 1837 1882	1834 1841 ——
H5	Jackson P.O. Box 318 Brownstown 47220	1816 Clark/Jefferson/ Washington	1882 1816 1882	1815 1817 ——
B3	Jasper 115 W. Washington St. Rensselaer 47978 *Record loss 1864.*	1835 (1838) Wabash New Purchase/ unorganized (Warren/White)	1882 1850 1882	1838 1864 ——
D7	Jay County Courthouse, 120 Court St. Portland 47371	1835 (1836) Adams New Purchase (Delaware/Randolph)	1882 1837 1882	1836 1837 1837
H6	Jefferson 300 E. Main St., Rm. 203 Madison 47250	1811 Clark/Dearborn/Knox	1882 1811 1882	1811 1811 1811
H5	Jennings P.O. Box 385 Vernon 47282	1817 Jackson/Jefferson	1882 1818 1882	1817 1818 1817
F4	Johnson 5 W. Jefferson Franklin 46131 *Record loss 1849 and 1874.*	1823 Delaware New Purchase	1882 1830 1882	1825 1821 1823
H2	Knox 101 N. 7th Vincennes 47591	1790 (Indiana county 1800) unorganized	1882 1806 1882	1783 1790 1801
	Knox County, NW Territory, was formed from non-county area in 1790. This included segments of present Illinois, Michigan, Ohio, Wisconsin, plus all of Indiana. Knox County became an Indiana territory in 1800, although much of the original county had been formed into other counties by that time. It became an Indiana county in 1816. Record loss 1814.			
B5	Kosciusko 121 N. Lake St. Warsaw 46580	1835 (1836) unorganized (Cass/Elkhart/ Grant)	1882 1830 1882	1834 1836 1836
A3	La Porte 813 Lincoln Way La Porte 46350	1832 St. Joseph/ unorganized	1882 1832 1882	1831 1832 1832
A6	Lagrange 105 N. Detroit Lagrange 46761	1832 unorganized (Allen/Elkhart)	1882 1832 1882	1832 1832 1832
A2	Lake 2293 N. Main St. Crown Point 46307	1836 (1837) Porter/ Newton	1882 1837 1882	—— —— ——
H4	Lawrence 1916 15th St. Bedford 47421	1818 Orange	1882 1818 1882	1819 1818 ——
E5	Madison P.O. Box 1277 Anderson 46016 *Record loss 1880.*	1823 Delaware New Purchase/ *Marion	1882 1853 1882	1822 1879
F4	Marion City-County Building 200 E. Washington St., Rm. W-122 Indianapolis 46204	1822 Delaware New Purchase	1882 1822 1882	1822 1822 1822
B4	Marshall 211 W. Madison St. Plymouth 46563	1835 unorganized (Cass/Elkhart/ St. Joseph)	—— 1836 ——	1834 1834 1837
H3	Martin P.O. Box 120 Shoals 47581	1820 Daviess/Dubois	1882 1820 1882	1820 1821 ——
C5	Miami 25 N. Broadway Peru 46970 *Record loss 1843.*	1832 Cass/ unorganized	1882 1843 1882	1836 1843 ——
G4	Monroe P.O. Box 547 Bloomington 47402	1818 Orange	1882 1818 1886	1817 1818 1854
E3	Montgomery P.O. Box 768 Crawfordsville 47933	1823 Wabash New Purchase/ *Parke/*Putnam	1882 1823 1882	1821 1822
F4	Morgan P.O. Box 1556 Martinsville 46151 *Record loss 1876.*	1822 Delaware New Purchase/ Wabash New Purchase	1882 1822 1899	1822 1822 ——

Map County Address	Date Formed Parent County/ies	Birth Marriage Death	Land Probate Court
Newton (old) (eliminated 1839)	1835 unorganized (St. Joseph/Warren/White)		
C2 Newton (present) P.O. Box 49 Kentland 47951	1859 Jasper	1882 1860 1882	1838 1860 1860
A6 Noble 101 N. Orange St. Albion 46701 *Record loss 1859.*	1835 (1836) unorganized (Allen/Elkhart/La Grange)	1882 1859 1882	1834 1854 —
H7 Ohio P.O. Box 185 Rising Sun 47040	1844 (1844) Dearborn	1882 1844 1882	1844 1844 —
J4 Orange Court Street Paoli 47454	1816 Gibson/Knox/Washington	1882 1816 1882	1816 1816 —
G3 Owen P.O. Box 146 Spencer 47460	1819 Daviess/Sullivan	1882 1819 1882	1819 1819 —
F2 Parke 116 W. High St., Rm. 204 Rockville 47872 *Record loss 1833.*	1821 Vigo/unorganized/Wabash New Purchase	1882 1829 1882	1816 1833 1833
K3 Perry 2219 Payne St. Tell City 47586	1814 Gibson/Warrick	1882 1814 1882	1815 1813 1815
J2 Pike Courthouse, 801 Main St. Petersburg 47567	1817 Gibson/Knox/Perry	1882 1817 1887	1817 1817 1817
A3 Porter 16 E. Lincoln Way Valparaiso 46383	1835 (1836) unorganized (St. Joseph)	1884 1836 1884	1833 1839 —
K1 Posey P.O. Box 606 Mount Vernon 47620	1814 Warrick/Knox/Gibson	1882 1814 1882	1812 1815 1815
B3 Pulaski 112 E. Main, Rm. 230 Winamac 46996	1835 (1839) unorganized (Cass/White)	1882 1839 1882	1840 1839 1839
F3 Putnam P.O. Box 546 Greencastle 46135	1822 Owen/Vigo/Wabash New Purchase	1882 1820 1882	1824 1825 —
Randolph (old) Ill. Territory, 1809	1790 (Indiana county, 1800) St. Clair—NW Territory		

Randolph County, NW Territory, was formed in 1795, from territorial St. Clair County. In 1800 Randolph became an Indiana territorial county. The present Randolph County was created in 1818. See below.

Map County Address	Date Formed Parent County/ies	Birth Marriage Death	Land Probate Court
E7 Randolph (present) Courthouse, 100 S. Main St. Winchester 47394	1818 Wayne	1882 1819 1882	1820 1819 —

Note also Randolph, Illinois Territory, above.

Map County Address	Date Formed Parent County/ies	Birth Marriage Death	Land Probate Court
Richardville	1844 (1844; changed to Howard, 1846) unorganized (Carroll/Cass/Miami)		
G6 Ripley P.O. Box 177 Versailles 47042	1816 (1818) Dearborn/Jefferson/*Jennings	1882 1818 1882	1818 1818 1818
F6 Rush P.O. Box 429 Rushville 46173	1822 Delaware New Purchase	— 1822 1823	1822 1822 1822
St. Clair Illinois Territory, 1809	1790 (Indiana county, 1800) unorganized		
A4 Saint Joseph 101 S. Main St. South Bend 46601	1830 unorganized (Carroll/Tippecanoe/Cass)	1882 1830 1882	1830 1830
J5 Scott 1 E. McClain Ave. Ste. 120 Scottsburg 47170	1820 Clark/Jackson/Jefferson/Jennings/Washington	1882 1820	1819 1820
F5 Shelby P.O. Box 198 Shelbyville 46176	1822 Delaware New Purchase	1882 1822 1882	1822 1822 —
K3 Spencer P.O. Box 12 Rockport 47635	1818 Perry/Warrick	1882 1818 1882	1818 1818 —
B3 Starke 53 E. Washington St. Knox 46534	1835 (1850) St. Joseph/unorganized (Starke/Cass/White)	1894 1840 1894	1850 1850
A7 Steuben 55 S. Public Sq. Courthouse Annex Angola 46703	1835 (1837) unorganized (LaGrange)	— 1832 —	1836 1845 —
G2 Sullivan P.O. Box 370 Sullivan 47882 *Record loss 1850.*	1817 Knox	1882 1850 1880	1850 1844 —
H7 Switzerland 212 W. Main Vevay 47043	1814 Dearborn/Jefferson	1882 1814 1882	1814 1814
D3 Tippecanoe P.O. Box 1665 Lafayette 47901	1826 Wabash New Purchase/unorganized	1882 1826 1882	1826 1825 1827
D4 Tipton 101 E. Jefferson Tipton 46072	1844 (1844) Adams New Purchase/unorganized (Cass/Hamilton/Miami)	— 1844 1882	1844 1844 1853
F7 Union 26 W. Union St. Liberty 47353	1821 Fayette/Franklin/Wayne	— 1821 —	1821 1821
K2 Vanderburgh P.O. Box 3556 Evansville 47708	1818 Gibson/Posey/Posey/Warrick	1882 1818 1882	1818 1821

Map	County Address	Date Formed Parent County/ies	Birth Marriage Death	Land Probate Court
E2	Vermillion 1 Courthouse Sq. Newport 47966	1824 Parke/unorganized/ Wabash New Purchase	1882 1824 1882	—— —— ——
G2	Vigo P.O. Box 8449 Terre Haute 47807	1818 Sullivan	1882 1818 1882	1816 1818 ——
	Wabash 1 W. Hill St. Wabash 46992 *Record loss 1870.*	1832 (1835) Adams New Purchase (Grant)/unorganized (Cass)	—— 1835 1899	1835 1847 ——
C5	Wabash New Purchase Eliminated 1835	1820 unorganized/*Monroe/*Owen/ *Vigo/*Parke		
D2	Warren 125 N. Monroe, Ste. 11 Williamsport 47993	1827 Wabash New Purchase/ unorganized (Vermillion) *Fountain/	1882 1827 1882	1830 1829 1827
K2	Warrick 1 County Sq., Rm. 200 Boonville 47601	1813 Knox	1882 1813 1882	1813 1814 1813
J4	Washington 99 Public Sq. Salem 47167	1814 Clark/Harrison	1882 1815 1882	1814 1814 1814
	Wayne 301 E. Main Richmond 47375 *Note also Wayne County below.*	1811 Clark/Dearborn/Knox	1882 1811 1882	1816 1812 1811
E7	Wayne—NW Territory	1796 (eliminated 1800) Knox/unorganized		

Wayne County, NW Territory, was formed in 1796 from territorial Knox County and unorganized area. This included portions of modern Illinois, Michigan, Ohio, and Wisconsin. Wayne County outside NW Territory was eliminated in 1800. In 1803 Wayne County, Indiana Territory, was created from territorial Knox and St. Clair County and unorganized area, including parts of today's Illinois, Indiana, Wisconsin, and most of Michigan. In 1811 Wayne County, Indiana Territory, was created from Clark, Dearborn, and Knox counties. This became an Indiana state county in 1816.

Map	County Address	Date Formed Parent County/ies	Birth Marriage Death	Land Probate Court
C6	Wells 102 W. Market St., Ste. 201 Bluffton 46714	1835 (1837) Adams New Purchase (Allen/Delaware/Randolph)	1883 1837 1883	1838 1838
C3	White P.O. Box 350 Monticello 47960	1834 Wabash New Purchase (Carroll)	1882 1834 1882	1834 1835 1834
B6	Whitley 101 W. VanBuren St. Columbia City 46725	1835 (1838) unorganized (Allen/Elkhart/ Grant)/*Huntington	1838	1813 1839 1882

Iowa

CAROL L. MAKI AND MICHAEL JOHN NEILL

From 1671 through 1689 the Iowa region was claimed for France by Sieur Saint-Lusson, Daniel de Greysolon Sieur de Luth (Du Luth), Robert Cavalier Sieur de la Salle, and Nicolas Perrot. Several jurisdictional changes occurred in Iowa's early history. France ceded Iowa to Spain in 1762, although it was returned in 1800 preceding the Louisiana Purchase in 1803, which made it United States territory. As part of the United States, Iowa was first included in the Illinois Territory (1808) and then the Missouri Territory (1812). Migrating groups from the states began the first settlements in 1832. Before statehood was established in 1846, these settlements were included in the Michigan Territory (1834), Wisconsin Territory (1836), and finally its own territory in 1838.

Prior to 1800, the only residents of the Iowa Territory were Native Americans and French. Julien DuBuque, a French Canadian, began mining lead in 1788 near present-day Dubuque, employing some of the normally unfriendly Fox tribal members in his mines. In 1796 DuBuque received a grant of land, including the lead mines, from the Spanish governor of Louisiana; the Spanish government gave additional grants. Louis Honore Tesson obtained 6,000 acres in 1799 in the present Lee County, and Basil Giard acquired land a year later in Clayton County. Meriwether Lewis and William Clark spent time near the Missouri River in Iowa in 1804. On 23 August 1805, the explorer Zebulon Pike raised the first American flag in Iowa, flying the stars and stripes from an area now on the southern edge of Burlington. A U.S. Army detachment from St. Louis built Fort Madison in 1808. Five years later, the fort was abandoned and burned by the departing troops whose exodus was caused by Chief Black Hawk and the War of 1812.

The year 1816 included the establishment of Fort Armstrong on Rock Island. Settlers from the East arrived as early as 1820. Danish immigrants settled in Lee County in 1832. A year later settlements were established by pioneers from Tennessee, Kentucky, Missouri, Illinois, Ohio, and Indiana.

With the creation of the Iowa Territory in 1838 came a great influx of settlers. The first territorial capital was established at Burlington. The new Iowans in the 1840s included Scandinavians, Dutch, Germans, Irish, Scots, and Welsh. New Englanders arrived in 1840, Quakers in 1841, and Mormons migrated across Iowa in 1846, the year Iowa became a state. The following year immigrants from the Netherlands settled at Pella. A large number of families migrated from Ohio to Iowa in 1854. From 1850 through 1880, there was a mass migration of Germans to the state. Migration from Iowa also occurred during this period, with a large exodus to California as a result of the gold rush, beginning in 1849.

The steamboat industry peaked from 1850 to 1877, while the first railroad in the state was completed in 1855. Both had significant influence on the settlement of the state. By 1860 the state population was 674,913. Ten years later it was 1,194,020.

Most of the immigrants settling in Iowa during the latter part of the nineteenth century were from northwestern Europe. They could purchase land cheaply but found the thick prairie sod difficult to improve for farming. Because of the need for heavy equipment and cooperative drainage plans, farming was much more commercial than family-oriented. The commercial aspect necessitated an extensive railroad network, resulting in high freight prices and a response in the form of the Grange Movement rebelling against the railroads. Financial depressions in 1873, 1893, and the

1930s greatly affected Iowa. As the twentieth century brought more efficient farming methods for mass production, many of the families who had owned farms moved to the cities. Today, farming continues to be an important aspect of the economy and exists with a sizable number of urban industries as well as the still rural ones like the community-owned Amana Colonies.

Vital Records

The Iowa vital records system originated on 1 July 1880, with legislation establishing a State Board of Health. Marriages were recorded in the counties prior to 1880, typically beginning when the county started keeping other records as well. Early birth records contain only minimal data—name, date, place, and names of parents. Death certificates prior to 1904 do not include the names of the parents of the deceased.

It is estimated that between 1880 and 1921 only about fifty percent of the births and deaths were registered. However, because of a provision for delayed birth registration, almost 470,000 delayed birth records have been filed with the Bureau of Vital Statistics.

All county vital records in Iowa are accessible to the public by personal inspection or by a written request to the clerk of the district court in the county where the event occurred. State vital records are not open to the public. Copies of certificates, however, are issued to grandparents, parents, children, a spouse, brothers or sisters, legal guardians, or respective legal representatives. An applicant must have a direct and tangible interest in any specified record and must have the ability to present a direct lineal relationship to the registrant. The purpose for which a certificate is needed should also be indicated. For the proper forms and fee schedule, contact the Iowa Department of Public Health, Bureau of Vital Records/Statistics, Lucas State Office Bldg., First Floor, Des Moines, IA 50319 <www.idph. state.ia.us>. According to the Iowa Bureau of Vital Statistics, counties do not have the authority to have birth, death, and marriage records between the years 1921 to 1941.

The State Historical Society of Iowa (see Archives, Libraries, and Societies), in cooperation with the Genealogical Society of Utah, is involved in a statewide county records microfilming project. Records included in this project are vital statistics, probate, and land. Copies of these microfilms, with an index to records filmed in each county, are available for use at the State Historical Society of Iowa's libraries, and many are now in the Family History Library (FHL) in Salt Lake City. The state historical society's website contains a listing of county records contained in its microfilm collection. State vital records, seventy-five years old or older, are now available, with some limitations, at the Iowa State Archives, a division of the State Historical Society of Iowa.

Many of the local chapters of the Iowa Genealogical Society (see Archives, Libraries, and Societies) have publications of vital records in their respective counties. A statewide publication listing, with ordering information, is available through the state society on its website.

Census Records

Federal

Population Schedules
- Indexed—1840, 1850, 1860, 1870, 1880. 1900, 1910, 1920, 1930
- Soundex—1880, 1900, 1920

Industry and Agriculture Schedules
- 1850, 1860, 1870, 1880

Mortality Schedules
- 1850, 1860, 1870, 1880

The State Archives at the State Historical Society of Iowa does hold, in addition to the above-mentioned census records, the manuscript state copies of the 1850, 1860, and 1870 federal censuses for Iowa, but they are only available for use on microfilm. The microfilmed state copies, however, make it possible to compare the microfilm edition of the federal copy from the National Archives for handwriting, spelling errors, completeness of the copy, or other problems suspected from the entry. Federal censuses for Iowa have been indexed through 1930, either in print, CD-ROM format, or online subscription services (see pages 3 and 17).

Territorial and State

In *Iowa History Sources: Census Data for Iowa*, No. 1 (Iowa City: State Historical Society of Iowa, 1973), author Loren N. Horton states, "Iowa is rich in the number of censuses taken, probably because legislative apportionment was based upon them during the nineteenth century. This was a period of rapid migration into the area and rapid disposal of public lands; therefore it was thought necessary to have a census taken almost every election in order to maintain fairness in distributing legislative seats."

Although Iowa did indeed enumerate its population frequently both in special and regular censuses, not all counties complied each time. Some enumerations are only for specific cities. Also, many of the censuses that were actually completed no longer exist. Because of this complexity, any research in these records should be preceded by obtaining the aforementioned publication by Loren N. Horton and the *Iowa Special Census* microfilm register from the research library of the State Historical Society of Iowa at Des Moines.

Taking into consideration that not all years include all counties, or all townships of a county, and that in fact some are very limited, the following census enumerations are available for Iowa.

The Wisconsin Territorial Census for 1836 includes the original counties of Dubuque and Des Moines, Iowa. This is indexed, printed, microfilmed, and available at the State Historical Society of Iowa. A microfilm copy of the territorial census of 1836 is also held by the National Archives—Central Plains Region (see page 12) and may also be found in "The Territorial Census for 1836," *Collections of the State Historical Society of Wisconsin*, volume 13, edited by Reuben Gold Thwaites (Madison, Wisc.: Democrat Printing Co., State Printer, 1895: 247-70).

Most of the following heads of households census enumerations have been indexed in some form. They are held in manuscript form by the State Archives at the State Historical Society of Iowa and are available for research on microfilm. They are listed by year and county: 1838–Van Buren; 1844–Keokuk; 1846–Louisa, Polk, and Wapello; 1847–Boone, Clinton, Davis, Louisa, Marion, Polk, Scott, Van Buren, and Wapello; 1849–Benton, Boone, Clinton, Louisa, Madison, Poweshiek, Scott, Van Buren, and Washington; 1851–Cedar, Clinton, Decatur, Guthrie, Iowa, Johnson, Madison, Mahaska, Page, Pottawattamie, Poweshiek, Scott, and Washington; 1852–forty-five counties included; 1853–Warren County for Allen, Greenfield, Lynn, and Richland townships only; 1854–fifty-two counties included; 1859–Carroll and Sac.

For the 1847 Iowa state census, additional details are indicated for some members of The Church of Jesus Christ of Latter-day Saints. The enumeration of its members in Pottawattamie includes the standard information but adds a count of wagons and guns; number of family members ill, aged, or infirm; and number oxen, cattle, and horses. It is thought that the extended census information was part of a preparation for moving these families westward.

Clinton in Clinton County is enumerated for 1887 in two bound volumes. The following are Iowa Special Censuses on microfilm: 1881–Mason City, Cerro Gordo County; 1888–Algona, Kossuth County; 1889–Cherokee, Cherokee County; 1889–North part of Des Moines, Polk County; 1891–Emmetsburg, Emmet County; 1891–Spencer, Clay County; 1891–Villisca, Montgomery County; 1892–Carroll, Carroll County; 1892–Eagle Grove, Wright County; 1892–Estherville, Emmet County; 1892–Jefferson, Greene County; 1892–Tama, Tama County; 1893–Mystic, Appanoose County; 1893–Hampton, Franklin County; 1893–Ames, Story County; 1893–Bloomfield, Davis County; 1893–Nevada, Story County; 1893–West Union, Fayette County; 1895–Independence, Buchanan County; 1896–Oelwein, Fayette County; 1897–New Hampton, Chickasaw County.

Although taken in 1863, 1869, 1873 and 1875, the returns are not known to be extant. Henry County Genealogical Society (P.O. Box 81, Mount Pleasant, IA 52641) has located and printed the 1863 and 1869 censuses for their county only.

The state censuses for 1856, 1885, 1895, 1905, 1915, and 1925 include name, age, sex, color, birthplace, and occupation (age sixteen and up) for each member of each household. Additional information, listed by year of enumeration, is also listed:

1856—voter; native/naturalized/alien; owner of land; years in state; marital status.

1885—marital status; house number and street in towns, smallest legal description if rural; county of birth if born in Iowa; nativity of parents; foreign/native; alien who has/has not taken out first papers.

1895—marital status; births and deaths in household in 1894; county of birth if born in Iowa; nativity of parents; foreign/native; naturalized; Civil War service, including company, regiment and state; Mexican War soldiers, including regiment and state.

1905 and 1915—marital status; birthplace of parents; owner of home or farm, with value; naturalized; years in United States/Iowa; military service in Civil, Mexican, or Spanish War.

1925—marital status; birthplace of parents; names of parents, including maiden name of mother, place of birth and marriage; age of parents, if living; house number and street in cities and towns; years in United States/Iowa; amount for which each listed property owner's house was insured.

No statewide index exists for the censuses of 1856, 1885, 1895, 1905, 1915, or 1925. Indexes, however, for counties, portions of counties, and some towns are becoming available through individuals, chapters of the Iowa Genealogical Society, *Hawkeye Heritage*, or the staff of the State Historical Society of Iowa.

All extant state censuses have been microfilmed and are available for research and purchase at the State Historical Society of Iowa. Most years are available through interlibrary loan from the organization's branch in Iowa City.

Background Sources

Regional historical sources are most frequently found through local groups or individuals who have a working knowledge of the town or county records. It is possible to contact these people through historical or genealogical societies in the area, or to use the query columns in their periodicals or through the appropriate county genealogy mailing list at <http://lists.rootsweb.com>.

Many of the local chapters of the Iowa Genealogical Society (see Archives, Libraries, and Societies) have reprinted county histories, some with indexes. Most of them must be ordered

directly through the local chapter. In addition, the following material includes useful background on Iowa history and its residents:

Dawson, Patricia, and David Hudson, comps. *Iowa History and Culture: A Bibliography of Materials Published Between 1952 and 1986.* Ames, Iowa: State Historical Society of Iowa in association with Iowa State University Press, 1989. Professional librarians spent more than ten years surveying Iowa's printed and unpublished dissertations and papers of historical accounts for this bibliography for the state of Iowa. Although family histories are not included, genealogical information may be located in the county, town, and church histories, in the biographies, and through the extensive name and subject indexes. Items in the Table of Contents such as "claim clubs," "pioneer life," and "defunct schools" could be helpful in developing an understanding of the historical context surrounding individuals and families.

Eckhardt, Patricia, comp. *Historical Organizations in Iowa, Iowa History Sources No. 2.* Iowa City: Iowa Historical Department, Division of the State Historical Society, 1982.

Iowa Genealogical Society. *Surname Index.* 5 vols. Des Moines: Iowa Genealogical Society, 1972–90. Includes a total of 149,000 surnames being researched by society members.

Morford, Charles. *Biographical Index to the County Histories of Iowa.* Vol. 1. Baltimore: Gateway Press, 1979. Provides surname indexes to numerous county histories.

Peterson, William, J. *Iowa History Reference Guide.* Iowa City: State Historical Society, 1952.

Sopp, Elsie L. *Personal Name Index to the 1856 City Directories of Iowa.* Gale Genealogy and Local History Series. Vol. 13. Detroit: Gale Research Co., 1980.

Suggested references regarding migration to Iowa and its settlement include:

Bogue, Allan G. *From Prairie to Cornbelt: Farming on the Illinois and Iowa Prairies in the 19th Century.* Chicago: University of Chicago Press, 1963.

Riley, Glenda. *Frontierswomen: The Iowa Experience.* Ames, Iowa: Iowa State University Press, 1983.

Maps

Among the standard map references for Iowa, in addition to the numerous county atlases for all areas of the state, is Alfred Theodore Andreas's *Illustrated Historical Atlas of the State of Iowa, 1875* (1875; reprint; Iowa City: State Historical Society, 1970), which superbly illustrates towns and farms, specifically locating patrons to the publication. An indexed patron's list with place of residence, county and state of birth, and year of emigration is included.

The earliest Sanborn Fire Insurance map (see page 5) of Iowa is from 1883. The State Historical Society of Iowa publishes and sells *Fire Insurance Maps of Iowa Cities and Towns: A List of Holdings,* compiled by Peter H. Curtis and assisted by Richard S. Green and Edward N. McConnell (Iowa City: Iowa State History Department, 1983), which lists the society's collection. All fire insurance maps (Sanborn and others) have been compiled into one microfilm collection that is at both branches of the State Historical Society research library, the University of Iowa, and the Library of Congress. Of the approximately 4,000 Iowa maps included in both locations of the State Historical Society of Iowa library, the Des Moines branch has original plat maps created by the territorial land surveyors.

Newberry Library's *Checklist of Printed Maps of the Middle West to 1900,* 11 vols. (Boston: G. K. Hall, 1980) lists all known pre-1900 plat maps and plat books for the state of Iowa. The *Atlas of Historical County Boundaries: Iowa* (New York: Charles Scribner's Sons, 1998) may also be helpful.

Current county maps for Iowa can be ordered by sending check or money order to the Iowa Department of Transportation <www.dot.state.ia.us/sitemap.htm>. The maps are fairly easy to read, divided by townships and sections, and show highways, railroads, cities and towns, and rivers and streams.

Land Records

Public-Domain State

Iowa was a public-domain state with one principal meridian, which was established in Arkansas in 1815. Original land disposition was made by the federal government and its agents. There were nine land districts in Iowa, the first two with offices at Burlington and Dubuque in 1838.

However, over 20,000 settlers were in Iowa prior to the first land sales and thus had no legal title to their claims. To prevent speculators and latecomers from buying such improved lands at land office auctions, the settlers and speculators formed claims clubs to rig the auctions on grounds of first settlement.

Patents, tract books, and township plats are available at the Bureau of Land Management Eastern States Office (see page 6). Holdings for Iowa land records at the National Archives—Central Plains Region (see page 12) include abstracts of military warrants. More federal military bounty land warrants were used in Iowa than any other state. It is estimated that half of Iowa was purchased with these authorizations. Locations on warrants for some or all acts from 1842 to 1855 are for the district offices of Chariton, Kanesville, Council Bluffs, Decorah, Osage, Des Moines, Fort Des Moines, Dubuque, Marion, Burlington, Fairfield, Fort Dodge, Iowa City, and Sioux City. Other records of the register and receiver are held for these same counties.

Records of homesteads including certificates, receipts, and entries, are held for Des Moines, Fort Dodge, and Sioux City.

Following the federal disbursement of land in Iowa, land purchases and sales were handled by the recorder of the respective county government, beginning with the establishment of that particular county.

Acquisitions of the Iowa State Archives that should be of great interest to the genealogist include land office copies of plats (in color) based on original land surveys (ca. 1835–60). These twelve volumes, transferred from the secretary of state's vault, cover the entire state and include notes on Native American villages and trails, old roads, and pioneer dwellings. The "Auditor of State Abstracts of Original Land Entries" (1847–59) has been microfilmed and is available to researchers. The cooperative microfilming project of the Genealogical Society of Utah and the State Historical Society of Iowa have provided the preservation of land conveyances for almost every county; these records are available at the State Historical Society of Iowa's Des Moines research library. Numerous tract books, receipt books, series of county plat books, etc., are available for genealogical research in Iowa. Other references include:

Bogue, Allan G. "The Iowa Claims Clubs: Symbols and Substance," *Mississippi Valley Historical Revue* 45 (1958): 231-35.

Lokken, Roscoe L. *Iowa Public Land Disposal.* Iowa City: State Historical Society of Iowa, 1942.

Shambaugh, Benjamin F., ed. *Constitution and Records of the Claim Association of Johnson County, Iowa.* Iowa City: University of Iowa Press, 1894.

Snedden, Howard E. "Auditor's Transfer Books: A Valuable Iowa Land Research Tool," *Hawkeye Heritage* 24 (Autumn 1989): 141-45. The Transfer Books, created in 1866, are sources of property transfers, arranged by land description instead of by grantor or grantee. The entries include the names of the parties involved and the transaction dates, and reference either deed books or plat books, which will vary with county. The Transfer Books are currently being microfilmed as well.

Swierenga, Robert P. *Pioneers and Profits: Land Speculation on the Iowa Frontier.* Ames, Iowa: Iowa University Press, 1968.

Federal land patents in Iowa can be searched via the Bureau of Land Management's website at <www.dot.state.ia.us/sitemap. htm>.

Following the federal disposal of land in Iowa, land purchases and sales were handled by the recorder of the respective county government, beginning with the establishment of that particular county. The State Historical Society of Iowa lends pre-1940 county plat (landownership) maps on microfilm. Map holdings vary greatly by county.

Probate Records

Matters of probate, including wills, administrator or executor bonds, inventories, and guardianships, are kept by the clerk of the county district court. The Genealogical Society of Utah and the State Historical Society of Iowa are jointly microfilming probate records at the county level. In the case of Scott County, packets of original probate files in addition to the court's record books are included in the microfilming project. Full particulars on which counties and which records have been microfilmed can be obtained from the library in Des Moines or through the FHL catalog (see pages 12-13).

Court Records

The first instrument of government formulated in Iowa country is said to be the Miners' Compact, drawn up by the lead miners in 1830. When the Iowa Territory was established in 1838, three district courts were created that continued until statehood in 1846 when the three districts became one. In 1849 this district was divided into northern, middle, and southern divisions.

Considerable reorganization took place through 1907. Holdings at the National Archives—Central Plains Region include files from the District of Iowa (1845–82); Northern District (1850–1959); and Southern District (1842–1959).

At the county level, criminal and civil court records are filed with the county clerks. A few Iowa court records have been, and are being, transferred to the State Archives in Des Moines. A recent acquisition of interest to genealogists is the Supreme Court of Iowa Order Books, beginning with the formation of the Iowa Territory in 1838, in four volumes through 1858. Order Book A contains twenty-one naturalizations between 1840 and 1851.

Naturalizations that are part of the District Court Records at the county level are being microfilmed. Naturalizations for most counties have been filmed and are available at the State Historical Society of Iowa research libraries and through the FHL.

Tax Records

The tax rolls for personal property and real estate were kept by the auditor or the treasurer of each county. A few of these records have been microfilmed and are available at the State Historical Society of Iowa. Original county tax rolls are usually not transferred.

Old age pension tax is a resource in Iowa that genealogists should consider. A 1934 directive to collect an old-age assistance tax was based on a list of all persons over twenty-one years of age. Although the tax was discontinued in 1936, the information

included could be important: name, address, sex, date of birth, place of birth, and names of both parents. Many counties have had these lists microfilmed and they are available through the FHL.

Cemetery Records

Many of the local chapters of the Iowa Genealogical Society have publications of cemetery records in their respective counties that can be ordered through the chapter. A statewide publication listing is available through the state society. A large number of cemetery transcription collections as well as records of funeral homes, casket lists, and obituary indexes are held by the FHL.

Church Records

Predominant church groups in Iowa include Catholic, Methodist, Lutheran, and Baptist. Less in size, but equally important in religious history in the state are the Quakers, Mormons, Mennonites, and Congregationalists. The first church building in Iowa, a Methodist Church built of logs, was constructed in Dubuque in 1834. A year later the Catholics erected a parish building in the same city. In 1843 the "Iowa Band" of Congregational and Presbyterian clergy began ministering to the settlers in Iowa. In 1854 a small group of the Community of True Inspiration arrived from Germany, settling along the Iowa River in the mid-section of the state. A year later additional members of their group joined them, establishing the unique Amana colonies of present-day Iowa.

For an extensive bibliography on religion and religious groups in Iowa, see Peterson (1952) and Dawson and Hudson (1989), both described in Background Sources.

The microfilming project of the Genealogical Society of Utah and the State Historical Society of Iowa has preserved a large number of church baptismal and marriage records. The state society also has impressive collections of original religious records from various Iowa organizations. The University of Iowa, Iowa State University, and other educational institutions within the state have additional manuscript collections of church records.

Military Records

Military records at the State Archives, a division of the State Historical Society of Iowa, include the State Adjutant General's records of Iowa volunteers in the Mexican War, Civil War, and Spanish-American War. Included among those records are regimental muster rolls, enlistment papers, roster books, reports, pay books, and correspondence with indexes for some of these

records. Index entries can be copied for a fee. There are no pension records for Iowa volunteer units. Records of the Grand Army of the Republic posts for many Iowa communities are available at the state archives. Casualty files for World War I and II have information, and sometimes photographs, of individual servicemen. Published sources include:

Iowa Adjutant General's Office. *Persons Subject to Military Duty, ca. 1862–1920*. 94 microfilm reels. Salt Lake City: Genealogical Society of Utah, 1978.

Iowa Adjutant General's Office. *Roster and Record of Iowa Soldiers in the War of the Rebellion: Together with Historical Sketches of Volunteer Organizations, 1861–1866*. 6 vols. Des Moines: E. H. English, State Printer, 1908–11.

Revolutionary War Soldiers and Patriots Buried in Iowa. Marceline, Mo.: Walworth, ca. 1978.

Snedden, Howard E. "A Unique Iowa Resource: The G.A.R. Card Index File," *Hawkeye Heritage* 21 (Summer 1986): 70:1.

———. "A Neglected Source: A Case in Point: The Civil War Draft Rolls of Iowa's Fifth Congressional District," *Hawkeye Heritage* 19 (Winter 1984): 185-89.

Although covering only the southwest quarter of the state, "consolidated lists" of eligible men are available with names and descriptions of men drawn for the draft, as well as an interesting array of additional genealogical information. As indicated by the author, remarks such as "Gone to Nebraska City," "In Holmes Co., Ohio," or "deserted across the plains" will certainly give direction to research. These lists are part of Record Group 110, Provost Marshall General's Bureau (Civil War) at the National Archives.

United States Adjutant General's Office. *Index to Compiled Service Records of Volunteer Union Soldiers Who Served in Organizations from the State of Iowa*. Washington, D.C.: National Archives, 1964.

The State Historical Society of Iowa lends the Civil War Roster and Index for all Iowa regiments from its Iowa City library.

Periodicals, Newspapers, and Manuscript Collections

Periodicals

Iowa has several valuable historical periodicals. The State Historical Society of Iowa has published the *Annals of Iowa*, a scholarly quarterly in three series (1863–74, 1882–83, 1893-present); *Iowa Historical Record* (1885–1902); the *Iowa Journal*

of History and Politics, renamed *Iowa Journal of History* (1903–61); and the *Palimpsest,* now titled the *Iowa History Illustrated,* a popular quarterly, published continuously since 1920. Volume and cumulative indexes are available. *Hawkeye Heritage,* the publication of the Iowa Genealogical Society, contains a wealth of local information from various parts of the state.

Newspapers

The *Du Buque Visitor,* Iowa's first newspaper, was published in 1836 at Dubuque, followed a year later by *The Western Adventurer* at Montrose. The State Historical Society of Iowa has been collecting the newspapers of the state extensively for quite some time. Currently archived are over 22,000 reels of microfilm. Papers cataloged as part of the United States Newspaper Project are on the OCLC database and can be obtained through interlibrary loan from either the Des Moines or Iowa City facilities. Suggested references include the following:

Cheever, L. D., comp. *Newspaper Collection of the State Historical Society of Iowa.* Iowa City: State Historical Society of Iowa, 1969. An update file to this listing is available at the State Historical Library in Iowa City.

Iowa Pilot Project of the Organization of American Historians, The Library of Congress, United States Newspaper Project. *A Bibliography of Iowa Newspapers, 1836–1976.* Iowa City: Iowa State Historical Department, 1979.

Petersen, W. J. *The Pageant of the Press, A Survey of 125 Years of Iowa Journalism.* Iowa City: Iowa State Historical Society, 1962.

Pitman, Edward F. *Index to Bound Newspapers in Iowa State Department of History and Archives.* Des Moines: State of Iowa, 1947.

Available for purchase from the State Historical Society of Iowa Library (Iowa City) is the *Bibliography of Iowa Newspapers, 1836–1976* (Iowa State Historical Department, 1979).

Manuscripts

Civil War diaries, a Bond of Proper Conduct, papers of an 1866 Indian agent, and a witness to a presidential assassination are just a few of the items found in the Manuscript Department of the State Historical Society of Iowa. In *Guide to Manuscripts* (Iowa City: State Historical Society of Iowa, 1973), compiler Katherine Harris lists numerous genealogical treasures in this collection. The book, which is very descriptive and well organized, is still only a sampling of the scope of the material available. A few examples are an 1840 bond of apprenticeship for Anne Brophy's sixteen-year-old son as apprentice mariner for five years; the 1841 proper conduct papers that allowed Francis and Maria Reno to be free African Americans without paying a bond; three pages written by E. H. Sampson, a guard at Ford's Theatre the night Abraham Lincoln was shot; fifty-three folders and nine packages

of records from Grace Episcopal Church, Cedar Rapids (1850–1967); the papers of Leander Clark, special Indian agent for the Sac and Fox in Tama County (1866–74); and numerous Civil War diaries, many without names. The collection also includes various county government and court papers, vital records, property deeds, maps, photographs, and family genealogies.

Another large manuscript collection is located at the State Archives in Des Moines. Numerous finding aids exist for these manuscripts although a published guide does not. Included in the collection are early land records, manuscript Civil War records for Iowa (muster rolls, clothing books, regimental reports, correspondence, volunteer enlistment), and records of schools and other institutions. This repository also has papers of private and public individuals, photographs, diaries, and journals. The record books of the Iowa Service Star Legion, which include nearly 1,100 completed questionnaires and photographs of World War I servicemen from Iowa, are an excellent example of a unique source.

Excellent manuscript collections will also be found in the following libraries: University of Iowa, Iowa State University, Luther College, Loras College, Grinnell College, and Morningside College (see Archives, Libraries, and Societies).

In many cases, manuscript collections in adjacent states should also be seriously considered in tracing families. The James J. Hill papers, located at the James J. Hill Library, St. Paul, Minnesota, are an excellent example. Hill is most widely known as the "Empire Builder" who created the giant Great Northern system from the St. Paul and Pacific Railroad and controlled railroads and property in Iowa. There is considerable Iowa material within this collection, most of it in twenty-six archival boxes labeled "Iowa Properties Papers." Because of the diversity of the Hill enterprises, there is a broad spectrum of original source material. The papers of the Lehigh Supply Company, for example, provide information on boarding houses and miners' incomes and expenditures.

Iowa Territorial Papers (1838–46) are held at the National Archives—Central Plains Region (see also Wisconsin—Manuscripts—Draper Manuscripts).

Archives, Libraries, and Societies

State Historical Society of Iowa Library
600 E. Locust
Des Moines, IA 50319
www.iowahistory.org

This statewide organization encompasses all the state historical operations, including the historical libraries (at the Des Moines address and at Iowa City—see below); State Archives (including manuscript, maps, school and institutional records, and photographs); museum; and membership and development

of publications. The extensive holdings of the research library at the Des Moines location are the largest in the state. The staff is very responsive to written requests for general information, and the society's website contains several bibliographies and finding aids (see list of publications under Periodicals).

State Historical Society of Iowa
Research Library
402 Iowa Ave.
Iowa City, IA 52240
www.iowahistory.org

The second largest research collection in the state is located at the Iowa City branch of the State Historical Society's research facilities. Holdings include local, state, and national histories; biographies; government documents, and current historical periodicals not all identical to the facility at Des Moines. Microfilm holdings are loaned between the collections. Of specific interest to genealogists are county histories, state census data, cemetery records, atlases, and plat books. Iowa newspapers, beginning in 1836, can be found in 10,000 bound volumes and 12,000 microfilm rolls (microfilm available through interlibrary loan). Fire insurance maps include more than 700 Iowa communities. Over 100,000 photographic images can be located by standard subject headings, geographical designations, or the portrait index.

Iowa Genealogical Society
P.O. Box 7735
Des Moines, IA 50322
www.iowagenealogy.org

Maintains an extensive genealogical reference library (shelf list available), publishes *Hawkeye Heritage* and a member newsletter, and publishes in cooperation with its chapters a wide variety of genealogical reference works, primarily Iowa vital records. State and national speakers are featured at an annual conference. The society is also placing county research guides on its website. The society has a genealogical library at 628 E. Grand Ave., directly across the street from the Iowa State Historical Building.

Newberry Library
60 W. Walton St.
Chicago, IL 60610
www.newberry.org

Although in Illinois, this repository should be considered a source for Iowa research. According to Peggy Tuck Sinko, author of *Guide to Local and Family History at the Newberry Library* (Salt Lake City: Ancestry, 1987), "The Iowa holdings of The Newberry Library are surpassed in size, scope, and quality only by the library's Illinois collection." The Iowa collection includes considerable genealogical and local history material, plus a number of rare books and manuscripts included in the Graff Collection.

Resources of Iowa research can be found in a multitude of other locations in the state. County/city level archival programs exist, for example, in Dubuque and both Polk and Scott counties. See the following to locate other valuable resource collections in the state of Iowa.

2003 Iowa Library Directory. Des Moines: State Library of Iowa, 2003 <www.silo.lib.ia.us/for-ia-libraries/directories/>.

Horton, Loren H., ed. *Historical Organizations in Iowa.* Iowa History Sources, No. 2. Iowa City: Iowa Historical Department, Division of State Historical Society, 1982.

Ludwig, Cherie, comp. *Iowa Genealogical and Historical Resources by County.* Iowa State Historical Department, Division of Historical Museum and Archives, 1978.

Special Focus Categories

African American
In the 1840s only slightly more than 300 African Americans were living in Iowa. Free African Americans were discouraged, if not totally forbidden, from migrating to the state by a ruling in April 1839. It stated that any African American, "black," or "mulatto" must provide "a fair certificate of actual freedom under a seal of a judge and give bond of $500 as surety against becoming public charges" before being permitted to settle in Iowa. After 1865, however, the African-American population in the state tripled, most migrating from Missouri and other Mississippi and Ohio river areas. Very few histories of African Americans in Iowa exist at this time. William J. Peterson's *Iowa History Reference Guide* (see Background Sources) lists numerous periodical articles and some books for African-American history in Iowa. The following are a brief sampling of those articles.

Bergmann, Leola Nelson. "The Negro in Iowa," *Iowa Journal of History* 46 (January 1948): 3-90.

Gallaher, Ruth A. "Slavery in Iowa," *Palimpsest* 28 (May 1947): 158-60.

Van Ek, Jacob. "Underground Railroad in Iowa," *Palimpsest* 2 (May 1921): 129-43.

Additional suggestions for reference on African-American history in Iowa include:

Iowa Bystander, 1894–1987, Des Moines. Renamed *New Iowa Bystander* in 1971, this newspaper was established for the African-American community in Iowa in 1894 by I. W. Williamson, Billy Colson, and Jack Logan. Some years are available on microfilm.

Schweider, Dorothy, Joseph Hraba, and Elmer Schweider. *Buxton: Work and Racial Equality in a Coal Mining Community.* Ames,

Iowa: Iowa State University Press, 1987. Buxton, which existed as an "integrated community" coal camp in south-central Iowa during the 1900s, was referred to as "the black man's utopia in Iowa."

Native American

In 1781 the wife of Peosta, a Fox warrior, reported the discovery of lead deposits in the Iowa country. Seven years later Julien Dubuque, a fur trader, obtained sanction from the Indians to work lead mines near what is now Dubuque. The following timeline of the Native Americans in Iowa will provide a guideline to their disbursement within and beyond the state.

1824: Half-Breed Tract established in present Lee County

1825: Neutral lines established between Sioux, Sac, and Fox

1830: Neutral ground is established between Sioux, Sac, and Fox

1832: Black Hawk War terminates in cession of strip of lands west of Mississippi River known as Black Hawk Purchase; Winnebago tribe is given part of neutral ground

1833: Title to Black Hawk Purchase is transferred to United States Government; Ottawa, Pottawattomie, and Chippewa tribes are given lands in what is now southwestern Iowa

1834: "Half-breeds" are given fee simple title to Half-Breed Tract by act of Congress

1836: Sac and Fox cede Keokuk's Reserve of the United States

1837: Sac and Fox cede to the United States 1,250,000 acres of land known as the second Black Hawk Purchase

1838: Chief Black Hawk dies at his home near the Des Moines River in Davis County

1842: Sac and Fox cede all remaining lands in Iowa

1843: Sac and Fox vacate lands east of line passing north and south through the Red Rocks of Marion County

1845: Sac and Fox withdraw from Iowa

1846: Pottawattomie relinquish lands in western Iowa

1848: Removal of Winnebago tribe begins

1851: Sioux cede lands in northern Iowa

1857: Spirit Lake Massacre: Sioux attack settlers and kill thirty; small band of Sac and Fox return, permitted to buy eighty acres of land in Tama County; members of these tribes still live on a semi-reservation north of the village of Tama

1862: Blockhouses erected in northwestern Iowa for protection against the Sioux

See the following for Native American research in Iowa:

Rafert, Stewart. "American-Indian Genealogical Research in the Midwest: Resources and Perspectives," *National Genealogical Society Quarterly* 76 (September 1988): 212-24.

Other Ethnic Groups

The following sources are valuable in gaining an understanding of various ethnic groups in Iowa from both a historical and genealogical standpoint.

Foreman, Grant. "English Emigrants in Iowa," *Iowa Journal of History* 44 (October 1946): 385-420.

Calkin, Homer L. "The Coming of the Foreigners," *Annals of Iowa* 43 (April 1962). This issue of *Annals* deals exclusively with foreigners including those immigrants from Germany, Scandinavia, and the United Kingdom.

Christensen, Thomas P. "A German Forty-eighter in Iowa," *Annals of Iowa* 26 (April 1945): 245-53.

———. *A History of Danes in Iowa.* New York: Arno Press, 1979.

Van der Zee, Jacob. *The Hollanders of Iowa.* Iowa City: State Historical Society of Iowa, 1912.

Wick, Barthinius Larson. *The Amish Mennonites: A Sketch of Their Origins, and of Their Settlement in Iowa, with Their Creed in an Appendix.* Iowa City: State Historical Society, 1984.

———. "The Earliest Scandinavian Settlement in Iowa," *Annals of Iowa* 29 (October 1948): 468-72.

Luther College, Koren Library, Decorah, Iowa 52101, holds over 20,000 Norwegian manuscripts and 1,000 volumes of Norwegian American newspapers.

County Resources

For some counties there are two "Date Formed" years listed. The first is the year the county was created; the second is the year it was fully organized if the date differs from the year of creation.

Under the heading "Parent County/ies," the name/s listed may be the county or counties from which the respective county was formed or it may be names by which the county was originally known. "Unorganized" in this same column denotes that the county was formed from non-county lands. The county name in parentheses is the county to which the unorganized land may have been attached at that time. Counties listed with an asterisk (*) are those in which you may also find records concerning the county listed. It may have been "attached" to those county/ies for some period of time.

Iowa county governments recorded few vital statistics earlier than 1880. Marriage record registration began in many areas with the organization of the county. It is estimated that between 1880 and 1921, only about fifty percent of the births and deaths were registered. Birth, marriage, death, and probate records are usually found in the office of the clerk of courts at the county seat. Land transactions are in the county recorder's office.

The FHL online catalog was used to compile most record state dates. Researchers are encouraged to contact the courthouse or local genealogical society in the county of interest.

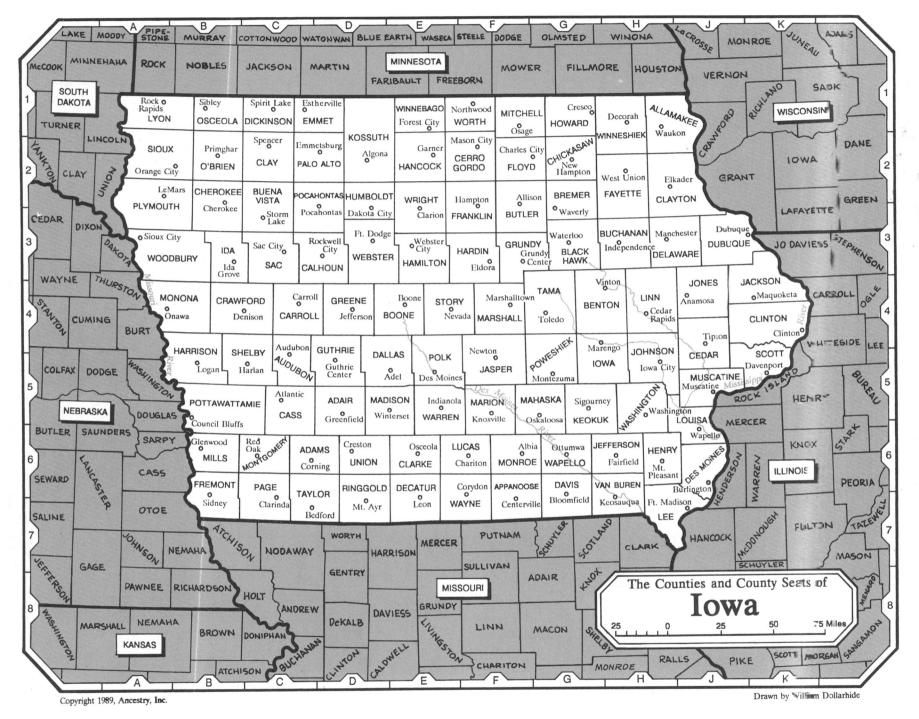

The Counties and County Seats of **Iowa**

25   0   25   50   75 Miles

IOWA

221

Drawn by William Dollarhide

IOWA

Map	County Address	Date Formed Parent County/ies	Birth Marriage Death	Land Probate Court
C5	Adair 400 Public Sq. Greenfield 50849	1851 (1854) Pottawattomie/ unorganized (Dallas/Mahaska /Monroe/Polk) *Cass	1880 1854 1880	1854 1857 1887
C6	Adams David and 9th Corning 50841	1851 (1853) Pottawattomie	1880 1855 1880	1853 1868 1857
H1	Allamakee 110 Allamakee St. Waukon 52172	1847 (1849) unorganized (Clayton)	1880 1849 1880	1851 1854 1849
F7	Appanoose 201 N. 12th St. Centerville 52544	1843 (1846) unorganized (VanBuren)/ *Davis	1880 1842 1880	1850 1846 1851
C5	Audubon 318 Leroy, Ste. 4 Audubon 50025	1851 (1855) Pottawattomie/unorganized (Dallas/Mahaska/ Monroe/Polk) *Cass	1880 1856 1880	1853 1871 1855
	Bancroft	1851 (abolished 1855) unorganized (Delaware/Polk)/ *Boone		
G4	Benton P.O. Box 549 Vinton 52349	1837 (1846) Dubuque/ *Jackson/*Linn	1880 1852 1880	1847 1856 1860
G3	Black Hawk 316 E. 5th St. Waterloo 50703	1843 (1847; 1853) Buchanan/ *Delaware/*Benton	1880 1853 1880	1853 1853 1853
E4	Boone 201 State St. Boone 50036	1846 (1849) unorganized (Linn)/ *Polk	1880 1848 1880	1849 1865 1867
G2	Bremer 415. E. Bremer Ave. Waverly 50677	1851 (1853) unorganized (Delaware/Polk)/*Buchanan	1880 1853 1880	1852 1852 1853
H3	Buchanan 210 5th Ave. NE P.O. Box 317 Independence 50644	1837 Dubuque/*Delaware	1880 1848 1880	1846? 1851 1852
C2	Buena Vista P.O. Box 220 Storm Lake 50588	1851 (1858) unorganized (Delaware/Polk)/*Woodbury	1880 1877 1880	1869 1871 1877
	Buncombe	1851 (changed to Lyon, 1861) *Woodbury		
F3	Butler P.O. Box 325 Allison 50602	1851 (1854) unorganized (Delaware/Polk)/*Buchanen *Blackhawk	ca. 1874 1854 1880	1854 1864 ?
D3	Calhoun 416 4th St. Rockwell City 50579	1851 (1855) unorganized (Delaware/Polk)/*Greene	1880 1857 1880	1855 1873 1860?
C4	Carroll P.O. Box 867 Carroll 51401	1851 (1855) Pottawattomie/ unorganized (Dallas/ Mahaska/Monroe/Polk)/ *Shelby/*Guthrie	1880 1855 1880	1855 1856 1855?
C5	Cass 5th W. 7th St. Atlantic 50022	1851 (1853) Pottawattomie	1880 1853 1880	1853 1864 1873?
J4	Cedar 400 Cedar St. Tipton 52772	1837 Dubuque	1880 1840 1880	1838 1839 1839
F2	Cerro Gordo 220 N. Washington Mason City 50401	1851 (1855) unorganized (Delaware/Polk)/*Floyd	1880 1855 1880	1855 1857 1880?
B2	Cherokee 520 W. Main St. Cherokee 51012	1851 (1858) unorganized (Delaware/Polk)/*Woodbury	1880 1866 1880	1856 1859 1872
G2	Chickasaw Prospect St. New Hampton 50659	1851 (1853) unorganized (Delaware/Polk)/*Fayette	1880 1853 1880	1851 1854 1853
E6	Clarke 100 S. Main St. Osceola 50213	1846 (1851) unorganized (Kishkekosh)	1880 1852 1880	1849 1853 1854
C2	Clay 215 W. 4th Spencer 51301	1851 (1858) unorganized (Delaware/Polk)/*Woodbury	1880 1866 1880	1858 1870 1880?
H2	Clayton 111 High St. Elkader 52042	1837 Dubuque	1880 1865 1880	1839 1840 1850
K4	Clinton 1900 N. 3rd Clinton 52732	1837 (1841) Dubuque/ *Scott	1880 1840 1880	1840 1851 1859
	Cook	1836 (eliminated 1838) Des Moines/*Muscatine		
B4	Crawford 1202 Broadway Denison 51442	1851 (1855) Pottawattomie unorganized (Dallas/Mahaska/ Monroe/Polk)/*Shelby	1880 1853 1880	1855 1867 1868
	Crocker	1870 (abolished 1871) Kossuth		
D5	Dallas 801 Court St. Adel 50003	1846 (1847) unorganized (Mahaska)/ *Polk	1880 1847 1880	1850 1851 1855
G6	Davis Bloomfield 52537	1843 (1844) unorganized (VanBuren)	1880 1844 1880	1847 1844 1844

IOWA

Map	County Address	Date Formed Parent County/ies	Birth Marriage Death	Land Probate Court
E6	Decatur 207 N. Main St. Leon 50144	1846 (1850) unorganized (Appanoose)/ *Davis	1880 1874 1880	1851 1871 1871
H3	Delaware 301 E. Main/P.O. Box 527 Manchester 52037	1837 (1841) Dubuque	1880 1851 1880	1847 1853 1857?
J6	Des Moines 513 N. Main St. Burlington 52601	1834 (Michigan Territory) unorganized	1880 1835 1880	1837 1835 1835
C1	Dickinson 1802 Hill Ave. Spirit Lake 51360	1851 (1857) unorganized (Delaware/Polk)/*Woodbury	1880 1871 1880	1861 1861 1880?
J3	Dubuque 720 Central Ave. Dubuque 52001 *No death records 1917–41; no birth record June 1940–September 1941.*	1834 (Michigan Territory) unorganized	1880 1835 1880	1834 1835 1834
D1	Emmet 609 1st Ave. N. Estherville 51334	1851 (1859) unorganized (Delaware/Polk)/ *Boone/*Webster	1880 1876 1880	1876 1877 1859
H2	Fayette Vine Street West Union 52175	1837 (1850) Dubuque/ *Clayton	1880 1851 ca. 1860	1851 1859 1859
F2	Floyd 101 S. Main St. Charles City 50616	1851 (1854) unorganized (Delaware/Polk)/*Fayette/ *Chickasaw	1880 1880 1880	1855 1855 1880?
	Fox	1851 (changed to Calhoun, 1853) unorganized (Delaware/Polk)		
F2	Franklin 12 First Ave. NW Hampton 50441	1851 (1856) unorganized (Delaware/Polk)/*Fayette/ *Chickasaw/*Hardin	1880 1855 1880	1855 1855 1856
B6	Fremont P.O. Box 610 Sidney 51652	1847 (1849) unorganized (Appanoose)	1880 1848 1880	1849 1880 1850
D4	Greene 114 N. Chestnut Jefferson 50129	1851 (1854) unorganized (Delaware/Polk)/*Dallas	1880 1854 1880	1854 1854 1889?
F3	Grundy 706 G. Ave. Grundy Center 50638	1851 (1856) unorganized (Delaware/Polk)/*Buchanen/ *Blackhawk	1875 1856 1880	1863 1869 1871
D5	Guthrie 200 N. 5th St. Guthrie Center 50115 *Courthouse fire in 1963.*	1851 (1851) unorganized (Dallas)	1880 1852 1872	1852 1859 1855
E3	Hamilton 2300 Superior St. Webster City 50595	1857 Webster	1880 1857 1880	1854 1865 1868
E2	Hancock 855 State St. Garner 50438	1851 (1858) unorganized (Delaware/Polk)/ *Boone/*Webster	1880 1873 1880	1857 1876 1858
F3	Hardin 1215 Edgington Ave. Eldora 50627	1851 (1853) unorganized (Delaware/Polk)/*Marshall	1880 1853 1880	1849 1854 1853
B4	Harrison 111 N. 2nd Ave. Logan 51546	1851 (1853) Pottawattomie	1880 1853 1880	1853 1853 1853
H6	Henry 100 E. Washington St. Mt. Pleasant 52641	1836 Des Moines	1880 1836 1880	1837 1837 1837
	Howard	1816 (became Missouri Territory) St. Louis/Washington/ unorganized (St. Charles)		
G1	Howard 137 N. Elm St. Cresco 52136	1851 (1855) unorganized (Delaware/Polk)/*Floyd	1880 1875 1880	1855 1873 1873
	Humboldt (old)	1851 (abolished 1855) unorganized (Delaware/Polk)*Boone		
D2	Humboldt (present) 203 Main P.O. Box 100 Dakota City 50529 *Abolished 1855; recreated 1857 from Kossuth/Webster.*	1851* unorganized (Delaware/Polk)/*Boone	1880 1858 1880	1855 1859 ?
B3	Ida 401 Moorehead St. Ida Grove 51445	1851 (1859) unorganized (Delaware/Polk)/*Woodbury	1880 1868 1880	1856 1870 1875
H5	Iowa P.O. Box 126 Marengo 52301	1843 (1845) Keokuk/*Johnson	1880 1847 1880	1847 1848 1851
K4	Jackson 201 W. Platt, Ste. 1 Maquoketa 52060	1837 Dubuque	1880 1847 1880	1838 1838 1839
F5	Jasper P.O. Box 944 Newton 50208	1846 (1846) unorganized (Mahaska)	1880 1846 1880	1847 1846 1846
H6	Jefferson P.O. Box 984 Fairfield 52556	1839 (1839) Henry	1880 1839 1880	1838 1838 1840
H5	Johnson 913 S. Dubuque St. Iowa City 52240	1837 (1838) Cook/Dubuque/Muscatine/ *Cedar	1880 1839 1880	1839 1839 1839
J4	Jones P.O. Box 109 Anamosa 52205	1837 (1839) Dubuque/*Jackson	1880 1840 1880	1841 1844 1848

223

Map County Address	Date Formed Parent County/ies	Birth Marriage Death	Land Probate Court
G5 Keokuk 101 S. Main Sigourney 52591	1837 (1844) Dubuque/ unorganized/*Cedar/ *Johnson/*Washington	1880 1844 1880	1844 1844 1844
Kishkekush	1843 (1845; changed to Monroe, 1846) unorganized (Henry)/ *Jefferson/*Wapello		
D1 Kossuth 114 W. State St. Algona 50511	1851 (1856) unorganized (Delaware/Polk)/ *Boone/*Webster	1880 1857 1880	1855 1856 1869?
H7 Lee 933 Ave. H Ft. Madison 52627 and Keokuk 52632 *County has two courthouses. Call for their respective holdings.*	1836 Des Moines	1880 1837 1880	1830 1841 1849
H4 Linn 930 1st St. SW Cedar Rapids 52401	1837 (1839) Dubuque/ *Jackson	1880 1840 1880	1841 1840 1840
J6 Louisa 117 S. Main St. Wapello 52653	1836 Des Moines	1880 1842 1880	1839 1838 1839
F6 Lucas 916 Braden Ave. Chariton 50049	1846 (1849) unorganized (Kishkekosh)	1880 1849 1880	1849 1850 1854
A1 Lyon 206 S. 2nd Ave. Rock Rapids 51246	1851 (1872) unorganized (Delaware/Polk)/*Woodbury	1880 1872 1880	1862 1885 1874
E5 Madison P.O. Box 152 Winterset 50273	1846 (1849) unorganized (Mahaska)	1880 1849 1880	1850 1852 1852
G5 Mahaska 106 S. 1st St. Oskaloosa 52577	1843 (1844) unorganized (Washington)	1880 1844 1880	1845 1844 1844
F5 Marion P.O. Box 497 Knoxville 50138	1845 unorganized	1880 1845 1880	1846 1845 1854
F4 Marshall 1 E. Main St. Marshalltown 50158	1846 (1849) unorganized (Linn)/ *Jasper	1880 1850 1880	1850 1851 1854
B6 Mills 418 Sharp St. Glenwood 51534	1851 (1851) Pottawatomie	1880 1880 1880	1853 1852 1888
F1 Mitchell 508 State St. Osage 50461	1851 (1854) unorganized (Delaware/Polk)/*Fayette/ *Chickasaw	1880 1855 1880	1854 1855? 1855?
B4 Monona 610 Iowa Ave. Onawa 51040	1851 (1854) Pottawattomie/unorganized (Dallas/Mahaska/Monroe/ Polk)/*Harrison	1880 1856 1880	1858 1860 1861?
F6 Monroe 10 Benton Ave. E. Albia 52531	1843 (1845) unorganized (Henry)/ *Jefferson/*Wapello	1880 1845 1880	1847 1848 1847
C6 Montgomery 105 Coolbaugh St. Red Oak 51545	1851 (1853) Pottawattomie/*Adams	1880 1855 1880	1854 1868 1890?
J5 Muscatine 401 E. 3rd St. Muscatine 52761	1836 Des Moines	1880 1837 1880	1838 1838 1839
B2 O'Brien 115 S. Hayes Primghar 51245	1851 (1860) unorganized (Delaware/Polk)/*Woodbury	1880 1860 1880	1857 1880? 1870
B1 Osceola 300 7th St. Sibley 51249	1851 (1872) unorganized (Delaware/Polk)/*Woodbury	1880 1872 1880	1869 1872 1873
C6 Page 112 E. Main St. Clarinda 51632	1847 (1852) unorganized (Appanoose)	1880 1852 1880	1854 1857 ?
D2 Palo Alto 1010 Broadway Emmetsburg 50536	1851 (1858) unorganized (Delaware/Polk)/ *Boone/*Webster	1880 1860 1880	1858? 1864 1870
A2 Plymouth 215 4th Ave. S.E. Le Mars 51031	1851 (1858) unorganized (Delaware/Polk)/*Woodbury	1880 1860 1880	1856 1871 1869
D2 Pocahontas 99 Court Sq. Pocahontas 50574	1851 (1859) unorganized (Delaware/Polk)/ *Boone/*Webster	1880 1859 1897	1861 1867 1867
E5 Polk 111 Court Ave. Des Moines 50309	1846 (1846) unorganized (Mahaska)	1880 1846 1880	1846 1846 1846
B5 Pottawattomie 227 S. 6th St. Council Bluffs 51501 and Avoca 51521 *County has two courthouses. Call for their respective holdings.*	1848 unorganized (Dallas/Mahaska/ Monroe/Polk)	1880 1848 1880	1849 1846 1876
G5 Poweshiek 302 E. Main St. Montezuma 50171	1843 (1848) Keokuk/*Iowa/*Johnson/ *Mahaska	1880 1848 1880	1843 1849 1869
D7 Ringgold 109 W. Madison Mt. Ayr 50854	1847 (1855) unorganized (Appanoose)/ *Taylor	1880 1855 1880	1855 1858 1855
Risley	1851 (abolished 1853) unorganized (Delaware/Polk)		
C3 Sac 100 NW State St. Sac City 50583	1851 (1856) unorganized (Delaware/Polk)/*Woodbury/ *Greene	1880 1864 1880	1856 1857 1869

IOWA

Map	County Address	Date Formed Parent County/ies	Birth Marriage Death	Land Probate Court
K5	Scott 416 West 4th Davenport 52801	1837 Cook/Dubuque/Muscatine	1880 1838 1880	1838 1838 1838
C5	Shelby 612 Court St. Harlan 51537	1851 (1853) Pottawattomie	1880 1853 1880	1854 1869 1869
A2	Sioux 210 Central Ave. SW Orange City 51041	1851 (1860) unorganized (Delaware/Polk)/*Woodbury	1880 1871 1880	1856 1870 1871
	Slaughter	1838 (changed to Washington, 1839) Henry/Louisa/Muscatine/ unorganized		
E4	Story 900 6th St. Nevada 50201	1846 (1853) unorganized (Linn)/ *Polk/*Boone	1880 1854 1880	1853 1855 1865
G4	Tama 100 W. High St. Toledo 52342	1843 (1853) Benton/*Linn	1880 1853 1880	1853 1854 1850
C7	Taylor 405 Jefferson St. Bedford 50833	1847 (1851) unorganized (Appanoose)	1880 1851 1880	1855 1859 1875?
D6	Union 300 N. Pine St. Creston 50801	1851 (1853) Pottawattomie/ unorganized (Dallas/ Mahaska/Monroe/Polk)	1880 1855 1880	1854 1854 1854
H6	Van Buren P.O. Box 475 Keosauqua 52565	1836 Des Moines	1880 1837 1880	1837 1841 1837
	Wahkaw	1851 (changed to Woodbury, 1853) unorganized (Delaware/Polk)		
B6	Wapello 101 W. 4th St. Ottumwa 52501	1843 (1844) unorganized (Henry)/ *Jefferson	1880 1844 1880	1844 1844 1844
E5	Warren 301 N. Buxton, Ste. 202 Indianola 50125	1846 (1849) unorganized (Mahaska)	1880 1849 1880	1849 1850 1849
H5	Washington P.O. Box 889 Washington 52353	1838 Henry/Louisa/Muscatine/ unorganized	1880 1839 1880	1839 1838 1868
F6	Wayne P.O. Box 435 Corydon 50060	1846 (1851) unorganized (Appannose)/ *Davis	1880 1851 1880	1851 1851 1873
D3	Webster 703 Central Ave. Fort Dodge 50501	1853 (1853) Risley/Yell	1880 1853 1880	1856 1855 1864
E1	Winnebago 126 S. Clark St. Forest City 50436	1851 (1857) unorganized (Delaware/Polk)/ *Boone/*Webster	1880 1890 1880	1873 1858 1900?
H1	Winneshiek 201 West Main Decorah 52101	1847 (1851) unorganized (Clayton)	1880 1851 1880	1851 1852 1851
A3	Woodbury 620 Douglas St. Sioux City 51101	1851 (1853) unorganized (Delaware/Polk)	1880 1854 1880	1855 1856 1900?
F1	Worth 1000 Central Ave. Northwood 50459	1851 (1857) unorganized (Delaware/Polk)/*Fayette/ *Chickasaw/*Floyd/*Mitchell	1880 1858 1880	1857 1897 1863
E2	Wright 115 N. Main St. Clarion 50525	1851 (1855) unorganized (Delaware/Polk)/ *Boone/*Webster	1880 1855 1880	1855 1855 1857
	Yell	1851 (abolished 1853) unorganized (Delaware, Polk)		

Kansas

**MARSHA HOFFMAN RISING, CG, FUGA, FASG
AND MARY CLEMENT DOUGLASS, CGRS**

ansas derives its name from a tribe of plains native peoples, the "Kansa," who lived in earth lodges along the Missouri, Kansas, and Blue rivers in the northeastern section of the state. Kansas, which was a segment of the vast area known as the Louisiana Purchase, became part of the United States in 1803. With the passage of the Kansas-Nebraska Act in 1854, it became the Kansas Territory. On 29 January 1861 Kansas was admitted as a free state and became the thirty-fourth state in the Union.

Kansas was first designated as permanent "Indian territory" and it became the home for many of the displaced tribes from the states of Illinois, Indiana, Ohio, and Missouri as well as the remaining indigenous plains people. In 1825 the Kansa and Osage tribes were induced to give up part of their eastern Kansas lands to make way for those from the east: the Shawnee, Kickapoo, Delaware, Wea, Piankeshaw, and others. By 1846 nineteen reservations had been established within the boundaries of what is now Kansas. The first mission for Native Americans in what is now Kansas was Mission Neosho, established in 1824. A Methodist mission was founded for the benefit of the Shawnee in 1829.

It did not take long for the restless white settlers to desire permanent homes and farms in Kansas. This settlement, however, was spurred not so much by natural westward expansion as by the determination of both pro-slavery and anti-slavery factions to achieve a majority population. This struggle became an important part of the peopling of Kansas, and the genealogist with early Kansas settlers will want to become familiar with the details.

Passage of the Kansas-Nebraska Act in 1854 only accentuated the difficulties, and this early civil war ultimately turned the Kansas Territory into "bleeding Kansas." As each faction attempted to establish a majority, fraud became common. As an example, the 1855 Kansas state census showed 53 voters in the seventh district, but three months later, 253 votes were cast. From 200 to 300 men from Missouri went into the seventh district of Kansas Territory in wagons and horseback on the day preceding the election. They were armed with pistols and other weapons and intended to vote to secure the election of pro-slavery members to the territorial legislature. These examples are typical of the stuffing of ballot boxes by residents of Missouri who were hoping to create a slave state. In 1859 slavery was prohibited by the Wyandotte Constitution, but this law did not go into effect until statehood in 1861. Kansas became a strong Republican force when it entered the Union. For the settler of Kansas, this period was a long, bloody, and difficult one. Bushwhackings, burnings, lootings, and murder became an inevitable part of life. Graphic testimony is offered in the *Reports of the Special Committee* (see Background Sources) and in the stories reported in surviving newspapers published along the Kansas-Missouri border and in eastern newspapers such as the *New York Tribune*.

The first act of the Kansas territorial legislature on 30 August 1855 was to designate thirty-three counties in the eastern section of the territory. The second act created Marion and Washington counties, and a third created Arapahoe County out of territory that would later become part of the territory of Colorado.

Kansas experienced its greatest population expansion at the end of the Civil War when peace brought development of the

prairie lands. The construction of railroads and the availability of cheap lands through both the railroad companies and the federal government brought many settlers to the area until 1867. The Homestead Act was available only to Union veterans, giving Kansas a distinctly Yankee flavor. Kansas was not always hospitable; pioneers were visited by prairie fires, droughts, blizzards, dust storms, grasshopper plagues, cyclones, and floods. Many would-be settlers retreated saying, "In God We Trusted; In Kansas We Busted." Some early settlers returned to the safety of the east. The settlers who remained and those who came later established the farms, communities, and businesses that shaped Kansas history.

Vital Records

The recording of births and deaths began at the statewide level in July 1911. Marriage records are on file from 1 May 1913 as are divorces from 1 July 1951. These records are located in the Kansas Department of Health and Environment, Office of Vital Statistics, Curtis State Office Bldg., 1000 Southwest Jackson, Ste. 120, Topeka, KS 66612-2221 <www.kdhe.state.ks.us/vital>. The most current fee (2004) for these certificates was $12 for birth, marriage, and divorce documents, and $13 for death certificates. Divorces that occurred prior to 1951 are in the office of the clerk of the district court in which the case was filed.

Territorial records of marriages and deaths located in Kansas newspapers from 1854 to 1861 were published in several issues of volume 18 of the *Kansas Historical Quarterly* (1960). Births and deaths were published in volume 19 (August and September 1961), and marriages were published in volume 21 (Summer 1955): 445-86. Reprints are available from the Midwest Historical Genealogical Society, Box 1121, Wichita, KS 67201, and Jefferson County Genealogical Society, P.O. Box 174, Oskaloosa, KS 66066. The *First Bicentennial Report of the State Board of Agriculture* also lists some vital statistics taken in the territory. Before statewide registration, some births and deaths were kept at the county level. Compliance was inconsistent and sporadic. The researcher should consult the Historical Records Survey—Kansas, entitled *Guide to Public Vital Records in Kansas,* which lists the location of vital records *not* held by the Bureau of Vital Statistics. It is divided into type of record—birth, marriage, death, and divorce—and then by county.

As recently as 1987, Kansas law was changed to allow access to records of births, marriages, and deaths that occurred between 1885 and 1913. The Kansas State Historical Society is currently involved in a cooperative microfilming project with the Genealogical Society of Utah. As of 2000, thirty counties have had their records filmed. The film is available at the Kansas State Historical Society, Center for Historical Research (see Archives, Libraries, and Societies). Published indexes, abstracts, and transcriptions of vital records from a number of sources are in the collections at the society as well.

Census Records

Federal

Population Schedules
- Indexed—1860, 1870, 1880, 1900, 1910, 1920, 1930
- Soundex—1880, 1900, 1910 (Miracode)

Mortality Schedules
- 1860, 1870, 1880 (indexed)

Industry and Agriculture Schedules
- (Industry) 1860, (Agriculture) 1870, 1880

The research center at the Kansas State Historical Society has all the federal population censuses for Kansas, as well as the 1880 and 1900 Soundex and the 1910 Miracode (see pages 3 and 17).

Territorial and State
The census enumerations that were completed between 1855 and 1859, inclusive, are actually voters lists. The researcher must note that some voters boycotted elections, making the lists by no means complete. The 1857 Census of Shawnee, Native and Adopted is available in the state archives department at Kansas State Historical Society.

The 1860 Kansas territorial census was taken as part of the federal census. Two copies of it exist. The original copy was sent to Washington, with a transcription retained by the state. Both copies have been indexed and are available for research at the Kansas State Historical Society, Center for Historical Research, making it possible to check inconsistencies between the two returns. A county census was completed at the time of application for county organization. Many of these are extant, some housed at the Kansas State Historical Society, which can provide a list of availability.

Kansas completed state censuses in 1865, 1875, 1885, 1895, 1905, 1915, and 1925. They have been microfilmed, are available for research, and have been partly indexed by the Kansas State Historical Society. A list of those indexed is available from the society. The statistical rolls of the Board of Agriculture contain enumerations for the years 1873 and 1877, 1896 to 1904 (incomplete), 1918, 1920 to 1924, 1925 (taken as part of the state census), 1926 to 1936, and from 1950 to 1979. These rolls only included the head of household until 1955. As with all census records, these must be used with caution as they are not entirely complete, but they are a good source for recent data.

Native American Censuses

Also available at the Kansas State Historical Society are:

Enrollment cards of the Five Civilized Tribes (1898–1914): Cherokee, Chickasaw, Choctaw, Creek, and Seminole.

Indian census rolls (1885–1940), primarily for tribes with a Kansas connection.

Background Sources

Anderson, Lorene, and Alan W. Farly. "Bibliography of Town and County Histories of Kansas," *Kansas Historical Quarterly* 21 (Autumn 1955): 513-51.

Andreas, Alfred Thayer (with William G. Cutler). *The History of the State of Kansas.* 2 vols. Chicago: A. T. Andreas, 1883. Reprinted in 1976 with an index of names from the 15,000 sketches found in the original volumes, this provides important access to early county and community histories.

Barry, Louise. *The Beginnings of the West: Annals of the Kansas Gateway to the American West, 1540–1854.* 1972. Reprint. St. Louis: The Patrice Press, 1988. Chronological exploration in encyclopedia format of the pre-territorial lives and times of those who lived in Kansas.

Cutler, William G. *History of the State of Kansas.* 2 vols. Chicago: A. T. Andreas, 1883.

Collections of the Kansas State Historical Society. 17 vols. Topeka: Kansas State Historical Society, 1881–1928. Historical documents for the state.

Napier, Rita, ed. *A History of the Peoples of Kansas.* Lawrence, Kans.: University of Kansas, Continuing Education, 1985. These scholarly essays discuss ethnic and minority group experience in the nineteenth and twentieth centuries.

Owen, Jennie, and Kirche Mechem, eds. *The Annals of Kansas 1886–1925.* 2 vols. Topeka: Kansas State Historical Society, 1954, 1956. This is a continuation of Wilder's book (see below).

Report of the Special Committee Appointed to Investigate the Troubles in Kansas with the Views of the Minority of Said Committee— Report No. 200 to the 34th Congress. Washington, D.C.: Cornelius Wendell, 1856. This book was indexed in a two-volume separate publication by Robert Hodge, *An Index to the Report of the Special Committee Appointed to Investigate the Troubles in Kansas,* vol. 1 (A–L) and vol. 2 (M–Z), published by the author (Vicksburg, Va., 1984). Testimonials and voting records regarding the slavery question in the settlement of Kansas.

Richmond, Robert W. *Kansas: A Land of Contrasts.* 3d ed. Arlington Heights, Ill.: Forum Press, 1989.

Rydjord, John. *Kansas Place Names.* Norman, Okla..: University of Oklahoma Press, 1972.

Shortridge, James R. *Peopling the Plains: Who Settled Where in Frontier Kansas.* Lawrence: University Press of Kansas, 1995. With a large number of maps and census data, the author provides an exceptional cultural geography detailing the origins and thus the ethnic diversity of nineteenth and early twentieth century settlers.

Socolofsky, Homer E., and Virgil W. Dean. *Kansas History: An Annotated Bibliography.* New York: Greenwood Press, 1992. The bibliography has 4,565 separate entries, a chronology, and indexes.

Socolofsky, Homer E., and Huber Self. *Historical Atlas of Kansas.* Norman: University of Oklahoma Press, 1972.

Stratton, Joanna L. *Pioneer Women: Voices from the Kansas Frontier.* New York: Simon and Schuster, 1981. Diaries of women in the early period of Kansas settlement.

Wilder, Daniel W. *The Annals of Kansas.* 1886. Reprint ed. Topeka: Kansas State Historical Society, 1975. Covers the pre-1886 era in Kansas. A new edition is in progress.

Maps

Robert W. Baughman's *Kansas in Maps,* first published in 1969 by the Kansas State Historical Society, contains ninety maps. It was reprinted in 1988 by the Patrice Press in St. Louis.

A good series of maps showing the expansion and development of Kansas counties was published in Kansas State Historical Society's volume 8 of *Transactions.* These maps were later reprinted by Kansas Genealogical Society, in Dodge City, in the *TreeSearcher* (April 1966–January 1967).

The map collection at Kansas State Historical Society includes 21,000 maps and architectural drawings. The maps were produced by government agencies, railroads, map publishers, and individuals. Researchers may request information regarding specific geographic locations and time periods, including the Kansas Dead Town List for those towns no longer in existence.

Indispensable for finding locations of rural cemeteries, churches, land holdings, township and range lines, section numbers, water courses, and other structures are the General Highway Maps (by county name), available from the Kansas Department of Transportation, Bureau of Transportation Planning, 915 Harrison, Rm. 754, Docking State Office Bldg., Topeka, KS 66612-1568 <www.ksdot.org/maps/main.html>. These maps are inexpensive, about $2 per county.

Land Records

Public-Domain State

Kansas was surveyed on the rectangular survey system and was first officially opened for white settlement in 1854. Some of the early patent books for Kansas counties have been microfilmed by and are available through the Family History Library (FHL) in Salt Lake City.

Kansas owes much of its growth to the passage and enactment of the Homestead Law, passed in 1862 and effective 1 January 1863. It offered "free" land to those who would live on and cultivate a tract. In order to make a claim, the individual had to (1) be twenty-one years old or head of a family, (2) be a United States citizen or have declared intention to become one, (3) *not* already own 320 acres of land, (4) *not* abandon land owned by him in the same state or territory, and (5) intend to use the homestead for himself and his family.

There were four classes of public lands opened for settlement. First, those owned by the federal government; second, those owned by institutions of higher learning; third, the common-school lands; and fourth, the railroad lands. The state was divided into nine land districts, and offices opened in twenty-five towns, including Larned (Pawnee County), Oberlin (Decatur County), Topeka (Shawnee County), Kirwin (Phillips County), Independence (Montgomery County), Concordia (Cloud County), Salina (Saline County), Wakeeney (Trego County), Wichita (Sedgwick County), and Cherokee Strip lands and Osage Indian trust lands. (See Socolofsky and Self, *Historical Atlas of Kansas* in Background Sources.) Land was also sold through the railroad offices of the Missouri, Kansas, and Texas Railway (headquarters at Parsons, Kansas), Atchison, Topeka, and Santa Fe (headquarters in Topeka), and Kansas Division, Union Pacific Railroad (headquarters in Kansas City).

The Kansas State Historical Society has the Kansas tract books (on microfilm), plats, and tract maps, and the purchases from the Dodge City land office. They also have the land sales of the Santa Fe Railroad (mostly central Kansas) and the Kansas Town and Land Company (Rock Island Railroad), which sold land in Colorado, New Mexico, and Nebraska as well as in Kansas. National Archives—Central Plains Region (see page 12) has Bureau of Land Management records for the states of Kansas, Iowa, and Nebraska, 1840–1915.

After initial purchase from the federal government, land records are located at the county level in register of deeds office.

Probate Records

Many probate records located at the county level are in the district court. One can expect to find an index to probate court papers, court records, executor's bonds, letters of testamentary, inventories, sale bills, guardian and curators' records, and court appointments. Usually the probate minute books, probate court records, and case files are also available. The researcher can check for the application letters for administration, executors and guardians, administrators and guardian's bonds, appraisement of estate, names and oaths of witnesses, sale bills, settlement records, orders of publication, term docket books, and wills and record of wills.

Court Records

The district court has general jurisdiction in all matters, both civil and criminal. Naturalization records may be filed here as well as other courts of record. This court also holds jury lists, witness claims, alimony records, patent rights, judgments, and attorneys of records.

Tax Records

For the most part, tax records remain at the local level. Assessment and tax rolls are kept permanently by the County Treasurer's office.

Cemetery Records

Two national cemeteries were established in Kansas: Leavenworth National Cemeteries, P.O. Box 1694, Leavenworth, KS 66048, and Fort Scott National Cemetery, P.O. Box 917, Fort Scott, KS 66701.

There is no central registry of cemetery locations in Kansas. The Woman's Kansas Day Club completed a project to identify and locate many Kansas cemeteries. The project's results are at the Kansas State Historical Society, which has additional collections of published cemetery inscriptions, though not comprehensive, listed in their card catalog.

The Register of Deeds in each county is often able to assist in locating cemeteries. Certain maps distributed by the Kansas Department of Transportation show the location of known cemeteries in relation to county roads.

Online there are several sources for locating ancestors' burial sites in Kansas. For example, *Cemeteries in Kansas, 1906* <www.kshs.org/genealogists/vital/cemetery.htm> includes cemeteries published in the *Transactions of the Kansas State Horticultural Society*, vol. 28 (1906): 317-83. This list was part of a report authorized by the 1903 legislature that contains the text of the report as well as the listing of cemeteries. While no names of people buried are included, the information identifies specific cemeteries by county, township, or city if known, and the size

of the cemetery in acres. See also Kansas GenWeb at <http://skyways.lib.ks.us/genweb> for cemetery listings by county.

Church Records

The earliest churches were established among the native tribes settled in Kansas long before it was organized as a territory. The Methodist, Baptist, Society of Friends, Roman Catholic, Presbyterian, and Congregational churches all had early missions that grew as the white settlers immigrated. Records of the Quakers can be found at Friends University in Wichita; Methodists at Baker University in Baldwin City; Mennonite at Bethel College in Newton; Lutheran, especially Swedish, at Bethany College in Lindsborg. Forsyth Library at Fort Hays University in Hays, KS 67601, holds numerous ethnic and religious group records. Volga German records here are outstanding.

The Kansas State Historical Society solicits church rolls, membership lists, records, and histories. The published material is located in the library; the unpublished material is located in the manuscript department. A few church records have been microfilmed.

Military Records

The records of the Kansas Adjutant General through World War II are located at the Kansas State Historical Society. Few are indexed. Virtually nothing has survived from the Territorial Militia, which was pro-slavery. The records of the unofficial "Free State Forces" are extant at the Kansas State Historical Society as are the records of the Kansas Adjutant General from 1861 to World War I. The Daughters of the American Revolution, John Haupt Chapter, have indexed the Kansas Civil War and Indian War militia. An index to the Kansas Adjutant General's report (1861–65) and a list of military men who received a bonus in World War I exist at the state archives. A list of soldiers killed in battle in Kansas regiments is given in Andreas' *History of Kansas*, 180–208 (see Background Sources).

Post-Civil War veteran's census records include the 1883 index to pensioners, veterans, their widows and orphans, and the 1930 veteran's census. The original Grand Army of the Republic Post Records are in the Kansas State Historical Society Library.

Good biographical information is available on Spanish-American and World War I veterans in the manuscript department of the Kansas State Historical Society. The Adjutant General report entitled *Index to Kansas Troops in the Volunteer Service of the United States in the Spanish and Philippine Wars* is also available for research. The Kansas State Historical Society holds the photostatic copies of World War I enlistment and discharge papers of Kansas military personnel (see also Cemeteries). The Kansas State Archives has a list of military men who received a World War I bonus. World War I Alien Registration cards for Kansas and World War II Selective Service 4th Registration cards of men born on or after 28 April 1877 and on or before 16 February 1897 are at the National Archives—Central Plains Region (see page 12).

World War II library holdings at the Kansas State Archives include honor rolls for selected counties. Archives records list Kansas citizens who served. Arranged by draft board, it is not indexed. Records of Kansas POW hospitals and camps are on microfilm and information on Camp Concordia may be found in its collections, as are Veteran Enrollments for 1883, 1889, and 1930 and records of the Kansas State Soldiers Home are in State Archives holdings. Portions of these records are on microfilm.

Periodicals, Newspapers, and Manuscript Collections

Periodicals

The Kansas State Historical Society publishes *Kansas History: A Journal of the Central Plains*, formerly called *Kansas Historical Quarterly* (1948–present). A directory to historical and genealogical societies is published annually, indicating more than twenty genealogical periodicals published in the state. The issues for 1931–77 are being digitized for online access.

Newspapers

The Kansas State Historical Society holds a superior collection of Kansas newspapers. Since the historical society was founded by newspaper editors, they have copies of the vast majority of the newspapers published in Kansas. Their current goal is to microfilm all pre-1930 holdings. The newspapers are now available on interlibrary loan, and may be purchased from the society with a list of holdings available online at <www.kshs.org/library/news.htm>.

The researcher will find an excellent reference in Aileen Anderson, ed. and comp., *Kansas Newspapers: A Directory of Newspaper Holdings in Kansas* (Kansas Library Network Board, 1984).

Manuscripts

In addition to newspapers, the Kansas State Historical Society has a diverse and rich manuscript collection, including letters, diaries, journals, and photographs of early pioneers. Although there is no comprehensive guide to the manuscripts at the Kansas State Historical Society, there are finding guides to major and individual collections online at <www.kshs.org/research/collections/resourceguide.pdf>. A useful source is the original manuscripts and biographies of over 800 Kansas women

collected by Lila Day Monroe, source material for *Pioneer Women* (see Background Sources). Among the other materials at the society are records of the Atchison, Topeka, and Santa Fe Railroad, including pay rolls, the papers of Indian missionaries, Isaac McCoy (1808–74) and Jotham Meeker (1825–64), and the papers of William Clark, superintendent of the St. Louis Indian Superintendency that have been microfilmed. The state archives department in the society holds state prison records from the 1860s to the 1980s.

Genealogists with ancestors in the medical professions may be interested in the *Comprehensive Index to Kansas Physicians and Midwives, 1887–1900*, and *Index to Obituaries from the Kansas Medical Journal, 1889–1966*. Both indexes were prepared by the Kansas State Historical Society. The material included is representative of the type of information included in its entire collection.

Several necrology indexes for hereditary and fraternal organizations are at the Kansas State Historical Society. They cover from the 1870s to the 1940s and give members' name and date of death. Organizations include Knights of Pythias, Ancient Order of United Workmen, Grand Lodge of Kansas, Masons, Odd Fellows, Modern Woodmen of America, and Grand Army of the Republic.

A recent publication (1987) entitled *A Guide to Special Collections in Kansas* describes over 300 repositories including collections in university, public, and school libraries. It is available from the Special Collections Department, Ablah Library, Wichita State University, Wichita, KS 67208.

Archives, Libraries, and Societies

Kansas State Historical Society
6425 SW Sixth St.
Topeka, KS 66612
www.kshs.org

The Center for Historical Research at the society is comprised of three sections: Library, State Archives, and Manuscripts. The society has published a listing of historical societies, genealogical societies, and museums throughout Kansas, which includes their addresses, hours of operation, and general descriptions of their collections. Interested individuals may purchase a copy from the Kansas State Historical Society.

Most extant territorial records, including census enumerations, are retained here. The researcher should review the specific category of records of interest for exact information. Included are territorial records pertaining to John Brown, the New England Emigrant Aid Company, and territorial military records as well as information about early settlers and pioneers.

Kansas Genealogical Society
Village Square Mall Lower Level, 2601 Central
P.O. Box 103
Dodge City, KS 67801
www.dodgecity.net/kgs/catalog/kgsearch01.html

The society serves as home for the Kansas Daughters of the American Revolution Library.

Topeka Genealogical Society
P.O. Box 4048
Topeka, KS 66604

In each April issue, the *Topeka Genealogical Society Quarterly* publishes a listing of all the material on Kansas that has been published by the genealogical societies within the state during the year. This has been an annual listing since 1979. Back issues may be obtained from the society.

Wichita State University
Ablah Library Special Collections
1845 Fairmount
Wichita, KS 67260-0068
http://specialcollections.wichita.edu/

The collections include online digitized maps and other Kansas material, especially on the aircraft industry.

University of Kansas
Kenneth Spencer Research Library, Kansas Collection
1450 Poplar Lane
Lawrence, KS 66045-1616
http://spencer.lib.ku.edu/kc/

Among its holdings are the Sanborn Fire Insurance Maps.

Iola Public Library
2186 Madison
Iola, KS 66749
www.iola.lib.ks.us/

The Raymond L. Willson Genealogy Collection here is an extensive collection that includes 2700 books and 8000 reels of microfilm. Books are arranged by state, with those not specific to a state in the first section. A complete set of Kansas census microfilm is available, along with a large selection of census microfilm from other states. Most interlibrary loan of genealogical material comes from this library.

A listing of Kansas genealogical societies for various counties can be found online at Kansas GenWeb <http://skyways.lib.ks.us/genweb/society/index.html>.

County Resources

The "County Address" indicates the address of the county courthouse in the county seat where inquiries regarding land (registry of deeds), probate (probate judge), and court (clerk of

the district court) can be addressed. The county clerk at the same address holds birth and death records before statewide recording. Those years with an asterisk (*) are not complete. Those years with a dagger (†) are held either in book or microfilm form at the Kansas State Historical Society. Marriage records are held by the probate judge. The year indicated is the first known record continuing to the present. Sources for this information include the Kansas State Historical Society and the *Guide to Public Vital Records in Kansas* as indicated by the society.

Land, probate, and court records in Kansas generally begin with the organization of the county, although there will be individual county variations. Records created soon after county organization may be incomplete. The "Date Formed" indicates when that occurred, although for some counties the date of government organization actually took place after legislative formation. In those cases the dates in parentheses are those for

when the records begin. County seat names in parentheses are original names or county seats no longer functioning.

The appearance of a question mark (?) indicates that the information was not available, while dashes (——) indicate that no records are known to exist in this category.

The Kansas GenWeb's project <http://skyways.lib.ks.us/genweb> includes county sites with street addresses or post office boxes of county courthouses and names of key personnel.

Information on land, probate, and court records was taken from the WPA Historic Records Survey, Kansas Counties, KSHS (for counties with question marks only). For other counties, information was verified at the respective county office. Addresses and dates of formation were taken from the National Association of Counties <www.naco.org>. Every county was also checked against the KSHS online collection of local history records on microfilm.

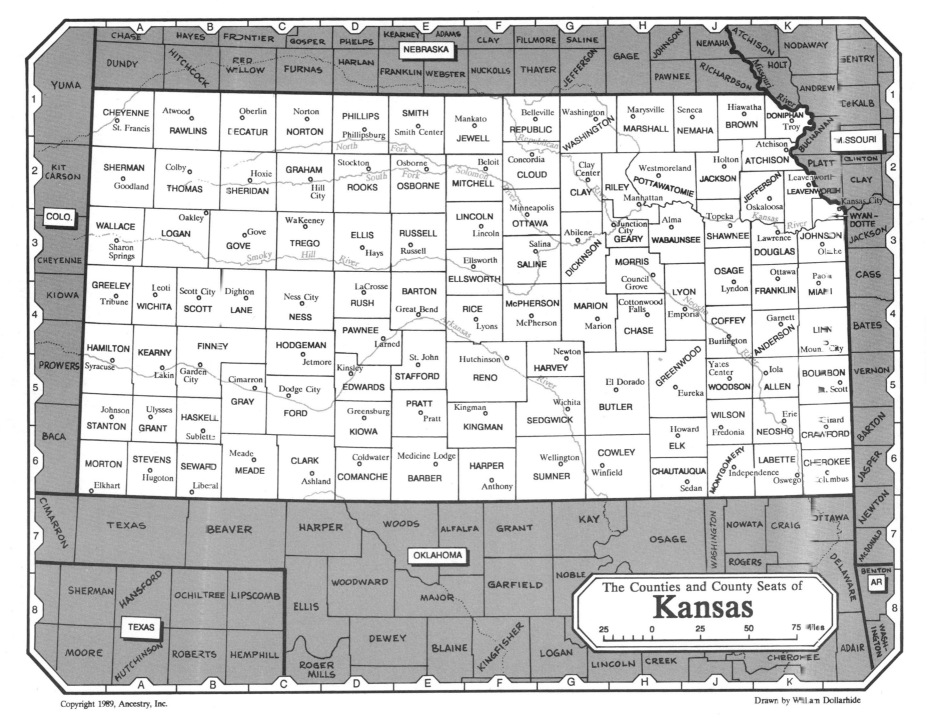

The Counties and County Seats of

Kansas

KANSAS

Drawn by William Dollarhide

Map	County Address	Date Formed Parent County/ies	Birth Marriage Death	Land Probate Court
K5	Allen 1 N. Washington Iola 66749-2841	1855 original	—— 1856 ——	1861† 1858 1858
	Iola city clerk has birth, death, and burial records.			
K4	Anderson 100 E. Fourth Ave. Garnett 66032-1500	1855 original	1892–94* 1857–1913 1892–94*	1857 1855 1860
	Arapahoe	1855 (became part of the territory of Colorado, 1861)		
K2	Atchison 423 N. Fifth St. Atchison 66002-1800	1855 original	1891–1911* 1855 1891–1911	1855 1855 1858
E6	Barber (Barbour) 120 E. Washington St. Medicine Lodge 67104-1421	1873 Peketon Territory	1891–1911 1874 1899–1911	1867 1867 1874
E4	Barton 1400 Main St. Great Bend 67530-4037	1872 Peketon Territory	1898–1911 1872 1892–1911	1872 1872 1873
K5	Bourbon 210 S. National Fort Scott 66701	1855 original	—— 1855 ——	1856 1855 1857
	Breckenridge	1855 (renamed Lyon, 1862) original		
J1	Brown 601 Oregon St. Hiawatha 66434-2241	1855 original	1885–1911*† 1857 1885–1911*†	1858 1857 1859
	Incomplete. No records extant for 1891–1906. †Records for 1907–11 at KSHS			
	Buffalo	pre-1880 (renamed Garfield, 1887) unorganized		
G5	Butler 205 W. Central El Dorado 67042	1855 original	1886–1911 1861 1886–1911	1860 1869 1860
	Calhoun	1855 (renamed Jackson, 1859) original		
	Early marriages of Calhoun County, Kansas Territory, are in Holton, Jackson County, Kansas.			
H4	Chase P.O. Box 547 Cottonwood Falls 66845-0547	1859 Wise/Butler	1885–1912 1860 1885–1911	1859 1859 1866
H6	Chautauqua 215 Chautauqua Sedan 67361	1875 Godfrey/Howard	1886–1911* 1870 1896–98; 1910–11*	1875 1875 1871
K6	Cherokee P.O. Box 14 Columbus 66725-0014 (formerly Center, Centralia)	1855 (as McGee; renamed , 1866) original	1894–1911 1867 1893–1911	1866 1866 1868
A1	Cheyenne P.O. Box 985 Saint Francis 67756-0985	1886 unorganized	—— 1886 ——	1886 1886 1886
C6	Clark P.O. Box 886 Ashland 67831-0886	1885 Peketon Territory (reorganized from Ford County)	1904–11 1885 1904–11	1885 1885 1885
G2	Clay P.O. Box 98 Clay Center 67432-0098	1866 original	1885–1911* 1864 1885–1911	1866 1868 1868
	Incomplete. Birth records extant for 1885–1900 and 1906–1911 only.			
F2	Cloud 811 Washington Concordia 66901-3415	1860 (as Shirley; renamed 1866)	1885–1910 1867 1885–1911	1867 1867 1868
J4	Coffey 110 S. Sixth Burlington 66839-1798	1859 original	1885–1908*† 1858 1886–1910*	1858 1857 1858
D6	Comanche 201 S. New York/P.O. Box 776 Coldwater 67029-0776	1885 Peketon Territory	1891–1908 1885 1891–1905	1885 1885 1885
H6	Cowley P.O. Box 741 Winfield 67156-9631	1867 (1885) (as Hunter; renamed Cowley, 1870)	1885–1911 1870 1885–1911	1870 1870 1871
K6	Crawford P.O. Box 249 Girard 66743-0249	1867 Cherokee/ Bourbon	1887–1912 1867 1887–1911	1867 1870 1867
	Davis	1855 (renamed Geary, 1889) original		
B1	Decatur P.O. Box 28 Oberlin 67749-0028	1873 (1879) unorganized	1889–1910 1880 1885–1910	1879 1900 1880
G3	Dickinson 109 E. First St. Abilene 67410	1857 original	1892–1911 1867 1892–1911	1861 1861 1882
K1	Doniphan P.O. Box 278 Troy 66087-0278	1855 original	1896–1911 1855 1895–1911	1856 1857 1858
	Dorn	1855 original		
	Dorn was divided 1867 into present counties of Neosho and Labette.			
K3	Douglas 1100 Massachusetts Lawrence 66044-3064	1855 original	1885–1907 1863 1885–97	1856 1856 1863
	Records destroyed 21 August 1863 in Quantrill's raid. Some marriage records reconstructed.			
D5	Edwards 312 Massachusetts Ave. Kinsley 67547-1090 (Petersburg, Peter's City)	1874 Kiowa (Petersburg, Peter's City)	1902–11* 1875 1902–11*	1874 1874 1874
H6	Elk P.O. Box 606 Howard 67349-0606	1875 Howard	1885–1911 1875 1885–1911	1906 1906 1906
	Courthouse burned 1906			

Map	County / Address	Date Formed / Parent County/ies	Birth / Marriage / Death	Land / Probate / Court
M1	[illegible] / 1204 Fort St. / Hays 67601-3873	1867 / unorganized	1886–1911 / [illegible] / 1885–1912	1871 / 1047 / 1860
F3	Ellsworth / 210 N. Kansas Ave. / Ellsworth 67439-3109	1867 / unorganized / Peketon Territory	1884–1911* / 1886–1911* / ——	1867 / 1867 / 1867
	*Incomplete. Birth records extant for 1884–95 and 1907–11 only. Death records extant for 1886–93 and 1907–11 only.			
B5	Finney / 311 N. Ninth St. / Garden City 67846-5312	1873 (as Sequoyah; renamed 1883) / Peketon Territory	1885–1910 / 1884 / 1886–1910*	1873 / 1873 / 1885
	Foote	1881 (renamed Gray, 1887) / unorganized		
C5	Ford / 100 Gunsmoke St. / Dodge City 67801-4456	1873 / Peketon Territory	1892–1911*† / 1874 / 1892–1911*†	1873 / 1873 / 1874
	*Incomplete. Records extant for 1892–1904 and 1905–11 only. †Records for 1905–11 at KSHS.			
K4	Franklin / 315 S. Main / Ottawa 66067-2331	1855 / original	1892–1910 / 1858 / 1892–1911	1857 / 1856 / 1859
	Garfield	pre-1880 (as Buffalo; renamed 1887; became part of Finney, 1893) / unorganized		
H3	Geary / 139 E. Eighth St. / Junction City 66441-2554	1855 (as Davis; renamed 1889) / original	1905–11 / 1857 / 1871–1911	1858 / 1857 / 1861
	Godfrey	1855 (renamed Seward, 1861; then Howard) / original		
B3	Gove / 520 Washington / Gove 67736-0128	1886 / unorganized	1892–1911 / 1886 / 1892–1911	1886 / 1886 / 1887
C2	Graham / 410 N. Pomeroy St. / Hill City 67642-1649	1880 / unorganized	1892–1911* / 1880 / 1892–1911*	1880 / 1880 / 1880
	*Incomplete. Records extant for 1892–1904 and 1910–11 only.			
A5	Grant / 108 S. Glenn / Ulysses 67880-2551	1888	1890–1926 / 1888–1912* / 1888–1909*	1888 / 1888
B5	Gray / P.O. Box 487 / Cimarron 67835-0487	1881 (as Foote; renamed 1887) / unorganized	—— / 1887 / ——	1886 / 1885 / 1887
	County clerk has tax rolls from 1889.			
A4	Greeley / 208 Harper St./Box 277 / Tribune 67879-0000	1873 (1889) / unorganized	1896–1904 / 1887 / 1897–1905	1886 / ? / 1880
H5	Greenwood / 311 N. Main / Eureka 67045-1321	1862 / original	1885–1911 / 1859 / 1885–1911	1857 / 1865 / 1880
A5	Hamilton / 219 N. Main/P.O. Box 1167 / [illegible] 67878 / (Hollidaysburg)	1873 (1886) / unorganized	1896–1911*† / 1886 / 1896–1911*	1884 / 1886 / 1885
F6	Harper / 201 N. Jennings / Anthony 67003-2748	1873 / Peketon Territory	1892–1910* / 1878 / 1891–1913	1873 / 1873 / 1878
G5	Harvey / 800 N. Main St., Box 687 / Newton 67114	1872 / Sedgwick	1886–1911 / 1872 / 1886–1911	1862 / 1872 / 1872
B5	Haskell / P.O. Box 518 / Sublette 67877-0518 / (Santa Fe)	1887 / Finney	1888–97 / 1887 / 1888–1904*	1887 / 1887 / 1886
C5	Hodgeman (Hageman) / 500 Main/P.O. Box 247 / Jetmore 67854-0247 / (Buckner)	1879 / Peketon Territory	—— / 1880 / ——	1879 / 1887 / 1880
	Howard	1855 (as Godfrey; renamed Seward, 1861; then Howard, 1867) / original		
	Howard was abolished in 1875 when it was divided into Elkland and Chautaugua.			
	Hunter	1867 (renamed Cowley, 1870) / original		
J2	Jackson / 400 New York / Holton 66436-1787	1855 (organized, 1857 as Calhoun: renamed 1859) / original	1892–1911*† / 1855 / 1892–1911*†	1857 / 1857 / 1861
	*Incomplete. Extant for 1892 and 1902-1911 only. †Records for 1892 at KSHS.			
K2	Jefferson / 300 W. Jefferson / Oskaloosa 66066-0321	1855 / original	1892–98* / 1855 / 1892–98*	1854 / 1855 / 1858
F1	Jewell / 307 N. Commercial St. / Mankato 66956-2025 / (Jewell City)	1867 (1870) / unorganized	1886–94 / 1871 / 1886–94	1870 / 1870 / 1872
K3	Johnson / 111 S. Cherry / Olathe 66061-3441	1855 / original	—— / 1857 / ——	1857 / 1857 / 1858
	Kansas	1873 (abolished 1883; became Morton) / unorganized		
A5	Kearny (Kearney) / 305 N. Main St. / Lakin 67860-0086	1873 (abolished 1883) (1889) / Peketon Territory	1911 / 1888 / 1911-13	? / 1886 / 1888
F5	Kingman / 130 N. Spruce / Kingman 67068	1869 (1874) / Reno	1885–1911 / 1875 / 1885–1911	1890 / 1878 / 1878
D6	Kiowa / 211 E. Florida / Greensburg 67054-2211	1867 (abolished 1875; re-created, 1886) / Peketon Territory/Edwards	—— / 1886 / ——	1879 / 1886 / 1886

KANSAS

Map	County Address	Date Formed Parent County/ies	Birth Marriage Death	Land Probate Court
K6	Labette 501 Merchant Oswego 67356	1867 Dorn/Neosho	1885–96 1867 1885–93	1867 1868 1865
B4	Lane 144 S. Lane/P.O. Box 788 Dighton 67839-0788	1886 Peketon Territory/ unorganized	1888–1911 1886 1888–1911*	1886 1886 1886
K2	Leavenworth 300 Walnut St. Leavenworth 66048-2725	1855 original	1887–1911* 1855 1887–1911*	1856 1855 1855
F3	Lincoln 216 E. Lincoln Ave. Lincoln 67455-2058 (Lincoln Center)	1870 unorganized	1886–1910 1871 1885–1910	1871 1871 1871
K4	Linn P.O. Box 350 Mound City 66056-0350	1855 original	1885–1911* 1855 1885–1911*	1857 1856 1859
A3	Logan 710 W. Second St. Oakley 67748-1251 (Russell Springs)	1881 (as Saint John; renamed 1887) Wallace unorganized	1911 1888 1911	1885 1885 1888
	Lykins (see Miami)	1855 (renamed Miami, 1861) original		
J4	Lyon 402 Commercial St. Emporia 66801-4000	1855 (as Breckenridge, renamed 1862) (1859) original	1886–1911 1856 1885–1911	1859 1859 1858
	Madison *Madison was divided 1861–64 into Breckenridge (later Lyon) and Greenwood.*	1855		
G4	Marion P.O. Box 219 Marion 66861	1855 (1860) Peketon Territory	1881–1911* 1865 1885–1911	1865 1863 1867
H1	Marshall 1201 Broadway Marysville 66508-1844	1855 original	1885–1911 1856 1885–1911	1855 1855 1858
	McGee	1855 (renamed Cherokee, 1866) (see Cherokee)		
F4	McPherson P.O. Box 676 McPherson 67460-0676	1870 Peketon Territory	1887–1911 1870 1885–1900	1870 1870 1871
	Assessor's records for 1897–98 and returns for 1910–11 are available.			
B6	Meade P.O. Box 278 Meade 67864-0278 (Skidmore, Meade Center)	1873 (abolished 1883) (1885) Peketon Territory	1886–1911 1886 1886–1911	1885 1885 1885
K4	Miami 201 S. Pearl St. Paola 66071-1756 (Peoria Village)	1855 (as Lykins; renamed 1861) original	1885–1911 1857 1885–1911	1855 1857 1858
F2	Mitchell P.O. Box 190 Beloit 67420 (Willow Springs) *†Records held by city clerk.*	1867 (1870) unorganized	1891–1911† 1871 1891–1911†	1870 1870 1871
J6	Montgomery 217 E. Myrtle/P.O. Box 446 Independence 67301	1869 Wilson	1888–1911* 1870 1887–1911	1870 1870 1870
H3	Morris 501 W. Main Council Grove 66846 *Death records held by city clerk.*	1855 (as Wise) original	—— 1859 ——	1859 1856 1860
A6	Morton P.O. Box 1116 Elkhart 67950-1116	1873 (1886) (became part of Seward, 1883; reorganized, 1886) Kansas	1911 1887 1911	1887 1887 1887
J1	Nemaha P.O. Box 186 Seneca 66538	1855 original	1883–1904 1857 1883–1904	1855 1857 1859
K6	Neosho P.O. Box 138 Erie 66733	1855 as Dorn (1864) original	1892–1905 1864 1892–1905	1866 1867 1867
C4	Ness 202 W. Sycamore St. Ness City 67560-1558	1867 (abolished 1874) (1880) unorganized/ Peketon Territory	—— 1880 ——	1880 1880 1880
C1	Norton P.O. Box 70 Norton 67654	1872 unorganized	1885–1911 1873 1885–1911	1872 1872 1874
J3	Osage 717 Topeka Ave. Lyndon 66451-9792	1859 (1855 as Weller) original	1885–1911 1860 1885–1911	1859 1861 1861
E2	Osborne 423 W. Main St. Osborne 67473-2301	1871 unorganized	1900–09 1872 1900–09	1871 1872 1872
	Otoe	1860 (abolished 1867) original		
F3	Ottawa 307 N. Concord St. Minneapolis 67467-2140 (Markley Mills)	1866 Saline	1885–1911† 1866 1885–1911†	1866 1866 1869
D4	Pawnee 715 Broadway Larned 67550	1872 Peketon Territory	1880–1911 1873 1897–1911	1872 1872 1873
	Peketon Territory	1854 (no population; abolished 1867) original		
D1	Phillips 301 State St. Phillipsburg 67661-1941	1872 unorganized	—— 1872 ——	1872 1872 1873

236

Map	County Address	Date Formed Parent County/ies	Birth Marriage Death	Land Probate Court
H?	Pottawatomie 207 N. First Westmoreland 66549	1855 original	1885–1911 1885 1885–1911	1857 1857 1862
E5	Pratt P.O. Box 885 Pratt 67124-0885	1879 Peketon Territory	1888–1900 1879 1880–1900	1879 1879 1879
B1	Rawlins 607 Main St. Atwood 67730-1839 (Kelso and Pragg)	1873 (1881) unorganized	—— 1881 ——	1881 1881 1881
F5	Reno 206 W. First St. Hutchinson 67501-5204	1872 Peketon Territory	1890–1911 1872 1890–1911	1870 1873 1871
F1	Republic 1815 M St. Belleville 66935-2242	1868 original	1885–1911 1869 1885–1911	1868 1868 1871
F4	Rice 101 W. Commercial St. Lyons 67554-2727 (Atlanta and Brookdale)	1871 Peketon Territory	1895–1911* 1872 1892–1911	1871 1871 1872
	Richardson (see Wabaunsee)	1855 (renamed Wabaunsee, 1859) original		
H2	Riley 110 Courthouse Plaza Manhattan 66502-0125	1855 original	1885–1909*† 1856 1885–1909*†	1857 1857 1859
	*Records incomplete. Extant for 1885–86 and 1892–1909 only. †Records for 1892–1909 at KSHS.			
D2	Rooks 115 N. Walnut St. Stockton 67669-1663	1872 unorganized	1888–1901 1873 1888–1901	1872 1872 1873
D4	Rush P.O. Box 220 LaCrosse 67548-0220	1874 unorganized/ Peketon Territory	1895–1911 1876 1886–1911	1874 1874 1875
E3	Russell 400 Main P.O. Box 113 Russell 67665-0113	1867 (1872) unorganized (Fossil Station)	1885–1911* 1872 1885–1911*	1872 1872 1872
	St. John	1881 (renamed Logan, 1887)		
F3	Saline 300 W. Ash St. Box 5040 Salina 67401-5040	1859 original	1885–1915* 1860 1885–1915*	1859 1859 1865
	Sequoyah Some records are in Ford County.	(renamed Finney, 1883)		
B4	Scott 303 Court St. Scott City 67871-1157	1886 unorganized	1904–11 1886 1906–11	1886 1886 1886
G6	Sedgwick 525 N. Main, Rm. 320 Wichita 66603-3731	1870 Hunter/Otoe/Peketon Territory	1884–1911* 1870 1884–1911*‡	1870 1870 1870
	*Birth records extant for 1884–89 and 1908–11 only. Death records extant for 1884–87 and 1908–11 only. ‡Death records for 1908–11 at Wichita Historical Office.			
	Seward (old)	1855 (as Godfrey; renamed 1861; renamed Howard, 1867) original		
B6	Seward (present) 415 N. Washington, Ste. 116 Liberal 67901-3462	1886 unorganized	—— 1886 1892	1886 1886 1886
J3	Shawnee 200 SE Seventh Topeka 66603	1855 original	1894–1910 1856 1894–1910	1855 1859 1858
B2	Sheridan P.O. Box 899 Hoxie 67740-0899	1880 unorganized	1886–1911 1878 1887–1910	? 1881 1873
A2	Sherman 813 Broadway Goodland 67735	1886 unorganized	1888–1911‡ 1886 1888–1911‡	1888 1886 1887
	‡Records at office of Goodland city clerk.			
	Shirley	1860 (renamed Cloud, 1867) original		
E1	Smith 218 S. Grant St. Smith Center 66967	1872 unorganized	1891–96 1872 1891–96	1872 1875 1872
E5	Stafford 209 N. Broadway St. John 67576	1879 Peketon Territory	1886–93 1879 1886–89	1879 1879 1879
A5	Stanton 201 N. Main Johnson 67855 (Veteran)	1887 unorganized	1887–1910* 1887 1889–1910*	1887 1887 1887
A6	Stevens 200 E. Sixth St. Hugoton 67951-2655	1886 unorganized	—— 1886 ——	1886 1886 1886
G6	Sumner 500 N. Washington Wellington 67152-4064	1871 Hunter/Peketon Territory	1885–1911* 1871 1885–1891*	1871 1871 1880
	*Birth records extant for 1885–91 and 1910–11 only.			
B2	Thomas 300 N. Court St. Colby 67701-2421	1885 unorganized	1889–1910 1886 1886–1910	1885 1885 1885
C3	Trego 216 N. Main St. WaKeeney 67672-2189	1879 unorganized	1899–1911* 1879 1899–1911*	1879 1879 1880
H3	Wabaunsee 215 Kansas St. Alma 66401-9797	1855 (as Richardson; renamed 1859) original	1892–1911 1856 1892–1911	1859 1857 1860

Map	County Address	Date Formed Parent County/ies	Birth Marriage Death	Land Probate Court
A3	Wallace P.O. Box 70 Sharon Springs 67758-0070	1868 (abolished 1879; 1889) unorganized	1891–1911 1880 1891–1911	1884 1885 1884
G1	Washington 214 C Street Washington 66968-1928	1855 (1860) original	1887–1911 1861 1885–1911	1860 1857 1872
	Weller	1855 (renamed Osage, 1859) Original		
A4	Wichita 206 S. Fourth Leoti 67861 (Bonasa)	1886 unorganized	1887–1909* 1887 1885–1909	1885 1887 1887

Map	County Address	Date Formed Parent County/ies	Birth Marriage Death	Land Probate Court
J5	Wilson 615 Madison St. Fredonia 66736-1340	1865 original	1885–1909 1864 1889–1911	1866 1869 1866
	Wise	1855 (renamed Morris, 1859) original		
J5	Woodson 105 W. Rutledge St. Yates Center 66783-1237	1855 original	1885–1911 1859 1885–1911	1858 1864 1864
K3	Wyandotte Unified City-Cty Gov. 701 N. 7th St. Kansas City 66101-3035	1855 (1859) original	1885–1911 1859 1885–92	1859 1857 1859

Kentucky

WENDY BEBOUT ELLIOTT, Ph.D., FUGA

Few American settlers had moved into the region of present-day Kentucky prior to the completion of the western portion of the border survey between Virginia and North Carolina in 1748. When the French and Indian War (Seven Years War) ended, the Ohio River was designated as the boundary between settlers and native inhabitants. Kentucky came under the jurisdiction of Augusta County, Virginia. Fincastle County, Virginia, was organized in 1772 to include all of present-day Kentucky with Harrodsburg designated the county seat. The following year the McAfee brothers and others surveyed land along the Salt River. In 1774, James Harrod founded Harrodsburg as the first permanent English settlement in Kentucky by a group that arrived via the Ohio River.

That same year Richard Henderson purchased from the Native Americans all land lying between the Ohio, Kentucky, and Cumberland rivers for his Transylvania Company. John Finley's stories of Kentucky land precipitated Daniel Boone's subsequent exploration. Boone blazed the trail from the Cumberland Gap (at the junction of present-day Virginia, Kentucky, and Tennessee) to the interior. This path between the Cumberland Gap and central Kentucky became known, through the Transylvania Company's publicity, as the Wilderness Road. In 1775 the Transylvania Company established Boonesborough as its headquarters.

During the Revolutionary War, the Virginia government virtually ignored the settlements in Kentucky. The resulting lack of military assistance and isolation from the eastern portion of Virginia led to troubles with native tribes and precipitated a desire among the settlers for Kentucky to achieve statehood. Between 1784 and 1790, nine conventions met at Danville demanding separation from Virginia; however, none of these attained success in gaining a division.

Congress admitted the Commonwealth of Kentucky to the Union as the fifteenth state on 1 June 1792 after the first constitution was drafted on 3 April of that year. Established as a commonwealth state, Danville became its first capital. Early settlers included Revolutionary War veterans staking claims to bounty-land grants. Scots-Irish, German, and English individuals and families from Virginia, Maryland, North Carolina, Pennsylvania, and Tennessee soon joined the veterans in Kentucky.

The disputed southern boundary between Kentucky and Tennessee remained unsettled until 1820 when Kentucky accepted the faulty Walker Line, drawn too far north of 36° 30', between the Cumberland Gap and the western Tennessee River. Several sections of the Line remained questionable until surveyors conducted another survey in 1859. Since families who lived in the disputed area did not know in which state they resided, records are frequently located in both states. Due to changing county boundaries and divisions, Kentucky counties affected include (west to east) Trigg, Christian, Todd, Logan, Simpson, Allen, Monroe, Cumberland, Clinton, Wayne, McCreary, Whitley, Knox, and Bell.

Ideology over the slave issue divided the populace before and during the Civil War. Many large landowners supported slavery, but the small farmers and mountain families did not. Officially, Kentucky, the birthplace of Abraham Lincoln, was neutral during the Civil War only until September 1861, when it actively began support of the Union, even though the Confederate States continued to act as if Kentucky were one of theirs.

Following the Civil War, tobacco and coal became leading commodities in Kentucky's economy. Kentucky's bluegrass pastures have produced an exceptional number of thoroughbred horses, leading to worldwide recognition in horse racing. Fort Knox, originally Camp Knox, began as a permanent military post and later became an official U.S. gold depository. In the twentieth century Fort Campbell served as a major training center for military recruits.

Genealogical research in the state is aided by excellent research facilities and printed materials on Kentucky's early settlement.

A source for legal issues is J. Barbour and John D. Carroll. *The Kentucky Statutes: Containing All General Laws Including Those Passed at Session of 1894.* Louisville: Courier-Journal Job Printing, 1894. It is a must for understanding early regulations for land and taxation.

Vital Records

Although compliance was never complete, birth and death records for Kentucky begin as early as 1852 when statewide registration was first enacted. The requirement continued for only ten years. Some births and deaths were recorded (1874–79, 1892–1910), but observance remained sporadic.

A few larger cities maintained separate birth and death records prior to 1911, but these too are incomplete. Louisville (1898–1911), Covington (1890–1911), Newport (1890–1911), and Lexington (1906–11) are four cities with registered births in their respective city health departments.

The Kentucky Department for Libraries and Archives and the Kentucky Historical Society (see Archives, Libraries and Societies) have early records for 1852 to 1910, arranged by counties. Jeffery M. Duff's *Inventory of Kentucky Birth, Marriage and Death Records, 1852–1910,* rev. ed. (Frankfort, Ky.: Department for Libraries and Archives, 1988), lists what is available by year and county at both of the repositories. Other repositories, including the Filson Library (see Archives, Libraries, and Societies) and the Family History Library (FHL) in Salt Lake City, have some copies. No statewide index has been compiled for these early records, although the Kentucky Historical Society has a card index of both births and deaths for 1852 to 1862. Some early records, which have been indexed by county, appear in various issues of the Kentucky Historical Society's *Register.*

Birth and death registration was enacted statewide on 1 January 1911 and generally adhered to by 1920. Indexes to births and deaths after 1911 are microfilmed; however, the actual records are not. Certificates of births and deaths after 1911 are only available at the Office of Vital Statistics, Department of Health Services, 275 E. Main St., Frankfort, KY 40601. The microfilmed index can be used at the Kentucky Historical Society, the University of Kentucky Library, the Filson Library, and the FHL. Delayed registrations of birth are maintained by the Office of Vital Statistics.

Kentucky marriage records usually begin about the time of the respective county's establishment or within a few years of that date. Some counties have marriage records for dates prior to organization. Fayette, Jefferson, and Lincoln counties have marriage records as early as 1785. The respective county clerk has jurisdiction over marriage records. Beginning in 1958 statewide registration was required. Originals are filed in the counties and duplicates are available at the Office of Vital Statistics. The Office of Vital Statistics maintains an index to marriage records from 1958. Licenses and bonds may be filed separately from certificates. An index to Kentucky marriage, divorce, and death records is online at <http://ukcc.uky.edu/~vitalrec>.

Published marriage records for Kentucky include the following:

Antoniak, Eleanor, indexer. *Kentucky Marriage Records.* Baltimore: Genealogical Publishing Co., 1983. Lists all marriages published in the *Register of Kentucky* but does not include records for all counties.

Clift, G. Glenn, comp. *Kentucky Marriages, 1797–1865.* 1974. Reprint. Baltimore: Genealogical Publishing Co., 1987. Newspaper marriage notices previously published in *The Register of the Kentucky Historical Society.* Alphabetical by county and alphabetical within each county by groom's surname.

Kentucky's state legislature granted divorces from 1792 through 1849. Between 1849 and 1958, divorces were usually recorded by the circuit courts in the respective counties. Some early original circuit court records are available at the Kentucky Department for Libraries and Archives. The records of early divorces are included in the Acts of the General Assembly of the Commonwealth of Kentucky. These volumes, and a few microfilm copies of circuit court records, are available at the Kentucky Historical Society and Kentucky Department for Libraries and Archives. Statewide registration commenced in 1958. Divorces granted after statewide registration are available through the Office of Vital Statistics at the above address.

Census Records

Federal

Population Schedules
- Indexed—1810, 1820, 1830, 1840, 1850, 1860, 1870, 1880, 1900, 1910, 1920, 1930
- Soundex—1880, 1900, 1910 (Miracode), 1920

Industry and Agriculture Schedules
• 1850, 1860, 1870, 1880

Mortality Schedules
• 1850, 1860, 1870, 1880

Slave Schedules
• 1850, 1860

Union Veterans Schedules
• 1890 (part)

Earlier U.S. censuses for Kentucky were destroyed, but published tax lists serve as a replacement for the lost 1790 and 1800 censuses. For substitutes, see these works:

Clift, Garrett Glenn. *"Second Census" of Kentucky, 1800: A Privately Compiled and Published Enumeration of Tax Payers Appearing in the 79 Manuscript Volumes Extant of Tax Lists of the 42 Counties of Kentucky in Existence in 1800.* 1954. Reprint. Baltimore: Genealogical Publishing Co., 1982. Names of taxpayers are arranged alphabetically. Shows name, county, and date of tax list.

Early Kentucky Tax Records. Baltimore: Genealogical Publishing Co., 1987. Taken from the *Register of the Kentucky Historical Society* (see Periodicals) and indexed by Carol Lee Ford.

Heinemann, Charles Brunk. *"First Census" of Kentucky, 1790.* Baltimore: Genealogical Publishing Co., 1981. Privately compiled list of taxpayers arranged alphabetically assists in locating the proper county of residence. Provides name, county, and date of tax list. This volume includes a map by Bayless Hardin depicting Kentucky in 1792, with the 1818 Jackson Purchase also noted.

Only returns for sixty-five Kentucky counties remain of the 1890 Union veterans and widows schedule of the federal census of Kentucky. Extracts and indexes for many of Kentucky's censuses have been compiled and published. Original or microfilm copies of the federal census returns are available at the Kentucky Department for Libraries and Archives. Several Kentucky indexes to censuses predate those published by AISI.

State School Census
Kentucky infrequently enumerated public school students beginning in 1888. Scattered records are at the office of the respective county Board of Health or Board of Education. These are restricted if held by the school board but are not if held by the county clerk. Some are maintained by the Kentucky Department for Libraries and Archives and the Kentucky Historical Society.

Background Sources

Many county and state histories are available for Kentucky. Because Virginia was its parent state, some early Kentucky history through 1792 is recorded in Virginia documents. Everton's "Sources of Genealogical Information in Kentucky" can be accessed at <www.everton.com/usa/ky.htm>. For other genealogical resources on the Internet for Kentucky, see <www.personal.umich.edu/~cgaunt/kentucky.html>.

Historical material pertaining to Kentucky can be found in many excellent publications. A few include these:

Allen, William B. *A History of Kentucky.* 1872. Reprint. Ann Arbor: University Microfilms, 1973.

Bryant, Ron D. *Kentucky History: An Annotated Bibliography.* Westport, Conn.: Greenwood Press, 2000.

Chinn, George Morgan. *Kentucky, Settlement and Statehood, 1750–1800.* Frankfort, Ky.: Kentucky Historical Society, 1975.

Clark, Thomas D. *Kentucky: Land of Contrast.* New York: Harper & Row, 1968.

Coleman, John Winston. *A Bibliography of Kentucky History.* Lexington: University of Kentucky Press, 1949. Kentucky histories written prior to 1949 are listed in this bibliography.

Collins, Lewis, and Richard H. Collins. *History of Kentucky.* 2 vols. 1874. Reprint. Frankfort, Ky.: Kentucky Historical Society, 1979.

Filson, John. *The Discovery, Settlement, and Present State of Kentucky.* Wilmington, Del.: James Adams, 1784.

Harrison, Lowell, and Klotter, James. *A New History of Kentucky.* Lexington: University Press of Kentucky, 1997. Includes an extensive bibliography. Replaces Dr. Clark's classic work cited above.

Hogan, Roseann Reinemuth. *Kentucky Ancestry: A Guide to Genealogical and Historical Research.* Salt Lake City: Ancestry, 1992. A good reference book.

Kincaid, Robert Lee. *The Wilderness Road.* Harrogate, Tenn.: Lincoln Memorial University Press, 1955.

Kleber, John, Harrison, Lowell, and Klotter, James, eds. *The Kentucky Encyclopedia.* Lexington: University Press of Kentucky, 1992.

Littell, William. *The Statute Laws of Kentucky to 1816.* 5 vols. Frankfort, Ky.: William Hunter, 1809–19. Most important work concerning Kentucky laws.

Van Every, Dale. *Forth to the Wilderness, 1754–1774.* New York: Mentor Books, American Library, 1962. A good brief history of the struggle to conquer the Appalachians and settle the western frontier. Available in paperback.

Maps

One of the earliest known maps printed of Kentucky is John Filson's for 1784. A later detailed map of Kentucky watercourses (22 x 46 inches) is published and sold by the Kentucky Cabinet for Economic Development, Maps and Publications Office, Division of Research, 133 Holmes St., Frankfort, KY 40601. This office maintains a large collection of maps and atlases available for purchase.

Helpful in locating early land grants is Luke Munsell's map printed in 1819 entitled "Map of the State of Kentucky together with parts of Indiana and Indian Territories." A copy of this map can be obtained from the Library of Congress, Photoduplication Service, Washington, DC 20540.

The Kentucky Libraries and Archives (see Archives, Libraries, and Societies) houses a collection of Kentucky maps for the period 1784–1818, including agency-sponsored late nineteenth- and early twentieth-century maps, but this collection is largely unprocessed. Maps for the state are also available at the Kentucky Historical Society, University of Kentucky Library, and the Filson Library. These collections include state, county, and city maps. For historical maps of Kentucky counties, see <www.abraxis.com/beegee/Genealogy/Kentucky/Maps/kymaps.htm>.

Cadastral maps show landowners, drawn from official registers, and used in conjunction with the appropriation of taxes, which list quantity, value, and ownership of real estate. Maps are included in:

DenBoer, Gordon. *Atlas of Historical County Boundaries: Kentucky.* Edited by John H. Long. New York: Charles Scribner's Sons, 1995. Contains data on 126 counties and includes 629 maps.

Field, Thomas P. *Guide to Kentucky Place Names.* Revised edition. Lexington: Kentucky Geological Survey, 1991. This updated edition replaces Rennick's 1984 compilation.

Rennick, Robert M. *Kentucky Place Names.* Lexington: University Press of Kentucky, 1984. A survey of Kentucky places was undertaken in 1971. This volume was published to publicize and stimulate interest in the survey. It catalogs approximately one-fourth of presently known places, usually only the largest, best known, and/or most important.

Stephenson, R. W. *Land Ownership Maps.* Washington, D.C.: Library of Congress, 1967. Contains maps of thirty-five Kentucky counties.

U.S. Geological Survey Maps (see page 5) for Kentucky are helpful in locating cemeteries.

Land Records

State-Land State

All early property in Kentucky was historically under Virginia's jurisdiction. In May 1779, Virginia passed an act that divided its western lands, including Kentucky County, which consisted of all of the present-day state. Just eighteen months later, Kentucky County was discontinued, and Fayette, Lincoln, and Jefferson counties were organized from it. The only extant land entries for this time are those in Land Entry Books of Jefferson and Lincoln counties, but these include some Kentucky County records. Originals are kept by the county clerk of Jefferson County and are entitled "Land Entry Book No. A." Lincoln County records are at the Kentucky Land Office in Frankfort.

Like many other colonies prior to the Revolutionary War, Virginia had plenty of land, but little money. After the French and Indian War ended in 1763, Virginia found it necessary to pay the troops in bounty-land warrants. Military warrants were issued for military service and treasury warrants could be purchased. Warrants were issued authorizing surveys of property. The procedure was ineffective, for it did not require a survey of the land prior to the issuance of the warrant. Instead, Virginia law required that the person locate his land wherever he chose and then survey the property at his own cost. Unfortunately, the surveys were not reliable as most were not adept at surveying, and their attempts to do so sometimes resulted in conflicts in title and loss of the land.

Original surveys, patents, warrants, and grants as well as indexes are filed in the Secretary of State's Land Office, Rm. 148, Capitol Bldg., Frankfort, KY 40601. It has the complete set of original documents for the Kentucky land grant records, including caveats and wills. The Kentucky Historical Society and Kentucky Department for Libraries and Archives have microfilm and photo copies of these records. Some records may be recorded in adjacent Tennessee counties due to the resurvey of Walker's Line in 1859.

Land and property records for Kentucky include deeds, entries, warrants, surveys, mortgages, and indexes to these documents. Under the Kentucky Court of Appeals, which served as a court of record, deed books were maintained beginning in 1796. The first twenty-six books are designated as books A through Z for the period 1796 to 1835, although earlier deeds and documents, some dated as early as 1775, are recorded therein.

Within these twenty-six volumes are documents for residents of Virginia, Pennsylvania, Maryland, New York, New Jersey, and Louisiana, as well as some foreign countries. Books A through C comprise, for the most part, documents relating to the period 1775 through 1796, but other books also include early records.

When the Green River country opened, a law enacted in 1795 provided that each head of household would receive the maximum of 200 acres at the rate of $30 per hundred acres. The "In Fee Simple" title to the property was not to be given to the landholder until the price of the land was completely paid.

The following printed sources deal with Kentucky land records:

Brookes-Smith, Joan E. *Index for Old Kentucky Surveys and Grants.* Frankfort, Ky.: Kentucky Historical Society, 1975. Alphabetically arranged from the microfilm collection at the Kentucky Historical Society, the book includes volume number, original survey number, name, acreage, county, watercourse, survey date, original book and page, grantee, grant, and original book and page.

———. *Master Index: Grants Which Were in What Is Now Kentucky.* Frankfort, Ky.: Kentucky Historical Society, 1975. Compiled from thousands of original documents, includes original survey number, individual's name, acreage, county where filed, location on watercourse, survey, grantee to whom land was later transferred, date, book, and page.

———, comp. *Master Index: Virginia Surveys and Grants, 1774–1791.* Frankfort, Ky.: Kentucky Historical Society, 1976. Contains data pertaining to bounty-land grants for service against the French and Indians. Includes Acts of the General Assembly of Kentucky pertaining to original land titles. Alphabetically arranged, includes Kentucky Historical Society volume number, original survey number, name, acreage, county, watercourse, survey date, original book and page, grantee, grant date, and original book and page.

Cook, Michael L., and Bettie A. Cook. *Kentucky Court of Appeals Deed Books.* 4 vols. Evansville, Ind.: Cook Publications, 1985. A series of nine volumes of *Kentucky Records Series,* the Deed Books cover a nearly forty-year span (from 1796–1803, 1803–11, 1811–21, and 1821–35). Volume 4 also includes state supreme court records for the district of Kentucky (1783–89).

———. *Fincastle & Kentucky County Virginia-Kentucky Records & History.* Vol. 1. Kentucky Records Series. Vol. 18. Evansville, Ind.: Cook Publications, 1987. Contains all known extant records for these counties, plus all acts of the Virginia legislature pertaining to Kentucky prior to 1792. Includes land entries for Lincoln and Jefferson counties pertaining to Kentucky County and Fincastle County land records.

Jillson, Willard Rouse. *The Kentucky Land Grants: A Systematic Index to All of the Land Grants Recorded in the State Land Office at Frankfort, Kentucky, 1782–1924.* 2 vols. 1925. Reprint. Baltimore: Genealogical Publishing Co., 1971. Vol. 1 [Part 1] lists Kentucky land grants; Virginia grants (1782–92); Old Kentucky grants (1793–1856); Grants south of Green River (1797–1866); Tellico Grants (1803–

53); Kentucky land warrants (1816–73); Grants West of Tennessee River (1822–58); and Grants south of Walker's line (1825–1923). Vol. 2 (Part 2) contains warrants for headrights (1827–49; one page) and grants in county court records (1836–1924). Originally published as Filson Club Publication Number 33.

———. *Old Kentucky Entries and Deeds: A Complete Index to All of the Earliest Land Entries, Military Warrants, Deeds and Wills of the Commonwealth of Kentucky.* 1926. Reprint. Baltimore: Genealogical Publishing Co., 1987. This work is a companion volume to *Kentucky Land Grants* and indexes land records for the commonwealth of Kentucky. Records abstracted include manuscript documents of early civil land entries, military warrants, and state land office entries as well as first deeds, wills, and powers of attorney (relative to land) that were filed with the clerk of the court of appeals at Frankfort. Each section is arranged alphabetically and must be searched separately. Originally published as Filson Club Publication Number 34.

Sutherland, James F., comp. *Early Kentucky Landholders, 1787–1811.* Baltimore: Genealogical Publishing Co., 1986. Reprinted in 2000. A valuable tool for tracking elusive Kentucky land records. Contains data on over 17,000 landholders, representing forty-six of the fifty-four Kentucky counties extant in 1811.

Once county jurisdiction was established, land was to be surveyed and recorded at the county clerk's office. In most cases, original county land and property records are maintained by the respective county clerk's office, but microfilm copies are available at the Kentucky Department for Libraries and Archives, the University of Kentucky Library, Kentucky Historical Society, Filson Library, and the FHL. Some published land records are available in local, regional, historical, or genealogical society collections or libraries.

Probate Records

County probate records are filed at the respective county courthouse usually under the county clerk's jurisdiction. Probate records include wills, estates, administrators, executors, inventories, settlements, sales, accounts, guardianship, orphans, insolvent estates, bastardy, apprentices, and insanity. Documents pertaining to probate are recorded in volumes containing records of administrations, court proceedings, court minutes, estates, executors, guardians, inventories, probates, sales, settlements, and/or wills. Records may be filed under various titles. Loose papers are usually kept in folders or tied together in packets. Early estate records are frequently recorded along with regular proceedings of the county court. Circuit court records include

inherited estate disputes. Some counties have transcribed early wills. The Kentucky Historical Society and the Filson Library have collections of these.

Some transcribed or microfilm copies of original probate records are available at the Kentucky Department for Libraries and Archives, Kentucky Historical Society, University of Kentucky Library, Filson Library, and the FHL. Some wills and inventories are recorded in book J of the books maintained by the Kentucky Court of Appeals (1780–88). These have been abstracted by Michael and Bettie Cook (see Land Records).

Some of the 120 Kentucky county courthouses have suffered record loss because of fire or other accidents. Even though fire may have destroyed records pertinent to the county in which research is being conducted, some records were re-recorded and other sources such as newspapers and church records may fill the void. Research must encompass several years beyond the time of the destruction of records.

Two sources are the following:

Jackson, Ronald, comp. *Index to Kentucky Wills to 1851.* Bountiful, Utah: Accelerated Indexing System, 1977.

King, Junie Estelle Stewart. *Abstracts of Early Kentucky Wills and Inventories.* 1933. Reprint. Baltimore: Genealogical Publishing Co., 1969.

Court Records

The first constitution gave judicial powers to the Kentucky Court of Appeals. Other courts of record in Kentucky included superior, county, chancery, quarterly, circuit, justice of peace, police, district, quarter sessions, oyer and terminer, and general. Court records include dockets, minutes, case files, and orders. Land, tax, and probate matters may be included in Kentucky court records. Most court records are maintained at the respective county courthouse. Some original records are maintained in books, while other court-related documents are filed in folders in boxes or cabinets. Many of the books containing court records have been microfilmed and some have been abstracted and published. The great majority of data, however, is filed in boxes, cabinets, and folders and has not been copied in any form.

Courts and their jurisdiction have altered over time in Kentucky. Some early courts are no longer extant. Some have undergone name or jurisdictional changes. Early records may be filed in volumes or containers that may be mistitled, making it necessary to examine all court records for a county. County courts maintained jurisdiction over most matters, both civil and criminal, until 1852 when quarterly or circuit courts began handling criminal cases. Some circuit courts handled major civil and criminal matters as well as divorces. The circuit courts also served as appellate courts. Matters involving large sums of money were usually heard by the courts of quarter sessions from before statehood through the state's first ten years.

Microfilmed copies of most county court records are at the Kentucky Department for Libraries and Archives. Many transcribed records are available at the University of Kentucky Library, the Kentucky Historical Society, Filson Library, and the FHL. Some published or transcribed records are at local and regional libraries.

Ireland, Robert M. *The County Courts in Antebellum Kentucky.* Lexington: University of Kentucky Press, 1972. Includes data concerning court procedures and types of records created.

Richardson, William C. *An Administrative History of Kentucky Courts to 1850.* Frankfort, Ky.: Kentucky Department for Libraries and Archives, 1983.

Tax Records

One of the most valuable sources for early Kentucky to date is its tax records. Most counties have yearly tax records from the date of organization. Some early tax schedules list watercourse, value and acreage of real estate, men over age twenty-one, young men between the ages of sixteen and twenty-one, slaves, and horses. Extant county tax schedules from the date of organization of the county through 1892 have been microfilmed for most counties and are available from the Kentucky Department for Libraries and Archives and the FHL. Numerous original tax records from 1892 are available at the Kentucky Department for Libraries and Archives. The Kentucky Historical Society has tax records to 1875.

Kentucky tax lists are arranged by county and date. Within the counties, residents within its districts are grouped together and names usually arranged under the beginning letter of the surname, although these are not in strict alphabetical order. Some early tax records have been published and are available in research libraries (see Census Records).

Cemetery Records

Many collections of cemetery records are available for Kentucky. A Kentucky cemetery records database is available through the Kentucky Historical Society website. In 1977 the Kentucky Historical Society began computerizing extant cemetery records for the state. Cemetery tombstone transcriptions are included in the Ardery collection (see Manuscripts). The main repositories for cemetery compilations are the Kentucky Historical Society, University of Kentucky Library, Filson Library, Daughters of the American Revolution (DAR) Library in Washington, D.C., local libraries, and the FHL. Kentucky regional libraries and some other large genealogical libraries outside the state have

collections of Kentucky cemetery transcriptions. In addition, publications pertaining to Kentucky and Kentuckians frequently contain cemetery records for the state. An Internet source of cemetery names and locations is <www.gac.edu/~kengelha/uscemeteries/kentucky.html>. (See also)

Coyle, Malle B., and Lorena Eubanks. *Kentucky Cemetery Records*. Lexington, Ky.: Kentucky Society, Daughters of the American Revolution, 1960.

Johnson, Robert Foster. *Wilderness Road Cemeteries in Kentucky, Tennessee, and Virginia*. Owensboro, Ky.: McDowell Publications, 1981.

Wilson, V., M. B. Coyle, L. C. Mallows, and I. B. Gaines. *Kentucky Cemetery Records*. 5 vols. Florence, Ky.: Daughters of the American Revolution, 1960–72. The Coyle and Eubanks volume cited above is part of this series.

Church Records

Church membership of early Kentuckians include Baptist, Church of Christ, Episcopal, Lutheran, Methodist, Presbyterian, and Roman Catholic. Some church records were published, others were microfilmed, some are housed in church repositories, but many remain in the local church. Church records and histories may be found in periodicals pertaining to Kentucky. Repositories include the DAR Library, the FHL, Kentucky Historical Society, University of Kentucky Library, and Filson Library. The original Shane Manuscript Collection, which pertains to Kentucky Presbyterians, is housed at Presbyterian Historical Society, 425 Lombard St., Philadelphia, PA 19147. It has been microfilmed and is available at other libraries. Catholic families also settled in Ohio River communities. After the Civil War, an increasing number of Irish moved to the state. Generally, Roman Catholic parish and diocese records are maintained locally.

Although Internet sources provide names and locations, few include any genealogical data. Church profiles can be accessed online at <www.church-profiles.com/ky/ky.html>.

See also *Kentucky Bible Records*, 6 vols., from files of the Genealogical Records Committee, Kentucky Society of Daughters of the American Revolution. Volume 4 was compiled by Malle B. Coyle and Anne W. Fitzgerald for the Kentucky Records Research Committee (Florence, Ky.: Kentucky State Society Daughters of the American Revolution, 1966). Volume 5 was compiled by Malle B. Coyle and Lorena C. Eubanks (1981). Each volume is individually indexed. Most entries include only name, date, and name and address of the owner of the Bible at the time of publication. These are available at the Kentucky Historical Society and have been microfilmed by FHL. Local genealogical groups publish Kentucky Bible records in genealogical publications such as *Bluegrass Roots*, and *Kentucky Ancestors* (see Periodicals).

Military Records

Kentucky men served in all U.S. military conflicts. As with other states, many types of military records—service, pension, and bounty land—are maintained by the National Archives in Washington, D.C., and its regional centers (see pages 11-12). The Military Records and Research Branch, Kentucky Department of Military Affairs, 1121 Louisville Rd., Frankfort, KY 40601, maintains military service records from the Revolutionary War to the present. The Kentucky Department for Libraries and Archives and the Kentucky Historical Society have strong collections that cover service as well as pension and bounty-land records.

Although sparsely settled at the time, men from Kentucky served in the Revolutionary War. Many of the state's later residents served for Virginia and were allotted Kentucky land for their service. Anderson C. Quisenberry's *Revolutionary Soldiers in Kentucky* (Baltimore: Genealogical Publishing Co., 1968) covers a broad scope of service records. Names of many early Kentuckians and others who later obtained land grants in Kentucky can be found in records of the George Rogers Clark military expedition. A chronological compilation of name, rank, dates of enlistment and discharge, and payment is included in Margery Heberling Harding, *George Rogers Clark and His Men: Military Records, 1778–84* (Frankfort, Ky.: Kentucky Historical Society, n.d.). Civil War rosters for Kentuckians who served in the Union and Confederate armies have been indexed and are available at the Kentucky Department for Libraries and Archives. Kentucky provided its Confederate veterans and widows with pensions, which can be located through the Kentucky Historical Society and Kentucky Department for Libraries and Archives. Alice Simpson, *Index of Kentucky Confederate Pension Applications* (Frankfort, Ky.: Division of Archives and Records Management, Department for Libraries and Archives, 1978) is helpful in locating these materials in Kentucky.

The Kentucky Historical Society has indexed rosters for Revolutionary Soldiers buried in Kentucky and Kentuckians who served in the Mexican War (1846–48). The University of Kentucky and Kentucky Historical Society house the state Sons of the American Revolution organization papers, and Eastern Kentucky State University published rosters of Civil War regiments from Kentucky.

Military Records and Research Branch, Kentucky Department of Military Affairs, 1121 Louisville Rd., Frankfort, KY 40601 maintains records for the Department of Military Affairs. These holdings are discharge documents for over 300,000 Kentucky veterans from all conflicts from World War I through Desert Storm and historical records of all Kentucky militia and National Guard units from statehood to date. Some military

group records can be accessed through online subscription databases (see page 17).

The following is a brief selected list of published works on Kentucky military records:

Alfaro, Armando J. *The Paper Trail of the Civil War in Kentucky, 1861–1865*. Frankfort, Ky: Stuff Publications, ca 2001.

Burns, Annie Walker. *Abstracts of Pension Papers of Soldiers of the Revolutionary War, War of 1812, and Indian Wars Who Settled in Kentucky*. 20 vols. Washington, D.C.: the author, 1935-present.

Clift, G. Glenn. *The "Cornstalk" Militia of Kentucky, 1792–1811*. 1957. Reprint. Baltimore: Genealogical Publishing Co., 1982. Includes a history of the militia and lists of commissioned officers.

Cook, Michael L. *Index to Report of the Adjutant General of the State of Kentucky*. 4 vols. Owensboro, Ky.: Cook and McDowell Publications, 1979–82. Both volumes (Union and Confederate) of the original report are covered by these indexes.

Kentucky Adjutant General. *Kentucky Soldiers of the War of 1812*. Kentucky Adjutant General's Report, 1891. Reprint. Nashville: Byron Sistler and Associates, 1992. Includes full name index and names of over 25,000 men who served. Probably the best single source of information on Kentucky veterans.

Kentucky Pension Roll of 1835: Report from the Secretary of War—in Relation to the Pension Establishment of the U.S. Baltimore: Southern Book Co., 1959. Taken from the U.S. Pension Roll of 1835, this provides a comprehensive list of pensioners residing in Kentucky that year.

Lynn, Stephen D. *Confederate Pensioners of Kentucky: Pension Applications of the Veterans and Widows, 1912–1946*. Nashville: Byron Sistler and Associates, 2000. Alphabetical list of 4,7000 Confederate pensioners. Data includes name, military unit, date and place of birth, and death information. Widow's data lists both married and maiden names, date and place of birth, date and place of marriage, husband's names, military unit, date and place of birth, and date and place of death.

_____. *Confederate Soldiers of Kentucky: A Roster of Veterans, 1861–1865*. Nashville: Byron Sistler and Associates, 2002. Most complete list. Names taken from various sources, including the Report of the Adjutant General of Kentucky, pension files, Confederate Home records, records of Veterans' organization, and others.

Taylor, P. F. *A Calendar of the Warrants for Land in Kentucky for Service in the French and Indian War*. Baltimore: Genealogical Publishing Co., 1967. Good source for records of early military land warrants.

Wilson, Samuel M. *Catalogue of Revolutionary Soldiers and Sailors to Whom Land Bounty Warrants Were Granted by Virginia*. Baltimore: Genealogical Publishing Co., 1967.

Periodicals, Newspapers, and Manuscript Collections

Periodicals

Several statewide, regional, and local genealogical publications are available for Kentucky. Most can be found at the Kentucky Historical Society, the University of Kentucky Library, the Filson Library, regional libraries, or the FHL. The Durrett Collection includes numerous rare books, manuscripts, published sources, and documentary records concerning settlement of Kentucky and the Ohio River Valley; it is a must for any researcher with early Kentucky roots. The Filson Club, founded by Reuben T. Durrett and others, is part of the Durrett collection, which was created to collect and maintain primary source materials on the state of Kentucky and its people. This material has been digitized and is available through the American Memory website of the Library of Congress: *The First American West: The Ohio River Valley, 1750–1820* at <http://memory.loc.gov/ammem/award99/icuhtml/fawhome.html>. Some local libraries maintain copies pertaining to their area. Many genealogical publications are maintained in the Kentucky Genealogical Society's collection housed at the Kentucky Libraries and Archives online at <www.kdla.ky.gov>.

Statewide or regional publications include the following:

Bluegrass Roots (1973-present). Frankfort, Ky.: Kentucky Genealogical Society.

The Bulletin (1968-present). Newsletter only. Owensboro, Ky.: West-Central Kentucky Family Research Association.

The East Kentuckian: Journal of Genealogy and History (1965–95). Lexington: published privately by Clayton R. Cox.

Filson Historical Quarterly (1926-present). Louisville: Filson Historical Society.

Kentucky Ancestors (1965-present). Frankfort, Ky.: Kentucky Historical Society.

Kentucky Family Records (1969-present). Owensboro, Ky.: West-Central Kentucky Family Research Association.

The Kentucky Genealogist (1959–86). Louisville: James R. Bentley, ed.

Kentucky Kinfolk (1985–94). Lexington: Kentucky Tree-Search.

Kentucky Pioneer Genealogy and Records (1979–85). Evansville, Ind.: Cook and McDowell Publications.

The Longhunter (1978-present). Bowling Green, Ky: Southern Kentucky Genealogical Society.

The Register of the Kentucky Historical Society (1903-present). Frankfort, Ky.: Kentucky Historical Society. A subject index is available for the first forty-three volumes.

South Central Kentucky Historical and Genealogical Society Quarterly (1974-present). Glasgow, Ky.: South Central Kentucky Historical and Genealogical Society. Changed name to *Traces* in 1982.

Tree Shaker (1982-present). Ashland, Ky.: Eastern Kentucky Genealogical Society.

Two sources combine information from noted periodicals for Kentucky:

Klotter, James, ed. *Genealogies of Kentucky Families from the Register of the Kentucky Historical Society and the Filson History Quarterly.* 4 vols. Frankfort, Ky.: Kentucky Historical Society, 1981. This indexed set includes all genealogies printed in the publications since 1903.

Trapp, Glenda K., and Michael L. Cook. *Kentucky Genealogical Index.* Vol. 1. Evansville, Ind.: Cook Publications, 1981. Every-name index to individuals mentioned in leading Kentucky genealogical publications through 1980.

Newspapers

The University of Kentucky Library is the major state repository for newspapers for the state. It participates in the United States newspaper project with holdings available from an online database. The Kentucky Union List of 14,000 titles of early Kentucky papers, identified by a recent project, is presently being microfilmed. When complete, all titles will be available through interlibrary loan. Many old Kentucky newspapers are archived at the American Antiquarian Society in Worcester, Massachusetts. A reliable Internet resource for modern newspapers is Kentucky Newspapers at <www.usnpl.com/kynews.html>.

The Kentucky Gazette, a Lexington newspaper, published news for most early Kentucky counties. Microfilm copies are available at many libraries in and out of the state and at the University of Kentucky Library in Lexington.

The *Louisville Courier* has been indexed for the years 1917 to 1977.

Some original and microfilmed newspapers are also available at the Kentucky Historical Society, the Filson Library, Louisville Free Public Library, and the Lexington Public Library. The FHL and some regional libraries also have copies on microfilm.

Other helpful sources include:

Clift, G. Glenn, comp., ed. *Kentucky Obituaries, 1787–1854.* Reprint, Baltimore: Genealogical Publishing Co., 1984. Compiled from publications of *The Register of the Kentucky Historical Society,* from newspapers housed in the Lexington Public Library, from *The Kentucky Gazette*, and from *The Reporter.* Arranged chronologically.

Green, Karen Mauer. *The Kentucky Gazette: Genealogical and Historical Abstracts.* 2 vols. Baltimore: Gateway Press, 1903 05. Volume 1 covers 1787–1800; volume 2 covers 1801–2000. These volumes are extracts of names, events, and dates from *The Kentucky Gazette* and include entries for people from many Kentucky counties. Volumes are individually indexed; each has separate indexes for persons and places.

Manuscripts

The largest collections of manuscripts, many on microfilm, are at the University of Louisville, Western Kentucky University in Bowling Green, Kentucky Historical Society, University of Kentucky Library, and the Filson Library. Manuscript collections pertaining (all or in part) to Kentucky and Kentuckians include, among many, the following:

The Ardery Collection contains abstracts of Kentucky and Virginia court, land, and Bible records as well as family history and correspondence. It is housed at the University of Kentucky Library, has been microfilmed, and is available through the FHL. See also:

Ardery, Julia H. *Kentucky Records.* 2 vols. Baltimore: Genealogical Publishing Co., 1969.

The Barton Collection is also housed at the University of Kentucky Library. Most material in this collection pertains to Pendleton County, although other counties and states are represented. It is available on microfilm at the Kentucky Historical Society, the Kentucky Department for Libraries and Archives, and through the FHL.

The Draper Manuscripts, located at the State Historical Society of Wisconsin (see Wisconsin—Manuscripts for a guide), contain a wealth of information concerning Kentucky and Kentuckians. This exceptional collection of historical material has been microfilmed (134 reels) and is available for purchase or for interlibrary loan from that repository. Locally, the entire Draper collection is available on microfilm at the Kentucky Historical Society, the Kentucky Department for Libraries and Archives, and the University of Kentucky. The FHL has a complete set on microfilm.

The DAR Collection includes transcriptions of Bible, cemetery, church, marriage, death, obituary, and probate records. It is housed at the DAR Library (see page 13) with microfilm copies of the originals available through the FHL.

The Shane Manuscript collection is available at the Western Kentucky University and Kentucky Historical Society.

In addition to *The Guide to Kentucky Archival and Manuscript Repositories,* cited under Archives, Libraries, and Societies, see also:

Brookes-Smith, Joan E. *Kentucky Historical Society: Microfilm Catalog: Excerpted Manuscripts.* 2 vols. Frankfort, Ky.: Kentucky Historical Society, 1975.

Clift, G. Glenn. *Guide to the Manuscripts of the Kentucky Historical Society.* Frankfort, Ky.: Kentucky Historical Society, 1955.

Talley, William M. *Talley's Northeastern Kentucky Papers.* Fort Worth, Tex: American Reference Publishers, 1971.

Archives, Libraries, and Societies

Kentucky Department for Libraries and Archives
Public Records Division
300 Coffee Tree Rd.
Frankfort, KY 40601
www.kdla.net

The department serves as the statewide repository for microfilmed county records from the earliest date for all 120 counties. Some counties, without sufficient space, store either their original early or modern records here as well. Consequently research using original records for many counties can be conducted entirely at this repository. Correspondence with the department and the appropriate counties is recommended to clarify specific holdings.

A valuable research tool is the Kentucky Department for Libraries and Archives' *The Guide to Kentucky Archival and Manuscript Repositories* (Frankfort, Ky.: Public Records Division, 1986). This compilation, available online, is based on data gathered by the Kentucky Guide Project. It contains an overview of 285 Kentucky repositories and their holdings.

Kentucky Historical Society
100 W. Broadway
Frankfort, KY 40601
http://history.ky.gov

For a detailed description of some holdings in the Kentucky Historical Society Library, consult Joan E. Brookes-Smith, *Kentucky Historical Society Microfilm Catalog,* vols. 3–4 (Frankfort, Ky.: Kentucky Historical Society, 1981) or see descriptions online.

An older and outdated finding aid for names and addresses of over 300 Kentucky genealogical and historical societies is the Kentucky Historical Society's *Directory of Historical Organizations and Speakers Bureau* (Frankfort, Ky.: Historical Confederation of Kentucky and Kentucky Historical Society, 1988). A reprinted edition is expected.

Kentucky Genealogical Society
(not a statewide organization)
P.O. Box 153
300 Coffee Tree Rd.
Frankfort, KY 40602-0153
www.kygs.org

University of Kentucky
Division of Special Collections and Archives
Margaret King Library
Lexington, KY 40506
www.uky.edu/Libraries/Special

Filson Library
1310 S. Third St.
Louisville, KY 40205
www.filsonhistorical.org

Special Focus Categories

African American

Both the Filson Library and the Kentucky Historical Society have extensive manuscripts and indexes of their collections, many of which include African-American families who migrated both as slaves and during Reconstruction. Kentucky served a dual role during slavery: stations of the Underground Railroad were established within the state, but at the same time, slaves were bought and sold. By 1860 nearly twenty percent of the state's population had African-American ancestry, which included slaves, free African Americans, and former slaves. However, the 1850 state constitution required that African Americans who were freed after passage of the new constitution leave the state within thirty days.

Judicial records for African Americans in Kentucky, for misdemeanors and petty crimes, can usually be found at the local level. Circuit courts heard cases for felonious crimes.

Beginning with the end of the Civil War, registrations of African-American marriages were maintained by county clerks. Marriages performed earlier but not recorded by civil authority were allowed to be post-recorded and filed under "Declarations" after 1865.

The Freedman's Bureau established schools, hospitals, and assistance for the poor and veterans. Freedman's Bureau records are both state and national. Federal Freedman's Bureau records include some genealogical information in the lists of refugees, freedmen, and abandoned lands as well as some marriage records. Little of genealogical value is recorded in the state level records.

In Kentucky some records for African Americans are maintained separately; these include marriage, vital records, school records, and tax lists. (See also Virginia—African American).

County Resources

Early Kentucky vital records, beginning from the dates indicated and until 1911, are held by the Kentucky Department of Libraries and Archives (see Vital Records). Land and probate records may be available at the office of the county clerk or at the Kentucky Department for Libraries and Archives.

Legal enactment dates for counties often vary from effective date of organization and beginning of record maintenance. The latter date is the one reflected in the following chart. Inventory sheets from the Kentucky Department for Libraries and Archives and the Kentucky Historical Society were used for beginning dates of some records. Land records may pre-date county organization because records were transferred from the parent county.

Dates given for court records may apply to one of many court records located in the county seat (see Court Records). Not all records are extant from the first date given.

For all records, it is advisable to direct correspondence to the county official at the county courthouse address listed in the following chart to determine present location and availability of records. In many cases, the Kentucky Department for Libraries and Archives will hold either the original or microfilm records.

The Historical Records Survey, *Guide to Public Vital Records in Kentucky* (Louisville: Historical Records Survey, 1942) was used to extract some information found in the following county listing. County formation information comes from Wendell Holmes Rone, Sr., *An Historical Atlas of Kentucky and Her Counties* (Mayfield, Ky.: Mayfield Printing Co., 1965). It contains photographs, chronologically arranged maps, and historical data from 1772 through 1856. Campbell and Kenton counties have two county courthouses.

Additional sources used to provide the most up-to-date information for courthouse addresses and to verify county formation data include: <www.kysos.com/ADMIN/LANDOFFI/kycounties.asp>, <www.naco.org>, and <www.uky.edu/KentuckyAtlas/kentucky-counties.html>. The most current phone numbers for Kentucky county courthouses are available through <www.kysos.com/Elecfil/Genelectionfiles/countyclerk.asp>. This website provides names of county clerk, telephone number, fax number, address, while some include online contact data. Additionally, some telephone calls to courthouses helped determine dates and addresses when sources showed conflicting information.

Microfilmed county records in the Family History Library collection were used to confirm dates of extant records for each Kentucky county. Although in some cases one or more published works cover a broader period, dates shown reflect those of original documents microfilmed in the county repository. In a few cases, the earliest date may be for an order book or survey rather than more substantial court minutes or deeds.

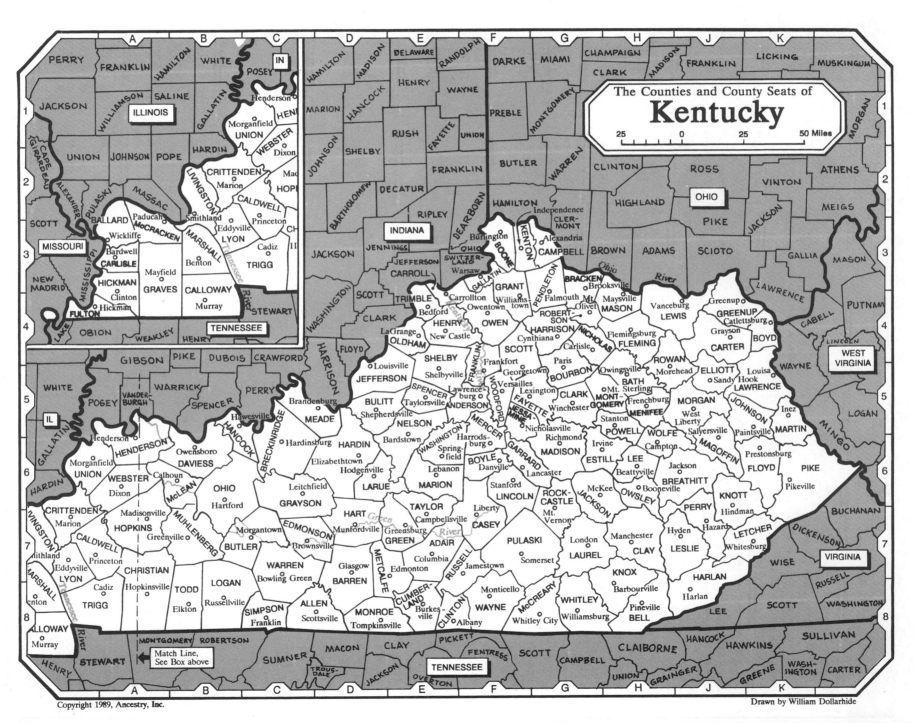

The Counties and County Seats of
Kentucky

25   0   25   50 Miles

Drawn by William Dollarhide

KENTUCKY

Map County Address	Date Formed Parent County/ies	Birth Marriage Death	Land Probate Court
F7 Adair 424 Public Sq. Columbia 42728-1431	1802 Green	1852 1802 1852	1801 1804 1802
D8 Allen 201 W. Main St./P.O. Box 336 Scottsville 42164-0336	1815 Barren/Warren	1852 1815 1852	1816 1815 1826
F5 Anderson 151 S. Main St. Lawrenceburg 40342-1192	1827 Franklin/Mercer/ Washington	1852 1827 1852	1827 1827 1827
A2 Ballard 424 Court St./P.O. Box 145 Wickliffe 42087-0145	1842 Hickman/McCracken	1853 1853 1853	1842 1842 1842
D7 Barren 117-1A N. Public Sq. Glasgow 42141	1799 Green/Warren	1852 1799 1852	1798 1798 1798
H5 Bath Main Street/P.O. Box 609 Owingsville 40360-0609	1811 Montgomery	1852 1811 1852	1811 1811 1811
H8 Bell P.O. Box 157 Pineville 40977-0157	1867 Knox/Harlan	1874 1867 1874	1867 1869 1867
F3 Boone 2950 E. Wash. Sq./P.O. Box 874 Burlington 41005-0874	1799 Campbell	1852 1799 1852	1799 1800 1799
G5 Bourbon 310 Main St./P.O. Box 312 Paris 40361-0312	1786 Fayette	1852 1786 1852	1786 1786 (wills) 1780
K4 Boyd 2800 Louisa St./P.O. Box 523 Catlettsburg 41129-0523	1860 Carter/Lawrence/ Greenup	1859 1860 1859	1860 1860 (wills) 1860
F6 Boyle 321 W. Main St. Danville 40422-1848	1842 Mercer/Lincoln	1852 1852 1852	1842 1842 1800
G3 Bracken 116 W. Miami St./P.O. Box 147 Brooksville 41104-0147	1797 Campbell/Mason	1852 1797 1852	1797 1797 1797
J6 Breathitt 1137 Main St. Jackson 41339-1194	1839 Clay/Estill/ Perry	1852 1852 1852	1873 1873 1838
C6 Breckinridge P.O. Box 538 Hardinsburg 40143-0538	1800 Hardin	1852 1860 1852	1800 1800 (wills) 1803
D5 Bullitt 149 N. Walnut St./P.O. Box 6 Shepherdsville 40165-0006	1797 Jefferson/Nelson	1854 1797 1854	1797 1797 1797
C7 Butler 110 N. Main St./P.O. Box 449 Morgantown 42261-0449	1810 Logan/Ohio	1853 1810 1853	1810 1810 1811
C2 Caldwell 100 E. Market St. Princeton 42445-1596	1809 Livingston	1852 1808 1852	1809 1809 1809
B4 Calloway 101 S. Fifth St. Murray 42071-2569	1821 Hickman	1852 1823 1852	1822 1836 1856
G3 Campbell 340 York St. Newport 41071-1682 and Alexandria 41001	1795 Harrison/Mason/Scott	1852 1795 1852	1795 1795 1791
A3 Carlisle P.O. Box 176 Bardwell 42023-0176	1886 Ballard	1911 1886 1904	1886 1886 1886
E3 Carroll 440 Main St. Carrollton 41008-1064	1838 Gallatin/Henry/Trimble	1852 1836 1852	1795 1838 1838
J4 Carter 300 W. Main St. Grayson 41143-1298	1838 Greenup/Lawrence	1852 1838 1852	1838 1835 1838
F6 Casey P.O. Box 310 Liberty 42539-0310	1807 Lincoln	1852 1807 1852	1807 1806 1807
A8 Christian 511 S. Main St. Hopkinsville 42240-2300	1797 Logan	1852 1797 1852	1797 1797 1797
G5 Clark 34 S. Main St./P.O. Box 4060 Winchester 40392-4060	1793 Bourbon/Fayette	1852 1793 1852	1793 1793 1793
H7 Clay 316 Main St. Manchester 40962-1265	1807 Madison/Floyd/Knox	1852 1807 1852	1799 1830 1809
E8 Clinton 212 Washington St. Albany 42602-1263	1836 Wayne/Cumberland	1852 1852 1852	1848 1863 1864
B2 Crittenden 107 S. Main St. Marion 42064-1563	1842 Livingston	1852 1842 1852	1842 1833 1842
E8 Cumberland P.O. Box 275 Burkesville 42717-0275	1799 Green	1852 1799 1852	1799 1815 1820
B6 Daviess P.O. Box 609 Owensboro 42302-0609	1815 Ohio	1853 1815 1853	1815 1812 1822
C7 Edmonson P.O. Box 830 Brownsville 42210-0830	1825 Grayson/Hart/Warren	1852 1843 1852	1825 1824 1824

KENTUCKY

Map	County Address	Date Formed Parent County/ies	Birth Marriage Death	Land Probate Court
J5	Elliott P.O. Box 225 Sandy Hook 41171-0225	1869 Carter/Lawrence/ Morgan	1874 1874 1874	1869 1966 1958
H6	Estill P.O. Box 59 Irvine 40336-0059	1808 Clark/Madison	1852 1808 1852	1808 1808 1808
G5	Fayette 162 E. Main St. Lexington 40507-1334	1780 Kentucky (Va.)	1852 1803 1852	1787 1789 1787
H4	Fleming Court Sq./P.O. Box 324 Flemingsburg 41041-0324	1798 Mason	1852 1798 1852	1798 1798 1798
K6	Floyd P.O. Box 1089 Prestonsburg 41653-1089	1800 Fleming/Mason/ Montgomery	1852 1803 1854	1806 1812 1808
F5	Franklin P.O. Box 338 Frankfort 40602-0338	1795 Woodford/Mercer/ Shelby	1852 1795 1852	1795 1795 1795
A4	Fulton P.O. Box 126 Hickman 42050-0126	1845 Hickman	1852 1845 1852	1845 1845 1845
F3	Gallatin P.O. Box 1309 Warsaw 41095-0616	1799 Franklin/Shelby	1852 1799 1852	1799 1799 1799
F6	Garrard 15 Public Sq. Lancaster 40444-1057	1797 Madison/Lincoln/ Mercer	1789 1797 1852	1797 1797 1797
F4	Grant 101 N. Main St. Williamstown 41097-1107	1820 Pendleton	1852 1820 1852	1820 1820 1820
A3	Graves 101 E. South St. Mayfield 42066-2324	1824 Hickman	1852 1887 1852	1887 1882 1858
C6	Grayson 10 Public Sq. Leitchfield 42754-1199	1810 Hardin/Ohio	1852 1852 1852	1896 1856 (wills) 1906
E7	Green 203 W. Court St. Greensburg 42743-1552	1793 Lincoln/Nelson	1852 1793 1852	1793 1793 1794
J4	Greenup P.O. Box 686 Greenup 41144-0686	1804 Mason	1852 1803 1852	1811 1822 1807
B5	Hancock P.O. Box 146 Hawesville 42348-0146	1829 Daviess/Ohio/ Breckinridge	1852 1829 1852	1829 1820 (wills) 1834
D6	Hardin P.O. Box 1030 Elizabethtown 42702-1030	1793 Nelson	1852 1793 1852	1793 1793 1793
J8	Harlan P.O. Box 670 Harlan 40831-0670	1819 Knox	1852 1820 1852	1820 1829 1821
G4	Harrison 190 W. Pike St. Cynthiana 41031-1242	1794 Bourbon/Scott	1852 1794 1852	1794 1794 1794
D7	Hart P.O. Box 277 Munfordville 42765-0277	1819 Hardin/Barren	1852 1852 1852	1783 1819
A6	Henderson P.O. Box 374 Henderson 42419-0374	1799 Christian	1852 1806 1852	1797 1799 (wills) 1816
E4	Henry P.O. Box 615 New Castle 40050-0615	1799 Shelby	1852 1800 1852	1799 1765 1803
A4	Hickman 110 E. Clay St. Clinton 42031-1296	1821 (1822) Caldwell/Livingston	1852 1822 1852	1822 1822 1822

Although Hickman was created in 1821, county administration didn't become effective until 1822.

Map	County Address	Date Formed Parent County/ies	Birth Marriage Death	Land Probate Court
A7	Hopkins 10 S. Main St./P.O. Drawer 737 Madisonville 42431-2588	1807 Henderson	1852 1806 1852	1807 1800 (wills) 1808
G6	Jackson P.O. Box 700 McKee 40447-0399	1858 Rockcastle/Owsley/ Madison/Clay/Estill/Laurel	1858 1858 1858	1858 1859 1858
D5	Jefferson 527 W. Jefferson St./ P.O. Box 33033 Louisville 40202-2850	1780 Kentucky (Va.)	1852 1781 1852	1783 1784 1780
F5	Jessamine 101 N. Main St. Nicholasville 40356-1270	1799 Fayette	1852 1799 1852	1799 1799 1799
K5	Johnson 124 Court St. Paintsville 41240-1607	1843 Floyd/Morgan/ Lawrence	1852 1843 1852	1843 1843 1843
F3	Kenton P.O. Box 1109 Covington 41012-1109 and Independence 41051	1840 Campbell	1852 1840 1852	1840 1840 1840
J7	Knott P.O. Box 446 Hindman 41822-0446	1884 Perry/Breathitt/ Floyd/Letcher	1911 1884 1911	1883 1891 1888
H8	Knox 401 Court Sq. Barbourville 40906-1463	1800 Lincoln	1852 1800 1852	1800 1803 1800
D6	Larue 209 W. High St. Hodgenville 42748-1563	1843 Hardin	1852 1843 1852	1843 1843 1843

252

Map	County Address	Date Formed Parent County/ies	Birth Marriage Death	Land Probate Court
G7	Laurel 101 S. Main St. London 40741-2308	1026 1826 Whitley/Clay/Knox/ Rockcastle	1852 1826 1852	1826 1817 1826
K5	Lawrence 122 S. Main Cross St. Louisa 41230-1393	1822 Floyd/Greenup	1852 1822 1852	1822 1821 1822
H6	Lee P.O. Box 551 Beattyville 41311-0551	1870 Owsley/Breathitt/ Wolfe/Estill	1874 1870 1874	1870 1870 1870
J7	Leslie P.O. Box 916 Hyden 41749-0916	1878 Clay/Harlan/Perry	1878 1878 1878	1879 1873 1866
K7	Letcher 156 Main St./P.O. Box 58 Whitesburg 41858-7286	1842 Perry/Harlan	1852 1842 1852	1842 1866 1866
H4	Lewis P.O. Box 129 Vanceburg 41179-0129	1807 Mason	1852 1807 1852	1807 1807 1807
F6	Lincoln 102 E. Main St. Stanford 40484-1279	1780 Kentucky (Va.)	1852 1781 1852	1780 1781 1780
K5	Livingston P.O. Box 400 Smithland 42081-0400	1798/1799 Christian	1852 1799 1852	1800 1799 1798
	Although Livingston was created 13 Dec 1798, county administration didn't become effective until 21 May 1799.			
B8	Logan 229 W. 3rd St./P.O. Box 358 Russellville 42276-0358	1792 Lincoln	1852 1790 1853	1792 1795 1793
B3	Lyon P.O. Box 310 Eddyville 42038-0310	1854 Caldwell	1853 1854 1853	1854 1847 1854
G6	Madison 101 W. Main St. Richmond 40475-1415	1786 Lincoln	1852 1786 1852	1787 1787 1786
J6	Magoffin P.O. Box 530 Salyersville 41465-0530	1860 Floyd/Johnson/ Morgan	1860 1860 1860	1860 1860 1860
E6	Marion 120 W. Main St. Lebanon 40033-1245	1834 Washington	1852 1852 1852	1863 1863 1863
B3	Marshall 1101 Main St. Benton 42025-1498	1842 Calloway	1852 1848 1852	1848 1848 1848
K5	Martin P.O. Box 460 Inez 41224-0460	1870 Lawrence/Floyd/ Pike/Johnson	1903 1871 1905	1870 1861 1870
H4	Mason P.O. Box 234 Maysville 41056-0234	1789 Bourbon	1852 1789 1852	1789 1791 1789
A2	McCracken P.O. Box 609 Paducah 42002-0609	1825 Hickman	1852 1825 1852	1825 1825 1825
G8	McCreary P.O. Box 699 Whitley City 42653-0699	1912 Wayne/Pulaski/Whitley	1912 1912 1912	1915 1912 1912
B6	McLean P.O. Box 57 Calhoun 42327-0057	1854 Muhlenberg/Daviess/ Ohio	1854 1854 1854	1854 1847 1854
D5	Meade P.O. Box 614 Brandenburg 40108-0614	1824 Hardin/Breckinridge	1852 1824 1852	1824 1824 1824
H5	Menifee P.O. Box 123 Frenchburg 40322-0123	1869 Powell/Wolfe/Bath/ Morgan/Montgomery	1874 1869 1874	1869 1870 1869
F6	Mercer P.O. Box 426 Harrodsburg 40330-0426	1786 Lincoln	1852 1774 1852	1779 1779 1786
E7	Metcalfe P.O. Box 25 Edmonton 42129-0025	1860 Monroe/Adair/Barren/ Cumberland/Green	1860 1867 1861	1868 1865 1868
D8	Monroe P.O. Box 188 Tompkinsville 42167-0188	1820 Barren/Cumberland	1852 1863 1852	1863 1861 1862
H5	Montgomery P.O. Box 414 Mount Sterling 40353-0414	1797 Clark	1852 1852 1852	1797 1797 1841
J5	Morgan P.O. Box 26 West Liberty 41472-0026	1823 Floyd/Bath	1852 1823 1852	1823 1823 1823
B7	Muhlenberg P.O. Box 525 Greenville 42345-0525	1799 Christian/Logan	1852 1802 1852	1798 1801 1799
E5	Nelson P.O. Box 312 Bardstown 40004-0312	1785 Jefferson	1852 1785 1852	1784 1785 1785
G4	Nicholas P.O. Box 227 Carlisle 40311-0227	1800 Bourbon/Mason	1852 1800 1852	1800 1800 1796
B6	Ohio P.O. Box 85 Hartford 42347-0085	1799 Hardin	1852 1799 1852	1798 1799 1799
E4	Oldham 100 W. Jefferson St. La Grange 40031-1189	1824 Henry/Shelby/ Jefferson	1852 1824 1852	1824 1824 1823
F4	Owen 135 W. Bryan St./P.O. Box 338 Owenton 40359-1440	1819 Scott/Franklin/ Gallatin/Pendleton	1852 1819 1852	1819 1819 1819

Map	County Address	Date Formed Parent County/ies	Birth Marriage Death	Land Probate Court
H6	Owsley P.O. Box 500 Booneville 41314-0500	1843 Clay/Estill/Breathitt	1843 1852 1852	1844 1930 1923*

*This is the date of the earliest existing record. Records are not on microfilm.

Map	County Address	Date Formed Parent County/ies	Birth Marriage Death	Land Probate Court
G3	Pendleton P.O. Box 112 Falmouth 41040-0112	1799 Bracken/Campbell	1852 1799 1852	1798 1799 1799
J7	Perry P.O. Box 150 Hazard 41702-0150	1821 Clay/Floyd	1852 1821 1852	1821 1901 1831
K6	Pike P.O. Box 631 Pikeville 41502-0631	1822 Floyd	1852 1822 1852	1788 1839 1822
H5	Powell P.O. Box 548 Stanton 40380-0548	1852 Clark/Estill/Montgomery	1852 1852 1852	1864 1864 1864
F7	Pulaski P.O. Box 724 Somerset 42501-0724	1799 Green/Lincoln	1852 1799 1852	1799 1801 1799
G4	Robertson P.O. Box 75 Mount Olivet 41064-0075	1867 Bracken/Nicholas/ Harrison/Mason	1874 1867 1874	1868 1864 1867
G6	Rockcastle 205 E. Main St., #6 P.O. Box 365 Mount Vernon 40456-2211	1810 Pulaski/Lincoln/ Knox/Madison	1852 1852 1852	1865 1855 1873
J5	Rowan 627 E. Main St. Morehead 40351-1390	1856 Fleming/Morgan	1856 1880 1856	1866 1853 1880
F7	Russell P.O. Box 579 Jamestown 42629-0579	1826 Cumberland/Adair/Wayne	1852 1826 1852	1825 1826 1826
F4	Scott 101 E. Main St. Georgetown 40324-1794	1792 Woodford	1852 1837 1852	1793 1796 1792
E5	Shelby P.O. Box 819 Shelbyville 40066-0819	1792 Jefferson	1852 1792 1852	1792 1794 1804
C8	Simpson P.O. Box 268 Franklin 42134-0268	1819 Allen/Logan/Warren	1852 1852 1852	1819 1882 1816
E5	Spencer 2 W. Main St./P.O. Box 544 Taylorsville 40071-0544	1824 Shelby/Bullitt/ Nelson	1852 1824 1852	1824 1824 1824
E6	Taylor 203 N. Court St. Campbellsville 42718-2298	1848 Green	1852 1848 1852	1848 1848 1848
B8	Todd P.O. Box 307 Elkton 42220-0307	1820 Christian/Logan	1852 1820 1852	1820 1820 1820
C3	Trigg P.O. Box 1310 Cadiz 42211-1310	1820 Christian/Caldwell	1852 1820 1852	1820 1820 1820
E4	Trimble P.O. Box 262 Bedford 40006-0262	1837 Henry/Oldham/Gallatin	1852 1837 1852	1837 1837 1837
C1	Union P.O. Box 119 Morganfield 42437-0119	1811 Henderson	1852 1811 1852	1811 1811 1823
C7	Warren 429 E. 10th St./P.O. Box 478 Bowling Green 42101-0478	1797 Logan	1852 1797 1852	1797 1796 1796
E5	Washington P.O. Box 446 Springfield 40069-0446	1792 Nelson	1852 1792 1852	1792 1792 1792
F8	Wayne P.O. Box 565 Monticello 42633-0565	1801 Pulaski/Cumberland	1852 1801 1852	1800 1801 1802
A6	Webster P.O. Box 19 Dixon 42409-0019	1860 Hopkins/Union/Henderson	1874 1860 1874	1860 1860 1860
G8	Whitley Main Street/P.O. Box 8 Williamsburg 40769-0008	1818 Knox	1852 1818 1852	1818 1818 1818
H6	Wolfe P.O. Box 400 Campton 41301-0400	1860 Owsley/Breathitt/ Powell/Morgan	1861 1861 1861	1860 1885 1818
F5	Woodford 103 S. Main St. Versailles 40383-1298	1789 Fayette	1852 1789 1852	1789 1789 1789

Louisiana

BETH A. STAHR, CGRS, AND SHARON SHOLARS BROWN

Although Hernando de Soto explored this region for Spain in the years 1541 and 1542, the colony of Louisiana was not founded until 1699, by two brothers from France, Pierre Le Moyne d'Iberville and Jean Baptiste Le Moyne de Bienville. Its boundaries stretched as far east as the Perdido River, about halfway between present-day Mobile, Alabama, and Pensacola, Florida, westward to the Red and Calcasieu rivers, next door to Spanish territory; and extended north all the way to Canada, which was a French possession. The vast boundaries of colonial Louisiana included part or all of at least ten states: Alabama (western part), Arkansas, Illinois, Kentucky, Louisiana (eastern part), Minnesota, Mississippi, Missouri, Oklahoma, and Tennessee.

France reigned over the Louisiana colony from 1699 until all North American holdings were lost in 1763, at the end of the Seven Years War. All French territory east of the Mississippi River, which included the Florida parishes, went to Great Britain, and all French territory west of the Mississippi went to Spain.

There is one quirk in this division important to the genealogist. New Orleans, on the east bank of the Mississippi River, should have gone to Great Britain but went to Spain instead. The kings of France and Spain were cousins, and together they connived to keep New Orleans out of the hands of Great Britain, their common enemy. They convinced the British negotiators that New Orleans was on the west bank and not the east.

The Spanish ruled its part of Louisiana from 1763 to 1800, when it was forced by Napoleon to relinquish control. It is important to note, however, that even though Louisiana was once again a French possession, there was no change of affairs. Spanish officials continued to govern the colony while Napoleon secretly negotiated with Thomas Jefferson to sell Louisiana to the United States. For this reason, researchers seeking people who lived in colonial Louisiana between 1800 and 1803 should begin in the Spanish records, not the French.

Thus, for nearly 300 years Louisiana was one of the areas in the world most sought after by the three major powers of Europe: Spain, France, and Great Britain. Spain explored it first but withdrew in favor of richer lands farther south in Mexico, Central America, and South America. Then France settled the land, but its decaying monarchy had little regard for the colony, while it was obvious that the French statesmen who were interested in it had never dealt with the vast fields upon which their policies were to operate. They did not comprehend the great extent of the country and were entirely ignorant of the means necessary for the successful cultivation of their lower Mississippi colony. Great Britain had no plans to give up its portion of the territory, but rather tried to obtain the French part as well.

The struggle for Louisiana was finally won, not by one of the European nations, who had plotted and fought for its permanent control for so long, but by the infant nation that rose up on the eastern shores of North America. The United States took possession of Louisiana in December 1803 and began preparing the colony, which had never known a working democracy, for statehood.

In 1812 war broke out between England and the United States, with Great Britain planning the conquest of Louisiana. Its objective failed when the Battle of New Orleans was lost. Less

than four months later, Louisiana celebrated its third anniversary as an American state.

Vital Records

The civil recording of births, marriages, and deaths did not begin in earnest until the early twentieth century. Although laws were passed in the late nineteenth century requiring that vital events be recorded, there was little compliance until later. Prior to that time it was the responsibility of the churches to maintain this data.

The Roman Catholic Church dominated Louisiana until the Louisiana Purchase in 1803. In fact, it was the only church in Louisiana until that time. The Catholic churches throughout the state kept registers of christenings, marriages, and burials, and were the recorders of Louisiana's early vital records. For important published works relating to marriages, see Church Records below and the following:

DeVille, Winston. *The New Orleans French, 1720–1733: A Collection of Marriage Records Relating to the First Colonists of the Louisiana Province.* Baltimore: Genealogical Publishing Co., 1973.

Forsyth, Alice D. *Louisiana Marriages, 1784–1806.* New Orleans: Polyanthos, 1977.

———, and Ghislaine Pleasonton. *Louisiana Marriage Contracts: 1725–1758.* New Orleans: Polyanthos, 1980.

Mills, Elizabeth Shown. *Natchitoches Church Marriages, 1818–1850. Translated Abstracts from Registers of St. François des Natchitoches, Louisiana.* Vol. 6. Cane River Creole Series. Tuscaloosa, Ala.: Mills Historical Press, 1985.

In the first part of the twentieth century many states, including Louisiana, began requiring civil registration of vital records. The earliest city in Louisiana to exact civil registrations was New Orleans in 1790; however, registrations were only randomly made until the twentieth century. It was not until 1914 that civil recording began statewide. As of 2003, the Louisiana State Archives (see Archives, Libraries, and Societies) holds Orleans Parish birth records over 100 years old, Orleans Parish marriage records over fifty years old, and statewide death records over fifty years old. Researchers may visit the State Archives in Baton Rouge or order records by mail for a fee (presently $5).

Some parish health departments have alphabetical birth and death indexes for their areas. These are not, however, complete listings of all births and deaths of that parish. Copies of these vital records can be ordered from Vital Records Registry, Louisiana Department of Health and Hospitals Office of Public Health, P.O. Box 60630, New Orleans, LA 70160 <www.dhh. state.la.us>. There are a few births (1790) and deaths (ca.

1803) recorded prior to 1914, but the majority of the records start in that year. One must either show proof of kinship as a direct descendant or provide proper authorization to obtain a copy of any of these records. As of July 1999, birth certificates are also available through the Parish Clerks of Court.

Census Records

Federal

Population Schedules
- Indexed—1810, 1820, 1830, 1840, 1850, 1860, 1870, 1880, 1900, 1910, 1920, 1930
- Soundex—1880, 1900, 1910, 1920, 1930

Industrial and Agricultural Schedules
- 1850, 1860, 1870, 1880

Mortality Schedules
- 1850, 1860, 1870, 1880

Slave Schedules
- 1850, 1860

Union Veterans Schedules
- 1890

After the 1803 purchase of Louisiana, it became an American possession; therefore, the first federal census report taken for the state was 1810.

Caution should be used particularly with relying on any census indexes (see page 3) for Louisiana, as many French and Spanish names were transcribed wrong for the census and numerous omissions exist. Many of these population schedules have been published:

Ardoin, Robert B. L. *Louisiana Census Records: 1810–1820.* 3 vols. Vols. 1 and 2 (Baltimore: Genealogical Publishing Co., 1970–72); and vol. 3 (New Orleans: Polyanthos, 1977). These cover more than fourteen of the early settled parishes.

Childs, Marleta, and John Ross, eds. *North Louisiana Census Reports.* Vol. 2: 1830 and 1840 Schedules of Caddo. Claiborne and Natchitoches Parishes. Vol. 3: 1850 and 1860 Schedules of Union Parish. New Orleans: Polyanthos, Inc., 1977.

As early as 1860 the federal government began attempts to identify Native Americans. In 1900 and 1910 it created a special Indian schedule. The first page was the same as the population census, the only difference being that it had "Indian Population" as its heading. The second page provided for such important information as tribal affiliation, the tribe

of each parent, the amount of Indian blood, and—if not full-blooded—their precise racial mixture. These schedules will be found at the end of the ward or district in which the Native American resided.

Some of the supplemental census schedules taken by the federal government are available for Louisiana at Duke University, Durham, North Carolina. Copies may also exist in Louisiana, but to date they have not been found. Louisiana's mortality schedules (1850–80) are on microfilm at the National Archives, Washington, D.C., microfilm T655.

Colonial

During the colonial period Louisiana shifted from French to Spanish control. Not until after the 1803 purchase of Louisiana did it become an American possession; therefore, the first federal census report taken for the state was 1810. But the French and Spanish were diligent scribes, and many censuses exist for Louisianians. Some of the censuses for the colony's inhabitants are listed below:

French Period

Maduell, Charles R., Jr., comp. and trans. *Census Tables for the French Colony of Louisiana, 1699–1732.* Reprint. Baltimore: Clearfield Publishing Co., 2000. Includes the following:

> December 1699—Census of the Inhabitants of the first settlement on the Gulf Coast, Fort Maurepas.
>
> 25 May 1700—Census of the officers, petty officers, sailors, Canadians, freebooters, and others located at Biloxi as of 25 May 1700.
>
> 1704—List of marriageable girls who arrived aboard the *Pelican* at Biloxi in the year 1704.
>
> 1 August 1706—Census of the inhabitants of Fort Louis de la Louisianne at Mobile, taken by Nicolas de la Salle.
>
> 1 August 1706—Census of families and inhabitants of Louisiana, taken by Nicolas de la Salle.
>
> 1711—Census of Fort Louis de la Mobile from the map of 1711.
>
> 25 October 1713—List of officers commissioned at Fort Louis, Biloxi.
>
> October 1713—Persons mentioned in the colony by Antoine de la Mothe Cadillac.
>
> 26 June 1721—Census of the inhabitants in the area of Biloxi and Mobile, as reported by Le Sieur Diron.
>
> 24 November 1721—General census of all the inhabitants of New Orleans and environs, as reported by Le Sieur Diron.
>
> 1 May 1722—Census of the inhabitants of Natchitoches, Fort St. Jean Baptist, taken for Le Sieur Diron, General of the Troops.
>
> 13 May 1722—Census of the inhabitants of the concessions along the Mississippi River; reported by Le Sieur Diron.

> 1722—Officials of the colony at Fort Louis, Biloxi, appointed in 1722.
>
> 8 April 1723—Some colonists of Louisiana mentioned in a letter by de La Chaise.
>
> 18 October 1723—Some colonists of Louisiana mentioned in a letter by de La Chaise.
>
> 12 November 1724—Census of inhabitants of German villages located ten leagues above New Orleans along the river, under command of D'Arensbourg.
>
> 20 December 1724—Census of inhabitants along the Mississippi River from New Orleans to Ouacha, or the German villages.
>
> March 1725—Census of the inhabitants of Dauphin Island, along the Mobile River, Cat Island, and Penscagoula (Pascagoula), compiled by M. Gorty.
>
> January 1726—General census of all the inhabitants of the colony of Louisiana, including the entire coast bordering the Gulf of Mexico, from Mobile to New Orleans, and the colonies along the Mississippi River, including the region known as Illinois.
>
> October 1726—List of those persons requesting "Negroes" from the company.
>
> 1 July 1727—Census of New Orleans as reported by M. Perier, commander general of Louisiana; also continuation of the census of M. Perier, being the inhabitants in the environs of New Orleans, along the river.
>
> 9 June 1730—List of persons massacred at Natchez, 28 November 1729, as reported by R. P. Philibert, Capuchin priest.
>
> 1731—List of property owners of New Orleans on the map published by Gonichon in 1731; census of inhabitants along the Mississippi River, unsigned, initialed N. S.; and list of landowners located along the Mississippi River from its mouth to the German villages, with indications of how they acquired the land. Date mentioned "after 1731."
>
> January 1732—Census of the inhabitants and property owners of New Orleans; and census of the inhabitants of Illinois, both unsigned but initialed N. S.

For this time period see also Jacqueline K. Voorhies, *Some Late Eighteenth Century Louisianians, 1758–1796* (Lafayette, La.: University of Southwestern Louisiana, 1973).

Spanish Period

Hill, Roscoe R. *Descriptive Catalogue of the Documents relating to the History of the United States in the Papeles Procedentes de Cuba deposited in the Archivo General de Indias.* 1916. Reprint. New York: Kraus Reprint Corporation, 1965. Lists the following:

Legajo 34

> 1795—Census of Baton Rouge and Manchak.

Legajo 81

1770—Reports of Eduardo Nugent and Juan Kelly on the number of inhabitants and livestock in the districts of Atakapas, Natchitoches, Opelousas, and Rapides.

Legajo 117

1784 (?)—Census of the German Coast.

Legajo 121

1790—Census of Ouachita.

Legajo 142

1805—Census of Baton Rouge.

Legajo 187-b

1766—List of inhabitants of Pointe Coupee; census of Pointe Coupee; list of Cote des Allemands; general census of Pointe Coupee; general census of Villere at Allemands.

Legajo 188-1

1772—Left Bank of the Mississippi from Bayou de Placaminas to Ile au Marais; 1773 Rapides; 1774 "negroes and mulattoes" at Natchitoches.

Legajo 188-2

1771—Census of Atakapas and Opelousas.

Legajo 189-2

1776 (dated wrong, 1766)—Census of parish of St. Charles (Allemands).

Legajo 193

1782—Census of Baton Rouge; 1786 census of Baton Rouge; 1798 census of the district of Nueva Feliciana; census of the district of la Metearie.

Legajo 198

1785—Census of Avoyelles.

Legajo 201

1788 and 1789—Census of Rapides; 1789 census of Natchitoches.

Legajo 205

1772—Census of Rapides.

Legajo 211

1795 (slaves)—Census of Primer Cote des Allemand; census of the second and third wards of New Orleans; census of slaves at Allemands, Atakapas, Natchitoches; 1796 census of the Quartier de la Metairie of New Orleans.

Legajo 212

1795 (slaves)—General census of slaves of New Orleans and masters who contributed to indemnity for slaves lost at Pointe Coupee; 1778 census of the third ward of New Orleans; 1803 census of Pointe Coupee.

Legajo 216

1799—Census of Allemands and Atakapas; general census of New Orleans.

Legajo 218

1774—Census of Atakapas.

Legajo 220

1803—Census of Atakapas (six documents).

Legajo 227-r

1790—*Recensements de la Pointe Coupee et Fausse Riviere.*

Legajo 2351

1777—Census of Louisiana.

Legajo 2357

1771—Census of Louisiana.

Legajo 2358

1777—Census of Atakapas and Opelousas.

Legajo 2360

1786—Census of Atakapas and Opelousas.

Legajo 2361

1787—Census of Pointe Coupee.

Legajo 2364

1796—Census of Opelousas.

Almost all of these censuses from the Spanish archives have been published in English by Voorhies (see above) and by Elizabeth Shown Mills in *Natchitoches Colonials: Censuses, Military Rolls and Tax Lists, 1722–1803* (Chicago: Adams Press, 1981).

From 1721 to 1773, the city of Nuestra Señora del Pilar de los Adaes served as the Spanish capital of Texas. This presidio was located in present-day Natchitoches Parish, near Robeline, Louisiana. Abandoned in 1773, its inhabitants relocated to San Antonio, Texas. By 1779 many of these people moved back closer to their old home of Adaes and reestablished the mission at Nacogdoches, Texas. Yearly census reports exist for Nacogdoches for the years 1792 to 1806, and 1809. Many Louisiana ancestors can be found on these enumerations. See "Census Reports of the Village of Nuestra del Pilar de Nacogdoches," Bexar Archives, University of Texas Archives, Austin, Texas. (Copies can also be found in the Robert Bruce Collection, vol. 18, 71-284, Ralph W. Steen Library, Special Collection, Stephen F. Austin University, Nacogdoches, Texas.)

Background Sources

Researchers interested in Louisiana have a number of excellent histories, archival guides, and source references available to them. The following are particularly useful:

French Period

Conrad, Glenn R., and Carl A. Brasseaux, eds. *A Selected Bibliography of Scholarly Literature on Colonial Louisiana and New France.* Lafayette, La.: Center for Louisiana Studies, 1982.

——. *First Families of Louisiana.* 2 vols. Baton Rouge: Claitor's Publishing Division, 1970.

De Ville, Winston. *Gulf Coast Colonials: A Compendium of French Families in Early Eighteenth Century Louisiana.* Reprint. Baltimore: Genealogical Publishing Co., 1995. Giraud, Marcel. *Histoire de la Louisiane française.* 4 vols. Paris: Presses Universitaires de France, 1953–1974. The first volume of this series has been translated into English and is available as Joseph C. Lambert, trans., *A History of Louisiana,* vol. 1: *The Reign of Louis XIV, 1698–1715* (Baton Rouge: Louisiana State University Press, 1974).

Leland, Waldo G. *Guide to Materials for American History in the Libraries and Archives of France.* Washington, D.C.: Carnegie Institute, 1932.

Robichaux, Jr., Albert J. *German Coast Families: European Origins and Settlement in Colonial Louisiana.* Rayne, La.: Hébert Publications, 1997.

Spanish Period

Bancroft Library. *Spain and Spanish America in the Libraries of the University of California.* 2 vols. Berkeley, Calif.: University of California, 1928 and 1930.

Bolton, Herbert Eugene. *Guide to Materials for the History of the United States in the Principal Archives of Mexico.* Washington, D.C.: Carnegie Institute, 1913.

Buckely, Eleanor Claire. "The Aguayo Expedition into Texas and Louisiana, 1719–1721," *The Quarterly of the Texas State Historical Association* 9 (July 1911).

Castañeda, Carlos E. *Our Catholic Heritage in Texas.* 6 vols. 1936–50. Reprint. New York: Arno Press, 1976.

Cox, Isaac Joslin. "The Louisiana-Texas Frontier," *The Quarterly of the Texas State Historical Association* 10 (July 1906): 0-10.

Cuba. *Documents Pertaining to the Floridas Which Are Kept in Different Archives of Cuba. Appendix No. 1: Official List of Documentary Funds of the Floridas—New Territories of the States of Louisiana, Alabama, Mississippi, Georgia, and Florida.* Kept in the National Archives. Havana, 1945.

Haggard, J. Villasano. *Handbook for Translators of Spanish Historical Documents.* Austin, Tex.: University of Texas, 1941.

Hill, Roscoe J. *Descriptive Catalogue of the Documents Relating to the History of the United States in the Papeles Procedentes de Cuba, deposited in the Archivo General de Indias, Seville.* Washington, D.C.: Carnegie Institute, 1916.

Holmes, Jack D. L. *A Guide to Spanish Louisiana, 1762–1806.* New Orleans: Louisiana Collection Series, 1970.

Notre Dame University. *Guide to the Microfilm Edition of the Records of the Diocese of Louisiana and the Floridas, 1576–1803.* Notre Dame, Ind.: Pub. the committee, 1967

Statehood

Carter, Clarence E. *The Territory of Louisiana, 1803–1812.* In *The Territorial Papers of the United States.* 28 vols. Washington, D.C.: Government Printing Office, 1940.

Foote, Lucy B. *Bibliography of the Official Publications of Louisiana, 1803–1934.* Baton Rouge: Hill Memorial Library, Louisiana State University, 1942.

Korn, Bertram Wallace. *The Early Jews of New Orleans.* Waltham, Mass.: American Jewish Historical Society, 1969.

Laws of the United States of America, from the 4th of March 1789 to the 4th of March 1815. Washington, D.C.: R. C. Weightman. Philadelphia: W. John Duane, 1815.

Mills, Elizabeth Shown, and Gary B. Mills. *Tales of Old Natchitoches.* Vol. 3. Cane River Creole Series. Natchitoches: Association for the Preservation of Historic Natchitoches, 1978.

Nolan, Charles A. *A Southern Catholic Heritage.* Vol. 1: 1704–1813. New Orleans: Archdiocese of New Orleans, 1976.

Poret, Ory G. *History of Land Titles in the State of Louisiana.* Baton Rouge: Louisiana Department of Natural Resources, 1972.

Guides

DeVille, Winston. "Louisiana." *Genealogical Research: Methods and Sources,* ed. Kenn Stryker-Rodda. Vol. 2. Rev. ed. Washington, D.C.: American Society of Genealogists, 1983.

——. *Mississippi Valley Mélange: A Collection of Notes and Documents for the Genealogy and History of the Province of Louisiana and the Territory of Orleans.* Ville Platte, La.: the author, 2000.

Hamer, Collin B. *Genealogical Materials in the New Orleans Public Library's Louisiana Division and City Archives.* New Orleans: Friends of the New Orleans Public Library, 1998. Also available at <http://nutrias.org/~nopl/guides/genguide/ggcover.htm>.

Maps

Most of the larger libraries (public and university) have excellent map collections. Superb maps can be found in the many historic and archive collections throughout the state; for example, the Historic New Orleans Collection in that city's French quarter

includes the Bouligny Family Papers and the d'Auberville-Bouligny Family Papers, which document life during both the French and Spanish colonial regimes in Louisiana and have an extensive cartographic collection numbering more than 400 items.

Maps created during Louisiana's changing regimes, by Spanish, French, and American sovereignty give information beyond that obtained from documents and books: the Pierre Clement de Laussat Papers and the Claude Perrin Victor Papers are good examples. Maps of the antebellum era reveal the settlement of population and the growth of transportation systems throughout the state. The Vieux Carré Survey describes each property in the French Quarter of New Orleans, including drawings, photographs, and a chain of title to property. These also are a part of the Historic New Orleans Collection, one of many repositories in Louisiana.

The State Land Office located in the State Land and Natural Resources Building in Baton Rouge has all of the original and official field notes, survey plats, and maps made by early U.S. surveyors in Louisiana. Plat maps (showing ownership) can also be found in each parish, in the clerk of courts office located in the parish courthouse. An important new book chronicling Louisiana maps is:

Lemmon, Alfred E. *Charting Louisiana: Five Hundred Years of Maps.* New Orleans: Historic New Orleans Collection, 2003.

Land Records

Public-Domain State

One of the most fantastic real estate deals of all time was made in 1803 when the infant United States acquired 544 million acres from France for the sum of $15 million. The land of the famous Louisiana Purchase was bought for approximately three cents per acre.

By the Act of March 26, 1804, Congress divided Louisiana into two parts: the territory of Louisiana and the territory of Orleans. The territory of Louisiana consisted of that area above the 33rd degree latitude, and the territory of Orleans covered that part below the 33rd latitude, or what is now essentially the state of Louisiana.

The governor and his legislative council used the powers granted by the act to divide the territory of Orleans into twelve counties: Acadia, Attakapas, Concordia, German Coast, Iberville, Lafourche, Natchitoches, Opelousas, Orleans, Ouachita, Pointe Coupee, and Rapides.

In 1807 the territory was redivided into nineteen parishes. These boundaries followed the old ecclesiastical boundaries used by the Spaniards. When Louisiana became a state in 1812 the state constitution referred to both counties and parishes. By the

time of the 1845 state constitution the term "counties" had been dropped and Louisiana became the only state to use the term "parishes."

An act of congress of 2 March 1805 gave three important provisions:

First, it allowed individuals to obtain legal possession of their land or to acquire land. Congress appointed district land registers and opened the United States District Land Office in New Orleans for the eastern division of the territory of Orleans and a land office at Opelousas for the western division of the territory of Orleans. Later, for the convenience of inhabitants, other land offices were opened in Ouachita, Natchitoches, and Greensburg. These land districts are still used today for identifying land by districts.

Second, inhabitants with French, Spanish, or British land grants had to appear before a board of commissioners with their proof of ownership. If approved by the board, the evidence was then forwarded on to Washington, D.C.

Third, surveyors were to go to the territory of Orleans to establish a system of subdividing the vacant public lands. By 1807 the United States surveyors had established a meridian and base line. Thus Louisiana land measurements changed from metes and bounds to section, township, and range.

Colonial grants can be found in various Louisiana parishes and in France, Spain, and England. As has been shown, after the Louisiana Purchase people had to prove their landownership. *American State Papers: Documents Legislative and Executive of the United States,* 32 vols., *Public Lands,* 7 vols. (Washington, D.C.: Gales and Seaton, 1832–61) is the best source for these re-patented lands. A guide to these papers is Phillip W. McMullin, *Grassroots of America* (Salt Lake City: Gendex Corp., 1972).

The state land office and the offices of clerks of courts in the parish courthouses have state and federal tract books listing the original landowners. These books are not in alphabetical order; the land record itself will have to be obtained from the State Land Office in Baton Rouge or from the National Archives Division, Bureau of Land Management, Suitland, MD 20409 (see page 12). The Louisiana State Land Office provides an online brochure by Ory G. Poret, "History of Land Titles in the State of Louisiana" at <www.state.la.us/slo/default.htm>.

Land records may be found in notarial records or deeds. Each of the early communities had its own notary public that drafted wills, deeds, marriage contracts, and all estate papers. These transactions were filed loosely, and numbered consecutively as they happened, regardless of the type of record. Many of these records are now in the clerk's office in the parish courthouse, some are in the state archives in Baton Rouge, and the Notarial Archives of New Orleans are in the Civil Courts Building in New Orleans. Other land records in the courthouses will be found in the conveyance books.

Probate (Succession) Records

The succession record of Louisiana is much like the probate file of other states; if a will exists, which is rare in early Louisiana, it is filed with the succession. This is indeed a rich source for genealogists. The family meeting is one of the most important documents found in a succession. These are meetings held by family members and friends to discuss the estate and the fate of the minor heirs (should there be any). They name each person attending, give their relationship to the deceased and the minors, and give the ages of the children. If there are married daughters, they give the names of their husbands, and the name of the widow and any former spouses with their maiden names. Other documents found in a succession are notes owed the deceased by others, an inventory of all property and movables, a complete listing of all heirs (with maiden names of the females and spouses of the married daughters), ages of all minor heirs, date of death of the deceased, appraisal of all property, and a listing of the disbursement of said property.

If the heirs of the deceased are not known, the succession is called a "vacant succession." The testimonies of acquaintances either identify the missing heirs or state that there are none. If there are heirs then the succession is left open until they are located. In this case the ancestral data compiled can be overwhelming. Succession records for many Louisiana parishes have been microfilmed by the Genealogical Society of Utah and are available on microfilm at the Family History Library (FHL) in Salt Lake City.

Court Records

Under the French regime provincial power was held by the governor and the superior council, while the *cabildo*, or council, served the Spanish. A group of men was appointed to serve on the council who acted in a manner similar to a court of law but did not have the power of legislature. Most of the records created by, or sent to, the *cabildo* are still in New Orleans and are part of four collections:

Superior Council Records. Housed at the Mint Building in New Orleans, this collection, from the French period, is an important resource for families in all corners of the colony. The files contain not only the judicial records of the city of New Orleans, but also those of all the outposts whose cases were appealed to New Orleans. Translated and very brief abstracts of these records were serialized in volumes 1-23 of the *Louisiana Historical Quarterly*.

Spanish Judicial Archives. This is a group of legal suits prosecuted at the various settlements and sent to New Orleans for final disposition in the Spanish era. These records are located in the Louisiana State Museum in the Old U.S. Mint Building

at New Orleans. Between 1923 and 1949, translated abstracts of these records were published in the *Louisiana Historical Quarterly*.

Black Boxes. This is another Spanish collection housed at the Louisiana State Museum. Americans acquired these documents in 1803 and packed them away in black wooden boxes, hence the name. The museum has translated abstracts to these records, and a guide to this collection was printed over several years in the quarterly *New Orleans Genesis*.

Minutes of the Cabildo. These are the records created by the Spanish governing body. Translations of these documents are available at most major libraries (public and university) in Louisiana. Some of the original records belonging to this collection can be found at the New Orleans Public Library, Tulane University, and Louisiana State University.

For a better understanding of the court system and its laws of the nineteenth and twentieth centuries, see Albert Tate Jr., "The Splendid Mystery of the Civil Code of Louisiana," *Louisiana Review* 2, no. 2 (1974). See also Coleman Lindsey, *The Courts of Louisiana* (n.p., n.d.). To conduct genealogical research in the parish courthouse, it is necessary to know that the clerk of court's office has most of the records needed: notarial, marriage, divorce, will, succession, deeds, civil suits, discharge papers, and so on.

Tax Records

Tax records are a valuable but little-used source. Almost everything was taxed: household and personal goods, livestock, slaves, and property. Tax lists can be used as a substitute census, to create complete neighborhoods for a neighborhood study, establish relationships, locate land, and so on. Unfortunately, most of these lists no longer exist in Louisiana, but those that are extant are usually found in the tax assessor's office in the parish courthouse.

Cemetery Records

The recording of cemetery inscriptions in Louisiana has long been a project of the Daughters of the American Revolution (DAR) and numerous genealogical societies. See Lela Cullon, *Louisiana Tombstone Inscriptions*, 11 vols. (Baton Rouge: Louisiana DAR, 1957–60). Genealogical publications continually print these inscriptions in their issues. Card indexes exist for some New Orleans cemeteries and can be found at the Louisiana State Museum Library (see Archives, Libraries, and Societies) or on microfilm at FHL.

Church Records

As previously stated, the Roman Catholic Church was the only church in Louisiana until the 1803 Louisiana Purchase. Historian James D. Hardy Jr. wrote that colonial Louisianians had to "be baptized, married and have their children baptized, and be buried as Catholics. A marriage performed anywhere but a Catholic Church was invalid, and the parties were living in sin. Their children were illegitimate...and their [marriage] contracts were unenforceable at law. Babies not given baptism were not people, and their births were unrecorded" (quoted in Winston DeVille, *Gulf Coasts Colonials* [Baltimore: Genealogical Publishing Co., 1968], page 11).

New recording requirements of the Catholic Church in the early nineteenth century created a virtual goldmine of genealogical data. Not only did the priest list the name or names of the persons involved and their parents, but he now named both sets of grandparents, place of nativity of each, and, as always, the maiden names of the females. Many church records still exist from both the French and the Spanish eras. Those of genealogical value are parish church registers and the bishops' records. Under the French, colonial Louisiana was part of the Diocese of Quebec. During the Spanish period the Diocese of Havana served Louisiana until 1793. At this time the Diocese of Louisiana and the Floridas was founded, with New Orleans as its see. For most of the colonial period the genealogist need not be concerned with the bishop's records; but between 1793 and 1803 this changed, and very valuable information can be found for this decade. One of the main sets of records within the bishop's files is the dispensations. These are mostly marital dispensations that ask for the church's permission to marry even though some impediment existed, for example, if the couple were first or second cousins or if one of the intended was not of the Catholic faith. Many Catholic Church registers have been translated and abstracted. Researchers should note that the abstracts for the registers are not always complete or accurate. See particularly:

Archdiocese of New Orleans. *Sacramental Records of the Roman Catholic Church of the Archdiocese of New Orleans.* Vol. 1, 1718–1750. Vol. 2, 1751–1771. Vol. 3, 1772–1783. Vol. 4, 1784–1790. Vol. 5, 1791–1795. Vol. 6, 1796–1799. Vol. 7, 1800–1803. Vol. 8, 1804–1806. Vol. 9, 1807–1809. Vol. 10, 1810–1812. Vol. 11, 1813–1815. Vol. 12, 1816–1817. Vol. 13, 1818–1819. Vol. 14, 1820–1821. Vol. 15, 1822–1823. Vol. 16, 1824–1825. Vol. 17, 1828–1829. Vol. 18, 1826–1827. Vol. 19, 1830–1831. New Orleans: Archdiocese of New Orleans, 1987-2003. These books may be ordered online at <www.archdiocese-no.org/archives/page5.htm>.

Diocese of Baton Rouge. *Catholic Church Records.* Vol. 1a revised. *Acadian Records, 1707–1749.* Vol. 1b revised, 1722–1769. Vol. 2, 1770–1802. Vol. 3, 1804–1819. Vol. 4, 1820–1829. Vol. 5, 1830–1839. Vol. 6, 1840–1847, Vol. 7, 1848–1852. Vol. 8, 1853–1857. Vol. 9, 1858–1862. Vol. 10, 1863–1867. Vol. 11, 1868–1870. Vol 12, 1871–1873. Vol. 13, 1874–1876. Vol. 14, 1877–1879. Vol. 15, 1880–1882. Vol. 16, *1883 Census Tables for the French Colony of Louisiana, 1699–1732–1885.* Vol. 17, *1886–1888.* Vol. 18, *1889–1891.* Vol. 19, *1892–1894.* Vol. 20, *1895–1896.* Baton Rouge: Diocese of Baton Rouge, 1978–2003. These books may be ordered online at <www.diobr.org/departments/Archives/published_sacramental_records.htm>.

Hébert, Donald. *South Louisiana Records.* Vol. 1, 1794–1840. Vol. 2, 1841–1850. Vol. 3, 1851–1860. Vol. 4, 1861–1870. Vol. 5, 1871–1875. Vol. 6, 1876–1880. Vol. 7, 1881–1885. Vol. 8, 1886–1890. Vol. 9, 1891–1895. Vol. 10, 1896–1899. Vol. 11, 1900–1903. Vol. 12, 1904–1920. Rayne, La.: Hébert Publications, 1978–85. These books may be ordered online at <www.hebertpublications.com/default.htm>.

Hébert, Donald. *Southwest Louisiana Records.* Vol. 1A, 1750–1800. Vol. 1B, 1801–1810. Vol. 2A, 1811–1818. Vol. 2B, 1819–1825. Vol. 2C, 1826–1830. Vol. 3, 1831–1840. Vol. 4, 1841–1847. Vol. 5, 1848–1854. Vol. 6, 1855–1860. Vol. 7, 1861–1865. Vol. 8, 1866–1868. Vol. 9, 1869–1870. Vol. 10, 1871–1872. Vol. 11, 1873–1874. Vol. 12, 1875–1876. Vol. 13, 1877–1878. Vol. 14, 1879–1880. Vol. 15, 1881–1882. Vol. 16, 1883–1884. Vol.17, 1885–1886. Vol. 18, 1887. Vol. 19, 1888. Vol. 20, 1889. Vol. 21, 1890. Vol. 22, 1891. Vol. 23, 1892. Vol. 24, 1893. Vol. 25, 1894. Vol. 26, 1895. Vol. 27, 1896. Vol. 28, 1897. Vol. 29, 1898. Vol. 30, 1899. Vol. 31, 1900. Vol. 32, 1901–1902. Vol. 33, 1903–1953. Vol. 34, 1901–1902. Vol. 35, 1903. Vol. 36, 1904. Vol. 37, 1905. Vol. 38, 1906. Vol. 39, 1907. Vol. 40, 1908. Vol. 41. 1909. Vol. 42, 1910. Vol. 43, 1911. Vol. 44, 1912. Vol. 45, 1913. Vol. 46, 1914. Vol. 47, 1915. Rayne, La.: Hébert Publications, 1976–2003. These books may be ordered online at <www.hebertpublications.com/default.htm>.

Mills, Elizabeth Shown. *Natchitoches, 1729–1803. Abstracts of the Catholic Church Registers of the French and Spanish Post of St. Jean Baptiste des Natchitoches in Louisiana.* Vol. 2. Cane River Creole Series. New Orleans: Polyanthos, 1977.

———. *Natchitoches, 1800–1826. Translated Abstracts of Register Number Five of the Catholic Church, Parish of St. François des Natchitoches in Louisiana.* Vol. 4. Cane River Creole Series. New Orleans: Polyanthos, 1980.

Two important guides to Catholic Church records are:

Hébert, Donald. *Guide to Church Records in Louisiana, 1720–1975.* Rayne, La.: Hébert Publications, 1975.

Nolan, Charles E. *A Southern Catholic Heritage.* Vol. 1, *1704–1813.* New Orleans: Archdiocese of New Orleans, 1976.

Military Records

Many military records exist for Louisiana soldiers. For the colonial period a valuable collection is at the General Military Archives, Segovia, Spain. This voluminous archives has service records on all soldiers of the Spanish military from 1680 to 1920, listing much genealogical data, such as the soldier's name, rank, sometimes a description, the names of his parents, and other information.

Two compiled lists of Louisiana soldiers serving in the American Revolution are these:

Churchill, E. Robert, comp., *Soldiers of the American Revolution under Bernardo De Galvez*. Five copies of this book were originally printed: one was placed in the Sons of the American Revolution Library housed in the Howard-Tilton Library at Tulane University, Louisiana; one was deposited in the DAR Library in Washington, D.C.; a third copy can be found in the Library of Congress.

Mills, Elizabeth Shown. *Natchitoches Colonials: Censuses, Military Rolls, and Tax Lists, 1722–1803*. Tuscaloosa, Ala.: Mills Historical Press, 1981.

The National Archives has many original military records for Louisiana, many of which have been microfilmed, for example: War of 1812–M229, 3 rolls; Florida War of 1836–M239; War of 1836–38–M241; Confederate War Index–M378, 31 rolls; Military Service Records–M320, 414 rolls. See also:

Mills, Gary B. *Civil War Claims*. Vol. 1. *An Index to Cases Filed with the Southern Claims Commission*. Laguna Hills, Calif.: Aegean Park Press, 1980.

Confederate Pensions were first issued to Confederate veterans and their widows by the State of Louisiana in 1898. The Louisiana State Archives (see Archives, Libraries, and Societies) has the original and microfilmed applications. Researchers can search an online index to the applications and can request photocopies by mail at <www.sec.state.la.us/archives/gen/cpa-index.htm>.

Periodicals, Newspapers, and Manuscript Collections

Periodicals

Many periodicals and quarterlies have been printed through the years, for example: *The Louisiana Genealogical Register* (compiled and published by the state genealogical society), *The New Orleans Genesis*, the *Natchitoches Genealogist*, and others.

Newspapers

The earliest known Louisiana newspaper was *Le Moniteur*, published in New Orleans, but only a few issues still exist.

Numerous guides have been compiled to Louisiana newspapers. See, for instance:

McMullan, Theodore N. *Louisiana Newspapers, 1794–1961*. Baton Rouge: Louisiana State University Library, 1965.

Louisiana State University created the Louisiana Newspaper Project, which first catalogued and then microfilmed extant Louisiana newspapers. These microfilms are available in the LSU Libraries (Middleton and Hill Memorial libraries) and other libraries throughout the state. Some libraries will loan the film through Interlibrary Loan. For more information see the Louisiana Newspaper Project website at <www.lib.lsu.edu/special/frames/llmvc.html>.

Manuscripts

The manuscript collections of the large libraries, college and university libraries, and archives throughout the state are numerous. Most of these institutions have guides to their holdings. See listings for these institutions below.

Archives, Libraries, and Societies

State of Louisiana Division of Archives
Records Management, and History
3851 Essen Lane
P.O. Box 94125
Baton Rouge, LA 70804
www.sec.state.la.us/archives/archives/archives-index.htm

The Archives Research Library provides public access to books on the history of Louisiana as well as Louisiana vital records, NARA microfilms of the federal census for Louisiana and passenger manifests for the Port of New Orleans, Confederate Pension Applications for Louisiana, military service records, assessment records, and records from the State Land Office and colonial documents.

State Library of Louisiana
Louisiana Section
701 N. Fourth St.
Baton Rouge, LA 70802
www.state.lib.la.us/Dept/LaSect/index.htm

The Louisiana Section of the Louisiana State Library includes a complete historical collection of Louisiana State Documents, historical photographs, genealogical and historical books, telephone books and city directories, major Louisiana newspapers on microfilm and maps.

Louisiana State University
Hill Memorial Library
Baton Rouge, LA 70803-3300
www.lib.lsu.edu/special

Hill Memorial Library houses the Special Collections and University Archives of Louisiana State University. The Louisiana and Lower Mississippi Valley Collections include books, periodicals, maps, prints, pamphlets, Louisiana state documents, and microfilm of Louisiana newspapers.

Tulane University
Special Collections of Howard-Tilton Memorial Library
Jones Hall
New Orleans, LA 70118
http://specialcollections.tulane.edu

Tulane University Libraries' Special Collections Departments include the University Archives, the Hogan Jazz Archive, and the Rare Books collection. Of special interest to genealogists are the Louisiana Collection, the Southeastern Architectural Archive, which documents the architectural and urban history of New Orleans from 1830 to the present, and Manuscripts Department, with notable collections on the Civil War, Jewish Studies, women, medicine, politics, Carnival, waterways, and literature.

Williams Research Center
of the Historic New Orleans Collection
410 Chartres St.
New Orleans, LA 70130
www.hnoc.org

The Williams Research Center provides access to scholarly collections focusing on New Orleans, Louisiana, and the Gulf South.

New Orleans Public Library
City Archives and Louisiana Division Special Collections
Main Library
219 Loyola Ave.
New Orleans, LA 70112
http://nutrias.org/~nopl/spec/speclist.htm

The Louisiana Division houses the New Orleans City Archives (1769-present), the records of the Orleans Parish civil courts (1804–1926) and criminal courts (1830–1931), and manuscripts collections, including the Louisiana Photograph Collection, the Carnival Collection, the Map Collection, the Menu Collection, the Rare Vertical File, and the Rare Book Collection.

Louisiana State Museum
The Historical Center, Old U.S. Mint
400 Esplanade Ave.
New Orleans, LA 70116
http://lsm.crt.state.la.us/site/mintex.htm

The Historical Center houses maps and documents of early French and Spanish colonial records. Researchers must make appointments to use these resources.

The New Orleans Notarial Archives Research Center
1340 Poydras St., Ste. 360
New Orleans, LA 70112
www.notarialarchives.org

Because Louisiana law is based on Napoleonic (Civil) Law, the notary held a prominent role Louisiana society, preparing property transactions, loans, wills, marriage contracts, partnerships, building contracts, adoptions, probates, and so on. By law, notaries were required to maintain an archive of the records they created and provide for their maintenance after their death. In 1867, the Louisiana Legislature created a central repository, the Office of the Custodian of Notarial Records for the Parish of Orleans. The records of New Orleans notaries include property transactions from the French period (1731–58), Spanish period (1768–1803), and American period. Because families often used the same notary through multiple generations, the notarial records can be a rich source for those researching in New Orleans.

Louisiana Genealogical and Historical Society
P.O. Box 3454
Baton Rouge, LA 70821
www.rootsweb.com/~la-lghs

As the state genealogical society, in addition to publishing *The Louisiana Genealogical Register*, it holds an all-day seminar every April. It has no permanent headquarters.

In addition to the major repositories listed above, researchers should take note of the collections available at the following academic libraries:

University of New Orleans Lakefront Campus
Louisiana & Special Collections Department
Earl K. Long Library
New Orleans, LA 70148
http://library.uno.edu/bysubject/laspecoll.html

University of Louisiana at Lafayette
Center for Louisiana Studies
P.O. Box 40831
Lafayette, LA 70504
www.louisiana.edu/Academic/LiberalArts/CLS

Northwestern State University
The Cammie G. Henry Research Center
Watson Memorial Library
913 College Ave.
Natchitoches, LA 71497
www.nsula.edu/watson_library/CGHRC.HTM

Louisiana Tech University
Prescott Memorial Library
Special Collections, Manuscripts, and Archives
Ruston, LA 71272-0046
www.latech.edu/tech/library/gscmaint.htm

Nicholls State University
Ellender Memorial Library
Archives and Special Collections
P.O. Box 2028
Thibodaux, LA 70310
http://server.nicholls.edu/library

Southeastern Louisiana University
Linus A. Sims Memorial Library
Center for Southeast Louisiana Studies
SLU 10730
Hammond, LA 70402
www.selu.edu/Academics/Depts/RegionalStudies

Those researching in New Orleans should be aware of the extensive archival collections available not listed above. The Greater New Orleans Archivists have provided this online listing of archival repositories <http://nutrias.org/gnoa/norepos.htm>.

Special Focus Categories

Immigration

New Orleans served as a major immigration port until the Civil War. Many nineteenth-century European immigrants traveled to New Orleans and then continued up the Mississippi River to settle in the Midwest.

Passenger lists for New Orleans have been microfilmed by the NARA for the years 1820–1902 (series M259; 1820–50 included on Gulf Coast Ports Index, series M334 [NARA site says 1820-74, not 1850]; 1853–99 indexed on series T527), 1900–45 (series T905 [series says 1910–45]; 1900–52 indexed on series T618). Researchers should be aware that the indexes are not complete, and that many passengers whose names appear on the manifests are not found in the microfilmed indexes. It also appears that some manifests were lost before the lists were microfilmed. The Works Projects Administration (WPA) transcribed passenger manifests for the years 1813–70. All seven volumes are available at the Louisiana State Museum Historical Center in New Orleans. Volumes 1-4 and 6 are available at the NARA in Washington, D.C. Volumes 1-3 are microfilmed on NARA series M2009. Quarterly Abstracts and State Department Abstracts for some years are also available on National Archives microfilm.

The New Orleans Public Library has microfilm of nineteenth-century ship passenger lists. Glen Conrad published most of those for the French period as *First Families of Louisiana*, 2 vols. (Baton Rouge: Claitor Publishing Co., 1970). A publication covering some of the lists from the middle period of the colonial era was done by Winston DeVille, *Louisiana Recruits, 1752–1758* (New Orleans: Polyanthos, 1973).

African American

An impressive array of primary source materials exists, in addition to the census materials cited above, in both parish offices and at the Louisiana State University collections in Baton Rouge (see page 15 for information on *Black Genesis* for a partial listing). In addition, a major ethnic group in Louisiana, the *Creoles de couleur*, have a unique place in its history. See Gary B. Mills, *The Forgotten People: Cane River's Creoles of Color* (Baton Rouge, Louisiana State University Press, 1977).

The Amistad Research Center, located in the Howard-Tilton Memorial Library of Tulane University, provides resources on the African Diaspora, human relations, and civil rights. See <www.tulane.edu/~amistad>.

The New Orleans Public Library has an online guide to African-American genealogy sources in its Louisiana Division at <http://nutrias.org/~nopl/guides/black.htm>.

The library also has an African American Resource Center, separate from the City Archives and Louisiana Division Special Collections at <http://nutrias.org/~nopl/info/aarcinfo/aarcinfo.htm>.

Native American

Native peoples occupied Louisiana long before the first white explorers arrived. Many tribes have resided within and roamed across the state throughout the years. Louisiana's present Native American population includes Choctaw, Chitimacha, Tunica-Biloxi, Houma, and Coushatta. Many records in Louisiana, both church and civil, have recorded native inhabitants by their ethnic designation.

See pages 15-16 and U.S. Court of Claims, *No. 12742: The Choctaw Nation of Indians v. The United States* (Washington, D.C.: n.p., ca. 1895).

Parish Resources

Parishes, not counties, are the political jurisdictions for recording marriage and court records in Louisiana as well as land (termed conveyances), and probate (termed successions). Parish clerks hold the majority of these records, while some cities have these functions divided among register of conveyances and district court clerks. The Genealogical Society of Utah has filmed court, property, notarial, probate, tax, and vital records for many Louisiana parishes, which are available through the FHL. The Louisiana Section of the State Library of Louisiana has some of the information on parish formation.

As of July 1999, birth certificates are available through the State Office of Vital Records and Parish Clerks of Court. Contact information for the Parish Clerks of Court is available at <www.sos.Louisiana.gov/admin/admin-births.htm>. Land, probate, court, and other vital records may also be found at different addresses than those shown in the following table (see Archives, Libraries, and Societies).

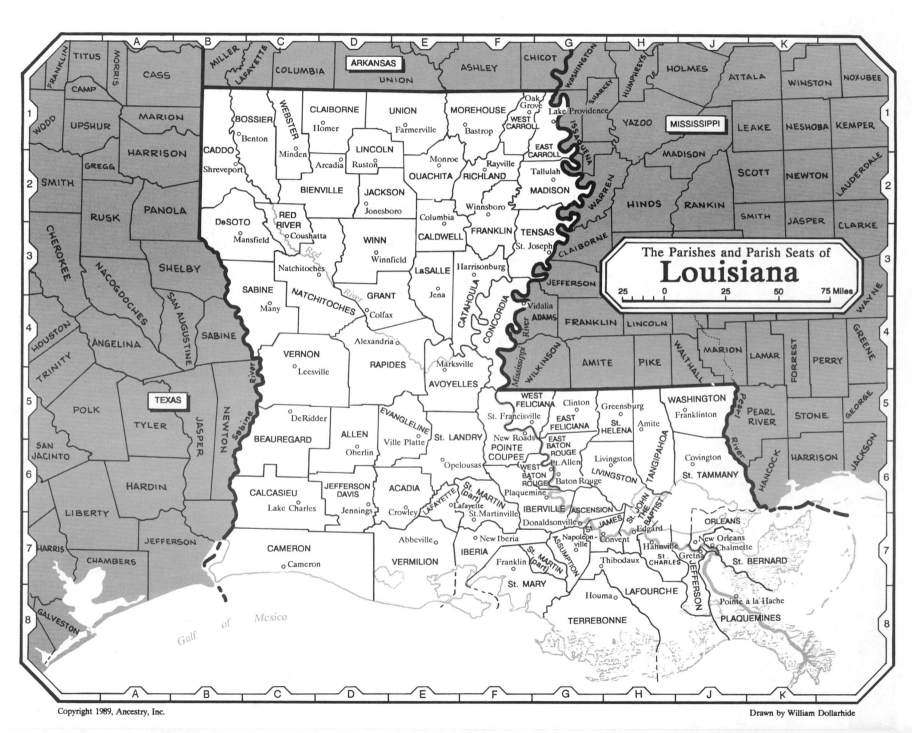

The Parishes and Parish Seats of
Louisiana

25 0 25 50 75 Miles

LOUISIANA

Drawn by William Dollarhide

Map	County / Address	Date Formed / Parent County/ies	Birth Marriage Death	Land Probate Court
F4	Acadia	1886	—	1886
	Courthouse Cir.	St. Landry	1886	1886
	Crowley 70527		—	1886
D5	Allen	1912	—	1886
	400 W. Sixth Ave.	Calcasieu	1913	1913
	Oberlin 70655		—	1913
G6	Ascension	1807	—	1770
	300 Houmas St.	St. James	1763	1800
	Donaldsville 70346		—	1800
G7	Assumption	1807	—	1788
	4809 Louisiana Hwy. 1	original	1800	1788
	Napoleonville 70390		—	1788
F4	Avoyelles	1807	—	1808
	301 N. Main St.	original	1808	1856
	Marksville 71351	(reorganized 1873)	—	1856
	Baton Rouge	(see East Baton Rouge and West Baton Rouge)		
C5	Beauregard	1913	—	1913
	214 W. First St.	Calcasieu	1913	1913
	DeRidder 70634		—	1913
C2	Bienville	1848	—	1848
	100 Courthouse Dr.	Claiborne	1848	1848
	Arcadia 71001			1848
C1	Bossier	1843	—	1843
	204 Burt Blvd.	Claiborne	1843	1843
	Benton 71006			1843
B1	Caddo	1838	—	1835
	501 Texas St.	Natchitoches	1835	1835
	Shreveport 71163-1127			1835
C6	Calcasieu	1840	—	1910
	1000 Ryan St.	St. Landry	1910	1910
	Lake Charles 70601		—	1910
E2	Caldwell	1838	—	1838
	200 Main St.	Catahoula/Ouachita	1838	1838
	Columbia 71418-1737			1838
C7	Cameron	1870	—	1870
	119 Smith Cir.	Calcasieu/Vermillion	1870	1870
	Cameron 70631			1870
	Carroll	1832		
		Ouachita/Concordia		
	Divided into East Carroll and West Carroll			
F3	Catahoula	1808	—	1900s
	301 Bushley St.	Harrisonburg	1900s	1900s
	Harrisonburg 71340		—	1900s
D1	Claiborne	1828	—	1850
	512 Main St.	Natchitoches	1850	1850
	Homer 71040		—	1850
	Record loss, 1949.			
F4	Concordia	1805	—	1850
	4001 Carter St.	Avoyelles	1840	1850
	Vidalia 71373		—	1850
B2	De Soto	1843	—	1843
	210 Texas St.	Natchitoches/Caddo	1843	1843
	Mansfield 71052-0038		—	1843
G6	East Baton Rouge	1810	—	1782
	222 St. Louis St.	original	1840	1782
	Baton Rouge 70821		—	1782
G1	East Carroll	1877	—	1832
	400 First St.	Carroll	1832	1832
	Lake Providence 71254		—	1832
G5	East Feliciana	1824	—	1824
	12305 St. Helena St.	Feliciana	1824	1824
	Clinton 70722		—	1824
E5	Evangeline	1911	—	1911
	200 Court St.	St. Landry	1911	1911
	Ville Platte 70586		—	1911
	Feliciana	1810		
		original (from Spanish West Florida)		
	Divided into East Feliciana and West Feliciana, 1824.			
F2	Franklin	1843	—	1843
	6500 Main St.	Catahoula/Ouachita/Madison	1843	1843
	Winnsboro 71295		—	1843
D3	Grant	1869	—	1880
	200 Main St.	Rapides/Winn	1880	1880
	Colfax 71417		—	1880
F7	Iberia	1868	—	1868
	300 Iberia St.	St. Martin/St. Mary	1868	1868
	New Iberia 70562		—	1868
G7	Iberville	1807	—	1770
	58050 Meriam St.	Assumption/Ascension	1770	1807
	Plaquemine 70765		—	1807
D2	Jackson	1845	—	1880
	500 E. Court St.	Claiborne/Ouachita/Union	1880	1880
	Jonesboro 71251		—	1880
J7	Jefferson	1825	—	1825
	200 Derbigny St.	Orleans	1825	1825
	Gretna 70054		—	1825
D6	Jefferson Davis	1913	—	1913
	300 State St.	Calcasieu	1913	1913
	Jennings 70546		—	1913
E6	Lafayette	1823	—	1823
	800 S. Buchanan St.	St. Martin	1823	1823
	Lafayette 70501			1823
H8	Lafourche	1807	—	1808
	303 W. 3rd St.	original	1808	1808
	Thibodaux 70301		—	1808
E3	LaSalle	1910	—	1910
	1050 Courthouse St.	Catahoula	1910	1910
	Jena 71342		—	1910
D1	Lincoln	1873	—	1873
	100 W. Texas Ave.	Bienville/Jackson/	1873	1873
	Ruston 71270	Union/Claiborne	—	1873

Map County Address	Date Formed Parent County/ies	Birth Marriage Death	Land Probate Court
H6 Livingston 20180 Iowa St. Livingston 70754	1832 St. Helena	—— 1875 ——	1875 1875 1875
G2 Madison 100 N. Cedar St. Tallulah 71282	1838 Concordia	—— 1866 ——	1839 1850 1882
F1 Morehouse 100 E. Madison St. Bastrop 71221	1844 Ouachita	—— 1870 ——	1844 1870 1870
C3 Natchitoches 200 Church St. Natchitoches 71457	1807 original	—— 1729 ——	1732 1732 1732
J7 Orleans 421 Loyola Ave. New Orleans 70112	1807 original	—— 1718 ——	1832 1805 1805
E2 Ouachita 300 St. John St. Monroe 71210	1807 original	—— 1805 ——	1805 1805 1805
K8 Plaquemines Pointe a la Hache 70082	1807 original	—— 1807 ——	1807 1807 1807
F5 Pointe Coupee 201 E. Main St. New Roads 70760-0290	1807 original	—— 1735 ——	1780 1780 1780
D4 Rapides 700 Murray St. Alexandria 71309	1807 original	—— 1864 ——	1864 1864 1864
C2 Red River 615 E. Carroll St. Coushatta 71019	1871 Caddo/Bossier/ Bienville/DeSoto/ Natchitoches	—— 1871 ——	1871 1871 1904
F2 Richland 100 Julia St. Rayville 71269	1869 Ouachita/Carroll/ Franklin/Morehouse	—— 1869 ——	1869 1869 1869
C3 Sabine 400 S. Capitol St. Many 71449	1843 Natchitoches	—— 1843 ——	1843 1843 1843
K7 St. Bernard 1100 W. St. Bernard Hwy. Chalmette 70044	1807 original	—— 1800s ——	1800s 1800s 1800s
H7 St. Charles 15045 River Rd. Hahnville 70057	1807 original	—— 1739 ——	1734 1734 1734
H5 St. Helena 369 Sitman St. Greensburg 70441	1810 original	—— 1804 ——	1804 1804 1804
G7 St. James 5800 Hwy. 44 Convent 70723	1807 original	—— 1846 ——	1809 1809 1809
H6 St. John the Baptist 2393 Hwy. 18 Edgard 70049	1807 original	—— 1772 ——	1770s 1770s 1770s
E5 St. Landry 118 S. Court St. Opelousas 70570	1807 original	—— 1756 ——	1760s 1760s 1760s
F6 St. Martin 415 S. Main St. St. Martinville 70582	1807 original	—— 1756 ——	1760 1700s 1800s
F8 St. Mary 500 Main St. Franklin 70538	1811 Assumption	—— 1800 ——	1800 1800 1800
J6 St. Tammany 701 N. Columbia St. Covington 70433	1810 St. Helena/Orleans	—— 1812 ——	1810 1812 1812
H6 Tangipahoa 100 N. Bay St. Amite 70422	1869 Livingston/St. Tammany/ St. Helena/Washington	—— 1869 ——	1869 1869 1869
G2 Tensas Courthouse Sq. Hancock St. St. Joseph 71366	1843 Concordia	—— 1843 ——	1843 1843 1843
G8 Terrebonne 7856 Main St. Houma 70361	1822 La Fourche	—— 1820 ——	1820 1820 1820
E1 Union 100 E. Bayou St. Farmerville 71241	1839 Ouachita	—— 1839 ——	1839 1839 1839
E7 Vermillion 100 N. State St. Abbeville 70510	1844 Lafayette	—— 1885 ——	1885 1885 1885
C4 Vernon 201 S. Fourth St. Leesville 71496	1871 Nachitoches/Rapides/Sabine	—— 1890 ——	1871 1871 1871
J5 Washington Washington at Main St. Franklinton 70438	1819 St. Tammany	—— 1897 ——	1897 1897 1897
C1 Webster 410 Main St. Minden 71058	1871 Claiborne/Bossier/Bienville	—— 1871 ——	1871 1871 1871
G6 West Baton Rouge 850 Eighth St. Port Allen 70767	1807 Baton Rouge	—— 1793 ——	1800s 1800s 1800s
F1 West Carroll 305 E. Main St. Oak Grove 71263	1877 Carroll	—— 1877 ——	1833 1850 1898
F5 West Feliciana 4789 Prosperity St. St. Francisville 70775	1824 Feliciana	—— 1879 ——	1811 1900 1900
D3 Winn 119 W. Main St. Winnfield 71483	1851 Natchitoches/Rapides/ Catchoula	—— 1886 ——	1886 1886 1886

Maine

ALICE EICHHOLZ, Ph.D., CG

Maine, geographically the largest New England state, for nearly half of its history was part of Massachusetts. The region, which first came to be known as the Province of Maine, was granted to Sir Ferdinando Gorges and Capt. John Mason in 1622. Wealthy merchants began the first settlements, followed by religious dissenters who moved from Massachusetts and New Hampshire to what is still referred to as "Downeast." Attempts by the Massachusetts Bay Colony to expand its boundaries into Maine began by the 1640s. Absorption of the province by Massachusetts was completed in the following decade, although the official purchase from an heir of Gorges was not made until 1677. In the seventeenth century, Puritan settlers in the former Province of Maine were often forced to retreat back to Massachusetts Bay Colony settlements because of conflict with Native Americans, the influence of the French, the threat of war, and the different climate. In time, the previously abandoned parts of Maine were eventually resettled, with expansion by the Scots-Irish (1718), Germans at Waldoboro (1740), and, after 1752, French Huguenots, Acadians, French-Canadians, and Irish.

After the American Revolution, settlement was encouraged in hopes of generating revenue to counter the tremendous cost of the war to the new state of Massachusetts. Many people from Massachusetts and New Hampshire, including Revolutionary soldiers, settled in Maine, assumed the land was theirs for the taking, and found themselves in disputes with original proprietors. They came to make use of Maine's natural resources to support their families, found an interior wilderness, and, as did other settlers to the rest of northern New England, a harsh environment. Until statehood was achieved in 1820, Maine was a political part of Massachusetts. Manufacturing, shipbuilding, fishing, and mining all added to considerable economic growth following statehood. By the mid-nineteenth century, a good portion of the state was settled, although some areas still remain sparsely populated today. Following the Civil War, textiles, leather, and lumber industries began to replace family farming, as a reason for migrations to the state, until the textile industry moved south by the end of the century. Emergence of hydroelectric power, agri-business, and tourism all influenced Maine's economy and settlement in the twentieth century. Today Maine attracts new residents and vacationers for its quality of life.

Geographically, Maine is vast and mountainous. The population is concentrated along the coast, with its islands and bays; along the border with New Hampshire; and in the lower third of the state along the Kennebec and Penobscot rivers. More than half of its land mass reaches above New Hampshire's northern latitude and remains chiefly wilderness. Political divisions in Maine are perhaps the most diverse in New England. There are 433 towns, twenty-two cities, thirty-six plantations, three "Indian" voting districts, twelve unorganized but populated townships, and approximately two hundred land divisions unpopulated and identified only by township and range. Border disputes existed with Maine's neighbors to the east and north in Canada. The same piece of land an ancestor lived on might be identified differently because borders, counties, and names changed. Genealogical research in Maine is challenging principally because of the numerous governmental changes affecting the way records have been kept.

Vital Records

Maine has the most uneven group of vital records in all of New England. One reason is that the first settlements were dilatory in recording vital events as was the custom of other Massachusetts communities. Only five towns (Biddeford, Kittery, Kennebunkport, York, and Wells) have such seventeenth-century records. By the eighteenth century, over 200 towns picked up the habit and followed it reasonably well until Maine became a separate state in 1820. Following statehood, records were not consistently kept at first, but most towns have good records of marriage intentions, if not marriage records themselves, and some births. Few deaths are recorded in town records.

After 1864, state legislation required that town clerks forward births, deaths, and marriages to the secretary of state. There was never total compliance to this although all those that were sent *before* 1892 (for about eighty towns) are available at the Maine State Archives (see Archives, Libraries, and Societies).

By 1892, the State Board of Vital Statistics was established by the legislature as the depository for returns of vital events, and mandatory recording became a reality. The Maine State Archives presently holds the original 1892–1922 birth, death, and marriage records. Certified copies of records for that time period can be obtained there. The archives also has the birth, death, and marriage records on microfilm (1922–55) with a helpful bride's index (1892-present), groom's index (1956-present), and death index (1955-present). Certified copies of all vital records after 1922 may be obtained from the Maine Department of Human Services, Office of Data Research and Vital Statistics, 11 State House Station, Augusta, ME 04333 <www.state.me.us/dhs/bohodr/ovrpage.htm>.

A number of other repositories in Maine (see <www.state.me.us/sos/arc/geneology> [sic "geneology"]) hold microfilm copies of the pre-1892 records, as do the Family History Library (FHL) in Salt Lake City and the New England Historic Genealogical Society (see page 13). Online indexes are available for marriages (1892–1996, excluding 1967–76) and deaths (1960–96) on the Maine State Archives website at <www.state.me.us/sos/arc/geneology> and at <www.ancestry.com> (see page 17).

The New England Historic Genealogical Society, additionally, has microfilm copies of some additional reels through 1955, and death records through 1970. The FHL, too, has some microfilm of post-1892 records, but they are not as current as those at the Maine State Archives, which are updated regularly from the Office of Data Research and Vital Statistics files.

Marriages for the early statehood period were sometimes recorded at the county level, as mandated by the legislature in 1828. Such records have not yet been fully assessed, although some are on microfilm at Maine State Archives. The most complete listing of available Maine vital records continues to be the updated Microfilm List of Maine Town and Census Records (1980), distributed by the Maine State Archives. Recently funded by a grant from the National Historic Records Commission, the Maine State Archives will be broadening its scope to survey all of Maine's town records. In the Town Resources section at the end of this chapter, details from the most recent update are included to guide the researcher in finding vital records.

A few of Maine's vital records have been published. A project undertaken by the Maine Historical Society issued printings of all pre-1892 vital records for eighteen towns, which included sources outside the town clerk's office—diaries, church records, newspapers, gravestone information, family records, Bibles, and private records. Transcripts of town records for York 1681–1891 were published serially in *New England Historical and Genealogical Register* (1955–69).

Census Records

Federal

Population Schedules
- Indexed—1790, 1800, 1810, 1820, 1830, 1840, 1850, 1860, 1870, 1880, 1900, 1910, 1920, 1930
- Soundex—1880, 1900, 1920

Industry and Agriculture Schedules
- 1850, 1860, 1870, 1880

Mortality Schedules
- 1850, 1860, 1870, 1880

Union Veterans Schedules
- 1890

Although Maine was part of Massachusetts until the 1820 census, for research purposes the National Archives catalogs the 1790, 1800, and 1810 federal censuses under Maine. The 1800 censuses for some towns in Hancock and Kennebec indicate where the person resided before immigrating to Maine. A date of emigration is given for some people in Kennebec although this was not consistently noted for Hancock. See Walter Goodwin Davis, "Part of Hancock County, Maine, in 1800," *New England Historical and Genealogical Register* 105 (1951): 204-13, 276-91. All of the above census records are at the Maine State Archives on microfilm, and are widely available at other repositories and online through Internet subscription databases (see page 17).

York County is incomplete on the 1800 census, half of Oxford County is missing in 1810, and Houlton Plantation returns are missing for Washington County, 1820.

State

In 1837 a state census enumerating heads of households was taken, but only Bangor, Portland, and unincorporated towns

survive on microfilm at the Maine State Archives. The Maine Historical Society (see Archives, Libraries, and Societies) holds the volume enumerating the town of Eliot.

Background Sources

In addition to the town histories that have been published for Maine, there are other excellent publications as well.

Atwood, Stanley B. *The Length and Breadth of Maine*. 1946. Reprint. Orono, Maine: University of Maine, 1973. The original place-name guide for Maine.

Clark, Charles E. *The Eastern Frontier: The Settlement of Northern New England, 1610–1763*. Hanover, N.H.: University Press of New England, 1987. Focuses primarily on Maine.

———, James S. Leamon, and Karen Bowden, eds. *Maine in the Early Republic*. Hanover, N.H.: University Press of New England, 1989. Essays by twelve local history professors cover the period following the Revolution to statehood in 1820.

Denis, Michael J. *Maine Towns and Counties: What Was What, Where and When*. Oakland, Maine: Danbury House Books, 1981. An indexed, updated survey of place-names.

Frost, John E. *Maine Genealogy: A Bibliographic Guide*. Portland: Maine Historical Society, 1985. A superb listing including printed probate records, maps, town histories, and numerous other sources. Organized by topic with thorough citations to expedite interlibrary loan research.

Haskell, John D. *Maine: A Bibliography of Its History*. 1977. Reprint. Hanover, N.H.: University Press of New England, 1983. Excellent focus on printed and published historical materials.

Noyes, Sybil, Charles T. Davis, and Walter G. Davis. *Genealogical Dictionary of Maine and New Hampshire*. 1928–39. Reprint. Baltimore: Genealogical Publishing Co., 1972, 1976, 1979. An excellent attempt at compiling family genealogies comprising every family established in New Hampshire and Maine by 1699, this is one of the first inclusive volumes with strong references to original source material. The information is available through an online subscription database <www.ancestry.com> (see page 17).

Pope, Charles H. *The Pioneers of Maine and New Hampshire, 1623–1660*. 1908. Reprint. Baltimore: Genealogical Publishing Co., 1973. Focuses on earliest period, not on all families as does Noyes et al. above.

Williamson, William D. *The History of the State of Maine*. 2 vols. Hallowell, Maine: Glazier, Master and Smith, 1839.

A guide to research in the state can be found in John Eldridge Frost, "Maine Genealogy: Some Distinctive Aspects," *The New England Historical and Genealogical Register* 131 (October 1977): 243-66, which includes a list of individual and multifamily genealogies. It is reprinted in Ralph J. Crandall, ed., *Genealogical Research in New England* (Baltimore: Genealogical Publishing Co., 1984).

Maine Families in 1790, vols. 1-8, published by Picton Press in Camden, Maine, between 1988 and 2000, is an ongoing project of the Maine Genealogical Society and several contributors, including Ruth Gray and Joseph C. Anderson II, CG, FASG. The eight volumes cover over 2000 comprehensive three-generation studies of families living in Maine at the time of the 1790 census. See <www. pictonpress.com>.

Maps

One superb map can be extensively used for research and traveling, detailing town divisions, geographical details, road surface types, routes of transportation, and locations of cemeteries. This map is the *Maine Atlas and Gazetteer*, which is published in updated versions by DeLorme Publishing of Freeport, Maine <www. delorme.com>.

A bicentennial project edited by Gerald E. Morris entitled *The Maine Bicentennial Atlas and Historical Survey* (Portland: Maine Historical Society, 1976) is a superb composite of historical maps from the earliest grants and charters to the present. Railroad, lumbering, mining, recreation, population changes, court regions, and election districts illustrate the depth of this resource for genealogical purposes.

Atwood's *Length and Breadth of Maine* (see Background Sources) includes helpful maps of towns. Maine State Archives has a computerized index of its fine map collection for Maine after statehood, but it is the Massachusetts State Archives (see Massachusetts—Archives) that holds the important lotting maps for the pre-statehood development of Maine. Included in many of the maps are location of residences and names of owners.

Saco Valley Publishing, 76 Main St., Fryeburg, ME 04037, has been reprinting excellent county editions of nineteenth-century maps indicating occupants' names for each structure.

Land Records

State-Land State

Maine obtained provincial status in New England under royal grants from England. In 1677 the Massachusetts Bay Colony purchased the area in Maine below the Kennebec River. The area east of the river became part of Massachusetts in 1691. As part of Massachusetts, the process of creating town grants for proprietors followed that of other Massachusetts towns (see Massachusetts—

Land Records). All deeds before 1737 for the settled area in Maine have been transcribed verbatim and published in eighteen volumes entitled *York Deeds, 1642–1737* (Portland, Maine: Maine Historical Society, 1887–1910), available at most major libraries with a collection of New England materials.

Following the Revolution in 1783, under the auspices of the Massachusetts General Court, a Committee for the Sale of Eastern Lands began to survey and sell remaining unorganized portions of the state to help pay for the cost of the war. Land was disposed of in lotteries, tax sales, street grants, patents, and a few war grants. All the original papers for the Eastern Lands are held in the Massachusetts State Archives (see Massachusetts), and there is a limited card index. Additionally, they have been published in *The Maine Historical and Genealogical Recorder*, vols. 4-8. Between 1824 and 1891, the Maine Land Office took over the work of the Massachusetts Committee for the Sale of Eastern Lands and distributed public land after separation from Massachusetts. Records are located at the Maine State Archives and include maps, field notes, and deeds starting with 1794 (as Massachusetts deeds). A brochure entitled "Land Office Records in the Maine State Archives" is available from the archives. Land grant applications from Revolutionary War veterans are also available.

Land transactions are recorded on the county level and are available at the county deed office.

Probate Records

The county seat is where an executor or petitioner would go to commence probate, adoption, or guardianship proceedings. The earliest of Maine's wills have been published in William Sargent's *Maine Wills, 1650–1760* (1887; reprint, Baltimore: Genealogical Publishing Co., 1972), which covers the entire state since there was only one place for instituting probate proceedings. William D. Patterson's *Probate Records of Lincoln County, Maine, 1760–1800* (1895; reprint, Camden, Maine: Picton Press, 1991) extends Sargent by including all probate records, not just wills, and all of eastern Maine to 1789 when Hancock and Washington counties were set off from Lincoln. There were five probate courts by 1800.

Since probate records include more than wills, John E. Frost has been compiling the earlier material to complement the wills. *Maine Probate Abstracts, 1687–1800* (Salt Lake City: Microfilm Service Corp., 1986–87) is a microfiche edition of all York County probate records for the time period and not just wills. It is presently available at Maine Historical Society, the Maine State Library, New England Historic Genealogical Society, and the FHL. Maine State Archives holds the Somerset County probate records. Joseph Crook Anderson II's two-volume work, *York County, Maine Will Abstracts, 1801–1858* (Camden, Maine:

Picton Press, 1997) brings Frost's work forward fifty years for York County wills and includes a comprehensive every-name index.

Court Records

An extensive array of courts has existed in Maine since the beginning of the settlements in the early 1600s. Jurisdictional changes are quite complicated. A detailed publication of the early records can be found in *Province and Court Records of Maine*, 6 vols. (Portland, Maine: Maine Historical Society, 1928), as well as on microfilm through the FHL. All of the original court records for York County are at Maine State Archives. Counties formed from York after 1760 (Cumberland and Lincoln) and 1789 (Washington) from York were also under Massachusetts jurisdiction, although these records appear not to have been microfilmed. Most extant court records to 1929 for all counties except Lincoln can be found at the Maine State Archives. Later court records after 1929 continue to be received by the archives. Lincoln County court records are at the courthouse in Wiscasset.

Before statehood, Maine's court of appeals was the Massachusetts Superior Court of Judicature (1692–1780). This also served as the original court for some other cases such as murders. Records for this court are filled as "Suffolk Files" at the Massachusetts State Archives (see Massachusetts) where they are indexed. The supreme judicial court replaced the superior court of judicature after 1780. According to the Massachusetts State Archives, their holdings include circuit court records for this court for Maine counties through 1793.

Online access to some private held indexes to court records can be found through Maine GenWeb <www.rootsweb.com/%7Eusgenweb/me/mecourt.html>.

Tax Records

Maine participated in the U.S. Direct Tax of 1798, although the surviving lists do not cover the entire state. Landowners, renters, land and title boundaries, acreage, dwellings, value, and tax due are included in the lists. These records can substitute for some missing towns on the 1800 census (see Massachusetts—Census Records and Tax Records). What survives is on microfilm with a printed inventory at the New England Historic Genealogical Society in Boston and the Maine State Archives.

The Maine State Archives has the 1837 Surplus Tax Census for Bangor, Portland, and the areas that were unincorporated at that time. Other tax lists exist throughout the years of Maine's history, both before and after statehood. No survey has been done to catalog these. Reading through town meeting records may unearth what was recorded in the early nineteenth century. Later tax lists may be located at town offices.

Cemetery Records

Numerous transcripts of Maine cemeteries have been made, principally by the Maine Old Cemetery Association and Daughters of the American Revolution (DAR) state and local chapters. There is a continuous indexing project of the transcripts being conducted by the Maine Old Cemetery Association. It is not only indexed but microfilmed and contains upwards of 200,000 people who were buried in Maine between 1650 and 1970. All of York County is now completed. This alphabetical surname indexing project is held on microfilm at the Maine State Library in Augusta, with originals at the Farmingdale center of the FHL in Maine. It can be accessed for a nominal fee by mail requests addressed to the Maine State Library. The Revolutionary War Soldiers' graves project and a similar project underway for Civil War Soldiers' graves are included.

The Maine Historical Society, the New England Historic Genealogical Society, Maine State Library, and Bangor Public Library all have a complete set of DAR transcripts (see page 13). In addition, the New England Genealogic Historical Society's continues to add cemetery transcriptions for all of New England and the online database open to members at <www.newenglandancestors.org> (see page 13).

Church Records

Few church records have been published or microfilmed for Maine, making them a major untapped source for genealogical research. No complete survey of what exists has been made, but the Congregational Church was the largest denomination and its records were usually quite comprehensive. According to John Frost, "Genealogy in Maine: A Pragmatic Approach," *Family History in the Northeast*, vol. 1, Hartford '83 Conference (Hartford, Conn.: Connecticut Society of Genealogists, 1983) records for over two dozen Congregational churches are located at Maine Historical Society, as well as thirteen Baptist, three Universalist, and ten Quaker meetings.

Literally hundreds more church records probably exist in various repositories or the churches themselves. The most likely genealogical material can be found in the lists of memberships with letters of admission or dismissal and the baptisms.

A few church records, such as those from the Church of Christ in Buxton, have been published in book form (1763–1817), and others, such as those from Wells, are in periodicals such as *New England Historical and Genealogical Register*. Some of Maine's church records are also being added to the New England Genealogic Historical Society's database online <www.newenglandancestors.org>.

Military Records

For service in wars before statehood, refer to Massachusetts—Military Records. However, a few printed sources have attempted to extract Maine soldiers from the Massachusetts holdings, notably Charles J. House, *Names of Soldiers of the American Revolution who Applied for State Bounty...in Land Office* (1893; reprint, Baltimore: Genealogical Publishing Co., 1967); Charles A. Flagg, *An Alphabetical Index of Revolutionary Pensioners Living in Maine* (1920; reprint, Baltimore: Genealogical Publishing Co., 1967); and Carleton and Sue Fisher, *Soldiers, Sailors and Patriots of the Revolutionary War—Maine* (Louisville: National Society of Sons of the American Revolution, 1982).

The adjutant general's holdings for Maine, which include militia on state service in wars, published yearly reports on Civil War soldiers. World War I and II reports are held at Maine State Archives. The Spanish-American War service records are also held at the state archives but are not published.

Maine State Archives has a card index of each Civil War soldier and grave records for Revolutionary, Civil War, and War of 1812 soldiers, as well as service records through World War I. In addition, there are listings of veterans by town of those who served in World War II, Korea, and Vietnam.

Periodicals, Newspapers, and Manuscript Collections

Periodicals

Maine has some excellent periodical sources from the nineteenth century presently in publication. Historical resources include *Maine Genealogist and Biographer* (1875–78), primarily for Kennebec County; *The Maine Historical and Genealogical Recorder* (1884–98), for Cumberland and York counties; *Bangor Historical Magazine* (1885–95), for Penobscot Valley; *Sprague's Journal of Maine History* (1913–26), published in Dover, Maine; and finally, what is known as *Maine Genealogies* but is actually called *Genealogical and Family History of the State of Maine* (1909), 4 vols., which has been made somewhat obsolete by later research. Present periodicals include these:

Downeast Ancestry, published six times a year (1977–88; now becoming available online through a number of websites).

Maine Historical Society Quarterly, Maine Historical Society (see Archives, Libraries, and Societies); articles on Maine history, available through membership.

Maine Genealogist, formerly *Maine Seine*, Maine Genealogical Society (see Archives, Libraries, and Societies); publication available through membership.

Newspapers

Local library and historical societies as well as the Maine Historical Society and Maine State Library have indexes to various newspaper vital statistics. The largest collection of microfilmed newspapers can be found at the University of Maine's Folger Library at Orono, which has a computer printout of listings with their holdings. They also supply a typescript, "Maine Newspapers in the Smaller Maine Public Libraries." An online article on Maine newspapers, their location, and genealogical usefulness by Russell Farnham, CG, can be found through membership subscription to <www.newenglandancestors.org>.

Manuscripts

Although it does not include acquisitions in the last forty years, Elizabeth Ring, *A Reference List of Manuscripts Relating to the History of Maine,* 3 vols. (Orono, Maine: University of Maine, 1938–41) is an excellent source. Volume 1 covers towns and manuscript materials related to them; volume 2 covers maps and collections of individuals, including the extensive collections at the Maine Historical Society of professional genealogists; and volume 3 is an index.

Both the Maine Historical Society and Maine State Library have excellent manuscript and single copy typescript collections for research in Maine genealogy.

Archives, Libraries, and Societies

Maine State Archives
84 State House Station
Augusta, ME 04333
www.state.me.us/sos/arc/genealogy

Maine State Archives is the state's official repository for state governmental records, beginning with 1639 court records and including many war and genealogical records for the state. It is the only central location in the state for vital records before 1892. In addition it holds all census records, adjutant general's records, most court records, Maine land office records, a few county marriage returns, and the updated microfilm collection of extant Maine town records. Researchers will find the Maine Historical Records Repository Guide on the Maine State Archives website <www.state.me.us/sos/arc/mhrab/repos/dirpage1.htm>.

Maine State Library
64 State House Station
Augusta, ME 04333
www.state.me.us/msl

Located at the Maine Cultural Center. The east wing of the building houses the Maine State Library, which has the largest collection of town histories and family genealogies in the state, microfilm holdings of newspapers, town reports after 1902, and the two collections of cemetery indexes.

Maine Historical Society Library
485 Congress St.
Portland, ME 04101
www.mainehistory.org

Open to nonmembers for a nominal fee, this superior collection includes extensive printed works on state and family history, and manuscripts (see above). Its website includes access to an ongoing, online genealogical discussion forum to post and retrieve queries <www.mainehistory.org/cgi-bin/discus/discus.cgi>.

Maine Genealogical Society
P.O. Box 221
Farmington, ME 04938
www.rootsweb.com/~megs/MaineGS.htm

The society has local chapters in the state and statewide meetings as well as the bimonthly publication *Maine Seine. Maine Families in 1790* is published in multiple volumes and sold by the society, along with vital records of Mount Desert and the records of Rev. Edward Carter. The organization's library is presently at Cutler Memorial Library in Farmington.

University of Maine at Orono
Raymond H. Folger Library
Special Collections Dept.
Orono, ME 04469
www.library.umaine.edu

In addition to focusing heavily on Orono, the collection has state, county, and town histories as well as special collections of various Maine families.

For a complete listing of repositories in the state that offer some records related to family history, see <www.mainemuseums.org/focusidx.htm>.

Special Focus Categories

Immigration

Although Portland, Maine, was a port of entry itself, with indexes to passengers arriving 1893 up to 1954 in the National Archives collection with copies at National Archives—Northeast Region (see page 11), many Maine residents are descendants of the Irish and other nationalities who passed through immigration in the ports of Boston and New Brunswick (see Massachusetts—Immigration).

Native American

The Maine Bureau of Indian Affairs records are located at the Maine State Archives. They contain some tribal census information. See also:

Ray, Roger B. *The Indians of Maine and the Atlantic Provinces.* Portland, Maine: Maine Historical Society, 1972.

French-Canadian

Maine State Library. *Genealogy of French Canada, Acadia, and Franco-America at the Maine State Library.* Augusta, Maine: the author, 1977.

Baxter, Angus. *In Search of Your Canadian Roots.* Baltimore. Genealogical Publishing Co., 1989.

See also New Hampshire—Archives, Libraries, and Societies.

County Resources

Since Maine was part of Massachusetts for a long time, it should be expected that it would conform to a similar system for recording deeds, probates, and vital records. Such is the case. Deeds and probates were filed at the county seat and vital records at the town office. However, in Maine, marriages were to be submitted to the county clerk as mandated by the legislature in 1828, although the practice was never uniform and the results have not been completely assessed. The following chart reports what has been found regarding marriage returns on a county basis and where they are located (either at the Maine State Archives or with the county clerk). The Town Resources that follow will also have marriage records.

Map	County Address	Date Formed Parent County/ies	Marriage	Land Probate
C12	Androscoggin 2 Turner St. Auburn 04210-5978	1854 Cumberland/Oxford/ Kennebec/Lincoln	1851–84 Maine State Archives	1854 1854
G3	Aroostook Court St., Box 787 Houlton 04370 *Previous deeds dealing with Washington County land from 1808, now in Aroostook, are located here as well.*	1839 Washington	1839–92 county clerk	1839 1839*
B14	Cumberland 142 Federal St. Portland 04101-4151 *Fire loss; 1900-08 index survived.*	1760 York	See Portland Under Towns	1760 1908*
B8	Franklin 38 Main St. Farmington 04938	1838 Cumberland/Kennebec/ Oxford/Somerset	1848–91 county clerk	1838 1838
H11	Hancock 60 State St. Ellsworth 04605	1789 Lincoln	1842–91 county clerk	1790 1790
D12	Kennebec 95 State St. Augusta 04330	1799 Lincoln	1828–87 Maine State Archives	1799 1799
F13	Knox 62 Union St. Rockland 04841	1860 Lincoln/Waldo	1859–87 Maine State Archives	1860 1860
D13	Lincoln High St. Wiscasset 04578	1760 York	1760–1865 county clerk	1763
B11	Oxford 26 Western Ave. South Paris 04281-1417	1805 York/Cumberland	1830–75 Maine State Archives	1805 1805
G8	Penobscot 97 Hammond St. Bangor 04401-4996	1816 Hancock	1827-88 Maine State Archives	1814 1816
E7	Piscataquis 51 E. Main St. Dover-Foxcroft, 04426-1306	1838 Penobscot/Somerset	1839–89 Maine State Archives	1838 1838
D13	Sagadahoc 752 High Bath 04530-2436 *Includes Lincoln County earlier deeds.*	1854 Lincoln	1852–87 Maine State Archives	1826* 1854
C8	Somerset Corner and High Streets Skowhegan 04976-9801	1809 Kennebec	1828–89 county clerk	1804 1830
F11	Waldo 73 Church St. Belfast 04915-1705 *Includes Hancock deeds covering Waldo land before county formation.*	1827 Hancock	1828–87 Maine State Archives	1789* 1827
K10	Washington Court St./P.O. Box 297 Machias 04654	1789 Lincoln	1827–90 Maine State Archives	1783 1783
A15	York 1 Court St. Alfred 04002	1652 original	1771–94; 1833–87 county clerk	1642 1689

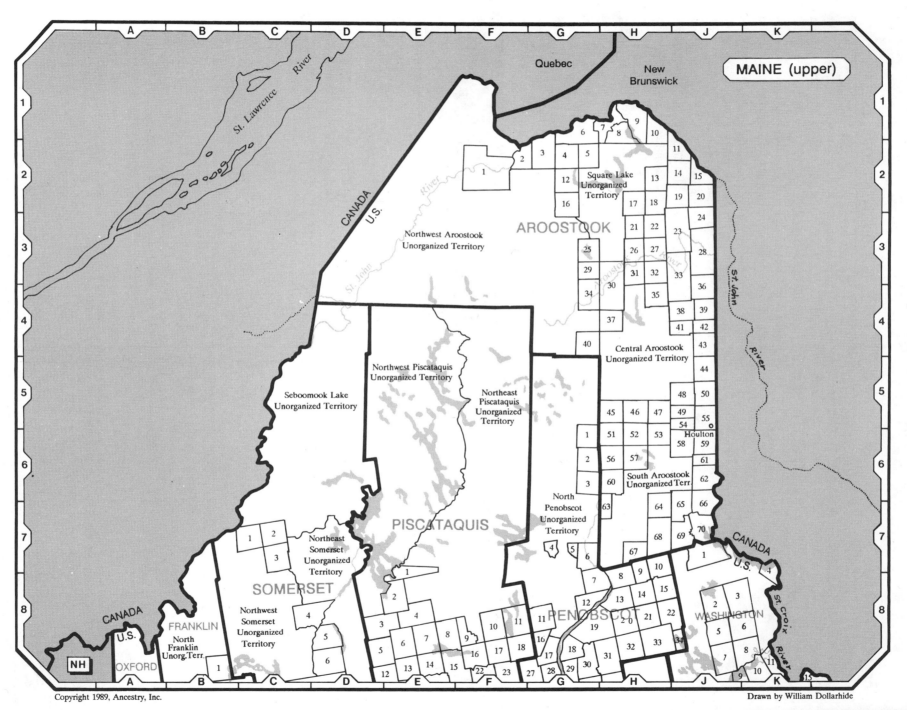

MAINE (upper)

Quebec

New Brunswick

AROOSTOOK

Northwest Aroostook
Unorganized Territory

Square Lake
Unorganized
Territory

Central Aroostook
Unorganized Territory

Northwest Piscataquis
Unorganized Territory

Northeast
Piscataquis
Unorganized
Territory

Seboomook Lake
Unorganized Territory

PISCATAQUIS

North
Penobscot
Unorganized
Territory

South Aroostook
Unorganized Terr.

Houlton

Northeast
Somerset
Unorganized
Territory

SOMERSET

Northwest
Somerset
Unorganized
Territory

FRANKLIN

North
Franklin
Unorg.Terr.

PENOBSCOT

WASHINGTON

NH

OXFORD

CANADA
U.S.

MAINE

276

Drawn by William Dollarhide

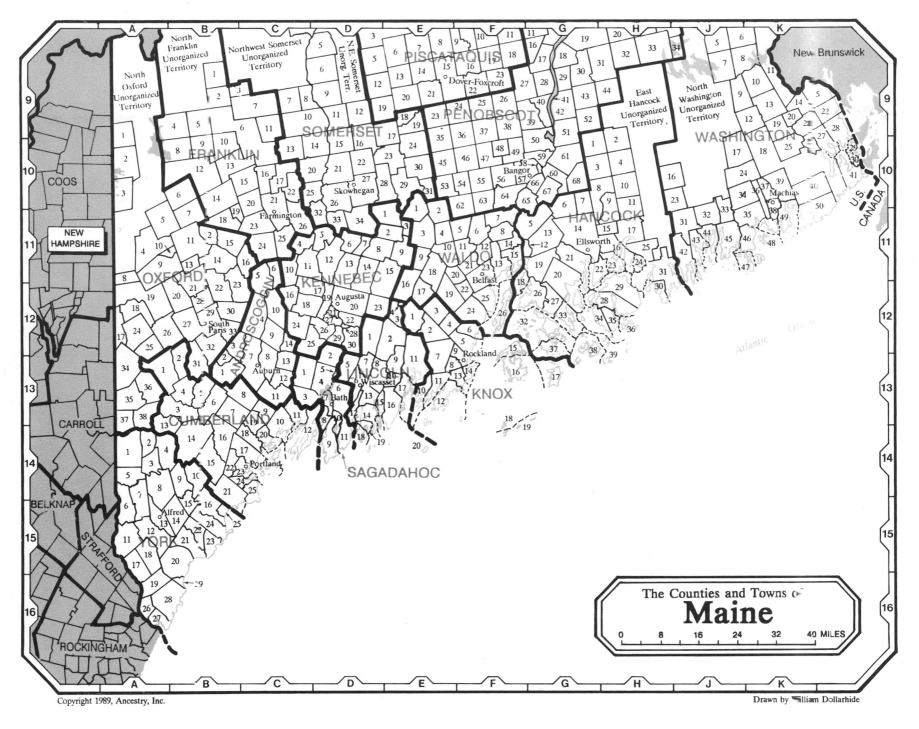

The Counties and Towns of
Maine

0   8   16   24   32   40 MILES

MAINE

Drawn by William Dollarhide

Town Resources

Town meeting records have an abundance of information about New England ancestors. Maine is no exception, although some may not be located at the town clerk's office. The ongoing project for locating and microfilming Maine's town records continues under the auspices of the Maine State Archives. The addresses are from the Secretary of State's website <www.state.me.us/sos/cec/elec/clerk.htm#a>. Those in the chart below are from the 2003 list online. Some towns operate out of town clerk's homes and change with annual elections. Microfilm information from "Maine Town and Census Records" and "Public Records Repositories in Maine," published by the Maine State Archives, provide the dates for record sources. There may be more recent additions to their collection, but they have not yet been cataloged.

"Date Formed" indicates the year the town was organized with its present county listed underneath (see County Resources

for previous county jurisdictions). The numbers in parentheses following the county corresponds to the town's number on the state map. Many towns have their vital records interspersed with the town meeting records while others have separate books for vital records. No distinction has been made in this chart, but both sources cited above do. The purpose here is simply to indicate the first year a researcher might expect to find town and vital records in either the Maine State Archives microfilm collection, the town clerk's office (indicated by an asterisk *), or in the Maine State Archives.

Unfortunately, fire has claimed many records since they were too often held in private homes. A question mark (?) suggests that information is incomplete or uncertain. Dates of records earlier than formation indicate the town holds records of parent towns. Some dates are considerably later than town organization, indicating that either the records are lost or have been destroyed by fire.

Town Address	Date Formed County (Map)	Vital Records	Town Records
Abbott 133 Main St./P.O. Box 120 Abbott 04406	1827 Piscataquis (13)	1900	1900*
Acton 35 H Rd. Acton 04001	1830 York (6)	1830	1830
Adams	(see Crawford)		
Addison 334 Water St./P.O. Box 142 Addison 04606	1797 Washington (45)	1834*	1824*
Albany 1420 Hunts Corner Rd. Albany 04217	1803 Oxford (19)	–1892	?
Albion 22 Main St./P.O. Box 287 Albion 04910	1804 Kennebec (9)	1802	1802
Alexander 50 Cooper Rd. Alexander 04694	1825 Washington (13)	1784	?
Alfred 16 Saco Rd./P.O. Box 129 Alfred 04002	1808 York (13)	1803	1824
Allagash Plantation 1063 Allagash Rd. Allagash 04774	1885 Aroostook (1)	1892	1892*
Alna 2263 Alna Rd./P.O. Box 265 Alna 04535	1794 Lincoln (7)	1795	1795
Alton 131 Hudson Rd. Alton 04468-9721	1844 Penobscot (39)	1859	1844*
Amherst 638 Airline Rd. Ellsworth 04605	1831 Hancock (3)	1783	1850*
Amity HC 61, Box 3A Calais Rd. North Amity 04471	1836 Aroostook (62)	1862	1862
Andover Stillman Rd./P.O. Box 219 Andover 04216	1804 Oxford (5)	1795	?
Anson P.O. Box 297 North Anson 04911	1798 Somerset (20)	1798	1798
Appleton 2915 Sennebec Rd. Union 04862	1829 Knox (3)	1774	1820
Argyle (unorganized)	Penobscot (40)	1876	?
Arrowsic 26 Mosquito Run Arrowsic 04530	1841 Sagadahoc (10)	1741	1892*

Town Address	Date Formed County (Map)	Vital Records	Town Records
Arundel 468 Old Limerick Rd. Kennebunkport 04046	1915 York (22)	1916	1916
Ashland (Dalton 1869–76) 17 Bridgham St./P.O. Box 910 Ashland 04732	1862 Aroostook (30)	1863*	?
Athens 226 Dorset Hill Rd. Athens 04912	1803 Somerset (16)	1900	1900*
Atkinson 102 N. Stagecoach Rd. Dover-Foxcroft 04426	1819 Piscataquis (22)	1766	1888*
Auburn 45 Spring St. Auburn 04210	1842 Androscoggin (7)	1751	1840
Augusta 16 Cony St. Augusta 04330	1797 Kennebec (20)	1780	1900?*
Aurora 15 Silsby Rd. Aurora 04408	1831 Hancock (4)	1945	——
Avon 60 Mt. Blue Rd. Avon 04966	1802 Franklin (15)	1766	1917
Baileyville 63 Broadway St. Baileyville 04694	1828 Washington (11)	1861	?
Baldwin 534 Pequawket Trail West Baldwin 04091	1802 Cumberland (13)	1802	1802
Bancroft 18 School House Rd. Wytopitlock 04497	1878 Aroostook (69)	1892	1910*
Bangor 73 Harlow St. Bangor 04401	1791 Penobscot (57)	1775	1812
Bar Harbor (Eden 1913) 93 Cottage St. Bar Harbor 04609	1796 Hancock (29)	1796	1798
Baring Plantation RR1, Box 290 Baring 04694	1825 Washington (14)	1892	1892*
Barnard Plantation 	1834 Piscataquis (9)	1921	1921*
Bath 55 Front St. Bath 04530	1781 Sagadahoc (7)	1757	1750*
Beals 11 Big Pond Rd. Beals 04611	1925 Washington (47)	1925	1925*
Beaver Cove Plantation 14 Coveside Rd./P.O. Box 1108 Greenville 04441	1975 Piscataquis (1)	1975	1975*
Beddington 1951 State Hwy. 193 Beddington 04622	1833 Washington (16)	1792	1844*
Belfast 131 Church St. Belfast 04915	1773 Waldo (23)	1773	1773
Belgrade RR 2/P.O. Box 912 Belgrade 04917	1796 Kennebec (12)	1758	1906*
Belmont 299 Fenwick Rd. Belmont 04952	1814 Waldo (22)	1855	?
Benedicta 144 Sweden St., Ste. 1 Caribou 04736	1873 Aroostook (63)	1928	1949*
Benton 1279 Clinton Ave. Benton 04901	1842 Kennebec (2)	1841	?
Berwick Sullivan Sq./P.O. Box 696 Berwick 03901	1713 York (17)	1701	1701
Bethel 19 Main St./P.O. Box 1660 Bethel 04217	1796 Oxford (9)	1745	1796*
Biddeford 205 Main St./P.O. Box 586 Biddeford 04005	1653 York (24)	1653	1653
Bingham Main St./P.O. Box 136 Bingham 04920	1812 Somerset (11)	1812	1812*
Blaine Main St./P.O. Box 190 Blaine 04734	1874 Aroostook (42)	1892	1942*

Town Address	Date Formed County (Map)	Vital Records	Town Records
Blanchard Plantation	1831 Piscataquis (5)	1831	1831*
Blue Hill Main St./P.O. Box 412 Blue Hill 04614	1789 Hancock (20)	1785	1789?*
Boothbay 1011 Wiscasset Rd., Box 106 Boothbay 04537	1764 Lincoln (14)	1763	1763*
Boothbay Harbor 11 Howard St. Boothbay Harbor 04538	1889 Lincoln (19)	1763	1889*
Bowdoin Route 125/P.O. Box 35 Bowdoinham 04287	1788 Sagadahoc (1)	1763	1788*
Bowdoinham 13 School St. Bowdoinham 04008	1762 Sagadahoc (4)	1776	1900*
Bowerbank RR 2 Bowerbank Rd./P.O. Box 360 Dover-Foxcroft 00426	1839 Piscataquis (8)	1832	1966*
Bradford 1 Wilder Davis Rd./P.O. Box 26 Bradford 04410	1831 Penobscot (26)	1862	1819
Bradley 165B Main St./P.O. Box 517 Bradley 04411	1835 Penobscot (61)	1805	1770
Bremen P.O. Box 171 Medomak 04551	1828 Lincoln (17)	1756	1828?
Brewer 80 N. Main St. Brewer 04412	1812 Penobscot (66)	1770	1743
Bridgewater 467 US Hwy. 1, P.O. Box 215 Bridgewater 04735	1858 Aroostook (43)	1894	1950*
Bridgton One Chase Common Bridgton 04009	1794 Cumberland (1)	1785	1794
Brighton Plantation P.O. Box 126 Athens 04912	1816 Somerset (12)	1840	1816
Bristol 1268 Bristol Rd./P.O. Box 147 Bristol 04539	1765 Lincoln (16)	1765	1765
Brooklin Rt. 175/P.O. Box 219 Brooklin 04616	1849 Hancock (33)	1835	1849
Brooks 9 Veteran's Hwy./P.O. Box 5 Brooks 04921	1816 Waldo (11)	1892	1930*
Brooksville 1 Town House Rd. Brooksville 04617	1817 Hancock (26)	1818	1966
Brookton Township Main St., HCR #1, Box 101 Forest City, ME 04413	1883 (repealed 1941) Washington	?	?
Brownfield Main St./P.O. Box 100 Brownfield 04010	1802 Oxford (35)	1802	1800?
Brownville 27 Church St./P.O. Box 659 Brownville 04414	1824 Piscataquis (10)	1812	?
Brunswick 28 Federal St., Ste. 2 Brunswick 04011	1737 Cumberland (11)	1735	1735
Buckfield 34 Turner St./P.O. Box 179 Buckfield 04220	1793 (as Buckstown) Oxford (30)	1700	179–?
Bucksport Main St., P.O. Drawer X Bucksport 04416	1792 Hancock (5)	1775	1800
Burlington 64 Woodsman Mill Rd. Lincoln 04417	1832 Penobscot (31)	1769	1840
Burnham 20 Miles Hill Rd./P.O. Box 55 Burnham 04922	1824 Waldo (1)	1821	1824?
Buxton 185 Portland Rd. West Buxton 04093	1772 York (10)	1773	1740
Byron 486 Swift River Rd. Byron 04275	1833 Oxford (6)	1814	1814
Calais 11 Church St./P.O. Box 413 Calais 04619	1809 Washington (15)	1824	1809

Town Address	Date Formed County (Map)	Vital Records	Town Records
Cambridge 8 Ham Hill Rd. Cambridge 04920	1834 Somerset (18)	1792	1834*
Camden 29 Elm St./P.O. Box 1207 Camden 04843	1791 Knox (6)	1783	1783
Canaan Main St./P.O. Box 68 Canaan 04924	1788 Somerset (28)	1776	1880?
Canton 28 Cross St./P.O. Box 669 Canton 04221	1821 Oxford (16)	1818*	?
Cape Elizabeth 320 Ocean House Rd./P.O. Box 6260 Cape Elizabeth 04107	1765 Cumberland (25)	1765	1765
Cape Porpoise	(see Kennebunkport)		
Caratunk Plantation P.O. Box 98 Caratunk 04925	1840 Somerset (6)	1854	1854
Caribou 25 High St. Caribou 04736	1859 Aroostook (23)	1848	1848
Carmel Main Rd., P.O. Box 114 Carmel 04419	1811 Penobscot (55)	1760	1964*
Carrabassett Valley 1001 Carriage Rd. Carrabassett Valley 04947	1972 Franklin (7)	?	1972*
Carroll Plantation 306 Osgood Rd. Carroll Plantation 04487	1845 Penobscot (22)	1928	1928*
Carthage 740 River Rd. Carthage 04224	1826 Franklin (18)	1812	1826
Cary Plantation 1846 US Hwy. 1 Cary Plantation 04471	1858 Aroostook (61)	1862	1972*
Casco P.O. Box 60 Casco 04015	1841 Cumberland (5)	1841	1873*
Castine 67 Court St./P.O. Box 204 Castine 04421	1796 Hancock (18)	1796	1796
Castle Hill Pulcifur Rd./P.O. Box 500 Mapleton 04757	1903 Aroostook (31)	1855	1940?*
Caswell Plantation 1020 Van Buren Rd. Limestone 04750	1879 Aroostook (20)	1898	1945*
Centerville 31 Mitton Mountain Rd. Centerville 04623	1842 Washington (34)	1770	?
Central Hancock (unorganized)	Hancock (15)		
Central Somerset (unorganized)	Somerset (10)		
Chanderville	(see Detroit)		
Chapman Pulcifur Rd./P.O. Box 500 Mapleton 04757	1824 (1879) Aroostook (35)	1868	?
Charleston 405 East Rd./P.O. Box 231 Bradford 04410	1811 Penobscot (25)	1809	1809
Charlotte 9 Hatton Lane Charlotte 04666	1825 Washington (21)	1816	1821
Chelsea 560 Togus Rd. Chelsea 04345	1850 Kennebec (22)	1782	1851*
Cherryfield P.O. Box 58 Cherryfield 04622	1816 Washington (31)	1854	1842?
Chester Pea Ridge Rd., RR 3, Box 1866 Lincoln Center 04458	1834 Penobscot (12)	1788	1862*
Chesterville 409 Dutch Gap Rd. Chesterville 04938	1802 Franklin (25)	1788	1803
China 571 Lakeview Dr. China 04358	1796 (as Harlem; renamed 1818) Kennebec (15)	1785	1785
Clifton 135 Airline Rd. Clifton 04428	1848 (Me. and N.H., 1849) Penobscot (68)	1848	1860*
Clinton Baker St./P.O. Box 219 Clinton 04927	1795 Kennebec (1)	1797	1892

MAINE

Town Address	Date Formed County (Map)	Vital Records	Town Records
Codyville Plantation Rt. 6 Topsfield 04490	1845 Washington (3)	1892	1922*
Columbia 106 Epping Rd. Columbia 04623	1796 Washington (32)	1752	1752
Columbia Falls 205 Main St./P.O. Box 100 Columbia Falls 04623	1863 Washington (33)	1863	1796
Connor Township 144 Sweden St., Ste. 1 Caribou 04736	1877 (1883) Aroostook (19)		
Cooper 73 Cooper Hwy. Cooper 04657	1822 Washington (19)	1878	1907*
Coplin Plantation 8269 Carrabassett Rd./P.O. Box 319 Stratton 04982	1895 Franklin (2)	1895	?
Corinna 8 Levi Stewart Dr. Corinna 04928	1816 Penobscot (35)	1797	?
Corinth 31 Exeter Rd./P.O. Box 309 East Corinth 04427	1811 Penobscot (37)	1785	1811*
Cornish Maple St./P.O. Box 400 Cornish 04020	1794 York (2)	1857*	?
Cornville 100 Wood Rd. Cornville 04976	1798 Somerset (22)	1772	1794*
Coxhall	(see Lyman)		
Cranberry Isles 1892 Main St./P.O. Box 15 Islesford 04646	1830 Hancock (36)	1783	1830?*
Crawford RR 1, Box 1045 Crawford 04694	1828 Washington (12)	1827	1901
Criehaven (unorganized)	Knox (19)		
Crystal 272 Crystal Rd./P.O. Box 383 Island Falls 04747	1901 Aroostook (56)	1854	1923*
Cumberland 290 Tuttle Rd. Cumberland 04021	1821 Cumberland (18)	1720	1821*
Cushing 279 Cushing Rd. Cushing 04563	1789 Knox (11)	1735	1845*
Cutler 2655 Cutler Rd./P.O. Box 236 Cutler 04626	1826 Washington (50)	1844	1843?*
Cyr Plantation HCR 63 Box 64B Van Buren 04785	1870 Aroostook (14)	1892	1892*
Dallas Plantation Dallas Hill Rd./P.O. Box 460 Rangeley 04970	1845 Franklin (5)	1892	1921*
Dalton	(see Ashland)		
Damariscotta 27 Church St./P.O. Box 218 Damariscotta 04543	1848 Lincoln (10)	1848	1864*
Danforth Center St./P.O. Box 117 Danforth 04424	1860 Washington (1)	1860	1936*
Dayton 221 Waterhouse Rd. Dayton 04005	1854 York (15)	1832	1832
Deblois 1012 Rt. 193 Deblois 04622	1852 Washington (23)	1855*	1852*
Dedham US Rt. 1, RR 3, Box 760 Holden 04429	1837 Hancock (6)	1787	1932*
Deer Isle P.O. Box 46 Deer Isle 04627	1789 Hancock (32)	1768	1789*
Denmark Rt. 117/P.O. Box 109 Denmark 04022	1807 Oxford (36)	1807*	1807*
Dennistown Plantation Main St., Box 126 Dennistown 04945	1895 Somerset (1)	1840	1910*
Dennysville King St., RR 1, Box 287 Dennysville 04628	1818 Washington (26)	1790*	1818*

MAINE

Town Address	Date Formed County (Map)	Vital Records	Town Records
Detroit 35 S. Main St. Detroit 04929	1828 Somerset (31)	1/80	1780
Dexter 23 Main St./P.O. Box 313 Dexter 04930	1816 Penobscot (23)	1761	1816*
Dickeyville	(see Frenchville)		
Dixfield 46 Main St./P.O. Box 808 Dixfield 04224	1803 Oxford (15)	1803	1803
Dixmont P.O. Box 100 Dixmont 04932	1807 Penobscot (62)	1800	1906*
Dover-Foxcroft 152 E. Main St. Dover-Foxcroft 04426	1822/1812 (merged 1915) Piscataquis (15)	1792	1800s?
Dresden P.O. Box 30 Dresden 04342	1794 Lincoln (5)	1771	1771
Drew Plantation HCR 60, Box 35 Wytopitlock 04497	1921 Penobscot (10)	1853	?
Durham 630 Hallowell Rd. Durham 04222	1789 Androscoggin (11)	1744	1961*
Dutton	(see Glenburn)		
Dyer Brook 864 Dyer Brook Rd. Dyer Brook 04747	1891 Aroostook (52)	1895	?
E Plantation P.O. Box 94 Blaine 04734	1898 Aroostook (41)	?	1966*
Eagle Lake RR 1, Box 2338 Eagle Lake 04739	1870 Aroostook (12)	1867	1890*
East Central Franklin	Franklin (unorganized)		
East Central Washington	Washington (unorganized)		
East Livermore	(see Livermore Falls)		
East Machias P.O. Box 117 East Machias 04630	1826 Washington (39)	1709	1823*
East Millinocket 53 Main St. East Millinocket 04430	1907 Penobscot (5)	1907	1907*
East Thomaston	(see Rockland)		
Eastbrook Rt. 200 N, RFD #1, Box 467 Eastbrook 04634	1837 Hancock (11)	1892	1892*
Easton 3 Station Rd./P.O. Box 127 Easton 04740	1865 Aroostook (36)	1892	1896*
Eastport 78 High St. Eastport 04631	1798 Washington (30)	1778	?
Eddington 906 Main St. Eddington 04428	1811 Penobscot (60)	1802	1805*
Eden	(see Bar Harbor)		
Edgecomb 803 Boothbay Rd. Edgecomb 04556	1774 Lincoln (13)	1774*	1774*
Edinburg 711 Edinburg Rd. Edinburg 04448	1835 Penobscot (28)	1835	?
Edmunds Township RR 1, Box 91 Edmonds 04628	(see Argyle) Penobscot		
Eliot 141 State Rd. Eliot 03903	1810 York (26)	1810	1810
Elliotsville Plantation	1835 Piscataquis (4)	1913	1960*
Ellsworth 1 City Hall Plaza/P.O. Box 586 Ellsworth 04605	1800 Hancock (14)	1800?*	1933*
Embden Embden Pond Rd./P.O. Box 659 North Anson 04958	1804 Somerset (14)	1783	1783
Enfield Hammett Rd./P.O. Box 429 West Enfield 04433	1835 Penobscot (18)	1857*	1940*
Etna Shadowlane Rd./P.O. Box G Etna 04434	1820 Penobscot (54)	1742	1900?*

Town Address	Date Formed County (Map)	Vital Records	Town Records
Eustis 88 Main St./P.O. Box 350 Stratton 04982	1871 Franklin (1)	1871	?
Exeter 1220 Stetson Rd./P.O. Box 59 Exeter 04435	1811 Penobscot (36)	1808	1808
Fairfax	(see Albion)		
Fairfield 19 Lawrence Ave./P.O. Box 149 Fairfield 04937	1788 Somerset (34)	1788	1788*
Falmouth 271 Falmouth Rd. Falmouth 04105	1718 Cumberland (17)	1718	1718
Farmingdale 289 Maine Ave. Farmingdale 04345	1852 Kennebec (27)	1852	1852*
Farmington 153 Farmington Falls Rd. Farmington 04938	1794 Franklin (21)	1741	1794*
Fayette RFD 3, Box 2180 Fayette 04349	1795 Kennebec (10)	1785	1795*
Forks Plantation Route 201/P.O. Box 77 West Forks 04985	1895 Somerset (5)	?	?
Fort Fairfield 227 Main St./P.O. Box 350 Fort Fairfield 04742	1858 Aroostook (28)	1847	1858*
Fort Kent 416 W. Main St. Fort Kent 04743	1869 Aroostook (6)	1892	1900*
Fox Isle	(see North Haven)		
Foxcroft	(see Dover-Foxcroft)		
Frankfort 48A Main Rd. South/P.O. Box 218 Frankfort 04438	1789 Waldo (8)	1903	1934*
Franklin 74 Hog Bay Rd. Franklin 04634	1825 Hancock (17)	1813*	1813*
Freedom 71 Pleasant St., P.O. Box 88 Freedom 04941	1813 Waldo (9)	1777	1813*
Freeport 30 Main St. Freeport 04032	1789 Cumberland (10)	1795	1789*
Frenchboro 69 Sunset Dr. Frenchboro 04635	? Hancock (39)		
Frenchville (Dickeyville) 283 US Rt. 1/P.O. Box 97 Frenchville 04745	1869 Aroostook (7)	1869	1869
Friendship Main St./P.O. Box 207 Friendship 04547	1807 Knox (10)	1769	1824*
Fryeburg 2 Lovewell's Pond Rd. Fryeburg 04037	1777 Oxford (34)	1777	1777
Gardiner 6 Church St. Gardiner 04345	1803 Kennebec (29)	1800	?
Garfield Plantation 75 Hacker Farm Rd./P.O. Box 191 Ashland 04732	1895 Aroostook (34)	1892	1958
Garland 30 Jones Rd. Garland 04939	1811 Penobscot (24)	1854	1936*
Georgetown 50 Bay Point Rd./P.O. Box 436 Georgetown 04548	1716 Sagadahoc (11)	1757	1757
Gilead 14 Depot St. Gilead 04217	1804 Oxford (8)	1757	1804?
Glenburn 144 Lakeview Rd. Bangor 04401	1822 Penobscot (49)	1800	1822*
Glenwood Plantation Springer Rd./P.O. Box 29 Wytopitlock 04497	1867 Aroostook (64)	1866*	1866*
Gorham 270 Main St. Gorham 04038	1764 Cumberland (15)	1721	1733
Gouldsboro Main St./P.O. Box 68 Prospect Harbor 04669	1789 Hancock (31)	1772	1772

MAINE

Town Address	Date Formed County (Map)	Vital Records	Town Records
Grand Falls Plantation	1878 Penobscot (44)	?	?
Grand Isle 366 Main St./P.O. Box 197 Grand Isle 04746	1869 Aroostook (10)	1892	1869
Grand Lake Stream Plantation Water St./P.O. Box 98 Grand Lake Stream 04637	1897 Washington (7)	?	?
Gray 6 Shaker Rd. Gray 04039	1778 Cumberland (7)	1700?*	1778*
Great Pond Plantation 1348 Great Pond Rd./P.O. Box 104 Aurora 04408	1895 Hancock (2)	1894	1950*
Greenbush 132 Military Rd./P.O. Box 210 Olamon 04467	1834 Penobscot (42)	1774	?
Greene 220 Main St./P.O. Box 510 Greene 04236	1788 Androscoggin (9)	1748	1788*
Greenfield *Deorganized 1993.	1834* Penobscot (52)	1850	1848
Greenville 10 Minden St./P.O. Box 1109 Greenville 04441	1836 Piscataquis (2)	1820	1831*
Greenwood 9 Bird Hill Rd./P.O. Box 180 Greenwood 04255	1816 Oxford (20)	1797	1813
Guilford 4 School St./P.O. Box 355 Guilford 04443	1816 Piscataquis (14)	1770	1816*
Hallowell 1 Winthrop St. Hallowell 04347	1771 Kennebec (21)	1761	1761
Hamlin HCR 62, Box 33 Van Buren 04785	1870 Aroostook (15)	1892	?
Hammond Plantation Burnt Brown Rd./P.O. Box 133 Hammond 04730	1886 Aroostook (48)	1864	1885*
Hampden 106 Western Ave. Hampden 04444	1794 Penobscot (64)	1892	1794*
Hampton	(see Aurora)		
Hancock Hancock Point Rd., P.O. Box 68 Hancock 04640	1828 Hancock (16)	1828	1828
Hanover 21 Ferry Rd./P.O. Box 70 Hanover 04237	1843 Oxford (10)	1807	?
Harlem	(see China)		
Harmony Main St./P.O. Box 14 Harmony 04942	1803 Somerset (17)	1764	1764
Harpswell Mountain Rd./P.O. Box 39 Harpswell 04066	1758 Cumberland (12)	1769	1900*
Harrington P.O. Box 142 Harrington 04643	1797 Washington (44)	1851	1837*
Harrison Main St./P.O. Box 300 Harrison 04040	1805 Cumberland (2)	1805	1805
Hartford Rt. 140/P.O. Box 220 Canton 04221	1798 Oxford (23)	1800	1798*
Hartland 21 Academy St./P.O. Box 280 Hartland 04943	1820 Somerset (23)	1772	1820*
Haynesville HC 60, Box 730, Ferry Rd. Haynesville 04446	1876 Aroostook (65)	1892	?
Hebron 78 Paris Rd. Hebron 04238	1792 Oxford (33)	1700	1700
Hermon P.O. Box 6300 Hermon 04402	1816 Penobscot (56)	1872	?
Hersey P.O. Box 677 Patten 04765	1873 Aroostook (51)	1862	1862
Hibberts Gore (Unorganized)	Lincoln (4)		
Highland Plantation 130 Howard Hill Rd. N. New Portland 04961	1871 Somerset (7)	1972	1972*

MAINE

Town Address	Date Formed County (Map)	Vital Records	Town Records
Hiram 25 Allard Cir. Hiram 04030	1814 Oxford (38)	1815	1804*
Hodgdon 179 Hodgdon Mill Rd. Hodgdon 04730	1832 Aroostook (59)	1837	1950*
Holden 570 Main Rd. Holden 04429	1852 Penobscot (67)	1756	1852
Hollis Rt. 35/P.O. Box 9 Hollis Center 04042	1798 York (9)	1781	1781
Hope 441 Camden Rd. Hope 04847	1804 Knox (4)	1795	?
Houlton 21 Water St. Houlton 04730	1831 Aroostook (55)	1892	1923*
Howard	(see Willimantic)		
Howland 8 Main St./P.O. Box 386 Howland 04448	1826 Penobscot (17)	1798	1911*
Hudson 2334 Hudson Rd. Hudson 04449	1825 Penobscot (38)	1856	1887*
Huntressville	(see Lowell)		
Indian Island Reservation 197 Penobscot Ave. Millinocket 04462	1962? Penobscot (41)	1962	1940?
Indian Township Passamaquoddy Reservation P.O. Box 301 Princeton 04668	1970 Washington (8)	?	
Industry 1033 Industry Rd. Industry 04938	1803 Franklin (22)	1738	1803*
Island Falls 68 Houlton Rd./P.O. Box 100 Island Falls 04747	1872 Aroostook (57)	1910	1910*
Islandport	(see Long Island Plantation)		
Isle Au Haut Main St./P.O. Box 106 Isle au Haut 04645	1874 Knox (17)	1875*	1951*
Isleboro 150 Main St./P.O. Box 76 Islesboro 04848	1789 Waldo (26)	1789*	1789*
Jackman 365 Main St./P.O. Box 269 Jackman 04945	1895 Somerset (3)	1892	1883
Jackson P.O. Box 393 Brooks 04921	1818 Waldo (5)	1809	1818
Jay 99 Main St. Jay 04239	1795 Franklin (24)	1779	1779
Jefferson P.O. Box 77 Jefferson 04348	1807 Lincoln (2)	1757	1757
Jonesboro Station Rd./P.O. Box 86 Jonesboro 04648	1809 Washington (35)	1766	1918
Jonesport P.O. Box 489 Jonesport 04649	1832 Washington (46)	1872	1854
Joy	(see Troy)		
Kenduskeag 4010 Broadway/P.O. Box 308 Kenduskeag 04450	1852 Penobscot (48)	1852	1852
Kennebec	(see Manchester)		
Kennebunk 1 Summer St. Kennebunk 04043	1820 York (21)	1729	1850
Kennebunkport P.O. Box 566 Kennebunkport 04046	1653 York (23)	1678	1678
Kilmarnock	(see Medford)		
Kingfield 38 School St. Kingfield 04947	1816 Franklin (11)	1816	1816
Kingman (unorganized)	Penobscot (9)		
Kingsbury Plantation Pickle Ridge Rd./P.O. Box 144 Springfield 04479	1836 Piscataquis (12)	1836	1836
Kingville	(see Troy)		

MAINE

Town Address	Date Formed County (Map)	Vital Records	Town Records
Kirkland	(see Hudson)		
Kittery 200 Rogers Rd. Ext. P.O. Box 808 Kittery 03904	1652 York (27)	1674	1440
Knox 10 Abbott Rd. Knox 04986	1819 Waldo (10)	1777	1820
Lagrange Bennoch Rd. P.O. Box 11 Lagrange 04453	1832 Penobscot (27)	1833	1832
Lake View Plantation 77 Village Rd. Lake View Plantation 04463	1892 Piscataquis (11)	1892	1905
Lakeville RR 1, Box 786 Springfield 04487	1868 Penobscot (33)	1862	1940
Lamoine 606 Douglas Hwy. Lamoine 04605	1870 Hancock (23)	1849	1870
Lebanon P.O. Box 430 E. Lebanon 04027	1767 York (11)	1765	1765
Lee 29 Winn Rd. Lee 04455	1832 Penobscot (20)	1780	1780
Leeds Rt. 106/P.O. Box 206 Leeds 04263	1801 Androscoggin (10)	1785	1801
Levant Townhouse Rd./P.O. Box 220 Levant 04456	1813 Penobscot (47)	1769	1920
Lewiston City Clerk's Office, 27 Pine St. Lewiston 04240	1795 Androscoggin (8)	1750	1795
Liberty 7 Water St./P.O. Box 116 Liberty 04949	1827 Waldo (17)	1864	1856
Ligonier	(see Albion)		
Limerick 55 Washington St. Limerick 04048	1787 York (3)	?	?
Limestone 93 Main St. Limestone 04750	1869 Aroostook (24)	1862	1861
Limington 425 Sokokis Ave. P.O. Box 240 Limington 04049	1792 York (4)	1792	1792
Lincoln 63 Main St. Lincoln 04457	1829 Penobscot (19)	1829	1829
Lincoln Plantation HCR 10, Box 325 Errol, NH 03579	1875 Oxford (1)	1890	1875
Lincolnville 493 Hope Rd. Lincolnville 04849	1802 Waldo (24)	1786	1802
Linneus 1185 Hodgdon Mills Rd. Linneus 04730	1836 Aroostook (58)	1784	1840
Lisbon 300 Lisbon St. Lisbon 04252	1799 Androscoggin (12)	1782	1799
Litchfield 2400 Hallowell Rd. Litchfield 04350	1795 Kennebec (25)	1785	1785
Littleton 1536 US Hwy. 1 Littleton 04730	1856 Aroostook (50)	1892	?
Livermore 10 Crash Rd. Livermore 04253	1795 Androscoggin (5)	1762	1795
Livermore Falls 2 Main St. Livermore Falls 04254	1843 Androscoggin (6)	1892	1844
Long Island Plantation P.O. Box 263 Long Island 04050	1857 Hancock (?)	1900	1900
Lovell Rt. 5/P.O. Box 236 Center Lovell 04016	1800 Oxford (24)	1785	1800
Lowell 24 W. Old Main Rd. Lowell 04493	1837 Penobscot (30)	1854	1900

287

Town Address	Date Formed County (Map)	Vital Records	Town Records
Lubec 40 School St. Lubec 04652	1811 Washington (41)	1819	1820
Ludlow 13 Cunliffe Rd. Ludlow 04761	1864 Aroostook (49)	1840	1840
Lyman 11 South Waterboro Rd. Lyman 04002	1778 York (14)	1850	1850
Lyndon	(see Caribou)		
Machias 70 Court St./P.O. Box 363 Machias 04654	1784 Washington (38)	1773	1773
Machiasport Route 92/P.O. Box 267 Machiasport 04655	1826 Washington (49)	1859	1966
Machisses	(see East Machias)		
Macwahoc Plantation HC 62, Box 752 Macwahoc 04451	1851 Aroostook (67)	1851	1851
Madawaska 328 St. Thomas St., Ste. 101 Madawaska 04756	1869 Aroostook (9)	1871	1869
Madison 26 Western Ave./P.O. Box 190 Madison 04950	1804 Somerset (21)	1939	1892
Madrid 1368 Rangeley Rd. Phillips 04966	1836 Franklin (10)	1789	1956
Magalloway Plantation HCR 10, Box 293 Errol, NH 03579	1883 Oxford (2)	1952	1952
Maine	(see Clifton)		
Manchester P.O. Box 18 Manchester 04351	1850 Kennebec (19)	1808	1850
Mansel	(see Tremont)		
Mapleton Pulcifur Rd./P.O. Box 500 Mapleton 04757	1878 Aroostook (32)	1864	?
Mariaville 11 Whispering Pine Dr. Mariaville 04605	1836 Hancock (8)	1875*	1836*
Mars Hill 15 W. Ridge Rd. Mars Hill 04758	1867 Aroostook (39)	1786	1880*
Marshfield P.O. Box 142 Machias 04654	1846 Washington (37)	1821	1846*
Masardis 26 School St. Masardis 04759	1839 Aroostook (37)	1818*	1930*
Matinicus Isle Plantation 254 South Rd./P.O. Box 198 Matinicus Island 04851	1840 Knox (18)	1891	1840
Mattawamkeag 327 Main St./P.O. Box 260 Mattawamkeag 04459	1860 Penobscot (8)	1860	1860*
Maxfield 231 River Rd. Maxfield 04453	1824 Penobscot (16)	1825	1825
Mechanic Falls 108 Lewiston St./P.O. Box 130 Mechanic Falls 04256	1893 Androscoggin (2)	1893*	1893*
Meddybemps Rt. 191, Box 102A Meddybemps 04657	1841 Washington (20)	1936	1946*
Medford 1015 Medford Center Rd. Medford 04463	1824 Piscataquis (18)	1844	?
Medway School St., HCR 86/Box 320 Medway 04460	1875 Penobscot (6)	1850	1875*
Mercer W. Sandy River Rd., RFD 2 Box 899 Norridgewock 04957	1804 Somerset (32)	1769	?
Merrill U.S. Rt. 2/P.O. Box 239 Smyrna Mills 04780	1895 Aroostook (46)	1893*	1938*
Mexico 134 Main St./P.O. Box 251 Mexico 04257	1818 Oxford (12)	1818*	1818*
Milbridge 22 School St./P.O. Box 66 Milbridge 04658	1848 Washington (43)	1848	1848

MAINE

Town Address	Date Formed County (Map)	Vital Records	Town Records
Milburn	(see Skowhegan)		
Milford 26 Davenport St./P.O. Box 336 Milford 04461	1833 Penobscot (51)	1864	1952*
Millinocket 197 Penobscot Ave. Millincoket 04462	1901 Penobscot (4)	1898*	1901*
Milo Pleasant St./P.O. Box 218 Milo 04463	1823 Piscataquis (17)	1802	1823
Milton (unorganized)	Oxford (13)		
Minot 329 Woodman Hill Rd./P.O. Box 154 Minot 04258	1823 Androscoggin (3)	1786	1802*
Monhegan Plantation P.O. Box 87 Monhegan 04852	1839 Lincoln (20)	1841	1841
Monmouth 859 Main St./P.O. Box 270 Monmouth 04259	1792 Kennebec (24)	1800s	1888
Monroe 11 Back Brooks Rd. Monroe 04951	1818 Waldo (6)	1778	1820*
Monson 10 Tenney Hill Rd./P.O. Box 308 Monson 04464	1822 Piscataquis (6)	1635	1920*
Montgomery	(see Troy)		
Monticello U.S. Rt. 1/P.O. Box 99 Monticello 04760	1846 Aroostook (44)	1860	1860
Montville 892 S. Mountain Valley Hwy. Montville 04941	1807 Waldo (18)	1785	1785
Moose River 727 Main St. Moose River 04945	1852 Somerset (2)	late 1800s*	1900
Moro Plantation R.R. 1, Box 1969 Smyrna Mills 04780	1850 Aroostook (45)	1896	1922
Morrill 107 Weymouth Rd. Morrill 04952	1855 Waldo (20)	1781	1855
Moscow 404 Stream Rd. Moscow 04920	1816 Somerset (9)	1771	1816*
Mount Chase Rt. 159/P.O. Box 318 Patten 04765	1864 Penobscot (1)	1871*	1951*
Mount Desert 21 Sea St./P.O. 248 Northeast Harbor 04662	1789 Hancock (28)	1806	1900*
Mount Vernon 1997 North Rd. Mount Vernon 04352	1792 Kennebec (11)	1775	1797*
Naples Lambs Mill Rd./P.O. Box 1757 Naples 04055	1834 Cumberland (4)	1834	1834*
Nashville Plantation 968 Portage Rd./P.O. Box 433 Ashland 04732	1889 Aroostook (29)	1889*	1889*
New Canada 27 Thibeault Rd. New Canada 04743	1881 Aroostook (5)	1892*	1892*
New Charleston	(see Charleston)		
New Gloucester 385 Intervale Rd./P.O. Box 82 New Gloucester 04260	1774 Cumberland (8)	1771	1700
New Limerick 11 Old Station Rd./P.O. Box 121 New Limerick 04761	1837 Aroostook (54)	1892*	1861
New Portland 8 Bennet Hill Rd./P.O. Box 564 New Portland 04954	1808 Somerset (13)	1770	1836*
New Sharon 47 Main St./P.O. Box 7 New Sharon 04955	1794 Franklin (26)	1797	1800*
New Sweden 50 Station Rd. New Sweden 04762	1895 Aroostook (18)	1872*	?
New Vineyard 20 Lake St./P.O. Box 262 New Vineyard 04956	1802 Franklin (17)	1892*	?
Newburgh 2660 Western Ave. Hampden 04444	1819 Penobscot (63)	1828	1814*

289

MAINE

Town Address	Date Formed County (Map)	Vital Records	Town Records
Newcastle 94 River Rd./P.O. Box 386 Newcastle 04553	1753 Lincoln (8)	1754	1754
Newfield P.O. Box 62 West Newfield 04095	1794 York (5)	1897*	1900*
Newport 23 Water St. Newport 04953	1814 Penobscot (45)	1858	1835*
Newry 422 Bear River Rd. Newry 04261	1805 Oxford (4)	1805	1805
Nobleboro 192 U.S. Hwy. 1/P.O. Box 168 Nobleboro 04555	1788 Lincoln (9)	1914	1788
Norridgewock 16 Perkins St./P.O. Box 7 Norridgewock 04957	1788 Somerset (26)	1674	1674
North Berwick 21 Main St./P.O. Box 422 North Berwick 03906	1831 York (18)	1831	1831
North Haven Main St./P.O. Box 400 North Haven 04853	1846 Knox (15)	1802	1802
North Yarmouth 10 Village Sq. Rd. North Yarmouth 04097	1732? Cumberland (19)	1720*	1732*
Northfield HCR 71, Box 224 Machias 04654	1838 Washington (24)	1798	1938*
Northport 16 Beech Hill Rd. Northport 04849	1796 Waldo (25)	1896*	?
Northwest Hancock (unorganized)	Hancock (1)		
Norway 19 Danforth St. Norway 04268	1797 Oxford (27)	1700	1856*
Number 14 Plantation 793 Cooper Hwy. Cooper 04657	1895 Washington (25)	1875	
Number 21 Plantation P.O. Box 693 Princeton 04668	1895 Washington (9)	1892*	1899*
Oakfield P.O. Box 10 Oakfield 04763	1897 Aroostook (53)	1882	1897*
Oakland 3 Fairfield St./P.O. Box 187 Oakland 04963	1873 Kennebec (6)	1873*	1873*
Ogunquit 23 School St./P.O. Box 2122 Ogunquit 03907	1980 York (29)	1871*	?
Old Orchard Beach 1 Portland Ave. Old Orchard Beach 04064	1883 York (25)	1883*	1883*
Old Town 150 Brunswick St. Old Town 04468	1840 Penobscot (50)	1820	1840*
Orient Old Rt. 1/P.O. Box 180 Orient 04471	1856 Aroostook (66)	1892	?
Orland 23 School House Rd./P.O. Box 67 Orland 04472	1800 Hancock (13)	1765	1792*
Orono 59 Main St./P.O. Box 130 Orono 04473	1806 Penobscot (59)	1806	1806
Orrington 29 Center Dr./P.O. Box 159 Orrington 04474	1788 Penobscot (65)	1643	1643
Osborn Rt. 179, HCR 31/Box 2980 Ellsworth 04605	1895 Hancock (10)	1938*	?
Otis Rt. 180, RR 4/Box 167AA Otis 04605	1835 Hancock (7)	1835	1835
Otisfield 403 State Otisfield 04270	1798 Oxford (31)	1798*	1798*
Owl's Head 224 Ash Point Dr./P.O. Box 128 Owls Head 04854	1921 Knox (14)	1921*	1921*
Oxbow Plantation 812 Oxbow Rd. Oxbow Plantation 04764	1895 Aroostook (40)	1940*	1940*

MAINE

Town Address	Date Formed County (Map)	Vital Records	Town Records
Oxford P.O. Box 153 Oxford 04270	1829 Oxford (32)	1829	1892*
Palermo P.O. Box 78 Palermo 04354	1804 Waldo (16)	1908*	1831*
Palmyra 778 Main St./P.O. Box 6 Palmyra 04965	1807 Somerset (30)	1800	1807*
Paris 33 Market Sq. South Paris 04281	1793 Oxford (29)	1795	1793
Parkman 771 State Hwy. 150 Parkman 04443	1822 Piscataquis (20)	1782	1822*
Parsonsfield 62 Federal Rd./P.O. Box 30 Kezar Falls 04047	1785 York (1)	1762	1774
Passadumkeag 15 Pleasant St./P.O. Box 75 Passadumkeag 04475	1835 Penobscot (29)	1844	1935*
Patten 21 Katahdin St./P.O. Box 260 Patten 04765	1841 Penobscot (2)	1821	1841*
Pembroke 71 Front St. Pembroke 04666	1832 Washington (27)	1831	1832*
Penobscot P.O. Box 4 Orland 04472	1787 Hancock (19)	1732	1880*
Pepperrellborough	(see Saco)		
Perham 206 High Meadow Rd. Perham 04766	1878 Aroostook (21)	1855	1897*
Perkins (unorganized)	Sagadahoc (5)		
Perry 71 Front St. Perry 04667	1818 Washington (18)	1780	1965
Peru 81 Peru Center Rd. P.O. Box 429 Peru 04290	1821 Oxford (14)	1813	1821
Phillips 1368 Rangeley Rd./P.O. Box 66 Phillips 04966	1812 Franklin (13)	1763	1812
Phillipsburg	(see Hollis)		
Phippsburg 1042 Main Rd. Phippsburg 04562	1814 Sagadahoc (9)	1825	1814
Pittsfield 8 Park St. Pittsfield 04967	1819 Somerset (29)	1815	1815
Pittston Rt. 126/Box 9A Gardiner 04345	1779 Kennebec (30)	1785	1785
Pleasant Point Indian Reservation Rt. 190/P.O. Box 343 Perry 04667	Washington (29)		
Pleasant Ridge Plantation Pleasant Ridge Rd./P.O. Box 151 Bingham 04920	1895 Somerset (8)	1852	1852
Plymouth Rt. 7/P.O. Box 130 Plymouth 04969	1826 Penobscot (53)	1795	1932*
Poland Rt. 26/P.O. Box 38 Poland 04273	1795 Androscoggin (1)	1780	1734
Port Watson	(see Brooklin)		
Portage Lake 7 School St./P.O. Box 255 Portage Lake 04768	1895 Aroostook (25)	1875	1875
Porter 71 Main St. Porter 04060	1807 Oxford (37)	1892*	1829*
Portland 389 Congress St., Rm. 203 Portland 04101	1786 Cumberland (23)	1712	1786
Pownal P.O. Box 95 Pownal 04069	1808 Cumberland (9)	1800	1800
Pownalborough	(see Wiscasset)		
Prentiss Plantation 144 Pickle Ridge Rd./P.O. Box 144 Springfield 04487	1858 Penobscot (15)	1841	1900*

Town Address	Date Formed County (Map)	Vital Records	Town Records
Presque Isle 12 Second St. Presque Isle 04769	1859 Aroostook (33)	1859	1892
Princeton 15 Depot Sq./P.O. Box 408 Princeton 04668	1832 Washington (10)	1861	1960
Prospect 958 Bangor Rd. Stockton Springs 04981	1794 Waldo (14)	1756	1889*
Putnam	(see Washington)		
Randolph 121 Kinderhook St. Randolph 04346	1887 Kennebec (28)	1898*	1922*
Rangeley 15 School St./P.O. Box 1070 Rangeley 04970	1855 Franklin (4)	1795	1855*
Rangeley Plantation South Shore Dr./P.O. Box 493 Rangeley 04970	1895 Franklin (8)	1910*	1900*
Raymond 401 Webbs Mill Rd. Raymond 04071	1803 Cumberland (6)	1745	1803*
Readfield 8 Old Kents Hill Rd. Readfield 04355	1791 Kennebec (17)	1777	1790*
Reed Plantation Rt. 171/P.O. Box 92 Wytopitlock 04497	1878 Aroostook (68)	1892*	1800*
Richmond P.O. Box 159 Richmond 04357	1823 Sagadahoc (2)	1782	1823*
Ripley 1084 Main St. Ripley 04930	1816 Somerset (19)	1783	1892*
Rockabema	(see Moro Plantation)		
Robbinston P.O. Box 44 Robbinston 04671	1811 Washington (22)	1857	1886*
Rockland 270 Pleasant St. Rockland 04841	1848 Knox (9)	1803	1854*
Rockport 101 Main St./P.O. Box 10 Rockport 04856	1891 Knox (5)	1783	1783
Rome 60 Ladd Rd. Rome 04963	1804 Kennebec (5)	1776	1776
Roque Bluffs 572 Johnson Cove Rd. Roque Bluffs 04654	1891 Washington (48)	1892*	1891*
Roxbury P.O. Box 24 Roxbury 04275	1835 Oxford (7)	1892*	?
Rumford 145 Congress St. Rumford 04276	1800 Oxford (11)	1800	1800*
Sabattus 190 Middle Rd./P.O. Box 190 Sabbattus 04280	1840 Androscoggin (13)	1892	1700*
Saco 300 Main St. Saco 04072	1762 York (16)	1717	1867*
St. Agatha 419 Main St./P.O. Box 110 St. Agatha 04772	1899 Aroostook (8)	1889	1889
St. Albans 7 Water St./P.O. Box 100 St. Albans 04971	1813 Somerset (24)	1785	1914*
St. Francis R1 Main Rd./P.O. Box 98 St. Francis 04774	1870 Aroostook (2)	1892*	1892*
St. George 3 School St./P.O. Box 131 Tenants Harbor 04860	1803 Knox (12)	1737	1803*
St. John Plantation 1825 St. John Rd. St. John Plantation 04743	1870 Aroostook (3)	1885*	1950*
Sandy River Plantation P.O. Box 589 Rangeley 04970	1905 Franklin (9)	1895	1905
Sanford 919 Main St. Sanford 04073	1768 York (12)	1769	1661

Town Address	Date Formed County (Map)	Vital Records	Town Records
Sangerville 1 Town Hall Ave./P.O. Box 188 Sangerville 04479	1814 Piscataquis (21)	1793	1814*
Scarborough 259 US Rt. 1/P.O. Box 360 Scarborough 04070	1658 Cumberland (21)	1725	1725
Searsmont Rt. 131/P.O. Box 56 Searsmont 04973	1814 Waldo (19)	1854	1814*
Searsport P.O. Box 499 Searsport 04974	1845 Waldo (13)	1801	1845
Sebago 406 Bridgton Rd. Sebago 04029	1826 Cumberland (3)	1892*	?
Sebasticook	(see Benton)		
Sebec 805 Milo Rd./P.O. Box 57 Sebec 04481	1812 Piscataquis (16)	1813	1794*
Seboeis Plantation 1134 Seboeis Rd. Seboeis 04448	1895 Penobscot (11)	1890*	1890*
Sedgwick 337 Graytown Rd./P.O. Box 40 Sedgwick 04676	1789 Hancock (27)	1792	1789*
Shapleigh 22 Back Rd./P.O. Box 26 Shapleigh 04076	1785 York (7)	1785	1785
Sherman 36 School St./P.O. Box 96 Sherman Mills 04776	1862 Aroostook (60)	1800	1904*
Shirley P.O. Box 147 Shirley 04485	1834 Piscataquis (3)	1797	1896*
Sidney 2986 Middle Rd. Sidney 04330	1792 Kennebec (13)	1772	1700*
Skowhegan 225 Water St. Skowhegan 04976	1823 Somerset (27)	1803	1814*
Smithfield P.O. Box 165 Smithfield 04978	1840 Somerset (33)	1775	1775
Smyrna U.S. Rt. 2/P.O. Box 239 Smyrna Mills 04780	1839 Aroostook (47)	1869	1869
Solon P.O. Box 214 Solon 04979	1809 Somerset (15)	1764	1804*
Somerville 665 Patricktown Rd. Somerville 04348	1858 Lincoln (3)	1798	1853*
Sorrento 79 Pomola Ave. Sorrento 04677	1895 Hancock (24)	1859*	1940*
South Berwick 180 Main St. S. Berwick 03908	1814 York (19)	1763	1763
South Bristol 470 Clarks Cove Rd. Walpole 04573	1915 Lincoln (15)	1916	1916
South Franklin (unorganized)	Franklin (19)		
South Oxford (unorganized)	Oxford (19)		
South Portland 25 Cottage Rd./P.O. Box 9422 South Portland 04116	1895 Cumberland (24)	1748	1748
South Thomaston 125 Spruce Head Rd./P.O. Box 147 South Thomaston 04858	1848 Knox (13)	1780	1780
Southeast (unorganized)	Piscataquis (23)		
Southport 361 Hendricks Hill Rd./Box 149 Southport 04576	1842 Lincoln (18)	1842	1842
Southwest Harbor P.O. Box 745 Southwest Harbor 04679	1905 Hancock (35)	1905	1905
Springfield P.O. Box 43, Rt. 6 Springfield 04487	1834 Penobscot (21)	1834	1834*
Stacyville P.O. Box 116, Route 11 Sherman Station 04777	1883 Penobscot (3)	1860	1860
Standish 175 Northeast Rd. Standish 04084	1785 Cumberland (14)	1770	1785

Town Address	Date Formed County (Map)	Vital Records	Town Records
Starks RFD 1/Box 469 Starks 04911	1795 Somerset (25)	1787	1796*
Stetson 3 Lakins Rd./P.O. Box 85 Stetson 04488	1831 Penobscot (46)	1803	1900
Steuben 294 U.S. Rt. 1 Steuben 04680	1795 Washington (42)	1769	1795*
Stockholm 63 School St./P.O. Box 10 Stockholm 04783	1991 Aroostook (13)	1897*	1891*
Stockton Springs Main St./P.O. Box 339 Stockton Springs 04981	1857 Waldo (15)	1832	1857*
Stoneham 22 Butters Hill Rd./P.O. Box 91 East Stoneham 04231	1834 Oxford (18)	1837	1912*
Stonington Main St./P.O. Box 9 Stonington 04681	1897 Hancock (37)	1897*	1897*
Stow 710 Stow Rd. N. Fryeburg 04037	1833 Oxford (17)	1830*	1830*
Strong Church Hill/P.O. Box 34 Strong 04983	1801 Franklin (16)	1779	1779
Stroudwater	(see Westbrook)		
Sullivan 1888 U.S. Hwy. 1 West Sullivan 04689	1789 Hancock (25)	1745	1745
Summit (unorganized)	Penobscot (43)		
Sumner 633 Main St., Rt. 219 West Sumner 04292	1798 Oxford (22)	1733	?
Surry 741 North Bend Rd./P.O. Box 147 Surry 04684	1803 Hancock (21)	1790	1803*
Swan's Island 1 Post Office Plaza/P.O. Box 100 Swan's Island 04685	1897 Hancock (38)	1850*	1839*
Swanville 6 Town House Rd., Rt. 131 Swanville 04915	1818 Waldo (12)	1812	1814*
Sweden 393 Black Mountain Rd. Sweden 04040	1813 Oxford (26)	1953*	1953*
Talmadge 3 Talmadge Rd. Waite 04492	1875 Washington (5)	1850	1850*
Temple P.O. Box 516 Temple 04984	1803 Franklin (20)	1784	1803*
Thomaston Knox St./P.O. Box 299 Thomaston 04861	1777 Knox (8)	1775	1776*
Thompsonborough	(see Lisbon)		
Thorndike P.O. Box 10 Thorndike 04986	1819 Waldo (4)	1776	1819*
Topsfield P.O. Box 59 Topsfield 04490	1838 Washington (2)	1834	1860*
Topsham 22 Elm St. Topsham 04086	1764 Sagadahoc (3)	1892*	1926*
Townsend	(see Southport)		
Tremont P.O. Box 65 Bernard 04612	1848 Hancock (34)	1825	1848*
Trenton 59 Oak Point Rd. Trenton 04605	1789 Hancock (22)	1786	1786
Troy 129 Rogers Rd. Troy 04987	1812 Waldo (2)	1840	1812*
Turner Turner Center Rd./P.O. Box 157 Turner 04282	1786 Androscoggin (4)	1740	1785*
Twombly (unorganized)	Penobscot (32)		
Union Common Rd./P.O. Box 186 Union 04862	1786 Knox (2)	1789	1788*
Unity (unorganized)	Kennebec (3)		
Unity 4 Clifford Common/P.O. Box 416 Unity 04988	1804 Waldo (3)	1797	1804*

Town Address	Date Formed County (Map)	Vital Records	Town Records
Upton 207 Mill Rd. Upton 04261	1860 Oxford (3)	1893	1830*
Usher	(see Stoneham)		
Van Buren 65 Main St. Van Buren 04785	1881 Aroostook (11)	1838	1881*
Vanceboro 9 Winchester Way/P.O. Box 33 Vanceboro 04491	1874 Washington (4)	1814*	1938*
Vassalboro Main St./P.O. Box 129 N. Vassalboro 04962	1771 Kennebec (14)	1764	1764
Veazie 1084 Main St. Veazie 04401	1853 Penobscot (58)	1852	1853*
Verona 16 School St./P.O. Box 1940 Bucksport 04416	1861 Hancock (12)	1900*	1955*
Vienna 328 Town Howe Rd. Vienna 04360	1802 Kennebec (4)	1752	1802*
Vinalhaven P.O. Box 815 Vinalhaven 04863	1789 Knox (16)	1785	1785
Wade P.O. Box 189 Washburn 04786	1913 Aroostook (26)	1899*	1949*
Waite Rt. 1, P.O. Box 29 Waite 04492	1876 Washington (6)	1892*	?
Waldo 54 Gurney Hill Rd. Waldo 04952	1845 Waldo (21)	1892*	?
Waldoboro 1600 Atlantic Hwy./P.O. Box J Waldoboro 04572	1773 Lincoln (11)	1778	1778
Wales 302 Center Rd. Wales 04280	1816 Androscoggin (14)	1759	1836*
Wallagrass P.O. Box 10 Wallagrass 04781	1870 Aroostook (4)	1866	1866
Waltham Rt. 179, HC 31/Box 2250 Ellsworth 04605	1833 Hancock (9)	1850*	1890*
Warren 167 Western Rd. Warren 04864	1776 Knox (7)	1795	1776*
Warsaw	(see Pittsfield)		
Washburn 1287 Main St. Washburn 04786	1861 Aroostook (27)	1898	1912*
Washington 40 Old Union Rd./P.O. Box 408 Washington 04574	1811 Knox (1)	1800	1811*
Waterboro 24 Townhouse Rd. East Waterboro 04030	1787 York (8)	1787	1787
Waterford Route 35, Valley Rd. Waterford 04088	1797 Oxford (26)	1762	1798*
Waterville 1 Common St. Waterville 04901	1802 Kennebec (7)	1813	1802*
Wayne Lovejoy Pond Rd., RR 1/Box 515 Wayne 04284	1798 Kennebec (16)	1773	1773
Webster	(see Sabbatus)		
Webster Plantation P.O. Box 144 Springfield 04487	1856 Penobscot (14)	1840	1920*
Weld 78 Dixfield Rd. Weld 04285	1816 Franklin (14)	1766	1844*
Wellington 3 Water St./P.O. Box 40 Harmony 04942	1828 Piscataquis (19)	1823	1823
Wells 208 Sanford Rd./P.O. Box 147 Wells 04090	1653 York (20)	1695	1700*
Wesley 4650 Airline Rd., Rt 9 Wesley 04654	1833 Washington (17)	1840	1832*
West Bath 219 Fosters Point Rd. West Bath 04530	1844 Sagadahoc (8)	1845	1914*
West Central Franklin	Franklin (unorganized)		

Town Address	Date Formed County (Map)	Vital Records	Town Records
West Forks Plantation Rt. 201/P.O. Box 5 West Forks 04985	1893 Somerset (4)	1898	1898*
West Gardiner 318 Spears Corner Rd. Gardiner 04345	1850 Kennebec (26)	1848	?
West Paris 25 Kingsbury St./P.O. Box 247 West Paris 04289	1957 Oxford (28)	1958*	1958*
West Pittston	(see Randolph)		
West Waterville	(see Oakland)		
Westbrook 2 York St. Westbrook 04092	1814 Cumberland (22)	1800	1718*
Westfield 6 Main St./P.O. Drawer C Westfield 04787	1905 Aroostook (38)	1892*	1894*
Westmanland Plantation 1055 Westmanland Rd. Westmanland 04783	1895 Aroostook (17)	1892	1940
Weston R.R. 1/P.O. Box 128 Danforth 04424	1835 Aroostook (70)	1814	1835*
Westport 6 Fowles Point Rd. Westport 04578	1828 Lincoln (12)	1761	1761
Whitefield 36 Townhouse Rd./P.O. Box 58 Whitefield 04353	1809 Lincoln (1)	1748	1748
Whiting Rt. 1/P.O. Box 101 Whiting 04691	1825 Washington (40)	1814	1817*
Whitney (unorganized)	Penobscot (34)		
Whitneyville HCR 71/Box 825 Machias 04654	1845 Washington (36)	1861	1890*
Willimantic RR 2/Box 134 Guilford 04443	1881 Piscataquis (7)	1859	1881*
Wilton 158 Weld Rd./P.O. Box 541 Wilton 04294	1803 Franklin (23)	1765	1765
Windham 8 School Rd. Windham 04062	1762 Cumberland (16)	1789	1823
Windsor P.O. Box 179 Windsor 04363	1809 Kennebec (23)	1797	1797
Winn 883 Route 2 Winn 04495	1857 Penobscot (13)	1872	1892*
Winslow 16 Benton Ave. Winslow 04901	1771 Kennebec (8)	1771	1771
Winter Harbor 23 Harbor Rd./P.O. Box 98 Winter Harbor 04693	1895 Hancock (30)	1895	1895
Winterport 20 School St./P.O. Box 559 Winterport 04496	1860 Waldo (7)	1860	1860*
Winterville Plantation RR 1/Box 2280-24 Quimby 04739	1895 Aroostook (16)	1876	1884*
Winthrop 15 Town Hall Lane Winthrop 04364	1771 Kennebec (18)	1720	1800*
Wiscasset 51 Bath Rd./P.O. Box 328 Wiscasset 04578	1760 Lincoln (6)	1752	1752
Woodland 843 Woodland Center Rd. Woodland 04736	1880 Aroostook (22)	1874	1875*
Woodstock 26 Monk Ave./P.O. Box 317 Bryant Pond 04219	1815 Oxford (21)	1814	1815
Woodville Rt. 116, HCR 65/Box 5058 Lincoln 04457	1895 Penobscot (7)	1900*	1930*
Woolwich 13 Nequasset Rd. Woolwich 04579	1759 Sagadahoc (6)	1756	1760
Wyman (unorganized)	Franklin (3)		
Yarmouth 200 Main St. Yarmouth 04096	1849 Cumberland (20)	1830	1849
York 186 York St. York 03909	1652 York (28)	1715	1897*

Maryland

ROGER D. JOSLYN, CG, FUGA, FGBS, FASG

In 1632 Maryland was granted to George Calvert, formerly secretary of state under King James I of England. However, since Calvert had converted to Catholicism in 1625 and so could not hold public office, the Maryland Charter was issued to his son Cecilius, alias Cecil, Second Baron Baltimore, in 1632. Nevertheless, it was Cecil's younger brother, Leonard, who brought the first colonists aboard the *Ark* and the *Dove*, landing in March 1634 at St. Clements Island near the future capital at St. Mary's. Named for Henrietta Maria, wife of King Charles I, the colony was called Maria's Land or Mariland.

Agriculture and trading were quickly established with the help of friendly Native Americans, slaves from Africa, and laborers who worked off their passage to the new land. The Europeans had good relations with the original inhabitants, although by the end of the century many Native Americans had perished from disease, war, or liquor, or in some cases, had integrated with other groups.

A significant point in Maryland's history was the passage of the Act of Toleration in 1649, which encouraged settlement by many non-conformists, not only Catholics (in Calvert, Charles, and Saint Mary's counties) but also dissenters from Virginia (in Anne Arundel County) and Friends (Quakers). The Protestant Revolution in England, however, spread unrest to Maryland, and the Crown overthrew the proprietary government in 1689. The Anglican Church was established as the state church of Maryland, and the capital moved to a more central location at Annapolis. With the conversion of the young Lord Baltimore to Protestantism, the proprietorship was restored in 1715. In 1781 Catholics were disfranchised and barred from public office,

but Jesuit Fathers continued to quietly serve a growing Catholic populace despite laws forbidding them to celebrate the Mass or perform the sacraments. A number of early Maryland gentry unions occurred through Catholic-Protestant marriages.

The earliest settlements congregated in southern Maryland, on the Western Shore, in Anne Arundel, Calvert, Charles, and Saint Mary's counties. By 1695, this included Prince George's County, which until 1748 stretched from Pennsylvania to Virginia, where Virginia fur traders had settled at Kent Island prior to Calvert's immigrants' arrival in 1634. On Maryland's Eastern Shore, Somerset County bordered Virginia, from which colony came the first settlers, soon joined by emigrants from St. Mary's and new arrivals from Britain. By the 1680s, Baltimore County, along the waterways of the Patapsco and Gunpowder rivers, was created. Because of an uncertain border, evidence of settlers in western Kent and southern and western Sussex counties in Delaware is found in Maryland records until the time of the Revolutionary War.

In the eighteenth century, settlers left the Chesapeake region and began building homes among the hills and valleys of western Maryland. Beginning in the 1730s, Germans from bordering Pennsylvania counties poured into what were then Baltimore and Frederick counties; some Quaker groups came about this time from New Jersey. In the mid-1700s, many settlers came from Pennsylvania, and servants, felons, and Jacobite rebels numbered heavily among the eighteenth-century emigrants from Britain, with the Jacobites sold as laborers. Migrations out of Maryland in the eighteenth century included Catholics from St. Mary's into Kentucky, and Moravians, most of whom went to

Winston-Salem, North Carolina, in the 1760s, where they could obtain free land. Other Germans, Ulster-Scots, and Quakers went south to Virginia and the Carolinas. With the completion of the National Road in 1818, migration westward through and out of Maryland was greatly increased. The building of the country's first railroad, the Baltimore and Ohio, as well as a canal system along the Potomac River, also increased mobility within and out of the state.

British warships visited the Chesapeake in 1777, and there was a sizable number of Loyalists among the populace, but no major battles were fought in Maryland during the American Revolution. The state was, however, the site for much action during the War of 1812. Although Maryland was loyal to the Union during the Civil War, there was much sympathy for the South in southern Western Shore counties and among the upper classes, and many fought for the Confederacy. After the war, many African-American Southerners fled to Maryland from their devastated homes. About this same time a large influx of Germans and eastern Europeans began to pour through Baltimore, one of the major eastern ports.

Vital Records

In 1640 the Maryland Assembly provided for the recording of births, marriages, and burials by the clerk of "Every Court"; banns were to be posted three days before a marriage, but very few of these records exist. Those that do are indexed at the Maryland State Archives. When the Anglican Church became the official church of the colony in 1692, the parishes were instructed to register the births, marriages, and deaths of all residents except African Americans. Every county formed by 1770 has at least one pre-Revolution parish register, and many of these include African Americans.

The clerks of the county circuit courts were to record births and deaths beginning in 1865, but compliance was very poor. The City of Baltimore started recording births and deaths in 1875 and the counties in 1898. This arrangement of county and city recording merged into a state system in 1972. The first place to check for Maryland births (1898–1998), including those for Baltimore City (1875–1978), is the Maryland State Archives, which has microfilm of records and indexes. The state archives also has Maryland death records for 1898 to 1987 (indexes 1898–1968), with Baltimore City deaths for 1875 to 1987 (indexes 1875–1971). Birth and death records, but not corresponding indexes, are restricted—births for one hundred years and deaths for twenty years. The state archives can certify births through 1924 and deaths through 1987. County civil marriage records from 1914 through 1950 are at the state archives but are indexed only to 1930. Further information, restrictions, and fees are found online at <www.mdarchives.

state.md.us>. Maryland births from April 1898 with City of Baltimore births from January 1875, Maryland deaths occurring less than twenty years ago, and Maryland marriages from June 1951 are also available from the Division of Vital Records, State Department of Health and Mental Hygiene, 6550 Reisterstown Rd. Plaza, Baltimore, MD 21215-0020. Further instructions, restrictions, fees, and downloadable forms are online at <www.mdpublichealth.org/vsa/html/apps.html>. The fee is currently $12 and a self-addressed, stamped envelope should be sent with each record request. Access at the Division of Vital Records is more restrictive than at the Maryland State Archives. Earlier marriages, usually from the 1770s to 1919, are either with the clerk of the circuit court where the license was issued or at the Maryland State Archives. The latter also has microfilm of most of these records, with an incomplete general index to records and licenses (1650–95, 1777–1886) for the counties of Anne Arundel, Caroline, Charles, Dorchester, Frederick, Kent, Prince George's, and Somerset; there is also an index to licenses for Baltimore City and County (1777–1851). Among the published marriage licenses or "marriage records" are those for the counties of Anne Arundel, Baltimore, Caroline, Carroll, Frederick, Harford, Montgomery, Somerset, Washington, Wicomico, and Worcester. Three volumes of *Maryland Marriages* (1634–1820), compiled by Robert Barnes (Baltimore: Genealogical Publishing Co., 1975–93), were gathered from church and estate as well as public records. A similar compilation by F. Edward Wright is *Maryland Eastern Shore Vital Records* and *Supplement*, 6 vols. (Silver Spring and Westminster: Family Line Publications, 1982–2001), which covers births, marriages, and deaths (1648–1825) from church and court records.

At the Maryland State Archives are microfilms of early county vital records and a card file indexing some pre-state records kept in the counties, from the 1600s for Charles, Kent, Somerset, and Talbot counties; births (1804–77) and deaths (1865–80) for Anne Arundel County; births (1898–1923) and deaths (1898–1916) for Calvert County; births (1865–73) for Kent County; and deaths (1898–1916) for Annapolis. Another state archives index covers implied marriages from court, land, and probate records (1674–1851), while other indexes cover vital records substitutes for various time periods from Bible, cemetery, and church records. Evidence of marriages found in Revolutionary War pension files was included in Newman's *Maryland Revolutionary Records* (see Military Records).

Although a few separations were granted, there were no divorces in Maryland before the Revolutionary War. From that time until 1842, they were granted by the state legislature; see Mary Keysor Meyer, *Divorces and Names Changed in Maryland by Act of the Legislature, 1634–1854* (1970; reprint, Baltimore: Genealogical Publishing Co., 1972). Records of later divorces are with the clerk of the circuit court where the divorce was granted or at the state archives.

Many adoption files, accessible prior to 1 June 1947, are at the state archives.

Census Records

Federal

Population Schedules
- Indexed—1790, 1800, 1810, 1820, 1830, 1840, 1850, 1860, 1870, 1880, 1900, 1910, 1920, 1930
- Soundex –1880, 1900, 1920

Industry and Agriculture Schedules
- 1850, 1860, 1870, 1880

Mortality Schedules
- 1850, 1860 (1850 and 1860 indexed), 1870, 1880 (1870 and 1880 indexed for Eastern Shore)

Slave Schedules
- 1850, 1860 (both indexed)

Union Veterans Schedules
- 1890 (indexed)

Microfilm of the federal censuses and corresponding book and microfilm indexes as well as indexed mortality schedules are at the Maryland State Archives, the Maryland State Law Library, and elsewhere (see pages 3 and 17). An index to the 1860 slave schedules was compiled by Ralph Clayton in the *Maryland Genealogical Society Bulletin* 25 (1984): 92-112. Missing schedules include 1790 for Allegany, Calvert, Somerset, and part of Dorchester counties (destroyed); 1800 for Baltimore County (never taken); and 1830 for Montgomery, Prince George's, Queen Anne's, Saint Mary's, and Somerset counties.

Non-population census schedules are at the state archives, which also has the original 1880 population schedules.

Colonial

A 1776 census was taken to determine population and is indexed at the Maryland State Archives, but it is not available for all counties. A 1778 "census" is a list of males over eighteen who in some counties signed the Oath of Fidelity, and in others, those who did not. Of the few extant lists, those for nine counties were published by Gaius Marcus Brumbaugh in *Maryland Records: Colonial, Revolutionary, County and Church From Original Sources*, 2 vols. (1915–28; reprint, Baltimore: Genealogical Publishing Co., 1985). See also Bettie Stirling Carothers' compilations, *1776 Census of Maryland*, and *1778 Census of Maryland* (Lutherville, Md.: n.p., 1972). Both versions of the 1778 census published by Brumbaugh and Carothers contain transcription errors. Brumbaugh also published some of the 1778 Oaths of Fidelity (also

indexed at the Maryland State Archives); others were compiled and published in two volumes by Bettie Stirling Carothers (Lutherville, Md.: the author, 1975–78). A police census taken in Baltimore in 1868 is in the Baltimore City Archives.

Among census substitutes are *Maryland Rent Rolls Baltimore and Anne Arundel Counties, 1700–1707, 1705–1724*, from the *Maryland Historical Magazine* (Baltimore: Genealogical Publishing Co., 1976). See Tax Records for other lists.

Background Sources

J. Thomas Scharf, *History of Maryland*, 3 vols. (1879; reprint with new index, Hatboro, Pa.: Tradition Press, 1967), is one of the major standard histories of the state. More modern and excellent works include Suzanne Ellery Greene Chappelle and others, *Maryland: A History of Its People* (Baltimore: Johns Hopkins University Press, 1986); and Robert J. Brugger, *Maryland: A Middle Temperament, 1634–1980* (Baltimore: Johns Hopkins Press, 1988). Hester Dorsey Richardson, *Side-Lights on Maryland History With Sketches of Some Families*, 2 vols. (1913), was reprinted in one volume by Tidewater Publishing of Cambridge, Maryland, 1967.

Matthew Page Andrews's *Tercentenary History of Maryland*, 4 vols. (Chicago and Baltimore: The S. J. Clarke Publishing Co., 1925), is really one volume of history and three of "mug book" biographies of twentieth-century Marylanders. Other "mug book" compilations, all of which must be used with caution, are *Portrait and Biographical Record of the Eastern Shore of Maryland* (New York: Chapman, 1898); *Men of Mark in Maryland*, 4 vols. (Washington, D.C.: B.F. Johnson, Inc., 1907–12); *Genealogical and Memorial Encyclopedia of the State of Maryland*, 2 vols., edited by Richard H. Spencer (New York: The American Historical Society, 1919).

Other useful works include Richard Walsh and William Lloyd Fox, eds., *Maryland: A History, 1632–1974* (Baltimore: Maryland Historical Society, 1974); Clayton C. Hall, *The Lords of Baltimore and the Maryland Palatinate* (Baltimore: J. Murphy Co., 1902); and Harry Wright Newman, *The Flowering of the Maryland Palatinate: An Intimate and Objective History of the Province of Maryland to the Overthrow of the Proprietary Rule in 1654* (1961; reprint, Baltimore: Genealogical Publishing Co., 1985). Newman also wrote on the manor system: *Seigniory in Early Maryland* (Washington, D.C.: Descendants of Lords of the Maryland Manors, 1949).

While seemingly limited in coverage, *A Biographical Dictionary of the Maryland Legislature, 1635–1789*, by Edward C. Papenfuse and others, 2 vols. (Annapolis, Md.: Johns Hopkins University Press, 1979–85) is quite useful since it covers a lot of persons and families not found in other published works.

Two excellent works detailing large groups of persons are Grace L. Tracey and John P. Dern, *Pioneers of Old Monocacy: The Early Settlement of Frederick County, Maryland, 1721–1743* (Baltimore: Genealogical Publishing Co., 1987), and Robert W. Barnes, *Baltimore County Families, 1659–1759* (Baltimore: Genealogical Publishing Co., 1989), the latter of which also contains a very useful bibliography. Not to be overlooked is Peter Wilson Coldham's *Settlers of Maryland, 1679–1783*, consolidated ed. (Baltimore: Genealogical Publishing Co., Inc., 2002). Local histories for Maryland's twenty-three counties have been published (see pages 4-5). Many books and articles have also been written on the histories of Maryland's cities and towns.

Guides

For excellent background reading, see the chapter on Maryland by John Frederick Dorman, FASG, in Milton Rubincam, ed., *Genealogical Research: Methods and Sources*, vol. 1, rev. ed. (Washington, D.C.: The American Society of Genealogists, 1980), 271-80. Also helpful is *A Guide to Genealogical Research in Maryland*, 5th ed., by Henry C. Peden, Jr. (Baltimore: Maryland Historical Society, 2001). An inexpensive guide is George K. Schweitzer's *Maryland Genealogical Research* (Knoxville, Tenn.: the author, 1991).

Marion K. Kaminkow, *Maryland A to Z: A Topographical Dictionary* (Baltimore: Magna Carta Book Co., 1985) has a useful bibliography for the state and for each county. Henry Gannett, *A Gazetteer of Maryland and Delaware*, 2 vols. (1904; reprint in one vol., Baltimore: Genealogical Publishing Co., 1979), and Mary Keysor Meyer, *Genealogical Research in Maryland: A Guide*, 3d ed. (Baltimore: The Maryland Historical Society, 1983) are also useful.

Eleanor P. Passano, *An Index to the Source Records of Maryland: Genealogical, biographical, historical* (1940; reprint, Baltimore: Genealogical Publishing Co., 1984) indexes 20,000 Maryland surnames in published and manuscript works, as well as various types of record sources, located in the Maryland Historical Society, Library of Congress, Library of the Daughters of the American Revolution (DAR), Johns Hopkins University, and the Library of the Diocese of Maryland in Baltimore (now at the George Peabody Library). Richard J. Cox and Larry E. Sullivan, eds., *Guide to the Research Collections of the Maryland Historical Society* (Baltimore: The Maryland Historical Society, 1981) is available from the society (see also the work by Pedley under Manuscripts).

An online guide to state and county records can be found on the website of the Maryland State Archives at <www.mdarchives.state.md.us/msa/refserv/html/series.html>. Several guides to genealogical research in specific counties have been published, such as for Carroll, Howard, Montgomery, and Washington counties, and those by Donna Valley Russell for Allegany, Frederick, and Garrett counties.

Maps

Reprints of county topographical maps are available from the Maryland Department of Natural Resources, Maryland Geological Survey, 2300 St. Paul St., Baltimore, MD 21218 <www.mgs.md.gov>. A good collection of maps, atlases, and plats is at the Maryland State Archives, many of which are indexed by place and some by names of tracts and owners. Early maps of Maryland are in Russell Morrison, and others, *On the Map* (Chestertown, Md.: Washington College, 1983). Other fine and useful maps are at the Maryland Historical Society. Mary Ross Brown, *An Illustrated Genealogy of the Counties of Maryland and the District of Columbia* (Silver Spring, Md.: the author, 1967) includes maps that show the county changes and also ward maps of Baltimore for 1850, 1860, 1870, and 1880. Atlases have been published for some of the counties, and county maps are to be found in most county histories.

For the best study of mapping in Maryland, see Edward C. Papenfuse and Joseph M. Coale, III, *Atlas of Historical Maps of Maryland, 1608–1908*, revised with the new title *The Maryland State Archives Atlas of Historical Maps of Maryland, 1608–1908* (Baltimore: Johns Hopkins University Press, 1982, 2003).

Land Records

State-Land State

The Maryland State Archives has land patents (from 1634) with indexes; quitrents (yearly payments to Lord Baltimore, similar to property taxes), 1749–61 (incomplete); rent rolls (the record of these payments), 1639–1776 (incomplete); debt books (yearly compilations by Lord Baltimore's agent, giving the name of each tract and the amount owed), 1735–73; certificates of survey, 1705 to date; and warrants and assignments, 1634–1842. A separate index covers private and proprietary manors as found in the patent records. See Elizabeth Hartsook and Gust Skordas, *Land Office and Prerogative Court Records of Colonial Maryland* (1946; reprint, Baltimore: Genealogical Publishing Co., 1968, 1989).

Beverly W. Bond's "The Quitrent System in Maryland," *Maryland Historical Magazine* 5 (1910): 350-65 describes the system whereby a rent was paid on land to the proprietor, and in volumes 19-26 of the same journal were published some rent rolls. Other rent rolls are in the Calvert Papers at the Maryland Historical Society, and some have been published for Anne Arundel, Baltimore, Dorchester, Kent, Prince George's, Somerset, Talbot, and Worcester counties.

Other background information is found in Clarence P. Gould, *The Land System in Maryland, 1720–1765* (Baltimore: Johns Hopkins Press, 1913); Paul H. Giddens, "Land Policies and Administration in Colonial Maryland, 1753–1769," *Maryland*

Historical Magazine 28 (1933): 142-71; and Canville D. Benson, "Notes on the Preparation of Conveyances by Laymen in the Colony of Maryland," *Maryland Historical Magazine* 60 (1965): 3-34.

Prior to 1683, land was granted to those who transported settlers to the colony. The names of such immigrants found in the land patents (1633–80) are listed in Gust Skordas, ed., *The Early Settlers of Maryland* (1968; reprint, Baltimore: Genealogical Publishing Co., 2002).

Other early land records have been published in separate volumes or in journals. For the names of Revolutionary soldiers to whom land in Allegany County was granted in 1781, see J. Thomas Scharf's *History of Western Maryland*, 2 vols. (1882; reprint, Baltimore: Regional Publishing Co., 1968). The names given to tracts by their original owners are important because most have been retained and are a way of tracing a piece of property. The Maryland State Archives has an index to tract names, and Donna Valley Russell's "Finding Land Tracts," *Western Maryland Genealogy* 3 (1987): 26-29 provides helpful background on the subject.

Deeds, mortgages, and bills of sale are recorded in the county circuit court, where standard indexes are also available. Mortgages were often recorded separately in later years. Microfilms of all county land records are available at the Maryland State Archives, which also has the original record books and indexes of many counties. At some courthouses there are microfilms of earlier records that have been transferred to the Maryland State Archives. A law enacted in 1784 required that abstracts of county deeds be sent to Annapolis. The extant records pertain mostly to counties whose early land records were destroyed, such as Calvert and Saint Mary's.

Early deeds could be recorded in both county courts and Provincial and General courts. Indexes to the latter for 1658 to 1815, by name of person or tract, are available at the state archives.

Among the published abstracts of land records are those for the counties of Anne Arundel, Baltimore, Calvert, Cecil, Charles, Dorchester, Frederick, Kent, Prince George's, Somerset, Talbot, Wicomico, and Worcester.

Probate Records

Before 1777 estates were recorded in the Prerogative Court, thus the records are "complete" despite courthouse fires and other losses at the county level. These include wills, inventories, accounts, balances of final distribution, and testamentary proceedings, all indexed at the state archives. For the 41 volumes of Prerogative Court wills (now at the Maryland State Archives and described in the work by Hartsook and Skordas cited under Land Records), see James M. Magruder, Jr., comp., *Index of Maryland Colonial Wills, 1634–1777*, 3 vols. (1933; reprint in one vol., with additions by Louise E. Magruder, Baltimore: Genealogical Publishing Co., 1986). The wills through 1743 were abstracted by Jane Baldwin Cotton in *The Maryland Calendar of Wills*, 8 vols. (1904–28; reprint, Baltimore, Genealogical Publishing Co., 1968), and continued in eight more volumes by F. Edward Wright from 1744 through 1777 (Westminster, Md.: Family Line Publications, 1994–97). Abstracts of later wills were also made by Annie Walker Burns, comp., *Abstracts of Maryland Wills* (Books 24–38, 1744–73), 15 parts (Annapolis, Md.: the author, 1938–45), although these abstracts are filled with errors, and by James M. Magruder, Jr., comp., *Maryland Colonial Abstracts: Wills, Accounts and Inventories, 1772–1777*, 5 vols. (1934–39; reprint in one vol., Baltimore: Genealogical Publishing Co., 1968). See also *Index to Inventories of Estates, 1718–1777* (Annapolis, Md.: Hall of Records Commission, 1947), and the following works compiled by Vernon L. Skinner, Jr., published by Family Line Publications of Westminster, Md.: *Abstracts of the Inventories of the Prerogative Court of Maryland* (1718–77), 17 vols. (1981–88); *Abstracts of the Inventories and Accounts of the Prerogative Court of Maryland, 1685–1718*, 11 vols. (1992–97); *Abstracts of the Administration Accounts of the Prerogative Court of Maryland* (1718–77) (1995–99); and *Abstracts of the Balance Books of the Prerogative Court of Maryland* (1755–77), 3 vols. (1995–97) covering Libers 2-7. For Liber 1 of the Balance Books, covering 1751 to 1755, see Debra Smith Moxey, comp., *Maryland Balance Book* (Madison, Md.: Dorchester Roots, 1993).

After 1777 probates were recorded in the county Orphans' Court. Indexes to wills kept in courthouses have been published for the counties of Allegany, Anne Arundel, Baltimore, Calvert, Cecil, Charles, Frederick, Garrett, Harford, Howard, Kent, Prince George's, Saint Mary's, Somerset, and Washington. Abstracts of many county wills have been published, including Anne Arundel, Caroline, Dorchester, Frederick, Harford, Kent, Montgomery, Prince George's, Queen Anne's, Saint Mary's, Somerset, Talbot, Washington, Wicomico, and Washington. The twenty volumes for Baltimore County (1783–1845), compiled by Annie Walker Burns, should be checked with original records for accuracy. Leslie and Neil Keddie published earlier Baltimore County wills for 1666 to 1760 (Salisbury, Md.: Family Tree Bookshop, 2002). Some abstracts are found in journals, such as those for Frederick County in *Western Maryland Genealogy*, as are indexes, such as that for Carroll County in the *Carrolltonian* (1984). Other county estate records that have been published include administrations, inventories, guardianship bonds, and distributions.

While some early original will books and other record volumes of estate records have been retained in the counties, most of these have been transferred to the state archives and are also available there on microfilm. Microfilms of early records are found in a few of the counties.

Court Records

In many cases, efforts to recover the early proprietary records of Maryland, which were privately kept by the Calvert family, have been successful, although some material has disappeared. The earliest surviving proprietary and royal papers for the period 1637 to 1785 were published in *Calendar of Maryland State Papers No. 1 The Black Books* (1943; reprint, Baltimore: Genealogical Publishing Co., 1967). At the Maryland State Archives are various records of and indexes to the provincial and general court (1658–1805) and the chancery (equity) court (1668–1851). An index to depositions from a variety of sources (1668–1789) was published in the *Maryland Historical Magazine* 23 (1928): 101-54, 197-242, 293-343. Other early court and related records have been published and indexed, such as provincial and county records from 1637 to the 1780s in seventy-two volumes of *The Archives of Maryland*, now online at the state archives' website. For the colonial period, see Debbie Hooper, *Abstracts of Chancery Court Records of Maryland, 1669–1782* (Westminster, Md.: Family Line Publications, 1996). One interesting sample of information from county court records is Millard Millburn Rice, ed., *This Was the Life: Excerpts from the Judgment Records of Frederick County, Maryland, 1748–1765* (1979; reprint, Baltimore: Clearfield Co., 2002). Some court records have been published for the counties of Caroline, Carroll, Charles, Montgomery, and Somerset.

Many twentieth-century court records are still in the counties, with earlier records or copies in the state archives. In the Orphans' Court, the clerk of which is the register of wills, are wills and other estate records. Taxes and road surveys are in the commissioner's office. A wonderful guide to the county court records in the counties and the Maryland State Archives (original documents, record books, and microfilm) is Morris L. Radoff, Gust Skordas, and Phebe R. Jacobsen, *The County Courthouses and Records of Maryland, Part II: The Records* (Annapolis, Md.: The Hall of Records Commission, 1963). Following a discussion of each type of record, a county-by-county listing covers what is available. Courthouse fires and other losses of records are mentioned. The guide also has pictures of the various types of indexing systems found throughout the counties. It should be noted, however, that much material has been transferred from the counties to the state archives since the publication of the work, and updated information should be sought in Annapolis.

Tax Records

Available at the Maryland State Archives with index is a Maryland tax assessment of 1783, which is "more complete" than the 1776 or 1778 "censuses" (see Census Records). Robert W. Barnes and Bettie Stirling Carothers abstracted the *1783 Tax List of Baltimore County, Maryland* (Lutherville, Md.: Bettie Stirling

Carothers, 1978), but while it has some omissions, it serves as an index to photocopies of the originals published as *Maryland Tax List, 1783: Baltimore County* from the collection of the Maryland Historical Society (Philadelphia: Historic Publications, 1970). The counties of Calvert, Cecil, Harford, and Talbot are covered by Bettie Carothers, comp., *1783 Tax List of Maryland, Part I* (Lutherville, Md.: the compiler, 1977). Furthermore, there is a two-part index to the 1783 list, one by names of property owners, the other by names of the tracts, online at the state archives' website.

The earliest tax records are to be found among the proprietary papers, dating from the 1630s. Some early tax records have been published, such as Raymond B. Clark, Jr., and Sara Seth Clark, comps., *Baltimore County, Maryland Tax Lists, 1699–1706* (Washington, D.C.: Raymond B. Clark, Jr., 1964). At the Maryland State Archives is a tax list for St. Anne's Parish, Anne Arundel County (1764–66). Also here are the surviving 1798 U.S. direct tax records for Anne Arundel County (indexed), Baltimore County and City, and the counties of Caroline, Charles, Harford, Prince George's, Queen Anne's, Saint Mary's, Somerset, and Talbot. Separate volumes of the 1798 U.S. Direct Tax lists have been published for Baltimore, Carroll, and Somerset counties. Richard J. Cox edited *A Name Index to the Baltimore City Tax Records, 1798–1808, of the Baltimore City Archives* (Baltimore: Baltimore City Archives and Records Management Office, 1981).

Cemetery Records

The *Directory of Maryland's Burial Grounds*, by the Genealogical Council of Maryland (Westminster, Md.: Family Line Publications, 1996), provides the location of public and private cemeteries.

The Maryland State Archives has indexes to cemetery records for various time periods. Some have been published in the *Maryland Genealogical Society Bulletin* and other journals and in individual works covering large parts of Anne Arundel, Baltimore, Carroll, Cecil, Dorchester, Frederick, Garrett, Harford, Kent, Prince George's, Queen Anne's, Saint Mary's, Somerset, Washington, Wicomico, and Worcester counties. A great number of grave marker inscriptions have been transcribed by members of the Maryland DAR and will be found at the Maryland Historical Society and the DAR Library in Washington, D.C. See also Helen W. Ridgely, *Historic Graves of Maryland and the District of Columbia* (1908; reprint, Baltimore: Genealogical Publishing Co., 2002).

Church Records

A search for church records should begin with Edna A. Kanely, comp. and ed., *Directory of Maryland Church Records*

(Westminster, Md.: Family Line Publications, 1987), arranged by county and giving a range of dates of available records for over 2,600 churches with mailing addresses. Somewhat dated but still quite useful is the list in Passano (see Background Sources). Also helpful are Percy G. Skirven, *First Parishes of the Province of Maryland* (Baltimore: The Norman, Remington Co., 1923), and Abdel Ross Wentz, *History of the Maryland Synod* (Harrisburg, Pa.: n.p., 1920).

The largest collection of church records is at the Maryland Historical Society, with a consolidated index, and many are at the Maryland State Archives, which has various original and microfilmed records, many with indexes. Some church records have been published in the *Maryland Genealogical Society Bulletin* or in individual books, such as those for St. Paul's in Baltimore and for many German churches in the western counties.

Although Catholicism is very important to the history of Maryland, the disfranchisement of Catholics after the establishment of the Anglican Church in 1692 largely contributed to the lack of record keeping prior to the Revolutionary War. One source for Saint Mary's County in the 1700s, however, is Timothy J. O'Rourke's *Catholic Families of Southern Maryland* (1980; reprint, Baltimore: Genealogical Publishing Co., 1985). Records of the German churches and the Society of Friends are very good. The latter were early settlers of Maryland, along with Anglicans and Catholics. Phebe R. Jacobsen's *Quaker Records in Maryland* (Annapolis, Md.: Hall of Records Commission, 1966) is an excellent guide to the original and microfilmed Friends' records at the Maryland State Archives. Some Quaker records were published in Kenneth Carroll, *Quakerism on the Eastern Shore* (Baltimore: Maryland Historical Society, 1970), and other records are at the Maryland Historical Society, the state archives, and the Friends Historical Library in Swarthmore, Pennsylvania.

Military Records

The Maryland State Archives has an incomplete index to colonial muster and payroll records for the period 1732 to 1772, as well as various records and indexes for the later wars and military units. Muster and payrolls of colonial Maryland militia are included in Murtie June Clark's *Colonial Soldiers of the South, 1732–1774* (Baltimore: Genealogical Publishing Co., 1983). Also helpful is Henry C. Peden, Jr., *Colonial Maryland Soldiers and Sailors, 1634–1734* (Westminster, Md.: Willow Bend Books, 2001). The National Archives—Mid-Atlantic Region has microfilms of the Revolutionary War military service (with index) and pension records (arranged alphabetically), the index to War of 1812 and Spanish-American War service records, and name indexes to Union and Confederate soldiers in the Civil War. Lists of Revolutionary War muster rolls were published in volume 18 of *Archives of Maryland* (1900; reprint, Baltimore: Genealogical

Publishing Co., 1972). Helpful for Revolutionary research are Raymond B. Clark, Jr., *Maryland Revolutionary Records: How to Find Them & Interpret Them* (St. Michaels, Md.: the author, 1976); S. Eugene Clements and F. Edward Wright, *Maryland Militia in the Revolutionary War* (Westminster, Md.: Family Line Publications, 1987); and Harry Wright Newman, comp., *Maryland Revolutionary Records: Data Obtained from 3,050 Pension Claims and Bounty Land Applications* (1938; reprint, Baltimore: Genealogical Publishing Co., 1987). Much manuscript material is located through *An Inventory of Maryland State Papers, Volume I, The Era of the American Revolution, 1775–1789*, edited by Edward C. Papenfuse and others (Annapolis, Md.: Hall of Records Commission, 1977). For Marylanders on the other side, see Richard Arthur Overfield's *The Loyalists of Maryland During the American Revolution*, thesis, University of Maryland (Ann Arbor: University Microfilms, 1968), and M. Christopher New, *Maryland Loyalists in the American Revolution* (Centerville, Md.: Tidewater, 1996).

For the nineteenth century, helpful published references include William M. Marine, *The British Invasion of Maryland, 1812–1815* (1913; reprint, Hatboro, Pa.: Tradition Press, 1965; and Baltimore: Genealogical Publishing Co., 1977); F. Edward Wright, *Maryland Militia, War of 1812*, 7 vols. (Silver Spring: Family Line Publications, 1979–85); Thomas Huntsberry, *Western Maryland, Pennsylvania and Virginia Militia in Defense of Maryland, 1805 to 1815* (Baltimore: the author, 1983); L. Allison Wilmer and others, *History and Roster of Maryland Volunteers, War of 1861–5*, 2 vols. (1898; reprint, Westminster, Md.: Family Line Publications, 1987); William W. Goldsborough, *The Maryland Line in the Confederate Army 1861–1865*, 2d ed. (1900; reprint with index, Port Washington, N.Y.: Kennikat Press, 1972); and Daniel P. Hartzler, *Marylanders in the Confederacy* (Silver Spring: Family Lines Publications, 1986).

World War I participants from Maryland are found in a list compiled by the Maryland War Records Commission (Baltimore, 1933). The War Records Division of the Maryland Historical Society compiled five volumes of *Maryland in World War II, Register of Service Personnel* (1965). Some military history is available at the State of Maryland Military Department, Room B14, Fifth Regiment Armory, 219 29th Division St., Baltimore, MD 21201-2288.

Periodicals, Newspapers, and Manuscript Collections

Periodicals

The Maryland Historical and Genealogical Bulletin was published privately in twenty-one volumes from 1930 to 1950. *The*

Maryland Genealogical Society Bulletin has been published by the Maryland Genealogical Society since 1960 and has included the usual fare of genealogical records, including marriage licenses, cemetery and Bible records, wills, militia lists, naturalizations, railroad employees, slave lists, and vital records, as well as compiled genealogies.

Maryland Historical Magazine has been published by the Maryland Historical Society since 1906 and has included much historical and genealogical material. Like many other historical magazines, the *Maryland Historical Magazine* stopped publishing genealogical material for some years. In 1980 Genealogical Publishing Company issued two volumes of *Maryland Genealogies: A Consolidation of Articles from the Maryland Historical Magazine.*

The Maryland and Delaware Genealogist was introduced in 1959 by Raymond B. Clark, Jr., and his mother, Sara Seth Clark, who published the standard abstracts of records and genealogies. *The Maryland Original Research Society of Baltimore Bulletin* was published in Baltimore from 1906 to 1913 and included lists of early settlers, genealogies, cemetery and family Bible records, militia lists, oaths of fidelity, and so forth. A reprint in one volume, edited by Albert Levin Richardson, was published in 1979 by Genealogical Publishing Company.

Western Maryland Genealogy, published by GenLaw Resources, Box 9187, Gaithersburg, MD 20898-9187 <www.genlawresources.com> covers Allegany, Carroll, Frederick, Garrett, Montgomery, and Washington counties. Considerable Maryland material, including genealogies, newspaper abstracts, tax lists, records of servants, and other source records, can also be found in the *National Genealogical Society Quarterly* (see page 13).

Newspapers

One of the first places to hunt for a Maryland newspaper is *Newspapers in Maryland Libraries: A Union List,* by Eleanore O. Hofstetter and M. S. Eustis (Baltimore: Maryland Department of Education, Division of Library Development, 1977). The Maryland State Archives has many newspapers, as well as guides to and abstracts from them. See also *Newspapers of Maryland: A Guide to the Microfilm Collection of Newspapers in the Maryland State Archives* (Annapolis, Md.: Maryland State Archives, 1990).

Newspaper abstracts have been published for several localities, especially for Baltimore. These include three works by Robert Barnes: *Marriages and Deaths from Baltimore Newspapers, 1796–1816; Marriages and Deaths from the Maryland Gazette, 1727–1839* (Baltimore: Genealogical Publishing Co., 1973, 1978); *Gleanings From Maryland Newspapers, 1727–95,* 4 vols. (Lutherville, Md.: Bettie Carothers, 1975–76); and Thomas L. Hollowak's two-volume *Index to Marriages and Deaths in The (Baltimore) Sun, 1837–1850 ... 1851–1860* (Baltimore: Genealogical Publishing Co., 1978). Abstracts of obituaries and marriages in *The Sun* and *Sun Almanac* for 1861 to 1915 were continued in volumes by Joseph C. Maguire, Jr., Francis P. O'Neill, and Walter E. Arps, Jr. Other large-scale compilations are those by F. Edward Wright: *Western Maryland Newspaper Abstracts 1786 ... 1810,* 3 vols.; and, with I. Harper, *Maryland Eastern Shore Newspaper Abstracts ... (1790–1834),* 8 vols. (Silver Spring: Family Line Publications, 1981–87). See also Karen Mayer Green, comp., *The Maryland Gazette, 1727–1761: Genealogical and Historical Abstracts* (Galveston, Texas: Frontier Press, 1990). The *Gazette* was Maryland's first newspaper and also included news about Delaware, Pennsylvania, and Virginia. Other newspaper items, mostly marriage and death notices, have been published for the counties of Allegany, Caroline, Carroll, Cecil, Frederick, Harford, Montgomery, and Washington.

Manuscripts

Avril J. M. Pedley, comp., *The Manuscript Collections of The Maryland Historical Society* (Baltimore: Maryland Historical Society, 1968) supplements the Cox/Sullivan Guide (see Background Sources) and is updated in the *Maryland Historical Magazine* by notes of subsequent additions to the manuscript collection.

Indexes to many special collections, including the Calvert family collection (at the Maryland Historical Society) and other private papers, state documents, and census and election records, as well as guides to photograph collections, are at the Maryland State Archives.

Archives, Libraries, and Societies

Maryland State Archives
350 Rowe Blvd.
Annapolis, MD 21401
www.mdarchives.state.md.us

In a beautiful building that opened in 1986, the Maryland State Archives, formerly the Hall of Records, is the central place for original source record research. Generally, one can expect to find all colonial governmental records as well as those from statehood up to 1900 and in many cases much later, as it is the official depository for all "state" records created before 28 April 1788, and for noncurrent records of state agencies, counties, and towns. Some service is available by mail; write for details and fees. *Bulletin No. 17: A Guide to the Index Holdings of the Maryland State Archives* is available for a nominal fee. The state archives sells microfilm of newspapers (see Newspapers). *The Archives of Maryland* and several hundred other volumes of governmental records and historical publications are available on the state archives' website at <www.mdarchives.state.md.us/megafile/msa/speccol/sc2900/sc2908/html/index.html>.

Maryland Genealogical Society

201 W. Monument St.

Baltimore, MD 21201-4674

www.mdgensoc.org

Not a library, the society is the publisher of the *Maryland Genealogical Society Bulletin* (see Periodicals).

Maryland State Law Library

361 Rowe Blvd.

Annapolis, MD 21401-1697

www.lawlib.state.md.us

Primarily a law library, it also has a large collection of useful books, maps, newspapers, the federal censuses and 1850 mortality schedules, and other items on microfilm. A guide to the library's genealogical holdings is available for a nominal fee.

Maryland Historical Society

201 W. Monument St.

Baltimore, MD 21201-4674

www.mdhs.org

The society provides a free list of genealogists or, for a fee, will have a professional genealogist check their indexed holdings. The society publishes the *Maryland Historical Magazine* (see Periodicals). In 1883, it also began *The Archives of Maryland*, now published by the Maryland State Archives, which sells back issues. See also the published guide to the society's collection under Background Sources.

George Peabody Library of Johns Hopkins University

17 E. Mount Vernon Pl.

Baltimore, MD 21202

Formerly the Peabody Institute Library, it is best known for its British collection of over 2,500 published English and Welsh parish registers and British and German heraldry. While its Maryland collection is not strong, the library has a wide variety of published material, including periodicals, for New England and the Mid-Atlantic regions.

Baltimore City Archives

211 E. Pleasant St., Rm. 201

Baltimore, MD 21202

This archives has a name index to the municipal records (1756–1938), compiled by the Works Progress Administration (WPA); indexes to Port of Baltimore ships' passenger lists kept by the city (1833–66) and those from the National Archives (1820–1909); and the index to naturalizations in the U.S. circuit and district courts for Maryland (Baltimore City) (1797–1951). These indexes can be searched for a fee of $4 per request. Other useful records here, dating from 1729, include maps, tax records from 1798, an 1868 police census (incomplete), and voter registrations (1838, 1839, 1868, and 1877–89). For more detail, consult William G. LeFurgy, *The Records of A City: A Guide to the Baltimore City Archives* (Baltimore: City Archives and Records Management Office, 1984).

Special Focus Categories

Immigration

Ships' passenger lists for the Port of Baltimore (1891–1948; earlier lists are in Washington, D.C.) and indexes to passenger lists for 1820 to 1952 are at the National Archives—Mid-Atlantic Region and the Maryland Historical Society. The index (1820–1909) is also available at the Baltimore City Archives. For the early period, see Michael H. Tepper, ed., *Passenger Arrivals at the Port of Baltimore, 1820–1834*, transcribed by Elizabeth P. Bentley (Baltimore: Genealogical Publishing Co., 1982). Harry Wright Newman's *To Maryland from Overseas* (1982; reprint, Baltimore: Genealogical Publishing Co., 2002) lists some Jacobite rebels who were sold into service in Maryland. For the colonial period, see also Peter Wilson Coldham, *The King's Passengers to Maryland and Virginia* (Westminster, Md.: Family Line Publications, 1997).

Naturalization

Naturalizations granted in U.S. district and circuit courts in Maryland (Baltimore) are available on microfilm at the National Archives—Mid-Atlantic Region in Philadelphia, with an index for the years 1797 to 1951. Some early naturalization petitions were destroyed by fire. The index is also available at the Baltimore City Archives and Maryland Historical Society. The Maryland State Archives has index/abstract cards for these courts (1797–1906), as well as indexes for 1925 to 1951 and for the naturalization of soldiers (1918–23). Other naturalization records are available at the Maryland State Archives and in the county courthouses. Citizenship was granted in the provincial period (1634–1776) by the court, legislature, or the governor and council, and these records are indexed at the Maryland State Archives. See also Jeffrey A. and Florence Leone Wyand, *Colonial Maryland Naturalizations* (Baltimore: Genealogical Publishing Co., 1975) for records of naturalizations (1660–1775). Additional naturalizations from 1733 from Maryland Commission Book 82 were abstracted and published in *Maryland Historical Magazine*, vols. 26 and 27 (1931–32). Robert Andrew Oszakiewski compiled two volumes of *Maryland Naturalization Abstracts*, covering Baltimore County and City (1784–1851), the County Court of Maryland (1779–1851), and the U.S. Circuit Court for Maryland (1790–1851) (Westminster, Md.: Family Line Publications, 1995–96). The Maryland State Archives also has an index to naturalizations (1781–1906), granted by the General Courts of the Eastern and Western Shores and in certain county courts. There are separate indexes for naturalizations in Baltimore City (1793–1933) and Baltimore County (1872–1902). Records for some counties have been published, such as those for Frederick County (1785–1850) and for Washington County prior to 1880.

African American

The Maryland State Archives has sale statistics, manumission records, certificates of freedom, and lists of slave owners for most counties with some limited indexes. Maryland African Americans who helped colonize Liberia and other places in Africa are discussed by Penelope Campbell in *The Maryland State Colonization Society, 1831–1857* (Urbana: University of Illinois Press, 1971). A very useful guide is *Researching Black Families at the Hall of Records*, by Phebe R. Jacobson (Annapolis, Md.: Hall of Records Commission, 1984).

Not much has been published about slavery in Maryland, but two authors provide studies from the two ends of the era: Raphael Cassimere, Jr., *The Origins and Early Development of Slavery in Maryland, 1633 to 1715* (thesis, Lehigh University; Ann Arbor: University Microfilms, 1975), and Charles Lewis Wagndt, *Mighty Revolution: Negro Emancipation in Maryland, 1862–1864* (Baltimore: Johns Hopkins Press, 1964). Published records include Paul Heinegg, *Free African Americans of Maryland and Delaware: From the Colonial Period to 1810* (Baltimore: Clearfield Co., 2000); Jerry M. Hynson, *Maryland Freedom Papers.* Vol. 1: Anne Arundel County, Vol. 2: Kent County, Vol. 3: 1832–1860 (Westminster, Md.: Family Line Publications, 1996, 1997, 2001); Hynson's *Free African Americans of Maryland 1832, Including Allegany, Anne Arundel, Calvert, Caroline, Cecil, Charles, Dorchester, Frederick, Kent, Montgomery, Queen Anne's, and Saint Mary's Counties* (Family Line Publications, 1998); Mary K. Meyer, *Free Blacks in Harford, Somerset, and Talbot Counties, Maryland, 1832* (Mt. Airy, Md.: Pipe Creek Publications, 1991); and Marsha Lynne Fuller, *African American Manumissions of Washington County, Maryland* (Hagerstown, Md.: Desert Sheik, 1997).

Native American

There is little published material about Native Americans in Maryland. A general history is *Indians of Early Maryland* by Harold R. Manakee (Baltimore: Maryland Historical Society, 1959), and a more specific study is James A. McAllister's *Indian Lands in Dorchester County, Maryland: Selected Sources, 1669 to 1870* (Cambridge, Md.: the author, 1962).

Ethnic Groups

A number of books have been published about Maryland Friends (Quakers), Germans, and Jews. Some Quaker resources have been discussed above under Church Records. Among those covering the Germans are *The Maryland Germans: A History*, by Dieter Cunz (1948; reprint, Port Washington, N.Y.: Kennikat Press, 1972) and *The Pennsylvania-German in the Settlement of Maryland*, by Daniel Wunderlich Nead (1914; reprint, Baltimore: Genealogical Publishing Co., 1985). For Jews, see "The Jews of Baltimore [to 1830]," in *American Jewish Historical Quarterly*, vols. 64 and 67, and *Generations*, the journal of the Jewish Historical Society of Maryland, published since 1978.

County Resources

Maryland has twenty-three counties and the city of Baltimore, which is not under county jurisdiction. At the courthouses are recorded transfers of land, estates, and other records. The first column below indicates the map coordinate. In the second column is the name of the county with the mailing address of the county circuit court clerk, where deeds, mortgages, vital records, divorces, naturalizations, and other matters are recorded. In the third column is the date the county was created and the name or names of the parent county or counties. The date the earliest land deed was recorded appears in the fourth column. In the last column is the date when Orphans' Court records begin, followed by the mailing address of that court's clerk and the register of wills, if different from the circuit court clerk. While some records are available in the counties, most original and/or microfilm copies of land, estate, vital, and court records have been transferred to the Maryland State Archives. As new county records are created, they will continue to be microfilmed and sent to the state archives. Other county offices not included below may have different mailing addresses.

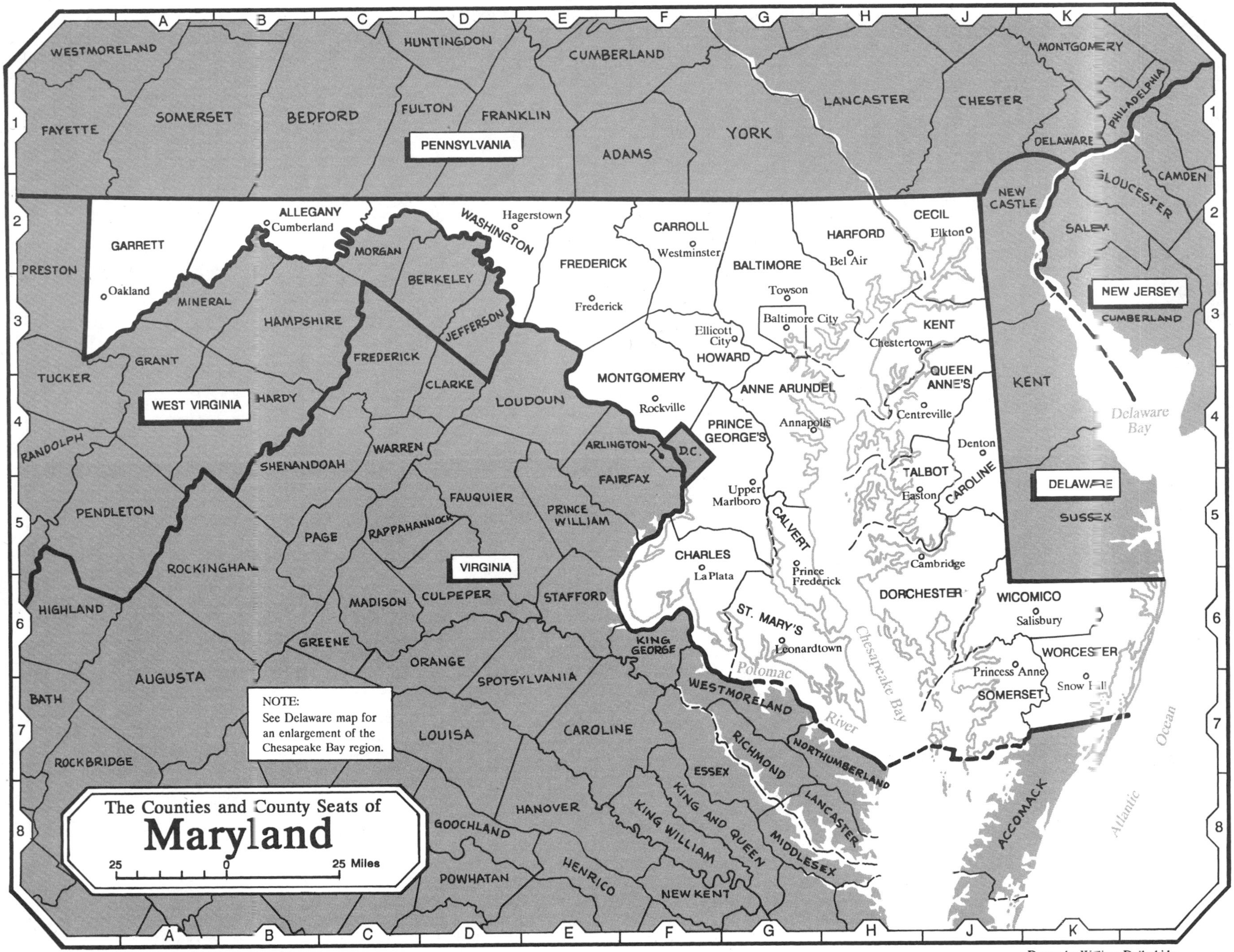

The Counties and County Seats of
Maryland

25   0   25 Miles

NOTE:
See Delaware map for
an enlargement of the
Chesapeake Bay region.

Drawn by William Dollarhide

307

MARYLAND

Map	County Circuit Court	Date Formed Parent County/ies	Deeds	Orphans' Court
B2	**Allegany** 30 Washington St. Cumberland 21502	1789 Washington	1791	1790
	A courthouse fire in 1893 destroyed marriage records for 1791–1847 and naturalizations for 1892–1893.			
G4	**Anne Arundel** P. O. Box 2395 Annapolis 21404-2395	1650 original	1653	1777 7 Church Cir. Annapolis 21401-2368
	The courthouse was destroyed by fire in 1704, with the loss of all but three court record volumes. Deeds before 1699 were lost, but there are five volumes of re-recorded deeds.			
G2	**Baltimore** 401 Bosley Ave. Towson 21204-4403	by 1659/60 original	1661	1666
G2	**Baltimore City** Land Records Division 100 N. Calvert St., Rm. 610 Baltimore 21202-3417	1851 Baltimore Co.	1851	1851 111 N. Calvert St. Baltimore 21202
G5	**Calvert** 175 Main St. Prince Frederick 20678	1654 original called Patuxent until 1658	1882	1882
	Most records were destroyed when the courthouse burned in 1882, but some deeds dating back to 1840 were re-recorded. Abstracts of deeds sent to Annapolis beginning in 1784 and provincial court deeds/land office records also make up for some of the destroyed records.			
J4	**Caroline** 109 Market St. P. O. Box 356 Denton 21629-0356	1773 Dorchester/ Queen Anne's	1774	1774 109 Market St. P. O. Box 416 Denton 21629-0416
F2	**Carroll** 55 N. Court St., Rm. G-8 P. O. Box 190 Westminster 21157-0190	1837 Baltimore/ Frederick	1837	1837 55 N. Court St., Rm. 104 Westminster 21157
	Most early papers of the county court have been lost.			
J2	**Cecil** 129 East Main St. Elkton 21921	1674 Baltimore	1674	1675
	Many early court records have disappeared.			
F6	**Charles** 200 Charles St. P. O. Box 3060 La Plata 20646-3060	1658 original	1658	1665 5200 Charles St. P. O. Box 3080 La Plata 20646-3080
H6	**Dorchester** 206 High St. P. O. Box 583 Cambridge 21613-0583	1669 Somerset/ Talbot	1669	1852 206 High St. Cambridge 21613
	There are gaps in the court records. Some were probably lost in a fire in 1852.			
E2	**Frederick** 100 W. Patrick St. Frederick 21701	1748 Baltimore/ Prince George's	1748	1751
	There were two major fires, but no major loss of records.			
A2	**Garrett** 203 S. 4th St. P. O. Box 447 Oakland 21550-0447	1872 Allegany	1873	1872 313 E. Alder St., Rm. 103 Oakland 21550
H2	**Harford** 20 West Cortland St. Bel Air 21014	1773 Baltimore	1773	1774
	Some records were destroyed in a fire in 1858.			
F3	**Howard** 8360 Court Ave. Ellicott City 21043	1850 Anne Arundel	1839	1840
	The county was formed in 1838 as Howard District of Anne Arundel Co., but did not gain full county status until 1850.			
J3	**Kent** 103 North Cross St. Chestertown 21620-1511	by 1642 original	1648	1674
	A courthouse fire in 1720 destroyed some records.			
F3	**Montgomery** 50 Maryland Ave. Rockville 20850	1776 Frederick	1777	1777
	A southern section of the county was set off in 1788 to form the District of Columbia.			
	Patuxent	1654 (renamed Calvert, 1658) original		
G5	**Prince George's** 14735 Main St. P. O. Box 1600 Upper Marlboro 20773-1600	1696 Calvert/Charles	1696	1698 5303 Chrysler Way P. O. Box 1729 Upper Marlboro 20773-1729
J4	**Queen Anne's** 100 Courthouse Sq. Centreville 21617	1706 Dorchester/ Talbot/Kent	1707	1706 107 North Liberty St. P. O. Box 59 Centerville 21617-0059
G6	**Saint Mary's** 41605 Court House Dr. P. O. Box 676 Leonardtown 20650-0676	1637 original original	1827	1658 41605 Court House Dr. P. O. Box 602 Leonardtown 20650-0602
	The courthouse was destroyed by fire in 1831. Some deeds were re-recorded back to 1781, and abstracts of deeds sent to Annapolis beginning in 1784 also make up for some of the records that were destroyed.			
J7	**Somerset** 30512 Prince William St. P. O. Box 279 Princess Anne 21853-0279	1666 original	1665	1664 30512 Prince William St. Princess Anne 21853
	The courthouse burned in 1831, but the records were saved.			
H5	**Talbot** 11 N. Washington St. Easton 21601	by 1661/2 original	1662	1668 P. O. Box 816 Easton 21601-0816
	Many court records have been lost.			

Map	County Circuit Court	Date Formed Parent County/ies	Deeds	Orphans' Court
D2	Washington 95 W. Washington St Hagerstown 21740 *Some records were lost in a courthouse fire in 1871.*	1776 Frederick	1777	1777
J6	Wicomico North Division and Main St. P. O. Box 806 Salisbury 21801-0806	1867 Somerset/ Worcester	1867	1866 North Division and Main St. P. O. Box 787 Salisbury 21801-0787
K6	Worcester 1 W. Market St., Rm. 104 Snow Hill 21863- 1074	1742 Somerset	1742	1742 1 West Market St. Rm. 102

Massachusetts

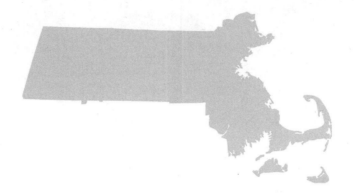

ALICE EICHHOLZ, Ph.D., CG

The Pilgrims landed on the outermost reaches of Cape Cod in 1620, considerably north of their original destination in Virginia. Providence would have it that they would create their colony based on the experimental ideals of religious freedom and self-government in a colder climate than they had expected. Plymouth Colony's development, and that of its neighbor to the near north, the Massachusetts Bay Colony, established ten years later, set a course for new models regarding the concept of community, political life, and records. During the "Great Migration" between 1620 and 1643, an estimated 20,000 people left England and settled in these two colonies that eventually merged, in 1691, to become the Province of Massachusetts.

Massachusetts was the stepping-stone for numerous other settlements that developed along the New England coast and for thousands of immigrants who came in waves across the Atlantic over the next four centuries. Settlements grew first along the shores, then along the riverbanks, and later out of the forests rich with furs and lumber. These settlements existed in contrast to those of the native inhabitants, and contained within themselves festering differences of opinion regarding religious and political views.

Some of those who dissented from their neighbors' views set out to begin their own communities, moving farther and farther west in the colony and sometimes immigrating to other locations, including most of the Eastern seaboard. They often took with them ideas about government and record keeping from their former Massachusetts communities.

Settlement continued steadily based on the mostly peaceful accord between natives, represented particularly by agreement with Massasoit, chief of the Wampanoags, and settlers. All that changed in 1675 when Massasoit's son King Phillip (Metacom) declared open warfare, raiding fifty towns in southeastern and central settlements. A year later, the resulting death (including King Phillip's) and destruction in towns ended the warfare, but confidence in settlement was not restored. The Peace of Utrecht in 1713 brought sweeping changes to the political and economic enterprises in Europe, marking the beginning of Great Britain's colonial and commercial power, and stepping up the pace of immigration again.

In the next two decades more and more towns were established as the population grew in all of lower New England. Warfare reared its influence again in a long series of French and Indian wars throughout all the colonies, sending settlers scrambling for safety back from the frontiers to the more securely established towns.

By the time of the American Revolution, nearly everyone still in Massachusetts could trace their ancestry to one of those 20,000 people in the first major immigration. Many of the French Huguenots, Irish, and Scots-Irish who had emigrated before the American Revolution married into the English families who had arrived earlier. There were also a few Portuguese and some Germans in the early development of the colonies, but it was not until later that these ethnic groups immigrated in large numbers.

Long known for disagreements with the Crown, Massachusetts, with its ideals and strong voice, became a catalyst for the American Revolution. Minutemen and Loyalists, sometimes in the same family, served their respective causes,

supported on both sides by family members and former neighbors who had settled throughout the New England colonies. The conclusion of the war found some former New Englanders in the provinces of Canada or the Port of New Orleans for their loyal opposition, and an even larger number of patriots moved to the newly developing frontiers in northern New England and New York. Maine, which remained part of the state of Massachusetts even after the colonies gained their independence, became a separate state in 1820.

The Commonwealth of Massachusetts was soon in the midst of the Industrial Revolution, which brought people with more cultural and linguistic differences to the growing state economy. A glimpse of this expanding immigration could be seen as early as the mid-seventeenth century when hundreds of Scottish prisoners—cheap labor for the ironworks in Braintree and Lynn—arrived in Boston's harbor. A steady stream of immigrants to Boston's port continued over the next two centuries, fueled by the Irish Potato Famine in the 1840s and 1850s, which provided the Industrial Revolution with a labor force previously unavailable in New England. Many other ethnic groups soon followed.

Massachusetts citizens were catalysts for another war of Northern ideals. The state sent its sons, and some daughters, to the southern battlefields of the Civil War. Industrial development continued to flourish, but by the end of the nineteenth century, New York City eventually outdistanced Massachusetts as a port for immigration. Despite that fact, the industrial development and ethnic diversity of Massachusetts have had a profound impact on life in New England, leaving records of a rich history.

Vital Records

No state in the Union can boast the depth and breadth of vital records sources that are available in Massachusetts. Starting with the arrival of the Pilgrims, vital events have been diligently, if not completely, recorded, preserved, and published. Spurred by legislative order, over 200 (out of 364) towns had all their vital records to 1850 published. The volume (or volumes) in this Systematic Series for each town is divided into births, marriages, and deaths, then alphabetized by surname and, finally, given name.

Some town vital records published before and after legislative order were printed verbatim, and then indexed, making them more valuable than those in the Systematic Series for research purposes since original family groupings remain as recorded. Other towns' vital records have been published or microfilmed since the Systematic Series. Original manuscript volumes of the Systematic Series are at the Massachusetts Archives at Columbia Point (see Archives, Libraries and Societies). Transcriptions of vital records for several western Massachusetts towns are in the Corbin Collection and those for the Braintree area are

in the Sprague Collection, both at the New England Historic Genealogical Society (see Archives, Libraries, and Societies). The latter's website and online store provide access to this material either through membership subscription to the online database or for purchase on microfilm or CD-ROM.

A listing indicating which towns have published vital records is that by Hanson and Rutherford in their chapter on Massachusetts research (see Background Sources). A code for locating vital records throughout different collections, individual publications, or the Systematic Series can be found in Marcia D. Melnyk's *Genealogist's Handbook for New England Research* (4th ed.; Boston: The New England Historic Genealogical Society, 1999). Several towns, however, have published vital records since these lists were created. The year in which vital record registration begins for a town is indicated in the Town Resources section.

Microfiche of vital records for more than 275 towns can be purchased from Archive Publishing (formerly Holbrook Research Institute), 1462 W. 1670 N., Provo, UT 84604 <www.archivepublishing.com>. Those fiches of original records are listed in a microfiche eighth edition (2000) of "Bibliography of Massachusetts Vital Records 1620–1895," available from the company's website, which provides complete information on this periodically expanding resource. Microfiche of individual towns' published Systematic Series is also available from the company.

Even though recording of vital events in towns was widespread in Massachusetts, the practice was still not universal. Most of the Systematic Series of published vital records additionally relied on documented material culled from other sources, such as church records, cemetery inscriptions, and family Bibles.

No statewide index exists that includes all the towns' records for vital events before 1841. This makes it necessary to know the appropriate town in which to locate a record before that date. However, the IGI (see pages 12-13), the membership online database for New England Historic Genealogical Society (see Archives, Libraries, and Societies), and the subscription database at Ancestry.com (see page 17) have extensive collections of Massachusetts vital records from the Systematic Series and other sources offered through their websites. These sources cannot be considered complete, but using them may be helpful in locating or eliminating towns as potential targets for vital records research when the only information known is simply "born in Massachusetts."

Some early vital records were filed by county instead of town for Suffolk, Middlesex, Essex, Plymouth (marriages only), and Hampshire (from private papers). See Michael S. Hindus' *The Records of the Massachusetts Superior Court and Its Predecessors* (Boston: Archives Division, Office of the Secretary of the Commonwealth, 1977) for a listing.

Beginning in 1841 the state mandated that a copy of each event recorded in a town or city be sent to the Secretary of the Commonwealth, which means that *two* sources exist for each event after that date: the town (or city) and the state. However, some towns were not in compliance until the late 1840s. At present, the indexes for 1841 to 1910 are in bound, ledger-style books, arranged in five-year periods, except for the first, which covers 1841 through 1850. The records are available at Massachusetts Archives. Boston records after mandatory recording do not begin in the ledger books until 1848, but all the city's vital records from 1630 are extant at Boston City Archives, 30 Millstone Rd., Hyde Park, MA 02136 <www.cityofboston.gov/archivesandrecords>. Published Boston vital records include births, deaths, marriages (1630–99); births (1700–1800); and marriages (1700–51, 1752–1809); and deaths (1700–99) (as *Deaths in the Town of Boston* [Boston: New England Historic Genealogical Society, 1999], two volumes compiled by Robert J. Dunkle and Ann S. Lainhart using multiple sources). A CD-ROM version of Clifford L. Stotts' *Vital Records of Springfield, Massachusetts to 1850* (Boston: New England Historic Genealogical Society, 2002) includes the town vital records, twenty-one cemeteries, ten churches, and eleven newspapers, among others.

As of 1 January 1896, the Massachusetts Registry of Vital Records and Statistics, 150 Mt. Vernon St., Dorchester, MA 02125-3105 <www.state.ma.us/dph/bhsre/rvr/vrrsrch.htm> is the repository for copies of town or city recorded vital records. The facility is open to the public, but marriage and birth records may be restricted. As with the bound ledger-style volumes for the 1841 to 1910 period, indexes continue in five-year periods, separated into births, marriages, and deaths. Records and indexes are transferred to the Massachusetts Archives every five years. Until individual death certificates were used in the 1900s, the name of the cemetery does not appear in the state copy, but it may be found in the town or city copy.

The 1841 to 1910 vital records ledger books and indexes for the state are open to the public and available on microfilm and in book form at the New England Historic Genealogical Society and through the Family History Library (FHL). Still, verifying the original copy at the town clerk's office is extremely important since the bound books are secondary sources and therefore subject to errors in transcription or omission from the original.

A statewide index to divorces after 1952 is available at the Registry of Vital Records and Statistics, but no records are kept there (see Court Records for location of divorces prior to 1922 and Probate Records for those filed after that date). A descriptive sheet entitled "Massachusetts Divorce Records," by Roger D. Joslyn, which originally appeared in the *Massachusetts Genealogical Council Newsletter*, may still be available from the council at P.O. Box 5393, Cochituate, MA 01778-5393 <http://home.comcast.net/~massgencouncil>.

Census Records

Federal

Population Schedules
- Indexed—1790, 1800 (incomplete), 1810, 1820, 1830, 1840, 1850, 1860, 1870, 1880, 1900, 1910, 1920, 1930
- Soundex—1880, 1900, 1920

Industry and Agriculture Schedules
- 1850, 1860, 1870

Mortality Schedules
- 1850, 1860, 1870, 1880

Union Veterans Schedules
- 1890

All of the Massachusetts federal census records and indexes are available as online images from subscription databases (see page 17). Microfilm of all federal census records is available at the New England Historic Genealogical Society, and other major repositories. The Massachusetts Archives holds original state copies and microfilm copies of the federal population, mortality, industry, and agriculture schedules. Original schedules for 1850, 1860, and 1870 are available for research; the original 1880 schedule is available if the microfilm is not clear. The Daughters of the American Revolution (DAR) have prepared an indexed transcript of the 1850 Massachusetts mortality schedule, a copy of which is at the New England Historic Genealogical Society. The 1890 Veterans enumeration and all other federal census records are available on microfilm at the National Archives—Northeast Region both in Boston (Waltham) and Pittsfield (see page 11).

The 1800 census does not include enumerations for Boston or much of Suffolk County, but the published 1798 U.S. Direct Tax for Boston may be helpful (see Tax Records).

State

Massachusetts conducted two state census enumerations (1855 and 1865), which contain information similar to the federal schedules. The originals are at the Massachusetts Archives and some transcripts with indexes have been published. Towns completed are in Essex, Middlesex, and Plymouth counties and available at the archives. This makes it possible to follow a family in the census records for every five-year period between 1850 and 1870, a critical time given immigration and Industrial Revolution mobility.

Background Sources

Colony, town, county, and state histories abound for Massachusetts. An exhaustive list of even the most helpful would

be beyond the scope of this book. The book loan program at the New England Historic Genealogical Society publishes a catalog in book and online formats of what circulates from its collection, with an extensive listing for Massachusetts. Periodical sources (see Periodicals) contain a great quantity of material on families, customs, and history of the state and New England in general.

Two comprehensive series provide a good background of understanding about both the Massachusetts Bay and Plymouth Colonies: Nathaniel B. Shurtleff and David Pulsifer, eds., *Records of the Colony of New Plymouth in New England, 1620–1691*, 12 vols. (Boston: W. White, 1855–61), and Nathaniel B. Shurtleff, ed., *Records of the Governor and Company of the Massachusetts Bay*, 5 vols. (Boston: W. White, 1853–54). Eugene Aubrey Stratton, *Plymouth Colony: Its History & People 1620–1691* (Salt Lake City: Ancestry, 1986) provides a good social history with a genealogical perspective and includes biography, customs, history, and annotated bibliography on printed material covering the colony. For later periods and locations, social history publications by Gloria L. Main and Laurel Thatcher Ulrich are important.

The following will be helpful in developing a more comprehensive history of the Bay State:

Hart, Albert Bushnell, ed. *Commonwealth History of Massachusetts, Colony, Province and State, 1605–1930*. 5 vols. 1927–30. Reprint. New York: Russell and Russell, 1967. Provides an excellent history from disputed colonial claims through the last major immigration period in the twentieth century.

Haskell, John D. *Massachusetts: A Bibliography of Its History*. 1976. Reprint. Hanover, N.H.: University Press of New England, 1983. Somewhat dated, but it surveys a broad scope of local historical material including those published in academia. Family genealogies are not included.

Following list includes three classic compilations of genealogical material for the state:

Anderson, Robert Charles. *The Great Migration Begins: Immigrants to New England, 1620–1633*. 3 vols. Boston: New England Historic Genealogical Society, 1996. A continuing project of comprehensively researched details of families of the earliest immigrants to the colonies. Available in CD-ROM version.

____ et al. *The Great Migration: Immigrants to New England 1634–1635*. 3 vols. Boston: New England Genealogic Biographical Society, 1999–2003. Extends the ongoing project through 1635 and surnames beginning with "H." Future volumes are planned.

Pope, Charles Henry. *Pioneers of Massachusetts, a Descriptive List, Drawn from the Records of the Colonies, Towns and Churches and from Other Contemporaneous Documents*. 1900. Reprint. Baltimore: Genealogical Publishing Co., 2003. Similar to Savage (below) with important differences. The introduction is essential reading.

Savage, James. *A Genealogical Dictionary of the First Settlers of New England, Showing Three Generations of Those Who Came Before May 1692*. 1860–62. Reprint. Baltimore: Genealogical Publishing Co., 1986. Arranged alphabetically by male settlers in New England before 1692. Some documentation is provided for original sources and it is cross-indexed. Now available on CD-ROM (Digital Editions, 2000) and open access online at <www.usgennet.org/usa/topic/newengland/savage>.

Society of Mayflower Descendants. *Mayflower Families Through Five Generations: Descendants of the Pilgrims Who Landed at Plymouth, Massachusetts, December, 1620*. 21 vols. Plymouth, Mass.: Society of Mayflower Descendants, 1975-present with addenda. See <www.mayflower.org/book.htm>. Not all passengers or their descendants have yet been covered in this ongoing series. Volume 3 is known to be quite unreliable. Recent publications by the society include *Mayflower Families in Process*, a series of four-generation booklets for each *Mayflower* passenger. Issued by surname of the passenger, they can be obtained from the society (see Archives, Libraries, and Societies). A few of these have been extended to five generations in separate publications.

In addition to those already cited, a very limited list of other examples of social history includes:

Cook, Edward M. *The Fathers of the Towns: Leadership and Community Structure in Eighteenth-Century New England*. Baltimore: Genealogical Publishing Co., 1976.

Jones, Douglas Lamar. *Village and Seaport: Migration and Society in Eighteenth Century Massachusetts*. Hanover, Mass.: University Press of New England, 1981. A study of Beverly and Wenham in Essex County.

Lockridge, Kenneth A. *A New England Town: The First Hundred Years, Dedham, Massachusetts, 1636–1736*. New York: W.W. Norton, 1985. A good example of use of historical material for understanding social history.

Thompson, Roger. *Sex in Middlesex: Popular Mores in a Massachusetts County, 1649–1699*. Amherst, Mass.: University of Massachusetts Press, 1986. Informative study on the American family.

In addition to Melnyk's *Handbook* discussed under Vital Records, research guides for the state include:

Blatt, Warren. *Resources for Jewish Genealogy in the Boston Area*. Boston: Jewish Genealogical Society of Greater Boston, 1996.

Crandall, Ralph J., ed. *Genealogical Research in New England*. Baltimore: Genealogical Publishing, Co., 1984.

Davis, Charlotte P. *Directory of Massachusetts Place Names, Current and Obsolete*. Lexington, Mass.: Bay State News,

1988. Compiled by the state DAR, this lists 4,000 cities, towns, villages, and other sections, all cross-indexed.

Galvin, William Francis. *Historical Data Relating to Counties, Cities and Towns in Massachusetts.* 5th ed. Boston: New England Historic Genealogical Society, 1997. This substitutes for a place-name index for towns and cities, indicating towns no longer in existence and those that spawned new towns by division.

Gardner-Wescott, Katherine A., ed. *Massachusetts Sources, Part I: Boston, New Bedford, Springfield, Worcester.* Boston: Massachusetts Society of Genealogists, 1988. This is the first part of an excellent series detailing each repository and the extent of materials held. Both public and private records are included.

Hanson, Edward W., and Homer Vincent Rutherford. "Genealogical Research in Massachusetts: A Survey and Bibliographical Guide." *The New England Historical and Genealogical Register* 135 (July 1981): 163-98. Covers in good detail many of the abnormalities in the Massachusetts public records, and lists some basic town histories as well as single and multi-ancestor genealogies.

Lainhart, Ann S. *A Researcher's Guide to Boston.* Boston: New England Historic Genealogical Society, 2003. An excellent guide to obvious and surprise sources for researching in this important port city.

Sibbison, Wendy. *Directory for Research on the Pioneer Valley, Massachusetts: Franklin, Hampshire and Hampden Counties.* Greenfield, Mass.: Greenfield Community College, 1983. Focuses on western Massachusetts.

Wright, Carroll D. *Report on the Custody and Condition of the Public Records of Parishes, Towns and Counties.* Boston: Wright & Potter, State Printers, 1889–1910.

Maps

Maps are critical to genealogical research. The Massachusetts Archives has published an eighteenth-century (1794–95) series of maps for the majority of Massachusetts towns, as well as a series originally done in 1831 that might be found in other libraries. Numerous town histories contain excellent maps that indicate dwelling places and owners at different points in town history.

As with most New England states, an *F.W. Beers Atlas* for each Massachusetts county was published in the 1870s. Major research libraries have generally printed copies of these folio-sized maps, which indicate residences, owners, schools, roads, churches, and cemeteries. The series has been reissued by Piper Publishing, 13 Church Rd., Easton, CT 06612 <www.piperpublishing.com> in CD-ROM format.

Excellent map collections of town lots and earlier land distribution exist at the Massachusetts Archives. Good printed maps are available for research at the New England Historic Genealogical Society and many town offices. Saco Valley Printing, 421 Main St., Fryeburg, ME 04037 <http://home.gwi.net/~lkane/home.html> has printed versions of nineteenth-century maps for New England, such as the Beers collection, many including structures and owners' names.

Land Records

State-Land State

Land ownership in Massachusetts descended initially from colony to proprietor and eventually to private ownership by individuals. The colonies of Plymouth and Massachusetts Bay were legally based on charters or patents from England to a company of business or trading associates. The general court for each colony (see Court Records), acting as a legislative body, established towns by granting blocks of land to a group of proprietors. The primary obligation of the proprietors was to divide the land among the settlers in the town based on family size, wealth, or both. Part of the land was held by town proprietors for the common good. See Roy Akagi, *The Town Proprietors of the New England Colonies* (1924; reprint, Gloucester, Mass.: P. Smith, 1963), or the *Great Migration Newsletter* (see Periodicals) for a discussion of the role of local proprietors in the development of towns.

Land was surveyed and plats drawn to identify who had a proprietorial share in each piece of land in town. The land itself was not actually sold in the early stages of town development. Having the use of a house lot and acreage for farming included a proprietorial right in the enterprise of the town and to further divisions of town land. See Stratton, *Plymouth Colony*, and Lockridge, *A New England Town* (both cited in Background Sources), and *Great Migration Newsletter* (see Periodicals) for examples of the land acquisition process in individual towns. Native Americans, with a different concept and understanding of land from that of the colonists, often relinquished their land claims to colonists who found the land a desirable location for a town or useful for hunting, trapping, or farming. For an excellent discussion of differing perceptions of land, see William Cronon, *Changes on the Land* (see Native American).

Successive divisions of town land occurred, since not all the land was divided at one time. As families grew and newcomers arrived, shares of additional divisions were allocated to more people. Influx of the Great Migration period (1620–43), overcrowding, the desire for more land, and disagreements among inhabitants over religious, social, and political concerns all forced the development of new towns, and the process of land acquisition was repeated. Those who wished to form a new town petitioned the general court and the land was granted to the

proprietors to divide as fit the needs of the new town. Published grants before county formation (1643 in Massachusetts Bay, 1685 in Plymouth) are found among the records of the colony (see Shurtleff and Pulsifer, *Records ... New Plymouth*, and Shurtleff, *Records ... Massachusetts Bay*, cited in the *Background Sources*).

When a county system became established, land transactions became part of the county's records. Eventually, land was sold by proprietors to individuals and between individuals. Proprietors continued to keep records on "common and undivided lands" in a town, some well into the nineteenth century.

Deeds are recorded in the earliest records of the counties. Those for Suffolk County (1640–97), York County (Maine) (1641–1737), and some of Plymouth Colony (1620–51) have been published. A series of abstracts for the latter continues in the revived *Mayflower Descendant* (see Periodicals). Essex County Registry of Deeds has put images from its first ten volumes available online at <www.salemdeeds.com>.

Deeds are the purview of the county registry of deeds. Grantor and grantee indexes are available with date of recording, and sometimes the location (or town) is listed in the index, although this practice is not uniform. The first fourteen volumes of Suffolk County deeds, entitled *Suffolk Deeds* (1640–97) (Boston: City Printers, 1880–1906) have, in addition to the grantor and grantee indexes, an every-name index. Original deeds through 1799 have an every-name index at the registry office. These every-name indexes indicate all names in addition to grantors/grantees found in the deeds, such as witnesses and abutters. Most of the original Suffolk deeds are now in the basement at the Massachusetts Archives instead of the registry office.

In New England fashion, deeds generally indicate the residence of, and sometimes occupations for, both sets of parties and describe the land in either lot numbers, divisions, metes, and bounds, or abutters—sometimes all four. There are conveyances, or legal transactions, for property, personal possessions, pews in churches, sale and manumissions of slaves, indentures, mortgages, pre-nuptial agreements, and dower rights. Some conveyances for cemetery plots can be found in nineteenth- and twentieth-century transactions.

Deeds are available at the relevant county seat, usually on microfilm if not the originals. There is usually a general deed index across deed books, although early deed books may also have their own index in each volume. While the usual location for deeds is the county seat, larger counties were later divided up into districts to make the registry more convenient to the seller. The County Resources section below clarifies the later divisions in counties. The New England Historic Genealogical Society and the FHL have large microfilm collections of land records from early settlement through mid-nineteenth-century and later for some registries.

A frequently overlooked solution to genealogical problems, particularly in New England states, is the use of information in land records. Articles for such problem-solving abound in major periodicals (see Periodicals). For two excellent examples of this technique using Massachusetts records, see the following articles:

Dearborn, David C. "The Family of William Curtis of Danvers, MA." In *A Tribute to John Insley Coddington*, edited by Neil D. Thompson and Robert C. Anderson, 31-46 (New York: Association for Promotion of Scholarship in Genealogy, 1980).

Greene, David L. "Salem Witches I: Bridget Bishop," *The American Genealogist* 57 (1981): 129-38.

Probate Records

By the time the Great Migration occurred, probate proceedings had already begun to apply to those with even minor personal property in England. Puritans pursued the practice with some vigor, but certainly not universally. Whether the person died with a will or without (intestate), complete probate proceedings were not automatic.

Probate records in Massachusetts are reasonably intact, but there are still gaps. In all cases there are two groups of records of concern: the original papers brought to court (such as original wills, affidavits of all kinds, and receipts from heirs) and those papers that were actually recorded in county probate books. Both of these exist in abundance for the state.

In Massachusetts the probate court jurisdictions follow county lines. Probate records have been published for Essex County (1635–81), Bristol County (1687-1745; 1745–62); Middlesex (1649–75, in process); wills for Suffolk County (1639–70); and indexes for the counties of Essex (1638–1841), Middlesex (1648–1909), Norfolk (1793–1900), Plymouth (1686–1881), Suffolk (1636–1910), and Worcester (1731–1910), many of which are also available for purchase in a CD-ROM format. Ruth Wilder Sherman and Robert S. Wakefield's *Plymouth Colony Probate Guide* (Warwick, R.I.: Plymouth Colony Research Group, 1983) is an alphabetical list of probate records (1620–91) and where they can be found for over 800 people who died in the colony.

Each probate court has its own record books, with indexes of its original files usually arranged by file number. The Massachusetts Archives, however, holds original probate files for Suffolk County (1636–1894), Middlesex County (1648–1871), Plymouth County (1686–1881), and Essex County (1638–1882, partially in storage). Probate record books to the mid-nineteenth century are generally on microfilm through the FHL, but most of the original files are only at the probate court office or the Massachusetts Archives. One exception is Middlesex County files, which *are* available on microfilm from the FHL and the Boston Public Library. Expanding microfilm collections at both

repositories include record books for Middlesex, Suffolk, and Hampshire counties, among others.

Beginning in 1922 divorces fell under the jurisdiction of both the superior court and probate court of the county (see Court Records). However, almost all cases after that date have been heard in probate court.

Court Records

During the seventeenth century, both colonies' court systems included, from highest authority to the lowest: the colony's general court, a court of assistants, inferior quarter courts, and local magistrates. The general court met quarterly to create laws to insure religious, peaceful government; it was composed of chosen freemen of the colony, the governor, deputy-governor, and assistants. Functioning somewhat as an executive session of the general court, the governor, deputy-governor, and assistants formed the court of assistants, which met more regularly, carried out general court business, and heard jury cases. Individually, assistants acted as local magistrates (justices of the peace) for civil suits in their respective towns. Additionally, magistrates who were not assistants were eventually added as the judicial need in towns arose.

Inferior quarter courts of first instance, later called county courts, were established in 1636 and were composed of the magistrates with a jury. This court's functions included civil actions, criminal actions, and administrative concerns. The three-tier court system (individual magistrates, county courts, court of assistants) continued until reorganization in 1692 after Plymouth Colony and Massachusetts Bay Colony merged by executive order of the English Crown. Previous county court functions were divided between a court of general sessions (criminal actions) and a common pleas court (civil actions) for each county, with one superior court of judicature (1692–1780) overseeing the entire colony. The latter became the supreme judicial court after 1780, handling appeals from lower courts and originating actions in some capital offenses. The separate county sessions and common pleas courts were reorganized into county superior courts in 1859.

Comprehensive discussions of the court system can be found in George Lee Haskins, *Law and Authority in Early Massachusetts: A Study in Tradition and Design* (New York: Archon Books, 1968), and Catherine S. Menand, *A Research Guide to the Massachusetts Courts and Their Records* (Boston: Massachusetts Supreme Judicial Court, Archives and Records Preservation, 1987). Michael S. Hindus's *Law in Colonial Massachusetts, 1630–1800*, in *Publications of Colonial Society of Massachusetts*, vol. 62. (Boston: Colonial Society of Massachusetts, 1984), lists various courts, their periods of operation and what kinds of records were kept. An earlier publication by Hindus (see Vital Records) indicates what might be found and where. However, with the transfer

of pre-1860 judicial records to the Judicial Archives at the Massachusetts Archives and much post-1859 material presently being held in storage, the Hindus listing is now very much dated and needs to be used accordingly.

Essex (1636–83), Suffolk (1671–80), Hampshire (1639–1702), and Plymouth (1686–1859 on searchable CD-ROM, produced by New England Historic Genealogical Society) county court records have been published, as well as those for Massachusetts Bay (1628–86) and Plymouth (1633–91) colonies. The Plymouth County court records are taken from the record books at the Pilgrim Society (see Archives, Libraries, and Societies) and are being indexed. The Hampshire County court records can be found in William Pynchon papers, Joseph H. Smith, ed. *Colonial Justice in Western Massachusetts, 1639–1702* (Cambridge, Mass.: Harvard University Press, 1961). Essex County Quarterly Court records, currently held at the Peabody Essex Institute (see Archives, Libraries, and Societies), are published in their nine-volume publication with an index. Microfilm copies are at the Massachusetts Archives. See also online sources at <http://etext.lib.virginia.edu/salem/witchcraft>. Those unpublished for 1687–98 are also at the Peabody Essex Institute with a typescript index by the Works Progress Administration (WPA). *Mayflower Descendant* (see Periodicals) has serially indexed the Suffolk County Inferior Court (common pleas). The surviving Suffolk Quarterly Court records are published in volumes 29 and 30 of *Publications of the Colonial Society of Massachusetts* (Boston: the society, 1933) and on microfilm at the state archives.

Towns issued "warnings out" to those poor for whom they would not assume responsibility. Although instituted by towns, the warnings were recorded in the county seat in Massachusetts. Those for Worcester County have been published. See Francis Blake, *Worcester County Warnings Out, 1737–1788* (1899; reprint. Camden, Maine: Picton Press, 1992). Others may also be in print or available online.

Seventeenth-century divorces were granted by the court of assistants until 1692 when authority transferred to the governor and council. The state's constitution gave that authority to the supreme judicial court in 1785. The county superior courts took over divorce cases from the supreme judicial court in 1887 and began sharing that authority with probate courts in 1922.

Tax Records

Tax records can be found at both the local and state levels. Massachusetts Archives has tax returns for 1768 and 1771, published as Bettye Hobbs Pruit, ed., *The Massachusetts Tax Valuation List of 1771* (1978; reprint, Camden, Maine: Picton Press, 1998). The archives also has some tax valuations for 1775 through 1778. The Massachusetts State Library holds them for 1780, 1783–84, 1791–93, 1800–101, and 1810–11.

Other tax lists may still be available at the town office. Boston's list for 1821 has been published in Lewis B. Rohrbach, *Boston Taxpayers in 1821* (1822; reprint, Camden, Maine: Picton Press, 1988), with a new index.

The U.S. Direct Tax of 1798 remains extant for most counties. See Michael H. Gorn, ed., *An Index and Guide to the Microfilm Edition of the Massachusetts and Maine Direct Tax Census of 1798* (Boston: New England Historic Genealogical Society, 1979). The surviving originals are at the New England Historic Genealogical Society (with a CD-ROM version available for purchase) and accessible on microfilm there and through the FHL.

Cemetery Records

Cemeteries are maintained by towns, churches, families, and later, private enterprises. Records for many of Boston's cemeteries have been published, in some cases as part of larger collections of death records (see Vital Records).

The state DAR annual volumes of cemetery records, including Bible, family, and church records transcribed by local chapters, are helpful but there is no central repository for maintaining them, as is often the case for other states. Copies of some of the volumes from the DAR are at the New England Historic Genealogical Society.

Periodicals and repositories throughout the state have many examples of published transcriptions; the most notable, such as the Corbin Collection (see Vital Records) are held in the Berkshire Athenaeum (see Archives, Libraries, and Societies) and New England Historic Genealogical Society. The Systematic Series of town vital records (see Vital Records) included some information from gravestones. Many of these are added regularly to the society's searchable database (see page 13) open to members at <www.newenglandancestors.org>. CR-ROM editions of the Corbin Collection are also available through the society's publications.

Church Records

One expects an ample supply of church records in a state whose history is so interwoven with religious principles and dissension, and such is the case in Massachusetts. Many exist in either published form by themselves or in numerous periodicals or noted in several collections of inventories. Some early church records of vital events were included in the Systematic Series (see Vital Records) and are included in published versions (book and CD-ROM) of individual towns. Church records in Massachusetts often contain other genealogical information such as admissions and dismissals, which could indicate migration. Original records not held by the church itself are often deposited in central denominational libraries. The Corbin Collection (see Vital Records) includes many church records for the western part of the state. An extensive collection on CD-ROM by Robert J. Dunkle and Ann S. Lainhart, *The Records of the Churches of Boston* (Boston: New England Historic Genealogical Society, 2002) includes entries from nineteen churches in the city.

The following will guide the researcher to finding the appropriate records in Massachusetts for some of the historically largest or prominent denominations:

Baptist. Southern (1800-1960) and American Baptist (1699-1872) church records for Boston are on microfilm at the Southern Baptist Historical Library and Archives in Nashville, Tennessee <www.sbhla.org> and American Baptist-Colgate Historical Library, Rochester, New York <www.crds.edu/abhs>.

Congregational. See Harold F. Worthley, *Inventory of the Records of Particular (Congregational) Churches of Massachusetts Gathered 1620-1805* (Cambridge, Mass.: Harvard University Press, 1970) and the Congregational Library, 14 Beacon St., Boston, MA 02108 <www.14beacon.org>.

Episcopal. See WPA, *Inventory of Church Archives of Massachusetts: Protestant Episcopal Church*, which was produced in 1942, and the Diocesan Library and Archives, 138 Tremont St., Boston, MA 02111 <www.diomass.org>.

Jewish. Records can be found at the American Jewish Historical Society Library, 160 Herrick Rd., Newton Centre, MA 02459 <www.ajhs.org>, which is located at Hebrew College.

Methodist. See the Boston University School of Theology Library, 745 Commonwealth Ave., Boston, MA 02215 <www.bu.edu/sth/library> for Methodist records.

Roman Catholic. See James M. O'Toole, "Catholic Church Records: A Genealogical and Historical Resource," *Register* 132 (1978): 251-63, and Archives of the Archdiocese of Boston, 2121 Commonwealth Ave., Brighton, MA 02135 <www.rcab.org/archives/welcome.htm>.

Society of Friends (Quakers). See Rhode Island—Archives—Rhode Island Historical Society, and Peabody Essex Institute (see Archives, Libraries, and Societies).

Unitarian-Universalist. See *An Inventory of the Universalist Archives in Massachusetts*, compiled by the WPA in 1942, and Andover-Harvard Divinity School Library, 45 Francis Ave., Cambridge, MA 02138-1994 <www.hds.harvard.edu/library>.

Military Records

Armed conflict was as much a part of Massachusetts history as religious dissension. Military sources are just as plentiful as for church records, but great quantities of them have been published.

Original extant records, with card file index of service records (1643–1783), are at Massachusetts Archives, as well

as some materials related to Shays' Rebellion, the War of 1812, and the Spanish American War. The Massachusetts Military Museum and Archives, 44 Salisbury St., Worcester, MA, 01609 <www.state.ma.us/guard/Museum/museum.htm> holds documents of the Massachusetts National Guard from 1636, material related to Massachusetts Volunteer regiments in the Civil War, archives of the Office of the Adjutant General, and military records of Massachusetts's soldiers and sailors (1775–1940). Military records of Massachusetts's veterans (1941–present) are at the Office of the Adjutant General, Military Records Branch, 239 Causeway St., Boston, MA 02114.

The records in print for earlier periods of conflict are covered in George M. Bodge's *Soldiers in King Philip's War* (1896; reprint, Baltimore: Genealogical Publishing Co., 1967). There are also five volumes jointly published by the Society of Colonial Wars in the Commonwealth of Massachusetts and New England Historic Genealogical Society: Mary E. Donahue, ed., *Massachusetts Officers and Soldiers, 1702–1722* (1980); Myron O. Stachiw, ed., *Massachusetts Officers and Soldiers, 1723–1743: Dummer's War to the War of Jenkins' Ear* (1980); Robert E. Mackay, ed., *Massachusetts Soldiers in the French and Indian Wars, 1744–1755* (1978); Nancy S. Voye, ed., *Massachusetts Officers in the French and Indian Wars, 1748–1763* (1975); and Doreski, Carole, ed., *Massachusetts Officers and Soldiers in the Seventeenth Century Conflicts* (1982).

Massachusetts Soldiers and Sailors of the Revolutionary War (Boston: Commonwealth of Massachusetts, 1896–1908) is comprised of seventeen volumes. An additional twenty thousand names were found after publication and entered on cards, which are on microfilm at Massachusetts Archives and New England Historic Genealogical Society. A fully searchable CD-ROM version is available through <www.ancestry.com>. Each listing is alphabetical by occurrence of the name in a muster roll, report, or pay file, etc., along with a town residence of the individual if it was obvious in the original record. No attempt was made to determine whether more than one record for the same name, in either the volumes or on cards, is actually for the same person.

Numerous materials are available for Loyalist research in Massachusetts. One of the many comprehensive biographical studies is David E. Mass, ed., *Divided Hearts: Massachusetts Loyalists, 1765–1790, A Biographical Directory* (Boston: New England Historic Genealogical Society, 1980).

For the War of 1812, see *Records of the Massachusetts Volunteer Militia Called Out by the Governor of Massachusetts to Suppress a Threatened Invasion during the War of 1812–14* (Boston: Adjutant General's Office, 1913). For the Civil War, see *Massachusetts Soldiers, Sailors, and Marines in the Civil War* (Norwood, Mass.: Norwood Press, 1932).

In addition to the Adjutant General's Office, many towns have memorials to their residents who served in later wars. Records are generally kept at the town or city clerk's office.

Periodicals, Newspapers, and Manuscript Collections

Periodicals

Many periodicals are published concerning Massachusetts families and history. Among the more frequently used are:

The New England Historical and Genealogical Register, published since 1847 by the society, serves all of New England and sets a standard for professional research with genealogies, local history, vital, church, and cemetery records and important book reviews. Each volume has an every-name annual index. A cumulative index across volumes is available as well as a more complete index in book form, online from the society or through subscription databases (see page 17), and in CD-ROM format.

The American Genealogist (TAG), P.O. Box 398, Demorest, GA 30535-0398 <www.americangenealogist.com> is an independent quarterly founded by Donald Lines Jacobus in 1922. Its primary focus is New England.

Great Migration Newsletter, in a category of its own, is available by subscription or published in groups of back issues from <www.newenglandancestors.org>. It includes articles on a variety of topics, including the settlement of early New England towns, migration patterns, seventeenth-century passenger lists, church records, and land records.

Essex Institute Historical Collections (1859–1993) and *Essex Antiquarian: A Quarterly Magazine Devoted to the Biography, Genealogy, History and Antiquities of Essex County, Massachusetts* (1897–1909) cover considerable primary and secondary source material for Essex County.

The Mayflower Descendant: A Quarterly Magazine of Pilgrim Genealogy and History (1899–1936; 1985-present) is published by the Massachusetts Society of Mayflower Descendants (see Archives, Libraries, and Societies). It is indexed in separate volumes with a consolidated index for 1899–1936.

The Mayflower Quarterly (1935-present), published by the General Society of Mayflower Descendants (see Archives, Libraries, and Societies) primarily serves as a news magazine for members with articles on the Pilgrim experience and some researched genealogies.

Periodicals focused specifically on local genealogy are:

The Essex Genealogist (Essex, Mass., 1980-present), published by the Essex Society of Genealogists, Inc., P.O. Box 313, Lynnfield, MA 01940-0313 <www.esog.org>.

Berkshire Genealogist (1978-present) is a quarterly devoted to western Massachusetts, published by the Berkshire Family History Association, P.O. Box 1437, Pittsfield, MA 01201 <www.berkshire.net/~bfha>.

Other periodicals, no longer being published, that contain historical material include:

The Historical Collections of Danvers Historical Society, Danvers, Mass.; 1913–67.

The Dedham Historical Register, Dedham, Mass.: 1890–1903.

The Medford Historical Register, Medford, Mass.: 1898–1940.

Newspapers

Since 1704, Massachusetts newspapers have included some notices of deaths and marriages. A good number of these newspapers have been indexed in either published or typescript form. The New England Library Association's Bibliography Committee has produced *A Guide to Newspaper Indexes in New England* (Lynnfield, Mass.: the committee, 1978), which is extremely helpful. The *American Genealogical-Biographical Index* (see Connecticut—Background Sources), now also in CD-ROM format, includes an index to the genealogical column of the defunct *Boston Evening Transcript* (see below).

For ninety years, the *Boston Pilot* ran an advertising service for Irish immigrants searching for missing friends and family members. The advertisements have been published in either a six-volume set (covering years 1831–70) or CD-ROM format (for years 1831–1920), by Ruth-Ann M. Harris and B. Emer O'Keefe, eds., *The Search for Missing Friends: Irish Immigrant Advertisements placed in the* Boston Pilot, *1831–1920* (Boston: New England Historic Genealogical Society, 1991–2002).

The largest collection of microfilm copies of newspapers in the state can be found at the Boston Public Library at Copley Square, the American Antiquarian Society, the State Library of Massachusetts (see Archives, Libraries, and Societies for all three). But perhaps the most important newspaper for genealogical purposes, and one which should not be overlooked in Massachusetts research, is the *Boston Evening Transcript*. Between 1895 and 1941, it offered a genealogical column of queries, answers, and notes. Indexes to these valuable columns are available at the Boston Public Library and other New England repositories along with indexes of a similar column in the *Hartford Times* (see Connecticut—Newspapers).

Manuscripts

Rich manuscript sources exist in many excellent repositories in the state. In the eastern portion of the state are the following key collections: the New England Historic Genealogical Society; Massachusetts Archives; Massachusetts Historical Society, which has a catalog of seven volumes; and the Peabody Essex Institute, Old Colony Historical Society in Taunton <www.oldcolonyhistoricalsociety.org> and Old Sturbridge Village <www.osv.org>.

There are several collections in the western portion of the state, the largest of which are at the Berkshire Athenaeum and Connecticut Valley Historical Museum (see Archives, Libraries, and Societies for addresses).

Archives, Libraries, and Societies

New England Historic Genealogical Society
101 Newbury St.
Boston, MA 02116-3087
www.newenglandancestors.org

Founded in the mid-nineteenth century, the society is an extremely active center for New England family research, with an extensive collection of local and family histories, educational programs, and superior publications, including *The New England Historical and Genealogical Register*, a quarterly periodical, and *New England Ancestors* (formerly *Nexus*), now a quarterly magazine, both distributed to the membership. Library facilities of open stacks (except for manuscripts and rare books) and massive microfilm collections of New England town and vital records are available on a per-day basis (free for members). The book loan department makes materials available by mail to members for a small fee, with an online catalog listing circulating books. A research service is available to the general public for a fee.

Massachusetts Archives at Columbia Point
220 Morrissey Blvd.
Boston, MA 02125
www.state.ma.us/sec/arc/arcidx.htm

The Massachusetts Archives holds all state copies of vital records (1841–95); passenger lists for the Port of Boston (1848–91), including a new index expected to go online; federal census records (state copies, 1850–70, with 1880 on microfilm) with all supplemental federal schedules and state censuses for 1855 and 1865; legislative records from the General Court with land grants, petitions, tax records (1643–1787); Eastern land records for the settlement of Maine; human service institution records; all military records for the state through the Revolution; and Judicial Archives beginning with colony era courts to mid-nineteenth century courts (see Court Records).

State Library of Massachusetts
341 State House, Beacon St.
Boston, MA 02133
www.state.ma.us/lib

Its genealogical collection includes extensive newspaper collections and indexes, town and county histories, town and county maps and atlases, and city directories back to 1787. See Kenneth E. Flower, *A Guide to Massachusetts Genealogical Material in the State Library of Massachusetts* (Boston: Massachusetts State Archives, 1978) or the online catalog.

MASSACHUSETTS

Boston Public Library

Copley Sq.
700 Boylston St.
Boston, MA 02117
www.bpl.org

The Social Science Department, Newspaper, and Microtext departments have important collections for genealogical research. The first holds family genealogies and vertical file material not found elsewhere. The newspaper department has over 260 newspapers, including the *Boston Evening Transcript* and indexes, although they are not limited to Boston or Massachusetts. Microtext has an extensive collection of census records for New England; copies of National Archives' Boston ship passenger arrival lists (1820–91), and indexes (1848–90) (see Immigration); probate records for Middlesex, Suffolk, and Hampshire counties; Suffolk Court of Common Pleas; and town records, newspapers, and city directories from over 200 cities and towns in the United States. See the website for further description of holdings in various departments.

Connecticut Valley Historical Museum
Library and Archives

Springfield Library Genealogy Department
220 State St.
Springfield, MA 01103
www.quadrangle.org/CVHM.htm

Serving the western portion of the state extremely well, this collection (formerly at the Springfield Public Library) holds an excellent local archives starting in 1636 for Springfield and vicinity. This is one of the better collections of ethnic materials available—French Canadian, Irish, and African American.

Berkshire Athenaeum

1 Wendell Ave.
Pittsfield, MA 01202
www.berkshire.net/PittsfieldLibrary/

The Local History and Genealogy Department holds the Cooke Collection of eighteenth- and nineteenth-century church and cemetery records as well as abstracts of newspaper notices of marriages and deaths, the personal records of ministers, and vital records that supplement the Systematic Series (see Vital Records). Other collections include files of research notes collected by local researchers, and a three-by-five card file of vital records and notes throughout the state and the northeast. This includes Connecticut, Vermont, and Hudson Valley, New York, as well, since the area was a major conduit for movement north and west. The Berkshire Family History Association, P.O. Box 1437, Pittsfield, MA 01201 <www.berkshire.net/~bfha/index.htm> has a close relationship with the Local History and Genealogy Department of the Athenaeum, and provides a research service in the collections for its members.

Peabody Essex Museum

East India Sq.
132-134 Essex St.
Salem, MA 01970
www.pem.org

Formerly the Essex Institute, this is the largest collection of Essex County original source material. There is a good collection of published genealogies and town histories for Essex County. This private library, available with an annual membership or for a daily fee, has the pre-1800 Essex County Court records (see Court Records). See website for details of holdings and accessibility.

General Society of Mayflower Descendants

P.O. Box 3297
Plymouth, MA 02361-3297
www.mayflower.org

The society is the national headquarters for the state organizations of descendants of Mayflower Pilgrims. It publishes the *Mayflower Quarterly* and the five-generation project (see Background Sources). A research library is available. The Massachusetts Society of Mayflower Descendants, 100 Boylston St., #750, Boston, MA 02116-4610 <www.massmayflower.org> also has a useful library.

Massachusetts Historical Society

1154 Boylston St.
Boston, MA 02215-3695
www.masshist.org/welcome

Although not a genealogical library, the collection includes rare books, personal papers, manuscripts, particularly the Thwing Collection of Early Bostonians (most of which is now available on CD-ROM from the society and New England Historic Genealogical Society), and rare books focusing particularly on Boston, Massachusetts, and New England.

Pilgrim Hall Museum

75 Court St.
Plymouth, MA 02360
www.pilgrimhall.org

While its collections are historical, not genealogical, the museum library holds the Plymouth County Court Record Books from 1686–1859. Otherwise, the collection focuses on the Pilgrim experience in Plymouth.

American Antiquarian Society

185 Salisbury St.
Worcester, MA 01609
www.americanantiquarian.org

Its superior collection, specializing in printed sources of American history prior to 1877, also includes a fine newspaper collection.

Special Focus Categories

Immigration

Both immigration and naturalization records abound for Massachusetts since Boston was a major port of entry for hundreds of millions of people seeking refuge, food, land, and religious and political freedom from points across the Atlantic. Smaller ports existed in other towns both north and south of Boston's wharfs. The seventeenth- and nineteenth-century records are well organized, but few of the eighteenth-century records are as easily accessed.

Early Immigration. While literally hundreds of published lists exist, the most definitive resource to use for those known lists for the 1620–1700 period is Filby and Meyer's *Passenger and Immigration Lists Index*, which is also available in online subscription databases for volumes published to 2003 (see page 17). However, the researcher *must* refer to the primary source after using the index, since the index is derived from other published indexes of original lists and not the primary material itself.

1800-Present. The nineteenth century brought massive numbers of immigrants to Massachusetts, creating a much more heterogeneous population than a century earlier. Fortunately, many passenger lists have been indexed for the period.

The Massachusetts Archives has an alphabetical card index to the Port of Boston passenger lists (1848–91), called the state list. The archives is computerizing this card file, which was about half complete (2004). The National Archives—Northeast Region (covering both Boston and Pittsfield—see page 11) both have passenger lists from both Massachusetts and other ports (1820–ca. 1954). The National Archives in Washington, D.C., has copies of the Boston lists for 1820 to 1891 (Record Group 36, M277), though some gaps in coverage appear in the microfilm copy of the lists. The microfilm index to passenger lists made by the National Archives in Washington, D.C., for 1848 to 1891 (Record Group 36, M265) used the *state* lists to create their index for arrivals at the port of Boston. Consequently, people might appear on the microfilmed federal index and the state list at the Massachusetts Archives, but not on the federal lists.

The National Archives in Washington, D.C., also has an index to passenger lists for arrivals at Boston from 1902 to 1920 (Record Group 85, T521; T617), book indexes to the Boston passenger lists by date of arrival from 1899 to 1940 (Record Group 85, T790), and passenger lists themselves 1891 to 1943 (Record Group 85, T843). These records groups are being added to the online Immigration Records searchable database at Ancestry.com <www.ancestry.com> (see page 17).

Boston was only one port of entry open for immigrants to Massachusetts. There are lists for other ports in the state as well, generally covered by the National Archives index in Record Group 36 (M334) Atlantic, Gulf, and Great Lakes ports (1820-91) (see page 14).

In the Boston area, the Boston Public Library has microfilm copies of all the federal passenger lists beginning in 1820, as well as other immigration material.

Naturalization

The WPA developed an index of naturalizations found in numerous city, county, state, and federal courts in New England for the period 1786 to 1906, which are Soundexed and microfilmed, and made available through National Archives (see pages 11-12). The abstract cards used to create that microfilm for all of New England are at the National Archives—New England Region in Waltham, Massachusetts. For the period 1906–70s, the abstract cards and an index for naturalization petitions from federal courts in Massachusetts (1906–1950s) have been moved to the National Archives—Northeast Region as well. In addition to the abstract cards and index, New England's regional branch holds dexigraphs of the actual records (originals at Massachusetts Archives), making it possible to check accuracy of the abstracts and index. Some have declarations of intention attached, which may give more information about the immigrant.

Massachusetts Archives holds abstracts for state and local courts (1885–1931 with separate annual indexes), and also Essex County naturalization records (1901–1982). Current petitions and index cards for the federal courts are at Immigration and Naturalization Service, U.S. Department of Justice, JFK Federal Bldg., Government Center, Boston, MA 02203.

African American

From colonial beginnings, African Americans (slave and free) were recorded in the same town and county records as white settlers. The terms "black," "slave," "Negro," and "colored" are often included in Massachusetts seventeenth- and eighteenth-century primary source material including land, probate, court, and vital records, for example. An annotated version of the 1754 Massachusetts slave census is presently being produced by Melinde Lutz Sanborn. Records of both slaves and free African Americans are found in numerous repository collections for pre-revolutionary Massachusetts (see pages 14-15). However, little has been done to extract the information to make it more usable for genealogical research. One major exception is Joseph Carvalho, *Black Families in Hampden County, Massachusetts, 1650–1855* (Boston: New England Historic Genealogical Society and the Institute on Massachusetts Studies, Westfield State College, 1984), which is an excellent study including families who migrated to Hampden County. See also:

Daniels, John. *In Freedom's Birthplace: A Study of the Boston Negroes.* 1914. Reprint. New York: Arno Press, 1969.

Moore, George H. *Notes on the History of Slavery in Massachusetts.* 1866. Reprint. New York: Negro University Press, 1968.

Pierson, William D. *Black Yankees: The Development of an Afro-American Subculture in Eighteenth Century New England.* Amherst: University of Massachusetts Press, 1988.

Smith, James Avery. *History of the Black Population of Amherst, Massachusetts, 1728–1870.* Boston: New England Historic Genealogical Society, 1999.

Native American

For centuries before the Pilgrims' arrival, several tribes of Native Americans lived in what is now Massachusetts. In the early stages of European settlement, friendly relations existed. Following the migration, conflicts continued to escalate through the last part of the seventeenth century, the most well known of which is King Philip's War with the Wampanoag of Plymouth Colony. Before the end of the conflicts in the mid-eighteenth century, significantly fewer native inhabitants were left in the area, many having died of smallpox or been killed, chased farther to the north or west, or sold into slavery. See Howard S. Russell, *Indian New England Before the Mayflower* (Hanover, N.H.: University Press of New England, 1980); William Cronon, *Changes on the Land: Indians, Colonists, and the Ecology of New England* (New York: Hill and Wang, 1983); and websites related to Natick Praying Indians.

Other Ethnic Groups

The large Irish and French-Canadian immigration in the mid-nineteenth century preceded the influx of eastern and southern European groups to Boston Harbor in the late nineteenth and early twentieth centuries. Latino and Southeast Asian immigrants are more recently arrived.

The Irish American Research Association, P.O. Box 619, Sudbury, MA 01776 <http://tiara.ie/index.html>, commonly known as TIARA, is a group that promotes cooperative research for both Protestant and Catholic Irish (see also New Hampshire—American Canadian Genealogical Society; and Rhode Island—American French Genealogical Society). The American Jewish Historical Society (see Church Records—Jewish) is an excellent resource for research on Jewish immigration.

County Resources

The following is a guide to beginning dates and locations of Massachusetts deeds, probates, and court records. Inquiries for land records should be addressed "Registry of Deeds" at the county (or district) seat. In some counties, division of the Registry of Deeds became necessary to make the location closer to the land involved in the transaction. Some registries have websites. Make sure the deed information sought falls in the appropriate district for the time period and geography involved.

The "Probate Court Clerk" at the county seat should be addressed for probate records; and "Clerk of Courts" for civil court records. As with other New England states, the New England Genealogic Historical Society has an extensive microfilm collection of county resources for Massachusetts.

Map	County	Date Formed Parent County/ies	Land Probate Court
J6	Barnstable Main Street Barnstable 02630	1685 as Barnstable County of Plymouth Colony	1827* 1686 1686

Fire destroyed nearly all early deed books and probate files, but probate books survived. Although the official deed books only begin in 1827, many deeds were re-recorded back to about 1783, though these are far from complete.

Map	County	Date Formed Parent County/ies	Land Probate Court
A3	Berkshire 44 Bank Row Pittsfield 01201	1761 Hampshire	1761 1761 1761

Divided into three districts in 1788. The above office is the "parent" county seat, encompassing all the Berkshire towns between 1761–88. After that it was still the probate office for the county, but only the registry of deeds for the Middle District (see Town Resources for towns in each of Berkshire's three registry of deeds districts).

	Berkshire Northern District 65 Park St. Adams 01220		1788
	Berkshire Southern District Great Barrington 01230		1788

Map	County	Date Formed Parent County/ies	Land Probate Court
G5	Bristol 11 Court St. Taunton 02780	1685 as Bristol County of Plymouth Colony	1685 1685 1685

The county seat was Bristol until 1746 when succeeded by Taunton. The Taunton seat divided into three districts in 1837 with the above remaining as probate office but only registry of deeds for the Northern District (see Town Resources for towns in each of Bristol's registry of deeds districts).

	Bristol Southern District 25 N. Sixth St. New Bedford 02740		1837
	Bristol Fall River District 441 N. Main St. Fall River 02720		1837

Map	County	Date Formed Parent County/ies	Land Probate Court
H7	Dukes 81 Main St. Edgartown 02539	1683 (as a New York County) 1695 (as a Mass. County)	1686 1696 1665

Records from 1665 deal with Martha's Vineyard.

Map	County	Date Formed Parent County/ies	Land Probate Court
H2	Essex 32 Federal St. Salem 01970	1643 original	1637 1635 1684

The county was divided into two districts in 1869. The above office is the "parent" county seat. After that it remained the probate office for the county, but the registry of deeds for only the Southern District (see Town Resources for towns in each of the registry of deeds districts). This registry also has all the "old" Norfolk County (1637–1714) and Ipswich Series Deeds, 1640–94, two of which have been transcribed by George Sanborn for the manuscript collection at New England Historic Genealogical Society. Essex court records to 1800 are at the Peabody Essex Museum (see Archives, Libraries, and Societies).

	Essex Northern District 381 Common St. Lawrence 01840		1869
B2	Franklin 425 Main St. Greenfield 01310	1811 Hampshire	1787* 1812 1812

*Earlier deeds for land now in Franklin County are at Springfield (see Hampden County). Abstracts of these deeds recorded at the Springfield registry from 1663–1786 are at Greenfield. Deeds for 1787-present are in Greenfield; between 1787–1812 they were recorded at the Deerfield registry, which was transferred to Greenfield in 1812. Probates before 1812 for towns now in Franklin County are at Northampton (see Hampshire County).

B4	Hampden 50 State St. Springfield 01103	1812 Hampshire	1636* 1812† 1812†

*Although not established as Hampden County until 1812, Springfield was the registry for Hampden's parent county, Hampshire, which was divided into three registries—Deerfield, Springfield, and Northampton—in 1787. Deerfield registry was transferred to Greenfield when Franklin County was established in 1811 (see Franklin and Hampshire). All deeds for land originally in Hampshire as well as Franklin and Hampden before their county division from Hampshire are located at the Springfield registry.
†Probates before 1812 for towns covered now by Hampden County are at the Hampshire Probate Office in Northampton. The bulk of the pre-1812 court records are also in Northampton.

C3	Hampshire 33 King St. Northampton 01060	1662 Middlesex	1812* 1660 1677

*In 1787 three registry offices were created (Deerfield, Springfield, and Northampton) for Hampshire County corresponding with what eventually became the three present counties of Franklin, Hampden, and Hampshire, respectively. All deeds for the Northampton registry before it became what is now Hampshire County are located at the Springfield registry.

F2	Middlesex 208 Cambridge St. Cambridge 02141	1643 original	1649* 1654* 1643

*Until 1649, records were kept in Boston. The county was divided into two districts in 1855. The above office is the "parent" county seat, encompassing all the Middlesex towns between 1643–1855. After that it was still the probate office for the county, but the registry of deeds for only the Southern District (see Town Resources for towns in each of Middlesex's two registry of deeds districts).

	Middlesex Northern District 360 Gorham St. Lowell 01852		1855
K7	Nantucket 16 Broad St. Nantucket 02554	1695 Dukes	1695 1706 1721
	Norfolk "Old" Essex County Courthouse 32 Federal, Salem 01970	1643 (abolished 1680) original	1637–1714

Exeter, Salisbury, Hampton, Haverhill, Dover, and Portsmouth (formerly Strawbery Banke) were in this county until it was abolished. All but Salisbury and Haverhill are now in New Hampshire. Probate and deed records for these towns in this period are located here.

G4	Norfolk 649 High St. Dedham 02026	1793 Suffolk	1793 1793 1793

Plymouth County towns of Hingham and Hull were part of Norfolk County from 1793–1803.

H5	Plymouth 11 S. Russell St. Plymouth 02360	1685 as Plymouth County of Plymouth Colony	1620 1633 1630

Plymouth Colony divided into three counties in 1685. The entire colony joined with Massachusetts Bay Colony in 1691 to form the commonwealth. All earlier records that apply to Plymouth Colony are at the county commissioner's office above, bound in a separate series. The present probate and registry of deeds office is at the same address. Court records (1686–1859) are at the Pilgrim Society, Court Street, Plymouth, MA 02360.

H3	Suffolk 24 New Chardon St., P.O. Box 9660 Boston 02114	1643 original	1639 1636 1671

In 1793 all that was Suffolk County except Boston, Chelsea, Hingham, and Hull became Norfolk County.

E3	Worcester 2 Main St. Worcester 01608	1731 Middlesex/Suffolk	1731 1731 1731

Worcester divided into two registries for deeds only in 1884 (see Town Resources for those towns that fall under this Worcester district registry after that date).

	Worcester Northern District 84 Elm St. Fitchburg 01420		1884

WASHINGTON

WINDHAM

HILLSBOROUGH

ROCKINGHAM

VERMONT

CHESHIRE

NEW HAMPSHIRE

RENSSELAER

Atlantic

Ocean

NEW YORK

Greenfield

ESSEX

FRANKLIN

MIDDLESEX

Salem

COLUMBIA

Pittsfield

Boston

SUFFOLK

HAMPSHIRE

BERKSHIRE

Northampton

WORCESTER

← See Box Below

Worcester

Springfield

HAMPDEN

NORFOLK

CONNECTICUT

RHODE
ISLAND

Taunton

PLYMOUTH

DUTCHESS

LITCHFIELD

PROVIDENCE

Plymouth

BRISTOL

Cape Cod Bay

HARTFORD

TOLLAND

WINDHAM

KENT

BRISTOL

Barnstable

NEWPORT

BARNSTABLE

Nantucket Sound

NEW LONDON

WASHINGTON

ESSEX

DUKES

Edgartown

MIDDLESEX

Massachusetts Bay

Nantucket

Cambridge

* = NORFOLK

NANTUCKET

Boston

SUFFOLK

Dedham

NORFOLK

PLYMOUTH

The Counties and Towns of

Massachusetts

0   10   20   30   40   50 Miles

MASSACHUSETTS

324

Copyright 1989, Ancestry, Inc.

Drawn by William Dollarhide

Town Resources

The *Historical Data Relating to Counties, Cities and Towns in Massachusetts*, cited in Background Sources above, provides some of the information that follows. Addresses are "Town Hall," unless otherwise indicated, and come from the most recent list of town clerks distributed by the secretary of state <www.state.ma.us/sec/ele/eleclk/clkidx.htm>. The second column lists the date the town was established and, in parentheses, former names or towns from which it was formed. The third column lists county and, if relevent, the registry of deeds district is indicated under the county.

Early records of town meetings have been published for a number of Massachusetts towns. See Ann S. Lainhart, "Town Records," *Essex Genealogist* 10 (February 1990): 3-10, for a list and discussion. Some are interspersed in the original vital record books on microfiche distributed by Archive Publishing, 57 Locust St., Oxford, MA 01540. Those for Middlesex County towns are at the Boston Public Library, New England Historic Genealogical Society, or can be acquired through Early Massachusetts Records, Inc., 1154 Boylston, Boston, MA 02215. A descriptive guide to the collection was published in 1976 and can be obtained from that address.

The researcher should assume that vital records, whether in separate books or in town records, begin with the formation of the town, as do the town records. See parent towns for earlier records; and the county (see County Resources) for beginning dates of deeds, probates, and court records. Clerks respond to inquiries regarding vital records, since most have indexes available, but unindexed town records with details of town life (officers, tax lists, freeman's lists, cattle and hog marks, voting lists, warnings out, overseers of the poor accounts, school records, etc.) must be searched in person either on microfilm or at the town's office.

Town Address	Date Formed County (Map)	Vital Records
Abington 500 Gliniewicz Way, No. Abington 02351	1712 Bridgewater	Plymouth (2)
Acton 472 Main St., Acton 01720	1735 Concord	Middlesex (24) Southern
Acushnet 122 Main St., Acushnet 02743	1860 Fairhaven	Bristol (19) Southern
Adams 8 Park, Adams 01220	1778 (East Hoosuck)	Berkshire (7) Northern
Agawam 36 Main, Agawam 01001	1855 W. Springfield	Hampden (14)
Alford 5 Alford Center Rd., Alford 01230	1773 Great Barrington	Berkshire (23) Southern
Amesbury 62 Friend, Amesbury 01913	1668 Salisbury	Essex (2) Southern
Amherst 4 Boltwood Ave., Amherst 01003	1759 Hadley	Hampshire (10) Northampton
Andover 36 Bartlet St., Andover 01810	1646	Essex (20) Northern
Aquinnah 65 State Rd., Aquinnah 02535	1855 (formerly Gay Head)	Dukes (1)
Arlington 730 Massachusetts Ave. Arlington 02174	1807 Cambridge (West Cambridge, 1867)	Middlesex (32) Southern
Ashburnham 32 Main St., Ashburnham 01430	1765 (Dorchester-Canada)	Worcester (3) Northern
Ashby 895 Main St. Ashby 01431	1767 Ashburnton/Fitchburg/ Townsend	Middlesex (1) Southern
Ashfield 412 Main St. Ashfield 01330	1765 (Huntstown Plantation)	Franklin (17) Greenfield (Deerfield)
Ashland 101 State St. Ashland 01721	1846 Framingham/Holliston/ Hopkinton	Middlesex (51) Southern
Athol 584 Main St., Athol 01331	1762 (Payquage Plantation)	Worcester (4) Worcester
Attleboro City Hall, 77 Park St. Attleboro 02703	1694 Rehoboth	Bristol (4) Northern
Auburn 104 Central St. Auburn 01501	1778 (named Ward until 1837) Leicester/Oxford/ Sutton/Worcester	Worcester (45) Worcester
Avon 65 E. Main St. Avon 02322	1888 Stroughton	Norfolk (20)
Ayer 1 Main/P.O. Box 308 Ayer 01432	1871 Groton/Shirley	Middlesex (18) Southern

Town Address	Date Formed County (Map)	Vital Records
Barnstable 367 Main St., Hyannis 02601	1638	Barnstable (5)
Barre 2 Exchange St./P.O. Box 418 Barre 01005	1753 Worcester (Rutland District, 1774; named Hutchinson until 1776)	Worcester (19)
Becket 557 Main St., Becket 01223	1765 (No. 4 Plantation)	Berkshire (22) Middle
Bedford 10 Mudge Way, Bedford 01730	1729 Billerica/Concord	Middlesex (21) Southern
Belchertown 2 Jabish St., Belchertown 01007	1761 (Cold Spring Plantation)	Hampshire (19) Northampton
Bellingham 2 Mechanic St., Bellingham 02019	1719 Dedham/Mendon/Wrentham	Norfolk (11)
Belmont 455 Concord Ave. Belmont 02178	1859 Waltham/Watertown/ West Cambridge (Arlington)	Middlesex (36) Southern
Berkley 1 N. Main St., Berkley 02780	1735 Dighton/Taunton	Bristol (11) Northern
Berlin 23 Linden St., Berlin 01503	1784 Bolton/Marlborough	Worcester (27) Worcester
Bernardston 38 Church St., Bernardston 01337	1762 (as Falltown Plantation)	Franklin (6) Greenfield (Deerfield)
Beverly City Hall, 191 Cabot St. Beverly 01915	1668 Salem	Essex (24) Southern
Billerica 365 Boston Rd., Billerica 01821	1655	Middlesex (13) Northern
Blackstone 15 St. Paul St., Blackstone 01504	1845 Mendon	Worcester (60) Worcester
Blandford 102 Main St. Blandford 01008	1741 (Suffield Equivalent) (Glasgow)	Hampden (2) Springfield
Bolton 633 Main St., Bolton 01740	1738 Lancaster	Worcester (2) Worcester
Boston 1 City Hall Sq., Rm. 241, Boston 02201	1630	Suffolk (4)

Boston
The following towns became part of Boston on the date indicated: East Boston (1637), South Boston (1804), Roxbury (1868), Dorchester (1870), Brighton (1874), Charlestown (1874), West Roxbury (1874), and Hyde Park (1912).

Town Address	Date Formed County (Map)	Vital Records
Bourne 24 Perry Ave. Buzzards Bay 02532	1884 Sandwich	Barnstable (1)

Town Address	Date Formed County (Map)	Vital Records
Boxborough 29 Middle Rd. Boxborough 01719	1783 Harvard/Littletown/Stow	Middlesex (23) Southern
Boxford 28 Middleton Rd. Boxford 01921	1694	Essex (13) Southern
Boylston 221 Main St., Boylston 01505	1786 Shrewsbury	Worcester (26) Worcester
Bradford (became part of Haverhill, 1897)	1675 Southern	Essex
Braintree 1 JFK Memorial Dr., Braintree 02184	1640 Boston	Norfolk (24)
Brewster 2198 Main St., Brewster 02631	1803 Harwich	Barnstable (8)
Bridgewater 64 Center Sq., Bridgewater 02324	1656	Plymouth (16)
Brighton (became part of Boston 1874)	1817 Cambridge	Suffolk
Brimfield 21 Main St., Brimfield 01010	1714 Original	Hampden (21) Springfield
Brockton City Hall, 45 School St. Brockton 02401	1821 Bridgewater (North Bridgewater)	Plymouth (1)
Brookfield 6 Center St., Brookfield 01506	1673	Worcester (40) Worcester
Brookline 333 Washington St., Brookline 02147	1705 Boston	Norfolk (28)
Buckland 17 State St. Shelburne Falls 01370	1779 No-town Plantation/ Charlemont	Franklin (11) Greenfield (Deerfield)
Burlington 29 Center St., Burlington 01803	1799 Woburn	Middlesex (22) Southern
Cambridge City Hall, 51 Inman St. Cambridge 02139	1631 (Newe Towne)	Middlesex (37) Southern
Canton 801 Washington St., Canton 02021	1797 Stoughton	Norfolk (18)
Carlisle 66 Westford St. Carlisle 01741	1780 Acton/Billerica/ Chelmsford/Concord	Middlesex (20) Northern

MASSACHUSETTS

Town Address	Date Formed County (Map)	Vital Records
Carver 108 Main St., Carver 02330	1790 Plympton	Plymouth (22)
Charlemont 157 Main St., Charlemont 01339	1765	Franklin (9) Greenfield (Deerfield)
Charlestown (became part of Boston 1874)	1630	Suffolk
Charlton 37 Main St., Charlton 01507	1754 Oxford	Worcester (43) Worcester
Chatham 549 Main St., Chatham 02633	1712 (Manamoit Village)	Barnstable (10)
Chelmsford 50 Billerica Rd., Chelmsford 01824	1655	Middlesex (12) Northern
Chelsea City Hall, 500 Broadway Chelsea 02150	1739 Boston (Winnissimet/ Rumney Marsh/Pullin Point)	Suffolk (3)
Cheshire 80 Church St. Cheshire 01225	1793 Adams/Lanesborough/ Windsor/New Ashford District	Berkshire (10) Northern
Chester 15 Middlefield Rd., Chester 01011	1765 (Murrayfield)	Hampden (1) Northampton
Chesterfield 422 Main St., Chesterfield 01012	1762 (New Hingham Plantation)	Hampshire (6) Northampton
Chicopee City Hall, 274 Front St. Chicopee 01013	1848 Springfield	Hampden (8)
Chilmark 401 Middle Rd., Chilmark 02535	1694	Dukes (2)
Clarksburg 111 River Rd., Clarksburg 01247	1798	Berkshire (2) Northern
Clinton 242 Church St., Clinton 01510	1850 Lancaster	Worcester (25) Worcester
Cohasset 41 Highland Ave., Cohasset 02025	1770 Hingham	Norfolk (27)
Colrain 55 Main Rd., Colrain 01340	1761	Franklin (4) Greenfield (Deerfield)
Concord 22 Monument Sq., Concord 01742	1635 (Musketequid)	Middlesex (25) Southern
Conway 32 Main St. Conway 01341	1767 Deerfield	Franklin (18) Greenfield (Deerfield)
Cummington 33 Main St., Cummington 01026	1779 No. 5 Plantation	Hampshire (2) Northampton
Dalton 462 Main St., Dalton 01226	1704 (Ashuelet Equivalent)	Berkshire (13) Middlesex
Dana (became part of Petersham, 1927)	1801 Greenwich/Hardwick/ Petersham	Worcester Worcester
Danvers 1 Sylvan St. Danvers 01923	1752 Salem (Salem Village/ Middle Parishes)	Essex (22) Southern
Dartmouth 400 Slocum Rd. S. Dartmouth 02714	1652 (Acushena/Ponaganesett/ Coaksett)	Bristol (17) Southern
Dedham 26 Bryant St., Dedham 02026	1636	Norfolk (5)
Deerfield 8 Conway St., S. Deerfield 01373	1677	Franklin (19) Greenfield (Deerfield)
Dennis 485 Main St., S. Dennis 02660	1793 Yarmouth	Barnstable (7)
Dighton 979 Somerset Ave., Dighton 02715	1712 Taunton	Bristol (10) Northern
Dorchester (became part of Boston, 1870)	1630 original	Suffolk
Douglas 29 Depot St., Douglas 01516	1746 (New Sherbourn)	Worcester (57) Worcester
Dover 5 Springdale Ave., Dover 02030	1784 Dedham	Norfolk (3)
Dracut 62 Arlington St., Dracut 01826	1702	Middlesex (6) Northern
Dudley 40 Schofield Ave., Dudley 01570	1732 Oxford	Worcester (55) Worcester
Dunstable 511 Main, Dunstable 01827	1673	Middlesex (4) Northern
Duxbury 878 Tremont St., Duxbury 02332	1637	Plymouth (15)
East Bridgewater 175 Central/Box 387 Bridgewater 02333	1823 Bridgewater	Plymouth (12)
East Brookfield 101 Depot Sq., East Brookfield 01515	1920 Brookfield	Worcester (41)

Town Address	Date Formed County (Map)	Vital Records
East Longmeadow 60 Center Sq., East Longmeadow 01028	1894 Longmeadow	Hampden (17)
Eastham 2500 State Hwy., Eastham 02642	1646 (Nawsett)	Barnstable (12)
Easthampton 50 Payson Ave., Easthampton 01027	1785 Northampton/Southampton	Hampshire (16) Northampton
Easton 136 Elm St., N. Easton 02334	1725 Norton	Bristol (3) Northern
Edgartown 70 Main St., Edgartown 02539	1671 (Great Harbour)	Dukes (6)
Egremont 171 Egremont Plain Rd./P.O. Box 56 South Egremont 01258	1760	Berkshire (24) Southern
Enfield (became part of Belchertown/ New Salem/Pelham/Ware, 1938)	1816 Belchertown/Greenwich	Hampshire Northampton
Erving 12 E. Main St., Erving 01344	1838	Franklin (15) Greenfield
Essex 30 Martin St., Essex 01929	1819 Ipswich	Essex (17)
Everett City Hall, 484 Broadway Everett 02149	1870 Malden	Middlesex (39) Southern
Fairhaven 40 Center St., Fairhaven 02719	1812 New Bedford	Bristol (20) Southern
Fall River City Hall, 1 Government Center Fall River 02722	1803 Freetown (Troy, 1834)	Bristol (14) Northern
Falmouth 59 Town Hall Sq., Falmouth 02540	1694	Barnstable (3)
Fitchburg 718 Main St., Fitchburg 01420	1764 Lunenberg	Worcester (9) Northern
Florida 60 South St. Drury 01343	1805 Barnardstone's Grant/ Bullock's Grant	Berkshire (4) Northern
Foxborough 40 South St. Foxborough 02035	1778 Stoughton/Walpole/ Wrentham/Stoughtonham now called Sharon	Norfolk (16)
Framingham 150 Concord St., Framingham 01702	1675	Middlesex (49) Southern

Town Address	Date Formed County (Map)	Vital Records
Franklin 150 Emmons, Franklin 02038	1778 Wrentham	Norfolk (12)
Freetown 3 N. Main St., Assonet 02702	1683	Bristol (15) Northern
Gardner City Hall, 95 Pleasant St. Gardner 01440	1785 Ashburnham/Templeton/ Westminister/Winchendon	Worcester (7) Worcester
Gay Head	1855 (renamed Aquinnah)	Dukes (1)
Georgetown 1 Liberty St., Georgetown 01833	1838 Rowley	Essex (9) Southern
Gill 325 Main Rd., Gill 01376	1793 Greenfield	Franklin (14) Greenfield (Deerfield)
Gloucester City Hall, 9 Dale Ave., Gloucester 01930	1642 (Cape Ann)	Essex (18) Southern
Goshen 42 Main St., Goshen 01032	1781 Chesterfield	Hampshire (3) Northampton
Gosnold 28 Tower Hill Rd., Cuttyhunk 02713	1864 Chilmark	Dukes (7)
Grafton 30 Providence Rd., Grafton 01519	1735 (Hassanamisco)	Worcester (48) Worcester
Granby 250 State St., Granby 01033	1768 South Hadley	Hampshire (18) Northampton
Granville 707 Main St., Granville 01034	1754	Hampden (12) Springfield
Great Barrington 334 Main St., Great Barrington 01230	1761 Sheffield	Berkshire (25)
Greenfield 14 Court Sq., Greenfield 01301	1753 Deerfield	Franklin (13) Greenfield (Deerfield)
Greenwich (became part of Hardwick/New Salem/Petersham/Ware, 1938)	1754 (Quabbin plantation)	Hampshire Northampton
Groton 173 Main St., Groton 01450	1655	Middlesex (10) Southern
Groveland 183 Main St., Groveland 01830	1850 Bradford	Essex (8) Southern
Hadley 100 Middle St., Hadley 01035	1661 (New Plantation)	Hampshire (9) Northampton
Halifax 499 Plymouth St., Halifax 02338	1734 Middleborough/Pembroke/ Plympton	Plymouth (17)

Town Address	Date Formed County (Map)	Vital Records
Hamilton 577 Bay Rd., Hamilton 01936	1793 Ipswich	Essex (16) Southern
Hampden 625 Main St., Hampden 01036	1878 Wilbraham	Hampden (19)
Hancock 3650 Hancock Rd., Hancock 01237	1776 (Jericho Plantation)	Berkshire (5) Northern
Hanover 550 Hanover St., Hanover 02339	1727 Abington/Scituate	Plymouth (4)
Hanson 542 Liberty St., Hanson 02341	1820 Pembroke	Plymouth (13)
Hardwick 307 Main St., Gilbertson 01037	1739 (Lambstown Plantation)	Worcester (20) Worcester
Harvard 13 Ayer Rd., Harvard 01451	1732 Groton/Lancaster/Stow	Worcester (17) Worcester
Harwich 732 Main St., Harwich 02645	1694 (Stauckett)	Barnstable (9)
Hatfield 59 Main St., Hatfield 01038	1670 Hadley	Hampshire (8)
Haverhill City Hall, 4 Summer St. Haverhill 01830	1641	Essex (4) Southern
Hawley 8 Pudding Hollow Rd., Hawley 01339	1792 (No. 7 Plantation)	Franklin (10) Greenfield (Deerfield)
Heath 1 E. Main St., Heath 01346	1785 Charlemont	Franklin (3) Greenfield (Deerfield)
Hingham 210 Center St. Hingham 02043	1635 (Barecove)	Plymouth (6) (Norfolk 1793–1803)
Hinsdale 39 South St., Hinsdale 01235	1804 Partridgefield/Dalton	Berkshire (14) Middle
Holbrook 50 N. Franklin St., Holbrook 02343	1872 Randolph	Norfolk (25)
Holden 1196 Main St., Holden 01520	1741 Worcester	Worcester (23) Worcester
Holland 27 Sturbridge Rd. Holland 01550	1783 South Brimfield (Wales)	Hampden (23) Springfield
Holliston 703 Washington St., Holliston 01746	1724 Sherborn	Middlesex (54) Southern
Holyoke City Hall, 536 Dwight St. Holyoke 01040	1850 West Springfield	Hampden (6)
Hopedale 78 Hopedale St., Hopedale 01747	1886 Milford	Worcester (51) Worcester
Hopkinton 18 Main St., Hopkinton 01748	1715 (Moguncoy)	Middlesex (53) Southern
Hubbardston 7 Main St., Hubbardston 01452	1767 Rutland	Worcester (12) Worcester
Hudson 78 Main St., Hudson 01749	1866 Marlborough/Stow	Middlesex (47) Southern
Hull 253 Atlantic Ave. Hull 02045	1644	Plymouth (7) (Norfolk 1793–1803)
Huntington 24 Russell Rd. Huntington 01050	1773 Murrayfield (Norwich)	Hampshire (12) Northampton
Ipswich 25 Green St., Ipswich 01938	1634 (Aggawam)	Essex (15) Southern
Kingston 26 Evergreen St., Kingston 02360	1726 Plymouth	Plymouth (19)
Lakeville 346 Bedford St., Lakeville 02347	1853 Middleborough	Plymouth (20)
Lancaster 695 Main St., Lancaster 01523	1653	Worcester (16) Worcester
Lanesborough 83 N. Main St. Lanesborough 01237	1765 (New Framingham Plantation)	Berkshire (9) Northern
Lawrence City Hall, 200 Common St. Lawrence 01840	1847 Andover/Methuen	Essex (34) Northern
Lee 32 Main St., Lee 01238	1777 Great Barrington	Berkshire (21) Middle
Leicester 3 Washburn Sq., Leicester 01524	1714	Worcester (34) Worcester
Lenox 6 Walker St., Lenox 01240	1767 Richmont	Berkshire (17) Middle
Leominster City Hall, 25 W. St., Leominster 01453	1740 Lancaster	Worcester (14) Northern
Leverett 9 Montague Rd., Leverett 01054	1774 Sunderland	Franklin (24) Greenfield (Deerfield)

MASSACHUSETTS

Town Address	Date Formed County (Map)	Vital Records
Lexington 1625 Massachusetts Ave., Lexington 02173	1713 Cambridge	Middlesex (27) Southern
Leyden 16 W. Leyden Rd., Leyden 01301	1784 Bernardston	Franklin (5) Greenfield (Deerfield)
Lincoln 16 Lincoln Rd., Lincoln 01773	1754 Concord/Lexington/Weston	Middlesex (26) Southern
Littleton 37 Shattuck Rd. Littleton 01460	1715 (Nashoba)	Middlesex (19) Southern (Northern 1856–60)
Longmeadow 20 Williams St., Longmeadow 01106	1783 Springfield	Hampden (15) Springfield
Lowell City Hall, 375 Merrimack St. Lowell 01852	1826 Chelmsford	Middlesex (7) Northern
Ludlow 488 Chapin St., Ludlow 01056	1774 Springfield	Hampden (9) Springfield
Lunenburg 17 Main St. Lunenburg 01462	1728 Turkey Hills and land belonging to Woburn/Dorchester/and Boardman's Farm	Worcester (10) Northern
Lynn 3 City Hall Sq., Lynn 01901	1635 (Saugust)	Essex (31) Southern
Lynnfield 55 Summer St., Lynnfield 01940	1782 Lynn	Essex (26) Southern
Malden City Hall, 200 Pleasant St. Malden 02148	1649	Middlesex (34) Southern
Manchester 10 Center St., Manchester 01944	1645 Salem	Essex (25) Southern
Mansfield 6 Park Row, Mansfield 02048	1770 Norton	Bristol (2) Northern
Marblehead 188 Washington St., Marblehead 01945	1633	Essex (29) Southern
Marion 2 Spring St., Marion 02738	1852 Rochester	Plymouth (26)
Marlborough City Hall, 140 Main St. Marlborough 01752	1660	Middlesex (48) Southern
Marshfield 870 Moraine St. Marshfield 02050	1640 (Green's Harbour) (Rexhame)	Plymouth (9)
Mashpee 16 Great Neck Rd. North, Mashpee 02649	1763	Barnstable (4)
Mattapoisett 16 Main St., Mattapoisett 02739	1857 Rochester	Plymouth (27)
Maynard 195 Main St., Maynard 01754	1871 Stow/Sudbury	Middlesex (41) Southern
Medfield 459 Main St., Medfield 02052	1650 Dedham	Norfolk (9)
Medford City Hall, 85 George P. Hassett Dr. Medford 02155	1630	Middlesex (33) Southern
Medway 155 Village St., Medway 02053	1713 Medfield	Norfolk (7)
Melrose City Hall, 562 Main St. Melrose 02176	1850 Malden	Middlesex (31) Southern
Mendon 20 Main St./P.O. Box 54 Mendon 01756	1667	Worcester (52) Worcester
Merrimac 2 School St., Merrimac 01860	1876 Amesbury	Essex (1) Southern
Methuen 41 Pleasant St., Methuen 01844	1725 Haverhill	Essex (11) Northern
Middleborough 20 Center St., Middleborough 02346	1669 (Namassackett)	Plymouth (21)
Middlefield 188 Skyline Trail Middlefield 01243	1783 Becket/Chester/Washington/Partridgefield/Worthington/Prescott's Grant	Hampshire (4)
Middletown 48 S. Main St. Middletown 01949	1728 Andover/Boxford/Salem/Topsfield	Essex (21) Southern
Milford 52 Main St., Milford 01757	1780 Mendon	Worcester (53) Worcester
Millbury 127 Elm St., Millbury 01527	1813 Sutton	Worcester (46) Worcester
Millis 900 Main St., Millis 02054	1885 Medway	Norfolk (8)
Millville 8 Central St., Millville 01529	1916 Blackstone	Worcester (59) Worcester

Town Address	Date Formed County (Map)	Vital Records
Milton 525 Canton St., Milton 02186	1662 Dorchester	Norfolk (21)
Monroe 3-C School St., Monroe 01350	1822 Rowe/The Gore	Franklin (1) Greenfield
Monson 110 Main St., Monson 01057	1760 Brimfield	Hampden (20) Springfield
Montague 1 Ave. A, Turners Falls 01376	1754 Sunderland	Franklin (21) Greenfield (Deerfield)
Monterey 435 Main St., Monterey 01245	1847 Tyringham	Berkshire (26) Southern
Montgomery 161 Main St. Montgomery 01085	1780 Westfield/Norwich/ Southampton	Hampden (4) Springfield
Mount Washington 118 East Rd. Mount Washington 01258	1779 (Tauconnuck Mountain plantation)	Berkshire (29) Southern
Nahant 334 Nahant Rd., Nahant 01908	1853 Lynn	Essex (33) Southern
Nantucket 16 Broad St. Nantucket 02554	1687 (Sherburn, 1713) (Tuckannock, 1795)	Nantucket
Natick 13 E. Central St., Natick 01760	1650	Middlesex (50) Southern
Needham 1471 Highland Ave., Needham 02192	1711 Dedham	Norfolk (2)
New Ashford 188 Mallery Rd., New Ashford 01237	1781	Berkshire (6) Northern
New Bedford City Hall, 133 Williams St. New Bedford 02740	1787 Dartmouth	Bristol (18) Southern
New Braintree 20 Memorial Dr., New Braintree 01531	1751 Harwick/Brookfield	Worcester (29) Worcester
New Marlborough P.O. Box 99, Mill River 01259	1759	Berkshire (31) Southern
New Salem 15 S. Main St., New Salem 01355	1753	Franklin (26) Greenfield (Deerfield)
Newbury 25 High Rd., Newbury 01950	1635 (Wessacucon)	Essex (7) Southern
Newburyport City Hall, 60 Pleasant St. Newburyport 01950	1764 Newbury	Essex (6) Southern
Newton City Hall 1000 Commonwealth Ave. Newton 02159	1691 (Cambridge Village/ Now Cambridge)	Middlesex (46) Southern
Norfolk 1 Liberty Lane, Norfolk 02056	1870 Franklin/Medway/Walpole/Wrentham	Norfolk (13)
North Adams City Hall, 10 Main St., North Adams 01247	1878 Adams	Berkshire (3)
North Andover 400 Osgood St., North Andover 01845	1855 Andover	Essex (12) Northern
North Attleborough 43 S. Washington St. North Attleborough 02760	1887 Attleborough	Bristol (1)
North Brookfield 185 N. Main St., North Brookfield 01535	1812 Brookfield	Worcester (31) Worcester
North Reading 235 North St., North Reading 01864	1853 Reading	Middlesex (15) Southern
Northampton City Hall, 210 Main St. Northampton 01060	1656	Hampshire (14)
Northborough 63 Main St., Northborough 01532	1766 Westborough	Worcester (28) Worcester
Northbridge 7 Main St., Whitinsville 01588	1772 Uxbridge	Worcester (49) Worcester
Northfield 69 Main St., Northfield 01360	1714 (Squakeag Plantation)	Franklin (7) Greenfield (Deerfield)
Norton 70 E. Main St., Norton 02766	1710 Taunton	Bristol (5) Northern
Norwell 345 Main St./P.O. Box 295 Norwell 02061	1849 Scituate (South Scituate, 1888)	Plymouth (5)
Norwood 566 Washington St., Norwood 02062	1872 Dedham/Walpole	Norfolk (6)
Oak Bluffs 56 School St./P.O. Box 2490 Oak Bluffs 02557	1880 Edgartown (Cottage City)	Dukes (5)
Oakham 2 Coldbrook Rd., Oakham 01068	1762 Rutland	Worcester (21) Worcester
Orange 6 Prospect St. Orange 01364	1783 Athol/Royalston/Warwick/ Ervingshire tract	Franklin (16) Greenfield (Deerfield)

MASSACHUSETTS

Town Address	Date Formed County (Map)	Vital Records
Orleans 19 School Rd., Orleans 02653	1797 Eastham	Barnstable (11)
Otis 1 N. Main St. Otis 01253	1773 Tyringham Equivalent (Loudon, 1810)	Berkshire (28) Middle
Oxford 325 Main St., Oxford 01540	1693	Worcester (44) Worcester
Palmer 4417 Main St., Palmer 01069	1752 (The Elbows Plantation)	Hampden (10) Springfield
Paxton 697 Pleasant St., Paxton 01612	1765 Leicester/Rutland	Worcester (33) Worcester
Peabody City Hall, 24 Lowell St. Peabody 01960	1855 Danvers (South Danvers, 1868)	Essex (27) Southern
Pelham 351 Amherst Rd., Amherst 01002	1743 (New Lisburn tract)	Hampshire (11) Northampton
Pembroke 100 Center St., Pembroke 02359	1712 Duxbury	Plymouth (14)
Pepperell 1 Main St., Pepperell 01463	1753 Groton	Middlesex (3) Southern
Peru 3 W. Main Rd., Hinsdale 01235	1771 (Partridgefield, 1806)	Berkshire (15) Middle
Petersham 3 S. Main St., Petersham 01366	1754 (Nichewoag Plantation)	Worcester (11) Worcester
Phillipston 50 On the Common Phillipston 01331	1786 Athol/Templeton (Gerry, 1814)	Worcester (5) Worcester
Pittsfield City Hall, 70 Allen St., Pittsfield 01201	1761 (Pontoosuck Plantation)	Berkshire (12) Middle
Plainfield 344 Main St. Plainfield 01070	1785 Cummington	Hampshire (1) Northampton
Plainville 142 South St., Plainville 02762	1905 Wrentham	Norfolk (15)
Plymouth 11 Lincoln St., Plymouth 02360	1620	Plymouth (23)
Plympton 5 Palmer Rd., Plympton 02367	1707 Plymouth	Plymouth (18)
Prescott (became part of Pelham and New Salem, 1938)	1822 Pelham/New Salem	Worcester
Princeton 6 Town Hall Dr., Princeton 01541	1759 Rutland	Worcester (13) Worcester
Provincetown 260 Commercial St., Provincetown 02657	1727	Barnstable (15)
Quincy City Hall, 1305 Hancock, Quincy 02169	1792 Braintree/Dorchester	Norfolk (23)
Randolph 41 S. Main St., Randolph 02368	1793 Braintree	Norfolk (22)
Raynham 53 Orchard St., Raynham 02767	1731 Taunton	Bristol (7) Northern
Reading 16 Lowell St., Reading 01867	1644 Lynn	Middlesex (16) Southern
Rehoboth 148 R Peck St., Rehoboth 02769	1645 (as Seacunk)	Bristol (9) Northern
Revere City Hall, 281 Broadway Revere 02151	1846 Chelsea (North Chelsea)	Suffolk (1)
Richmond 1529 State Rd., Richmond 01254	1765 (Richmont)	Berkshire (16) Middle
Rochester 1 Constitution Way, Rochester 02770	1686 (Scippicam)	Plymouth (24)
Rockland 242 Union St., Rockland 02370	1874 Abington	Plymouth (3)
Rockport 34 Broadway, Rockport 01969	1840 Gloucester	Essex (19) Southern
Rowe 321 Zoar Rd., Rowe 01367	1785 (Myrefield)	Franklin (2) Greenfield (Deerfield)
Rowley 139 Main St., Rowley 01969	1639	Essex (10) Southern
Roxbury (annexed to Boston, 1868)	1630	Suffolk
Royalston 13 The Common, Royalston 01368	1765 (Royalshire tract)	Worcester (1) Worcester
Russell 65 Main St., Russell 01071	1792 Westfield/Montgomery	Hampden (3)
Rutland 250 Main St., Rutland 01543	1714 (Naquag tract)	Worcester (22) Worcester
Salem City Hall, 93 Washington St., Salem 01970	1630	Essex (28) Southern
Salisbury 5 Beach Rd., Salisbury 01950	1639 (Colchester)	Essex (3) Southern

Town Address	Date Formed County (Map)	Vital Records
Sandisfield 66 Sandisfield Rd., Sandisfield 01255	1762 (No. 3 Plantation)	Berkshire (32) Southern
Sandwich 145 Main St., Sandwich 02563	1638	Barnstable (2)
Saugus 298 Central St., Saugus 01906	1815 Lynn	Essex (30) Southern
Savoy 720 Main Rd., Savoy 01256	1797	Berkshire (8) Northern
Scituate 600 Chief Justice Cushing Way Scituate 02066	1633	Plymouth (8)
Seekonk 100 Peck St., Seekonk 02771	1812 Rehoboth	Bristol (8) Northern
Sharon 90 S. Main St., Sharon 02067	1765 Stoughton (Stoughtonham)	Norfolk (17)
Sheffield 21 Depot Sq., Sheffield 01257	1733	Berkshire (30) Southern
Shelburne 51 Bridge St., Shelburne Falls 01370	1768 Deerfield	Franklin (12) Greenfield (Deerfield)
Sherborn 19 Washington St., Sherborn 01770	1674	Middlesex (52) Southern
Shirley 7 Keady Way, Shirley 01464	1753 Groton	Middlesex (9) Southern
Shrewsbury 100 Maple Ave., Shrewsbury 01545	1720	Worcester (36) Worcester
Shutesbury 1 Cooleyville Rd., Shutesbury 01072	1761 (Roadtown Plantation)	Franklin (25) Greenfield (Deerfield)
Somerset 140 Wood St., Somerset 02726	1790 Swansea	Bristol (13) Northern
Somerville City Hall, 93 Highland Ave. Somerville 02143	1842 Charlestown	Middlesex (38) Southern
South Hadley 116 Main St., South Hadley 01075	1753 Hadley	Hampshire (17) Northampton
Southampton 8 East St., Southampton 01073	1753 Northampton	Hampshire (15) Northampton
Southborough 17 Common St., Southborough 01772	1727 Marlborough	Worcester (38) Worcester
Southbridge 41 Elm St., Southbridge 01550	1816 Charlton/Dudley/Sturbridge	Worcester (54) Worcester454
Southwick 454 College Hwy., Southwick 01077	1770 Westfield	Hampden (13) Springfield
Spencer 157 Main St., Spencer 01562	1753 Leicester	Worcester (32) Worcester
Springfield City Hall, 36 Court St., Springfield 01103	1641	Hampden (16) Springfield
Sterling 1 Park St., Sterling 01564	1781 Lancaster	Worcester (15) Worcester
Stockbridge 6 Main St., Stockbridge 01262	1739 (Indian Town Plantation)	Berkshire (20) Middle
Stoneham 35 Central St., Stoneham 02180	1725 Charlestown	Middlesex (29) Southern
Stoughton 10 Pearl St., Stoughton 02072	1726 Dorchester	Norfolk (19)
Stow 380 Great St., Stow 01775	1683 (Pompositticut Plantation)	Middlesex (40) Southern
Sturbridge 308 Main St., Sturbridge 01566	1738 (New Medfield tract)	Worcester (42) Worcester
Sudbury 322 Concord Rd., Sudbury 01776	1639	Middlesex (42) Southern
Sunderland 12 School St., Sunderland 01375	1714 (Swampfield)	Franklin (23) Greenfield (Deerfield)
Sutton 4 Uxbridge Rd., Sutton 01527	1714	Worcester (47) Worcester
Swampscott 22 Monument Ave., Swampscott 01907	1852 Lynn	Essex (32) Southern
Swansea 81 Main St. Swansea 02777	1667 Rehoboth (Wannamoisett)	Bristol (12) Northern
Taunton City Hall, 15 Summer St., Taunton 02780	1639 (Cohannett)	Bristol (6) Northern
Templeton 9 Main St. Baldwinville 01436	1762 (Narragansett No. 6 Plantation)	Worcester (6) Worcester
Tewksbury 1009 Main St., Tewksbury 01876	1734 Billerica	Middlesex (8) Northern
Tisbury 51 Spring St., Vineyard Haven 02568	1671 (Middletowne)	Dukes (4)
Tolland 241 W. Granville Rd., Tolland 01034	1810 Granville	Hampden (11) Springfield

Town Address	Date Formed County (Map)	Vital Records
Topsfield 8 W. Common St., Topsfield 01983	1648 Ipswich	Essex (14) Southern
Townsend 272 Main St., Townsend 01469	1732	Middlesex (2) Southern
Truro 24 Town Hall Rd., Truro 02666	1709 (Pawmett tract)	Barnstable (14)
Tyngsborough 25 Bryants Lane, Tyngsborough 01879	1789 Dunstable	Middlesex (5) Northern
Tyringham 16 Main Rd., Tyringham 01264	1762 (No. 1 Plantation)	Berkshire (27) Middle
Upton 1 Main St. Upton 01568	1735 Hopkinton/Mendon/ Sutton/Uxbridge	Worcester (50) Worcester
Uxbridge 21 S. Main St., Uxbridge 01569	1727 Mendon	Worcester (58) Worcester
Wakefield 1 Lafayette St., Wakefield 01880	1812 Reading (South Reading)	Middlesex (45) Southern
Wales 3 Hollow Rd. Wales 01081	1762 Brimfield (South Brimfield)	Hampden (22) Springfield
Walpole 135 School Rd., Walpole 02081	1724 Dedham	Norfolk (10)
Waltham City Hall, 610 Main St., Waltham 02154	1738 Watertown	Middlesex (45) Southern
Ware 126 Main St., Ware 01082	1761 (Ware River Parish)	Hampshire (20) Northampton
Wareham 54 Marion Rd., Wareham 02571	1739 Rochester/Agawam Plantation	Plymouth (25)
Warren 48 High St. Warren 01083	1742 Brimfield/Brookfield/ Kingsfield (Western-1834)	Worcester (39) Worcester
Warwick 12 Athol Rd., Warwick 01364	1763 (Roxbury Canada Plantation)	Franklin (8) Greenfield (Deerfield)
Washington 8 Summit Hill Rd., Washington 01223	1777 (Hartwood Plantation)	Berkshire (18) Middle
Watertown 149 Main St., Watertown 02472	1630	Middlesex (35) Southern
Wayland 41 Cochituate Rd. Wayland 01778	1780 Sudbury (East Sudbury, 1835)	Middlesex (43) Southern
Webster 350 Main St., Webster 01570	1832 Dudley/Oxford	Worcester (56) Worcester
Wellesley 525 Washington St., Wellesley 02181	1881 Needham	Norfolk (1)
Wellfleet 300 Main St., Wellfleet 02667	1763 Eastham	Barnstable (13)
Wendell 270 Wendell Depot Rd. Wendell Depot 01380	1781 Shutesbury/Ervingshire	Franklin (22) Greenfield (Deerfield)
Wenham 138 Main St., Wenham 01984	1643	Essex (23) Southern
West Boylston 120 Prescott St., West Boylston 01583	1808 Boylston/Holden/Sterling	Worcester (24) Worcester
West Bridgewater 65 N. Main St., West Bridgewater 02379	1822 Bridgewater	Plymouth (10)
West Brookfield 2 E. Main St., West Brookfield 01585	1848 Brookfield	Worcester (30) Worcester
West Newbury 381 Main St., West Newbury 01985	1819 Newbury (Parsons)	Essex (5) Southern
West Springfield 26 Central St., West Springfield 01089	1774 Springfield	Hampden (7) Springfield
West Stockbridge 9 Main St., West Stockbridge 01266	1774 Stockbridge	Berkshire (19) Southern
West Tisbury 1059 State Rd., West Tisbury 02575	1892 Tisbury	Dukes (3)
Westborough 34 W. Main St., Westborough 01581	1717 Marlborough	Worcester (37) Worcester
Westfield City Hall, 59 Court St., Westfield 01085	1669 Springfield	Hampden (5) Springfield
Westford 55 Main St., Westford 01886	1729 Chelmsford	Middlesex (11) Northern
Westhampton 1 South Rd., Westhampton 01027	1778 Northampton	Hampshire (13) Northampton
Westminster 3 Bacon St., Westminster 01473	1759 (Narragansett No. 2)	Worcester (8) Northern
Weston Town House Rd., Weston 02193	1713 Watertown	Middlesex (44) Southern
Westport 816 Main St. Westport 02790	1787 Dartmouth	Bristol (16) Southern

MASSACHUSETTS

Town Address	Date Formed County (Map)	Vital Records
Westwood 580 High St., Westwood 02090	1897 Dedham	Norfolk (4)
Weymouth 75 Middle St., Weymouth 02189	1635 (Wessaguscus)	Norfolk (18)
Whately 218 Chestnut Plain Rd., Whately 01093	1771 Hatfield	Franklin (20) Greenfield (Deerfield)
Whitman 54 South Ave., Whitman 02188	1875 Abington/E. Bridgewater (South Abington)	Plymouth (11)
Wilbraham 240 Springfield St., Wilbraham 01095	1763 Springfield	Hampden (18) Springfield
Williamsburg 141 Main St., Haydenville 01039	1771 Hatfield	Hampshire (7) Northampton
Williamstown 31 North St., Williamstown 01267	1765 (as West Hoosuck Plantation)	Berkshire (1) Northern
Wilmington 121 Glen Rd., Wilmington 01887	1730 Reading/Woburn	Middlesex (14) Northern
Winchendon 109 Front St., Winchendon 01475	1764 (Ipswich Canada Plantation)	Worcester (2) Worcester
Winchester 71 Mount Vernon St. Winchester 01890	1850 Medford/Woburn/ W. Cambridge	Middlesex (30) Southern
Windsor 3 Hinsdale Rd., Windsor 01270	1771 (Gageborough)	Berkshire (11) Northern
Winthrop 1 Metcalf Sq., Winthrop 02152	1846 Chelsea (N. Chelsea)	Suffolk (2)
Woburn City Hall, 10 Common St., Woburn 01801	1642 (Charlestowne Village)	Middlesex (28) Southern
Worcester City Hall, 455 Main St., Worcester 01608	1684 (Quansigamond Plantation)	Worcester (35) Worcester
Worthington 160 Huntington Rd., Worthington 01098	1768 (No. 3 Plantation)	Hampshire (5)
Wrentham 100 Stonewall Blvd., Wrentham 02093	1673 (Wollonopaug)	Norfolk (14)
Yarmouth 1146 Route 28 S. Yarmouth 02664	1639 (Mattacheeset)	Barnstable (6)

Michigan

ARLEIGH P. HELFER JR. AND CAROL L. MAKI

W ater dominated Michigan's early history. The Great Lakes, the numerous inland lakes, and the extensive arrangement of rivers were means of transportation, sources of food supply, determinants of the climate, battlegrounds, the impetus for industry, and a strong force in the settlement patterns. Immigration was accelerated by the opening of the Erie Canal in 1825. Diverse soils and vast mineral deposits added their influence to the development of the area. Proximity to Canada also played a large part in the early exploration of the state.

The first French explorers arrived in the area between 1618 and 1622 and found approximately 15,000 Native Americans. For generations, the nations of the Chippewa or Ojibway, Potawatomi, Miami, Ottawa, Menominee, and Huron or Wyandot had held claim to the land.

The first European explorer thought to have actually visited the area that is now Michigan was Etienne Brule. Brule was sent from Canada by Samuel de Champlain, late in 1618 or early the following year. Another French Canadian, Jean Nicolet, ventured into the area in 1634. The rationalization for French exploration of the land included adventure, visions of wealth and empire, and determination of their missionaries. Catholic missions were established at Sault Ste. Marie in 1668 and at St. Ignace in 1671. French forts were built in the late seventeenth century. The French-Canadian families were brought by the fur trading industry and lived in or near the forts. They raised large families and enough crops for their own use.

The earliest permanent settlement was made at Fort Pontchartrain (now Detroit) in 1701. It was established by Antoine de la Mothe Cadillac. He arrived with a small group of followers to develop trade on the Great Lakes and defend the (then French) territory from the English.

During the eighteenth century, Michigan was involved in international wars, as the French, the English, and the Americans fought for supremacy in the area. Many native tribes were involved in these battles. The British flag flew over Michigan from 1760 to 1796, although the United States had actually been ceded the area in 1783. Michigan was defined, although not named, in the Northwest Ordinance of 1787. From 1796 to 1800, Michigan was governed under the auspices of the Northwest Territory. At that time the principal population settlements were at Detroit and Mackinac Island, and most inhabitants were of French ancestry. English and Scots-Irish were most prevalent in the merchant class. Along the Raisin River, south of Detroit, was a community of French farmers. From 1800 to 1803, Michigan was considered both Indiana Territory and Northwest Territory, but from 1803 to 1805 it was completely included in Indiana Territory. On 11 January 1805, Michigan Territory was established. The War of 1812 put Michigan in British hands for a second time, but it returned to the United States in 1813.

Michigan then became a lumbering and mining site. The new industries brought new people and new settlements. The first land office opened in 1818, but the difficulty of traveling to the territory hindered extensive migration. It was considered more dangerous to attempt to navigate Lake Erie than the Atlantic Ocean.

Federally funded lighthouses and harbor improvements, steam navigation on the Great Lakes, and the completion of

the Erie Canal were instrumental in increasing the flow of Americans to Michigan. New Englanders and descendants of New Englanders, having previously migrated to New York, began moving to the area. New roads within the state and others connecting to adjacent states made Michigan even more accessible. For the most part, settlers came from New York, Ohio, and Indiana. They were not the very rich or the very poor and were typically farmers, generally young, and usually married.

There were, in addition to Yankees, several communities of settlers with German or Irish ancestry, many Quakers, and a few Southerners. The number of foreign-born immigrants was small before statehood.

In 1835 a state government was created, but the Toledo War delayed the actual statehood process. The "war" involved a border dispute between Michigan and Ohio, which led to mobilization of armed men. There were no fatalities, and Ohio received the disputed land, with Michigan receiving as compensation the land that is now the Upper Peninsula. Although the state government was already functioning during that period, Congress officially declared Michigan a state on 26 January 1837.

Lumber, copper, and iron-ore industries became a major attraction for immigrants between the 1840s and 1880s, augmenting the population with Irish, Finns, Norwegians, Swedes, Italians, and Poles. A group of religious refugees from Holland brought their skilled crafts and farming experience.

By the beginning of the twentieth century, when the iron had been heavily worked and the forests cut, the automobile industry generated a new commodity for Michigan's economy, bringing eastern Europeans and African Americans from the South. The Detroit area, the site of Cadillac's settlement, remains the most densely populated in the state.

Vital Records

Marriages, recorded in the county where they occurred, are the earliest public vital records in Michigan because of a marriage registration law that was enacted in 1805. A later law required marriages to be collected by the county clerk after 1 April 1867 and forwarded to the Secretary of State. Births and death records for each county, with copies also sent to the state, began no later than January 1867, although registration of all vital records was certainly not enforced. A 1905 law was much more effective. Divorce records began in 1897.

Photocopies of these registrations can be ordered from the Michigan Department of Community Health, Vital Records Requests, P.O. Box 30721, Lansing, MI 48909 <www.michigan.gov/mdch>.

All death, marriage, and divorce records, and those birth records more than 100 years old are public records, and photocopies of them are available to any individual or agency upon written application and payment of the fee. Birth records fewer than 100 years old are available only to the individual to whom the record pertains, the parent(s) named on the record, any heir, legal guardian, or any legal representative of an eligible person. "Heir" generally is interpreted as any descendant with a blood relationship to the individual. Relationship to the person named on the birth record, and date and place of death for that person must be supplied when requesting such a birth certificate.

Official forms, all available online, are required to request a certified copy of any vital record (non-certified copies for genealogical research are not available.) Non-refundable fees for any type of copy are the following: first record request, including a standard three-year search—$20; duplicates of certified copies—$5 each; additional years searched per record request—$4 per year.

Marriages registered before mandatory recording (1867) in some counties (see County Resources) may be ordered from the appropriate county clerk. Charges for searches and/or copies will vary from county to county but must not exceed the state fees. Some township clerks also recorded births and deaths.

The Michigan Department of Community Health offers the Genealogical Death Indexing System (GENDIS), which provides Internet access (see address above) to selected death records at its website. The data (individual's name, date of death, father's surname, and county of death) have been obtained from microfilmed death ledgers and transcribed by genealogical society members. GENDIS contains well over 200,000 records from 1867 to 1897, with additions planned.

Microfilm copies of indexes to specific groups of Michigan vital records are at the Library of Michigan, State Archives of Michigan, Burton Historical Collection of the Detroit Public Library, and the Allen County Public Library in Fort Wayne, Indiana (see Archives, Libraries, and Societies for location of all four repositories):

Michigan. State Department of Public Health. *Index of Death Records, 1867–1914.* 13 reels.

Michigan. State Department of Public Health. *Index to Marriage Records, 1872–1921.* 21 reels.

The government archive records at the Burton Historical Collection include the forms for Wayne County Marriage Returns. Completed by a minister or civil authority, the forms were sent to the county clerk between 1818 and 1888, although most are dated 1860 to 1877. The forms include the date of the marriage and names of the bride and groom with their color, residence, age, place of birth, and occupation.

Census Records

Federal

Population Schedules
- Indexed—1820 (six counties and Detroit), 1830, 1840, 1850, 1860, 1870, 1880, 1900, 1910, 1920, 1930
- Soundex—1880, 1900, 1910, 1920

Industry and Agriculture Schedules
- 1850, 1860, 1870, 1880

Mortality Schedules
- 1850, 1860, 1870, 1880

Union Veterans Schedules
- 1890

A complete set of federal population and supplemental schedules are available on microfilm at the State Archives of Michigan/Library of Michigan along with available AISI indexes (see page 3). Other repositories in the state have population schedules, Soundex, and indexes, while the Burton Historical Collection in Detroit and the Allen County Public Library in Fort Wayne, Indiana, hold those for Michigan and numerous other states as well.

Territorial and State

Numerous state and territorial censuses were taken in Michigan, although few are extant. In 1710 the French compiled the first Michigan census. The 1710 census and numerous others through the year 1792 are of the Detroit area, for the most part. Fort Saint Joseph had a census taken in 1780 (*Michigan Pioneer and Historical Collections*, vol. 10, 1908, 406-07), as did Wayne County in 1796, which was printed in *National Genealogical Society Quarterly* 64 (1981): 185-94. A tax list of Wayne County in 1802 and a list of residents of Detroit in 1805 may be considered early enumerations of Michigan population. Sources discussing the state censuses more comprehensively include Donna Valley Russell's *Michigan Censuses 1710–1830 Under the French, British, and Americans* (Detroit: Detroit Society for Genealogical Research, 1982) and "State Censuses of Michigan: A Tragedy of Lost Treasures," *Family Trails* 6 (Summer/Fall, 1978).

Microfilm copies of the state census schedules for 1845, 1854, 1864, 1874, 1884, and 1894 are held by the State Archives of Michigan; some are partial and/or incomplete. The Library of Michigan in Lansing and the Allen County Public Library in Fort Wayne, Indiana, also hold Michigan territorial and state census records as early as 1827. Prior to 1884 the state census names only the head of the household. The 1884 census, however, will identify those in each household that have married within the census year, giving the month of and the location of the marriage.

There are also mortality schedules included in the 1884 and 1894 state censuses. A special Civil War Veteran Census was taken by the state in 1888; the manuscript of this census is at the state archives. See State Archives Circular No. 9, *State Census Records in the State Archives,* available from the archives.

McGinnis's publication (see Background Sources) has a county-by-county listing of the state and territorial censuses that do exist. A list and location of schedules is also available from Bentley Historical Library, University of Michigan (see Archives, Libraries, and Societies).

Background Sources

The numerous county histories and many volumes of *Michigan Pioneer and Historical Collections* are suggested as sources of early local history. The latter, frequently listed as *Michigan Historical Collections,* was published between 1877 and 1929 by the Pioneer Society of the State of Michigan. Included in the forty volumes are proceedings of the society, biographical sketches, obituaries, genealogies, and other historical material. A finding aid to the *Collections* was originally developed by the Works Progress Administration (WPA): Michigan Historical Society, *Classified Finding List of the Collections of the Michigan Pioneer and Historical Society* (Detroit: Wayne University Press, 1952).

Two sources for genealogical information and research in the state of Michigan are:

Callard, Carol, ed. *Sourcebook of the Michigan Census, County Histories and Vital Records.* Lansing, Mich.: Library of Michigan, 1987.

McGinnis, Carol. *Michigan Genealogy Sources and Resources.* Baltimore: Genealogical Publishing Co., 1987.

The above two sources provide information on the availability of vital and government records. McGinnis's has sections on genealogical collections and historical and genealogical societies, arranged by county.

Maps

A John Farmer 1855 Wayne County plat map was the first Michigan map to show land ownership. H. F. Walling's 1873 atlas for the entire state was reprinted in 1977 by The Bookmark, in Knightstown, Indiana. Many county maps indicating ownership were published as part of the 1876 centennial. Extensive map collections are available at the Library of Michigan and the Burton Historical Collection.

Consult Robert W. Karrow's *Checklist of Printed Maps of the Middle West to 1900* (Chicago: The Newberry Library, n.d.). This fourteen-volume set lists all known pre-1900 plat maps and plat books for eleven states, including Michigan.

The earliest Sanborn map (see page 5) for Michigan is the year 1868 for the community of Lansing.

Land Records

Public-Domain State

Private land claims based on grants made prior to U.S. sovereignty are found for Mackinac and Detroit. These records are in the National Archives (see pages 11-12). Most were "ribbon farms," very narrow but very long to ensure river frontage. Consult Silas Farmer's *History of Detroit and Wayne County and Early Michigan* (Detroit: Silas Farmer and Co., 1890) or D. B. Reynolds's *Early Land Claims in Michigan* (Lansing, Mich.: Michigan Department of Conservation, 1940) for information on private land claims.

The first public-domain land was purchased by settlers in Michigan in 1818. The Ordinance of 1785 had provided the methods for dividing and selling the recently ceded regions. The land was first surveyed into six-mile-square townships, each containing thirty-six sections. The townships were surveyed from an east-west line called a "base line" and a north-south line called a "principal meridian." These public domain lands were offered, at the first land office, in Detroit, for $2 per acre, with a minimum purchase required. "Installment plans" were available. In 1820 the cost per acre was lowered to $1.25, with "cash only" and a minimum purchase of eighty acres. Land was usually paid for with silver, gold, bank notes, or drafts. A "patent," usually signed by a clerk, for the U.S. President, would be sent to the landowner, giving title to the previously federal property. A "pre-emption law" in 1841 gave the "squatters" the right to purchase 160 acres at a minimum price.

Federal land patents can be checked online at <www.glorecords.blm.gov>. Microfilm copies of the federal land patent records are also at the Michigan State Library. These provide information on the first ownership of all federal lands in the state. The State Archives of Michigan has the original state land patent records. It is necessary to have an exact legal description of the property to utilize either of these valuable sources.

The State Archives of Michigan has numerous records of land transactions. They include the following sources of information (not inclusive) under various departments: tract books of swamp lands purchases, original maps prepared by federal surveyors that show cultural and physical features as they existed between about 1815 and 1855, abstracts of land grants ca. 1837 to 1900, surveys of private claims as early as 1807, and land tract books from 1818 to 1962. See Circular No. 2, *Land Records*, published by the State Archives of Michigan, for more complete information.

Subsequent land transactions, no longer under federal control, are recorded in the appropriate county registrar's office.

Deeds for southeastern Michigan's "Toledo Strip," encompassing portions of Monroe, Lenawee, and Hillsdale counties, may have been recorded in Ohio and Michigan.

The State Archives of Michigan indicates that a long-range goal of publishing "First Land Owners" volumes for each of the counties has been undertaken by either the Michigan Genealogy Council or Col. Paul Peck. To date, about thirteen have been completed.

Probate Records

Probate records are the responsibility of the probate court office or the office of the probate judge in each county. There is no state index to these records, but see County Resources for earliest records available. Some probate court records, estate case files in particular, have been deposited at the state archives or at a regional depository. Consult State Archives Circular No. 6, *Probate Court Records*, for a listing of counties and dates of these original and microfilmed files.

Court Records

County circuit court records are kept by the county clerk or the circuit court clerk in the appropriate county office. There are no state indexes to these records. See State Archives Circular No. 37, Circuit Court Records, for more information.

National Archives—Great Lakes Region (see page 12) holds federal district court records as follows: Eastern District (Flint), 1895–1962; Bay City, 1894–1962; Detroit, 1837–1962; Western District (Grand Rapids), 1863–1962; and Marquette, 1878–1962. An inventory of holdings is available at the archives in Chicago. Documentation of shipwrecks on the Great Lakes, filed in the admiralty case files, is included in these records.

Tax Records

Property tax records at the county level usually date back to the first land records. Either the county treasurer or the register of deeds is the custodian of these records.

Numerous early tax assessment and general tax rolls are available at the Michigan State Archives. Organized by county, the records include the name of the owner or occupant of the property, legal description and number of acres, value of land and personal estate, and amount of tax levied. There are tax rolls for some counties for the late 1830s, but most are for the last half of the nineteenth century. A complete list of these extensive rolls can be obtained from the State Archives Circular No. 1, *Tax/Assessment Rolls at the State Archives*. This circular also lists those tax rolls kept at the archives regional depositories (see Archives,

Libraries, and Societies). Because of the complicated nature of tax records, in-person research at the archives is encouraged.

National Archives—Great Lakes Region in Chicago (see page 12) holds numerous federal personal property and corporate tax assessment lists for the state of Michigan.

Cemetery Records

The Library of Michigan in Lansing and the Burton Historical Collection have over 1,000 books of transcribed or published tombstone readings from Michigan cemeteries. To locate a cemetery in the state, consult the *Michigan Cemetery Compendium* (Spring Arbor, Mich.: HAR-AL, 1979). It lists most cemeteries in Michigan.

Church Records

The earliest religious denomination in Michigan was the Roman Catholic Church, established through a mission in 1668 at Sault Ste. Marie. Ste. Anne's, in Detroit, has parish records beginning in 1703. The Moravians, the first Protestant group in Michigan, assembled in Mount Clemens in the late 1770s. They were followed by Congregationalists in 1800 and the first Michigan Methodist minister in 1803.

Michigan Historical Collections in Ann Arbor holds large collections from the Presbyterian Church and the Protestant Episcopal Church, in addition to other denominations. Dutch Reformed Church records are at Calvin College and Seminary Library in Grand Rapids; Finnish church records are deposited at the Finnish-American Historical Archives at Suomi College in Hancock. The Upjohn Library at Kalamazoo College in Kalamazoo has a large collection of Baptist archive material.

Many early Detroit churches have their records deposited at the Burton Historical Collection–Detroit Public Library. The records for the Central Methodist Church and St. Paul's Cathedral begin in 1820. The St. Joseph, Michigan Catholic Mission records of 1720 to 1772 are at this repository.

The Michigan Historical Records Survey, WPA, completed an *Inventory of the Church Archives of Michigan*, and many of the church records from this inventory were published from 1936 through 1942. Several unpublished inventories are held by the Burton Historical Collection–Detroit Public Library.

Military Records

The State Archives of Michigan is the repository for military records in the state. Mail and e-mail <archives@michigan. gov> inquiries are answered. The Descriptive Rolls of Michigan Units (1838–1919) are available for certain individuals serving in

a Michigan unit during that time period. Their files also include records of fraternal organizations for veterans of the Civil War and the Spanish-American War. Muster rolls of these organizations include names of members and their military history. A census taken of Civil War veterans in 1888 includes county, name of soldier, rank, military unit, and post office address. The state archives has extensive information on the Veterans' Facility, initially called the Soldier and Sailors' Home. It was established for Civil War veterans, but now serves veterans of all wars in which the United States has been involved. Records, many of which are indexed, span a period of 1885 to 1986. Individuals in those records were inhabitants of the facility: wives, widows, and mothers of veterans, and ex-nurses. The case files may include complete application forms with military and family information.

The State Archives of Michigan has no pension records for Civil War veterans (see National Archives holdings, page 9). It does have, however, a file of grave registrations gathered by the Civil War Centennial Observance Commission. The forms, filed by county and by name of soldier, include name, enlistment and service records, place and date of birth and death, name and location of cemetery, and additional remarks. They also have Muster Rolls of the Grand Army of the Republic Posts in Michigan. The archives has portraits of Civil War Soldiers, indexed by unit and by surname.

In the state archives' collection classified as Civil War Manuscripts, certificates, diaries, discharges, journals, letters, and miscellaneous documents can be found. The following published finding aids can be obtained from the state archives for their military collections: Archival 1, *Records of the Michigan Military Establishment, 1838–1941*; Archival 15, *Records of the Grand Army of the Republic, Michigan Department*; Archival 17, *Records of the Michigan Veteran's Facility*; Circular No. 20, *Civil War Manuscripts*. Check for online State Archive indexes at its website.

The Burton Historical Collection holds extensive records for Civil War soldiers, but they are not cross indexed. One group of their records is for U.S. General Hospital (1864–65), which includes a register of sick and wounded soldiers taken to Harper, St. Mary's, and the Post Hospitals in Detroit.

George H. Brown, as Adjutant General, published *Record of Service of Michigan Volunteers in the Civil War, 1861–1865*, often referred to as *Michigan Soldiers and Sailors* (Kalamazoo, Mich.: Ihling Brothers and Everard, 1903–15). This forty-six volume set includes an alphabetical index. An index compiled by Colman C. Vaughn lists Michigan individuals who served in the Civil War: *Alphabetical General Index to Public Library Sets of 85,271 Names of Michigan Soldiers and Sailors Individual Records* (Lansing, Mich.: Wynkoop, Hallenbeck, Crawford, Co., 1915).

The state archives also has unpublished indexes for the Spanish-American War and World War I.

Periodicals, Newspapers, and Manuscript Collections

Periodicals

The *Detroit Society for Genealogical Research Magazine*, published by the society, with a mailing address at the Burton Historical Collection of the Detroit Public Library, has been published since 1937. It is not limited to Detroit but also publishes family histories and source material for the entire state, as well as states or areas from which Michigan residents came: New York, New England, Pennsylvania, and Canada, particularly Ontario and Quebec.

Also see:

Quigley, Maud. *Index to Michigan Research Found in Genealogical Periodicals*. Grand Rapids: Western Michigan Genealogical Society, 1979.

Michigan History. Published bimonthly by Bureau of History, Michigan Department of State, this contains state history articles, book reviews, and information pertinent to historical research.

Newspapers

Michigan's first newspaper, *The Michigan Essay or Impartial Observer*, was published in Detroit on 31 August 1809 for one single edition. Continuous newspaper publishing began in July of 1817 with the *Detroit Gazette*. The most important articles in this English-language publication were also printed in French on the last page. The Library of Michigan has an extensive collection of microfilmed Michigan newspapers, which are available for use at the library or through interlibrary loan to other Michigan libraries. The Bentley Historical Library in Ann Arbor and the Detroit Public Library also have large Michigan newspaper collections. Following are two references that may be helpful in locating newspapers:

Brown, Elizabeth Reed. *A Union List of Newspapers Published in Michigan Based on the Principal Newspaper Collections in the State with Notes Concerning Papers Not Located*. Ann Arbor: University of Michigan, Department of Library Science, 1954.

Michigan Newspapers on Microfilm, With a Description of the Michigan Newspapers on Microfilm Project. 4th ed. Lansing, Mich.: Michigan Bureau of Library Services, 1973.

Manuscripts

Included in the genealogical and historical collections of the University Archives and Historical Collections of Michigan State University, Main Library EG13, East Lansing, MI 48824-1048, are numerous original papers, diaries, and manuscripts.

Significant in the latter category are the John Harvey Kellogg papers, the REO Motor Company records, the Land Grant Research Collection, and the Hackley and Hume papers, business records and personal papers associated with the lumber industry.

The Burton Historical Collection has over twelve million items in its manuscript archives. Bernice Cox Sprenger's *Guide to the Manuscripts in the Burton Historical Collection, Detroit Public Library* (Detroit: Burton Historical Collection, 1985) details these personal papers and records of churches, businesses, and organizations. Examples of genealogically important items listed in this collection include the Charles Kanter Papers' record book of an early Detroit German-American bank; the book indicates the German birthplaces of depositors. The papers of the Children's Aid Society for 1860 to 1942 could be an important resource for tracing a Detroit ancestry, especially since the organization functioned as an orphan home and an adoption agency. Also at this library is the Register of Prisoners for the House of Corrections (Detroit); the Register (1861–1983), indexed, gives the place of birth of each prisoner. See also Draper Manuscripts in Wisconsin—Manuscripts.

Archives, Libraries, and Societies

State Archives of Michigan
702 W. Kalamazoo St.
P.O. Box 30740
Lansing, MI 48909-8240
www.michigan.gov/hal

Original material generated by government offices at the state and/or local level, census records, tax assessment rolls, military records and photographs are among the extensive holdings. It also has some naturalization files, correctional facility records, school records, and depression era agency files. At least sixty-three information circulars on various topics are distributed by the archives; a listing of these is available online from their website. The circulars act as finding aids to their extensive collection. Some of these are described in the various sections of this chapter. The reading room is inside the Michigan Historical Center, which asks to be contacted at <archives@michigan.gov> prior to visits.

Library of Michigan
Michigan Library and Historical Center
Abrams Historical Collection
702 W. Kalamazoo St.
P.O. Box 30007
Lansing, MI 48909-7507
www.michigan.gov/hal

Holdings here, alleged to be one of the ten largest genealogy collections in the country, include books, microforms, manuscripts, newspapers, surname index, Centennial and Sesquicentennial Certificate applications, and diaries. Records are housed in a new building with card catalog on at least 100 computer terminals. All private and local governmental collection citations are available in the "Answer Online Catalog" <http://opac.libofmich.lib.mi.us/screens/opacmenu.html> and can also be reached from its main website. Limited reference service is available by mail.

Burton Historical Collection
Detroit Public Library
5201 Woodward Ave.
Detroit, MI 48202
www.detroit.lib.mi.us/burton/burton_index.htm

Considered the largest collection in Michigan, it includes diverse and extensive holdings of original, printed, and micrographic historical and genealogical material. The emphasis of the collection is on Detroit and Michigan, beginning with the seventeenth century. Refer to Joseph Oldenburg's *A Genealogical Guide to the Burton Historical Collection–Detroit Public Library* (Salt Lake City: Ancestry, 1988). The library has established a $10 per day fee for non-residents of Detroit to access its special collections.

Allen County Public Library
Fred J. Reynolds Historical Genealogy Collection
P.O. Box 2270
900 Webster St.
Fort Wayne, IN 46801-2270
www.acpl.lib.in.us

As the second largest genealogical repository in North America (see Indiana–Archives, Libraries, and Societies), the collection includes significant Michigan source material as described in sections of this chapter.

Michigan Historical Collections
Bentley Historical Library
University of Michigan
1150 Beal Ave.
Ann Arbor, MI 48109-2113
www.umich.edu/~bhl

The focus for genealogical work in this collection is original source materials for Michigan history, with emphasis on Washtenaw County. Specific materials include city directories, plat books for the lower peninsula, newspapers, and church records for almost all Protestant denominations, including discontinued churches.

Regional Depository Archives

Genealogical research in Michigan must include the regional repositories. Each facility includes many of the following in their collections: Michigan military records, manuscripts and diaries, microfilmed newspapers, county and local history books, family genealogies, cemetery records, records of the Daughters of the American Revolution (DAR), maps and atlases, church records, city directories, federal and state census records, and assessment and tax rolls. Contact the individual library for hours; limited replies are given to written queries.

Clarke Historical Library
Central Michigan University
300 E. Preston St.
Mt. Pleasant, MI 48859
www.clarke.cmich.edu

Resources of particular interest to genealogists in this repository include records of Native Americans in Michigan, extensive material on Isabella County, and the James Jesse Strang Mormon Collection. (Strang, a follower of Joseph Smith, who was expelled from the church by Brigham Young, formed the Strangite sect in Wisconsin and Michigan.) This also has been designated a Federal Depository Library.

Archives and Regional History Collections
Western Michigan University
1903 W. Michigan Ave.
Kalamazoo, MI 49008-5353
www.wmich.edu/library/depts/archives

This collection includes township and county records from Allegan, Barry, Berrien, Branch, Cass, Calhoun, St. Joseph, Kalamazoo, Kent, Muskegon, Ottawa, and Van Buren counties, and over 8,000 catalogued photographs.

Archives and Historical Collections
Michigan Technological University
1400 Townsend Dr.
Houghton, MI 49931
www.lib.mtu.edu

This depository is responsible for Gogebic, Ontonagon, Houghton, Keweenaw, Baraga, and Iron counties; it currently holds vital records for Houghton and Keweenaw counties, but has inventories for and will be acquiring records of the other counties. Special collections include those of the Michigan Technological University and the Copper County Historical Collection, the latter containing records of the mining companies and benevolent societies.

Michigan Room,
Grand Rapids Public Library
111 Library St. N.E.
Grand Rapids, MI 49503
www.grapids.lib.mi.us

This library has local history books, microforms, newspapers, cemetery records, manuscripts, diaries, and considerable material on Kent County history and people.

Other Libraries

There are literally dozens of local libraries with historical and/or genealogical collections and genealogical societies in the state (see McGinnis—Background Sources). The scope of material in the majority of the libraries is very impressive, including books, microforms, original local manuscripts, church and cemetery records, maps, photographs, family genealogies, newspapers, diaries, and oral histories. Most Michigan public libraries also have a state-sponsored subscription to the online Ancestry Library Edition databases, (see page 17) the searching of which is restricted to library locations.

Genealogical and Historical Societies

Numerous organizations of this type exist at both the state and county level in Michigan. Most of them are affiliated with the Michigan Genealogical Council, c/o P.O. Box 80953, Lansing, MI 18908-0953. A list of its member societies, their addresses, and, in some cases, their websites can be obtained on the Internet <www.rootsweb.com/roots-l/USA/mi/research.html>.

Special Focus Categories

Naturalization

Beginning in the 1840s and burgeoning near the end of the century, immigrants from northern and eastern Europe journeyed to Michigan for employment opportunities and religious freedom. Naturalization records for Michigan are organized by county, twenty-five of which have indexes. Declarations of intentions are usually arranged by surname while other documents for the citizenship process are chronological. Records for over twenty of Michigan's counties are cataloged by the State Archives of Michigan, thirteen of which are available online. See State Archives Circular No. 10 or their website for a current list

African American

Among the 500 residents in Detroit in 1796, both Native American and African American slaves are listed along with some free African Americans. During the 1840s and 1850s, several religious denominations in Michigan crusaded against slavery; the "Underground Railroad" assistance to fleeing slaves included a well-established course through the state to Canada. Some African Americans chose to settle in Michigan. In February of 1855 the state legislature passed a "personal liberty law" to block the recovery of escaped slaves who were in Michigan. Southerners who attempted to retrieve their slaves in Michigan were met with delay and violence.

In the twentieth century, large numbers of African Americans, displaced by agri-business in the south, gravitated to Detroit for employment opportunities in the automotive industry.

For additional information and background, see African-American family manuscripts at the Burton Historical Collection: Malcolm Dade (1831–1976), Northcross Family (1899–1973), and the Pelham Family (1851–1948).

Also see:

Banner, Melvin E. *The Black Pioneer in Michigan.* Midland, Mich.: Pendall Publishing Co., 1973.

Larrie, Reginald. *Black Experiences in Michigan History.* Lansing, Mich.: Michigan History Division, Michigan Department of State, 1975.

State Archives of Michigan. Circular No. 29, *African-Americans.* Lansing, Mich., 2002.

Native American

Michigan had a Native American population of 15,000 to 20,000 when the first French explorers entered the state in the 1600s. Early in 1825 President Monroe proposed the removal of the indigenous population from Michigan. In August of that year the first treaty was signed with the Sioux, Winnebago, and Chippewa tribes.

In the early 1800s the Miami nation moved outside the present boundaries of Michigan. The Huron were first given a southeastern Michigan tract of land and then moved to 4,996 acres along the Huron River. The tribe eventually left Michigan when an 1842 treaty surrendered all their property rights in that state.

The Potawatomi Indian nation ceded its final reservations in Michigan to the United States by the Treaty of Chicago in 1833, agreeing to move to assigned lands west of the Mississippi. Beginning in 1838 members of the tribe started westward, first to Missouri, then to Iowa, and finally to Kansas. However, significant numbers of the tribe did not leave Michigan and eluded the government agents or escaped during the journey to the west to return to Michigan.

The State Archives of Michigan catalogs a variety of documents relating to Native Americans in the state (Circular No. 30). A finding aid in their reading room details the holdings and how to use them.

The Burton Historical Collection has the 1908 census of the Chippewa Indians of Michigan, known as the Durant Roll. It names "all persons and their descendants who were on the roll of the Ottawa and Chippewa Tribe in 1870 and living on March 4, 1907." The census lists each name, relationship to the head of the family, age, sex, band within the tribe, and place of residence.

The National Archives—Great Lakes Region (see page 12) has sizable holdings of the Bureau of Indian Affairs, including census and annuity rolls for Michigan beginning in the 1880s. Their collection includes financial records for individual Indians at the Mackinac Agency and correspondence from the Mount Pleasant Indian School.

National Archives Record Group 75, Records of the Bureau of Indian Affairs, includes correspondence, documents relating to negotiation of treaties, letter books, and special files. Records of the Superintendent of Indian Affairs for Michigan (1814–51) are on seventy-one rolls of microfilm designated as M1 in Record Group 75. Record Group 11, U.S. Government, General Records, M668, includes the actual ratified Indian treaties (1722–1869).

For additional information, see A. Felch, "The Indians of Michigan and the Cession of Their Lands to the United States by Treaties," *Michigan Pioneer and Historical Collections,* 16 (1894–95): 274-97.

Other Ethnic Groups

The French were the first Europeans to inhabit present-day Michigan. Christian Denissen's *Genealogy of French Families of the Detroit River Region, 1701–1911,* 2 vols., edited by Harold F. Powell (Detroit: Detroit Society for Genealogical Research, 1976) was revised in 1987 to include families through 1937. The Burton Historical Collection holds typed transcriptions of twenty-two volumes of French Notarial Records for Montreal (1682–1822) and four volumes of the Detroit Notarial Records (1737–95). Included are business contracts, indentures, apprentice and servant contracts, and fur trade transactions. Michigan French-Canadian descendants definitely should attempt to utilize the extensive available Canadian provincial and religious records in all repositories.

Membership in the French-Canadian Heritage Society of Michigan includes chapter meetings, five newsletters per year and the quarterly journal, *Michigan's Habitant Heritage.* The organization's collection is housed at the Mount Clemens Public Library <www.macomb.lib.mi.us/mountclemens>. Its mailing address has changed several times in recent years; the latest information about it is available at <www.fchsm.habitant.org>.

The Polish Genealogical Society of Michigan can be contacted in care of the Burton Collection at the Detroit Public Library. Internet-based information is available at <www.pgsm.org>.

Michigan attracted a large number of immigrants. Entries for collections on various groups can be found in all of the repositories' holdings. One example is in the Michigan Historical Collections in Ann Arbor, which holds letters sent by Swedish immigrants to entice others to come, as well as Swedish-language newspapers published in Michigan. *Ethnic Groups in Detroit* (Wayne State University, Department of Sociology and Anthropology: Detroit, 1951) was published as part of the city's 250th anniversary. Included is a discussion of forty-three ethnic groups.

County Resources

Records at the county level are the responsibility of different offices. The office of the county clerk has birth, death, and marriage records. The register of deeds has land records, and the office of the probate judge has probate files. Circuit court offices or office of the county clerk: circuit court records.

Callard's *Sourcebook...* (see Background Sources) provides a bibliography of relevant titles for each of the eighty-three Michigan counties. It is available for $6 from the Department of Management and Budget, Office Services Division Publications, State Secondary Complex, 7481 Crowner Dr., P.O. Box 30026, Lansing, MI 48909.

For some counties on the chart, there are two years listed for "Date Formed." The first is the year the county was created, the second is the year it was fully organized, if it differs from the creation year. Under the heading "Parent County/ies," the name/s listed may be the county or counties from which the respective county was formed, or it may be names by which the county was originally known. "Unorganized" denotes that it was formed from non-county lands. A county name in parentheses is the county to which the unorganized land may have been attached at that time. An asterisk (*) under "Parent County" indicates those locations in which you may also find records for the listed county. The * county may have been "attached" to the listed county for some period of time. The date listed for each category of record is the earliest record known to exist in that county. It does not indicate that there are numerous records for that year and certainly does not indicate that all such events that year were actually registered.

Callard (1987) and McGinnis (1987), described in Background Sources, and more recent online resources, were used for the following guide to county information.

Each county has its own policies regarding the number of genealogists allowed to conduct research concurrently and whether or not children are permitted in the records area. It would be wise to check these rules with the county office in advance of an on-site visit.

Some Michigan counties provide Internet search capability for selected vital records. Such availability can be determined by checking the county's website, a list of which can be found at <www.michigan.gov/emi>. Look for the "Local Government" link under the "More State Web Sites" section.

The Counties and County Seats of
Michigan
25 0 25 50 75 100 Miles

Drawn by William Dollarhide

Map	County / Address	Date Formed / Parent County/ies	Birth Marriage Death	Land Probate Court
	Aischum	1840 (renamed Lake, 1843) Mackinac/*Ottawa		
F7	Alcona 106 5th St. P.O. Box 308 Harrisville 48740-0308	1840 (1869) (as Negwegon; renamed 1843) *Mackinac/*Alpena/ *Cheboygan/*Iosco	1869 / 1869 / 1869	1869 / 1869 / 1872
C4	Alger 101 Court St. Munising 49862-1103	1885 Schoolcraft	1884 / 1887 / 1884	1884 / 1889 / 1885
J5	Allegan 113 Chestnut St. Allegan 49010-1332	1831 (1835) Barry/unorganized	1867 / 1836 / 1867	1835 / 1839 / 1837
E7	Alpena 720 W. Chisholm St. Alpena 49707-2453	1840 (1857) (as Anamickee; renamed 1843) Mackinac/*Cheboygan	1869 / 1871 / 1871	1858 / 1858 / 1871
	Anamickee	1840 (renamed Alpena, 1843) Mackinac/unorganized (Saginaw)		
E5	Antrim 208 E. Cayuga St. P.O. Box 520 Bellaire 49615-0520	1840 (1863) (as Meegisee; renamed 1843) Mackinac *Grand Traverse	1866 / 1866 / 1867	1867 / 1863 / 1867
G7	Arenac 120 N. Grove St. Standish 48658-0747	1831 (1883) unorganized land *Saginaw *Arenac was eliminated in 1857 and recreated 1883 from Bay County.*	1883 / 1883 / 1883	1882 / 1883 / 1883
B2	Baraga 16 N. Third St. L'Anse 49946-1002	1875 Houghton	1875 / 1875 / 1875	1875 / 1876 / 1875
J5	Barry 220 W. State St. Hastings 49058-1849	1829 (1839) unorganized land *St. Joseph/*Kalamazoo	1867 / 1839 / 1867	1834 / 1862 / 1850
G7	Bay 515 Center Ave. Bay City 48708-5125	1857 Midland/Saginaw/Arenac	1867 / 1867 / 1867	1835? / 1857 / 1883
F4	Benzie 448 Court Place P.O. Box 398 Beulah 49617-0398	1863 (1869) Leelanau *Grand Traverse	1868 / 1869 / 1868	1854 / 1870 / 1869
K4	Berrien 811 Port St. (Mail) or 701 Main St. (Walk-in) St. Joseph 49085-1183	1829 (1831) unorganized land *Cass	1867 / 1831 / 1867	1831 / 1834 / 1833
	Bleeker	1861 (renamed Menominee, 1863) unorganized		
K6	Branch 31 Division St. Coldwater 49036-1904	1829 (1833) unorganized * St. Joseph	1867 / 1833 / 1867	1833 / 1833 / 1833
	Brown	1818 unorganized land *Became part of Wisconsin Territory in 1836; now Wisconsin.*		
J6	Calhoun 315 W. Green St. Marshall 49068-1518	1829 (1833) unorganized *St. Joseph/*Kalamazoo	1867 / 1833 / 1867	1833 / 1835 / 1867
K5	Cass 120 N. Broadway P.O. Box 355 Cassopolis 49031-1302	1829 (1829) unorganized	1867 / 1830 / 1867	1829 / 1829 / 1831
	Charlevoix (old)	1840 (as Keskkauko; renamed 1843; became part of Emmet, 1853)		
E6	Charlevoix (present) 203 Antrim St. Charlevoix 49720-1368	1869 Antrim/Emmet/Otsego *Recreated 1869 from Antrim/Emmet/Otsego.*	1868 / 1868 / 1868	1869 / 1881 / 1869
D6	Cheboygan 870 S. Main St. P.O. Box 70 Cheboygan 49721-0070	1840 (1853) Mackinac	1867 / 1867 / 1867	1854 / 1854 / 1884
	Cheonoquet	1840 (renamed Montmorency, 1843) Mackinac/unorganized		
C6	Chippewa 319 Court St. Sault Ste. Marie 49783-2183	1826 Michilimackinac	1869 / 1827 / 1869	1826 / 1828 / 1860?
G6	Clare 225 W. Main St. P.O. Box 438 Harrison 48625-8336	1840 (1871) (as Kayakee; renamed 1843) Mackinac *Midland/*Isabella/*Mecosta	1871 / 1871 / 1871	1865 / 1872 / 1871
H6	Clinton 100 E. State St. P.O. Box 69 St. Johns 48879-1582	1831 (1839) unorganized land *Kent	1867 / 1839 / 1867	1837 / 1840 / 1860?
	Crawford	1818 (Michigan Territory) unorganized land *Became part of Wisconsin Territory in 1836; now Wisconsin.*		
F6	Crawford 200 W. Michigan Ave. Grayling 49738-1746	1840 (1879) (as Shawono; renamed 1873 1843) Mackinac *Cheboygan/*Iosco/*Antrim/*Kalkasa	1863 / 1873 / 1873	1863 / 1881 / 1881
D4	Delta 310 Ludington St. Escanaba 49829-4057	1843 (1861) Mackinac/unorganized land	1867 / 1867 / 1867	1843 / 1843 / 1869
	Des Moines	1834 unorganized *Became part of Wisconsin Territory in 1836; now Iowa.*		
C3	Dickinson 705 S. Stephenson Ave. P.O. Box 609 Iron Mountain 49801	1891 Iron/Marquette/ Menominee	1891 / 1891 / 1891	1891 / 1891 / 1891
	Dubuque	1834 unorganized *Became part of Wisconsin Territory in 1836; now Iowa.*		

Map	County Address	Date Formed Parent County/ies	Birth Marriage Death	Land Probate Court
J6	Eaton 1045 Independence Blvd. Charlotte 48813-1855	1837 unorganized *Kalamazoo/*St. Joseph	1867 1838 1867	1835 1835 1837
D6	Emmet 200 Division St. Petoskey 49770-2486	1840 (1853) (as Tonedagana; renamed 1843) Mackinac	1867 1867 1867	1853 1867 1867
	Forest	1913 (abolished) Cheboygan/Presque Isle		
H7	Genesee 900 S. Saginaw St. Flint 48502-1428	1835 (1836) Lapeer/Saginaw/Shiawassee *Oakland	1867 1867 1867	1819 1836 1835
G6	Gladwin 401 West Cedar Ave. Gladwin 48624-2058	1831 (1875) unorganized *Saginaw/*Midland	1875 1875 1875	1886 1889 1880
C1	Gogebic 200 N. Moore St. Bessemer 49911-1052	1881 Ontonagon	1887 1887 1887	1887 1887 1887
E5	Grand Traverse 400 Boardman Ave. Traverse City 49684-2542	1851 Omeena	1856 1853 1867	1853 1875 1882
H6	Gratiot 214 E. Center St. Ithaca 48847-0437	1831 (1855) unorganized *Saginaw/*Clinton	1867 1867 1867	1847 1867 1867
K6	Hillsdale 29 N. Howell St. Hillsdale 49242	1829 (1835) unorganized *Lenawee	1867 1835 1867	1835 1835 1846
B2	Houghton 401 E. Houghton Ave. Houghton 49931-2016	1845 Marquette/Ontonagon/ Schoolcraft	1867 1855 1867	1848 1872 1848
G8	Huron 250 E. Huron Ave. Bad Axe 48413-1139	1840 (1859) Sanilac *St. Clair/*Tuscola	1867 1867 1867	1837 1861 1867
J7	Ingham 341 S. Jefferson St. Mason 48854-1652	1829 (1838) Shiawassee/Washtenaw	1867 1837 1867	1835 1835 1839
H6	Ionia 100 W. Main St. Ionia 48846-1651	1831 (1837) Michilimackinac *Kent	1867 1837 1867	1836 1835 1845
F7	Iosco 422 Lake St. P.O. Box 778 Tawas City 48764-0778	1840 (1857) unorganized *Cheboygan/*Saginaw	1867 1858 1867	1840 1859 1859
	Iowa	1830 Crawford *Became part of Wisconsin Territory in 1836; now Wisconsin.*		
C2	Iron 2 S. Sixth St. Crystal Falls 49920-1435	1885 Marquette/ Menominee	1895 1895 1895	1855 1886 1895
G6	Isabella 200 N. Main St. Mount Pleasant 48858-2390	1831 (1859) unorganized/Michilimackinac Saginaw/*Ionia/*Midland	1867 1859 1867	1838 1859 1880
	Isle Royale	1875 (attached to Houghton, 1885; Abolished, became part of Keweenaw, 1897) Keweenaw *Disbanded 1885, attached to Houghton; Eliminated in 1897; absorbed by Keweenaw.*		
J6	Jackson 312 S. Jackson St. Jackson 49201-1338	1829 (1832) Washtenaw/unorganized	1867 1867 1867	1830 1834 1830?
J5	Kalamazoo 201 W. Kalamazoo Ave. Kalamazoo 49007-3726	1829 (1830) unorganized *St. Joseph	1867 1831 1867	1824 1830 1847
F6	Kalkaska 605 N. Birch St. Kalkaska 49646-0780	1840 (1871) (as Wabassee; renamed 1843) *Grand Traverse/*Antrim	1871 1871 1871	1853 1874 1871
	Kanotin	1840 (renamed Iosco, 1843) unorganized *Mackinac		
	Kautawaubet (Kautawbet)	1840 (renamed Wexford, 1843) Mackinac		
	Kayakee (Kaykakee)	1840 (renamed Clare, 1843) Mackinac/unorganized *Saginaw		
H5	Kent 300 Monroe NW Grand Rapids 49503-2206	1831 (1836) Michilimackinac	1867 1845 1867	1860 1898 1854
	Keskkauko (Keshkauko, Reshkauko)	1840 (renamed Charlevoix, 1843) Mackinac		
A3	Keweenaw HC1, Box 607 Eagle River 49924-9700	1861 Houghton	1869 1869 1869	1861 1866 1861
G5	Lake 800 Tenth St. Baldwin 49304-7970	1840 (1871) Mackinac *Mason/*Newaygo	1870 1870 1870	1872 1872 1871
H8	Lapeer 255 Clay St. Lapeer 48446-2205	1822 (1835) Oakland/St. Clair/unorganized	1867 1831 1867	1835 1838 1835
E5	Leelanau 301 E. Cedar St. Leland 49654-1107	1840 (1863) Mackinac *Grand Traverse	1867 1867 1867	1851 1882 1879
K7	Lenawee 425 N. Main St. Adrian 49221-2103	1822 (1826) Monroe	1867 1853 1867	1827 1827 1870
J7	Livingston 200 E. Grand River Ave. Howell 48843-7041	1833 (1836) Shiawassee/Washtenaw/ *Oakland	1867 1836 1867	1834 1837 1837
C5	Luce 407 W. Harrie St. Newberry 49868	1887 Chippewa/Mackinac	1887 1887 1887	1887 1888 1887

Map	County Address	Date Formed Parent County/ies	Birth Marriage Death	Land Probate Court
C6	Mackinac 100 N. Marley St. St. Ignace 49781-1457	1818 Wayne	1873 1867 1873	1785 1851 1808
J8	Macomb 40 N. Main St. Mt. Clemens 48043-2306	1818 Wayne	1867 1819 1867	1818 1849 1818
F5	Manistee 415 Third St. Manistee 49660-1606	1840 (1855) Mackinac *Ottawa/*Grand Traverse	1867 1867 1867	1868 1881 1855
	Manitou	1855 (abolished 1895) Emmet/Leelanau		

In 1861 the county government was disorganized, and Manitou was attached to Mackinac. In 1865 it was attached to Leelanau, then again attached to Mackinac in 1869. Finally, in 1895, Manitou was abolished and was absorbed by Charlevoix and Leelanau counties.

Map	County Address	Date Formed Parent County/ies	Birth Marriage Death	Land Probate Court
C3	Marquette 234 W. Baraga Ave. Marquette 49855-4751	1843 (1848) Chippewa/Houghton *Houghton	1867 1850 1867	1851 1854 1852
G4	Mason 304 E. Ludington Ave. Ludington 49431-2121	1840 (1855) (as Notipekago; renamed 1843)Mackinac *Ottawa	1867 1867 1867	1840 1855 1867
G5	Mecosta 400 Elm St. Big Rapids 49307-1849	1840 (1859) Mackinac/Oceana *Kent/*Newaygo	1867 1859 1867	1867 1867 1859
	Meegisee	1840 (renamed Antrim, 1843) Mackinac		
D3	Menominee 839 Tenth Ave. Menominee 49858-3000	1861 (as Bleeker; renamed 1863) unorganized	1863 1867 1860	1850 1868 1861
	Michilmackinac	1818 (renamed Mackinac, 1837) Wayne		
G6	Midland 220 W. Ellsworth St. Midland 48640-5194	1831 (1850) Saginaw/unorganized	1867 1867 1867	1855 1856 1839
	Mikenauk	1840 (renamed Roscommon, 1843) Mackinac/unorganized		
	Milwaukee	1834 (1835) Brown		

Became part of Wisconsin Territory in 1836; now in Wisconsin.

Map	County Address	Date Formed Parent County/ies	Birth Marriage Death	Land Probate Court
F6	Missaukee 111 S. Canal St. P.O. Box 800 Lake City 49651-0800	1840 (1871) Mackinac *Manistee/*Grand Traverse/ *Wexford	1870 1871 1870	1871 1871 1872
K7	Monroe 106 E. First St. Monroe 48161-2115	1817 Wayne	1874 1818 1867	1806 1817 1805
H6	Montcalm 211 W. Main St. P.O. Box 368 Stanton 48888-0368	1831 (1850) Michilimackinac/unorganized *Ionia	1867 1867 1867	1838 1855 1860?

Map	County Address	Date Formed Parent County/ies	Birth Marriage Death	Land Probate Court
E7	Montmorency P.O. Box 789 Atlanta 49709-0789	1840 (1881) (as Cheonoquet; renamed 1843) Mackinac/unorganized *Cheboygan/*Alpena	1881 1881 1881	1943 1943 1940
H4	Muskegon 990 Terrace St. Muskegon 49442-3395	1859 Ottawa/unorganized	1867 1867 1867	1839 1867 1856
G5	Newaygo 1087 Newell St. P.O. Box 885 White Cloud 49349-8795	1840 (1851) Oceana/Mackinac *Kent/*Ottawa	1867 1851 1867	1840 1880 1893
	Negwegon (Neewago)	1840 (renamed Alcona, 1843) unorganized *Mackinac		
	Notipekago (Nontipekago)	1840 (renamed Mason, 1843) Mackinac *Ottawa		
J8	Oakland 1200 N. Telegraph Rd. Pontiac 48341-1032	1820 Macomb	1867 1827 1867	1821 1822 1826
G4	Oceana 100 State Street P.O. Box 653 Hart 49420	1831 (1851) Michilimackinac *Kent/*Ottawa	1867 1867 1868	1846 1900 1859
F7	Ogemaw 806 W. Houghton Ave. West Branch 48661-1278	1840 (1875) unorganized *Mackinac/*Iosco/*Cheboygan	1879 1876 1876	1876 1877 1876

In 1867 Ogemaw was abolished and absorbed by Iosco. In 1873 it was re-created from part of Iosco.

Map	County Address	Date Formed Parent County/ies	Birth Marriage Death	Land Probate Court
	Okkuddo (Okkudo)	1840 (renamed Otsego, 1843) Mackinac		
	Omeena	1840 (abolished , 1853; became part of Grand Traverse) Mackinac		
B1	Ontonagon 725 Greenland Rd. Ontonagon 49953-1423	1843 (1848) Chippewa/Mackinac *Houghton	1868 1853 1868	1850 1853 1854
G5	Osceola 301 W. Upton Ave. Reed City 49677-1149	1840 (1869) (as Unwattin ; renamed 1843) Mackinac *Mason/*Newaygo/*Mecosta	1869 1869 1870	1853 1870 1870
F7	Oscoda 310 Morenci St. P.O. Box 399 Mio 48647-0399	1840 (1881) Mackinac *Iosco/*Cheboygan/*Alpena/ *Alcona	1880 1881 1880	1850 1881 1881
E6	Otsego 225 W. Main St. Gaylord 49735-1372	1840 (1875) (as Okkuddo; renamed 1843) Mackinac *Cheboygan/*Alpena/*Antrim	1875 1895 1875	1864 1876 1875
H5	Ottawa 414 Washington St. Grand Haven 49417-1473	1831 (1837) Michilimackinac/unorganized *Kent	1866 1848 1867	1834 1844 1839

Map	County Address	Date Formed Parent County/ies	Birth Marriage Death	Land Probate Court
E7	Presque Isle 151 E. Huron Ave. Rogers City 49779-1318	1840 (1871) Mackinac *Cheboygan/*Alpena	1871 1872 1871	1856 1874 1872
	Reshkauko (see Keskkauko)			
F6	Roscommon 500 Lake St. Roscommon 48653-7664	1840 (1875) (as Mikenauk; renamed 1843) Mackinac *Cheboygan/*Midland	1874 1877 1874	1875 1875 1875
H7	Saginaw 111 S. Michigan Ave. Saginaw 48602-0000	1822 (1835) St. Clair/unorganized *Oakland	1867 1867 1867	1836 1800? 1843
H8	St. Clair 201 McMorran Blvd. Port Huron 48060-4006	1820 (1821) Macomb	1868 1837 1868	1821 1828 1833
K5	St. Joseph 125 W. Main St. P.O. Box 189 Centreville 49032-0189	1829 (1829) unorganized	1867 1832 1867	1830 1832 1842
G8	Sanilac 67 W. Sanilac Ave. Sandusky 48471-1060	1822 (1848) St. Clair/unorganized *Lapeer/*Oakland	1867 1867 1867	1834 1857 1850
C5	Schoolcraft 300 Walnut St. Manistique 49854-1495	1843 (1871) Chippewa/Mackinac Houghton/ Marquette/*Houghton/	1870 1870 1870	1871 1874 1881
	Shawono (Shawano, Shawona)	1840 (renamed Crawford, 1843) Mackinac		
H7	Shiawassee 208 N. Shiawassee St. Corunna 48817-1447	1822 (1837) Oakland/St. Clair/unorganized *Genesee	1867 1867 1867	1836 1840 1848
	Tonedagana	1840 (renamed Emmet, 1843) Mackinac		
H8	Tuscola 440 N. State St. Caro 48723	1840 (1850) Sanilac *Saginaw	1867 1851 1867	1850 1852 1887
	Unwattin	1840 (renamed Osceola, 1843) Mackinac *Ottawa		
J5	Van Buren 212 Paw Paw St. Paw Paw 49079	1829 (1837) unorganized *Lenawee/*Cass	1867 1836 1867	1836 1837 1844
	Wabassee	1840 (renamed Kalkaska, 1843) Mackinac		
	Washington	1867 (declared unconstitutional) Marquette		
J7	Washtenaw P.O. Box 8645 Ann Arbor 48107-8645	1822 (1826) Wayne/Oakland	1867 1833 1867	1835 1827 1835
J8	Wayne (excl. Detroit) 201 City County Bldg. Detroit 48226	1796 original	1867 1842 1867	1703 1797 1818
	In 1796 Wayne County was created as part of the Northwest Territory; in 1815 it became part of the Michigan Territory.			
J8	Wayne (Detroit only) 1151 Taylor St. Detroit 18202		1867 1867	
F5	Wexford 432 E. Division St. Cadillac 49601-1970	1840 (1869) (as Kautawaubet; renamed 1843) Mackinac *Manistee/*Grand Traverse	1867 1864 1867	1869 1869 1869
	Wyandot	1840 (abolished 1853; became part of Cheboygan) Mackinac		

Minnesota

CAROL L. MAKI AND MICHAEL JOHN NEILL

Minnesota has been claimed by four nations since the first Europeans explored its terrain. Nine different territories or government subdivisions of the United States have maintained jurisdiction over its land. Understanding its multiple dominions and authorities is essential in researching early Minnesota residents.

With the erection and blessing of a great wooden cross at Sault de Ste. Marie on 14 June 1671, Simon Francois Daumont, Sieur de St. Lusson, claimed for the king of France an area that included present-day Minnesota. French exploration followed, forts were built, and the fur trading industry created economic and family relationships between the French and the Native Americans.

In 1762 France secretly ceded to Spain the Minnesota country west of the Mississippi River, which resulted in the twin cities of St. Paul and Minneapolis briefly being French and Spanish. History intervened the following year when territory east of the river and free navigation on it was acquired by England by the Treaty of Paris. By proclamation, northeastern Minnesota was forbidden trade and settlement. In 1774 that same area became part of the Province of Quebec and ten years later a United States territory. It remained unorganized until the Northwest Territory was created in 1787 and became part of the Indiana Territory in 1800. A northwestern section of the future state remained English until 1818. The southwestern section was Spanish until 1800 when it was ceded to France for another three years. It then became part of the District of Louisiana and subsequently the Louisiana Territory from 1804 to 1812.

The northeastern section of Minnesota, which had been Indiana Territory, became part of the Illinois Territory in 1809 and Michigan Territory in 1818. The balance of the state was in Missouri Territory from 1812 through 1821, but unorganized from then until 1834 when all of Minnesota country was attached to Michigan Territory. This temporary arrangement lasted two years. It became the Wisconsin Territory in 1836.

Two years later Minnesota divided again and placed the country west of the Mississippi River with Iowa Territory until 1846. The eastern section remained part of Wisconsin Territory until 1848. On 29 May of that year, Wisconsin obtained statehood, with the western border being essentially the St. Croix River. This left Minnesota as an abandoned area without any organized government. The Stillwater Convention of 1848, despite a couple of false starts, produced a document organizing the Minnesota Territory. In March of 1849 Congress passed the proposal, and Minnesota finally came into existence. Included was part of what is now eastern North and South Dakota. Minnesota was admitted to the Union as the thirty-second state in May of 1858.

Early settlement in Minnesota was affected by several factors, including the fur trading industry, the Catholic missions, and the military, which all brought white settlers to the area. The first American military post was the primitive Cantonment New Hope near Mendota. Established in 1819 by Col. Henry Leavenworth and the Fifth United States Infantry, the camp was later renamed Camp Coldwater and moved to higher ground in the spring of 1820. Shortly thereafter it was replaced by a permanent stone fort originally called Fort St. Anthony, but

changed to Fort Snelling in 1825. The fort became a nucleus from which early Minnesota settlements evolved. Refugees from the Selkirk Colony in Canada tried to make new homes on or near the military reservation, and French-Canadian traders and voyagers settled their families at Mendota across the river from the fort. Indian treaties in 1837 opened an area in 1838 between the Mississippi and St. Croix rivers, the first available Minnesota real estate. The logging industry and the evolving sawmills established a St. Croix River valley community, the second focus of white settlement in Minnesota. On the east bank of the Mississippi River at St. Anthony Falls, the third center of pre-territorial population developed, eventually becoming the city of Minneapolis.

Treaties of Traverse des Sioux and Mendota in 1851 opened the territory west of the Mississippi River to settlers, and the Rock Island Railroad opening in 1854 brought many new Americans. Later, the Homestead Act of 1862 was a very positive incentive for immigration to Minnesota.

Minnesota immigrants from 1820 through 1890 were from the British Isles, Germany, and Scandinavia, for the most part, although there were small groups of Czech and Polish farmers and those from Switzerland, the Netherlands, and Belgium. All these groups continued to arrive in Minnesota after 1890, but beginning in 1890 and continuing through 1920 there was also a new group of immigrants—those without financial means to purchase property but eager to fill the employment opportunities in the new industries and in the transportation systems. Their nationalities varied, many coming from the Russian and Austro-Hungarian empires. Immigrants also included Italians, Greeks, Russian-Germans, Poles, Jews, Ukrainians, and Finns.

Vital Records

Legislation that ordered recording of county vital records was passed in 1870. In some counties marriage registrations began before that date, but these early records are somewhat incomplete. Researchers may request birth, death, or marriage records from the office of the court administrator or clerk of district court in the respective county courthouse. Some counties have recently begun to transfer their birth, death, and marriage records to the office of the county recorder.

In 1907 the Minnesota Vital Records law was enacted, giving the state the responsibility of keeping birth and death records. This office has birth records starting in 1900 and death records starting in 1908. The Minnesota Historical Society (see Archives, Libraries, and Societies) has an online death certificate index that currently runs from 1908 to 1996 <http://people.mnhs.org/dci>. There is no statewide marriage index until 1958 and the statewide divorce index begins in 1970, but these two statewide indexes only provide verification of the marriage or divorce. The

specific county where the event occurred will also need to be contacted. More information (including current fees) can be obtained from the Minnesota Department of Health, Section of Vital Statistics, Attention: Office of the State Registrar, P.O. Box 9441, Minneapolis, MN 55440 <www.health.state.mn.us/forms.html>.

Some limited county vital records registers have been transferred to the Minnesota Historical Society Research Center (see Archives, Libraries, and Societies), although access may be restricted. The center holds justice of the peace (marriage) records from some counties and coroner's inquest (death) registers. Other alternate sources for vital records may include local genealogical societies that have transcribed and indexed vital records and obituaries from their respective counties. The *Minnesota Genealogical Journal* (Roseville, Minn.: Park Genealogical Books, 1984) <www.parkbooks.com> has transcriptions of marriages from several Minnesota counties. This publication has also printed extractions of marriage records, which include Minnesota people in Pierce and St. Croix counties, Wisconsin.

The Works Progress Administration (WPA) Historical Records Survey of township vital records was published in *Guide to Public Vital Statistics Records in Minnesota*. Many of these records have since been transferred to the Minnesota Historical Society.

Township records may include some vital statistics. Deaths and births may have been reported to townships or cities from 1870 through 1953. If these records are extant (and many are not), they will frequently contain more information than the county or state record. Many of these locally created vital records are at the Minnesota Historical Society Research Center. Township records may also include the clerk's minute books and township road records, indicating names of residents. If they exist, justice of the peace records are likely to be in these materials as well.

School records, rather than vital registrations, can often be used to help determine the age of an individual. Many of these are at the Minnesota Historical Society Research Center.

Census Records

Federal

Population Schedules
- Indexed—1850, 1860 (Minnesota Historical Society), 1870, 1880, 1890 (limited), 1900, 1910, 1920, 1930
- Soundex—1880, 1900, 1920

Industry and Agriculture Schedules
- 1850, 1860, 1870, 1880

Mortality Schedules
- 1850, 1860, 1870, 1880

Union Veterans Schedules
- 1890

Although not a state at the time, Minnesota residents were enumerated in 1850 as part of the regular federal enumeration process. Both the 1850 and 1860 schedules have printed indexes in addition to those widely available online (see pages 3 and 17). See Patricia C. Harpole and Mary D. Nagle, *Minnesota Territorial Census, 1850* (St. Paul: Minnesota Historical Society, 1972), and Dennis Meissner, *Guide to the Use of the 1860 Minnesota Population Census Schedule and Index* (St. Paul: Minnesota Historical Society, 1978).

Much of the Minnesota 1870 federal census was destroyed. Only the schedules for Stearns, Steele, Stevens, St. Louis, Todd, Wabasha, Wadena, Waseca, Washington, Watonwan, Wilkin, Winona, and Wright counties still exist. However, a duplicate of the entire census retained by the Minnesota Historical Society was microfilmed. There are, therefore, two versions of the 1870 federal census for the state of Minnesota. The extant 1890 federal census includes one page of Rockford Township in Wright County. A state copy for the 1890 federal return of Rockville Township, Stearns County, is at Minnesota Historical Society Research Center.

The extensive early logging industry in Minnesota may make it difficult to locate ancestors involved in that particular labor force. Some may be counted in the lumber camps or at the numerous boarding houses in the river cities and towns. It is also important to note that the steamboat crews on the rivers were often enumerated in the city in which the boat was temporarily docked.

Federal non-population schedules for Minnesota for 1860 to 1880 (agriculture, manufacturing, mortality, and social statistics) can be purchased through the Minnesota Historical Society order department.

Territorial

Minnesota inhabitants were first enumerated in the Michigan Territory 1820 census and the 1836 census of the Wisconsin Territory. A census of the Minnesota Territory was ordered in 1849, which included the name of head of household and number of males and females in that household. See Wiley R. Pope, *Minnesota Genealogical Index*, vol. 1 (St. Paul: Minnesota Family Trees, 1984) and Minnesota (Territory), Legislative Assembly, *Journal of the House of Representatives, First Session of the Territory of Minnesota, 1850*, Appendixes C and D, 195-215.

A very incomplete 1853 Minnesota census exists for limited areas. Some schedules are only head of household, number of children, and total number in household, but a few include all names of inhabitants. The state census for heads of household in 1855 has been largely lost. The published schedule for Wright County has survived, as have manuscript copies for the counties of Chisago, Doty, and Superior. Winona, however, has an unusual "inhabitants by building" enumeration for that year.

The 1857 Minnesota territorial census was mandated for statehood qualification and apparently included fictitious names in seven counties to boost the population. See Arthur L. Finnell, "Southwest Minnesota's 1857 State Census: Notes on a Forgery," *Minnesota Genealogist 17* (June 1986): 76-78, and Robert J. Forrest, "Mythical Cities of Southwestern Minnesota," *Minnesota History 14* (September 1933): 243-62. The census includes name, age, sex, color, birthplace, voting status of male (native or naturalized), and occupation of each male over the age of fifteen. This census has been indexed by last name and a microfilm edition is available.

State

State censuses were also taken in 1865, 1875, 1885, 1895, and 1905. Each of the state census enumerations includes all members of the household. In 1865, "Soldier in service on June 1, 1865" was included. The 1875 census gives the birthplaces of father and mother. The 1895 and 1905 censuses may be especially helpful to the genealogist as they include the length of time an individual has lived in the state and the district. Microfilmed copies of the state censuses are at the Minnesota Historical Society in St. Paul. They may be purchased or obtained on interlibrary loan through the society.

The 1918 Alien Registration and Declaration of Holdings, under the auspices of the Minnesota Commission of Public Safety, is an alternate source for locating an immigrant ancestor in Minnesota in the twentieth century. The registration forms, completed by non-citizen adults in the state in February 1918, are filed by county. These registrations have been indexed and microfilmed and are at the Minnesota Historical Society and available through interlibrary loan through the FHL. Questions on the form include place of birth, years in the country, port of entry, date of arrival, occupation, name of spouse, and names of children. Originals of these forms are at the Minnesota Historical Society.

Alternates to census records in determining the location of a particular ancestor at a particular time include city directories, especially in St. Paul (from 1856) and Minneapolis (from 1859). Some are in original form; others are on microfilm at the Minnesota Historical Society.

Background Sources

Local history resources in Minnesota include the printed and archival collections of the Minnesota Historical Society, the library of the Minnesota Genealogical Society (see Archives,

Libraries, and Societies), other private and public libraries, and county and local historical and genealogical societies. Each of these has unique material for research. The following sources are recommended:

Brook, Michael. *Reference Guide to Minnesota History, A Subject Bibliography of Books, Pamphlets and Articles in English.* St. Paul: Minnesota Historical Society, 1974. Arranged by subject and indexed.

———, and Sarah P. Rubenstein. *A Supplement to Reference Guide to Minnesota History: A Subject Bibliography, 1970–80.* St. Paul: Minnesota Historical Society, 1983. Arranged by subject and indexed.

Folwell, William Watts. *A History of Minnesota.* 4 vols. St. Paul: Minnesota Historical Society, 1921–30.

Kirkeby, Lucille L. *Holdings of Genealogical Value in Minnesota's County Museums.* Brainerd, Minn.: the author, 1986. This organizes the local historical societies by county, lists their hours, and gives descriptions of collections that would be of interest to a family researcher.

Minnesota Historical Society. *Genealogical Resources of the Minnesota Historical Society: A Guide.* St. Paul: Minnesota Historical Society Press, 1989.

Pope, Wiley R. *Tracing Your Ancestors in Minnesota: A Guide to Sources.* St. Paul: Minnesota Family Trees, various years. This is a series of research guides for Minnesota genealogical research. The first volume is a general statewide guide, but other volumes cover specific sections of the state. The sectional guides list resources in the county government centers, the Minnesota Historical Society, regional research centers, and county historical repositories.

Upham, Warren, and Rose Barteaw Dunlap, comps. *Collections of the Minnesota Historical Society.* Vol. 14. St. Paul: Minnesota Historical Society, 1912. This is an 892-page index of Minnesota biographies (1655–1912). The sources include 250 national and state printed biographical collections, Minnesota pamphlets, histories and military records of the state, magazines and journals, personal memoirs, scrapbooks, and state newspapers. A brief biographical sketch plus the reference from which the data was extracted is provided for each individual.

Warren, Paula Stuart. *Minnesota Genealogical Reference Guide*, 3d ed. St. Paul: Warren Research and Publishing, 1997.

Warren, Paula Stuart, and Ann H. Peterson. *An Introduction to Minnesota Research Sources.* St. Paul: Minnesota Genealogical Society, 1988.

Warren, Paula Stuart. "Genealogical Research in Minnesota," *National Genealogical Society Quarterly* 77 (March 1989): 22-42. A valuable, concise Minnesota guide to research.

Maps

A. T. Andreas, *An Illustrated Historical Atlas of the State of Minnesota* (Chicago: the author, 1874) was the first county atlas of Minnesota. It includes the county maps, cities and townships, illustrations of private homes and businesses in the state, portrait sketches of important citizens, and statistical information. The original atlas is quite scarce, with the only existing copies sometimes available through dealers of rare books. It has, however, been republished as Winona County Historical Society's *Atlas of the State of Minnesota, Andreas, 1874* (Evansville, Ind.: Unigraphic, 1976), providing an excellent genealogical reference tool. A companion to it is Paul J. Ostendorf's *Every Person's Name Index to An Illustrated Historical Atlas of the State of Minnesota* (Winona, Minn.: St. Mary's College, 1979).

County atlases for Minnesota include maps for the respective county and for townships within that county. The names of property owners are frequently included on these maps. The Minnesota Historical Society has microfilmed many of these atlases, which makes them accessible on interlibrary loan.

Library of Congress Fire Insurance Maps in the Library of Congress; Plans of North American Cities and Towns Produced by the Sanborn Map Company (Washington D.C.: Library of Congress, 1981) states that the earliest map of this type for Minnesota is for 1884. There is, however, a Sanborn map for the city of St. Paul for 1875; this map is located at the map library of the Minnesota Historical Society.

The map collection of the Minnesota Historical Society consists of over 35,000 individual maps and 1,300 atlases, the majority of these for Minnesota and the Midwest. The society is a five-state regional depository for the U.S. Geological Survey maps (see page 5). It has extensive collections of Minnesota territory and state maps, county and city maps, and fire insurance maps of over 950 Minnesota towns and cities. There are random maps and plat maps in the county records at the Minnesota Historical Society Research Center. The map library of the Wilson Library at the University of Minnesota, Minneapolis, is an outstanding cartographic repository, not restricted to Minnesota. It includes worldwide maps and associated material. For further information, see the following references:

Treude, Mai. *Windows to the Past: A Bibliography of Minnesota County Atlases.* Minneapolis: University of Minnesota, Center for Urban and Regional Affairs, 1980.

Upham, Warren. *Minnesota Geographic Names: Their Origin and Historic Significance.* 1920. Reprint. St. Paul: Minnesota Historical Society, 1969. This is also online at <http://mnplaces.mnhs.org/upham>.

The Minnesota Department of Transportation, Room B-20, St. Paul, MN 55155, provides a series of current state, county, and city maps.

Land Records

Public-Domain State

Minnesota is a public-domain state, with twelve General Land Office (GLO) districts, the first opening in 1848 at Falls Saint Croix River, Wisconsin. However, pioneers were staking their claims long before that. Immediately following the tribal treaties of 1838, the European settlers built homes and sawmills, logged the white pine, and generally took possession of land that was not legally available. The federal government was, apparently, exceedingly slow to begin land surveys in the territory. The pressure of settlers and investors finally resulted in that process in 1847. The Pre-Emption Act of 1841 allowed home-seekers to purchase up to 160 acres of surveyed public lands at $1.25 per acre.

Numerous land records are held by the Minnesota Historical Society including records of the state auditor; land department's state land sale correspondence, sales and accounting records; and U.S. General Land Office files comprised of correspondence, accounting records, and location records (which include homestead records and preemption sales). The earliest records are for the Stillwater district, beginning in 1848. The Minnesota Historical Society Research Center also has duplicates of the records of the U.S. Surveyor General's Office and a list of lands allotted to the White Earth Reservation in 1901. *A Guide to the Records of Minnesota's Public Lands* (St. Paul: Minnesota Historical Society, 1985), by George Kinney and Lydia Lucas, indicates holdings at the research center. The Bureau of Land Management (BLM) website (see page 6) allows researchers to search federal land patents for Minnesota and other states.

At the county level in Minnesota, land records are kept by the county recorder. This office will have deed and mortgage records, grantor-grantee indexes, township and village plats, and various records pertaining to power of attorney, contracts, and leases.

Probate Records

The probate office in county courthouses will usually have all those records pertaining to estates and wills, guardianships, juvenile court records, and insanity records. Probate case files for Freeborn, Pope, Washington, and Winona counties are at the Minnesota Historical Society Research Center. This repository also holds probate summary volumes (not the files) for numerous other counties in the state. Probate records will frequently pre-

date death records in Minnesota counties. They may also help locate the out-of-Minnesota death record of an ancestor.

Court Records

The first term of the district court in Minnesota convened in the second floor of John McKusick's store on 1 June 1847 in Stillwater.

The district court may include civil and criminal cases with indexes, coroner's records, professional registrations, and oaths and bonds. Civil cases may include monetary suits, change of name, divorce, garnishments, and adoptions. The district court records for Wright County at Minnesota Historical Society Research Center include, for example, court minutes (1858–1929); criminal case files and dockets (1858–1928); judgment dockets (1857–66); and register of civil actions (ca. 1879–99). The court records at this repository vary considerably by county and type of record. Some counties have not transferred any of these files but retain them at the district court office in the county seat.

Tax Records

The Minnesota Historical Society holds large numbers of county property tax records, filed under the respective county. Some of the tax records are for specific municipalities. No determination has been made concerning tax record holdings in the county courthouse.

Cemetery Records

The Minnesota Genealogical Society's Cemetery Project is a compilation of the names and sites of all cemeteries in Minnesota, indicating which have been transcribed and where the transcription can be located. Many cemetery records have been published in the *Minnesota Genealogist*, the quarterly publication of that society. Several regional groups have published records of their local cemeteries. See also Wiley R. Pope, *Minnesota Cemeteries in Print: A Bibliography of Minnesota Published Cemetery Inscriptions, and Burials, etc.* (St. Paul: Minnesota Family Trees, 1988), Minnesota Historical Society Research Center for the WPA papers for cemeteries in Minnesota, and Wiley R. Pope, *Minnesota Cemetery Locations* (St. Paul: Minnesota Family Trees, 1988).

Church Records

Detailed background on Minnesota church history is found in numerous published denominational histories. The religion of

the European settlers was first brought to Native Americans in what is now Minnesota by the Catholic missionaries and the French explorers. In 1656 Groseilliers and Radisson built a chapel at Prairie Island, near present-day Hastings. The Mission of St. Michael the Archangel was established at Fort Beauharnois on Lake Pepin (Mississippi River) in 1727.

In June of 1839, the Right Reverend Mathias Loras, first Bishop of Dubuque, Iowa, visited Mendota (then known as St. Peter's), finding 185 Catholics among the French, English, and Sioux. Arrangements were made for the establishment of a parish. James Michael Reardon's *The Catholic Church in the Diocese of St. Paul, from Earliest Origin to Centennial Achievement* (St. Paul: North Central Publishing Co., 1952) provides background on the development of this parish.

Sacramental records for all parishes within the Roman Catholic Archdiocese of St. Paul and Minneapolis are presently being microfilmed. The staff will provide limited research upon written request directed to Steven Granger, Archivist, Archdiocese of St. Paul and Minneapolis, 226 Summit Ave., St. Paul, MN 55102.

For Catholic parishes in Minnesota (and North and South Dakota), there is the Minnesota Historical Society collection for the Archdiocese of St. Paul and Minneapolis parish questionnaires and related papers. The questionnaires were from the 1930s and 1940s; however, additions were made through the 1970s when the collection was microfilmed.

During the 1850s the number of churches increased rapidly in the new territory with at least fifteen congregations in St. Paul, eight in Minneapolis, and seven in St. Anthony by 1859. Episcopal, Presbyterian, Methodist, Baptist, Congregational, and Catholic were the most prevalent at that time. Chisago Lakes and Vasa, both Scandinavian settlements, had Lutheran churches in the mid-1850s. Quakers were active in Minneapolis at this time, while the first Jewish service was held in St. Paul in 1856.

Numerous church records are deposited at the Minnesota Historical Society. Some are originals; some are microfilms. There are significant collections for Quakers, the Episcopal Church, and the United Church of Christ. Anne A. Hage's *Church Records in Minnesota: A Guide to Parish Records of Congregational, Evangelical, Reformed, and United Church of Christ Churches, 1851–1981* (Minneapolis: Minnesota Conference, United Church of Christ, 1983) helps in locating record sources.

Luther Seminary in St. Paul is the archives repository of the Region Three Archives of the Evangelical Lutheran Church in America and for some American-Lutheran Church records. The seminary is at 2481 Como Ave., St. Paul, MN 55108 <www.luthersem.edu/archives>. An historical reference is Emeroy Johnson, *A Church Is Planted: The Story of the Lutheran Minnesota Conference, 1851–1876* (Minneapolis: Lutheran Minnesota Conference, 1948).

Microfilmed records of the Minnesota Conference of the old Augustana Synod (Swedish-American) are at the American Swedish Institute in Minneapolis. Archives of the Minnesota South District of the Lutheran Church–Missouri Synod are at Concordia College in St. Paul. There are records of Swedish-American Lutheran Churches at Gustavus Adolphus College, Folke Bernadotte Memorial Library, St. Peter, Minnesota.

The WPA Minnesota Papers "Historical Records Survey, Churches," held by the Minnesota Historical Society, gives information on locations of individual church records in the 1930s and limited histories of the congregations. The papers are filed by county, name of community, and church.

The Minnesota Historical Society Research Center has guidebooks to the center's *Minnesota Historic Resources Survey* completed between 1973 and 1979 and organized by county and 300 historic organizations on seven reels of microfilm. The guidebooks indicate location of church records in local historical societies or other manuscript repositories. The state archives section has secretary of state notebooks for articles of incorporation of churches and religious organizations.

Military Records

Initial research on a Minnesota volunteer in the Civil War should include the two-volume Board of Commissioners on Publication of History in Civil and Indian Wars' *Minnesota in the Civil and Indian Wars, 1861–1865* (St. Paul: Pioneer Press Co., 1890–93 and 1891–99). The first volume includes regimental rosters and narratives. The second contains reports and correspondence. *Minnesota in the Civil and Indian Wars: An Index to the Rosters* was compiled in 1936 for the Minnesota Historical Society by the WPA and is available on microfilm at the society.

The society's reference library has an incomplete file "in progress" of veterans of these periods of warfare, including those who moved to Minnesota after the wars. The information, which may include residence, death date, widow's name, pension file number, regiment, and company, has been accumulated from a variety of sources, including the 1890 Federal Census of Veterans, pension registers, names of participants in GAR parades, the reports noting deaths during the years, and a few biographical sketches.

The Minnesota Historical Society Research Center holds numerous diaries of Civil War veterans, some regimental records, Grand Army of the Republic records, microfilms of service cards for Minnesota State Militia in federal military service in the Civil War, and Civil War Pension Registers of letters sent from the Adjutant General for 1877 through 1949. The name of the veteran, date of the letter, and amount awarded is included on

the cards. Board of Auditors files at the research center includes minutes and registers of claims and certificates relating to the Dakota Conflict (Sioux uprising) of 1862.

World War I military service cards for people who entered the service through the Minnesota National Guard are also at the research center along with photographic copies of original draft lists, induction lists, and soldiers' bonus records. This file includes over 120,000 bonus applications for Minnesota soldiers, marines, sailors, and medical personnel who served in World War I. It is *not* indexed, but the fifty-one questions on the application include name, place and date of birth, names and residence of nearest relative, draft information, present residence and occupation, name of employer, business address, name and address of parents at time of enlistment, length of residence in Minnesota, and marital status. The Minnesota Historical Society also has bonus records for World War II on microfilm.

The Public Safety Commission Gold Star Roll Records at the Minnesota Historical Research Center pertain to men and women from Minnesota who died in World War I. The four-page form includes biographical information and *may* include family photographs, letters, and clippings.

Other military records at the Minnesota Historical Society Research Center include Camp Ripley records for 1842 to 1843, Mexican border service payroll records from the early twentieth century, Minnesota soldiers' home records beginning in 1891, membership applications for the Sons of the American Revolution, and information from the Mexican-American and Spanish American wars.

Periodicals, Newspapers, and Manuscript Collections

Periodicals

The *Minnesota Genealogist*, quarterly publication of the Minnesota Genealogical Society (see Archives, Libraries, and Societies), includes a variety of genealogical articles, cemetery readings, newspaper and vital records extractions, book reviews, queries, and miscellaneous information of interest to the Minnesota researcher. Indexes are available through the society.

Minnesota History usually contains three to four full-length historical articles. It is indexed and published quarterly by the Minnesota Historical Society.

Newspapers

An excellent source for the historical development of Minnesota's newspapers is George S. Hage, *Newspapers on the Minnesota Frontier, 1849–50* (St. Paul: Minnesota Historical Society, 1967). The Minnesota Historical Society was chartered in 1849 as a repository for these territorial "day-books of history." On

28 April 1849, the first issue of the *Minnesota Pioneer* was published by James Madison Goodhue. By 14 July of that year Minnesota had three newspapers, all printed in St. Paul. The *St. Anthony Express*, the earliest newspaper in what is now Minneapolis, was first printed in 1851. The prime objective of these early papers was to attract settlers to the territory.

There are two reference sources available for locating information in the *Minnesota Pioneer*. The *Minnesota Pioneer Index* is a card file located at the Minnesota Historical Society that covers the newspaper through 4 Sept 1851. The *Minnesota Genealogical Journal* includes important extractions from the same newspaper through 4 April 1854. Obituaries, probate notices, lists of arrivals at St. Paul hotels, and letters remaining at the post office are covered.

The Minnesota Biography File is an extensive ongoing alphabetical card file index citing obituaries and other biographical details from newspapers, serials, books, and microfilmed scrapbooks in the collection at the Minnesota Historical Society.

Both Minneapolis and St. Paul city libraries have printed contemporary indexes of their respective major newspapers. The Minnesota regional research centers and local historical and genealogical groups may have indexing projects of community newspapers underway.

Two other sources are the Babcock Newspaper Index to articles in Minnesota newspapers (1849–58), which is a card index located at Minnesota Historical Society Research Center and the University of Minnesota, and the Immigration History Research Center's *Newspapers on Microfilm* (St. Paul: Immigration History Research Center, 1978). The latter is for ethnic newspapers.

Manuscripts

The Minnesota Historical Society has manuscript collections for almost every aspect of Minnesota territorial and state history. Many of these are listed in three guides:

Kane, Lucile M., and Kathryn A. Johnson, comps. *Manuscript Collections of the Minnesota Historical Society, Guide Number Two.* St. Paul: Minnesota Historical Society, 1955.

Lucas, Lydia A., comp. *Manuscripts Collections of the Minnesota Historical Society.* St. Paul: Minnesota Historical Society, 1977.

Nute, Grace Lee, and Gertrude W. Ackermann, comps. *Guide to the Personal Papers in the Manuscripts Collections of the Minnesota Historical Society.* St. Paul: Minnesota Historical Society, 1935.

Significant collections at the Minnesota Historical Society include the historical records of the Northern Pacific and Great Northern railways (1854–1970). Personnel files are limited. The Mission File Index, developed by Grace L. Nute, is an index

to copies of manuscript materials about missionaries and pre-twentieth century life in Minnesota.

The Minnesota Historical Society also has an immense number of fur trade papers. These are described, although not inclusively, in Bruce M. White, *The Fur Trade in Minnesota; An Introductory Guide to Manuscript Sources* (St. Paul: Minnesota Historical Society Press, 1977).

Manuscript collections of value can be found at the Iron Range Research Center, Minnesota Regional Research Centers (see Archives, Libraries, and Societies), Immigration History Research Center of the University of Minnesota, and university and religiously affiliated libraries in the state. Some repositories have printed guides or bibliographies.

Archives, Libraries, and Societies

Minnesota Historical Society

345 Kellogg Blvd. W.
St. Paul, MN 55101
www.mnhs.org

The Minnesota Historical Society has been collecting, preserving, and interpreting the history of Minnesota since 1849, which makes the society older than the state it represents. Now located at the Minnesota History Center, the center also includes the Minnesota State Archives <www.mnhs.org/preserve/records/index.html>. See Minnesota Historical Society Library and Archives Division, *Genealogical Resources of the Minnesota Historical Society: A Guide* (St. Paul: Minnesota Historical Society Press, 1989) for an excellent guide to the multitude of sources in their collection. This handbook alphabetically lists resources, cross-referenced, with a description of contents, location within the society's departments, and means of access.

At the above location are the audio-visual library (genealogists will appreciate the photograph collection of approximately 200,000 images, indexed by subject and name); the map library; the newspaper library (over 3 million issues of approximately 6,500 newspapers); reference library (over 500,000 books, pamphlets, periodicals, microforms, and documents); the largest collection of published Minnesota materials; extensive holdings on railroads, Canadian history, the fur trade, Scandinavians, and Native Americans in Minnesota; and publication offices.

With the integration of the Minnesota State Archives into the historical society, state archives records here include those created by state or local governments in Minnesota. There is an on-going program of transferring these records to the Minnesota Historical Society's system of research centers (see below). The collection is immense, covering a broad spectrum of Minnesota history beginning in 1849. Representative of the collections to be found are the State Board of Auditors for the adjustment of claims

for war expenditures (1862–68); Supreme Court Naturalization Records (1858–1906); and Stillwater State Prison (1853–1976). References to numerous items at this location are included under various subjects covered in this chapter.

Manuscript collections at the historical society encompasses over 6,000 collections, including diaries, letters, account books, scrapbooks, business papers, and personal papers of politicians and farmers.

Minnesota Genealogical Society

5768 Olson Memorial Hwy.
Golden Valley, MN 55422
www.mngs.org

Membership includes the quarterly *Minnesota Genealogist* and the *MGS Newsletter*. Meetings are held quarterly, with state and national speakers. The Minnesota Genealogical Society Library at 1101 Fort Rd. (West 7th St.), St. Paul, MN 55116, contains over 3,000 reference books, research materials on Indian and Metis groups, and the books and research materials of several of the branches of the society. The society also has an extensive number of special interest groups focusing on a wide variety of ethnic research concentrations.

The Minnesota Genealogical Society office and library are staffed by volunteers, and hours are limited. Classes are provided for beginning and advanced genealogists.

Iron Range Research Center

801 SW Hwy. 169, Ste. 1
Chisholm, MN 55719
www.ironrangeresearchcenter.org

Located at the Iron Range Interpretative Center with a full-time library and archives staff, it is designated as the government records repository for Iron Range communities and includes manuscripts, oral histories, and photographs, immigration and naturalization information, and a mining accident index.

Minnesota Regional Research Centers

This network was originally established by the Minnesota Historical Society. James E. Fogerty states in *Preliminary Guide to the Holdings of the Minnesota Regional Research Centers* (St. Paul: Minnesota Historical Society, 1975) that its purpose was to expand research possibilities within the state by collecting and preserving sources at various locations in the state. See also James Fogerty, *Manuscript Collection of the Minnesota Regional Research Centers: Guide Number 2* (St. Paul: Division of Archives and Manuscripts, Minnesota Historical Society, 1980).

The centers, which are located on the campuses of, and now associated with, colleges and universities in the state, concentrate on topics of regional importance. They are not all staffed on a full-time basis. Material varies at individual centers from information on the Stephen H. Long expedition of 1823 to the account of an auto trip from Minnesota to California and

back in 1929. There are oral history interviews and such items as the register of a nineteenth century inn on the Mississippi River.

The Minnesota Historical Society (see above) serves the counties of Dodge, Fillmore, Goodhue, Houston, Mower, Olmsted, Wabasha and Winona counties. Other centers and the counties they cover include:

Central Minnesota Historical Center

Centennial Hall, Rm. 148
St. Cloud State University
St. Cloud, MN 56301

Serves Aitkin, Benton, Chisago, Crow Wing, Isanti, Kanabec, Mille Lacs, Morrison, Pine, Sherburne, Stearns, Todd, Wadena, and Wright counties.

North Central Minnesota Historical Center (closed)

Some collections are now held by the Beltrami County Historical Society and some are held by the Minnesota Historical Society. The center formerly served Beltrami, Cass, Clearwater, Hubbard, Itasca, Koochiching, and Lake of the Woods counties.

Northeast Minnesota Historical Center

University of Minnesota–Duluth
Library 375
Duluth, MN 55812

Serves Carlton, Cook, Lake, and St. Louis counties.

Northwest Minnesota Historical Center

Livingston Lord Library
Minnesota State University–Moorhead
Moorhead, MN 56560

Serves Becker, Clay, Kittson, Mahnomen, Marshall, Norman, Otter Tail, Pennington, Polk, Red Lake, Roseau, and Wilkin counties.

Southern Minnesota Historical Center

Minnesota State University–Mankato
Mankato, MN 56001

Serves Blue Earth, Brown, Fairbault, Freeborn, Le Sueur, Martin, Nicollet, Rice, Sibley, Steele, Waseca, and Watonwan counties.

Southwest Minnesota Historical Center

Southwest State University
Marshall, MN 56258

Serves Cottonwood, Jackson, Kandiyohi, Lac Qui Parle, Lincoln, Lyon, McLeod, Meeker, Murray, Nobles, Pipestone, Redwood, Renville, Rock, and Yellow Medicine counties.

West Central Minnesota Historical Center

University of Minnesota–Morris
Morris, MN 56267

Serves Big Stone, Chippewa, Douglas, Grant, Pope, Stevens, Swift, and Traverse counties.

Special Focus Categories

Immigration

The only direct immigration to Minnesota would have been across the United States-Canadian border by land, railroad, or waterways. According to the Immigration and Naturalization Service, St. Paul, it was not until 1890 that port of entry records were kept for people entering from Canada. Passenger lists were not required on the lakes and rivers of Minnesota although some lists do exist. They may be found in diaries, letters, records of ship personnel, newspapers, or shipping company business papers. Their rarity makes them an uncommon source for genealogical research. For extensive information on the availability of river vessel records, see Ann H. Peterson's comprehensive "Finding River People on Western Waters," *National Genealogical Society Quarterly* 78 (Dec. 1990): 245-61. Although focused on crews of steamboats, her listed sources could be helpful for research involving Midwest river travel. (See also Vermont—Immigration).

Naturalization

Naturalization records are located at the district court office of the county or at the Minnesota Historical Society Research Center (see Archives, Libraries, and Societies). Availability varies by county and will continue to shift as more counties transfer their files to the center. Supreme court naturalization records (1858–1906) are found at the center. After 1906, naturalization was granted by the U.S. Federal District Court.

African American

Minnesota counted very few African Americans in the population prior to the Civil War. Those who were in the state were basically in two groups, either servants of officers at Fort Snelling or engaged in the fur trading industry. The latter, hired mainly by the fur companies in St. Louis, were some of the earliest African Americans in Minnesota. The Minnesota territorial census of 1849 listed forty free persons of African descent, thirty of those living in St. Paul in seven family groups. After 1860 the African-American population increased twofold, including over 500 men, women, and children arriving by steamboats from St. Louis to St. Paul in May of 1863. The Minnesota Historical Society has numerous manuscript collections pertaining to African Americans in Minnesota. Some of these have been documented in various articles in *Minnesota History*. See also:

Spangler, Earl. *Bibliography of Negro History: Selected and Annotated Entries, General and Minnesota.* Minneapolis: Ross and Haines, 1963. Excellent bibliography.

Taylor, David Vassar. "The Blacks." In *They Chose Minnesota: A Survey of the State's Ethnic Groups.* Edited by June Drenning

Holmquist. St. Paul: Minnesota Historical Society Press, 1981, 73-91. Excellent history of the African Americans in Minnesota, including detailed endnotes.

———. *Blacks in Minnesota: A Preliminary Guide to Historical Sources*. St. Paul: Publications of the Minnesota Historical Society, 1976.

Native American

Minnesota's two major native nations were the Dakota (or Sioux), originally from the southern prairie, and the Ojibway (or Chippewa) of the northern pine forests, both semi-nomadic societies based on hunting and gathering. In 1805 the United States purchased a small parcel of land in Minnesota for a military post, Fort Snelling. All other land belonged to the Native Americans. Intertribal fighting for northern Minnesota existed until 1825 when the Dakota and Ojibway agreed to a tribal diagonal demarcation almost across the center of the state.

Massive cessions of Native American land to European settlement began in Minnesota country in 1837 when an area between the St. Croix and Mississippi rivers was relinquished by the Dakota and Ojibway. After the chiefs signed the treaty, they headed north to the lands for which they thought they had given only timber rights. It was not until 1849 that they realized they had indeed sold their native land.

In 1847 land west of the Mississippi in central Minnesota was provided by treaty for the Winnebago and Menominee, although neither tribe ever occupied the area. Four years later, at Traverse des Sioux and Mendota, the Dakota signed treaties that gave the United States most of southern Minnesota. In treaties of 1854, 1855, 1863, and 1866, the Ojibway gave up much of their northern Minnesota land.

During the 1850s and 1860s, the Dakota treaties brought about a tragic and sorrowful chapter of Minnesota history. The reservations were not established as promised, and the various bands refused to move to the provisional reserves in the mid-1850s. Land annuity payments, the restriction of reservation life, and the nonexistence of promised agricultural aid led many Dakota families to return to their original lands, now the homes of European settlers. In 1857 settlers were killed in Spirit Lake, Iowa, and in Jackson County, Minnesota. A treaty in 1858 providing for Dakota self-government and land allotments failed, resulting in the Sioux Conflict of 1862, after which many either fled to the Dakota Territory or Canada or were moved to Crow Creek (now South Dakota). The unsatisfactory conditions at Crow Creek resulted in many deaths before the tribe was moved to Nebraska in 1866.

Minnesota's Ojibway were not involved in armed conflict with the white settlers, but the United States acquired most of their land and tried to confine them to reservations within the state. Small inter-tribal treaty parcels were consolidated, and some Ojibway refused to move to these larger reservations.

By 1980 there were nearly twice as many Native Americans in Minnesota as when the Europeans first visited this area. The metropolis of St. Paul and Minneapolis has the third largest urban concentration of Native Americans in the United States. The Ojibway in the northern part of the state occupy one of the few unallotted and unceded reservations in the country.

For an excellent explanation of the Native Americans in Minnesota in the twentieth century, see Mitchell E. Rubenstein and Alan R. Woolworth, "The Dakota and Ojibway," in *They Chose Minnesota: A Survey of the State's Ethnic Groups*, edited by June Drenning Holmquist (St. Paul: Minnesota Historical Society Press, 1981), 17-35. An article specifically directed at the family researcher of Native American records is Virginia Rogers, "The Indians and the Metis: Genealogical Sources on Minnesota's Earliest Settlers," in *Minnesota History* (Fall 1979): 286-96. Rogers has directed her research on Ojibway born prior to 1850, including the use of Canadian genealogical volumes and extensive study of missionary manuscript sources. These include early parish records, with baptisms at St. Ignace de Michilimackinac as early as 1712.

Helpful aids at the Minnesota Historical Society include the society's *Chippewa and Dakota Indians: A Subject Catalogue of Books, Pamphlets, Periodical Articles, and Manuscripts in the Minnesota Historical Society* (St. Paul: Minnesota Historical Society, 1969) and their original source material: U.S. Office of Indian Affairs, Chippewa Annuity Rolls (1849–1935); U.S. Office of Indian Affairs, Sioux Annuity Rolls (1849–1935); White Earth Indian Reservation, Saint Columba Parish Register (1853–1933); and Philip C. Bantin, *Guide to Catholic Indian Mission and School Records in Midwest Repositories* (Milwaukee, Wis.: Marquette University Libraries, Department of Special Collections and University Archives, 1984).

Other Ethnic Groups

Nineteenth-century French Canadians as fur traders, as lumbermen, and as priests in the Catholic Church were the first immigrants to Minnesota. Later other French Canadians followed, locating their new homes in the river valleys. The first French-Canadian communities at Fort Snelling and Mendota were both at the junction of the Mississippi and Minnesota rivers. Minnesota has a larger French-Canadian population in the late twentieth century than any state outside of New England.

Of the approximately thirty-two million total immigrants to the United States from 1820 through 1950, it is estimated that at least one million made their way to or through Minnesota. They came to the state for the available land; they came with tickets purchased for them by earlier U.S. immigrants; and they came to the support and security of ethnic communities already established in the counties and small towns. Most came via Canada and the Red River trails, up the Mississippi on steamboats, and overland. Eventually they arrived by train.

Excellent and thorough discussions of all the immigrant groups to Minnesota can be found in June Drenning Holmquist, *They Chose Minnesota: A Survey of the State's Ethnic Groups* (St. Paul: Minnesota Historical Society Press, 1981).

There are several research repositories for ethnic groups in Minnesota. The Immigration History Research Center was founded in 1965 at the University of Minnesota (311 Andersen Library, 222-21st Ave. S., St. Paul, MN 55114 <www1.umn.edu/ihrc>). Its dual purpose is to encourage the study of the role of immigration and to collect the records of twenty-four American ethnic groups originating from Eastern, Central, and Southern Europe and the Near East. The collection includes newspapers, books, and periodicals. The center also has records of churches, cultural societies, political, and fraternal organizations, in addition to the personal papers of some immigrants. The American Letters (1880–1964), a microfilmed collection of some 15,000 letters sent by immigrants to friends and relatives in Finland is an example of the type of items in the collection.

The Norwegian-American Historical Association, St. Olaf College, Northfield, MN 55057 <www.naha.stolaf.edu> has a collection on immigration including letters, diaries, business records, family histories, photographs, oral histories, and obituary and newspaper indexes, including the Rowberg file, which contains more than 175,000 newspaper clippings. Their website has online versions of some society periodicals and publications.

The Minnesota Historical Society (see Archives, Libraries, and Societies) has a large collection of Norwegian immigration materials including guidebooks written for prospective emigrants, about 10,000 manuscripts, an excellent printed and periodical collection for Swedish-Americans, and several ethnic collections that include artifacts and manuscripts listed in the society's *Historic Resources in Minnesota: A Report on their Extent, Location, and Need for Preservation* (St. Paul: Minnesota Historical Society, 1979).

The American Swedish Institute, 2600 Park Ave., Minneapolis, MN 55407 <www.americanswedishinst.org> focuses on the settlement of Swedes in America. Its collection includes family and personal papers, oral history, correspondence and record books of Swedish immigrant organizations, Bibles, genealogies, photographs, and microfilm copies of Swedish church records in Minnesota.

The emphasis of the Celtic Collection, O'Shaughnessy Library, College of Saint Thomas, 2115 Summit Ave., St. Paul, MN 55105 <www.stthomas.edu/libraries/special/celtic.htm> is on Welsh, Scottish, and Irish history, folklore, language, and literature.

marriage; county recorder—land records; office of the probate judge—probate files; and office of the court administrator—criminal and civil court records. Although years for birth, marriage, and death records indicated in the following chart are the earliest located in that county, not all records may start at that date and there may be different starting dates for different records within the county. The earliest year for probate records may be probate files or wills. Court records may be civil and/or criminal. In some counties, the earlier criminal files may be found in the civil court files.

For some counties there are two years for date of formation listed. The first is the year the county was created. The second is the year it was fully organized if it differs from the creation year. Under the heading "Parent County/ies," the name/s listed may be the county or counties from which the respective county was formed, or it may be names by which the county was originally known. "Unorganized" denotes that it was formed from non-county areas. A county name in parentheses is the county to which the unorganized land may have been attached at that time. Counties listed with an asterisk (*) are not parent counties but other counties in which you may also find records for the respective county since it may have been "attached" to that county for some period of time.

The files of the Minnesota Historical Society Research Center and the following have been consulted for county information:

Dalquist, Alfred J. *Minnesota Genealogical Journal.* Brooklyn Park, Minn.: Park Genealogical Book Co., 1984–87.

Pope, Wiley R. *Tracing Your Ancestors in Minnesota: A Guide to the Sources.* Vols. 1–8. St. Paul: Minnesota Family Trees, 1980–88. This source draws heavily on the WPA guides that were developed fifty years ago. Record sources have changed in the interim.

The Minnesota Legislative Manual, 1989–90. St. Paul: Election Division, Secretary of State, 1989.

What follows is a guide to the various record sources and is not to be considered a definitive explanation for the peculiarities of each county's holdings.

County addresses were obtained from the Minnesota Department of Health [online], Center for Health Statistics, "Addresses of County Registrars/Recorders" at <www.health.state.mn.us/index.html>.

County Resources

Records at the county level are the responsibility of the following offices: office of the court administrator—birth, death, and

MINNESOTA

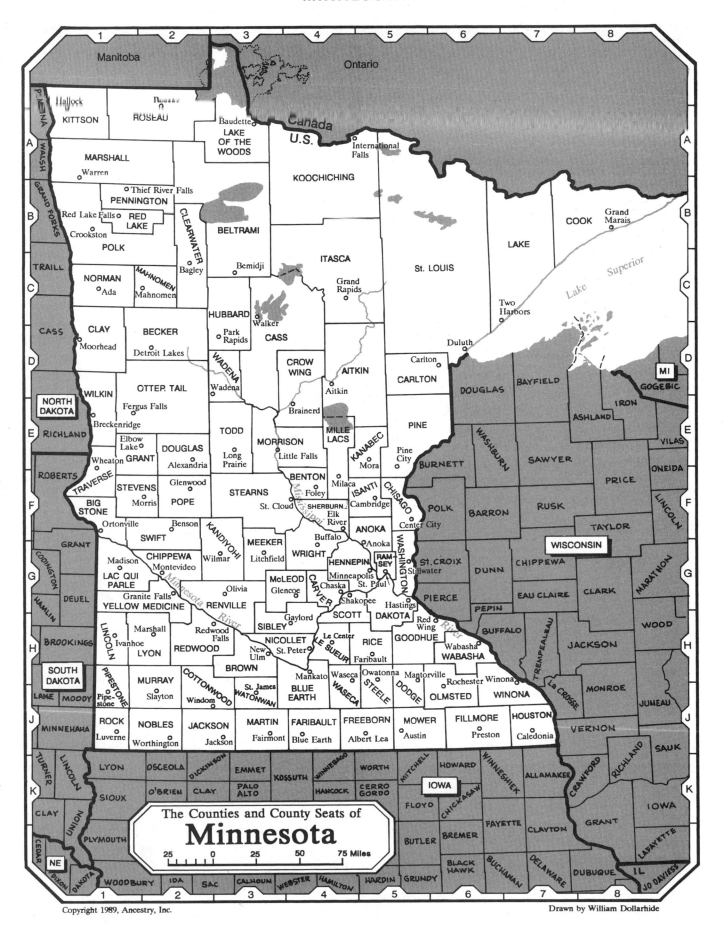

The Counties and County Seats of

Minnesota

25   0   25   50   75 Miles

Drawn by William Dollarhide

Map	County Address	Date Formed Parent County/ies	Birth Marriage Death	Land Probate Court
D4	Aitkin 209 2nd St. NW Aitkin 56431 *Aitkin County was spelled Aiken until 1872*	1857 (1885) Pine/Ramsey 1887/ *Crow Wing/*Morrison	1874 1885 1885	1872 1890 1862
	Andy Johnson	1862 (as Toombs; renamed 1862; disestablished, 1864; renamed Wilkin, 1868) Pembina *Stearns/*Crow Wing/*Douglas		
F5	Anoka 325 E. Main St. Anoka 55303	1857 Ramsey	1870 1858 1870	1857 1858 1858
D2	Becker 915 Lake Ave. Detroit Lakes 56501	1858 (1871) Cass/Pembina/ *Stearns/*Crow Wing/*Douglas 1871	1871 1871	1872 1872 1871
B3	Beltrami 619 Beltrami Ave. NW Bemidji 56601	1866 (1897) Itasca/Pembina/Polk/ unorganized *Becker	1896 1897 1896	1874 1896 1897
F4	Benton 531 Dewey St. Foley 56329	1849 St. Croix/unorganized	1865 1850 1867	1850 1852 1850
	Big Sioux	1857–58 (abolished 1858) Brown		
F1	Big Stone 20 SE 2nd St. Ortonville 56278	1862 (1881) Pierce *Renville/*Stevens	1881 1881 1881	1873 1881 1881
J3	Blue Earth 204 S. Fifth St. Mankato 56001	1853 Dahkota	1870 1865 1870	1853 1858 1854
	Breckenridge	1858–62 (renamed Clay, 1862) Pembina		
B3	Brown Box 248 New Ulm 56073	1855 (1856) Blue Earth	1870 1857 1870	1857 1856 1857
	Buchanen	1857–61 (abolished 1861; became part of Pine) Pine *Chisago/*St. Louis		
D5	Carlton 301 Walnut Ave. Carlton 55718	1857 (1870) Pine/St. Louis	1870 1871 1870	1870 1870 1871
G4	Carver 600 E. Fourth St. Chaska 55318	1855 (1855) Hennepin/Sibley	1870 1856 1870	1856 1857 1854
D3	Cass Walker 56484	1851 (1872) (1897) Dakota/Pembina/Mahkato/ Wahnahta (abolished 1876) *Benton/*Stearns/*Crow Wing/*Morrison	1896 1897 1896	1864 1897 1888
	Disestablished 1876; became part of Crow Wing; reorganized, 1897.			

Map	County Address	Date Formed Parent County/ies	Birth Marriage Death	Land Probate Court
G2	Chippewa 629 N. 11th St. Montevideo 56265	1862 (1869) Davis/Pierce *Renville	1870 1870 1870	1870 1872 1870
F5	Chisago 313 N. Main Center City 55012	1851 (1852) Ramsey/Washington	1870 1858 1870	1852 1857 1858
D1	Clay 807 11th St. North Moorhead 56560	1858 (as Breckenridge; renamed 1862) (1872) *Stearns/*Crow Wing/ *Douglas/*Becker	1872 1872 1872	1864 1872 1872
C2	Clearwater 213 Main Ave. North Bagley 56621	1902 Beltrami	1898 1903 1903	1903 1903 1903
B8	Cook 411 W. 2nd St. Grand Marais 55604	1874 (1897) Lake/ *St. Louis	1897 1897 1897	1892
H2	Cottonwood 900 Third Ave. Windom 56101	1857 (1873) Brown *Redwood/*Watonwan	1871 1871 1871	1871 1871 1871
D4	Crow Wing 326 Laurel St. Brainerd 56401	1857 (disestablished 1858) (1866) (disestablished 1867) (1871) Ramsey *Morrison	1873 1871 1874	1857 1874 1871
	In 1858 Crow Wing was disorganized and attached to Morrison; in 1866 it was fully organized; again disestablished in 1867 and attached to Morrison; in 1871 it was fully organized.			
H5	Dakota 1560 Hwy., 55 West Hastings 55093	1849 (1853) unorganized *Ramsey	1870 1853 1870	1852 1863 1853
	Davis	1855 (abolished 1862; became part of Chippewa and Lac Qui Parle) Cass/Nicolet/Pierce/Sibley *Stearns		
J5	Dodge 22 E 6th St. Mantorville 55955	1855 (1855) Rice/unorganized	1870 1858 1870	1856 1857 1859
	Doty	1855 (renamed Newton, 1855; abolished 1856; became part of St. Louis) Itasca		
E2	Douglas 305 Eighth Ave. W. Alexandria 56308	1858 Cass/Pembina	1870 1870 1870	1862 1868 1867
J4	Faribault P.O. Box 130 Blue Earth 56013	1855 (1857) Blue Earth	1870 1870 1870	1854 1858 1870
J6	Fillmore 101 Fillmore St. Preston 55965	1853 Wabasha	1870 1856 1870	1853 1857 1856

Map County Address	Date Formed Parent County/ies	Birth Marriage Death	Land Probate Court
J5 Freeborn 111 S. Broadway Albert Lea 56007	1855 (1857) Blue Earth/Rice	1870 1857 1870	1854 1866 1857
H5 Goodhue 509 W. 5th St. Red Wing 55066	1853 (1854) Dakota/Wabasha	1870 1854 1870	1853 1854 1854
E1 Grant 10 Second St. NE Elbow Lake 56531	1868 (1883) Stevens/Traverse/Wilkin *Douglas	1877 1869 1879	1872 1875 1872
G4 Hennepin 300 S. Sixth St. Minneapolis 55487	1852 (1852) Dakota *Ramsey	1870 1853 1870	1848 1855 1853
J7 Houston P.O. Box 29 Caledonia 55921	1854 Fillmore	1870 1854 1870	1856 1867 1857
C3 Hubbard 301 Court St. Park Rapids 56470	1883 (1887) Cass *Wadena	1885 1884 1887	1883 1884 1884
F5 Isanti 555 18th Ave. SW Cambridge 55008	1857 (disestablished 1858; reorganized, 1871) Ramsey/ *St. Louis/*Anoka	1873 1871 1873	1857 1868 1880
C4 Itasca 123 Fourth St. N.E. Grand Rapids 55744	1849 (1857) (disestablished 1858; reorganized, 1891) *Washington/*Benton/ *Chisago/*Crow Wing/*Morrison/ *St. Louis/*Aitkin	1893 1891 1894	1868 1898 1891
J2 Jackson Box 209 Jackson 56143	1857 (1866) (abolished, Sioux uprising 1862) Brown *Martin	1870 1868 1870	1866 1867 1871
E5 Kanabec 18 N. Vine Mora 55051	1858 (1881) Pine/ *Chisago	1880 1885 1880	1859 1888 1882
G3 Kandiyohi 400 Benson Ave. SW Wilmer 56201	1858 (1871) Davis/Meeker/Pierce/ Renville (disbanded 1866) (see Monongalia)	1870 1880 1870	1858 1867 1871
A1 Kittson 410 S. 5th St. Hallock 56728	1878 (1897) (see Pembina) *Polk	1877 1881 1881	1879 1899 1897
A4 Koochiching 715 Fourth St. International Falls 56649	1906 Itasca	1906 1906 1906	1907 1907 1907
Lac Qui Parle (old)	1862–68 (disbanded) Davis/Pierce/*Renville		
G1 Lac Qui Parle (present) P.O. Box 132 Madison 56256	1871 (1873) Redwood	1872 1872 1872	1871 1868 1885
B7 Lake 601 3rd Ave. Two Harbors 55616	1856 (1891) (see St. Louis OLD) *Benton/*St. Louis	1891 1888 1891	1874
A3 Lake of the Woods P.O. Box 808 Baudette 56623	1922 Beltrami	1922 1923 1923	1896 1923 1922
I14 Le Sueur 88 S. Park Ave. Le Center 56057	1853 Dakota	1870 1854 1870	1856 1853 1853
Lincoln (old)	1861–68 (disbanded) Renville/*McLeod		
H1 Lincoln (present) P.O. Box 119 Ivanhoe 56142	1873 (1881) Lyon/ *Redwood	1879 1879 1879	1874 1878 1880
H2 Lyon 607 West Main Marshall 56258	1868 (1870) (1875) Redwood (abolished 1873)	1874 1871 1874	1870 1890 1875
G3 McLeod 2389 Hennepin Ave. N. Glencoe 55336	1856 Carver/Sibley	1870 1865 1870	1856 1864 1867
Mahkahto	1849–51 (disbanded) unorganized/*Ramsey		
C2 Mahnomen P.O. Box 380 Mahnomen 56557	1906 Norman	1907 1907 1907	1904 1907 1907
Manomin	1857–58 (disbanded) Ramsey *St. Louis/*Anoka/*Hennepin (eliminated 1869)		
A1 Marshall 208 East Colvin Ave. Warren 56762	1879 (1881) Kittson/ *Polk	1884 1881 1884	1882
J3 Martin 201 Lake Ave. Fairmont 56013	1857 Brown/Faribault	1870 1862 1870	1857 1864 1861
G3 Meeker 325 N. Sibley Litchfield 55355	1856 (1866) Davis (abolished 1856) *Carver	1869 1859 1869	1856 1858 1858
Midway	(eliminated 1858)		
E4 Mille Lacs 635 2nd St. SE Milaca 56353	1857 (1860) Ramsey/ *Morrison	1871 1868 1872	1849 1875 1861
Monongalia	1861 (1861)–1865 (disbanded) Davis/Pierce/unorganized *Stearns, *Meeker (consolidated with Kandiyohi 1870)		

See Arthur L. Finnell, The Extant Records of Monongalia County, Minnesota, 1858–1870. Marshall, Minn.: Finnell-Richter and Assoc. 1980.

MINNESOTA

Map	County Address	Date Formed Parent County/ies	Birth Marriage Death	Land Probate Court
E3	Morrison 213 1st Ave. S. E. Little Falls 56345	1856 (1856) Benton	1870 1866 1870	1856 1860 1857
J5	Mower 201 1st St. NE Austin 55912	1855 (1856) Rice	1870 1870 1870	1856 1877 1858
H2	Murray 2500 28th St. Slayton 56172	1857 (1879) Brown/*Redwood/ *Watonwan/*Cottonwood	1873 1872 1873	1873 —— 1879
	Newton	(see Doty; eliminated 1856)		
H4	Nicollet 510 S. Minnesota Ave. Saint Peter 56082	1853 Dakota	1870 1852 1870	1853 1862 1850
J2	Nobles 315 10th St. Worthington 56187	1857 (1870) Brown/ *Martin	1869 1872 1870	1872 1873 1874
C1	Norman 16 E. 3rd Ave. Ada 56510	1881 Polk	1881 1882 1881	1885 1882 1882
J6	Olmsted 151 4th St. SE Rochester 55902	1855 (1855) Fillmore/Rice/ Wabasha/unorganized	1871 1855 1871	1855 1864 1858
D2	Otter Tail P.O. Box 867 Fergus Falls 56537	1858 (1870) Cass/Pembina/ *Stearns/*Crow Wing/ *Douglas	1871 1869 1871	1867 1872 1871
	Pembina	1849 (1852)–1853 (abolished; changed to Kittson, 1878) unorganized/Benton/ *Morrison/*Crow Wing/ *Douglas/*Becker/*Clay		
B1	Pennington Box 616 Thief River Falls 56701	1910 Red Lake	1910 1910 1910	1880 1910 1910
	Pierce	1853–62 (disbanded) *Nicolet		
E5	Pine 315 6th St. Pine City 55063	1856 (1857) (disestablished 1871 1858; reorganized, 1871) Chisago/Ramsey/ Chisago	1871 1871	1875 1871
H1	Pipestone 416 S. Hiawatha Ave. Pipestone 56164	1857 (1879) Brown/*Big Sioux/ (exchanged name with Rock, 1862) *Redwood/*Watonwan/ *Cottonwood/*Rock	1877 1879 1877	1879 1880 1879
B1	Polk P. O. Box 397 Crookston 56716	1858 (1879) Pembina/*Crow Wing/ *Douglas/*Polk/ *Clay	1873 1873 1873	1873 1877 1879
F2	Pope 130 E. Minnesota Ave. Glenwood 56334	1862 (1866) Cass/Pierce/unorganized	1868 1869 1870	1866 1867 1868
G5	Ramsey 15 W. Kellogg Blvd. Room 286 Saint Paul 55102	1849 St. Croix OLD/ unorganized	1870 1849 1870	1844 1849 1849
B1	Red Lake 124 N. Main St. Red Lake Falls 56750	1896 (1897) Polk	1897 1897 1897	1873 1897 1897
H2	Redwood P.O. Box 130 Redwood Falls 56283	1862 (1865) Brown	1864 1865 1869	1865 1877 1868
G3	Renville 500 E. DePue Olivia 56277	1855 (1866) Nicollet/Pierce/ Sibley	1870 1867 1870	1864 1893 1870
H5	Rice 320 NW 3rd St. Faribault 55021	1853 (1855) Dakota/ Wabasha	1870 1856 1870	1853 1858 1858
J1	Rock 204 E. Brown Luverne 56156	1857 (1874) Brown/*Big Sioux (exchanged name with Pipestone, 1862) *Martin/*Nobles	1870 1872 1870	1871 1873 1874
A2	Roseau 606 5th Ave. SW Roseau 56751	1894 (1897) Beltrami/ Kittson	1895 1895 1895	1892 1894 1895
	St. Croix	(eliminated 1849)		
	St. Louis (old)	1855 (changed to Lake, 1856) (see Superior)		
C5	Saint Louis (present) 100 N. 5th Ave. W. Duluth 55802	1856 (1857) Itasca/Newton/ *Benton	1870 1870 1870	 1869
G4	Scott 200 W. 4th Ave. West Shakopee 55379	1853 Dahkota	1871 1856 1871	1853 1853
F4	Sherburne 13880 Hwy. 10 Elk River 55330	1856 (1862) Benton	1870 1858 1870	1856 1857 1861
H4	Sibley 400 Court St. Gaylord 55334	1853 (1854) Dakota/ *Hennepin	1870 1865 1870	1855 1895 1866
F3	Stearns 705 Courthouse Sq. Saint Cloud 56302	1855 (1855) Cass/Nicollet/ Pierce/Sibley	1870 1870 1870	1855 1859 1857
J5	Steele 630 Florance Ave. Owatonna 55060	1855 (1856) Blue Earth/LeSueur/ Rice	1870 1856 1870	1856 1858 1856

364

Map	County Address	Date Formed Parent County/ies	Birth Marriage Death	Land Probate Court
F1	Stevens 5th and Colorado P.O. Box 107 Morris 56267	1862 (1871) Pierce/unorganized/ *Stearns/*Douglas/ *Pope	1872 1869 1872	1871 1875 1870
	Superior	1855 (changed to St. Louis-OLD) Itasca		
F2	Swift P.O. Box 110 Benson 56215	1870 (1897) Chippewa/*Pope/ *Kandiyohi	1871 1871 1870	1871 1873 1874
E3	Todd 215 1st Ave. South Long Prairie 56347	1855 (1873) Cass/*Stearns/ *Morrison	1869 1867 1870	1867 1876 1868
	Toombs named Andy Johnson —1862	1858 Pembina		
F1	Traverse 702 Second Ave. N Wheaton 56296	1862 (1881) Pierce/unorganized/ *Chippewa/*Stearns/ *Douglas/*Pope	1881 1881 1881	1872 1880 1881
H6	Wabasha 625 Jefferson Ave. Wabasha 55981	1849 (1853) unorganized/ *Washington	1870 1865 1870	1853 1856 1860
D3	Wadena P.O. Box 415 Wadena 56482	1858 (1881) Cass/Todd/ *Crow Wing/*Morrison	1873 1873 1880	1873 1889 1881
	Wahnahta	1849—51 (eliminated)		
J4	Waseca 300 N. State St. Waseca 56093	1857 Steele	1870 1857 1870	1856 1871 1857
G5	Washington 14949 62nd St. N., Ste. 275 Stillwater 55082	1849 St. Croix (old)/ unorganized	1870 1843 1870	1856 1849 1847
J3	Watonwan Box 518 St. James 56081	1860 (1871) Brown/ *Blue Earth	1870 1867 1870	1859 1890 1885
E1	Wilkin 300 S. 5th St. Breckenridge 56520	1868 (1872) (see Andy Johnson) *Otter Tail	1880 1884 1885	1871 1888 1884
J7	Winona 74 West 3rd Winona 55987	1854 Fillmore/ Rice	1870 1854 1870	1853 1856 1855
G4	Wright 10 2nd St. N.W. Buffalo 55313	1855 (1855) Cass/ Sibley	1868 1856 1868	1856 1854 1858
G2	Yellow Medicine 415 9th Ave. Granite Falls 56214	1871 (1874) Redwood	1872 1872 1872	1861 1874 1872

Mississippi

KATHLEEN STANTON HUTCHISON

The first written record in Mississippi history was made in 1540 when the Spaniard Hernando de Soto and his men crossed its boundaries to discover the Mississippi River. Yet long before these first Europeans came, there were Native Americans who existed in this natural habitat with its gentle climate, fertile soil, and plentiful food environment. Mississippi was home to many tribes; in the early days Mississippi had a larger population of Native Americans than any other state in the Southeast. Some of the major tribes include the Natchez on the lower Mississippi, the Chickasaw in the north and northeast, and the Choctaw in the central and southern part.

Mississippi history may be divided into four distinct jurisdictional periods: French Colonial (1699–1763), British Provincial (1763–79), Spanish Provincial (1779–98), and American Territorial and Statehood (1798-present). The year 1699 saw the French establish the colony of Biloxi, the first permanent settlement in this part of the Lower Mississippi Valley. Later this colony was moved to Mobile, and Natchez was established as the seat of government in 1716. Toward the end of the Seven Years War (or French and Indian War) in 1763, France ceded this province to Britain, beginning the immigration of Protestant, land-loving British, a stark contrast with the remaining Roman-Catholic French. Sixteen years later in 1779, the British yielded control of the Natchez District to the Spanish, who remained until pro-American sentiment prevailed.

When Mississippi Territory was formed in 1798 by the U.S. Congress, the territory included lands north of the 31st parallel and south of Tennessee, lying between the Chattahoochee and Mississippi rivers. During this period there were only two significant regions of settlement: the Natchez District, found in the southern part of the state along the Mississippi River, and the St. Stephens District in the eastern section on the Tombigbee River. At the time, Spain controlled the Gulf Coast and the Choctaw, Creek, and Chickasaw tribes owned more land than did the white settlers, who numbered fewer than 5,000 in 1798.

With the opening of the territory in that year, there was a surge of immigration that sparked a recurring division and formation of county boundaries. The fact that the present state of Alabama was part of Mississippi Territory occasionally causes confusion for the researcher. The present Alabama counties of Washington, Madison, Baldwin, Clarke, Monroe, Mobile, and Montgomery were organized as counties in Mississippi Territory. County names have been duplicated in Mississippi and Alabama of these except for Baldwin and Mobile counties. The coastal area of Mississippi Territory was part of British West Florida (1763–79) and later of Spanish West Florida (1779–1810) until after the War of 1812. Actually, the land encompassing the Mississippi counties of Hancock, Harrison, and Jackson was made a part of Mississippi Territory in 1812, following the West Florida Revolution of 1810.

Ambiguous application of land grant distribution through the Treaty of Paris in 1783 and Pinckney Treaty of 1795, coupled with politics of the era, produced a sometimes-muddled trail of land titles. Early Mississippi history may be characterized as one of white settlers moving onto lands that were previously owned by natives. The acquisition of this land by treaties is more fully explained in Goodspeed's *Biographical and Historical Memoirs of Mississippi* (see Background Sources for additional references).

Some of the problems encountered with these treaties may be better understood by reviewing Clarence Edwin Carter, comp. and ed., *Territorial Papers of the United States: The Territory of Mississippi*, vol. 6 (Washington, D.C.: Government Printing Office, 1938).

The thrust of immigration and settlement pushed the territory toward statehood in 1817. In 1832, through treaties made with the Choctaw and Chickasaw, all land in the present state of Mississippi was opened for settlement. Offering opportunities for a richer life, the divergent cultures from the past came together as one. Cotton became king, and the state of Mississippi flourished at an astonishing pace for decades preceding the Civil War, aided by the labors of many African Americans, both slave and free.

Mississippi voted to secede from the Union on 9 January 1861, putting into motion events that led to Mississippi's involvement in the Civil War. The harsh period of Reconstruction that followed the war left a long-standing bitterness that further strengthened Mississippi's political stand regarding states' rights. The Jim Crow laws, legislation put into effect by the white electorate, guaranteed that the freed slaves would continue in a condition of servitude, poverty, and ignorance. Sharecropping sprang into being for African Americans and whites alike, leading once again to an economic dependence on cotton. Because of its persistence in clinging to an agricultural society, Mississippi was well into the twentieth century before attempting to join an industrialized America. The records created after 1940 reflect the political, economic, and cultural changes that dramatically altered Mississippi life.

Vital Records

By law, the State of Mississippi was not required to keep birth or death certificates until 1 November 1912. Birth and death records since 1912 have been kept by the Mississippi State Department of Health, Vital Records, P.O. Box 1700, Jackson, MS 39215 <www.msdh.state.ms.us/phs/index.htm>. The department responds to mail requests; however, the requests must be submitted on the appropriate required form, which can be obtained from the website.

The Mississippi Department of Archives and History (see Archives, Libraries, and Societies) maintains microfilm copies of marriage records held in the county courthouses. The records held are often sporadic depending upon the years of courthouse fires. The Mississippi Genealogical Society, *Survey of Mississippi Courthouses* (Jackson, Miss.: the society, 1957), although outdated, provides important holdings information about surviving court records kept in each courthouse. In addition to the marriage records in each county, there is a statewide index listed by groom's name on microfilm for those marriages prior to

1926. This index includes name of the bride and groom, date marriage took place or when the license was secured, name of the county, and book and page number of the marriage record. Also, some counties have original marriage records indexed by bride's name. After the Civil War, separate books for African American marriages were kept, although when looking for *any* marriage in Mississippi, *all* marriage volumes in the county should be checked.

Before 1859, divorce proceedings were introduced as private bills in the legislature. References to these are found in *Index to Session Acts*, an unpublished guide found in the Mississippi Department of Archives and History. Since 1859, divorce proceedings are filed in the chancery clerk's office of the county in which the divorce took place. Copies of these later records are not found at the state archives.

Census Records

Federal

Population Schedules
- Indexed—1820, 1830 (part), 1840, 1850, 1860 (part), 1870, 1880, 1900, 1910, 1920, 1930
- Soundex—1880, 1900, 1910, 1920

Industry and Agriculture Schedules
- 1850, 1860, 1870, 1880

Mortality Schedules
- 1850, 1860, 1870, 1880

Slave Schedules
- 1850, 1860 (part)

Union Veterans Schedules
- 1890

In 1817 Mississippi became the twentieth state to enter the union; therefore, the first federal population census available is that of 1820. Variations of this census appear in three printed forms, none of which include slave or miscellaneous information. Both the *Mississippi 1820 Census* and the *Mississippi 1830 Census* have been published by Irene and Norman Gillis, Shreveport, Louisiana. Enumerations for Pike County are missing in 1830, but the Gillis index used extant tax records to supplement their index. Transcriptions are subject to error and should be used simply as a *guide* to the original records. A significant addition to the 1840 census supplies the names and ages of pensioners. Schedules are missing for Hancock, Sunflower, and Washington counties in 1860. By 1870, with slavery abolished, all African Americans, natives, and Chinese were included, along with

information regarding citizenship. With the destruction of the 1890 population schedules, only the schedules enumerating Union veterans are available for Mississippi.

Aside from those indexes produced by AISI (see page 3) two other indexes include Irene S. Gillis, comp., *Mississippi 1850 Census Surname Index*, 3 vols. (Shreveport: the compiler, 1972), and Kathryn Rose Bonner, comp., *Mississippi 1860 United States Census Index*, 3 vols. (Mariana, Ark.: the compiler, n.d.).

Microfilm copies of all federal census schedules and the original state copies of the 1850 through 1880 schedules are located at the Mississippi Department of Archives and History. Some of the original agriculture and industry schedules were lost after microfilming. Scattered reels of census schedules are available at other repositories in the state. Microfilm copies of federal censuses for Mississippi are available through national organizations (see pages 3-4).

Colonial

An early census of the Natchez District, taken in 1792 from the Spanish Provincial records, has been printed in Dunbar Rowland, *History of Mississippi, The Heart of the South*, 4 vols. (Chicago: S. J. Clark Publishing Co., 1925). Other censuses from the Spanish Colonial period (1784, 1787, 1788, and 1794) can be found in the *Papeles Procedentes de Cuba* (The Cuban Papers) located at the General Archives of the Indies in Seville, Spain. See Roscoe R. Hill, *Descriptive Catalogue of the Documents Relating to the History of the United States in the Papeles Procedentes de Cuba* (Washington, D.C.: Carnegie Institute of Washington, 1916).

Territorial and State

Territorial census reports were authorized by the legislature of Mississippi Territory at different intervals from 1798 until 1817. A useful start with territorial census information may be found in Norman E. Gillis, *Early Inhabitants of the Natchez District* (Shreveport: the author, 1963). Although the information was gathered from secondary sources, it still remains a helpful tool. The original records are housed at the Mississippi Department of Archives and History. These census records are available for research purposes at the Mississippi Department of Archives and History and for purchase on microfilm from Underground Vaults & Storage, Inc., P.O. Box 1723, Hutchinson, KS 67504-1723.

One other special census, known as the "Armstrong Roll of 1831" (see Alabama—Census Records), was taken following the signing of the Choctaw "Treaty of Dancing Rabbit Creek," the last major land concession made by the Native Americans to the Europeans. Some of the information on this roll includes names of the Choctaw tribal members, whites who married Choctaw natives, and slaves.

An indirect source giving census information is the Educable Children Records, a census of school-age children taken by county. Although the Mississippi Department of Archives and History has some of these records, many are still located at each county superintendent of education's office. These records are arranged at the archives by county with no index available.

Background Sources

To begin researching Mississippi records, there are three publications of particular note that provide useful overviews of resources in the state. See Richard S. Lackey, "Mississippi" in Kenn Stryker-Rodda, ed., *Genealogical Research Methods and Sources*, vol. 2, rev. ed. (Washington, D.C.: American Society of Genealogists, 1983): 188-218; Ruth Land Hatten, "Genealogical Research in Mississippi," *National Genealogical Society Quarterly* 76 (March 1988): 25-51; Anne S. Lipscomb, Kathleen S. Hutchison, *Tracing Your Mississippi Ancestors* (Jackson, Miss.: University Press of Mississippi, 1994). For a broad historical account of the development of Mississippi, consult Richard A. McLemore, *A History of Mississippi*, 2 vols. (Jackson, Miss.: University and College Press of Mississippi, 1973). All four were consulted as resources in developing this chapter.

An excellent interpretive history is John Ray Skates, *Mississippi: A Bicentennial History* (New York: W. W. Norton & Co., and Nashville: American Association for State and Local History, 1979). It contains a good, short bibliographic essay at the end that suggests other Mississippi history to read.

In the later part of the nineteenth century, an historical and biographical compilation of information about Mississippi was put together in Goodspeed's *Biographical and Historical Memoirs of Mississippi*, 2 vols. (Chicago: Goodspeed Publishing Co., 1891), reproduced by Bell and Howell (Wooster, Ohio: Micropublishers, Micro Photo Division, n.d.). Information for these volumes was taken from oral histories, but the publication offers a genuine "flavor" of Mississippi.

With eighty-two counties in the state, it would be impractical to formulate a listing of all local histories. For a current listing, see P. William Filby's *A Bibliography of American County Histories* (see page 4).

Original folders of the Works Progress Administration (WPA) county files, completed in the late 1930s, provide an introspective view of a county through a variety of sources found in each folder. Both the folders and a microfilm copy are at the Mississippi Department of Archives and History. The Mississippi Library Commission, 1221 Ellis Ave., Jackson, MS 39209-7328, has microfilm copies as well.

The Biographical Index found at the Mississippi Department of Archives and History is a card index to information on Mississippians during the territorial and early statehood days. It is also available online at the archives website. The genealogical sources indexed include territorial census and tax rolls, secretary of state's register of commissions (lists of state and county office

holders), select Mississippi newspaper notices, and Goodspeed's *Memoirs*, cited previously. Also indexed are Mississippi soldiers who participated in the War of 1812 and the Mexican War.

For the best explanation of Mississippi military participation, see Dunbar Rowland, *Military History of Mississippi, 1803–1898* (1898; reprint, Spartanburg, S.C.: Reprint Co., 1978). James F. Brieger, *Hometown Mississippi* (Jackson, Miss.: Town Square Books, Inc., 1997), provides an extensive listing of Mississippi places with a brief historical passage and can be important in locating communities that no longer exist.

Maps

Historical maps found at the Mississippi Department of Archives and History can be accessed through the archives' chronological listing, which is arranged by date and situation of the map. Included in this list are numerous maps dating from 1500 to 1984. This selection contains all accessioned maps, including some produced by governmental agencies such as the U.S. Geological Survey (see page 5) and the Mississippi State Highway Department. Sanborn fire insurance maps (see page 5) help identify location of structures.

County highway maps, produced by the Mississippi Department of Transportation, Map Sales Office, P.O. Box 1850, Jackson, MS 39215-1850, are available for a nominal fee. These maps are useful when trying to locate cemeteries in the state (see Cemetery Records).

Information in respect to state and federal legislation of land is covered in the Mississippi Historical Records Survey, *State and County Boundaries of Mississippi* (Jackson, Miss.: Historical Records Survey, 1942). This publication presents, in summary form, all the laws affecting the boundaries of the state of Mississippi, the counties in the state, and the judicial districts that were changed either by law, treaty, or proclamation. Another publication not to be overlooked is *Atlas of Historical County Boundaries* (New York: Simon & Schuster, 1993) which is inclusive of all counties both existing and extinct in the state of Mississippi.

The 1895 atlas of Mississippi can be found online at <www.livgenmi.com/1895/>.

Land Records

Public-Domain State

At different times, early Mississippi land records were granted by four different jurisdictions: France, Britain, Spain, and the state of Georgia. These four all owned parts of Mississippi before the area became part of the United States in 1798. Ownership of land based on a grant from a former jurisdiction is called a private land claim, and each landowner of these claims was required to file it with the federal government after Mississippi came under U.S. jurisdiction. These private land claim records are on microfilm (RG 28 SG 1) at the Mississippi Department of Archives and History and can be accessed by consulting the department's guide, "Index to Private Claims and Field Notes in Mississippi." Further information is given in E. K. Kirkham, *The Land Records of America ...* (see page 6) and *Guide to Genealogical Research in the National Archives* (see page 11).

Mississippi is a public land state, which means that initial (first-grant) disposition of public owned land after 1798 became the responsibility of the federal government under the General Land Office (GLO), now the Bureau of Land Management (BLM). Types of records contained here are field notes and surveys, tract books, official monthly abstracts, patents, and entry records. For the individual buying land directly from the United States government, the transaction was recorded in local federal land offices, and the legal description was entered into tract books. Mississippi's eight land office districts and the chronological periods of operation within the state of Mississippi, as described in Harry P. Yoshpe and Philip P. Brower, *Preliminary Inventory of Land Entry Papers...*, No. 22 (see page 6), were the following:

St. Stephens (the district east of the Pearl River) was the first opened land office district (26 December 1806–17), and it was also the first closed. The district was located in what is now Washington County, Alabama. Transactions covered those for the southeastern district, including land Georgia ceded to the federal government in 1798 and 1802. Augusta became the land office serving the area.

The Washington land office (Adams County, or district west of the Pearl River) covered land including Choctaw sales of individual reserves (1807–61).

The federal land office at Huntsville, Alabama (1810-present), was created for the purpose of managing those lands acquired by treaties with the Chickasaw in 1805 and Cherokee in 1806; the office is located in Madison County, Alabama. See Marilyn Davis Barefield, comp., *Old Huntsville Land Office Records and Military Warrants, 1810–1854* (Easley, S.C.: Southern Historical Press, 1985).

Between 1827 and 1836, the Jackson land office (Hinds County) was located at Mt. Salus and regulated land sales in west-central Mississippi.

The office at August (Perry County) was moved to Paulding (Jasper County) in 1860–61, having jurisdiction over lands in the lower portion of east-central Mississippi (1820–59).

The Columbus district (Lowndes County) encompassed lands in the northern portion of east-central Mississippi (1833–61).

The Chocchuma land office (now Grenada County) was located in the Choctaw District on the Yalobusha River (1833–40).

It moved to Grenada after 1840 where it continued operating until 1860, serving land in the vicinity of northwest Mississippi.

The Pontotoc office (Pontotoc County) served lands roughly in the extreme northeast of Mississippi (1836–61). By 1869, all were consolidated to one in Jackson.

When the land offices closed in Mississippi, the land records were sent to the BLM (see page 6); however, the original field notes and plat books are housed at the secretary of state's office. Inquiries may be sent to the Public Lands Division, 401 Mississippi St., Jackson, MS 39205. This office is open to those who want to do research, but there is a fee for research done by the staff.

The best genealogical information pulled from the first-grant land records may be found in the various types of entry records. The private land claim, as previously explained, was the entry record that recorded claims to land from foreign governments. Military bounty land was issued as a reward for military service. "Credit" entries were simply those lands purchased with the intent of paying later, and the "Cash" entries signified those lands sold after 1820 when land was sold for cash only. Those lands given by the government for specific reasons were called donation entries. Homestead entries were created under the Homestead Act of 1862, which gave certain stipulations to settlers in exchange for land. An aid in deciphering these records may be found in Richard S. Lackey, "Credit Land Sales, 1811–1815: Mississippi Entries of the Pearl" (master's thesis, University of Southern Mississippi, 1975: 185-222); and Robert V. Haynes, "Disposal of Lands in Mississippi Territory," *Journal of Mississippi History* 24 (1962): 226-52.

Another type of land transaction involves the buying and selling of property among private citizens (subsequent sales). In Mississippi, these transactions are recorded as deeds at the county courthouse and filed by the chancery clerk; both the Mississippi Department of Archives and History and the Family History Library (FHL) in Salt Lake City have large collections of these land records on microfilm, filed by county.

The Mississippi Department of Archives and History has copies of records taken from both the land commissioner's office (first-grants) and the offices of chancery clerks (subsequent sales). The congressional records in the archives provide a considerable amount of information about land legislation, including petitions from individuals, land companies, and state and local governments regarding land claims from 1795 to 1872. Located in these documents are also copies of treaties with Native Americans regarding land cessions. Other information is dispersed throughout the provincial, territorial, state, and federal records found in the collection. The map file includes extensive land surveys for the area of the lower Mississippi Valley.

The documentation of ownership of land offers valuable information to the researcher, but it can be a complicated process in Mississippi. For a better working knowledge in the use

of such records, see Elizabeth Shown Mills, "Backtracking Hardy Hunter: A Case Study of Genealogical Problem Solving Via the Preponderance of Evidence Principle," *Association of Professional Genealogists Quarterly* 1 (Spring 1986): 1-19; continued in 1 (Summer 1986): 1-20; and her "Land Titles: A Neglected Key to Solving Genealogical Problems—A Case Study," *Louisiana Genealogical Register* 31 (June 1984): 103-23.

Probate Records

Although Mississippi Territory had influences from different European countries, it was English law that it looked to for guidance even from the beginning; this law separated courts of law and equity as Mississippi distinguished the chancery court from the circuit court.

Courts of probate were originally created by the state constitution in 1817 as "orphans' courts," with responsibilities encompassing probate matters and guardianship. By 1832, the actual name had become "probate court" and was administered by the "chancery clerk." An amendment passed in 1857 abolished all chancery courts, with probate function then coming under the jurisdiction of the circuit courts. And so it remained until 1869 when the chancery courts were reinstated.

The chancery court in Mississippi encompasses a wide range of duties. One responsibility of the clerk of the chancery court was to act as judge of probate, keeping records of wills and testaments that are probated. Other functions include claims against an estate being administered; taking proof of wills and admitting wills to probate; and appointing guardians for minors, people of unsound minds, and convicts. These records are on file at the county courthouse, and many are also on microfilm at the Mississippi Department of Archives and History.

Record books are only one source of material in Mississippi. Loose papers associated with the estate are also located in some county courthouses, with scattered microfilm copies at the Mississippi Department of Archives and History.

Court Records

It is important to make the distinction that probate records are maintained by the chancery court, but that the chancery court has additional responsibilities for other records. These tasks include keeping official records of land titles, mortgages, and other documents customarily recorded at the courthouse.

The term "circuit" developed in 1817 when the state set up judges to rotate in a particular geographic area to make determinations in civil matters. These courts have not deviated greatly from their earliest mission. Marriage licenses, voter registrations, declarations and naturalizations, criminal court minutes, and in some cases the coroner's book are maintained

by the circuit court. These records are available to the public at the county courthouse and may also be found on microfilm at the Mississippi Department of Archives and History and through the FHL.

Tax Records

Local county courthouses maintain original tax records, both real and personal. Microfilm copies of the earlier records are found in the Mississippi Department of Archives and History, where the collection is extensive but nevertheless has gaps. Some counties, though not many, have published selected years of tax rolls.

Cemetery Records

The card catalog at the Mississippi Department of Archives and History provides access to the numerous cemetery books that have been published for many counties throughout the state. Another card index of value provides volume-by-volume access to *Mississippi Cemetery and Bible Records,* an ongoing publication project by the Mississippi Genealogical Society since 1949. Individual volumes, without the card index, are on the shelves of many local libraries throughout the state.

The Bible and Cemetery Records Collection, prepared by the Daughters of the American Revolution (DAR), is very useful but is not thoroughly indexed. Although records of individual cemeteries are scattered throughout these compilations, some volumes concentrate on the cemeteries of one county, such as Hinds, Adams, or Bolivar.

Another source to consult is the Genealogical and Cemetery File, which consists of an upright file of folders arranged by county and includes, among other items, unpublished cemetery records donated to the archives by researchers.

To facilitate the process of finding a cemetery in the state, the typescript of "State Cemeteries" located at the Mississippi Department of Archives and History lists public and private cemeteries, giving section, township, and range. This finding aid and the WPA cemetery list, a typescript listing of public and private cemeteries by county, which also includes the section, township, and range, can be used in conjunction with county maps (see Maps). There is a cemetery index available online at the state archives website as well. Also on microfilm are the Mississippi grave registrations, which could help in the location of a veteran who was buried in Mississippi. However, this list is not complete.

All of the above resources are available at the Mississippi Department of Archives and History (see Maps for location of cemeteries in the state).

Church Records

The Spanish Dominion brought the strong influence of Catholicism into colonial Mississippi, but Mississippi as a territory witnessed the development of other organized religions that were predominantly Protestant faiths. In actuality, the priest left with the Spanish when the U.S. officially claimed Mississippi Territory, leaving only a handful of Catholic families in the area. For a general interpretation of this period, see James J. Pillar, "Religious and Cultural Life, 1817–1860," in McLemore, *A History of Mississippi,* vol. 1, 378-410, cited in Background Sources.

In 1798 the remaining Roman Catholic populace was occasionally administered to by priests from Louisiana and Mobile. More specific information about Catholic records in colonial and territorial times may be found in Elizabeth Shown Mills, "Spanish Records: Locating Anglo and Latin Ancestry in the Colonial Southeast," *National Genealogical Society Quarterly* 73 (December 1985): 243-61; and in *Records of the Diocese of Louisiana and the Floridas, 1576–1803,* 12 reels (South Bend, Ind.: University of Notre Dame Archives Microfilm Publications, 1967).

There was no real growth in the church until after the 1840s when there was a rush of Irish immigrants into the state. A separate diocese was created in 1837, located in Natchez, but ultimately was moved to Jackson. Archival material housed in the Catholic Diocese of Jackson Archives (P.O. Box 2248, 237 East Amite St., Jackson, MS 39225-2248) includes clipping files (1850-present); papers of all prior bishops of the Mississippi Catholic Church (1837-present); property deeds and microfilmed sacramental record books of all parishes in the diocese; national Catholic directories (1843-present); and books dealing with Mississippi history and Southern church history.

Although no churches experienced rapid expansion during territorial and early statehood days, the Methodist Church became the largest antebellum religious group. See Gene R. Miller, *A History of North Mississippi Methodism, 1820–1900* (Nashville, Tenn.: Parthenon Press, 1966) for a general history of this denomination. The J. B. Cain Archives of Mississippi Methodism (Millsaps-Wilson Library, Millsaps College, Jackson, MS 39210) contains an archival collection that features the history and development of the Methodist Church in Mississippi from the Methodist Episcopal Church to the United Methodist Church. The materials include church histories, manuscript items from the early nineteenth century, various conference minutes beginning in 1817, and some periodicals. Most of these materials do not circulate, but photocopy services are available depending on the condition of the item. The Archives and History Center of the United Methodist Church, Drew University, Madison, NJ 07940, also holds a significant records collection.

Beginning in 1791 the Baptist Church in Mississippi showed early signs of strength after the preacher Richard Curtis brought together the first group of Baptists at Coles Creek near Natchez. The Mississippi Baptist Association was formed as early as 1806 with a total of six churches and 706 members. Now it claims the largest membership in the state. For a broad overview, see Richard A. McLemore, *A History of Mississippi Baptists, 1780–1970* (Jackson, Miss.: Mississippi Baptist Convention Board, 1971), and Gordon A. Cotton, *Of Primitive Faith and Order: A History of the Mississippi Primitive Baptist Church, 1780–1974* (Raymond, Miss.: Keith Press, 1974). Historical materials focusing on the development of the church are housed at the Mississippi Baptist Historical Commission, Mississippi College Library, P.O. Box 4024, Clinton, MS 39058. The collection contains minutes of churches, a clipping file that includes some biographical data relating to preachers and other church leaders dating to the late eighteenth century, local histories, association minutes, Baptist convention minutes, newspapers and newsletters, photographs, and other select church-related records. There are no restrictions on use of the materials.

The formation of the Presbyterian Church in 1800 is attributed to three missionaries who were sent by the Synod of the Carolinas to preach: James Hall, William Montgomery, and James Bowman. The first established Presbyterian Church in Mississippi was Bethel at Uniontown in Jefferson County. The Synod of Mississippi was formed in 1835. For information on the synod, see Walter B. Posey, *The Presbyterian Church in the Old Southwest, 1778–1838* (Richmond, Va.: John Knox Press, 1952), and "Documentary Material Relating to the Early History of the Presbyterian Church in Mississippi," *Journal of the Presbyterian Historical Society* 21 (December 1943): 196-200. Some historical records may be found in the Belhaven College, Hood Library, 1500 Peachtree St., Jackson, MS 39202. There are no restrictions on the use of the materials. Other records may be located through the Historical Foundation of the Presbyterian and Reformed Churches, Assembly Dr., Box 849, Montreat, NC 28757.

Episcopal Church services were held in the Mississippi region in 1790. However, the first church, named Christ Church (at Church Hill in Jefferson County) was not organized until 1815 when it was founded by Adam Cloud. The Episcopal Diocese of Mississippi was organized in 1826 with churches located in Church Hill, Natchez, Port Gibson, and Woodville. No central repository exists for these church records. For more detail, see Nash K. Burger and Charlotte Capers, "Episcopal Clergy of Mississippi, 1790–1940," *Journal of Mississippi History* 8 (April 1946): 59-66.

The Lutheran Church was the last Protestant church to organize in the state. The New Hope Lutheran Church was first formed, in 1846, near Sallis in Attala County. However, in 1855, when there were nine Lutheran churches, the Mississippi Synod was assembled as part of the United Synod of the South. The repository for the Southern states is the Lutheran Theological Southern Seminary, 4201 N. Main St., Columbia, SC 29203-5898.

In addition to records found in local churches, researchers should look at the WPA publication *Guide to Vital Statistics Records in Mississippi,* vol. 2, *Church Archives* (Mississippi Historical Records Survey, 1942). Compiled by Donna Pannell, *Church Records in the Mississippi Department of Archives and History* (1986), a bound computer printout, lists available materials such as manuscript papers, journals, minutes, and organization records found in both the library and the manuscript section of the department. The manuscripts index is also available online at the Mississippi Department of Archives and History website.

Military Records

Revolutionary War. At the beginning of the Revolutionary War, the region that was later to become Mississippi Territory was a province of Great Britain. In 1779 a patriot by the name of James Willing led attacks along the Mississippi, confiscating and destroying property belonging to the British. The significance of this action foreshadows later events that led to the Spanish taking control of British West Florida. Primary source material regarding these events may be uncovered through the British Provincial records found in the Mississippi Department of Archives and History. Of special interest is the Fifth Series (covering America and the West Indies), 582-97. Another helpful source from the National Archives is the Oliver Pollack Papers from Record Group 360, Records of the Continental Congress. These records were obtained in London through the British Public Record Office. For a better understanding of the period, see Robert V. Haynes, *The Natchez District and the American Revolution* (Jackson, Miss.: University Press of Mississippi, 1976).

Veterans of the Revolutionary War pioneered their way into this land, and some can be traced through *Family Records: Mississippi Revolutionary Soldiers,* published by the Mississippi Society of the DAR. Information found here is not considered official proof but does offer good leads to what may otherwise have been lost. This publication does have errors, but it is well indexed. Because Mississippi was not part of the United States at the time, the Mississippi Department of Archives and History has no official Revolutionary War records on file. The grave registrations, however, include Revolutionary soldiers who are buried in Mississippi (see Cemetery Records).

War of 1812. Research about the War of 1812 in Mississippi should begin with Eron O. M. Rowland's article, "Mississippi Territory in the War of 1812," found in volume four (Centenary Series) of Dunbar Rowland, ed., *Publications of the Mississippi Historical Society* (Jackson, Miss.: the society,

1921). The Mississippi Department of Archives and History has available copies of National Archives microfilm of both index and service records for Mississippians who served in this war. In addition, grave registrations should be checked (see Cemetery Records).

Mexican War. For an overview of the Mexican War as it related to Mississippi, see Lynda J. Lasswell, "First Regiment of Mississippi Infantry in the Mexican War" (master's thesis, Rice University, 1969). National Archives microfilm of Mississippians' service records for the war is available at the Mississippi Department of Archives and History, along with Mississippi grave registrations (see Cemetery Records).

Civil War. Of particular value are the chapters in Rowland's *Military History...* (see Background Sources). They include the numerical listing of the state's units that served in the army of Northern Virginia, and the other listing of those that served in the Western Theater of Operations, Army of Tennessee. For a publication citing original materials pertaining to the Civil War, see Patti Carr Black and Maxyne Madden Grimes, comps., *Guide to Civil War Source Material in the Department of Archives and History, State of Mississippi* (Jackson, Miss.: Mississippi Department of Archives and History, 1962).

National Archives microfilm of Mississippi Confederate military records, which include both muster rolls and some pension applications, are found at the Mississippi Department of Archives and History. The military record gives the name, rank, and organization of Mississippi soldiers who served in the Confederate States Army; the pension application, made by the veteran or widow of a veteran, gives more genealogical data. There is also a listing of Union volunteers from Mississippi. All of these compilations are indexed. The state archives also has a microfilm copy of "Selected Records of the War Department Relating to Confederate Prisoners of War, 1861–1865," which is part of the War Department Collection of Confederate Records, Record Group 109.

Some county courthouses conducted and kept an enumeration of confederate soldiers in 1907. The Vicksburg National Military Park, Park Historian, 3201 Clay St., Vicksburg, MS 39183-3495, has a listing of all known Union soldiers buried in their National Military Cemetery along with some family members who were buried there after 1866. This list is available at the park and at the Old Courthouse Museum in Vicksburg. Confederate soldiers are buried at the Cedar Hill Cemetery, whose office has recorded lot purchasers beginning in 1840 and has a listing arranged alphabetically by state of Confederate soldiers buried there. Inquiries may be addressed to P.O. Box 150, Vicksburg, MS 39180.

Later Wars. With privacy restrictions placed on some later military records, availability becomes more difficult. Some records found in the Mississippi Department of Archives and History include World War I records (which include an alphabetical typescript index of Mississippi veterans). The National Archives—Southeast Region (see page 12) has World War I draft registration cards. The state's archives has an alphabetical index to Mississippi soldiers who fought in the Korean Conflict (Record Group 33), and in Official Records, Mississippians killed in World War I, World War II, the Korean Conflict, and the Vietnam Conflict. Grave Registrations for those buried in Mississippi include the following wars: Revolutionary War, War of 1812, Indian Wars, Mexican War, Civil War, Philippine Insurrection, World War I, World War II, and the Korean Conflict. Though helpful, the source is not exhaustive.

Periodicals, Newspapers, and Manuscript Collections

Periodicals

A selected listing of genealogical and historical periodicals for Mississippi includes the following:

Publications of the Mississippi Historical Society (1898–1914), published by the society (see Archives, Libraries, and Societies). Additional publications from the society continued to 1925 before *The Journal of Mississippi History* (1939-present), P.O. Box 571, Jackson, MS 39205, published by the organization, began.

Family Trails (1977–90), published quarterly by the Historical and Genealogical Association of Mississippi (see Archives, Libraries, and Societies).

Mississippi Coast Historical and Genealogical Society Quarterly (1968-present), P.O. Box 513, Biloxi, MS 39533.

Mississippi Genealogical Exchange (1955–87), P.O. Box 16609, Jackson, MS 39211.

Mississippi Genealogy and Local History (1969–70; 1974–79).

There are many good periodicals and newsletters published by local historical societies throughout the state. A listing of these organizations is kept at the Mississippi Department of Archives and History. Nancianne Parkes Suber offers valuable information through her newspaper genealogical column "Family Trees," which appears weekly in the state newspaper *Clarion-Ledger*.

Newspapers

More than 2,000 newspaper titles have been published in Mississippi since the first paper, the *Mississippi Gazette*, appeared in Natchez in 1799. With the completion of the Mississippi Newspaper Project, a grant initiated by the Mississippi Department of Archives and History and funded by the National Endowment for the Humanities, surviving titles were identified,

located, and microfilmed for preservation and research purposes. General bibliographic information was gathered along with detailed holdings data for courthouses, museums, and all types of libraries throughout the state. This information may be accessed through OCLC, a national online database found in many public and academic libraries (see page 12), or through the *Mississippi Union List of Newspapers* (Jackson, Miss.: Mississippi Department of Archives and History, 1990). See also George Lewis's reference guide, *Mississippiana: Union List of Newspapers* (Jackson, Miss.: Mississippi Library Commission, 1971).

Since newspapers record documented events including births, deaths, and marriages, they are a source that should not be overlooked by researchers. Some have been indexed in Betty Couch Wiltshire, *Marriages and Deaths from Mississippi Newspapers, 1837–63*, vol. 1 (Bowie, Md.: Heritage Books, 1987); *1801–50*, vol. 2 (ca. 1989); and *1813–50*, vol. 3 (ca. 1989); vol. 4 (1850–61); *Mississippi Newspaper Obituaries, 1862–75* (Carrolton, Miss.: Pioneer Publishing Co., 1994); vol. 2 (1876–85). Furthermore, some titles of newspapers are the only surviving documentation of the existence of a community or town.

Manuscripts

The Private Manuscript Collection found at the Mississippi Department of Archives and History consists of private papers from the 1700s to the present donated to the archives by families and individuals. Genealogical information is scattered throughout the collection; however, access can be a problem. The in-house finding aid is arranged alphabetically by title, which is usually the name of the donor, and contains a brief description of the papers. This narrative can also be searched online by using key words. The types of materials located consist of letters, business papers, plantation journals, diaries, church and minute books and records, and even school and bank reports. The photograph collection encompasses some 50,000 images and portraits, architecture, scenes, and events. The WPA county collection is also found here. Access is provided through a card file arranged alphabetically by subject.

Archives, Libraries, and Societies

Mississippi Department of Archives and History
P.O. Box 571
200 North Street
Jackson, MS 39201
www.mdah.state.ms.us

Major holdings of the department are outlined in its 1977 catalog, compiled by Tomas W. Henderson and Ronald E. Tomlin, *Guide to the Official Records in the Mississippi Department of Archives and History*, which lists collections by record group

number and itemizes county records available on the premises in microfilm form. Holdings acquired since 1977 have been described in the archives' annual and biennial reports. Some records are restricted (for example, those of the insane asylums and charity hospitals), but an archivist will usually provide a copy of available data on a specific individual. The department offers online finding aids and indexes that include newspapers on microfilm, film collections, personal records (manuscripts), the biographical index, and the cemetery index. See <www.mdah.state.ms.us/arlib/find.html>.

Mississippi Historical Society
200 North St.
Jackson, MS 39201
www.mdah.state.ms.us/admin/mhistsoc.html

Historical and Genealogical Association of Mississippi
618 Avalon Rd.
Jackson, MS 39206

Mississippi Genealogical Society
P.O. Box 5301
Jackson, MS 39296-5301

L.W. Anderson Genealogical Library
William Carey College
P.O. Box 1647
Gulfport, MS 39502
www.wmcarey.edu

Lauderdale County Department of Archives and History
P.O. Box 5511
Meridian, MS 39302
www.lauderdalecounty.org/archivespage2.htm

University of Southern Mississippi
McCain Library and Archives
Hattiesburg, MS 39410
www.lib.usm.edu

Among the largest holdings in the state of printed sources, not limited to Mississippi specifically, are located here.

Millsaps College
Millsaps-Wilson Library
1701 N. State St.
Jackson, MS 39210
www.library.millsaps.edu/library

Mississippi College
Mississippi Baptist Historical Collection
Leland Speed Library
101 West College St.
P.O. Box 4047
Clinton, MS 39058
www.mc.edu/campus/library

Mississippi State University, Special Collections

P.O. Box 5408
Mississippi State, MS 39762-5408
www.library.msstate.edu

Microfilm of the collection's newspapers is available through interlibrary loan.

University of Mississippi, Archives and Special Collections

John Davis Williams Library
University, MS 38677
www.olemiss.edu/depts/general_library/files/archives

A general summary of the holdings found in the above institutions is found in the publication compiled and edited by Sandra E. Boyd and Julia Marks Young, *Mississippi's Historical Heritage: A Directory of Libraries, Archives, and Organizations* (Hattiesburg, Miss: Society of Mississippi Archivists, 1990). The publication provides an alphabetical listing of institutions by county, their current address, and a general summary of published and unpublished historical materials.

A directory of Mississippi libraries with listings by category and place can be found online at <www.mlc.lib.ms.us/directory/index.htm>.

Special Focus Categories

Immigration

The ports of New Orleans and then Mobile were main ports of entry for those nineteenth-century immigrants who later came to settle in Mississippi. Gulfport, Harrison County, served as port of entry in the twentieth century.

National land passports were issued to those passing through Native American lands or foreign-held land. Occasionally they give a description of the person and an explanation for the reason of passage. For publication of these types of passports pertaining to Mississippi, see Dorothy Williams Potter, *Passports of Southeastern Pioneers, 1770–1823: Indian, Spanish and Other Land Passports for Tennessee, Kentucky, Georgia, Mississippi, Virginia, North and South Carolina* (Baltimore: Gateway Press, 1982).

Naturalization

Before 28 September 1906, all naturalization proceedings took place in any state court. Access to these earlier records may be obtained through the typescript index created by the WPA in 1942, "Index to Naturalization Records in Mississippi Courts, 1798–1906." Preparation of this index involved a massive combing of courthouse records in both chancery and circuit courts that located some material that had previously been considered lost. This index gives information leading to the location of declarations of intention, petitions, and minutes, noting the administration of oaths of allegiance.

Following 1906, the federal district courts conducted all naturalization matters. These records are housed at the National Archives—Southeast Region (see page 12).

African American

Materials previously described in this chapter may be used in African-American genealogical research. In addition, there are other resources for the study of both free and slave African-American families in Mississippi's history. See Vernon L. Wharton, *The Negro in Mississippi, 1865–1890* (Chapel Hill: University of North Carolina Press, 1947) for a classic study of that time period. There are the more specialized collections that are associated with African-American history or genealogy, and then there are areas in scattered collections that reveal a variety of useful information. An extensive compilation of manuscript, photograph, and sound collections found in the state archives is found in Anne L. Webster, *African Americans: A Mississippi Sourcebook* (Carrolton, Miss.: Pioneer Publishing Co., 2001).

A voluminous collection also housed at the National Archives contains the papers pertaining to the Bureau of Refugees, Freedmen, and Abandoned Lands (RG 105), commonly referred to as the Freedman's Bureau Collection. The Mississippi Department of Archives and History has a microfilm copy of these records and has created the only existing index for Mississippi labor contracts found within the collection. This bureau supervised issues relating to refugees, freedmen, and abandoned property. The labor contracts have been digitally indexed by plantation, planter's name, freedman's name, and county. The researcher should be aware of the fact that there were approximately 300,000 freed slaves, but the index provides only 36,000 names. Not all freedmen entered into labor contracts. Another segment of the Freedman's Bureau includes the custody papers of the abandoned property owned by Confederates. Signed loyalty oaths or presidential pardons are held here if the property was restored to an individual.

The researcher should also consider slave enumerations in the federal censuses, the slave schedules of 1850 and 1860, and later censuses when each person in the household was named and "race" indicated. In addition, county records of all kinds reveal some African-American genealogical information interspersed in tax rolls and marriage, probate (some records specifically noting names and ages of slaves in the estate), and court records. The distinction of race, however, was not always marked in some of these records.

Other information may be gathered from school censuses, plantation journals, church records, cemetery records, and even newspapers. For a recently published guide to African-American press materials, see Julius E. Thompson, *The Black Press in Mississippi, 1865–1985: A Directory* (West Cornwall, Conn.: Locust Hill Press, 1988). With an intended historical purpose,

this work directly renders a listing of newspapers, magazines, and newsletters printed by African Americans in Mississippi from 1865 to 1985.

One collection that focuses on the African-American population is the Slave Impressments—Confederacy. These records are located at the National Archives (RG 109) and are hard to access since they are not indexed, microfilmed, or published. For the years 1864 through 1865, this material gives a physical description, identification of the owner, the slave's value, and the date and name of person to whom the slave was sent for work detail.

The WPA ex-slave narrative project has particular genealogical interest. Mississippi was one of several states where the WPA conducted interviews with these freedmen. These interviews have been published (see page 15) and are available at the Mississippi Department of Archives and History. Apart from these narratives, the manuscript collection at the department also contains oral histories of historical as well as genealogical value. Another collection found in the state archives library, with a limited finding aid, is the Alfred Stone Papers, which encompass a large compilation of published materials pertaining to African-American history.

The Newsfilm Collection draws together a more recent historical period of unedited news footage for the years 1954 to 1971. The significance of this collection is found in the documentation of the Civil Rights Movement in Mississippi including events like the arrival of the Freedom Riders, the Capitol Street Boycott, lunch counter sit-ins, demonstrations, James Meredith's enrollment at the University of Mississippi, and the desegregation of schools. The Coleman Library at Tougaloo College near Jackson maintains a significant collection focusing on the history of the Civil Rights Movement in Mississippi. Private papers of some Civil Rights leaders are found here along with papers from the NAACP Legal Defense Fund, the Lawyers Committee for Civil Rights Under Law, and the Lawyers Constitutional Defense Committee.

Another repository of special interest is the University of Mississippi Blues Archives, which houses an extensive collection of historical materials pertaining to the blues. In addition to the recordings there is extensive biographical information on blues musicians including interviews, posters, and photographs.

Native American

Mississippi records relating to Native Americans did not give actual names until the nineteenth century. For a good explanation of the structure of kinship, see Charles M. Hudson, *Southeastern Indians* (Knoxville: University of Tennessee Press, 1976), 185-96. Census records such as the "Armstrong Roll of 1831" (see Census Records) is a good place to begin, along with the papers kept by the Bureau of Indian Affairs (see page 16). The Mississippi Department of Archives and History has some of the Bureau of Indian Affairs records on microfilm. There is also a select collection of genealogical sources located at the Choctaw reservation. Inquiries may be directed to Tribal Historian, Mississippi Band of the Choctaw, Box 6010, Philadelphia, MS 39350.

Treaties are another genealogical source to be considered. See Charles J. Kappler, comp., *Indian Affairs: Laws and Treaties, 1779–1803*, vol. 2. (1904; reprint, New York: Interland Publishing Co., 1972). A valuable source with listings of Choctaw names is found in the master's thesis by Samuel James Wells, "Choctaw Mixed Bloods and the Advent of Renewal" (University of Southern Mississippi, 1987). A copy of the printed form or microfilm may be found at the Mississippi Department of Archives and History. Early native trading post records are found in the papers of Panton, Leslie, and Company, a multi-reel microfilm edition covering 1738–1853, which is available at the archives.

A bibliography of works published on the Choctaw is Clara Sue Kidwell and Charles Roberts, *The Choctaw: A Critical Bibliography* (Bloomington: Indiana University Press, 1960). See also Sharon Sholars Brown, "The Jena Choctaw: A Case Study in the Documentation of Indian Tribal Identity," *National Genealogical Society Quarterly* 75 (September 1987): 180-93, and Arthur H. DeRosier, *The Removal of the Choctaw Indians* (Knoxville: University of Tennessee Press, 1970).

Many records relating to Native Americans were created by early colonial Americans as found in the Provincial Records (RG 24-26—see Provincial Records, below), in the Mississippi Department of Archives and History. However, evidence found in the records provides mostly background understanding of native and colonist relations.

Provincial Records

These original records are divided according to the historical powers that ruled Mississippi during its early development. The French Provincial Records covering the French Dominion date from 1678–1763 and are housed in Paris, France, at the Archives du Ministers du Colonies, Series C13a. A description of these papers may be found in the *Fifth Annual Report of the Mississippi Department of Archives and History, 1905–06*, 61–151. For a translation of these records, see *Mississippi Provincial Archives French Dominion, 1729–1748*, 5 vols. (Baton Rouge: Louisiana State University Press, 1927–84).

The English provincial records, dating from 1763 through 1783, cover the term of British Dominion and are at the British Public Records Office in London. For a listing of these records, see Charles M. Andrews, *Guide to the Materials for American History to 1783 in the Public Record Office of Great Britain*, 2 vols. (Washington, D.C.: Carnegie Institute, 1965).

The Spanish provincial records are located in Seville, Madrid, and Simancas in Spain. Transcripts and microfilm copies

of selections of all of these colonial records are found at the Mississippi Department of Archives and History and are known as the Provincial Records (RG 24–26).

County Resources

Microfilm and original copies of a large, although incomplete, collection of Mississippi county records are in the collection held by the Mississippi Department of Archives and History. Microfilm copies are also generally available through the FHL. Researchers will still want to consult county courthouses for those materials that have either not been transferred or microfilmed, including—but not limited to—marriage licenses, probate files, court records, etc.

In 1798 when Mississippi became a territory, Adams, Pickering, and Washington counties were organized. Pickering was renamed Jefferson in 1802. As new counties were formed in the territory, some counties in both Alabama and Mississippi duplicated names from territorial days. For a visual representation of this county formation problem, see William Thorndale and William Dollarhide, *Map Guide to U.S. Federal Census Records, 1790–1920* (Baltimore: Genealogical Publishing Co., 1987).

Dates in the chart that follows indicate those materials jointly held by the Mississippi Department of Archives and History and the FHL. Known record losses from fires and other causes are indicated.

Deeds, probate records, and marriages may be found at the chancery clerk at the county courthouse. Microfilmed marriage books for both whites and African Americans (see Vital Records) are indicated, in that order, under "Marriages." Court records may be found in the appropriate clerk's office at the courthouse. Updated listing of contact information for county chancery clerks can be found at <www.mslawyer.com/mssc/chanclk.html>

Many sources for Mississippi research are available online and are increasing in quantity through the state's US GenWeb project. <www.rootsweb.com/usgenweb/ms/msfiles.htm> (see page 16).

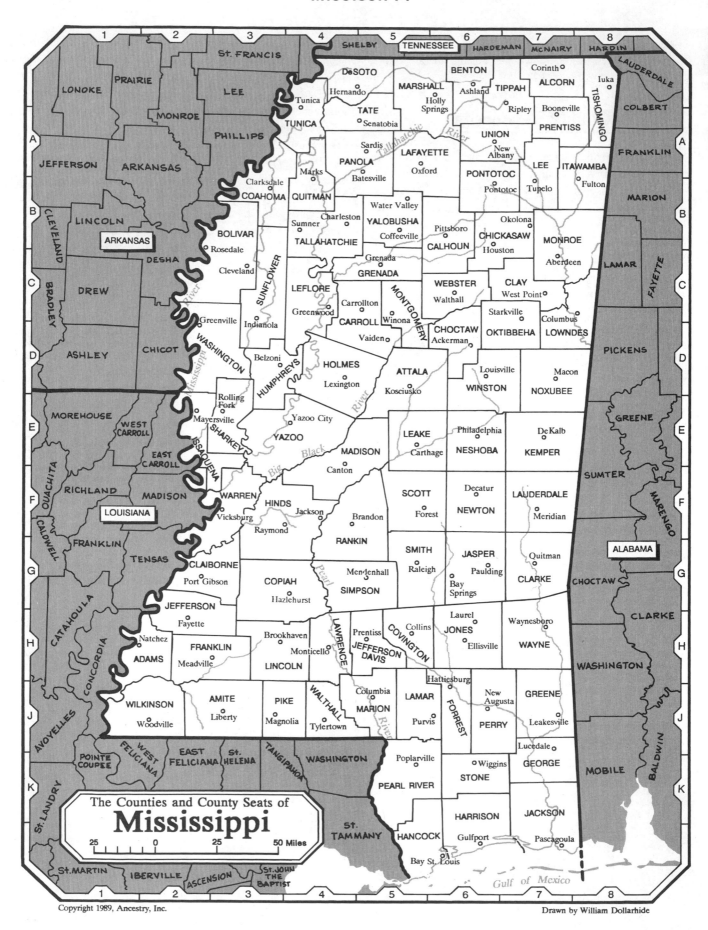

The Counties and County Seats of
Mississippi

25 0 25 50 Miles

Drawn by William Dollarhide

Map	County Address	Date Formed Parent County/ies	Birth Marriage Death	Land Probate Court
H2	Adams Natchez 39120-1008 *Some early records are Spanish.	1799 Natchez District	——— 1802/1866 ———	1780 1800 1701*
A7	Alcorn Corinth 38834-0069 *Record loss, 1917.*	1870 Tippah/Tishomingo	——— 1876/1871 ———	1870 ? 1881
J3	Amite Liberty 39645-0680	1809 Wilkinson	1809/1866	1810 1809 1809
D5	Attala 230 W. Washington St. Kosciusko 39090 *Record loss, 1858 and 1896.*	1833 Choctaw cession, 1830	——— 1892/1892 ———	1858 1858 1858
	Bainbridge	(renamed Covington) Lawrence/Wayne		
A6	Benton Ashland 38603-0218	1870 Marshall/Tippah	——— 1870/1909 ———	1870 1871 ?
B3	Bolivar Rosedale 38769-0698 and Cleveland 38732	1836 Choctaw cession, 1830	——— 1866 ———	1836 1861? 1836
B6	Calhoun Pittsboro 38951-0008 *Record loss, 1922.*	1852 Lafayette/Yalobusha	——— ? ———	? ? ?
D5	Carroll 1 Pinson Sq. Carrollton 38917 and Vaiden 39176	1833 Choctaw cession, 1830	——— 1834/1915 ———	1834 1834 1834
B6	Chickasaw 101 N. Jefferson St. Houston 38851 and Okalona 38860 *Record loss, 1863.*	1836 Chickasaw cession, 1832	——— 1863/1863 ———	1836 1863 1863
D6	Choctaw Ackerman 39765-0250	1833 Choctaw cession, 1830	——— 1881/1881 ———	1880 1879 1881

Record loss, 1888. Chester was the first county seat but suffered several fires. No records from that period extant.

Map	County Address	Date Formed Parent County/ies	Birth Marriage Death	Land Probate Court
G2	Claiborne 410 Main St. Port Gibson 39150	1802 Jefferson	——— 1802/1805 ———	1802 1802 1805
G7	Clarke Quitman 39335-0616	1833 Choctaw cession, 1830	——— 1853/1865 ———	1834 1837 1867?
C7	Clay West Point 39773-0815	1871 (as Colfax; renamed 1876) Chickasaw/Lowndes/Oktibbeha	——— 1872 ———	1872 1872 1872

Map	County Address	Date Formed Parent County/ies	Birth Marriage Death	Land Probate Court
B3	Coahoma 5 First St./P.O. Box 579 Clarksdale 38614 and Friars Point 38631	1836 Choctaw cession, 1830	——— 1849/1849	1839 1856? ?
	Colfax	1871 (renamed Clay, 1876) Chickasaw/Lowndes/Oktibbeha		
G3	Copiah Hazlehurst 39083-0551	1823 Choctaw cession, 1820	1823	1823 1823 1856?
H5	Covington Collins 39428-1679 *Record loss, 1904.*	1819 (as Bainbridge; renamed) Lawrence/Wayne	——— 1904/1904 ———	1853 1854 1857
A4	DeSoto 2535 Hwy. 51 S Hernando 38632 *Record loss, 1940.*	1836 Chickasaw cession, 1832	1845/1866	1836 1836 1854
J6	Forrest Hattiesburg 39401-1310	1906 Perry	1906	1906 1906 ?
H2	Franklin Meadville 39653-0297 *Record loss, 1877.*	1809 Adams	——— 1825/1825 ———	1842* 1842 1836
K7	George 355 Cox St. Lucedale 39452	1910 Greene/Jackson	1910/1910	1910 1910 1910
J7	Greene Leakesville 39451-0460 *Record loss, 1875.*	1811 Amite/Franklin/Wayne	1874/1910	1876 1878 1898
C5	Grenada Grenada 38520-1280	1870 Carroll/Yalobuska/ Choctaw/Tallahatchie	——— 1870/1880 ———	1834* 1870 1870

*Earlier records from parent counties are included.

Map	County Address	Date Formed Parent County/ies	Birth Marriage Death	Land Probate Court
K5	Hancock P.O. Box 429 Bay St. Louis 39520 *Record loss, 1853.*	1812 Mobile District	1853	1853 1853 1853
H6	Harrison P.O. Box CC Gulfport 39501 *Record loss, 1916.*	1841 Hancock/Jackson/Perry	1841/1907	1841 1853 ?
F3	Hinds Raymond 39154-0686 and Jackson 39201	1821 Choctaw cession, 1820	1870/1871	1870 1823 1854*

*Index and partial records begin 1854 with fragments earlier.

Map	County Address	Date Formed Parent County/ies	Birth Marriage Death	Land Probate Court
D4	Holmes Lexington 39095-0239	1833 Yazoo	1884	1833 1833 ?

Map	County Address	Date Formed Parent County/ies	Birth Marriage Death	Land Probate Court
D3	Humphreys Belzoni 39038-0547	1918 Holmes/Washington/ Yazoo/Sunflower	—— 1918? ——	1918? 1918? 1918?
E2	Issaquena Mayersville 39113-0027	1844 Washington	—— 1866	1843 1849 1849
B8	Itawamba Fulton 38843-0776	1836 Chickasaw cession, 1832	—— 1837 ——	1836 1854 1854
K7	Jackson Pascagoula 39567-0998 *Record loss, 1875.*	1812 Mobile District	—— 1875	1875 1874 1875
G6	Jasper Paulding 39348-1047 and Bay Springs 39422 *Indexes available for earlier dates. Record loss, 1932.*	1833 Choctaw cession, 1830	—— 1906/1906	1904* 1904*
H2	Jefferson Fayette 39069-0145 *Record loss, 1904.*	1799 (as Pickering; renamed 1802) Natchez District	—— 1805/1869 ——	1798 1805 1802
H5	Jefferson Davis Prentiss 39474-1137	1906 Covington/Lawrence	—— 1906/1906	1906 1906 1906
H6	Jones Ellisville 39437-1468 and Laurel 39440 *Record loss.*	1826 Covington/Wayne	—— 1882/1888	1828 1894 1857
E7	Kemper DeKalb 39328-0188 *Record loss, 1882.*	1833 Choctaw cession, 1830	—— 1912/1912 ——	1881 1881 1881
A5	Lafayette Oxford 38655-1240	1836 Chickasaw cession, 1832	—— 1850/1876	1836 1836 1836
J5	Lamar Purvis 39475-1240 *Includes former Marion County records. Record loss, 1934.*	1904 Marion/Pearl River	—— 1903 ——	1836* 1901 ?
F7	Lauderdale Meridian 39301-1587	1833 Choctaw cession, 1830	—— 1839/1870	1837 1849 1856
H4	Lawrence Monticello 39654-1160 *Record loss.*	1814 Marion	—— 1818/1910 ——	1815 1836 1815
E5	Leake Carthage 39051-0072	1833 Choctaw cession, 1830	—— 1836 ——	1834 1852 1844
B7	Lee Tupelo 38801-1785	1866 Itawamba/Pontotoc	—— 1867/1867 ——	1867 1867 1867
C4	Leflore Greenwood 38930-0250 *Includes records from parent counties.*	1871 Carroll/Sunflower/Tallahatchie	1844/1894 ——	1837* 1845* ?
H3	Lincoln Brookhaven 39601-555	1870 Franklin/Lawrence/ Copiah/Pike/Amite	1893/1893	1894 1893 ?
D7	Lowndes Columbus 39701-1364	1830 Monroe	—— 1830/1881 ——	1830 1830 1837
F4	Madison Canton 39046-0404	1828 Yazoo	1830	1828 1828 1828
J5	Marion 215 Broad St., Columbia 39429	1811 Amite/Wayne/Franklin	—— 1812/1908	1821? 1812 1812
A5	Marshall Holly Springs 38635-0219 *Two early deed books missing.*	1836 Chickasaw cession, 1832	1836	1856* 1836 1839
B7	Monroe Aberdeen 39730-0578	1821 Chickasaw cession, 1816	—— 1821 ——	1821 1825 1825
C5	Montgomery Winona 38967-0071 *Record loss, 1903.*	1871 Carroll/Choctaw	1891/1901	1871 1872 1872
E6	Neshoba 401 Beacon St. Philadelphia 39350	1833 Choctaw cession, 1830	—— 1877/1895	1835 1837 1859
F6	Newton Decatur 39327-0068 *Record loss, 1877 and 1910*	1836 Neshoba	—— 1872/1876 ——	1876 1876 1876
D7	Noxubee Macon 39341-0147	1833 Choctaw cession, 1830	—— 1834/1834 ——	1834 1834 1834
D7	Oktibbeha 101 E. Main St. Starkville 39759 *Record loss, 1880.*	1833 Choctaw cession, 1830	—— 1861/1861 ——	1834 1880 1836
A4	Panola 151 Public Sq. Sardis 38666 *Record loss, 1886.*	1836 Chickasaw cession, 1832	—— 1871/1884 ——	1836 1845 1836
K5	Pearl River Poplarville 39470-0569	1890 Hancock/Marion	—— 1890/1909 ——	1890 1899 1890
J6	Perry New Augusta 39462-0198 *Record loss, 1877.*	1820 Greene	—— 1877/1892	1862 1889 ?
	Pickering	1799 (renamed Jefferson, 1802) Natchez District		

380

Map	County Address	Date Formed Parent County/ies	Birth Marriage Death	Land Probate Court
J4	Pike 218 E. Bay St. Magnolia 39652 *Record loss, 1882.*	1815 Marion	—— 1882/1882 ——	1882 1882 1002
B6	Pontotoc Pontotoc 38863-0209	1836 Chickasaw cession, 1832	—— 1849/1880 ——	1836 1836 1872?
A7	Prentiss Booneville 38829-0477 *Earlier deeds from parent county. Record loss, 1912.*	1870 Tishomingo	—— 1870 ——	1836* 1870 1872
B4	Quitman 230 Chestnut St. Marks 38646	1877 Panola/Coahoma/Tunic/ Tallahatchie	—— 1877/1877 ——	1877 1878 1878
F4	Rankin 305 Government St. Brandon 39042	1828 Hinds	—— 1828 ——	1824 1828 1819
F5	Scott Forest 39074-0630	1833 Choctaw cession, 1830	—— 1872/1865 ——	1835 1835 1867?
E3	Sharkey Rolling Fork 39159-0218	1876 Washington/Issaquena	—— 1876 ——	1876 1877 1877
G4	Simpson Mendenhall 38114-0637 *Plat (Tract) book from 1832. Record loss, 1840, 1872.*	1824 Choctaw cession, 1820	—— 1872/1872 ——	1872* 1872 1872
G5	Smith Raleigh 39153-0160 *Record loss, 1892, 1915.*	1833 Choctaw cession, 1830	—— 1912 ——	1892 1893 ?
K6	Stone Wiggins 39577-0007 *Records not on microfilm.*	1917 Harrison	—— ? ——	1917? 1917? 1917?
	Sumner	1874 (renamed Webster, 1882) Montgomery/Choctaw		
C3	Sunflower Indianola 38751-0998 *Record loss, 1870.*	1844 Bolivar/Washington	—— 1871/1871 ——	1817* 1884 1844
B4	Tallahatchie Charleston 38921-0350 *and* Sumner 38957 *Record loss at Sumner, 1908.*	1830 Choctaw cession, 1830	—— 1856/1880 ——	1835 1834 1841
A4	Tate 201 S. Ward St. Senatobia 38668 *Transcripts from parent counties available.*	1873 Marshall/Tunica/DeSoto	—— 1873/1873 ——	1873* 1873 1873
A6	Tippah Ripley 38663-0099 *Record loss, 1863.*	1836 Chickasaw cession, 1832	—— 1858/1888 ——	1836 1855 1849
A8	Tishomingo 1008 Battleground Dr. Iuka 38852	1836 Chickasaw cession, 1832	—— 1842/1866 ——	1036 1836 1856
A4	Tunica Tunica 38676-0639	1836 Chickasaw cession, 1832	—— 1858 ——	1836 1839 1839
A6	Union New Albany 38652-0847 *School Commissioner Minutes 1846–59. Record loss, 1882.*	1836 Pontotoc/Tippah	—— 1878/1892 ——	1872 ? ?
J4	Walthall Tylertown 39667-0351	1914 Marion/Pike	—— 1914/1914 ——	1913 1913 1913
F3	Warren Vicksburg 39180-0351	1809 Natchez District	—— 1846/1860 ——	1810 1810 1810
D2	Washington Greenville 38701-0309	1827 Warren/Yazoo	—— 1891/1858 ——	1828 1839 ?
H7	Wayne 609 Azalea Dr. Waynesboro 39367 *Record loss, 1892.*	1809 Washington	—— 1881 ——	? 1879 ?
C6	Webster Walthall 39771-0398	1874 (as Sumner; renamed 1882) Montgomery/Choctaw	—— 1874/1909 ——	1873 1874 1879
J1	Wilkinson Woodville 39669-1284	1802 Adams	—— 1804/1823 ——	1803 1808 1822
D6	Winston Louisville 39339-0069	1833 Choctaw cession, 1830	—— 1834/1908 ——	1835 1834 1856
B5	Yalobusha Water Valley 38965-0664 *and* Coffeeville 38922	1833 Choctaw cession, 1830	—— 1847/1866 ——	1834 1834 1834
E4	Yazoo Yazoo City 39194-1106	1823 Choctaw cession, 1820	—— 1845 ——	1824 1834 1867?

Missouri

MARSHA HOFFMAN RISING, CG, FUGA, FASG
AND PAMELA BOYER PORTER, CGRS, CGL

Missouri became the twenty-fourth state with its admission to the Union on 10 August 1821. Its central location, navigable waterways, and variable terrain attracted settlers from every part of the country as well as from abroad. Missouri was settled by people from New England, the Ohio Valley, the Appalachian region, and the upper South, as well as from Germany and other European nations.

Four major migrations influenced Missouri's settlement. The first began during Spanish and French control when each encouraged American settlement due to their fear of British encroachment. A colony came with Colonel George Morgan and settled near New Madrid. This is known as the first distinctly American settlement. In 1797 Moses Austin helped develop a sizable settlement at Mine au Breton, and in 1798 Daniel Boone was offered 1,000 arpents of land if he would move to Missouri and bring new settlers with him. This group settled in 1798 in what is now the area of St. Charles County. That same year a group of German-Swiss from North Carolina settled near the Whitewater Creek bottoms in present-day Cape Girardeau and Bollinger counties.

The second wave of settlers came with the acquisition of the territory by the United States in 1803. The population of the state grew from 10,000 people in 1804, to over 65,680 by 1821 when the state was admitted to the Union. During this time period, boundaries were changing rapidly, and the researcher will find it necessary to follow these changes in order to locate required records.

The third major wave was from 1820 through 1860 when the Ohio-Mississippi-Missouri river system and the extension of the Cumberland Road to the Mississippi River brought thousands of immigrants from the upper South and lower Midwest into Missouri, pushing the frontier to the Kansas border. Kentucky contributed the largest number of settlers during this period, followed by Tennessee, Virginia, Ohio, Indiana, and Illinois. The mountaineers from middle or east Tennessee and North Carolina were especially attracted to the Ozarks. Many of the Missouri and Mississippi river settlements were established by Southerners who maintained their political sympathies, attitudes about slavery, and Democratic politics. They settled along the Mississippi River well north of St. Louis and across the Missouri Valley. Kentucky contributed a large proportion of settlers to the middle prairie regions, while the people from Ohio, Indiana, and Illinois concentrated along the northern border and the Mississippi River. During this period, Germany also contributed a large number of settlers who settled in St. Louis and along the river counties to the west.

The researcher working in this time and place should also be familiar with the rapidly changing county boundaries and names. Much of the land purchased during this period was through the federal land offices located in strategic positions throughout the state. The first land offices were established in 1818 at Jackson, Franklin, and St. Louis.

Immigration, for all intents and purposes, came to a standstill during the Civil War; but with peace, the fourth wave of settlers arrived. With the help of the railroads, Europeans as well as pioneers from the prairie states of Ohio, Indiana, Illinois, and Iowa provided the major portion of newcomers. Northerners outnumbered Southerners nearly two to one. They occupied

most of the remaining land north of the Missouri River, along the Kansas border, and along the Osage and Springfield plains. During this period the cities of St. Louis, Kansas City, Joplin, Springfield, and Jefferson City also grew rapidly. By 1890 the population of Missouri had reached 2,679,185.

Vital Records

No vital records were kept on the state level before 16 August 1909. For birth records filed after that date, requests should be made to Missouri Department of Health and Senior Services, Bureau of Vital Records, P.O. Box 570, Jefferson City, MO 65102. The 2004 search fee for a birth record was $15, which includes one certified copy of the record, if found. The Bureau of Vital Statistics also maintains certificates of Missouri deaths less than fifty years old. A $10 search fee includes one certified copy of the death record, if found. The application for copies of birth or death certificates can be downloaded from the Missouri Vital Records website at <www.dhss.mo.gov/BirthAndDeathRecords/birthdeath.pdf>.

A 2004 House bill transferred all death records more than fifty years old to the Missouri State Archives. Plans are to digitize the more than two million certificates and eventually to make them available online. For the latest information about access to death records in the care of Missouri State Archives, see <www.sos.mo.gov/archives/resources/birthdeath/>

A non-compulsory birth registration law was adopted in Missouri in 1863 and provided that county recorders of deeds could record births upon request. These births are recorded in the regular deed books (or in marriage books) and are not indexed. Registration was sporadic.

In the city of St. Louis, deaths were recorded from 1850–1910 and births from 12 July 1870 through 1910. It is estimated that only about 60 percent of the births and deaths that occurred during this period were recorded. These St. Louis City birth and death registers have been microfilmed and are available through Missouri State Archives. Certified birth or death certificates from 1870 to the present in the City of St. Louis can be requested by writing to St. Louis City Vital Records/Recorder of Deeds, City Hall, Room 126, 1200 Market St., St. Louis, MO 63103. Request forms are available for download from <www.stlouis.missouri.org/citygov/recorder/vitalrecords.html>. The fee in 2004 was $10. Kansas City also has intermittent early birth and death records (1874–1910). The 2004 fee was $3 per search and $3 per copy, and the address for inquiry is Kansas City Vital Records, 2400 Troost Ave., Ste. 1200, Kansas City, MO 64108. For more information, see the website at <www.kcmo.org/health.nsf/web/birth?opendocument>.

In 1883 Missouri passed a state law requiring the recording of births and deaths at the county level. Ten years later this law was inadvertently repealed. At any rate, compliance was poor. Most counties do have these registers, but there is enormous variation as to how complete and/or comprehensive they are. "A Guide to Public Vital Statistics Records in Missouri" (deaths) was published in the Missouri State Genealogical Association Journal in the fall issue of 1984. The Historical Records Survey, Guide to Public Vital Statistics in Missouri (St. Louis: Historical Records Survey, 1941), will also aid the researcher.

The ongoing volunteer Missouri Birth and Death Records Database project abstracts births, stillbirths, and deaths recorded before 1909 and places them online at <www.sos.state.mo.us/archives/resources/birthdeath>. Many of these records are also available on microfilm through Missouri State Archives (see Archives, Libraries, and Societies) and the Family History Library (FHL) in Salt Lake City.

Some indexes or abstracts of Missouri vital records, including St. Louis death records (1850–1908), are online at Ancestry.com (see page 17). Many of these early county vital records have been microfilmed and are available through the Missouri State Archives or the FHL.

Marriage records are held by the county recorder of deeds. Prior to 26 June 1881, no marriage license was required; the marriage was recorded at any convenient courthouse.

Divorce records are held by the clerk of the circuit court of the county in which the divorce occurred, except in the City of St. Louis, where they are held by the City Circuit Court Clerk, Civil Courts Building, 10 N. Tucker Blvd., St. Louis, MO 63101; and in Kansas City by the Civil Records Department, Jackson County Courthouse, 415 E. 12th St., Kansas City, MO 64106.

Certified statements of marriage or dissolution of marriage from 1 July 1948 to the present can be ordered from the Bureau of Vital Records, P.O. Box 570, Jefferson City, MO 65102. The $10 fee includes a search for one five-year period. For more information see the bureau's website (address above). Certified copies of marriage or divorce records can be obtained only from the appropriate recorder of deeds or circuit clerk office.

Census Records

Federal

Population Schedules
- Indexed—1830, 1840, 1850, 1860, 1870, 1880, 1900, 1910, 1920, 1930
- Soundex—1880, 1900, 1910, 1920

Industry and Agriculture Schedules
- 1850, 1860, 1870, 1880

Mortality Schedules
- 1850, 1860, 1870, 1880

Slave Schedules
- 1850, 1860

Union Veterans Schedules
- 1890 (all except Daviess and Dekalb counties; some inadvertently included Confederate veterans)

The censuses for the years 1810 and 1820 are lost for all districts. All the remaining population censuses (except for 1890) have survived. The State Historical Society of Missouri in Columbia (see Archives, Libraries and Societies) holds microfilmed copies of all available federal population censuses for Missouri and will make available censuses through 1880 to Missouri residents on interlibrary loan. Mid-Continent Public Library in Independence also holds microfilmed copies of all federal censuses and Soundexes for Missouri and will loan these to Missouri libraries. The Missouri State Archives (see Archives, Libraries, and Societies) holds microfilmed copies of all federal censuses for Missouri including the Soundex. The Missouri State Archives knows of no state copies of the federal population schedules that survived the capitol building fire of 1911. It does hold the original federal supplement to the 1880 population census, which enumerated the "defectives, delinquents, and dependents." Called Supplemental Schedules Numbers 1–7, this part of the census enumerated those labeled "Insane, Idiots, Deaf-mutes and Blind, Homeless Children, Prisoners, Paupers and Indigents." Institutions were inventoried as well as private households. Since the county or state listed was the one of legal residence, the listing for the inhabitants of various institutions will give their last residence before moving into the institution. The Missouri Historical Society in St. Louis has the original agriculture, industry, slave, and mortality schedules. The State Historical Society of Missouri in Columbia has microfilmed copies of these supplemental schedules.

Territorial and State

Censuses were taken during the territorial period in 1814, 1817, and 1819, but only statistical summaries remain. There are listings of heads of families of New Madrid for 1797 and 1803. Heads of families were enumerated for St. Charles in 1817 and 1819 only. Some of the early Spanish censuses of Upper Louisiana have been retrieved from the archives in Seville, Spain, and were published in Louis Houck's *The Spanish Regime in Missouri*, 2 vols. (Chicago: R.R. Donnelley and Sons, 1909). This publication is an excellent documentary history of the time period between 1770 and 1804.

Although Missouri conducted a number of state censuses, most of the individual schedules are lost; only the statistical abstracts remain. The state did compile a census corresponding to the 1840 U.S. census. Nine of those enumerations survived the capitol building fire of 1911. These are for the counties of New Madrid, Newton, Pike, Randolph, Ray, Shelby, Stoddard, Warren, and Rives (now Henry). The originals are located in the Missouri State Archives. A few listings remain for the state censuses of 1844, 1852, 1856, and 1868. Most of these are statistical abstracts only. The state census of 1876 exists for about one-fifth of Missouri's counties. The originals of many censuses remain in the counties, but microfilmed copies have been made by Missouri State Archives and can be searched at its facility. Schulyer County took a special census in 1880. These censuses are not individual enumerations, but by age group similar to the federal population schedules before 1850. They include the number of deaf, dumb, blind, insane, as well as the number of livestock and some agricultural items.

A query using the term "census" in the Missouri State Archives local records inventory database (<www.sos.mo.gov/CountyInventory/index.asp>) will determine extant state censuses for each county. Bear in mind that Missouri State Archives has not completed inventories of all counties, so this database is incomplete.

Background Sources

The following publications will be helpful to the Missouri researcher:

Parrish, William E., gen. ed. *A History of Missouri*. 5 vols. Columbia, Mo.: University of Missouri Press, 1971–97.

Gerlach, Russell L. "Population Origins in Rural Missouri," *Missouri Historical Review* 71 (October 1976): 1-21.

———. *Settlement Patterns in Missouri: A Study of Population Origins, with a Wall Map*. Columbia: University of Missouri Press, 1986.

Houck, Louis. *History of Missouri: From the Earliest Explorations and Settlements until the Admission of the State Into the Union*. 3 vols. Chicago: R.R. Donnelley and Co., 1908.

March, Daniel. *The History of Missouri*. 4 vols. New York: Lewis Historical Publishing Co., 1967. Volumes 3 and 4 contain personal and family records.

Meyer, Duane. *The Heritage of Missouri*. Columbia, Mo.: University of Missouri Press, 1967.

Ohman, Marian M. "Missouri County Organization, 1812–1876," *Missouri Historical Review* 76 (April 1982): 253-81.

———. *A History of Missouri's Counties, County Seats, and Courthouse Squares*. Columbia, Mo.: University of Missouri-Columbia Extension Division, 1983.

Porter, Pamela Boyer and Ann Carter Fleming. *Research in Missouri*. Arlington, Va.: National Genealogical Society, 1999. One of the *NGS Research in the States Series*.

Schroeder, Walter A. *Bibliography of Missouri Geography.* Columbia, Mo.: University of Missouri-Columbia Extension Division, 1977. An excellent annotated listing of geographic materials including atlases. A must for the serious researcher.

Shortridge, James R. "The Expansion of the Settlement Frontier in Missouri," *Missouri Historical Review* 75 (October 1980): 64-90.

Maps

One of the best publications for Missouri maps is Milton D. Rafferty, *Historical Atlas of Missouri* (Norman, Okla.: University of Oklahoma Press, 1981). Detailed county maps showing cemeteries, houses, churches, schools, and all county roads are available from the Missouri Department of Transportation, Transportation Planning, 2217 St. Mary's Blvd., Jefferson City, MO 65102. The cost is minimal. Ward maps of St. Louis and Kansas City have been microfilmed by the National Archives and are available at National Archives facilities or major research facilities.

Other maps that will be helpful to the Missouri researcher are:

Campbell, R. A. *Gazetteer of Missouri.* St. Louis: R.A. Campbell, 1874.

Ramsey, Robert L. *Our Storehouse of Missouri Place Names.* 1952. Reprinted. Columbia, Mo.: University of Missouri Press, 1991.

Selby, Paul O. "A Bibliography of Missouri County Histories and Atlases," 2d ed. Kirksville, Mo.: *Bulletin of the Northeast Missouri State Teachers* College. Vol. 66, No. 12 (1966.)

Wetmore, Alphonso. *Gazetteer of the State of Missouri.* St. Louis: C. Keemle, 1837.

Land Records

Public Domain State

Land in Missouri was granted by the three nations of France, Spain, and the United States. The original papers, as well as microfilmed copies, of the Spanish and French land grants are retained by the Missouri State Archives. Recording by the United States government of clear land titles granted by the Spanish and French governments actually began in St. Louis on 16 September 1805. An index to the land grants was published privately by Betty Harvey Williams in 1977 as *Index to French and Spanish Land Grants Recorded in Registers of Land Titles in Missouri, Books A, B, C, D, E.* The St. Louis Genealogical Society published *Index to the Minutes of the first and second Board of Land Commissioners, Missouri, 1805–1812 and 1832–1835* (1981; reprint, St. Louis: St. Louis Genealogical Society, 1998). The original minutes are housed in the Missouri State Archives.

Two good printed sources that describe the attempts to settle the early land conflicts are *Missouri Land Claims* (1835; reprint, New Orleans: Polyanthos, 1976) and Walter Lowrie, *Early Settlers of Missouri as Taken From Land Claims in the Missouri Territory* (1834; reprint, Easley, S.C.: Southern Historical Press, 1986). The former publication, beginning in 1812, is the 1832 report from the Commissioner of the General Land Office (GLO) to the 24th Congress. The latter publication contains records compiled and indexed from the *American State Papers.*

The United States began granting land in Missouri from its Land Offices in 1818. For a brief history of locations and land policies in Missouri, see "Missouri's Public Domain: United States Land Sales, 1819–1922," *Archives Information Bulletin,* vol. 2, no. 3 (July 1980), produced by the Office of the Missouri Secretary of State. An *Index of Purchasers of U.S. Land Sales in Missouri, 1818–1846* (vols. 1-3) and *Springfield Land Office Abstracts, 1835–1846,* can be obtained from the Ozarks Genealogical Society, P.O. Box 3945, Springfield, MO 65808. The original records of the United States Land Sales have been microfilmed on seventeen rolls and are located in Record Group 5 at the Missouri State Archives. A complete name index is on each roll. They are available for purchase at $15 per reel.

If the researcher knows the land description of the property of interest, copies of the original land patents granted by the United States government can be obtained from United States Department of the Interior, Bureau of Land Management, Eastern States Land Office (see Introduction). A search of the Bureau of Land Management General Land Office Records online database <www.glorecords.blm.gov> can provide the information needed to order land entry files from NARA (see pages 11-12).

The Missouri State Archives also holds other land records of interest to the genealogical researcher: an alphabetical index to War of 1812 military lands of north Missouri; the Savannah Land Grant Pre-emption Grants from 1845 through 1857 (indexed); the Platte Purchase records (with an index available at the archives); the Land Office Reports, microfilmed copies of *American State Papers,* volumes 1 through 8; and the United States General Land Office Reports, 1828–59. Other records of interest, which are indexed, include the township school lands, seminary lands, saline lands, and swamp lands, all of which were patented by the state.

Each county has a recorder of deeds. Here the researcher can expect to find the direct and indirect index to deeds, a transcript

of deeds, warranty deeds, administrator's deeds, quit claim deeds, sheriff's deed records, index to mortgages, mortgages, school fund mortgage records, chattel mortgages, deeds of trust, patent records, plat books, the index to marriage records, marriage records, applications for marriage licenses, records of certificates of marriage, records of marriage of persons of color (from 1865 to the twentieth century in separate registers), and military discharge papers. Note that in Missouri, all marriage records are held by the recorder of deeds (see Vital Records section).

Probate Records

These are retained at the county level although many have been microfilmed by the Genealogical Society of Utah, in cooperation with the Missouri State Archives and the Missouri Supreme Court. Fortunately for the genealogist, a special emphasis is placed on microfilming the estate files. One can expect to find an index to probate court papers, court records, executor's bonds, letters of testamentary, inventories, sale bills, guardian and curators' records, and court appointments. Usually the probate minute books, probate court records, and case files are also available. The researcher can check for the application letters for administration, executors and guardians, administrators and guardian's bonds, appraisement of estate, names and oaths of witnesses, sale bills, settlement records, orders of publication, term docket books, wills, and records of wills. A searchable index for St. Louis City probate files from 1802 to 1900 is available online at Missouri State Archives at <www.sos.mo.gov/archives/stlprobate>. In addition, St. Louis probate case files up to 1865 have been digitized and are available as .pdf files on this same website.

Court Records

Clerk of the County Court. In this office in each county is located an index to common pleas, records of all extant proceedings, chancery minute books, records of births and deaths, county court records, right-of-way and road records, as well as surveyor's records (including field notes and plats made by the county surveyor). This office usually holds the county treasurer's notes, bonds and commissions, records of marks and brands, wolf scalps, stray notices, real estate assessments, and tax books. The researcher needs to be aware that in some counties, early terms for this court included "Chancery" or the "Court of Common Pleas."

Clerk of the Circuit Court. This office holds the direct index to records such as divorces, debt, dissolution of partnerships, adoptions, judgment, and tax fee books, including direct and indirect indexes. It also retains the index to criminal records and criminal files of the circuit court. Adoptions are under the jurisdiction of the circuit court. Naturalization records, including petitions, declarations of intention, certificates, certificates

of allegiance, and granting of citizenship are also located in the clerk's office, as well as an index to civil case files. Some naturalization records have been found with the deeds.

The strategic location and history of St. Louis make it truly a gateway to many American families. To aid researchers in locating specific cases or subjects, the Missouri State Archives and the American Culture Studies Program at Washington University in St. Louis cooperated to produce an online searchable database of all St. Louis Circuit Court cases—civil, criminal, and chancery actions—that have been archivally processed (currently 1808–32, with a few selected cases after 1832). To read about the St. Louis Circuit Court Historical Records Project or search its database, see the website at <www.stlcourtrecords.wustl.edu>.

Federal records that pertain to Missouri citizens are located at the National Archives—Central Plains Region (see page 12). The U.S. circuit and district court records beginning as early as 1822 include case file indexes, records books, dockets, and judgment books that have been microfilmed.

Tax Records

The Missouri Historical Society has some original tax records; others can be found in the Western Historical Manuscript Collection at the University of Missouri, but most extant records remain in the office of the clerk of the county court. The Missouri State Archives has microfilmed some tax records. A researcher can determine which county tax records exist by searching the Archives Local Records Inventory Database <www.sos.mo.gov/CountyInventory> and then looking at the Archives Roll-by-Roll Listing by County <www.sos.mo.gov/archives/resources/county/croll.asp> to find out if the records are available on microfilm.

Prior to 1850, purchasers of the federal lands in Missouri were exempt from land taxes for five years after purchase. If one finds an ancestor on a Missouri tax list with livestock, etc., but no land being taxed, the individual may have purchased his land from the government within the preceding five years.

Some early delinquent tax lists were sent to the state auditor's office and are now located in the Capitol Fire Documents held by the Missouri State Archives (see Manuscripts below).

Cemetery Records

The following national cemeteries are located in Missouri:

Springfield National Cemetery, 1702 E. Seminole St., Springfield, MO 65804. The names of all known soldiers buried there, including those transferred from towns throughout southwest Missouri, were published in *Ozar'kin*, published by the Ozarks Genealogical Society in the four issues of volume 8 (1986). There is also an online index to burials at <www.interment.net/data/us/mo/greene/springnat>.

Jefferson Barracks National Cemetery, 2900 Sheridan Rd., St. Louis, MO 63125 <www.cem.va.gov/nchp/jeffersonbarracks. htm>. A computerized grave locater kiosk is available at the cemetery's Administration Building, and an online index to burials is available at <www.interment.net/data/us/mo/stlouis/jeffbarr>.

Jefferson City National Cemetery, 1024 E. McCarty St., Jefferson City, MO 65101. The researcher may contact Jefferson Barracks National Cemetery for information, or access an online index to burials at <www.interment.net/data/us/mo/cole/ jeffcitynat>.

Missouri State Veterans Cemetery in Higginsville, 20109 Business Hwy. 13, Higginsville, MO 64037. An incomplete index of burials can be found online at <www.interment.net/data/us/ mo/lafayette/vets>.

Missouri State Veterans Cemetery in Springfield, 5201 S. Southwood Rd., Springfield, MO 65804. Researchers can find an incomplete online index at <www.interment.net/data/us/mo/ greene/vets>.

St. James Missouri Veterans Home Cemetery, 620 N. Jefferson, St. James, MO 65559. This cemetery includes burials from the Civil War era forward.

Missouri State Veterans Cemetery in Bloomfield, 17357 Stars and Stripes Way, Bloomfield, MO 63825. Information about this cemetery that opened in October 2003 can be found online at <www.mvc.dps.mo.gov/Cems/Bloom_Home.htm>.

Missouri State Veterans Cemetery in Jacksonville, 1479 County Road 1675, Jacksonville, MO 65260. See <www.mvc. dps.mo.gov/Cems/Jacks_Home.htm> for information about this newer cemetery that opened in 2003.

There is no central registry for cemeteries located in Missouri. The Daughters of the American Revolution (DAR) have compiled and published numerous inscriptions of cemeteries throughout the state. Many of these records have been microfilmed and are available through the Family History Library. Elizabeth Gorrell Kot's and Shirley Pugh Thomson's *Missouri Cemetery Inscription Sources: Print and Microfilm* (Vallejo, Calif.: Indices Publishing, 1995) includes FHL microfilm and microfiche numbers.

An Index to the Cemetery Locations in the Missouri Ozarks is available from the Ozarks Genealogical Society (see Land Records for address) for $20. The publication covers a forty-one-county area south of the Missouri River, listing over 5,000 cemeteries by name and location.

Church Records

Church records that have been microfilmed by the Missouri State Archives can be located by searching for the term "church records on microfilm" in the archives' online catalog at <www. msa.library.net>. Church microfilm rolls are not available for purchase, without written consent of the individual church, and must otherwise be used at the Missouri State Archives. The

Western Historical Manuscript Collection at the University of Missouri campuses located in Columbia, St. Louis, Rolla, and Kansas City holds some church records. These can be located by using the online catalog of the relevant collection (see Manuscripts). The Western Historical Manuscript Collection–Columbia also holds photographs and histories of churches throughout the state, which were gathered in the Missouri Extension Homemakers Association's "Sacred Stones and Stained Glass Project." Most church records in Missouri are scattered and remain in private hands.

Military Records

The best source for these records is the Missouri State Archives. Many of the records previously held by the Office of the Adjutant General have been transferred, from the War of 1812 up through World War II. Service records are indexed and maintained for the following wars: War of 1812, Indian Wars (1832–38), Seminole War (1837) Mormon War (1838), Iowa or Honey War (1839), Mexican War (1846–47), and Civil War—both Union and Confederate. Confederate pension applications and application for admission to the Confederate Homes are also among these holdings. Accumulated files number approximately one-half of the reported 40,000 men who served from Missouri. Alphabetical indexes for the Spanish-American War (1898) are also extant. An online searchable database of information extracted from service cards of more than 500,000 Missourians who served in the military from territorial times through World War I is available at <www.sos.mo.gov/archives/soldiers>. Record Group 133 includes World War II Reports of Separation, arranged alphabetically. Records subsequent to World War I remain in the Office of the Adjutant General, Archives, 2302 Militia Dr., Jefferson City, MO 65101.

The Loyalty Oaths (often called "The Ironclad Oath") administered after the Civil War can sometimes be located in local historical societies, county offices, in manuscript collections (see below), or among various record groups of Missouri State Archives. An index to the Missouri portion of the National Archives' microfilmed *Union Provost Marshals' File of Papers Relating to Individual Citizens* is available online at <www.sos. mo.gov/archives/provost>. These papers, dated from 1861 to 1866, include some oaths of allegiance to the United States, correspondence, provost marshal court papers, orders, passes, paroles, transportation permits, and claims for compensation for property used or destroyed by the military. Researchers can check the online index and then contact the State Archives for information about obtaining copies of the microfilmed records.

A list of the Revolutionary War soldiers buried in Missouri is not complete, but was published in the *Missouri State Genealogical*

Society Quarterly, vol. 5 (1985), nos. 3 and 4; and vol. 6, no. 2. The known 1812 soldiers buried in Missouri were published in the same quarterly, vol. 6, nos. 1 and 2.

Periodicals, Newspapers, and Manuscript Collections

Periodicals

Statewide and locally, many genealogical periodicals are published in Missouri. Both the *Missouri Historical Review* and the *Missouri State Genealogical Association Journal* cover the state on a broader spectrum. Indexes for *Missouri Historical Review* from its inception in 1906 to July 1976 are available for purchase from the State Historical Society of Missouri. Active local organizations can be contacted regarding their current publications as well as activities. To determine available material of a local nature, refer to the *Directory,* published by State Historical Society of Missouri (see Archives, Libraries, and Societies below).

Newspapers

The State Historical Society of Missouri in Columbia holds the most complete newspaper collection. The earliest extant is the *Missouri Gazette* (1808–14), which has been microfilmed. The society periodically updates and publishes *Missouri Newspapers on Microfilm at the State Historical Society of Missouri,* available from the society for $14. The society will loan its microfilmed newspapers through the interlibrary loan system.

Several early newspapers have been abstracted for their genealogical material. These include *The Liberty Tribune, The Springfield Advertiser, The St. Louis Christian Advocate, Death Records from Missouri Newspapers, 1810–1857, Death Records of Missouri Men,* and *Death Records of Missouri Pioneer Women.* These have been privately published and are available in many libraries.

The State Historical Society of Missouri in Columbia has indexed some of its newspapers, particularly those located in the Mid-Missouri geographic area. Newspapers that are indexed are listed on the society's website at <www.system.missouri.edu/shs/newscardfiles.html>. Those researching a topic or an ancestor may contact the society to request a copy of the list of index roll numbers needed to order the appropriate roll of index cards through interlibrary loan. Missouri Historical Society in St. Louis has a unique obituary clippings collection that began more than one hundred years ago. This collection concentrates on newspapers published in the eastern part of the state. St. Louis Public Library offers an online index to obituaries in St. Louis newspapers <www.slpl.lib.mo.us/libsrc/obit.htm> from 1880 to 1921, 1942 to 1945, and 1992 to 2002, with other years being added periodically. The St. Louis Mercantile Library (see

Archives, Libraries, and Societies) holds the clipping file of the now-defunct *St. Louis Globe-Democrat* newspaper.

Manuscripts

The University of Missouri Western Historical Manuscript Collection (WHMC) at Columbia and the State Historical Society of Missouri created a joint collection of manuscript holdings in 1963, which is located at 23 Ellis Library, University of Missouri, Columbia, MO 65201. In 1968, branches of the Western Historical Manuscript Collection were created at University of Missouri campuses in Kansas City, Rolla, and St. Louis. WHMC-Columbia houses the records of the Missouri Historical Records Survey (1936–42), available on microfilm, which includes transcriptions of early court records. Each WHMC collection focuses primarily on a Missouri region—Columbia on Mid-Missouri, Kansas City on western Missouri, Rolla on southern Missouri and the Ozarks, and St. Louis on the eastern area. Collections include frontier and pioneer life, genealogy, travel and description, women, architecture, and many other topics. WHMC-Columbia maintains a card-file index of collections at all four branches. Indexes to the holdings of any or all of the branches can be searched online at <www.system.missouri.edu/whmc/search.html>. The records that survived the devastating fire of the capitol building in 1911 were combined into a collection at the State Historical Society of Missouri called the Capitol Fire Documents, which has been indexed and microfilmed. The collection consists of 13 reels of the index and 242 reels of documents. The original records and microfilmed copies are in the Missouri State Archives. The State Historical Society in Columbia has a copy of all the film.

The House and Senate journals are also in the Missouri State Archives. They have been microfilmed and are available for on-site research or purchase. Items of interest in the records of the General Assembly are private acts, early divorces, petitions, compensation for individuals, etc.

Federal records that pertain to Missouri citizens are located at the National Archives—Central Plains Region at 2306 E. Bannister Rd., Kansas City, MO 64131. Various Missouri federal records and finding aids are described online at <www.archives.gov/facilities/mo/kansas_city/holdings.html> in *Guide to Archival Holdings at NARA's Central Plains Region (Kansas City).*

Archives, Libraries, and Societies

Missouri Historical Society Library and Research Center
225 S. Skinker Blvd.
P.O. Box 11940
St. Louis, MO 63112
www.mohistory.org

The Missouri Historical Society was founded in 1866, and since that time has been collecting published and manuscript

materials focusing on the history of St. Louis, the state of Missouri, and the nineteenth-century American West. The collections include notable holdings regarding the colonial and territorial periods, the American fur trade, western travel and exploration, steamboats and river transportation in the Mississippi Valley, the Civil War, and the 1904 St. Louis World's Fair. Much of the library's catalog is now accessible online at the website. In addition, the library's on-site "Information File" indexes numerous local published sources, and the Archives Card Catalog indexes the manuscript collections.

State Historical Society of Missouri

1020 Lowry St.

Columbia, MO 65201

www.system.missouri.edu/shs/

Located in the Ellis Library, University of Missouri–Columbia, this is a public institution that holds federal population censuses, newspapers, county histories, genealogies, city directories and county atlases in its wide collection. A former print publication of the society entitled *Directory of Local Historical Societies, Museums, and Genealogical Societies in Missouri* is now being maintained online at <www.system.missouri.edu/shs/DirectoryMap.htm>. The directory lists addresses, hours, special collections, and publications of these various organizations, most of which exist on a county level and publish their own materials.

Missouri State Archives

P.O. Box 1747

Jefferson City, MO 65102

www.sos.mo.gov/archives

Located at 600 West Main in Jefferson City, this is the official repository for state materials. The archives has an extensive microfilm collection of county records (see County Resources below). In addition to original records, it houses some county histories, cemetery records, genealogies, and other published local records. The Research Room and Online Resources website at <www.sos.mo.gov/archives/resources/resources.asp> provides information about the records it holds and its online resources, including a searchable catalog.

Mercantile Library

Thomas Jefferson Library Bldg.

8001 Natural Bridge Rd.

St. Louis, MO 63121

www.umsl.edu/mercantile

Now located on the campus of University of Missouri—St. Louis, Mercantile Library was formed in 1846. It houses an excellent rare book and manuscript collection emphasizing Western Americana, travel and exploration, and Missouri history. The Herman T. Pott National Inland Waterways Library and the John W. Barriger III National Railroad Library reside within the Mercantile Library.

Mid-Continent Public Library Genealogy and Local History Branch

317 W. 24 Hwy

Independence, MO 64050

www.mcpl.lib.mo.us/branch/ge/

This impressive genealogy and history collection includes microfilm and textual research materials for Missouri and surrounding states. More than 6,000 genealogy and local history books are available nationwide by interlibrary loan through Mid-Continent's circulating collection.

St. Louis County Library

1640 S. Lindbergh Blvd.

St. Louis, MO 63131

www.slcl.org/slcl/sc/index.html

Special Collections contains holdings of the St. Louis Genealogical Society and the National Genealogical Society as well as the genealogical and local history materials of St. Louis County Library. The 20,000-plus books of the National Genealogical Society's circulating collection are available by interlibrary loan to the general public through their local libraries.

Missouri State Genealogical Association

P.O. Box 833

Columbia, MO 65205

www.mosga.org

This is the statewide genealogical organization, although many counties have their own local genealogical societies. MoSGA publishes the *Missouri State Genealogical Association Journal* on a quarterly basis.

National Park Service

Wilson Creek National Battlefield Park

Springfield, MO 65807

Mailing address: 6424 West Farm Rd. 182

Republic, MO 65738-9514

www.nps.gov/wicr

An excellent new and expanded Civil War library opened in April 2003 and is available to the public Tuesday through Saturday.

St. Louis Genealogical Society

P.O. Box 43010

St. Louis, MO 63143

www.stlgs.org

The largest genealogical society in the state with 2900 members, the society hosts a well-attended annual conference, monthly meetings, and Computer Interest Group meetings that are open to the public. Its library is housed in the St. Louis County Library (see above). The society office at 4 Sunnen Dr., Ste. 140, St. Louis, MO, also holds some resources.

Special Focus Categories

Territorial Records

Many of the best sources for the early time period of Missouri history are inventoried in *Genealogical Research: Methods and Sources*, vol. 2, revised edition published by the American Society of Genealogists in 1983. Many of the colonial records are housed in the Missouri Historical Society in St. Louis (see Archives, Libraries and Societies). Most of the early civil records and manuscripts concerning early colonial and St. Louis families are also there. The Chouteau Papers, which include the records of the American Fur Trading Company, and the papers of the French and Spanish colonial archives are just two of the society's major holdings. Real estate transactions from the St. Louis colonial archives were copied, in both French and English, into volumes maintained by the recorder of deeds in St. Louis. These volumes are indexed and microfilmed copies are available at the Missouri State Archives (see Archives, Libraries, and Societies). The researcher may also be assisted by the three-volume Historical Records Survey publication, *Early Missouri Archives* published in 1941.

Original and microfilmed copies of the French and Spanish Land Grant papers are held at the Missouri State Archives. The papers have been partially indexed (see Land Records). A must for pre-statehood research is *Index to the Minutes of the first and second Board of Land Commissioners, Missouri, 1805–1812 and 1832–1835* (1981; reprint, St. Louis: St. Louis Genealogical Society, 1998).

The Missouri State Archives holds microfilmed copies of the early court records of Randolph County, Illinois; the Kaskaskia Manuscripts (1718–1841); as well as the Randolph County Circuit Clerk papers. Copies of the Cahokia Parish Records, now St. Clair County, Illinois (1784–1809), are also held by the Missouri State Archives. Many of the early settlers traveled back and forth across the Mississippi River with great ease and may have recorded marriages and baptisms with whichever priest or county office was in the area in which they were trading or visiting. The researcher should check in both Missouri and Illinois for records of these early pioneers.

Two sources helpful to the genealogist working in this time period are *The American State Papers: Documents Legislative and Executive of the Congress of the United States*, 38 volumes, indexed in *Grassroots of America*, edited by Philip W. McMullen and published in 1972 by Gendex Corporation in Salt Lake City. The genealogist will be particularly interested in the section that pertains to public lands. The researcher should also consult Clarence Edwin Carter's *The Territorial Papers of the United States*, vol. 13, Territory of Louisiana-Missouri, 1803–06, vol. 14 1806–14, Territory of Missouri, vol. 15, 1815–21 (Washington; General Services Administration, 1951). All are indexed. These publications are located in major genealogical and historical collections as well as most university libraries.

The Missouri Judicial Records collection at the State Archives includes case files and papers of hearings before the Territorial Court (1804–20) and the Missouri Supreme Court (1821-present). A microfilmed index is available at the archives. Most of the records have not been microfilmed but they are available for on-site use. The state supreme court database online at <www.sos.mo.gov/archives/judiciary/supremecourt> indexes and abstracts criminal and civil court cases that were appealed to the territorial and state Supreme Court of Missouri up to 1857, and a partial listing of cases to 1871. Other territorial records available at the Missouri State Archives are found in Record Group 1, Territorial Records of Louisiana and Record Group 2. These consist of some early tax lists, licenses for fur traders, and other miscellaneous records.

African American

Although Missouri was a slave-holding state, the geography determined where slaves were present in significant numbers. The slave population was distributed along the Mississippi and Missouri rivers. The greatest concentration was in the area called "Little Dixie" because it was settled by Southerners before the Civil War. The core area of "Little Dixie" includes the present-day counties of Howard, Cooper, Boone, Callaway, Audrain, Randolph, Monroe, Ralls, and Pike. The best general history for Missouri's African-American population is Lorenzo J. Greene, Gary R. Kremer, and Anthony F. Holland, *Missouri's Black Heritage* (1980; reprint, Columbia, Mo.: University of Missouri Press, 1993). The slave schedules for 1850 and 1860 for Missouri are extant and available on microfilm through the National Archives (see pages 11-12).

County Resources

County records are retained at the local county level. The Missouri State Archives is making an extensive effort to microfilm many of these county records. A microfilm reel entitled *A Roll by Roll Listing of County Records on Microfilm* is available from the Missouri State Archives, or it can be viewed at the State Archives website <www.sos.mo.gov/archives/resources/county/croll.asp>. This enables the researcher to ascertain the exact number of the reel desired. Microfilmed copies of county records are currently available at $15 per roll. Instructions and an order form can be accessed at <www.sos.mo.gov/forms/archives/arch1.pdf>.

An ongoing project of the Missouri Local Records Preservation Program compiles inventories of local records by county. The searchable Local Records Inventory Database can be found at the state archives website <www.sos.mo.gov/CountyInventory/index.asp>.

Note that in Missouri all marriage records are held by the

recorder of deeds, even though they are listed here with other vital records sources. The year given is the earliest recorded, but there was no official requirement until 1881. Those birth and death records that do exist before statewide recording began in 1909 are held at the clerk of the county court in the county seat. The time period these cover is indicated below.

A Missouri State Archives Birth and Death Records Database at <www.sos.mo.gov/archives/resources/birthdeath> abstracts births, stillbirths, and deaths recorded before 1909 at the county level that are available on microfilm at the archives.

Dates given in the chart are the earliest ones for which records are held in a particular category. The researcher should be aware that this does not mean all records in that category are extant. For instance, there may be letters of administration for a county as early as 1833, but the guardianships may not begin until 1845, nor are all the early records indexed. A ~

before the date indicates that the date could not be established. A * indicates that records for this county and time period are incomplete.

Dates for available records were verified with the state archives website listing "Guide to County and Municipal Records on Microfilm" at <www.sos.mo.gov/archives/resources/county/croll.asp>. These were cross-checked with the Local Records Inventory Database <www.sos.mo.gov/CountyInventory/index.asp> and the Birth and Death Records Database <www.sos.mo.gov/archives/resources/birthdeath/>. When these dates conflicted, the county courthouse was contacted.

Correspondence may be addressed to the recorder of deeds, probate clerk, clerk of the circuit court, or clerk of the county court at the county courthouse as indicated below. Street addresses are necessary for some larger counties.

The Counties and County Seats of
Missouri

25   0   25   50   75 Miles

Drawn by William Dollarhide

Map	County Address	Date Formed Parent County/ies	Birth Marriage Death	Land Probate Court
D1	Adair 100 W. Washington Kirksville 63501 *Courthouse burned 1865.*	1841 Macon	1883–93 1841	1841 1841 1841
B1	Andrew Savannah 64485	1841 Platte Purchase	1883–95 1841 1883–93	1841 1841 1841
	Arkansas	1806 (abolished 1819; became Arkansas Territory) New Madrid		
B1	Atchison 400 S. Washington Rock Port 64482	1845 Platte Purchase/Holt	1883–93 1845 1883–93	1845 1845 1845
D5	Audrain 101 N. Jefferson Mexico 65265	1836 Callaway/Monroe/Ralls	1883–86 1837 1883–86	1837 1837 1837
H3	Barry 700 Main Cassville 65625	1835 Greene	1883–85 1837 1883–85	1835 1835 1872
G2	Barton 1004 Gulf Lamar 64759 *Courthouse burned 1862.*	1855 Jasper	1883–96 1866 1883–99	1857 1866 1866
E2	Bates 1 N. Delaware Butler 64730 *Courthouse burned 1861.*	1841 Van Buren (now Cass)	1883–1907 1860 1883–93	1839 1845 1858
E3	Benton 316 Van Buren Warsaw 65355 *State census of 1876.*	1835 Pettis/Greene	1883–90 1839 1883–90	1837 1836 1835
G7	Bollinger 204 High St. Marble Hill 63764 *Courthouse burned 1866, 1884.*	1851 Cape Girardeau/Madison/ Stoddard/Wayne	1883–91 1865 1883–92	1851 1866 1866
D5	Boone 801 E. Walnut Columbia 65201	1820 Howard	—— 1821 ——	1821 1821 1821
C1	Buchanan St. Joseph 64501	1838 Platte Purchase	—— 1839 1883–93	1839 1839 1839
H7	Butler Poplar Bluff 63901	1849 Wayne	1883–93 1878 1883–93	1849 1849 1849
C2	Caldwell Kingston 64650 *Courthouse burned 1860, 1896.*	1836 Ray	—— 1860 ——	1835 1856 1859
D5	Callaway Fulton 65251 *State census of 1844 and 1876.*	1820 Boone/Howard/ Montgomery	1883–88 1821 1883–88	1821 1821 1821
F4	Camden 1 Court Cir. Camdenton 65020 *Courthouse burned 1902. Some deeds were re-recorded in 1902.*	1841 (as Kinderhook; renamed 1843) Benton/Morgan/Pulaski	—— 1902 ——	1849 1902 1902
G8	Cape Girardeau 1 Barton Sq. Jackson 63755 *State census 1868 and 1876. Almost all county records up to 1990 are now in custody of the Cape Girardeau County Archive Center, 112 E. Washington, Jackson, MO 63755 <www.showme.net/CapeCounty/archive/>.*	1812 original	1883–93 1805 1883–93	1805 1805 1815
C3	Carroll 8 S. Main Carrollton 64633	1833 Ray	1883–85 1833 1883–90	1833 1833 1833
H6	Carter Van Buren 63965	1859 Oregon/Reynolds/Ripley/ Shannon	—— 1861 ——	1845 1859 1866
E2	Cass Harrisonville 64701 *State census of 1876.*	1835 (as Van Buren; renamed 1849) Jackson	1883–1903 1836 ——	1837 1835 1835
F3	Cedar Stockton 65785	1845 Dade/St. Clair	1883–89 1845 1883–86	1845 1845 1845
C4	Chariton 306 S. Cherry St. Keytesville 65261 *County Court records burned 1861; courthouse burned 1864, 1973.*	1820 Howard	1883–87 1821 1883–87	1826 1861 1820
G3	Christian 100 W. Church St. Ozark 65721 *Courthouse burned 1865; state census of 1876.*	1859 Greene/Taney/Webster	1840–1904 1866 1883–84	1861 1864 1865
	Clark	1818 (abolished 1819 when it became part of Arkansas Territory)		
B5	Clark (present) 111 E. Court St. Kahoka 63445 *Records incomplete. Birth records extant for 1830–40 and 1883–92 only.*	1836 Lewis	1830–92; 1836 1883–92	1833 1836 1837
D2	Clay Administration Bldg. Liberty 64068	1822 Ray	1883–84 1822 1883–84	1822 1821 1822
C2	Clinton 207 N. Main Plattsburg 64477 *Records incomplete. Birth records extant for 1863–79 and 1883–88 only.*	1833 Clay	1863–88; 1847 1883–88*	1833 1833 1836
E5	Cole 311 E. High Jefferson City 65101	1820 Cooper	1883–1906 1821 1883–1906	1821 1834 1821
D4	Cooper 200 Main St. Boonville 65233	1818 Howard	1883–94 1819 1883–89	1819 1819 1821

Map	County Address	Date Formed Parent County/ies	Birth Marriage Death	Land Probate Court
F6	Crawford 302 Main Steelville 65565 *Death records extant for 1883–91 and 1942–43. Courthouse burned 1873, 1884.*	1829 Gasconade	1879–1903 1829 1883–91*	1832 1832 1831
G3	Dade Greenfield 65661 *Courthouse burned 1863.*	1841 Barry/Polk	1883–85 1863 1883–85	1841 1841 1846
F4	Dallas 102 S. Cedar St. Buffalo 65622 *Courthouse burned 1863, 1864, 1867, 1955.*	1841 (as Niangua; name changed 1844) Polk	1883–1908 1867 1883–1924	1867 1867 1867
C2	Daviess 102 N. Main Gallatin 64640 *State census of 1876.*	1836 Ray	1883–91 1837 1883–91	1838 1890 1837
	Decatur	(see Ozark; name changed from Ozark 1843; changed back to Ozark 1845)		
C2	DeKalb 109 W. Main Maysville 64469 *Death records extant for 1883–91 and 1942–43. Courthouse burned 1878.*	1845 Clinton	1883–93 1845 1883–91*	1836 1877 1856
F6	Dent 400 N. Main Salem 65560 *Courthouse burned during Civil War and 1866; earlier deeds recreated.*	1851 Crawford/Shannon	1883–84 1851 1883–84	1851 (1866) 1866 1866
	Dodge	1849/50 (abolished 1853; see Putnam)		
H4	Douglas Ava 65608 *Courthouse burned 1882, 1886.*	1857 Ozark	—— 1877 1886–94	1858 1886 1886
J8	Dunklin Court Sq. Kennett 63857 *Courthouse burned during Civil War and 1872; deeds 1872–76 recreated.*	1845 Stoddard	—— 1872 ——	1859 1865 1872
E6	Franklin 300 E. Main Union 63084 *State census of 1876.*	1818 St. Louis	1862–92 1819 ——	1819 1819 1819
E6	Gasconade 119 E. First St. Hermann 65041	1820 Franklin	1867–96 1822 1883–96	1821 1825 1821
B2	Gentry 200 W. Clay St. Albany 64402 *Courthouse destroyed by windstorm 1883. Incomplete sporadic records before 1885.*	1845 Clinton	1883–93 1885 1883–93	1885* 1885* 1885*
G3	Greene 940 Boonville Springfield 65802 *Courthouse burned 1861; state census of 1844 and 1876.*	1833 Crawford/Wayne	1883–1901 1833 1883–1902	1833 1830 1833
B3	Grundy 700 Main St. Trenton 64683 *Records incomplete. Birth records extant for 1847–66 and 1883–93 only.*	1841 Livingston	1847–93* 1841 1883–93	1841 1863 1841
B2	Harrison 1505 Main St. Bethany 64424 *Courthouse burned 1874.*	1845 Daviess	1883–89 1845 1883–93	1845 1853 1845
	Hempstead	1818 (abolished 1819; became part of Arkansas Territory) New Madrid		
E3	Henry Clinton 64735	1834 (as Rives; renamed 1841) Lillard (now Lafayette)	1883–90 1835 scattered	1835 1834 1835
F3	Hickory Hermitage 65668 *Courthouse burned 1852, ~1860, and 1881.*	1845 Benton/Polk	1883–98 1872 1883–89	1846 1845 1845
B1	Holt 102 W. Nodaway Oregon 64473 *Courthouse burned 1965; state census of 1876.*	1841 (as Nodaway; renamed 1841) Platte Purchase	1883–89 1841 1883–89	1841 1837 1841
D4	Howard 1 Courthouse Sq. Fayette 65248 *Courthouse burned 1886, 1975; state census of 1876.*	1816 St. Charles/St. Louis	1883–93 1816 1883–88	1816 1818 1816
H5	Howell 1 Courthouse West Plains 65775 *Courthouse burned 1866.*	1857 Oregon	1883–95 1867 1883–95	1866 1862 1857
F7	Iron 250 S. Main St. Ironton 63650 *State census of 1876.*	1857 Madison/Reynolds/ St. Francois/Washington/ Wayne	1883–96 1857 1883–87	1814 1857 1857
D2	Jackson 415 E. 12th St. Kansas City 64106 *and* 200 S. Main Independence 64050	1826 Lillard (now Lafayette)	1883–95 1827 1883–93	1827 1828 1828
G2	Jasper 302 S. Main Carthage 64836 *Courthouse burned 1863.*	1841 Barry	1883–1900 1841 1883–97	1841 1841 1841
E7	Jefferson Hillsboro 63050	1818 St. Louis/Ste. Genevieve	1883–92 1825 1883–92	1819 1820 1819
E3	Johnson 300 N. Holden Warrensburg 64093	1834 Lillard (now Lafayette)	1883–94 1835 1883–94	1832 1835 1835
	Kinderhook	1841 (changed to Camden 1843) Benton/Pulaski/Morgan		

Map	County / Address	Date Formed / Parent County/ies	Birth / Marriage / Death	Land / Probate Court
D5	Knox Edina 63537	1845 Scotland	1883–1939 1045 1003–93	1845 1845 1845
F4	Laclede Laclede County Government Center Lebanon 65536	1849 Camden/Pulaski/Wright	1883–93 1855 ——	1849 1848 1845
D3	Lafayette 1001 Main Lexington 64067	1820 (as Lillard; renamed 1825) Cooper	—— 1821 ——	1820 1821 1821
	Lawrence	1815 (abolished 1819; became part of Arkansas Territory) New Madrid		
G3	Lawrence 1 Courthouse Sq. Mt. Vernon 65712 *Courthouse burned 1895.*	1845 Barry/Dade	1883–93 1845 1883–93	1845 1843 1845
B5	Lewis Monticello 63457	1833 Marion	1883–87 1833 1883–87	1833 1833 1833
D6	Lincoln Troy 63379	1818 St. Charles	—— 1825 1883–84	1819 1820 1819
C4	Linn Linneus 64653 *Records incomplete. Birth records extant for 1822–88 and 1907 only.*	1837 Chariton	1822–1907* 1857 1883–87	1836 1840 1837
C3	Livingston 700 Webster St. Chillicothe 64601	1837 Carroll	1883–91 1837 1883–90	1837 1837 1837
H2	McDonald Pineville 64856 *Courthouse burned 1863; deeds before 1863 recreated. State census of 1876.*	1849 (as Seneca) Newton	1856–94 1865 ——	1853 1865 1855
C4	Macon 101 E. Washington Macon 63552	1837 Chariton/Randolph	1883–93 1837 1883–93	1837 1838 1837
G7	Madison 1 Courthouse Sq. Fredericktown 63645	1818 Cape Girardeau/ Ste. Genevieve	1883–1900 1821 1883–1900	1819 1821 1827
F5	Maries 211 Fourth St. Vienna 65582 *Courthouse burned 1868.*	1855 Osage/Pulaski	1883–84 1869 1883 only	1855 1866 1866
C5	Marion Palmyra 63461 *Also births 1927–30 and deaths 1927–30.*	1826 Ralls	1883–90* 1827 1883–89*	1827 1827 1827
B3	Mercer 802 Main St. Princeton 64673 *Courthouse burned 1898.*	1845 Grundy	1883–94 1898 1883–94	1846 1849 1868
E4	Miller 256 High St. Tuscumbia 65082	1837 Cole/Pulaski	1883–91 1837 1883–1904	1837 1837 1837
H8	Mississippi Charleston 63834 *Courthouse burned 1891, 1997.*	1845 Scott	—— 1845 ——	1823 1845 1845
E4	Moniteau California 65018 *State census of 1876.*	1845 Cole/Morgan	1883–94 1845 1883–87	1845 1845 1845
C5	Monroe 300 N. Main Paris 65275 *Courthouse burned 1861.*	1831 Ralls	1883–85 1831 1883–85	1831 1832 1831
D6	Montgomery Montgomery City 63361 *Courthouse burned 1864, 1901; copies of the original early deeds are at Jones Abstract Company in Montgomery City. State census 1876.*	1818 St. Charles	—— 1864 ——	1839 1889
E4	Morgan 100 E. Newton St. Versailles 65084 *Records incomplete. Birth records extant for 1841–63 and 1883–86 only. Courthouse burned 1887.*	1833 Cooper	1841–86 1833 1883–86	1837 1834 1833
H8	New Madrid New Madrid 63869	1812 original	—— 1847 ——	1805 1800 1805
H2	Newton Neosho 64850 *Courthouse destroyed during Civil War.*	1838 Barry	1883–85 1865 1883–85	1839 1839 1939
	Niangua	1841 (renamed Dallas, 1844) Polk		
B1	Nodaway 305 N. Main Maryville 64468	1845 Andrew	1883–90 1845 1883–93	1845 1845 1845
H6	Oregon Alton 65606 *Records incomplete. Marriage records extant for 1845–61 and 1877 only.* †Court records extant for 1845–59 and 1872 only. *Courthouse burned 1863 during Civil War.*	1845 Ripley	1883–90 1845–77* 1883–89	1845 1854 1845–72†
E5	Osage Linn 65051 *Courthouse burned 1880 and 1922; state census of 1876.*	1841 Gasconade	1883–98 1841 1883–94	1841 1841 1841
H4	Ozark Gainesville 65655 *Courthouse burned 1858 or 1859, 1865, 1934, and 1937.*	1841 (renamed Decatur, 1843; renamed Ozark, 1845) Taney	1884–90 1858 1887–89	1858 1865 1858
J8	Pemiscot 610 Ward Ave. Caruthersville 63830 *Courthouse burned 1882. Deed index from 1833 survived fire.*	1851 New Madrid	1883–84 1882 ——	1881 1865 1883

Map County Address	Date Formed Parent County/ies	Birth Marriage Death	Land Probate Court
F8 Perry 321 N. Main Perryville 63775 *State census of 1876.*	1820 Ste. Genevieve	1883—94 1830 1883—94	1821 1821 1821
E3 Pettis Sedalia 65301	1833 Cooper/Saline	1883—85 1833 1883—85	1833 1833 1833
F5 Phelps 200 N. Main Rolla 65401 *State census of 1876.*	1857 Crawford	1883—90 1857 1883—90	1857 1858 1857
C6 Pike Bowling Green 63334 *Courthouse burned 1864 and 1915.*	1818 St. Charles	1883—84 1825	1819 1825 1819
C1 Platte 415 Third St. Platte City 64079 *Courthouse destroyed 1861 during Civil War.*	1838 Platte Purchase	1883—87 1839 1883—87	1839 1839 1839
F3 Polk Bolivar 65613	1835 Greene	1872—1900 1836 1883—90	1837 1835 1836
F5 Pulaski 301 Historic 66 East Waynesville 65583 *Courthouse burned 1903.*	1833 Crawford	—— 1903 ——	1903 1833 1834
B4 Putnam Unionville 63565	1845 Adair/Sullivan	1878—1907 1849 1887—1907	1847 1853 1855
C6 Ralls New London 63459	1820 Pike	1883—93 1821 1883—86	1821 1821 1821
C4 Randolph Huntsville 65259	1829 Chariton/Ralls	1883—89 1829 1883—89	1841 1829 1858
Courthouse burned 1882 and 1955. Deed index from 1829 survived fire.			
D2 Ray Richmond 64085	1820 Howard	1883—90 1820 1883—89	1820 1821 1821
G6 Reynolds Centerville 63633	1845 Shannon	1883—86 1872 1883—86	1872 1872 1872
Courthouse burned 1862, 1871; state census of 1876.			
H7 Ripley Doniphan 63935	1833 Wayne	1883—97 1833 1883—93	1833 1856 1867
Courthouse burned during Civil War and 1898.			
Rives	1834 (see Henry)		
D7 St. Charles 201 N. Second St. P.O. Box 99 St. Charles 63302	1812 original	1867—90 1807 ——	1804 1805 1808
City Clerk has birth and death records 1883—1952.			

Map County Address	Date Formed Parent County/ies	Birth Marriage Death	Land Probate Court
F3 St. Clair 655 Second St. Osceola 64776 *Courthouse burned 1861 and 1864.*	1841 Rives (now Henry)	1883—1903 1855 1883—90	1841 1865 1841
F7 St. Francois Farmington 63640 *State census of 1876.*	1821 Jefferson/Ste. Genevieve/ Washington	1883—93 1836 1883—90	1822 1822 1822
E7 St. Louis (City) 1200 Market St. St. Louis 63103	1804 (1764) (1876 became independent city separate from St. Louis County)	1825—* 1766 1825—*	1766 1766 1766
On August 22, 1876, St. Louis City separated from St. Louis County and began keeping its own records, also retaining all original St. Louis County records before 1876. **Public Vital Records before State Recording: City of St. Louis Vital Records Division, City Health Department, 634 N. Grand Blvd., St. Louis, MO 63103. Some births and deaths were recorded back as far as 1825, but they are far from complete.*			
E7 St. Louis County 41 S. Central Ave. Clayton 63105	1812 original	1883—* 1876— 1883—*	1876 1876 1876
Note that all records of St. Louis County prior to 1876 are held by the City of St. Louis (see listing above). **Public Vital Records before state recording: Vital Records Division, County Health Department, 111 S. Meramec, Clayton, MO 63105.*			
F7 Ste. Genevieve Ste. Genevieve 63670	1812 original	1883—92 1807 1883—92	1804* 1807 1804
State census 1868. *Also Misc. Records (Concessions, Contracts, Deeds, Slave Deeds) 1761— .			
D3 Saline 101 W. Arrow Marshall 65340 *Courthouse burned 1864 during Civil War.*	1820 Cooper	1883—85 1835 1883—85	1821 1821 1821
B4 Schuyler Lancaster 63548 *State census 1880.*	1845 Adair	1883—93 1845 1883—91	1845 1845 1846
B5 Scotland 117 S. Market Memphis 63555	1841 Clark/Lewis/Shelby	1883—89 1841 1883—89	1836 1842 1841
G8 Scott 131 S. Winchester Benton 63736 *State census of 1876.*	1821 New Madrid	1883—86 1840 1883—86	1822 1825 1822
G6 Shannon Eminence 65466 *Courthouse burned during Civil War, 1871, 1895, and 1938.*	1841 Ripley	—— 1881 ——	1859 1869 1872
C5 Shelby Shelbyville 63469 *Courthouse burned 1891.*	1835 Marion	1883—87 1835 1883—87	1835 1836 1835
H8 Stoddard 316 S. Prairie Bloomfield 63825 *Courthouse burned 1864 during Civil War.*	1835 New Madrid	1883—87 1863 1883—86	1835 1835 1835

Map	County Address	Date Formed Parent County/ies	Birth Marriage Death	Land Probate Court
H3	Stone 108 E. Fourth St. Galena 65656	1851 Taney	—— 1851 ——	1854 1848 1851
B4	Sullivan 109 N. Main Milan 63556 *Courthouse burned 1908. *Also birth records 1883–92.*	1845 Linn	1835–71* 1845 1883–99	1845 1849 1845
H4	Taney 266-A Main St. Forsythe 65653 *Courthouse burned 1885.*	1837 Greene	—— 1885 ——	1881 1888 1887
G5	Texas 210 N. Grand Ave. Houston 65483 *Courthouse burned or damaged ~1850, destroyed during Civil War, burned 1881 and 1930. State census of 1876.*	1845 Shannon/Wright	1883–87 1855 1883–90	1843 1870 1858
	Van Buren	1835 (see Cass)		
F2	Vernon 100 W. Cherry Nevada 64772 *Courthouse burned 1863 during Civil War.*	1855 Bates	1883–97 1855 1883–1904	1855 1855 1856
D6	Warren 104 W. Main Warrenton 63383	1833 Montgomery	1883–89 1833 1884–94	1833 1833 1833

Map	County Address	Date Formed Parent County/ies	Birth Marriage Death	Land Probate Court
F6	Washington 102 N. Missouri Potosi 63664 *Records incomplete. Death records extant for 1883–95 and 1974–76 only. Courthouse burned 1907.*	1813 Ste. Genevieve	1883–95 1815 1883–1976*	1813 1813 1819
G7	Wayne 109 Walnut Greenville 63944 *Courthouse burned 1853 or 1854 and 1892; some deeds re-recorded.*	1818 Cape Girardeau/Lawrence	—— 1892 ——	1849 1869 1893
G4	Webster 100 Crittenden St. Marshfield 65706 *Courthouse burned 1863 during Civil War; damaged by tornado 1880. State census of 1868, 1876.*	1855 Greene	1883–93 1855 1883–84	1854 1856 1855
B2	Worth Fourth & Front St. Grant City 64456 *Courthouse burned 1866. State census of 1876.*	1861 Gentry	1883–93 1861 1883–93	1849 1861 1861
B4	Wright 125 Court Sq. Hartville 65667 *Courthouse burned 1862 and 1863 during Civil War and 1896; damaged by tornado in 1888.*	1841 Pulaski	—— 1897 ——	1853 1853 1895

Montana

DWIGHT A. RADFORD

The first wave of migration and settlement into Montana began when gold was discovered in Bannack (1862) and Alder Gulch (1863), south of Butte. Montana became a fusion of frontiers that included settlers who had originally gone to California and Oregon in the 1850s. Settlers from the east, southern-born Civil War veterans, and foreign-born immigrants, including those from Europe and China all arrived in the same time period.

Montana was created as a territory in 1864. The area was formed from Washington Territory west of the Continental Divide and Nebraska Territory east of the Continental Divide. Statehood was granted in 1889.

After 1865, cargo and people destined for the gold camps arrived in Montana by steamboat up the Missouri River. Steamers usually left St. Louis or Sioux City in late March or early April and arrived at Fort Benton, Montana, between May and July. The Mullan Road began in Fort Benton and continued to the mines some 100 to 200 miles away. In 1867 the total number of people entering and leaving Montana by way of the Missouri River and Mullan Road routes was about 5,000.

Beginning in 1869 Montana territorial officials began advertising for settlers. An agent in New York was contracted to print pamphlets on the territory for distribution in Germany and Scandinavian countries. According to the 1870 U.S. census, Montana's population consisted of 18,306 whites, 1,949 Chinese, and 183 African Americans. The estimated Native American population was 19,300. By 1872 the Montana Immigration Society was established in Helena, and by 1875 another immigration society was holding meetings in Bozeman. The agent for Bozeman was commissioned to bring immigrants into Big Horn and Yellowstone counties.

By 1883 the Northern Pacific Railroad was completed. From 1882 to 1883 the railroad sent out 2.5 million pieces of literature advertising land for sale. Immigrants from northern Europe were sought as they could adapt to the climate and conditions of Montana, though only a few came. An English colony was established in Helena and the Yellowstone Valley in 1882; a few French came to Missoula County; and a few Dutch families settled in the Gallatin Valley in 1893. The most notable settlement was that of Finnish lumbermen east of Missoula in 1892. Italians and Germans settled in Fergus and Park counties, and many Germans came from North Dakota and Canada.

The cattlemen of Montana were primarily English and Scottish, although they drove cattle owned by the Germans. The sheepmen were also from the British Isles.

American migrations included 506 individuals from Ripon, Wisconsin. This group of 115 families settled near Billings in 1882. Many southerners came to the state and settled in the Bitterroot Valley. Settlers arriving from Oregon drove cattle.

The smelters and mills of the Anaconda Copper Mining Company in Anaconda and Great Falls at first drew Scandinavian and Irish workers to the area. After 1900 a heavy influx of workers from the Balkan countries arrived. The Montana coal mines of Cascade, Carbon, and Musselshell counties were worked by the Irish, Poles, and Italians.

Vital Records

Prior to 1895 there were no legal requirements for keeping birth records in Montana. In 1895 the Legislative Assembly passed a law requiring all physicians and midwives to keep a register of all births. All pre-1907 birth records are filed with the county clerk in the county where the child was born (see County Resources). Montana began recording births and deaths on the state level in 1907. It was not until about 1915 that mandatory registration of births became more complete. By 1922 about 90 percent of the births were being registered.

The 1895 law governing births also pertained to deaths. At that time the registration of deaths was the responsibility of clergymen, coroners, physicians, sextons, and undertakers. Registration of deaths on the state level began in 1907. By 1910 the registration of deaths reached about 90 percent. It was not until about 1915 that the registration of Montana deaths became reasonably complete.

Certified copies of birth and death certificates dated 1907 and later can be obtained from the Office of Vital Statistics, Montana Department of Health and Human Services, DPHHS Building, 111 N. Sanders, P.O. Box 4210, Helena, MT 59604-4210 <www.dphhs.state.mt.us>. Montana deaths (1954–98) are also indexed at <www.ancestry.com> (see page 17).

Marriage and divorce records are not available through the Office of Vital Statistics. These records may be obtained from the clerk of the district court in the county where the license or decree was issued. Divorces were registered on the state level beginning in July 1943. The Family History Library (FHL) in Salt Lake City has microfilm copies of county marriages.

Census Records

Federal

Population Schedules
- Indexed—1870, 1880, 1900, 1910, 1920, 1930
- Soundex—1880, 1900, 1920

Industrial and Agricultural Schedules
- 1870, 1880

Mortality Schedules
- 1870, 1880

Union Veterans Schedules
- 1890 (indexed)

In 1860 the area of Montana that lies east of the Continental Divide was part of Nebraska Territory. Persons residing in this area were enumerated in the unorganized part of Nebraska Territory. The only exceptions to this were two trading posts, Fort Alexander and Fort Union, which were enumerated with unorganized Dakota. The area of Montana west of the Continental Divide was enumerated as the Bitterroot Valley and the Ponderay Mountains in Spokane County, Washington Territory.

A "census" of miners taken during 1862 to 1863 can be found in "List of Early Settlers: A List of All Persons (Except Indians) Who Were in What Is Now Montana During the Winter of 1862–63, Which Was the First Winter After the Gold Mines of This Region Had Become Noised Abroad," *Contributions to the Historical Society of Montana*, vol. 1. (Helena, Mont.: Rocky Mountain Publishing Co., 1876).

Yellowstone National Park was created in 1872, and all residents of the area were enumerated in the Wyoming census for 1880.

Background Sources

The Montana Historical Society (see Archives, Libraries, and Societies) publishes books that can be valuable historical works. Their "Main Street" series is exceptional in taking one community and recounting its history. In this series towns include historic Virginia City (vol. 1), Glendive (vol. 2), Lewistown (vol. 3), Hamilton (vol. 4), Kalispell (vol. 5), and Missoula (vol. 6).

Burlingame, Merrill G. and K. Ross Toole, eds. *A History of Montana.* 3 vols. New York: Lewis Historical Publishing Co., 1957. Volumes one and two are a history of Montana. Volume three provides valuable biographical sketches.

Brown, Mark H. *The Plainsmen of the Yellowstone: A History of the Yellowstone Basin.* New York: G. P. Putnam's Sons, 1961. A history of the Yellowstone Basin, it includes early maps of the area and maps of the Crow and Cheyenne reservations.

Fritz, Harry W., Mary Murphy, and Robert R. Swartout. *Montana Legacy: Essays on History, People and Places.* Helena: Montana Historical Society, 2002. Celebrates the diversity of Montana with articles ranging from the fur trade to more modern issues such as power deregulation.

Hamilton, James McClellan. *History of Montana from Wilderness to Statehood.* 2d ed. Edited by Merrill G. Burlingame. Portland, Ore.: Binfords and Mort, 1970. A state history with illustrations, maps, portraits, and references.

Koury, Michael J. *The Military Posts of Montana.* Bellevue, Nebr.: Old Army Press, 1970. Introduction to the army posts of Montana, including Camp Cooke, Fort C.F. Smith, Fort Shaw, Fort Ellis, Camp Baker, Fort Logan, Fort Benton, Fort Custer, Fort Keogh, Fort Missoula, Fort Maginnis, and Fort Assiniboine.

Merrian, Harold Guy. "Ethnic Settlement of Montana," *Pacific Historical Review* (June 1943). A brief overview of the immigration of foreign-born settlers into Montana.

Richards, Dennis L. *Montana's Genealogical and Local History Records, A Selected List of Books, Manuscripts, and Periodicals.* Detroit: Gale Research Co., 1981. One of the best guides to history and genealogical works. Lists historical and genealogical sources for the territorial and state periods of Montana.

Spence, Clark C. *Montana: A Bicentennial History.* States and the Nations series. New York: W. W. Norton and Co., 1978. History of the state with illustrations, maps, and photographs.

Swartout, Jr., Robert R. and Harry W. Fritz. *Montana Heritage: An Anthology of Historical Essays.* Helena: Montana Historical Society, n.d. A collection of articles from the *Montana Magazine of Western History* concerning little-considered topics such as women, American Indians, and various immigrant groups.

Wolle, Muriel Vincent Sibell. *Montana Pay Dirt: A Guide to Mining Camps of the Treasure State.* Denver: Sage, 1963. Contains maps, illustrations, and a selected bibliography.

Maps

Maps can be very useful in conducting Montana research, especially in light of the now extinct communities. Several kinds of maps are available which can help in locating land, mining claims, ghost towns, or ranches.

The U.S. Geological Survey topographical maps (see page 5) for Montana can be ordered through the USGS website <www.usgs.gov> or the Montana office at 3162 Bozeman Ave., Helena, MT 59601. Topographical maps for Montana can also be found online at <www.topozone.com/>.

The libraries in the state designated by the U.S. Geological Survey as map depository libraries are the Montana Historical Society; Montana State University–Billings <www.msubillings.edu>; Montana State University–Bozeman <www.montana.edu>; Montana Tech at the University of Montana, Butte <http://mtech.edu>; Montana State University–Northern, Havre <www.msun.edu>; Montana State Library, Helena; and the University of Montana, Missoula <www.umt.edu>.

The state lacks a historical atlas; however, Roberta Cheney, *Names on the Face of Montana*, rev. ed. (Missoula, Mont.: Mountain Press, 1987) can prove helpful in locating places during specific time periods.

Land Records

Public-Domain State

Montana federal land offices were originally located in Bozeman, Glasgow, Great Falls, Helena, Kalispell, Lewistown, Miles City, and Missoula. All of these offices were eliminated by 1950, leaving Billings as the only land office at present.

The land entries for the Montana area (1800–1908) are filed by state, land office, kind of entry, and certificate number. There is no name index prior to 1908 for Montana. To access a federal land entry either the certificate number or the legal description of the land such as range, township, and section must be known. The description can be obtained from the county recorder of deeds. Lands that went to patent after the twentieth century can be found on the Bureau of Land Management (BLM) website <www.glorecords.blm.gov>. Public land records can be accessed through the Department of the Interior. Major federal land records include survey plats and field notes, tract books, register's returns, case files or land-entry papers, and patent records. The survey plats, tract books, and patent records prior to 1908 are available at the BLM Montana/Dakotas State Office, 5001 Southgate Dr., P.O. Box 36800, Billings, MT 59107 <www.mt.blm.gov>.

Patent records after 1908 and case files or land-entry papers prior to 1908 are available through the National Archives system (see page 11). Both the Seattle and Denver centers hold Montana research materials. The case files are the most important genealogically as they often contain military papers, naturalization records, and other documentation.

Subsequent land transactions after the initial federal grant are filed with the respective county clerk and recorder.

Probate Records

Probate courts in Montana existed from 1864 to 1889. These courts had jurisdiction over adoptions, marriages, probates, and various civil suits and criminal matters. After 1889 jurisdiction was transferred to the district courts. Montana probate records are filed at the county courthouses.

Court Records

The Montana court records system has records of genealogical value. These records are found in the district courts, probate courts, and the state supreme court.

District courts are districtwide courts that serve as major trial courts. Their jurisdictions cover appeals, criminal cases, debts, divorces, guardianships, juvenile matters, naturalizations, and probates (since 1889).

Probates courts were disbanded in 1889 when their functions were transferred to the district courts. Prior to that time their jurisdiction covered minor civil and criminal matters, marriages, and probates.

The supreme court served as a statewide appellate court. Microfiche copies of state supreme court dockets are available

through interlibrary loan for cases dating from 1868 to approximately 1983. Supreme court records are on microfiche at the Montana Historical Society (see Archives, Libraries, and Societies).

The court records can be obtained on the county level at the courthouses in the clerk of court's office.

Tax Records

Property taxes in Montana consisted of the name of the individual and a description of the property. Delinquent tax records included the delinquency date, penalty, interest, and amount due. Tax records are arranged by range, township, and section number, and can be obtained by contacting the clerk and recorder at the county courthouse. The National Archives has the records for the Bureau of Internal Revenue (1864–72) for Montana Territory. These are also on microfilm at the FHL.

Cemetery Records

Montana does not have a complete listing of all known cemeteries, nor does it have an agency over cemeteries. Some cemetery records are kept by the county clerk and recorder; in other cases, the county has a cemetery board that is responsible for record keeping. Many cemeteries have no records, and others kept records only of who purchased the lot and the name of the individual buried there. The policy varies with each cemetery. Some Montana genealogical societies have transcribed cemetery records in their counties. The website <www.interment.net> has a growing collection of indexes to Montana graveyards.

Church Records

Church records in Montana vary according to denomination. Many churches transferred memberships, thus making it possible to trace the migration of a family. Before 1900 the largest religious groups were the Roman Catholic, Methodist, Episcopal, and Presbyterian churches. Each group arrived during the territorial period to proselytize among the Native Americans and the miners. Minority faiths included various Latter-day Saint movements, Baptist, Brethren, Hutterites, Lutheran, and Disciples of Christ.

Many denominational histories are on file at the University of Montana, Mansfield Library, Missoula. These include Assemblies of God, Baptist, Brethren Church, Catholic, Disciples of Christ, Episcopal, Hutterite, Methodist, Latter-day Saint, and Presbyterian faiths.

Patricia M. McKinney's *Presbyterianism in Montana: Its First Hundred Years, 1872–1972* (Helena: Thurbers, n.d.) provides a list of churches in Montana including Native American congregations both extant and defunct.

There are two Roman Catholic dioceses in Montana and records can be obtained by contacting the diocese. These include the Diocese of Great Falls–Billings, 121 23rd St. South, P.O. Box 1399, Great Falls, MT 59403 <www.dioceseofgfb.org> and the Diocese of Helena, 515 N. Ewing, P.O. Box 1729, Helena, MT 59624 <www.diocesehelena.org>. They will advise as to the location of parish registers.

Latter-day Saints living in Idaho crossed into Montana to obtain employment. They began freighting goods and produce from Idaho and Utah into Montana in the late 1870s. As early as 1880 Montana politicians took advantage of popular prejudice in trying to eliminate the Mormon vote in some precincts. Montana was not an official church missionary field until 1896. All ward, branch, and mission records are on file at the FHL.

Also on microfilm at the FHL are branch records from the Reorganized Church of Jesus Christ of Latter Day Saints (RLDS Church, now Community of Christ) with original records at the World Church Archives in Independence, Missouri. A now-defunct Utah Mormon sect was the Morrisites, who migrated to Montana. Their history can be found in C. Leroy Anderson's *Joseph Morris and the Saga of the Morrisites* (Logan, Utah: Utah State University Press, 1981).

The first Mennonite mission was established on the Northern Cheyenne Reservation at Bushy in 1904. In 1906 the Lame Deer mission was established eighteen miles away. Other Cheyenne communities asked the Mennonite missionaries to preach to them, and over 500 Cheyennes were baptized when the missions first opened. The Montana Mennonite congregations are part of the General Conference Mennonite Church. A history of this movement is found in Lois R. Habegger's *Cheyenne Trails: A History of Mennonites and Cheyennes in Montana* (Newton, Kans.: Mennonite Publication Office, 1959).

The Methodist Church reached Montana in 1864 as miners brought their faith to the gold mines. For a history of Methodism in Montana, see Doris Whithorn's *Bicentennial Tapestry of the Yellowstone Conference* (Livingston, Mont.: The Livingston Enterprise, 1984). A major records repository for the United Methodist Church is located at the Montana Conference Depository, Paul M. Adams Memorial Library, Rocky Mountain College, Billings, MT 59101 <http://library.rocky.edu>.

In the last quarter of the nineteenth century, members of the Church of the Brethren began to settle in Idaho and then moved up the Snake River Valley into Montana. Many congregations were established in Idaho and Western Montana

between 1895 and 1910. The history of this settlement entitled *The Brethren Along the Snake River: A History of the Brethren in Idaho and Western Montana* (Elgin, Ill.: The Brethren Press, 1966), by Roger Sappington, should be referred to when searching and identifying congregations in western Montana.

Military Records

Many original military records for the state of Montana are on file at the Montana Historical Society archives in Helena. These include the Spanish American War, World War I and World War II, records and early National Guard enlistment records. These records are filed on 60,000 cards arranged alphabetically by surname. The information on these cards includes name, service number, place of enlistment and date, age at entrance, rate, home address, service record history, remarks, and discharge information.

The Montana GenWeb Project website (see page 16) includes indexes for soldiers in the Spanish American War and the 1940 Montana National Guard. Additional sources are continually added.

Periodicals, Newspapers, and Manuscript Collections

Periodicals

Montana: The Magazine of Western History is published quarterly by the Montana Historical Society. Available through the society are two published volumes of indexes to their magazine, one covering 1951 to 1990 and the other 1991 to 2000.

An important but defunct publication is *Contributions to the Historical Society of Montana with its Transactions,* published irregularly between 1876 and 1940. Copies are available at the Montana Historical Society. It is an excellent source of history and genealogy. An excellent source for information on newspapers, city and county records, cemetery records, church records, military records, and indexes to local histories and other books, magazines, and newsletters is *The Montana Historical and Genealogical Data Index,* which was compiled by Paulette Parpart and Donald Spritzer.

The best way to access the numerous local historical and genealogical periodicals published in Montana is through the Montana State Genealogical Society's website (see Archives, Libraries, and Societies).

Newspapers

The Montana Historical Society has the largest collection of newspapers in the state. The guide to the collection is *A Union List of Montana Newspapers in Montana Repositories,* which

also covers other libraries in the state. Many newspapers are on microfilm at Montana State University and the University of Montana. Links to Montana newspapers can be accessed through the Montana GenWeb Project (see page 16) and the website <http://newslink.org/mtnews.html>. The Montana Historical Society provides a comprehensive index to obituaries from Montana newspapers (1864–1900). However, indexes after 1900 are not complete.

Manuscripts

Since 1865 the Montana Historical Society has collected manuscripts for the state and other areas. Manuscripts cover areas such as agriculture, banking, early exploration, fur trading, government, the military, mining, and Native Americans, and can be accessed through its own database or the National Union Catalog of Manuscripts (see page 11).

Other repositories with important manuscripts are the following: Butte-Silver Bow Public Archives, P.O. Box 81, 17 W. Quartz St., Butte, MT 59703 <www.mtech.edu/silverbow/archives.htm> which houses both municipal and private papers and records concerning Butte; the Cascade County Society and Archives, Paris Gibson Sq., 1400 1st Ave., North Great Falls, MT 59401; and the Historical Museum at Fort Missoula, Bldg. 322, Fort Missoula, MT 59801 <www.ohwy.com/mt/y/yachimu.htm>.

Archives, Libraries, and Societies

Montana Historical Society
225 N. Roberts
P.O. Box 201201
Helena, MT 59601-1201
www.montanahistoricalsociety.org

The Montana Historical Society has served as the official archives for the records of the state of Montana since 1969. In that capacity, it has obtained state and territorial records from 1864 to the present. Box and folder-level inventories are available for processed manuscripts and state records through a keyword searchable database.

Montana State Genealogical Society
P.O. Box 555
Chester, MT 59522
www.rootsweb.com/~mtmsgs

The society's website also has valuable links to local societies statewide.

The Montana GenWeb Project <www.rootsweb.com/~mtgenweb> has links and databases to essential resources for Montana genealogical research. Additionally, the Montana State Library website provides a shared online catalog and

library directory for libraries throughout the state <http://montanalibraries.org>.

Special Focus Categories

Immigration

Most of the foreign immigrants who settled in Montana arrived through the port of New York, although immigrants also came from Canada. The ports of entry from Canada were Sweetgrass, Gateway, and Roosville. Sweetgrass was established as a port of entry in 1903, Gateway in 1908, and Roosville in 1930.

The Montana ports of entry are filed with the Seattle passenger lists, which have been microfilmed and are at the National Archives and the FHL. Additional information on persons entering through Montana ports-of-entry may be found in the St. Albans, Vermont District records (so-called, see Vermont—Immigration), which are indexed.

Naturalization

Naturalization records are available from the county clerk of the district court in which the naturalization was recorded. Microfilm of naturalization records of many counties is available at the Montana Historical Society.

Native American

Some Native American Agency records are microfilmed and can be examined through the National Archives—Pacific Alaska Region (Seattle) (see page 12); FHL in Salt Lake City; and the University of Montana in Missoula, Montana. These agency records are very important and should not be overlooked when conducting Native American research.

Billings Area Office, Billings, Montana (1912–52). These records document the activities of the federal government as trustee of tribal lands and resources. Record sources include general decimal files, grazing leases, and records concerning education, health, tribal enactments, irrigation, land transactions, forestry, soil conservation, agricultural extension, and road construction.

Blackfeet Agency, Browning, Montana (1875–1959). Records include general correspondence, grazing permits, oil and gas production reports, census records, birth and health records, ledgers, abstracts of accounts of individual Indians, tribal council records, records concerning education, road, forestry, irrigation, credit, welfare, and rehabilitation programs. This agency was established in 1855 for the three bands of the Siksika Native Americans.

Crow Agency, Crow Agency, Montana (1874–1959). This agency was established in 1869 and administered the affairs of the Mountain and River Crows. The River Crows were originally under the control of the Fort Peck Agency, but they gradually came under the control of the Crow Agency. Record sources include general correspondence and decimal files, student case files, school censuses, tract books, maps of the Crow reservations, grazing leases, building plans, annuity payrolls, ledgers for accounts of individual Indians, records of goods issued to Indians, census rolls, Indian court dockets, records concerning irrigation, forestry, Civilian Conservation Corps, and road programs.

Flathead Agency, St. Ignatius, Montana (1875–1960). Records include general correspondence and decimal files; correspondence; reports and censuses concerning schools; grazing permits; leases; records concerning allotments and land transactions, and other records concerning land, irrigation, Civilian Conservation Corps, engineering, and road and forestry programs; ledgers for accounts of individual Indians; census reports; records concerning relief, welfare projects and cases; Indian police and court records; credit program files; tribal accounts; and annuity payrolls. This agency was established in 1854 principally for the Flathead, Upper Pend d'Oreille, and Kutenai tribes. Lower Kalispells moved onto the Flathead Reservation in 1887, and the Spokane moved to the reservation in 1894. In time, the distinctions became ignored and all were known as Flatheads.

Fort Belknap Agency, Harlem, Montana (1877–1969). Records include general correspondence and decimal files, correspondence concerning education, school reports and applications, grazing permits, leases, ledgers for accounts of individual Indians, correspondence and reports about health and welfare, census rolls, family history cards, traders' licenses, police and court records concerning roads, land sales, Civilian Conservation Corps work, and financial matters. This agency was established in 1873 and had jurisdiction over the Gros Ventre and Upper Assiniboine along the Milk River.

Fort Peck Agency, Popular, Montana (1871–1959), formally known as the Milk River Agency. Agency records include general correspondence and decimal files, school reports, records of 4-H activities, grazing permits, mining leases, ledgers for accounts of individual Indians, credit rehabilitation ledgers, industrial status reports, census records, medical reports, registers of Indians, birth and death records, welfare relief case files, tribal council records, and records concerning land allotments and sales, forestry and range management, irrigation, and road construction. This agency had jurisdiction over the Lower Assiniboine and Sioux, principally Yanktonai, Native Americans.

"Indian Schools" were set up to further the education of the Native American youth. Two important schools whose records should not be overlooked are the Chemawa Indian School in Chemawa, Oregon, and the Fort Shaw School in Cascade County, Montana. These schools attracted students from many states. (For a more detailed account of the Chemawa Indian School, see Oregon—Native American section.) The Fort Shaw

School was established in Fort Shaw in 1892 as a non-reservation school and closed in 1910. Its records consist of letters received, registers of pupils, rosters of employees, and cashbooks. A major Native American Collection is the James McLaughlin Papers. Major James McLaughlin was an Indian agent for some time in the Dakotas, Montana, and Wyoming Territory. He kept careful records of his dealings with many tribes. His papers include Native American family data and locations of specific families. Many families had become scattered during their subsequent relocation to reservations. The James McLaughlin Papers, therefore, are an excellent source for locating many of these scattered families. This collection consists of 30,000 pages with an index containing 15,675 cross-reference cards.

A guide to the James McLaughlin Papers is published and entitled *Guide to the Microfilm Edition of the Major James McLaughlin Papers* by Rev. Louis Pfaller (Richardson, N.Dak.: Assumption College, 1969).

A very important Native American collection for Montana, as well as Idaho, Oregon, and Washington, is the Pacific Northwest Tribes Missions Collection of the Oregon Province Archives of the Society of Jesus (1853–1960). This massive collection of Jesuit records includes births, marriages, deaths, censuses, land records, church records, histories, and newspaper clippings. The following tribes are recorded in these records: Blackfoot, Cheyenne, Coeur d'Alene, Colville, Crow, Flathead, Kalispell, Kootenai, Nez Perce, Spokane, and Umatilla.

These records are on microfilm with a copy at the FHL and the originals at the Crosby Library, Gonzaga University, Spokane, Washington, which is where the Oregon Province Archives is now located. For a guide to the microfilm collection, see Robert C. Carriker and Eleanor R. Carriker, *Guide to the Microfilm Edition of the Pacific Northwest Tribes Missions Collection of the Oregon Province Archives of the Society of Jesus* (Wilmington, Del.: Scholarly Resources, 1987).

Other Ethnic Groups

The discovery of gold in Montana brought many Chinese into the region during the early 1860s. These Chinese were from the province of Kwangtung around the Canton area. The 1870 U.S. census of Montana Territory counted 1,943 Chinese, representing about ten percent of the total population. By 1880 the number had declined to 1,765, but by 1890 had risen to 2,532.

By the 1870s there were a number of Chinese mining operations in western Montana. As placer mining declined during the late 1870s and 1880s, the Chinese moved into other fields such as railroad construction and business, which served not only the Chinese population but the white majority as well. Montana's largest communities of Chinese were in Butte and Helena.

The most important institution in the Chinese community was the Joss House, or Temple, which served the religious (Confucianism) as well as the social needs of the community. Butte's Chinatown had two Joss Houses. Another important institution was the Masonic temple.

The Chinese contributed much to the development of Montana, especially in the building of the Northern Pacific Railroad, which opened the state up to further development. However, little remains of Montana's Chinese era. The failure of the community was due to racism, discriminatory laws, and immigration laws, as well as the shortage of Chinese female emigrants in western America. For an excellent treatment of Montana's Chinese, see "Kwangtung to Big Sky: The Chinese in Montana, 1864–1900," *Montana: The Magazine of Western History* 1 (Winter 1988): 38. The best method of researching the Chinese in Montana is county sources such as land, tax and court records, and federal census enumerations.

County Resources

County seats in Montana are the location of the county clerk and recorder (vital records and deeds) and the clerk of the district court (probate and court records). The latter includes civil and criminal files and naturalizations. The Montana Association of Counties website <www.discoveringmontana. com/maco> has links to each county with updated contact information.

Starting dates of records and dates for the formation of counties were taken from Dennis Lee Richards' work (see Background Sources).

British Columbia

Alberta

Saskatchewan

Canada
U.S.

DIVIDE

Counties and county seats:

LINCOLN — Libby

FLATHEAD — Kalispell

GLACIER — Cut Bank

TOOLE — Shelby

LIBERTY — Chester

HILL — Havre — Chinook

Malta — VALLEY — Glasgow

Scobey — DANIELS

Plentywood — SHERIDAN

PONDERA — Conrad

BLAINE

PHILLIPS

ROOSEVELT — Wolf Point

WILLIAMS

NORTH DAKOTA

RICHLAND — Sidney

McKENZIE

SANDERS — Thompson Falls

LAKE — Polson

TETON — Choteau

CHOUTEAU — Fort Benton

MINERAL — Superior

LEWIS AND CLARK

Great Falls

CASCADE

Stanford

FERGUS — Lewistown

PETROLEUM — Winnett

GARFIELD — Jordan

McCONE — Circle

DAWSON — Glendive

PRAIRIE

Dagmar / Dawson

GOLDEN VALLEY

CLEARWATER

MISSOULA — Missoula

POWELL

Helena

MEAGHER

White Sulphur Springs

JUDITH BASIN

WHEATLAND — Harlowton

MUSSELSHELL — Roundup

ROSEBUD

Terry

SIOUX

SLOPE

GRANITE — Philipsburg — Deer Lodge

Hamilton

BROADWATER — Townsend

GOLDEN VALLEY — Ryegate

Hysham

TREASURE

Miles City

CUSTER — Forsyth

FALLON — Baker

BOWMAN

IDAHO

RAVALLI

DEER LODGE — Anaconda — Butte

JEFFERSON — Boulder

SILVER BOW

GALLATIN — Bozeman

SWEET GRASS — Big Timber

Livingston

STILLWATER — Columbus

YELLOWSTONE — Billings

Hardin

BIG HORN

POWDER RIVER — Broadus

CARTER — Ekalaka

HARDING

MADISON — Virginia City — Dillon

BEAVERHEAD

PARK

CARBON — Red Lodge

BUTTE

SOUTH DAKOTA

LAWRENCE

LEMHI

VALLEY

CUSTER

BOISE

ELMORE

CAMAS

BLAINE

BUTTE

JEFFERSON

MADISON

TETON

BINGHAM

BONNEVILLE

TETON

Yellowstone National Park

PARK

WYOMING

HOT SPRINGS

FREMONT

BIG HORN

SHERIDAN

JOHNSON

CAMPBELL

CROOK

WESTON

NATRONA

CONVERSE

NIOBRARA

CUSTER

Rivers: Flathead River, Clark Fork, Bitterroot River, Missouri, Teton River, Milk River, Musselshell, Yellowstone, Bighorn, Little Bighorn

The Counties and County Seats of
Montana

25 0 25 50 75 100 Miles

Drawn by William Dollarhide

Map	County Address	Date Formed Parent County/ies	Birth Marriage Death	Land Probate Court
B6	**Beaverhead** 2 S. Pacific Dillon 59725-2799	1865 original	1901 1877 1901	1865 1865 1865
	Land was added from Madison County in 1907, and again in 1911.			
	Big Horn	1865 (Split into Dawson, 1869 and Custer, 1877)		
G6	**Big Horn (modern)** 121 Third St./P.O. Box 908 Hardin 59034-0908	1913 Rosebud/Yellowstone	1909 1913 1909	1913 1913 1913
F2	**Blaine** 400 Ohio/Box 278 Chinook 59523-0278	1912 Chouteau	1907 1912 1907	1912 1912 1912
	Land was added from Phillips County in 1915.			
D5	**Broadwater** 515 Broadway St. Townsend 59644-2397	1897 Jefferson/Meagher	1894 1897 1903	1897 1897 1897
F6	**Carbon** 17 W. Eleventh/P.O. Box 887 Red Lodge 59068-0887	1895 Park/Yellowstone	1904 1895 1895	1895 1895 1895
K6	**Carter** 214 Park St., P.O. Box 315 Ekalaka 59324-0315	1917 Fallon	1915 1917 1915	1917 1917 1917
D4	**Cascade** 415 Second Ave. N. Great Falls 59401	1887 Chouteau/Meagher/ Lewis and Clark	1892 1888 1893	1887 1887 1887
E2	**Chouteau** 1308 Franklin, Box 459 Fort Benton 59442-0459	1865 original	1895 1882 1895	1865 1865 1865
J5	**Custer** 1010 Main St. Miles City 59301-3419	1877 Big Horn	1895 1877 1896	1877 1877 1877
J1	**Daniels** 213 Main St./P.O. Box 247 Scobey 59263-0247	1920 Sheridan/Valley	1913 1920 1920	1920 1920 1920
K3	**Dawson** 207 W. Bell Glendive 59330-1694	1869 Big Horn	1895 1882 1895	1869 1869 1869
B5	**Deer Lodge** 800 S. Main Anaconda 59711-2999	1865 original	1903 1865 1895	1865 1865 1865
	Edgerton	1865 (renamed Lewis and Clark, 1867)		
K5	**Fallon** 10 W. Fallon, P.O. Box 846 Baker 59313-0846	1913 Custer	1908 1912 1918	1913 1913 1913
F3	**Fergus** 712 Main St. Lewistown 59457-2562	1885 Meagher	1904 1885 1904	1885 1885 1885
	Land was added from Chouteau County in 1907.			
A2	**Flathead** 800 S. Main St. Kalispell 59901-5400	1893 Missoula	1896 1892 1907	1893 1893 1893
D6	**Gallatin** 311 W. Main St. Bozeman 59715-4576	1865 original	1895 1865 1895	1865 1865 1865
H3	**Garfield** Leavit St./P.O. Box 7 Jordan 59337-0007	1919 Dawson	1911 1919 1917	1919 1919 1919
B1	**Glacier** 512 E. Main St. Cut Bank 59427-3016	1919 Teton	1919 1910 1919	1919 1919 1919
F5	**Golden Valley** P.O. Box 10 Ryegate 59074-0010	1920 Musselshell/Sweet Grass	1919 1892 1920	1920 1920 1920
B4	**Granite** 220 N. Sansome/P.O. Box 925 Philipsburg 59858-0925	1893 Deer Lodge	1895 1892 1895	1893 1893 1893
	Land was added from Missoula County in 1943.			
E1	**Hill** 315 Fourth St. Havre 5950-3999	1912 Chouteau	1898 1912 1897	1912 1912 1912
C5	**Jefferson** 201 Centennial/Box H Boulder 59632-0249	1865 original	1895 1866 1895	1865 1865 1865
E4	**Judith Basin** 31 First Ave./Box 427 Stanford 59479-0427	1920 Cascade/Fergus	1920 1920 1920	1920 1920 1920
A3	**Lake** 106 Fourth Ave. East Polson 59860-2125	1923 Flathead/Missoula	1923 1923 1923	1923 1923 1923
C4	**Lewis and Clark** 316 N. Park/P.O. Box 1724 Helena 59624-1724	1865 (as Edgerton; renamed 1867) original	1895 1865 1895	1867 1867 1867
D2	**Liberty** 111 First St. E./Box 459 Chester 59522-0459	1920 Chouteau/Hill	1920 1920 1920	1920 1920 1920
A1	**Lincoln** 512 California Ave. Libby 59923-1942	1909 Flathead	1897 1896 1897	1909 1909 1909
3	**McCone** 1004 Ave. C/P.O. Box 199 Circle 59215-0199	1919 Dawson/Richland	1919 1919 1919	1919 1919 1919
C6	**Madison** 110 W. Wallace/Box 278 Virginia City 59755-0278	1865 original	1903 1864 1903	1865 1865 1865
D4	**Meagher** P.O. Box 309 White Sulphur Springs 59645-0309	1867 Gallatin	1895 1866 1895	1867 1867 1867
A3	**Mineral** 300 River St./P.O. Box 550 Superior 59872-0550	1914 Missoula	1914 1887 1914	1914 1914 1914

Map	County / Address	Date Formed / Parent County/ies	Birth Marriage Death	Land Probate Court
B4	Missoula / 200 W. Broadway / Missoula 59802-4292	1865 original; added Powell, 1915	1895 / 1865 / 1895	1865 / 1865 / 1865
	Land was added from Powell County in 1915.			
G5	Musselshell / 506 Main St. / Roundup 59072-2498	1911 / Fergus/Yellowstone	1911 / 1895 / 1911	1911 / 1911 / 1911
E6	Park / 414 E. Callender / Livingston 59047-2799	1887 / Gallatin	1889 / 1887 / 1892	1887 / 1887 / 1887
G4	Petroleum / 201 E. Main/P.O. Box 226 / Winnett 59087-0226	1925 / Fergus	1916 / 1925 / 1915	1925 / 1925 / 1925
G2	Phillips / 314 2nd Ave. W./P.O. Box 360 / Malta 59538-0360	1915 / Blaine/Valley	1914 / 1915 / 1917	1915 / 1915 / 1915
C2	Pondera / 20 Fourth Ave., S.W. / Conrad 59425-2340	1919 / Chouteau/Teton	1910 / 1919 / 1913	1919 / 1919 / 1919
J6	Powder River / P.O. Box 270 / Broadus 59317-0270	1919 / Custer	1919 / 1915 / 1919	1919 / 1919 / 1919
C5	Powell / 409 Missouri Ave. / Deer Lodge 59722-1084	1901 / Deer Lodge	1907 / 1901 / 1907	1901 / 1901 / 1901
	Land was added from counties Deer Lodge in 1903 and Missoula in 1915.			
J4	Prairie / 217 W. Park/Box 125 / Terry 59349-0125	1915 / Custer/Dawson/Fallon	1915 / 1915 / 1915	1915 / 1915 / 1915
A5	Ravalli / 215 S. Fourth / Hamilton 59840-2853	1893 / Missoula	1911 / 1893 / 1911	1893 / 1893 / 1893
3	Richland / 201 W. Main / Sidney 59270-4087	1914 / Dawson	1914 / 1914 / 1912	1914 / 1914 / 1914
K2	Roosevelt / 400 2nd Ave. South / Wolf Point 59201-1600	1919 / Sheridan	1919 / 1913 / 1919	1919 / 1919 / 1919
H4	Rosebud / P.O. Box 47 / Forsyth 59327-0047	1901 / Custer	1893 / 1901 / 1900	1901 / 1901 / 1901
A3	Sanders / 1111 Main St./P.O. Box 519 / Thompson Falls 59873-0519	1906 / Missoula	1915 / 1906 / 1915	1906 / 1906 / 1906
K1	Sheridan / 100 W. Laurel Ave. / Plentywood 59254-1699	1913 / Valley	1911 / 1913 / 1911	1913 / 1913 / 1913
C5	Silver Bow / 155 W. Granite / Butte 59701-9256	1881 / Deer Lodge	1878 / 1881 / 1890	1881 / 1881 / 1881
	Land was again added from Deer Lodge in 1917.			
F6	Stillwater / 400 Third Ave N./Box 970 / Columbus 59019-0970	1913 / Carbon/Sweet Grass (1915)/ Yellowstone	1887 / 1913 / 1907	1913 / 1913 / 1913
	Land was added from Sweet Grass in 1915.			
E5	Sweet Grass / 200 W. First Ave./P.O. Box 888 / Big Timber 59011-0888	1895 / Meagher/Park/Yellowstone	1895 / 1895 / 1895	1895 / 1895 / 1895
C3	Teton / 110 S. Main/P.O. Box 610 / Choteau 59422-0610	1893 / Chouteau	1897 / 1893 / 1919	1893 / 1893 / 1893
D1	Toole / 226 1st St. South / Shelby 59474-1920	1914 / Hill/Teton	1912 / 1914 / 1912	1914 / 1914 / 1914
H5	Treasure / 307 Rapelje/P.O. Box 392 / Hysham 59038-0392	1919 / Rosebud	1919 / 1919 / 1919	1919 / 1919 / 1919
H2	Valley / 501 Sq. Court, Box 1 / Glasgow 59230-2405	1893 / Dawson	1907 / 1893 / 1907	1893 / 1893 / 1893
E5	Wheatland / 201 A Ave. NW / P.O. Box 1903 / Harlowton 59036-1903	1917 / Meagher/Sweet Grass	1908 / 1917 / 1909	1917 / 1917 / 1917
K4	Wibaux / 200 S. Wilbaux/Box 199 / Wibaux 59353-0199	1914 / Dawson/Fallon (1919)	1914 / 1914 / 1914	1914 / 1914 / 1914
G5	Yellowstone / 217 North. 27th St. / P.O. Box 35000 / Billings 59107-5000	1883 / Custer/Gallatin	1884 / 1887 / 1884	1883 / 1883 / 1883
	Land was added from the Crow Indian Reservation in 1885.			

Nebraska

MARSHA HOFFMAN RISING, CG, FUGA, FASG, AND DWIGHT A. RADFORD

Nebraska was part of the Louisiana Purchase acquired from France in 1803. Before the 1860s most pioneers passed through Nebraska along the Platte River Valley on their way to Oregon and California. The first serious attempts to form Nebraska Territory were begun in 1851, but territorial status was not achieved until three years later. Nebraska Territory was created in 1854 as a result of the Kansas-Nebraska Act, a political compromise regarding the expansion of slavery. Although this act officially opened the area for white settlement, the real impetus to organizing the territory was the building of a Pacific railroad, not colonization. At that time Nebraska Territory extended to the Canadian border. The center of government was located in Omaha, which sits on the Missouri River. As the population grew, migration worked its way westward along the rivers, such as the Platte, and via the rapidly developing railroads.

The first federal land office was established in 1854, but it was not until after the Civil War that extensive settlement began. This led to Nebraska's admission to the United States on 1 March 1867. The Homestead Acts of 1862 and 1866 governed the disposal of the public land in Nebraska, but these acts did not account for the large migration to the state. The settlement of Nebraska required a new view of the economics of an unfamiliar geography and an advance in technology. The former obstacle was overcome by the cattle ranchers whose animals grazed the vast prairie, and the technology that came with the invention of farming implements. These agricultural innovations included barbed wire, the steel plow, the spring harrow, and windmills—inventions that did not come into widespread usage until the years between 1870 and 1890. It was during that period that the

Great Plains experienced a tremendous growth in population. By 1880 the years of good weather and new productivity in farming equipment had brought the population growth in Nebraska to more than 450,000.

Not only farmers but merchants, capitalizing on expanding markets, moved to Nebraska and created small towns, especially along the developing railroads. In fact, between 1860 and 1870, the city population of Nebraska increased over 400 percent, an indication that not everyone in Nebraska lived on farms.

Both natives and foreigners were attracted by the government land acts, advertising by the railroads and steamship companies, and immigration efforts by the federal government. European groups that settled Nebraska include individuals and families from Russia, Bohemia, Germany, Sweden, Denmark, and the British Isles.

Years of unprecedented growth and frontier expansion soon gave way to negative repercussions. Abysmal living conditions, inflated land prices, low profits on produce, and poor weather brought a reversal of fortunes and mounting dissatisfaction with economic and political conditions. From this discontent came the agrarian political movements.

Genealogical research in Nebraska must be completed at both the state and county level. Few statewide Nebraska indexes exist, but the survival of records across the state is good. The researcher will find it necessary to do a great deal of family research at the county level where the individual family resided. The purpose of the Nebraska State Historical Society and Genealogical Society of Utah's joint project is to microfilm specific county records in order to make these resources more widely available.

Vital Records

The statewide requirement for registration of births and deaths began in late 1904 and for marriages and divorces in 1909. However, compliance was not complete for several years. The available records can be ordered from the Nebraska Department of Health and Human Services, 301 Centennial Mall, P.O. Box 95065, Lincoln, NE 68509-5065 <www.hhs.state.ne.us/ced/nevrinfo.htm>.

With the exception of some delayed birth registrations located in the office of the county clerk, Nebraska did not record births and deaths at the county level. The Nebraska State Historical Society (see Archives, Libraries, and Societies) has both the Omaha birth registry (1869–1907) and the Omaha death registry (1873–1915). These as well as most of the early vital records are incomplete for the beginning years of registration. Divorce records before 1909 are at the county clerk of the district court.

Several county genealogical societies have compiled indexes to the early marriage records. The Nebraska State Historical Society (see Archives, Libraries, and Societies) and the Family History Library (FHL) maintain microfilm copies for research, including a large number of county registers.

Census Records

Federal

Population Schedules
- Indexed—1860, 1870, 1880, 1900, 1910, 1920, 1930
- Soundex—1880, 1900, 1920

Industry and Agriculture Schedules
- 1860, 1870, 1880

Mortality Schedules
- 1860, 1870, 1880

Union Veterans Schedules
- 1890 (indexed)

The Nebraska State Historical Society has copies of the federal schedules and the 1860 to 1880 agriculture, industry, and mortality schedules.

Territorial and State

The Nebraska State Historical Society has the original enumerations for the territorial censuses. Territorial censuses are available for 1854, 1855, and 1856 and are indexed in *Nebraska and Midwest Genealogical Records* and at <www.ancestry.com> subscription databases. A few counties were recorded in censuses taken in 1867, 1874, 1875, 1878–79. Lancaster County was indexed and published in the *Historical Records of Lancaster County Nebraska*, Series 3, vols. 1–13 (Lincoln, Nebr.: Genealogical Records Committee of the Deborah Avery Chapter of the Daughters of the American Revolution [DAR], under sponsorship of the Nebraska State Historical Society, 1939).

Microfilm copies of the 1885 state census are at the Nebraska State Historical Society, the National Archives, and the FHL. Schedules include names of all members of the household and agricultural, industrial, and mortality schedules. An index is included in the 1890 Census Substitute database on <www.ancestry.com>.

School Censuses

Required by law, school censuses are taken every year in Nebraska. Some of these are available at the Nebraska State Historical Society and some can be found on Nebraska's USGenWeb <www.rootsweb.com/~negenweb/> archives, as well as on microfilm at the FHL.

Background Sources

The best printed sources for the territorial period are the following:

Territorial Papers of the United States Senate—Nebraska, 1853–1867. Record Group 46, Reel 16. This publication is available in many historical societies and university libraries.

White, John B., comp. *Published Sources on Territorial Nebraska.* Vol. 23, Nebraska State Historical Society Publications. Lincoln, Nebr.: Nebraska State Historical Society, 1956. This may be purchased from the society for $3.

U.S. Department of State. *State Department Territorial Papers, Nebraska, December 31, 1854–March 27, 1867.* Washington, D.C.: National Archives and Records Service, General Services Administration, 1955. This publication is available on NARA microfilm M228.

Published sources for Nebraska are the following:

Berry, Myrtle D. "Local Nebraska History—A Bibliography," *Nebraska History* 26 (April-June 1945): 104-15.

Compendium of Historical Reminiscence and Biography of Western Nebraska Containing...Biographical Sketches of Hundreds of Prominent Old Settlers. Chicago: Alden Publishing, 1909 and 1912 (1912 contains the entire state). A classic work that includes some early pioneers, it is especially valuable since many of them contributed to the information directly.

History of the State of Nebraska. 2 vols. Reprinted with index by Raymond E. Dale. Lincoln, Nebr.: Nebraska State Historical Society, 1962. Originally published by A. T. Andreas in 1882 in Chicago. Reprinted with index in 1975 (often referred to as "Andreas") and available online at <www.kancoll.org/books/andreas_ne/hon_cnty.html>.

Luebke, Frederick C. *Ethnicity on the Great Plains.* Lincoln, Nebr.: University of Nebraska Press, 1980. Provides background on the ethnic groups who immigrated to Nebraska between 1865 and 1890.

Mattes, Merrill J. *The Great Platte River Road: The Covered Wagon Main Line via Fort Kearny to Fort Laramie.* Lincoln, Nebr.: University of Nebraska Press, 1987. An in-depth study of the border towns, trail routes, river crossings, Indian encounters, stage stations, military posts, and North Platte Valley landmarks along the Great Platte River Road to Oregon and California.

Nebraska State Genealogical Society. *Nebraska: A Guide to Genealogical Research.* Lincoln, Nebr.: the society, 1984.

Olson, James C., and Ronald C. Naugle. *History of Nebraska.* 3d ed. Lincoln, Nebr.: University of Nebraska Press, 1997. Originally created to mark the territorial centennial of Nebraska and revised for the statehood centennial, it is standard text for college students and general reader on Nebraska history.

Perkey, Elton A. *Perkey's Nebraska Place Names.* Rev. ed. Lincoln, Nebr.: J&L Co., 1995. Brief sketches of place-names organized by county showing location, founding, and naming of each place.

Many counties have published county histories and have donated copies to the Nebraska State Historical Society. See <www.nebraskahistory.org/lib-arch/services/refrence/la_pubs/sources4.htm>.

Maps

The Nebraska State Historical Society holds the Sanborn Fire Insurance Maps for Nebraska. The society has an excellent collection of early county atlases covering most of the state, including some 500 county atlases or plat books from 1885 to about 1947. For a listing, see Nebraska County Atlases/Platbooks at <www.nebraskahistory.org/databases/atlas.shtml>. See also:

Everts and Kirk. *The 1885 Official State Atlas of Nebraska.* Reprinted in 1976 with 10,000-name index by Margie Sobotka. Fremont, Nebr.: Eastern Nebraska Genealogical Society, 1976.

Land Records

Public-Domain State

Nebraska is a public domain state in which land was initially granted by the federal government. The first homestead claim in the United States was made on 1 January 1863, nine miles west of Beatrice in Gage County by Daniel Freeman. His homestead is now the location of Homestead National Monument (see <www.nps.gov/home>). The Homestead National Monument is currently working on obtaining microfilm copies of the National Archives Homestead case files. Many of these early homesteaders in Nebraska were Civil War veterans from the northern states of Ohio, New York, Pennsylvania, Illinois, Indiana, and Iowa, eager to obtain the inexpensive farmland available from the federal government.

Land was dispersed in Nebraska through several land offices. Those in operation throughout the nineteenth century were the following: Omaha City (1854), Brownsville (1857), Nebraska City (1857), Dakota City (1857), Beatrice (1868), Lincoln (1868), Grand Island (1868), West Point (1869), Lowell (1872), North Platte (1872), Norfolk (1873), Bloomington (1874), Niobrara (1875), Neligh (1881), Valentine (1882), McCook (1882), Sidney (1886), Chadron (1886), O'Neill (1888), Alliance (1890) and Broken Bow (1890). These land offices lasted until 1933, when the last one closed at Alliance.

The current work on this essential subject in Nebraska research is Russell C. Lang's *Original Land Transfers of Nebraska: How the West Was Almost Given Away* (Baltimore: Gateway Press, 2001). This work focuses on the original land transfers and settlement process (1866–85). The references in Lang's work are particularly noteworthy. In addition, a helpful reference from Nebraska State Historical Society is "U.S. Government Land Laws in Nebraska, 1854–1907," by James E. Porter (see <www.nebraskahistory.org/lib-arch/services/refrence/la_pubs/landlaw7.htm>).

The Nebraska State Historical Society has records from the land offices and microfilmed copies of all the tract books. Some of these entries are indexed. If the exact land description is known, land patents for Nebraska may be obtained from the Bureau of Land Management (BLM) Wyoming State Office, 5353 Yellowstone Rd., Box 1828, Cheyenne, WY 82003-1828 <www.wy.blm.gov>.

Railroads acquired nearly a tenth of Nebraska land from the federal government and sold it cheaply to settlers to encourage settlement and the development of commerce. The original homestead may have first been farmed by early homesteaders but was acquired from the railroad at an early date. For this reason, it is best to track the title chain back using the exact land description in the register of deed's office before going to the federal records. Most of the original records of railroad land sales were destroyed by fire, but the Nebraska Historical Society holds land records of the Burlington and Missouri River Railroad in Nebraska. An index to the oil and gas patents from 1908 is online at the BLM website <www.glorecords.gov>, where patents can be examined by state, county, or land description. This database does not include all lands that went to patent for Nebraska as it does for some other states.

After the first land purchase from the government, transfers of land are located in the individual county in the register of

deeds office. Here the researcher can search deeds, indexed by grantee-grantor, mortgages, and cemetery record deed books. Some offices hold the register of entries made at the land office in Lincoln under the Homestead Act of 1862. Many abstracts and claims are also located at the county level. Some county deeds are on microfilm at the Nebraska State Historical Society and the FHL.

Probate Records

Probate records are located in the office of the clerk of the county court. These records may include wills, estate records, guardianships, bonds, and probate books. Although adoption records are located in this office, they are closed to the public. Some counties have their probate records on file at the Nebraska State Historical Society, and microfilm copies of many are at the FHL.

Court Records

In the office of the clerk of the district court, available records include felony cases, cases of appeal, divorce cases, civil cases, and naturalization records. The naturalization records should include declarations of intention, petitions for naturalization, and second or final papers. The Nebraska State Historical Society has many county naturalization records. Many are also on microfilm at the FHL.

Tax Records

Many tax records are still held at the county level; many taken before 1912 have been sent to the Nebraska State Historical Society. The society is continually collecting county records. At present they have tax records for about half of the counties and assessment records for many others, all for various periods of time. The researcher should contact the Public Records at the Nebraska State Historical Society to learn of its holdings for a particular county before contacting the county. County tax records, real and personal, are located in the office of the county treasurer at the county seat.

Cemetery Records

Many cemetery inscriptions located in Nebraska have been transcribed with the records housed at the Nebraska State Historical Society. Online sources include the USGenWeb Project with a growing list of tombstone transcripts for Nebraska at <www.usgenweb.org> and <www.interment.net>, which has a growing selection for Nebraska counties.

The DAR Library in Washington, D.C., holds a multi-volume collection from over 150 cemeteries located in Nebraska.

The National Cemetery in Nebraska is the Fort McPherson National Cemetery, HCO 1 Box 67, Maxwell, NE 69151.

Church Records

The Nebraska State Historical Society holds a number of early church records in its manuscript division. For a complete list of the counties, communities, inclusive dates, and name of the church, the society's website should be consulted for a reference guide. Included in the collection are records from selected churches representing Baptist, Presbyterian, Congregational, Lutheran, Evangelical United Brethren, Methodist, Episcopal, and Society of Friends denominations.

The Roman Catholic Church arrived in Nebraska Territory by way of the Jesuits, who were in the area as early as 1838. The first church in the territory was in Omaha and was founded in 1856. Today the state is served by three dioceses: the Archdiocese of Omaha, the Diocese of Lincoln, and the Diocese of Grand Island. Each has its own website and contact information for individual parishes. The search for records should start here. The Archdiocese of Omaha, 100 N. 62nd St., Omaha, NE 68132 <www.archomaha.com> covers Antelope, Boone, Boyd, Burt, Cedar, Colfax, Cuming, Dakota, Dixon, Dodge, Douglas, Holt, Knox, Madison, Merrick, Nance, Pierce, Platte, Sarpy, Stanton, Thurston, Washington, and Wayne counties. The Diocese of Lincoln, P.O. Box 80328, Lincoln, NE 68501-0328 <www.dioceseoflincoln.org> covers thirty-five counties and portions of five more split by the river: Adams, Butler, Cass, Chase, Clay, Dawson (south), Devel (south), Dundy, Fillmore, Franklin, Frontier, Furnas, Gage, Gosper, Hall (south), Hamilton, Harlan, Hayes, Hitchcock, Jefferson, Johnson, Kearney, Keith (south), Lancaster, Lincoln (south), Nemaha, Nuckolls, Otoe, Pawnee, Perkins, Phelps, Polk, Red Willow, Richardson, Saline, Saunders, Seward, Thayer, Webster, and York. The Diocese of Grand Island, P.O. Box 1531, 311 W. 17th St., Grand Island, NE 68802 <www.gidiocese.org> covers thirty counties and five more split by the river: Arthur, Banner, Box Butte, Blaine, Brown, Buffalo, Cherry, Cheyenne, Custer, Dawes, Dawson (north), Devel (north), Garden, Garfield, Grant, Greeley, Hall (north), Hooker, Howard, Keith (north), Keya Paha, Kimball, Lincoln (north), Logan, Loup, McPherson, Morrill, Rock, Scotts Bluff, Sheridan, Sherman, Sioux, Thomas, Valley, and Wheeler counties.

The Episcopal Church historically had clergy serving the Indian Territory from Ft. Kearney; the first parish was organized in Omaha in 1856. Today the state is served by the Episcopal Diocese of Nebraska, 109 N. 18th St., Omaha, NE 68102

<www.episcopal-ne.org>. The diocesan website has contact information for all the parishes in the state.

A large number of German and Scandinavian immigrants brought their Lutheran faith to Nebraska. There are two main Lutheran denominations in Nebraska: Evangelical Lutheran Conference of America (ELCA) and Lutheran Church–Missouri Synod. The Nebraska Synod of ELCA, 4980 S. 118th St., Ste. D, Omaha, NE 68137-2220 <www.elca.org> provides contract information for all congregations in the Nebraska Synod. The Lutheran Church–Missouri Synod in Nebraska, 152 S. Columbia Ave., P.O. Box 407, Seward, NE 68434-0407 <www.ndlcms.org> provides similar information for all their congregations in the district. The websites are the first place to start in the search for Lutheran records. Both denominations may have to be contacted to determine which denomination an ancestor's congregation may belong to now.

The search for records of the Methodist or Evangelical United Brethren Church starts with the Nebraska United Methodist Church Historical Center. The official repository for the archives of the Nebraska Annual Conference of the United Methodist Church is at Nebraska Wesleyan University, Cochrane Woods Library, 5000 St. Paul Ave., Lincoln, NE 68504-2794 <www.nebrwesleyan.edu>. The registers are at the FHL.

Although there are several Presbyterian denominations in Nebraska, it is the Presbyterian Historical Society in Philadelphia (operated by the Presbyterian Church, USA) that collects research materials for all branches of Presbyterianism. A large collection of congregational registers for Nebraska is available; they have been microfilmed and are at the FHL. Nebraska synods are served by the Lakes and Prairies Synod <www.lakesandprairies.org> serving the Central Nebraska region and the synod of the Rocky Mountains <www.synodrm.org>. Each website provides links to the local presbyteries and contact information for local congregations.

Both The Church of Jesus Christ of Latter-day Saints (LDS) and the Community of Christ (formerly the Reorganized Church of Jesus Christ of Latter-day Saints, or RLDS Church) have had missionaries and members in the state. Records for both denominations have extensive collections on microfilm at the FHL.

The search for Seventh-day Adventist records should start with the Nebraska Conference (1878–1981) and the institutions operated by that jurisdiction. Today the state is served through the Kansas-Nebraska Conference, 3440 Urish Rd., Topeka, KS 66614-4601 <www.ks-ne.org>.

Military Records

The Nebraska State Historical Society has specialized collections concerning military veterans and microfilm of the government records. The following are examples.

Among the more specialized collections not produced by the U.S. Government are the records of the Grand Army of the Republic (GAR). The Grand Army of the Republic Membership Rosters (the Nebraska Department of the Grand Army of the Republic Membership Files) give the name of each member, dates of military service, the unit and state from which he served, GAR post number, and Nebraska post office address of union Civil War Veterans. The GAR Burial Records consist of an alphabetical file of Civil War veterans buried in Nebraska that lists the military unit of service, date of death, place of burial, and often the place of birth.

"Rosters of Nebraska Soldiers in the Civil War (1861–65)" were published in Andreas's 1882, *History of Nebraska* (see Background Sources). It includes rosters of those persons serving in Nebraska units and Indian Campaigns on the Plains (1861–69). These rosters list names, dates of service, Nebraska residence, and remarks. These have been included in a database at <www.ancestry.com> as "Nebraska Volunteers, 1861–69."

"Rosters of Soldiers, Sailors, and Marines (1887–1925)" were printed and published by the secretary of state from information furnished by county clerks and assessors. These rosters give name, unit designation, and post office address. An online database at <www.ancestry.com> covers "Nebraska Resident Military Roster on June 1, 1891," which includes a roster of soldiers, sailors, and marines from the War of 1812, Mexican War, and the Civil War who resided in the state on that date.

The war service cards for the 1898 Spanish-American War provide name, birthplace, age or birth date, residence, dates of service and assigned unit of Nebraskans. Included in these records are the enlistment and service records for Nebraskans who served in the Philippine War and the Insurrection that followed (1898–1902). World War I service cards are also available and provide name, serial number, residence, age or birth date, and dates of service of Nebraskans. A World War II servicemen index cites references to Nebraska servicemen from local newspapers in the state.

Periodicals, Newspapers, and Manuscript Collections

Periodicals

Nebraska History is published quarterly by the Nebraska State Historical Society. It has quality articles on a large array of Nebraska topics of history and culture. The society publishes an index (1959–79). Another important journal is *Nebraska Ancestree,* a quarterly that is published by the Nebraska State Genealogical Society. It contains genealogical data such as

cemetery readings, early marriage records, newspaper abstracts, and queries. Back issues of its earlier publication may be available, such as *Nebraska and Midwest Genealogical Records*, vols. 1–22, published from 1923–44.

Many of the genealogical societies in Nebraska publish monthly newsletters.

Newspapers

The Nebraska State Historical Society has over 32,000 reels of Nebraska newspapers on microfilm dating from the territorial period to the present. The newspapers at the society have been cataloged as part of the Nebraska Newspaper Project, which currently has over 3,000 Nebraska newspaper titles. An inventory of the society's newspaper collection can be accessed online through IRIS, the University of Nebraska–Lincoln Libraries online catalog at <www.iris.unl.edu/screens/opacmenu.html>. IRIS can be searched by keyword, subject, title, and name of the newspaper.

The Nebraska State Historical Society also has various published and unpublished newspaper indexes. A listing is available on the society's website <www.nebraskahistory.org/databases/newspapers.shtml>. The Nebraska State Newspaper Project, started in the 1980s as a project to index Nebraska newspapers, currently consists of over 200,000 names and is part of the Nebraska GenWeb Project <www.rootsweb.com/~nenews/NSHS/nshsnews.htm>.

The *Omaha World-Herald* Clipping File, a subject and biographic file with 400,000 subject files (including over five million clippings between 1907 and 1983), is held at the Douglas County Historical Society, General Crook House, 5730 N. 30th St., #11B, Omaha, NE 68111-1657 <www.omahahistory.org>.

Manuscripts

The Nebraska State Historical Society has over 15,000 feet of archival material gathered from private sources. These manuscript collections represent the records of businesses, organizations, associations, churches, private educational institutions, and personal papers of individuals and families. The society's website provides reference to these collections by type: business, organizational, church, family/individual, and political.

Archives, Libraries, and Societies

Nebraska State Historical Society
P.O. Box 82554
1500 R St.
Lincoln, NE 68501-2554
www.nebraskahistory.org

Resources of the society consist of the library, public records, manuscripts, moving images/sound, photographs, and reference. The holdings are described in various sections of this chapter. Many published and unpublished family histories and biographical accounts of Nebraskans in various formats are included. The website has extensive links to resources for the state.

Nebraska State Genealogical Society
Box 5608
Lincoln, NE 68505
www.rootsweb.com/~nesgs

County record source guides are published by the society along with its quarterly *Nebraska Ancestree* and newsletter. The society's library is housed in the Beatrice Public Library.

The State DAR Library
Lue R. Spencer Genealogical Library,
Edith Abbott Memorial Library
2nd and Washington Streets
Grand Island, NE 68801

Holdings include DAR cemetery records of Nebraska and originals of Nebraska DAR Ancestors Registry.

American Historical Society of Germans from Russia
631 D St.
Lincoln, NE 68502
<www.ahsgr.com>

The society's collection includes special indexes, obituaries, and materials relating to Germans from Russia.

There are currently over forty-six genealogical societies and 150 historical societies operating in Nebraska. The Nebraska GenWeb Project website is an excellent resource for links to archives, libraries, and societies statewide <www.rootsweb.com/~negenweb>. The "Nebraska Libraries Catalog" page on the University of Nebraska–Lincoln website provides access to academic libraries, public libraries, and other libraries throughout the state <www.unl.edu/libr/othrcats/othrneb.html>.

Special Focus Categories

Naturalization

A card index to pre-1906 naturalizations for all the counties in Nebraska, western Iowa, and some counties in eastern Iowa in the 1930s and 1940s was compiled as a Works Progress Administration (WPA) project. This index has been microfilmed and can be searched at the Nebraska State Historical Society. Each card contains the name, country of origin, date of naturalization, and the court, county, and state of naturalization. The name of the state does not appear on cards for many

Nebraska counties. The reverse side contains the type of naturalization and the volume and page number where the record is located. This index includes only those who received their final papers in Nebraska. It does not report those who only declared their intention in Nebraska. The Nebraska State Historical Society has over eighty percent of the naturalization records for the counties in the state from the district courts. The FHL and the society have large collections of U.S. District Court records (National Archives) on microfilm.

Native American

There are four tribes historically in Nebraska that have tribal offices today—Omaha, Santee Sioux, Ponca, and Winnebago. Each has its own reservation served through the State of Nebraska Commission on Indian Affairs, the state's liaison between the tribal governments and state government <www.indianaffairs.state.ne.us>. Other tribes on the border with other states are served from reservations and agencies elsewhere.

The U.S. Government generated many records on the Nebraska tribes, although only the four tribes with headquarters in Nebraska will be mentioned here. Agency records include censuses, school records, and enrollment records. Most of these records are at the National Archives in Washington D.C. and the NARA in Kansas City (see page 12); however, a few are also at the NARA in Denver and in Fort Worth. The FHL has microfilm for many of them as well.

Some tribes, like the Santee Sioux, were relocated twice prior to being relocated in Nebraska, so their records cover agencies in several states. Outlined in the following chart are the Indian agency, years of the particular collection, the NARA location, and the existence of post-1885 censuses.

Ethnic Groups

Czech bibliographical materials can be found in the archives at the Nebraska State Historical Society and in general stacks at Love Library on the University of Nebraska campus, which has a policy of not assisting in genealogical queries. These materials must be searched by the individual.

A special census of Germans from Russia living in Lincoln (1913–14) is available on microfilm at the Nebraska State Historical Society and the American Historical Society of Germans from Russia. A transcription is also on the Internet at <www.webbitt.com/volga/gn.lincoln.htm>.

Tribe	Agency	DC/NARA	Census
Omaha	Upper Missouri Agency (1824–37)	DC	no
Omaha	Council Bluffs Agency (1837–56)	DC	no
Omaha	Omaha (Winnebago) Agency (1867–1946)	DC/KC	yes
Omaha	Nebraska Agencies (1876–80)	DC	no
Ponca	Upper Missouri Agency (1824–59)	DC	no
Ponca	Paqwnee (Ponca) Agency (1871–1964)	DC/FTW	yes
Ponca	Santee Sioux (Flandreau) (1892–1957)	KC	yes
Santee Sioux	Saint Peters Agency (to 1870)	DC	no
Santee Sioux	Santee Sioux Agency (1871–76)	DC/KC	yes
Santee Sioux	Nebraska Agencies (1876–80)	DC	no
Santee Sioux	Flandreau School (1873–1951)	DC/KC	yes
Santee Sioux	Winnebago and Yankton (1867–1955)	DC/KC	yes
Winnebago	Wind River Agency (1898–1955)	DEN	yes
Winnebago	Prairie du Chien Agency (1824–42)	DC	no
Winnebago	Turkey River Subagency (1842–46)	DC	no
Winnebago	Winnebago Agency (1826–76)	DC	no
Winnebago	Nebraska Agencies (1876–80)	DC	no
Winnebago	Omaha (Winnebago) Agency (1861–1955)	KC	yes

County Resources

The Nebraska State Historical Society has a microfilming partnership with the Genealogical Society of Utah to preserve county records. The county marriage registers have been among the first completed with naturalization and deed records in process. The available microfilm can be viewed at the Nebraska State Historical Society and the FHL. The Nebraska State Genealogical Society has published *Research Guides for Genealogical Data* for the majority of Nebraska's counties. This ongoing project will publish additional guides in the future.

Current links to each county's government can be found at the State of Nebraska website <www.nebraska.gov/counties.phtml>. In the chart below, dates in parentheses indicate the year the county was organized as opposed to the year it was formed. "Original" counties were established in 1854 when territorial government was created. "Unorganized" land refers to counties added later from land not organized under territorial government.

The dates for records on the following chart are based on a comparison of the catalog of the Nebraska Historical Society, the Family History Library Catalog, the various county inventories produced by the Nebraska Genealogical Society, and the USGenWeb site for Nebraska. The source for county formations is *Nebraska: A Guide to Genealogical Research* by the Nebraska State Genealogical Society, which references three standard works in compiling its data. The years for records were taken from various county guides produced by the society.

The county clerk can be expected to hold county commissioners' minutes, notary records, and delayed birth registrations. Other records of interest to the researcher include military discharges, voter registrations, estray notices, marks and brands, physician's registers, farm and ranch names, and school registers. A few county commissioners' minutes are at the Nebraska State Historical Society.

Few births or deaths were kept before statewide recording (see Vital Records). Marriages are at the county clerk, deeds are at the register of deeds, and probates are at the clerk of the county court, as are court records dealing with civil matters.

The Counties and County Seats of

Nebraska

25   0   25   50   75 Miles

NEBRASKA

416

Copyright 1989, Ancestry, Inc.

Drawn by William Dollarhide

Map	County Address	Date Formed Parent County/ies	Birth Marriage Death	Land Probate Court
B6	Adams 500 W. Fifth, Rm. 109 Hastings 68901-7509	1867 unorganized	—— 1872 ——	1871 1871 1872
H3	Antelope 501 Main St. Neligh 68756-1466	1871 unorganized	—— 1876 ——	1871 1871 1871
C4	Arthur 205 First St./P.O. Box 126 Arthur 69121-0126 *Earlier records attached to McPherson County	1887 (1913*) McPherson	—— 1914 ——	1913 1913 1913
A4	Banner 204 State St./P.O. Box 67 Harrisburg 69345-0067	1888 Cheyenne	—— 1883 ——	1889 1889 1889
	Blackbird Indian Reservation *Became Omaha Reservation in 1857 and Thurston County in 1889. From 1884–89 administered by Dakota County.*			
E2	Blaine P.O. Box 136 Brewster 68821-0136	1885 unorganized	—— 1883 ——	1886 1886 1886
H4	Boone 222 S. Fourth St. Albion 68620-1247	1871 unorganized	—— 1872 ——	1871 1871 1871
A2	Box Butte P.O. Box 678 Alliance 69301-0678	1886 Dawes	—— 1887 ——	1887 1887 1887
G1	Boyd 401 Thayer St./P.O. Box 26 Butte 68722-0026	1891 unorganized	—— 1892 ——	1891 1891 1891
E2	Brown 148 W. Fourth Ainsworth 69210	1883 unorganized	—— 1883 ——	1887 1883 1880
F5	Buffalo 1512 Central/P.O. Box 1270 Kearney 68848-1270	1855 (1870) unorganized	—— 1872 ——	1870 1874 1871
K3	Burt 111 N. 13th St./P.O. Box 87 Tekamah 68061-0087	1854 original	—— 1861 ——	1857 1858 1858
J4	Butler 451 N. 5th St./P.O. Box 289 David City 68632-0289	1857 unorganized	—— 1869 ——	1857 1856 1859
	Calhoun	1856 (renamed Saunders, 1862) Lancaster		
K5	Cass 346 Main St. Plattsmouth 68048-1957	1854 original	—— 1855 ——	1855 1855 1856
J2	Cedar 101 Broadway/P.O. Box 47 Hartington 68739-0047	1855 unorganized	—— 1872 ——	1857 1857 1857
C6	Chase 921 Broadway/P.O. Box 1299 Imperial 69033-1299 *Attached for administrative purposes to Frontier County until 1877, then to Hayes County until 1886.	1886 Keith*	—— 1887 ——	1887 1887 1886
D2	Cherry 365 N. Main/P.O. Box 120 Valentine 69201-0120	1883 Sioux	—— 1883 ——	1882 1883 1883
A4	Cheyenne 1000 10th St./P.O. Box 217 Sidney 69162-0217	1867 Lincoln	—— 1870 ——	1871 1871 1871
G6	Clay 111 W. Fairfield Clay Center 68933-1499	1871 unorganized	—— 1871 ——	1872 1871 1872
J4	Colfax 411 E. Eleventh St. Schuyler 68661-1940	1869 Platte	—— 1869 ——	1869 1869 1860
J3	Cuming 200 S. Lincoln/P.O. Box 290 West Point 68788-0290	1855 unorganized	—— 1866 ——	1869 1869 1862
E4	Custer 431 S. Tenth St. Broken Bow 68822-2001	1877 unorganized (originally Kountze County)	—— 1883 ——	1880 1877 1877
J2	Dakota 1600 Broadway/P.O. Box 39 Dakota City 68731-0039	1855 unorganized	—— 1856 ——	1855 1858 1857
A2	Dawes 451 Main St. Chadron 69337-2697	1885 Sioux	—— 1886 ——	1885 1886 1877
E5	Dawson 700 N. Washington/P.O. Box 370 Lexington 68850-0370	1860 (1871) unorganized	—— 1873 ——	1871 1871 1870
B5	Deuel 718 3rd/P.O. Box 327 Chappel 69129-0327	1889 Cheyenne	—— 1889 ——	1886 1889 1888
J2	Dixon 302 3rd St./P.O. Box 546 Ponca 68770-0546	1856 Dakota	—— 1861 ——	1862 1858 1860
J4	Dodge 435 N. Park Fremont 68025	1854 original	—— 1856 ——	1857 1867 1856
K4	Douglas 1819 Farman St. Omaha 68102	1854 original	1869 1856 1873	1854 1855 1855
C6	Dundy 102 7th Ave. W./P.O. Box 506 Benkelman 69021-0506	1873 (1884) unorganized	—— 1873 ——	1873 1873 1873
	Emmett	1867 (changed to Knox, 1873; originally called L'Eau Qui Court, 1867)		

Map	County Address	Date Formed Parent County/ies	Birth Marriage Death	Land Probate Court
H6	Fillmore 900 G St./P.O. Box 307 Geneva 68361-0307	1856 (1871) from Saline	—— 1871 ——	1872 1872 1871
	Forney	1854 (renamed Nemaha, 1855) original		
F6	Franklin 405 15th Ave./P.O. Box 146 Franklin 68939-0146	1871 unorganized	—— 1872 ——	1871 1872 1872
D6	Frontier P.O. Box 40 Stockville 69042-0040	1872 unorganized	—— 1873 ——	1872 1872 1872
E6	Furnas 912 R St./P.O. Box 387 Beaver City 68926-0387	1873 unorganized	—— 1876 ——	1873 1873 1873
J6	Gage 612 Grant St./P.O. Box 429 Beatrice 68310-0429	1855 unorganized (Beatrice)	1890 1860 1890	1858 1855 1857
B4	Garden 611 Main St./P.O. Box 486 Oshkosh 69154-0486	1909 Deuel	—— 1910 ——	1887 1910 1910
F3	Garfield 250 S. 8th/P.O. Box 218 Burwell 68823-0218	1884 Wheeler	—— 1884 ——	1884 1884 1884
E6	Gosper 507 Smith St./P.O. Box 136 Elwood 68937-0136	1873 (1881) unorganized	—— 1873 ——	1875 1873 1873
C3	Grant 105 E. Harrison St./P.O. Box 139 Hyannis 69350-0139	1887 unorganized	—— 1888 ——	1888 1888 1888
G4	Greeley Courthouse Sq./P.O. Box 287 Greeley 68842-0287	1871 unorganized	—— 1871 ——	1870 1871 1871
	Greene	1855 (renamed Seward, 1862) Cass		
G5	Hall 121 S. Pine St. Grand Island 68801-6076	1858 unorganized	—— 1868 ——	1858 1859 1867
H5	Hamilton 1111 Thirteenth St., Ste. 1 Aurora 68818-2017	1867 unorganized	—— 1870 ——	1871 1871 1871
F6	Harlan 706 W. 2nd St./P.O. Box 698 Alma 68920-0698	1871 Lincoln	—— 1873 ——	1871 1871 1871
D6	Hayes Troth St./P.O. Box 370 Hayes Center 69032-0370	1877 unorganized	—— 1886 ——	1877 1877 1877
D6	Hitchcock 229 E. D St./P.O. Box 248 Trenton 69044-0248	1873 unorganized	—— 1888 ——	1873 1873 1873
G2	Holt 204 N. 4th/P.O. Box 329 O'Neill 68763-0329	1862 (as West; renamed 1876) unorganized	—— 1878 ——	1862 1862 1862
D3	Hooker 303 NW 1st St./P.O. Box 184 Mullen 69152-0184	1889 unorganized	—— 1889 ——	1889 1903 1889
G4	Howard 612 Indian/P.O. Box 25 Saint Paul 68873-0025	1871 Hall	—— 1872 ——	1871 1871 1871
	Izard	(renamed Stanton, 1862)		
	Jackson	1855 (renamed Fillmore, 1856) Original		

Far west corner of Nebraska; later divided into Chase, part of Hayes, Perkins, Dundy, and Hitchcock. Census for 1870 is found in Lincoln enumeration.

Map	County Address	Date Formed Parent County/ies	Birth Marriage Death	Land Probate Court
J6	Jefferson 411 Fourth St. Fairbury 68352-2513	1856 (1864) unorganized	—— 1864 ——	1864 1864 1864

Was established in 1856 as Jefferson County. Present-day Jefferson County, to the east, was designated as Jones County. When Nebraska was admitted to the Union in 1867, Jefferson and Jones Counties were united as Jefferson. In 1870 Jefferson was again separated. The area that was originally called Jones took the name Jefferson and retained the old county records. The original Jefferson became known as Thayer County.

Map	County Address	Date Formed Parent County/ies	Birth Marriage Death	Land Probate Court
K6	Johnson 351 Broadway/P.O. Box 416 Tecumseh 68450-0416	1857 Nemaha	—— 1858 ——	1859 1867 1862
	Johnston	1855 (renamed Saline, 1856)		
	Jones	(abolished 1867; became Jefferson) unorganized		
F6	Kearney 424 N. Colorado/P.O. Box 339 Minden 68958-0339	1860 (1872) unorganized	—— 1872 ——	1872 1873 1873
C4	Keith 511 N. Spruce/P.O. Box 149 Ogallala 69153-0149	1873 Cheyenne	—— 1873 ——	1873 1873 1873
E1	Keya Paha 310 Courthouse Dr./P.O. Box 349 Springview 68778-0349	1884 Brown	—— 1885 ——	1881 1884 1884
A4	Kimball 114 E. Third St. Kimball 69145-1456	1888 Cheyenne	—— 1889 ——	1886 1889 1886
H2	Knox 206 Main St./P.O. Box 166 Center 68724-0166	1857 as L'Eau Qui Court* 	—— 1869 ——	1857 1857 1857

*Name changed to Knox 1873.

Map	County Address	Date Formed Parent County/ies	Birth Marriage Death	Land Probate Court
	Kountze	(changed to Custer, 1877)		

Map	County Address	Date Formed Parent County/ies	Birth Marriage Death	Land Probate Court
J5	**Lancaster** 555 S. Tenth St., Rm 110 Lincoln 68508-2803	1855 unorganized	—— 1866 ——	1858 1866 1863
	L'Eau Qui Court	(renamed Knox, 1873) unorganized		
D5	**Lincoln** 301 N. Jeffers St. North Platte 69101-3932	1860 (as Shorter; renamed 1866) unorganized	—— 1862 ——	1868 1868 1866
D4	**Logan** P.O. Box 8 Stapleton 69163-0008	1885 unorganized	—— 1885 ——	1885 1885 1885
	Loup (old)	1855 (abolished 1856; became part of Madison, Izard, Monroe, Platte) Burt		
F6	**Loup (present)** 408 4th St./P.O. Box 187 Taylor 68879-0187	1883 unorganized	—— 1883 ——	1883 1883 1883
H3	**Madison** 110 Clara Davis Dr./P.O. Box 290 Madison 68748-0290	1856 (1867) unorganized	—— 1868 ——	1867 1867 1867
	McNeale	1855 (abolished 1856; became part of Madison) Burt		
D4	**McPherson** 5th & Anderson/P.O. Box 122 Tryon 69167-0122	1887 (1890) unorganized	—— 1890 ——	1890 1890 1890
H4	**Merrick** 1510 18th St./P.O. Box 27 Central City 68826-0027	1858 unorganized	—— 1869 ——	1858 1858 1858
	Monroe	1856 (abolished 1860; became part of Platte) Loup		
A3	**Morrill** 6th & Main St./P.O. Box 610 Bridgeport 69336-0610	1908 Cheyenne	—— 1909 ——	1909 1909 1909
H4	**Nance** 209 Esther St./P.O. Box 338 Fullerton 68638-0338	1879 Monroe	—— 1893 ——	1878 1879 1879
K6	**Nemaha** 1824 N St. Auburn 68305-2342	1855 (as Forney; renamed 1855) unorganized	—— 1855 ——	1855 1855 1855
H6	**Nuckolls** 150 S. Main/P.O. Box 366 Nelson 68961-0366	1860 (1871) unorganized	—— 1872 ——	1869 1871 1871
K5	**Otoe** 1021 Central Ave./P.O. Box 249 Nebraska City 68410-0249	1854 Pierce	—— 1855 ——	1854 1855 1855
K6	**Pawnee** 625 6th St./P.O. Box 431 Pawnee City 68420-0131	1855 unorganized*	—— 1858 ——	1855 1855 1855

Attached to Richardson for judicial purposes until 1856.

Map	County Address	Date Formed Parent County/ies	Birth Marriage Death	Land Probate Court
C5	**Perkins** 200 Lincoln Ave./P.O. Box 156 Grant 69140-0156	1887 Keith	—— 1888 ——	1887 1887 1887
F6	**Phelps** 715 5th Ave./P.O. Box 404 Holdrege 68949-0404	1873 unorganized	—— 1877 ——	1873 1886 1873
	Pierce (old)	1854 (abolished 1855) original		
H2	**Pierce (present)** 111 W. Court St. Pierce 68767-1224	1870 unorganized	—— 1879 ——	1856 1856 1856
H4	**Platte** 2610 Fourteenth St. Columbus 68601-4960	1856 Monroe	—— 1858 ——	1856 1856 1857
H4	**Polk** Courthouse Sq./P.O. Box 276 Osceola 68651-0276	1856 (1870) Butler	—— 1871 ——	1870 1870 1870
D6	**Red Willow** 502 Morris Ave. McCook 69001-2006	1873 unorganized	—— 1873 ——	1879 1873 1873
K6	**Richardson** 1700 Stone St. Falls City 68355-2025	1854 (1855) original	—— 1855 ——	1855 1855 1855
F2	**Rock** 400 State St./P.O. Box 367 Bassett 68714-0367	1888 Brown	—— 1884 ——	1888 1888 1887
J6	**Saline** 215 S. Court/P.O. Box 865 Wilber 68465-0865	1855 (1867) original	—— 1866 ——	1867 1867 1866

Originally named Johnston when created in 1855 from organized lands. Absorbed into Saline County in 1856.

Map	County Address	Date Formed Parent County/ies	Birth Marriage Death	Land Probate Court
K4	**Sarpy** 1210 Golden Gate Dr. Papillion 68046-3088	1857 Douglas	—— 1857 ——	1857 1857 1857
J4	**Saunders** 433 N. Chestnut/P.O. Box 610 Wahoo 68066-1863	1856 (as Calhoun; renamed 1862) unorganized	—— 1866 ——	1856 1866 1866
A3	**Scotts Bluff** 1825 Tenth St. Gering 69341-2444	1888 Cheyenne	—— 1889 ——	1889 1889 1889
J5	**Seward** 529 Seward St./P.O. Box 190 Seward 68434-0190	1856 (as Greene; renamed 1862) unorganized	—— 1869 ——	1856 1856 1856

Map	County / Address	Date Formed / Parent County/ies	Birth Marriage Death	Land Probate Court
B2	Sheridan 301 E 2nd/P.O. Box 39 Rushville 69360-0039	1885 Sioux	—— 1885 ——	1885 1894 1885
F2	Sherman 630 O St./P.O. Box 456 Loup City 68853-0456	1871 unorganized	—— 1873 ——	1871 1871 1871
	Shorter	1860 (renamed Lincoln, 1861) unorganized		
A2	Sioux 325 Main St./P.O. Box 158 Harrison 69346-0158	1867 (1886) Izard	—— 1887 ——	1882 1908 1886
	Attached to Cheyenne County for administrative purposes until 1886. Boundaries defined in 1877.			
J3	Stanton 804 Ivy St./P.O. Box 347 Stanton 68779-0347	1865 (as Izard; renamed 1862) Dodge	—— 1869 ——	1862 1862 1862
	Taylor *Unorganized county in western section enumerated as part of Lincoln in 1870 census. Taylor became the counties of Garden, Deuel, and parts of Morrill and Cheyenne.*			
H6	Thayer 225 N. 4th St./P.O. Box 208 Hebron 6837-02080	1867 (as Jefferson; renamed 1872) Jefferson	—— 1871 ——	1871 1871 1870
D3	Thomas 503 Main St./P.O. Box 226 Thedford 69166-0226	1887 unorganized	—— 1887 ——	1887 1887 1887
J3	Thurston 106 S. 5th St./P.O. Box G Pender 68047-0138	1855 (as Blackbird; renamed 1889) Burt	1917 1855 1917	1882 1895 1886
	From 1857–89, Thurston was part of the Omaha Reservation.			
F4	Valley 125 S. Fifteenth Ord 68862	1871 unorganized	—— 1871 ——	1871 1871 1871
K4	Washington 1555 Colfax St./P.O. Box 466 Blair 68008-0466	1854 original	—— 1856 ——	1857 1855 1855
J3	Wayne 510 Pearl St./P.O. Box 248 Wayne 68787-0248	1867 unorganized	—— 1871 ——	1871 1871 1869
G6	Webster 621 N. Cedar St. Red Cloud 68970-2300	1871 unorganized	—— 1871 ——	1872 1872 1871
	West	1860 (renamed Holt, 1862) unorganized		
G3	Wheeler 3rd & Main/P.O. Box 127 Bartlett 68622-0127	1877 unorganized	—— 1917 ——	1917 1917 1917
	Courthouse fire 1917.			
H5	York 510 Lincoln Ave. York 68467-2963	1855 (1870) Seward	—— 1870 ——	1870 1870 1870

Nevada

NELL SACHSE WOODARD AND DWIGHT A. RADFORD

Beginning in the 1820s, trailblazers such as Jedediah S. Smith, Peter Skene Ogden, Kit Carson, and Gen. John C. Fremont crossed Nevada's miles of trackless wilderness, laying the footpaths for pioneers who would follow in the next two decades. The Donner Party followed the Humboldt and Truckee rivers in the winter of 1846 on the way to their historic and tragic encampment in the Sierras. By 1848, lands encompassing Nevada were ceded to the United States by Mexico. The Mormon Station, the first permanent settlement at what is now Genoa in the Carson Valley, was established at the same time Utah Territory was formed in 1850. The territory included all of the present state of Utah, Nevada (except the southern tip that was in New Mexico Territory), the western third of Colorado, and a small corner of southwestern Wyoming.

The decade that followed brought the discovery of gold and silver and the opening of the Comstock Mine in Virginia City in 1859. Carson City was founded the same year with a burgeoning population of gold-seekers, many from California and Europe.

The Comstock Mine brought about the settlement of the state and its rapid economic growth. Nevada became a territory in 1861, and three years later was incorporated into the United States as the thirty-sixth state. When the Comstock Lode petered out, Nevada suffered a severe economic depression until minerals were discovered at Tonopah in 1900.

Near the turn of the twentieth century, an expansion of the sheep farming industry was attempted for improvement of a slackened economy. What it produced was an active conflict between cattlemen and sheepmen, which proved to be grist for many popular movies about the west. The Taylor Grazing Act settled the conflict by dividing the open range in 1934. The sheep industry was also responsible for increasing the ethnic diversity of the population, bringing English, Scots, Mexicans, Irish, Chinese, and Basques to the state.

In modern times, the state has been traversed by three major continental railroads and several airline companies. With the advent of legalized gambling in 1931, its two principal cities—Reno and Las Vegas—became meccas for the nation's gamblers, and then augmented their already established eminence by granting marriages and divorces for people in a hurry who could not quickly obtain a decree in their own state.

In addition to its gambling interests, the state still carries on mining and, in recent decades, has become a magnet for recreational purposes, particularly with mountain resorts and skiing, or boating at Lake Mead, an adjunct to Boulder Dam. Nevada has extensive farming that, for the most part, is irrigated. The state also contributed its share of inhabitants for the wars in which the United States has been engaged and has been the site of much nuclear testing since the advent of the first atomic bomb during World War II.

Vital Records

Birth and death records are at the Nevada State Department of Human Resources, Health Division, Office of Vital Records and Statistics, 505 E. King St., Carson City, NV 89701 <www.health2k.state.nv.us>. These records date from 1911 to the

present. Some counties have available birth and death registers beginning in 1887, a few of which have been deposited with the Office of Vital Records and Statistics. Most of those that still exist are in the county recorder's office. None of the pre-1911 birth and death records are included in the statewide index, which begins in 1911 and has restricted access.

Although vital statistics are held by county recorders or health officers, those officers are restricted by law from providing certified copies of such documents. Only the Office of Vital Records and Statistics can provide certified copies of birth or death records. Abbreviated birth certificates, which contain birth date, sex, race, and birthplace of the person, are provided. An applicant for a copy of a birth or death certificate must have a direct and tangible interest in the matter recorded. The only available sources for births before 1887 are the extant newspapers or church baptismal records (see Church Records).

County coroners issued burial certificates based on death certificates issued by physicians. If no physician had been in attendance, it was the duty of the county coroner, based on the facts of the death, to file all physicians' certificates and memoranda of burial permits issued and turn them over to the successor in office. Incorporated cities required burial permits from the county coroner's offices (1879 and 1911). These exist for Virginia City and Gold Hill (1879–87) and Carson City (1893–96). Nevada State Library and Archives, Division of Archives and Records (see Archives, Libraries, and Societies), has the Ormsby County Coroner's burial permit register (1893–96), which includes Carson City's permits and Storey County's coroners' records. There is a compilation of names from the coroner's records at the Nevada State Library. The Family History Library (FHL) in Salt Lake City has some county birth and death records on microfilm.

The Office of Vital Records and Statistics also has marriage and divorce records after 1969. Prior to that date, marriage records are located in the county recorder's office where the license was originally obtained. Nevada marriage indexes can be found in two formats available to the public. A large collection of marriages is found on the CD-ROM index "Arizona, California, Idaho and Nevada (1850–1951) Marriage Index" through <www.genealogy.com>. The second is an online index, part of the "Western States Historical Marriage Records" on BYU-Idaho Family History Center's website <http://abish.byui.edu/specialCollections/fhc/FamilyHistory.htm>. These latter indexes currently cover from the beginning of county marriage records to about 1900 with some extending to the 1930s. The FHL has microfilm copies of the county marriages.

Divorce records from 1862 are kept by individual county clerk's offices. The indexes of divorce records for the territorial period for Carson County and both Utah and Nevada territories are at the Nevada State Library and Archives, Division of Archives and Records.

Census Records

Federal

Population Schedules
- Indexed—1850 (part of Utah Territory), 1860 (part of Utah Territory), 1870, 1900, 1910, 1920, 1930
- Soundex—1880, 1900, 1920

Industry and Agriculture Schedules
- 1870, 1880

Mortality Schedules
- 1850 (part of Utah Territory), 1860 (part of Utah Territory), 1870, 1880

Union Veterans Schedules
- 1890

For census purposes, the counties of Carson, Humboldt, and St. Mary's were in Utah Territory in 1860. All of the Nevada federal censuses through 1910 are available on microfilm in the Nevada State Library, the Nevada Historical Society, and the Las Vegas Family History Center (FHC).

The mortality, industry (1870, 1880), and agriculture (1870) schedules are located at the Nevada Historical Society. The Nevada State Library has the 1880 agriculture schedule and a typescript of the 1870 mortality schedule, which is indexed. AISI publishes indexes to all the population and mortality schedules (see pages 3-4).

Territorial and State
The Nevada State Library and Archives has a partial census for the territory for 1862 and 1863; there is a full one available for 1875. The 1875 census includes all members of the household and is published in the *Appendix to Journals of Senate and Assembly, of the Eighth Session of the Legislature of the State of Nevada, 1877* (vols. 2 and 3) and the microfiche index. These are available in the Las Vegas FHC as well.

Background Sources

Balboni, Alan. *Beyond the Mafia: Italian Americans and the Development of Las Vegas.* Reno: University of Nevada Press, 1996. An authoritative account with 150 oral interviews illustrating the impact of Italian Americans on the growth and evolution of Las Vegas.

Carlson, Helen S. *Nevada Place Names: A Geographical Dictionary.* Reno: University of Nevada Press, 1974.

Dunbar, Andrew J., and Dennis McBride. *Building Hoover Dam: An Oral History of the Great Depression.* Reno: University of

Nevada Press, 2001. An account of the people who built the dam living in the tightly controlled confines of Boulder City, contrasted with the opposite environment in nearby Las Vegas.

Ford, Jean, Betty J. Glass, and Martha B. Gould, eds. *Women in Nevada History: An Annotated Bibliography of Published Sources.* Reno: Women's History Project, 2000. A bibliographic index of information from 425 books and publications covering 1881 to 1998.

Greene, Diane E. *Nevada Guide to Genealogical Records.* Baltimore: Clearfield Co., 2000. Provides a comprehensive guide to Nevada's records and where they are located.

Greene, Diane E., and Gary E. Elliott, eds. *Nevada: Readings and Perspectives.* Reno: Nevada Historical Society, 1997. Forty-five articles that focus on the diverse aspects of Nevada history. Some are classics from the *Nevada Historical Society Quarterly.*

Hulse, James W. *The Silver State.* 2d ed. Reno: University of Nevada Press, 1998. A textbook used at the college level, it provides a manageable overview of the state's history in a readable format.

James, Ronald M., and C. Elizabeth Raymond. *Comstock Women: The Making of a Mining Community.* Reno: University of Nevada Press, 1997. A collection of fourteen essays recounting Nevada's past from women's perspectives.

Miranda, M. L. *A History of Hispanics in Southern Nevada.* Reno: University of Nevada Press, 1997. Documents the contribution of Hispanics in mining, railroads, ranching, industry, and urban life. A pioneering study in previously neglected field of research.

Maps

A wide variety of maps are offered by the Nevada Department of Transportation, Map Sales, Room 206, 1263 S. Stewart St., Carson City, NV 89712 <www.nevadadot.com>. The department's website has quad maps online for review. They will send a catalog and price list of available maps.

The United States Geological Survey will supply any of its maps for a nominal fee (see page 5). The state office is at 333 W. Nye Lane, Room 203, Carson City, NV 89706.

Land Records

Public-Domain State

Nevada was among the states that received federal land grants. On 1 January 1863 the Homestead Act, passed by the U.S. Congress, became effective. The first U.S. District Land Office

was opened in Carson City, Nevada, in 1862; additional ones followed at Auston (1867), Belmont (1868), Elko (1872), Eureka (1873), and Pioche (1874). In addition to those records held by the National Archives (see pages 11-12), the Bureau of Land Management (BLM) Nevada State Office, 1340 Financial Blvd., Box 12000, Reno, NV 89502 <www.nv.blm.gov> has records involving transactions through Nevada's land offices. The Nevada State Library and Archives has Carson County (Utah Territory) land records and land patents for the state. Land office grants are indexed on the BLM website <www.glorecords.blm.gov>.

The Comstock Mine's minerals, including gold and silver, were claimed in 1859. The result was the first influx of population into the state that would continue until the substantial depletion of its mineral resources late in the nineteenth century. Mining dominated the economy and politics of the state for a half century. In 1866 alone, there were 200 mining districts that acted roughly as a court system in that they recorded deeds, transferred titles to claims, drew abstracts, and recorded a variety of land instruments. Documents related to mining and minerals may be found on the county level at the Nevada State Library and Archives.

The archives has mining corporation papers (1861–1926). Those after 1926 are at the Nevada Secretary of State's Office. Other holdings at the archives include state mine inspection records (1909–74) for operating mines. These records include information regarding name, county and mine supervisor, licenses of hoist operators (1922–71), and mining accidents, both fatal and nonfatal (1909–71).

In each individual county in Nevada, records pertaining to land after initial grant are usually located in the respective office of the county recorder.

Probate Records

Probate records for Nevada are located at the office of the county clerk of the respective county and include guardianships, estate files, and the like.

Court Records

Shortly after the territory of Nevada came into being on 2 March 1861, President Lincoln named James Nye as governor and appointed three newly designated federal district judgeships. The bulk of the cases involved the handling of litigation regarding mines and mining, but there were some criminal cases as well.

In general, the modern court system follows the pattern of the other southwestern states. There are four levels of jurisprudence, beginning with the municipal court, which handles only civil cases against city/local ordinances. Currently there are twenty-three

judges of these courts. The next step upward is the justice court, composed of sixty-two judges. They also have jurisdiction over civil cases, but this includes injunctions in domestic problems as well. This level is followed by the district court, which has thirty-four judges. These courts handle both civil and criminal cases, divorces, probate, minors, and appeals from the lower courts. The highest court is the Nevada State Supreme Court, made up of five justices who hear appeals from the lower courts, review district court cases, and accept writs.

Each level of the court system has its own offices, clerks, and records maintenance. Thus if a case is pursued at any of these courts, the search must be made in the office holding jurisdiction over the respective records. The Administrative Office of the Courts, Supreme Court Building, 201 S. Carson, Ste. 250, Carson City, NV 89701-4702, will provide the proper court and its address.

Tax Records

The county courthouse where the property was located is the best place to search for tax records. The tax assessment rolls are also at the same place. The assessment rolls are published annually in the local newspapers and should be on file where the newspapers are currently held, either the actual newspaper or the microfilm. The Nevada State Library and Archives, Division of Archives and Records, holds duplicate assessment rolls for all counties (1891–92), and Ormsby County's assessment rolls (1862–1950).

The FHL has the Internal Assessment Lists for the Nevada Territory (1863–66) on microfilm and the Nevada GenWeb (see page 16) Project is transcribing and indexing these online.

Cemetery Records

Cemetery records for almost every county in the state of Nevada can be found on microfilm through the FHL and at the Las Vegas FHC. Volume one of Richard B. Taylor's *The Nevada Tombstone Record Book* (Las Vegas: Nevada Families Project, 1986) covers most of Southern Nevada with the promise that volume 2 will cover the rest of the state when it is published. The website <www.interment.net> has a growing collection of tombstone transcripts as does the Nevada GenWeb Project (see page 16).

Church Records

Historically, Nevada was built on the lure of mineral wealth; the populace shifted with each succeeding strike. Establishing churches and bringing religion to this transient group of people was not only difficult but was compounded by the fire destruction of numerous early frame churches. The Church of Jesus Christ of Latter-day Saints (Mormon), Roman Catholic, Methodist, Episcopalian, Congregationalist, and Jewish congregations all

have had some historical part in the establishment of religion in Nevada. A description of early churches is found in Marjorie A. Hanes, *Early Nevada Churches* (Reno: Nevada State Society, Daughters of the American Revolution, 1974). Today the largest denominations in the state are the Roman Catholic Church and The Church of Jesus Christ of Latter-day Saints.

Research into Episcopal records is made easy by the fact that the parish records for 1862 to 1969 for the diocese have been deposited at the Nevada Historical Society. The church is served by the Nevada Diocese of Reno, 515 Court St., P.O. Box 1121, Reno, NV 89504-1221 <http://dmla.clan.lib.nv.us/docs/museums/reno/his-soc.htm>. The Roman Catholics are served by two dioceses, in Las Vegas and Reno: Diocese of Las Vegas, 336 Cathedral Way, P.O. Box 18316, Las Vegas, NV 89114-8316 <www.lasvegas-diocese.org>; and Diocese of Reno, 2905 Arlington, Ste. 200, Reno, NV 89501 <www.catholicreno.org>.

The records of The Church of Jesus Christ of Latter-day Saints for Nevada have been microfilmed and are found in the FHL and are also available at its Las Vegas FHC.

The United Methodist Church in Nevada is served by the Desert Southwest District, 1550 E. Meadow Brook Ave., Ste. 200, Phoenix, AZ 85014-4040 <www.desertsw.org>.

Military Records

In 1861 the Union was able to raise a volunteer regiment of infantry that served with California troops. In 1862 headquarters were established at Fort Churchill for the military district of Utah and Nevada, and in 1863 six companies of cavalry and a like number of infantry outfits were raised. These Union soldiers did not serve outside their own region. The militia was under the jurisdiction of the legislature. The National Archives has indexes of the army volunteers for the state; these are also available through the FHL and <www.ancestry.com>.

Although the Nevada State Library and Archives has service records for World War I through 1972 and copies of discharge papers, access is restricted to the person of record or immediate family. The FHL has microfilm of the WWI Draft Registration Cards, while <www.ancestry.com> has indexed the cards online for the entire state.

Periodicals, Newspapers, and Manuscript Collections

Periodicals

Nevada Historical Society Quarterly is published by the Nevada Historical Society. The Nevada Historical Society's website has an online index to this publication by author, title, and subject. Another important publication is *The Prospector*, published

since 1976 by Clark County Genealogical Society (see Archives, Libraries, and Societies).

Newspapers

Newspapers for a great many cities are on microfilm at the Nevada State Library, Nevada Historical Society, and the University of Nevada in both Reno and Las Vegas. The University of Nevada Las Vegas Libraries website (see Archives, Libraries, and Societies) has a database inventory of these newspapers on microfilm. The database provides access by title, county, and city. The website also has links to indexes and current newspapers.

The *Territorial Enterprise* had its advent at Genoa in 1858 but was shortly moved to Carson City and then to Virginia City. Mark Twain used this newspaper to cut his journalistic teeth, so these publications were not just politics and mining but literary endeavors as well.

The *Silver Age* superseded the *Enterprise* at Carson City. *The Daily Independent* began publishing in Carson City in 1863, but it did not survive after October 1864. *The Daily Evening Post* was also a short-lived publication. A number of early papers were started only to end or to move from one location to another. A standard reference to those and subsequent undertakings is Richard E. Lingenfelter and Karen Rix Gash, *The Newspapers of Nevada: A History and Bibliography, 1854–1979* (Reno: University of Nevada Press, 1984).

Manuscripts

The Nevada Historical Society, a major historical depository, has an excellent collection of old newspapers, manuscripts, and diaries. The Nevada Historical Society's "Russell McDonald Collection," indexed on the society's website, has biographical information on state officials and other prominent Nevada residents.

"Nevada Women's History Project" <www.nevadawomen.org> provides biographies and source material (published and unpublished) for manuscript collections in the state.

A special collection at the University of Nevada at Las Vegas contains major historical records, manuscripts, diaries, and photographs, especially of Clark County.

Outside the state, a researcher should consult the Bancroft Library of the University of California at Berkeley, California (see California), as well as the Utah State Archives and the Utah State Historical Society (see Utah). All of these have important historical manuscript materials, particularly for the territorial and pre-state eras.

Archives, Libraries, and Societies

Nevada State Library and Archives
401 N. Stewart St.
Carson City, NV 89701
http://dmla.clan.lib.nv.us/docs/nsla

This institution includes the state's library and archives, each with good research collections, although the archives concerns itself with statewide oriented research material. A library directory for the state can be found on its website under Nevada Library Directory and Statistics."

Nevada Historical Society
1650 N. Virginia St.
Reno, NV 89503
http://dmla.clan.lib.nv.us/docs/museums/reno/his-soc.htm

University of Nevada Las Vegas Libraries
4505 South Maryland Pkwy.
Las Vegas, NV 89154
www.library.nevada.edu/index.html

Las Vegas Nevada Regional Family History Center
509 S. Ninth St. (no mail inquiries)
Las Vegas, NV 89101

A branch of the FHL, it is large enough to collect a variety of materials for research pertaining to Nevada.

Nevada State Genealogical Society
Box 20666
Reno, NV 89515-0666
www.rootsweb.com/~nvsgs

Clark County Genealogical Society
P.O. Box 1929
Las Vegas, NV 89125-4099
www.rootsweb.com/~nvccngs

The largest county genealogical society in the state; it publishes *The Prospector.*

Special Focus Categories

Native American

Historically, there have been four major tribes occupying lands in present-day Nevada: Northern and Southern Paiute, the Shoshone, and the Washo. Today, there are twenty-three reservations although most of the state's native people have never lived on one. The reservations and small colonies scattered throughout Nevada often make research somewhat difficult.

The Inter-Tribal Council of Nevada <www.itcn.org> represents twenty-six tribes, communities, and organizations in the Nevada and Great Basin region, including Te-Moak Tribe of Western Shoshone (in four bands); the Washoe Tribe of Nevada/California; various Paiute tribes, reservations, and colonies; and the Goshutes of Nevada and Utah. The Inter-Tribal Council of Nevada does not conduct genealogical research; however, their member links provide important contact information. It should

be noted that many of Nevada's Native Americans lived on state boundaries. Consequently, records may be in government agencies and in censuses outside Nevada.

The agencies in Nevada are currently divided into the Eastern Nevada Agency and Western Nevada Agency. Most of the older agency records are at the FARC San Francisco (see California—Native American).

Other Ethnic Groups

Nevada has a large foreign-born population whose history is covered in Wilbur S. Shepperson, *Restless Strangers: Nevada's Immigrants and Their Interpreters* (Reno: University of Nevada Press, 1970). The book draws from newspaper accounts, interviews, and census records.

The Yugoslavians and the Basques are two important ethnic groups in the history of Nevada. The following will provide helpful background material on them: Adam S. Eterovich, *Yugoslavs in Nevada, 1859–1900* (San Francisco: R and E Research Associates, 1973), and William A. Douglass and Jon Bilbao, *Amerikanuak, Basques in the New World* (Reno: University of Nevada Press, 1975). The Basque Studies Library at the University of Nevada, Reno, holds a large collection of Basque-related material for Nevada, Oregon, and Idaho. It maintains the most comprehensive collection for Basque Studies outside of Europe.

County Resources

The following chart indicates what vital, land, probate, and court records are in each county. The dates indicated are the first known records for each county. County records may still be with the county, at the Nevada State Library and Archives, and/or on microfilm at the FHL. Some data from Greene's work (See Background Sources) was also used.

In Nevada, the county recorders hold land records, except in two cases where the county assessor's office handles them. County clerks have probate records, and the clerk of the courts maintains court records. Current contact information to the individual counties can be found on the website "Nevada County and City Information" <www.sos.state.nv.us/county/countymap.htm>. A list of what record types can be found and which office handles them can be found on the Nevada State Library and Archives website.

Drawn by William Dollarhide

The Counties and County Seats of
Nevada

25 0   25   50   75   100 Miles

NEVADA

Map	County Address	Date Formed Parent County/ies	Birth Marriage Death	Land Probate Court
	Carson	1854 (abolished 1861; became part of Washoe, Churchill, Storey, Lyon, Douglas, and Humboldt) Utah Territory		
	As part of Utah Territory, it included Carson City, Genoa, and Virginia City, *but it was abolished when Nevada Territory counties were formed.*			
E2	Carson City City Hall, 885 E. Musser St. Carson City 89701-4775	1861 Ormsby	1887 1887 1887	1855 1864 1864
	Ormsby County was consolidated with Carson City, 1969, to form an independent city.			
D3	Churchill 155 N. Taylor St. Fallon 89406	1861 original	1888 1864 1885	1864 1904 1904
J7	Clark 200 S. Third St. Las Vegas 89155	1909 Lincoln	1909 1909 1909	1909 1909 1909
	District Health Department, 625 Shadow Lane, Las Vegas, has births and death *from 1955 for Las Vegas.*			
E2	Douglas 1594 Esmeralda St./P.O. Box 218 Minden 89423	1861 original	1885 1862 1887	1855 1887 1887
	In 1859, the county was part of Millard County, Utah, then added to Carson County.			
B6	Elko 571 Idaho St. Elko 89801-3715	1869 Lander	1887 1869 1887	1869 1869 1869
G4	Esmeralda P.O. Box 517 Goldfield 89013-0517	1861 original	1887 1871 1887	1863 1881 1864
D5	Eureka P.O. Box 667 Eureka 89316-0677-3150	1873 Lander/White Pine	1887 1870 1887	1873 1873 1873
	Added part of White Pine County in 1881.			
A3	Humboldt 50 W. Fifth St. Winnemucca 89445	1861 original	1887 1862 1887	1861 1863 1869
D4	Lander 315 S. Humboldt St. Battle Mountain 89820-1982	1862 Humboldt/Churchill	1887 1863 1887	1862 1862 1862
G6	Lincoln P.O. Box 90 Pioche 89043	1866 Nye	1887 1871 1887	1865 1855 1873
E2	Lyon 27 S. Main St. Yerington 89447-2571	1861 original	1887 1861 1887	1862 1867 1867
E3	Mineral P.O. Box 1450 Hawthorne 89415-1450	1911 Esmeralda	1911 1911 1911	1911 1911 1911
F5	Nye P.O. Box 153 Tonopah 89049-0153	1864 Esmeralda	1887 1864 1887	1864 1864 1864
	Ormsby	1861 (became part of Carson City, 1969) original		
	Pahute	1864 (abolished 1871; became part of Lincoln and later Clark) Arizona Territory		
C3	Pershing P.O. Box 820 Lovelock 89419-0820	1919 Humboldt	1919 1919 1919	1919 1919 1919
	Roop	1870 (annexed to Washoe, 1883)		
	St. Mary's	1860 (abolished 1869; became Elko)		
D2	Storey P.O. Box D Virginia City 89440-0139	1861 original	1887 1862 1887	1859 1886 1861
B2	Washoe P.O. Box 11130 Reno 89520-0027	1861 original	1887* 1862 1887*	1870 1870 1870
	At Washoe County Health Department, 1001 East Ninth Street, Reno 89520.			
D7	White Pine 801 Clark St. Ely 89301-1994	1869 Lander	1887 1884 1887	1885 1885* 1869
	Courthouse fire, 1885.			

New Hampshire

GEORGE F. SANBORN JR., FASG, AND ALICE EICHHOLZ, Ph.D., CG

The first permanent European settlements in what is now New Hampshire occurred along the Piscataqua River in 1623, when two groups of families associated with the Fishmonger's Company of London settled on Dover Neck and Little Harbor (now part of Portsmouth). It is highly probable that European fishermen had visited the Isles of Shoals and adjacent parts of the mainland for many years prior to 1623. Following these two settlements, towns sprang up in Exeter (1637) and Hampton (1638). For many years, New Hampshire consisted of these four communities. As their populations grew, the large tracts of land that comprised the four towns were subdivided until they included the many coastal communities seen today. The lands not claimed by the towns were covered by various patents granted to English entrepreneurs, whose heirs were still struggling over the titles decades later.

New Hampshire was a Royal Province until 1771 except for two short periods, 1642 to 1679 and 1690 to 1692, when it was under the control of Massachusetts. New Hampshire, as a Royal Province, was in the peculiar position of geographically separating the two parts of the Massachusetts Bay Colony: present-day Maine and Massachusetts. People began migrating at a very early date from Middlesex and Essex counties, Massachusetts, into the seacoast area and the Merrimack River Valley, while settlers from Connecticut and central and western Massachusetts were pushing their way up into what is now Cheshire County, with many settling as far inland as the interior parts of Grafton County.

A significant number of Ulster Scots settled in south central New Hampshire in 1718 and again in 1723. They had close familial ties with other Ulster Scots settlements in New England and Cherry Valley, and on the New York frontier, southwest of Albany. Originally settling in the old town of Londonderry, they spread out to found numerous other towns across the southern tier of New Hampshire.

Settlement of the interior of New Hampshire was affected largely by two waves of migrations. People from the seacoast were primarily responsible for settling the Lakes Region, the Upper Merrimack Valley, and "along the edge of Maine," whereas settlers from southern New England were primarily responsible for settling western and southwestern New Hampshire, with a mixture of both groups peopling the North Country. The settlers with seacoast origins had a further tendency to continue westward out of New Hampshire.

By the middle of the nineteenth century, French-Canadians began to move southward into New Hampshire to work in the mill towns and in the lumber industry. Migration from Quebec and later from the Maritime Provinces became very heavy between 1880 and 1920 and now accounts for over one-third of New Hampshire's population. Large numbers of Irish settlers came to the larger towns and cities following the potato famine and now comprise a significant portion of the population, while migrations of other ethnic groups to particular areas, often to work in specific trades, have added to the rich mosaic of New Hampshire's population. Such groups include the Poles of Franklin and the Greeks of Manchester and Laconia, as well as the Italians brought to New Hampshire to work as masons or road builders.

Vital Records

The town or city clerk's office is the place where vital events are officially recorded in New Hampshire. Today each town or city sends copies of its vital events to the New Hampshire Department of State, Division of Vital Records and Health Statistics, 29 Hazen Dr., Concord, NH 03301 <www.sos.nh.gov/vitalrecords/index.html>. Statewide compilation, however, did not begin until a law was passed in 1866 requiring the secretary of state to make a report of all vital events for each of the towns. Total compliance with the law was not accomplished until the 1880s, and even then the practice of sending a copy of the vital event to the secretary of state was not uniform. By 1905, when the Bureau of Vital Records was established, regular statewide recording became a reality.

A statewide compilation, gathered from earlier town vital records, generated the alphabetical arrangement which exists today in the card file at the bureau and in the microfilm collections at the New England Historic Genealogical Society (see Massachusetts) and the Family History Library (FHL). This alphabetical compilation is incomplete since some towns did not send all their pre-1905 vital records to the bureau. It is therefore important to check the town clerk's official records directly if no event is found in the bureau's compilation.

Births that were recorded before 1901 and deaths, marriages, and those divorce records from the 1870s to 1948 can be personally searched at the bureau. The current price for a copy, in person or by mail, is $12; phone orders are accepted at an additional charge if a credit card is used (see Court Records).

A computerized statewide system for recording birth records is being created. When finished, it will be possible to obtain a birth record for anyone in New Hampshire at any of the participating town or city clerk's offices. Statutory restrictions to records will still remain, however.

The alphabetical arrangement of the compilation at the bureau and consequently on microfilm requires some explanation. The system used was an early version of Soundex. Vital records are broken down into type of event (birth, marriage, and death) and time period, and then by the first and third letter of the last name to determine the proper card file drawer in which to search for the event. Cards exist for grooms, but brides before 1947 are on a separate microfilm index since they are not included on separate cards in the compilation. After 1901 for births and 1947 for deaths, marriages, and divorces, a researcher has to demonstrate a direct interest in the event to view or receive a copy of the record.

Children not named at birth later had their names added in the town or city office records. This practice, particularly prevalent in the last half of the nineteenth century, meant that the name eventually given did not always get sent to the state compilation. French-Canadian families might have used the baptismal names of "Joseph" or "Marie" in the copy sent to the state.

There are printed versions of New Hampshire vital records for some towns including Colebrook (1873–86), Croydon (to 1900), Danville (1760–1886), Dover (1640–1850), Hampton (to 1900), Hampton Falls (to 1899), Keene (1742–1881), Laconia marriages (1826–92), Londonderry (to 1910), and South Hampton (1743–1886). A large number of typescripts of southeastern town vital records were prepared by Priscilla Hammond and others and are located at the New Hampshire Historical Society (see Archives, Libraries, and Societies), with some at the New England Historic Genealogical Society. Town reports, generated by each town every year, include vital records for residents during the previous year. The printed reports are available both at the individual town (or city) clerk's office, but a complete set for all towns is at the New Hampshire State Library (see Archives, Libraries, and Societies).

When the microfilming project of New Hampshire town records was completed, an every-name card index created by the Works Progress Administration (WPA) for town records kept before approximately 1850 was microfilmed as well. Births, deaths, and marriages were included in the records as early as 1640 although there is no consistency, and they are far from complete. The original card index is held by the New Hampshire State Library. Both the town records and the WPA index are available on microfilm at the New England Historic Genealogical Society and through the FHL. A notable omission in the index is the town of Exeter, which was completely overlooked.

Census Records

Federal

Population Schedules

- Indexed—1790, 1800 (part), 1810, 1820 (part), 1830, 1840, 1850, 1860, 1870, 1880, 1900, 1910, 1920, 1930
- Soundex—1880, 1900, 1920

Industry and Agriculture Schedules

- 1850, 1860, 1870, 1880

Mortality Schedules

- 1850, 1860, 1870, 1880

Union Veterans Schedules

- 1890

Part of the 1800 and 1820 census records for New Hampshire are no longer in existence. Towns in Rockingham County in 1800 not included are Atkinson, Greenland,

Hampton, Hampton Falls, Londonderry, Northampton, Pelham, Plaistow, Salem, Seabrook, Stratham, and Windham. Strafford County towns missing from that census are Alton, Barnstead, Brookfield, Effingham, Gilmanton, Middleton, New Durham, Ossipee, Tuftonboro, Wakefield, and Wolfeborough. *The 1798 U.S. Direct Tax* has been found for nine of these towns (published by Heritage Books): Alton, Brookfield, Effingham, Middleton, New Durham, Ossipee, Tuftonboro, Wakefield, and Wolfeborough. This is an excellent alternative source to the lost census returns (see Tax Records). *Heads of Family at the Second Census of the United States Taken in the Year 1800* was privately published by John Brooks Threlfall (Madison, Wisc.: the author, 1973). Except for the missing towns, the entire census enumerations are in this volume, which is distributed through Adams Press in Chicago, Illinois.

All the census records for 1820 for Grafton County and parts of Rockingham (Gosport, Greenland, New Castle, Newington, Portsmouth, and Rye) are lost. Only Center Harbor, Gilford, Moultonborough, New Hampton, and Sanbornton records are available for Strafford County.

The original population returns (1850, 1860, 1870, and 1880 for the entire state, and 1840 for Rockingham, Merrimack, and Strafford county towns) are now held by the New Hampshire Division of Records Management and Archives (see Archives, Libraries, and Societies).

With large numbers of French-Canadians in the state by the time of the 1850 census, care should be taken to use alternate spellings when using any indexes. The New Hampshire State Library (see Archives, Libraries, and Societies) and the New England Historic Genealogical Society (see page 13) hold microfilm copies of all extant census records for the state.

Provincial

For the provincial period, various enumerations, primarily for tax purposes, exist for the years 1732, 1744, 1767, and 1776. All originals are available at the New Hampshire Records and Archives, and except for 1732, appear in the multi-volume set of *New Hampshire State Papers* (see Background Sources). There are reprints of some with additional material used for supplements. It should be noted that none of the following listings are censuses in strict terms:

Holbrook, Jay Mack. *New Hampshire Residents, 1633–1699.* Oxford, Mass.: Holbrook Research Institute, 1979. For Dover, Exeter, Portsmouth, Hampton (and Kingston), Isles of Shoals. An alphabetical listing compiled from tax lists, land grants, probates, church records, and other sources. Each listing gives the original source for checking accuracy.

———. *New Hampshire 1732 Census.* Oxford, Mass.: Holbrook Research Institute, 1981. Lists 3,500 heads of household by town with number of males over age sixteen enumerated and covers a period of years, not just 1732.

———. *New Hampshire 1776 Census.* Oxford, Mass.: Holbrook, 1976. Over 9,000 males listed by place of residence and whether for or against revolution. Original spellings are used.

Background Sources

Town histories are abundant, particularly for southwestern towns of New Hampshire, with over 100 containing excellent genealogies of families stretching the generations back to the point of debarkation. The largest collections are held by the New Hampshire State Library and the New Hampshire Historical Society, located next door to each other (see Archives, Libraries, and Societies for addresses).

Jeremy Belknap, *The History of New Hampshire*, 3 vols. (1784–96) is an excellent history of the state including the complicated and conflicting land grants up to 1796. It has been reprinted many times and is available on microfilm. The second edition (1812) included all three volumes, but John Farmer revised the first two volumes in one (Dover, Del.: n.p., 1831), with copious notes added to the text. This one-volume edition was reprinted in 1862. Volume 3 of the 1812 edition has been recently reprinted as Gary T. Lord, ed., *Belknap's New Hampshire History: An Account of the State in 1792* (Hampton, N.H.: Peter Randall, 1973), with a new introduction and notes on this classic perspective of New Hampshire history.

Copeley, William. *Index to Genealogies in New Hampshire Town Histories.* Concord, N.H.: New Hampshire Historical Society, 1988. Updated and comprehensive, this index lists any family for whom more than three generations are covered in New Hampshire published town histories.

Hanrahan, E. J., ed. *Hammond's Check List of New Hampshire History.* Somersworth, N.H.: New Hampshire Publishing Co., 1971. This bibliography of published New Hampshire history has been superseded by Haskell and Bassett (see below), but some items were not carried over.

Haskell, John D., and T. D. Seymour Bassett, eds. *New Hampshire: A Bibliography of Its History.* Hanover, N.H.: University Press of New England, 1979. A scholarly bibliography, it indicates background sources of value to genealogists.

Hunt, Elmer M. *New Hampshire Town Names and Whence They Came.* Peterborough, N.H.: Noone House, 1970. This gazetteer provides a good place-name index indicating etymology.

New Hampshire State Papers. 40 vols. Concord and Manchester, N.H., 1867–1943. Although published under various titles, its official title is *Documents and Records Relating to New Hampshire, 1623–1800,* as described in R. Stuart Wallace,

"The State Papers? A Descriptive Guide," *Historical New Hampshire* 31 (1976): 119-28. Published versions of numerous records are included in the extensive forty-volume collection. Probate (to 1771), town, and military records are among them. Wallace's descriptive guide can provide a general overview.

Noyes, Sybil, Charles T. Libby, and Walter G. Davis. *Genealogical Dictionary of Maine and New Hampshire.* 1928–29. Reprint. Baltimore: Genealogical Publishing Co., 1983. This is a highly creditable attempt at compiling family genealogies of every family established in New Hampshire and Maine by 1699.

Turner, Lynn Warner. *The Ninth State: New Hampshire's Formative Years.* Chapel Hill: University of North Carolina Press, 1983. Covered in this readable text are the events and developments after the Revolution.

Excellent county histories and gazetteers can aid in locating particular family surnames and providing good background for local research. Some notable ones are:

Child, Hamilton. *Child's Cheshire County Gazetteer, 1736–1885.* Syracuse, N.Y.: Journal, 1885.

———. *Child's Grafton County Gazetteer, 1709–1886.* Syracuse, N.Y.: Journal, 1886.

Hurd, D. Hamilton. *History of Hillsborough County, New Hampshire.* Philadelphia, Pa.: J. W. Lewis & Co., 1885.

Merrill, Georgia Drew. *History of Carroll County.* 1889. Reprint. Somersworth, N.H.: New Hampshire Publishing Co., 1972.

———. *History of Coos County.* 1888. Reprint. Somersworth, N.H.: New Hampshire Publishing Co., 1971.

Guides that will be helpful for genealogical research in the state include:

Dearborn, David C., "New Hampshire Genealogy: A Perspective," *The New England Historical and Genealogical Register* 130 (October 1976): 244-58. An interesting perspective on migration is included.

Melnyk, Marcia D., ed. *Genealogist's Handbook for New England Research.* 4th ed. Boston: New England Historic Genealogical Society, 1999. Major collections, repositories, and town formation information are presented.

Towle, Laird C., and Ann M. Brown. *New Hampshire Genealogical Research Guide.* Bowie, Md.: Heritage Books, 1983. Details of resources available are provided.

Maps

New Hampshire is a state with excellent map sources, making it possible to follow migration trails with the use of political divisions and geographic features. David A. Cobb, *New Hampshire Maps to 1900: An Annotated Checklist* (Concord, N.H.: New Hampshire Historical Society, 1981), helps to identify and locate many maps for research purposes.

An excellent, currently published atlas for the entire state is *The New Hampshire Atlas and Gazetteer* published by DeLorme Publishing in Freeport, Maine. It is continually updated and has excellent cartography of New Hampshire features, including roads (indicating type of surface) and geological features. Earlier versions contain markings for structures, some cemeteries, and churches. Although it is slightly oversized for easy carrying, its usefulness outweighs this hindrance.

Statewide nineteenth-century maps are also excellent. D. H. Hurd and Co., *Town and City Atlas of the State of New Hampshire* (Boston, 1892) indicates occupants' names for structures and treats each town on a separate page with close-up maps for more populated areas. Saco Valley Publishing, 76 Main St., Fryeburg, ME 04037, has been reprinting excellent county editions of these in a handy notebook size.

Early folio-size maps were published by H. F. Wallings and Charles H. Hitchcock in *Atlas of the State of New Hampshire* (New York, 1877). Although individual structures are not shown on these maps, such detail can be found on the large county maps done by Wallings, Chase, and others in the 1850s.

As with other New England states, obtaining a copy of the town's lotting map (the way land was divided before being granted or sold) can be extremely beneficial in solving genealogical problems. The most comprehensive collection of these can be found at the New Hampshire Records and Archives. The layouts are catalogued by town, and include the numbering process of lots and, in many cases, name of the original proprietor, which can help backtrack land holdings and provide a chain of title for problem solving. Many of these are found in the *New Hampshire State Papers* (see Background Sources) as well.

Land Records

State-Land State

All New Hampshire deeds for the provincial period before 1771 were filed in Exeter, or the Ipswich deeds and the Old Norfolk County deeds in Salem, Massachusetts. Microfilms and original books of the first 100 volumes of those filed in Exeter, called Province Deeds, now reside, along with a card file index, at the New Hampshire Records and Archives. Microfilm copies of the card file index and the actual deeds are also located at the New England Historic Genealogical Society (see page 13).

Counties were formed in 1769, with each county seat becoming the location for recording land transactions in that county. In actuality, however, the practice did not begin until 1771, except for Strafford County, which, due to delays in constructing a new courthouse, did not commence until 1773. Indexes at county offices are in grantor and grantee volumes,

by time period, and often include the name of the town where the land is located. Since there are numerous towns in each county, this detail in the index can be helpful in searching land held by those with a common surname. When details of property description are given in the deed, they usually follow the "metes and bounds" survey system or identify the lot by number.

New Hampshire Records and Archives holds the original books and an index to Rockingham County deeds (1771–1824), which includes transactions in Strafford County (1771–73). Early books of Grafton County Deeds (through volume 116) are available on microfilm at the New Hampshire Records and Archives, as is the index to those deeds (1773–1870). The original volumes are housed at the Grafton County courthouse in North Haverill (see County Resources). For all other counties, deeds are available in the books or microfilms at the county seat. Microfilm copies of deed books to about 1850 for most counties are at the FHL, with a growing collection of the same also at the New England Historic Genealogical Society.

Because of geographic and boundary considerations, some early deeds involving land transactions in the Cheshire County area might have been recorded in Massachusetts. Consequently, Hampden County Courthouse in Springfield (see Massachusetts—County Resources) should be consulted. Conversely, it is possible that land granted by New Hampshire in what is now Vermont may be mentioned in the Province Deeds.

Probate Records

Probate records covering the colonial period (1636–1771), originally filed in Portsmouth and Exeter, are in the collection at the New Hampshire Records and Archives; abstracts have been published in volumes 31–39 of the *New Hampshire State Papers* (see Background Sources). These volumes are being added to the online subscription database at <www.ancestry.com>. Probate records for residents of towns along the Massachusetts border may be found in Massachusetts counties. For those in Rockingham County, see *Essex County (Mass.) Probate Index, 1636–1840* (see Massachusetts—Probate Records).

After the formation of counties, probates were filed at county seats. All probate records, except for Coos County (whose records were burned prior to 1887), are extant.

Microfilm copies of many are at the FHL and the New England Historic Genealogical Society (see page 13). Published abstracts include Helen F. Evans, *Abstracts of Probate Records of Strafford County New Hampshire, 1771–1799* (Bedford, N.H.: the author, 1973); *Abstracts of the Probate Records of Rockingham County [New Hampshire], 1771–1799* (Bowie, Md.: Heritage Books, 2000), also available on CD-ROM; and Nicholas G. Copadis et al, *Hillsborough County Register of Probate Index, 1771–1884* (Nashua, N.H.: n.p., 1973).

Abstracts and indexes are only the tip of the iceberg in probate records, however. Not all material in the probate file was recorded in probate books. Consequently, a probate search is not complete without surveying the materials in the original files. Original files that include letters, affidavits, bills, receipts, original wills, and inventories are at New Hampshire Records and Archives for Rockingham, Cheshire, and Grafton counties. Other counties retain their originals.

Court Records

Each county, in addition to having a registry of probate and of deeds, has court records. At different times inferior courts of common pleas, superior courts, and courts of general sessions of the peace existed to deal with civil and criminal cases, equity, and naturalizations. The superior court records include naturalization records.

Divorces, although indexed beginning in the 1870s at the Bureau of Vital Records, are all filed at the county superior court. Some earlier ones are in legislative petitions.

The province court records to 1771 are card indexed at the New Hampshire Records and Archives. After that time, the county seat traditionally housed court records. In a few cases, card indexes to plaintiff and defendant are available to guide the search. Original county court records now at the New Hampshire Records and Archives instead of the county seat include Grafton (1773–1899), Hillsborough (to 1880), Merrimack (to 1870), Rockingham (1772–1860), Strafford (1773–1850), and Sullivan (to 1880). Microfilm of Grafton, Merrimack, and Strafford court record copy and docket books are at the New Hampshire State Library. *New Hampshire State Papers*, vol. 40, contains court records from the Dover-Portsmouth Quarterly Court (1640–92) and there are some general court records and indexes both at the New Hampshire Records and Archives and on microfilm at the FHL for the colonial period. After statehood, the court system became established along county lines. The only court records that have been abstracted or published for the post-colonial period are Laura Penny Hulslander's abstracts of *Strafford County Inferior Court Records, 1773–83* (Bowie, Md.: Heritage Books, 1990).

Tax Records

No thorough survey has yet been attempted to locate all the annual tax lists for New Hampshire towns. They can be found in manuscript collections in public libraries, in town clerk's offices among the pages of the annual town meeting minutes, and at the archives and other repositories. Both residents and nonresidents who owned property or businesses might be listed on the annual assessment, which would indicate the number of voting-age males as polls, and such items as the type and acreage

of land, animals, and milling products. Following annual tax lists can provide important clues for ages of males (nearly always ages twenty-one to fifty and occasionally sixteen to sixty) and for men moving to or leaving a town, since non-landowners were listed as well, although a few officials were usually exempt.

One important collection of tax records, which has been microfilmed from the originals held at the New Hampshire Records and Archives, is the multi-volume nonresident tax lists (1849–74). Some printed tax lists are listed under Census Records.

In 1798 a U.S. direct tax was ordered. Heritage Books has printed the returns that have been located for nine New Hampshire towns located at that time in Strafford County.

Cemetery Records

Few cemetery records have been published; most exist in manuscript form in various repositories. There is an extensive typescript collection augmented annually by the local chapters of the DAR. A copy of each volume is deposited at the New Hampshire Historical Society, whose growing collection of cemetery inscriptions from all sources is being microfilmed. There are numerous typed and indexed cemetery transcriptions at the New Hampshire Historical Society, including many for southeastern towns.

Contributions to genealogical periodicals often contain cemetery inscriptions, and an increasing number of cemetery records have been published by local historical societies in recent years.

The New Hampshire Old Gravestone Association' website <www.rootsweb.com/~nhoga> has a Master Burial Site Index, which attempts to list all known burial sites in the state. It does not include transcriptions of graves at those sites.

Church Records

The New Hampshire Historical Society has an excellent manuscript collection of original church records, and a typescript collection of church records that indicates when members were admitted, the date and reason for leaving the church, baptisms, marriages, and burials. The society's online catalog provides a listing by town at <http://nhhistory.library.net>. A considerable number of church records published in *The New Hampshire Genealogical Record* have been recently indexed and reprinted by Heritage Books of Bowie, Maryland.

The American Baptist Historical Society, 1106 S. Goodman St., Rochester, NY 14620, and the Historical Commission of the Southern Baptist Convention, 910 Commerce St., Ste. 400, Nashville, TN 37203, both have a microfilm collection of some early church records from New Hampshire towns. They are available for purchase.

Military Records

Because men tended to enroll in service units close to their homes and with neighbors, using military lists can be helpful in tracing migration patterns. Muster rolls, pay receipts, and other service records are complete for New Hampshire residents from the colonial period through the Civil War and are available in three published collections.

Ayling, August D. *Revised Register of the Soldiers and Sailors of New Hampshire in the War of Rebellion, 1861–1866.* Concord, N.H., 1895.

New Hampshire State Papers. Vols. 5-6, 14, 16. Include records of those who served in the French and Indian Wars for New Hampshire. Vols. 14-17 include "Rolls of Documents Relating to Soldiers in the Revolutionary War." Indexes available (see Background Sources).

Potter, Chandler E. *The Military History of the State of New Hampshire, 1623–1861.* 2 vols. 1866, 1868. Reprint (2 vols. in 1). Baltimore: Genealogical Publishing Co., 1972.

The New Hampshire Records and Archives has Civil War enlistment papers in a microfiche edition, which is also available at the New England Historic Genealogical Society.

The New Hampshire Historical Society has a name index and abstracts in seventy-one volumes of all New Hampshire residents who received pensions, regardless of residence. A microfilm of these volumes and index is at the New England Historic Genealogical Society. The original applications and records are in Washington, D.C., at the National Archives, with microfilm copies in Waltham, Massachusetts, at the New England Branch (see pages 11-12).

Periodicals, Newspapers, and Manuscript Collections

Periodicals

The New Hampshire Genealogical Record (Dover, N.H., 1903–10), originally short-lived (only seven volumes were published), has been revived under the auspices of the New Hampshire Society of Genealogists. Publication resumed in July 1990. It is devoted to compiled genealogies, source records, book reviews, and the like.

The New Hampshire Historical Society has published *Historical New Hampshire* since 1944 in quarterly editions as a magazine of state and local history.

The Granite Monthly, a sixty-two-volume magazine published between 1877 and 1930, does not concentrate on family history but is a rich source of local and state history and includes some marriage records and other genealogical data. It is indexed in Jacobus (see page 10).

NEW HAMPSHIRE

American-Canadian Genealogist is the quarterly publication distributed to members of the American-Canadian Genealogical Society in Manchester (see Archives, Libraries, and Societies), publishing materials and articles concentrating on Canadian, American (Quebec and New England, principally) research.

Newspapers

No newspapers were published in New Hampshire before the 1750s, although items referring to residents before that date may be found in Massachusetts newspapers (see Massachusetts—Newspapers). For the provincial period, the Boston Athenaeum's *Index of Obituaries in Boston Newspapers, 1704–1800*, 3 vols. (Boston, 1968), may prove helpful.

The New Hampshire Historical Society is the principal repository for pre-1900 newspapers in the state, holding what remains extant of the Granite State's newspapers beginning with the *New-Hampshire Gazette* in 1758 until 1900. The society had a grant to microfilm the most fragile pre-1900 newspapers in its collection. Post-1900 newspapers are often on microfilm at the New Hampshire State Library along with some pre-1900 microfilms. Original newspapers between 1900 and 1945 may not be used.

Hammond, Otis G. *Notices from the New Hampshire Gazette, 1765–1800*. Lambertville, N.J.: Hunterton House, 1971. Vital events appearing in the first newspaper and a valuable place-name index are included.

Manuscripts

The three major sources of collections in New Hampshire can be found at the New Hampshire Records and Archives, New Hampshire State Library, and New Hampshire Historical Society.

Baker Library at Dartmouth College in Hanover, New Hampshire, has a significant manuscript collection, but other helpful collections exist around the state as well, notably three: the Dimond Library at the University of New Hampshire in Durham; the Exeter Historical Society, Exeter, New Hampshire; and the Agnes Bartlett Collection on Portsmouth families, available on microfilm at the New Hampshire Historical Society and New England Historic Genealogical Society. The latter institution is also the repository for some of the finest New Hampshire genealogical manuscripts and original source records, rivaling the New Hampshire Historical Society.

Archives, Libraries, and Societies

New Hampshire Division of Records Management and Archives
71 S. Fruit St.
Concord, NH 03301
www.state.nh.us/state/

Often referred to as the New Hampshire Records and Archives, this office holds the provincial (court, probate, and deed) records before 1771 (and some after that date), maps, military records, and state copies of the federal censuses. Many records were published in the *New Hampshire State Papers* (see Background Sources), including original records before 1771 that are cataloged and accessible in the archives. Additionally, this office has many original town records, all legislative petitions, and a guide to its resources on the website.

New Hampshire Historical Society
30 Park St.
Concord, NH 03301
www.nhhistory.org

The society includes a library, museum, and gift shop with superb collections of New Hampshire research materials and a large collection of local history and family genealogies. Microfilm copies of the Province Deeds and Probate records are located here. A strong point is the magnificent manuscript collection and pre-1900 newspapers on microfilm. The website provides an online catalog of its holdings.

New Hampshire State Library
20 Park St.
Concord, NH 03301
www.state.nh.us/nhsl

All the microfilm collections for town records, post-1900 original newspapers, and census records are housed here, as is the WPA index to town records (see Vital Records and Town Resources). The website provides a "Town Records Index" of its holdings for New Hampshire towns.

New Hampshire Society of Genealogists
P.O. Box 2316
Concord, NH 03302
www.nhsog.org

Semi-annual state meetings are held. The society publishes a newsletter of current events and news, and *The New Hampshire Genealogical Record*, a journal of scholarly articles, compiled genealogies, and abstracts of records. Among its current projects, the society is attempting to document genealogies of all families in the 1790 census (similar to *Maine Families in 1790* and *Vermont Families in 1790*). In addition, a family register for all individuals and families known to have lived in New Hampshire before 1901 is maintained by the society. Inquiries concerning the family register can be sent by mail or e-mail from the website.

435

American-Canadian Genealogical Society Library
4 Elm St.
Manchester, NH 03102
Mailing Address: P.O. Box 6478
Manchester, NH 03108-6478
www.acgs.org

    This unique repository has an extensive microfilm collection of early Canadian original source material. It is one of the only major sources of French-Canadian research in the United States and serves both the Maritimes and Lower Canada (Quebec). The society publishes *American-Canadian Genealogist*. Individual help is offered the researcher both onsite and through mail or e-mail inquiry for a fee.

Special Focus Categories

Immigration

New Hampshire was not a significant port of immigration, even though thirty-two of its miles are on the Atlantic coast. In addition to a sizable French-Canadian and Atlantic-Canadian migration from the north, many of Massachusetts' immigrants found their way to New Hampshire for work in manufacturing in the late nineteenth century. The collections of the American-Canadian Genealogical Society Library, New Hampshire Historical Society, and New Hampshire State Library are excellent sources for research.

Native American

The early history of New Hampshire is filled with conflict between settlers and Native Americans. Little remains in the provincial records for reclaiming specific family information on native inhabitants who lived in New Hampshire or participated in those conflicts, beginning in 1675 with King Philip's War. Those who survived were eventually pushed west and north into Canada. See Vermont—Native Americans or pages 15-16 for possible resources.

County Resources

New Hampshire deeds and probates are recorded on the county level. An act forming counties was passed in 1769, but the Province continued to record deeds and probates until 1771. Strafford did not organize as quickly as the other original counties, beginning its functions in 1773. After 1771, deeds are located at the county registry of deeds and probate records are located at the county registry of probate. Both registries are located at the county seat, but sometimes in different buildings. All addresses are from the New Hampshire Government Resources website <www.nh.gov/government/local.html> and Melnyk's *Genealogist's Handbook for New England Research*, 4th ed. (see Background Sources). Deeds and probate records on microfilm at the New Hampshire Historical Society and at the New Hampshire Division of Records and Archives go through 1771, with Rockingham County deeds at the archives through 1824. At the FHL and the New England Historic Genealogical Society they go from inception to ca. 1850. Later records are only available at the appropriate county office unless otherwise indicated in the following chart.

Map County Address	Date Formed Parent County/ies	Birth Marriage Death	Land Probate Court
G4 Belknap 64 Court St. Laconia 03246 *County courthouse has copies of Strafford County deeds covering land that became part of Belknap after formation in 1840.*	1841 Strafford/Merrimack	1841	1841
E5 Carroll P.O. Box 163 (deeds) P.O. Box 419 (probate) Ossipee 03864	1841 Strafford/Grafton	1841	1841
K2 Cheshire 33 West St. (deeds) 12 Court St.(probate) Keene 03431	1771 original	1771	1771
B5 Coos 55 School St. Lancaster 03584 **Fire damaged thirty-three volumes of the pre-1887 deeds and all of the probate records before that date. Damaged deeds were transcribed when possible and are retained in the courthouse. Seven volumes of Grafton deeds relating to Coos County before formation are kept in a separate series with separate indexes covering 1772–1803.*	1803 Grafton	1803*	1887
E3 Grafton 3785 Dartmouth College Hwy. North Haverill 03774	1771 original	1773	1773
J3 Hillsborough 19 Temple St. (deeds) 30 Sprinig St. (probate) Nashua 03060 *There is a published index to the 1771–1884 probates.*	1771 original	1771	1773
H3 Merrimack 163 N. Main St. Concord 03301	1823 Rockingham/Hillsborough	1823	1823
J5 Rockingham 10 Rt. 125 Brentwood 03833 Mailing address: P.O. Box 896 Kingston 03848	1771 original	1630	1639
H5 Strafford Justice and Admin. Bldg. County Farm Rd. Dover 03820	1773 original	1769	1769
H2 Sullivan 24 Main St. Newport 03773 *Early deeds were damaged by fire. A separate series of "burned deeds," consisting of copies of surviving portions of the burned volumes with a separate index, is at the registry.*	1827 Cheshire	1827	1827

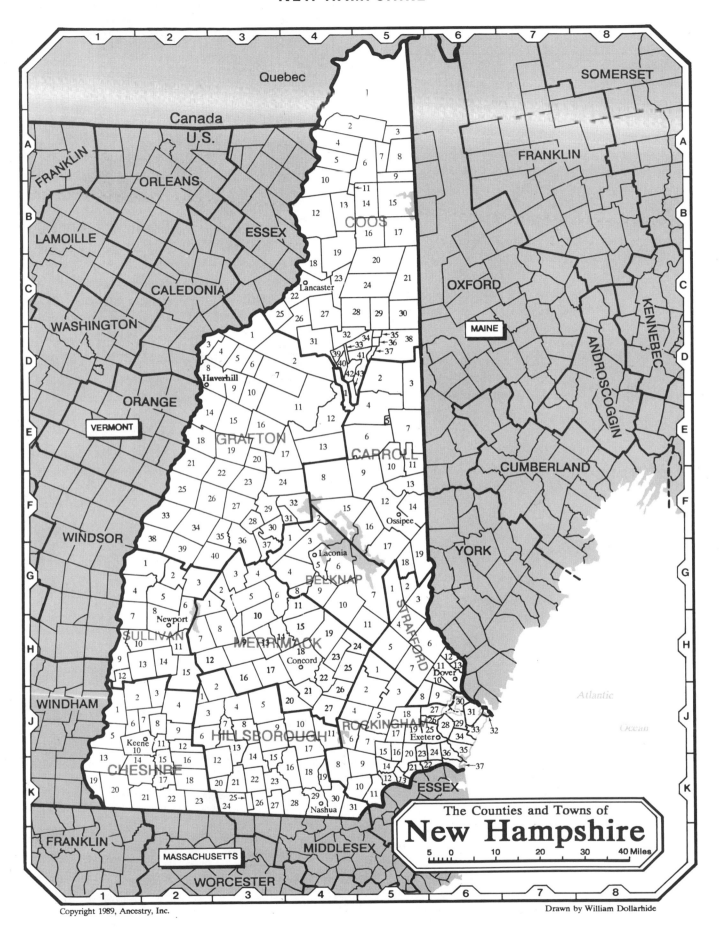

The Counties and Towns of
New Hampshire

5 0   10   20   30   40 Miles

Drawn by William Dollarhide

Town Resources

The WPA index, located at the New Hampshire State Library, on microfilm at the New England Historic Genealogical Society, and through the FHL, provides an unusual statewide index of town records to approximately 1850, which includes vital records. (A notable omission in the index is the town of Exeter, which was inadvertently overlooked.) Town officers, tax records, warrants, minutes and accounts of town meetings, cattle and sheep marks, voting lists, warnings out, and militia are usually found at town clerks' offices, although the information and availability varies greatly from town to town. A thorough search for genealogical material must include the record holdings of the appropriate town.

On the chart below, addresses are from the New Hampshire Secretary of State <www.state.nh.us/sos/clerks.htm> for town/city clerks as of 2004. Most will not do research but usually indicate what materials they have available. The date for formation in the second column usually indicates the beginning of the town records, and therefore when vital records began to be recorded (see Vital Records). "Other Names" indicates names used earlier in the towns history or, in the case of "from," the town from which it was formed. The third column lists the town's parent county and its number on the state map. The parent county/ies are listed on the second line of the third column.

To determine what deed and probate records exist for each town, find the name on the town list, note the date of formation, county, and parent counties. Then refer to the county chart to see where the originals are located. For the entire state before 1771, both deeds and probate records are held at New Hampshire Records and Archives. This means that to extend the research back through all possible records in the geographic area encompassing the county before 1771, the province original deeds and original probate records need to be searched as well.

Town Address	Date Formed Other Names	County (Map) Parent County
Acworth Box 193, Acworth 03601	1735/36 Burnet	Sullivan (13) Cheshire
Albany 1972 Rt. 16, Conway 03818 *Originally in Grafton County until 1810, then in Strafford until Carroll was created.*	1766 Burton	Carroll (6) Grafton/Strafford
Alexandria 45a Washburn Rd., Bristol 03222	1753	Grafton (36)
Allenstown 16 School St., Allenstown 03275	1722	Merrimack (26) Rockingham
Alstead P.O, Box 65, Alstead 03602	1735/36 No. 4/Newton	Cheshire (2)
Alton 1796 P.O. Box 637, Alton 03809	Belknap (7) New Durham Gore	Strafford
Amherst P.O. Box 960, Amherst 03031	1728 Narragansett No. 3	Hillsborough (16)
Andover P.O. Box 61, Andover 03216	1751 Emerystown	Merrimack (5) Hillsborough
Antrim P.O. Box 517, Antrim 03440	1777 Cumberland	Hillsborough (3)
Ashland P.O. Box 517, Ashland 03217	1868 from Holderness	Grafton (31)
Atkinson 21 Academy St., Atkinson 03811	1767 from Plaistow	Rockingham (12)
Atkinson and Gilmanton Grant	unincorporated	Coos (3)

Town Address	Date Formed Other Names	County (Map) Parent County
Auburn P.O. Box 309, Auburn 03032	1845 from Chester	Rockingham (6)
Barnstead P.O. Box 11, Barnstead 03225	1727	Belknap (11) Strafford
Barrington 41 Province Lane, Barrington 03825	1722	Strafford (7)
Bartlett RR 1 Box 50, Intervale 03845	1790 Strafford	Carroll (4) Grafton/Coos
Bath P.O. Box 165, Bath 03740	1761	Grafton (8)
Bean's Grant	unincorporated	Coos (40)
Bean's Purchase	unincorporated	Coos (38)
Bedford 24 N. Amherst Rd., Bedford 03110	1733/34 Narragansett No. 5	Hillsborough (17)
Belmont P.O. Box 310, Belmont 03220 *Belmont inherited the original Gilmanton town records when the towns separated.*	1859 from Upper Gilmanton	Belknap (9) Strafford
Bennington 7 School St., Unit 101, Bennington 03442	1842 from Hancock/Deering/Greenfield	Hillsborough (7)
Benton 110 Flanders Rd., Benton 03785	1764 from Coventry	Grafton (15)
Berlin City Clerk Main St., Berlin 03570	1771 Maynesborough	Coos (24) Grafton

Town Address	Date Formed Other Names	County (Map) Parent County
Bethlehem P.O. Box 189, Bethlehem 03574	1774	Grafton (2)
Boscawen 116 N. Main St., Boscawen 03303	1732 Contoocook	Merrimack (14) Hillsborough
Bow 10 Grandview Rd., Bow 03304	1727	Merrimack (21) Rockingham
Bradford P.O. Box 607, Bradford 03221	1735/36 New Bradford/Bradfordton	Merrimack (12) Hillsborough
Brentwood 1 Dalton Rd., Exeter 03833	1744 from Exeter	Rockingham (19)
Bridgewater P.O. Box 419, Bridgewater 03264	1788 from New Chester	Grafton (30)
Bristol 230 Lake St., Bristol 03222	1819 from Hill & Bridgewater	Grafton (37)
Brookfield P.O. Box 756, Brookfield 03872	1794 from Middleton	Carroll (18) Strafford
Brookline P.O. Box 336, Brookline 03033	1769	Hillsborough (27)
Cambridge	1773 (unincorporated)	Coos (17) Grafton
Campton 1307 NH Rte 175, Campton 03223	1761	Grafton (24) Strafford
Canaan Box 38, Church Rd., Canaan 03741	1761	Grafton (34)
Candia 74 High St. Candia 03034	1763 from Chester Charmingfare	Rockingham (4)
Canterbury P.O. Box 500, Canterbury 03224	1727	Merrimack (15) Rockingham
Carroll P.O. Box 88, Twin Mountain 03595	1772 Breton Woods	Coos (31) Grafton
Center Harbor P.O. Box 140 Center Harbor 03226	1797 from New Hampton, "Moultonborough Addition"	Belknap (2) Strafford
Chandler's Purchase	1835 (unincorporated)	Coos (33)
Charlestown Box 834, Railroad St., Charlestown 03603	1735	Sullivan (9) Cheshire
Chatham 1681 Main Rd., Chatham 03813	1767	Carroll (3) Strafford/Coos/ Grafton
Chester P.O. Box 275, Chester 03036	1720	Rockingham (7)
Chesterfield P.O. Box 64, Chesterfield 03443	1735 No. 1	Cheshire (13)
Chichester 54 Main St., Chichester 03263	1727	Merrimack (23) Rockingham
Claremont City Clerk 58 Tremont Sq., Claremont 03743	1764	Sullivan (7) Cheshire
Clarksville 408 NH Rt. 145, Clarkesville 03592	1792 Dartmouth College Grant	Coos (2) Grafton
Colebrook 10 Bridge St., Colebrook 03576	1762 Dryden	Coos (5) Grafton
Columbia P.O. Box 157, Colebrook 03576	1762 Preston/Cockburntown	Coos (10) Grafton
Concord City Clerk 41 Green St., Concord 03301	1659 Penacock/Rumford	Merrimack (18) Rockingham
Conway 1634 E. Main, Conway 03813	1765	Carroll (7) Strafford/Grafton
Cornish Box 183, Cornish Flat 03746	1763	Sullivan (4) Cheshire
Crawford's Purchase and Crawford's Notch	1834 (unincorporated)	Coos (39)
Croydon 879 NH Rt. 10, Croydon 03773	1763	Sullivan (5) Cheshire
Cutt's Grant	unincorporated	Coos (42)
Dalton 741 Dalton Rd., Dalton 03598	1784 from Littleton	Coos (25) Grafton
Danbury 23 High St., Danbury 03230	1795 from Alexandria	Merrimack (3) Grafton
Danville P.O. Box 11, Danville 03819	1760 from Kingston Hawke	Rockingham (16)
Deerfield P.O. Box 159, Deerfield 03037	1766 Nottingham	Rockingham (2)
Deering 762 Deering Center Rd., Deering 03244	1774	Hillsborough (4)

Town Address	Date Formed Other Names	County (Map) Parent County
Derry 14 Manning St., Derry 03038	1827 from Londonderry	Rockingham (9)
Dixville RFD 1, Dixville Notch 03576	unincorporated	Coos (6) Grafton
Dix's Grant	unincorporated	Coos (7)
Dorchester 369 N. Dorchester Rd., Dorchester 03266	1761	Grafton (26)
Dover City Clerk City Hall, 288 Central Ave., Dover 03820 *Not formally granted as a town.*	1623*	Strafford (11)
Dublin P.O. Box 62, Dublin 03444	1749 Monadnock	Cheshire (16)
Dummer 1420 East Side River Rd., Dummer 03588	1773	Coos (16) Grafton
Dunbarton 1011 School St., Dunbarton 03301	1735 Gorhamstown/Starkstown	Merrimack (20) Hillsborough
Durham 15 Newmarket Rd., Durham 03824	1732 Dover Parish	Strafford (9)
East Kingston 24 Depot Rd., E. Kingston 03827	1738 Kingston	Rockingham (23)
Easton 62 Mountainview Rd., Easton 03580	1876	Grafton (10)
Eaton P.O. Box 118, Eaton Center 03832	1766	Carroll (11) Strafford
Effingham P.O. Box 48, S. Effingham 03882	1749	Carroll (14) Strafford
Ellsworth 12 Ellsworth Pond Rd., Campton 03223	1769 Trecothick	Grafton (20)
Enfield P.O. Box 373, Enfield 03748	1761	Grafton (39)
Epping 157 Main St., Epping 03042	1741/42 from Exeter	Rockingham (18)
Epsom P.O. Box 10, Epsom 03234	1727	Merrimack (25) Rockingham
Errol P.O. Box 100, Errol 03579	1774	Coos (15) Grafton
Erving's Grant	unincorporated	Coos (11)
Exeter 10 Front St., Exeter 03833 *Not formally granted as a town.*	1638*	Rockingham (25)
Farmington 356 S. Main St., Farmington 03835	1798 from Rochester North Rochester	Strafford (4)
Fitzwilliam P.O. Box 504, Fitzwilliam 03447	1752 Monadnock No. 4	Cheshire (22)
Francestown P.O. Box 67, Francestown 03043	1772	Hillsborough (8)
Franconia P.O. Box 900, Franconia 03580	1764 Indian Head/Morristown	Grafton (7)
Franklin City Clerk 316 Central St., Franklin 03235	1828 Pemigewasset	Merrimack (6) Rockingham
Freedom P.O. Box 457, Freedom 03836	1831 N. Effingham	Carroll (13) Strafford
Fremont P.O. Box 20, Fremont 03044	1764 from Exeter Poplin	Rockingham (17)
Gilford 47 Cherry Valley Rd. Gilford 03246	1812 Gunstock Parish of Gilmanton	Belknap (6) Strafford
Gilmanton P.O. Box 550, Gilmanton 03837	1727	Belknap (10) Strafford
Gilsum 14 Spring St., Gilsum 03448	1752 Boyle	Cheshire (7)
Goffstown 16 Main St., Goffstown 03045	1733/34 Narragansett No. 5	Hillsborough (10)
Gorham 20 Park St., Gorham 03581	1779 from Shelburne	Coos (29) Grafton
Goshen P.O. Box 58, Goshen 03752	1791 Sunapee	Sullivan (11) Cheshire
Grafton P.O. Box 297, Grafton 03240	1761	Grafton (40)
Grantham P.O. Box 135, Grantham 03753	1761	Sullivan (2) Cheshire
Greenfield P.O. Box 16, Greenfield 03047	1791 Lyndefield Addition	Hillsborough (13)
Greenland P.O. Box 100, Greenland 03840	1721 from Portsmouth	Rockingham (29)

Town Address	Date Formed Other Names	County (Map) Parent County
Greenville P.O. Box 354, Greenville 03048	1872	Hillsborough (26)
Green's Grant	unincorporated	Coos (36)
Groton 63-1 N. Groton Rd., Hebron 03241	1761 Cockermouth	Grafton (27)
Hadley's Purchase	unincorporated	Coos (43)
Hale's Location	unincorporated	Carroll (5)
Hampstead 11 Main St./P.O. Box 298 Hampstead 03841	1749 Timberlane Parish of Haverill, Massachusett	Rockingham (14)
Hampton 100 Winnacunnet Rd., Hampton 03842	1638	Rockingham (35)
See Lane Memorial Library's website at <www.hampton.lib.nh.us/genealog/> for searchable databases of Hampton family records from a variety of sources.		
Hampton Falls 1 Drinkwater Rd. Hampton Falls 03844	1726 from Hampton Hampton Falls Parish or Fallside Parish from 1712	Rockingham (36)
Hancock P.O. Box 6, Hancock 03449	1779	Hillsborough (6)
Hanover P.O. Box 483, Hanover 03755	1761	Grafton (33)
Harrisville P.O. Box 284, Harrisville 03450	1870 Twitcheville	Cheshire (12)
Hart's Location 5 Forest Rd., Hart's Location 03812	1722	Carroll (1) Grafton
Haverhill 2975 Dartmouth College Hwy. N. Haverhill 03774	1763 Lower Coos	Grafton (14)
Hebron HC 58, Box 286, E. Hebron 03232	1792 from Cockermouth	Grafton (28)
Henniker 2 Depot Hill Rd., Henniker 03242	1735/36 No. 6	Merrimack (16) Hillsborough
Hill P.O. Box 251, Hill 03243	1753 New Chester	Merrimack (4) Grafton
Hillsborough P.O. Box 1699, Hillsborough 03244	1735/36 No. 7	Hillsborough (2)
Hinsdale P.O. Box 31, Hinsdale 03451	1753	Cheshire (19)
Holderness P.O. Box 203, Holderness 03245	1751	Grafton (32) Strafford
Hollis 7 Monument Sq., Hollis 03049	1746	Hillsborough (14)
Hooksett 16 Main St. Hooksett 03106	1822 Chester Woods/ Rowe's Corner	Merrimack (27) Hillsborough
Hopkinton P.O. Box 446, Contoocook 03229	1735/36 No. 5	Merrimack (17) Hillsborough
Hudson 12 School St., Hudson 03051	1746 Nottingham West	Hillsborough (30)
Jackson P.O. Box 336, Jackson 03846	1800 New Madbury/ Adams	Carroll (2) Strafford/ Coos/Grafton
Jaffrey 10 Goodnow St., Jaffrey 03452	1749 Rowley, Canada	Cheshire (18)
Jefferson 84 Stage Hollow Rd., Jefferson 03583	1765	Coos (27) Grafton
Keene City Clerk 3 Washington St., Keene 03431	1733 Upper Ashuelot	Cheshire (10)
Kensington 95 Amesbury Rd., Kensington 03833	1737	Rockingham (24)
Kilkenny	1774 (unincorporated)	Coos (23) Grafton
Kingston P.O. Box 657, Kingston 03848	1694	Rockingham (20)
Laconia City Clerk P.O. Box 489 Laconia 03246	1855 from Meredith/Gilford/Gilmanton Meredith Bridge	Belknap (5)
Lancaster 25 Main St., Lancaster 03584	1763	Coos (22) Grafton
Landaff P.O. Box 125, Landaff 03585	1764	Grafton (9)
Langdon 5 Walker Hill Rd., Alstead 03602	1787	Sullivan (12) Cheshire
Lebanon City Clerk 51 N. Park St., Lebanon 03766	1761	Grafton (38)
Lee 7 Mast Rd., Durham 03824	1766	Strafford (8)

Town Address	Date Formed Other Names	County (Map) Parent County
Lempster P.O. Box 33, Lempster 03605	1735/36 No. 9/Dupplin	Sullivan (14) Cheshire
Lincoln P.O. Box 39, Lincoln 03251	1764	Grafton (11)
Lisbon 46 School St., Llisbon 03585	1763 Chiswick/Gunthwaite	Grafton (5)
Litchfield 2 Liberty Way, Ste 3, Litchfield 03051	1729 Naticock	Hillsborough (19)
Littleton 125 Main St., Littleton 03561	1764 Lisbon	Grafton (1)
Livermore	1876 (unincorporated)	Grafton (12)
Londonderry 50 Nashua Rd., Ste 100, Londonderry 03053	1722	Rockingham (8)
Loudon P.O. Box 7837, Loudon 03301	1773 from Canterbury	Merrimack (19) Rockingham
Lowe and Burbank Grant	unincorporated	Coos (32)
Lyman 65 Parker Hill, Lyman 03585	1761	Grafton (4)
Lyme P.O. Box 342, Lyme 03768	1761	Grafton (25)
Lyndeborough P.O. Box 164, Lyndeborough 03082	1735	Hillsborough (14)
Madbury	1755	Strafford (10)
Manchester City Clerk 904 Elm St. Manchester 03101	1735 Harrytown/Tyngsborough/ Derryfield	Hillsborough (11)
Marlborough P.O. Box 425 Marlborough 03455	1752 Monadnock No. 5/Oxford/ New Marlborough	Cheshire (15)
Marlow P.O. Box 231, Marlow 03456	1753 Addison	Cheshire (3)
Martin's Location	unincorporated	Coos (35)
Mason 16 Darling Hill Rd., Mason 03048	1749 No. 1	Hillsborough (26)
Meredith 41 Main St., Meredith 03253	1748 Palmer's Town/New Salem	Belknap (3) Strafford
Merrimack P.O. Box 27, Merrimack 03054	1746 from Nashua	Hillsborough (18)
Middleton 182 Kings Hwy., Middleton 03887	1749	Strafford (2)
Milan P.O. Box 158, Milan 03588	1771 from Paulsborough	Coos (20) Grafton
Milford 1 Union Sq., Milford 03055	1794 from Munson	Hillsborough (23)
Millsfield P.O. Box 48, Errol 03579	1774	Coos (14) Grafton
Milton P.O. Box 180, Milton 03851	1802 from Rochester	Strafford (3)
Monroe P.O. Box 63, Monroe 03771	1854 from Lyman	Grafton (3)
Mont Vernon P.O. Box 417, Mont Vernon 03057	1803 from Amherst	Hillsborough (15)
Moultonborough P.O. Box 15, Moultonborough 03254	1763	Carroll (15) Strafford
Nashua City Clerk City Hall, 229 Main St., Nashua 03061	1746 Dunstable	Hillsborough (29)
Nelson 7 Nelson Common Rd., Nelson 03457	1752 Monadnock No. 6/Packersfield	Cheshire (9)
New Boston P.O. 250, New Boston 03070	1735/36	Hillsborough (9)
New Castle P.O. Box 367, New Castle 03854	1693 from Portsmouth	Rockingham (32)
New Durham P.O. Box 207, New Durham 03855	1749 Cocheco Township	Strafford (1)
New Hampton P.O. Box 538, New Hampton 03256	1765 Moultonborough Addition	Belknap (1) Strafford
New Ipswich 661 Turnpike Rd., New Ipswich 03071	1735/36	Hillsborough (24)
New London P.O. Box 314, New London 03257	1753 Heidleberg/ Alexandria Addition	Merrimack (1) Hillsborough
Newbury P.O. Box 253 Newbury 03255	1753 Dantzig/Hereford/ Fisherfield	Merrimack (7) Cheshire/ Hillsborough
Newfields P.O. Box 300, Newfields 03856	1849 from Newmarket	Rockingham (26)

NEW HAMPSHIRE

Town Address	Date Formed Other Names	County (Map) Parent County
Newington 205 Nimble Hill Rd., Newington 03801	1764	Rockingham (30)
Newmarket 186 Main St., Newmarket 03857	1727 from Exeter	Rockingham (27)
Newport 15 Sunapee St., Newport 03773	1753 Grenville	Sullivan (8) Cheshire
Newton P.O. Box 375, Newton 03858	1749 from South Hampton	Rockingham (21)
North Hampton P.O. Box 141 North Hampton 03862	1738 from Hampton North Hill/North Parish of Hampton	Rockingham (34)
Northfield 21 Summer St., Northfield 03276	1780 from Canterbury	Merrimack (11) Rockingham
Northumberland 2 State St., Groveton 03582	1761 Stonington	Coos (18) Grafton
Northwood 818 First NH Turnpike, Northwood 03261	1773 from Nottingham	Rockingham (1)
Nottingham P.O. Box 114, Nottingham 03290	1722	Rockingham (3)
Odell	unincorporated	Coos (13)
Orange 76 Eastman Rd. Orange 03741	1769 Cardigan/Bradford/Middletown/ Liscomb	Grafton (35)
Orford 59 Archery Town Rd., Orford 03777	1761	Grafton (21)
Ossipee Box 67, Center Ossipee 03814	1785 New Garden	Carroll (12) Strafford
Pelham 6 Main St., Pelham 03076	1746	Hillsborough (31) Rockingham
Pembroke 311 Pembroke St. Pembroke 03275	1728 Lovewell's Town/ Suncock/Buckstreet	Merrimack (22) Rockingham
Peterborough 1 Grove St., Peterborough 03458	1737/38	Hillsborough (12)
Piermont 573 Rt. 25C, Piermont 03779	1764	Grafton (18)
Pinkham's Grant & Pinkham's Notch	unincorporated	Coos (37)
Pittsburg 526 Main St., Pittsburg 03592	1840 Indian Stream	Coos (1) Grafton
Pittsfield P.O. Box 98, Pittsfield 03263	1782 from Chichester	Merrimack (24) Rockingham
Plainfield P.O. Box 380, Meriden 03770	1761	Sullivan (1) Cheshire
Plaistow 145 Main St., Plaistow 03865	1749 from Haverhill, Massachusetts	Rockingham (13)
Plymouth 6 Post Office Sq., Plymouth 03264	1763 New Plymouth	Grafton (29)
Portsmouth City Clerk 1 Junkins Ave., Portsmouth 03801	1631 Piscataqua/Strawberry Banke	Rockingham (31)
Randolph 130 Durand Rd., Randolph 03570	1772 Durand	Coos (28) Grafton
Raymond 4 Epping St., Raymond 03077	1764 from Chester as Freetown	Rockingham (5)
Richmond 105 Old Homestead Hwy., Richmond 03470	1735 Sylvester, Canada	Cheshire (21)
Rindge P.O. Box 11, Rindge 03461	1736/37 from Rowley, Canada	Cheshire
Rochester City Clerk 31 Wakefield St., Rochester 03867	1722	Strafford (6)
Rollinsford P.O. Box 309, Rollinsford 03869	1849 from Somersworth	Strafford (13)
Roxbury 404 Branch Rd., Roxbury 03431	1812 from Marlborough	Cheshire (11)
Rumney P.O. Box 275, Rumney 03266	1761	Grafton (23)
Rye 10 Central Rd., Rye 03870	1726 from Portsmouth	Rockingham (33)
Salem 33 Geremonty Salem 03079	1750 North Parish of Methuen Massachusetts	Rockingham (11)
Salisbury P.O. Box 180 Salisbury 03268	1736/37 Baker's Town/ Stevenstown/Gerrishtown	Merrimack (10) Hillsborough
Sanbornton P.O. Box 124, Sanbornton 03269	1748	Belknap (4) Strafford

443

Town Address	Date Formed Other Names	County (Map) Parent County
Sandown P.O. Box 583, Sandown 03873	1756 from Kingston	Rockingham (15)
Sandwich P.O. Box 194, Center Sandwich 03227	1763	Carroll (8) Strafford
Sargent's Purchase	unincorporated	Coos (41)
Seabrook P.O. Box 476 Seabrook 03874	1768 from Hampton Falls/ South Hampton	Rockingham (37)
Second College Grant	unincorporated	Coos (8)
Sharon 432 RT 123, Sharon 03458	1791 from Peterborough	Hillsborough (20)
Shelburne 881 North Rd., Shelburne 03581	1769	Coos (30) Grafton
Somersworth City Clerk 157 Main St., Somersworth 03878	1754 from Dover	Strafford (12)
South Hampton 3 Hilldale Ave. S. Hampton 03827	1742 from Amesbury and Salisbury, Massachusetts	Rockingham (22)
Springfield P.O. Box 22, Springfield 03284	1769 Protectworth	Sullivan (3)
Stark 1189 Stark Hwy., Stark 03582	1774 Percy	Coos (19) Grafton
Stewartstown P.O. Box 119, W. Stewartstown 03597	1770	Coos (4) Grafton
Stoddard 2175 RT 9, Stoddard 03464	1752 Monadnock No. 7/Limerick	Cheshire (4)
Strafford P.O. Box 169, Strafford 03815	1820	Strafford (5)
Stratford P.O. Box 366, N. Stratford 03590	1762 Woodbury	Coos (12) Grafton
Stratham 10 Bunker Hill Ave., Stratham 03885	1715/16	Rockingham (28)
Success	1773 (unincorporated)	Coos (21) Grafton
Sugar Hill P.O. Box 574, Sugar Hill 03585	1962 from Lisbon	Grafton (6)
Sullivan 522 South Rd., Sullivan 03431	1787	Cheshire (8)
Sunapee P.O. Box 303, Sunapee 03782	1768 Saville/Wendell	Sullivan (6) Cheshire
Surry 358 Pond Rd., Surry 03431	1769	Cheshire (6)
Sutton P.O. Box 487, South Sutton 03273	1749 Perrystown	Merrimack (8) Hillsborough
Swanzey P.O. Box 10009, Swanzey 03446	1733	Cheshire (14)
Tamworth P.O. Box 279, Tamworth 03886	1766	Carroll (9) Strafford
Temple P.O. Box 69, Temple 03084	1750 Peterborough Slip	Hillsborough (21)
Thompson and Meserve's Purchase	unincorporated	Coos (34)
Thornton 16 Merrill Access Rd., Campton 03223	1763	Grafton (17)
Tilton 257 Main St. Tilton 03276	1869 from Sanbornton East Sanbornton	Belknap (8)
Troy P.O. Box 249, Troy 03465	1815 from Marlborough	Cheshire (17)
Tuftonboro P.O. Box 98, Tuftonboro 03816	1750	Carroll (16) Strafford
Unity 13 Center Rd., Unity 03773	1753 Buckingham	Sullivan (10) Cheshire
Wakefield 2 High St. Sanbornville 03872	1749 Ham's-town/East-town/ Watertown	Carroll (19) Strafford
Walpole P.O. Box 756, Walpole 03608	1736 Bellowstown	Cheshire (1)
Warner P.O. Box 265 Warner 03278	1735/36 New Amesbury/ Jennesstown/Waterloo/Ryetown	Merrimack (9) Hillsborough
Warren P.O. Box 66, Warren 03279	1763	Grafton (19)
Washington 7 Halfmoon Pond Rd. Washington 03280	1735/36 Monadnock No. 8/ New Concord/Camden	Sullivan (15) Cheshire
Waterville Valley P.O. Box 500, Waterville Valley 03223	1829 Waterville	Grafton (13)

New Mexico

KAREN STEIN DANIEL, CG, AND MARGARET WINDHAM

Among the western states, New Mexico is unique. Before the first presidio, or military post, was erected in Alta, California, New Mexico had celebrated its sesquicentennial; it would see its bicentennial even before Brigham Young would gaze upon the valley of the Great Salt Lake.

As early as 1540, Coronado traveled across New Mexico from Arizona, going as far north as Kansas. Four decades later, Rodriquez explored what is now New Mexico, with Espejo and Oñate expeditions following suit. In 1598, Oñate established the first Spanish settlement in the Rio Grande Valley. Santa Fe was established in the early seventeenth century, bringing the Spanish-speaking population to 2,400 by 1680. That same year Native Americans revolted, reclaiming their homeland, but by 1693 New Mexico had been reconquered and reoccupied.

Over a century passed before Mexico revolted against Spain in 1821, gaining its independence, with the area that is now New Mexico included in the newly independent country. In 1844 New Mexico land was divided into three districts: Central, Northern, and Southeastern. Six years later, in 1850, the Central District was divided into the counties of Santa Fe, Santa Ana, and San Miguel; the Northern District was divided into Rio Arriba and Taos counties; and the Southeastern District was divided into Valencia and Bernalillo.

United States expansionism had been one of the factors provoking the Mexican War in 1846, with General Kearny occupying Santa Fe. When the war ended in 1848, Mexico ceded the Guadalupe Hidalgo Treaty territories, including almost all of the southwestern lands, and New Mexico became a part of the United States. Two years later, in 1850, Congress created the Territory of New Mexico, setting up a territorial government within a year. The Gadsden Purchase in 1854 established the present southern border of New Mexico. In 1877 telegraph lines were erected from New Mexico to San Diego, providing the communication needed for more settlement.

The reason for New Mexico's early settlement was simply that it was easily reached by anyone coming from the Spanish and Mexican strongholds via the Rio Grande. Important as a means of travel, the river was not only lifeblood for the weary traveler, but it also insured the growth of crops. Not only were the citizens of New Mexico forced to defend themselves against marauding natives as well as aggressive Texans who looked wistfully to the west for expansion, they had to endure their own indifferent public officials as well. From the founding of Santa Fe in 1610, the inhabitants of New Mexico waited 302 years for the benefits of statehood.

New Mexico entered the Union in 1912 as the population reached 300,000, with many of the people living on small land holdings. In recognition of the entry of the state into the modern technological world, the county of Los Alamos came into being in March 1949. It was there during World War II, with the development of the atom bomb, that the country prepared to bring the war to its eventual conclusion.

Today New Mexico is a mixture of cultures and political philosophies, a center for both nuclear, technological research, and new-age living set on a backdrop of Native American and Mexican cultures.

Vital Records

New Mexico's vital records are divided between a statewide index for births and deaths and county clerks' offices where marriage records are filed. Statewide recording began in 1920, although some earlier records may be found, including those found as part of real estate transactions in some counties. Additionally, there are some delayed certificates of birth from 1866 to 1895 and some death certificates beginning in 1889.

Access to the statewide index of births and deaths is available through the New Mexico Department of Health, New Mexico Vital Records, P.O. Box 26110, Santa Fe, NM 87502, or in person at 1105 S. Saint Francis Dr. in Santa Fe <www.health.state.nm.us>. The non-refundable fee for a birth certificate search and copy is $10, and $5 for a death certificate search and copy. Birth and death records are restricted and issued only to immediate family members or others demonstrating "a tangible legal interest." Birth records are closed for 100 years, and death records for fifty years.

The New Mexico Death Index Project (1899–1940), an online resource available to researchers at <www.rootsweb.com/~usgenweb/nm/nmdi.htm> is a volunteer effort to locate names in preparation for ordering death certificates from the New Mexico Department of Health. The index contains first and last names, middle initials (and corrected information), date and county of death, and age. Additionally, the Genealogical Society of Utah has microfilmed certificates of death (1889–1945), with deaths for Native Americans listed separately. These are available through the Family History Library (FHL) in Salt Lake City.

Requests for marriage records should go to the county clerk in the county where the license was issued. Some marriage records are also located at the New Mexico State Records Center and Archives (see Archives, Libraries, and Societies); detailed lists for the various counties may be accessed through the "Online Archive of New Mexico" at <http://elibrary.unm.edu/oanm>. This online archive also includes some coroner, inquest, and justice of the peace records for the various counties.

Divorces are filed through the district court serving the county in which the divorce was granted. Records before 1912 are located in court dockets at the New Mexico State Records Center and Archives.

Census Records

Federal

Population Schedules
- Indexed—1850, 1860, 1870, 1880, 1900, 1910, 1920, 1930
- Soundex—1880, 1900, 1920

Union Veterans Schedules
- 1890

In addition to sources for all federal censuses (see pages 2-4), microfilmed population schedules and available printed indexes of all New Mexico federal censuses are located at the New Mexico State Records Center and Archives, and the Special Collections Library (see Archives, Libraries, and Societies). The Albuquerque Genealogical Society is in the process of compiling an every-name index to the 1910 census for each New Mexico county. Completed counties are published and available at the Special Collections Library.

Available in print is:

Windham, Margaret Leonard, ed. *New Mexico 1850 Territorial Census.* 4 vols. Albuquerque: New Mexico Genealogical Society, 1976.

Native American Schedules
Native American schedules prior to 1880 are incomplete and contain inaccuracies. From 1885 to 1940, Native American censuses were taken regularly but not annually. Surviving records vary by tribe. The researcher should consult National Archives sources for details (see pages 11-12).

Colonial and State
Numerous Spanish and Mexican colonial censuses can be found at the New Mexico State Records Center and Archives. Originals are in Spanish, but the following have been published:

Olmsted, Virginia L., comp. *Spanish and Mexican Censuses of New Mexico, 1750 to 1830.* Albuquerque: New Mexico Genealogical Society, 1981.

____, trans. and comp. *Spanish and Mexican Colonial Censuses of New Mexico, 1790, 1823, 1845.* Albuquerque: New Mexico Genealogical Society, 1979. (Contains corrections of the 1975 edition, as well as new material.)

Copies are available at the Special Collections Library at the University of New Mexico, Family History Centers in Albuquerque, and many other locations.

The New Mexico State Records Center and Archives also holds the 1885 state census, which was actually a federally taken census and includes all members of the household. Some schedules are missing and others are illegible. It is available through the Special Collections Library at the University of New Mexico, the National Archives, the FHL, and other locations.

Background Sources

The newest and most definitive genealogical guide for New Mexico researchers is:

Daniel, Karen Stein. *Genealogical Resources in New Mexico.* 2d ed. Albuquerque: New Mexico Genealogical Society, 1999. Offers researchers a comprehensive discussion and bibliography for the state and provides additional information on repositories, record groups and collections, and societies.

For historical background, the most definitive sources are:

Bancroft, Hubert Howe. *History of Arizona and New Mexico, 1530–1888.* San Francisco: History Publishing, 1888.

Twitchell, Ralph Emerson. *The Leading Facts of New Mexican History.* 2 vols. 1911. Reprint. Albuquerque: Horn and Wallace, 1963.

An overview of the state can be obtained by using the extensive bibliography of:

Beck, Warren A. *New Mexico: A History of Four Centuries.* Norman, Okla.: University of Oklahoma Press, 1962.

Other useful sources include:

Lamar, Howard Robert. *The Far Southwest, 1846–1912: A Territorial History.* New Haven, Conn.: Yale University Press, 1966.

Myers, Christine. *New Mexico Local and County Histories: A Bibliography.* Albuquerque: New Mexico Library Association, 1983.

Roberts, Calvin A., and Susan A. Roberts. *A History of New Mexico.* Revised edition. Albuquerque: University of New Mexico Press, 1991.

Simmons, Marc. *New Mexico: An Interpretive History.* 1977. Reprint. Albuquerque: University of New Mexico Press, 1988.

Twitchell, Ralph Emerson. *The Spanish Archives of New Mexico.* 2 vols. 1914. Reprint, New York: Arno Press, 1976.

Tyler, Daniel. *Sources for New Mexican History, 1821–1848.* Santa Fe: Museum of New Mexico Press, 1984.

Those with Hispanic heritage will also want to consult:

Chávez, Fray Angélico. *Origins of New Mexico Families: A Genealogy of the Spanish Colonial Period.* Revised. Santa Fe: Museum of New Mexico Press, 1992.

Esquibel, José Antonio, and John B. Colligan. *The Spanish Recolonization of New Mexico: An Account of the Families Recruited at Mexico City in 1693.* Albuquerque: Hispanic Genealogical Research Center of New Mexico, 1999.

Platt, Lyman D. *Hispanic Surnames and Family History.* Baltimore: Genealogical Publishing Co., 1996.

Ryskamp, George R. *Finding Your Hispanic Roots.* Baltimore: Genealogical Publishing Co., 1997.

Ryskamp, George R. *Tracing Your Hispanic Heritage.* Riverside, Calif.: Hispanic Family History Research, 1984.

Maps

The following atlas and place-name indexes exist for New Mexico research:

Beck, Warren, and Ynez D. Haase. *Historical Atlas of New Mexico.* Norman, Okla.: University of Oklahoma Press, 1969.

Julyan, Robert. *The Place Names of New Mexico.* Rev. ed. Albuquerque: University of New Mexico Press, 1998.

Pearce, T. M. *New Mexico Place Names: A Geographical Dictionary.* Albuquerque: University of New Mexico Press, 1965.

Land Records

Public-Domain State

New Mexico was admitted as a territory on 9 September 1850 and became a state on 6 January 1912. When it became a part of the United States, it became a public-domain land state.

The New Mexico State Records Center and Archives has large holdings of land records going back to 1693. Spanish and Mexican land grants date from that period. The original records are in Spanish, but some have been translated. Researchers will want to consult:

Oczon, Annabelle M. "Land Grants in New Mexico: A Selective Bibliography," *New Mexico Historical Review* 57 (January 1982).

Salazar, J. Richard, ed. and comp. *Calendar to the Microfilm Edition of the Land Records of New Mexico: Spanish Archives of New Mexico, Series I, Surveyor General Records and the Records of the Court of Private Land Claims.* Santa Fe: New Mexico State Records Center and Archives, 1987.

Information regarding homestead lands for New Mexico is located at the United States Bureau of Land Management (BLM), New Mexico State Office, 1474 Rodeo Rd., Santa Fe, NM 87505 (mailing address: P.O. Box 27115, Santa Fe, NM 87502-0115) <www.nm.blm.gov>. This office maintains public land records on microfiche for New Mexico, Kansas, Texas, and Oklahoma, including copies of original patents, tract books, and plats. They also hold topographic maps.

The National Archives and Records Administration—Rocky Mountain Region, P.O. Box 25307, Denver, CO 80225-0307 <www.nara.gov/regional/denver.html> maintains retired records from federal agencies and courts in New Mexico, including tract books, abstracts, registers, canceled land entry case files, survey plats, private land claim plats within Pueblo land grants, and plats and field notes of the Surveyor General.

Deed books from 1850 exist for most counties, as well as mining deeds from 1850 to 1920. Both sets are generally indexed. A large body of land records for the counties is available at the New Mexico State Records Center and Archives, as well as within the respective counties, where complete records are maintained by the county clerk. Additional land records can be found at the University of New Mexico, Center for Southwest Research, in Albuquerque. The "Online Archive of New Mexico" <http://elibrary.unm.edu/oanm> is particularly helpful for locating various manuscript collections, including land records, within the state.

Probate Records

Many early probates may be found at the New Mexico State Records Center and Archives. Formal probate records are filed by the district court that serves a particular county, or by informal probate in the county clerk's office. The size and complexity of the estate determines whether it would be handled as a formal or informal practice.

There are thirteen judicial districts in the state, each covering one or more counties. In order to locate the work of the probate court, write to the clerk of the respective court in the county of focus for the research problem. Addresses found under Court Records (see below) apply to probate records as well. However, the county clerk's office may need to be contacted since laws change from time to time.

Court Records

New Mexico's courts begin with actions close to the people. Magistrate courts handle civil cases such as tort, contract, and real property rights, among others. Probate courts are courts of limited jurisdiction with no jury trials. They hear informal probate matters and uncontested estate cases. Metropolitan and municipal courts handle city violations. Court records before 1912 are archived at the New Mexico State Records Center and Archives and can be located through the "Online Archive of New Mexico" at <http://elibrary.unm.edu/oanm>.

The next level above these local courts is the district courts, which are arranged into thirteen districts as listed below. These are courts of general jurisdiction, including probate and divorce actions, as well as jury trials.

First Judicial District includes Santa Fe, Los Alamos, and Rio Arriba counties: Court Clerk, P.O. Box 2268, Santa Fe, NM 87504 <www.firstdistrictcourt.com>.

Second Judicial District includes Bernalillo County: Court Clerk, 400 Lomas NW, Albuquerque, NM 87102 <www.cabq.gov/cjnet/dst2alb>.

Third Judicial District includes Doña Ana County: Court Clerk, 201 W. Picacho, Ste. A, Las Cruces, NM 88005 <http://thirddistrictcourt.com/clerksoff1.htm>.

Fourth Judicial District includes Guadalupe, Mora, and San Miguel counties: Court Clerk, P.O. Box 1540, Las Vegas, NM 87701-1540; 420 Parker Ave., Ste. 5, Santa Rosa, NM 88435.

Fifth Judicial District includes Lea, Eddy, and Chaves counties: Court Clerk, P.O. Box 1776, Roswell, NM 88202-1776; 102 N. Canal, Ste. 240, Carlsbad, NM 88220; Box 6-C, Lovington, NM 88260 < www.fifthdistrictcourt.com/loc.htm>.

Sixth Judicial District includes Grant, Hidalgo, and Luna counties: Court Clerk, 700 S. Silver, Deming, NM 88030; P.O. Box 608, Lordsburg, NM 88045; P.O. Box 2339, Silver City, NM 88061.

Seventh Judicial District includes Catron, Sierra, Socorro, and Torrance counties: Court Clerk, P.O. Box 78, Estancia, NM 87016; P.O. Drawer 1129, Socorro, NM 87801; P.O. Box 3009, Truth or Consequences, NM 87901.

Eighth Judicial District includes Colfax, Union, and Taos counties: Court Clerk, P.O. Box 310, Clayton, NM 88415; P.O. Box 150, Raton, NM 87740.

Ninth Judicial District includes Curry and Roosevelt counties: Court Clerk, 109 W. First St., Ste. 207, Portales, NM 88130; 700 N. Main, Ste. 11, Clovis, NM 88101.

Tenth Judicial District includes Quay, De Baca, and Harding counties: Court Clerk, P.O. Box 1067, Tucumcari, NM 88401; P.O. Box 910, Fort Sumner, NM 88119; P.O. Box 1002, Mosquero, NM 87733.

Eleventh Judicial District includes McKinley and San Juan counties: Court Clerk, 201 W. Hill St., Rm. 4, Gallup, NM 87301; 103 S. Oliver Dr., Aztec, NM 87410; 920 Municipal Dr., Farmington, NM 87401 <www.eleventhdistrictcourt.state.nm.us>.

Twelfth Judicial District includes Lincoln and Otero counties: Court Clerk, 100 New York Ave., Rm. 209, Alamogordo, NM 88310-6937; P.O. Box 725, Carrizozo, NM 88301.

Thirteenth Judicial District includes Sandoval, Cibola, and Valencia counties: Court Clerk, 100 Avenida de Justicia, Bernalillo, NM 87004; P.O. Box 758, Grants, NM 87020; P.O. Box 1089, Los Lunas, NM 87301.

Above the district courts, the state's Supreme Court reviews death penalty cases and necessary writs and may review cases from the courts of appeal. Located in Santa Fe, this is the court of last resort and has superintending control over inferior courts. The courts of appeal hear mandatory review of death penalty cases and may review other criminal cases and extraordinary writs.

Tax Records

The New Mexico State Records Center and Archives holds property tax records for the entire state beginning in the 1870s

and continuing, in some cases, to approximately 1929. From 1884 to 1912, these records have been microfilmed and are also retained at the Special Collections Library. The remaining portion consists of original documents. A comprehensive list of tax record holdings, including some poll tax lists, for the New Mexico State Records Center and Archives may be accessed through the "Online Archive of New Mexico" at <http://elibrary.unm.edu/oanm>.

Individual counties have property tax books from 1913 to the present.

Internal Revenue Assessments Lists for the Territory of New Mexico (1862–70 and 1872–74) exist on one roll of National Archives microfilm M781, Record Group 58. This roll is retained at the Special Collections Library.

Cemetery Records

Many cemetery abstracts have been published by the New Mexico Genealogical Society (see Archives, Libraries, and Societies) and others, and may be found at the Special Collections Library, the New Mexico State Records Center and Archives, and other locations. Researchers should refer to Dorothy A. Brylinski and Ann L. Mossman, comps. and eds., *New Mexico Genealogist Comprehensive Index*, volumes 1-38, 1962–1999 (Albuquerque: New Mexico Genealogical Society, 2000); and *New Mexico Cemeteries: A Genealogical Guide*, at the Special Collections Library. The latter is an ongoing cemetery project to identify all known cemeteries and private grave sites in the state, as well as to create an index of cemetery names and locations. Online lists and abstracts also exist at RootsWeb and other sites (see page 16). Burial lists are online for Fort Bayard National Cemetery at <www.interment.net/data/us/nm/grant/ftbaynat> and Santa Fe National Cemetery at <www.interment.net/data/us/nm/santafe/santanat/index.htm>.

Catholic Church sacramental records also offer extensive documentation of burials. The Fray Angélico Chávez History Library and the New Mexico State Records Center and Archives also maintain necrology files.

Church Records

The early population of New Mexico was generally both Spanish-speaking and Catholic. As such, the sacramental records of the towns and villages present an important avenue of research and may provide the names of several generations within one document. Catholic Church sacramental records (baptisms, marriages, and burials) are rich in vital record information and may prove a valuable alternative in cases where vital records are closed to the public.

The New Mexico State Records Center and Archives, the Special Collections Library, the FHL, and other locations maintain some early Catholic records from the Archives of the Archdiocese of Santa Fe. Some records for the Diocese of Las Cruces have also been filmed by the FHL. The Hispanic Genealogical Research Center of New Mexico has published and is currently abstracting records for publication from the Diocese of Gallup. A wealth of Catholic records has been published by the New Mexico Genealogical Society and others. Records generally begin in the late 1600s and continue to 1955, and may include baptisms, marriages, burials, and census records, among others. Some records exist for Native Americans. Researchers should begin by referring to the online source, "Locating Catholic Church Records in New Mexico," at <www.nmgs.org> and the *New Mexico Genealogist Comprehensive Index*, volumes 1-38, 1962–1999 (Albuquerque: New Mexico Genealogical Society, 2000). Reference should also be made to Chávez, Fray Angélico, *Archives of the Archdiocese of Santa Fe, 1678–1900*. (St. Paul, Minn.: North Central Publishing Co., 1957).

For Protestant records, consult the local churches in the area where the ancestor lived. Some manuscript and other holdings can be found at the New Mexico State University Library and the University of New Mexico. Check the "Online Archive of New Mexico" at <http://elibrary.unm.edu/oanm>. For Presbyterian Church records, consult the Menaul Historical Library of the Southwest in Albuquerque, 301 Menaul Blvd. NE, Albuquerque, NM 87107 <www.menaulschool.com/histlib/>.

Military Records

The New Mexico Records Center and Archives, as well as other repositories, have holdings of the Spanish, Mexican, and Territorial Archives including military records for those respective eras.

Begin by consulting:

Calendar of the Microfilm Edition of the Spanish Archives of New Mexico, 1621–1821. Reprint. Santa Fe: State of New Mexico Records Center, 1987.

Jenkins, Myra Ellen. *Calendar of the Microfilm Edition of the Mexican Archives of New Mexico, 1821–46*. Santa Fe: State of New Mexico Records Center, 1970.

Jenkins, Myra Ellen, and J. Richard Salazar. *Calendar to the Microfilm Edition of the Territorial Archives of New Mexico*. Santa Fe: New Mexico Records Center and Archives, 1974.

Territorial records include the Indian Wars of the 1850s, Union militia muster rolls, some Confederate records, and records of the Spanish American War. *Compiled Service Records*

of *Volunteer Union Soldiers Who Served in Organizations from the Territory of New Mexico* are found on forty-six rolls of microfilm as NARA–M427; and *Index to Compiled Service Records of Volunteer Soldiers Who Served in Organizations from the Territory of New Mexico* is found on four rolls of microfilm as NARA–M242. Both collections are located at the Special Collections Library and the Family History Library. New Mexico supplied men for Teddy Roosevelt's famed "Rough Riders." For rosters and regimental information, contact the City of Las Vegas and Rough Riders Memorial Museum, P.O. Box 160, Las Vegas, NM 87701.

The New Mexico Records Center and Archives has records of the Grand Army of the Republic, Department of New Mexico for the period 1861–1903, manuscript collection 1960-044. They also have a large collection of New Mexico Adjutant General Records (1847–[ongoing]), as manuscript 1973-019. This collection contains records of the Adjutant General, National Guard, and Office of Military Affairs (1847–1988) and include enlistment and discharge papers, casualty records, muster rolls, annual reports, and other records for the Civil War, Indian wars, Spanish-American War, World Wars I and II, Korean War, and Vietnam War. A finding aid is available online at <http://elibrary.unm.edu/oanm/NmAr/nmar%231973-019>. The New Mexico State Records Center and Archives also has Civilian Conservation Corps, New Mexico District Records, 1935–1942, as manuscript 1959-030, containing approximately 11,000 names cards for enrollees, with name, birth date, family information, camp assignments, and discharge information. The World Wars I and II Collection (1910–56), manuscript 1959-233, contains obituaries of New Mexico servicemen, as well as photostats of New Mexico servicemen's discharge records.

The Special Collections Library has microfilm rolls for New Mexico and some Colorado posts in Returns from Military Posts, 1800–1916 (NARA–M617), as well as the New Mexico rolls from Organization Index to Pension Files of Veterans Who Served Between 1861 and 1900 (NARA–T289). They also maintain New Mexico, World War I Selective Service System Draft Registration Cards (1917–1918) on sixteen rolls of microfilm. Consult the "Online Archive of New Mexico" at <http://elibrary.unm.edu/oanm> for further military collections in the state.

For veteran burials in New Mexico under federal jurisdiction, see Cemetery Records.

Periodicals, Newspapers, and Manuscript Collections

Periodicals

The *New Mexico Historical Review* has been published since 1926 by University of NM, 1013 Mesa Vista Hall, Albuquerque, NM 87131-1186 <www.unm.edu/~nmhr>. It is a fully indexed magazine of history that genealogists will find particularly helpful for background information and bibliographies.

La Crónica de Nuevo México is published by the Historical Society of New Mexico, P.O. Box 1912, Santa Fe, NM 87504 <www.hsnm.org>.

The *Colonial Latin American Historical Review* is published quarterly by the Spanish Colonial Research Center, NPS, Zimmerman Library, University of New Mexico, Albuquerque, NM 87131 <www.unm.edu/~clahr>.

The *New Mexico Genealogist* is published by the New Mexico Genealogical Society, P.O. Box 8283, Albuquerque, NM 87198-8283 <www.nmgs.org>. Published quarterly for over forty years.

Herencia is the quarterly journal published by the Hispanic Genealogical Research Center of New Mexico, P.O. Box 51088, Albuquerque, NM 87181 <www.hgrc-nm.org>.

Quipu is a free newsletter published by the New Mexico State Records Center and Archives, 1205 Camino Carlos Rey, Santa Fe, NM 87505 <www.nmcpr.state.nm.us/pubs/publications_forms.htm>.

Newspapers

The New Mexico Newspaper Project, completed in 1996, was the culmination of the microfilming of hundreds of New Mexico newspapers from the 1840s to the present. This includes many small, obscure, and short-lived papers, as well as papers from the mining camps. At least one newspaper was filmed for each New Mexico county. The complete set of this project, including some 600 rolls, is available at the University of New Mexico in Albuquerque, microform and periodical section, lower level. The University of New Mexico also holds numerous other papers, both from inside and outside the state, not part of the original project. The researcher can access holdings through the University of New Mexico at <www.unm.edu/libraries.html>. An excellent collection of microfilmed New Mexico newspapers is also to be found at the New Mexico Records Center and Archives, and microfilmed newspapers from the Territorial Period can be found at the Special Collections Library. Manuscript collections in the state may also contain collections of newspapers or newspaper clippings.

Vital records for many years of Albuquerque newspapers have been abstracted by the Albuquerque Genealogical Society (formerly Genealogy Club of Albuquerque) and are available at the Special Collections Library.

Consult the following:

Grove, Pearce, Becky J. Barnett, and Sandra J. Hansen, eds. *New Mexico Newspapers: A Comprehensive Guide to Bibliographical Entries and Locations.* Albuquerque: University of New Mexico Press, 1975.

New Mexico Newspaper Project. *Newspaper Holdings in New Mexico Institutions.* Dublin, Ohio: OCLC, 1997.

New Mexico Newspaper Project. *The University of New Mexico Library Newspaper Holdings.* Dublin Ohio: OCLC, 1997.

Manuscripts

The "Online Archive of New Mexico" is a major finding aid for four of the state's major archival repositories and can be accessed at <http://elibrary.unm/edu/oanm>. Contributing repositories include the Center for Southwest Research at the University of New Mexico, the Fray Angélico Chávez History Library at the Palace of the Governors, the New Mexico State Records Center and Archives, and the Rio Grande Historical Collections of New Mexico State University. The "Online Archive" contains descriptive information about the collections housed at these facilities, including an inventory, a collection summary, contents list, and other information. Not every manuscript collection housed at these facilities is included in this source, and researchers may need to contact the individual repository regarding other collections, or review their individual websites and online catalogs.

See also:

Beers, Henry Putney. *Spanish and Mexican Records of the American Southwest, A Bibliographical Guide to Archive and Manuscript Sources.* Tucson: University of Arizona Press, 1979.

Ferris, Kathlene, ed. *Guide to Manuscript Collections in the Center for Southwest Research.* Albuquerque: University of New Mexico, 1990.

Archives, Libraries, and Societies

New Mexico State Records Center and Archives
1205 Camino Carlos Rey
Santa Fe, NM 87505-9860
www.nmcpr.state.nm.us

As the main repository of government documents within the state, it participates in the "Online Archive of New Mexico." Among its holdings are land grant documents; Spanish (1621–1821), Mexican (1821–46), and Territorial (1846–1912) Archives; statehood records; Archives of the Archdiocese of Santa Fe records; governors' papers; judicial and private papers. Publishes *Quipu.*

New Mexico State Library
1209 Camino Carlos Rey
Santa Fe, NM 87505-9860
www.stlib.state.nm.us

The library provides access to state and federal sources; Southwest collections, including Hispanic and Native American; newspapers; vertical files; and clipping files.

New Mexico Genealogical Society
P.O. Box 8283
Albuquerque, NM 87198-8283
www.nmgs.org

Publishes *New Mexico Genealogist.*

Historical Society of New Mexico
Box 1912
Santa Fe, NM 87504
www.hsnm.org

Publishes *La Cronica.*

Center for Southwest Research
Special Collections Department, General Library
University of New Mexico
Albuquerque, NM 87131-1466
www.unm.edu/~cswrref/enghome.html

Major research center for New Mexico, the Southwest, and the American West; participating repository of the "Online Archive of New Mexico"; land grant and Native American collections; vertical files; family histories; inventories and bibliographies.

Special Collections Library
Albuquerque-Bernalillo County Library System
423 Central Ave. NE (at Edith)
Albuquerque, NM 87102
www.cabq.gov/library/specol.html

This is the main genealogical research library in New Mexico. Specialties include Southwestern reference; microform and CD-ROM collections; all New Mexico censuses; special Native American censuses; extensive New Mexico and U.S. genealogical collections.

Fray Angélico Chávez History Library
P.O. Box 2087
120 Washington Ave.
Santa Fe, NM 87504-2087
www.palaceofthegovernors.org

This research library collects materials to document the history of New Mexico, the Southwest, American West, and Meso-America. It is a participating repository of the "Online Archive of New Mexico" and maintains vertical files and newspaper clippings.

Rio Grande Historical Collections
New Mexico State University Libraries
P.O. Box 30006, MSC 3475
Las Cruces, NM 88003-8006
http://lib.nmsu.edu

A participating repository of the "Online Archive of New Mexico," its holdings include Southwest collections on Native Americans, cowboys, cattle industry, farming, overland trails, borderlands, and the Western Women Collection.

National Hispanic Cultural Center
1701 4th SW (at Avenida César Chávez)
Albuquerque, NM 87102
www.nhccnm.org

A library and genealogy research center, its holdings include rare books, archival and genealogical collections, and microform collections.

Hispanic Genealogical Research Center of New Mexico
P.O. Box 51088
Albuquerque, NM 87181
www.hgrc-nm.org

Publishes *Herencia*.

Special Focus Categories

Native American

Native to New Mexico are the Jicarilla and Mescalero Apache; the Navajos, part of the Navajo Nation of New Mexico, Arizona, and Utah; the various Pueblo tribes; and the Ute Indians, part of the Ute Mountain Reservation of New Mexico, Colorado, and Utah. Federal records of the Bureau of Indian Affairs are located in NARA Record Group 75. Among the records located at the National Archives and Records Service—Rocky Mountain Region, Denver, Colorado (see page 12) are records of the Albuquerque Area Office (1877–1989); Consolidated Ute Agency (1878–1952); Gallup Area Office (1913–68); Jicarilla Agency (1890–1966); Mescalero Agency (1874–1946); Navajo Agencies beginning in 1933; Pueblo Agencies beginning in 1869; Shiprock Boarding School (1944–52); and others. Records located at the National Archives and Records Service—Pacific Region, Laguna Niguel, California (see page 12), are Eastern Navajo Agency, Crownpoint, Arizona (1909–44), and Shiprock-San Juan Training School and Agency (Navajo), New Mexico (1903–55), along with others.

See also Daniel's *Genealogical Resources in New Mexico* (see Background Sources), which offers a comprehensive bibliography of primary and secondary sources for each of the New Mexico tribes.

Some manuscript collections of various Native American records can be found within the state by consulting the "Online Archive of New Mexico" <http://elibrary.unm.edu/oanm>.

Various records of the different tribes, including census records, have been microfilmed by the FHL.

County Resources

The county clerk's office in the county seat will have land records, including deeds, mining records, surveys, and plats; marriage records; and some probate records. Military discharges, liens, mortgages, powers of attorney, and miscellaneous affidavits may also be found there. Probate records may be found in the district clerk's office. Counties may have offices in towns other than the county seat, but these retain no permanent custody of records.

Some counties have Territorial and Mexican era records in their custody, and this will explain record holdings earlier than formal organization of the county. Earlier records should be available at the New Mexico State Records Center and Archives. Consult the "Online Archive of New Mexico" <http://elibrary. unm.edu/oanm> for holdings. Former county seats are in parentheses below the address.

For official county information, please consult:

Vigil-Giron, Rebecca, Secretary of State, compiler. *New Mexico Blue Book 1999–2000*. Santa Fe: Office of the Secretary of State, 1999, or consult the New Mexico Secretary of State's website <www.sos.state.nm.us> for updated and additional information.

For additional county information, please consult:

Brylnski, Dorothy A. and Ann L. Mossman. *New Mexico Genealogist Comprehensive Index Volumes 1-38, 1962–1999*. Albuquerque: New Mexico Genealogical Society, 2000.

Daniel, Karen Stein. *Genealogical Resources in New Mexico*. 2d ed. Albuquerque: New Mexico Genealogical Society, 2002.

Julyan, Robert. *The Place Names of New Mexico*. Rev. ed. Albuquerque: University of New Mexico Press, 1998.

Villegas, Jose L., compiler. *Marriage Register Inventory*. Santa Fe: New Mexico State Records Center and Archives, 1998.

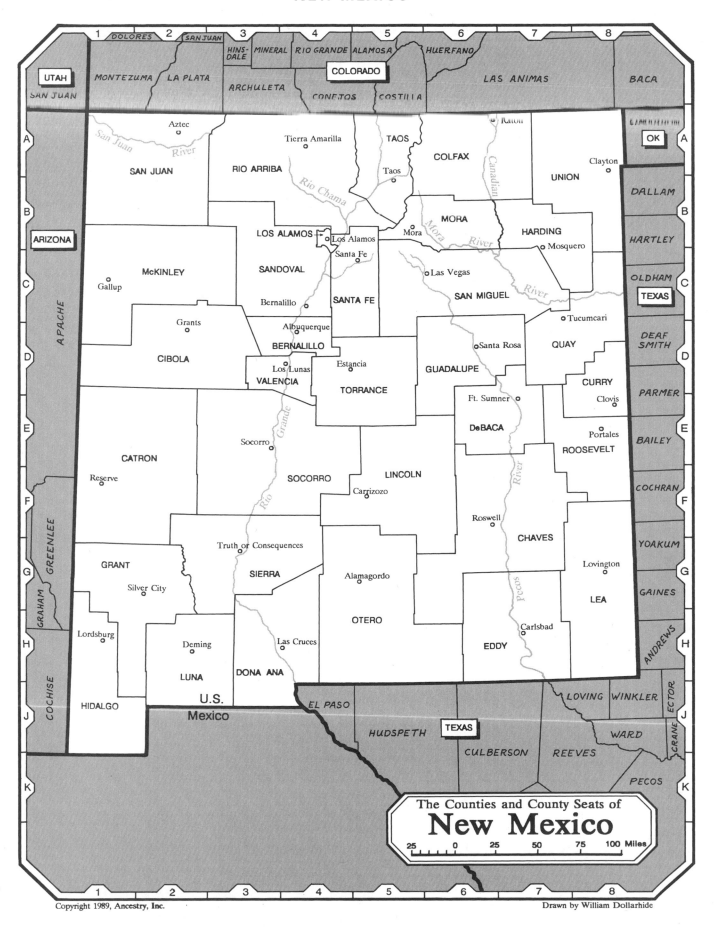

The Counties and County Seats of
New Mexico

Drawn by William Dollarhide

Map County Address	Date Formed Parent County/ies	Birth Marriage Death	Land Probate District Court#
Arizona Part of Gadsden Purchase.	1859 (became part of Dona Ana, 1861–62) Tubac		
D4 Bernalillo One Civic Plaza NW Albuquerque 87102 *Libro Matrimonios (1885–1903) available at the New Mexico State Records Center and Archives*	1852 original	—— 1885	1873 1861 #2
E2 Catron P.O. Box 197 Reserve 87830	1921 Socorro	—— 1921 ——	1921 1921 #7
F7 Chaves 401 N. Main St. Roswell 88201 *Holds some territorial records.*	1889 Lincoln	—— 1891	1887 1900 #5
D2 Cibola 515 W. High St. Grants 87020-2526	1981 Valencia	—— 1981 ——	1981 1981 #13
A6 Colfax P.O. Box 159 Raton 87740 *(Elizabeth Town, 1869; Cimarron 1872; Springer 1882). Typescript (1877–1907) available at the New Mexico State Records Center and Archives.*	1869 Mora/Taos	—— 1869	1864 1884 #8
D8 Curry 700 N. Main St., Ste 7 Clovis 88101-6664	1909 Quay/Roosevelt	—— 1905	1903 1909 #3
E7 DeBaca P.O. Box 347 Fort Sumner 88119-0347	1917 Chaves/Guadalupe/ Roosevelt	—— 1917 ——	1917 1917 #10
H3 Dona Ana 251 W. Amador Ave., Rm 103 Las Cruces 88005 (Mesilla, 1856) *Part of Gadsden Purchase, 1854.*	1852 Original	—— 1869	1803 1833 #3
H7 Eddy P.O. Box 850 Carlsbad 88221 *Marriage Certificates (1891–1921) available at the New Mexico State Records Center and Archives.*	1889 Lincoln	—— 1891	1884 1912 #5
G1 Grant P.O. Box 898 Silver City 88062 *(Pinos Altos, 1869–72). Register of Marriages (1868–1872) available at the New Mexico State Records Center and Archives.*	1868 Dona Ana	—— 1868 ——	1872 1887 #6
D6 Guadalupe 420 Parker Ave. Santa Rosa 88435-2361	1891 Lincoln/San Miguel	—— 1895 ——	1893 1907 #4
B7 Harding P.O. Box 1002 Mosquero 87733-1002	1921 Mora/Union	—— 1921	1921 1921 #10
J1 Hidalgo 300 S. Shakespeare St. Lordsburg 88045-1927	1919 Grant	—— 1920	1879 1920 #6
G8 Lea P.O. Box 1507 Lovington 88260 *Also has transcribed records from parent counties starting 1913.*	1917 Chaves/Eddy	—— 1917	1918 1917 #5
F5 Lincoln P.O. Box 338 Carrizozo 88301 *(Rio Bonito, formerly called Los Placitas then Lincoln, 1869–70) County clerk has complete indexes for all records.*	1869 Socorro/Dona Ana	—— 1882	1869 1881 #12
B4 Los Alamos 2300 Trinity Dr./P.O. Box 30 Los Alamos 87544-0030	1949 Sandoval/Santa Fe	—— 1949	1949 1950 #1
H2 Luna 700 S. Silver Deming 88030-4173 *Applications for Marriage Licenses (1909–1912) available at the New Mexico State Records Center and Archives.*	1901 Dona Ana/Grant	—— 1901 ——	pre-1901 1901 #6
C1 McKinley P.O. Box 1268 Gallup 87305	1899 Bernalillo/Valencia/ San Juan/Ria Arriba	—— 1901	1901 1901 #11
B6 Mora P.O. Box 360 Mora 87732-0580	1860 Taos	—— 1891 ——	1861 1920s #4
H5 Otero 1000 New York Ave. Alamogordo 88310	1899 Dona Ana/Lincoln/ Socorro	—— 1899 ——	1890s 1890s #12
D7 Quay P.O. Box 1225 Tucumcari 88401	1903 Guadalupe/Union	—— 1893	1903 1892 #10
A3 Rio Arriba P.O. Box 158 Tierra Amarilla 87575 *and* P.O. Box 1256 Espanola 87532-1256	1852 original	—— 1884 ——	1852 1852 #1
E8 Roosevelt 101 W. First Portales 88130	1903 Chaves/Guadalupe	—— 1903 ——	1892 1903 #9
C3 Sandoval P.O. Box 40 Bernalillo 87004-0040 *Record loss, 1926.*	1903 Bernalillo	—— 1926 ——	1926 1926 #13
A1 San Juan 100 S. Oliver Dr. Aztec 87410	1887 Rio Arriba/Taos	—— 1887	1887 1909 #11

Map	County Address	Date Formed Parent County/ies	Birth Marriage Death	Land Probate District Court#
C6	San Miguel 500 W. National Las Vegas 87701 (San Miguel 1852–64)	1852 original	—— 1888 —	1887 1859 #4

Marriage Certificates (1912–14) available at the New Mexico State Records Center and Archives.

Map	County Address	Date Formed Parent County/ies	Birth Marriage Death	Land Probate District Court#
	Santa Ana (Pina Blanca 1852–76)	1850 (became part of Bernalillo, 1876) original		
C4	Santa Fe 102 Grant/P.O. Box 1985 Santa Fe 87501	1852 original	—— 1900* —	1848 1894 #1

*Marriage Record A (1863–99) available at the New Mexico State Records Center and Archives.

Map	County Address	Date Formed Parent County/ies	Birth Marriage Death	Land Probate District Court#
G3	Sierra 300 Date St. Truth or Consequences 87901	1884 Socorro/Dona Ana/Grant	—— 1865 —	1884 1884 #7

(Hillsborough, 1884; Truth or Consequences, originally called Hot Springs) Marriage Licenses, Book B (1865–82) and Marriage Certificates (1887–1931) available at the New Mexico State Records Center and Archives.

Map	County Address	Date Formed Parent County/ies	Birth Marriage Death	Land Probate District Court#
E3	Socorro P.O. Box 1 Socorro 87801 (Limitar 1854–67)	1850 Original	—— 1885 —	1912* 1912* #7

*Original records before 1912 are at the New Mexico State Record Center and Archives. Roll 1, book A, pages 479–495 (1863–65) available at the New Mexico State Records Center and Archives.

Map	County Address	Date Formed Parent County/ies	Birth Marriage Death	Land Probate District Court#
A5	Taos 105 Albright St., Ste. D Taos 87571	1852 original	—— 1905* —	1880s 1912 #8

*Marriage Register A-1 (1863–1905) available at the New Mexico State Records Center and Archives.

Map	County Address	Date Formed Parent County/ies	Birth Marriage Death	Land Probate District Court#
D5	Torrance Ninth and Allen/P.O. Box 48 Estancia 87016	1903 Lincoln/San Miguel/ Socorro/Santa Fe/Valencia/ Bernalillo	—— 1910 —	1910 1909 #7
A7	Union P.O. Box 430 Clayton 88415	1893 Colfax/Mora/San Miguel	—— 1894 —	1894 1911 #8
D3	Valencia P.O. Box 969 Los Lunas 87031	1852 original	—— 1869 —	1880s 1870 #13

Original territorial records were filed at Valencia, 1852–72; Tome, 1872–74; Belen, 1874–76. Registro Matrimonios (1869–1905) and Marriage Certificates (1885–1912) available at the New Mexico State Records Center and Archives.

New York

ROGER D. JOSLYN, CG, FUGA, FGBS, FASG

In 1609 Henry Hudson explored the river that bears his name, and in the 1620s the Dutch West India Company established settlements at Fort Orange (Albany) and Manhattan, influencing immigration by other northern Europeans. The English, mostly settlers from New England, came to Long Island, where the boundary between New Netherland and New England had to be settled by treaty in 1650. The Dutch claimed New Netherland from the Connecticut to the Delaware rivers but were overthrown in 1664 by the English, who renamed the colony for the Duke of York. The Dutch staged a brief comeback in 1673, but after a year, New York reverted to English control.

By the time of the Revolutionary War, New Englanders had crossed westward into the eastern counties of New York, and settlers from Long Island and New Jersey had migrated to the lower Hudson valley. Huguenots had settled in New York City, New Rochelle, and elsewhere in the late 1600s, and Ulster-Scots came to the lower Hudson valley and settled in Orange and Ulster counties. The first major immigration of Germans to New York was in 1710, when 847 Palatine families settled in the Hudson Valley.

The American Revolution was a major part of New York's history. The British occupied New York City and controlled all of Long Island and part of Westchester County. This provided a refuge for many Loyalists, including some from New Jersey, while patriots fled to Connecticut from Long Island and from elsewhere up the Hudson. Major battles were fought upstate and every effort was made to prevent the British from taking control of the Hudson Valley and dividing the colonies.

Up to the time of the Revolutionary War, New York had been slower to expand beyond its original settlements than most of the other colonies. Much of the land had been held by only a few people, and Native Americans threatened settlement west of the Hudson and Mohawk valleys. After the war, however, New York grew dramatically. Migrations and immigrations increased at a rapid pace, with only a slight interruption during the War of 1812. Immigration was fueled particularly by Europeans sailing into the port of New York. The state became the principal gateway for those heading west, mostly from New England to the Great Lakes and beyond, although a great number of people remained, as families made "chain migrations" across New York (see David Paul Davenport, "The Yankee Settlement of New York, 1783–1820," *Genealogical Journal*, 17 [1988–89]: 63-88, especially 70). Important to settlement were the Old Military Tract and St. Lawrence Ten Towns in the north; the Military Tract, Chenango Ten Towns, and Boston Ten Towns in the central region; and the Phelps-Gorham and Holland purchases further west. Travel was greatly enhanced by the completion of the Erie Canal in 1825, by which one could get from New York City to Buffalo in less than three weeks. The Hudson River was linked with Lake Champlain by a canal in the northeast and with the Delaware River by another in the southeast. By the mid-1800s, a busy system of stage lines and a network of railroads carried migrants, business people, and goods over the entire state, which promoted growth of cities and villages along their paths.

In the nineteenth century, immigrants swarmed through the port of New York, particularly the Irish and Germans in the

mid-1800s, followed by Italians, Poles, Jews, and others by the turn of the century. Large numbers of African Americans came north after the Civil War and even more so after the world wars; a notable Puerto Rican immigration came after World War II. Today, one-third of New York City's population is foreign-born.

New York had disputed areas with Massachusetts in Columbia County and over six million upstate acres (mostly west of Seneca Lake), with Connecticut in Dutchess County, and with Vermont over the counties of Gloucester, Cumberland, and part of Charlotte. Earlier, New York lost two of its original twelve counties to Massachusetts: Cornwall in 1686 (which eventually became land in Maine) and Dukes in 1692. There was also disagreement over borders with New Jersey and Pennsylvania. Staten Island, long claimed by New Jersey, was not fully relinquished until 1855.

Under the Reorganization Act of 7 March 1788, New York was divided into 120 towns (not townships), many of which were already in existence. (In parts of New York, particularly in the west, land was often *surveyed* into townships, and many people today still use the term colloquially.) The number of towns and cities has increased greatly since 1788. A town may have villages (incorporated), hamlets, and other communities included in its own governments.

Since 1 January 1898, the modern city of New York has been comprised of five boroughs with coterminous counties (but Bronx did not have its own county until 1914). While often identified synonymously with the state of New York, the city is an entity of its own, and some state laws concerning record keeping do not apply.

Vital Records

Not until the mid-nineteenth century was any attempt made by the state of New York to mandate the keeping of vital records. This makes the use of "substitutes," such as church, cemetery, census, and newspaper records, that much more important. A few vital records were entered into some early town records on Long Island and later in some towns along the eastern border, the latter evidently by New England settlers bringing with them a long-standing tradition of such practice. The mass migration into New York just after the Revolution, however, took place at a time when vital event recording slacked off greatly, even in New England.

The earliest items that might be classified as civil vital records in New York were marriage licenses, issued from 1639 to 1783. Names of the parties and the date of the license were published in *Names of Persons for Whom Marriage Licenses Were Issued by the Secretary of the Province of New York, Previous to 1784* (1860; reprint with supplements as *New York Marriages Previous to 1784*, Baltimore: Genealogical Publishing Co., 1968). This work did not include all the important information in related marriage bonds, which date from 1664, the majority of which were filed after 1700. Most of the bonds were destroyed or damaged in the 1911 fire at the New York State Library (see Archives, Libraries, and Societies). From those that survived, Kenneth Scott compiled *New York Marriage Bonds, 1753–1783* (New York: Saint Nicholas Society of the City of New York, 1972). Some records of marriages performed by justices of the peace have survived, of which a few have been published in *Tree Talks* and *The New York Genealogical and Biographical Record* (see Periodicals).

In 1847 a law was enacted requiring school districts to keep records of births, marriages, and deaths. While the law was not a complete failure, compliance was scattered, and some towns that began to record vital events quickly stopped. Those records that were kept are incomplete, and the latest that records were kept was 1852, as the law was repealed in 1853. Originals of a few of these records are still with the town and county clerks or have been placed in historical societies. Some records have been published in *Tree Talks* and in the Cemetery, Church, and Town Records volumes compiled by the Daughters of the American Revolution (DAR) in the State of New York (see Cemetery Records). Also useful for the nineteenth century are the marriages and deaths listed in the 1865 and 1875 New York state censuses for the census period ending 31 May of those years (the 1865 census also included deaths of officers and enlisted men). Marriages and deaths were also recorded in the 1855 state census but without names. The statistics of births, marriages, and deaths for each household recorded in the 1825, 1835, and 1845 censuses can sometimes be used to advantage (see Census Records).

Another attempt by the state to require the keeping of vital records was made in 1880, and this law is the basis for the recording of births, marriages, and deaths in New York today. The record was made in the town, village, or city in which the event took place and, after being recorded there (in ledger volumes), the original certificate was sent to Albany, where alphabetical indexes of names are arranged by event and then by year. Today, the original certificate is forwarded to the Department of Health, with the local registrar keeping a duplicate copy. Each index entry lists the name, date of event, place, and certificate number; no maiden names or marital status are shown for deaths, and ages at death are given only from 1940. Marriages are indexed by the name of each party, but there is no cross-referencing except for 1908 to 1914 and since 1944, when the first four letters of the spouse's surname are included. Since compliance with the 1880 law was slow, many events were not recorded.

Copies of vital record certificates, marked "for genealogical research only," can be issued at the state or local level for the current fee of $22 each. This applies only to births recorded at least seventy-five years ago and to marriages and deaths recorded

fifty years ago and earlier. Indexes to these records are available at the New York State Archives in Albany, the National Archives—Northeast Region in New York City, the Onondaga County Public Library in Syracuse, the Rochester Public Library, and the Buffalo and Erie County Public Library, all of which also have a list of local registrars from which copies of the records may be obtained. Copies can also be obtained from the New York Department of Health, Vital Records Section, Genealogy Unit, P.O. Box 2602, Albany, NY 12237-2602 <www.health.state. ny.us/nysdoh/consumer/vr.htm>, but a long delay for a response is likely because of the large backlog of requests. Certified copies of birth, marriage, and death certificates, at the local or state level, are currently $30 each.

Some cities kept vital records earlier than those sent to Albany under the 1880 law. These include Albany, Buffalo, Rochester, Syracuse, Utica, Yonkers, and New York City. For Albany, Buffalo, and Yonkers, birth and death records before 1914 and marriages before 1908 should be sought from those cities' registrars of vital statistics, as copies were not sent to the state until those years. For the period 1908 through about 1935, marriages were also recorded with the county clerk, although some counties do not have these records for all of this time period.

Copies of vital records for New York City are not duplicated in Albany except for those areas annexed to the cities of New York or Brooklyn after 1880, such as Staten Island (Richmond County), the present Queens County, and certain parts of Bronx and Kings counties, and only up until the consolidation of Greater New York City on 1 January 1898. For early vital records of New York City (Manhattan, Brooklyn, Queens, Bronx, and Staten Island), contact the New York City Municipal Archives (see Archives, Libraries, and Societies). Births through 1909, marriages through 1937, and deaths through 1948 can be obtained by mail for $15 each ($6 if the certificate number is known), or one may visit the archives and search indexes and microfilms of the records for a $5 daily search fee (copies of desired records would then be an additional $6 each). Later birth and death records should be obtained from the New York City Department of Health, Bureau of Vital Records, 125 Worth St., New York, NY 10013 <www.nyc.gov/html/doh>; the current cost is $15 for each record. Marriage records for all of New York City after 1937 should be obtained from the Office of the City Clerk, 1 Centre Street, New York, NY 10007. The current fee is $10 if the license number is provided, or $15 for a one-year search and copy of the record if found. Indexes to New York City marriage licenses (1908–51), arranged by borough, are available at the Municipal Archives. Printed New York City vital records indexes (from 1888 for Manhattan and from 1898 for the other boroughs) are available at the New York Public Library for births and deaths through 1982 and for marriages through 1937. The New York Genealogical and Biographical Society also has these indexes, but for births and deaths through 1965 (see Archives,

Libraries, and Societies). For more detail about availability of New York City vital records, see *Genealogical Resources in New York* under Background Sources.

While there is no contemporary, comprehensive guide to New York State vital records, a nearly complete inventory of what existed in the early 1940s was compiled by the Historical Records Survey, *Guide to Public Vital Statistics Records in New York State (Including New York City)*, 3 vols. (Albany, N.Y.: Historical Records Survey, 1942). This guide includes existing records for the period 1847 to 1852.

Since 1847, divorce actions in New York have been handled in the Supreme Court for the county in which the divorce was heard. New York divorce files, however, are sealed for 100 years. In colonial times, petitions for divorce had to be made to the governor or legislature, and only a few were granted. The Court of Chancery granted divorces from 1787 to 1847. These older records are in the state archives or for the downstate counties at the New York County Clerk's Office, Division of Old Records, 31 Chambers St., Rm. 703, New York, NY 10007 (see Charles Farrell, comp., "Index to Matrimonial Actions 1787–1840, New York County Clerk's Office," *The New York Genealogical and Biographical Record*, 129 [1998]: 81-88). See also Matteo Spalletta, "Divorce in Colonial New York," *The New-York Historical Society Quarterly* 39 (1955): 422-40.

Census Records

Federal

Population Schedules
- Indexed—1790, 1800, 1810, 1820, 1830, 1840, 1850, 1860, 1870, 1880, 1890 (fragment), 1900, 1910, 1920, 1930
- Soundex—1880, 1900, 1920

Industrial and Agricultural Schedules
- 1820 (industrial only), 1850, 1860, 1870, 1880

Mortality Schedules
- 1850, 1860, 1870, 1880

Union Veterans Schedules
- 1890 (indexed)

Microfilms of the federal censuses for New York, 1790 to 1930, and corresponding book and microfilm indexes are available in several places throughout the state and country (see pages 3-4). There are three published indexes for the 1800 census. The 1850 index published by AISI covers only half of the towns for Westchester County, as the other half were indexed in error from the 1860 census (see David L. Kent and John C. Baskin, *Westchester County, New York, the Index to That Half of*

Westchester County Omitted from the Accelerated Indexing Systems Index to the 1850 Federal Census of New York [Austin, Tex.: the authors, 1993]). Some counties have their "short form" copies of the 1880 census, which serve as complete indexes (by district) to that census (see the Douglas-Yates guide mentioned below). Within the state, the National Archives—Northeast Region (see page 11) has complete sets of these records, as do the New York Public Library, the New York State Library, and the Onondaga County Public Library (see Archives, Libraries, and Societies). The New York Genealogical and Biographical Society has the census through 1920 for New York. Most of these collections include the 1910 street indexes to enumeration districts for the New York City boroughs of Manhattan, Bronx, Brooklyn, and Staten Island. Many libraries with genealogical collections have microfilms of most or all the censuses for their particular county and often for surrounding counties. Several early New York censuses have been published, many in *Tree Talks*, some in *The New York Genealogical and Biographical Record,* and in the volumes by Ralph Van Wood for Cayuga, Herkimer, Oneida, and Ontario counties. Two enumerations were taken in New York City in 1870. Parts of the enumerations for the towns of Eastchester (Westchester County) and Brookhaven (Suffolk County) are among the few surviving schedules of the 1890 federal census. A recount of the 1890 enumeration for New York City (Manhattan and West Bronx), called the "Police Census" (since it was taken by the city police)—which is available at the Municipal Archives, The New York Public Library, and The New York Genealogical and Biographical Society—fills part of the void of the destroyed federal census. Damaged and missing censuses include the following:

- **1810:** Cortland and part of Broome County—missing
- **1860:** Chenango and Columbia counties—damaged
- **1880:** Suffolk County and New York City Wards 21 and 22—damaged

The corresponding federal mortality, agricultural, industry/manufacturing, and other schedules are available at the state library, and microfilms of these records are also at the New York Genealogical and Biographical Society and the Queensborough Library in Jamaica, Long Island.

Colonial and State

Some important censuses were taken in colonial New York, some of which have been extracted and published (see Background Sources). Others have been published in journals such as *The New York Genealogical and Biographical Record* and the *National Genealogical Society Quarterly.*

Of almost greater value in New York than the federal are the state censuses, taken every ten years from 1825 to 1875, in 1892, and again in 1905, 1915, and 1925; pre-1825 state censuses and state copies of those for 1855 to 1905 were destroyed in the 1911

state library fire. Most of the censuses that have survived can be found with the county clerk, although some are with the county historian or in other locations. For a list of the whereabouts of these censuses, consult Marilyn Douglas and Melinda Yates, compu., *New York State Census Records, 1790–1925*, Bibliography Bulletin 88 of the New York State Library (Albany, N.Y.: 1981), which has some errors and omissions. The state library and the New York Genealogical and Biographical Society have microfilms of almost all the surviving state censuses. The New York Public Library has most microfilms for 1855 and for almost all of the surviving state censuses for the New York City and Long Island counties and Westchester County.

Indexes have been prepared for some of the state censuses and are usually found with the county historian or at the county historical society. Some of these indexes are mentioned in the Douglas-Yates guide; others are listed in David Paul Davenport's "The State Censuses of New York, 1825–75," *Genealogical Journal* 14 (1985–86): 172-97, and in Laura LeBarron, "Finding Aids at The NYG&B Library for New York State Censuses," *The NYG&B Newsletter* 8 (1997): 11-13, 19-21.

The Douglas-Yates guide also shows the existence of the county copies of the federal censuses available locally, which are useful for checking against the federal copies as microfilmed by the National Archives. The state copies of the federal census perished in the 1911 New York State Library fire.

The 1825, 1835, and 1845 state censuses are similar to pre-1850 federal censuses in that only the name of the head of the household is listed, although there is valuable information about the composition of the household, its agriculture and commerce, and so forth. Beginning in 1855, every person is listed, with his or her relationship to the head of the household, and, if a native New Yorker, the county of birth is shown. Years of residency in the town or city in which enumerated are also given, as is citizenship status for adult males. The 1865 census dropped the years' residency column but added ones for parents of how many children and number of times married. It also listed active and veteran servicemen. Later state censuses provide similar information, although the schedules for 1892 listed only name, sex, color, age, country of birth, whether or not a U.S. citizen, and occupation. The date and court of naturalization for naturalized citizens was a feature of the 1925 census. For more details, consult the Douglas-Yates guide.

The surviving 1790 state census schedules for Albany County were compiled by Kenneth Scott in *New York: State Census of Albany County Towns in 1790* (Baltimore: Genealogical Publishing, 1975; reprint, Baltimore: Clearfield Co., 1991). In his work, Scott also compared these schedules with the 1790 federal census for Albany County.

At one time, the state library had some original census records, but these have all been returned to their original

jurisdictions. For example, the schedules for Albany County are now in the County Hall of Records, 250 South Pearl Street, Albany, NY 12202.

Background Sources

New York State abounds in published history, so much so that only a few representative titles can be listed here. These include Alexander C. Flick, ed., *History of the State of New York,* 10 vols. (1933–37; reprint, Port Washington, N.Y.: Kennikat Press, 1962); David M. Ellis and others, *A History of New York State,* rev. ed. (Ithaca, N.Y.: Cornell University Press, 1967); Bruce Bliven, Jr., *New York: A Bicentennial History* (New York: Norton, 1981); and Michael G. Kammen, *Colonial New York: A History* (New York: Scribners, 1975). *The Empire State: A History of New York,* ed. by Milton M. Klein (Ithaca, N.Y.: Cornell University Press, and Cooperstown, N.Y.: New York State Historical Association, 2001) provides a good general history.

For the earlier period, one should not overlook Edmund B. O'Callaghan, ed., *Documentary History of the State of New-York,* 4 vols. (Albany: n.p., 1849–51), which concerns the seventeenth and eighteenth centuries but is not indexed. Various lists of persons from these volumes were reprinted as *Lists of Inhabitants of Colonial New York* (Baltimore: Genealogical Publishing Co., 1989).

O'Callaghan also edited *Calendar of Historical Manuscripts in the Office of Secretary of State, Albany, N.Y.,* 2 vols. (1865–66; reprint, Ridgewood, N.J.: Gregg Press, 1968). Volume 1 covers the Dutch period (1630–64) and volume 2 covers the English (1664–1776). Some of the manuscripts were lost or damaged in the New York State Library fire in 1911. O'Callaghan translated, sometimes incorrectly, a great many of the Dutch documents, but most remained unpublished. With Berthold Fernow, he edited the fifteen-volume *Documents Relative to the Colonial History of the State of New-York* (1853–87; reprint, New York: A.M.S. Press, 1969). The first ten volumes were compiled from records in Amsterdam, Paris, and London, with volume 11 serving as the index. Volumes 12–14 cover documents found in New York State, and volume 15 covers the Revolutionary War (see Military Records). Since the 1970s, the surviving original Dutch and English material up to 1700 is being published in the series titled *New York Historical Manuscripts,* although some of the volumes to date, under various editors and publishers, have included material not in O'Callaghan's *Calendar,* such as the Brooklyn Dutch Church records and records of the New Amsterdam notary Salomon Lachaire.

Major genealogical compilations for New York include David M. Riker, *Genealogical and Biographical Directory to Persons in New Netherland, from 1613 to 1674,* 4 vols. (Salem, Mass.: Higginson Books, 1999), also published by Family Tree Maker on CD-ROM as *New Netherland Vital Records, 1600s* (1999); Henry Z. Jones, Jr., *The Palatine Families of New York: A Study of the German Immigrants Who Arrived in Colonial New York in 1710,* 2 vols. (Universal City, Calif.: the author, 1985) and Mr. Jones's subsequent volumes on the Palatines; and Frank J. Doherty's in-progress series, *Settlers of the Beekman Patent Dutchess County, New York,* 7 vols. to date (Pleasant Valley, N.Y.: the author, 1990–). More recent scholarship and reinterpretations of New York history are found in articles in *New York History, The New-York Historical Society Quarterly* (defunct), and *The William and Mary Quarterly* (see Virginia).

Much of the state's regional history consists of three- or four-volume works, the first two or three volumes of which are the "history" and the rest "mug" books. The term mug book refers to those printed sources that present pictures and biographies of those who subscribed to the publication. The latter are useful for clues about families, but they are not always factual. A long list of works on regional New York history and genealogy is found in Austin's "Genealogical Research in Upstate New York" (see under Guides below).

Guides

For a good overview, see the New York chapters in *Genealogical Research: Methods and Sources,* vol. 1, rev. ed., edited by Milton Rubincam (Washington, D.C.: The American Society of Genealogists, 1980). Kenn Stryker-Rodda wrote on "New Netherland, Long Island, Staten Island, and the Hudson Valley Counties" (pp. 168-95) and Mary J. Sibley on "Upstate New York," updated by Gerald J. Parsons (pp. 195-220). This work is out of print, but is still a very useful guide.

George K. Schweitzer, *New York Genealogical Research* (Knoxville, Tenn: the author, 1995) is a good, inexpensive New York guide. Also useful is the Family History Library's *Research Outline* for New York, #31069, 2d ed. (Salt Lake City: the library, 1997).

Kate Burke, *Searching in New York: A Reference Guide to Public and Private Records* (Costa Mesa, Calif.: ISC Publications, 1987) includes libraries, hospitals, and so forth, and is useful for adoptees. Some information is not current or sufficiently detailed.

John Austin, "Genealogical Research in Upstate New York, An Informal Finding List of Published Materials" (Glens Falls, N.Y.: the author, 1983) is out of print but a very useful guide to items in *Tree Talks,* abstracts of and indexes to wills, and so forth.

Gateway to America: Genealogical Research in the New York State Library, 2d ed., rev. (Albany, N.Y.: The New York State Library, 1982) is available from the library for $3. While this publication is dated, it does provide a printed guide to many of the basic genealogical materials in the library. More updated, single-sheet guides on several topics, such as vital records, adoption,

probate records, and so forth are available at the library and on its website.

Guide to Records in the New York State Archives (Albany, N.Y.: State Archives, 1993) should be supplemented by the archives' online catalogue.

"Research in Progress in New York History," a feature in *New York History* indexing books and articles since 1952, was continued in 1968 as *Research and Publications in New York State History*, published by the University of the State of New York, but was discontinued in the early 1970s.

Gordon L. Remington's *New York State Towns, Villages, and Cities: A Guide to Genealogical Sources* (Boston: New England Historic Genealogical Society, 2002) provides an excellent gateway into many basic records, including local histories, church registers and cemetery inscriptions, and the town clerk's registers of Civil War soldiers and sailors (see Military Records).

Estelle M. Guzik, ed., *Genealogical Resources in New York* (New York: Jewish Genealogical Society, 2003) is the best guide to most nineteenth- and twentieth-century New York City sources (not state sources, as implied by the title), as well as New York City-area Jewish research (the newer edition has a narrower focus than the first edition, published in 1989 under the title *Genealogical Resources in the New York Metropolitan Area*). It should be supplemented by Rosalie Fellows Bailey, *Guide to Genealogical and Biographical Sources for New York City (Manhattan), 1783–1898* (1954; reprint Baltimore: Clearfield Co., 1998, with introduction by Harry Macy, Jr.), which while somewhat outdated, is very useful for identifying many other and earlier records, some covering more than just Manhattan.

J. H. French, *Gazetteer of the State of New York* (1860; reprint with additional indexes, Baltimore: Genealogical Publishing Co., Inc., 1995) is the best and most useful of several gazetteers. For a modern list of New York places, consult *Gazetteer of the State of New York* (Albany, N.Y.: New York State Department of Health, 1995). Also see Gordon Remington's *New York State Towns, Villages, and Cities*.

Herbert F. Seversmith and Kenn Stryker-Rodda, *Long Island Genealogical Source Material*, National Genealogical Society Special Publication 24, 2d printing (Washington, D.C.: National Genealogical Society, 1980) is an excellent bibliography of about 850 published and manuscript sources in 125 libraries throughout the country.

Rosalie Fellows Bailey, *Dutch Systems in Family Naming: New York-New Jersey*, National Genealogical Society Special Publication 12, 3d printing (Washington, D.C.: National Genealogical Society, 1978) covers a difficult subject superbly, for which also see Kenn Stryker-Rodda's "New Netherland Naming Systems and Customs," *The New York Genealogical and Biographical Record* 126 (1995): 35-45.

Maps

The first place to obtain a map is in each county, usually in the county treasurer's office for a dollar or two. Most maps are large enough to show all county roads, and a further benefit is that most show the towns in different colors, making them easily distinguishable. Many more maps can be found at the courthouse in the county clerk's or tax offices. They can be useful for locating a specific piece of property; but the further back in time, the fewer maps will be available. A map is sometimes included with a recorded deed. More detailed maps are available for cities, villages, and towns, and a good place to look for these would be local libraries. U.S. topographical maps are useful for locating cemeteries. Excellent map collections are at the New York Public Library, the New York State Library, and the New-York Historical Society.

Numerous county maps are found in county histories and county atlases. For a list of these, see Albert Hazen Wright, *A Check List of New York State County Maps Published, 1779–1945* (Ithaca, N.Y.: Cornell University, 1965).

On a larger scale, David H. Burr's *An Atlas of the State of New York* (New York: David H. Burr, 1829) and Joseph R. Bien's *Atlas of the State of New York* (New York: J. Bien & Co., 1895) are useful; the latter work depicts original patent and lot boundaries. For patents (1624–1800), and a series of maps showing county formations and migration routes, consult the excellent *Richards Atlas of New York State*, 2d ed., edited by Robert J. Rayback (Phoenix, N.Y.: Frank E. Richards, 1965). *New York: Atlas of Historical County Boundaries*, compiled by Kathryn Ford Thorne and edited by John H. Long (New York: Simon & Schuster, 1993) is helpful for following county boundary changes, but be aware of the glaring error for Dutchess County (see *The American Genealogist*, 69 [1994]: 251-52). Other historical maps of New York are online at <www.sunysb.edu/libmap/nymaps.htm>.

The New York State Center for Geographic Information, P.O. Box 2062, Albany, NY 12220-0062 <www.nysgis.state.ny.us> has a good collection of paper and digital maps for sale, and its website is linked to online digital images of the U.S. Geological Survey quadrangle maps.

Accurate maps of historical changes in towns, cities, and villages are few. Useful exceptions are David Kendall Martin, "The Districts of Albany County, New York, 1772–1784," *The NYG&B Newsletter* 1 (1990): 9, 12-13, which covers only one section of the province, but with maps that help show that county's divisions prior to the creation of towns in 1788; and Marjory B. Hinman, *The Creation of Broome County, New York* (Windsor, N.Y.: the author, 1981), with clear, useful maps of early nineteenth-century town boundaries in Broome and predecessor counties. For New York City, see Harry Macy, Jr., "Before the Five-Borough City: The Old Cities, Towns and Villages That

Came Together to Form 'Greater New York,'" *The NYG&B Newsletter* 9 (1998): 3-6.

Land Records

State-Land State

The *Calendar of N.Y. Colonial Manuscripts Indorsed Land Papers..., 1643–1803* (1864; reprint, Harrison, N.Y.: Harbor Hill Books, 1987) lists documents relating to applications for land patents and other government grants, including warrants or descriptions of surveys, warrants for patents, returns of surveys, certificates, petitions, affidavits, and claims. Microfilm of the material is at the New York State Archives along with the land patents (which are also on microfilm at the New York Genealogical and Biographical Society). The Secretary of State Deeds, dating from colonial times and including some private conveyances up to about 1775 (fewer to about 1830) and mostly for property in New York City and adjacent areas), are on microfilm at the state archives and the New York Genealogical and Biographical Society, with the usual grantor and grantee indexes. Charles F. Grim's *An Essay Towards an Improved Register of Deeds, City and County of New York to December 31, 1799 "Inclusive"* (New York: Gould, Banks & Co., 1832) indexes those Secretary of State Deeds pertaining to New York City property.

Abstracts of early deeds for Kings and Westchester counties have been published in *The New York Genealogical and Biographical Record,* beginning in volumes 48 and 50 respectively. Fred Q. Bowman, *Landholders of Northeastern New York, 1739–1802* (Baltimore: Genealogical Publishing Co., 1983) covers the counties of Clinton, Essex, Franklin, Warren, and Washington.

Isaac N. P. Stokes' superb *Iconography of Manhattan Island, 1498–1909,* 6 vols. (1915–28; reprint, New York: Arno Press, 1967) is based heavily on land records and includes detailed maps. It is well indexed.

Bounty land in the central part of the state was awarded by lottery to New York Revolutionary War soldiers, although most sold their allotments rather than settled on them. The successful drawers are listed in *The Balloting Book, and Other Documents Relating to Military Bounty Lands in the State of New York* (Albany, N.Y.: Packard & Van Benthuysen, 1825).

To help understand the settlement of western New York, see Orsamus Turner, *History of Pioneer Settlement of Phelps and Gorham's Purchase and Morris' Reserve* (1851; reprint with supplements and indexes by LaVerne C. Cooley and George E. Lookup, Interlaken, N.Y.: Heart of the Lakes Publishing, 1976). Turner also wrote *Pioneer History of the Holland Land Purchase of Western New York* (1849; reprint with Cooley's index, Interlaken, N.Y.: Heart of the Lakes Publishing, 1976, and Bowie, Md.: Heritage Books, 1991). See also William Chazanof, *Joseph Ellicott and the Holland Land Company: The Opening of Western*

New York (Syracuse, N.Y.: Syracuse University Press, 1970); Ruth L. Higgins, *Expansion in New York with Especial Reference to the Eighteenth Century* (1931; reprint, Philadelphia: Porcupine Press, 1974); and William Wyckoff, *The Developer's Frontier: The Making of the Western New York Landscape* (New Haven, Conn.: Yale University Press, 1988). Microfilm of the archives of the Holland Land Company is available at the Daniel E. Reed Library, State University at Fredonia, Fredonia, NY 14063; Research Guide No. 55 explains these records. Karen E. Livsey's *Western New York Land Transactions, 1804–1824, ...1825–1835,* 2 vols. (Baltimore: Genealogical Publishing Co., 1991, 1996) is an index to early Holland Company sales. Other land company records are in the state library in Albany and scattered among various repositories.

In the counties are deeds and mortgages and corresponding indexes to each type of record (published indexes covering into the nineteenth century are available for New York and Albany counties). These records in the county clerk's offices begin mostly with the formation of the county, but sometimes colonial deeds were recorded in town records, and some counties have copies or abstracts of deeds originally recorded in their parent county/counties pertaining to land now in the "child" county. Also, many land transactions were not recorded in earlier times since there was no state law strongly requiring such until 1823. (The recording of deeds was required in new counties in northern, central, and western New York from the 1790s and in New York City from 1811. Mortgages were required to be recorded from 1753.) Additionally, it may have been a long way to the courthouse, or the family moved on before the document could get recorded. Furthermore, with some New York lands in dispute, deed holders were reluctant to bring them in for recording. Many early New Yorkers simply leased land from individuals or families who held vast acreage. Evidence of residency in those cases might be found in the private papers of manorial families such as the Livingstons, Van Rensselaers, and Van Cortlandts. Unfortunately, there is no guide to the location of all manorial records, but very helpful is Henry B. Hoff, "Manors in New York," *The NYG&B Newsletter* 10 (1999): 55-58, 11 (2000): 13-17; also Sung Bok Kim's *Landlord and Tenant in Colonial New York* (Chapel Hill: University of North Carolina Press, 1978) includes an excellent overview and a good bibliography. The Livingston papers are available at the J. Pierpont Morgan Library in New York City and are on microfilm at the Family History Library; the Van Rensselaer papers are in the state library in Albany.

Probate Records

Estate records have been handled in New York in the Surrogate's Court since 1787 when a system of county Surrogate's courts was established. Prior to that time most estates were handled

in New York City, the capital until 1797. Abstracts of most of the earlier records are found in *Abstracts of Wills on File in the Surrogate's Office, County of New York, 1665–1800,* in volumes 25–41 of the New-York Historical Society Collections (New York, 1892–1909), usually referred to as "New York Wills," and in Berthold Fernow, comp. and ed., *Calendar of Wills on File and Recorded in the Offices of the Court of Appeals, of the County Clerk at Albany and of the Secretary of State, 1626–1836* (1896; reprint, Baltimore: Genealogical Publishing Co., 1967). Only the first of these includes letters of administration, but both contain errors (the former set actually includes two volumes of corrections and additions, and Fernow's work omits hundreds of wills, for which one should consult the complete, typewritten index at the New York State Archives and State Library). Also, there is some overlap between these sources, so both should be consulted. (The New-York Historical Society series is available on CD-ROM from Heritage Books of Bowie, Md.) Other material has been published in abstract form in Kenneth Scott, *Genealogical Data from New York Administration Bonds, 1753–1799,* volume 10 of the New York Genealogical and Biographical Society Collections (New York, 1969); *Genealogical Data from Further New York Administration Bonds, 1791–1798,* vol. 11 of the New York Genealogical and Biographical Society Collections (New York, 1971); *Genealogical Data from Administration Papers in the New York State Court of Appeals in Albany* (New York: National Society of Colonial Dames of the State of New York, 1972); *Records of the Chancery Court, Province and State of New York: Guardianships, 1691–1815* (New York: Holland Society of New York, 1971); and, with James A. Owre, *Genealogical Data from Inventories Of New York Estates, 1666–1825* (New York: New York Genealogical and Biographical Society, 1970). Scott also published articles on New York wills, guardianships, and inventories in the *National Genealogical Society Quarterly,* 51:90; 54:98, 246; 55:119; and 56:51. Original wills ca. 1665 to 1738 are available on microfilm at the state archives, The New York Genealogical and Biographical Society, and elsewhere; most filed (original) and recorded wills prior to 1787 are at the state archives (although most estates were apparently settled without going through probate at all).

Before 1787, some wills were recorded in the counties and occasionally in town records. See Gustave Anjou, *Ulster County, N.Y. Probate Records,* 2 vols. (New York: the author, 1906), covering records 1663 to 1766 and 1792 to 1827, and the two volumes by William S. Pelletreau, *Early Long Island Wills of Suffolk County, 1691–1703,* and *Early Wills of Westchester County New York from 1664 to 1784* (New York: Francis P. Harper, 1897, 1898). Pelletreau's former work does not include those in Suffolk County sessions records (for which see Thomas W. Cooper, *The Records of the Court of Sessions of Suffolk County in the Province of New York 1670–1688* [Bowie, Md.: Heritage Books, 1993]) or a few in early county deed books. Better abstracts of the

Westchester County wills are found in Pelletreau's *Abstracts of Wills on File* (see also below for Westchester County). Other early New York will abstracts have been published in *The New York Genealogical and Biographical Record,* such as those for Kings County, mostly from deeds (1661–1719), in volume 47; Montgomery County (1787–1831), in volumes 56–57; Tioga County (1799–1847), in volumes 57–58; Queens County wills from deeds (1683–1744), in volume 65; Dutchess County wills in volume 61; and Westchester County wills (1787–99), in volumes 55–57 and 67. For the period 1688 to 1690, New York was part of the Dominion of New England, and during that time estates valued at over £50 were to be probated in Boston. Seventeen wills of New York residents were brought to Boston, and abstracts of these are found in volumes 12 and 13 of *The American Genealogist.*

Beginning in 1830, a New York law required that the petition for probate include a list of each legal heir—whether or not there was a will, and whether or not heirs were named in the will—their relationship to the deceased, and their residences. This is often the single most important document in an estate file, but it is not generally found in the record books.

Most counties have consolidated indexes to all estate matters including wills, administrations, guardianships, and so forth. In some counties, however, the types of estates may be indexed separately. Likewise, all the documents pertaining to a particular estate may not be filed together but separately according to type of action such as bonds, accounts, and inventories, and thereunder by date of filing. Many counties have particularly separated the original wills—many early ones are not on file—from the rest of the documents pertaining to an estate. Some early letters of administration give the relationship of the administrator to the deceased, and some early letters of guardianship provide the date of birth of the minor.

A New York law permits clerks of the surrogate court to impose a stiff fee (currently $90) to search for an estate over twenty-five years old (Surrogate's Procedure Act Section 2402, item 14), and the cost of copies of the documents can be extra. Some indexes to wills, administrations, and guardianships, and some abstracts of these records for many counties can be found in the state library, the New York Public Library, the New York Genealogical and Biographical Society, and in other libraries. Many such indexes and abstracts were prepared by the late Gertrude A. Barber of New York City or by one of her sisters, Ray C. Sawyer and Minnie Cowen. The indexes and abstracts serve as guides only and should be verified in the original record books and files. Abstracts of New York state wills to about 1830 with an all-name index by W. A. D. Eardeley at the Brooklyn Historical Society are also helpful. Abstracts of wills and letters of administration and guardianship have also been published in *Tree Talks* and other journals.

Two excellent guides for New York estates should be consulted: Harry Macy, Jr., "New York Probate Records Before 1787," *The NYG&B Newsletter* 2 (1991): 11-15; and Gordon L. Remington, *New York State Probate Records: A Genealogist's Guide to Testate and Intestate Records* (Boston: New England Historic Genealogical Society, 2002). See also the state archives' Information Leaflet #3 on Probate Records, available on the archives' website.

Court Records

The county clerk is the keeper of most civil and criminal trial court records, naturalizations, copies of marriage records (1908–ca. 1935), censuses (county copies of the federal census and the state censuses), as well as deeds and mortgages. Estate matters are recorded with the clerk of the county Surrogate's Court (see Probate Records), but before 1847 cases involving property of minor heirs and incompetents were often heard in the Court of Chancery. The *Inventory of the County Archives of New York State,* taken by the Historical Records Survey, 6 vols. (Albany and New York: WPA, 1937–40) was published only for Albany, Bronx, Broome, Cattaraugus, Chautauqua, Chemung, Kings, Richmond, and Ulster counties. Unpublished survey forms are at the New York State Archives, excluding those for the five counties of New York City, which are in that city's Municipal Archives (see Archives, Libraries, and Societies).

Much state court record material is at the state archives and the Old Records Division of the New York County Clerk's Office. An excellent guide to some of these records is James D. Folts and others, *"Duely & Constantly Kept:" A History of the New York Supreme Court, 1691–1847 and An Inventory of Its Records (Albany, Utica, and Geneva Offices), 1797–1847* (Albany, N.Y.: New York State Court of Appeals and the New York State Archives and Records Administration, 1991). Federal court records are at the National Archives—Northeast Region, covering the U.S. district and circuit courts in New York for various periods from 1789 to 1967 and early admiralty courts from 1685 to 1838.

Tax Records

Scattered town and precinct tax records for a few years in the 1770s and 1780s and nearly complete lists for the whole state (1799–1804) are at the New York State Archives and New York State Library—Manuscripts and Special Collections, although for the latter period the surviving 1804 rolls cover only delinquent taxes of nonresidents. New York City tax records are at the Municipal Archives (see Archives, Libraries, and Societies) and, for 1699 to 1734, on microfilm at the New York Genealogical and Biographical Society. Some early assessment rolls have been published in *The New York Genealogical and Biographical Record,*

such as those for New York City, 1730, in volume 95; New Rochelle, 1767, in volume 107; and Ulster County (1709–21) in volume 62. See also volumes 43-44 of the New-York Historical Society's *Collections* for New York City assessments (1695–99). A few counties such as Ontario have retained their early tax records, but most do not have them until about 1850 or even later. Many old tax lists are to be found in manuscript collections. Dutchess County is fortunate to have a long series of eighteenth century tax records. See Clifford M. Buck, *Dutchess County, NY, Tax Lists 1718–1787 with Rombout Precinct by William Willis Reese,* edited by Arthur and Nancy Kelly (Rhinebeck, N.Y.: Kinship, 1990).

Some of the 1798 U.S. Direct Tax records survive for New York. Two published examples are David Kendall Martin, "A 1798 United States Assessment List for Northern New York State [Plattsburgh]," *The New York Genealogical and Biographical Record* 113 (1982): 93-102, and C. R. Carey, "Town of Deer Park 1798 Assessment Records," *Orange County Historical Society Publication No. 8* (Goshen, 1978–79): 13-25. Later federal tax records for New York are at the National Archives—Northeast Region. One early federal tax list was published for New York City: *The Income Record: A List Giving the Taxable Income for the Year 1863, of Every Resident of New York* (New York: The American News Co., 1865).

One list of published New York tax records is Roger D. Joslyn, "New York State Censuses and Tax Lists," *The NYG&B Newsletter* 9 (1998): 17-19. Henry's B. Hoff's "Pre-1750 New York Lists: Censuses, Assessment Rolls, Oaths of Allegiance, and Other Lists," also in the *Newsletter* 3 (1992): 20-22, includes earlier published tax lists.

Cemetery Records

In 1999 The Association of Municipal Historians of New York State published their compilation *New York State Cemeteries Name/Location Inventory, 1995–1997* (Bowie, Md.: Heritage Books), which will help in finding the majority of cemeteries in the state.

The largest number of New York cemetery records (the bulk of which are actually transcriptions of cemetery marker inscriptions) is found in the multi-volume collection of the Daughters of the American Revolution in the State of New York Cemetery, Church, and Town Records, located at the New York State Library, the New York Public Library, and the DAR Library in Washington, D.C. Scattered volumes are found in other libraries including many local libraries in the area in which a particular cemetery is located. To determine which cemeteries have been covered, consult *Revised Master Index to the New York State Daughters of the American Revolution Genealogical Records Volumes,* Books 1 and 2, prepared by the General Peter

Gansevoort Chapter, Albany, New York (Zephyrhills, Fla.: Mrs. Jean D. Worden, 1998). There is also a master card catalog index to the collection, arranged by place, at the state library. While these DAR collections are useful, it is unfortunate that most of the cemetery inscriptions have been alphabetized, thus destroying important clues based on the location of the grave markers.

Some counties have had many or nearly all of their cemetery records published. These include Dutchess, Genesee, Putnam, Ulster, and Washington counties. Another large published collection is *Some Cemeteries of the Between-the-Lakes Country*, 3 vols. (Trumansburg, N.Y.: Chief Taughannock Chapter, DAR, 1974), covering parts of the counties of Seneca, Schuyler, and Tompkins. The Orange County Genealogical Society is publishing that county's cemetery records, a volume for each town. Published cemetery records are also found in *Tree Talks*, *The New York Genealogical and Biographical Record*, and other genealogical journals. Many transcriptions are in manuscript form such as those by Gertrude A. Barber and her sisters, Ray C. Sawyer and Minnie Cowen. Local libraries and historical societies throughout the state are likely to have collections of cemetery records for their areas. For the New York City area, see Carolee Inskeep's *The Graveyard Shift: A Family Historian's Guide to New York City Cemeteries* (Orem, Utah: Ancestry Publishing, 2000).

Church Records

Particularly useful as vital records substitutes among the surviving New York church records are those of the Dutch Reformed, Lutheran, Anglican, and Quaker groups. For a general background about colonial New York churches, consult *Ecclesiastical Records, State of New York*, 7 vols. (Albany, N.Y.: James B. Lyon, 1901–05, 1916). Volume 7 is an index.

For the records themselves, see *Guide to Vital Statistics Records in New York State Churches (Exclusive of New York City)*, 2 vols. (Albany, N.Y.: Historical Records Survey, 1942), and *Guide to Vital Statistics Records in the City of New York, Boroughs of the Bronx, Brooklyn, Manhattan, Queens, Richmond. Churches*, 5 vols. (New York: Historical Records Survey, 1942). There are also several volumes arranged by denomination. These guides, although dated, are still useful for learning what existed and where. An excellent modern guide is Richard Haberstroh, *The German Churches of Metropolitan New York: A Research Guide* (New York: The New York Genealogical and Biographical Society, 2000).

The largest collection of New York church records is probably that of the Daughters of the American Revolution in the State of New York Cemetery, Church, and Town Records (see Cemetery Records above). Scattered volumes may be found in local libraries for the area in which a particular church is located. To determine what records have been covered, consult the *Revised Master Index* (see Cemetery Records). A card catalog at the New York State Library indexes this collection by county and thereunder by town, village, or other municipality.

Another large collection was commissioned by the New York Genealogical and Biographical Society and is known by the name of its editor, Royden Woodward Vosburgh. Its 101 volumes cover mostly Dutch, German-Lutheran, and Presbyterian records, but not all are indexed. Besides the New York Genealogical and Biographical Society, these volumes are available at the Connecticut State Library and on microfilm at the New York Public Library, the Family History Library, and in other libraries (see "The Vosburgh Collection of New York Church Records," *The NYG&B Newsletter* 9 [1998]: 53-55). Arthur C. M. Kelly and Jean D. Worden have published abstracted church records including some that were also done by Vosburgh.

For western and central New York there is a collection of microfilmed church records compiled by the Study Center for Early Religious Life in Western New York at Ithaca College; the study center is now defunct, but the collection is available at the Department of Manuscripts and University Archives, Cornell University, Ithaca, NY 14853-5310. A published list of the records is available.

Quakers are treated in John Cox, Jr., "Quaker Records in New York," *The New York Genealogical and Biographical Record* 45 (1914): 263-69, 366-73. Some Quaker records are published such as those for New York City and Long Island in volume 3 of William Wade Hinshaw's *Encyclopedia of American Quaker Genealogy* (1940; reprint, Baltimore: Genealogical Publishing Co., 1969, 1991), and Shirley V. Anson and Laura M. Jenkins, comps., *Quaker History and Genealogy of the Marlborough Monthly Meeting, Ulster County, N.Y. 1804–1900+* (Baltimore: Gateway Press, 1980). See also Loren V. Fay, ed., *Quaker Census of 1828* (Rhinebeck, N.Y.: Kinship, 1989). Original and full copies of New York state Quaker records from 1663, formerly in New York City, are now at the Friends Historical Library, Swarthmore College, Swarthmore, PA 19081, and many microfilms and abstracts are at the New York Genealogical and Biographical Society (see Suzanne McVetty, "Records of the Society of Friends (Quakers), New York Yearly Meeting," *The NYG&B Newsletter*, 8 [1977]: 27-31, and the subsequent "1998 Additions to the NYG&BS Microfilm Collection," also in the *Newsletter*, 9 [1998]: 50-52). A "Map of the Meetings constituting New-York Yearly Meeting of Friends," 12, by Dr. Shadrach Ricketson, is found facing page 263 in volume 45 of *The New York Genealogical and Biographical Record* (1914).

A very helpful guide for Jewish genealogical sources in the New York City area is *Genealogical Resources in New York* (see Background Sources). Harry Macy, Jr. has authored several

helpful articles on New York City church records in *The NYG&B Newsletter*.

Many church records, mostly early and particularly for Long Island, New York City, and the Hudson River Valley, have been published in *The New York Genealogical and Biographical Record*, with a large collection of unpublished records maintained by the New York Genealogical and Biographical Society and by other repositories with manuscript collections.

Military Records

Most pre-twentieth-century New York military records are at the New York State Archives, although some were destroyed or damaged in the 1911 fire at the New York State Library. Other material, including indexes and other resources concerning the New York State Militia and National Guard, is at the New York State Military Museum and Veterans Research Center, 61 Lake Ave., Saratoga Springs, NY 12866 <www.dmna.state.ny.us/historic/mil-hist.htm>.

Volumes 2 and 3 of the *Annual Report of the State Historian* (Albany and New York, 1896, 1897) contain collected lists of colonial militia, reprinted by Genealogical Publishing Company of Baltimore as *New York Colonial Muster Rolls, 1664–1775*, 2 vols. (2000), in which the age, birthplace, and occupation are given for many soldiers. *Muster Rolls of New York Provincial Troops, 1755–1764*, volume 24 of the New-York Historical Society Collections (1892; reprint, Bowie, Md.: Heritage Books, 1990), edited by Edward F. DeLancy, is another transcript of many of the same records.

Berthold Fernow, *New York in the Revolution*, vol. 1 (New Orleans: Polyanthos, 1972; Baltimore: Clearfield Co., Inc., 2000), was originally volume 15 of *Documents Relative to the Colonial History of the State of New York* (Albany: Weed, Parsons and Co., 1887). Additional names are in *New York in the Revolution as Colony and State*, 2 vols., and *Supplement* (Albany, N.Y.: J. B. Lyon, 1901, 1904; reprint Baltimore: Genealogical Publishing Co. Inc., 1996), and in *Calendar of Historical Manuscripts Relating to the War of the Revolution*, 2 vols. (Albany, N.Y.: Weed, Parsons and Co., 1868). To find other documents in the state library and state archives, consult Stefan Bielinski, ed., *A Guide to the Revolutionary War Manuscripts in the New York State Library* (Albany, N.Y.: New York State American Bicentennial Commission, 1976). See also Milton M. Klein, comp., *New York in the American Revolution: A Bibliography* (Albany, N.Y.: New York State American Revolution Bicentennial Commission, 1974). A lot of Revolutionary War material burned in the 1911 state library fire, but the remaining charred fragments are at last being microfilmed and made available for research. The state archives is preparing a computerized name index to New York soldiers and other individuals mentioned in the surviving Revolutionary War manuscripts. Other Revolutionary War material sent to Washington before the 1911 fire should be sought in the National Archives (see *The New York Genealogical and Biographical Record*, 120 [1989]: 66).

There is much published and manuscript material on New York Loyalists. One of the best works is Harry B. Yoshpe, *Disposition of Loyalist Estates in the Southern District of the State of New York* (New York: Columbia University Press, 1939). Alexander C. Flick's *Loyalism in New York During the American Revolution* (New York: Columbia University Press, 1901) includes summary lists of Loyalist lands sold by the Commissioners of Forfeitures. Some Loyalist material is at the New York Public Library and the state archives.

Hugh Hastings, ed., *Military Minutes of the Council of Appointment of the State of New York, 1783–1821*, 4 vols. (Albany, N.Y.: J. B. Lyon, 1901–04), with volume 4 as an index, lists local officers and is useful for determining the area from which a War of 1812 soldier probably served when only his unit commander's name is known. Published material on New Yorkers in the War of 1812 is scarce, but one list put out by the New York (State) Adjutant General's Office is *Index of Awards on Claims of the Soldiers of the War of 1812* (1860; reprint, Baltimore: Genealogical Publishing Co., 1969). The original claims are at the state archives, which also has abstracts of War of 1812 payrolls.

Research into Civil War participants from New York should start with the excellent *The Union Preserved: A Guide to Civil War Records in the New York State Archives*, comp. By Daniel Lorello and ed. by Harold Holzer (Albany and New York: Fordham University Press and the New York State Archives Partnership Trust, 1999). This guide covers some material outside the state archives. There is a typescript index of Civil War participants from New York at the state archives, as well as an online database index at <www.archives.nysed.gov/a/researchroom/rr_mi_civilwar_dbintro.shtml>. If the regiment is known, see *Register of New York Regiments in the War of the Rebellion*, 43 vols., issued as supplementary reports to the *Annual Report* of the state adjutant general for 1893–1905 (Albany, N.Y.: J. B. Lyon and others, 1894–1906). The annual reports are indexed in Richard A. Wilt, *New York Soldiers in the Civil War…*, 2 vols. (Bowie, Md.: Heritage Books, 1999). A *Record of Commissioned Officers, Non-Commissioned Officers and Privates...in Suppressing the Rebellion*, 8 vols. (Albany, N.Y.: Comstock & Cassidy, 1864–68), and *Registers...the War of the Rebellion* (Albany, N.Y.: J. B. Lyon, 1894), not indexed by name, were compiled by the New York Adjutant General's Office. Frederick Phisterer, comp., *New York in the War of the Rebellion, 1861–1865*, 6 vols. (Albany, N.Y.: J. B. Lyon, 1912), lists officers only. The National Archives—Northeast Region and the state library have the microfilm index of compiled service records of New York volunteer soldiers in the Union army. The state archives has much material on the Civil War, including town clerk's registers, which often show the soldier's full name,

full date and place of birth, and names of parents, including mother's maiden name. Civil War soldiers and deaths of officers and enlisted men were also noted in the population schedules of the 1865 state census, and veterans or their widows were listed in a special 1890 census (see Census Records).

Richard H. Saldaña, *Index to the New York Spanish-American War Veterans, 1898*, 2 vols. (North Salt Lake City, Utah: AISI Publishers, 1987) is a reprint with an index of the original three-volume report issued by the state adjutant general in 1900, arranged by regiment. In addition, a card file of New York participants in this war should also be checked at the state archives, which also has World War I card files of New York state servicemen and navy nurses. Cards of the "old men," fourth draft registration for World War II for the five New York City boroughs arranged alphabetically are at the National Archives—Northeast Region (see Leslie Corn, "World War II Fourth Registration Draft Cards: A Newly-Released 20th-Century Resource for 19th-Century Research," *The NYG&B Newsletter*, 13 [2002]: 5-9).

Periodicals, Newspapers, and Manuscript Collections

Periodicals

The New York Genealogical and Biographical Record is the oldest continuing genealogical periodical in the state. Published since 1870, it is the quarterly of the New York Genealogical and Biographical Society and has printed numerous source records, compiled genealogies, and other fine articles concerning New York history and genealogy. Some of the journal's more extensive coverage has extended to New England and New Jersey. A name and article index to the *Record* (1870–1998) is available from the society on CD-ROM. For a subject index, see also *Master Index to this journal* (1870–1982) by Jean D. Worden (Franklin, Ohio: the author, 1983). The society is currently publishing the *Record* on CD-ROM.

The Central New York Genealogical Society began *Tree Talks* in 1961. Except for some information articles and book reviews, it is essentially a journal of mostly pre-1850 source records, arranged by county, with coverage for most of the state except New York City and Long Island, with concentration on upstate New York. Its contents include abstracts of censuses, wills, administrations, guardianships, marriages and deaths from newspapers, cemetery marker transcripts, church records, family Bibles, naturalizations, tax records, and town records. A published subject index for *Tree Talks* (1961–88) and an every-name index on CD-ROM (1961–2001) was published by Kinship.

The *Western New York Genealogical Society Journal* is the periodical of that organization. Published since 1974, it includes sources of records and other material pertaining to the eight western counties of Allegany, Cattaraugus, Chautauqua, Erie, Genesee, Niagara, Orleans, and Wyoming.

Source material for Saratoga, Warren, and Washington counties is covered in *The Patents*, a bimonthly begun in 1981 by the Northeastern New York Genealogical Society. Among the many periodicals covering one New York county are a series of "Valley Quarterlies" published by Arthur C. M. Kelly (60 Cedar Heights Rd., Rhinebeck, NY 12572 <www.kinshipny.com>), including *The Capital* (Albany and Rensselaer counties), *The Columbia* (Columbia County), *The Mohawk* (Montgomery and Schenectady counties), and *The Saratoga* (Saratoga County), all with abstracts of source records. A CD-ROM indexes these quarterlies through 1999, when publication of the journals was changed to a yearly format, now titled *Yearbooks*.

Janet W. Foley's *Early Settlers of New York State: Their Ancestors and Descendants*, 9 vols. (Akron, N.Y.: 1934–42; reprint in 2 vols. Baltimore: Genealogical Publishing Co., 1993) contains source records and queries with concentration on central and western New York.

De Halve Maen is the journal of the Holland Society of New York (<www.hollandsociety.com>), published since 1922. It contains articles about early Dutch in the state and has some genealogies tracing the origins of Dutch immigrants.

Important quarterlies with greater historical focus are *The New-York Historical Society Quarterly* (1917–80) and *New York History*, begun in 1919 by the New York State Historical Association in Cooperstown. The *Proceedings* (1902–17) of the association should also be mentioned.

Journals published outside the state should not be overlooked for New York material. These include *The New England Historical and Genealogical Register*, *National Genealogical Society Quarterly*, *The American Genealogist*, *The Genealogist*, *The Genealogical Magazine of New Jersey*, and *The Detroit Society for Genealogical Research Magazine*.

Newspapers

The "Newspaper Project" at New York State Library seeks to identify and preserve newspapers throughout the state. A list of what papers are available on microfilm is on the library's website. Also see *Bibliographies and Lists of New York State Newspapers: An Annotated Guide*, Bibliography Bulletin 87 of the New York State Library (Albany, 1981), available for $4, and *A Checklist of Newspapers in Microform in the New York State Library* (Albany, 1979), available for $3. Sylvia G. Faibisoff and Wendell Tripp, comps., *A Bibliography of Newspapers in Fourteen New York Counties* (Cooperstown, N.Y.: New York Historical Association, 1978) covers Allegany, Broome, Cayuga, Chemung, Chenango, Cortland, Delaware, Otsego, Schuyler, Seneca, Steuben, Tioga, Tompkins, and Yates counties.

Many New York libraries and historical societies have important collections of newspapers and often have abstracts of or indexes to newspaper items, mostly notices of marriages and deaths. Among the many published newspaper abstracts and indexes are the following:

Biebel, Frank A. *Index to Marriage and Death Notices in the New-Yorker Staats-Zeitung, 1836–1870.* New York: The New York Genealogical and Biographical Society, 2000.

Bowman, Fred Q. *10,000 Vital Records of Western New York, 1809–1850; ...of Central New York, 1813–1850; ...of Eastern New York, 1777–1834.* Baltimore: Genealogical Publishing Co., 1985, 1986, 1987; and *8,000 More Vital Records of Eastern New York State, 1804–1850.* Rhinebeck, N.Y.: Kinship, 1991. For a continuation of the latter book, see "1,100 Vital Records of Northeastern New York, 1835–1850" in volumes 118 and 119 of *The New York Genealogical and Biographical Record.*

DeGrazia, Laura Murphy and Diane Fitzpatrick Haberstroh, comps. *Irish Relatives and Friends from "Information Wanted" Ads in the Irish-American, 1850–1871.* Baltimore: Genealogical Publishing Co., Inc., 2001.

Gavit, Joseph. *American Deaths and Marriages, 1784–1829.* This is a microfilm of alphabetized abstracts from New York newspapers, for which Kenneth Scott prepared *Index to Non-principal Names.* New Orleans: Polyanthos, 1976.

Maher, James P., comp. *Index to Marriages and Deaths in the New York Herald 1835–1855, ...1856–1863,* and *...1864–1870,* 3 vols. to date. Baltimore: Genealogical Publishing Co., 1987, 2000 (vols. 1 and 3) and Alexandria, Va., 1992 (vol. 2). Coverage extends beyond the New York City area.

Reynolds, Helen W. *Notices of Marriages and Deaths...Published in Newspapers Printed in Poughkeepsie..., 1778–1825.* Volume 4 of Dutchess County Historical Society Collections. Poughkeepsie, N.Y., 1930. A card file at the Adriance Library, Poughkeepsie, takes these abstracts further into the nineteenth century.

Scott, Kenneth. *Genealogical Data from Colonial New York Newspapers (1726–1783).* Reprinted from *The New York Genealogical and Biographical Record.* Baltimore: Genealogical Publishing Co., 1982.

———, and Kristin Lunde Gibbons, eds. *The New-York Magazine Marriages and Deaths: 1790–1797.* New Orleans: Polyanthos, 1975.

Nineteenth-century marriage and death notices from the *New York Evening Post* and *Brooklyn Eagle,* both abstracted by Gertrude A. Barber, are also to be checked. For a more complete list of New York City and Long Island area abstracts, see Henry B. Hoff's "Marriage and Death Notices in New York City Newspapers" and "Marriage and Death Notices in Long Island Newspapers," *The NYG&B Newsletter* 2 (1991): 3-5 and 20-21, respectively.

Fully word-searchable online newspapers include *The New York Times* (1851–2001), available at major and academic libraries and through membership with The New York Genealogical and Biographical Society, and *The Brooklyn Daily Eagle* (1841–1902) at <www.asu.edu/lib/resources/db/eagle.htm>.

Manuscripts

An abundance of manuscript genealogical material is located in the New York State Archives, the New York State Library, the New York Genealogical and Biographical Society, and elsewhere. The following published guides outline other major collections:

Breton, Arthur J. *A Guide to the Manuscript Collections of The New-York Historical Society.* 2 vols. Westport, Conn.: Greenwood Press, 1972. Covers the society's newspaper, map, photo, and business record holdings.

Works Progress Administration (WPA). *Guides to Depositories of Manuscript Collections in New York State.* New York: Historical Records Survey, 1941–44.

Mango, Karin R., comp. *The Long Island Historical Society Calendar of Manuscripts: 1763–1783.* Brooklyn: Long Island Historical Society, 1980. Now called the Brooklyn Historical Society.

New York Historical Resources Center. *Guide to Historical Resources in...County, New York Repositories.* Ithaca, N.Y.: Cornell University Press, 1978–91. Sometimes called "the Red Books," this series has at least one volume for each county. Public records are not represented, and not all New York City and Long Island information was published. The material collected in these guides is now known as the Historical Documents Inventory and its data, sometimes updated and including some of what was not published, is available online through the state archives website (see Archives, Libraries, and Societies).

The New York Public Library Research Libraries Dictionary Catalog of the Manuscript Division. 2 vols. Boston: G. K. Hall, 1967.

Archives, Libraries, and Societies

New York State Archives
The State Education Department
Cultural Education Center, Rm. 11A36
Empire State Plaza
Albany, NY 12230
www.archives.nysed.gov

The New York State Archives was the last state archives to be established in the United States. It houses land and court records, military and tax records, New York state vital records

indexes, pre-settlement survey maps, and legislative records. See *Guide to Records in the New York State Archives* (1993) and the online catalog at the archives' website.

New York State Library
Cultural Education Center, 7th Floor
Empire State Plaza
Albany, NY 12230
www.nysl.nysed.gov

The state library has a large collection of published and manuscript material on New York, including genealogies and local histories, federal and state censuses, city directories, and periodicals. It is also one of the two depositories for the State of New York DAR collection. There is a published guide to the library called *Gateway to America* (see Background Sources). *The Eighth Annual Report of the New York State Education Department* and the *New York (State) State Library Annual Report 94th,* both for 1911, reported the loss and salvage following the library's disastrous fire that year. An annotated copy of the latter is in the manuscript division of the state library. (See Harry Macy, Jr., "The 1911 State Library Fire and Its Effect on New York Genealogy," *The NYG&B Newsletter,* 10 [1999]: 19-22.)

The New-York Historical Society
170 Central Park West
New York, NY 10024-5194
www.nyhistory.org

Probably best known to genealogists for its manuscript collection, The New-York Historical Society has newspapers, city directories, maps, original deeds and other documents, and prints and photographs. The guide to its manuscript collections is currently out of print. Some of the society's holdings were published in its *Collections* from 1811 to 1975. From 1917 to 1980, the society also published *The New-York Historical Society Quarterly,* revived in 2003 as *The New-York Journal of American History.*

The New York Public Library
5th Ave. and 42nd St.
New York, NY 10018
www.nypl.org/research/chss/grd/index.html

The New York Public Library is not only a tremendous library for New York research, but also contains substantial amounts of material on the rest of the country and the world. Besides genealogy and local history, the public library has newspapers, federal and state censuses, church records, city and telephone directories, and divisions for maps, manuscripts, Jewish, and other material. For the published and some of the manuscript material, see *Dictionary Catalog of the Local History and Genealogy Division,* 18 vols. (Boston: G. K. Hall, 1974), and four supplements. More current acquisitions are accessed through the library's online catalog at <catnyp.nypl.org>. Timothy Field Beard, a former reference librarian in the Local History and Genealogy Division, with Denise Demong compiled *How to Find Your Family Roots* (New York: McGraw Hill, 1977), which includes New York Public Library call numbers in its bibliography. A list of area researchers is available from the library on request.

The New York Genealogical and Biographical Society
122 East 58th St.
New York, NY 10022-1939
www.newyorkfamilyhistory.org

A private society, the New York Genealogical and Biographical Society publishes a newsletter (*The New York Researcher*) and a scholarly quarterly, *The New York Genealogical and Biographical Record.* Its library holds much New York State and related material, both for New England and the Mid-Atlantic states. For New York there are censuses, federal and state; land and probate records; a large manuscript collection of church, cemetery, Bible, and other records; and an extensive amount of published family and local histories. The library subscribes to many online databases and makes ProQuest, with the fully word-searchable *New York Times* (1851–2001), and HeritageQuest Online, available to its members through remote access. Nonmembers can use the library for a small fee, but only members have access to the stacks, manuscripts, and microforms. The library provides a list of area researchers.

Municipal Archives
Department of Records and Information Services
31 Chambers St.
New York, NY 10007
www.nyc.gov/html/records/home.html

Holdings of early New York City records are described in various sections of this chapter.

Onondaga County Public Library
447 South Salina St.
Syracuse, NY 13202-2494
www.ocpl.lib.ny.us

With one of the largest collections of genealogical material in the state, it has a fine collection of published works, manuscripts, and specialized indexes, including New York State vital records (see Vital Records).

Central New York Genealogical Society
Box 104, Colvin Station
Syracuse, NY 13205
www.rootsweb.com/~nycnygs

While the society does not maintain a library, it publishes *Tree Talks,* a very fine journal of abstracted source material.

Western New York Genealogical Society, Inc.

5859 S. Park Ave.

P.O. Box 338

Hamburg, NY 14075-0338

www.wnygs.org

The society's journal consists of many useful source records and articles about the eight counties it covers (see Periodicals). Volumes 1–28 of the journal (1974–2001) are available from the society on CD-ROM.

Among the other libraries in the state with large collections of New York material are the Brooklyn Historical Society (formerly Long Island Historical Society), 128 Pierrepont St., Brooklyn, NY 11201 <www.brooklynhistory.org>; Buffalo and Erie County Historical Society, 25 Nottingham Ct., Buffalo, NY 14216 <www.bechs.org>; Montgomery County Department of History and Archives, Old Courthouse, Railroad St., Fonda, NY 12068 <www.amsterdam-ny.com/mcha>; New York State Historical Association, West Lake Rd., P.O. Box 800, Cooperstown, NY, 13326-0800 <www.nysha.org>; the Long Island Division of the Queens Borough Public Library, 89-11 Merrick Boulevard, Jamaica, NY 11432 <www.queenslibrary.org/central/longisland/index.asp>; the Long Island Studies Institute at Axinn Library, at Hofstra University, 619 Fulton St., Hempstead, NY 11550-1090 <www.hofstra.edu/Libraries/LISI/LISI_genlinfo.cfm>; and Rochester Public Library, 115 S. Ave., Rochester, NY 14604 <www.rochester.lib.ny.us/>.

Special Focus Categories

Immigration

Microfilm lists of ships' passenger arrivals at the port of New York are at the National Archives—Northeast Region (1820–1952) and at the New York Public Library (1820–1910). The archives has name indexes for 1820 to 1846 and 1897 to 1948, and the public library has them for 1820 to 1846 and 1897 to 1943. A portion of the gap in the unindexed period (1847–97) has been filled by such publications as Ira Glazier, ed., *The Famine Immigrants...1846–1851*, 8 vols. (Baltimore: Genealogical Publishing Co., 1983–86); Robert P. Swierenga, comp., *Dutch Immigrants in U.S. Ship Passenger Manifests, 1820–1880*, 2 vols. (Wilmington, Del.: Scholarly Resources, 1983); Nils William Olsson and Erick Wiken, *Swedish Passenger Arrivals in the United States, 1820–1850* (Stockholm: The Royal Library of Sweden, 1995), No. LV of Acta Bibliothecae Regiae Stocholmiensis, combining two earlier works and adding more information); Ira A. Glazier and P. William Filby, eds., *Germans to America...1840–[1900]*, 70 vols. to date (Wilmington, Del.: Scholarly Resources, 1988–); Gary J. Zimmerman and Marion Wolfert, *German Immigrants...from Bremen to New York, 1847–1871*, 4 vols.

(Baltimore: Genealogical Publishing Co., 1985–93); Trudy Schenk and Ruth Froelke, *The Wuerttemberg Emigration Index*, 8 vols. to date (Salt Lake City: Ancestry, 1986–); Ira A. Glazier and P. William Filby, eds., *Italians to America 1880–[1900]*, 14 vols. to date (Wilmington, Del.: Scholarly Resources, Inc., 1992–); and Ira A. Glazier, ed., *Migration from the Russian Empire, 1875–1910*, 6 vols. to date (Baltimore: Genealogical Publishing Co., 1995–). For a critical evaluation of two of these works, see Gordon L. Remington, "Feast or Famine: Problems in the Genealogical Use of *The Famine Immigrants* and *Germans to America*," *National Genealogical Society Quarterly* 78 (1990): 135-46. Images of ships' passenger lists for Ellis Island, New York City (1892–1925) can be found online at <www.ellisislandrecords.org>.

Naturalization

County naturalization records are kept by the county clerk. U.S. court records are in federal buildings in Buffalo and Albany, with most downstate records to the 1940s or 1950s at the National Archives—Northeast Region. At the latter is a microfilm of a WPA-created card index, arranged by Soundex, for all naturalizations (but not declarations of intention) performed in all courts in all five New York City boroughs (1792–1906), together with dexigraphs (photostats) of the original records. Until the late 1800s and early 1900s, these records provide little information; upstate records up to the mid-1800s are generally more informative. For some early records, see two compilations by Kenneth Scott: *Early New York Naturalizations...1792–1840* (Baltimore: Genealogical Publishing Co., 1981) from federal, state, and local court records, and with Kenn Stryker-Rodda, *Denizations, Naturalizations and Oaths of Allegiance in Colonial New York* (Baltimore: Genealogical Publishing Co., 1975). See also "Naturalizations in Federal Courts, New York District, 1790–1828," by Mrs. Edward J. Chapin, in volume 97 of *The New York Genealogical and Biographical Record* (1966); Kenneth Scott, "New York City Naturalizations, 1795–1799," *National Genealogical Society Quarterly* 71 (1983): 280-83; and "List of Immigrants, 1802–1814" in the Emmet Collection in the New York Public Library manuscript department. The New York State Archives' Leaflet #6 on Naturalization & Related Records is available on its website. Also helpful is *Naturalization Records of New York State*, corrected edition (Syracuse, N.Y.: New York State Council of Genealogical Organizations Publication No. 1, 2001); Henry B. Hoff, "Published New York City Naturalizations," *The NYG&B Newsletter* 4 (1993): 4; and Leslie Corn, "New York State Supreme Court Naturalization Records in the New York County Clerk's Office/Division of Old Records," *The NYG&B Newsletter* 10 (1999): 59-62, 11 (2000): 6-11.

Related works in this category are Kenneth Scott and Rosanne Conway, *New York Alien Residents, 1825–1848* (Baltimore: Genealogical Publishing Co., 1978; reprint, Baltimore: Clearfield Co., 1991), and Kenneth Scott, "Resident

Aliens Enabled to Hold Land in New York State, 1790–1825," *National Genealogical Society Quarterly* 67 (1979): 42-57.

African American

The best bibliography of material on African-American families in New York is *Black Genesis* (see page 15). Not to be overlooked is the New York Public Library's Schomburg Center for Research in Black Culture, 515 Lenox Ave., New York, NY 10037, with its extensive collection.

Native American

The two major Native American groups in New York were the Iroquois Five (later Six) Nations and their enemies, the Algonquins. Other groups were in the southeast and on Long Island. Among several works on the subject, research can begin in H. Leon Abrams, Jr., *A Partial Working Bibliography on the Amerindians of New York* (Greeley, Colo.: University of Northern Colorado, Museum of Anthropology, 1979); Russell A. Judkins, ed., *Iroquois Studies: A Guide to Documentary and Ethnographic Records from Western New York and the Genesee Valley* (Geneseo, N.Y.: Department of Anthropology, State University of New York and the Geneseo Foundation, 1987); Barbara J. Sivertsen, *Turtles, Wolves and Bears: A Mohawk Family History* (Bowie, Md.: Heritage Books, 1996); *"We Are Still Here!": The Algonquian Peoples of Long Island Today* (1996) and *The Algonquian Peoples of Long Island from Earliest Times to 1700* (1997), both by John A. Strong and published by Empire State Books of Interlaken, N.Y.; and "Problems of American Indian Research in New York State," from a talk by Elma Patterson, Indian Affairs Specialist for the New York State Department of Social Services, *Western New York Genealogical Society Journal* 12 (1985): 107-12. While it focuses on the Oneidas, James D. Folts, "Before the Dispersal: Records of New York's Official Relations with the Oneidas and Other Indian Nations," *The Oneida Indian Journey: From New York to Wisconsin, 1784–1860,* ed. Laurence M. Hauptman and L. Gordon McLester III (Madison, Wis.: University of Wisconsin Press, 1999), 151-70, covers New York colony and state records that document all Indian nations in what is now New York State. See also E. M. Ruttenber, "Indian Geographical Names," issued as a supplement and bound in the back of the New York State Historical Association's *Proceedings* for 1906.

County Resources

Since 1919 New York has had a system of local historians who are appointed to collect and preserve old records. While each county, town, and village should have a historian, not all vacancies are always filled, and of those that are, the knowledge and helpfulness in answering inquiries varies. In most cases it is best to start with the county historian, whose office may contain original or transcribed county, church, cemetery, newspaper, and other material, and in some cases, specialized indexes to these and other types of records. See *Directory of New York State County and Municipal Historians* (n.p., 1991), available for $20 from Directory, RED #2, Box 228, Bath, NY 14810. A list of county historians can be found at <www.rie.net/~aplmys/cohistorians.html>.

Publication of town records is not widespread, with the exception of those for Queens (including Nassau), Suffolk, and Westchester counties. Various items from town records have been presented in *Tree Talks* (see Periodicals). See also Harold R. Nestler, *A Bibliography of New York State Communities: Counties, Towns, Villages* (Port Washington, N.Y.: Ira J. Friedman, 1968).

Some New York counties have set up record centers or archives such as are found in Broome, Cayuga, Montgomery, Ontario, Rockland, Ulster, Warren, Washington, Westchester, and other counties. While most initial inquiries about records should be made with the county clerk and county Surrogate's clerk, the information sought might actually now be housed in a county records center/archives. This practice will doubtless continue in New York, especially for older records.

All the counties in New York, past and present, are listed below. The first column indicates the map coordinates. The name of the county and the mailing address of the county clerk, who is in charge of deeds, mortgages, copies of marriage records (1908–ca. 1935), divorces, court records, state censuses, and other records, is in the second column. The year the county was created follows and, where applicable, the parent county or counties from which it was formed. The date the earliest deed was recorded is in the fourth column. County deeds and mortgages not found with the county clerk are also indicated here. The last column shows the date of the earliest county Surrogate Court record, followed by the mailing address of the county Surrogate's clerk, if not the same as that of the county clerk. Some counties have copies or abstracts of earlier deeds and wills from parent counties.

It should be kept in mind that the names of the parent county or counties are those from which the new county was first formed in the year indicated. Many changes took place later, at which times whole towns or parts of them were annexed to or from the newer county. For example, Yates County was created in 1823 from part of Ontario County; the following year, two towns were added to Yates from Steuben County. For the specifics of other changes, consult gazetteers, county directories, and county histories.

NEW YORK

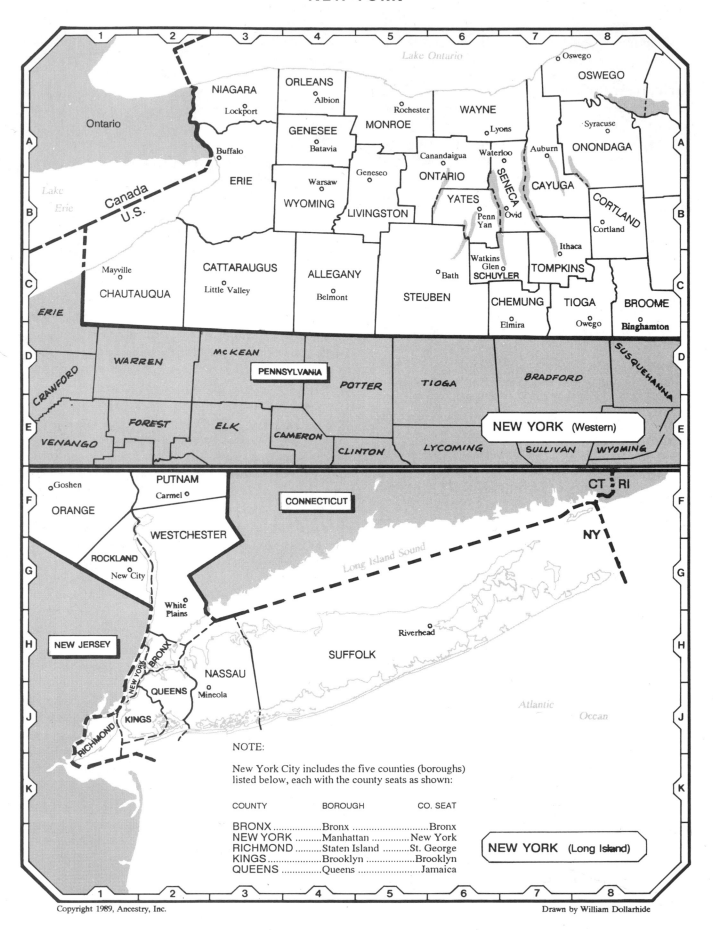

NOTE:

New York City includes the five counties (boroughs)
listed below, each with the county seats as shown:

COUNTY	BOROUGH	CO. SEAT
BRONX	Bronx	Bronx
NEW YORK	Manhattan	New York
RICHMOND	Staten Island	St. George
KINGS	Brooklyn	Brooklyn
QUEENS	Queens	Jamaica

NEW YORK (Long Island)

Drawn by William Dollarhide

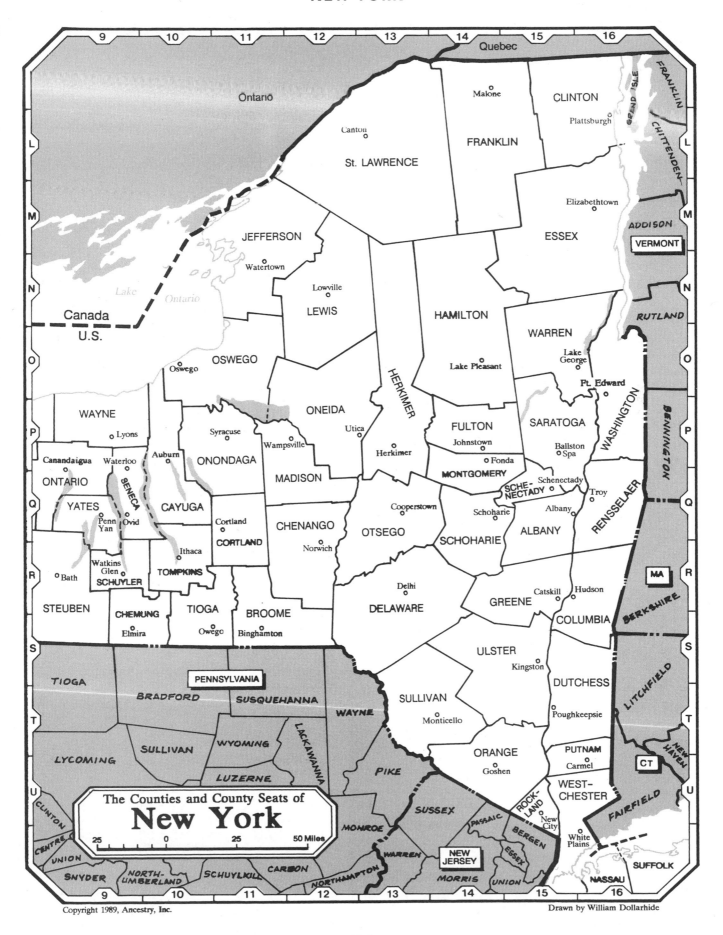

The Counties and County Seats of
New York

25   0   25   50 Miles

Drawn by William Dollarhide

Map County Address	Date Formed Parent County/ies	Deeds	Surrogate's Court
Q15 Albany 16 Eagle St., Rm. 128 Albany 12207-1019	1683 original	1656	1787 16 Eagle St. Albany 12207-1019
C4 Allegany 7 Court St. Belmont 14813-1039	1806 Genesee	1807	1807
H2 Bronx 851 Grand Concourse Rm. 118 Bronx 10451-2937	1914 New York (Westchester)	1914*	1914 851 Grand Concourse, Rm. 317

* At the City Register's Office, 1932 Arthur Ave., Rm 301, Bronx 10457

Map County Address	Date Formed Parent County/ies	Deeds	Surrogate's Court
S11 Broome 44 Hawley St./P.O. Box 2062 Binghamton 13902-2062	1806 Tioga	1806	1806 P.O. Box 1766 Binghamton 13901-1766
C3 Cattaraugus 303 Court St. Little Valley 14755-1028	1808 Genesee	1817	1817

Cattaraugus had no county government until 1817. Its records were first kept in Buffalo, but they were destroyed in 1813 when the British burned the courthouse. In 1812 Cattaraugus was annexed to Allegany County, and from 1814–17 county records for the eastern towns of Olean and Ischua were kept in Belmont and for the western town of Perry, in Buffalo.

Map County Address	Date Formed Parent County/ies	Deeds	Surrogate's Court
Q10 Cayuga 160 Genesee St. Auburn 13021	1799 Onondaga	1799	1799 153 Genesee St. Auburn 13021-3471
Charlotte	(see Washington)		
C1 Chautauqua 1 N. Erie St./P.O. Box 170 Mayville 14757-0170	1808 Genesee	1811	1811 3 N. Erie St. Mayville 14757

Chautauqua was attached to Niagara County until 1811, but records kept in Buffalo were burned by the British in 1813.

Map County Address	Date Formed Parent County/ies	Deeds	Surrogate's Court
S10 Chemung 210 Lake St. P.O. Box 588 Elmira 14902-0588	1836 Tioga	1836	1836 224 Lake St. P.O. Box 588 Elmira 14902-0588
R12 Chenango 5 Court St. Norwich 13815	1798 Herkimer/ Tioga	1798	1798
L16 Clinton 137 Margaret St. Plattsburgh 12901-2933	1788 Washington	1788	1790
R16 Columbia 560 Warren St. Hudson 12534	1786 Albany	1786	1787 401 Union St. Hudson 12534
Cornwall	1683 original		

Located in Maine, this county was transferred to Massachusetts in 1686, but no longer exists in name. See Collections of the Maine Historical Society, first series, vol. 5 (1857).

Map County Address	Date Formed Parent County/ies	Deeds	Surrogate's Court
Q11 Cortland 46 Greenbush St., Ste. 101 Cortland 13045-3702	1808 Onondaga	1808	1808 46 Greenbush St., Ste. 301 Cortland 13045-2725
Cumberland	1766 Albany		

Disallowed the year after it was formed, Cumberland was re-established in 1768 and ceased to exist 1777–78 when Vermont declared itself a republic.

Map County Address	Date Formed Parent County/ies	Deeds	Surrogate's Court
S13 Delaware P.O. Box 426 Delhi 13753-0426	1797 Ulster/ Otsego	1797	1797 3 Court St. Delhi 13753
Dukes	1683 original		

Dukes County was annexed to Massachusetts in 1692 (see Massachusetts).

Map County Address	Date Formed Parent County/ies	Deeds	Surrogate's Court
T15 Dutchess 22 Market St. Poughkeepsie 12601	1683 original	1718	1752 10 Market St. Poughkeepsie 12601

Almost uninhabited until 1701, Dutchess was administered by Ulster County from that time until at least 1713. Some older records, including marriages, 1908–35; state and federal censuses; tax records, 1854–1954; and the "Ancient Documents" series are at the County Records Center and Archives, 27 High St., Poughkeepsie 12601.

Map County Address	Date Formed Parent County/ies	Deeds	Surrogate's Court
B3 Erie 25 Delaware Ave. Buffalo 14202	1821 Niagara	1808	1800 92 Franklin St. Buffalo 14202

In 1813 the British burned the courthouse in Buffalo, then the seat of Niagara County, destroying records that also included Cattaraugus and Chautauqua counties.

Map County Address	Date Formed Parent County/ies	Deeds	Surrogate's Court
M15 Essex 7559 Court St. P.O. Box 247 Elizabethtown 12932-0247	1799 Clinton	1799	1803 100 Court St. P.O. Box 505 Elizabethtown 12932-0505
L14 Franklin 355 W. Main St./P.O. Box 70 Malone 12953-0070	1808 Clinton	1808	1809 355 W. Main St. Malone 12953
P14 Fulton 223 W. Main St. P.O. Box 485 Johnstown 12095-0485	1838 Montgomery	1838	1838 223 W. Main St. Johnstown 12095
A4 Genesee P.O. Box 379 Batavia 14021-0379	1802 Ontario	1803	1805 1 W. Main St. P.O. Box 462 Batavia 14020-0462
Gloucester	1770 Cumberland		

This county ceased to exist when Vermont declared itself a republic 1777–78.

Map County Address	Date Formed Parent County/ies	Deeds	Surrogate's Court
R15 Greene P.O. Box 446 Catskill 12414-0446	1800 Ulster/Albany	1800	1803 320 Main St. P.O. Box 469 Catskill 12414-0469
O14 Hamilton Rt. 8, Box 204 Lake Pleasant 12108	1816 Montgomery	1797	1861 White Birch Lane P.O. Box 780 Indian Lake 12842-0780

Hamilton remained attached to Montgomery County until 1838 and then briefly to Fulton County. Earlier surrogates' records are evidently in Montgomery, Fulton, and St. Lawrence counties. See Tree Talks 20 (1980): 166.

Map	County Address	Date Formed Parent County/ies	Deeds	Surrogate's Court
P10	Herkimer County Office Bldg. 109 Mary St., Ste. 111 Herkimer 13350-2923	1791 Montgomery	1804 1791-20*	1792 301 N. Washington St. P.O. Box 5550 Herkimer 13350-5550

*Deeds 1791–98 for what became Oneida County are in Utica.

Map	County Address	Date Formed Parent County/ies	Deeds	Surrogate's Court
M11	Jefferson 175 Arsenal St. Watertown 13601-2522	1805 Oneida	1805	1805
J2	Kings 360 Adams St., Rm. 189 Brooklyn 11201-3712	1683 original	1683*	1787 2 Johnson St., Rm. 109 Brooklyn 11201

* At the City Register's Office, 210 Joralemon St., Rm 2, Brooklyn 11201.
Many Surrogate's files before about 1870 are now at the NYC Archives and on microfilm at the Family History Library.

Map	County Address	Date Formed Parent County/ies	Deeds	Surrogate's Court
N12	Lewis 7660 State St., P.O. Box 232 Lowville 13367-0232	1805 Oneida	1805	1805 7660 State St. Lowville 13367
B5	Livingston 6 Court St. Geneseo 14454-1048	1821 Genesee/Ontario	1821	1821 2 Court St. Geneseo 14454
Q11	Madison P.O. Box 668 Wampsville 13163-0668	1806 Chenango	1806	1806 Court St. P.O. Box 607 Wampsville 13163-0607
A5	Monroe 39 West Main St. Rochester 14614	1821 Genesee/Ontario	1821	1824 541 Hall of Justice Rochester 14614
Q14	Montgomery P.O. Box 1500 Fonda 12068-1500	1772 Albany (called Tryon until 1784)	1777	1787 58 Broadway P.O. Box 1500 Fonda 12069-1500
H3	Nassau 240 Old Country Rd., Rm. 109 Mineola 11501	1899 	1899 Queens	1899 262 Old Country Rd. Mineola 11501
J2	New York 60 Centre St., Rm. 103B New York 10007-1402	1683 original	1654*	1665** 31 Chambers St., Rm. 402 New York 10007

* At the City Register's Office, 66 John Street, 13th Floor, New York 10038. Early records of the county clerk are in Division of Old Records, 31 Chambers Street, Rm 703.
**Pre-1830 Surrogate's files and inventories are not known to have survived.

Map	County Address	Date Formed Parent County/ies	Deeds	Surrogate's Court
A3	Niagara 175 Hawley St. P.O. Box 461 Lockport 14094-0461	1821 Genesee	1821	1821 175 Hawley St. Lockport 14094

Records for the period 1813–21 are in Buffalo, which was the county seat of Niagara until Erie was created; earlier records were destroyed when the British burned the Buffalo courthouse in 1813.

Map	County Address	Date Formed Parent County/ies	Deeds	Surrogate's Court
P12	Oneida 800 Park Ave. Utica 13501-2939	1798 Herkimer	1791-1885*	1798

* At the B-1 Records Center, 800 Park Ave., Utica 13501. Deeds 1886 to present are with the county clerk.

Map	County Address	Date Formed Parent County/ies	Deeds	Surrogate's Court
P11	Onondaga 401 Montgomery St., Rm. 200 Syracuse 13202	1794 Herkimer	1784	1796 401 Montgomery St., Rm. 209 Syracuse 13202-2173
A6	Ontario 20 Ontario St. Canandaigua 14424	1789 Montgomery	1789–1915*	1789–1926* 27 N. Main St.

*These records—and mortgages to 1920—are at the Ontario County Department of Records, Archives, and Information Management Services, 3051 County Complex Drive, Canandaigua 14424; later deeds and all indexes are at the county clerk's; later Surrogate's Court records are at the courthouse, Canandaigua 14424.

Map	County Address	Date Formed Parent County/ies	Deeds	Surrogate's Court
U14	Orange 255-275 Main St. Goshen 10924-1621	1683 original	1703	1787 30 Park Pl. Goshen 10924
A4	Orleans 3 S. Main St. Albion 14411-1449	1824 Genesee	1824	1824
O11	Oswego 46 E. Bridge St. Oswego 13126-2123	1816 Oneida/Onondaga	1791	1816 25 E. Oneida St. Oswego 13126
Q13	Otsego 197 Main St., P.O. Box 710 Cooperstown 13326-0710	1791 Montgomery	1791	1791 197 Main St. Cooperstown 13326-1129
U15	Putnam 40 Gleneida Ave. Carmel 10512	1812 Dutchess	1812	1812 44 Gleneida Ave.
J2	Queens 88-11 Sutphin Blvd., Rm.105 Jamaica 11435	1683 original	1683*	1787** 88-11 Sutphin Blvd., Rm. 700 Jamaica 11435

* At the City Register's Office, 144-06 94th Ave., Jamaica 11435.
** Most or all pre-1830 surrogate's files were lost or destroyed.

Map	County Address	Date Formed Parent County/ies	Deeds	Surrogate's Court
Q16	Rensselaer 105 Third St. Troy 12180	1791 Albany	1791	1794 72 Second St.
J1	Richmond 130 Stuyvesant Pl., 2nd Floor Staten Island 10301	1683 original	1683	1787 18 Richmond Terrace, Rm. 201 Staten Island 10301-1935
U15	Rockland 1 S. Main St., Ste. 100 New City 10956-3549	1798 Orange	1798	1798 1 S. Main St., Ste. 27D New City 10956-3549
L13	St. Lawrence 48 Court St. Canton 13617-2217	1802 Clinton/Herkimer/ Montgomery	1802	1803
P15	Saratoga 40 McMaster St. Ballston Spa 12020-1908	1791 Albany	1791	1791 30 McMaster St. Ballston Spa 12020
Q15	Schenectady 620 State St. Schenectady 12305	1809 Albany	1809	1809 612 State St. Schenectady 12305-2113

Map	County Address	Date Formed Parent County/ies	Deeds	Surrogate's Court
R14	Schoharie 300 Main St. P.O. Box 549 Schoharie 12157-0549	1795 Albany/Otsego	1795	1795 290 Main St. P.O. Box 669 Schoharie 12157-0669
R9	Schuyler 105 Ninth St., Box 8 Watkins Glen 14891	1854 Tompkins/Steuben/ Chemung	1854	1854 105 Ninth St.
B7	Seneca One Di Pronio Dr. Waterloo 13165	1804 Cayuga	1804	1804 44 W. Williams St. Waterloo 13165
C6	Steuben 3 E. Pulteney Sq. Bath 14810	1796 Ontario	1796	1796
H5	Suffolk 310 Center Dr. Riverhead 11901-3398	1683 original	1683	1787 320 Center Dr. Riverhead 11901
T13	Sullivan 100 North St. Monticello 12701 *A fire in 1909 destroyed will volumes 1-7 but all or most of the files survived.*	1809 Ulster	1809	1811
S10	Tioga 16 Court St. P.O. Box 307 Owego 13827-0307 *The explanation for the delay in the Surrogate's records is not fully known, but some estate records during this period may have perished in an early fire in Spencer, once the county seat.*	1791 Montgomery	1791	1798 20 Court St. P.O. Box 10 Owego 13827-0010
R10	Tompkins 320 N. Tioga St. Ithaca 14851	1817 Cayuga/Seneca	1817	1817 320 N. Tioga St. P.O. Box 70 Ithaca 14851-0070
	Tryon	(see Montgomery)		
S14	Ulster 244 Fair St. P.O. Box 1800 Kingston 12402-1800	1683 original	1684	1787
O15	Warren 1340 State Rt. 9 Lake George 12845	1813 Washington	1813	1813 1340 State Rt. 9 Lake George 12845-9803
P16	Washington 383 Broadway, Bldg. A Fort Edward 12828 *The eastern part of the county became a part of Vermont when it declared itself a republic in 1777–78.*	1772 Albany (called Charlotte until 1784)	1774	1787 383 Broadway, Bldg. C Fort Edward 12828
A6	Wayne 9 Pearl St. P.O. Box 608 Lyons 14489-0608	1823 Ontario/ Seneca	1823	1823 54 Broad St., Rm. 106 Lyons 14489
U15	Westchester 110 Dr. Martin Luther King Jr. Blvd. White Plains 10601 **These records, with indexes for 1680–1897, are held at the Records Center and Archives, 2199 Saw Mill River Rd., Elmsford, NY 10523. Later deed records are with the county clerk (address above).* ***Later Surrogate Court records are at 140 Grand St., 8th Floor, White Plains, NY 10601.*	1683 original	1667–1852*	files, 1775–1910; original wills through 1941; and record books, 1777–1895**
B4	Wyoming 143 N. Main St. Warsaw 14569	1841 Genesee	1841	1841 147 N. Main St. Warsaw 14569-1123
B6	Yates 417 Liberty St., Ste. 1107 Penn Yan 14527	1823 Ontario	1823	1823 108 Court St. Penn Yan 14527

North Carolina

JOHNI CERNY AND GARETH L. MARK

The first permanent English settlers in North Carolina were Virginians who heard glowing reports of fertile bottomlands, abundant timber resources, and an excellent climate. They moved into the Albemarle Sound area about 1650, purchasing land from the local Indian tribes. The Virginia Assembly also granted land along the Chowan and Roanoke rivers to Roger Green in 1653. By 1657, Nathaniel Batts had the first house—at the western end of Albemarle Sound.

English claims on North Carolina date to 1497 when John Cabot visited the New World and claimed the area for King Henry VII. These claims were the basis for Charles I's 1629 grant of "Carolana" to Sir Robert Heath, who failed to settle Carolina before the execution of Charles I in 1649. During the Commonwealth period in England, many citizens remained loyal to Charles II. At his ascension to the throne of England in 1660, eight men pressed their claims for a reward: Edward Hyde, Earl of Clarendon; George Monck, Duke of Albemarle; Lord William Craven; Lord John Berkeley; Lord Anthony Ashley Cooper, Earl of Shaftesbury; Sir George Carteret; Sir William Berkeley; and Sir John Colleton. Charles II granted Carolina to the eight Lords Proprietors in 1663. After the claims of Heath's successors had been disposed of, the grant was revised and extended in 1665.

Two factors heavily influenced the development of North Carolina. Its stormy coastline, known as the "graveyard of the Atlantic," does not include a natural harbor to promote commerce. The Cape Fear River is the only river that empties into the Atlantic Ocean, and its approaches are endangered by the Frying Pan Shoals. Except for a few Highland Scots, immigrants to North Carolina generally arrived by overland routes. The second factor influencing North Carolina's development was the presence of approximately 35,000 Native Americans. They taught the European settlers important agricultural techniques such as planting row crops and fertilizing plants. The Europeans also learned the natives' techniques of wilderness war. But the presence of the whites eventually destroyed the native civilization through disease, forceful removal to reservations, and war.

New Bern was founded in 1710 by colonists from Germany, Switzerland, and England under the leadership of Christopher de Graffenried. The colonists landed in Virginia and trekked overland to North Carolina, arriving too late to plant and harvest crops. The settlement survived and flourished, however, and New Bern became the largest town in North Carolina during the colonial period. The New Bern settlement, however, was located in the Tuscarora hunting grounds, and the Cary Rebellion in 1711 left the colonists open to attack. The Tuscarora Indian War (1711–15) was the result.

In 1729 the Lords Proprietors, except for John Carteret, Earl Granville, sold their shares in the provinces of North and South Carolina to King James II of England, ending the proprietary period. North Carolina was the most sparsely settled English colony in America at that time. The end of the proprietary period marked the beginning of a period of great expansion and growth. A steady stream of Scots-Irish and German immigrants traveled over the Great Wagon Road from Pennsylvania through the Shenandoah Valley of Virginia to North Carolina. The only significant migration that sailed directly to North Carolina was a small group of Highland Scots. The Moravians purchased nearly

100,000 acres in present-day Forsyth County from Earl Granville in 1753 and settled the tract they called "Wachovia."

The movement for independence from England was strong in North Carolina, and a provincial congress met in New Bern in 1774. Yet not all North Carolinians supported the revolution. The Highland Scots, in particular, remained loyal to the crown and recruited Loyalist military units.

In 1789, North Carolina ratified the United States Constitution and ceded its western lands, now known as Tennessee, to the federal government. The site for North Carolina's state capital was located and named Raleigh three years later. Dissatisfaction with the state constitution of 1776, which heavily favored the eastern counties and towns, resulted in the constitutional convention of 1835 and the adoption of a new state constitution.

North Carolina was not ardently secessionist in 1860, but when the federal government requested troops to quell the Southern rebellion, Governor John W. Ellis refused and North Carolina soon joined the Confederacy. North Carolina supplied about 125,000 troops to the Confederacy, more than any other southern state, and over 14,000 North Carolinians were killed in action.

After the Civil War, North Carolina rapidly developed as an industrial state. Governmental support fostered the growth of the textile, tobacco, and furniture industries for which North Carolina is known.

See Powell, *North Carolina through Four Centuries*, cited in Background Sources, for a more comprehensive history of the Tarheel State.

Vital Records

On 10 March 1913, the North Carolina General Assembly ratified an act requiring the registration of births and deaths in the state; virtually full compliance was achieved by 1920, with some delayed birth records for earlier dates eventually added. The indexes to these records are available in the county where the event took place or on microfilm at the North Carolina State Archives and the Family History Library (FHL) in Salt Lake City.

Copies of original birth certificates can be obtained from the North Carolina Department of Health and Human Services, Office of Vital Records, 1903 Mail Service Center, Raleigh, NC 27699-1903 <http://vitalrecords.dhhs.state.nc.us/vr/index.html>. The County Register of Deeds in the county where the birth was filed may be able to provide a copy of a birth certificate. The FHL has 305 reels of microfilm containing North Carolina Birth Certificates (1913–22).

Copies of death records can be obtained from the office of the County Register of Deeds and from the Office of Vital Records (cited above). The North Carolina State Archives also

has death certificates for those who died between 1913 and 1955 on microfilm in the Search Room. The microfilm collection of the FHL has death certificates (1906–94); still births (1814–1953); fetal deaths (1960–74), and an index (1906–67).

Most marriages performed before 1668 were not recorded. A 1669 law required that each marriage be registered, but based on the few events that were recorded, compliance was very low. Marriages could be solemnized by Church of England ministers or any member of the colony's council, including the governor; in 1741, the justices of the peace were extended the right to perform marriages. Citizens had to publish banns three times or obtain a marriage license; most marriages were by publication of banns. When the marriage was by license, the groom executed a marriage bond in the bride's county of residence; some marriage bonds have survived for about half of North Carolina's counties. *Index to Marriage Bonds Filed in the North Carolina State Archives* is a microfiche index to both brides and grooms of marriage bonds available at the North Carolina State Archives. The index may be used in the Search Room at the archives, and a copy is available through the FHL. See Archives, Libraries, and Societies for information about searches by mail at the North Carolina State Archives.

After 1868, the register of deeds in each county was given the task of issuing marriage licenses. These licenses and their accompanying certificates offer a wealth of information, including age when married, parents' names (if the parents were living), parents' residences, and consent when required. Marriage records from 1868 to 1962 are on file with the register of deeds in the county where the marriage took place. Most North Carolina marriage records dating from 1868 to 1950 have been microfilmed and are available at the North Carolina State Archives and the FHL. Marriage records dating from 1962 are available at the Division of Health Services.

The superior court in each county has granted divorce decrees since 1814. Details about divorces that were not included in court minutes are very valuable to researchers. They include "loose papers" that discuss reasons for the divorce, details of the family's composition, children's ages, and other information. Copies of pre-1868 divorce records are at the North Carolina State Archives; records dating from 1868 are available from each county's superior court clerk.

Census Records

Federal

Population Schedules
- Indexed—1790 (incomplete), 1800, 1810 (incomplete), 1820 (incomplete), 1830, 1840, 1850, 1860, 1870, 1890 (fragments), 1900, 1910, 1920, 1930

- Soundex—1880, 1900, 1910 (Miracode), 1920

Industry and Agriculture Schedules

- 1850, 1860, 1870, 1880

Mortality Schedules

- 1850, 1860, 1870, 1880

Union Veterans Schedules

- 1890

Slave Schedules

- 1850, 1860

The first federal census was taken in 1790, and all of North Carolina's enumerations have survived except Caswell, Granville, and Orange counties. The 1810 U.S. census of North Carolina is complete except for Craven, Greene, New Hanover, and Wake counties. The 1820 census is missing Currituck, Franklin, Martin, Montgomery, Randolph, and Wake counties. Those schedules surviving for the 1890 population schedules are South Point and River Ben townships in Gaston County and Township No. 2 in Cleveland County. The North Carolina State Archives has either bound original copies or microfilm copies of the extant federal censuses of North Carolina.

State

Apparently there was no colonial census of North Carolina, but tax records, used judiciously, may be substituted (see Tax Records). A census was conducted in 1775 by direction of the Continental Congress, and the enumeration of Pitt County has survived. See Jean Anderson, "The Census of 1775 as Seen in Pitt County, NC," *The North Carolina Genealogical Society Journal* 7, no. 4 (November 1981): 186-96. In 1784 the North Carolina General Assembly requested that a list of inhabitants be taken. Age and sex categories for whites and African Americans are included. Compliance was slow and apparently incomplete, with some counties not responding until 1786. There is some evidence that another census was conducted in 1787; the so-called 1784–87 state census may be two censuses intermingled. Extant portions of the 1784–87 state censuses are in Alvaretta K. Register, *State Census of North Carolina, 1784–1787*, 2d ed., rev. (1971; reprint, Baltimore: Genealogical Publishing Co., 1978). Additional portions of those censuses have been located since Register's publication. See Helen F. M. Leary, comp., "Bertie Co., N.C., 1787 State Census," *The North Carolina Genealogical Society Journal* 9, no. 1 (February 1983): 32-34, and Jonathan B. Butcher, "1787 Census Return for Pearson's Company, Rowan County, NC," *The North Carolina Genealogical Society Journal* 11, no. 4 (November 1985): 253-54.

Background Sources

An essential guide for research in North Carolina is Helen F. M. Leary and Maurice R. Stirewalt, eds., *North Carolina Research: Genealogy and Local History*, 2d ed. (Raleigh, N.C.: North Carolina Genealogical Society, 1996). In addition to being specific about the locations of sources, it provides excellent suggestions for research strategies and the interpretation of records in their historical context. See also Helen F. M. Leary, "A Master Plan for North Carolina Research," *National Genealogical Society Quarterly* 75 (1987):15-36.

A history of North Carolina by William S. Powell, *North Carolina Through Four Centuries* (Chapel Hill, N.C., and London, England: University of North Carolina Press, 1989) is a new standard textbook for college level work and very readable for the general public.

The laws of North Carolina are available in many publications. The most accessible is James Iredell, comp., *Laws of the State of North Carolina* (Edenton, N.C.: James Iredell, 1791), reprinted as *The First Laws of the State of North Carolina* (Wilmington, Del.: Michael Glazier, 1984).

The North Carolina Office of Archives and History has published several guides to its holdings, the most notable of which is *Guide to Research Materials in the North Carolina State Archives, Section B: County Records* (11th rev. ed., 2d printing, Raleigh, N.C.: North Carolina Department of Archives and History, 1997). It details both original and microfilmed records held by the agency and available for purchase on microfilm. A catalog of other publications is also available from the North Carolina State Archives.

The University of North Carolina Press offers excellent materials for placing ancestors in the context of local history within the state. Their catalog can be searched online at <http://uncpress.unc.edu>. Joe A. Mobley has edited a revised edition of the original five volume series of *The Way We Lived* (Chapel Hill, N.C. and London: University of North Carolina Press, 2003). The new publication includes all five original parts in one volume, with the fifth part extended thirty years in time: Elizabeth A. Fenn and Peter Wood, *Natives and Newcomers: North Carolina before 1770*; Harry T. Watson, *An Independent People: North Carolina, 1770–1820*; Thomas H. Clayton, *Close to the Land: North Carolina, 1820–1870*; Sydney Nathans, *A Quest for Progress: North Carolina, 1870–1920*; and Thomas A. Parramore, *Express Lanes & Country Roads: North Carolina, 1920–2001*.

Maps

Excellent maps, atlases, and gazetteers for North Carolina are readily available. The best gazetteer available for North Carolina

is William Stevens Powell, *The North Carolina Gazetteer: A Dictionary of Tar Heel Places* (Chapel Hill, N.C.: University of North Carolina Press, 1968). The *Gazetteer* includes historical definitions, derivations of place-names, and exact locations. It is cross-indexed well and gives references for the first use of place-names. An important historical publication is Richard Edwards, ed., *Statistical Gazetteer of the States of Virginia and North Carolina* (Richmond, Va.: Published for the Proprietor, 1856).

There are several excellent atlases and map guides available for North Carolina. James W. Clay, Douglas M. Orr, Jr., and Alfred W. Stuart, eds., *North Carolina Atlas: Portrait of a Changing Southern State.* (1975; reprint. Chapel Hill, N.C.: University of North Carolina Press, 2000) is perhaps the best atlas available. Fifteen North Carolina maps are included in William P. Cummings, *North Carolina in Maps* (3d printing, Raleigh, N.C.: State Department of Archives and History, 1992). See also Garland P. Stout, *Historical Research Maps: North Carolina Counties*, 5 vols. (Greensboro, N.C.: Garland P. Stout, 1973).

The North Carolina Office of Archives and History has revised David Leroy Corbitt, *The Formation of the North Carolina Counties, 1663–1943* (1950; reprint with supplementary data and corrections, Raleigh, N.C.: State Department of Archives and History, 1969). This guide is essential for determining the historical boundaries of North Carolina's counties.

Land Records

State-Land State

The availability of land in North Carolina drew thousands of settlers from Virginia, Pennsylvania, and Maryland during the mid-to-late 1700s. Until Colonel William Byrd of Westover surveyed the northern border of North Carolina, Virginia sometimes granted to its citizens land that belonged to North Carolina. Those grants may be found in Nell Marion Nugent, *Cavaliers and Pioneers, Abstracts of Virginia Land Patents and Grants*, 4 vols. (1934; reprint, Baltimore: Genealogical Publishing co., 1991).

The process of patenting land in North Carolina was not complex. Anyone wanting to patent land submitted an application (also called a land entry) to a land office. The land officer then issued a warrant. Land officers included the secretary of state (1669–1776), the agents of Earl Granville (1748–76), or the county entry taker (1778–present). The warrant was taken to a surveyor who surveyed the land and sketched a plat (map) of the claim. The plat was then filed in the land office or, after 1777, recorded by the county register of deeds, and a patent for the land was issued and recorded. Land grants and related indexes are available at the North Carolina State Archives (see Archives, Libraries, and Societies). If you write to the archives, furnish the full name of the grantee and the county in which the grant was made. Detailed instructions for requesting information by mail, fax or online, visit this section of the archive's website <www.ah.dcr.state.nc.us/sections/archives/arch/mail.htm>. The Granville grants and other miscellaneous papers have been indexed and can be accessed by *MARS*, a database of the North Carolina State Archives online at <www.ah.dcr.state.nc.us>; the Search Room at the archives has a card catalog of grants of deeds. The FHL has this collection on 522 reels of microfilm.

During the proprietary period (1663–1729) the Lords Proprietors relied on a headright system to distribute land grants. The standard headright of fifty acres per person established in Virginia was adopted in the Carolinas about 1697; before that time a sliding scale was used that granted one hundred acres to heads of families but only six acres to women servants when their terms expired. The governor was allowed to sell tracts of 640 acres or less to those without headrights, or who had used their headrights for free land. To keep people in North Carolina, the assembly forbade the sale of headrights until the claimant had been in the colony for two years. The proprietary land patents are available at the North Carolina State Archives and on microfilm at the FHL. See Margaret M. Hofmann, *Province of North Carolina, 1663–1729, Abstracts of Land Patents* (Roanoke Rapids, N.C.: the author, 1983) for abstracts from the Secretary of State's Land Grant Office, referencing over 25,000 surnames and places; and Caroline B. Whitley, *North Carolina Headrights: A List of Names, 1663–1744* (Raleigh, N.C.: North Carolina Office of Archives and History, Historical Publications Section, 2001) for headrights from published and manuscript sources.

Seven of the original proprietary shares were sold to King George II in 1729, and North Carolina became a royal colony. Only John Carteret, second Earl Granville, chose not to sell the share he had inherited. The Crown continued the headright system instituted by the Lords Proprietors, but modified the system in 1741 to again allow one hundred acres for the head-of-household. The Crown land office first opened in 1735, six years after the Crown purchased the province. Abstracts of Crown land patents are in Margaret M. Hofmann, *Colony of North Carolina, 1735–1764, Abstracts of Land Patents* and *Colony of North Carolina, 1765–1775, Abstracts of Land Patents* (Weldon, N.C.: Roanoke News Co., 1983–84).

The Granville District, an area that encompassed the upper half of present-day North Carolina, was created and partially surveyed in 1744 for John Carteret, second Earl Granville. Unlike the early proprietors, Granville owned all unsettled lands but had no right to govern the area. Earl Granville never visited North Carolina, but appointed agents there as representatives to grant land, collect rents, and conduct his business. The Granville land office opened in 1748. See Margaret M. Hofmann, *The Granville District of North Carolina, 1748–1763: Abstracts of Land Grants*, 5 vols. The titles of volumes four and five differ slightly from the first three; they are *The Granville District of North Carolina,*

1748–1763, and *Abstracts of Miscellaneous Land Office Records.* These publications are available at libraries with genealogical collections throughout the country. For an extensive list of these and other land record titles by the author, see <www.margaretmhofmann.com>. For more information about the Granville District, see Thornton W. Mitchell, "The Granville District and Its Land Records," *North Carolina Historical Review* 70 (April 1991): 103–129.

After the Revolutionary War, the state of North Carolina granted land formerly owned by the Crown and Earl Granville. A settler could claim as much as 640 acres of unsettled land for himself and an additional hundred acres for his wife and each minor child for a fee of two pounds ten shillings per hundred acres. If the amount of land claimed exceeded the above allotment, the additional land cost five pounds per hundred acres. Most of the state grants have been microfilmed and are available at the North Carolina State Archives and the FHL, along with grants made in Tennessee to veterans who served in the Revolutionary War.

When land was sold by individuals, the transaction generally was recorded in county deed books. Most deed books are partially indexed, but to facilitate research, most North Carolina counties also have general indexes to grantees and grantors. Descriptions of land follow the "metes and bounds" survey system (see page 6). Copies of deeds may be obtained from the county register of deeds, but many North Carolina county records have been microfilmed and are available at the North Carolina State Archives and the FHL. Additionally, many early North Carolina deed books have been abstracted and published. Copies of these publications may be found in libraries with genealogical collections.

Probate Records

Probate records are generally of two types: wills and estate records. Estate records include both recorded and "loose" documents relating to a decedent's estate, such as inventories, divisions of estates, sales of real or personal property, and other documents. Some of this material is recorded in bound books under various titles. Although bound books generally remain in the county, many have been microfilmed and are available at the North Carolina State Archives and the FHL. However, for each county there may be surviving original wills and loose estate papers that have been transferred to the North Carolina State Archives. They are filed by county alphabetically by the surname of the decedent, and may be examined in the Search Room of the archives.

North Carolina early wills were filed with the secretary of state prior to 1760. For summarized abstracts, see J. B. Grimes, *Abstracts of North Carolina Wills, 1690 to 1760* (reprint; Baltimore:

Genealogical Publishing Co., 1967), and William Perry Johnson, "Grimes Wills: Major Additions and Corrections," *Journal of North Carolina Genealogy* 11 (1965) and 12 (1966) and *North Carolina Genealogy* 13 (1967) and 14 (1968).

After 1760, wills were recorded in North Carolina counties, with the county court assuming the jurisdiction over probate matters from 1760 to 1868. After 1868, probate jurisdiction was transferred to the clerk of the superior court in each county. Some early probate records can be obtained from the clerk of the superior court in individual counties; however, pre-1868 original records have been sent to the North Carolina State Archives for preservation and copies of all records are available there. The FHL also has an extensive collection of wills and other probate records on microfilm. Thornton W. Mitchell, *North Carolina Wills: A Testator Index, 1665–1900,* 2 vols. (1987; rev. ed. Baltimore: Genealogical Publishing Co., 1992) is a statewide index to all known wills probated during that period.

Court Records

Court of Pleas and Quarter Sessions (ca. 1670–1868). The court of pleas and quarter sessions was the basic court of North Carolina's counties. As such, it was often called the county court or precinct court before 1739 and the inferior court after 1806.

The county court was presided over by justices of the peace and handled minor civil matters (usually dealing with indebtedness), misdemeanors, probate, levying and expending of local taxes, matters dealing with public works (buildings, roads, bridges, ferries, and mills), summoning and selection of jurors, and a host of other local matters. See Raymond A. Winslow, Jr., "The County Court," *The North Carolina Genealogical Society Journal* 10 (1984): 70–79 and 134–43, for an in-depth examination of the county court. The court of pleas and quarter sessions was abolished under the constitution of 1868, and the county superior court took over its functions.

The county court minutes often are not indexed but are one of the richest sources of genealogical information available. Gaps in local records may be filled in by examination of the Supreme Court of North Carolina case files (see below).

General Court (1670–1754). The general court, sometimes called the court of grand council, the grand court, and the Court of Albemarle, was the court of appeals for the county court. Additionally, the general court was the court of origin in all criminal cases punishable by loss of life or limb. The court often handled probate of large estates or estates that included land in several counties. Three district courts were added to the general court in 1739, and the court was replaced in 1754 by district courts.

District Courts (1754–1806). District courts, sometimes called district superior courts, replaced the general court in 1754. In 1782 district courts acquired jurisdiction over all equity cases. From 1771 to 1778 the district courts did not function. When the courts were reestablished in 1778, their probate authority was transferred to the county courts. District courts were replaced in 1806 by superior courts in each county.

Superior Court (1806–present). In 1806 each county received a superior court to share the judicial burden until the constitution of 1868 abolished the county court. Initially, superior courts heard cases involving large sums of money or serious criminal charges, and then took over all county-level court jurisdiction in 1868.

Court of Chancery (1663–1776). The governor and council were members of the court of chancery. During its period of operation, this court was the only court with jurisdiction over equity cases, such as division of land between partners, enforcement of contracts, and other non-criminal cases. In 1782 the North Carolina legislature vested jurisdiction over equity cases in the district courts. The equity system was abolished by the constitution of 1868.

Court of Conference (1799–1805) and Supreme Court of North Carolina (1805–present). The supreme court is the highest judicial level in the state. It was originally formed by the judges of the district superior courts, but election of supreme court justices began in 1818. Before the twentieth century, if a case was appealed to the supreme court, the entire case file was often transferred from the lower court to the supreme court. See Loren D. Austin, "Genealogy in North Carolina's Supreme Court Cases," *The North Carolina Genealogical Society Journal* 7 (August 1981): 124-32.

The North Carolina State Archives maintains most original pre-1900 court records, and microfilm copies are available at the FHL. See Leary, *North Carolina Research: Genealogy and Local History* (cited in Background Sources) for a more thorough discussion of North Carolina's court system. An information circular, "North Carolina Courts of Law and Equity Prior to 1868," is available online at <www.ah.dcr.state.nc.us>.

Tax Records

That all governments require money to operate was well known to those who established North Carolina's civil administration. They decided to follow existing methods of taxation by placing levies on people. Prior to 1777, people who were taxed were usually called taxables, tithables, or polls; in essence they were paying a head tax. A 1715 law enacted by the general assembly defined taxables as all free males sixteen years of age and over and all slaves, male and female, aged twelve and over. The law was revised in 1749 and included all white males aged sixteen and

over, as well as "negroes," "mulattoes," "mustees," or "octoroons" (offspring of a white and a "quadroon"), and all persons of mixed blood to the fourth generation, both male and female, who were twelve years of age and older.

Tax rules remained fairly constant from 1749 until 1777 when the state began applying different criteria, such as restricting the poll tax to freemen who did not own a minimum amount of property, exempting soldiers, changing the minimum age to twenty-one, or taxing only unmarried men. By 1784 the legislature settled on taxing freemen and male servants twenty-one and over and all slaves (male and female) between twelve and fifty. In 1801 all free males over fifty were exempted from the poll tax, and then in 1817 the exemption age was lowered to forty-five. A constitutional amendment in 1835 set age limits at twenty-one to forty-five for free males and twelve to fifty for slaves. The constitution of 1868 included all males between the ages of twenty-one and fifty. Poll taxes were abolished in North Carolina in 1970. Property taxes were levied in North Carolina from 1715 through 1722 and then abolished. They were reinstated in 1777 and remain in effect today. See Raymond A. Winslow, Jr., "Tax and Fiscal Records," *North Carolina Research* (see Background Sources).

North Carolina tax lists have survived better than those for many states. The lists date from the first decade of the eighteenth century to the present. Microfilmed copies of some of the surviving lists are available at the North Carolina State Archives and the FHL. Many transcriptions are found in the pages of North Carolina's periodicals. See also Clarence E. Ratcliff, *North Carolina Taxpayers, 1701–1786* (1987; rev. ed., Baltimore: Genealogical Publishing Co., 2002) and *North Carolina Taxpayers, 1679-1790* (1984; rev. ed., Baltimore: Genealogical Publishing Co., 2003).

Cemetery Records

An index of many pre-1914 gravestone inscriptions in North Carolina cemeteries is in the Search Room at the North Carolina State Archives. The FHL has a microfilm copy of the index, while both the North Carolina State Archives and the FHL have collections of cemetery records, arranged by county.

Church Records

Quakers. William Edmundson and George Fox were Quaker missionaries who brought the Society of Friends (Quakers) to North Carolina in 1672. The tide of Quaker migration from Pennsylvania, Maryland, and Virginia was enough to make the Society of Friends one of the larger religious groups in North Carolina during the eighteenth and early nineteenth centuries. By the start of the Civil War, the majority of Quaker families had moved to Ohio and Indiana where they hoped to escape the

effects of slavery and the conflict they thought it would cause. Quakers kept excellent records, and originals of the North Carolina monthly meeting minutes, and records are among the Quaker Collection at Guilford College Library in Greensboro, North Carolina. The collection consists of over 6,000 manuscript volumes of minutes and records from 1680 to the present. Early records from monthly meetings in East Tennessee, Georgia, and South Carolina that were affiliated with the North Carolina Yearly Meeting also are found there. Many North Carolina Quaker records are published in part in William W. Hinshaw, *Encyclopedia of American Quaker Genealogy*, vol. 1 (1936; reprint, Baltimore: Genealogical Publishing Co., 1994).

Church of England. The second denomination to establish a congregation in North Carolina was the Church of England in 1700. As elsewhere, that group became known as Episcopalians some years after the American Revolution. There are no surviving eighteenth-century Church of England parish registers for North Carolina.

Moravian. Known also as United Brethren, a group from Pennsylvania purchased nearly 100,000 acres in 1753 and called the tract "Wachovia." Their first three towns were Bethabara, Bethania, and Salem. They, like the Quakers, kept excellent records. Write to the Moravian Archives, Southern Province of the Moravian Church in America, Drawer M, Salem Station, Winston-Salem, NC 27108. The collection contains historical books and manuscripts concerning Moravians in North Carolina. Early congregational diaries have been translated and published in Adelaide L. Fries et al., eds., *The Records of the Moravians in North Carolina*, 11 vols. (Raleigh, N.C.: State Department of Archives and History, 1922–69). Also, C. Daniel Crews and Lisa D. Bailey, *Records of the Moravians in North Carolina*, vol. 12, 1856–66 (Raleigh, N.C.: State Office of Archives and History, 2000) includes material not presented in volume 11 that covers the same dates.

Baptists. The Baptists reached North Carolina during the mid-eighteenth century, and the Sandy Creek Church, called the "Mother of Southern Baptist Churches," was founded in 1755. Over the next two centuries, the Baptist Church became the leading religious denomination in the state. Baptist Church records do not offer the wealth of information found in Quaker or Moravian records, but useful historical details and migrational clues are sometimes found in their records. Many types of Baptist churches split off from the host denomination.

The principal depository of Baptist records is the Baptist Historical Collection of the Z. Smith Reynolds Library at Wake Forest University. Write to P.O. Box 7777, Reynolds Station, Winston-Salem, NC 27106. For records of the Free-Will Baptists, write to the Free-Will Baptist Historical Collection, Moye Library, Mount Olive Junior College, Mount Olive, NC 28365. Primitive Baptist records are found at the Primitive Baptist Library, 4023 N. NC Hwy. 87, Elon, NC 27244.

Other denominations. A plethora of religious groups exists in North Carolina today, but few of them were influential during the state's early history. The Presbyterians, Lutherans, and the Moravians constituted the largest minority denominations during the eighteenth and nineteenth centuries.

Presbyterianism came with the Highland Scots families who settled in the Cape Fear River area in the 1730s and the Scots-Irish who came down into North Carolina from Pennsylvania and Virginia. Write to the Presbyterian Historical Foundation, P.O. Box 847, Montreat, NC 27410.

Lutheranism came into North Carolina with the Germans who first arrived in Pennsylvania early in the eighteenth century and then moved into Virginia's Shenandoah Valley before continuing south to North Carolina, where they joined the descendants of the Germanna colonists from Orange and Spotsylvania counties of north-central Virginia. Write to Archives of the North Carolina Synod, P.O. Box 2049, Salisbury, NC 28144.

Military Records

North Carolina's war record begins with the Chowanoc Indian War (1675–77) and continues with the Tuscarora Indian War (1711–15), but virtually no records survive to tell of the participants. Then came the War of Jenkins' Ear (1739–44) and King George's War (1744–48) between England, France, and Spain. Some North Carolinians served in these wars, but only a few muster rolls remain. The French and Indian War began in 1755 and ended in 1763; that North Carolinians served in this war is certain, but little remains to document a soldier's service. The surviving muster rolls and militia officer lists are available at the North Carolina State Archives and are published in Murtie June Clark, *Colonial Soldiers of the South, 1732–1774* (1983; reprint, Baltimore: Genealogical Publishing Co., 1999).

Revolutionary War. Some of the original service records for the Revolutionary War were destroyed by fire, but those remaining are on file at the National Archives, compiled primarily from rosters and rolls of soldiers serving in North Carolina's militia units. See the published list of North Carolina soldiers in *Roster of Soldiers from North Carolina in the American Revolution* (1932; reprint, Baltimore: Genealogical Publishing Co., 1977). However, the comprehensive index to Revolutionary War Records on fifty-eight reels of microfilm is available at the National Archives and its branches, the FHL and its branches, and other selected libraries.

The new states were required to raise quotas of soldiers to serve in the Continental Line during the Revolutionary War, and land was offered as an inducement. North Carolinians who volunteered to serve for at least two years were given bounty-land

warrants that could be exchanged for land in what was to become Tennessee. The North Carolina State Archives has some fiscal records of soldiers serving in the Continental Line, but does not have service records.

Many North Carolinians remained loyal to the Crown during the Revolutionary War. See Murtie June Clark, *Loyalists in the Southern Campaign of the Revolutionary War* (Baltimore: Genealogical Publishing Co., 1980).

War of 1812. Information included in service records for the War of 1812 is similar to that in the same records of soldiers in the Revolutionary War. *Muster Rolls of the Soldiers of the War of 1812: Detached from the Militia of North Carolina, in 1812 and 1814* (1851; reprint, Baltimore: Genealogical Publishing Co., 1976) is the most comprehensive list available of soldiers from North Carolina. Unfortunately, *Muster Rolls* contains many errors and must be carefully verified in original records. There are War of 1812 pay vouchers for twenty-eight counties arranged alphabetically and an alphabetical list of all vouchers available in the Search Room of the North Carolina State Archives.

Civil War. Many service records are available at the North Carolina State Archives, including enlistment bounty payrolls. The most comprehensive publication on North Carolina's Confederate soldiers is Louis H. Manarin and Weymouth T. Jordan, comps., *North Carolina Troops, 1861–1865, A Roster*, 15 vols. (Raleigh, N.C.: State Department of Archives and History, 1981–present). Volume 15 was published in 2003. Others may follow. *North Carolina Troops* includes both unit histories and some excellent biographies.

North Carolina offered pensions to Confederate veterans and their widows beginning in 1885. The 1885 pension law offered pensions to veterans and widows of veterans disabled by the loss of a limb or an eye; an 1887 amendment provided pensions for widows of veterans who died of disease while serving the Confederacy. A new law was enacted in 1889 and revised in 1901 that required a twelve-month residence in North Carolina and required that widows had married the veteran before April 1865 to qualify for a pension. Original pension records and the accompanying index are available at the North Carolina State Archives; the index is available on microfilm at the FHL.

Spanish American War. A printed *Roster of the North Carolina Volunteers in the Spanish American War* is available in the Search Room of the North Carolina State Archives.

For a more in-depth look at how military, veterans', and pension records apply in North Carolina, see George Stevenson, "Military Records," and Raymond A. Winslow, Jr., "Military Service and Veterans Records" in Leary, *North Carolina Research: Genealogy and Local History* (see Background Sources).

Periodicals, Newspapers, and Manuscript Collections

Periodicals

A host of excellent periodicals regarding North Carolina genealogy have been or are currently being published, including *The North Carolina Genealogical Society Journal* (Raleigh, N.C.: North Carolina Genealogical Society, 1975–present) and *North Carolina Genealogy*, formerly *The North Carolinian* (Raleigh, N.C.: W. P. Johnson, 1955–75). These two periodicals provide an extensive array of instructive articles and transcriptions of original source material, making it important for the researcher to keep abreast of their contents. The North Carolina Office of Archives and History, the University of North Carolina at Chapel Hill, as well as the Genealogical Branch of the State Library of North Carolina, and the FHL have copies of these and other periodicals of interest to the researcher.

Newspapers

North Carolina Gazette, the first newspaper published in North Carolina, appeared in August 1751. See Raymond Parker Fouts, *Abstracts from the State Gazette of North Carolina* (1982, rev. and enlarged ed., Cocoa, Fla.: GenRec, 1997) for genealogical abstracts for the period 1792 to 1795. Other newspapers followed and are detailed in H. G. Jones and Julius H. Avant, *Union List of North Carolina Newspapers, 1751–1900* (Raleigh, N.C.: State Department of Archives and History, 1963). For updated information, see the *North Carolina Online Union List of Serials* (part of the OCLC Union List of Serials System), which covers the holdings of more than fifty libraries in North Carolina. It can be accessed via the Interlibrary Loan Subsystem of OCLC. Details of this service appear on the State Library website at <http://statelibrary.dcr.state.nc.us/tss/union.htm>.

The most extensive collection of early North Carolina newspapers on microfilm is at the North Carolina State Archives; however, many other public and academic libraries have newspapers on microfilm. See Roger C. Jones, comp., *Guide to North Carolina Newspapers on Microfilm: Titles Available from the Division of Archives and History*, (6th ed., rev., Raleigh, N.C.: Division of Archives and History, 1984). See also Alan D. Watson *An Index to North Carolina Newspapers, 1784–1789* (2d printing, Raleigh, N.C.: North Carolina Office of Archives and History, 1997).

For a list of the newspapers available on microfilm at the University of North Carolina, see <www.lib.unc.edu/reference/microforms/newsort.html>.

Manuscripts

There are superior manuscript collections in North Carolina with comprehensive guides that were published before libraries

and archives developed comprehensive online databases. University of North Carolina at Chapel Hill, Manuscripts Department at <www.lib.unc.edu/mss/inv.html> provides an updated alphabetical index that includes the *Southern Historical Collection*. Duke University, Rare Book, Manuscript and Special Collections Library <http://scriptorium.lib.duke.edu/specoll/collections.html> also provides an updated catalog.

The North Carolina State Archives holds important collections of private papers, including correspondence, diaries, and account books. See Barbara T. Cain with Ellen Z. McGrew and Charles E. Morris, *Guide to Private Manuscript Collections in the North Carolina State Archives* (4th printing, Raleigh, N.C.: North Carolina Office of Archives and History, 1999). Another important manuscript source comes from the Society of North Carolina Archivists, *Archival and Manuscript Repositories in North Carolina: A Directory* (Roanoke Rapids, N.C.: M. M. Hofmann, 1993); includes a list of 133 repositories, contact points, and holdings.

Another important manuscript source for North Carolina is the Draper Collection held by the State Historical Society of Wisconsin (see Wisconsin—Manuscripts). Microfilm copies of the collection may be found at University of North Carolina at Chapel Hill and the North Carolina State Archives, as well as other repositories.

Archives, Libraries, and Societies

North Carolina State Archives
North Carolina Division of Historical Resources
109 E. Jones St.
Raleigh, NC 27611
Mailing Address:
4614 Mail Service Center
Raleigh, NC 27699-4617
www.ah.dcr.state.nc.us/sections/archives/arch/default.htm

The North Carolina State Archives maintains and provides public access to a voluminous collection of original and microfilmed material that ranges from the sixteenth century to the present. It publishes *North Carolina Historical Review,* as well as many guides to their collections (see Background Sources) and other books. It houses more than 50,000 linear feet of materials, containing more than one million individual items. The North Carolina State Archives will perform searches for residents of North Carolina without charging a fee. Out-of-state residents must pay $20 for each letter sent, for which the archives staff will answer *one* question about a specific person. The fee must accompany each letter. Requests may be sent by U.S. Postal Service, fax, or e-mail. See <www.ah.dcr.state.nc.us/sections/archives/arch/mail.htm> for guidelines and details about how to phrase questions.

Other online features include MARS (Manuscript and Archives Reference System), a catalog containing descriptions of some of the records at the North Carolina State Archives. Also the *Guide to Research Materials in the North Carolina State Archives: County Records*, a listing of more than 9,000 bound volumes, 21,000 boxes, and over 24,000 reels of microfilmed county government records and documents (downloadable in PDF and Microsoft Word formats). Of great interest to genealogists is *Original County Estate Papers*, a listing of the names of persons whose estate documents are on file at the archives and the year the estate was probated.

Genealogical Services Branch,
Division of North Carolina State Library
109 E. Jones St.
Raleigh, NC 27611
Mailing Address:
4614 Mail Service Center
Raleigh, NC 27699-4617
www.ah.dcr.state.nc.us/sections/archives/arch/mail.htm

Located in the same building as the North Carolina State Archives, the Genealogical Services Branch includes an extensive array of published and printed sources for genealogical research, as well as microfilmed census records for many states. The library's catalog is on its website.

North Carolina Genealogical Society
P.O. Box 1492
Raleigh, NC 27602
www.ncgenealogy.org

The society publishes *The North Carolina Genealogical Society Journal* (see Periodicals) and has a useful website.

University of North Carolina
Chapel Hill, NC 27514

In addition to an extensive list of publications coming from the University of North Carolina Press, the university houses the following: the Southern Historical Collection, which can be browsed at <www.lib.unc.edu/mss/shcabout.html>; the North Carolina Collection Gallery, an exceptional and extensive collection of books, images, and museum pieces described at <www.lib.unc.edu/ncc/gallery.html>; and a tremendous Reference Section outlined at <www.lib.unc.edu/ncc/refdescrip.html>.

Duke University
William R. Perkins Library
Durham, NC 27701
www.lib.duke.edu

This fine collection focuses on, but is not limited to, the southeastern part of the state (see African American).

Smaller collections of genealogical and historical material exist throughout the state in local genealogical and public repositories. See Jo Ann Williford and Elizabeth F. Buford, eds., *A Directory of North Carolina Historical Organizations* (Raleigh, N.C.: Department of Cultural Resources for the Federation of North Carolina Historical Societies, 1982), for descriptions of member organizations. See also Society of North Carolina Archivists, *Archival and Manuscript Repositories in North Carolina: A Directory* (Roanoke Rapids, N.C.: M. M. Hofmann, 1993) for a list of 133 repositories, contact points, and holdings.

Special Focus Categories

African American

Duke University Library in Durham and the University of North Carolina Library at Chapel Hill have excellent collections of materials relating to African Americans in North Carolina, in addition to that available through the National Archives (see pages 11-12). The North Carolina Department of Archives and History and the Moravian Archives in Winston-Salem also have sources in their collections pertaining to African Americans and slavery. See Thornton W. Mitchell, comp., *Preliminary Guide to Records Relating to Blacks in the North Carolina State Archives*, Archives Information Circular, No. 17 (1980; revised, Raleigh, N.C.: State Department of Archives and History, 2001).

A basic guide to African American research in North Carolina is Ransom McBride, "Searching for the Past of the North Carolina Black Family in Local, Regional, and Federal Record Resources," *The North Carolina Genealogical Society Journal* 9 (May 1983): 66-77. See also Minnie K. Peebles, "Black Genealogy," *North Carolina Historical Review*, 55 (April 1978): 164-173.

Native American

By 1838 the majority of North Carolina's Native American population had been destroyed or relocated to other areas. The Tuscarora moved up to New York after the Tuscarora War (1711–15), and most of the remaining Cherokee were removed farther west between 1825 and 1842 to what would become Oklahoma. A significant number of tribal members who did not want to move hid out in the mountains of North Carolina and became the Eastern Band of Cherokee. Another group of Cherokees remained in the state by petitioning to become citizens. Certificates allowing them to stay were issued if they proved they could care for themselves.

Most Cherokee records were created and are presently maintained by the federal government. The National Archives has a register of Cherokees who petitioned to remain in the East, registers of Indians who decided to migrate to the West between 1817 and 1838, and the Cherokee census of 1835 (called the Henderson Roll). The census includes a list of members of the Cherokee Nation in North Carolina, Tennessee, Alabama, and Georgia. Consult also the *Eastern Cherokee Reservation Census Rolls, 1898 to 1939*, and other removal records available at the National Archives (see pages 11-12).

An Act of Congress approved on 1 July 1902 gave the U.S. Court of Claims jurisdiction over any claim arising from treaty stipulations that the Cherokees had against the United States and vice versa. Three suits were brought before the court and each was decided in favor of the Cherokees. The Secretary of the Interior was instructed to identify those persons of Cherokee descent entitled to a portion of the more than one million dollars appropriated by Congress for use in payment of claims.

The court established that payment was to be made to all Eastern and Western Cherokees who were alive on 28 May 1906 and who could establish that they were members or descendants of members of the Eastern Cherokee Tribe at the time the treaties were made before 1845. Claims were to be filed with the claims agent on or before 31 August 1907. By that deadline nearly 46,000 applications were on file, representing about 90,000 individual claimants. Roughly one-third of these were entitled to a share. Census lists and rolls compiled by other special agents between 1835 and 1884 were used to determine eligibility and create a new 1910 Eastern Cherokee Enrollment.

Congress authorized the allotment of land to the Five Civilized Tribes on 3 March 1893 and appointed a commission to determine who was eligible to receive land. Over 200,000 applications for land selection were received. Cherokee allotments began in 1903. Applicants were required to submit documents and affidavits as proof of Cherokee citizenship.

Some records pertaining to the Cherokees from North Carolina are housed at the Indian Archives in the Oklahoma Historical Society, Oklahoma City. The collection, which covers the Five Civilized Tribes, contains approximately three million pages of manuscripts and 6,000 bound volumes—the largest collection of Native American documents outside of the National Archives. (See Oklahoma—Archives, Libraries, and Societies.)

In addition to the sources described in the Introduction (see pages 15-16), Native American records are available at the North Carolina State Archives as detailed on their website at <www.ah.dcr.state.nc.us>.

County Resources

The Lords Proprietors planned three counties in Carolina in 1664: Albemarle, Clarendon, and Craven. Craven County lay in South Carolina, and Clarendon County was abandoned in 1667 after achieving a population of about 800. Albemarle County included too large an area to provide adequate local government, so it was subdivided into Berkeley, Carteret,

and Shaftesbury precincts about 1668. About 1681, the three original precincts were divided and renamed Chowan, Currituck, Pasquotank, and Perquimans precincts. By about 1689 the four precincts functioned as de facto counties. In 1696 Bath County was formed; it was divided into Archedale, Pamptecough, and Wickham precincts in 1705. The Provincial Government of North Carolina recognized the *de facto* status of the precincts and declared all precincts to be counties in their own right in 1739, and Albemarle and Bath counties were abolished.

Research in North Carolina county records can begin with the microfilmed North Carolina material at a central collection, such as the North Carolina State Archives, Allen County Public Library (see page 204), the FHL, or other repositories with the North Carolina Core Collection. However, county seats may still hold additional material, including original deed and will books. What follows is an outline of beginning dates of extant records of each county. When counties were formed in North Carolina, many county clerks copied appropriate records from the parent county. In other cases, records pertaining to the land and families of the new county were transferred wholesale. Most counties therefore have some records that pre-date the formation of the county. The register of deeds at the county seat holds land and vital records; the clerk of the superior court holds probate records and court records if they have not been transferred to the state archives in Raleigh. Land records may include deeds, grants, plats, and other miscellaneous items. Probate records include not only wills, but also loose estates records, most of which have not been microfilmed. Court records may include apprentice bonds, bastardy bonds, and officials' or constables' bonds in addition to dockets, fee and account books, and court minutes and orders. The beginning dates do not imply that all records are extant since some of North Carolina's county records have been lost due to fire and other causes.

County records information is quoted from *Guide to Research Materials in the North Carolina State Archives, Section B: County Records* (11th rev. ed., Raleigh, N.C.: North Carolina Department of Archives and History, 1997), describing more than 9,000 bound volumes, 21,000 boxes of loose records, and 24,000 reels of microfilm. County formation information is derived from the above *Guide*, David Leroy Corbitt, *The Formation of the North Carolina Counties, 1663–1943* (1950; 2d printing, Raleigh, N.C.: State Department of Archives and History, 1969); William Perry Johnson, "North Carolina Precincts and Counties, 1663–1911," *The North Carolinian* 2, no. 2 (June 1956): 165-72; and Helen F. M. Leary, ed., *North Carolina Research: Genealogy and Local History*, 2d ed. (Raleigh, N.C.: North Carolina Genealogical Society, 1996).

NORTH CAROLINA

Virginia counties (top, shaded): RUSSELL, WASHINGTON, SMYTH, WYTHE, BLAND, PULASKI, FLOYD, FRANKLIN, GRAYSON, CARROLL, PATRICK, HENRY, PITTSYLVANIA, CHARLOTTE, HALIFAX, LUNENBURG, MECKLENBURG, BRUNSWICK, GREENS-VILLE, DINWIDDIE, SUSSEX, SOUTHAMPTON, ISLE OF WIGHT, NANSEMOND, CHESAPEAKE, VIRGINIA BEACH

VIRGINIA

TENNESSEE — SULLIVAN, JOHNSON, CARTER

North Carolina counties and county seats:

ASHE — Jefferson; Sparta; ALLEGHANY; SURRY; Danbury; Dobson; STOKES; ROCKINGHAM — Wentworth; Yanceyville; CASWELL; Roxboro; PERSON; WATAUGA — Boone; WILKES — Wilkesboro; YADKIN — Yadkinville; FORSYTH — Winston-Salem; GUILFORD — Greensboro; Graham; Hillsborough; ORANGE; DURHAM — Durham; GRANVILLE; Oxford; Louisburg; Henderson; VANCE; WARREN — Warrenton; Halifax; NORTHAMPTON — Jackson; Winton; GATES — Gatesville; CAMDEN — Camden; CURRITUCK — Currituck; HERTFORD; PASQUOTANK — Elizabeth City; PERQUIMANS — Hertford; CHOWAN — Edenton; BERTIE — Windsor

AVERY — Newland; MITCHELL; Bakersville; CALDWELL — Lenoir; Taylorsville; ALEXANDER; DAVIE — Mocksville; IREDELL; Statesville; Lexington; DAVIDSON; RANDOLPH — Asheboro; ALAMANCE; CHATHAM — Pittsboro; FRANKLIN — Louisburg; Nashville; NASH; WAKE — Raleigh; Tarboro; EDGECOMBE; Williamston; MARTIN; Plymouth; WASHINGTON; Columbia; TYRRELL; DARE — Manteo

BURKE — Morganton; Marion; McDOWELL; Newton; CATAWBA; LINCOLN — Lincolnton; ROWAN — Salisbury; CABARRUS — Concord; Albemarle; STANLY; Troy; MONTGOMERY; MOORE; Carthage; Sanford; LEE; Lillington; HARNETT; JOHNSTON — Smithfield; WILSON — Wilson; Goldsboro; WAYNE; Snow Hill; GREENE; PITT — Greenville; BEAUFORT — Washington; HYDE — Swanquarter

RUTHERFORD — Rutherfordton; CLEVELAND — Shelby; GASTON — Gastonia; MECKLENBURG — Charlotte; POLK; Columbus; YORK; UNION — Monroe; ANSON — Wadesboro; RICHMOND — Rockingham; SCOTLAND — Laurinburg; HOKE — Raeford; Fayetteville; CUMBERLAND; SAMPSON — Clinton; DUPLIN — Kenansville; Kinston; LENOIR; Trenton; JONES; New Bern; CRAVEN; Bayboro; PAMLICO; CARTERET — Beaufort; ONSLOW — Jacksonville

ROBESON — Lumberton; BLADEN — Elizabethtown; PENDER — Burgaw; Whiteville; COLUMBUS; Wilmington; NEW HANOVER; BRUNSWICK — Southport

CHEROKEE

Match Line, See Box Below

South Carolina counties (shaded): GREENVILLE, SPARTANBURG, UNION, CHESTER, LANCASTER, CHESTERFIELD, MARLBORO, LAURENS, NEWBERRY, FAIRFIELD, GREENE, DARLINGTON, DILLON, MARION, HORRY, GEORGETOWN

SOUTH CAROLINA

Inset map (lower left):

TENNESSEE — ANDERSON, KNOX, JEFFERSON, GREENE, WASHINGTON, UNICOI, CARTER, ROANE, LOUDON, MONROE, BLOUNT, SEVIER, COCKE, MADISON — Marshall; Burnsville; YANCEY; MITCHELL; AVERY; Bakersville; Marion; McDOWELL; BUNCOMBE — Asheville; HAYWOOD — Waynesville; SWAIN; GRAHAM — Robbinsville; Bryson City; Sylva; JACKSON; Franklin; MACON; TRANSYLVANIA — Brevard; HENDERSON — Hendersonville; POLK — Columbus; RUTHERFORD — Rutherfordton; CHEROKEE — Murphy; CLAY — Hayesville

GEORGIA — FANNIN, UNION, TOWNS, RABUN
SOUTH CAROLINA — OCONEE, PICKENS, GREENVILLE, SPARTANBURG

The Counties and County Seats of NORTH CAROLINA

25   0   25   50 Miles

Pamlico Sound; Cape Hatteras; Cape Lookout; Cape Fear; Onslow Bay; Long Bay; Atlantic Ocean

Drawn by William Dollarhide

Map	County / Address	Date Formed / Parent County/ies	Birth / Marriage / Death	Land / Probate District Court #
E2	Alamance 124 W. Elm St. Graham 27253-1312	1849 Orange	1913 1853 ——	1793 1832 1849
	Albemarle *Divided into Carteret, Berkeley, and Shaftesbury precincts about 1668. Miscellaneous records, 1678-1737.*	1664 (abolished 1739 when its precincts were declared counties) original		
A2	Alexander 621 Liledoun Rd. Taylorsville 28681-0000 *Record loss, 1865.*	1847 Iredell/Wilkes/Caldwell	1913 1867 1913	1833 1847 1853
B1	Alleghany P.O. Box 366 Sparta 28675-0366 *Record loss, 1932.*	1859 Ashe	1914 1861 1914	1859 1859 1862
C5	Anson 114 N. Greene St., Rm. 30 Wadesboro 28170-2100 *Record loss, 1868. Records fragmented.*	1750 Bladen	1921 1741 1921	1749 1751 1771
	Archdale Precinct	1705 (renamed Craven Precinct about 1712) precinct of Bath		
A1	Ashe 150 Government Cir. Ste. 2500 Jefferson 28640-9378 *Record loss, 1865. Records fragmented.*	1799 Wilkes	1913 1828 1913	1778 1801 1805
A2	Avery P.O. Box 640 Newland 28657-0640	1911 Caldwell/Mitchell/Watauga	1914 1911 1914	1911 1911 1911
	Bath *Divided into Archedale, Pamptecough, and Wickham precincts, 1705.*	1696 (abolished 1739 when its precincts were declared counties) original		
J3	Beaufort P.O. Box 1027 Washington 27889-1027 *Records fragmented. Delayed birth certificates are available.*	1705 (as Pamptecough Precinct; renamed 1712; declared a county, 1739) precinct of Bath	—— 1847 ——	1695 1720 1744
	Berkeley Precinct	about 1668 (renamed Perquimans Precinct about 1681) precinct of Albemarle		
J2	Bertie P.O. Box 530 Windsor 27983-0530	1722 Chowan Precinct, Albemarle County	—— 1762 ——	1721 1728 1724
F5	Bladen P.O. Box 1048 Elizabethtown 28337-1048 *Record losses, 1800 and 1893. Also called Pelham Precinct.*	1734 (as Pelham Precinct; renamed 1734) New Hanover Precinct, Bath County	1913 1868 1913	1784 1766 1866
G6	Brunswick P.O. Box 249 Bolivia 28422-0249 *Record loss, 1865.*	1764 New Hanover/Bladen	1914 1804 1714	1764 1764 1782
C7	Buncombe 205 College St., Ste. 300 Asheville 28801-3001 *Record losses, 1830 and 1865. Records fragmented.*	1791 Burke/Rutherford	1887 1842 ——	1791 1815 1790
A3	Burke 200 Avery Ave. Morganton 28655-3103 *Record loss, 1865.*	1777 Rowan	1913 1780 1913	1770 1776 1755
	Bute *Records transferred to Warren and Franklin counties.*	1764 (abolished 1779) Granville	—— —— ——	1778 1760 1764
C4	Cabarrus Governmental Center P.O. Box 707 Concord 28025-0707 *Record loss, 1876.*	1792 Mecklenburg	1914 1792 ——	1784 1793 1793
A2	Caldwell 905 West Ave., N.W. P.O. Box 2200 Lenoir 28645-2200	1841 Burke/Wilkes	1914 1841 1914	1840 1830 1838
K1	Camden 117 N. NC 343 Camden 27921-0190 *Records fragmented.*	1777 Pasquotank	1913 1848 1913	1739 1766 1802
J5	Carteret 402 Courthouse Sq. Beaufort 28516-1898	1722 Craven Precinct, Bath County	1912 1746 1912	1721 1744 1723
	Carteret Precinct *Divided into Currituck and Pasquotank Precincts about 1681.*	about 1668 (abolished about 1681) precinct of Albemarle		
E1	Caswell P.O. Box 98 Yanceyville 27379-0098	1777 Orange	1913 1775 1913	1777 1771 1767
A3	Catawba P.O. Box 389 Newton 28658-0389	1842 Lincoln	1913 1843 1913	1837 1843 1843
E3	Chatham P.O. Box 87 Pittsboro 27312-0087	1770/1771 Orange	—— 1772 ——	1771 1771 1757
A8	Cherokee 75 Peachtree St. Murphy 28906-2947 *Record losses, 1865, 1895, and 1926.*	1839 Macon	1913 1837 1913	1838 1848 1846

Map County Address	Date Formed Parent County/ies	Birth Marriage Death	Land Probate District Court#
J2 Chowan P.O. Box 1030 Edenton 27932-1030	about 1668 (as Shaftsbury precinct)* precinct of Albemarle	1913 1747 1913	1678 1694 1715
Record loss, 1848. Records fragmented. ** Formed as Shaftsbury Precinct about 1681, it was renamed Chowan about 1681 and declared a county, 1739.*			
Clarendon	1664 (abolished 1667) original		
A8 Clay P.O. Box 118 Hayesville 28904-0118	1861 Cherokee	1913 1870 1913	1845 1862 1868
Record loss, 1870. Early records fragmented.			
A4 Cleveland P.O. Box 1210 Shelby 28150-1210	1841 Rutherford/Lincoln	1908 1851 1913	1792 1795 1838
F6 Columbus 111 Washington St. Whiteville 28472-3323	1808 Bladen/Brunswick	1913 1867 1913	1802 1808 1817
H4 Craven 406 Craven St. New Bern 28560-4911	1705 (as Archdale Precinct)* precinct of Bath	—— 1740 ——	1710 1737 1712
Formed as Archdale Precinct, it was renamed Craven about 1712 and declared a county in 1739.			
F4 Cumberland P.O. Box 1829 Fayetteville 28302-1829	1754 Bladen	1913 1800 1913	1752 1757 1755
K1 Currituck P.O. Box 39 Currituck 27929-0039 *Record loss.*	about 1681 (as a precinct; declared a county, 1739) Carteret Precinct, Albemarle County	1914 1851 1914	1735 1772 1799
K3 Dare P.O. Drawer 1000 Manteo 27954-1000	1870 Currituck/Tyrrell/Hyde	—— 1870 ——	1804 1832 1869
Davidson (Tenn.)	1783 Washington, Tenn.		
Ceded to the United States in 1790 as part of the Southwest Territory (later Tennessee).			
C3 Davidson P.O. Box 1067 Lexington 27292-1067 *Record loss, 1866.*	1822 Rowan	1914 1822 1914	1808 1817 1820
C2 Davie 123 S. Main St. Mocksville 27028-2464	1836 Rowan	1913 1851 1913	1792 1808 1829
Dobbs	1758 (abolished 1791) Johnston	—— 1785 ——	1746 ——
Divided into Glasgow and Lenoir counties, 1791.			
G5 Duplin P.O. Box 910 Kenansville 28349-0910 *Records fragmented.*	1750 New Hanover	1914 1755 1914	1754 1759 1784
E2 Durham 200 E Main St. Durham 27701-3649	1881 Orange/Wake	—— 1881 ——	1881 1875 1881
H2 Edgecombe P.O. Box 10 Tarboro 27886-0010	1741 Bertie	1914 1760 1914	1732 1730 1744
Land records prior to 1759 are among those of Halifax County.			
Fayette	1784 (abolished 1784) Cumberland		
Formation repealed 1784.			
C2 Forsyth 201 N. Chestnut, 5th Floor Winston-Salem 27101-4120	1849 Stokes	—— 1849 ——	1849 1845 1848
F2 Franklin 113 Market St. Louisburg 27549-2523	1779 Bute	1913 1789 1913	1781 1776 1774
A4 Gaston P.O. Box 1578 Gastonia 28053-1578 *Record loss, 1874. Records fragmented.*	1846 Lincoln	—— 1848 ——	1846 1839 1847
J1 Gates P.O. Box 148 Gatesville 27938-0148	1779 Chowan/Hertford/Perquimans	1913 1779 1913	1776 1762 1768
Glasgow	1791 (renamed Greene, 1799) Dobbs		
A8 Graham P.O. Box 575 Robbinsville 28771-0575	1872 Cherokee	1913 1873 1913	1789 1847 1864
F2 Granville P.O. Box 906 Oxford 25765-0906	1746 Edgecombe	1913 1758 1913	1746 1746 1742
Greene (Tenn.)	1783 Washington, Tenn.		
Ceded to the United States in 1790 as part of the Southwest Territory (later Tennessee).			
H3 Greene 229 Kingold, Ste. D Snow Hill 28580-1331 *Record loss, 1876. Records fragmented.*	1791 (as Glasgow; renamed 1799) Dobbs	1913 1875 1913	1857 1809 1861
D2 Guilford 301 W. Market St. P.O. Box 3427 Greensboro 27402-3427	1770/1771 Rowan/Orange	1913 1770 1913	1771 1771 1774
H2 Halifax P.O. Box 38 Halifax 27839-0038	1758 Edgecombe	1913 1770 1913	1716 1759 1759
E4 Harnett 301 W. Cornelius Harnett Blvd. Lillington 27546-0759 *Record losses, 1892 and 1894. Records fragmented.*	1855 Cumberland	1914 1892 1914	1855 1854 1875

Map	County Address	Date Formed Parent County/ies	Birth Marriage Death	Land Probate District Court#
	Hawkins (Tenn.)	1787 Sullivan, Tenn.		
	Ceded to the United States in 1790 as part of the Southwest Territory (later Tennessee)			
B7	Haywood 215 N Main St. Waynesville 28786-3869	1808 Buncombe	1913 1808 1913	1706 1803 1809
C8	Henderson 100 N. King St. Hendersonville 28792-5053	1838 Buncombe	1914 1838 1913	1835 1838 1838
J2	Hertford County Office Bldg. #1 P.O. Box 116 Winton 27986-0116	1759 Chowan/Bertie/ Northampton	1911 1868 1911	1862 1868 1830
	Record losses, 1830 and 1862. Records fragmented.			
E4	Hoke P.O. Box 120 Raeford 28376-0210	1911 Cumberland/Robeson	1911 1911 1911	1911 1911 1911
K3	Hyde P.O. Box 188 Swan Quarter 27885-0188	1705 (as Wickham Precinct; renamed 1712; declared a county, 1739) precinct of Bath	1877 1742 1877	1736 1745 1713
B3	Iredell P.O. Box 788 Statesville 28677-0788	1788 Rowan	1913 1788 1913	1788 1787 1786
	Record loss, 1854.			
B8	Jackson 401 Grindstaff Cove Rd. Sylva 28779-3250	1851 Haywood/Macon	——— 1853 ———	1853 1853 1853
	Records fragmented. Delayed birth certificates are available.			
F3	Johnston P.O. Box 1049 Smithfield 27577-1049	1746 Craven	1914 1746 1914	1748 1760 1759
	Records fragmented.			
H4	Jones P.O. Box 340 Trenton 28585-0340	1779 Craven	1914 1851 1914	1779 1760 1807
	Record loss, 1862.			
E3	Lee P.O. Box 1968 Sanford 27331-1968	1907 Chatham/Moore	1913 1908 1913	1908 1906 1908
H4	Lenoir P.O. Box 3289 Kinston 28501-3289	1791 Dobbs	1914 1791 1914	1737 1869 1874
	Record losses, 1878 and 1880. Records fragmented.			
A3	Lincoln 115 W. Main St. Lincolnton 28092-2601	1779 Tryon	1913 1779 1913	1763 1765 1771
	Records fragmented.			
B8	Macon 5 West Main St. Franklin 28734-3005	1828 Haywood	1913 1828 1913	1820 1830 1822
C7	Madison P.O. Box 579 Marshall 28753-0579	1851 Buncombe/Yancey	1913 1851 1913	1851 1851 1837
II3	Martin P.O. Box 668 Williamston 27892-0668	1774 Halifax/Tyrrell	1913 1872 1913	1774 1774 1809
	Records loss, 1884 Records fragmented.			
D7, A3	McDowell 60 East Court St. Marion 28752-4041	1842 Burke/Rutherford	1914 1842 1914	1813 1841 1822
B4	Mecklenburg 600 E. Fourth St. Charlotte 28321-2846	1762 Anson	1913 1783 1913	1762 1713 1774
D6, A2	Mitchell 26 Crimson Laurel Cir., #2 Bakersville 28705-9510	1861 Burke/Caldwell/McDowell/ Watauga/Yancey	1913 1861 1913	1789 1823 1861
	Record loss, 1907.			
D4	Montgomery P.O. Box 425 Troy 27371-0425	1779 Anson	1913 1779 1913	1769 1785 1807
	Record loss, 1835. Records fragmented.			
E4	Moore P.O. Box 905 Carthage 28327-0905	1784 Cumberland	1913 1851 1913	1787 1783 1784
	Record loss, 1889. Records fragmented.			
G2	Nash 120 W Washington St. #3072 Nashville 27856-1376	1777 Edgecombe	1913 1777 1913	1739 1770 1751
G6	New Hanover 320 Chestnut St., Rm. 502 Wilmington 28401-4068	1729 (as a precinct; declared a county, 1739) Craven Precinct, Bath County	1879 1741 1879	1729 1732 1738
	Records fragmented.			
H1	Northampton P.O. Box 808 Jackson 27845-0808	1741 Bertie	1917 1811 1917	1741 1759 1771
H5	Onslow 118 Old Bridge St. Jacksonville 28540-4229	1734 New Hanover Precinct, Bath County	1914 1745 1914	1712 1735 1732
	Record losses, 1752 and 1786.			
E2	Orange P.O. Box 8181 Hillsborough 27278-8181	1752 Bladen/Granville/Johnston	1913 1779 1913	1752 1752 1752
J4	Pamlico P.O. Box 776 Bayboro 28515-0776	1872 Beaufort/Craven	1913 1872 1913	1869 1872 1872
	Pamptecough Precinct	1705 (renamed Beaufort Precinct, 1712) precinct of Bath		

Map	County Address	Date Formed Parent County/ies	Birth Marriage Death	Land Probate District Court#
K2	Pasquotank P.O. Box 39 Elizabeth City 27907-0039	about 1681 (as a precinct; declared a county, 1739) Carteret Precinct, Albemarle County	1691 1691 1691	1666 1709 1737
	Pelham Precinct	1734 (renamed Bladen Precinct, 1734) New Hanover Precinct, Bath County		
G5	Pender P.O. Box 5 Burgaw 28425-0005	1875 New Hanover	1913 1875 1913	1875 1875 1875
K2	Perquimans P.O. Box 45 Hertford 27944-0045	about 1668 (as Berkeley precinct; renamed about 1681; declared a county, 1739) precinct of Albemarle	1659 1659 1913	1681 1709 1688
E1	Person 304 S. Morgan St., Rm. 212 Roxboro 275739-5245	1791 Caswell	.1913 1791 1913	1774 1792 1775
H3	Pitt 1717 W. Fifth St. Greenville 27834-1601 *Record loss, 1857. Records fragmented.*	1760 Beaufort	1913 1826 1913	1762 1836 1850
D8, A4	Polk P.O. Box 308 Columbus 28722-0308	1855 Henderson/Rutherford	—— 1855 ——	1830 1851 1847
D3	Randolph 707 McDowell Rd. P.O. Box 4728 Asheboro 27204-4728	1779 Guilford	1913 1779 1913	1779 1773 1772
D4	Richmond P.O. Box 504 Rockingham 28379-0504	1779 Anson	1914 1779 1914	1762 1772 1772
E5	Robeson 701 N. Elm St. Lumberton 28358-4891	1787 Bladen	1913 1803 1913	1782 1783 1795
D1	Rockingham 371 NC 65 Wentworth 27375-0206	1785 Guilford	1913 1785 1913	1785 1772 1786
C3	Rowan 130 West Innes St. Salisbury 28144-4365 *Record loss, 1865.*	1753 Anson	1913 1753 1913	1753 1743 1753
D8, A4	Rutherford 289 N. Main St. Rutherfordton 28139-2503 *Record loss, 1907.*	1779 Tryon	1913 1774 1913	1768 1782 1779
F4	Sampson County Office Bldg. 435 Rowan St. Clinton 28328-4729 *Record losses, 1865 and 1921.*	1784 Duplin	1913 1867 1913	1752 1778 1790
D5	Scotland P.O. Box 489 Laurinburg 28352-0489	1899 Richmond	1913 1900 1913	1900 1887 1887
	Shaftesbury Precinct	about 1668 (renamed Chowan Precinct about 1681) precinct of Albemarle		
C4	Stanly 201 S. Second St. Albemarle 28001-5741	1841 Montgomery	1913 1850 1913	1840 1839 1841
C1	Stokes P.O. Box 20 Danbury 27016-0020	1789 Surry	1913 1790 1913	1760 1753 1782
	Sullivan (Tenn.)	1779 Washington, Tenn. *Ceded to the United States in 1790 as part of the Southwest Territory (later Tennessee).*		
	Sumner (Tenn.)	1787 Davidson, Tenn. *Ceded to the United States in 1790 as part of the Southwest Territory (later Tennessee).*		
B1	Surry 118 Hamby Rd., Ste. 329 Dobson 27017-8820	1770 Rowan	1912 1778 1912	1771 1770 1770
A7	Swain P.O. 2321 Bryson City 28713-2321 *Record loss, 1879. Delayed birth certificates are available.*	1871 Jackson/Macon	—— 1871	1871 1871 1871
	Tennessee (Tenn.)	1788 Davidson, Tenn. *Ceded to the United States in 1790 as part of the Southwest Territory (later Tennessee).*		
C8	Transylvania 28 E. Main St. Brevard 28712-3728	1861 Henderson/Jackson	1913 1861 1913	1861 1861 1861
	Tryon	1768 Mecklenburg *Divided into Lincoln and Rutherford Counties in 1779. Records transferred to Lincoln County.*	—— ——	1769 1769
K3	Tyrrell P.O. Box 449 Columbia 27925-0049	1729 Bertie/Chowan, Currituck, Pasquotank precincts, Albemarle County	1913 1742 1913	1736 1739 1735
C4	Union 500 N. Main St., Rm. 921 Monroe 28112-4730	1842 Anson/Mecklenburg	1913 1842 1913	1842 1837 1843
F1	Vance 122 Young St. Ste. B Henderson 27536-4268	1881 Granville/Franklin/Warren	1913 1881 1913	1849 1881 1881
F3	Wake P.O. Box 550 Raleigh 27602-0550	1770 Cumberland/Orange/Johnston	—— 1770	1774 1770 1769

Map	County Address	Date Formed Parent County/ies	Birth Marriage Death	Land Probate District Court#
	Walton (Ga.)	1803 (abolished 1812)		
	Was a settlement of Georgia but was actually in North Carolina; see Walton (old) Georgia.			
G1	Warren P.O. Box 619 Warrenton 27589-0619	1779 Bute	1914 1779 1914	1764 1763 1769
	Washington District	1776 original		
	Ceded to the United States in 1790 as part of the Southwest Territory (later Tennessee).			
J3	Washington P.O. Box 1007 Plymouth 27962-1007	1799 Tyrrell	1912 1851 1912	1779 1795 1815
	Record losses, 1862, 1869, and 1881.			
A2	Watauga 842 W King St., Ste. 1 Boone 28607-3485	1849 Ashe/Caldwell/Wilkes/Yancey	1914 1873 1914	1830 1858 1873
	Record loss, 1873. Records fragmented.			
G4	Wayne P.O. Box 227 Goldsboro 27530-0227	1779 Dobbs	1913 1790 1913	1780 1776 1782
	Wickham Precinct	1705 (became Hyde Precinct, 1712) Bath		
B2	Wilkes 110 North St. Wilkesboro 28697-2428	1777 Surry/Washington District	1913 1778 1913	1741 1777 1761
G3	Wilson P.O. Box 1728 Wilson 27893-1728	1855 Edgecombe/Nash/ Johnston/Wayne	1913 1855 1913	1836 1840 1850
B2	Yadkin P.O. Box 146 Yadkinville 27055-0146	1850 Surry	1914 1850 1914	1793 1836 1845
D7, A2	Yancey Courthouse, Rm. 11 Burnsville 28714	1833 Buncombe/Burke	1913 1851 1913	1831 1838 1834

North Dakota

BETH H. BAUMAN AND MARSHA HOFFMAN RISING, CG, FUGA, FASG

The first Europeans in the area arrived the last part of the eighteenth century and were fur traders employed by the Missouri Fur Company. The peopling of the area quickly followed the first exploration with settlements in Selkirk Colony, on the Red and Assiniboine rivers, and the Pembina settlement. Both were established in 1812, but conditions were so difficult that by 1823 Selkirk had become part of the Hudson Bay Company settlement and Pembina had been abandoned.

The indigenous tribes of the Dakotas were the Mandans and Arikaras. Eastern tribes that were moved into the area included Hidatsas, Crows, Cheyennes, Creeks, Assiniboines, Yanktonai Dakotas, Teton Dakotas, and Chippewas. The smallpox epidemics in 1782 and 1786 wiped out three-fourths of the Mandans and half of the Hidatsas. The epidemic of 1837, probably introduced by the white fur traders, also had a devastating effect on the native population.

Composing the largest settlement at the Red River were the "half-breeds" (called *métis*) who were the offspring of European fathers (French, Canadian, Scottish, and English) and Native American mothers (Chippewa, Creek, Assiniboine). Many area residents claimed French-Chippewa ancestry. By 1850 more than half of the five to six thousand people living at Fort Garry were métis, with a large percentage being Canadian-born.

Settlers began moving into the region in 1849 with the organization of Minnesota Territory and the settlement of Iowa and Minnesota. This immigration brought a number of settlers to southeastern Dakota. Dakota Territory was created by an act of Congress on 2 March 1861 from the area that had previously been Nebraska and Minnesota territories. Overland migration to Montana brought settlers in conflict with the Native Americans, and several wagon trains were attacked. The government reacted by constructing a number of additional forts including Rice, Buford, Stevenson, Totten, and Ransom. Fort Pembina was established in 1870.

Steamboats improved transportation after 1871, but it was the railroads that truly opened North Dakota to the outside world. With the treaties signed by the Sioux in 1867 and 1868, the population of North Dakota increased from 16,000 people to 191,000 during the Dakota Boom years from 1879 to 1886.

Many of these settlers arrived in community groups: a group from Lansing, Michigan, settled in McIntosh County; a German-Russian group of fifty families settled Morton County; another of seventy-five families located in Emmons County; an Iowa colony settled in Logan County; and a group of 100 Pole families settled at Crystal Springs in Kidder County. For further information, see Harold E. Briggs, "The Great Dakota Boom, 1879–1886," *North Dakota Historical Quarterly* 4 (January 1930): 78-108.

Land could be purchased from either the Northern Pacific Railroad or directly from the federal government land offices under the Homestead or Timber Culture acts. The Pembina land office was opened in 1871; by 1890, under the 1841 pre-emption law 19,500 settlers had purchased three million acres. The speculation frenzy during the boom period was followed by retrenchment and abandonment. Those who stayed faced economic problems, drought, and low farm prices.

The genealogical researcher with ancestors in North Dakota should be aware of the three major themes in its history: 1) its remoteness, which resulted in late development and a

dependence on outside influences and economic changes; 2) the cool, sub-humid climate that required major adaptation by the immigrating families; and 3) an economy with low farm income and little manufacturing.

Major efforts encouraged immigration to North Dakota after statehood was obtained on 2 November 1889, creating a second population boom period. Articles describing mineral resources, timber, land, climate, livestock, and religious denominations were widely published. Of the approximately forty-five million acres of land, three-fourths were advertised as still susceptible to profitable tillage, and thirty million acres were still idle in 1892. Beginning in 1898 and ending with World War I, some 250,000 immigrants moved to the state, many of these foreign-born. Most of this settlement occurred along the Great Northern Railroad, the Missouri Plateau, and the Drift Prairie. Again, more people immigrated to the area than could be sustained, and later years brought more outward migration from the state.

Vital Records

A state law passed in 1893 made it mandatory to file vital records with township clerks. It was repealed in 1895 but reenacted in 1899.

The State Department of Vital Records was formed in 1923; all copies of prior birth and death information were required to be sent there. Copies of birth and death records beginning 1 July 1893 may be obtained from the North Dakota Department of Health, Division of Vital Records, 600 E. Blvd. Ave., Bismarck, ND 58505 <www.vitalnd.com>. Requests can be made from the website. Relationship information must be provided when requesting these records.

Marriage records generally date from county organization and can be obtained from the county judge of the county where the license was issued. Only marriage records after 1 July 1925 are on file at the Division of Vital Records in Bismarck.

All divorce proceedings are recorded by the clerk of the district court in each county.

Indexes to deaths from the turn of the twentieth century to present, marriages 1925 to present, and recent divorces in North Dakota are available in the State Historical Society Reading Room at the Heritage Center (see Archives, Libraries, and Societies).

The records from the Bureau of Indian Affairs include vital records such as birth, death, and marriage from the agencies of Fort Totten, Turtle Mountain, Standing Rock, and Fort Berthold. The National Archives—Central Plains Region (see page 12) maintains these records.

Census Records

Federal

Population Schedules

- Indexed—1850 as Pembina County, Minnesota Territory; 1860, as unorganized Dakota; 1870, as Dakota Territory; special 1885 (see below), 1900, 1910, 1920, 1930
- Soundex—1900, 1920

Industry and Agriculture Schedules

- Agriculture—1870, 1880

Mortality Schedules

- 1860, 1870, 1880 Indexed as Dakota Territory; 1885

Union Veterans Schedules

- 1890

The first federal census records available for this area can be found with the 1836 Iowa Territory census. North Dakota State Archives and Historical Research Library of the State Historical Society of North Dakota (see Archives, Libraries, and Societies) holds microfilmed copies of 1850 Pembina County Minnesota; 1860, 1870, and 1880 of Dakota Territory; the 1890 Union veterans and widows census; the 1900 census, including Soundex; and 1910 census. Dakota Territory agriculture schedules for 1870 and 1880 are on microfilm at the South Dakota State Historical Society.

State

The 1857 census for Pembina County, then part of Minnesota Territory, is located at the State Archives and Historical Research Library.

Part of the special, pre-statehood, federal 1885 census is available in print (see Collections under Background Sources). Only part of the indexing has been completed by AISI and is also available at <www.ancestry.com>. This schedule included a special veterans and mortality return. This and the unindexed 1915 and 1925 state censuses are available on microfilm at the State Archives and Historical Research Library and through interlibrary loan.

Native American

Several series of censuses were taken at the different reservations. Indexing is variable. Unless otherwise indicated, the State Archives and Historical Research Library retains these censuses:

- Fort Totten Reservation: 1885–1905, 1910–39
- Fort Berthold Reservation: 1889–93, 1895–1939
- Standing Rock Reservation: 1885–1913, 1915–39 (located at National Archives—Central Plains Region in Kansas City)

- Turtle Mountain Reservation: 1885–1905 (with Fort Totten Reservation), 1910–39
- Digger Indians: 1899–1904, 1915–20

Background Sources

Aberle, George. *Pioneers and Their Sons: 165 Family Histories.* 2 vols. Bismarck, N.Dak.: Tumbleweed Press, 1980.

Bye, John E. *Guide to Manuscripts and Archives.* Fargo, N.Dak.: North Dakota Institute for Regional Studies, 1985. An index is available at <www.discovernd.com/hist>.

Collections of the State Historical Society of North Dakota. 7 vols. Bismarck, N.Dak.: North Dakota Historical Society, 1906–25. Volume 4 (1913) contains a transcription of the 1885 census for some counties.

Hennesey, W. B. *Compendium of History and Biography of North Dakota.* Chicago: George A. Ogle & Co., 1900.

———. *History of North Dakota.* Bismarck, N.Dak.: Bismarck Tribune, 1910.

Lounsberry, Clement Augustus. *North Dakota History and People: Outlines of American History.* 3 vols. Chicago: S. J. Clarke, ca. 1916.

Miller, Michael M. *Researching Germans from Russia: An Annotated Bibliography.* Fargo, N.Dak.: North Dakota Institute for Regional Studies, 1987.

Robinson, Elwyn B. "The Themes of North Dakota History." *North Dakota History* 26 (January–October 1959): 5-24.

———. *History of North Dakota.* Lincoln, Nebr.: University of Nebraska Press, 1966.

Sherman, William C. and Playford V. Thorson, eds. *Plains Folks: North Dakota's Ethnic History.* Fargo, N.Dak.: North Dakota Institute for Regional Studies, 1988.

Ulvestad, Martin. *Norwegians in America.* 2 vols. (in Norwegian). This publication discusses Norwegian migration to North America, specifically North Dakota.

Wick, Douglas A. *North Dakota Place Names.* Bismarck, N.Dak.: Hedemarken Collectibles, 1988.

Williams, Mary Ann Barnes. *Origins of North Dakota Place Names.* Washburn, N.Dak.: the author, 1966.

Maps

The State Archives and Historical Research Library holds a one-reel microfilm index (Series 1121) to *Cartographic Records of North Dakota,* which are in the custody of the Bureau of Indian Affairs.

County plat books and atlases from 1884, including Andreas' *Historical Atlas of Dakota,* are housed at the archives as well as other repositories with North Dakota collections. A list of North Dakota county plat books and atlases is available at <www.discovernd.com/hist>.

See William C. Sherman, *Prairie Mosaic: An Ethnic Atlas of Rural North Dakota* (Fargo, N.Dak.: North Dakota Institute for Regional Studies, 1983), which will be most helpful, as will *Northwestern Gazetteer: Minnesota, North and South Dakota and Montana Gazetteer and Business Directory* (St. Paul: R. L. Polk and Co., 1914).

Land Records

Public-Domain State

The State Archives and Historical Research Library holds a few original records of the General Land Office (GLO) for North Dakota and a microfilmed copy of the Bureau of Land Management's (BLM) original tract books and survey plats (see Archives, Libraries, and Societies). The North Dakota Water Commission, State Office Building, 900 E. Blvd. Ave., Bismarck, ND 58505, maintains original township plats although patents and copies of tract books and plats are located at the BLM, P.O. Box 222, Billings, MT 59107. To search land patents, use the BLM website <www.glorecords.blm.gov>.

After initial purchase, the records of transfer of land at the county level remain in the office of the register of deeds. Most land records in North Dakota are extant at the county level from the time the county was organized.

Probate Records

The district court has original jurisdiction for probate and testamentary matters, the appointment and removal of administrators and guardians, and other probate action. Marriage licenses are issued by the county judge, who keeps those records on file. Request these records from the county clerk of court. Insanity records are also maintained in the office of the county judge.

Court Records

The State Archives and Historical Research Library (see Archives, Libraries, and Societies) holds some federal district court records for Dakota Territory from 1861 through 1889 on microfilm and some county level court records. However, the county's clerk of the district court is responsible for juvenile court records, naturalization records, coroner's juries and records, civil actions, jury lists, justice of the peace records,

liquor applications for medical use, judgment records, and criminal proceedings.

Tax Records

The county auditors have possession of the tax rolls in North Dakota. Some rolls date from statehood and/or organization of the county and may be available at the State Archives and Historical Research Library and the special collection at the Chester Fritz Library (see Archives, Libraries, and Societies).

Cemetery Records

The North Dakota Bureau of Vital Statistics holds an index to cemetery names (not individuals buried there), location, and date of organization of cemeteries in the state. Many cemetery transcripts have been compiled by local genealogical societies in separate publications or periodicals. They may be found in one of several North Dakota libraries.

Church Records

Predominant religious denominations in North Dakota history are Roman Catholic, Lutheran, Methodist, Episcopalian, and Presbyterian. Most extant records remain with the local church. Some records in manuscript, microfilm, or printed form can be found at the State Archives and Historical Research Library, the Chester Fritz Library, the North Dakota Institute for Regional Studies (see Archives, Libraries, and Societies), and the Family History Library (FHL).

Military Records

The Historical Research Library has the National Archives microfilm index to service records of Union soldiers in North Dakota.

The researcher should also check the *Official Roster of North Dakota Soldiers, Sailors and Marines in World War I, 1917–1918*, 4 vols. (Bismarck, N.Dak.: North Dakota State Historical Society, 1931). Other rosters exist for World War II and the Korean and Vietnam eras. Contact the Office of the Adjutant General, P.O. Box 551, Attention: SIDPERS, Bismarck, ND 58502.

Periodicals, Newspapers, and Manuscript Collections

Periodicals

North Dakota History (formerly *North Dakota Historical Quarterly*) is published by the State Historical Society of North Dakota. This is the major statewide periodical for historical material, publishing helpful background for research.

Newspapers

Newspapers from across the state have been collected at the State Archives and Historical Research Library since the turn of the century. All have been microfilmed and are available on interlibrary loan. An index of newspapers, arranged by county name and city name, is available.

Between 5 April 1931 and 28 October 1934, the *Fargo Forum* printed 173 profiles of pioneer women of North Dakota under the title "Quarter Sections and Wide Horizons." With few exceptions, all were living in Dakota Territory prior to statehood in 1889. The stories were written by Angela Boyelin, editor of the *North Dakota Clubwoman*.

A list of North Dakota newspapers available can be found on the State Historical Society of North Dakota website <www.discovernd.com/hist>.

Manuscripts

Three major manuscript collections exist in North Dakota. The first of these is located in the State Archives and Historical Research Library. David P. Gray's *Guide to Manuscripts* [of North Dakota] serves as a directory to the state historical society's manuscript collections and is available at <www.discovernd.com/hist>. Of note are the following groups of materials at the library:

Historical Data Project Biography (WPA) contains biographical information and consists of over 5,000 files gathered in the 1930s and organized by individual name and county. These files are microfilmed and available on interlibrary loan from the library.

The Necrology of North Dakota consists of six scrapbooks and obituaries from the years 1920 to 1926, and is held in the manuscript division of the state archives.

Photo Archives has over 60,000 black and white images from 1865 to present. Reprints can be made for a nominal fee.

Pioneer Mothers Project, indexed by individual name, was created by the North Dakota Federation of Women's Clubs in the 1930s and contains family histories, biographical entries, obituaries, and some lineage charts.

Chester Fritz Library's *Guide to Orin G. Libby Manuscript Collection* consists of three volumes, providing access to this second large group of materials on North Dakota. Volume one was compiled by John B. Davenport in 1975, volume two by Colleen A. Oihus in 1983, and volume three by Sandra J. Beidler in 1985.

The third collection includes a statewide biographical index of over 500 volumes and is located at the North Dakota Institute of Regional Studies.

Archives, Libraries, and Societies

State Archives and Historical Research Library
State Historical Society of North Dakota
12 E. Blvd. Ave.
Bismarck, ND 58505-0179
www.discovernd.com/hist

The archives and historical research library is operated as one unit by the State Historical Society of North Dakota and holds several categories of records that are discussed elsewhere. The staff will do a limited search in censuses and newspapers if specific information is known. *Guide to the North Dakota State Archives* (Bismarck, N.Dak.: State Historical Society of North Dakota, North Dakota Heritage Center, 1985) is available to assist in using the library's collection.

Many of the territorial records for the Dakotas are housed at the State Archives of North Dakota including Dakota Territorial Papers (1877–86), the Office of Indian Affairs Correspondence for the years 1824 through 1887, and the Indian Treaty negotiations between 1801 and 1869.

North Dakota State Library
Liberty Memorial Bldg.
Capitol Grounds
Bismarck, ND 58505
http://ndsl.lib.state.nd.us

The State Library holds printed volumes of source materials, as it is the primary library and coordinates the various libraries throughout the state. While its collection for genealogical research is limited, it does have county histories and other similar printed sources that circulate on interlibrary loan.

Chester Fritz Library
University of North Dakota
Grand Forks, ND 58202-9000
www.und.nodak.edu/dept/library

The family history room holds a variety of national and North Dakota printed source materials in addition to those cited in various sections above.

North Dakota Institute for Regional Studies
North Dakota State University Library
Fargo, ND 58105
www.lib.ndsu.nodak.edu

Manuscript sources here constitute one of the major collections in the state and include the Germans from Russia collection. They also have a biography index and access to the index for the *Fargo Forum* newspaper.

Bismarck-Mandan Historical and Genealogical Society
P.O. Box 485
Bismarck, ND 58502-0485
www.rootsweb.com/~ndbmhgs

As one of three genealogical societies producing publications, this association makes state research possible through the Historical Research Library. Other societies at Fargo (Red River Valley Genealogical Society <www.fargocity.com/~rrvgs/htmls/links.htm>) and Minot (Mouse River Loop Genealogical Society <www.mrlgs-nd.org>) have a more limited scope.

Bismarck Family History Center
1500 County W. Rd.
Bismarck, ND 58503

This is the main branch and one of eight family history centers of the FHL in North Dakota. Since the state has few archives and libraries that contain genealogical materials, the state's family history centers are an important resource for access to microfilm from the library in Salt Lake City (see Archives, Libraries, and Societies, p. 12)

The North Dakota State Genealogical Society website <www.rootsweb.com/~ndsgs> offers Internet addresses for other genealogical societies in the state.

Special Focus Categories

Naturalizations
Most of North Dakota's naturalization records have been transferred from the clerk of the district court offices in each county to the State Archives and Historical Research Library. These records represent the bulk of documentation pertaining to immigration and naturalization proceedings in the state. The records document individuals who became, or applied to become, citizens between 1873 and 1952. An index to all fifty-three county naturalization records can be found on the State Historical Society of North Dakota's website.

Ethnic Groups
North Dakota settlers who were immigrants to America came primarily from Norway and Canada, but others were from Germany, England, Ireland, Sweden, and Russia. By 1890 the foreign-born settlers made up forty-three percent of the population. These people, together with the children of foreign parents, actually comprised sixty-nine percent of North Dakota's families. In 1910, twenty-one percent of the residents were Norwegian, twenty percent were German (with about half of these from Russia), twelve percent were English and Celtic (Irish, Scottish, and Welsh), and five percent were descendants of earlier immigrants.

The Germans from Russia Heritage Society, 1008 E. Central Ave., P.O. Box 1671, Bismarck, ND 58501, has an in-depth collection of family files, obituaries, immigration records, and family and county histories for those with a German heritage

through Russia. Both North Dakota and national records are included. Another collection for this ethnic group is located at the North Dakota Institute for Regional Studies (see Archives, Libraries, and Societies), but, in addition, its biographical index identifies books and publications dealing with this group of immigrants.

The Bygdeboker (Bygde Books) that discuss Norwegian immigrants are located at the Chester Fritz Library and are available on interlibrary loan if they have been microfilmed.

See also Sherman and Thorson under Background Sources.

County Resources

The FHL holds the *Historical Records Survey of North Dakota* (Bismarck, N.Dak.: WPA, 1939). Although outdated, it remains a helpful guide. County records including land, court, tax, probate, and township records for North Dakota may be extant from time of formation. There may, however, be individual discrepancies, and the researcher will need to check with the local office for exact reference. The county judge holds marriage and probate records, the register of deeds holds land records, and the clerk of the district court holds civil court records. Details about county offices can be found on the Internet at <www. state.nd.us/sec/county_contacts/contacts>

Some records have been transferred to the State Archives and Historical Research Library (see State Historical Society website <www.discovernd.com/hist>). Since this is a continuing process, correspondence should be addressed to the county *first*, and if the records have been transferred, the letter will be forwarded. County offices can normally be addressed in care of the county courthouse; however, in the list below, addresses or post office boxes for registers of deeds are given.

For some counties on the chart there are two years listed for "Date Formed." The first is the year that the county was created; the second is the year it was fully organized if it differs from creation year. Under the heading "Parent County/ies," unorganized land denotes that it was formed from non-county lands, and counties listed with an asterisk (*) are those to which the county was at one time "attached" before organization.

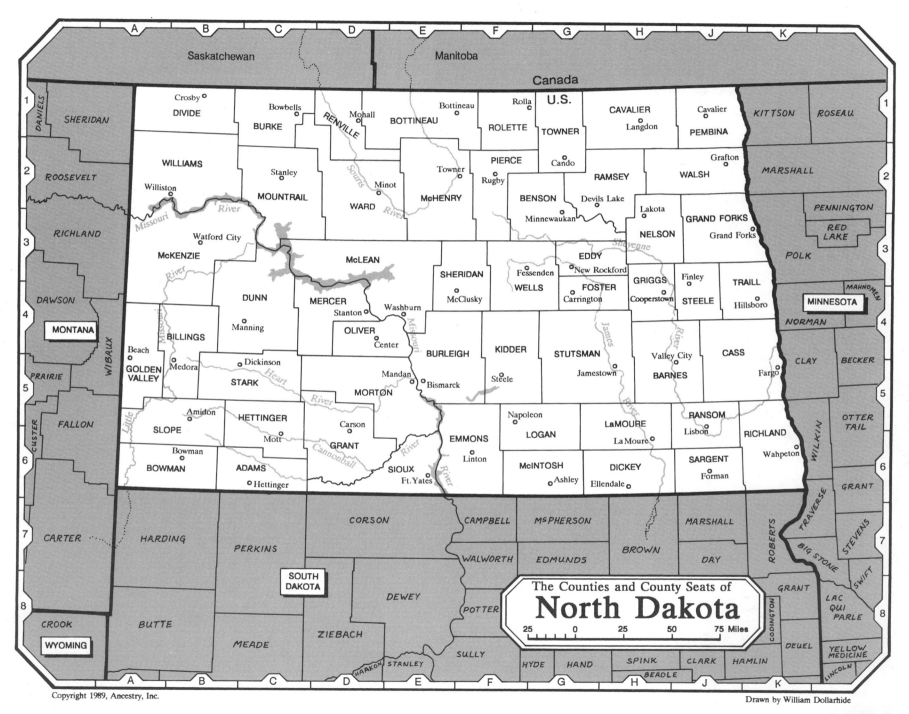

The Counties and County Seats of
North Dakota

25   0   25   50   75 Miles

NORTH DAKOTA

Drawn by William Dollarhide

Map	County Address	Date Formed Parent County/ies	Birth Marriage Death	Land Probate Court
C6	Adams P.O. Box 469 Hettinger 58639	1907 Hettinger	—— 1907	1907 1907 1907
	Allred	unorganized		

In 1896 Allred became a part of Billings; in 1901 Allred was re-created from Billings; in 1903 it was attached to Williams; and in 1905 it was abolished when it became part of McKenzie.

Map	County Address	Date Formed Parent County/ies	Birth Marriage Death	Land Probate Court
H5	Barnes Register of Deeds P.O. Box 684 Valley City 58072	1873 (as Burbank; renamed as Barnes, 1875) Pembina	1893–1910 1882 1893–1910	1875 1875 1875
G2	Benson 311 B Ave. Minnewaukan 58351	1883 Ramsey/De Smet	1903 1885 1903	1883 1883 1883
B4	Billings P.O. Box 138 Medora 58645	1879 (1886) unorganized/Howard	—— 1887 ——	1879 1879 1879
E1	Bottineau 314 W. Fifth Bottineau 58318	1873 (1884) Buffalo	—— 1884 ——	1884 1884 1884
A6	Bowman P.O. Box 379 Bowman 58623	1883 (1907) Billings	? 1907 ?	1883 1883 1883

In 1896 Bowman became part of Billings; in 1901 Bowman was re-created from Billings; in 1903 it was attached to Stark; and in 1907 it became fully organized.

Map	County Address	Date Formed Parent County/ies	Birth Marriage Death	Land Probate Court
	Buffalo	1864 (1871) Unorganized/Bruguier/Charles Mix *Bon Homme		

In 1873 Buffalo lost land to twenty-five counties in Dakota territory; in 1889 Buffalo became a county in the newly created state of South Dakota.

Map	County Address	Date Formed Parent County/ies	Birth Marriage Death	Land Probate Court
	Buford	1883 Wallette		

In 1891 Buford was attached to Ward; in 1892 it was abolished and became part of Williams.

Map	County Address	Date Formed Parent County/ies	Birth Marriage Death	Land Probate Court
	Burbank	1873 (renamed Barnes, 1875) Pembina		
C1	Burke P.O. Box 219 Bowbells 58721	1910 Ward	—— 1910 ——	1910 1910 1910
E5	Burleigh Clerk of District Court and Clerk of County Court 514 E. Thayer Ave. Bismarck 58501 and Register of Deeds 221 N. 5th St. Bismarck 58501	1873 Buffalo	—— 1898 1880; 1901*	1873 1873 1873
J5	Cass P.O. Box 2806 Fargo 58108 *1889–1920 at Fargo	1873 Pembina	—— 1872 1884–87*	1873 1873

Map	County Address	Date Formed Parent County/ies	Birth Marriage Death	Land Probate Court
H1	Cavalier 901 3rd St Langdon 58249	1873 (1884) Pembina	1884–1908 1887 1884–1908	1873 1873 1873
	De Smet	1873 (as French; renamed De Smet, 1875) Buffalo		

In 1887 De Smet was abolished and became part of Pierce.

Map	County Address	Date Formed Parent County/ies	Birth Marriage Death	Land Probate Court
H6	Dickey Register of Deeds P.O. Box 148 Ellendale 58436 *Incomplete	1881 La Moure/Ransom/ unorganized	1894–1900 1883 1894–1900*	1881 1881 1881
B1	Divide P.O. Box 68 Crosby 58730	1910 Williams	—— 1910 ——	1910 1910 1910
	Dunn (old)	1883 (became part of Stark, 1896) Howard		
C4	Dunn (present) P.O. Box 106 Manning 58642	1901 (1908) Stark	—— 1908 ——	1908 1908 1908
G3	Eddy 524 Central Ave. New Rockford 58356	1885 Foster	1889–1926 1887 1893–1907	1885 1885 1885
F6	Emmons P.O. Box 905 Linton 58552	1879 (1883) unorganized/Burleigh	1903 1888 1903	1879 1879 1879
	Flannery	1883 Wallette		

In 1891 Flannery was attached to Ward; in 1892 it was abolished and became part of Williams.

Map	County Address	Date Formed Parent County/ies	Birth Marriage Death	Land Probate Court
G4	Foster P.O. Box 257 Carrington 58421	1873 (1883) Pembina	—— 1883 ——	1873 1873 1873
A5	Golden Valley P.O. Box 596 Beach 58621	1912 Billings	—— 1912 ——	1912 1912 1912
J3	Grand Forks Register of Deeds P.O. Box 6 Grand Forks 58206	1873 (1875) Pembina	—— 1887* 1891*	1873 1873 1873

*Coroner's records and inquests for deaths; county judge has index to marriage certificates from 1875.

Map	County Address	Date Formed Parent County/ies	Birth Marriage Death	Land Probate Court
D6	Grant P.O. Box 258 Carson 58529	1916 Morton	—— 1916 ——	1916 1916 1916
H4	Griggs P.O. Box 326 Cooperstown 58425	1881 Foster/Burbank/Traill	1901–07 1883 1900–07	1881 1881 1881
	Gringras	1873 (renamed Wells, 1881) Buffalo		

Map County Address	Date Formed Parent County/ies	Birth Marriage Death	Land Probate Court
C6 Hettinger P.O. Box 668 Mott 58646	1883 (1907) Stark	—— 1907 ——	1883 1883 1883
Howard	1873 (abolished 1883; became part of Allred, Dunn, McKenzie, Wallace) unorganized		
F4 Kidder P.O. Box 66 Steele 58482	1873 (1881) Buffalo	1899–1907 1886 1885–1907	1873 1873 1873
H6 La Moure 202 4th Ave. N.E. La Moure 58458 *City auditor.	1873 (1881) Pembina	1903–23* 1887 1903–23*	1873 1873 1873
G6 Logan P.O. Box 6 Napoleon 58561	1873 (1884) Buffalo	1883–1923 1890 1883–1923	1873 1873 1873
E2 McHenry Register of Deeds P.O. Box 57 Towner 58788	1873 (1885) Buffalo	1889–1907 1905 1889–1907	1873 1873 1873
G6 McIntosh P.O. Box 179 Ashley 58413	1883 (1884) Logan/unorganized	1899–1908 1885 1899–1908	1883 1883 1883
McKenzie (old)	1883 (abolished 1896; became part of Billings 1897) Howard		
B3 McKenzie (present) Register of Deeds P.O. Box 523 Watford City 58854	(1901) 1905 Billings	1905–08 1906 1905–08	1905 1905 1905
In 1901 McKenzie was re-created but remained attached to Stark until it was fully organized in 1905.			
D3 McLean Register of Deeds P.O. Box 119 Washburn 58577	1883 Burleigh/Stevens/Sheridan	1884–1907 1887 1884–1907	1883 1883 1883
D4 Mercer P.O. Box 39 Stanton 58571 *Coroner's reports.	1875 unorganized	—— 1885 1909*	1875 1875 1875
D5 Morton 210 2nd Ave. N.W. Mandan 58554	1873 (1881) unorganized	1893–95 1882 1893–1908	1873 1873 1873
C2 Mountrail P.O. Box 69 Stanley 58784	1873 Buffalo	—— 1909 ——	1909 1909 1909
In 1891 Mountrail was attached to Ward; in 1892 it was abolished and became part of Ward; in 1909 it was re-created from Ward.			
H3 Nelson P.O. Box 565 Lakota 58344	1883 Foster/Grand Forks/Ramsey	? 1885 ?	1883 1883 1883
D4 Oliver P.O. Box 125 Center 58530	1885 Mercer	—— 1885 ——	1885 1885 1885
J1 Pembina Register of Deeds P.O. Box 147 Cavalier 58220 *Also births and deaths, 1899–1907.	1867 unorganized	1893–95* 1872 1893–95*	1867 1867 1867
F2 Pierce 240 S.E. 2nd St. Rugby 58368	1887 (1889) Bottineau/De Smet/McHenry/Rollette	1893–1903 1888 1893–1903	1887 1887 1887
G2 Ramsey P.O. Box 863 Devils Lake 58301	1873 (1885) Pembina	1903–09 1887 1903–09	1873 1873 1873
J5 Ransom Register of Deeds P.O. Box 666 Lisbon 58054 *Also coroner's records, 1883.	1873 (1881) Pembina	—— 1882 1892–1902*	1873 1873 1873
Renville (old)	1873 Buffalo (attached to Ward, 1891; abolished 1892; became part of Bottineau and Ward)		
D1 Renville (present) P.O. Box 68 Mohall 58761	1910 Ward	—— 1910 ——	1919 1919 1919
K6 Richland Register of Deeds P.O. Box 995 Wahpeton 58075 and Clerk of the County Court 413 3rd Ave. N. Wahpeton 58075 *Coroner's inquests.	1873 (1875) unorganized/Pembina	—— 1877 1883*	1873 1873 1873
F1 Rolette Register of Deeds P.O. Box 939 Rolla 58367	1873 (1884) Buffalo	1894–1929 1884 1894–1915	1873 1873 1873
J6 Sargent P.O. Box 176 Forman 58032 *Also coroner's inquests from 1899.	1883 Ransom/unorganized	—— 1886 1888*	1883 1883 1883
Sheridan (old)	1873 Buffalo (abolished 1892; became part of McLean)		
F3 Sheridan (present) P.O. Box 668 McClusky 58463	1908 McLean	—— 1909 ——	1909 1909 1909
E6 Sioux P.O. Box 345 Fort Yates 58538 *Superintendent of Indian reservation.	1914 Standing Rock Res.	1902* 1916 1902*	1915 1915 1915

Map	County Address	Date Formed Parent County/ies	Birth Marriage Death	Land Probate Court
B6	Slope P.O. Box II Amidon 58620	1914 (1915) Billings	—— 1915	1915 1915 1915
B5	Stark P.O. Box 130 Dickinson 58601	1879 (1883) Howard/Williams/unorganized	—— 1887 1893–94	1873 1873 1873
J4	Steele P.O. Box 275 Finley 58230	1883 Griggs/Traill	—— 1884 ——	1884 1884 1884
	Stevens	1873 Buffalo		

The original Stevens County was created in 1862 from unorganized land but was abolished in 1863. This Stevens County was attached to Ward in 1891 and was abolished in 1892 when it became part of McLean and Ward.

Map	County Address	Date Formed Parent County/ies	Birth Marriage Death	Land Probate Court
G5	Stutsman 511 2nd Ave. S.E. Jamestown 58401 *Clerk of district court.	1873 Pembina/Buffalo	—— 1884 1881*	1873 1873 1873
G1	Towner 315 Second St. Cando 58324	1883 (1884) Rolette/Cavalier	1903–07 1888 1903–27	1883 1883 1883
J4	Traill Register of Deeds P.O. Box 399 Hillsboro 58045 *Mayville only.	1875 Grand Forks/Burbank/Cass	—— 1880 1891*	1875 1875 1875

Map	County Address	Date Formed Parent County/ies	Birth Marriage Death	Land Probate Court
	Wallace	1883 Howard		

In 1896 Wallace was abolished and became part of Billings and Stark; in 1901 it was re-created from Billings and Stark but remained attached to Stark. In 1905 it was abolished again and became part of McKenzie.

Map	County Address	Date Formed Parent County/ies	Birth Marriage Death	Land Probate Court
	Wallette	1873 (abolished 1883; became part of Buford and Flannery) Buffalo		
J2	Walsh 600 Cooper Ave. Grafton 58237 *Filed in state records.	1881 Grand Forks/Pembina	—— 1882 ——	1881 1881 1881
D2	Ward Ward County Courthouse Minot 58701 *Coroner reports, clerk of district court.	1885 Renville/Stevens	—— 1888 1888*	1885 1885 1885
F3	Wells Register of Deeds P.O. Box 125 Fessenden 58438	1873 (as Gingras; renamed 1881) Buffalo	1893–1913 1887 1893–1913	1873 1873 1873
	Williams (old)	1873 (abolished 1892; became part of Mercer) unorganized		
B2	Williams (present) P.O. Box 2047 Williston 58801	1892 (1903) Buford/Flanery	—— 1892 ——	1890 1890 1890

Ohio

CAROL L. MAKI AND MICHAEL JOHN NEILL

René Robert Cavelier, Sieur de la Salle, the French explorer, traveled through Ohio land in 1667 and is thought to have been the first white person to see the Ohio River. Eighty years later, in 1747, the Ohio Company of Virginia was organized to colonize the Ohio River Valley, leading to the creation of the Ohio Land Company two years later. Great Britain gained control of the region following the French and Indian War in 1763, but lost it again in 1779.

The establishment of Northwest Territory in 1787 marked the beginning of a steady stream of migration. Scots-Irish from Virginia, Kentucky, and Pennsylvania settled mainly in Marietta in Washington County. New Englanders and Revolutionary War soldiers, most of them from Massachusetts and Connecticut, arrived in that same area. They were followed by settlers from Essex County, New Jersey, who located in Cincinnati in an area called the Symmes Purchase. French immigrants settled in Gallipolis, Gallia County, from 1790 through 1791. Additional Connecticut migrations occurred from 1796 to 1797, settling in the Connecticut Western Reserve. Others from Connecticut and Vermont settled in what became Geauga County three years later. Clermont County was the new home of settlers from Maine in 1796, the same year that emigrants from Scotland arrived in Montgomery County. In 1796 the Refugee Tract was established in Columbus for Canadians who sympathized with the American Revolution. Three years later Ohio Territory was created, followed in 1800 by the first Ohio territorial census and the opening of the first land offices at Marietta, Steubenville, Chillicothe, and Cincinnati. The territory became a state in 1803.

The influx of new settlers continued, with Germans and Welsh from Pennsylvania, plus additional migrations from Kentucky and Virginia. In 1803 Ohio obtained statehood. Three years later the United Society of Believers of Christ's Second Appearing (Shakers) migrated to Warren County. Germans settled in Brown and Tuscarawas counties from 1814 through 1824. The opening of the Erie Canal in 1825 was an opportunity for those in the northeastern United States to migrate to Ohio. The Mormons (see Church Records) arrived in Ohio in 1831. English and Irish emigrated to Ohio for railroad construction employment in the 1840s. By 1860, Ohio's extensive railroad construction provided more miles of track than any other state.

Ohio was intensely involved with the abolitionist movement prior to the Civil War, having considerable activity in the Underground Railroad along Lake Erie and the Ohio River. Following the Civil War, the state gained national political power, producing seven United States presidents. As an agricultural and industrial state, some early industries were barrel-making and meatpacking. The American Federation of Labor formed there in the 1880s. The industrialization and urbanization of Ohio brought new residents from eastern and southern Europe and African Americans from southern states. Mining became increasingly important with products of coal, limestone, and salt.

The twentieth century brought continued industrial strength under the power of capitalists like Benjamin F. Goodrich, Charles Franklin Kettering, and John D. Rockefeller. A multitude of Ohio manufacturers of this century have produced a diverse range of items from steam shovels to matches.

Vital Records

Ohio enacted a statute in 1856–57 that required birth, death, and marriage registration, a law that was generally disregarded. A later 1867 law again required registration of birth and death records. Some of these are extant. Two types of "death records" known to be in existence before 1867 are records of cholera deaths, registered during some epidemics, and veterans' deaths, representing only a small proportion of the deaths that occurred. The third law, which went into effect on 20 December 1908, set up the current recordkeeping system in Ohio.

For both birth and death registrations that exist prior to 20 December 1908, the county probate court is one place those records can be currently accessed. The Ohio Historical Society (see Archives, Libraries, and Societies) has a significant number of these records on microfilm as does the Family History Library (FHL) in Salt Lake City.

Birth records after 19 December 1908 to the present and death certificates from 1 January 1945 to the present are held by the Ohio Department of Health, Division of Vital Statistics, P.O. Box 15098, Columbus, OH 43215-0098 <www.odh.state.oh.us>.

The Ohio Historical Society holds copies of death certificates from 20 December 1908 through 31 December 1944, and currently has an online index for years 1913 to 1937 at <www.ohiohistory.org/dindex>. Indexes for later Ohio deaths (presently 1958–2000) are available through <www.ancestry.com>.

Some city health departments may have city birth and death records if separate records were kept.

Marriage records were kept by the office of the county probate clerks until 7 September 1949, when it became a state registration procedure. There is no statewide index of marriages before 7 September 1949. The statewide index to marriages begins with that date when certified abstracts of marriages were filed with the state. The Ohio Department of Health, Division of Vital Statistics will search indexes of these abstracts. However, certified copies of marriage records may only be obtained from the probate court of the county that issued the license (see County Resources).

Ohio marriages to approximately 1865 are included in the IGI (see pages 12-13) of the FHL. Marriage records in Ohio usually include the following information: names of bride and groom, date of marriage, county and possibly the specific location, officiating party, and ages and residences of the bride and groom.

The Ohio Historical Society and the Ohio Network of American History Research Centers (see Archives, Libraries, and Societies) are collecting centers for early birth, marriage, and death records and may be contacted regarding their holdings in addition to the county courthouse.

An index of some Ohio marriages is Marjorie Smith, ed., *Ohio Marriages, 1790–1897* (1977; reprint, Baltimore: Genealogical Publishing Co., 1986). The Ohio Genealogical Society has also published *Ohio Marriages Recorded in County Court Through 1820: An Index* (Mansfield, Ohio: the society, 1997). The information is extracted from the *Old Northwest Genealogical Quarterly*. Marriages, listed alphabetically by bride and groom, come from fifteen volumes of this periodical and begin in the early 1800s. This includes records from only nine counties.

Hamilton County has the jurisdiction for the registration of marriages for Cincinnati. However, many of those records were lost in a courthouse fire. Records that survived were indexed by the WPA and include applications, licenses, and returns. Genealogists have reconstructed marriage records from ministers' daybooks, original certificates, and newspaper accounts. Cincinnati was also a "Gretna Green" locale (meaning no questions were asked for marriages). Consequently, its marriage records should be checked for marriages not otherwise found in Ohio, Indiana, or Kentucky.

Reconstructed marriage records for Hamilton County have been published, as have marriage records for other counties.

Marriage records from family and local sources have also been collected by the Daughters of the American Revolution (DAR). The State Library of Ohio is the official depository for the state copies of DAR compilations. These records are listed in Carol W. Bell, *Master Index Ohio D.A.R. Genealogical and Historical Records*, vol. 1 (Westlake, Ohio: Mrs. Thomas B. Clark, 1985). Local genealogical societies have compiled numerous vital records indexes.

Since 1851, divorces have been handled by the county court of common pleas. Prior to 1851 the records can be found in the supreme court, the chancery court, or the court of common pleas, and then appealed through the legislature. See David G. Null's "Ohio Divorces, 1803–1852," *National Genealogical Society Quarterly* 69 (March 1981): 109-14, for a list of people granted divorces by the legislature between 1795 and 1852; and Carol Willsey Bell's, *Ohio Divorces: The Early Years* (Boardman, Ohio: Bell Books, 1994), which contains summaries of divorce cases from early county records through the 1860s.

Census Records

Federal

Population Schedules

- Indexed—1800 (Washington County only), 1810 (Washington County only—others burned 1812), 1820 (Franklin and Wood counties missing), 1830, 1840, 1850, 1860, 1870 (Cincinnati and Cleveland only), 1890 (fragment), 1900, 1910, 1920, 1930
- Soundex—1880, 1900, 1910 (Miracode), 1920

Industry and Agriculture Schedules

- 1850, 1860, 1870, 1880 (lists do not exist for all counties for each year); manufacturer's—1820 (very limited)

Mortality Schedules

- 1850 for counties H–W (published), 1860 all counties (published), 1870 (Seneca County only), 1880 (Adams to Geaugan counties only)

Union Veterans Schedules

- 1890

The Ohio Historical Society suggests that the duplicate tax lists of Ohio counties may be used as a substitute for the missing 1810 census. In addition to the indexes published by AISI (see pages 3-4), the 1850 and 1860 census records have been indexed and published by Lida Flint Harshman. The Ohio Genealogical Society (see Archives, Libraries, and Societies) has completed an every-name surname index from the original 1880 census it has in its possession. In addition to the online indexes through subscription services (see page 17), federal censuses for Ohio through 1870 are indexed in print form and available at Family History Centers and through several vendors.

The 1890 population census exists only for Cincinnati (Hamilton County) and Wayne Township (Clinton County) and is indexed in the microfilm index provided by the National Archives for the remaining 1890 census returns.

State

Ohio had no state census records. There are scattered county census records taken for militia purposes, plus personal and real estate tax lists, all of which have been incorrectly referred to as state census records. There are quadrennial enumerations taken every four years from 1803 to 1911 to determine voting districts. These include males (white only, prior to 1863) over twenty-one years of age residing in a county, showing address, race, occupation, and whether a freeholder of land. Not all counties are available for each four-year period, nor is each township for each county included. A list of the available records can be obtained from the Ohio Historical Society, where the enumerations are either on microfilm or in original form. This repository also holds "enumerations of school-aged youth" for selected years and counties.

The "Special Enumeration of Blacks Immigrating to Ohio, 1861–1863, by the Auditor of the State" (State Archives Series 2261) is microfilmed and can be purchased from the Ohio Historical Society Microfilm Department. The microfilm includes a four-part index, by name, previous residence, questionable names, and county of those African Americans who had migrated to the state between 1 March 1861 and 3 March 1863. Forty-seven counties scattered around the state responded with at least one name, resulting in a total of 1,375

names. The Ohio Genealogical Society (see Archives, Libraries, and Societies) has published many of these enumerations in its chapter's newsletters.

Background Sources

The Ohio Historical Society has an extensive collection of Ohio county histories, many of which are included in its Ohio County History Surname Index. An information sheet regarding the microfilmed edition and its index is available from the Ohio Historical Society.

For additional information see:

Bell, Carol Willsey. *Ohio Guide to Genealogical Sources.* Baltimore: Genealogical Publishing Co., 1988.

———. *Ohio Genealogical Guide.* 5th ed. Youngstown, Ohio: the author, 1990.

Bowman, Mary L. *Abstracts and Extracts of the Legislative Acts and Resolutions of the State of Ohio, 1803–1821.* Mansfield, Ohio: Ohio Genealogical Society, 1994. An additional volume printed in 1996 covers 1821–1831.

Colket, Meredith B., Jr. "Genealogical Material Relating to the Western Reserve." *National Genealogical Society Quarterly* 59 (1971): 281-82.

Dickore, Marie. "Genealogical Resources in the Cincinnati, Ohio Area." *National Genealogical Society Quarterly* 43 (1955): 1-5.

Fenley, Ann. *The Ohio Connection Formula for Finding Elusive Ancestors.* Dayton, Ohio: Ohio Connection, 1985.

Fess, Simeon D. *Ohio: A Four-Volume Reference Library on the History of a Great State.* Chicago: Lewis Publishing Co., 1937.

Gagel, Diane VanSkiker. *Ohio Courthouse Records.* Ohio Genealogical Society Research Guide Series, No. 1. Mansfield, Ohio: Ohio Genealogical Society, 1997.

Harter, Stuart, comp. *Ohio Genealogy and Local History Sources Index.* Fort Wayne, Ind.: the compiler, 1986.

Khouw, P., et al. *County by County in Ohio Genealogy.* Columbus, Ohio: State Library of Ohio, 1978.

Overton, Julie Minot. *Ohio Towns and Townships to 1900: A Location Guide.* Mansfield, Ohio: Ohio Genealogical Society, 2000.

Peters, Sunda Anderson and Kay Ballantyne Hudson, eds. *First Families of Ohio Roster, 1964–2000.* Mansfield, Ohio: Ohio Genealogical Society, 2001.

Robson, Charles, ed. *Biographical Encyclopedia of Ohio in the Nineteenth Century.* Cincinnati: Galaxy Publishing Co., 1876.

Sperry, Kip. *Genealogical Research in Ohio*. Baltimore: Genealogical Publishing Co., 1997.

Upton, Harriet Taylor. *History of the Western Reserve*. 3 vols. Chicago: Lewis Publishing Co., 1910.

Ohio has a very active statewide genealogical society, with local chapters throughout the state and several out-of-state chapters (see Archives, Libraries, and Societies). Contact the state or local groups for guidance in research for specific areas. The response is generally outstanding with letters answered promptly and courteously, sometimes being forwarded to possible "connections."

Maps

The earliest Sanborn insurance map for Ohio is an 1875 map for Zanesville, held by the Ohio Historical Society. Consult the Newberry Library, *Checklist of Printed Maps of the Middle West to 1800* (2 vols. Boston: G. K. Hall, 1980), although this is not an inclusive listing for maps in Ohio. It does not, for example include those held by the Western Reserve Historical Society (see Archives, Libraries, and Societies). Many academic and other libraries in Ohio have at least a partial collection of Sanborn maps on microfilm, and many libraries offer online access to Sanborn maps for the entire state of Ohio. Other excellent sources include:

Brown, Lloyd A. *Early Maps of the Ohio Valley: A Selection of Maps, Plans and Views Made by Indians and Colonials from 1673–1783*. Pittsburgh: University of Pittsburgh Press, 1959.

Kilbourn, John. *The Ohio Gazetteer, Or, Topographical Dictionary Containing A Description of the Several Counties, Towns, Etc.* Columbus, Ohio: J. Kilbourn, 1826.

Smith, Thomas H. *The Mapping of Ohio*. Kent, Ohio: Kent State University Press, 1977.

Walling, Henry F. *Atlas of the State of Ohio*. 1867. Reprint. Knightstown, Ind.: Bookmark, 1983. Delineates townships, railroads, roads, and geographical features as of 1868.

Land Records

Public-Domain State

Virginia, New York, Connecticut, and Massachusetts claimed portions of land in this part of Northwest Territory based on charters granted by the kings of England. In 1778 the congressional committee proposed that these states cede their western lands. New York ceded in 1781, Virginia in 1784, Massachusetts in 1785, and Connecticut in 1786 and 1800. Both Virginia and Connecticut reserved lands in Ohio as part of the cession compromise.

In 1784 the first congressional committee was appointed to prepare a plan for disposal of federal lands north of the Ohio River. The Land Act of 20 May 1785 set up a rectangular survey system (see page 6) reserving one section in each township of thirty-six sections for the support of public schools. Originally, section twenty-nine in each township was reserved for religious purposes until 1833, when Congress authorized the State of Ohio to sell these sections.

The following is a list and description of Ohio's land tracts, which were the basis of initial government-to-individual transfers of land:

Virginia Military District. Land in twenty-three Ohio counties from the Ohio River north between the Scioto and Little Miami rivers was reserved by Virginia to satisfy its military bounty warrants. One of the original nine major subdivisions in Ohio, it is the only one not using a rectangular survey system. In 1852 Virginia ceded all unclaimed lands to the federal government, which in turn ceded these remaining lands to Ohio in 1875. Soldiers' applications are filed in the Virginia State Library in Richmond (see Virginia). Volume four (in two parts) of Clifford Neal Smith's *Federal Land Series* (see page 6), deals exclusively with land in the Virginia Military District.

Connecticut Western Reserve. Fourteen northeastern counties starting at the Pennsylvania line, bordered by Lake Erie to the north, and west 120 miles, including the Fire Lands (see below), encompassed this agreement with Connecticut. Records are at the Connecticut State Library (see Connecticut), although the Western Reserve Historical Society has an extensive collection.

Fire Lands. This area, including the west end of the Connecticut Western Reserve, was given to Connecticut supporters of the American Revolution who suffered losses because of the destruction of nine Connecticut towns by the British and Tories.

Seven Ranges. Located in southeastern Ohio on the Ohio River, these were the first public lands to be surveyed in the United States.

Moravian Indian Grants. Three separate tracts of 4,000 acres each in Tuscarawas County were reserved in 1785 for the "use of the Christian Indians who formerly settled there, or the remains of that society." This was because of the slaughter of nine innocent Christian Native Americans in 1782, in retaliation for hostile raids on settlers in West Pennsylvania and Virginia.

Refugee Tract. Located in central Ohio, it runs forty-two miles east from the Scioto River and was granted to Canadian (1783) and Nova Scotian (1785) refugees who abandoned their settlements and fled to the United States to aid the colonial cause during the Revolutionary War.

Dohrman Tract. Arnold Henry Dohrman was granted this tract in 1787 to compensate for disallowed expenditures and his

humanitarian efforts as an agent of the United States for the revolutionary cause.

The Ohio Company. Over 1.5 million acres were negotiated from the federal government in southeastern Ohio in 1787 by the Ohio Company. But only 750,000 were included when the company failed to raise money for the whole piece (first purchase). A second purchase of over 200,000 acres was added in 1792. Records are at Marietta College Library, Marietta, Ohio.

Donation Tract. One hundred thousand acres were granted in 100-acre lots to any male, eighteen or older, who would settle on the land at the time of the conveyance. It was to be a buffer between the settlers in the Ohio Company and the native population.

Symmes Purchase. Known also as the Miami Purchase, it was acquired in 1794 and privately surveyed in southwestern Ohio from the Ohio River twenty-four miles northward between the Great Miami and the Little Miami Rivers. Fire has destroyed most of the records, although the Hamilton County Recorder's Office has two extant volumes.

French Grants. The first grant, in Scioto County on the Ohio River, consisted of 24,000 acres given to the French in 1795, who were swindled by the Scioto Company. An additional smaller grant was made in 1798.

U.S. Military District. Bounty land granted the Continental army officers and soldiers in 1796 containing 2.5 million acres was bounded north by the Greenville Treaty Line, east by the Seven Ranges, south by the Refugee Tract and Congress Lands, and west by the Scioto River.

Zane's Tracts. Three tracts of land, 640 acres each, were granted to Ebenezer Zane for laying out a road (Zane's Trace) from Wheeling, Virginia (now West Virginia) to Limestone (now Maysville), Kentucky.

Congressional Lands. After other sales and grants, Congress had two remaining tracts—one east of the Scioto River, one west of the Miami River.

The Auditor of the State, 88 E. Broad St., 5th Floor, Columbus, OH 43266-0541; the National Archives; and the BLM—Eastern States Office in Alexandria, Virginia (see page 6) all have records dealing with some aspect of government-to-individual transfers of land.

For explanations of greater detail, see William E. Peters, "Ohio Lands and Their History," *Bulletin of the History and Philosophy Society of Ohio* 15 (1957): 340-48; his *Ohio Lands and Their Subdivision*, 2d ed. (Athens, Ohio.: the author, 1918); and his seventeen-volume typescript, "Code of Land Titles in Ohio. A Compilation from Official Records of All Charters, Indian Treaties, Grants..." (1935). See also Kenneth Duckett, "Ohio Land Patents," *Ohio History* 72 (1963): 51-60. Available free from the state auditor and publisher are *Ohio Lands: A Short History*, a short information booklet, and *The Building of Ohio*, a small map showing all the land grants in Ohio.

Mayburt Stephenson Reigel's *Early Ohioans' Residences from the Land Grant Records* (Mansfield, Ohio: Ohio Genealogical Society, 1976) concerns some records that are in the state archives section of the Ohio Historical Society and not those in the custody of the auditor of the state. The author searched twenty-four volumes of records, including those for land offices at Cincinnati, Steubenville, Chillicothe, Canton-Wooster, Zanesville, and Marietta, plus the Refugee Tract and the Donation Tract Lands. The first mention of each name, in each place of residence, and in each land office, is listed. The place of residence may assist a genealogist in determining from where the ancestor migrated. Researchers must be aware in using this source that it includes very limited extractions from the twenty-four volumes.

Ellen T. Berry and David A. Berry, *Early Ohio Settlers: Purchasers of Land in Southeastern Ohio, 1800–1840* (Baltimore: Genealogical Publishing Co., 1984) also summarizes the records of the Marietta Land Office. The alphabetically arranged entry gives the date, name, and residence of the purchaser, and the location of the land. Also, see the following by the same authors and publisher: *Early Ohio Settlers, Purchasers of Land in South Western Ohio* (1986), which indexes the records of the Cincinnati Land Office, and *Early Ohio Settlers, Purchasers of Land in East and East Central Ohio* (1989). Carol Willsey Bell, *Ohio Lands: Steubenville Land Office, 1800–1820* (Youngstown, Ohio: the author, 1983), includes an every-name index to this series of records.

Marie Clark Taylor compiled two helpful books: *Ohio Lands South of the Indian Boundary Line* (Chillicothe, Ohio: the compiler, 1984) and *Ohio Lands: Chillicothe Land Office, 1800–1829* (Chillicothe, Ohio: the compiler, 1984).

The Bureau of Land Management Office has a searchable index of patents for Ohio on its website <www.glorecords.blm.gov> but the searchable database does not include sales of federal land made on credit before 1820.

The Newberry Library in Chicago has very good resources on land records and boundary disputes for Ohio. Included in its collection are works on the Scioto Land Company and the Ohio Company, plus the microfilmed Ohio Land Grant Records (1788–1820).

Once granted by the federal government, subsequent transactions involving that land are recorded at the county recorder's office in deed books.

Probate Records

The court of common pleas was responsible for probate and estate records beginning in 1797. Since 1851, probate functions have been under the jurisdiction of the probate court. Indexes are available in each probate office. Some probate records are

on microfilm at the Ohio Historical Society and the FHL. The county probate court holds guardianship, name changes, insanity proceedings, naturalization, marriage records from the beginning of the county, and birth and death records (1867–1908).

Adoptions in Ohio are processed through the probate court. Access to adoption records is restricted. For those prior to 1939, the probate court must be petitioned. From 1 January 1939 to 1 January 1964, adopted persons or their lineal descendants can obtain information from the supervisor of special records at the State Department of Health in Columbus (see Vital Records).

Indexes are available in each probate office, while some records are accessible on microfilm at the Ohio Historical Society and the FHL. An excellent source is Carol Willsey Bell, *Ohio Wills and Estates to 1850: An Index* (Columbus, Ohio: the author, 1981), which includes an excellent introduction, cites entries for records no longer in existence, and references documents in county courthouses. A county records manager, or similar office, has been created in some Ohio counties. This office may hold records generated by chancery courts, petition to partition land to settle an estate, probate journals, and probate case files.

Court Records

From the time of the Northwest Ordinance in 1787 until 1802, three judges held courts in Ohio Territory, but the records are scarce. In 1804, a year after statehood, the territory was organized as one district court at Chillicothe. Considerable reorganization, divisions, and transfers later occurred in the system.

Many other kinds of records are found in Ohio county court records. Vital records, naturalizations (in probate court after 1851), and military pension applications are examples of items possibly found in the county court of common pleas located at the county seat until 1851, and later in the state supreme court files. Land records, deeds, and miscellaneous volumes can at times include records of court proceedings.

Bell's *Ohio Guide to Genealogical Sources* (see Background Sources) details the various county court records that can be located at each county seat, many of which are available on microfilm through either the Ohio Historical Society or the FHL. The County Resources section in this chapter indicates only the first known court record of any kind for the county.

Some court records may be deposited at the Ohio Network of American History Research Centers. See David Levine, "Ohio's Court System," in Ohio Genealogical Society, *The Report* 20 (Winter 1980): 171-74.

Some holdings for the Ohio circuit court are at the National Archives—Great Lakes Region. Refer to its inventory for details on the northern division: Cleveland (1855–1962) and Toledo (1869–1962); and the southern division: Cincinnati (1803–1962), Columbus (1877–1962), and Dayton (1915–62).

Tax Records

Tax records for Ohio began as early as 1800. The archives section of the Ohio Historical Society has a collection of original Ohio tax lists from the state auditor's office. It includes lists from the county's organization to 1838, usually arranged by county and township. They are not indexed. Esther Weygandt Powell has included many of them in *Early Ohio Tax Records* (Akron, Ohio: the author, 1971), beginning about 1800. The book does not include all the tax lists at the archives, nor does it include tax lists for all counties. It does, however, provide an excellent source to document many early Ohio families. The reprint of this book (Baltimore: Genealogical Publishing Co., 1985) includes a surname index. County courthouses hold various tax records that have not been inventoried. They are in the office of the county auditor or the county records manager.

The FHL has microfilm copies of all known extant tax records (1800–38) for Ohio. AISI produced *Index to Ohio Tax Lists, 1800–10* (Bountiful, Utah: AISI, 1977) and Gerald Petty has compiled *Ohio 1825 Tax Duplicates* (Columbus, Ohio: Petty's Press, 1897). A similar volume by Petty for 1835 is also available.

The National Archives—Great Lakes Region (see page 12) retains numerous federal tax records for Ohio. These include assessment books (1867–73) and corporate and personal records for District 10–Toledo, and District 11–Columbus.

Cemetery Records

According to the Ohio Genealogical Society, the majority of Ohio counties have published cemetery records in one form or another. The society suggests contacting local societies or one of the major genealogical libraries in the state.

Ohio Cemeteries (Ohio Genealogical Society, 1978), edited by Maxine Hartmann Smith, is a listing comprising all known cemeteries included in several sources. It is organized by county and by township, alphabetically, with an index by cemetery name. Included are concise locations of the cemetery and publication information. *Ohio Cemeteries: Addendum* (Baltimore: Gateway Press, 1990), edited by Teresa L. M. Klaieber, includes updates and revisions to the previous volume. County chapters of the Ohio Genealogical Society can be contacted regarding cemetery information in their counties.

See also *Ohio Cemetery Records: Extracted from the "Old Northwest" Genealogical Quarterly* (Baltimore: Genealogical Publishing Co., 1984), which includes an every-name index by Elizabeth P. Bentley and covers northeastern and central Ohio, and the Ohio Adjutant General's Office, *Grave Registration of Soldiers Buried in Ohio* (Salt Lake City: Genealogical Society of Utah, 1958).

Church Records

Religion in Ohio was an early and important factor in settlement. The first Moravian mission was established in 1772. Presbyterians and Quakers were in the state at an early date, the latter having established forty-three monthly meetings and settlements between 1801 and 1883. The Presbyterians founded seventeen towns between 1784 and 1799. Baptists, Congregationalists, several reformed groups, Lutherans, Disciples of Christ, United Brethren, Methodists, and Catholics arrived prior to 1850. By 1890 the latter two denominations were the largest in the state. The Methodist circuit in Ohio was organized in 1798, with circuit riders traveling from log cabins to camp meetings across the territory. In 1831 members of The Church of Jesus Christ of Latter-day Saints migrated from New York to Kirtland in Lake County. No thorough survey exists of any of the holdings of individual churches in Ohio, although many are on microfilm through the FHL. The Ohio Genealogical Society is presently undertaking a church records survey.

Historical Records Survey for Ohio produced an *Inventory of the Church Archives of Ohio Presbyterian Churches* (Salt Lake City: Genealogical Society of Utah, 1967). Records of the Quakers in the Miami Valley and the Church of the Brethren of the Southern District of Ohio are available on microfilm through the FHL. Some Ohio Quaker records may be found in William Wade Hinshaw, *Encyclopedia of American Quakers* (Ann Arbor, Mich.: Edwards Brothers, 1936). The Western Reserve Historical Society has an extensive Shaker manuscript collection. Bluffton College in Bluffton, Ohio, has Mennonite records.

Military Records

There is a long list of published (printed and/or microfilmed) Ohio military records that are available through the FHL and throughout many genealogical libraries. These include records from the Civil War, Mexican War, American Revolution, War of 1812, Spanish-American War, and World War I. An excellent listing can be found in Bell's *Ohio Guide to Genealogical Sources* (see Background Sources).

Loyalist records are an important resource in Ohio. A large concentration of loyalist material is available at the Ohio Historical Society, the Blegen Library at the University of Cincinnati, and Miami University in Oxford, Ohio.

Ohio did not grant state pensions, but the office of the State of Ohio, Adjutant General's Department, Room 11, State House Annex, Columbus, OH 43266-0605, holds the records for those who served in the War of 1812 through the Vietnam era. The collection consists only of wartime records with no published indexes available across its holdings. The office does not hold information on national pension records. The Civil War index is on microfilm and is available through the FHL.

Information from service records will be supplied for an individual at no charge, but full name, birth date, and other available information should be submitted if possible. Records for the War of 1812 are sketchy. A sample provided by the adjutant general's department gave the roll of various companies, giving the service dates of the unit and the members of the company, with their rank. A service number for World War II and Korea is very helpful. For Vietnam, a social security number is necessary.

The Ohio Historical Society holds a number of Civil War regimental histories on microfilm that may be purchased from the society. The society also has a War of 1812 roster of Ohio soldiers that can be searched at its site. This database contains the names of 1,759 officers and 24,521 men who were enlisted in this war. A genealogically important and impressive, although not inclusive, resource is the "Graves Registration File" at the society, which includes several hundred microfilm reels with information on Ohio burial places for veterans through the Vietnam era. Microfilm cards state name, war of service, date of death and burial site, and occasionally additional details on military service or family. The society will search the reference for a fee.

Military records located at the county level may include soldiers' discharge and/or burial information.

Periodicals, Newspapers, and Manuscript Collections

Periodicals

Ohio History has been published by the Ohio Historical Society since 1887. It was previously called *Ohio Archaeological and Historical Quarterly* and *Ohio Historical Quarterly*. An online version through 2002 is available free at <http://publications.ohiohistory.org>.

The Report, Ohio Records and Pioneer Families, and *Civil War Genealogy Journal* are published by the Ohio Genealogical Society with excellent local history, problem-solving techniques, and original source material.

Also see:

Bell, Carol Willsey. *Ohio Genealogical Periodical Index: A County Guide.* Youngstown, Ohio: the author, 1987. Subject index to publications of genealogical and historical societies.

Newspapers

The *Centinel of the North-Western Territory* was published in Cincinnati ten years before Ohio became a state. Its first issue was dated 9 November 1793. This newspaper, and some issues of the *Chillicothe Gazette,* the oldest paper in continuous publication

west of the Alleghenies, are available at the Ohio Historical Society, along with a limited number of newspaper indexes.

Many local historical societies and public libraries have obituary files. The German Immigrant Society of Cincinnati has a clipping collection of 1,700 obituaries.

There have been several projects for the compilation and indexing of newspapers in Ohio. These are primarily done on an individual newspaper or county basis. Some may be obtained by contacting county historical or genealogical societies. A microfiche catalog of newspapers available at the Ohio Historical Society, published in 1990, may be purchased from the society.

Also consult Karen Mauer Green, *Pioneer Ohio Newspapers, 1802–1818* (Galveston, Tex.: Frontier Press, 1988), which is a compilation of abstracts of genealogical data and "mentions" of people from six Ohio newspapers. It includes articles from newly formed settlements in Indiana, Illinois, and Michigan. The book has an every-name, place-name, and subject index. Green has also published *Pioneer Ohio Newspapers, 1793–1810* (Galveston, Tex.: Frontier Press, 1986), which covers five early Ohio newspapers. The cities most prevalent in these indexes are Chillicothe, Cincinnati, Marietta, and Steubenville. Further information is in Stephen Gutgesell, *Guide to Ohio Newspapers, 1793–1973, Union Bibliography of Ohio Newspapers Available in Ohio Libraries* (Columbus, Ohio: Ohio Historical Society, 1974). The Ohio Historical Society provides microfilmed newspapers on an interlibrary loan basis. A catalog of available newspapers may be ordered from the society, and bibliographic information is available on its website.

Manuscripts

The manuscript division of the Ohio Historical Society includes as primary subjects: Northwest Territory and early statehood, the Civil War, religion, African Americans, women, labor, politics, and mass communication. Particularly notable are the Wilbur Siebert Collection, which includes American Loyalists and the Underground Railroad; land grants signed by George Washington and Thomas Jefferson; Henry O. Dwight's watercolor drawings of the Civil War; and Ohio AFL-CIO records. For details see Andrew D. Lentz, ed., *A Guide to Manuscripts at the Ohio Historical Society* (Columbus, Ohio: Ohio Historical Society, 1972).

Kermit J. Pike, *A Guide to the Manuscripts and Archives of the Western Reserve Historical Society* (Cleveland, Ohio: Western Reserve Historical Society, 1972) surveys this excellent collection including oral histories of Western Reserve women.

The Ohio Genealogical Society's manuscript collection includes Bible records and First Family of Ohio applications, the latter proving ancestry in Ohio prior to 1820.

See also Draper Manuscripts under Wisconsin— Manuscripts.

Ohio Network Centers (see page 528) should be contacted for their pertinent manuscript collections.

Archives, Libraries, and Societies

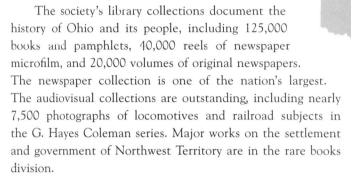

Ohio Historical Society

Archives Library Division
1985 Velma Ave.
Columbus, OH 43211
www.ohiohistory.org

The society's library collections document the history of Ohio and its people, including 125,000 books and pamphlets, 40,000 reels of newspaper microfilm, and 20,000 volumes of original newspapers. The newspaper collection is one of the nation's largest. The audiovisual collections are outstanding, including nearly 7,500 photographs of locomotives and railroad subjects in the G. Hayes Coleman series. Major works on the settlement and government of Northwest Territory are in the rare books division.

The society houses (at the above address) the State Archives of Ohio, with more than 30,000 cubic feet of state and local government records. The society's website contains a number of online databases, including the Ohio Death Certificate Index (1913–37), a searchable database of Ohio Civil War flags, and an Ohio newspaper bibliography. The society also serves the central Ohio counties as part of the Ohio Network of American History Research Centers. The academic journal *Ohio History* is published by the society and has been indexed from 1887 to 2000. The *Directory of Historical Organizations in Ohio* can be obtained from the society as well.

State Library of Ohio

Genealogy Division
274 E. First St.
Columbus OH 43201
http://winslo.state.oh.us/services/genealogy/index.html

The Genealogy Division holds microfilm; printed, typescript, and manuscript collections, including family and local histories; atlases; cemetery records; city directories; military records; censuses and census indexes; and transcribed records provided by the Ohio chapters of the DAR. See "The State Library of Ohio," in the Ohio Genealogical Society's *The Report* 23 (Winter 1983): 187-88, for a description of the holdings of the State Library of Ohio.

Ohio Genealogical Society

713 S. Main St.
Mansfield, OH 44907
www.org.org

Membership includes a quarterly, *The Report*, and the monthly *OGS Newsletter*. The society also publishes two additional quarterlies: *Ohio Records and Pioneer Families*, and the *Ohio Civil War Genealogy Journal*, available through a

separate subscription. The society has annual meetings, 100 county chapters, the Families of Ohio lineage society, and publishes various items of genealogical and historical interest. This library contains over 15,000 volumes, family vertical files, Bible records, ancestors cards, manuscript files, census microfilm, and a broad variety of other valuable resources for research in Ohio. A response to a written request for general and specific information is answered promptly, cordially, and very thoroughly.

Western Reserve Historical Society
10825 East Blvd.
Cleveland, OH 44106
www.wrhs.org

Its extensive manuscript collection (published guide available by mail) is supplemented by an equally extensive microfilm collection of federal census returns, Shaker records, and the National Archives Revolutionary War pension records. The society also has an extensive collection of printed Ohio material. The society serves as the network center (see below) for its area and charges a per-day fee for nonmembers.

Ohio Network of American History Research Centers

Established in 1970 to aid in the collection, preservation, and accessibility of research materials related to Ohio history, the network is composed of seven institutions—Ohio's two largest historical societies and five state universities. A central feature of the network is the division of the entire state into seven distinct geographical areas for research. Each center also collects county records for its area, but the amount of material available may vary greatly from county to county.

Archives Services
University of Akron Libraries
Polsky Bldg.
Akron, OH 44325-1702
Serves Region 1—East Central Ohio

Center for Archival Collections
Jerome Library
Bowling Green State University
Bowling Green, OH 43403-0175
Serves Region 2—Northwest Ohio

Archives and Rare Books Department
Blegen Library—8th Floor
University Libraries
University of Cincinnati
Cincinnati, OH 45221-0113
Serves Region 3—Southwest Ohio

Archives—Library Division
Ohio Historical Society
1985 Velma Ave.
Columbus, OH 43211
Serves Region 4—Central Ohio

Archives and Special Collections
Alden Library
Ohio University
Athens, OH 45701-2978
Serves Region 5—Southeast Ohio

Western Reserve Historical Society
10825 East Blvd.
Cleveland, OH 44106
Serves Region 6—Northeast Ohio

Special Collections and Archives
Paul Laurence Dunbar Library
Wright State University Library
Dayton, OH 45435-0001
Serves Region 7—West Central Ohio

For information about the network and service of its centers, contact either the specific center or headquarters at the Ohio Historical Society.

Special Focus Categories

African American
Consult the following when researching African Americans in Ohio:

Alilunas, Leo. "Fugitive Slave Cases in Ohio Prior to 1850," *Ohio State Archaeological and Historical Quarterly* 69 (1940): 160-84. See other issues of this particular periodical for additional articles on African Americans in Ohio.

Fuller, Sara, ed. *The Ohio Black History Guide.* Columbus, Ohio: Ohio Historical Society, 1975.

Gerber, David Allison. *Black Ohio and the Color Line, 1860–1915.* Urbana: University of Illinois Press, 1976.

Hickock, Charles Thomas. *The Negro in Ohio, 1802–1870.* 1896. Reprint. New York: AMS Press, 1975.

Nitchman, Paul E. *Blacks in Ohio.* 7 vols. Ft. Mead, Md.: the author, 1987.

Turpin, Joan. *Register of Black, Mulatto and Poor Persons in Four Ohio Counties, 1791–1861.* Bowie, Md.: Heritage Books, 1985.

Wesley, Charles Harris. *Ohio Negroes in the Civil War.* Publications of the Ohio Civil War Centennial Commission, no. 6. Columbus, Ohio: Ohio Historical Society, 1962.

The Archives—Library Division of Ohio Historical Society publishes *Selected Bibliography of Black History Sources at the Ohio Historical Society* and holds the state auditor's "Special Enumeration of Blacks Immigrating to Ohio, 1861–1863," State Archives Series 2261, and the *Palladium of Liberty*, the state's first African-American newspaper (see Census Records section for information on 1863 census of African Americans).

The Afro-American Museum, Wilberforce, Ohio 45385, is the first national museum of its kind.

Native American

Twelve to fifteen thousand native inhabitants were said to have been living in Ohio country when the first European settlers arrived. The Miami lived in the western part of Ohio, and the Wyandotte were in the northwest. The Huron, the Ottawa, and the Seneca were also in the northwest. The Shawnee tribe was located in the lower Scioto Valley, the Delaware in the Muskingum Valley, the Tuscarora in the northeastern section of that valley, and the Mingo occupied the east.

In the mid-1700s, the French and the English began their long struggle for possession of the region. The English victory was followed by the battles of the American Revolution; the native inhabitants of Ohio were tragically involved in both of these wars. When the bloodshed was over between the two European factions, the contest for the land began in earnest between white and native. By the end of the Revolutionary War, still unwilling to give up their domain, the natives struggled to maintain their lands for twelve long years. In the summer of 1794, at the battle at Fallen Timbers, Anthony Wayne and his well-trained troops totally defeated the Native Americans of Ohio. The following year, in August of 1795, a treaty was negotiated—the final step in taking away native homelands. The last group of Native Americans left northwestern Ohio in 1833.

See Stewart Rafert, "American-Indian Genealogical Research in the Midwest: Resources and Perspectives," *National Genealogical Society Quarterly* 76 (September 1988): 212-24. See also Wisconsin—Native American Records.

Other Ethnic Groups

The introductory section of this chapter identified some of the various ethnic groups that settled in Ohio. Western Reserve Historical Society is notable in its collection of materials on the ethnic immigrants to Ohio. Two helpful sources are:

Maxwell, Fay. *Irish Refugee Tract Abstract Data and History of Irish Acadians.* Columbus, Ohio: Maxwell Publications, ca. 1974.

Smith, Clifford Neal. *Early Nineteenth Century German Settlers in Ohio, Kentucky and Other States.* McNeal, Ariz.: Westland Publications, 1984.

County Resources

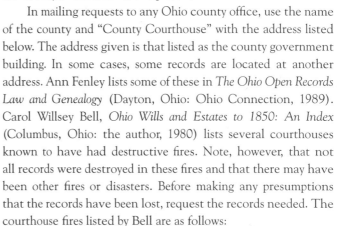

Ohio generally does not have any birth and death records prior to 1867. From 1867 to 1908 birth and death records were recorded at the probate court office in the county where the event occurred. After 1908 the event was recorded at the county's health department and also with the Vital Records Office in Columbus. A marriage record before 1949 (see Vital Records) will be found in the probate court office of the county where the event occurred. Deeds will be found in the county recorders office from the county's formation to the present.

In mailing requests to any Ohio county office, use the name of the county and "County Courthouse" with the address listed below. The address given is that listed as the county government building. In some cases, some records are located at another address. Ann Fenley lists some of these in *The Ohio Open Records Law and Genealogy* (Dayton, Ohio: Ohio Connection, 1989). Carol Willsey Bell, *Ohio Wills and Estates to 1850: An Index* (Columbus, Ohio: the author, 1980) lists several courthouses known to have had destructive fires. Note, however, that not all records were destroyed in these fires and that there may have been other fires or disasters. Before making any presumptions that the records have been lost, request the records needed. The courthouse fires listed by Bell are as follows:

Adams, 1910; Belmont, 1980; Brown, 1977; Champaign, 1948; Columbiana, 1976; Crawford, 1831; Delaware, 1835; Fayette, 1828; Franklin, 1879; Fulton, before 1860; Gallia, 1981; Hamilton, 1814, 1849, 1884; Henry, 1847; Licking, 1875; Monroe, 1840, 1867; Seneca, 1841; and Trumbull, 1895.

The following list of counties indicates the county seat; the year the county was created; if different, the year it was fully organized for record keeping (in parentheses); and the parent county from which it was formed. Under parent county are some county names with an (*) to indicate that records may also be found there since the county may have been "attached" to those other counties for some period in its history.

The date listed for each record category is the earliest record known to exist in that county. It does not indicate that there are numerous records for that year and certainly does not indicate that all such events that year were actually registered. In some cases there may be lapses in records after the beginning year listed. For example, Adams County has birth and death records beginning in 1888, but only through 1893.

In addition to sources used for all states (see page 16), information for the County Resources section was obtained from Bell's *Ohio Guide to Genealogical Sources* (see Background Sources) and the following:

Fenley, Ann. *Ohio Open Records Law and Genealogy.* Dayton, Ohio: Ohio Connection, 1989.

OHIO

The Counties and County Seats of
Ohio

Drawn by William Dollarhide

Map	County Address	Date Formed Parent County/ies	Birth Marriage Death	Land Probate Court
H3	Adams 110 W. Main West Union 45693	1797 Hamilton/Washington	1888 1910 1888	1797 1849 ——
C2	Allen 301 N. Main St. Lima 45802	1820 (1831) Shelby/Logan *Mercer	1867 1831 1867	1831 1835 1831
C5	Ashland W. Second St. Ashland 44805	1846 Huron/Lorain/Richland/Wayne	1867 1846 1867	1846 1846 1846
A8	Ashtabula 25 W. Jefferson St. Jefferson 44047	1808 (1811) Geauga/Trumbull	1867 1812 1867	1798 1811 ——
G6	Athens Athens 45701	1805 Washington	1867 1817 1867	1792 1800 1807
D2	Auglaize 201 Willipie St. Wapakoneta 45895	1848 Allen/Mercer	1867 1848 1867	1835 1852 1848
E8	Belmont 101 W. Main St. St. Clairsville 43950	1801 Jefferson/Washington	1867 1803 1867	1800 1804 1804
H2	Brown Georgetown 45121	1818 Adams/Clermont	1867 1818 1867	1818 1817 1818
G1	Butler 101 High St. Hamilton 45012	1803 Hamilton	1856 1803 1856	1803 1851 1803
D7	Carroll 119 Public Sq. Carrollton 44615	1833 Columbiana/Harrison/ Jefferson/Stark/Tuscarawas	1867 1833 1867	1826 1833 1833
E3	Champaign 200 N. Main Urbana 43078	1805 Franklin/Greene	1867 1805 1867	1806 1804 1805
E3	Clark P.O. Box 1008 Springfield 45502	1818 Champaign/Greene/Madison	1867 1818 1867	1818 1818 1818
H2	Clermont 76 S. Riverside Batavia 45103	1800 Hamilton	1856 1801 1856	1800 1810 1801
G3	Clinton 46 S. South St. Wilmington 45177	1810 Highland/Warren	1868 1817 1867	1806 1810 1810
C8	Columbiana 105 S. Market St. Lisbon 44432	1803 Jefferson	1867 1803 1867	1798 1803 1803
E6	Coshocton 349 1/2 Main St. Coshocton 43812	1810 (1811) Muskingum/Tuscarawas	1867 1811 1867	1800 1811 1811
C4	Crawford 112 E. Mansfield St. Bucyrus 44820	1820 (1826) Delaware *Seneca*/*Sandusky/*Huron	1866 1831 1860	1816 1831 1831
B6	Cuyahoga 2905 Franklin Blvd. NW Cleveland 44113	1808 (1810) Geauga	1867 1810 1868	1810 1811 1823
E1	Darke Fourth and Broadway Greenville 45331	1809 (1817) Miami	1867 1817 1867	1822 1818 1817
B1	Defiance 500 Court St. Defiance 43512	1845 Henry/Paulding/Williams	1867 1845 1867	1823 1845 1845
E4	Delaware 91 N. Sandusky Delaware 43015	1808 Franklin	1867 1835 1867	1807 1812 1818
B5	Erie 323 Columbus Ave. Sandusky 44870	1838 (1838) Huron/Sandusky	1856 1838 1856	1837 1838 1838
F5	Fairfield 210 E. Main, Rm. 301 Lancaster 43130	1800 Ross/Washington	1867 1803 1867	1801 1803 1801
F3	Fayette 110 E. Court Washington Courthouse 43160	1810 Highland/Ross	1867 1810 1868	1810 1810 1882
E4	Franklin 373 S. High St. Columbus 43215	1803 Ross/unorganized	1867 1803 1867	1800 1805 1803
A2	Fulton 210 S. Fulton Wauseon 43567	1850 Henry/Lucas/Williams	1867 1864 1867	1835 1853 1850
H5	Gallia Locust St. Gallipolis 45613	1803 Washington	1864 1803 1867	1803 1803 1811
B7	Geauga Chardon 44024	1806 Trumbull	1867 1803 1867	1795 1806 1806
F2	Greene 45 N. Detroit St. Xenia 45385	1803 Hamilton/Ross/	1869 1803 1870	1798 1803 1802
E7	Guernsey 801 E. Wheeling Ave. Cambridge 43725	1810 Belmont/Muskingum	1867 1810 1867	1802 1812 1810
G1	Hamilton 1000 Main St. Cincinnati 45202	1790 original	1863 1808 1881	1787 1790 1844
C3	Hancock 300 S. Main Findlay 45840	1820 (1828) Logan/Delaware *Wood	1867 1828 1867	1820 1828 1828

OHIO

Map	County Address	Date Formed Parent County/ies	Birth Marriage Death	Land Probate Court
D3	Hardin Kenton 43326	1820 (1833) Logan/Delaware	1867 1833 1867	1831 1830 1833
E7	Harrison Cadiz 43907	1813 Jefferson/Tuscarawas	1867 1813 1867	1812 1813 1814
B2	Henry 660 N. Perry Napoleon 43545	1820 (1834) Logan/Shelby *Wood/*Williams	1867 1847 1867	1846 1847 1847
G3	Highland P.O. Box 825 Hillsboro 45135	1805 Adams/Clermont/Ross	1867 1805 1868	1804 1809 1805
F5	Hocking 1 E. Main St. Logan 43138	1818 Athens/Ross/Fairfield	1867 1818 1867	1818 1819 1818
D6	Holmes 1 E. Jackson St. Millersburg 44654	1824 (1825) Coshocton/Tuscarawas/Wayne	1867 1821 1867	1808 1825 1825
B5	Huron 2 E. Main St. Norwalk 44857	1809 (1815) Portage/Geauga *Cuyahoga	1867 1818 1867	1809 1815 1818
H5	Jackson Jackson 45640	1816 Athens/Gallia/Ross/Scioto	1867 1816 1867	1816 1819 1816
D8	Jefferson 301 Market St. Steubenville 43952	1797 Washington	1867 1803 1867	1795 1798 1803
D5	Knox 106 E. High St. Mt. Vernon 43050	1808 Fairfield/Franklin	1867 1808 1867	1808 1808 1808
A7	Lake 47 N. Park Place Painesville 44077	1840 (1840) Cuyahoga/Geauga	1867 1840 1867	1839 1853 1840
J5	Lawrence 1 Veterans Sq. Ironton 45638	1815 (1817) Gallia/Scioto	1864 1817 1867	1818 1846 1817
E5	Licking Courthouse Sq. Newark 43055	1808 Fairfield	1875 1809 1875	1800 1875 1809
D3	Logan P.O. Box 429 Bellefontaine 43311	1818 Champaign	1867 1818 1867	1810 1851 1804
B5	Lorain 308 Second St. Elyria 44035	1822 (1824) Cuyahoga/Huron/Medina	1867 1824 1867	—— 1840 1824
A3	Lucas 800 Adams St Toledo 43624	1835 Wood/Sandusky	1867 1835 1868	1808 1835 1835
F3	Madison 1 N. Main St. London 43140	1810 Franklin	1867 1810 1888	1810 1810 1810
C8	Mahoning 120 Market St. Youngstown 44503	1846 Columbiana/Trumbull	1856 1846 1856	1795 1846 1847
D4	Marion 100 N. Main St. Marion 43302	1820 (1824) Delaware	1867 1824 1867	1821 1825 1824
C6	Medina 93 Public Sq. Medina 43302	1812 (1818) Portage	1867 1818 1867	1818 1818 1818
G6	Meigs Second St. Pomeroy 45769	1819 Athens/Gallia	1867 1819 1867	1819 1820 1819
D1	Mercer 101 N. Main Celina 45822	1820 (1824) Darke/Shelby	1867 1838 1867	1823 1824 1824
E2	Miami 215 W. Main St. Troy 45373	1807 Montgomery	1853 1807 1867	1807 1807 1804
F7	Monroe 101 N. Main St. Woodsfield 43793	1813 (1815) Belmont/Guernsey/ Washington	1867 1866 1867	1836 1840 1818
F2	Montgomery 451 W. Third St. Dayton 45402	1803 Hamilton	1867 1803 1866	1805 1803 1803
F6	Morgan 19 E. Main St. McConnelsville 43756	1817 (1819) Guernsey/Muskingum/ Washington	1867 1819 1867	1795 1819 1819
D4	Morrow 48 E. High St. Mt. Gilead 43338	1848 Delaware/Knox/ Marion/Richland	1867 1848 1867	1848 1848 1848
E6	Muskingum 401 Main St. Zanesville 43701	1804 Fairfield/Washington	1867 1804 1867	1800 1804 1804
F7	Noble Caldwell 43724	1851 Guernsey/Monroe/Morgan/ Washington	1867 1851 1867	1851 1851 1851
B4	Ottawa 315 Madison St. Port Clinton 43452	1840 Erie/Lucas/Sandusky	1867 1840 1869	1820 1840 1840
C1	Paulding 115 N. Williams St. Paulding 45879	1820 (1839) Shelby/Darke *Williams/*Wood	1867 1839 1867	1835 1842 1839
F5	Perry New Lexington 43764	1818 Fairfield/Muskingum/ Washington	1867 1818 1867	1818 1817 1818

OHIO

Map	County Address	Date Formed Parent County/ies	Birth Marriage Death	Land Probate Court
F4	Pickaway Circleville 43113	1810 Fairfield/Franklin/Ross	1867 1810 1867	1810 1810 1810
G4	Pike 100 E. Second Waverly 45690	1815 Adams/Ross/Scioto	1867 1815 1867	1799 1817 1815
B7	Portage 203 W. Main Ravenna 44266	1808 Trumbull	1867 1808 1867	1795 1803 1809
F1	Preble Eaton 45320	1808 Butler/Montgomery	1867 1808 1867	1805 1808 1808
C2	Putnam 245 E. Main St. Ottawa 45875	1820 (1834) Shelby/Logan *Wood/*Williams	1857 1834 1867	1830 1835 1834
C5	Richland 50 Park Ave., East Mansfield 44903	1808 (1813) Franklin *Knox	1856 1813 1890	1814 1813 1819
G4	Ross 2 N. Paint St. Chillicothe 45601	1798 Adams/Hamilton/Washington	1867 1798 1867	1797 1797 1798
B4	Sandusky 100 N. Park Fremont 43420	1820 Huron	1867 1820 1867	1822 1820 1820
H4	Scioto 602 Seventh St. Portsmouth 45662	1803 Adams	1856 1804 1856	1803 1810 1809
B4	Seneca 103 S. Washington St. Tiffin 44883	1820 (1824) Huron/Sandusky	1867 1841 1867	1821 1828 1824
D2	Shelby Sidney 45365	1819 Miami	1867 1824 1867	1819 1825 1819
C7	Stark 110 Central Plaza S., 5th Floor Canton 44702	1808 (1809) Columbiana/Muskingum	1867 1809 1867	1809 1810 1809
B7	Summit 209 S. High St. Akron 44308	1840 (1840) Medina/Portage/Stark	1866 1840 1870	1840 1839 1840
B8	Trumbull 160 High St., N.W. Warren 44483	1800 Jefferson/ Wayne County of Northwest Territory	1867 1803 1867	1795 1803 1807
D7	Tuscarawas 101 E. High Ave. New Philadelphia 44663	1808 Muskingum	1867 1808 1867	——— 1809 1808
D4	Union 5th & Court St. Marysville 43040	1820 Delaware/Franklin/ Logan/Madison	1867 1820 1867	1811 1820 1820
C1	Van Wert 101 E. Main St. Van Wert 45891	1820 (1837) Darke/Shelby *Mercer	1867 1840 1867	1824 1840 1837
G5	Vinton 100 E. Main St. McArthur 45651	1850 Athens/Gallia/Hocking/ Jackson/Ross	1867 1850 1867	1850 1852 1850
G2	Warren 320 E. Silver St. Lebanon 45036	1803 Hamilton	1867 1803 1867	1795 1803 1803
F7	Washington 205 Putnam St. Marietta 45750	1788 unorganized	1867 1789 1867	1788 1789 1790
C6	Wayne 428 W. Liberty Wooster 44691	1808 (1812) *Columbiana/*Stark	1867 1813 1867	1813 1817 1812
A1	Williams 1 Courthouse Sq. Bryan 43506	1820 (1824) Darke/Shelby *Wood	1867 1824 1867	1824 1825 1824
B3	Wood 1 Courthouse Sq. Bowling Green 43402	1820 Logan	1867 1820 1867	1820 1820 1823
C3	Wyandot 109 S. Sandusky Ave. Upper Sandusky 43351	1845 Crawford/Hancock/ Hardin/Marion	1867 1845 1867	1826 1845 1845

Oklahoma

WENDY BEBOUT ELLIOTT, Ph.D., FUGA

Oklahoma's background, formation, and organization are unique among the states. Developed out of "Indian Territory" (a name originating in the 1830s) and Oklahoma Territory (created in 1890), numerous jurisdictional and boundary changes are part of the state's history.

The region alternated between French and Spanish possession until 1803, when it became part of the United States' Louisiana Purchase from France. A few forts and settlements cropped up along the Red River as the area successively fell under the territorial jurisdiction of Louisiana (1805), Missouri (1812), and Arkansas (1819).

As early as 1804, efforts were made to negotiate the removal of southeastern tribes to west of the Mississippi River. The period of largest removal occurred between 1825 and 1842 when the federal government forced relocation to what eventually became western Arkansas and eastern Oklahoma. The region was established as a home, "as long as the grass shall grow and rivers run," for the Five Civilized Tribes (Creek, Cherokee, Chickasaw, Choctaw, and Seminole), who were displaced from their previous homes in the south and southeast by the U.S. government and its citizens. The routes traveled became known as the "Trail of Tears" because of the grief and loss experienced by Native Americans during their uprootings. Once relocated, the five tribes again set up their own governments as they had in their previous homes, established a newspaper, built towns, and organized schools and farms. Forts Gibson, Washita, and Towson were erected to protect the Native Americans from intruding U.S. citizens and raiding Plains tribes.

When the United States acquired the Republic of Texas in 1845, what would later become Oklahoma's panhandle ostensibly belonged to Texas. In 1850 Congress purchased the panhandle strip, but this "No Man's Land" remained separate from Indian Territory or any other territory or state. During the 1850s, railway companies pressured the government to open the unassigned lands in the panhandle strip, and in 1854 Congress confined Indian Territory only to present-day Oklahoma, excluding the panhandle strip. Prior to the Civil War, the Chickasaw and Choctaw nations leased the southwestern third of the present-day state to the United States as hunting grounds for the Plains tribes.

During the Civil War, internal dissension among the tribes arose as some members served the Union, while others supported the Confederate cause, and still others tried to stay neutral. A much larger percentage favored the Confederate cause, and the Five Civilized Tribes officially supported the Confederacy.

At the conclusion of the Civil War, the federal government, partly to make provision for free African Americans to own land and partly as a response to Native American support of the Confederacy, demanded a new set of treaties in 1866. These treaties reduced the original size of the reservations and permitted other tribes to be moved into the area. Within the next seventeen years, many other tribes were relocated to Oklahoma. The greater part of the Cherokee Outlet (along the northern border with Kansas) and a desirable tract in the center of Oklahoma remained "Unassigned."

Between 1865 and 1889, cattlemen, railroaders, soldiers, and settlers lived within Indian Territory's borders before

settlement was legally permitted. Some had taken advantage of the loopholes in the law allowing artisans and professionals to contract with tribes for labor.

In 1872 the first railroad was established through the area connecting Missouri, Kansas, and Texas. Indian Territory was called "the promised land" as it offered fine grazing land and the possibility of free land. Major trails such as the Chisholm, Great Western, East Shawnee, West Shawnee, Couch, Payne, and Plummer ran between cattle land in Texas and grazing and farmland in Kansas.

In April 1880, in defiance of federal authorities, David L. Payne crossed the Kansas/Oklahoma border and marched with a band of twenty-one "Boomers" (those who promoted opening of the territory for settlement) to the center of Indian Territory, commonly called "Oklahoma country." The trail they blazed was followed by other Boomers over the next five years.

A major settlement transition occurred in 1889. The previous sixty years had marked the arrival in Indian Territory of sixty-five different tribes, including the Five Civilized Tribes. However, agitation for opening these lands to nonnative settlement increased until the federal government purchased a clear title to the central tract, called "Unassigned Lands," and on 22 April 1889 the first official "run" for these homestead lands occurred. Prospective homesteaders lined up along the South Canadian River and Indian Territory boundary lines to await the signal to begin. Others, called "Sooners" (because they did not wait), jumped the gun. This contributed to many court cases where landownership was contested and also gave rise to the state's nickname—the Sooner State.

An estimated 50,000 people settled the tract in a day, marking the shift from native to nonnative settlement. Oklahoma City became a "tent colony" with more than 10,000 people. Other large towns settled that day were Guthrie, Kingfisher, and Norman.

Many "land run" trails into the area led southward from Kansas. These included the Wild Horse, Ponca, Black Bear, and Caldwell trails. Stage routes ran south from Kansas, west from Arkansas, and east from Fort Reno. The Butterfield Stage route left Fort Smith, Arkansas, and ran southwest to the Red River. A wagon road closely followed the North Canadian River through Potawatomie land. Through a joint effort of a number of railroad companies, a line was completed from Guthrie to Kingfisher and beyond to Seward.

The present-day state of Oklahoma was divided into two governmental divisions, Oklahoma Territory and Indian Territory, in May 1890. Indian Territory encompassed the eastern half of the state and the Cherokee Outlet along the Kansas border. Oklahoma Territory included the panhandle, called "No Man's Land," and an area that stretched from the southwestern section, including Greer County northeast to the Kansas border, called "Unassigned Lands." At this point county governments began to emerge in Oklahoma Territory.

During the 1890s cattlemen were prohibited from the practice of leasing grazing grounds from the tribes. Congress forced the Native Americans to accept individual land allotments for each member of their tribes instead of holding the land in common. The Dawes Commission was established in 1893 to register individual Native Americans, allot the land, and assist and supervise the government in changing from a tribal to a state organization. In response to vehement demand, additional tracts were opened for land runs or homesteading in 1891, 1892, 1893, 1895, 1901, 1904, and 1906.

By 1900 Oklahoma Territory had burgeoned to encompass more than the western half of the present state, while Indian Territory was dwindling to a smaller part of the eastern section. Greer County, formerly under Texas jurisdiction, became legally attached to Oklahoma Territory in 1896. In June 1906 Congress provided for the admission of Oklahoma Territory and Indian Territory to the Union as one state, if both nonnatives and natives approved. On 16 November 1907, President Theodore Roosevelt proclaimed Oklahoma the forty-sixth state. Oklahoma City supplanted Guthrie as the capital in 1910.

Mineral and ore deposits drew many settlers, some directly from Europe. Coal and petroleum products still represent a large portion of the state's output. With the spectacular rise of the petroleum industry, the state entered a prosperous era that helped it survive declines in the livestock industry and in the value of dry-farming produce. By the 1930s, six railroads served the state, converging in Oklahoma City.

The state's population of residents with Native American heritage remains one of the highest in the United States. The dual history of native relocation and nonnative settlement remains important in the use of records kept for genealogical research.

Vital Records

Statewide recording of births and deaths began in October 1908, although compliance was incomplete for several years in most counties and for as much as two decades or longer in others. Registration was mandated in 1917, but it was another decade before 90 percent compliance was attained. Although county clerks record births and deaths and provide information on request, certificates are available only from the Vital Records Section, State Department of Health, 1000 N.E. Tenth St., P.O. Box 53551, Oklahoma City, OK 73152 <www.health.state.ok.us/program/vital/brec.html>. Purpose and relationship statements are required. Early birth certificates contain much less information than those recorded currently.

Since statehood, marriage and divorce records are maintained by the clerk of the court in the county in which the

license was issued or divorce granted. Some marriage records are also available at the county level for Oklahoma Territory before statehood. Some of these have been published, such as Frances Murphy Bode, *Oklahoma Territory Weddings* (Geary, Okla.: Blaine County People and Places, Pioneer Book Committee, 1983), based on newspaper notices and county records for Blaine, Caddo, and Kingfisher counties. Numerous publications for marriage records are included in Laura Martin, *Oklahoma Marriages: A Bibliography* (Oklahoma City: Library Resources Division, 1996).

Tribal records at the Oklahoma Historical Society (see Archives, Libraries, and Societies) contain some earlier birth records in relationship to land allotments (see Land Records) as well as death records. Children of mixed marriages may be included in the births.

Some Native American and county vital records have been published by individuals and organizations. Several examples follow:

Ashton, Sharron Standifer. *Indians and Intruders.* 5 vols. Norman, Okla.: Ashton Books, 1996–2002. These publications include birth, marriage, and death records as well as numerous other abstracted records.

Bogle, Dixie. *Cherokee Nation Births and Deaths, 1884–1901.* Utica, Ky.: Cook and McDowell Publishers, 1980. Available at the Family History Library (FHL) in Salt Lake City as well as numerous other libraries.

Oklahoma Genealogical Society. *Index to Marriage Records, Oklahoma County, O. T., 1889 to 1907.* Oklahoma City: Oklahoma Genealogical Society, 1993.

Talkington, N. Dale. *Birth and Death Notices in Oklahoma and Indian Territories from 1871.* Houston, Tex.: the author, 1999. Abstracts of nearly 2000 records.

Tiffee, Ellen, and Gloryann Hankins Young. *Oklahoma Marriage Records, Choctaw Nation, Indian Territory.* 10 vols. Norman, Okla.: University of Oklahoma Press, 1969–78. Individually indexed, the data was abstracted from U.S. court records, second division for the period 1890 to 1907. Area covered includes today's counties of McCurtain, Latimer, Hughes (part), LeFlore, Bryan (part), Pittsburg, Choctaw, Atoka, Haskell, Pushmataha, and Coal (part). This set is available at the FHL as well as numerous other libraries.

Some marriage records for the Five Civilized Tribes and some other tribes are also at the Oklahoma Historical Society. Others are at the National Archives—Southwest Region (see page 12). Nonnative settlers whose marriages were recorded in U.S. Federal District Court records for Indian Territory are included. Marriage records (June 1890–1907) in Indian Territory may be located in the office of the court clerk in either Muskogee or Pittsburg counties. After 1895, marriage records may be found in county court clerk offices in Carter or Craig. Still others may be found in Atoka, Bryan, Latimore, and LeFlore counties. Creek County marriages may have been recorded in the cities of Bristow,

Drumright, Sapulpa, or Muskogee, the latter now in Muskogee County. There is no centralized index for these marriages.

Some indexes to marriage records are available online, such as those in the Chickasaw Nation at <www.chickasawhistory.com/m_index.htm>; and more than 2000 marriage notices taken from newspapers (1898–1906) for Old Greer County, Oklahoma Territory (today's Greer, Harmon, and Jackson counties) at <www.rootsweb.com/~okgreer/olgrmarr.html>.

Census Records

Federal

Population Schedules
- Indexed—1860 (partial), 1900, 1910, 1920, 1930
- Soundex—1900, 1910 (Miracode), 1920

Slave Schedules
- 1860 (partial)

Union Veterans Schedules
- 1890 (Oklaoma Territory and Indian Territory)

Those who were not Native American but who were residing in Indian Territory were enumerated in the federal census of 1860. These schedules are recorded under "Indian Lands" and follow the enumeration for Yell County, Arkansas, in the microfilm editions. Some Native Americans were also included in the slave schedules of 1860. See Sharron Standifer Ashton, "1860 Slave Schedules: Indian Lands West of Arkansas," *Oklahoma Genealogical Society Quarterly* 36 (June 1991): 67-71, and Frances Wood, *Indian Lands West of Arkansas (Oklahoma) Population Schedule of the United States Census of 1860* (n.p.: Arrow Printing Co., 1964).

In the 1890 and 1900 census enumerations, the present-day state was divided into Oklahoma Territory and Indian Territory. None of the population returns for 1890 survived, but returns for both territories in the special schedule enumerating Union veterans and widows of Union veterans of the Civil War in 1890 are available on one microfilm reel. The only extant population census enumerations for 1890 for Indian Territory is for the Cherokee Nation (see Census Records—Native American, below). An Internet site for an index to the 1890 Oklahoma Territorial Census is <www.ok-history.mus.ok.us/lib/1890/1890index.htm>.

Census enumerations for 1900 for both Oklahoma and Indian territories are on separate microfilm reels. Reel numbers for the area called "Oklahoma" follow those for Ohio but include only schedules for Oklahoma Territory counties, Oklahoma Territory Indian Reservations, and Indian military and naval jurisdictions. The 1900 census for Indian Territory is grouped separately in microfilm reels following the territories of Wyoming,

Alaska, and Hawaii. Indicating a final resolution to the dispute over jurisdiction of Greer County, which functioned as part of Texas between 1886 and 1896, Greer County was included in the 1900 Oklahoma Territory census. In 1910 the first federal census for the state of Oklahoma was enumerated.

Microfilm copies of all these federal census returns are at the Oklahoma Historical Society, National Archives, other major libraries, and the FHL.

Native American

• Cherokee—1880, 1890, 1896

The Cherokee Nation took its own censuses in 1880 and 1890, and according to the Indian Archives at the Oklahoma Historical Society, the censuses are considered fairly accurate. The originals are at the Indian Archives where microfilm copies are available for sale but not for interlibrary loan. Other repositories may have copies. In 1896, in association with the Dawes Commission in determining Cherokee citizenship, another census was taken but is not considered as accurate, with many claims of citizenship eventually overturned.

Other enumerations are included at the Indian Archives, Oklahoma Historical Society, and among the Bureau of Indian Affairs resources (see page 16). Some published censuses of Native Americans include:

Hook, Charlene. *1851 Census Drennen Roll of Cherokee and Court Claims Records.* Tulsa, Okla.: Indian Nations Press, 195–.

Wagner, Rosalie, comp. *Cherokee Nation 1890 Census, Index of Persons Living Under Permit in the Coo-Wee-Scoo-Wee and Delaware Districts.* Vinita, Okla.: Northeast Oklahoma Genealogical Society, 1986.

Territorial

An Oklahoma Territory census was taken in June 1890 for the seven territorial counties. Finding aids include a card index at the Oklahoma Historical Society and James W. Smith, *Smith's First Directory of Oklahoma Territory: For the Year Commencing August 1st, 1890* (Guthrie, Okla.: the author, 1890). Brian Basore, *Basore's Name Finding List for Smith's First Directory of Oklahoma Territory August 1, 1890* (Oklahoma City: Oklahoma History Society) is a helpful guide to the unindexed directory. In 1907 a census was recorded, but the only remaining schedule is for Seminole County.

Some school censuses are available at the respective county's superintendent of schools. These records may contain full name of student, birth date, and parents' names.

Background Sources

An understanding of the development of both Indian and Oklahoma Territories is essential in Oklahoma research. Sources include:

Baird, W. David, and Danney Goble. *The Story of Oklahoma.* Norman, Okla.: University of Oklahoma Press, 1994. Text was written for National Cowboy Hall of Fame.

Clark, Blue. *Lone Wolf v. Hitchcock: Treaty Rights and Indian Law at the End of the Nineteenth Century.* Lincoln: University of Nebraska Press, 1994. An easily understood description of laws, it is a good study of the topic that includes maps and bibliography.

Collins, Hubert E., ed. *Warpath and Cattle Trail.* Niwot, Colo.: University Press of Colorado, 1998. With a foreword by Hamlin Garland and introduction by William W. Savage, Jr., and James H. Lazalier, it discusses Cheyenne, Arapaho, and the Chisholm Trail.

Federation of Oklahoma Genealogical Societies. *Directory of Oklahoma Sources.* Oklahoma City: Federation of Oklahoma Genealogical Societies, 1993.

Gibson, Arrell Morgan. *Oklahoma: A History of Five Centuries,* 1965. Reprint. 2d ed. Norman, Okla.: Harlow Publishing Corp., 1981. A standard, well-known history.

Gittinger, Roy. *The Formation of the State of Oklahoma, 1803–1906.* 1917. Reprint. Norman, Okla.: University of Oklahoma Press, 1939. Relates the historical events under French, Spanish, and Mexican jurisdiction and the territorial periods.

Goble, Danney. *Progressive Oklahoma: The Making of a New Kind of State.* Norman, Okla.: University of Oklahoma Press, 1980.

Gray, Robert N. *The Cherokee Strip of Oklahoma: A Hundred Yesteryears.* Enid, Okla.: Sons and Daughters of the Cherokee Strip Pioneer Museum, 1992.

Hill, Luther B. *A History of the State of Oklahoma.* 2 vols. Chicago: Lewis Publishing Co., 1908. Details the history of the territories up to statehood.

Jackson, A. P., and E. C. Cole. *Oklahoma! Politically and Topographically Described.* Kansas City, Mo.: Miller and Hudson, 1885.

Littlefield, Daniel F. *The Chickasaw Freedmen: A People without a Country.* Westport, Conn.: Greenwood Press, 1980.

McReynolds, Edwin C., Alice Marriott, and Estelle Faulconer. *Oklahoma: A History of the State and Its People.* Rev. ed. Norman, Okla.: University of Oklahoma Press, 1971.

Morgan, H. Wayne, and Anne Hodges Morgan. *Oklahoma: A Bicentennial History.* New York: W. W. Norton, and Nashville: American Association for State and Local History, 1977. Includes a good bibliographic essay on various aspects of the state's history.

——. *Oklahoma: New Views of the Forty-Sixth State.* Norman, Okla.: University of Oklahoma Press, 1982.

Newson, D. Earl. *The Cherokee Strip: Its History and Grand Opening.* Stillwater, Okla.: New Forums Press, c1992. Includes maps and an index.

Parker, James W. *All Along the Chisholm Trail.* 2 vols. Yukon, Okla.: the author, 1988.

Reese, Linda Williams. *Women of Oklahoma, 1890–1920.* Norman, Okla.: University of Oklahoma Press, 1997.

Thoburn, Joseph B., and Wright, Muriel H. *Oklahoma: A History of the State and Its People.* 4 vols. 1929. Reprint. Tucson, Ariz.: W. C. Cox, 1974.

Wickett, Murray R. *Contested Territory: Whites, Native Americans, and African Americans in Oklahoma, 1865–1907.* Baton Rouge: Louisiana State University Press, 2000. Discusses Anglos, Native Americans, ex-slaves, and African Americans.

Zellner, William W., and Ruth L. Laird, eds. *Oklahoma: The First Hundred Years.* Ada, Okla.: Galaxy Publications, n.d.

Writings on Native American history and culture in the state are extensive, but a good place to start is with Angie Debo, *A History of the Indians of the United States* (Norman, Okla.: University of Oklahoma Press, 1970), which has a fine bibliography for more comprehensive reading. See also Debo's "Major Indian Record Collections in Oklahoma" in *Indian-White Relations: A Persistent Paradox,* edited by Jane Smith and Robert Kvasnicka (Washington, D.C.: Howard University Press, 1976). Debo also authored numerous other books on Native Americans.

Two reference works are Mary Huffman, comp., *The Five Civilized Tribes: A Bibliography* (Oklahoma City: Oklahoma Historical Society, Library Resources Division, 1991); and a dated but helpful study: Francis Paul Prucha, *Indian-White Relations in the United States: A Bibliography of Works Published, 1975–1980* (Lincoln, Nebr.: University of Nebraska Press, 1982). Other suggested readings include:

Carlson, L. A. *Indians, Bureaucrats, and Land.* Westport, Conn.: Greenwood Press, 1981. Concerns Oklahoma Native Americans and land policy.

Coffer, William E. [Koi Hosh]. *Phoenix: The Decline and Rebirth of the Indian People.* New York: Van Nostrand Reinhold, 1980.

Dickerson, Philip Jackson. *History of the Osage Nation: Its People, Resources, and Prospects: The Last Reservation to Open in the New State.* Pawhusk, Okla.: n.p., 1906.

Foreman, Grant. *Indian Removal: The Emigration of the Five Civilized Tribes.* 1953. Reprint. Norman, Okla.: University of Oklahoma Press, 1969.

King, Duane H., ed. *The Cherokee Indian Nation: A Troubled History.* Knoxville: University of Tennessee Press, 1979. Provides historical glimpses of the Cherokees before, during, and after removal.

LeMaster, Arlene. *Eastern Oklahoma Indians and Pioneers: Choctaw Nation, Indian Territory.* 3 vols. Poteau, Okla.: Family Heritage Resources, 1992.

Smith, Robert E., ed. *Oklahoma's Forgotten Indians.* Vol. 15 in the society's *Oklahoma Series.* Oklahoma City: Oklahoma Historical Society, 1981.

Tyler, Lyman S. *A History of Indian Policy.* Washington, D.C.: Government Printing Office, 1973. Details policy and its constant changes.

Wright, Muriel Hazel. *A Guide to the Indian Tribes of Oklahoma.* Norman, Okla.: University of Oklahoma Press, 1951.

For reading on the land runs, see:

Hoig, Stan. *The Oklahoma Land Rush of 1889.* Oklahoma City: Oklahoma Historical Society, 1984. Provides a historical overview of the land rush including its problems and opportunities.

Thiel, Sidney, comp. *The Oklahoma Land Rush.* Washington, D.C.: Historical Records Commission, n.d.

Wood, S. N. *The Boomers or the True Story of Oklahoma.* Topeka, Kans.: Bond and Neill, 1885.

Background reading in the role African Americans played in Oklahoma's settlement is available in several works (see also Special Focus Categories):

Aldrich, Gene. *Black Heritage of Oklahoma.* Edmond, Okla.: Thompson Book & Supply Co., 1973.

Baker, T. Lindsay, and Julie P. Baker. *The WPA Oklahoma Slave Narratives.* Norman, Okla.: University of Oklahoma Press, c1996.

Tolson, Arthur L. *The Black Oklahomans: A History, 1541–1992.* New Orleans: Edwards Print Co., 1994. This work includes a lengthy bibliography.

A guide for doing research in the Twin Territories is Bradford Koplowitz, *Guide to the Historical Records of Oklahoma* (Bowie, Md.: Heritage Books, 1990). This guide lists numerous records and repositories in which specific records are maintained for all counties, many municipalities, and five general repositories.

A helpful, although not completely current, publication for Oklahoma research is Patrick J. Blessing, *Oklahoma Records and Archives* (Tulsa, Okla.: University of Tulsa Publications in American Social History, No. 1, 1978). This guide includes maps and access information for vital records statewide. Record holdings described are those of the Secretary of State, Commissioner of Land Office, Department of Interior, State Election Board, WPA, Historical Records Surveys, Vital Statistics, miscellaneous, theses, dissertations, Public Works, and guides.

Some Internet sites that provide information on various aspects of Oklahoma history include <www.rootsweb.com/~okbeaver/NoMansLand/nomansld.htm>, <www.ok-history.mus.ok.us/okt/OKHistLinks.html>, and <www.rootsweb.com/~oknowata/OOO1.htm>.

Maps

Maps are particularly important in identifying the previous jurisdictions of the two territories that preceded present-day Oklahoma. The University of Oklahoma Library's Manuscripts Division (see Archives, Libraries, and Societies) and the Oklahoma State University Library at Stillwater, Oklahoma, maintain excellent collections for the state and its earlier territories. A *Guide to Cartographic Records in the National Archives* (Washington, D.C.: National Archives and Records Service, 1971) indicates availability of General Land Office (GLO) maps, which are particularly helpful for Oklahoma Territory.

County maps may be purchased from the Oklahoma Department of Transportation, Reproduction Branch, 200 N.E. 21st St., Oklahoma City, OK 73105-3204. Fees are minimal.

Some valuable compilations have been published including these:

Morris, John Wesley, ed. *Boundaries of Oklahoma*. Oklahoma City: Oklahoma Historical Society, 1980. Explains the changing borders within the territory and state.

——. *Ghost Towns of Oklahoma*. Norman, Okla.: University of Oklahoma Press, 1978.

——, Charles R. Goins, and Edwin C. McReynolds. *The Historical Atlas of Oklahoma*. 3d ed. Norman, Okla.: University of Oklahoma Press, 1986. Historical data and accompanying maps for the various developmental stages of the territory and state.

Oklahoma Department of Highways. *Town and Place Locations*. 1975. Oklahoma City, Okla.: Oklahoma Department of Highways, 1991. Alphabetically arranged listing showing place-name, county, section, township, and range. Includes towns and cities of today as well as towns that have vanished, names of known landmarks, road junctions, or railroad sidings. Lists over 4,200 places in Oklahoma.

Shirk, George H. *Oklahoma Place Names*. 1965. 2d ed. Norman, Okla.: University of Oklahoma Press, 1974. Alphabetically arranged, it begins with "A County" and concludes with "Zybra."

In addition to online sources for all states (see pages 16-17), various county maps are available on the Internet, such as <www.rootsweb.com/~okgreer/ogrmap.htm>.

Land Records

Public-Domain State

Before 1889, the first year Oklahoma was officially opened for nonnative settlement, many nonnatives contracted for labor with the Five Civilized Tribes in exchange for land tenancy. Land records for the nations were filed under their respective Bureau of Indian Affairs (BIA) agency.

After some areas were opened for nonnative settlement, the common holdings of the tribes were divided into individual allotments to tribal members, with the federal government remaining guardian over the allotments. This freed up other land that was then made available to nonnative settlers. No centralized repository exists for the land allotments given the natives, but original allotments for all but the Five Civilized Tribes are on microfilm at the Indian Archives at the Oklahoma Historical Society. Outright payments made for land in the Cherokee Outlet are included in this microfilm. Arrell Morgan Gibson, *Oklahoma: A History of Five Centuries* (1965; reprint, Norman, Okla.: University of Oklahoma Press, 1981), describes allotment history and details for several tribes.

Land allotments given to Native Americans between 1889 and 1906 freed more land for nonnatives. The Indian Archives at the Oklahoma Historical Society holds land descriptions and plat maps for some of these allotments, although originals are either at the BIA in Muskogee, Oklahoma, or the National Archives—Southwest Region (see page 12). Related publications include:

Chapman, B. B. "Cherokee Allotments in the Outlet," *The Chronicles of Oklahoma* 59 (Winter 1981–82): 401-21.

Cook, Fredrea, and Marlyn Hermann. *Forgotten Oklahoma Records: Cherokee Land Allotment Book*. Vol. 1. Cullman, Ala.: Gregath Co., 1981.

A majority of the nonnative settlers in the territory of Oklahoma obtained their lands through homestead claims. Case entry files, original tract books, and plat maps for homestead claims are maintained by the BLM (see page 6). Patents and copies of both tract books and plat maps are at the Bureau of Land Management, Box 27115, Santa Fe, NM 87502-0115. The Oklahoma Historical Society has seventy-two volumes of Oklahoma Federal Tract Books on microfilm that can be used in determining land descriptions to obtain homestead files. These are records of the homesteaders in Oklahoma Territory and a relatively few homesteaders (volume 63) for Ottawa and Delaware counties. Although not indexed by name, but by land description, a surname index has been compiled for each reel. A statewide index is currently being developed.

Helpful for those researching land records in the state is Oklahoma Historical Society's information about land records at <www.ok-history.mus.ok.us/lib/OKLND.htm>. A brief

overview of both Native American land records and Oklahoma's township and range coordinates based on present-day county boundaries is presented in E. Wade Hone, *Land & Property Research in the United States* (see page 5).

Homestead papers associated with the claim usually contain some genealogical information, including details such as age, birthplace, marital status, and number of family members, along with data concerning land use and improvements. If the homestead applicant was a naturalized citizen, or in the process of becoming one, the homestead files include a copy of the naturalization papers. If the homesteader was a Union veteran, the file may contain a copy of the discharge paper.

To locate homestead claims in the BLM records (see page 6), which were finalized prior to 1908, either the land description from the tract books (including county, township, range, etc.) or the date of entry and name of land office is required. For claims finalized after 1908, the number assigned to the case at the time that the land was patented is required. It is best to include a legal description of the property. In all cases, the full name of the homesteader must accompany the request for file copies.

A legal description of the land or the number assigned to the case may also be on file with the respective county clerk's office in which the land was originally located. These records are filed separately in the county but are usually fully indexed by landowner's name.

Land was, and continues to be, identified according to the rectangular survey method of measurement (see page 6). Records from Oklahoma's several local land offices (open from 1889–1927) are housed at the Division of Archives and Records, Oklahoma Department of Libraries (see Archives, Libraries, and Societies).

Since statehood in 1907, the respective clerk of the court or registrar maintains land and property transactions between individuals. Oklahoma land records usually include an abstract of title (property ownership) from the date of patent or first sale.

Many Oklahoma land records are microfilmed and available at the FHL, for example:

Philamathic Museum (Anadarko, Oklahoma). *Original Deeds and Government Sale Land Purchasers, 1901.* Microfilm. Salt Lake City: Filmed by the Genealogical Society of Utah, 1996. Subjects include Indians of North America, land tenure in Oklahoma, land and property records, and Caddo and Anadarko land and property records.

Published land records include works such as:

Chapman, Berlin Basil. *Oklahoma Territory and the National Archives: A Study in Federal Lands.* N.p.: 1982. Includes bibliographical references.

Garrison, Linda Norman, comp. and ed. *Successful Bidders of the Big Pasture Land Opening, 1906.* Lawton, Okla.: Southwest Oklahoma Genealogical Society, 1992.

Examples of online sites for Oklahoma lands include:

Landowners in Kingfisher County in 1906 at <www.rootsweb.com/~okkingfi/landowners.html>; or

Original owners in Lincoln County arranged by township at <www.rootsweb.com/~oklincol/first_names.html>.

Probate Records

Probate records filed with the various tribal governments and Indian Agencies for the Five Civilized Tribes and some other Native American tribes in Oklahoma are maintained by the Oklahoma Historical Society. Other tribes' records are in the National Archives—Southwest Region (see page 12).

Territorial probate records were processed and filed under the jurisdiction of the U.S. district court. Most original federal district court probate records are also in the National Archives—Southwest Region, although the Oklahoma Historical Society has some federal district court probate records on microfilm.

Some probate packets for the northern section of Cherokee Territory were filed in the U.S. district court. These are indexed and identified in the following volume:

Wever, Orpha Jewell. *Probate Records, 1892–1908, Northern District Cherokee Nation.* 2 vols. Vinita, Okla.: Northeast Oklahoma Genealogical Society, 1982–83.

Since statehood, the respective county clerk of the court has maintained probate records. County probate records may include some wills recorded during the territorial period.

Reliable sources include:

Oklahoma Genealogical Society. *Index to Probate, Oklahoma County, Oklahoma, 1895–1920.* Oklahoma City: Oklahoma Genealogical Society, 1983.

Oklahoma Historical Society. Indian Archives Division. *Probate Records for Saline District in the Cherokee Nation, 1886–1898.* Oklahoma City: Oklahoma Historical Society, 1976. Subjects in this publication are Cherokee Indians and nation, Oklahoma court, guardianship, land, property, probate, and native records.

Court Records

The western district of Arkansas at Fort Smith covered present-day Oklahoma as early as 1844. U.S. Federal District Courts served as the official criminal and civil courts for non-Native Americans until land was opened in 1889. Congress established federal courts at Muskogee in 1889 for crimes except those punishable by death or imprisonment. Cases for felonies were tried at either Fort Smith, Arkansas; Paris, Texas; or Fort Scott, Kansas. For nonnatives, the laws of Arkansas were applicable.

Between 1890 and 1895, federal law divided Indian Territory into the three judicial districts of South McAlester (Choctaw Nation), Ardmore (Chickasaw and Seminole nations), and Muskogee (Cherokee and Creek nations and the Quapaw Agency). Judges from these three jurisdictions heard all appellate cases, including those from Fort Smith, Paris, and Fort Scott. Until 1898, tribal courts continued hearing cases in which both parties were Native Americans. Thereafter, all persons in Indian Territory, no matter their race, were subject to federal laws and the laws of Arkansas.

In 1883 Congress changed the jurisdiction for the northern half of the western section of Indian Territory to that of the U.S. District Court of Kansas. The U.S. District Court, Northern District of Texas, was authorized to extend its jurisdiction to the southern half of the western part of Indian Territory.

During the first few years, a district court in Oklahoma Territory frequently served more than one county.

Most original, pre-statehood, district court records are in the National Archives—Southwest Region. Some are on microfilm at the Oklahoma Historical Society, Archives and Manuscripts Division.

Civil and criminal court records after statehood are available from the clerk of the court for the respective county. They maintain records such as proceedings, dockets, cases, and indexes to civil court matters. Jurisdiction may include probate, felony, civil, divorce, adoption, naturalization, small claims, licenses, juvenile, notary, minister's credentials, traffic, and misdemeanor cases. The appellate courts for Oklahoma are the state supreme court, court of appeals, and the court of criminal appeals.

Some early court records may include non-court related records. A volume stored in the basement of the Logan County courthouse contains the first court minutes, but the frontispiece lists a few marriages that occurred during that period. A few reference books include:

Bowen, Jeff. *Cherokee Citizenship Commission Docket Books, 1880–1884 and 1887–1889.* N.p.: the author, 1997.

Burton, Jeffrey. *Indian Territory and the United States, 1866–1906: Courts, Government, and the Movement for Oklahoma Statehood.* Norman, Okla.: University of Oklahoma Press, 1995.

Downs, Marion. *Chickasaw [Nation] Court Records.* Calera, Okla.: Bryan County Heritage Association, 2000. Includes Indian and county court records.

Ford, Jeanette W., comp. *Preliminary Inventory of the Records of the United States District Courts for Oklahoma.* Fort Worth, Tex.: National Archives, Central Plains Region, 1980.

Tax Records

Heavy spring rains with severe flooding in 1902 awakened Oklahoma's citizens to the need for better roads. Territorial laws placed responsibility with townships, and a road overseer was to be elected for each district. General property tax and some funds from liquor licenses collected by counties and townships were used to finance the building of public roads along section lines. A road tax was required, along with the requirement that all males between the ages of twenty-one and forty-five donate four eight-hour days a year to work on highways. Those who did not work or provide a substitute were fined $5 for each absence.

The county treasurer or assessor may have tax or assessment records. Some tax records are stored in museums, historical, and/or genealogical societies' repositories. Published tax records for Oklahoma are almost nonexistent. Some duplicated copies of county tax records are stored in the Oklahoma Department of Libraries, State Archives Division for security purposes but are not available for research. Koplowitz, *Guide to the Historical Records of Oklahoma* (cited in Background Sources), indicates location of county records, including those of tax and assessments.

Cemetery Records

The Oklahoma Historical Society Library has the state copies of cemetery transcriptions completed by the state DAR, although this group of compilations is by no means comprehensive. A card file index at the library lists cemeteries in the DAR collection and some other cemeteries that have been canvassed. The card index is alphabetical by name of county and indicates the cemetery.

Many other cemetery records exist that are not on the card file. Published records include some for Carter, Garfield, LeFlore, Murray, Muskogee, Payne, Roger Mills, Sequoyah, and Woodward counties. The FHL has *Cemetery Records of Oklahoma.* 9 vols. (Salt Lake City: Genealogical Society of Utah, 1959–62). Also see James W. Tyner and Alice Tyner Timmons, *Our People and Where They Rest,* 10 vols. (Norman, Okla.: University of Oklahoma, 1969–78), and Madeline S. Mills and Helen R. Mullenax, *Relocated Cemeteries in Oklahoma and Parts of Arkansas-Kansas-Texas* (Tulsa, Okla.: the authors, 1974). The newest guide is Barbara Pierce and Brian Basore, *Oklahoma Cemeteries: Bibliography of the Collections in the Oklahoma Historical Society.* (Oklahoma City: Oklahoma Historical Society, Library Resources Division, 1993.

Other publications include:

Chasteen, Jerri G. *Master Index to Our People and Where They Rest: An Index to 1,043 Old Cemeteries within the Boundary of the Old Indian Territory.* Pryor, Okla.: the author, 1995.

Lemley, Marie Perrin. "Cemetery Records of Oklahoma." Manuscript microfilmed by the Genealogical Society of Utah, 1993.

Lester, Gary W. *Cemetery Relocation Records of Grand and Eucha Lakes.* Braggs, Okla.: Green Leaf Creek, 1995.

Church Records

A Methodist Church was organized at Pecan Point, in present-day McCurtain County, in 1818. It was the first Protestant Church in the territory. Prior to statehood the largest numbers of citizens were Baptist, Roman Catholic, Disciples of Christ, or Methodist. Church records are among the most difficult to locate sources in Oklahoma. Some are on microfilm at the Oklahoma Historical Society; others are maintained by members of the congregation and are housed in private homes rather than in church repositories. Still others are stored in the respective church. Some church records are deposited in the denominations' archives. A Historical Records Survey inventory was created relating to various church records in the counties. See Works Projects Administration, Historical Records Survey. *Preliminary List of Churches and Religious Organizations in Oklahoma* (Oklahoma City: Historical Records Survey, 1942); and Oklahoma Historical Society. *Establishing Churches in the Cherokee Nation, 1866–1908.* Oklahoma City: Oklahoma Historical Society, 1976.

The Chronicles of Oklahoma (see Periodicals) frequently publishes articles concerning specific churches or denominations. An example is Walter N. Vernon, "Methodist Beginnings Among Southwest Oklahoma Indians," *The Chronicles of Oklahoma* 58 (1980): 392-411.

Numerous missions provided through the Presbyterian, Baptist, and Moravian churches were established to serve Native Americans. Both teachers and missionaries constituted part of the nonnative population in Indian Territory. Some records are on microfilm in the Archives and Manuscript Division of the Oklahoma Historical Society. Others are maintained by denominational archives.

Records for Methodists, Catholics, and Baptists are housed in state facilities:

United Methodist, Box 1138, Bristow, OK 74010.

Roman Catholic Chancery Office, 7501 N.W. Expressway, Oklahoma City, OK 73123.

Oklahoma Baptist University Library, Shawnee, OK 74801. Privately funded, the library collection contains some materials and histories of the Baptist Church.

Oklahoma City University, Oklahoma City, OK 73106. Founded in 1911 at Guthrie, it is affiliated with the Methodist Episcopal Church. After uniting with Epworth University, it was relocated to Oklahoma City.

Other church headquarters outside the state for denominations in Oklahoma include:

Southern Baptist Convention, 901 Commerce St. #750, Nashville, TN 37203.

Disciples of Christ Historical Society, 1101 Nineteenth Ave., South, Nashville, TN 37212.

See also the following works:

Burke, Bob. *Like a Prairie Fire: A History of the Assemblies of God in Oklahoma.* Oklahoma City: Oklahoma District Council of the Assemblies of God, 1994.

England, Stephen J. *Oklahoma Christians: A History of Christian Churches and of the Start of the Christian Church (Disciples of Christ) in Oklahoma.* N.p.: Bethan Press, 1975.

Gaskin, J. M. *Baptist Ministers in Oklahoma.* N.p., 1966.

Heiss, Willard C., William Wade Hinshaw, and Jeremiah Hubbard. *Hinshaw & Hubbard Oklahoma Quaker Records: Cherokee Monthly Meeting, New Hope Monthly Meeting, Siloam Monthly Meeting, Vera Monthly Meeting, Wyandotte Monthly Meeting and Marriages by J. Hubbard.* Kokomo, Ind.: Selby, 1991.

McKee, Wilma. *Growing Faith: General Conference Mennonites in Oklahoma.* Newton, Kans.: Faith and Life Press, 1988.

Routh, F. C. *The Story of Oklahoma Baptists.* Oklahoma City: Baptist General Convention, 1932.

West, C. W. *Missions and Missionaries of Indian Territory.* Muskogee, Okla.: Muskegee Publishing, 1990.

Military Records

Military records are available for Oklahoma prior to statehood. Bounty-land and military service records are located either at the National Archives or the Southwest Region branch in Fort Worth (see page 12). See also Odie B. Faulk, Kenny A. Franks, and Paul F. Lambert, eds., *Early Military Forts and Posts in Oklahoma* (Oklahoma City: Oklahoma Historical Society, 1978). For a historical perspective, see Brad Agnew, *Fort Gibson: Terminal on the Trail of Tears* (Norman, Okla.: University of Oklahoma Press, 1980), who argues that the troops served as a cultural buffer between whites and Indians. Names of soldiers who accompanied Native Americans during the federal government's forced removal of tribes can be found in U.S. Senate Document 512.

Confederate and Union service as well as other military service records are available from the National Archives (see pages 11-12). Some Civil War applications for pensions and pension records are extant at the Oklahoma Department of Libraries, State Archives Division (see Archives, Libraries, and Societies). Included are records for Confederate veterans (and their widows) who served elsewhere but were residents of Oklahoma when allocated pensions. These are filed numerically and indexed separately. See Oklahoma Board of Pension Commissioners, *Confederate Pension Applications for Soldiers and Sailors* (Oklahoma City: Archives and Records Division, Oklahoma Department of Libraries, n.d.). Data on a Confederate pension from Oklahoma may be obtained from the Oklahoma Department of Welfare, Capitol Office Bldg., Oklahoma City, OK 73103.

Index to Applications for Pensions from the State of Oklahoma Submitted by Confederate Soldiers, Sailors and their Widows (Oklahoma City: Oklahoma Genealogical Society, 1969), Special Publication No. 2, gives veteran's name, application number, and number of the reel for locating the pension file on microfilm.

Native American military units were part of Texas organizations, and are filed with those units, not as separate units for Indian Territory. Some confederate service records may be filed with the State Adjutant General's Office or the Oklahoma Historical Society, Archives and Manuscripts Division. See also Grant Foreman, *History of the Service and List of Individuals of the Five Civilized Tribes in the Confederate Army*, 2 vols. (Oklahoma City: Oklahoma Historical Society, 1948); and Frank Cunningham, *General Stand Watie's Confederate Indians*, with a foreword by Brad Agnew (1959. Reprint. Norman, Okla.: University of Oklahoma Press, 1998).

Other publications include N. Dale Talkington and Deone K. Pearcy, *Tributes of Blue: Obituaries of Civil War Union Soldiers and Sailors Buried in Oklahoma.* (Tehachapi, Calif.: T. P. Productions, 1996) and Oklahoma Genealogical Society Special Publication No. 15, *Veteran Burials in the State of Oklahoma* (Oklahoma City: Oklahoma Genealogical Society, 1999).

Online sources include the USGenWeb (see page 16) project for Oklahoma military records, and an online guide to Oklahoma Historical Society materials in its collection is available <www.ok-history.mus.ok.us/lib/military.htm>.

The Oklahoma Historical Society maintains a card file of veterans buried in Oklahoma. These data cards may include full name, birth date, death date, burial place, and military service unit data. The society also has incomplete records for the Confederate Home located in Ardmore, Oklahoma. Other records at the society include those contained in the Indian Archives section, such as muster rolls of the Indian Home Guard, which are on microfilm. These are arranged by tribe, then by unit.

A description of records held in the National Archives for World War I draft records is:

United States. Selective Service System. Oklahoma Historical Society. *Oklahoma, World War I Selective Service System Draft Registration Cards, 1917–1918.* National Archives Microfilm Publications, M1509. Washington, D.C.: National Archives, 1987–1988.

Periodicals, Newspapers, and Manuscript Collections

Periodicals

The Chronicles of Oklahoma is a valuable periodical published by the Oklahoma Historical Society since 1921. This ongoing series contains information about all aspects of life in the state and records created by and for its people. Volume 23 includes an article on the Edward Palmer Collection housed in the Carnegie Library in Enid, Oklahoma. Two cumulative indexes plus an annotated guide help locate individuals and subjects.

Chronicles of Oklahoma Cumulative Index. Vol. 1 (vols. 1–37, 1921–1959). Oklahoma City: Oklahoma Historical Society, 1961.

Chronicles of Oklahoma Cumulative Index. Vol. 2 (vols. 38–57, 1960–1979). Oklahoma City: Oklahoma Historical Society, 1983.

Welsh, Carol. *An Annotated Guide to the Chronicles of Oklahoma, 1921–1994.* Oklahoma City: Oklahoma Historical Society, 1996.

As many as fifty distinct publications are available for Oklahoma counties, regions, special interests, or the state. The Federation of Oklahoma Genealogical Societies publishes a quarterly *Newsletter*; and the *Oklahoma Genealogical Society Quarterly*, which began in 1961 (formerly called *The Bulletin*, beginning in 1955) as the publication for the Oklahoma Genealogical Society (see Archives, Libraries, and Societies for addresses). See also Mary Jackson Duffe, comp. *Oklahoma Genealogical Society Quarterly Subject Index, 1955–1990* (Oklahoma City: Oklahoma Genealogical Society, 1992), which lists records for counties, Native Americans, schools, churches, newspapers, and other categories.

Other periodicals for the state include *Dusty Trails*, a quarterly publication of the Genealogical Institute of Oklahoma, 3813 Cashion Place, Oklahoma City, OK 73112; *Prairie Lore*, a publication of the Southwestern Oklahoma Historical Society; *The Goingsnake Messenger*, a quarterly published by the Goingsnake District Heritage Association (Westville, Oklahoma); and *The Frontier Freedman's Journal: An African American Genealogical and Historical Journal of the South, Indian Territory, and the Southwest*, Angela Y. Walton-Raji, ed. <www.hometown.aol.com/angelaw859/ffj.html>.

Newspapers

The Oklahoma Historical Society has an extensive collection of newspapers published in Indian Territory, Oklahoma Territory, and the state of Oklahoma, dating back to the *Cherokee Advocate*, which ran from 1845 to 1901 in Tahlequah, Cherokee Nation, Indian Territory. Another newspaper was the *Indian Chieftain*, which was published between 1884 and 1900 in Vinita, Cherokee Nation, Indian Territory. Most are on microfilm (which can be purchased), and some indexes are available. A smaller collection is at the Oklahoma Department of Libraries (see Archives, Libraries, and Societies). The Muskogee Genealogical Society indexed all Muskogee newspapers. These index cards

are maintained by the Muskogee Public Library, Muskogee, OK 74401. See also:

Carter, L. Edward. *The Story of Oklahoma Newspapers, 1844–1984.* Muskogee: Published for the Oklahoma Heritage Association by Western Heritage Books, 1984.

Oklahoma Historical Society. *Index to Oklahoma Newspapers.* Oklahoma City: Oklahoma Historical Society, 2002 <www.ok-history.mus.ok.us/news/newsindex.html>.

Parker, Doris Whitehall. *Footprints on the Osage Reservation.* 2 vols. Pawhuska, Okla.: the author, 1984. These are newspaper abstracts for 1894 to 1907.

Pearcy, Deone K., and N. Dale Talkington, ed. *Oklahoma Death Notice and Obituary Index to* The Daily Oklahoman *(1947–1974).* Tehachapi, Calif.: T. P. Productions, 1992.

Ray, Grace. *Early Oklahoma Newspapers: History and Description of Publications from Earliest Beginnings to 1889.* Norman, Okla.: University of Oklahoma Press, 1928.

A brief history of newspaper publishing in Oklahoma is available online <www.ok-history.mus.ok.us/arch/news8.html>. The Margaret Carder Library in Mangum, Oklahoma, and the Oklahoma Historical Society have microfilm copies of the *Magnum Star, Sun Monitor,* and *Greer County Weekly.*

Manuscripts

Large manuscript collections pertaining to Oklahoma's history and people are housed at the Oklahoma Historical Society in the Archives and Manuscript Division, including the Indian Archives, which maintains an extensive manuscript collection of records pertaining to the state's Native Americans. The division consists of a large number of individual collections. Outstanding among them are the Grant Foreman Collection, principally dealing with the Five Civilized Tribes; the Joseph Thoburn Collection, concentrating on anthropology, archeology and history; and the Muriel Wright Collection, Wright being the former editor of *Chronicles of Oklahoma,* with correspondence dealing with Choctaw and Oklahoma history and families.

The WPA's Project S-149, Indian-Pioneer Papers (called the Indian-Pioneer History Collection), is located at both the Oklahoma Historical Society and the Western History Collection at the University of Oklahoma (see Archives, Libraries, and Societies). The project includes interviews of a large number of native and nonnative (both white and African-American) pioneers about their experiences and lives in Oklahoma. Included in these records are details of birth dates and places, parents' names, and other genealogically pertinent information. Each repository, however, has indexed this collection separately.

In addition to the University of Oklahoma, other university libraries in the state have significant collections. The Angie Debo Collection at Special Collections, Oklahoma State University

in Stillwater, contains the personal papers, correspondence, and recollections of this important professor of history in the state. In addition to Blessing, *Oklahoma Records and Archives,* and Koplowitz, *Guide to the Historical Records of Oklahoma* (both cited in Background Sources), which indicate general manuscript holdings, guides for specific manuscript collections include:

Ashton, Sharron Standifer. *Guide to Cherokee Indian Records Microfilm Collections: Archives and Manuscripts Division, Oklahoma Historical Society.* Norman, Okla.: Ashton Books, 1996.

Gibson, Arrell Morgan. *A Guide to Regional Manuscript Collections in the Division of Manuscripts, University of Oklahoma Library.* Norman, Okla.: University of Oklahoma Press, 1960.

Stewart, John, and Kenny Franks. *State Records, Manuscripts, and Newspapers at the Oklahoma State Archives and Oklahoma Historical Society.* Oklahoma City: State Department of Libraries and Oklahoma Historical Society, 1975.

An invaluable source is the Oklahoma Indian-Pioneer Papers collected during the 1930s by the WPA, which sponsored interviews with early settlers of the state. The collection includes nearly 11,000 oral histories preserved on microfiche. Several institutions hold copies, including the Oklahoma Historical Society, University of Oklahoma Libraries, and the McFarlin Library, University of Tulsa. In 2002, the Oklahoma Genealogical Society began publishing in its *Quarterly,* an alphabetically arranged list of the interviewees' names with volume and microfiche number. Surnames beginning with letters, A, B, and C have been completed with others to follow. Volunteer transcribers have also begun placing these histories on the Web at <http://www.rootsweb.com/~okgenweb/pioneer>.

Archives, Libraries, and Societies

Oklahoma Historical Society Museum and Library
Wiley Post Historical Bldg. Library Center
2100 N. Lincoln Blvd.
Oklahoma City, OK 73105-4997
www.ok-history.mus.ok.us

The society has a museum and a library with several major collections that do not circulate. It has federal census records, nearly 50,000 books including, but not limited to, the extensive collection of printed volumes belonging to the State Library of the Oklahoma Society of the National Society of the Daughters of the American Revolution (DAR), the collection of the Oklahoma Genealogical Society, and other standard genealogical reference materials. It has the largest collection of newspapers in the state, Oklahoma state records, and land records. The strength of its printed collections, however,

concerns the counties formed from Oklahoma Territory. It maintains a surname file, a good collection of family histories, marriage and cemetery records, military and pension records, and quarterlies from numerous organizations. The society has also produced several categorized guides to its invaluable collection. Some are listed in this chapter under specific topics such as newspapers and churches.

The Fred S. Bard Collection of genealogical material concerning pioneers and history is included in the library. See Oklahoma Historical Library, *Guide to the Oklahoma Historical Library* (Oklahoma City: Oklahoma Historical Society, 1993); and Oklahoma Historical Society. *Oklahoma State, County, and Town Records* (Oklahoma City: Oklahoma Historical Society, 2002). A brief online description is at <www.ok-history.mus. ok.us/lib/staterec.htm>.

The Archives and Manuscripts Division houses some records for the counties of Comanche, Greer, Johnston, Kiowa, Logan, Muskogee, Osage, Payne, Potawatomie, and Swanson. The Indian Archives section of the division maintains excellent resources for Native American research. The following list of microfilmed records is available:

Oklahoma Historical Society. *Indian Archives Division. Catalog of Microfilm Holdings in the Archives & Manuscripts Division Oklahoma Historical Society, 1976–1989: Native American Tribal Records and Special Collections*. Oklahoma City: Oklahoma Historical Society, 1989.

(See also Special Focus Categories).

University of Oklahoma Library

630 Parrington Oval
Monnet Hall, Rm 452
Norman, OK 73019
http://libraries.ou.edu

Genealogical materials, including histories and general reference materials for public use, are among the accessions for the library. Special interests are history of the West, development of the Trans-Mississippi West, and Native American cultures. Its Western History Collection includes the WPA Indian-Pioneer Papers (see Manuscripts). The library maintains more than 1,500 collections pertaining to Oklahoma, Native Americans, and western frontier history. The Manuscripts Division houses over 5,000 maps of Indian Territory, Oklahoma Territory, and the Trans-Mississippi West. It also has more than 1,000 sound recordings, including the Doris Duke Indian Oral History Collection and other interviews with Oklahoma's pioneers and leaders. Guides to the holdings are Donald L. Dewitt's two publications: *American Indian Resource Materials in the Western History Collections, University of Oklahoma* (Norman, Okla.: University of Oklahoma Press, 1990); and *Guide to Manuscript Collections: Western History Collections, University of Oklahoma* (Norman, Okla.: University of Oklahoma Press, 1994).

Oklahoma Department of Libraries
Division of State Archives and Records

200 NE 18th St.
Oklahoma City, OK 75105
www.odl.state.ok.us/oar

The agency holds the original permanent records generated by state government, including Confederate pension applications and transcripts of minutes of the boards of county commissioners for forty-seven counties (1886–89). The Records Center, a few blocks away at 125 N.E. 21st Street, maintains the non-permanent records for state government and has some records for Cleveland County. A small guide to the collection is Thomas W. Kremm, comp. and ed., *Guide to Special Collections of the Oklahoma State Archives* (Oklahoma City: Archives and Records Division, Oklahoma Department of Libraries, 1980).

Oklahoma Genealogical Society

P.O. Box 12986
Oklahoma City, OK 73157-2986
www.rootsweb.com/~okgs

It publishes the *Oklahoma Genealogical Society Quarterly* (see Periodicals) and special publications, including the *First Families of the Twin Territories,* Special Publication No. 13 (Oklahoma City: Oklahoma Genealogical Society, 1997). This work includes six pre-statehood maps.

The Oklahoma Territorial Museum

107 E. Oklahoma
Guthrie, OK 73044

It has a collection of early Oklahoma microfilmed records as well as a small collection of histories of the area.

Oklahoma City Public Library

131 Northwest Third St.
Oklahoma City, OK 73102
www.odl.state.ok.us/index.html

The library has a genealogical collection. On request, the staff will check family histories free of charge, and materials are available through interlibrary loan.

Thomas Gilcrease Institute of American History and Art

1400 Gilcrease Museum Rd.
Tulsa, OK 74127
www.gilcrease.org

Tulsa Genealogical Society Library

9072 E. 31st St.
P.O. Box 585
Tulsa, OK 74101-0585
www.tulsagenealogy.org

Five Civilized Tribes Museum
Federal Bldg., Agency Hill
Honor Heights Dr.
Muskogee, OK 74401
www.fivetribes.org

Many county and city libraries have some genealogical collections, and most counties have genealogical or historical societies. The Federation of Oklahoma Genealogical Societies, P.O. Box 2531, Ponca City, OK 74602, can help locate currently operating ones (also see page 13).

Special Focus Categories

Native American

Because of the federal government's removal policy, sixty-five different tribes have made their home in present-day Oklahoma. The sources for research are enormously varied from the kinds of materials generally associated with county-state record patterns. In addition to the sources held in the National Archives and its Southwest regional branch in Fort Worth (see page 12), materials for research on both natives and nonnatives who lived in the Twin Territories can be found at all agencies of the Bureau of Indian Affairs (see page 16), including those in Anadarko, Ardmore, Concho, Okmulgee, Pawhuska, Pawnee, Miami, Shawnee, Tahlequah, Talihina, Wewoka, and Stewart. What is covered here are some general categories of records found regarding Native Americans in the state. For a more extensive and detailed discussion, see Blessing, *Oklahoma Records and Archives*, and Koplowitz, *Guide to the Historical Records of Oklahoma* (both cited under Background Sources).

Research guides for specific Oklahoma Nations or tribes are available, such as:

Mooney, Thomas G. *Exploring Your Cherokee Ancestry: A Basic Genealogical Research Guide*. Tahlequah, Okla.: Cherokee National Historical Society, 1990.

Olsen, Monty. *Choctaw Emigration Records*. 2 vols. Calera, Okla.: Bryan County Heritage Association, 1990.

Sturtevant, William C. *A Seminole Sourcebook*. New York: Garland Publishing, 1987.

Some copies of census records on Native Americans are available at the Oklahoma Historical Society library and the FHL. These censuses are alphabetically arranged by BIA agency, then tribal name, and then date of enumeration. Since agency changes were made, a specific tribe may have been under the jurisdiction of two or more agencies. Beginning about 1916, the registration of individuals' names may be alphabetically arranged within the tribe's census schedule.

Land allotment records can be a valuable source of information about Native American ancestors. To obtain a parcel of land, each applicant had to include documentation of descent. Final rolls list those who received land allotments. When the land was to be sold or the individual had died, all heirs were identified since transfer of land required permission from all heirs. This data was usually registered in allotment or family registers. Later lists of heirs may be located in records entitled "Heirship Records." Each person is usually identified by age or birth date and relationship. Most allotted land eventually returned to tribal jurisdiction, for few individuals received patents to their holdings (see also Land Records).

Enrollment records, on which land allotments were based, were drawn up by the Dawes Commission for the Five Civilized Tribes. Under the Dawes Commission, information was abstracted onto data cards entitled *Enrollments Cards for the Five Civilized Tribes: 1898–1914* (Washington, D.C.: National Archives, 1981). Cards were made from both approved and rejected applications of Cherokee, Choctaw, Chickasaw, Creek, and Seminole tribe members. Microfilm of these packets and records is available at the Oklahoma Historical Society, the National Archives, and the FHL. Original applications are housed at the National Archives—Southwest Region in Fort Worth. A guide and index to these records is included in the Commission to the Five Civilized Tribes' publication, *The Final Rolls of Citizens and Freedmen of the Five Civilized Tribes in Indian Territory*, 2 vols. (Washington, D.C.: Government Printing Office, n.d.).

Another valuable source is the Guion Miller records, which are contained on 348 reels of microfilm entitled *Eastern Cherokee Applications of the U.S. Court of Claims, 1906–1909* (Washington, D.C.: National Archives, 1981). A separate index is available for this collection of court records for individuals who applied for government compensation for lands confiscated from the Eastern Cherokees during the 1800s, east of the Mississippi River. Claims include data with documentation showing claimant's lineage back to the Eastern Cherokee. It was also required that the claimant prove no other tribal affiliation. Billy Dubois Edgington and Carol Anne Buswell, transcribed and edited a comprehensive work, *Vital Information from the Guion Miller Roll (Court of Claims), 1906–1909* (Mill Creek, Wash.: Indian Scout Publications, 1998). This massive work is an alphabetical arrangement that includes surname, given names, Miller Roll application number, gender, married name of female applicant, birth year when available, birth state or territory, residence city, county, and state.

Second only to the National Archives in Native American research for Oklahoma is the Indian Archives Division of the Oklahoma Historical Society. Included are federal and state government records and private collections, particularly the extensive work of Grant Foreman (also see Manuscripts). The society's collection is listed and described in Lawrence Kelly, "Indian Records in the Oklahoma Historical Society Archives," *The Chronicles of Oklahoma* 54 (1976): 227-44. Other issues

include data relating to the Native Americans in Oklahoma and their records. Among many such articles are "Public Land Policy of the Five Civilized Tribes," 23 (1945): 107-18; "Provincial Indian Society in Eastern Oklahoma" 23 (1945): 323-37; and "Cherokee Allotments in the Outlet," 59 (1981): 401-21.

The Archives and Manuscripts Division of the Oklahoma Historical Society has approximately three million pages and 6,000 bound volumes from Indian Agencies in Oklahoma for 1870 through 1930. The archives is the national repository for records of the Cherokee, Chickasaw, Choctaw, Creek, and Seminole nations for the period 1860 through 1906. The archives also maintains agency records for Cheyenne, Pawnee, Quapaw, Chilocoo, Shawnee, Kiowa, and Arapaho as well as for the Cantonment agency. The Mekusukey Academy records and many special collections are also held there. There are 1,400 volumes of the Executive Library Cherokee Nation in the collection. The newspaper collection includes *The Cherokee Advocate* which began publication in 1844 in Indian Territory.

The Bureau of Indian Affairs, Muskogee Agency, 4th Floor, Federal Bldg., Muskogee, OK 74401, maintains records of the Cherokee and other tribes. The Cherokee Registration Office, P.O. Box 119, Tahlequah, OK, 74464, has records pertaining to the Cherokees. The Bureau of Indian Affairs, W.C.D. Office Complex, P.O. Box 368, Anadarko, OK 73005-0368, covers the Anadarko, Concho, Horton, Pawnee, and Shawnee Agencies.

The University of Oklahoma Library has many significant sources, including two manuscript collections for the Cherokee and the "Duke Indian Oral History Collection." A guide to the holdings is Donald L. Dewitt, *American Indian Resource Materials in the Western History Collections, University of Oklahoma* (Norman, Okla.: University of Oklahoma Press, 1990).

The Thomas Gilcrease Institute of American History and Art Library in Tulsa, Oklahoma, holds records pertaining to the Choctaw, Arapaho, and Cheyenne. The institute's older publication provides a guide to its collection: *A Guidebook to Manuscripts in the Library of the Thomas Gilcrease Institute of American History and Art* (Tulsa, Okla.: The Institute, 1969).

A few selected private collections in the Indian Archives Division, Oklahoma Historical Society, include transcripts of the Office of Commissioner Indian Affairs and Superintendent of the Five Civilized Tribes in the Grant Foreman transcripts, Frederick B. Severs Collection for the Creek Nation, Grant Foreman's numerous collections and WPA project interviews, John H. Adair Collection of early Cherokees, and the G. A. Root collection of newspaper clippings for Oklahoma Land openings.

Some Internet sites of interest include <www.choctawnation. com> and <www.rootsweb.com/~usgenweb/ok/nations/>.

The following publications include valuable source material:

Armstrong, K. M., and Bob Curry. *Chickasaw Rolls: Annuity Rolls of 1857–1860 and the "1855" Chickasaw District Roll of 1856.*
Bowie, Md.: Heritage Books, 1995. Includes transcribed enumerations but no index.

Baker, Jack D. *Cherokee Emigration Rolls, 1817–1835.* Oklahoma City: Baker Publishing Co., ca. 1977.

Bogle, Dixie. *Cherokee Nation Births and Deaths, 1884–1901.* Owensboro, Ky.: Cook and McDowell Publications, 1980. This publication was sponsored by the Northeast Oklahoma Genealogical Society and contains abstracts from two newspapers, *Indian Chieftain* and *Daily Chieftain.*

Bogle, Dixie, and Dorothy Nix. *Cherokee Nation Marriages, 1884–1901.* Owensboro, Ky.: Cook and McDowell Publications, 1980. This publication was sponsored by Abraham Coryell Chapter, National Society Daughters of the American Revolution, and it contains abstracts taken from *Indian Chieftain* newspapers.

Campbell, John Bert. *Campbell's Abstract of Creek Indian Census Cards and Index.* Muskogee, Okla.: Phoenix Job Printing, 1981.

———. *Campbell's Abstract of Seminole Indian Census Cards and Index.* Muskogee, Okla.: Oklahoma Printing, 1925.

Chase, Marybelle W., comp. *1842 Cherokee Claims: Tahlequah District.* Nashville: Tennessee State Library and Archives, 1989. This volume contains reproductions of handwritten records and is indexed.

———. *A Survey of Tribal Records in the Archives of the United States Government in Oklahoma.* N.p., n.d.

Corwin, Hugh D. *The Kiowa Indians: Their History and Life Stories.* Lawton, Okla.: author, 1958.

Gormley, Myra Vanderpool. *Cherokee Connections.* Reprint. 1995. Baltimore: Genealogical Publishing, 2003. Helpful description of sources with a brief bibliography.

Kelly, Lawrence. "Indian Records in the Oklahoma Historical Society Archives." *The Chronicles of Oklahoma* 54 (Summer 1976): 227-44.

Oklahoma Genealogical Society. *A Compilation of Records from the Choctaw Nation, Indian Territory.* Oklahoma City: Oklahoma Genealogical Society, ca. 1976.

Sober, Nancy Hope. *The Intruders: The Illegal Residents of Cherokee Nation, 1866–1907.* Ponca City, Okla.: Cherokee Books, 1991. Provides detailed background and eight appendixes with various lists of names, which are not included in the book's index. Well documented, the notes provide bibliographic reference material.

Other Ethnic Groups

A series entitled "Newcomers to a New Land" was sponsored by the Department of Libraries and the Oklahoma Library Association. These books analyze the role and impact of major

ethnic groups in the state. The following resource list includes some of the volumes in the series:

American Historical Society of Germans from Russia. Harvester (Oklahoma) Chapter. *German-Russian Heritage: Steppes to America.* N.p.: American Historical Society Germans from Russia, 1991.

Bernard, Richard. *The Poles in Oklahoma.* Norman, Okla.: University of Oklahoma Press, 1980.

Bicha, Karel D. *The Czechs in Oklahoma.* Norman, Okla.: University of Oklahoma Press, 1980.

Blessing, Patrick J. *The British and Irish in Oklahoma.* Norman, Okla.: University of Oklahoma Press, 1980.

Brown, Kenny L. *The Italians in Oklahoma.* Norman, Okla.: University of Oklahoma Press, 1980.

Burton, Arthur T. *Blacks, Buckskin and Blue: African American Scouts and Soldiers on the Western Frontier.* Austin, Tex.: Eaton Press, 1999.

Hale, Douglas. *The Germans from Russia in Oklahoma.* Norman, Okla.: University of Oklahoma Press, 1980.

Rohrs, Richard C. *The Germans in Oklahoma.* Norman, Okla.: University of Oklahoma Press, 1980.

Smith, Michael M. *The Mexicans in Oklahoma.* Norman, Okla.: University of Oklahoma Press, 1980.

Tobias, Henry J. *The Jews in Oklahoma.* Norman, Okla.: University of Oklahoma Press, 1980.

For Czechs in Oklahoma, see also:

Lynch, Russell Wilford. "Czech Farmers in Oklahoma," *Oklahoma A & M College Bulletin* 39, no. 13 (June 1942).

In addition to general sources for African American genealogical research (see pages 14-15), there are specific works for Oklahoma:

Franklin, Jimmie Lewis. *The Blacks in Oklahoma.* Norman, Okla.: University of Oklahoma Press, 1980.

———. *Journey Toward Hope: A History of Blacks in Oklahoma.* Norman, Okla.: University of Oklahoma Press, 1982. Both of Franklin's works include helpful bibliographies.

Tolson, Arthur L. *The Black Oklahomans* (see Background Sources).

Walton-Raji, Angela Y. *Black Indian Genealogy Research: African American Ancestors among the Five Civilized Tribes.* Bowie, Md.: Heritage Books, 1993. Includes appendixes with lists of freedman surnames on the five tribal rolls.

Williams, Nudie. "The Black Press in Oklahoma: The Formative Years, 1889–1907," *Chronicles of Oklahoma* 61 (Fall 1983): 308-19. Text and notes include most early newspapers for African Americans in Oklahoma.

County Resources

Oklahoma deeds, probates, and civil court records are located at the county clerk's or clerk of the courts office. Marriage records before statewide recording may be found at the county clerk's as well, but records of births and deaths are not available until statewide recording began. Official certificates come from the State Department of Health (see Vital Records). The State Election Board, Oklahoma Museum of Election History, Oklahoma City, OK 73105, holds precinct registers and/or other records for thirty-four counties.

The largest percentage of Oklahoma's extant public records were generated in the twentieth century and are generally intact. Send inquiries to the county official at the courthouse address for the appropriate county. Some dates in the following chart were obtained from Blessing, *Oklahoma Records and Archives,* and Koplowitz, *Guide to Historical Records of Oklahoma* (both cited in Background Sources). There are a few discrepancies in county record beginning dates between Koplowitz and Blessing; in such instances, Koplowitz's dates have been used.

Information for current addresses and zip codes for Oklahoma county courthouses came from <www.royaltydeeds.com/courthouses/oklahoma.htm>. Additional dates for earliest availability of county records and formation dates with previous jurisdictions were taken from the Family History Library website at <www.familysearch.org>. At the time of the land runs that opened Oklahoma for settlement, thirty judicial Recording Districts were designated as the transitional form of government just prior to statehood and county formation. The Recording District for the appropriate counties are listed in the middle column. Records for those districts may not be extant, however. Only dates for records under county jurisdictions were used; other published compilations are available and in many instances include earlier records.

The Counties and County Seats of
Oklahoma

25 0 25 50 75 100 Miles

OKLAHOMA

549

Map County Address	Date Formed Parent County/ies Recording District	Birth Marriage Death	Land Probate Court
K3 Adair P.O. Box 169 Stilwell 74960-0169	1907 Cherokee Nation Recording Dist. #6	1908 1907 1908	1907 1907 1907
F2 Alfalfa 300 S. Grand Cherokee 73728	1907 Woods	1908 1894 1908	1895 1892 1982
J5 Atoka 201 E. Court Atoka 74525	1907 Choctaw Nation	1908 1892 1908	1907 1897 1913
C1 Beaver P.O. Box 237 Beaver 73932-0237	1890 original	1908 1890 1908	1891 1890 1880
D4 Beckham P.O. Box 67 Sayre 73662-0067	1907 Roger Mills/Greer	1908 1907 1908	1900 1907 1895
F3 Blaine P.O. Box 138 Watonga 73772-0138	1892 original	1908 1892 1908	1893 1892 1887
H6 Bryan 402 W. Evergreen Durant 74701	1907 Choctaw Nation Recording Dist. # 25	1908 1902 1908	1903 1902 1902
F4 Caddo P.O. Box 68 Anadarko 73005-0068	1901 original	1908 1901 1908	1902 1891 1901
F3 Canadian P.O. Box 458 El Reno 73036-0458	1889 original	1908 1890 1908	1890 1890 1890
G5 Carter 1st and B St. SW/P.O. Box 1236 Ardmore 73402-1236	1907 Chickasaw Nation	1930 1895 1930	1907 1908 1895
K3 Cherokee 213 W. Delaware Tahlequah 74464	1907 Cherokee Nation Recording Dist. #6	1908 1907 1908	1906 1907 1907
J6 Choctaw 300 E. Duke Hugo 74743	1907 Choctaw Nation	1908 1907 1908	1907 1907 1907
A1 Cimarron P.O. Box 145 Boise City 73933-0145	1907 Beaver	1908 1908 1908	1904 1908 1908
G4 Cleveland 201 S. Jones Norman 73069	1889 unassigned lands	1908 1867 1893	1890 1889 1891
H5 Coal 4 N. Main St. Coalgate 74538	1907 Tobucksy County of Cherokee Nation	1908 1907 1908	1904 1907 1907
F5 Comanche 315 SW 5th St. Lawton 73501	1901 Kiowa/Comanche/Apache lands Witcha-Caddo lands	1906 1901 1906	1893 1901 1901
F5 Cotton 201 N. Broadway St. Walters 73572	1912 Comanche	1917 1912 1918	1912 1912 1912
K1 Craig 301 W. Canadian Vinita 74301	1907 Cherokee Nation Recording Dist. #3	1908 1902 1908	1907 1895 1907
H3 Creek 371 E. Lee Sapulpa 74067	1907 Creek Nation Recording Dists. #8 and #9	1908 1907 1908	1898 1907 1917
E3 Custer P.O. Box 300 Arapaho 73620-0300	1892 Cheyenne/Arapaho lands	1908 1894 1908	1899 1895 1896
Day	1892 (abolished 1907; now Ellis County area) Cheyenne/Arapaho lands		
K2 Delaware P.O. Box 309 Jay 74346-0309	1907 Cherokee Nation	1908 1911 1908	1905 1867 1868
E3 Dewey P.O. Box 268 Taloga 73667-0268	1892 Cheyenne/Arapaho	1908 1893 1908	1892 1894 1894
D3 Ellis 100 S. Washington/P.O. Box 197 Arnett 73832-0197	1907 Day/Woodward	1908 1892 1908	1889 1893 1900
F2 Garfield 114 W. Broadway Enid 73701	1893 Cherokee Outlet	1908 1893 1908	1893 1894 1907
G5 Garvin P.O. Box 926 Pauls Valley 73075-0926	1907 Chickasaw Nation Recording Dist. #17	1908 1907 1908	1906 1907 1893
F4 Grady 4th and Choctaw Ave. P.O. Box 1009 Chickasha 73018-1009	1907 Caddo/Comanche/ Chickasaw Nation	1908 1907 1908	1903 1907 1907
F2 Grant P.O. Box 167 Medford 73759-0167	1893 Cherokee Outlet	1908 1893 1908	1893 1893 1893
D4 Greer P.O. Box 2077 Mangum 73554-2077	(organized by Texas, 1886; became part of Oklahoma, 1896)	1912 1901 1912	1886 1901 1886
D5 Harmon 114 W. Hollis Hollis 73550	1909 Greer	1909 1909 1909	1909 1909 1909
D1 Harper P.O. Box 369 Buffalo 73834-0369	1907 Woodward	1908 1907 1908	1900 1907 1903
K4 Haskell 202 E. Main St. Stigler 74462	1907 Choctaw Nation Recording Dists. #12 and #14	1908 1907 1908	1905 1907 1909

OKLAHOMA

Map	County Address	Date Formed / Parent County/ies / Recording District	Birth Marriage Death	Land Probate Court
H4	Hughes 200 N. Broadway Holdenville 74848	1907 Creek Nation	1908 1907 1908	1907 1907 1907
D5	Jackson P.O. Box 515 Altus 73521-0515	1907 Greer	1908 1907 1908	1898 1907 1907
F6	Jefferson 220 N. Main St. Waurika 73573	1907 Comanche County/ Chickasaw Nation	1908 1907 1900	1907 1907 1907
H5	Johnston 403 W. Main Tishomingo 73460	1907 Chickasaw Nation Recording Dist. #22	1908 1907 1908	1907 1907 1907
G1	Kay P.O. Box 450 Newkirk 74647-0450	1895 Cherokee Outlet	1908 1893 1908	1893 1893 1893
F3	Kingfisher 100 S. Main/P.O. Box 118 Kingfisher 73750	1890 original	1908 1900 1908	1890 1900 1896
E4	Kiowa P.O. Box 73 Hobart 73651-0073	1901 Kiowa/Comanche/Apache/ Caddo/Wichita	1908 1901 1908	1901 1901 1901
K4	Latimer 109 N. Central St. Wilburton 74578	1902 Choctaw Nation	1908 1907 1908	1890 1906 1923
K4	Le Flore P.O. Box 218 Poteau 74953-0218	1907 Choctaw Nation Recording Dist. #14	1908 1897 1908	1908 1908 1908
H3	Lincoln P.O. Box 126 Chandler 74834-0126	1891 Iowa/Pottawatomie Shawnee/Sac-Fox lands	1908 1891 1900	1891 1893 1891
G3	Logan 301 E. Harrison Guthrie 73044	1889 original	1908 1890 1908	1894 1890 1890
G6	Love 405 W. Main St. Marietta 73448	1907 Chickasaw Nation	1908 1907 1908	1903 1907 1907
	Lovely By Arkansas Legislature. Abolished 1828.	1827		
F2	Major E. Broadway/P.O. Box 379 Fairview 73737-0379	1907 Woods	1908 1907 1908	1894 1894 1894
H6	Marshall Rm. 101 Madill 73446	1907 Chickasaw Nation Recording Dist. #22	1908 1907 1908	1907 1905 1907
K2	Mayes P.O. Box 97 Pryor 74361-0097	1907 Cherokee Nation	1908 1902 1908	1903 1907 1907
G4	McClain P.O. Box 629 Purcell 73080-0629	1907 Chickasaw Nation Recording Dist. #18	1908 1895 1883	1903 1895 1895
K6	McCurtain P.O. Box 1078 Idabel 74745-1078	1907 Choctaw Nation Recording Dist. #24	1908 1907 1908	1907 1917 1907
J4	McIntosh P.O. Box 110 Eufaula 74432-110	1907 Creek Nation	1905 1907 1905	1907 1907 1907
G5	Murray P.O. Box 442 Sulphur 73086-0442	1907 Chickasaw Nation	1908 1907 1908	1906 1907 1907
K3	Muskogee P.O. Box 1008 Muskogee 74401-1008	1907 Creek Nation	1908 1907 1908	1913 1907 1907
G2	Noble 300 Courthouse Dr./P.O. Box 409 Perry 73077-0409	1893 Cherokee Outlet	1908 1893 1908	1893 1893 1893
J1	Nowata 229 N. Maple St. Nowata 74048	1907 Cherokee Nation Recording Dist. #3	1908 1907 1908	1909 1908 1907
H3	Okfuskee P.O. Box 108 Okemah 74859-0108	1907 Creek Nation	1909 1907 1909	1907 1907 1907
G3	Oklahoma 320 N.W. Robert S. Kerr Oklahoma City 73102	1890 original	1908 1889 1908	1889 1890 1890
J3	Okmulgee P.O. Box 904 Okmulgee 74447-0904	1907 Creek Nation	1908 1907 1908	1907 1907 1907
H2	Osage P.O. Box 87 Pawhuska 74056-0087	1907 Osage Nation	1908 1907 1908	1906 1907 1897
K1	Ottawa 102 E. Central Miami 74354	1907 Cherokee Nation Recording Dists. #1 and #2	1908 1907 1908	1895 1907 1907
H2	Pawnee 500 Harrison Pawnee 74058	1892 Cherokee Outlet/ Pawnee Nation	1908 1897 1908	1894 1897 1897
G3	Payne 6th and Husband St./P.O. Box 7 Stillwater 74074-007	1890 Cherokee Outlet/ unassigned lands	1876 1894 1876	1884 1889 1895
J4	Pittsburg 115 E. Carl Albert Pkwy. McAlester 74501	1907 Choctaw Nation	1908 1890 1908	1907 1893 1901
H5	Pontotoc 13th and Broadway P.O. Box 1425 Ada 74820-1425	1907 Chickasaw Nation	1908 1907 1908	1906 1906 1907

551

OKLAHOMA

Map	County Address	Date Formed Parent County/ies Recording District	Birth Marriage Death	Land Probate Court
H4	Pottawatomie 325 N. Broadway Shawnee 74801	1891 Pottawatomie-Shawnee Nations	1908 1892 1908	1895 1892 1892
K5	Pushmataha 302 SW B St. Antlers 74523	1907 Choctaw Nation Recording Dist. #24	1917 1907 1917	1907 1904 1905
D3	Roger Mills P.O. Box 708 Cheyenne 73628-0708	1892 Cheyenne-Arapaho Nations	1908 1893 1908	1892 1907 1894
J2	Rogers 219 S. Missouri/P.O. Box 1210 Claremore 74018-1210	1907 Cherokee Nation	1915 1907 1915	1907 1909 1907
H4	Seminole P.O. Box 1180 Wewoka 74884-1180	1907 Seminole Nation Recording Dist. #13	1908 1907 1908	pre-1907 1909 1915
K3	Sequoyah 120 E. Chickasaw St. Sallisaw 74955	1907 Cherokee Nation Recording Dist. #11	1908 1907 1908	1907 1907 1907
F5	Stephens 101 S. 11th St. Duncan 73533	1907 Comanche County/ Chickasaw Nation	1908 1907 1908	1907 1917 1907
B1	Texas P.O. Box 197 Guymon 73942-0197	1907 Beaver	1908 1907 1908	1882 1907 1907
E5	Tillman P.O. Box 992 Frederick 73542-0992	1907 Kiowa Terr./Comanche counties	1917 1907 1917	1902 1907 1908
J3	Tulsa 500 S. Denver Ave. Tulsa 74103	1907 Creek/Cherokee Nations	1908 1907 1908	1907 1907 1907
J3	Wagoner 307 E. Cherokee/P.O. Box 156 Wagoner 74467-0156	1908 Cherokee Nation	1908 1907 1908	1906 1907 1907
J1	Washington 420 S. Johnstone Ave. Bartlesville 74003	1907 Cherokee Nation	1908 1907 1908	1900 1907 1907
E4	Washita P.O. Box 380 Cordell 73632-0380	1892 Cheyenne-Arapaho Nations	1908 1892 1908	1907 1903 1892
E2	Woods P.O. Box 386 Alva 73717-0386	1893 Cherokee Outlet	1908 1893 1908	1893 1893 1893
E2	Woodward 1600 Main St. Woodward 73801	1893 Cherokee Outlet	1908 1893 1908	1893 1894 1893

Oregon

DWIGHT A. RADFORD

The non-native settlement of Oregon began in 1829 when retired French-Canadian fur trappers from the Hudson Bay Company started farming on the banks of the Willamette River at Champoeg near present-day St. Paul. By the 1840s, American missionaries had established settlements in the Oregon Territory. Missions were sponsored by the Congregational, Presbyterian, Methodist, and Catholic churches.

Missionaries began encouraging emigration to Oregon in the early 1840s. Most of the early settlers in Oregon were farmers from the Mississippi, Missouri, and Ohio River valleys, who came in response to the invitation with the promise of free land and a better life. Between 1840 and 1860, 53,000 immigrants came to Oregon to make their homes. The Oregon Donation Land Act of 1850 provided from 160 to 320 acres of free land to white male settlers. Wives could receive an additional 160 to 320 acres in their own right.

The first city in Oregon, Willamette Falls, later called Oregon City, was established in 1829 by Dr. John McLoughlin, chief broker for the Hudson Bay Company. The city of Portland was started in 1844 when sixteen blocks were plotted out along the Willamette River bank. Portland became a place where wagons could meet seafaring ships during the California gold rush to exchange commodities. In 1850, gold was discovered in the Rogue River Valley, which led to the founding of Jacksonville in 1852. The town of Roseburg began in 1852 as a way station on the California-Oregon trail. Between 1847 and 1856, routes and settlements were plagued by warfare and conflict between natives and settlers in southern and northeastern Oregon. Statehood was obtained in 1859.

Gold mining in Baker and Grant counties during 1862 and 1865 brought prosperity to the entire region. More permanent to the economy were the cattle drives across the Cascades from the valleys to the mines to feed the workers. This gave rise to the cattle-baron empires and cattle towns such as Burns, Lakeview, and Prineville. The sheep industry followed the cattle empires in northeastern Oregon between the Dalles and the Umatilla and contributed to the growth of towns such as Condon, Heppner, and Pendleton.

European immigrants came to Oregon in the 1870s. Scandinavians drawn by fishing settled in coastal areas, and a large number of Finns settled at Astoria. Swiss immigrants settled at Tillamook and began the cheese industry in the area.

Portland became a major port and during the 1870s added wheat commodities, thus attaining status as one of the major wheat ports of the world. Portland's thriving economy drew a wide range of foreign immigrants including Chinese, Germans, Irish, Jews, Scandinavians, and Scots.

Vital Records

The State of Oregon began recording births and deaths in July 1903 and marriages in 1906. Divorce certificates were recorded at the state level beginning in 1925. These all may be obtained from Oregon Health Services, Center for Health Statistics, 800 NE Oregon St., Ste. 205, Portland, OR 97232; P.O. Box 14050, Portland, OR 97293-0050 <www.ohd.hr.state.or.us/chs/>.

The Oregon State Archives (through the online Oregon Historical Records Index <http://arcweb.sos.state.or.us/banners/genlist.htm>) and Oregon State Library (see Archives, Libraries, and Societies) have growing collections of vital records. The Oregon Historical Society (see Archives, Libraries, and Societies) has a complete death index and the later divorce and marriage indexes. Microfilmed vital records at the Family History Library (FHL) in Salt Lake City include death indexes (1903–2000) and marriages (1906–24) as well as some indexed county records.

Indexes to Oregon deaths (1903–98) and marriages (1906–20) are online through subscription database <www.ancestry.com>.

Census Records

Federal

Population Schedules
- Indexed—1850, 1860, 1870, 1880, 1900, 1910, 1920, 1930
- Soundex—1880, 1900, 1910 (by Genealogical Forum of Oregon)

Industry and Agriculture Schedules
- 1850, 1860, 1870, 1880

Mortality Schedules
- 1850, 1860, 1870, 1880

Union Veterans Schedules
- 1890 (indexed)

The Oregon State Archives, Oregon State Library, and Oregon Historical Society Library (see Archives, Libraries, and Societies) hold microfilm copies of federal Oregon censuses. The supplemental schedules are at the latter.

Territorial and State

Territorial and state census records reflect the rapid growth of the Oregon country. These census enumerations were taken in 1842, 1843, 1845, 1849, 1853, 1854, 1855, 1856, 1857, 1858, 1859, 1865, 1875, 1885, 1895, and 1905. Only portions of some of these enumerations have survived. Most of these censuses include only the name of the head of household, although the 1895 and 1905 censuses include some information on all members of the household. The state censuses are inventoried on the Oregon State Archives website as part of its "Oregon Historical Records Index" database. The FHL has microfilm copies of most Oregon state censuses.

Background Sources

Bailey, Barbara Ruth. *Main Street, Northeastern Oregon: The Founding and Development of Small Towns*. Portland: Oregon Historical Society, 1982. This volume examines all the towns founded within the northeastern section of Oregon except Baker and LaGrande.

Brandt, Patricia. *Oregon Biographical Index*. Corvallis: Oregon State University, 1976. This is an important publication that indexes forty-seven historical volumes, which are either entirely devoted to biographies or have large self-contained biographical sections.

Carey, Charles Henry. *History of Oregon*. Chicago: Pioneer History Publishing Co., 1922. Three volumes detailing the discovery, settlement, and development of Oregon country.

Clarke, S.A. *Pioneers of Oregon History*. Portland: J.K. Gill, 1905. This two-volume work deals with early exploration of the Oregon region, the Native American population, arrival of Protestant and Catholic missionaries, overland emigration, and the early political history of Oregon.

Douthit, Nathan. *Uncertain Encounters: Indians and Whites at Peace and War in Southern Oregon, 1820s–1860s*. Corvallis: Oregon State University Press, 2002. This major contribution to the study of native-emigrant relations of the Pacific Northwest focuses on the fifty-year period from the fur trade to the Rogue River War.

Gaston, Joseph. *The Centennial History of Oregon, 1811–1912; With Notice of Antecedent Explorations*. Chicago: S.J. Clarke Publishing Co., 1912. This two-volume work covers the history of the northwest Pacific coast, the fur-trading industry, founding of Portland, Indian wars, government, religion, agriculture and industry in Oregon, and politics. The second volume is dedicated to biographical sketches of Oregonians.

Genealogical Forum of Oregon. *Oregon Guide to Genealogical Sources*. Revised. 1998. Portland, Ore.: the author, 1998. The guide provides information on records deposited at various repositories throughout the state.

Hawthorne, Julian. *The Story of Oregon: A History with Portraits and Biographies*. Salt Lake City: Genealogical Society of Utah, 1964. Of this two-volume set, the most valuable portion is the autobiographical section in volume two. These autobiographies were contributed by a number of living residents of the state.

Hines, Harvey K. *An Illustrated History of the State of Oregon*. Chicago: Lewis Publishing Co., 1893. This history of Oregon contains full-page portraits and biographical material on many of the prominent citizens of the period.

Lang, Herbert O. *History of the Willamette Valley*. Salt Lake City: Genealogical Society of Utah, 1985. The purpose of this volume, which was originally published in 1885, was to arrange and preserve the scattered records and recollections of the Willamette Valley. The newspapers of the valley contributed information.

Portrait and Biographical Record of the Willamette Valley, Oregon: Containing Original Sketches of Many Well Known Citizens of the Past and Present. Chicago: Chapman Publishing Co., 1903. Provides excellent sketches of Willamette Valley residents. A great deal of genealogical information is provided in these biographies.

Portrait and Biographical Record of Western Oregon: Containing Original Sketches of Many Well-Known Citizens of the Past and Present. Tucson, Ariz.: W.C. Cox, 1974. This volume originally published in 1904 records biographies of the men who contributed to the development and progress of western Oregon. Many pioneers are listed.

Preston, Ralph N. *Historical Oregon: Overland Stage Routes, Old Military Roads, Indian Battle Grounds, Old Forts, Old Gold Mines*. Portland, Ore.: Binford & Mort, 1978. A compilation of historical maps of Oregon from the Lewis and Clark expedition map to modern maps.

Maps

Maps are essential in conducting onsite research, plotting mining claims, and in discovering cemeteries and towns. Several helpful maps are available for Oregon, including Ralph N. Preston's *Historical Oregon: Overland Stage Routes, Old Military Roads, Indian Battle Grounds, Old Forts, Old Gold Mines* (Portland, Ore.: Binford & Mort, 1978). This is an excellent collection of early Oregon maps beginning with the 1804 Lewis and Clark trail map to a present-day map of the state illustrating overland stage routes, old military roads, Indian battle grounds, old forts, and old mining areas.

A classic work now in its eighth edition is Philip L. Jackson and A. Jon Kimberling's *Atlas of the Pacific Northwest* (Corvallis: Oregon State University Press, 1993). A standard reference for Oregon, Washington, and Idaho, it includes 200 maps and graphs and eighteen essays on regional topics. Another excellent reference work that is also available on CD-ROM is James E. Meacham and Erik B. Steiner's *Atlas of Oregon* (Eugene, Ore.: University of Oregon Press, 2002).

Excellent local city and county maps can be obtained through the Oregon Department of Transportation, Transportation Development Division, Geographic Information Services Unit, 555 13th S. NE, Ste. 2, Salem, OR 97301-4178 <www.odot.state.or.us/home>.

The United States Geological Survey (USGS) has a catalog of its maps online at <www.usgs.gov>. The USGS office serving Oregon is at 1061 SE Cherry Blossom Dr., Portland, OR 97216.

Major libraries in Oregon have been designated by the USGS as map depository libraries. They include Southern Oregon State University in Ashland <www.sou.edu/library>; Central Oregon Community College in Bend <www.cocc.edu/library>; Oregon State University in Corvallis <http://osulibrary.orst.edu>; University of Oregon, in Eugene <http://libweb.uoregon.edu/index.php>; Pacific University in Forest Grove <http://library.pacificu.edu>; Oregon Institute of Technology in Klamath Falls <www.oit.edu/index.html?method=lbry>; Eastern Oregon State University in La Grande <http://pierce.eou.edu>; Linfield College in McMinnville <www.linfield.edu/library>; Western Oregon University in Monmouth <www.wou.edu/provost/library>; Lewis and Clark College in Portland <http://library.lclark.edu>; Portland State University in Portland <www.lib.pdx.edu>; Oregon Historical Society Library in Portland; and the Oregon State Library in Salem.

Land Records

Public-Domain State

Land records for the Oregon territorial period of 1844 to 1857 were kept with the territorial recorder. These records are indexed and are in the Oregon State Archives. Early settlers who were in Oregon by 1855 may have received grants called Donation Land Claims. Claims often provide valuable genealogical information such as a person's year and place of birth, date and place of marriage, given name of the wife, record of migration to Oregon, record of settlement on the land, citizenship, and names of witnesses and those who testified in behalf of the claimant.

Under the terms of an act of Congress approved on 27 September 1850, certain white and "half-breed" Native American settlers in Oregon Territory were entitled to land. This also applied to certain settlers arriving in the territory between 1 December 1850 and 1 December 1853. The number of acres granted to the settlers varied between 160 and 640 acres, depending upon marital status and date of settlement. Settlers were required to live on and cultivate the land for four years. Donation Claims, filed with each land office, have been abstracted, indexed, and published by the Genealogical Forum of Oregon. Indexing is both by name and geographical location. The Forum's published editions are available in many genealogical libraries. The Oregon State Archives has a microfilm copy of the U.S. Bureau of Land Management (BLM) Oregon Donation Land Claim Files as does the FHL.

Public Land Offices were opened in the following towns: Oregon City (pre-1855–1905); Winchester (1855–59); Roseburg (1860–unknown); Burns (1889–1925); Le Grande (1867–1925); Linkville (1873–77); Lakeview (1877–unknown); The Dalles (1875–unknown); and Portland (1905–25). Records generated through these land offices included cash entries, homestead final certificates, canceled homestead entries, timber-culture final certificates, canceled timber-culture entries, desert-land final certificates, canceled desert-land entries, town lots, Indian allotments, and notifications of settlers on unsurveyed lands to the surveyor general of Oregon. The Genealogical Forum of Oregon Library has a microfilm series of the BLM tract books, plat books, and survey notes for Oregon. These land office records are also on microfilm at the FHL.

In 1862, under the five-year Homestead Act, Congress provided for a gift of up to 160 acres to persons who would settle on and cultivate the lands and reside upon them for five years. This requirement was reduced to three years in 1912. The original Oregon homestead applications have been moved to the National Archives—Pacific Alaska Region (Seattle) (see page 12). They contain names of those persons whose claims were canceled. The indexes and record books have been microfilmed and are available through the FHL.

Subsequent land records, including deeds and mortgages, were recorded in each county beginning at the creation of the county. County deeds are at the Oregon State Archives and some are on microfilm at the FHL.

Probate Records

Probate records in Oregon were kept by county courts or circuit courts with large collections at the Oregon State Archives. For a listing of the probate records and where they are deposited, see the Oregon State Archives online database "Oregon Historical County Records Guide" (see County Resources). This site also provides explanations of what is covered in each record type held at the archives and what records are still deposited at the various county courthouses. The FHL also has a large collection of county probate records on microfilm.

Court Records

The Oregon court system is divided as follows: circuit courts, county courts, district courts, justice courts, municipal or city courts, and the supreme court.

Circuit courts are major trial courts. In Oregon they have countywide jurisdiction over criminal cases, probate matters, guardianships, divorces, and some administrative functions. County courts, where they exist, have countywide jurisdiction in juvenile cases, and in some probate matters. District courts have

countywide jurisdiction over minor criminal cases. Justice courts have concurrent countywide jurisdiction with circuit courts over minor criminal cases. Municipal or city courts have jurisdiction over municipal law violations or liquor control law violations. The supreme court has the final appellate jurisdiction for the entire state.

Most Oregon court records are either deposited at the state archives or remain at local county courthouses. These records and their locations are all inventoried on the Oregon State Archives website database "Oregon Historical County Records Guide" (see County Resources).

Tax Records

Some assessment or tax rolls from 1845 to 1900 are deposited at the Oregon State Archives, but most tax records are still at county courthouses. The archives also has a useful research tool from the state treasurer entitled, "Reports of Estates, 1903–1913," which contains the date of death and the names of heirs of those who died testate. This record is arranged by county, then by year.

Each county generated "Tax Lot Cards," which contain descriptions of real property and are used to track ownership, size of holding, and as a deed reference. These are inventoried on the Oregon State Archives website "Oregon Historical County Records Guide" (see County Resources).

Oregon counties are required to keep their tax rolls through 1905. All subsequent records must be kept for fifty years before they are destroyed. The exception to this is for years ending in zero or five, which are kept for research samples.

Cemetery Records

An important source in identifying and locating Oregon cemeteries is *Oregon Cemetery Survey* (Salem, Ore.: Oregon Department of Transportation, 1978). This volume records the location of every known cemetery in Oregon by utilizing modern highway maps of each county to show the location of each cemetery. A more comprehensive and contemporary work based on this earlier one is Dean H. Byrd, Stanley R. Clark, and Janice M. Healy's monumental *Oregon Burial Site Guide* (Portland, Ore.: Binford & Mort Publishing, 2001). It provides information on cemeteries missed in the 1978 work, and an easier indexing system.

Many cemetery transcriptions are on the Internet. These include <www.interment.net> with a growing selection and links to Oregon cemeteries and valuable links to Oregon sites that concern cemeteries; and "Oregon Cemetery Transcriptions" <www.rootsweb.com/~orpionpr/Cemeteries.html>. Links to various sites including preservation sites can

be found at the Oregon Historic Cemetery Association website at <www.oregoncemeteries.org>.

Local genealogical and historical societies have also indexed graveyards. Published versions are widely available, with some microfilmed records at the Oregon State Library.

Church Records

Before the turn of the twentieth century, the largest religious groups in Oregon were Roman Catholic, Methodist, Episcopal, Presbyterian, Baptist, and Christian Church. Most church registers are still housed at the original churches, though some records have been transferred to a central archive.

In 1834 Methodist missionaries led the settlement of the Willamette Valley in Marion County. Earl Howell's *Methodism in the Northwest* (Nashville: Parthenon Press, 1966) outlines the church's encounter in the Pacific Northwest. Early Methodist vital records are incomplete and scattered. Archives collections are located at Willamette University in Salem, Mark O. Hatfield Library, 900 State St., Salem, OR 97301 <http://library.willamette.edu>.

Presbyterians under the leadership of Marcus Whitman established churches in Walla Walla (now in Washington) in 1836. The first Presbyterian Church in present-day Oregon was in the home of William H. Gray on Clatsop Plains between Astoria and Seaside. The first service was given in 1846. The Oregon State Library has on file a WPA inventory of Presbyterian Churches in Oregon, indexed by the Presbyterian Historical Society in Philadelphia. These inventories consist of churches affiliated with the Presbyterian Church in the United States, United Presbyterian Church of North America, Cumberland Presbyterian Church, and Reformed Presbyterian Church, and are not complete. The inventories are in the form of questionnaires that asked for the date the congregation was organized and which church records are available, and they only list congregations in eleven Oregon counties. The Presbyterian Historical Society prepared four indexes: 1) by county name, 2) by place-name, 3) in chronological order according to the organizational date of the congregation, and 4) by church name. The indexes and the inventories are on microfilm at the FHL.

The first permanent Episcopalian minister was Rev. St. Michael Fackler, who came to Oregon City in 1847. The vital records of the Diocese of Eastern Oregon were gathered by its historian. These have been microfilmed and are at the Oregon State Library along with an index to baptisms from 1873 to 1956 extracted from the records and interfiled in the "Oregon Collection" catalog.

The Episcopal Diocese of Oregon, 11800 SW Military Lane, Portland, OR 97219 <www.diocese-oregon.org> has archives that include records of defunct parishes and diaries of bishops of the diocese dating back to 1841.

The Quakers arrived in Oregon prior to the Civil War and founded the first Friends Sunday School in Ashland during the early 1850s. No communities or meetings were developed until the 1870s due to the fact that Quaker families were scattered throughout the region. From the 1870s onward, the migration of Quaker families into Oregon was rapid, and the Oregon Yearly Meeting was established in 1893. Most of the early Oregon Friends were representatives of Orthodox, Gurneyite Quakerism. By 1890, there were slightly less than 1,000 Quakers in Oregon. For a history of Oregon's Quaker community, see Ralph K. Beebe's *A Garden of the Lord: A History of Oregon Yearly Meetings of Friends Church* (n.p., ca. 1968). A repository of Quaker records is at George Fox University, 414 N. Meridian St., Newberg, OR 97132 <www.georgefox.edu>.

Two Catholic priests arrived in what is now Oregon from Quebec in 1838. They established a mission at St. Paul, north of Salem, on what is called French Prairie, where Hudson Bay fur trappers had a settlement. The priests also traveled the Pacific Northwest, establishing missions and churches. The early Oregon Catholic records are well preserved and have been transcribed by Harriet Duncan Minnick in her seven volumes of *Catholic Church Records of the Pacific Northwest* (Portland, Ore.: Binford & Mort, 1972–1989). Catholic repositories include Diocese of Baker, 911 SE Armour St., Bend, OR 97702 (mailing address: P.O. Box 5999, Bend, OR 97708) <www.dioceseofbaker.org> and Archdiocese of Portland in Oregon, Archives, 2838 E. Burnside, Portland, OR 97214 <www.archdpdx.org>.

When Mormon missionaries first arrived in Oregon in 1857, they were met with great opposition. For this reason, missionary work was postponed until later in the century. In 1890 the establishment of the Oregon Lumber Company at Sumter Valley brought an influx of Mormon families into Oregon. The Amalgamated Sugar Factory, built in 1897, brought still more people to the state seeking employment. Thus, Malheur County has a large Mormon population dating back to the 1880s. Ward/branch and mission records of The Church of Jesus Christ of Latter-day Saints are deposited at the FHL. Today The Church of Jesus Christ of Latter-day Saints is one of the largest denominations in the state.

The Lutheran Church Missouri Synod, Northwest District, 1700 NE Knott St., Portland, OR 97212 <www.lcms.org> has archival holdings relating to the history of the denomination, biographical material, and congregational records.

Jewish settlers came to Oregon early. Oregon's first synagogue was the Congregation Beth Israel, organized in Portland in 1858. Other congregations soon followed, among them the Congregation Ahavath Achim, organized in Portland in 1911. This synagogue was composed of Sephardic Jews who came from Turkey and the island of Rhodes.

The Oregon Jewish Museum, 310 NW Davis St., Portland, OR 97209 <www.ojm.org/index.html> houses the archive of the Jewish Historical Society of Oregon, which includes a library collection of documents, photographs, and record books pertaining to Jewish life in Oregon as well as some synagogue and Hebrew school records, and transcripts of interviews with members of the local Jewish community.

Military Records

The Oregon State Archives has an extensive collection of early and more current military records of residents. This includes information from the Indian Wars and the Oregon National Guard. The collection at the state archives should be one of the first places to seek information about a soldier. Many Oregon soldiers spent their last years in the Oregon Soldiers Home in Roseburg. The state archives and the FHL have microfilm copies of these important records.

The Oregon GenWeb Project (see Archives, Libraries, and Societies) is another source for growing information on soldiers from Oregon serving in the military. It has a growing number of links and databases to soldiers from various wars and conflicts.

M. A. Parker and Edna Mingus' roster of volunteers from Oregon who served in the Civil War, *Soldiers Who Served in the Oregon Volunteers Civil War Period Infantry and Cavalry* (Portland, Ore.: Genealogical Forum of Oregon, 1961) provides the name of the soldier, rank, date of service, place of enlistment, place of birth, age, occupation, and company.

The Official Records of the Oregon Volunteers in the Spanish War and Philippine Insurrection by C.U. Gantenbein (Salem, Ore.: J.R. Whitney, State Printers, 1903) is a roster of soldiers providing age, place of birth, occupation, physical description, and time of service.

World War I records on file at the Oregon State Archives include an index to all World War I veterans who served from Oregon, World War I files from the state historian of the Defense Council, records of state bonuses, and loan applications of veterans. World War I files include some biographical questionnaires and are useful in genealogical research. The World War I Draft Registration Cards are available through the National Archives and at the FHL. Oregon State Archives has a casualty index to the Korean Police Action, 1950 to 1954, and an index to the Oregon State Reserve in World War II, 1940 to 1945.

Periodicals, Newspapers, and Manuscript Collections

Periodicals
The periodical collections at the Oregon State Library and at the Oregon Historical Society include publications of local and county historical societies in Oregon. Major Oregon periodicals include the *Oregon Historical Quarterly*, published by the Oregon Historical Society with an online index on the society's website; the *Bulletin*, published by the Genealogical Forum of Oregon, Inc.; and the *Oregon Genealogical Society Quarterly*, published by the Oregon Genealogical Society.

Newspapers
The largest Oregon newspaper collection on microfilm is at the University of Oregon's Knight Library, inventoried online at <http://libweb.uoregon.edu/govdocs/micro/papers.htm>. The second largest newspaper collection is at the Oregon Historical Society.

Manuscripts
The Oregon State Library has manuscripts in their microfilm collection. Betty Book's *Manuscripts on Microfilm at Oregon State Library* (reprinted by Genealogical Council of Oregon, 1990) provides the titles and major topic of each manuscript.

The WPA organized large quantities of documents. Included in these projects were unpublished county manuscripts, containing biographical sketches, church histories, cemetery information, interviews, town histories, etc. These are deposited at the University of Oregon and the Oregon State Library in Salem. The University of Oregon's Manuscript and Rare Book Collection, located in the Knight Library, also has a large number of manuscripts dealing with Oregon history and development.

The Oregon Historical Society has several biographical aids to assist the researcher. One such collection is the vertical file, consisting of newspaper clippings including 4,000 subjects on state and local history and 1,500 biographies and genealogies of prominent Oregonians. Also covered in these files are historic structures, ethnic groups, cities, counties, Portland neighborhoods, railroads, and maritime history. This collection is indexed. The library also has a "Biography Card File," which contains information from books, newspapers, scrapbooks, and Indian War pension papers.

Another collection at the Oregon Historical Society is the "Pioneer Card File" which provides data on early emigrants. The "DAR Card File" indexes material in the DAR books on file at the society.

The work compiled by the Oregon Daughters of the American Revolution (DAR) is on thirty-three rolls of microfilm at the FHL. The collection consists of Bible records, cemetery records, wills, marriage records, divorce records, records of pioneers, church records, donation land claims, compiled genealogies, and military records. It is divided by county and general Oregon state items.

Archives, Libraries, and Societies

Oregon State Archives
800 Summer St. NE
Salem, OR 97310
http://arcweb.sos.state.or.us/default.htm

The "Oregon Historical County Records Guide" database on its website provides access to a large number of original sources in its collections.

Oregon State Library
250 Winter St. NE
Salem, OR 97301-3950
www.osl.state.or.us/home

Oregon Historical Society
1200 SW Park Ave.
Portland, OR 97203
www.ohs.org

Genealogical Forum of Oregon, Inc.
P.O. Box 42567
Portland, OR 97242-0567
www.gfo.org

Oregon Genealogical Society
P.O. Box 10306
955 Oak Alley
Eugene, OR 97440-2306

University of Oregon
Knight Library, 2d Floor North
15th & Kincaid St.
Eugene, OR 97403
http://libweb.uoregon.edu

Southern Oregon Historical Society
106 Central Ave.
Medford, OR 97501
www.sohs.org

The Oregon GenWeb Project <www.rootsweb.com/~orgenweb/> and the Genealogical Council of Oregon <www.rootsweb.com/~orgco/mission.htm> provide information on statewide genealogical organization. The catalogs for major Oregon academic university and college libraries can be accessed through ORBIS <http://orbis.uoregon.edu>.

Special Focus Categories

Immigration

Immigrants arrived in Oregon from six ports: Astoria, Newport, North Bend, Portland, Reedsport, and Tillamook. Records concerning the port of Portland are on file at the National Archives—Pacific Alaska Region (Seattle) and include records of the Immigration and Naturalization Service, Portland Office, and the Portland Collector of Customs. No passenger lists for the port of Portland or the smaller ports have been found at this time.

Naturalization

Foreign-born residents could become naturalized in any court of record. Records created prior to 1906 may still be in the county. Some records were not kept in separate naturalization books, but in court journals or court minutes, making them difficult to locate. The Oregon State Archives has a large collection of citizenship records.

Native American

The history of Oregon's Native American population is similar to that of Washington. Coastal tribes were little affected by the Spaniards in California or the fur traders. However, from the mid-nineteenth century onward, the Native Americans of Oregon were rapidly dispossessed and placed upon reservations as follows: most of the Chinookan tribes were placed on the Warm Springs and Grande Ronde reservations and on Yakima Reservation in Washington; all of the Athapascan tribes were placed on the Siletz Reservation; the Umpqua went to the Grand Ronde; the Kusan and Yakonan tribes were placed on the Siletz Reservation; the Salishan population of Oregon was placed on the Grande Ronde and Siletz reservations; most of the Kalapooian peoples went to the Grand Ronde and a few on the Siletz; most of the Molala went to the Grande Ronde; the Klamath went to Klamath Reserve; the Modoc went mostly on the Klamath Reserve, but a few went to the Quapaw Reservation in Oklahoma; the Shahaptian tribes of Oregon went to the Umatilla Reservation; and the Northern Paiutes went to the Klamath Reservation.

For a more detailed history of each Oregon reservation and land definitions, see Jeff Zucker, *Oregon Indians: Culture, History and Current Affairs, An Atlas and Introduction* (Portland, Ore.: Oregon Historical Society, ca. 1983).

Many Native Americans converted to Catholicism, and the early parish and mission registers have been printed. An excellent source of Native American family genealogies is Charles E. McChesney et al., *Rolls of Certain Indian Tribes In Washington and Oregon* (Fairfield, Wash.: Ye Galleon Press, 1969).

Many Native American records are microfilmed and are on file at the National Archives—Pacific Alaska Region (Seattle); some are on file at the FHL. The following agency records are available:

Grand Ronde-Siletz Agency, Toledo, Oregon (1863–1954). Records include general correspondence and decimal files, school records, heirship cards, maps, annuity payrolls, ledgers

for accounts of individual Indians, vital statistics and census rolls, health reports, social service case files, court records, tribal constitutions, records concerning land allotments and sales, forestry, Civilian Conservation Corps work, and relief and rehabilitation. This agency was established in 1856 for Native Americans living on the Coast Reservation who had been moved from other parts of Oregon. The principal tribes under this agency were the Joshua, Sixes (Kwatami), Chetco, Rogue River, Chastacosta, and Klamath.

Klamath Indian Agency, Klamath Falls, Oregon (1865–1960). Records include general subject files, tribal election ballots, business committee and general council minutes, Klamath Loan Board files, records concerning irrigation, allotments and other land transactions, forestry, grazing, agricultural extension, accounts of individual Indians, law and order, annuities, and medical care. Klamath was made a full agency in 1872, with the Klamath, Modoc, "Snake," Pit River, and Shoshone tribes under its jurisdiction.

Portland Area Office, Portland, Oregon (1902–64). Records include program planning records, minutes of the Columbia Basin Inter-Agency Committee, correspondence and reports concerning schools, grazing permits, welfare case files, tribal constitutions, legal case files, allotment ledgers, records concerning land allotments and sales, land classification, heirship, forestry, irrigation, road construction, tribal welfare, and health.

Umatilla Indian Agency, Pendleton, Oregon (1862–1964). Records include general correspondence, school records, tribal rolls, records concerning farming and grazing leases, the Civilian Conservation Corps program, individual Indian accounts, land allotments, heirship, family histories, medical treatment, law enforcement, court cases, and economic and social surveys. This agency was established in 1861 for the Umatilla, Cayuse, and Walla Walla tribes. Other tribes were later transferred to this agency.

Warm Springs Indian Agency, Warm Springs, Oregon (1861–1952). Records include general correspondence, decimal files, school attendance records, land and survey field notes, a tract book, cattle sales reports, ledgers and abstracts of individual Indian accounts, appropriation land allotment ledgers, censuses, a family history record, individual Indian history cards, court dockets, birth and death registers, medical reports, tribal council records, records concerning lease payments, forestry, Civilian Conservation Corps programs, roads, and per capita payments. This agency was established in 1851 for the Warm Springs, Wasco, Tenino, John Day, and Northern Paiute tribes.

A valuable source for Native American research is the Chemawa Indian School records, a non-reservation school established in Forest Grove, Oregon, in 1880. In 1885 the school was moved to a site north of Salem known as Chemawa, where it has been called both Chemawa and Salem. The school is important because it enrolled students from all over the Pacific Northwest. The school records include general correspondence, decimal files, descriptive statements about children, applications for admission, attendance records, student health cards, student and graduate student case files, and ledgers for accounts of individual Indians. These school records are on file at the National Archives—Pacific Alaska Region (Seattle) and the FHL.

Another major source for Native American research is the Major James McLaughlin Papers.

Other Ethnic Groups

The southeast corner of Oregon has a large population of Basques, who arrived in the latter 1800s and early 1900s. Basques usually entered America at Ellis Island and drifted across the country. Principal Basque settlements in Oregon were McDermitt, on the northern Nevada border; Jordan Valley; Andrews, 125 miles south of Crane; Fields, 15 miles further south; and Ontario, Oregon, at the junction of the Malheur River and the Snake River.

In 1925 McDermitt was almost completely a Basque town, and by 1945 Jordan Valley had the largest Basque settlement in southeast Oregon with two-thirds of the population of Basque descent. The University of Nevada has major Basque collections, which include 12,000 volumes concerning the Basques in America. For more information, contact at the Basque Studies Program, University of Nevada, Getchell Library, Rm. 274, Reno, NV 89557 <www.library.unr.edu/depts/basqlib/Default.htm>.

During the 1880s, Oregon's Chinese population greatly increased as a result of extensive railroad construction in the area. Tension rose against the Asiatics in the Pacific Northwest. Shortly after the riots against Seattle and Tacoma's Chinatowns in November 1885, Portland held an anti-Chinese convention during which resolutions were adopted requiring the Chinese population to relocate to San Francisco within thirty days. The first group of Chinese laborers coming directly to Portland arrived in 1888.

The Chinese played a vital role in the development of eastern Oregon. Eastern Oregon's growth was dependent on the railroad and mining for which the Chinese provided the majority of labor. By 1857 the Chinese began moving north from California to Oregon to begin mining. Migrants began to move eastward from southern Oregon when gold was discovered on the Powder River in Oregon and the Salmon River in Idaho. By 1880 many Chinese mining companies were in operation at John Day in Grant County. Christopher Howard Edson's, *The Chinese in Eastern Oregon, 1860–1890* (San Francisco: R and E Research Associates, 1974) is an excellent study of the contributions of the Chinese community to the settlement and development of eastern Oregon.

A few Japanese entered Oregon between 1880 and 1890, but the greatest migration came during subsequent decades. Japanese immigrants generally worked as railroad hands, sawmill workers, and agricultural laborers. A total of 2,501 Japanese were recorded in the 1900 U.S. census of Oregon. By 1930 the Japanese population in Oregon had doubled. During World War II, hysteria swept America and Oregon's Japanese community came under suspicion. Many Japanese-Americans were relocated to camps in Idaho where they remained until the war was over.

County Resources

A major resource for identifying records and where they are deposited and used in developing the following county chart is the Oregon State Archives' online "Oregon Historical County Records Guide" <http://arcweb.sos.state.or.us/county/cphome.html>. It provides a map, history and guide to the status of each county's records. Consider it one of the first resources for seeking county records.

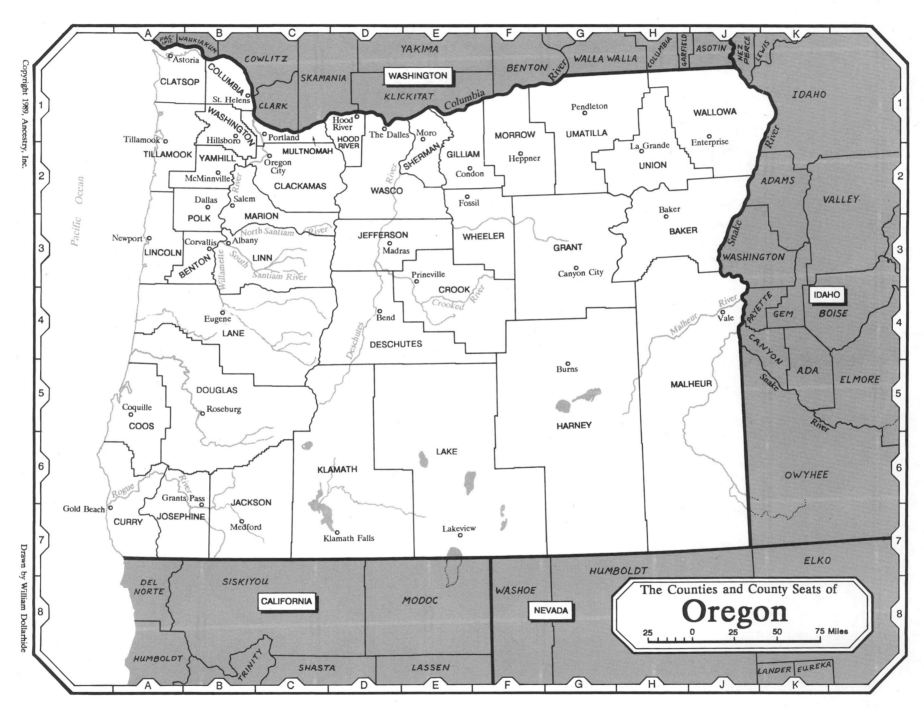

The Counties and County Seats of

Oregon

OREGON

562

25   0   25   50   75 Miles

Oregon counties and county seats labeled on map:

CLATSOP — Astoria
COLUMBIA — St. Helens
TILLAMOOK — Tillamook
YAMHILL — McMinnville
WASHINGTON — Hillsboro
MULTNOMAH — Portland
CLACKAMAS — Oregon City
POLK — Dallas
MARION — Salem
LINCOLN — Newport
BENTON — Corvallis
LINN — Albany
LANE — Eugene
DOUGLAS — Roseburg
COOS — Coquille
CURRY — Gold Beach
JOSEPHINE — Grants Pass
JACKSON — Medford
KLAMATH — Klamath Falls
LAKE — Lakeview
HOOD RIVER — Hood River
WASCO — The Dalles
SHERMAN — Moro
GILLIAM — Condon
JEFFERSON — Madras
WHEELER — Fossil
CROOK — Prineville
DESCHUTES — Bend
HARNEY — Burns
MORROW — Heppner
UMATILLA — Pendleton
UNION — La Grande
WALLOWA — Enterprise
GRANT — Canyon City
BAKER — Baker
MALHEUR — Vale

Bordering states/regions:

WASHINGTON
WAHKIAKUM
COWLITZ
CLARK
SKAMANIA
KLICKITAT
YAKIMA
BENTON
WALLA WALLA
COLUMBIA
GARFIELD
ASOTIN
NEZ PERCE
LEWIS
IDAHO
ADAMS
VALLEY
WASHINGTON
IDAHO — Boise
PAYETTE
GEM
CANYON
ADA
ELMORE
OWYHEE
ELKO
HUMBOLDT
WASHOE
NEVADA
LANDER
EUREKA
LASSEN
MODOC
SHASTA
TRINITY
SISKIYOU
DEL NORTE
HUMBOLDT
CALIFORNIA

Rivers labeled:

Pacific Ocean
Columbia River
Willamette River
North Santiam River
South Santiam River
Deschutes River
Crooked River
Rogue River
Snake River
Malheur River

OREGON

Map	County Address	Date Formed Parent County/ies	Birth Marriage Death	Deeds Probate Court
H3	Baker 1995 Third St Baker City 97814	1862 Wasco	1871 1862 1905	1862 1862 1882
B3	Benton 120 N.W. 4th Corvallis 97330	1847 Polk	1907 1850 1907	1851 1850 1849
	Champoeg	1843 (renamed Marion, 1849) original		
C2	Clackamas 906 Main St. Oregon City 97045	1843 original	1902 1848 1902	1850 1844 1845
A1	Clatsop 749 Commercial Astoria 97103	1844 Tuality District	1894 1851 1903	1849 1847 1847
B1	Columbia Courthouse St. Helens 97051	1854 Washington	1907 1854 1907	1850 1850 1854
A5	Coos 205 N. Baxter Coquille 97423	1853 Jackson/Umpqua	1888 1853 1906	1854 1852 1853
E4	Crook 300 E. Third Prineville 97754	1882 Wasco	1907 1882 1907	1864 1882 1882
A7	Curry 29821 Ellensburg Ave. Gold Beach 97444	1855 Coos	——— 1856 ———	1856 1856 1856
D4	Deschutes 1130 NW Harriman Bend 97701	1916 Crook	——— 1916 1916	1869 1916 1883
B5	Douglas 1036 S.E. Douglas Roseburg 97470	1851 Umpqua	1903 1852 1903	1851 1852 1852
E2	Gilliam 221 S. Oregon St. Condon 97823	1885 Wasco	1903 1885 1912	1871 1884 1859
G3	Grant 201 S. Humbolt Canyon City 97820	1864 Umatilla/Wasco	1894 1864 1915	1862 1864 1864
G6	Harney 450 N. Buena Vista Burns 97720	1889 Grant	——— 1889 ———	1871 1889 1885
D1	Hood River 309 State St. Hood River 97031-2093	1908 Wasco	1907 1908 1907	1861 1868 1875
B7	Jackson 10 S. Oakdale Medford 97501	1852 Lane	1906 1855 1906	1853 1853 1853
D3	Jefferson 75 SE "C" St. Madras 97741	1914 Crook	1886 1882 1886	1864 1883 1881
A7	Josephine 500 NW Sixth St. Grants Pass 97526	1856 Jackson	1906 1857 1906	1854 1848 1854
D6	Klamath 305 Main St. Klamath Falls 97601	1882 Lake	——— 1882 ———	1870 1882 1872
E6	Lake 513 Center St. Lakeview 97630 Land added from Grant County in 1885.	1874 Jackson/Wasco	——— 1875 ———	1870 1875 1874
B4	Lane 125 E. Eighth Eugene 97401	1851 Linn/Umpqua/Benton	1882 1852 1882	1854 1852 1852
A3	Lincoln 225 W. Olive St. Newport 97365	1893 Benton/Polk	1907 1893 1907	1865 1867 1855
C3	Linn 300 Fourth Ave. SW Albany 97321	1847 Champoeg	1903 1850 1903	1853 1850 1854
J6	Malheur 251 B St. W. Vale 97918	1887 Baker	1907 1880 1907	1863 1886 1861
B2	Marion 100 High St. N.E. Salem 97301	1843 (as Champoeg; renamed 1849) original	1871 1849 1907	1850 1843 1841
F1	Morrow 100 Court St. Heppner 97836	1885 Umatilla/Wasco	1905 1885 1905	1861 1885 1868
C1	Multnomah Records Center 1620 S.E. 190th Ave. Portland 97233	1854 Clackamas/Washington	1864 (Portland) 1855 1862 (Portland)	1849 1850 1849
B3	Polk 850 Main St. Dallas 97338	1845 Yamhill District	1903 1848 1903	1851 1847 1846
E2	Sherman 500 Court St. Moro 97039	1889 Wasco	1904 1889 1905	1859 1888 1870
A2	Tillamook 201 Laurel Ave. Tillamook 97141	1853 Clatsop/Yamhill/Polk	1903 1854 1903	1854 1859 1854
	Tuality	1843 (renamed Washington, 1849) Original		
G1	Umatilla 216 S.E. 4th Pendleton 97801	1862 Wasco	1890 1862 1892	1861 1863 1862

OREGON

Map	County Address	Date Formed Parent County/ies	Birth Marriage Death	Deeds Probate Court
	Umpqua	1851–63 (became part of Douglas, 1862) Benton		
H2	Union 1001 4th St. Ste. D La Grande 97850	1864 Baker	1905 1864 1905	1864 1864 1864
G1	Wallowa 101 S. River Enterprise 97828	1887 Union	1905 1879 1905	1875 1886 1887
D2	Wasco 511 Washington The Dalles 97058	1854 Marion/Clackamas/Linn	1865 1854 1865	1854 1854 1848

Map	County Address	Date Formed Parent County/ies	Birth Marriage Death	Deeds Probate Court
B1	Washington 155 N. First Hillsboro 97124	1843 (as Tuality District; renamed 1849) original	1907 1842 1903	1847 1842 1844
F3	Wheeler 701 Adams St. Fossil 97830	1899 Crook/Gilliam/Grant	1915 1896 1915	1865 1887 1888
B2	Yamhill 535 E. Fifth McMinnville 97128	1843 original	1871 1856 1875	1852 1849 1843

Pennsylvania

ROGER D. JOSLYN, CG, FUGA, FGBS, FASG

The Dutch first came to the area now known as Pennsylvania following Henry Hudson's exploration of the Delaware River, the state's waterway to the Atlantic, but they did little more than establish trading posts. Swedes arrived in 1638 and, with the Finns, who came about the same time, spilled over into what is now the Philadelphia area. The Dutch gained control of this New Sweden in 1655, but nine years later England conquered New Netherland, and Pennsylvania became a part of the Duke of York's new territory, which included New York, New Jersey, and Delaware. In 1673 and 1674 the Dutch regained control, but soon the colony was back under English rule.

None of these early settlements had a more lasting impression on Pennsylvania than did William Penn's colony. Chartered in 1681 by King Charles II to Penn, a Quaker, Pennsylvania received its new governor aboard the *Welcome* the following year. The new immigrants were primarily English Quakers, although some were of Welsh, Scottish, and Irish ancestry. Pennsylvania became a royal province briefly from 1692 to 1694, when Penn lost his power over the conflict between the proprietary and popular elements, but the colony then resumed under the proprietary government until the American Revolution. Penn and his descendants left a long-standing influence, especially in terms of governing, in dealing with the native population, and in providing a haven of religious tolerance.

Penn's "Holy Experiment" encouraged throngs of immigrants in the next century. The two largest groups were the Ulster-Scots (also referred to as the Scots-Irish), who first came in 1707 and in greater numbers from 1728 on, and the Germans, who first arrived in 1683. The Germans, mostly from the Rhine, included subgroups that characterize those who have become known, more culturally than ethnically, as the "Pennsylvania Dutch"— Lutherans, Reformed, Mennonites, Amish, Dunkers (Dunkards), Moravians, Roman Catholics, and Schwenkfelders. After an initial settlement in Germantown (now part of Philadelphia), they became a significant portion of the population in Montgomery, Lancaster, Northampton, Lehigh, Berks, Lebanon, and York counties. The Ulster-Scots settled first in Lancaster, Dauphin, and Chester counties, and then moved westward into the Cumberland Valley. Both groups eventually contributed to the settlement of southwestern Pennsylvania. The westward movements were made despite the Allegheny Mountains that diagonally divide the rectangular-shaped state, and early settlements tended to be made in the valleys, such as the Cumberland, Lebanon, and Lehigh. Other immigrants in the 1700s included Welsh (some of whom were Quakers), French (including Huguenots, later Acadians, and at the end of the century refugees from revolution-torn France and Haiti), Irish, Jews, and African Americans. In spite of the strong Quaker influence, slavery did exist in Pennsylvania, but of the 10,000 African Americans there in 1790, over half were free, and slavery was phased out in the early 1800s.

Most of Pennsylvania's western settlers had migrated from the eastern part of the province. Some came up from Maryland and Virginia, such as Ulster-Scots and Germans, many of whom had ventured south from Pennsylvania earlier. The Holland Land Company's territory extended into the northwestern part of Pennsylvania, where New Yorkers met Pennsylvanians coming north from Washington, Allegheny, and other southwestern counties.

It has generally been believed that the Penns dealt fairly with the Native Americans, peacefully acquiring additional territory through treaties and purchase; however, some historians question this. As settlers pushed westward, they forced the natives ahead of them, and the resulting hostilities peaked during the French and Indian War. This conflict caused Pennsylvania to create its first militia in order to defend the frontier settlements.

Connecticut claimed northeastern Pennsylvania and began sending settlers there in the 1750s. A bitter conflict ensued until Connecticut relinquished its claim through the Decree of Trenton in 1782. Other boundary disputes took place with New York and, in the southwest, with Virginia. The most famous, however, was the controversy between the Penns and Lord Baltimore. A temporary line was drawn with Maryland in 1739, but the fixed boundary was not settled until Charles Mason and Jeremiah Dixon's work was ratified in 1769, creating what became the historic slave/free state division between the North and South.

At the time of the Revolutionary War, Pennsylvania was the "keystone" between the northern and southern colonies since many important events took place in Philadelphia that shaped the emerging nation; in fact, the state's charter referred to the "Commonwealth" of Pennsylvania, to help express democracy. The British invaded Philadelphia and defeated the patriots at Germantown in 1776, but Pennsylvania is probably best remembered for the harsh winter of 1777–78 that Washington's poorly trained army spent at Valley Forge. During the War of 1812, Pennsylvanians were instrumental in Commodore Perry's victory on Lake Erie. (The "Erie Triangle," now Erie County, was purchased from Native Americans in 1792, to provide the state with a port on the lake. Pennsylvania's third port is Pittsburgh, whose early development was the result of its location on the Ohio River.) The Commonwealth was greatly involved in the Civil War, including the Battle of Gettysburg, a major turning point for the Union army.

In the nineteenth century Pennsylvania experienced the same growth through transportation systems of canals, roads, and railroads, as did the other mid-Atlantic states. Like its neighbors, Pennsylvania also received a large influx of new immigrants, such as Irish and Germans, followed by Italians, Poles, Scandinavians, Russians, Slovaks, and others. Many of these groups, as well as African Americans migrating north, took part in the tremendous industrial growth of the Commonwealth—in the steel production in Bethlehem and Pittsburgh, the coal mining around Scranton, Wilkes-Barre, and in western Pennsylvania, and the oil fields in the northwest.

Vital Records

Although a colonial law of 1682 provided for the recording of births, marriages, and burials in Pennsylvania, few if any of these events were ever entered in civil records. A new law in the mid-nineteenth century required the county register of wills to record these events, with copies sent to Harrisburg. These records, covering 1852 to 1854 but surviving and incomplete for only forty-nine counties, might still be found the courthouses, with duplicate returns at the Pennsylvania State Archives, where microfilms of many are available. Indexes to these records are arranged first by county, then by event, then by year. Microfilms of some of these records are also available at the Historical Society of Pennsylvania (see Archives, Libraries, and Societies), the Carnegie Library of Pittsburgh, and the State Library of Pennsylvania. Additionally, Closson Press of Apollo, Pennsylvania, has published the records for most of the extant counties. From 1860 through 1893, births and deaths were recorded in Philadelphia. Other cities, such as Allegheny, Easton, Harrisburg, Pottsville, Pittsburgh, and Williamsport, also maintained vital records later in the nineteenth century, although there are gaps in the records. Since 1885 the clerk of the orphans' court in each county has had the responsibility of recording marriages. Microfilms of some of these records are at the state archives and the Historical Society of Pennsylvania. Births and deaths in Pennsylvania were also recorded in the county orphans' courts (1893–1906), and here also may be found delayed registrations of birth for events occurring as far back as the 1860s. The state archives has microfilms of some of these records; the Philadelphia City Archives and the Historical Society of Pennsylvania have them for Philadelphia (1860–1915).

Statewide registration of births and deaths has occurred since 1906, although compliance with the law was scattered for at least the first ten years. To request these records, complete form H105.102 and submit it with the current fee of $4 for a birth record or $3 for a death record to Division of Vital Statistics, State Department of Health, Central Building, 101 S. Mercer St., P.O. Box 1528, New Castle, PA 16103-1528. Further instructions, fees, and downloadable forms are online at <www.health.state.pa.us>. Application can also be made at one of the following five Division of Vital Records branch offices: Health & Welfare Building, Rm 129, Foster St. and Commonwealth Ave., P.O. Box 90, Harrisburg, PA 17120-0090; Rm 902, 401 N. Broad St., Philadelphia, PA 19108; Rm 512, 300 Liberty Ave., Pittsburgh, PA 15222; 3832 Liberty St., Erie, PA 16509; or 100 Lackawanna Ave., Scranton, PA 18503.

Marriage licenses were not required in colonial Pennsylvania, but information from surviving marriage bonds (1743–90) was published in *Pennsylvania Archives*, series 2, volume 2, and reprinted with some other records as *Pennsylvania Marriages Prior to 1790* (Baltimore: Genealogical Publishing Co., 1984). These records provide the names of the couple and the date of the bond. See also "List of Marriage Licenses Issued in the Secretary's Office, from August 1755 through April 1759" in *Pennsylvania Genealogical Magazine* 21 (1960):

312-27. Many early church marriage records were published in *Pennsylvania Archives*, series 2, vols. 8 and 9, and reprinted as *Record of Pennsylvania Marriages Prior to 1810*, 2 vols. (Baltimore: Genealogical Publishing Co., 1987). The three-volume *Pennsylvania Vital Records* (Baltimore: Genealogical Publishing Co., 1983) reprints a number of articles containing births, baptisms, marriages, deaths, and divorces from *The Pennsylvania Magazine of History and Biography* and *The Pennsylvania Genealogical Magazine*.

Aside from the exceptions noted above and for marriages recorded from 1885 in the county Orphans' Courts, nineteenth-century civil vital records in Pennsylvania are practically non-existent. It is important, therefore, to make use of substitutes such as church and justice of the peace records, grave marker inscriptions and burial records, newspaper marriage and death notices, and censuses. John T. Humphrey compiled a series of *Pennsylvania Births* to 1800 for the counties of Berks, Bucks, Chester, Delaware, Lancaster, Lebanon, Lehigh, Montgomery, Northampton, Philadelphia, and York (various publishers, 1991–98) taken from over two hundred church registers and Quaker monthly meeting records. All but York County is also on CD-ROM: *Birth Index: Southeastern Pennsylvania, 1680–1800*, Family Tree Maker Family Archive #196 (Brøderbund, 1998).

Most Pennsylvania divorce records from 1804 are found in the county court of common pleas, where the prothonotary is usually the clerk with custody of the records. Only two divorces found in the Pennsylvania *Statutes at Large* exist for the colonial period—one granted in 1769 and a second voided in 1772. Divorces were granted, mostly for adultery, by the General Assembly during and following the Revolutionary War, for which one should consult *Statutes at Large of Pennsylvania*, beginning with volume 7. The assembly had jurisdiction from 1776 to 1847 (see Candy Crocker Livengood, *Genealogical Abstracts of Pennsylvania & the Statutes at Large* [Westminster, Md.: Family Line Publications, 1990], and also Joel Fishman, "A Bibliographical Description of the Legal Works Cited in Candy Livengood's *Genealogical Abstracts of the Laws of Pennsylvania & Statutes at Large* [1990]," *Western Pennsylvania Genealogical Society Quarterly* 22 [1996]: 6–7). The supreme court had concurrent jurisdiction of granting divorces from 1785 to 1804, and its records to 1801 were published in *Publications of the Genealogical Society of Pennsylvania* 1 (1898): 185-92, and reprinted in *Pennsylvania Vital Records* (see above), 425–31. A list of 383 divorces and annulments granted by the Pennsylvania Supreme Court (but not including many divorce petitions not granted) is found in Thomas L. Yoset, "Divorces Granted by the Pennsylvania Legislature (1770–1874)," *Crawford County Genealogy* 21 (1998): 53-82. The state archives has divorce papers (1786–1815) from the records of the Supreme Court. Philadelphia divorce dockets (1851–74) are in that city's archives.

Census Records

Federal

Population Schedules
- Indexed—1790, 1800, 1810, 1820, 1830, 1840, 1850, 1860, 1870, 1880, 1900, 1910, 1920, 1930
- Soundex—1880, 1900, 1910 (miracode), 1920

Industrial and Agricultural Schedules
- 1850, 1860, 1870, 1880

Mortality Schedules
- 1850, 1860, 1870, 1880 (1880 not indexed)

Veterans Schedules
- 1890

From the first federal census of 1790, the records are nearly complete for Pennsylvania, and microfilms of the federal copies are widely available at the National Archives—Mid-Atlantic Region (see page 11), the Pennsylvania State Archives, the Historical Society of Pennsylvania, the Pennsylvania State Library, the Carnegie Library of Pittsburgh (see Archives, Libraries, and Societies), and other libraries. Two enumerations were taken in Philadelphia in 1870; the second includes the street address. Gaps in the records are the following: 1800 (parts of Bedford and Westmoreland counties); 1810 (parts of Bedford, Cumberland, and Philadelphia counties); and 1820 (parts of Lancaster, Lehigh, Luzerne, and Monroe counties).

There are three published book indexes for the 1800 census and two for 1810. The 1850 census also has two indexes, one arranged by county. An all-name index to the 1850 to 1880 censuses for Pittsburgh and Allegheny City is at the Carnegie Library of Pittsburgh. For the 1910 Miracode, Philadelphia County is indexed apart from the rest of the commonwealth. The original schedules of the 1880 census, microfilmed by the National Archives, are now in the state archives. The state copies of the 1840 to 1870 censuses are no longer extant, but a few county copies are known to exist. Microfilm of the non-population and mortality schedules for 1850 to 1880 are at the state library and at the National Archives—Mid-Atlantic Region.

Pennsylvania took no state censuses, but an enumeration of taxpayers compiled every seven years from 1779 through 1863 is commonly called the Septennial Census. These records have only survived in small numbers and are available at the state archives and on microfilm at the Family History Library (FHL) at Salt Lake City.

Background Sources

Many of Pennsylvania's early government records were published in two groups. The first group contained the *Minutes of the Provincial Council* and *The Supreme Executive Council of Pennsylvania,* usually referred to as *The Colonial Records,* 16 vols. (1838–53; reprint, New York: A.M.S. Press, 1971). Beginning in 1852, the first of nine series of *Pennsylvania Archives* was published. The published archives include records concerning military service and pensions, land warrants, naturalizations, baptisms and marriages, tax lists, ships' lists, Native Americans, boundary disputes, Provincial Assembly journals, and actions of governors, as well as maps. Not all the volumes are indexed and some of the original material from which they were prepared is now gone, but there are helpful guides that should be consulted. Among these are Henry Howard Eddy and Martha L. Simonetti, eds., *Guide to the Published Archives of Pennsylvania* (Harrisburg, Pa.: Historical and Museum Commission, 1949; reprint, 1976); Sally A. Weikel, comp., *Genealogical Research in the Published Pennsylvania Archives* (Harrisburg, Pa.: State Library of Pennsylvania, 1976); Jean S. Morris, comp., *Use of the Published Pennsylvania Archives in Genealogical Research,* 2d ed. (Pittsburgh: Western Pennsylvania Genealogical Society, 2003); and Christine Crawford-Oppenheimer, *Lost in Pennsylvania? Try the Published Pennsylvania Archives,* Genealogical Society of Pennsylvania Special Publication No. 7 (Philadelphia, 1999). See also Frank B. Evans, "The Many Faces of the Pennsylvania Archives," *American Archivist* 27 (1964): 271, and Roland M. Baumann, "Dr. Sheuk's Missing Series of the Published Pennsylvania Archives," *Pennsylvania Magazine of History and Biography* 103 (1979): 415-31.

Norman B. Wilkinson, comp., *Bibliography of Pennsylvania History,* 2d ed., S.K. Stevens and Donald H. Kent, eds. (Harrisburg, Pa.: Pennsylvania Historical and Museum Commission, 1957) is a large work divided into sections for state, county, local, and topical history. A *Supplement* (Harrisburg, Pa.: Pennsylvania Historical and Museum Commission, 1957), edited by Carol Wall, was published in 1976. Updates through 1985, compiled by John B. B. Trussell, Jr., appeared in six volumes as *Pennsylvania Historical Bibliography* (Harrisburg, Pa.: Pennsylvania Historical and Museum Commission). The bibliography was continued through 1989 in *Pennsylvania History,* edited by Donna Munger, in volumes 56 and 57 (1989–90).

George P. Donehoo, *Pennsylvania: A History,* 11 vols. (New York: Lewis Historical Publishing Company, 1926) is one of the better large works, with volumes 5–11 containing biographical data. Philip F. Klein and Ari Hoogenboom, *A History of Pennsylvania,* 2d ed. (University Park, Pa., and London, England: The Pennsylvania State University Press, 1986), is another useful work. *Pennsylvania: A History of the Commonwealth,* ed. Randall M. Miller and William Pencak (Penn State Press and Pennsylvania Historical and Museum Commission, 2002), actually includes a chapter about Pennsylvania genealogy. Another excellent introduction to materials about the Commonwealth's history is *A Guide to the History of Pennsylvania,* by Dennis B. Downey and Francis J. Bremer (Westport, Conn.: Greenwood Press, 1993).

No study of Pennsylvania is complete without *The Papers of William Penn,* edited by Mary Maples Dunn and others, 5 volumes published in Philadelphia by the University of Pennsylvania Press, 1981–86. Each volume is indexed separately.

Other titles include Paul A. W. Wallace, *Pennsylvania, Seed of a Nation* (New York: Harper & Row, 1962); Joseph J. Kelley, Jr., *Pennsylvania: The Colonial Years, 1681–1776* (Garden City, N.Y.: Doubleday & Company, Inc., 1980), which has a useful bibliography; and works by Sylvester Kirby Stevens: *Pennsylvania, The Keystone State,* 2 vols. (New York: American Historical Co., 1956); *Pennsylvania, Birthplace of a Nation* (New York: Random House, 1964); and *Pennsylvania, The Heritage of a Commonwealth,* 4 vols. (West Palm Beach, Fla.: American Historical Co., 1968), of which volume 4 is biographical.

In Pennsylvania, as in other states, "mug" books (printed sources that present pictures and biographies of those who subscribed to the publication) are common and must be used with care. The largest set in Pennsylvania is the *Encyclopedia of Pennsylvania Biography,* published by Lewis Historical Publishing Company of New York in 32 volumes (1914–67). A somewhat better group is *Colonial and Revolutionary Families of Pennsylvania,* 17 vols. (1911–65; reprint, Baltimore: Genealogical Publishing Co., 1968).

Although covering a small, focused population, an excellent example in the biographical dictionary type of work is *Lawmaking and Legislators in Pennsylvania: A Biographical Dictionary,* two volumes to date, covering 1682–1756, edited by Craig W. Horle and others (Philadelphia: University of Pennsylvania Press, 1991–).

Guides

One of the best overviews is Milton Rubincam's chapter on Pennsylvania in *Genealogical Research: Methods and Sources,* vol. 1, rev. ed. (Washington, D.C.: The American Society of Genealogists, 1980).

Thomas F. Gordon, *A Gazetteer of the State of Pennsylvania* (1832; reprint, New Orleans, La.: Polyanthos, 1975) is helpful for the early period. A later, related work that is basic on the subject is A. Howry Espenshade, *Pennsylvania Place Names* (1925; reprint, Baltimore: Clearfield Publishing Co., 1991). Many places not named in these works can be located in *Pennsylvania Postal History* (Lawrence, Mass.: Quarterman Publications, 1976), by John L. Kay and Chester M. Smith, Jr.

How Pennsylvania Acquired Its Present Boundaries, by William A. Russ, Jr. (University Park, Pa.: Pennsylvania Historical Association, 1966) covers the colony's boundary disputes.

Kay Haviland Freilich's "Genealogical Research in Pennsylvania," *National Genealogical Society Quarterly* 90 (2002): 7-36, also available as National Genealogical Society Special Publication No. 68 (2003), provides an excellent introduction to the subject.

Pennsylvania Genealogical Research, by George K. Schweitzer, rev. ed. (Knoxville, Tenn.: the author, 1997) is a good, basic, inexpensive guide.

Pennsylvania Line: A Research Guide to Pennsylvania Genealogy and Local History, 4th ed. (Laughlintown, Pa.: Southwest Pennsylvania Genealogical Services, 1990), contains a wide variety of helpful information, such as place-names; maps of the counties, townships, and cities; and lists of available published and microfilmed books, newspapers, and censuses. A similar but much expanded work of this type will be published in 2004 by Closson Press.

For the western part of the Commonwealth, see Raymond Martin Bell, *Searching in Western Pennsylvania* (Detroit: Detroit Society for Genealogical Research, 1977), and Bell's *Mother Cumberland: Tracing Your Ancestors in South-Central Pennsylvania* (Bowie, Md.: Heritage Books, 1989); George Swetnam and Helen Smith, *A Guidebook to Historic Western Pennsylvania* (Pittsburgh: University of Pittsburgh Press, 1976); and the twelve papers from the "Come Home to Pennsylvania Conference," held in Pittsburgh in May 1983 and published in *Western Pennsylvania Genealogical Quarterly*, vols. 8 and 9 (1982).

John Daly has produced *Descriptive Inventory of the Archives of the City of Philadelphia* (Philadelphia: Department of Records, 1970), and, with Allen Weinberg, *Genealogy of Philadelphia County Subdivisions*, 2d ed. (Philadelphia: Department of Records, 1966), now available as *Philadelphia Maps, 1682–1982: Townships–Districts–Wards*, Genealogical Society of Pennsylvania Special Publication No. 6 (Philadelphia, 1996), which explains, with maps, the changes of the state's largest city/county.

Floyd G. Hoenstine, *Guide to Genealogical and Historical Research in Pennsylvania*, 4th ed. (Hollidaysburg, Pa.: the author, 1978), with supplements for 1985 and 1990, provides a surname index to many published works. Mr. Hoenstine's collection of over 3000 books, from which he created his *Guide*, is at the Blair County Genealogical Society, 431 Scotch Valley Rd., Hollidaysburg, PA 16648 <www.rootsweb.com/~pabcgs>, which sells his four-volume set for a small fee.

Maps

County road maps are available in most if not all courthouses. Older maps are published in county histories, county atlases, and in manuscript collections such as at the Historical Society of Pennsylvania, the state library, the Free Library of Pennsylvania (Logan Square, Philadelphia, 19103), the Carnegie Library at

Pittsburgh, and the Pennsylvania State Archives. For the latter see Martha L. Simonetti, comp., *Descriptive List of the Map Collection in the Pennsylvania State Archives*, edited by Donald H. Kent and Harry E. Whipkey (Harrisburg, Pa.: Pennsylvania Historical and Museum Commission, 1976), and online at < www.phmc.state.pa.us >. Useful city maps can sometimes be found in city directories. An interesting map showing the development of the Commonwealth's counties is available for a nominal fee from the Pennsylvania Historical and Museum Commission, Publication Sales Program, 400 N. St., Harrisburg, PA 17120-0053. See also Henry F. Walling and O. W. Gray, *1872 Historical Topographical Atlas of the State of Pennsylvania* (1872; reprint, Knightstown, Ind.: Bookmark, 1977), which has business directories and a place-name index. A wonderful publication, *The Atlas of Pennsylvania*, edited by David J. Cuff and others (Philadelphia: Temple University Press, 1989), goes beyond its maps in providing a "geographical encyclopedia."

Available at the state archives (with copies at the state library and the respective county recorders of deeds) are warrantee maps for twenty-four counties. Those for Fayette, Greene, and Washington were also published and indexed in volume 3 of *The Horn Papers* by W. F. Horn (New York: Hagstrom Co., 1945), but the preceding two volumes of text are mostly fiction (see *William & Mary Quarterly*, series three, 4 [1947]: 409-451). *Allegheny County Warrantee Atlas* was published by the Western Pennsylvania Genealogical Society (Pittsburgh, 1982; reprint 2003).

Land Records
State-Land State

The Land Records Office came into operation in 1682, keeping records about state boundaries, land granted by William Penn and the Commonwealth, and land still owned by Pennsylvania. Of greatest value are the warrants, surveys, and patents, including warrantee maps (see Maps), all available by mail for a modest fee from their current repository in the Pennsylvania State Archives. Research on Pennsylvania land is incomplete without consulting Donna Bingham Munger, *Pennsylvania Land Records: A History and Guide for Research* (Wilmington, Del.: Scholarly Resources, 1991).

Some of the earliest records of Pennsylvania grants are held by the Philadelphia City Archives and are indexed in *Warrants and Surveys of the Province of Pennsylvania including the Three Lower Counties 1759*, compiled by Allen Weinberg and Thomas E. Slattery (1965; reprint, Knightstown, Ind.: The Bookmark, 1975). The "Lower Counties" were those that are now the state of Delaware. Warrantees of land for several counties for 1733 to 1896 are listed in *Pennsylvania Archives*, 3d series, vols. 2, 3,

and 24–26, and are indexed in volumes 27–30; they are also now available on CD-ROM by Retrospect Publishing. See also William H. Egle, *Early Pennsylvania Land Records: Minutes of the Board of Property of the Province of Pennsylvania, 1687–1732* (Baltimore: Genealogical Publishing Co., 1976), reprinted from the *Pennsylvania Archives,* 2d series, vol. 19, for references to pre-1733 purchases.

The southwest corner of Pennsylvania was contested with Virginia, and many records for this area are to be found at the Virginia State Archives (Richmond) and at the University of West Virginia (Morgantown). For further research refer to "Virginia Claims to Land in Pennsylvania," in *Pennsylvania Archives* 3d series, vol. 3, 483–574; Boyd Crumrine, *Virginia Court Records in Southwestern Pennsylvania...1775–1780* (1902–5; reprint with index, Baltimore: Genealogical Publishing Co., 1974); and articles by Dr. Raymond Martin Bell in the *National Genealogical Society Quarterly* 45 (1957), and *The Virginia Genealogist* 7 (1963) and 11 (1967).

Settlers from Connecticut came to the Upper Delaware and Wyoming valleys claimed by that colony from about 1753 to 1782. The records of the Delaware Company have not survived, but see *The Susquehanna Company Papers* by Julian P. Boyd and Robert J. Taylor, 11 vols. (Wilkes-Barre, Pa.: Wyoming Historical and Geological Society; Ithaca, N.Y.: Cornell University Press, 1930–71); William Henry Egle, *Documents Relating to the Connecticut Settlement in the Wyoming Valley (of Pennsylvania)* (1890; reprint, Bowie, Md.: Heritage Books, 1990); and Donna Bingham Munger, "Following Connecticut Ancestors to Pennsylvania: Susquehanna Company Settlers," *The New England Historical and Genealogical Register* 139 (1985): 112-25. Other material is at the Connecticut State Library and the Wyoming Historical and Geological Society in Wilkes-Barre.

Land in the western part of the state, called the "Donation Lands," was offered to Revolutionary War soldiers of the Pennsylvania Line of the Continental Army. Also in this section of Pennsylvania were "Depreciation Lands," auctioned for the redemption of Revolutionary War Depreciation Certificates. The claims to these lands were published with maps in volumes 3 and 7 of *Pennsylvania Archives,* 3d series. A helpful discussion of both of these land groups by John E. Winner appeared in the *Western Pennsylvania Historical Magazine* 8 (1925): 1-11. See also "The Depreciation and Donation Lands," compiled by Nell Y. Herchenroether, in *Western Pennsylvania Genealogical Quarterly* 7 (1981): 127-33.

Most research in Pennsylvania land records will begin in the deeds and mortgages found with the recorder of deeds. Here will also be found the seller and buyer (grantor and grantee) indexes, sometimes arranged by the somewhat cumbersome Russell system (which is explained by William L. Iscrupe, "Using the Russell Index," *Western Pennsylvania Genealogical Society Quarterly* 30 [2004]: 34-36). In Pennsylvania, deeds and mortgages are more often than not indexed separately. Chattel mortgages are also found with the recorder of deeds. Most county deeds recorded to about 1850 and corresponding indexes are available on microfilm at the state archives and the Historical Society of Pennsylvania. Some unrecorded deeds may be found in courthouses, and many have found their way from private hands into archives, historical societies, and libraries. Keep in mind that in Pennsylvania, as elsewhere, a deed may have been recorded long after its execution and acknowledgment. In the southwestern part of the state, for example, some original deeds surfaced for recording when titles were being cleared for petroleum rights around the beginning of the twentieth century—some deeds dating over 100 years earlier. In earlier times many clerks were careful to copy German signatures into the deed books. This practice is of particular value, as in the text of the deed the name was usually anglicized.

Probate Records

The Pennsylvania General Assembly passed an act in 1682, which required the recording of wills and letters of administration. The first place to seek a will or other type of estate record in the Keystone State is with the county register of wills. Here researchers will find files of original papers pertaining to an estate as well as the record books in which were copied wills and letters of administration. In some counties the original papers may be arranged by type of document—will, bond, or account—and thereunder, by date of filing. Most microfilming of estate records has concentrated on will books, but the files must not be passed up even where there is a will. The clerk of the Orphans' Court in each county (who is often the register of wills) is responsible for keeping such records that concern the division of estates, guardians of minor children, and so forth. Indexes to records in both the register of wills and clerk of the Orphans' Court offices should both be checked, as often there will be action on an estate in both places. Most county indexes will lead to a docket book, which in turn will summarize the existing documents and record book entries. Besides the availability of many Pennsylvania estate records on microfilm and some in abstract form in periodicals such as *Publications of the Genealogical Society of Pennsylvania, Your Family Tree,* and the *Western Pennsylvania Genealogical Society Quarterly,* or in separate publications, published indexes for many counties are widely available, usually up to about 1900. Some of these indexes cover both wills and letters of administration and provide the year of the first action on the estate, the volume and page for the will or letters of administration, and the file number of the original papers, if a number has been assigned. Microfilms of the indexes and record books are at the Pennsylvania State Archives and the Historical Society of Pennsylvania, and many for the western counties are at the Carnegie Library of Pittsburgh.

In counties with large German populations, such as Berks, Lancaster, and York, it is common to find original wills written in German, with English translations.

Court Records

Sylvester K. Stevens and Donald H. Kent, *County Government and Archives in Pennsylvania* (Harrisburg, Pa.: Pennsylvania Historical and Museum Commission, 1947), while a bit dated, explains the responsibilities of the various county offices, with a good description of the county courts.

The prothonotary has been the clerk of the court of common pleas since 1707. Court records here include divorces, naturalizations, peddlers' licenses, registration of attorneys, oaths of county officers, equity, sheriff's sales, juror lists, some tax records, and some civil court records. Other court records are with the clerk of courts.

Among the few published court records for Pennsylvania is Diane E. Greene, *Cumberland County, Pennsylvania Quarter Sessions Dockets, 1750–1789* (Baltimore: Clearfield Company, Inc., 2000). Some court record abstracts have been published in various journals, such as *The Western Pennsylvania Historical Magazine*.

Other courts exist in Pennsylvania, although their jurisdictions are less likely to have genealogical impact. These include the supreme court (1722-present) and superior court (1895-present), with mostly appellate but some original jurisdiction. Federal court records are at the National Archives—Mid-Atlantic Region.

Tax Records

Late eighteenth-century state tax records for various counties, covering 1765 to 1791, were published in *Pennsylvania Archives*, 3d series, vols. 11-32; some of these lists were reprinted by Family Line Publications of Westminster, Maryland (now Heritage Books). The 1781 tax list for Washington County in volume 22 of the *Pennsylvania Archives* was actually taken in 1782 (see Jane M. Fulcher and Raymond Martin Bell, "Washington County, Pennsylvania Intestate Records, 1789–1806," *The Pennsylvania Genealogical Magazine* 31 [1979]: 51).

John "D" Stemmons and E. Diane Stemmons, comps., *Pennsylvania in 1780* (Salt Lake City: the compilers, 1978) indexes 1779 and 1780 tax lists published in the *Pennsylvania Archives*, 3d series, volumes 12-18 and 20-22, as well as unpublished lists for Northampton County 1780 and Westmoreland County (Connecticut, not Pennsylvania), 1776-80. An addendum to the Stemmons' work added lists for other counties, mostly for 1783.

Among the few surviving 1798 U.S. Direct Tax lists are those for Pennsylvania. They were microfilmed by the National Archives and are available at the Mid-Atlantic Region in Philadelphia, the Pennsylvania State Archives, and the Carnegie Library of Pittsburgh. Indexes have been published for several counties and those for western counties have been published. Some of the lists for Berks and Chester counties are missing.

Tax records are typically found in the county tax assessment offices but may also be in the county commissioners' office or with the prothonotary. The state archives has microfilms for some of these records (1715–1930s), and those of early lists for the western counties of Bedford, Crawford, Fayette, Washington, and others are at the Carnegie Library of Pittsburgh. Some assessment records have found their way into manuscript collections of county historical societies, the Historical Society of Pennsylvania, and the state archives, as well as the Philadelphia City Archives.

Cemetery Records

Large collections of cemetery records are located at the Historical Society of Pennsylvania, the Historical Society of Western Pennsylvania, the Carnegie Library of Pittsburgh, and at many local libraries and historical societies. The Pennsylvania State Library maintains the state's Daughters of the American Revolution cemetery collection (see page 7). Records for several Philadelphia funeral directors are in the Collections of the Genealogical Society of Pennsylvania (housed at the Historical Society of Pennsylvania).

The Genealogical Society of Pennsylvania microfilmed cemetery records throughout the commonwealth and is currently indexing cemetery records in their collections. Various compilations of cemetery inscriptions have been published, such as those for the western counties by Closson Press and Mechling Books.

Church Records

The Historical Records Survey produced an inventory of the church archives in Pennsylvania, but the only part published was for the Society of Friends (see below). Arranged by county, the inventory is located in the Pennsylvania State Archives. A good number of church records have been published individually and in periodicals such as *The Pennsylvania Genealogical Magazine* and *Western Pennsylvania Genealogical Society Quarterly*. Many copies exist in manuscript at the Historical Society of Pennsylvania, the Pennsylvania State Library (DAR collection), and in other libraries. A good portion of the published material concerns German churches and Quaker meetings.

Among the useful published works are *The Mennonite Encyclopedia*, 4 vols. (Hillsboro, Kans.: Mennonite Brethren

Publishing House, 1955–59); Howard Weigner Kriebel, *The Schwenkfelders in Pennsylvania, A Historical Sketch* (Lancaster: The Pennsylvania-German Society, 1904); Samuel Kriebel Brecht, ed., *The Genealogical Record of the Schwenkfelder Families* (New York and Chicago: Rand McNally & Company, 1923); *The Brethren Encyclopedia*, 3 vols. (Philadelphia: Brethren Encyclopedia, 1983); and *History of the Church of the Brethren of the Eastern District of Pennsylvania* (Lancaster: Era Printing Company, 1915), which has much genealogical material.

Some major religious bodies have libraries in the commonwealth with collections that include not only Pennsylvania church records, but those for other states as well. These include the following:

The collection at the Friends Historical Library, Swarthmore College, Swarthmore, PA 19081 <www.swarthmore.edu/ Library/friends> is defined in four publications: *Catalog of the Book and Serials Collections of the Friends Historical Library*, 6 vols. (Boston: G.K. Hall, 1982); *Guide to the Manuscript Collections of the Friends Historical Library* (Swarthmore, Pa.: Friends Historical Library, 1982); *Inventory of Church Archives: Society of Friends in Pennsylvania*, compiled by the Pennsylvania Historical Survey (Philadelphia: Friends Historical Association, 1941); and *Guide to the Records of Philadelphia Yearly Meeting*, compiled by Jack Eckert (Haverford, Pa.: Haverford College, 1989). The library has original and microfilmed Quaker records, mostly for Pennsylvania, New Jersey, New York, Maryland, and some for Virginia, including those for fourteen Pennsylvania meetings copied by Hinshaw but never published. See Ethel D. Williams, *Know Your Ancestors* (Rutland, Vt.: Charles E. Tuttle Company, 1960), p. 125-27, 136. While the basic meeting records are located at Swarthmore, other material can be found in the Quaker Collection at Magill Library at Haverford College, Haverford, PA 19041-1392 <www.Haverford.edu/ library/special>. Some Pennsylvania Quaker records have been published. The most significant are those in William Wade Hinshaw, *Encyclopedia of American Quaker Genealogy*, vol. 2, covering the two oldest monthly meetings in the Philadelphia area, and volume 4 covering three southwestern Pennsylvania monthly meeting records (1938 and 1946; reprint, Baltimore: Genealogical Publishing Co., 1969, 1991).

The Lancaster Mennonite Historical Society, 2215 Millstream Rd., Lancaster, PA 17602-1499 <www.lmhs.org> has a handout entitled *Genealogical Resources at the Lancaster Mennonite Historical Society*. A research fee is charged for mail inquiries. The society also publishes a quarterly, *Pennsylvania Mennonite Heritage*.

The Evangelical and Reformed Historical Society of the United Church of Christ, 555 W. James St., Lancaster, PA 17603 <www.erhs.info> loans microfilm of church records ($5 per reel), covering German churches in Adams, Berks, Bucks, Chester, Columbia, Dauphin, Lancaster, Lebanon, Lehigh,

Monroe, Montgomery, Northampton, Northumberland, Perry, Philadelphia, Schuylkill, and York counties, as well as a few for Maryland and Virginia.

Many German church records, particularly for the German Reformed and Evangelical Church, have been published in books and periodicals. Charles H. Glatfelder, in *Pastors and People: German Lutheran and Reformed Churches in the Pennsylvania Field, 1717–1793*, 2 vols. (Breingsville, Pa.: The Pennsylvania German Society, 1980, 1981), provides the location and history of the early churches and pastors of these two denominations. For a large collection of Evangelical records, see *Pennsylvania German Church Records* (births, baptisms, marriages, burials, etc.), reprinted from *Proceedings and Addresses of the Pennsylvania German Society*, 3 vols. (Baltimore: Genealogical Publishing Co., 1983).

The Presbyterian Historical Society, 425 Lombard St., Philadelphia, PA 19147 <http://history.pcusa.org/contents. html> has records of over 20,000 churches and has published the *Journal of Presbyterian History* since 1901. At the other end of the commonwealth, the Presbyterian Historical Society of Western Pennsylvania and the Reformed Presbyterian Historical Society in Pittsburgh have a variety of records, journals, and newspapers.

Two Methodist repositories are in Western Pennsylvania: Methodist Archives and History, 1238 Varner Rd., Pittsburgh, PA 15227, and United Methodist Archives of Western Pennsylvania, Allegheny College, 731 Park Ave., Meadville, PA 66335.

The Historical Society of Pennsylvania has a microfilm collection of Jewish synagogue and cemetery records; other related material is at the Philadelphia Jewish Archives Center, 18 S. 7th St., Philadelphia, PA 19106 <www.jewisharchives. net>. Other Jewish archives are at the Historical Society of Western Pennsylvania in Pittsburgh.

Western Pennsylvania parishes are served by the Catholic Archives and Records Center, Cardinal Dean Center, 4721 Fifth Ave., Pittsburgh, PA 15213 <www.DioPitt.org>.

Other important archives are kept by the Moravians at 66 West Church St., Bethlehem, PA 18018; the Schwenkfelders at Pennsburg, PA 18073; the Lutherans at Abdel Ross Wentz Library, Lutheran Theological Seminary at Gettysburg, 66 Seminary Ridge, Gettysburg, PA 17325–1795 <www.ltsg.edu/ wentz_lib/wentz.htm> and the Lutheran Theological Seminary, 7301 Germantown Ave., Philadelphia, PA 19119–1794 <www. ltsp.edu>; the Church of the Brethren (formerly Dunkards) at Elizabethtown College, One Alpha Dr., Elizabethtown, PA 17022–2298, and Juniata College, 1700 Moore St., Huntingdon, PA 16652; and the Brethren in Christ Church at Messiah College, One College Ave., Gratham, PA 17027.

Military Records

Because of the Quaker influence, Pennsylvania had no formal militia until the French and Indian War, when it became necessary to defend its citizens on the western frontier. Most original state military records up through the Vietnam War are in the Pennsylvania State Archives. Information from the time of World War II is restricted.

Many names of soldiers and sailors, from the time of the French and Indian War through the Mexican War, are found in the volumes of *Pennsylvania Archives*, particularly in the 2d, 5th, and 6th series, although research in these should be supplemented by records at the state archives and the National Archives. For the specific *Pennsylvania Archives* volumes, consult the guides listed under Background Sources. For this period, the following should also be mentioned:

Cope, Harry E., comp. *List of Soldiers and Widows of Soldiers Granted Revolutionary War Pensions by Commonwealth of Pennsylvania*, edited by Mrs. Daniel L. Whitehead. Greensburg, Pa.: Phoebe Bayard Chapter DAR, 1976. Indexes acts of the Pennsylvania General Assembly.

Laverty, Bruce. *Colonial Muster Rolls at the Historical Society of Pennsylvania*. Philadelphia: Historical Society of Pennsylvania, 1983. Reproduces copies of original rolls with name index.

Muster Rolls of the Pennsylvania Volunteers in the War of 1812–1814. Reprinted from *Pennsylvania Archives*. 2d series, vol. 12. Baltimore: Genealogical Publishing Co., 1967. Only officers are indexed.

Stevens, S. K. and others. *The Papers of Henry Bouquet (1755–65)*. 6 vols. Harrisburg, Pa.: Pennsylvania Historical and Museum Commission, 1951–94. Volume 7 is in preparation.

The following should be consulted for background reading:

Jackson, John W. *The Pennsylvania Navy, 1775–1781*. New Brunswick, N.J.: Rutgers University Press, 1974.

Kent, Donald H. *The French Invasion of Western Pennsylvania*. Harrisburg, Pa.: Pennsylvania Historical and Museum Commission, 1981.

Roach, Hannah Benner. "The Pennsylvania Militia in 1777," *The Pennsylvania Genealogical Magazine* 23 (1964): 161-229. Reprinted as pamphlets with name index, 1975.

Sipe, C. Hale. *The Indian Wars of Pennsylvania*. 2d ed., with *A Supplement*. Harrisburg, Pa.: Telegraph Press, 1931.

Trussell, John B. B., Jr. *The Pennsylvania Line: Regimental Organization and Operations, 1775–1783*. Harrisburg, Pa.: Pennsylvania Historical and Museum Commission, 1977.

Waddell, Louis M. and Bruce D. Bomberger. *The French and Indian War in Pennsylvania, 1753–1763: Fortification and Struggle*

During the War for Empire (Harrisburg, Pa.: Pennsylvania Historical and Museum Commission, 1996).

Much interesting material is located at the David Library of the American Revolution, River Rd., Box 48, Washington Crossing, PA 18977-0048 <www.dlar.org> which has a guide to its microform holdings: David J. Fowler, *Guide to the Sol Feinstone Collection of the David Library of the American Revolution* (Washington Crossing, Pa.: David Library, 1994).

Like the other Mid-Atlantic colonies, there were Loyalists in Pennsylvania, mostly in the southeastern part of the colony, many of whom left for England or Canada. Some are identified in Anne M. Ousterhouk, "Opponents of the Revolution Whose Pennsylvania Estates Were Confiscated," *Pennsylvania Genealogical Magazine* 30 (1978): 237-53. See also "Forfeited Estates Accounts" in *Pennsylvania Archives*, 6th series, vols. 12-13. For a detailed study, see Wilbur H. Siebert, "The Loyalists of Pennsylvania," *Ohio State University Bulletin* 24 (1920; reprint, Boston: Gregg, 1972). Copies of muster rolls of the Pennsylvania Loyalist Regiment are at the Public Archives of Canada and the Library of Congress.

Samuel P. Bates, *History of Pennsylvania Volunteers, 1861–65*, 5 vols. (Harrisburg, Pa.: B. Singerly, 1869–71) was reprinted by Broadfoot Publishing Company (Wilmington, Del., 1994) to include an every-name index. Also consult the National Archives microfilm *Index to Compiled Service Records of Volunteer Union Soldiers in Pennsylvania Organizations*, available at the National Archives—Mid-Atlantic Region and the Pennsylvania State Library. There is also a separate, every-name index in the state archives.

Antoinette J. Segraves compiled "A Guide to Pennsylvania Soldiers in the Mexican War," published in *The Pennsylvania Genealogical Magazine*, vols. 36-38 (1986–94).

Record of Pennsylvania Volunteers in the Spanish-American War, 1898, 2d ed. (Philadelphia: Wm. Stanley Ray, 1901) was compiled by the Pennsylvania Adjutant General's Office. The state archives has many records of the American Revolution, Civil War, Spanish-American War, and other military matters on its website at <www.digitalarchives.state.pa.us>.

The original cards for the fourth registration of the World War II draft, providing information on men ages forty-five through sixty-four in April 1942, are at the National Archives—Mid-Atlantic Region.

Soldier discharges since the Civil War are usually in the office of the county recorder of deeds, but are restricted. Veterans' grave and burial records are kept in the Office of the Director of Veterans' Affairs at the county courthouses, with copies at the state archives.

Periodicals, Newspapers, and Manuscript Collections

Periodicals

The Pennsylvania Genealogical Magazine, published by the Genealogical Society of Pennsylvania since 1948, has tended to focus on the Philadelphia area, with some coverage of New Jersey, Delaware, and Maryland, but in recent years the editors have strived for more inclusive coverage of the commonwealth. The first issue was numbered volume 16, as it succeeded the society's *Publications of the Genealogical Society of Pennsylvania,* started in 1895. Volumes 1–39 are available as Family Archives CD-ROM #213 (Brøderbund, 1998). *Genealogies of Pennsylvania Families,* 3 vols. (Baltimore: Genealogical Publishing Co., 1982), was reprinted from these two journals.

The Pennsylvania Magazine of History and Biography is the publication of the Historical Society of Pennsylvania. It contains excellent articles on Pennsylvania subjects, although mostly with a historical focus, and since 1936 without "genealogical" material. Volume 1 was published in 1877, and in 1954 the society issued a consolidated index to the first seventy-five volumes, *The Pennsylvania Magazine of History and Biography Index, volumes 1–75 (1877–1951)* (Philadelphia: Historical Society of Pennsylvania, 1954), edited by Eugene E. Doll; it does not include names from "genealogical" articles, however. Ian M. G. Quimby edited *The Pennsylvania Magazine of History and Biography Index, volumes 76–123 (1952–1999)* (Philadelphia: The Historical Society of Pennsylvania, 2001). Volumes 30 to 67 (1906–43) were reprinted by Johnson Reprint Corporation of New York in 1969. In 1981 Genealogical Publishing Company of Baltimore reprinted a volume of *Genealogies of Pennsylvania Families* from *The Pennsylvania Magazine.*

The Western Pennsylvania Genealogical Society has published the *Western Pennsylvania Genealogical Society Quarterly* since 1974. It is one of the more important regional journals since it covers a large area and has many fine articles and abstracts of source records.

Another journal that concerns the central and western parts of the commonwealth was *Your Family Tree* (1948–83). Besides queries, it featured abstracts of wills, tax lists, grave marker inscriptions, and newspaper items.

Publications of the Pennsylvania German Folklore Society was issued in twenty-eight volumes (1963–66), when it merged with the *Pennsylvania German Society Proceedings,* which since 1891 had produced sixty-three volumes. Many emigration and church records have been published in these periodicals.

More historical than genealogical, but still useful, is *Pennsylvania History,* published by the Pennsylvania Historical Association since 1934. A cumulative index for volumes 1-28 is available at the Genealogical Society of Pennsylvania.

Much Pennsylvania material has been published in the *National Genealogical Society Quarterly.* There are also numerous one-county, one-township, and regional publications that should not be overlooked.

Newspapers

In 1984 the Pennsylvania State Library published an updated *Pennsylvania Newspapers and Selected Out-of-State Newspapers,* originally compiled by Louis F. Rauco in 1976 and arranged by county, locality, and title. See also Glenora Rossell, ed., *Pennsylvania Newspapers: A Bibliography and Union List,* 2d ed. (Pittsburgh: Pennsylvania Library Association, 1978). This updates the earlier edition by Ruth Salisbury, but the most current information is available through Online Computer Library Center. The commonwealth sponsored a newspaper project to identify, catalog, preserve, and microfilm old newspapers. The state library, with the largest collection, makes microfilms available through interlibrary loan. Check the library's website for its newspaper holdings. Other excellent collections of newspapers are at the Free Library of Philadelphia, the Western Pennsylvania Genealogical Society, and the Carnegie Library of Pittsburgh.

Several volumes of newspaper abstracts have been published. Some representative titles are:

Duer, Clara E. *Pittsburgh Gazette Abstracts, 1786–1820.* 5 vols. Pittsburgh: Western Pennsylvania Genealogical Society, and Apollo, Pa.: Closson Press, 1986–95.

Hawbaker, Gary T., ed. *Runaways, Rascals, and Rogues: Missing Spouses, Servants and Slaves.* Hershey, Pa.: the author, 1987.

Hocker, Edward W. *Genealogical Data Relating to the German Settlers in Pennsylvania and Adjacent Territory: From Advertisements in German Newspapers Published in Philadelphia and Germantown, 1743–1800.* Baltimore: Genealogical Publishing Co., 1980.

Scott, Kenneth. *Genealogical Data from The Pennsylvania Chronicle, 1767–1774.* National Genealogical Society Special Publication No. 37. Washington, D.C.: National Genealogical Society, 1980.

An index of death and marriage notices from the *Public Ledger* of Philadelphia (1825–1875), created by volunteers of the Genealogical Society of Pennsylvania, is in that society's library and in other libraries.

Manuscripts

Many wonderful collections of manuscript material at the Historical Society of Pennsylvania are on microfilm at the FHL, such as those of Gilbert Cope, Alfred R. Justice, Israel D. Rupp, and many others. Nearly every repository in the commonwealth has extensive, helpful collections (see below). For a beginning guide to some of these, see Irwin Richman, comp., *Historical*

Manuscript Depositories in Pennsylvania (Harrisburg, Pa.: Pennsylvania Historical Museum Commission, 1965), which is arranged by place, and especially *Guide to the Manuscript Collections of the Historical Society of Pennsylvania* (Philadelphia: the society, 1991). *Catalogue of the Manuscript Collections in the Libraries of Western Pennsylvania*, by Joan O. Morris (Pittsburgh: the author, 2003), includes the Historical Society of Western Pennsylvania and the University of Pittsburgh Archives Center.

Archives, Libraries, and Societies

Pennsylvania State Archives

350 North St.
Harrisburg, PA 17120-0090
www.phmc.state.pa.us

The Pennsylvania State Archives holds various source materials, including vital records, censuses, maps, tax lists, military records, and state land records. See Robert M. Dructor, *Guide to Genealogical Sources at the Pennsylvania State Archives*, 2d ed. (Harrisburg, Pa.: Pennsylvania Historical and Museum Commission, 1998). This should be supplemented with these titles also published by the Historical and Museum Commission:

Suran, Frank M., comp. and ed. *Guide to the Record Groups in the Pennsylvania State Archives*. 1980.

Whipkey, Harry E., comp. *Guide to the Manuscript Groups in the Pennsylvania State Archives*. 1976.

Most updates, however, appear on the state archives' website. The commission also publishes a number of books on Pennsylvania. These are detailed in their catalog.

State Library of Pennsylvania

Bureau of State Library
333 Market St.
Harrisburg, PA 17126-1745
www.statelibrary.state.pa.us

Genealogies, local histories, maps, censuses, newspapers, periodicals, and city directories are at the state library. Of particular use is the Genealogical Surname Index, about which see Janice B. Newman in "Genealogical Research at the State Library of Pennsylvania," *Pennsylvania Genealogical Magazine* 35 (1988): 199-212. Also to be consulted is A *Guide to the Genealogy/Local History Section of the State Library of Pennsylvania* (Harrisburg, Pa.: State Library of Pennsylvania, 1989).

The Historical Society of Pennsylvania

1300 Locust St.
Philadelphia, PA 19107-5699
www.hsp.org

Founded in 1824, the historical society has published the *Pennsylvania Magazine of History and Biography* since 1877. See *Guide to the Manuscript Collections of the Historical Society of Pennsylvania*, 3d ed. (Philadelphia: Historical Society of Pennsylvania, 1991), and the society's online catalog. The society charges a research fee for mail inquiries.

In 2002, the collections of the Balch Institute for Ethnic Studies were merged with those of the HSP (see <www.balchinstitute.org>).

The Genealogical Society of Pennsylvania

215 S. Broad St., 7th Floor
Philadelphia, PA 19107-5325
www.libertynet.org/gspa

In 1892 a group of Historical Society of Pennsylvania members formed the adjunct Genealogical Society of Pennsylvania, which became a separate body. Beginning in 1895, the society produced *Publications of the Genealogical Society of Pennsylvania*, renamed *Pennsylvania Genealogical Magazine* in 1948. Helen Hutchinson Woodroffe compiled "A Genealogist's Guide to Pennsylvania Records." Beginning in volume 31 (1979), it is a listing of the county material in the Historical Society of Pennsylvania's extensive collection of materials and includes call numbers. This guide is also available with the same title as a separate publication of the society, edited by Marion F. Egge (Philadelphia, 1995). See also J. Carlyle Parker, comp., *A User's Guide to the Manuscript Collection of the Genealogical Society of Pennsylvania...Microfilmed by the Genealogical Department of Salt Lake City* (Turlock, Calif.: Marietta Publishing Co., 1986).

Historical Society of Western Pennsylvania

1212 Smallman St.
Pittsburgh, PA 15222-4200
www.pghhistory.org

Covering the western half of the commonwealth, the historical society has an extensive library and has published *The Western Pennsylvania Historical Magazine* (now *Pittsburgh History*) since 1918, with cumulative indexes for volumes 1-43 and 44-54.

Western Pennsylvania Genealogical Society

4400 Forbes Ave.
Pittsburgh, PA 15213-4080
www.wpgs.org

Formerly housed with the Historical Society of Western Pennsylvania, the Genealogical Society, covering twenty-six counties, publishes *Western Pennsylvania Genealogical Society Quarterly*, with volumes 1-25 available on CD-ROM, which also includes Allegheny County naturalizations (1788–1905) and *Lists and Indexes to the Legal, Court and Municipal Records of Allegheny County*. For a list of the society's holdings, see volumes 4 and 6 of the genealogical society's *Quarterly*.

The South Central Pennsylvania Genealogical Society, Inc.
P.O. Box 1824
York, PA 17405-1824
www.scpgs.org

This society has distinguished itself through the publication of many source records, including Bible records, tax lists, private vital records, cemetery inscriptions, and naturalizations.

Many Pennsylvania counties have fine historical and genealogical societies, which should be checked for their book and manuscript collections. These include Adams, Berks, Blair, Bucks, Chester, Crawford, Cumberland, Lancaster, and York counties. See also *Directory Pennsylvania 1990* by the Library Development of the State Library of Pennsylvania (Harrisburg, Pa.: 1990).

Special Focus Categories

Immigration

Two works take up the coming of Pennsylvania's first immigrants to the Penn colony: *Passengers and Ships Prior to 1684*, compiled and edited by Walter Lee Sheppard, Jr. (1970; reprint, Bowie, Md.: Heritage Books, 1985), which is a synthesis of passenger lists; and George E. McCracken, *The Welcome Claimants: Proved, Disproved and Doubtful* (1970; reprint, Bowie, Md.: Heritage Books, 1985).

The most important work on the mass immigration of Germans is Ralph B. Strassburger, *Pennsylvania German Pioneers*, edited by William J. Hinke, 3 vols. (1934; reprint of volumes 1 and 3, Baltimore: Genealogical Publishing Co., 1980; reprint of all three volumes, Camden, Maine: Picton Press, 1992), covering arrivals at Philadelphia of thousands of Palatines and others (1727–1808). Volume 2, which has facsimile signatures of the passengers who signed an oath to the province, was included in Picton's reprint, but not GPC's. See also the "Annotations" to this work by Dr. Friedrich Krebs in *The Pennsylvania Genealogical Magazine* 21 (1960): 235-48. Two other volumes, edited by Don Yoder, supplement Strassburger/Hinke: *Pennsylvania German Immigrants, 1709–1786* (Baltimore: Genealogical Publishing Co., 1984), reprinted from the Pennsylvania German Folklore Society *Yearbooks*, and *Rhineland Emigrants* (Baltimore: Genealogical Publishing Co., 1981), reprinted from *Pennsylvania Folklife*. The many fine publications concerning German immigrants by Annette Kunselman Burgert should not be overlooked.

Other early records were published in *Pennsylvania Archives*, 2d series, vol. 17, p. 521-667; Michael Tepper, ed., *Emigrants to Pennsylvania, 1641–1819* (Baltimore: Genealogical Publishing Co., 1975), consolidated from passenger lists published in *The Pennsylvania Magazine of History and Biography*; and Carl Boyer, III, ed., *Ship Passenger Lists: Pennsylvania and Delaware, 1641–1825* (Newhall, Calif.: the compiler, 1980).

Passenger lists for the port of Philadelphia (1800–1945) and indexes (1800–1948) are available at the National Archives—Mid-Atlantic Region. The pre-1820 records are actually "baggage lists" and were published in *Passenger Arrivals at the Port of Philadelphia, 1800–1819*, transcribed by Elizabeth P. Bentley and edited by Michael H. Tepper (Baltimore: Genealogical Publishing Co., 1986).

While not classified as immigration records, crew and vessel lists for the port of Philadelphia (1789–1880) are available in indexed typescript volumes at the Historical Society of Pennsylvania and the Free Library of Philadelphia, Logan Square, Philadelphia, PA 19103.

Naturalization

Most county naturalizations are in the office of the prothonotary, although some are in city or county archives, such as those for Philadelphia and Chester counties. A few of these records have been published, such as those for Allegheny (1798–1906), Bucks (1802–1906), Philadelphia (see below), and Westmoreland (1802–52). Provincial, state, and other records are in the state archives, including those of the supreme court, most of which were published in *Pennsylvania Archives*, 2d series, vol. 2, and reprinted as *Persons Naturalized in the Province of Pennsylvania, 1740–1773* (Baltimore: Genealogical Publishing Co., 1967, 1991). For other records at the archives, see Dructor's *Guide* listed under Archives, Libraries, and Societies.

Non-British subjects in Pennsylvania were required to take an oath to the province, and their names are found in Strassburger/Hinke noted above. Records of oaths of loyalty to Pennsylvania's Revolutionary government are found in Thompson Wescott, *Names of Persons Who Took the Oath of Allegiance to the State of Pennsylvania Between … 1777 and 1789* (1865; reprint, Baltimore: Genealogical Publishing Co., 1965). Many nineteenth-century Philadelphia records are located through P. William Filby, ed., *Philadelphia Naturalizations: Records of Aliens' Declarations of Intention and/or Oaths of Allegiance, 1789–1880* (Detroit: Gale Research Co., 1982), which reproduced an earlier compilation by the Historical Records Survey (1941). This should be used with Jefferson M. Moak's "The WPA Index of Naturalizations: An Explanation," *The Pennsylvania Genealogical Magazine* 36 (1989): 109-16.

Federal court naturalizations are at the National Archives—Mid-Atlantic Region in Philadelphia and cover petitions for courts in Philadelphia (1790–1991; indexed, 1795–1990), Pittsburgh (1820–1979; indexed, 1820–1990), Erie (1940–72), Harrisburg (1911–17), Scranton (1901–90), Wilkes-Barre (1943–72), and Williamsport (1909–13), as well as an index to the latter four courts (1901–90).

African American

Ruth E. Hodge's *Guide to African American Resources at the Pennsylvania State Archives* (Harrisburg: Pennsylvania Historical

PENNSYLVANIA

and Museum Commission, 2000) replaces an earlier work by David McBride. McBride also edited *Blacks in Pennsylvania History: Research and Educational Perspectives* (Harrisburg: Pennsylvania Historical and Museum Commission, 1983). Charles L. Blockson, *Pennsylvania's Black History* (Philadelphia: Portfolio Association, 1975) is another useful work. For other sources, see also the Pennsylvania chapter in *Black Genesis* (see page 15).

Native American

Among the tribes in Pennsylvania were the Lenni-Lenape (or Delaware) in the east, the Susquehannock and Shawnee along the Susquehanna River, and the Iroquois Five Nations who migrated down from New York in the west. See Paul A.W. Wallace, *Indians of Pennsylvania*, 2d ed. (1986), and his *Indian Paths of Pennsylvania* (1987), both published by the Pennsylvania Historical and Museum Commission, Harrisburg. (See also Kraft's *The Lenape* under New Jersey—Special Focus Categories.)

Other Ethnic Groups

John E. Bodnar, *Ethnic History in Pennsylvania: A Selected Bibliography* (Harrisburg: Pennsylvania Historical and Museum Commission, 1974) covers published and manuscript material. Also useful is David E. Washburn, comp. and ed., *The Peoples of Pennsylvania: An Annotated Bibliography of Resource Materials* (Pittsburgh: University for International Studies, University of Pittsburgh, 1981).

The "big three" colonial Pennsylvania immigrant groups have all been covered in great detail in published material. Some selected titles are the following:

William Wistar Comfort, *The Quakers* (University Park: Pennsylvania Historical Association, 1948), while brief, includes a helpful bibliography; see also Albert Cook Myers, *Immigration of the Irish Quakers into Pennsylvania, 1682–1750* (1902; reprint, Baltimore: Genealogical Publishing Co., 1969); and Hugh Barbour and J. William Frost, *The Quakers* (New York: Greenwood Press, 1988).

Emil Meynen, *Bibliography on German Settlements in Colonial North America, Especially on the Pennsylvania Germans and Their Descendants, 1683–1933* (1937; reprint, Gale Research Corp., 1966) is useful, and Russell Wieder Gilbert, *A Picture of the Pennsylvania Germans* (University Park: Pennsylvania Historical Association, 1962) has a bibliography.

John A. Hostetler, *Amish Society* (Baltimore: Johns Hopkins University Press, 1983) explains the beliefs and practices of this group.

For the Ulster-Scots, see Wayland F. Dunaway, *The Scotch-Irish of Colonial Pennsylvania* (1944; reprint, Baltimore: Genealogical Publishing Co., 1985); and Charles K. Bolton, *Scotch Irish Pioneers of Ulster and America* (1910; reprint, Baltimore: Genealogical Publishing Co., 1972).

For information on the early Swedes in Pennsylvania, see the titles listed under Delaware—Background Sources.

Another early immigrant group is covered in Albert Bernhardt Faust and Gaius Marcus Brumbaugh's *Lists of Swiss Immigrants in the Eighteenth Century in the American Colonies*, 2 vols. in one (1920–25; reprint, Baltimore: Genealogical Publishing Co., 1991).

While not one of the major three immigrant groups, the Welsh have received good treatment in print. See Thomas Allen Glenn, *Merion in the Welsh Tract* (1896; reprint, Baltimore: Genealogical Publishing Co., 1970) and *Welsh Families of Pennsylvania*, 2 vols. (1911–13; reprinted in one volume, Baltimore: Genealogical Publishing Co., 1970, 1991). Although known for unreliable publications, Charles H. Browning's *Welsh Settlement of Pennsylvania* (1912; reprint, Baltimore: Genealogical Publishing Co., 1970) is a worthwhile work. It also includes Welsh Quakers.

County Resources

The township is the basic political unit in the county and may have within its boundaries incorporated towns, boroughs, and cities, although these would have their own local governments.

The Commonwealth of Pennsylvania is comprised of sixty-seven counties and here may be found records of land, estates, taxes, vital records, divorces, naturalizations, voter registration, court records, and so forth. In 1952 an archives was started in Philadelphia, the oldest city archives in the country. John Daly compiled a *Descriptive Inventory* to its holdings in 1970. The first county archives was established in Chester County in 1982 and is considered the model for the Commonwealth. A number of other county archives are underway at various stages throughout Pennsylvania. For more detail about county office holdings, see the *County Records Survey, Record Series Inventory, 1985–86*, available on microfiche from the state archives, although Philadelphia is not included, and Monroe County follows Montgomery out of alphabetical sequence. This survey updates the inventories prepared by the Works Progress Administration (WPA), although the latter have greater detail. See also Stevens and Kent's *County Government Archives* cited under Court Records.

The first column below indicates the map coordinates. In the second column is the name of the county and the mailing address of the recorder of deeds, where deeds and mortgages are found. The third column shows the date of county formation, with the name or names of the parent county or counties. The fourth column gives the date the earliest deed was recorded. The last column gives the mailing address of the register of wills, if different from the recorder. Estate records are found in the register's office or orphans' court. (See Court Records for other county offices.)

577

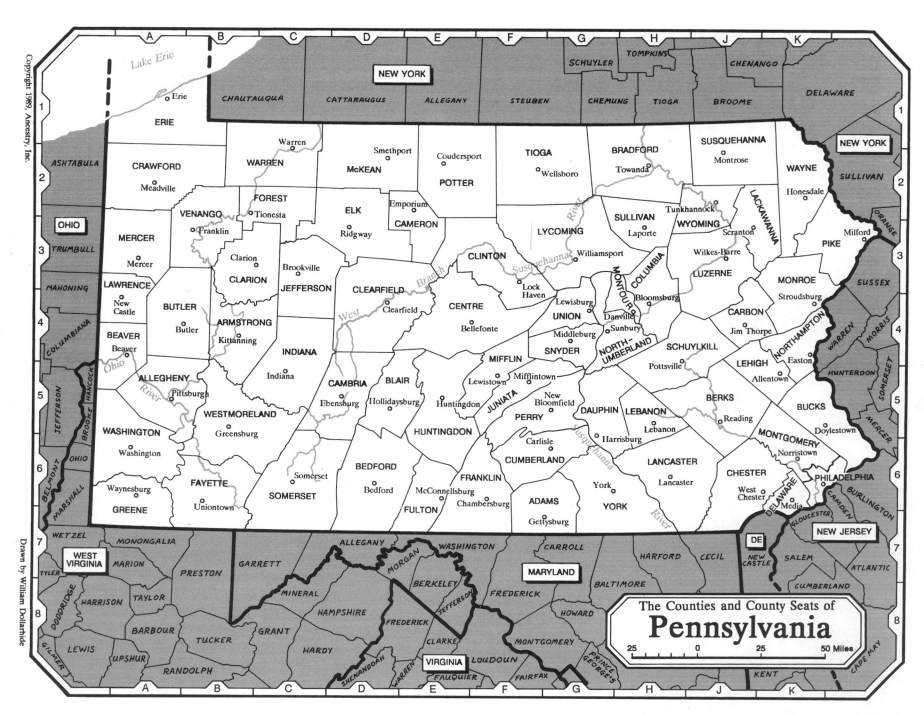

The Counties and County Seats of

Pennsylvania

25   0   25   50 Miles

Drawn by William Dollarhide

PENNSYLVANIA

Map	County Address	Date Formed Parent County/ies	Deeds	Register of Wills
G6	Adams Courthouse, Rm. 102 Gettysburg 17325-2398	1800 York	1800	1800
A5	Allegheny County Office Bldg. 542 Forbes Ave. Pittsburgh 15219	1788 Washington/ Westmoreland	1788	1789 City-County Building Pittsburgh 15219
B4	Armstrong Market St. Kittanning 16201	1800 Allegheny/ Lycoming/ Westmoreland	1805	1805
	Armstrong was attached to Westmoreland County until 1805.			
A4	Beaver 810 Third St., Bldg. B Beaver 15009-0537	1800 Allegheny/ Washington	1803	1800 801 Third St. Beaver 15009
	Beaver was attached to Allegheny County until 1803.			
D6	Bedford 200 South Juliana St. Bedford 15522-1714	1771 Cumberland	1771	1771
J5	Berks 633 Court St., 3d Floor Reading 19601-3594	1752 Chester/ Lancaster/ Philadelphia	1752	1752 633 Court St., 2d Floor
	There are unrecorded deeds back to 1717 on microfilm at the Historical Society of Pennsylvania.			
E5	Blair 423 Allegheny St. Hollidaysburg 16648-2022	1846 Huntingdon/ Bedford	1846	1846
H2	Bradford 301 Main St. Towanda 18848-1824	1810 (as Ontario) Luzerne/Lycoming (renamed and formally organized, 1812)	1812	1812
K5	Bucks 55 East Court St. Doylestown 18901	1682 original	1684	1683
B4	Butler 124 West Diamond St. P.O. Box 1208 Butler 16001-1208	1800 Allegheny	1804	1804
	Butler was attached to Allegheny County until 1803.			
D5	Cambria 200 South Center St. Ebensburg 15931	1804 Somerset/Bedford/ Huntingdon	1846	1819 P.O. Box 298 Ebensburg 15931-0298
	Cambria was attached to Somerset County until 1807.			
E3	Cameron 20 East Fifth St. Emporium 15834-1469	1860 Clinton/Elk/ McKean/Potter	1860	1863
J4	Carbon Hazard Sq. and Rt. 209 P.O. Box 87 Jim Thorpe 18229-0087	1843 Monroe/ Northampton	1843	1843 1 Hazard Sq. P.O. Box 286 Jim Thorpe 18229-0286
E4	Centre Willowbank Co. Office Bldg. 414 Holmes St Bellefonte 16823-1400	1800 Lycoming/Mifflin/ Northumberland/ Huntingdon	1801	1800 Willowbank Co. Office Bldg. 414 Holmes St., Ste. #2 Bellefonte 16823
J6	Chester 235 West Market St., Ste. 100 P.O. Box 100 West Chester 19380	1682 original	1688	1924 1714–1923* 2 North High St., Ste. 109 P.O. Box 2748 West Chester 19380-0991
	*Located at Chester County Archives and Records Service, Government Services Bldg., Ste. 80, 610 Westtown Rd., West Chester, PA 19382.			
B3	Clarion Main St. Clarion 16214	1839 Venango/Armstrong	1840	1840
D4	Clearfield 230 East Market St. P.O. Box 361 Clearfield 16830-0361	1804 Lycoming/ Huntingdon	1805	1823
	Not organized for judiciary purposes until 1822, Clearfield functioned as a part of Centre County.			
F3	Clinton Water and Jay Streets P.O. Box 943 Lock Haven 17745-0943	1839 Lycoming/Centre	1839	1839
H3	Columbia 35 West Main St. Box 380 Bloomsburg 17815-0380	1813 Northumberland	1813	1813
A2	Crawford 903 Diamond Sq. Meadville 16335	1800 Allegheny	1800	1800
G6	Cumberland 1 Courthouse Sq. Carlisle 17013	1750 Lancaster	1750	1750
H5	Dauphin Front & Market Sts., Rm. 102 P.O. Box 1295 Harrisburg 17108-1295	1785 Lancaster	1785	1785 Front & Market Sts., Rm. 103 Harrisburg 17101
K6	Delaware Govt. Admin. Bldg. #107 201 West Front St. Media 19063	1789 Chester	1789	1789
D2	Elk P.O. Box 314 Ridgway 15853-0314	1843 Jefferson/ McKean/Clearfield	1844	1844
A1	Erie 140 West 6th St., Rm. 121 Erie 16501	1800 Allegheny	1823	1823
	Erie was attached to Crawford County until 1803. A courthouse fire destroyed pre-1823 records.			

Map	County Address	Date Formed Parent County/ies	Deeds	Register of Wills
B6	Fayette 61 East Main St. Uniontown 15401-3514	1783 Westmoreland	1784	1784
C2	Forest 526 Elm St. P.O. Box 423 Tionesta 16353-0423 *Forest was attached to Jefferson County until 1857.*	1848 Jefferson/ (part of Venango; annexed 1866)	1857	1855
E6	Franklin 157 Lincoln Way East Chambersburg 17201-2211	1784 Cumberland	1784	1784
E6	Fulton North Second St. McConnellsburg 17233	1850 Bedford	1850	1851
A6	Greene 93 East High St. Waynesburg 15370	1796 Washington	1796	1796
E5	Huntingdon 223 Penn St. Huntingdon 16652	1787 Bedford	1786	1787
C4	Indiana 825 Philadelphia St. Indiana 15701-3934 *Indiana was attached to Westmoreland County until 1806.*	1803 Lycoming/ Westmoreland	1806	1803
C3	Jefferson 200 Main St. Brookville 15825-1236 *Jefferson was attached to Westmoreland County until 1806 and to Indiana County until 1830.*	1804 Lycoming	1828	1832
F5	Juniata P.O. Box 68 Mifflintown 17059-0068	1831 Mifflin	1831	1831
J3	Lackawanna North Washington Ave. Scranton 18503	1878 Luzerne	1878	1878
J6	Lancaster 50 North Duke St. Lancaster 17602-2805 *Some early court records have been transferred to the Lancaster County Historical Society, 230 N. President Ave., Lancaster, PA 17603.*	1729 Chester	1729	1729 50 North Duke St. P.O. Box 83480 Lancaster 16702-3480
A4	Lawrence County Government Center 430 Court St. New Castle 16101	1849 Beaver/Mercer	1849	1849
H5	Lebanon 107 Municipal Bldg. 400 S. 8th St. Lebanon 17042-6794	1813 Dauphin/ Lancaster	1813	1813 105 Municipal Bldg. 400 South 8th St. Lebanon 17042-6794
J4	Lehigh 17 S. 17th St., Rm. 350 Allentown 18101-2400	1812 Northampton	1812	1812 455 W. Hamilton St., Rm. 124 Allentown 18101-1614
J3	Luzerne 200 N. River St. Wilkes-Barre 18702-2685 *A flood in 1972 destroyed some estate files.*	1786 Northumberland	1787	1786
G3	Lycoming 48 W. 3d St. Williamsport 17701-6519	1795 Northumberland	1795	1795
D2	McKean 500 West Main St. P.O. Box 3426 Smethport 16749-3426 *Attached to Centre County until 1814 and to Lycoming County for judicial and elective purposes, McKean was not fully organized until 1826.*	1804 Lycoming	1827	1827 P.O. Box 202 Smethport 16749-0202
A3	Mercer Box 109, Courthouse North Diamond St. Mercer 16137-0109 *Attached to Crawford County until 1804.*	1800 Allegheny	1803	1804 Box 112, Courthouse Mercer 16137-0112
F5	Mifflin 20 North Wayne St. Lewistown 17044-1770	1789 Cumberland/ Northumberland	1789	1789
K3	Monroe Courthouse Sq. Stroudsburg 18360	1836 Pike/Northampton	1836	1836
K5	Montgomery P.O. Box 311 Norristown 19404-0311 * *Some early deed books are in the county archives (see below) and the county historical society.* † *Most records through the mid-1980s are in the Montgomery County Archives Center, 1880 Markley St., Norristown 19401.*	1784 Philadelphia	1784*	1784†
H3	Montour 29 Mill St. Danville 17821-1945	1850 Columbia	1850	1850
K4	Northampton 7th and Washington Streets Easton 18042-7401	1752 Bucks	1752	1752
G4	Northumberland 2d and Market Streets Sunbury 17801-3408	1772 Lancaster/Berks/ Bedford/Cumberland/ Northampton	1770	1771
	Ontario	(renamed Bradford, 1812)		
G5	Perry Center Sq., 25 W. Main St. P.O. Box 223 New Bloomfield 17068-0223	1820 Cumberland	1820	1820

Map	County Address	Date Formed Parent County/ies	Deeds	Register of Wills
K6	Philadelphia City Hall #154 Broad and Market Streets Philadelphia 19107-3200 (for deeds from 1952; earlier at City Archives)	1682 original	1684	1682 City Hall, Rm. 180 Philadelphia 19107 (for indexes) 3101 Market St. Philadelphia 19104 (for records)
	The city and county of Philadelphia were combined in 1854 and city and county offices merged in 1952. The orphans' court is in Room 415 of City Hall, and the City Archives is located at 3101 Market St., Ste. 150, Philadelphia 19104 <www.phila.gov/phils/carchive.htm>. E-mail: archives@phila.gov.			
K3	Pike 412 Broad St. Milford 18337	1814 Wayne	1814	1814 506 Broad St.
E2	Potter 1 East Second St. Coudersport 16915	1804 Lycoming	1806	1836
	Attached to Lycoming County until 1814 and to McKean County for judicial purposes, Potter was not fully organized until 1835.			
H4	Schuylkill 401 North Second St. Pottsville 17901	1811 Berks/Northampton (parts of Columbia and Luzerne added 1818)	1811	1811
G4	Snyder P.O. Box 217 Middleburg 17842-0217	1855 Union	1855	1855
C6	Somerset 300 North Center St., Ste. 400 Somerset 15501	1795 Bedford	1795	1795 111 North Center Ave., Ste. 170 Somerset 15501
H3	Sullivan Courthouse, Main St. Laporte 18626	1847 Lycoming	1848	1847
J2	Susquehanna 11 Maple St. P.O. Box 218 Montrose 18801-0218	1810 Luzerne	1812	1812
	Susquehanna was attached to Luzerne County until 1812.			
F2	Tioga 116 Main St. Wellsboro 16901-1410	1804 Lycoming	1806	1806
G4	Union 103 S. 2d St. Lewisburg 17837-1903	1813 Northumberland	1813	1813
B3	Venango 1168 Liberty St. Franklin 16323-1252	1800 Allegheny/ Lycoming	1805	1806
	Venango was attached to Crawford County until 1805.			
C2	Warren 204 4th St. Warren 16365-2318	1800 Allegheny/ Lycoming	1819	1820
	Attached to Crawford County until 1805 and then to Venango, Warren was formally organized in 1819.			
A6	Washington 100 W. Beau St. Washington 15301-4402	1781 Westmoreland	1781	1781 1 S. Main St. #1002 Washington 15301
K2	Wayne 925 Court St. Honesdale 18431-9517	1798 Northampton	1798	1798 925 Court St. Honesdale 18431-1996
B5	Westmoreland 2 North Main St., Ste. 503 Box 160 Greensburg, PA 15601	1773 Bedford	1773	1773 2 N. Main St., Ste. 301 Greensburg 15601-2405
J2	Wyoming 1 Courthouse Sq. Tunkhannock 18657-1216	1842 Luzerne	1842	1843
H6	York 28 East Market St. York 17401-1501	1749 Lancaster	1749	1749

Rhode Island

ALICE EICHHOLZ, Ph.D., CG

Named when Roger Williams referred to Aquidneck Island as the "isle of roses," bedecked by rhododendrons and owned by the native inhabitants, Rhode Island had its beginnings as a haven for religious dissenters expelled by Massachusetts Bay and Plymouth colonies. Williams's unceasing belief in religious freedom probably helped establish a long, collaborative relationship with the Narragansetts. In 1636, the only place he had to run was south, out of reach of both Massachusetts colonies and to a place not yet within the Puritan strongholds of Connecticut's colonies. He purchased from the native inhabitants what became Providence Plantations in 1637, and a group associated with Anne Hutchinson purchased Aquidneck Island in 1638. Renamed "Rhode Island," the area now encompasses Portsmouth, Middletown, and the city of Newport.

Geographically, the settlements might have met economic disaster had it not been for the enterprise of sea trade. Not having the rich natural resources that the other colonies had, a few wealthy planters in the eastern part of the colony capitalized on their excellent location relative to the sailing currents of the Atlantic. They developed import trade in sugar, fruit, rum, slaves, and exports from the other colonies to build an impressive plantation system. Throughout the state's history this industry has provided a highly mobile and much more ethnically diverse population in Rhode Island than can be found in the other New England states. Transients in town for a year or two were not uncommon as individuals from other New England locations broke loose from their moorings and headed to Newport for adventure and livelihood on the sea.

More and more land was purchased from the native inhabitants, and groups of Quakers from England and Jews from Portugal and Spain arrived in the colony, where they were accorded the status of freemen by the General Assembly. At the outbreak of King Philip's War in 1675, despite an attempt to remain neutral, Rhode Island and Providence Plantations were swept into the war when major battles were fought there. When this early battle of the colonial wars ended, more and more land was purchased from the indigenous tribes, and conflicts developed with both Massachusetts and Connecticut colonies over land claims.

The towns in Rhode Island remained reasonably separate and distinct groups that coexisted despite considerable differences. As such, no county system of government developed until the eighteenth century, and even then its function was chiefly for court proceedings. The General Assembly and the General Court dealt with the colonial matters usually conducted by counties.

During the Revolution, the British captured and occupied the Island of Aquidneck. The British Navy used Narragansett Bay as a strategic harbor, just as the United States Navy does today. Portuguese Jews, French settlers, and African slaves all found their way to Narragansett Bay in the seventeenth and eighteenth centuries. The port of Providence brought hundreds of Irish and French-Canadians in the nineteenth century, and Italians, Germans, Russians, and Poles in the early twentieth century.

Good collections of Rhode Island records, the indexing of early materials, and the short distance from one end of the state to another, all make Rhode Island an excellent site for genealogical research.

Vital Records

Although many vital events before 1853 were not recorded, those that were are fairly easy to locate. The General Assembly mandated that marriage intentions be recorded beginning in 1647, although the law was not enforced. More often, marriages were reported by ministers to town clerks. Births were often recorded in family groups at different times in a family's life, but not all births were recorded even when some in the family were. James N. Arnold's *Vital Record of Rhode Island, 1636–1850*, 21 vols. (Providence, R.I.: Narragansett Historical Publishing Co., 1891–1912), whose title is in the singular, is a compilation of Rhode Island research materials, the first six volumes of which are alphabetized extracts of vital events from town records. The volumes can usually be located at major research libraries holding New England resources and are at the Family History Library (FHL). Births, deaths, and marriages (both bride and groom listed separately) are recorded from the earliest settlement to 1850 and are organized according to county and town. More information is often given under the groom's entry. Some of the rest of the volumes contain vital events from sources other than the town records (see Church Records), although individual entries are documented, which makes it possible to check the original source. Towns, for the most part, still hold all of these originals in the clerk's office (see Town Resources).

Arnold's *Vital Record* stops in 1850, and since statewide reporting did not begin until 1853, vital events for the three years between 1850 and 1853 must be searched for in town records.

The Division of Vital Records, Rhode Island Department of Health, Rm 101 Cannon Bldg., 3 Capitol Hill, Providence, RI 02908-5097 <www.healthri.org/management/vital/home.htm> is responsible for the permanent filing of copies of vital events recorded in all Rhode Island towns from 1853 to the present. Mail or in-person requests can be made at the above address for births or marriages that occurred less than 100 years ago or deaths that occurred less than fifty years ago, with appropriate applications available on the website. The present fee is $15 for each record.

Vital events earlier than these cutoff time frames are available either in the town, at the Rhode Island State Archives (see Archives, Libraries, and Societies), or by microfilm at the Rhode Island Historical Society (see Archives, Libraries, and Societies), FHL, or New England Historic Genealogical Society (see page 13). Microfilm indexes exist to 1900 with computerized indexes to marriages and deaths to 1900 at the Rhode Island Historical Society.

A more recent publication of vital records is Alden G. Beaman's *Vital Records of Rhode Island, New Series* (Princeton, Mass.: the author, 1975–present), presently in thirteen volumes with more to follow published by his daughter. Using probates and gravestones, Beaman supplements Arnold with information on vital events not found in the town's vital records. This is an alphabetical arrangement for an entire county, with the town of residence indicated. Washington, Newport, and Kent counties are included in what has already been published.

Vital records for Providence from 1850 to 1945 are in print in thirty-two volumes, usually available at research centers with good New England collections or on microfilm.

Divorces were granted through all of the courts. Those granted between 1749 and 1900 are available at the Archives at the Judicial Records Center (see Court Records). After 1962 records can be obtained—with some restrictions—from Family Court, 22 Hayes Street, Providence, RI 02908, or by writing the Supreme Court Judicial Records Center.

Census Records

Federal

Population Schedules
- Indexed—1790, 1800, 1810, 1820, 1830, 1840, 1850, 1860, 1870, 1880, 1900, 1910, 1920, 1930
- Soundex—1880, 1900, 1920

Industry and Agriculture Schedules
- 1850, 1860, 1870, 1880

Mortality Schedules
- 1850, 1860, 1870, 1880

Union Veterans Schedules
- 1890

Provincial

Before obtaining statehood, Rhode Island took several censuses for a variety of purposes. These are supplemented by the freemen's lists indicating all those admitted to free status between 1747 and 1755. The originals and a card index are at the Rhode Island State Archives, but they have been published in Bruce C. MacGunnigle, *Rhode Island Freemen, 1747–1755* (Baltimore: Genealogical Publishing Co., 1977).

Some censuses were ordered as early as 1706, but the earliest extant census is for 1730, although only Portsmouth and part of South Kingston returns have been located. African Americans and whites are enumerated and identified as such in the lists transcribed by Mildred Mosher Chamberlain and published in *Rhode Island Roots* 7 (1981): 16-17 and 10 (1984): 1.

The 1774 census has survived for nearly all towns and has been indexed and published. Only New Shoreham (Block Island) is missing. Since this is a pre-Revolutionary War list, its value is in locating these families before the decline in population and

the economic and political changes caused by the war. Original returns are at Rhode Island State Archives, but their publication makes them more accessible. See John R. Bartlett, *Census of the Inhabitants of the Colony of Rhode Island and Providence Plantations* (1858; reprint, Baltimore: Genealogical Publishing Co., 1969).

A military census falls chronologically between the 1774 and 1782 census (see Military Records). The last census before the federal censuses begin can be found indexed in Jay Mack Holbrook's, *Rhode Island 1782 Census* (Oxford, Mass.: Holbrook Research Institute, 1979). Since returns for some of the towns were lost, this is a reconstructed census using original manuscripts and tax lists to replace those lost records. Returns for North Providence and Smithfield are not extant. There is a breakdown by age, sex, and race in the original manuscript, but Holbrook covers whites only (see also Military Records).

State

Rhode Island is the only New England state with extensive state census records taken every ten years between 1865 and 1935 (1895 is missing). Similar to the federal census, the Rhode Island State Archives has microfilm copies of all the state censuses with an every-name index to the 1865 state census and indexes to the 1875 and 1885 censuses. Microfilm copies of the 1865, 1875, and 1885 censuses are also at the Rhode Island Historical Society. See Maureen Taylor, "Rhode Island Local and State Censuses," available by membership subscription at <www.newenglandancestors.org>.

Background Sources

Comprehensive town histories with genealogies, abundantly found in other New England states, do not exist to the same extent in Rhode Island. Particularly for the seventeenth century, much of Rhode Island's local history is found in the town council records available in print (see Town Resources). However, there are good general history materials for the state, genealogical research guides, and compendium family genealogies such as:

Andrews, Charles M. *The Colonial Period of American History.* 2 vols. New Haven, Conn.: Yale University Press, 1938. Presents a good view of history useful to genealogists.

Arnold, Samuel Greene. *History of Rhode Island and Providence Plantations.* 2 vols. New York: D. Appleton & Co., 1859–60. Detailed chronological history of the state.

Austin, John O. *Genealogical Dictionary of Rhode Island.* 1887. Reprint. Baltimore: Genealogical Publishing Co., 1969. Comprehensive in its coverage of 485 families for three or four generations. No references are indicated, but the researcher can often surmise the source, and thus check the original. The reprint edition supplements the original and has corrections.

Bartlett, John Russell, ed. *Records of the Colony of Rhode Island and Providence Plantations in New England.* 7 vols. Providence, R.I.: A. Crawford Greene and Brother, 1856–62. A helpful edited transcript of the General Assembly proceedings.

Bridenbaugh, Carl. *Fat Mutton and Liberty of Conscience: Society in Rhode Island, 1636–1690.* Providence, R.I.: Brown University Press, 1974. A social history of the seventeenth century.

Coleman, Peter J. *The Transformation of Rhode Island, 1790–1860.* Providence, R.I.: Brown University Press, 1963. A comprehensive portrait of the effects of social and political life in the state during early statehood until the Civil War.

Fiske, Jane Fletcher. "Genealogical Research in Rhode Island." *The New England Historical and Genealogical Register* 136 (July 1982): 173-219. A superb guide to research in Rhode Island that follows the types of resources century-by-century. It is reprinted in Ralph J. Crandall, ed., *Genealogical Research in New England* (Baltimore: Genealogical Publishing Co., 1984).

Gannett, Henry. *A Geographic Dictionary of Connecticut and Rhode Island.* 2 vols. in 1. 1984. Reprint. Baltimore: Genealogical Publishing Co., 1987. Serves as a place-name guide for the state.

Genealogies of Rhode Island Families from the New England Historical and Genealogical Register. 2 vols. Baltimore: Genealogical Publishing Co., 1989. A second set of similar material is published from Rhode Island periodicals (see Periodicals).

Parks, Roger, ed. *Rhode Island: A Bibliography of Its History.* Hanover, N.H.: University Press of New England, 1985. An excellent, comprehensive bibliography.

Sherman, Ruth Wilder. *Peleg Burroughs' Journal, 1778–1798: The Tiverton, R.I. Years of the Humbly Bold Baptist Minister.* Warwick, R.I.: Rhode Island Genealogical Society, 1981. An extraordinary example of day-to-day living in the late eighteenth century, including genealogical information and social history.

Sperry, Kip. *Rhode Island Sources for Family Historians and Genealogists.* Logan, Utah: Everton, 1986. Alphabetical organization of source records that can be found, with basic research maps, in the state and in the FHL.

Taylor, Maureen A. *Research in Rhode Island.* Arlington, Va.: National Genealogical Society, 2001.

Maps

An excellent map of Rhode Island and Providence Plantations, 1636–65, makes clear the location and dates of purchase for all of the early settlements. Land disputes and dates of boundaries of resolution are included. A copy can be found in James Truslow

Adams, ed., *Atlas of American History* (New York: Charles Scribner's Sons, 1943). Two other excellent published map resources are John Hutchins Cady, *Rhode Island Boundaries, 1636–1936* (Providence, R.I.: State of Rhode Island and Providence Plantations, 1936), and Marion I. Wright and Robert J. Sullivan, *Rhode Island Atlas* (Providence, R.I.: Rhode Island Publications Society, 1982).

Perhaps the largest collection of maps in the state can be found at the Rhode Island Historical Society, although some of these are on microfilm through the FHL. A "Chronological Checklist of Maps in Rhode Island in the Rhode Island Historical Society Library," published in *Rhode Island Historical Collections* 11 (1918): 47-55, continues serially through the next several volumes. Among the more relevant to genealogical research are the Wallings Series and the *Beers' Atlas* of 1870, the first one produced for the state. Over 200 categories of maps are listed in the checklist.

Town offices usually have lot maps, although no statewide survey exists.

Land Records

State-Land State

From the beginning of the settlement, as in Connecticut and Vermont, land transactions in Rhode Island were filed in the town office in either proprietors' records or deed books. Indexes to the records are just as varied as they are in the rest of New England. Some grantor/grantee indexes are by surname only, some by surname and first initial instead of full name. Land was divided by proprietors in a pattern of lots. Metes and bounds were the usual land descriptions when the transaction did not involve an easily identified part of the lot or full lot.

One group of land records was recorded by the colony during the seventeenth century. Such transactions produced a multi-volume collection entitled "Rhode Island Land Evidence," which is located at the Rhode Island State Archives. Volume 1 has been abstracted and published as *Rhode Island Land Evidence*, vol. 1 (1921; reprint, Baltimore: Genealogical Publishing Co., 1970). Abstracts of volumes 2, 3, 4, and 5 have been printed in *Rhode Island Roots* (see Periodicals).

Some unindexed, unpublished deeds from the 1640s, which did not appear in the first volume of *Records of the Colony of Rhode Island* (see Background Sources), are at the Rhode Island Archives.

Probate Records

Unlike any other state in New England, from colonial times probate functions have been organized by town, not county or separate probate district. The town council, in addition to its normal function, handled probate matters in Rhode Island. Wills were accepted and challenged, executors authorized, administrators appointed, inventories ordered, and estates distributed, although the town council book, probate book, or will book differed from town to town. It was not until much later that a certain uniformity began to take hold in the recording procedures, dividing town functions into separate books instead of locating them on whatever blank parchment space was available in the office or home of a council member.

Court Records

Courts kept the only countywide records in Rhode Island, and that has been the case since the inception of counties in 1729. After 1729, a superior court of judicature (criminal) and inferior court of common pleas (civil) as well as a supreme court were established, similar to those in Massachusetts. Debts, divorces, and trespass claims are found within the court records for each county. Previous to 1729 the General Court of Trials existed for the entire state along with several lower courts. All the colonial court records from colonial and state courts from 1645 to 1900 are located at the Rhode Island Supreme Court Judicial Records Center, 5 Hill St., Pawtucket, RI 02860 <www.courts.state.ri.us/records/defaultrecords.htm>. Records are available for on-site research with some restrictions. Civil cases (1671–1900), criminal cases (1671–1900), divorces (1749–100), and naturalizations (1793–1974) are presently available for research.

Court records in print include records of the general court of trials: *Rhode Island Court Records: Records of the Court of Trials of the Colony of Providence Plantations*, 2 vols. (Providence, R.I.: Rhode Island Historical Society, 1920, 1922), which covers from 1647 to 1670; and Jane F. Fiske, *Gleanings from Newport Court Files, 1659–1783* (Boxford, Mass.: Genbooks, n.d.)

Tax Records

Tax records pre-date the Revolution and may be found at the town clerk's office, Rhode Island State Archives, or the Rhode Island Historical Society. The clerk's office usually has an inventory of tax list holdings. No other attempt has been made to catalog or inventory tax records, though when they exist on a year-by-year basis, they provide good evidence for the social status of a family and its presence in a town when no land is owned.

Cemetery Records

Rhode Island cemetery records exist in abundance. As with other New England states, the local DAR chapters have been

collecting gravestone inscriptions and indexing them in typed volumes annually. A complete set of their work can be found at the DAR Library in Washington and the Rhode Island Historical Society.

James N. Arnold gathered gravestone inscriptions from many Rhode Island cemeteries. Part of his collection of handwritten bound manuscripts is at the Rhode Island Historical Society, while the notebooks with card index are at the Knight Memorial Library, 275 Elmwood Ave., Providence, RI 02907.

Another excellent collection on microfilm at the Rhode Island Historical Society is the Benns Collection at the East Greenwich Public Library, 82 Pierce St., East Greenwich, RI 02818. Newport Historical Society (see Archives, Libraries, and Societies) has some cemetery records as well. David Dumas, "Rhode Island Grave Records," *Rhode Island Roots* 3 (1977): 1-6, is an excellent guide to locating many of the manuscript and typescript collections. The Historic Graves Commission for Rhode Island has devised a list of all cemeteries declared "historical." The Rhode Island State Archives holds the Graves Registration List, organized by town, of historical cemeteries.

Church Records

Quakers, Anglicans, and Baptists all managed to develop a strong presence in Rhode Island and Providence Plantations. Although church records never reach quite the comprehensiveness that is characteristic of Massachusetts in the seventeenth century, there are strong collections in the state, many still held and maintained by the local organization. A WPA survey of church records conducted in 1939 was updated to 1970 by the Rhode Island State Archives when the microfilming was completed for the FHL. Information may be obtained by a request addressed to the Rhode Island State Archives (see Archives, Libraries, and Societies).

Baptist. In a colony founded by Roger Williams, this is the historical home of the Baptists in this country. Since infant baptism was not practiced, the earliest church records have more social than genealogical value. The Newport Historical Society Library has some of these records. Ministers often carried their own records with them that included marriages. Some of these are printed in Arnold's *Vital Record* (see Vital Records). Later Baptist records can be found at the Rhode Island Historical Society and the local church.

Society of Friends. Arnold's volume 7 (see Vital Records) is devoted to the vital records for Narragansett and Rhode Island Friends. It is an index rather than a transcript of the records, and some of the valuable items such as witnesses to marriages are not included and need to be sought in the original records. Those for the settlements on the island of Rhode Island are at the Newport Historical Society. Rhode Island Historical Society's manuscript

department has a curator for the Friends materials for the rest of the colony. Many Rhode Island Quaker families migrated to Monmouth County, New Jersey, as well as Dutchess County, New York, and North Carolina. Some others moved with the sea trade to the Caribbean.

Episcopal. Three Episcopal congregations were established in Rhode Island by the early eighteenth century. Volume 10 of Arnold has the earliest extant baptisms and marriages for Trinity Church at Newport with the originals now at the Newport Historical Society. Wilkins Updike's *History of the Episcopal Church at Narragansett*, 3 vols. (Boston: D. B. Updike, 1907) is a complete transcription of that church's records from 1718 to 1774, whereas Arnold's volume 10 reports just the vital records for the church up to 1875.

Roman Catholic. Both French and Irish Catholic Churches developed in the nineteenth century. See Patrick T. Conley and Matthew J. Smith, *Catholicism in Rhode Island: The Formative Era* (Providence, R.I.: Diocese of Providence, 1976). Records can be located at the Diocesan Archives, 1 Cathedral Sq., Providence, RI 02903, or at the individual parishes. A few of the early Irish records are at the Chancery Archives of the Archdiocese of Boston (see Massachusetts—Church Records).

Military Records

Shipwrecks, privateering, slave trading, and smuggling were all part of everyday life in colonial Rhode Island. Many materials illustrative of military service concerning these events are housed at the Rhode Island State Archives, but there is no cumulative index. The first published material on military service in the state is Joseph J. Smith's *Civil and Military List of Rhode Island, 1647–1850*, 3 vols. (Providence, R.I.: Preston and Rounds, 1900–07), with a full index published in the last volume. Unfortunately, only officers are included for the Revolutionary War. George M. Bodge's *Soldiers of King Philip's War* (1906; reprint, Baltimore: Genealogical Publishing Co., 1976) deals with all of New England. However, Rhode Island was heavily involved in all of the colonial wars since it depended so heavily on sea trade with England and other European countries. Rhode Island State Archives material concerning the colonial wars is published by the Rhode Island Historical Society in Providence in three volumes by Howard M. Chapin, *Rhode Island in the Colonial Wars: A List of Rhode Island Soldiers and Sailors in King George's War, 1740–48; Rhode Island Privateers in King George's War, 1739–48;* and *Rhode Island Soldiers and Sailors in the Old French and Indian War, 1755–62.*

In a more complete form than Smith's, revolutionary records appear in volume 12 of Arnold and in Benjamin Cowell's *Spirit of '76 in Rhode Island* (1850; reprint, Baltimore: Genealogical Publishing Co., 1973). In addition, Mildred M. Chamberlain's

The Rhode Island 1777 Military Census (Baltimore: Genealogical Publishing Co., 1985) lists men in age categories 16–50, 50–60, and over 60, and whether they were able for service. But, since Portsmouth, Middletown, and Newport were occupied by the British at the time, no returns exist for those towns. Those for Exeter, Little Compton, and New Shoreham appear to be lost. A card file at the Rhode Island State Archives indexes men who served in the Revolution.

Adjutant General's Office records before 1865 are now located at the Rhode Island State Archives, although the report entitled *Annual Report...for the Year 1865, Official Register, Rhode Island Officers and Enlisted Men, U.S. Army and Navy, 2* vols. (Providence, R.I.: State Printer, 1893–95), is usually available in research libraries with New England collections and is the official register for the Civil War.

Military records for service from the Civil War through World War I can be obtained from the Adjutant General's Office, 1051 N. Main St., Providence, RI 02904.

Periodicals, Newspapers, and Manuscript Collections

Periodicals

Rhode Island Roots is the quarterly of the Rhode Island Genealogical Society. Transcriptions of early Rhode Island records and family genealogies are the focus of its material.

Rhode Island Genealogical Register is an independent journal (P.O. Box 585, East Princeton, MA 01517) devoted to publishing original source material for Rhode Island.

Several periodicals were published in the past including *The Newport Historical Magazine* (1880–84), *The Rhode Island Historical Magazine* (1844–87), *Rhode Island Historical Tracts* (1877–96), *Rhode Island Historical Society Collections* (1827–1914), *Rhode Island Historical Society Publications* (1893–1900).

Genealogical material from the old journals is reprinted in *Genealogies of Rhode Island Families from Rhode Island Periodicals*, 2 vols. (Baltimore: Genealogical Publishing Co., 1983).

Newspapers

The first newspaper, the *Gazette*, was published in Newport in 1732. Because of Rhode Island's unique position as one of the early "jumping off" points in a highly mobile community moving west and south, its newspapers tended to carry marriage and death notices for many former residents. Arnold's volumes 12 through 21 of *Vital Record* carry abstracts of many of these records.

The Rhode Island Historical Society is the official repository in the state for all published newspapers; however, abstracts of vital records from them may be found in several other repositories.

The Rhode Island Historical Society itself has some abstracts and indexes. One is a microfilm card index to the *Providence Journal* and the *Providence Bulletin*.

Manuscripts

Many town and city libraries have manuscript collections consisting of personal and business papers both from the broader community and professional genealogists. The three largest of these are at Rhode Island Historical Society, Newport Historical Society (see Archives, Libraries, and Societies), and Brown University, John Hay Library, 1 Prospect St., Providence, RI 02912, the latter being particularly strong in nineteenth-century material.

Archives, Libraries, and Societies

Rhode Island State Archives
337 Westminster St.
Providence, RI 02903
www.state.ri.us/archives

Service can be obtained by mail and appointment. The archives holds the state census records, military records, colonial petitions, and correspondence. Much of the material is also available on microfilm through the FHL.

Rhode Island Historical Society
121 Hope St.
Providence, RI 02906
www.rihs.org

The society's extensive holdings (federal and state census records, Quaker meeting records for all of New England, extensive gravestone records, and manuscripts) outlined in various sections of this chapter, are also described more fully on its website under "Research Library."

Rhode Island Genealogical Society
P.O. Box 433
Greenville, RI 02828
http://users.ids.net/~ricon/rigs.html

Its publication, *Rhode Island Roots*, is included quarterly with membership.

Newport Historical Society
82 Touro St.
Newport, RI 02840
www.newporthistorical.com

Library holdings include church, early town, and cemetery records for Newport and a good manuscript collection with ship logs.

Special Focus Categories

Immigration

Newport, Bristol and, to a lesser extent, Providence, were ports of entry for the slave trade (see African American, below) in the colony's early history and the choice for later immigrants. Immigration records are held by the National Archives and available regionally at the National Archives—Northeast Region (see page 11).

U.S. Customs Service passenger records for the ports of Providence (1820–67), Newport (1820–57), and Bristol and Warren (1820–71) are included in NARA microfilm publication M575 and are held regionally at the National Archives—Northeast Region (see page 11). *Index to Passengers Arriving at Providence, R.I., June 18, 1911–October 5, 1954* (NARA microfilm publication T518), as well as the passenger lists to 1943, are available on microfilm at the National Archives.

Naturalization

Naturalizations granted (1842–1904) by the Federal District Court at Providence are included in the Soundex cards for all of New England (1790–1906) held at the National Archives—Northeast Region (see Massachusetts—Naturalization). They were also granted by other courts, both at the county and state level, and can be hard to find. Court records previously at the Providence College Library have been moved to the superior court at the Rhode Island Judicial Records Center, 5 Hill St., Pawtucket, RI 02860. Both the Records Center and the Rhode Island State Archives have a personal name index to these records (1793–1900) on microfilm.

African American

As part of the "Triangular Slave Trade" with the South and the Caribbean, Rhode Island's economy was heavily reliant on slave trade. However, slavery waned in acceptance during the Revolutionary War. Despite the slave trade, Rhode Island had one of the first anti-slavery laws. Records of African Americans as both slaves and free citizens exist in abundance in Rhode Island, integrated in all varieties of public records. The Rhode Island State Archives has numerous collections that document the role of African-American soldiers in the Revolutionary War. Not much has been published, however. The Rhode Island Historical Society, in its large collection of manuscript material, has many records on African Americans.

Native American

Rhode Island's native population sold their land to the outcasts from Plymouth and Massachusetts Bay colonies to create the earliest settlements in the state. The early manuscript holdings in the Rhode Island State Archives contain information on Narragansetts and their descendants, who managed to stay in the state long after the demise, through either death or slavery after King Philip's War, of most other tribes in New England. "Indian" is a term found often in all categories of records for the state. As with African American slaves, natives often took the names of their owners or those to whom they were indentured, making it critical to follow white families of the same surnames. For excellent historical background, see Sydney S. Rider, *The Lands of Rhode Island as they were Known to Canonicus and Miantunnomu* (Providence, R.I.: the author, 1904).

Other Ethnic Groups

French, Jewish, and Portuguese communities have existed in the state from an early time. For Jewish research, Rhode Island Jewish Historical Society, 130 Sessions St., Providence, RI 02906 <www.dowtech.com/rijha> offers annual state and local meetings and projects. It publishes *Rhode Island Jewish Historical Notes* with a query column.

The early French were Huguenots soon integrated into Rhode Island's population. The American-French Genealogical Society, P.O. Box 830, Woonsocket, RI 02861 <www.afgs.org> is primarily concerned with French-Canadians who came for work in the nineteenth-century mills. Membership is open to French-Canadian or French researchers, but inquiries regarding the society's library are answered by mail for a per surname fee. The society provides *Je Me Souviens* with membership. See also Albert K. Aubin, *The French in Rhode Island* (Pawtucket, R.I.: American French Genealogical Society, 1981).

County Resources

The major genealogical use for counties in Rhode Island is the pursuit of court records and federal census returns. Before 1729 there were no county courts in Rhode Island. Two counties became incorporated in 1703: Providence and Newport. By 1750 all of Rhode Island's present counties existed, and no more developed after these were formed. Bristol became a county in 1746–47 when five towns, originally belonging to Massachusetts, were ceded to Rhode Island. Perhaps because the rest of the country is so oriented to counties, some of the vital records have been published in "county" groups, but the records themselves exist only on a town level.

Modern court records are at the superior court at the county seat; earlier ones have been moved (see Court Records).

Map	County Address	Date Formed Parent County/ies	Encompassed Towns
E7	Bristol Bristol 02809	1746/47 Bristol County Mass	Barrington, Bristol, Warren
E4	Kent East Greenwich 02818	1750 Providence	Coventry, East Greenwich, Warwick, West Greenwich, West Warwick
G6	Newport Newport 02840	1703 original	Jamestown, Little Compton, Middletown, Newport, New Shoreham (Block Island), Portsmouth, Tiverton
C3	Providence Providence 02903	1703 original	Burrillville, Central Falls, Cranston, Cumberland, East Providence, Foster, Glocester, Johnston, Lincoln, North Providence, North Smithfield, Pawtucket Providence, Scituate, Smithfield, Woonsocket
H3	Washington West Kingston 02892	1729 Narragansett Country	Charlestown, Exeter, Hopkinton, North Kingston, Narragansett, Richmond, South Kingston, Westerly

Town Resources

No other state has the emphasis on the town that Rhode Island enjoys. Town resources are extensive, and what follows is only a brief summary. In Rhode Island, the "town records" are usually found in the town council book or the town meeting records. Brigham's inventory (see Court Records), Fiske's article (see Background Sources), and the Works Progress Administration (WPA) Historical Records Survey for the state all contain excellent summaries of what records are available for each town. The chart that follows draws on that material. The first column lists town (or city) and address. All correspondence concerning deeds and probates should be directed to the town or city clerk at that address. Links to each town's website can be found on the Rhode Island Historical Society webpage at <www.rihs.org/links.htm>. Since so much of the early material is already in print, it is wise to consult those sources first. The second column lists the date formed and the parent town/s. There are no parent counties, as such, in Rhode Island. The "Date Formed" also indicates the year one can expect to find the *first* recorded vital records in that town. Fiske's article indicates which volume of Arnold (see Vital Records) corresponds to that town's vital records. The last column indicates the beginning dates that land and probate records can be found and where the court records for that town can be located.

Some early records for the four original towns, Portsmouth, Providence, Newport, and Warwick are in print. See also Marcia D. Melnyk, *Genealogist's Handbook for New England Research.* 4th ed. Boston: New England Historic and Genealogical Society, 1999.

Town Address	Date Formed Parent Town/s	Land Probate Court
Barrington 283 County Rd. Barrington 02806	1770 Barrington, Massachusetts	1770 1770 Bristol
Originally created in 1717 as Barrington, Massachusetts, it was ceded to Rhode Island in 1747 as part of the town of Warren. Barrington, Rhode Island, a new town, was set off from Warren in 1770. Barrington, Massachusetts records between 1717 and 1747 are in Bristol County; 1747–70 in the Warren town clerk's office. This office has the meeting records for the town since 1718.		
Bristol 10 Court St. Bristol 02809	1747 Bristol, Massachusetts	1747 1747 Bristol
Part of Plymouth Colony, 1681–86, then Bristol Co. Mass. Ceded to Rhode Island, 1747. See Taunton, Massachusetts, for earlier records.		
Burrillville 105 Harrisville Main St. Harrisville 02830	1806 Glocester	1806 1806 Providence
Central Falls 580 Broad St. Central Falls 02863	1895 (incorporated) Lincoln	1895 1895 Providence
Early Smithfield records are in this office.		
Charlestown 4540 S. County Trail Charlestown 02813	1738 Westerly	1738 1738 Washington
Coventry 1670 Flat River Rd. Coventry 02816	1741 Warwick	1741 1741 Kent
Cranston City Hall, 869 Park Ave. Cranston 02910	1754 Providence	1754 1754 Providence
Cumberland 45 Broad St./P.O. Box 7 Cumberland 02864	1747 Attleboro Gore, Massachusetts	1747 1747 Providence
Earlier records, 1692–1747, are in Bristol County, Massachusetts at Taunton.		
East Greenwich 125 Main St./P.O. Box 111 East Greenwich 02818	1677 (called Dedford or Deptford, 1686-89)	1679 1679 Kent
East Providence 145 Taunton Ave. E. Providence 02914	1862 Rehoboth/Seekonk, Mass.	1862 1862 Providence
See Rehoboth and Seekonk, Bristol County, Massachusetts, for earlier records.		
Exeter 675 Ten Rod Rd. Exeter 02822	1742 North Kingstown	1742 1742 Washington
Foster 181 Howard Hill Foster 02825	1781 Scituate	1781 1781 Providence
Glocester Main St./P.O. Box B Chepachet 02814	1731 Providence	1731 1731 Providence
Hopkinton 1 Town House Rd. Hopkinton 02833	1757 Westerly	1757 1757 Washington
Jamestown 93 Narragansett Ave. Jamestown 02835	1678 Native lands, Conanicut	1678 1678 Newport
Johnston 1385 Hartford Ave. Johnston 02919	1759 Providence	1759 1759 Providence
Probates to 1898 at Providence City Archives, Providence 02903.		
Lincoln 100 Old River Rd. Lincoln 02865	1871 Smithfield	1871 1871 Providence
Records before 1895 in Central Falls City Clerk's Office.		
Little Compton P.O. Box 226 Little Compton 02837	1682 (part of Plymouth Colony)	1747 1747 Newport
Became part of Rhode Island in 1747. Earlier records are at Plymouth Colony and Bristol County offices (see Massachusetts).		
Middletown 350 E. Main Rd. Middletown 02840	1743 Newport	1743 1743 Newport
Narragansett 25 Fifth Ave. Narragansett 02882	1901 South Kingstown District, 1888	1888 1901 Washington
Was a district before becoming a town; 1888–1901 records in S. Kingstown. Proprietor's records are in print: James Arnold, The Fones Record (1894; reprint, Baltimore: Genealogical Publishing Co., 1990).		
Newport City Clerk, 43 Broadway Newport 02840	1639 original	1639 1639 Newport
Records before 1783 at Newport Historical Society.		
New Shoreham P.O. Drawer 220 Block Island 02807	1661 (admitted to colony, 1664 as Block Island;) renamed, 1672	1672 1672 Washington
Part of Newport County until 1963.		

Town Address	Date Formed Parent Town/s	Land Probate Court
North Kingstown 80 Boston Neck Rd. Wickford 02852	1641 (renamed Kingstown, 1674; Rochester, 1686–89, North Kingstown after 1723)	1674 1674 Washington
Fire damaged all records in 1870; they are being restored.		
North Providence City Hall, 2000 Smith St. North Providence 02911	1765 Providence	1765 1765 Providence
North Smithfield 1 Main St. Slatersville 02876	1871 Smithfield	1871 1871 Providence
Pawtucket City Hall, 137 Roosevelt Ave. Pawtucket 02860	1862 Pawtucket, Mass., North Providence, R.I.	1862 1862 Providence
Incorporated 1885. See Seekonk, Bristol County Massachusetts, Northern District for earlier records.		
Portsmouth 2200 E. Main Rd., P.O. Box 155 Portsmouth 02871	1638 original	1636 1636 Newport
Pocasset proprietors' records are in manuscript form at New Bedford, Massachusetts Public Library.		
Providence 25 Dorrance St. Providence 02903	1636 original	1636 1636 Providence
Providence City Archives has earlier deeds and vital records for Providence and Johnston; probates to 1898		
Richmond 5 Richmond Townhouse Wyoming 02898	1747 Charlestown	1747 1747 Washington
Scituate 195 Danielson Pike N. Scituate 02857	1731 Providence	1731 1731 Providence
Smithfield 64 Farnum Pike Esmond 02917	1731 Providence	1731 1731 Providence
Records to 1870 are in city clerk's office, Central Falls 02863.		
South Kingstown 66 High St., P.O. Box 31 Wakefield 02879	1723 Kingstown	1674 1674 Washington
Kingstown divided into North and South in 1723. Records before that date were in North Kingston, but damaged in 1870. Copies are here.		
Tiverton 343 Highlands Road Tiverton 02878	1747 Dartmouth and Freetown, Mass.	1747 1747 Newport
Earlier records are in the Bristol County offices in Taunton, Massachusetts.		
Warren 514 Main St. Warren 02885	1747 Barrington, Rehoboth and Swansea, Mass.	1747 1747 Bristol
See Bristol County, Northern District, Taunton, Massachusetts, for earlier records.		
Warwick 3275 Post Rd. Apponaug 02886	1642 (as Shawomet; renamed, 1648) original	1642 1642 Kent
Westerly 45 Broad St. Westerly 02891	1669 (called Haversham, 1686–89) original	1669 1669 Washington
West Greenwich 280 Victory Hwy. West Greenwich 02816	1741 East Greenwich	1741 1741 Kent
West Warwick 1170 Main St. West Warwick 02893	1913 Warwick	1913 1913 Kent
Woonsocket City Hall, 169 Main St. Woonsocket 02895	1867 Cumberland/Smithfield	1867 1867 Providence
City Hall has copies of earlier deeds from parent towns beginning 1847.		

RHODE ISLAND

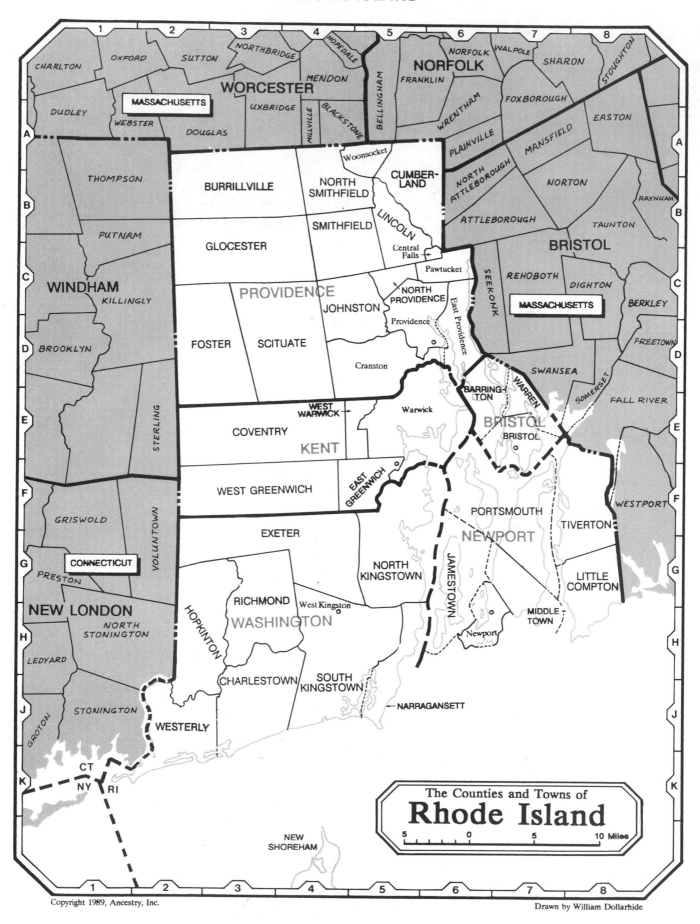

MASSACHUSETTS

CONNECTICUT

MASSACHUSETTS

The Counties and Towns of
Rhode Island

5   0   5   10 Miles

Drawn by William Dollarhide

South Carolina

JOHNI CERNY AND GARETH L. MARK

English claims on the area date to 1497 when John Cabot visited the New World and claimed the area for King Henry VII. These claims were the basis for Charles I's 1629 grant of "Carolana" to Sir Robert Heath, who failed to settle Carolina before the execution of Charles I in 1649. During the Commonwealth period in England, many citizens remained loyal to Charles II. At his ascension to the throne of England in 1660, eight men pressed their claims for a reward: Edward Hyde, Earl of Clarendon; George Monck, Duke of Albemarle; Lord William Craven; Lord John Berkeley; Lord Anthony Ashley Cooper, Earl of Shaftesbury; Sir George Carteret; Sir William Berkeley; and Sir John Colleton.

Charles II granted Carolina to the eight Lords Proprietors in 1663. After the claims of Heath's successors had been disposed of, the grant was revised and extended in 1665. The Great Plague of 1665, London's Great Fire of 1666, and war with the Dutch and French probably interfered with immediate settlement plans. Finally, in August 1669, three ships with over a hundred colonists sailed under the temporary command of Captain Joseph West and reached Barbados by November. Two of the original ships were lost in storms, but on 15 March 1670, the *Carolina* and a replacement ship anchored in what is now called Bull's Bay. Permanent settlement of South Carolina had finally begun.

The first settlement, called "Old Town," was on the western side of the Ashley River at its mouth. The original settlers were entitled to headright grants: 150 acres for each male over sixteen and a hundred acres for each female and each male under sixteen. Instead they chose security over land, surrounding their houses with a palisade and confining themselves to ten-acre plots. Their precaution proved wise when three Spanish frigates attacked the town in August 1670; fortunately, bad weather forced the Spanish to withdraw.

A new town was laid out at Oyster Point on the neck of land between the Ashley and Cooper rivers, with streets intersecting at right angles. One of the first pre-planned cities in North America, Charles Town was settled in 1680. Renamed Charleston in 1783, it was the only repository for South Carolina's public records until 1785 and remained the capital of South Carolina until the legislature moved the capital to Columbia in 1790.

South Carolinians first found economic stability in the deerskin trade, but the resulting encroachment on the territory of the Yemassee Indians led to war in 1715. South Carolina also was a leading producer of naval stores, such as pitch and tar. A welcome trade in the seventeenth century, it became a serious problem after the Yemassee Indian War since it attracted pirates to South Carolina's shores. Blackbeard, the most notorious pirate in the history of seafaring, sailed four ships toward Charles Town in June 1718, stopped ships at leisure, and took hostages whom he traded for medical supplies. The South Carolina assembly had repeatedly requested the crown to protect the province, and about half of the free white men—nearly 600 individuals—signed a petition to that effect in 1717. The ineffectual policies of the Lords Proprietors and their apparent inability to defend the colony led to further disaffection. When a rumor reached Charles Town in 1719 that the Spanish were readying a fleet to attack the city, revolution broke out. While not bloody, the revolution of 1719 nonetheless effectively ended the rule of the Lords Proprietors, and the crown established a provisional

royal government in 1721. When the crown bought out seven of the eight proprietors in 1729, South Carolina became a royal colony.

South Carolina is divided, culturally and topographically, into Up Country and Low Country. The topographical division runs along the fall line, from approximately Aiken to Columbia to Camden to Cheraw. Culturally, Charleston and the surrounding Tidewater region is the Low Country. Residents of the Low Country tended toward large rice or indigo plantations with great numbers of slaves. Residents of the Up Country tended to work small farms and in general had few slaves. The government was seated at Charleston, and residents of the Up Country often complained of unfair representation. This was based at least in part on the lack of local government.

During the three decades from the 1730s into the 1760s, the frontier families of the Up Country frequently rebelled against the provincial government. The Low Country elite promised representation, protection against outlaws and Indian attacks, and churches and schools, but they neglected to deliver on their promises. As a result of isolation, hardships, and a growing divergence from the Low Country, residents of the Up Country seldom bothered to travel to Charles Town, except to petition for land. The Stamp Act of 1765 imposed taxes on many official and unofficial papers—including not only legal documents but also playing cards—which greatly affected the pocketbooks of the Low Country planters. While they had the political power in South Carolina, residents of the Low Country needed the support, and numbers, of the Up Country frontiersmen to resist the Stamp Act. Some autonomy was granted in the District Circuit Court Act of 1769, which divided the province into seven judicial districts. About 1772, the first courts were held outside of Charleston. (See County/District Resources for a full explanation.)

The Revolutionary War found a deeply divided South Carolina. Charlestonians planned to resist the importation of tea, and the Boston Tea Party strengthened their resolve; Up Country Loyalists were equally resolved and attacked a fort at Ninety-Six in November 1775. The war raged throughout South Carolina for seven years. The British attacked Charleston in June 1776 but were forced to withdraw. Then, in July 1776, the Cherokee War broke out in the Up Country. Militia from South and North Carolina, Georgia, and Virginia defeated the tribe, and the northwest corner of South Carolina was ceded by the Cherokees in the treaty of May 1777. Between 1776 and 1779, Patriots and Loyalists fought skirmishes and continued marauding attacks on each other in the Up Country, although the Loyalists were largely suppressed. In May 1778, the British once again moved against Charleston, laying siege to the city. Charleston capitulated on 12 May 1780, and the British began moving into the Up Country, establishing a series of outposts. Meanwhile, the suppressed Loyalists began guerrilla raids on Patriot farms,

and local civil war broke out in several areas. The Patriots also formed guerrilla bands and harassed both the Loyalists and the British. Finally, the Patriot partisans began driving the British out of the Up Country, with major battles at Camden (May 1781), Ninety-Six (May–June 1781), and Eutaw Springs (September 1781); the British were so weakened that they and the Loyalists were forced to withdraw to Charleston. When the British finally evacuated Charleston on 14 December 1782, more than 4,000 Loyalists went with them.

Rice and indigo provided economic stability to South Carolina during much of the eighteenth century; the debts accrued during the Revolutionary War and the loss of bounties to support indigo production threatened to ruin the economy. Loyalists returning from exile in the Bahamas brought a new strain of cotton that thrived in the southeast. Then, in 1793, Eli Whitney improved the cotton gin. Within a decade, short-staple cotton transformed the Up Country into a prosperous region.

Like rice and indigo before it, cotton was a labor-intensive crop. A shortage of laborers led South Carolina to temporarily reopen the slave trade in 1803; 40,000 African Americans were imported in five years. As cotton pushed its way westward, political and journalistic battles over the slavery issue divided the United States into increasingly antagonistic factions. South Carolina and its neighbors felt threatened by the North's abolitionist movement, and when Abraham Lincoln was elected to the presidency, South Carolina called a secession convention on 17 December 1860. As the first state to secede, the first state to ratify the Constitution of the Confederate States of America, and the first state to fire shots during the Civil War, South Carolina received particularly harsh treatment when Union General William T. Sherman and his troops subdued her in 1864. Virtually destroyed, South Carolina faced difficult decades of racial and economic strife, but she recovered and today is a prosperous and healthy state.

Vital Records

A law mandating registration of all births and deaths in South Carolina was signed into law on 1 September 1914. Actual registration began in 1915, and South Carolina achieved ninety percent compliance within a few years. Original copies of birth and death certificates are filed with the state, and copies can be obtained by writing to South Carolina Department of Health and Environmental Control, Office of Vital Records and Public Health Statistics, 2600 Bull St., Columbia, SC 29201 <www.scdhec.net/vr>. The above office accepts Visa or MasterCard for payment for urgent requests made by phone. There is an additional fee for this service including postal costs.

Each South Carolina county has a copy of the state's records, and a few cities have records pre-dating the statewide

registration requirement: Charleston began keeping birth records in 1877 and death records in 1821, and Georgetown was authorized to establish a vital records registration system in 1883. The Church of England parishes created in 1706 recorded christenings, marriages, and burials, and these registers can serve as vital records for much of the colonial period (see Church Records).

South Carolina had no law requiring marriage licenses or registration until 1911. Assembly Act No. 70, "An Act to Require Marriage Licenses and Regulate Their Issuances," became effective on 1 July 1911. Licenses are on file with the judge of probate in each county. Prior to 1911, marriages were legal if performed according to canonical law; common law marriages also were recognized. Many churches recorded marriages, but when compared with the vast number of marriages that took place, the number of documented marriages is small. Marriage settlements, made by a widow and her second husband to protect the heirs of her first husband, and premarital agreements, not necessarily involving widows, were popular for a while. These records date from about 1760 to about 1890, and may be found in county conveyance books or the South Carolina Department of Archives and History and on microfilm at the Family History Library (FHL) in Salt Lake City. Newspapers accounts of marriages from 1732 to the present are a primary source of marriage documentation (see Newspapers).

Until 1949, divorce was illegal in South Carolina. Since then, divorces are the province of the county court, and all inquiries should be directed to the county clerk of court.

Census Records

Federal

Populations Schedules
- Indexed—1790, 1800 (see note below), 1810, 1820, 1830, 1840, 1850, 1860, 1870, 1880, 1900, 1910, 1920, 1930
- Soundex—1880, 1900, 1910, 1920

Industry and Agriculture Schedules
- 1850, 1860, 1870, 1880

Mortality Schedules
- 1850 (indexed), 1860 (indexed), 1870, 1880

Slave Schedules
- 1850, 1860

Union Veterans
- 1890

The South Carolina Department of Archives and History holds all of the federal census records either in original or microfilm form. Part of the 1800 census for Richland District is missing. The 1850 census of York and Lexington districts indicates county of birth as well as state for each person.

State

South Carolina did not conduct any full colonial censuses; there are fragments of state census returns available at the South Carolina Department of Archives and History. The 1829 state census of Fairfield and Laurens districts and the 1839 state census of Kershaw and Chesterfield districts are extant. The population returns for the 1869 state census are complete except for Clarendon, Oconee, and Spartanburg Counties. The 1875 state census returns are available for Clarendon, Newberry, and Marlboro Counties, as are partial returns for Abbeville, Beaufort, Fairfield, Lancaster, and Sumter counties. The original returns are found at the South Carolina Department of Archives and History; some of the returns have been published in South Carolina's historical and genealogical periodicals.

Background Sources

Successful research in South Carolina requires the researcher to be familiar with three things: (1) the cultural and topographical division of the state into Up Country and Low Country (see above), (2) the checkered history of local government formation (see County/District Resources), and (3) the laws of the state. The most comprehensive collection of South Carolina laws is found in Thomas Cooper and David J. McCord, eds., *The Statutes at Large of South Carolina*, 10 vols. (Columbia, S.C., 1836–41). See also John D. Cushing, comp., *The First Laws of the State of South Carolina* (Wilmington, Del.: Michael Glazier, 1981).

Robert M. Weir, *Colonial South Carolina: A History* (1983; reprint, Columbia, S.C.: University of South Carolina Press, 1997) covers South Carolina's colonial history. Researchers should consult Richard N. Coté, comp., *Local and Family History in South Carolina: A Bibliography* (Easley, S.C.: Southern Historical Press, 1981) for a comprehensive list of publications. See also John Hammond Moore, *Research Materials in South Carolina* (Columbia, S.C.: University of South Carolina Press, 1967).

Brent Howard Holcomb, *A Guide to South Carolina Genealogical Research and Records* (Columbia, S.C.: the author, 1986) and George K. Schweitzer, *South Carolina Genealogical Research* (Knoxville, Tenn.: the author, 1985), serve as guides for research in South Carolina.

No researcher can afford to overlook the "Combined Alphabetical Index" of the South Carolina Department of Archives and History, now called the "On-line Records Index" and accessible at <www.archivesindex.sc.gov>. The current version of the 293,212 items includes *Index to Multiple Record Series, ca. 1675–1929; Will Transcripts, 1782–1855; Colonial Land*

Grants, Confederate Pension Applications, 1919–1926; Plats for State Land Grants, 1784–1868; Legislative Papers, 1782–1866; Criminal Journals, 1769–1776. Not all series have been indexed to the same depth, and not all series cover the entire province or state; nonetheless, it is one of the most valuable resources available to genealogists. A link to an updated "Series List" of the records indexed appears on that webpage.

See also Charles H. Lesser, South Carolina Begins: The Records of a Proprietary Colony, 1663–1721 (Columbia, S.C.: The South Carolina Department of Archives and History, 1995), containing a detailed description of most of South Carolina's records before 1721 and instructions on their use.

Maps

The South Caroliniana Library of the University of South Carolina at Columbia has the best collection of early South Carolina maps (see also Manuscripts). The South Carolina Department of Archives and History publishes a pamphlet "The Formation of Counties in South Carolina," which can be purchased online at <www.state.sc.us/scdah/genealog.htm>.

See Suzanne Cameron Linder, Historical Atlas of the Rice Plantations along the ACE River Basin, 1860 (Columbia, S.C.: Department of Archives and History, 1995). The publication traces the lives, families, and property of plantation owners along Ashepoo, Combahee, and Edisto Rivers—the ACE Basin.

There is no gazetteer for South Carolina, but a useful substitute is Claude Henry Neuffer, ed., Names in South Carolina, 30 vols. (1954–83; reprint, 4 vols., Spartanburg, S.C.: Reprint Company, 1976–84). See also Joseph B. Martin III, "Guide to Presbyterian Ecclesiastical Names and Places in South Carolina, 1685–1985," South Carolina Historical Magazine, 90 (October 1989): 4–215; and Works Progress Administration, Palmetto Place Names (1945; reprint, Easley, S.C.: Reprint Company, 1975).

Robert Mills, Atlas of the State of South Carolina (1825; reprint, Easley, S.C.: Southern Historical Press, 1980), is fully indexed and mentions many landowners. Thorndale and Dollarhide (see page 3) illustrate the changing boundaries of South Carolina's districts and counties at each decennial census and includes census districts in 1790 and 1800 that were not legal polities. The Map of the States of North & South Carolina published in 1831 by Hinton & Simpkin & Marshall has been reproduced by Jonathan Sheppard Books (Box 2020, Albany, NY 12220).

Land Records

State-Land State

Land and property records, in combination with court records, are often the key to solving difficult research problems. South Carolina's colonial land records are among the most complete of the thirteen original colonies, probably because all records were maintained in Charleston, and Charleston was not destroyed during the Revolutionary War.

Land in South Carolina was granted by headright and bounty. Headrights were the "right" to free land of every "head" settling in the colony. Settlers who arrived with the first fleet were authorized headrights of 150 acres for every male aged sixteen and above and a hundred acres for every female and every male aged under sixteen. Heads-of-household could claim land for their slaves and servants as well as family members. Settlers who arrived after the first fleet and before 1756 were authorized fifty acres for each member of the household. After 1755, heads-of-household could receive a hundred acres plus an additional fifty acres for every other member of the household.

The prospective grantee first petitioned the Grand Council for a warrant (see Court Records). The petition had to be made in person by the head-of-household; he had to give his name, the number of acres requested, and the location of the land. While there was no requirement to request all of the land due to the family, the household had to have as many persons as claimed. Petitions occasionally include names and ages of spouses and children or other genealogically valuable information. The date of petition or application is often called the precept, warrant, or pursuant date. The petitions are found at the South Carolina Department of Archives and History in one of two sets of volumes: Records of the Grand Council (1671–92), in two volumes and Records of His Majesty's Council in twenty-seven volumes covering the entire colonial period. These twenty-nine volumes are in chronological order and are unindexed; the precept date is required to locate the petition. See also Alexander S. Salley Jr., and R. N. Olsberg, eds., Warrants for Land in South Carolina, 1672–1721 (Columbia, S.C.: University of South Carolina Press, 1977), and Alexander S. Salley, Jr., Records of the Secretary of the Province and the Register of the Province of South Carolina, 1671–1675 (Columbia, S.C.: Historical Commission of South Carolina, 1944).

After receiving a warrant, the prospective grantee carried it to a surveyor who surveyed the land and drew a plat, or map, of its boundaries. Recorded plats have important information including the following: the precept date, necessary to locate the original petition the survey (or certified) date; the recording date; and a full description of the land, including watercourses and location. Recorded plats are indexed in the Combined Alphabetical Index (see Background Sources).

When the plat was returned to the surveyor general's office, the prospective grant was checked against other plats to ensure that only one person was claiming the same land. If there were no problems, grant papers were sent to the governor for his signature and seal. Recorded grants are indexed in the Combined Alphabetical Index (see Background Sources). The FHL has South Carolina Land Plats, 1731–1861 (with indexes

covering 1688–1872), filmed on twenty-eight microfilm reels from original records at the Secretary of State's Office in 1955.

Once the land was finally granted, the owner was responsible for paying a quitrent. The first quitrent payment came due within two years on headright grants and within ten years on bounty land grants. The quitrent was a land tax that had its roots in English manorial society where "the land obligations due the manor, such as plowing and haying the lord's land, were computed to an annual money payment. Upon payment, the obligations were 'quit' for the year." The FHL has *South Carolina Land Grants, 1784–1882*, filmed from the original records and including a partial general index and some volumes indexed individually.

Another important land record is the memorial. From 1731 through 1775, those who had obtained land were tasked with preparing a memorial attesting to the location, quantity, names of adjacent landowners, and the boundaries of the land. Memorials also included a chain of title, often from the original patentee to the current owner. Original memorials are located at the South Carolina Department of Archives and History and are indexed in the Combined Alphabetical Index (see Background Sources). Some memorials have been microfilmed and are available at the FHL. The following published volumes are useful:

Esker, Katie-Prince Ward. *South Carolina Memorials, 1731–1776: Abstracts of Selected Land Records from a Collection in the Department of Archives and History*. 2 vols. New Orleans: Polyanthos, 1973–77.

Jackson, Ronald Vern, Gary Ronald Teeples, and David Schaefermeyer, eds., *Index to South Carolina Land Grants, 1784–1800*. Bountiful, Utah: Accelerated Indexing Systems, 1977.

Langley, Clara A. *South Carolina Deed Abstracts, 1719–1772*. 4 vols. Easley, S.C.: Southern Historical Press, 1983–84.

Lucas, Silas E., Jr., *An Index to Deed of the Province and State of South Carolina, 1719–1785, and Charleston District, 1785–1800*. Easley, S.C.: Southern Historical Press, 1977.

The boundary between South Carolina and North Carolina was first surveyed in 1772, and a final agreement was reached in 1815. Land previously thought to be in Mecklenburg and Tryon counties, North Carolina, was found to be in South Carolina. Records of both Carolinas should be examined for colonial inhabitants of the area encompassed by present-day Cherokee, Greenville, Spartanburg, and York Counties. See Brent Howard Holcomb, comp., *North Carolina Land Grants in South Carolina* (Greenville, S.C.: A Press, 1980).

In South Carolina, deeds are often called *mesne conveyances*, or conveyances, and are recorded in the office of the Register of Mesne Conveyance. Original records are found in each county's Clerk of Court office, and microfilmed copies of most pre-1865 records are available at the South Carolina Department of Archives and History, and the FHL.

Probate Records

Under the law of primogeniture during the colonial period the oldest living son, called the *heir at law*, inherited all of the land when the father died intestate (without leaving a will). If a will had been written, its content determined who would inherit. If there were no male heirs, all female heirs shared the land equally. South Carolina abolished primogeniture with a law that became effective on 1 May 1791. That law stated "If the intestate shall leave a widow and one or more children, the widow shall take one-third of the said estate, and the remainder shall be divided between the children, if more than one, but if only one, the remainder shall be vested in that one forever."

The division of intestate estates during the colonial period was based on an English statute of 1670, formally adopted into South Carolina law in 1712. The division of the estate after payment of all just debts and expenses was as follows: the widow, if any, received one-third of all real estate for life; the heir-at-law (eldest son) received the title to all real estate, including the widow's dower, which he inherited at her death; the widow received one-third of the personal property, and the children shared equally in the other two-thirds. If there were no widow, the children shared the personal property equally. If there were no children, the widow received one-half of the estate, and the other half was divided equally among the siblings of the deceased. Any property, real or personal, that was not bequeathed or devised in a valid will was divided according to the law.

Initially, the governor and the Grand Council were the only court of ordinary (probate) in the province; the secretary of the province also began functioning as a court of ordinary by 1692 (see Court Records). See Caroline T. Moore and Agatha Aimar Simmons, *Abstracts of the Wills of State of South Carolina, 1670–1800*, 4 vols. (Columbia, S.C.: R. L. Bryan, 1960–74); Caroline T. Moore, comp., *Records of the Secretary of the Province of South Carolina, 1692–1721* (Columbia, S.C.: R. L. Bryan, 1978); Brent Howard Holcomb, comp., *Probate Records of South Carolina*, 3 vols. (Easley, S.C.: Southern Historical Press, 1977); and Alexander S. Salley, Jr., "Abstracts from the Records, Court of Ordinary (Probate)," in *South Carolina Historical and Genealogical Magazine*, 8–13 (1907–12).

In 1781, the seven circuit court districts (see County/District Resources) were given courts of ordinary, but the only surviving records are those of Camden, Charleston, and Ninety-Six Districts. See Brent Howard Holcomb and Elmer O. Parker, comps., *Old Camden District Wills and Administrations, 1781–1787* (Easley, S.C.: Southern Historical Press, 1981); Brent Howard Holcomb, comps., *Ninety-Six District Journal of the Court of Ordinary, Inventory Book, Will Book, 1781–1786* (Easley, S.C.: Southern Historical Press, 1978); and Pauline Young,

comp., *Abstracts of Old Ninety-Six and Abbeville District: Wills, Bonds, Administrations, 1774–1860* (1950; reprint, Easley, S.C.: Southern Historical Press, 1977).

In 1785, the circuit court districts were subdivided into counties; courts of ordinary were established in functioning counties beginning in 1787. During the fifteen years that counties in circuit court districts existed, probate actions could be conducted in the courts of ordinary in both the county and its circuit court district. When the counties and districts were replaced by twenty-five districts (counties) in 1800, courts of ordinary were established in each district. Probate records from 1800 to the present and records of the counties and circuit court districts from 1785 to 1800 are found in the county's judge of probate office. See Martha Lou Houston, comp., *Indexes to the County Wills of South Carolina* (1939; reprint, Baltimore: Genealogical Publishing Co., 2003); and Charleston Free Library, *Index to the Wills of Charleston County, South Carolina, 1671–1868* (Baltimore: Genealogical Publishing Co., 1993); and Pauline Young, comp., *A Genealogical Collection of South Carolina Wills and Records*, 2 vols. (1955; reprint, Easley, S.C.: Southern Historical Press, 1984).

Many probate records are among the records of the equity court. Established in 1791 and mostly disbanded by 1821, the equity courts handled partitions of property, among other probate actions (see Court Records). Maps illustrating the equity court districts are found with a brief explanation of the equity court records in Brent Howard Holcomb, "South Carolina Equity Records," *The South Carolina Magazine of Ancestral Research*, 6 (1978): 235-38.

Probate documents created by county, equity and other courts have been microfilmed and can be searched at the Department of Archives and History in Charleston and the FHL and its various branches. See <www.state.sc.us/scdah/guide/ctyguide.htm> for a list of all county records available at the South Carolina Department of Archives and History.

Court Records

Genealogists often avoid searching court records, especially when they have not been indexed. Difficult and complex research problems cannot be solved without the clues and facts contained in court records, especially in the Southern states. South Carolina's complex court system, explained briefly here, should be studied thoroughly. See also Alexia J. Helsley & Michael Stauffer, *South Carolina Court Records: An Introduction for Genealogists* (Columbia, S.C.: The Department of Archives and History, 1993).

Grand Council/His Majesty's Council. While South Carolina was a proprietary and crown colony, its government was centralized, and all civil administration took place at Charleston. The Grand Council, composed of the governor and councilors,

sat as the General Court, the court of chancery (equity), the court of common pleas, the court of general sessions (assize), the court of admiralty, the court of probate, and the court of appeals. Eighteenth century restructuring led to appointments of judges for many of these courts. All records were created and maintained in Charleston, and the extant original records are at the South Carolina Department of Archives and History.

General Court. The General Court handled all cases that did not have a specific court; one of its important functions was hearing petitions for headright grants (see Land Records). The records of the general court are included in *Journals of the Grand Council* (1671-92) and *His Majesty's Council Journals* (1721-74), original records maintained at the South Carolina Department of Archives and History.

Court of Chancery. Established in 1721, the court of chancery handled equity cases (see Equity Circuit Courts). Prior to 1791, most cases were tried in Charleston, and all records were kept there. The South Carolina Department of Archives and History maintains the original records of the court of chancery, and there is an index to the extant cases. The court of chancery was replaced by equity circuit courts in 1791.

Equity Circuit Courts (1791–1821). The equity court, also called the chancery court, handled cases for which there were no remedies specified in South Carolina law. For example, the equitable division of a tract of land among heirs cannot be mandated in a law that would cover all cases; each division must take into account many variables, including the quality of the land.

Prior to 1791, most equity court cases were tried in the court of chancery in Charleston, and all records were kept there. An index to the extant cases and the records themselves are housed at the South Carolina Department of Archives and History.

In 1791, South Carolina was divided into three equity circuits: (1) the Upper Circuit included Ninety-Six and Washington Circuit Court districts and Spartanburg and Union counties in Pinckney Circuit Court District; (2) the Middle Circuit included the remaining counties in Pinckney Circuit Court District, plus all of Camden, Cheraws, and Orangeburgh Circuit Court districts; (3) the Lower Circuit included Beaufort, Charleston, and Georgetown Circuit Court districts.

Another division in 1799 produced four districts, each of which was divided in half; there were eight district seats. A further division in 1808 produced nine districts. By 1821, all districts/counties had their own equity court, except Cheraws District. In 1868, the equity or chancery court was combined with the court of ordinary or probate and became the court of probate.

Maps of the equity circuits are essential to understanding the locations of the districts. See Brent Howard Holcomb, "South Carolina Equity Records," *The South Carolina Magazine of Ancestral Research* 6 (1978): 235-38.

Known record locations include the following: Middle Circuit (1791–99) and Camden Circuit (1808–21) records are housed in Camden County, Lower Circuit (1791–99); Charleston Circuit (1808–21) records are housed in Charleston County; Columbia Circuit (1808–21) records are housed in Richland County; Western Circuit (1799–1808) and Pinckney Circuit (1808–21) records are housed in Union County. The records have not been positively located for Upper Circuit (1791–99); Southern, Northern, Eastern, and the lower half of Western circuits (1799–1808); and Cheraws, Georgetown, Ninety-Six, Orangeburgh, and Washington circuits (1808–21).

Court of Common Pleas. This is the civil court of South Carolina. A civil court handles all cases involving private citizens or organizations against private citizens or organizations. The court of common pleas was one of the functions of the grand council during most of the colonial period. Until 1772, the court of common pleas was held in Charleston, but by 1772 courts of common pleas had been established in each of the circuit court districts (see County/District Resources), with records maintained in Charleston until 1785. Each of the counties within the circuit court districts formed in 1785 was authorized a court of common pleas. The counties in Beaufort, Charleston, and Georgetown districts did not function, and the counties in Orangeburgh District only functioned until about 1791. From 1785 until 1800, courts of common pleas operated at both the county and district level; extant records of both must be examined. When districts (counties) were formed in 1800, each was authorized its own court of common pleas.

The records of the court of common pleas generally include guardianship records, such as petitions, reports, and orders; renunciations of dower; and Revolutionary War pension applications. The records will be found in the clerk of court's office. Most pre-1865 court of common pleas records have been microfilmed and are available at the South Carolina Department of Archives and History and the FHL.

Court of General Sessions of the Peace, Oyer and Terminer, Assize and General Gaol Delivery. This is the criminal court of South Carolina and is generally called the court of general sessions or court of assize. The court of general sessions was one of the functions of the grand council during most of the colonial period. Until 1772, the court of general sessions was held in Charleston; by 1772 courts of general sessions had been established in each of the circuit court districts (see County/District Resources), with records maintained in Charleston until 1785. Each of the counties within the circuit court districts formed in 1785 was authorized a court of common pleas. The counties in Beaufort, Charleston, and Georgetown districts did not function, and the counties in Orangeburgh District only functioned until about 1791. From 1785 until 1800, courts of general sessions operated at both the county and district level; extant records of both must be examined. When

districts (counties) were formed in 1800, each was authorized its own court of general sessions.

Court of Ordinary. During the colonial period, the governor acted as ordinary for the province of South Carolina, with power to grant probates and administrations; the secretary of the colony also began acting as an ordinary by 1692. Courts of ordinary were established in the circuit court districts in 1781 and in functioning counties within the circuit districts in 1787. When districts (counties) were formed in 1800, each was authorized its own court of ordinary. In 1868, the court of ordinary was combined with the court of equity (chancery) and became the court of probate.

Circuit Courts (1769–1800). Circuit courts were established by the South Carolina Assembly in 1769. Each circuit court district (see County/District Resources) was authorized a clerk of common pleas for its court of common pleas and a clerk of the Crown for its court of general sessions. Records of the circuit courts were maintained in Charleston until 1785. When the circuit court districts were abolished in 1800, their records were transferred to the district (county) with the circuit court district seat.

Precinct Courts. Precinct courts, also called county courts, were established in 1721. The five courts were held outside Charleston and staffed by local justices of the peace who tried minor criminal cases and civil suits. There are no extant records for the precinct courts according to the South Carolina Department of Archives and History.

County Courts. County courts were first established in 1785. The county courts were directed to maintain records of their proceedings, prove and record conveyances and renunciations of dower (see Land Records and Probate Records), license tavern-keepers, and levy taxes. Many county courts did not function until 1800, and others functioned only for a few years from 1785 to 1791. When districts (counties) were established in 1800, the county court became the primary judicial body in the district, with three offices: the register of mesne conveyance (see Land Records), the court of common pleas, and the court of general sessions.

Court records created by the County Court, Court of Common Pleas, Equity Court, District Court, Court of General Sessions, Probate Court, and Court of Magistrates and Freeholders have been microfilmed and can be searched at the Department of Archives & History in Charleston and the FHL. See <www.state.sc.us/scdah/guide/ctyguide.htm> for a list of all county level records available at the South Carolina Department of Archives & History. Most libraries and archives with genealogical collections have some printed abstracts of court records.

Tax Records

With the exception of a single tax list from 1733 and occasional lists of tax collectors, no colonial tax records of South Carolina have survived. Parishes and townships functioned as tax districts until 1800; circuit court districts and their counties also functioned as tax districts from 1785 to 1800. The known tax lists (1783–99) are as follows: Christ Church Parish (1784, 1786, 1788, 1793–99); Prince Frederick's Parish (1784, 1786); Prince George's Parish (1786–87); Prince William's Parish (1798); St. Andrew's Parish (1784–85, 1787, 1789, 1791, 1795); St. Bartholomew's Parish (1783–87, 1798); St. Helena's Parish (1798); St. James Goose Creek (1796); St. John's Berkeley Parish (1793); St. Luke's Parish (1798–99); St. Paul's Parish (1783, 1785–96, 1798–99); Ninety-Six District (1787); Orangeburgh District (1787); Lancaster County in Camden District (1797); and Lexington County in Orangeburgh District (1788). Many of these tax lists are incomplete. They are located at the South Carolina Department of Archives and History.

Most districts/counties have some tax records dating from 1800 to the present, with the majority of tax records dating from 1865. A fairly complete series from 1824, mostly of the Low Country districts, is available at the South Carolina Department of Archives and History and is indexed in the Combined Alphabetical Index (see Background Sources). The South Carolina Department of Archives and History has originals of most extant tax lists, and microfilmed copies of county tax records are available at the South Carolina Department of Archives and History and the FHL.

The best available substitutes for colonial tax lists are jury lists. The jury lists include men eligible to serve on juries and were compiled from tax lists. See Mary Bondurant Warren, comp., *South Carolina Jury Lists, 1718–1783* (Danielsville, Ga.: Heritage Papers, 1977). Ge Lee Corley Hendrix and Morn McKoy Lindsay, comps., *The Jury Lists of South Carolina, 1778–1779* (1975; reprint, Baltimore: Genealogical Publishing Co., 1980) is accepted as proof of the identity of Revolutionary War patriots.

Voter registration lists, 1867, 1868, and 1898 are another valuable substitute for tax records. The lists from 1867 and 1868 are particularly useful for African American research because the newly freed slaves registered to vote; many African Americans make their first appearance in the voter registration lists. Although voter registration was conducted by counties, the originals of the 1867, 1868, and 1898 lists are at the South Carolina Department of Archives and History; counties maintained copies for their records.

Directories for the city of Charleston date from 1782. These directories may help locate a Charleston ancestor who does not appear in other records. They are housed at the Charleston Library Society (see Archives, Libraries, and Societies).

Church Records

In the absence of early marriage and vital records, South Carolina church records play an important role in genealogical research. The Church of England (known later as the Protestant Episcopal Church) was established as the official state-supported church of South Carolina in 1706, with responsibility for recording births, christenings, marriages, and burials. Between 1706 and 1778, twenty-five parishes were established, including two for the Huguenots, who were allowed to use a French version of the Book of Common Prayer. All of the extant parish registers have been published; most have appeared in *The South Carolina Historical and Genealogical Magazine* or in book form. Extant records of the Protestant Episcopal Church may also be found in the Dalcho Historical Society, Episcopal Diocese of South Carolina, 1020 King St., Charleston, SC 29403. See also Margaretta, Leland, and Isabella G. Childs, "South Carolina Episcopal Church Records," *South Carolina Historical Magazine* 84 (October 1983): 250-63.

Quakers settled in South Carolina early; the first group was joined by emigrants from Ireland in the 1750s and by Quakers from Pennsylvania, North Carolina, New Jersey, New York, and Virginia after 1760. See William F. Medlin, *Quaker Families of South Carolina and Georgia* (N.p.: Ben Franklin Press, 1982). South Carolina Quaker records are included in William Wade Hinshaw, ed., *Encyclopedia of American Quaker Genealogy*, vol. 1 (1936; reprint, Baltimore: Genealogical Publishing Co., 1994).

French Huguenots began to settle permanently in South Carolina in 1685 when land grants were issued along the shoreline. While most of the group's early records have been lost, some publications speak of early members and their families. See *Transactions of the Huguenot Society of South Carolina*, (1888-present), the publication of the Huguenot Society of South Carolina, 25 Chalmers St., Charleston, SC 29401.

Presbyterians established their denomination in South Carolina during the early eighteenth century and later became associated with the Reformed Presbyterian Church. See *Inventory of the Church Archives of South Carolina Presbyterian Churches: 1969 Arrangement with Indexes* (South Carolina Historical Records Survey, Works Progress Administration, 1969). Write to the Historical Foundation of the Presbyterian and Reformed Churches, P.O. Box 847, Montreat, NC 29757, or Presbyterian College Library, Due West, SC 29325. See also Richard N. Cote, "South Carolina Religious Records: Presbyterian Records," *South Carolina Historical Magazine* 85 (April 1984): 145-52.

Lutherans also established themselves in South Carolina during the eighteenth century with the arrival of German and Swiss settlers. Early Evangelical Lutheran records are excellent genealogical resources. Write to Lutheran Theological Seminary Library, Columbia, SC 29203.

The first Roman Catholic parish was established at Charleston in 1789. Known for keeping excellent records of christenings, marriages, and burials, the church has preserved its registers at the Charleston Diocesan Archives, Chancery Office, 119 Broad St., P.O. Box 818, Charleston, SC 29402.

The Baptist Church is contemporary South Carolina's largest religious group, despite the fact that it was not established there until 1783. Write to South Carolina Baptist Historical Collection, James B. Duke Library, Poinsett Highway, Furman University, Greenville, SC 29613. A list of the church records available at the James B. Duke Library is found in the *Journal of the South Carolina Baptist Historical Society*, 3 (1977): 32-43. See also J. Glenn Clayton, "South Carolina Baptist Records," *South Carolina Historical Magazine* 85 (October 1984): 319-27.

Methodists arrived in South Carolina about the same time as the Baptists (1783). Methodist records include conference records, membership lists, and historical and biographical information. Write to South Carolina Methodist Conference Archives, Sandor Teszler Library, Wofford College, Spartanburg, SC 29301.

For a complete list of South Carolina's church records that have been microfilmed, see <www.state.sc.us/scdah/guide/rg900100.htm> at the Department of Archives and History website. The FHL also has a sizable collection of those records. The South Caroliniana Library of the University of South Carolina in Columbia houses some church records.

See also Richard N. Cote, "South Carolina Religious Records: Other Denominations," *South Carolina Historical Magazine* 86 (January 1985): 50-61. Cote's article discusses records of the following religious groups: African Methodist Episcopal Church; Congregational; Unitarian and Universalist Churches; the Christian Church (Disciples of Christ); French Protestant (Huguenot) Church; Jews; Lutheran Church; Roman Catholic Church; and Society of Friends (Quakers).

Cemetery Records

The Works Progress Administration (WPA) and the Daughters of the American Revolution (DAR) have compiled major collections of South Carolina tombstone inscriptions. Alexia J. Hensley, *Silent Cities, Cemeteries & Classrooms* (Columbia, S.C.: South Carolina Department of Archives and History, 1997) includes a bibliography of published cemetery inscriptions for South Carolina. See also Cote (1981), listed in Background Sources, who provides a listing of major published collections. Most South Carolina counties have historical or genealogical societies that have compiled cemetery records. Schweitzer has addresses for local historical and genealogical societies. Cemetery records are frequently published in the major genealogical periodicals of South Carolina (see Periodicals).

Military Records

Colonial Wars. South Carolina's military history began in 1670 when the Spanish attacked "Old Town." Frequent battles with the Spanish, French, and Indian tribes continued throughout the colonial period. Unfortunately, few records have survived to tell of the participants and the nature of their involvement. Leonardo Andrea compiled a list of soldiers who served in various military capacities between 1715 and 1772 in *South Carolina Colonial Soldiers and Patriots* (Columbia, S.C., 1952). See also Murtie June Clark, *Colonial Soldiers of the South, 1732–1774* (1986; reprint, Baltimore: Genealogical Publishing, Co., 1999). Mention of South Carolina soldiers may be found in works dealing with specific wars of a national or regional scope.

Revolutionary War. South Carolinians were heavily involved in the Revolutionary War on both sides. Although some records were destroyed, the Revolutionary War resources for South Carolina are quite rich.

Patriots who served in the Continental Line may be found by examining the National Archives microfilm publications (see page 9), which are available at the South Carolina Department of Archives and History and the FHL. Original pension records are available at the National Archives, but a published index (see page 9) is widely available.

South Carolina militia units that participated in the Revolutionary War are not included in the service records listed above. A recent compilation of Patriot records, including militia records, is Bobby Gilmer Moss, comp., *Roster of South Carolina Patriots in the American Revolution* (1983; reprint, Baltimore: Genealogical Publishing Co., 1994). See also Alexander S. Salley, Jr., comp., *South Carolina Provincial Troops in Papers of the First Council of Safety, 1775* (1900–02; reprint, Baltimore: Genealogical Publishing Co., 1999).

Loyalists may be found in Murtie June Clark, *Loyalists in the Southern Campaign of the Revolutionary War*, 3 vols. (1981; reprint, Genealogical Publishing Co., 1999). See also *South Carolina Royalist Troops, Muster Rolls, 1777–1783*, on two microfilm reels at the South Caroliniana Library in Columbia (see Archives, Libraries, and Societies).

Many South Carolinians can be found in the *Accounts Audited of Claims Growing Out of the Revolution* at the South Carolina Department of Archives and History. The *Accounts Audited* is indexed in the Combined Alphabetical Index (see Background Sources).

Stub indents are another important resource. When South Carolina paid claims for goods, services, or damages from the Revolutionary War, they were paid with certificates called indents. Rather like stub checkbooks, the certificates were in two parts: one part was issued to the claimant as compensation; the other part was a stub on which pertinent information, such as the

claimant's name, the nature of the claim, and the amount paid was recorded. The state retained the stub of the indents, and they are found at the South Carolina Department of Archives and History in Office of the Commissioners of the Treasury, *Stub Indents and Indexes, 1779–1791*, 22 vols. See also Alexander S. Salley Jr., ed., *Stub Entries to Indents Issued in Payment of Claims Against South Carolina Growing Out of the Revolution*, 12 vols. (Columbia, S.C.: University of South Carolina Press, 1910–27). Irregularly issued reprints may be available. See also Charles H. Lesser, *Sources for the American Revolution at the South Carolina Department of Archives and History* (Columbia, S.C.: South Carolina Department of Archives and History, 2000).

War of 1812. The National Archives has service records, pension files, and indexes to the War of 1812 service and pension records (see page 9). See also Virgil D. White, comp., *Index to War of 1812 Pension Files*, 3 vols. (Waynesboro, Tenn.: The National Historical Publishing Co., 1989). Extensive manuscript and microfilmed records of South Carolina units and soldiers of the War of 1812 are at the South Caroliniana Library in Columbia (see Archives, Libraries, and Societies). The Department of History & Archives has a card index of *South Carolina Pay Lists.*

Civil War. The military personnel records of the Confederate States of America, along with other confederate records captured by the Union Army, were taken to Washington and preserved by the War Department. Consequently, service records for South Carolina Confederate soldiers can be found in the National Archives. See the National Archives microfilm publications: *Compiled Service Records of Confederate Soldiers Who Served in Organizations from the State of South Carolina; Index to the Compiled Service Records of Confederate Soldiers Who Served in Organizations from the State of South Carolina;* and *(Service) Records Relating to Confederate Naval and Marine Personnel.* These three series are available at the National Archives and the South Carolina Department of Archives and History. See also Alexander S. Salley, Jr., comp., *South Carolina Troops in Confederate Service*, 3 vols. (Columbia, S.C.: R. L. Bryan, 1913–14, 1930). References to South Carolina regimental histories are found in C. E. Dornbusch, comp., *Military Bibliography of the Civil War*, vol. 2 (New York: New York Public Library, 1967): 84-90.

South Carolina enacted a pension law for indigent Confederate veterans in 1888. Subsequent revisions in 1895, 1896, 1900, 1903, and 1910 added widows of veterans and all veterans who gave service in any Confederate state. A complete revision in 1919 established the Confederate Pension Department and County Pension Boards. Virtually all veterans and their widows qualified for pensions, but everyone receiving or wishing to receive a pension had to reapply. The reapplications are at the South Carolina Department of Archives and History and are indexed in the "Card File Index of 1919–1926 South Carolina Confederate Pension Applications" at the Department.

See also Patrick J. McCawley, *Guide to Civil War Records: A Guide to the Records in the South Carolina Department of Archives & History* (Columbia, S.C.: The Department of Archives and History, 1994); Alexia Jones Hensley, *South Carolina's African American Confederate Pensioners, 1923–1925* (Columbia, S.C.: Department of Archives and History, 1998) detailing the activities and some personal information of a group of African Americans during the Civil War; and Patrick J. McCawley, *Selected Civil War Bibliography* (Columbia, S.C.: Department of Archives & History, 1998), listing over 450 titles published from 1863 to 1996.

Mexican War. The Palmetto Regiment took part in the campaign in the Valley of Mexico. Jack Allen Meyer, *South Carolina in the Mexican War: A History of the Palmetto Regiment of Volunteers, 1846–1917* (Columbia, S.C.: Department of Archives and History, 1996) chronicles the formation of the regiment's companies, includes rosters of soldiers, maps tracing the routes they took, and the swords and medals awarded to the soldiers upon their return.

Periodicals, Newspapers, and Manuscript Collections

Periodicals

Like most other states, South Carolina historical and genealogical organizations publish excellent periodicals including *South Carolina Historical Magazine* (Charleston, S.C.: South Carolina Historical Society, 1900-present), *Carolina Herald* (Greenville, S.C.: Carolina Genealogical Society, 1974-present). See "Index of the Carolina Herald Online" at <www.scgen.org/herald.htm> and *Transactions of the Huguenot Society of South Carolina* (Charleston, S.C.: The Huguenot Society of South Carolina, 1888-present). Two important private publications are *The South Carolina Magazine of Ancestral Research* (Columbia, S.C.: Brent Howard Holcomb, 1973-present) and *Carolina Genealogist* (Danielsville, Ga.: Mary B. Warren, 1969–84). The South Carolina Department of Archives and History and the FHL have these and other periodicals pertaining to South Carolina genealogy.

Newspapers

South Carolina's newspaper history began with the publication of the first issue of the *South Carolina Gazette* in 1732. The largest collection of South Carolina newspapers is found at the South Caroliniana Library; the Charleston Library Society and the South Carolina Department of Archives and History have slightly smaller collections (see Archives, Libraries, and Societies for addresses). See a complete list of newspapers at the South Carolina Department of Archives and History online at <www.state.sc.us/scdah/guide/rg900200.htm>. See also John H. Moore,

South Carolina Newspapers (Columbia, S.C.: University of South Carolina Press, 1988).

Newspapers are an important source of South Carolina vital records because marriage and death notices appeared in most newspapers. Newspaper extracts have been regularly published in *The South Carolina Magazine of Ancestral Research* and *South Carolina Historical Magazine* (see Periodicals). Dozens of published books of newspaper extracts are available. A bibliography is found in George K. Schweitzer, *South Carolina Genealogical Research* (Knoxville, Tenn.: the author, 1985): 114-19.

Manuscripts

There are two major manuscript collections of South Carolina genealogical material. Leonardo Andrea compiled a vast collection of research notes tracing families during their residence in South Carolina as well as tracking them back to earlier residences and forward as they migrated south and west. The Leonardo Andrea Collection is available on microfilm at the FHL. Motte Alston Read collected information on colonial South Carolina families from court records, deeds, church records, newspapers, and other sources. The Motte Alston Read Collection is housed at the South Carolina Historical Society and is available on microfilm at the FHL.

The largest collection of South Carolina manuscripts is housed at the South Caroliniana Library of the University of South Carolina in Columbia. The Manuscript Division holds over 1.3 million manuscripts, including church records, letters, Bible records, and numerous other public and private records. A short list of finding aids to the manuscript collection appears online at <www.sc.edu/library/socar/mnscrpts/findaids.html> with instructions to contact the library for information not available online. See Allen H. Stokes, Jr., comp., *A Guide to the Manuscript Collection of the South Caroliniana Library* (Columbia, S.C.: South Caroliniana Library, 1982).

Archives, Libraries, and Societies

South Carolina Department of Archives & History

8301 Parklane Center
Columbia, SC 29223
www.state.sc.us/scdah

Publishes *The New South Carolina State Gazette*. The South Carolina Department of Archives and History collects non-current public records, including county and district records, colonial and state records, federal census records and indexes, colonial land records indexes, military records, and a large microfilm collection of genealogical and historical information. The Department of Archives and History also produces the Combined Alphabetical Index (see Background Sources), which can be accessed online at <www.archivesindex.sc.gov>.

Currently, the online version of 293,212 items includes *Index to Multiple Record Series, ca. 1675–1929; Will Transcripts, 1782–1855; Confederate Pension Applications, 1919–1926; Plats for State Land Grants, 1784–1868; Legislative Papers, 1782–1866; Criminal Journals, 1769–1776.* Other record categories included in the online index will be referenced in various sections of this chapter. The Archives & History website does not feature scanned images of historical or genealogical documents. Copies of documents and limited search requests can be ordered by e-mail <www.state.sc.us/scdah/refquery.htm>. The holdings of the South Carolina Department of Archives & History appear in *A Guide to Local Government Records in the South Carolina Archives* (Columbia, S.C.: University of South Carolina Press, 1988). An updated version of that publication appears online at <www.state.sc.us/scdah/guide/guide.htm>.

South Carolina Genealogical Society

P.O. Box 16355
Greenville, SC 29606-16355
www.scgen.org/index.htm

Publishes *The Carolina Herald.*

South Carolina Historical Society

100 Meeting St.
Charleston, SC 29401
www.schistory.org

Publishes *South Carolina Historical Magazine.* The South Carolina Historical Society maintains a library with a large collection of genealogical and historical records and publications. An extensive online catalog of manuscripts, books, and family histories (60,000 records) can be searched at <www.schistory.org/searchcatalogue.htm>.

South Caroliniana Library

University of South Carolina
Columbia, SC 29208
www.sc.edu/library/socar/index.html

The library has a Book Division with over 75,000 volumes in book or microform and a Manuscript Division with over 1.3 million manuscripts (see Manuscripts). The Division holds unpublished genealogical files documenting connections among families of South Carolina and beyond with collections of Leonardo Andrea, Bessie Lee Garvin, and Louise K. Crowder. A short list of finding aids to the genealogy collection appears online at <www.sc.edu/library/socar/mnscrpts/findaids.html> with instructions to contact the library for information not available online.

Charleston Library Society

164 King St.
Charleston, SC 29401
www.sciway.net/lib/cls_home.html

The Charleston Library Society, the third oldest library in the United States, was founded in 1748 and began collecting books, magazines, and pamphlets by subscription. Although virtually destroyed in 1778, the collection has been rebuilt and includes some valuable eighteenth-century newspapers, as well as Charleston City Directories dating from 1782.

Special Focus Categories

Immigration

Passenger lists for the Port of Charleston are at the National Archives (see Introduction): series M575 includes arrivals (1820–28); series M334 is an index.

African American

African Americans arrived with the first ships in 1670, and were the majority of South Carolina's population, as slaves, from about 1708 to the eve of the Revolutionary War. When the 1820 U.S. Census was conducted, African Americans were again in the majority, a position they retained until the 1920s. They brought many important skills with them to South Carolina; as agriculturists, herdsmen, and watermen, they made a significant contribution to the planter society of South Carolina.

Researchers cannot afford to overlook the Voter Registration Lists of 1867 and 1868. African Americans in South Carolina gained temporary control of the state through their voting majority; many recently freed slaves made their first appearance in the Voter Registration Lists.

Lists of free persons of color, slave lists, plantation records, personal and family records, bills of sale, account books, indentures, and a variety of similar records attest to African Americans in South Carolina. The South Carolina Department of Archives and History, College of Charleston, South Carolina Historical Society, University of South Carolina, and Winthrop College have important collections of these types of records and manuscripts. Not every South Carolina district or county created or preserved each type of record listed above. In fact, the number of local records attesting to a specific slave is small when compared with those available for people who were not enslaved. The best sources of information about slaves are district (county) estate and property records. See James Rose and Alice Eichholz, *Black Genesis* (1978; reprint, Baltimore: Genealogical Publishing Co., 2003).

Kenneth M. Stampp, Professor Emeritus, University of California at Berkeley offers one of the best discussions of antebellum plantation records as the introduction to "Records of Ante-Bellum Southern Plantations from the Revolution Through the Civil War," Series J: Selections from the Southern Historical Collections, Part 3: South Carolina, available online at <www.lexisnexis.com/academic/guides/southern_hist/plantations/plantj3.asp>.

Other useful publications include:

Begley, Paul R., Alexia J. Helsley, and Steven D. Tuttle. *African American Genealogical Research.* Rev. ed. Columbia, S.C.: Department of Archives and History, 1997.

Cody, Cheryll Ann. "Naming, Kinship and Estate Dispersal: Notes on Slave Family Life on a South Carolina Plantation, 1786–1833," *William & Mary Quarterly*, 3d Series. 39 (1982): 192-211.

Helsley, Alexia Jones, *South Carolina's African American Confederate Pensioners, 1923–1925* (Columbia, S.C.: Department of Archives and History, 1998).

Helsley, Alexia Jones and Patrick J. McCawley, *The Many Faces of Slavery* (Columbia, S.C.: Department of Archives and History, 1999), discusses manumission, contracts, maroons, religion, miscegenation, and family relationships.

County/District Resources

Districts/Counties, 1800-present. In 1800, the nine circuit court districts and thirty-seven counties were abolished and replaced by twenty-five districts. Some of the new districts were identical with counties in districts established between 1785 and 1799; other districts were new polities entirely. As the highest level of local government, all twenty-five districts had equal status and record-keeping functions. The original districts expanded and divided between 1800 and 1867 to become thirty districts. Under the new constitution adopted in 1868, districts were renamed counties.

The forty-six present-day counties in South Carolina trace their lineage to the formation of districts in 1800. Although many can trace their geographical lineage to 1785, and some can trace their records lineage to 1785, any listing of counties that provides a formation date pre-1800 misses the essential point that the pre-1800 counties were not the highest level of local government. Before 1800, all counties were counties in circuit court districts; residents could conduct their business in either the county or the circuit court district, and researchers must check the records of both. A complete listing of the counties of South Carolina and their records is found on the following chart, Districts and Counties, 1800–Present.

The listing of Districts/Counties includes all districts and counties in existence from 1800 to the present and refers to the county, or county and circuit court district from which the district was formed. Some counties functioned before 1800, and the date those counties began functioning is recorded. The beginning dates for land, probate, and court records are the first indicated for the type of record specified in each county's courthouse and may include records of an earlier polity. Many records were destroyed, particularly near the end of the Civil War, and many other records are fragmentary; dates given for the first record do

not imply that all records from that date are extant. Residents of the Up Country counties often recorded records when they acquired local government, so some of the records pre-date the formation of local governments.

Counties in Districts. In 1785, the seven circuit court districts were subdivided into thirty-three counties. Inferior courts were established in some of the counties, and record-keeping began at the local level. However, the circuit court districts continued to function, and many local actions were conducted at the district seat instead of the county seat. Three districts—Beaufort, Charleston, and Georgetown—were allowed to postpone the formation of county governments, and their counties never functioned. The residents of Orangeburgh District also preferred district government to county government, and three of the four counties in that district were not used from 1791 through 1799.

While many present-day counties were established geographically between 1785 and 1799, the counties created during that period did not keep records or function as local governments equally. The county did not become the highest level of local government throughout South Carolina until 1800. For a complete listing of counties established and abolished between 1785 and 1799, see the following chart, Counties in Districts, 1785–1800.

The listing of counties in circuit court districts includes every county formed between 1785 and 1800. Counties abolished in 1800 are identified, and the location of their extant records is detailed.

Circuit Court Districts, 1769–1800. Circuit court districts were established in 1769 and began holding court by about 1772. Originally there were seven districts: Beaufort, Camden, Charleston, Cheraws, Georgetown, Ninety-Six, and Orangeburgh. Pinckney and Washington circuit court districts were added in 1791. The chart of circuit court districts that follows details the extant records of the nine circuit court districts created in 1769 and 1791 and where the extant records are located. The counties formed in each district are identified.

Townships. One of the early and genealogically important actions of the provincial (royal) government was the Township Act of 1731; additional townships were authorized in 1761. The act authorized eleven townships containing 20,000 acres each, and agents were sent to Europe to recruit families as settlers. The families were offered inducements such as free transportation to South Carolina, free provisions for one year, and free land. The townships neither created nor kept records; their functions were solely geographical. Townships, like parishes, were used for some tax districts and appeared as locators in grants and conveyances. The townships are included in the listing of Townships and Parishes.

Parishes. In 1706, the province of South Carolina established the Church of England as the official state-supported church. The twenty-five parishes established from 1706 through 1778 recorded vital records and became districts for the proportioning and election of representatives in 1716; parishes were also used as tax districts. They functioned as geographic locators in grants and conveyances, but did not necessarily replace the proprietary counties in that function; some grants and conveyances mention the parish, some the proprietary county, and some give both. The parishes are included in the listing of Townships and Parishes.

Proprietary Counties. The first division of South Carolina into local polities occurred in 1682 when Berkeley, Colleton, and Craven proprietary counties were established; Carteret was added in 1685 and renamed Granville in 1708. These counties neither created nor kept records; their function was geographical. The proprietary counties served as districts for the assignment and election of representatives until 1716, militia duty, and general reference in land grants and conveyances (deeds). The proprietary counties were superseded by circuit court districts in 1769, but continued to be used as geographical references until the formation of counties within the circuit court districts in 1785. The forty-six current counties in South Carolina are listed with their proprietary counties in the Proprietary Counties chart that follows.

Successful research in South Carolina requires an understanding of the unique and complex development of its local government and jurisdictions. Unlike the other twelve British colonies, South Carolina did not form counties or towns during the colonial period. The South Carolina Department of Archives and History publishes a free pamphlet, "The Formation of Counties in South Carolina," which traces the evolution of political subdivisions in the state. The department also publishes a set of ten guide maps illustrating the development of parishes, districts, and counties. Information in the following tables is quoted from South Carolina Department of Archives and History, *A Guide to Local Government Records in the South Carolina Archives* and the guides by Schweitzer (1985) and Holcomb (1964), all listed under Background Sources, and Thorndale and Dollarhide, *Map Guide* (see page 3).

For up-to-date information and changes to the county record holdings of the South Carolina Department of Archives and History, see the online version of *A Guide to Local Government Records in the South Carolina Archives* at <www.state.sc.us/scdah/guide/guide.htm>.

The Counties and County Seats of

South Carolina

NORTH CAROLINA

GEORGIA

SOUTH CAROLINA

Copyright 1989, Ancestry, Inc.

Drawn by William Dollarhide

606

25   0   25   50 Miles

South Carolina counties and county seats:

Oconee — Walhalla
Pickens — Pickens
Greenville — Greenville
Spartanburg — Spartanburg
Cherokee — Gaffney
York — York
Anderson — Anderson
Laurens — Laurens
Union — Union
Chester — Chester
Lancaster — Lancaster
Chesterfield — Chesterfield
Marlboro — Bennettsville
Abbeville — Abbeville
Greenwood — Greenwood
Newberry — Newberry
Fairfield — Winnsboro
Kershaw — Camden
Lee — Bishopville
Darlington — Darlington
Florence — Florence
Dillon — Dillon
Marion — Marion
Horry — Conway
McCormick — McCormick
Saluda — Saluda
Edgefield — Edgefield
Lexington — Lexington
Richland — Columbia
Sumter — Sumter
Clarendon — Manning
Williamsburg — Kingstree
Georgetown — Georgetown
Aiken — Aiken
Calhoun — St. Matthews
Orangeburg — Orangeburg
Barnwell — Barnwell
Bamberg — Bamberg
Allendale — Allendale
Dorchester — St. George
Berkeley — Moncks Corner
Charleston — Charleston
Colleton — Walterboro
Hampton — Hampton
Jasper — Ridgeland
Beaufort — Beaufort

Rivers: Savannah River, Santee River, Pee Dee, Lynches, Wateree R., Black River, Edisto River, North Fork, South Fork, Little Pee Dee

North Carolina counties (shaded): Cherokee, Clay, Macon, Swain, Graham, Jackson, Haywood, Transylvania, Henderson, Polk, Rutherford, Cleveland, Gaston, Mecklenburg, Cabarrus, Union, Anson, Stanly, Montgomery, Richmond, Scotland, Moore, Hoke, Cumberland, Harnett, Sampson, Robeson, Bladen, Columbus, Brunswick

Georgia counties (shaded): Towns, Rabun, Habersham, White, Hall, Stephens, Franklin, Banks, Hart, Madison, Elbert, Jackson, Clarke, Oglethorpe, Barrow, Oconee, Walton, Newton, Morgan, Greene, Wilkes, Lincoln, McDuffie, Columbia, Richmond, Taliaferro, Warren, Jasper, Putnam, Hancock, Glascock, Jefferson, Burke, Monroe, Jones, Baldwin, Washington, Screven, Bibb, Wilkinson, Johnson, Emanuel, Jenkins, Twiggs, Peach, Houston, Dooly, Pulaski, Laurens, Dodge, Wheeler, Montgomery, Toombs, Tattnall, Evans, Bryan, Bulloch, Effingham, Chatham, Liberty, Wilcox, Telfair

Districts and Counties, 1800-present

Map	District/County (1800-present) Address	Date Formed Parent District Functioned From	Birth Marriage Death	Land Probate Court
C3	Abbeville P.O. Box 574 Abbeville 29620-0579	1800 Abbeville in Ninety Six District 1911 1785	1916 1911 1911	1791 1772 1791
	Record loss, 1873. Records of Ninety-Six Circuit Court District are housed in Abbeville County.			
D5	Aiken 828 Richland Ave. W. Aiken 29801-3834	1871 Edgefield/Barnwell/ Orangeburg/Lexington	1915 1911 1915	1872 1872 1871
E6	Allendale P.O. Box 190 Allendale 29810-0190	1919 Barnwell/ Hampton	1919 1919 1919	1919 1919 1919
B2	Anderson P.O. Box 8002 Anderson 29620-8002	1826 Pendleton	1915 1911 1915	1826 1826 1826
	Records of Pendleton County in Ninety-Six and Washington Districts and Pendleton District are housed in Anderson County.			
F6	Bamberg P.O. Box 149 Bamberg 29003-0149	1897 Barnwell	1915 1911 1915	1897 1897 1897
	Records of Orangeburgh Circuit Court District, Court of Common Pleas, are housed in Bamberg County.			
E6	Barnwell 57 Wall St. Barnwell 29812-1584	1800 Winton County in Orangeburgh District 1785 (Winton County)	1915 1911 1915	1800 1800 1800
	Records of Winton County (1785–91) in Orangeburgh Circuit Court District are housed in Barnwell County.			
G8	Beaufort P.O. Drawer 1228 Beaufort 29901-1228	1800 Beaufort District 1772 (Beaufort District)	1915 1911 1915	1863 1865 1865
	Record loss, 1865. Beaufort District absorbed the four counties in Beaufort Circuit Court District.			
H6	Berkeley 223 N. Live Oak Dr. Moncks Corner 29461-3707	1882 Charleston	1915 1911 1915	1883 1883 1881
F4	Calhoun Courthouse Annex, Ste. 108 Saint Matthews 29135-1452	1908 Lexington/ Orangeburg	1915 1911 1915	1908 1908 1908
H7	Charleston 2 Courthouse Sq. Charleston 29401-0000	1800 Marion/Washington Counties in Charleston District; 1680	1915 1911 1915	1671 1671 1700
	Records of Charleston Circuit Court and Equity Circuit Districts and the Province of South Carolina (1671–1785) are housed in Charleston County.			
	Charleston (City)		1871 1871 1821	1858 1790 1774
	Records are in Charleston County.			
D1	Cherokee 210 N. Limestone St. Gaffney 26340-3136	1897 Union/York/ Spartanburg	1915 1911 1915	1897 1897 1897
L1	Chester P.O. Drawer 580 Chester 29706-0580	1800 Chester County in Pinckney District 1785 (in Camden District)	1915 1911 1915	1786 1787 1785
H2	Chesterfield 200 W. Main St. Chesterfield 29709-0529	1800 Chesterfield County in Cheraws District 1785	1915 1911 1915	1861 1865 1823
	Record loss, 1865. Records fragmented.			
G5	Clarendon P.O. Box 486 Manning 29102-0486	1855 Sumter 1785–1800	1915 1911 1915	1856 1856 1856
	Record loss, 1911. Records of old Clarendon County in Camden Circuit Court District lost, 1801.			
G7	Colleton P.O. Box 157 Walterboro 29488-0002	1800 Colleton/Bartholomew/Berkeley Counties in Charleston District	1915 1911 1915	1802 1865 1807
	Record losses, 1805, 1865. Records fragmented.			
H3	Darlington 1 Public Sq., Rm 210 Darlington 20532-3213	1800 Darlington County in Cheraws District 1785	1915 1911 1915	1803 1783 1801
	Record loss, 1806.			
J3	Dillon P.O. Box 449 Dillon 29536-0449	1910 Marion	1915 1911 1915	1910 1910 1910
G6	Dorchester 201 Johnson St. St. George 29477-2412	1897 Berkeley/ Colleton	1915 1911 1915	1897 1897 1897
D4	Edgefield 215 Jeter St. Edgefield 29824-1133	1800 Edgefield County in Ninety-Six District 1785	1915 1911 1915	1786 1785 1785
F3	Fairfield P.O. Drawer 60 Winnsboro 29180-0060	1800 Fairfield County in Camden District 1785	1915 1911 1915	1784 1787 1785
J3	Florence 180 N. Irby St. Florence 29501-3456	1888 Marion/Darlington/ Clarendon/Williamsburg	1915 1911 1915	1889 1889 1889
J5	Georgetown P.O. Drawer 421270 Georgetown 29440-0000	1800 Kingston/Winyah/ Williamburg Counties in Georgetown District 1772 (Georgetown District)	1915 1911 1915	1862 1862 1783
	Record loss, 1865. Records fragmented.			
C1	Greenville 301 University Ridge, Ste. 100 Greenville 29601-3674	1800 Greenville County in Ninety-Six District 1786	1915 1911 1915	1784 1787 1786

Map	District/County (1800-present) Address	Date Formed Parent District Functioned From	Birth Marriage Death	Land Probate Court
C3	Greenwood 528 Monument Greenwood 29646-2643	1897 Abbeville/ Edgefield	1915 1911 1915	1897 1897 1897
F7	Hampton 201 Jackson St. W. Hampton 29924-0000	1878 Beaufort	1915 1911 1915	1878 1878 1878
K4	Horry P.O. Box 288 Conway 29526-0288	1801 Georgetown	1915 1911 1915	1803 1799 1803
	Formed from the territory of Kingston County (non-functioning) in Georgetown Circuit Court District.			
F8	Jasper 103 Elm St. Ridgeland 29526-5116	1912 Beaufort/ Hampton	1915 1912 1915	1912 1912 1912
G3	Kershaw 515 Walnut St. Camden 29020-3623	1800 Kershaw County in Camden District 1791	1915 1911 1915	1787 1782 1783
	Records of Camden Circuit Court and Equity Circuit districts are housed in Kershaw County.			
G2	Lancaster P.O. Box 1809 Lancaster 29720-1809	1800 Lancaster County in Camden District 1785	1915 1911 1915	1762 1820 1800
	Record loss, 1865. Records fragmented. Some Camden Circuit Court District conveyance records are included.			
D2	Laurens P.O. Box 445 Laurens 29360-0445	1800 Laurens County in Ninety-Six District 1785	1915 1911 1915	1774 1766 1789
G3	Lee P.O. Box 387 Bishopville 29010-0387	1902 Darlington/Kershaw/ Sumter	1915 1911 1915	1902 1902 1902
E4	Lexington 212 S. Lake Dr. Lexington 29072-3437	1804 Orangeburg	1915 1911 1915	1839 1809 1800
	Record losses, 1839, 1865. Records fragmented. *Formed from territory of Lexington County (non-functioning) in Orangeburgh District.*			
J3	Marion P.O. Box 183 Marion 29571-0183	1800 Liberty County in Georgetown District 1800	1915 1800 1915	1800 1790 1800
	Marriage records: 1800—59 (incomplete), 1911-present.			
J2	Marlboro P.O. Box 419 Bennettsville 29512-0419	1800 Marlboro County in Cheraws District 1785	1915 1788 1915	1786 1787 1785
	Marriage records: 1788—1819 (incomplete), 1911-present.			
C4	McCormick Rt. 2, Box 84-AAA McCormick 29835-9612	1916 Abbeville/ Greenwood	1916 1916 1916	1916 1916 1916
E3	Newberry P.O. Box 156 Newberry 29108-0156	1800 Newberry County in Ninety-Six District 1785	1915 1911 1915	1776 1776 1776
A2	Oconee 415 Pine St. Walhalla 29691-2145	1868 Pickens	1915 1911 1915	1868 1868 1868
F5	Orangeburg P.O. Box 9000 Orangeburg 29116-9000	1800 Lewisburg/Lexington/ Orange Counties in Orangeburgh District 1772 (Orangeburgh District)	1915 1911 1915	1824 1864 1824
	Record loss, 1865. Records fragmented.			
	Pendleton	1800 Pendleton County in Washington District 1789 (in Ninety-Six District)	—— —— ——	1790 1790 1790
	Abolished when divided into Anderson and Pickens Districts, 1826. Records transferred to Anderson District, Anderson County.			
B1	Pickens 222 McDaniel Ave. Pickens 29671-2759	1826 Pendleton	1915 1911 1915	1828 1828 1823
F3	Richland P.O. Box 192 Columbia 29201-0192	1800 Richland County in Camden District 1785	1915 1911 1915	1865 1787 1793
	Record loss, 1865. Records fragmented. Records of Columbia Equity Circuit District are housed in Richland County.			
D4	Saluda 108 S. Rudolph SE Saluda 29130-1744	1896 Edgefield	1915 1911 1915	1896 1896 1896
D1	Spartanburg 366 N. Church St. Spartanburg 29303-3637	1800 Spartanburg County in Pinckney District 1785 (in Ninety-Six District)	1915 1911 1915	1784 1787 1785
G4	Sumter 13 E. Canal St. Sumter 29150-4925	1800 Clarendon/Claremont/Salem Counties in Camden District 1785 (Clarendon/Claremont Counties in Camden District)	1915 1911 1915	1801 1774 1795
	Record loss, 1801, destroyed records of Clarendon and Old Claremont Counties. Records fragmented.			
D2	Union P.O. Box 703 Union 29379-0000	1800 Union County in Pinckney District 1785 (in Ninety-Six District)	1915 1911 1915	1778 1777 1785
	Records of Western and Pinckney Equity Circuit Districts are housed in Union County.			
J5	Williamsburg P.O. Box 330 Kingstree 29556-0330	1804 Georgetown	1915 1911 1915	1806 1802 1806
	Formed from territory of Williamsburg County (non-functioning) in Georgetown Circuit Court District.			
E1	York P.O. Box 66 York 29745-0066	1800 York County in Pinckney District 1785 (in Camden District)	1915 1911 1915	1786 1786 1786
	Records of Pinckney Circuit Court District are housed in York County.			

Counties in Districts, 1785-1800

County (1785–1800)	Circuit Court Districts	Date Formed Parent County/ies
Abbeville *Functioned from 1785.*	Ninety Six	1785 original
Bartholomew Non-functioning county. Area absorbed by Colleton District, 1800.	Charleston	1785 original
Berkeley Non-functioning county. Area absorbed by Colleton District, 1800.	Charleston	1785 original
Chester Functioned 1785–91. Area absorbed by Pinckney District, 1791.	Camden	1785 original
Chester Functioned from 1791.	Pinckney	1791 removed from Camden District
Chesterfield Functioned from 1785.	Cheraws	1785 original
Claremont Functioned 1785–1800. Area absorbed by Sumter District, 1801.	Camden	1785 original
Clarendon Functioned from 1785. Area absorbed by Sumter District, 1801.	Camden	1785 original
Colleton Non-functioning county. Area absorbed by Colleton District, 1800.	Charleston	1785 original
Darlington Functioned from 1785.	Cheraws	1785 original
Edgefield Functioned from 1785.	Ninety-Six	1785 original
Fairfield Functioned from 1785.	Camden	1785 original
Granville Non-functioning county.	Beaufort	1785 original
Greenville Functioned 1786–95. Area absorbed by Washington District, 1795.	Ninety-Six	1786 Indian lands
Greenville Functioned from 1795.	Washington	1795 removed from Ninety-Six District
Hilton Non-functioning. Area absorbed by Beaufort District, 1800.	Beaufort	1785 original
Kershaw Functioned from 1791.	Camden	1791 Fairfield/Lancaster/ Richland Counties in Camden District
Kingston Non-functioning county. Area absorbed by Georgetown District, 1800, and reformed as Horry District, 1801.	Georgetown	1785 original
Lancaster Functioned from 1785.	Camden	1785 original
Laurens Functioned from 1785.	Ninety-Six	1785 original
Lewisburg Functioned from 1785. Area absorbed by Orangeburg District, 1800.	Orangeburgh	1785 original
Lexington Functioned from 1785. Area absorbed by Orangeburg District, 1800, and reformed as Lexington District, 1804.	Orangeburgh	1785 original
Liberty Non-functioning county. Renamed Marion District, 1800.	Georgetown	1785 original
Lincoln Non-functioning county. Area absorbed by Beaufort District, 1800.	Beaufort	1785 original
Marion Non-functioning county. Area absorbed by Charleston District, 1800.	Charleston	1785 original
Marlboro Functioned from 1785.	Cheraws	1785 original
Newberry Functioned from 1785.	Ninety-Six	1785 original
Orange Non-functioning county. Area absorbed by Orangeburg District, 1800.	Orangeburgh	1785 original
Pendleton Functioned 1789–95. Area absorbed by Washington District, 1795.	Ninety-Six	1789 original
Pendleton Functioned from 1795.	Washington	1795 removed from Ninety-Six District
Richland Functioned from 1785.	Camden	1785 original
Salem Functioned 1792–1800. Area absorbed by Sumter District, 1800.	Camden	1792 Clarendon/Claremont Counties in Camden District
Shrewsbury Non-functioning county. Area absorbed by Beaufort District, 1800.	Beaufort	1785 original

County (1785–1800)	Circuit Court Districts	Date Formed Parent County/ies
Spartanburg *Functioned 1785–91. Area absorbed by Pinckney District, 1791.*	Ninety-Six	1785 original
Spartanburg *Functioned from 1791.*	Pinckney	1791 removed from Ninety-Six District
Union *Functioned 1785–91. Area absorbed by Pinckney District, 1791.*	Ninety-Six	1785 original
Union *Functioned from 1791.*	Pinckney	1791 removed from Ninety-Six District
Washington *Functioned 1785–91. Area absorbed by Charleston District, 1800.*	Charleston	1785 original

County (1785–1800)	Circuit Court Districts	Date Formed Parent County/ies
Williamsburg *Non-functioning county. Area absorbed by Georgetown District, 1800, and reformed as Williamsburg District, 1804.*	Georgetown	1785 original
Winton *Functioned 1785–1800. Remaining records, 1785–91, in Barnwell County. Renamed Barnwell District, 1800.*	Orangeburgh	1785 original
Winyah *Non-functioning county. Area absorbed by Georgetown District, 1800.*	Georgetown	1785 original
York *Functioned 1785–91. Area absorbed by Pinckney District, 1791.*	Camden	1785 original
York *Functioned from 1791.*	Pinckney	1791 removed from Camden District

Circuit Court Districts, 1769-1800

Circuit Court District (1769–1800) Records Repository (Counties in District)	Date Formed Parent District	Land Probate 1790 Census District(s)
Beaufort (Granville, Hilton, Lincoln, Shrewsbury)	1769 original	— — — District
Camden Kershaw/Lancaster (Chester, Clarendon, Claremont, Fairfield, Lancaster, Richland, York)	1769 original	1784 1781 1782 by county
Charleston Charleston (Bartholomew, Berkeley, Colleton, Marion, Washington)	1769 original	1671 1671 1671 Parishes
Cheraws (Chesterfield, Darlington, Marlboro)	1769 original	— — — Counties
Georgetown Georgetown (Kingston, Liberty, Williamsburg, Winyah)	1769 original	— — 1783 Parishes

Circuit Court District (1769–1800) Records Repository (Counties in District)	Date Formed Parent District	Land Probate 1790 Census District(s)
Ninety-Six Abbeville (Abbeville, Edgefield, Greenville, Laurens, Newberry, Pendleton, Spartanburg, Union)	1769 original	1784 1782 1777 Counties
Orangeburgh (Lewisburg, Lexington, Orange, Winton)	1769 original	— — 1787 North and South
Pinckney York (Chester, Spartanburg, Union, York) *Counties enumerated in Camden and Ninety-Six Districts in 1790.*	1791 Ninety-Six	— — —
Washington (Greenville, Pendleton) *Counties enumerated in Ninety-Six District in 1790.*	1791 Ninety-Six functioned from 1795	— — —

Townships and Parishes

Parish/Township	Established	Location	Proprietary County/District
All Saints Parish	1778	near Georgetown	Georgetown District
Amelia Township	1731	Congaree and Santee Rivers	Orangeburgh District
Belfast Township	1761	Stevens and Long Cane Creeks	Edgefield and Abbeville Districts
Boonesborough Township	1761	Long Cane Creek, Saluda and Little rivers	Abbeville District
Christ Church Parish	1706	Wando River	Berkeley
Fredericksburgh Township	1731	Wateree River	Sumter and Kershaw Districts
Hillsborough Township	1761	Long Cane Creek	Abbeville District
Kingston (King's Town) Township	1731	Waccamaw River	Horry District
Londonborough Township	1761	Stevens Creek of Savannah River	Edgefield District
New Windsor Township	1731	Savannah River	Barnwell and Edgefield Districts
Orange Parish	1778	St. Matthew's	Orangeburgh District
Orangeburgh Township	1731	South Edisto or Pon Pon River	Orangeburgh District
Prince Frederick's Parish	1734	upper Prince George's	Craven
Prince George's Parish	1721	between Santee and Pee Dee Rivers	Craven
Prince William's Parish	1745	upper St. Helena's	Granville
Purrysburgh	1731	Savannah River	Beaufort District
Queensborough Township	1731	Pee Dee River and Lynch's Creek	Georgetown and Marion Districts
Saxegotha (Saxe-Gotha) Township	1731	Congaree River	Lexington District
St. Andrew's Parish	1706	Ashley River	Berkeley
St. Bartholomew's Parish	1706	near St. Helena	Colleton
St. David's Parish	1768	St. Mark's and Prince Frederick's	Craven
St. Denis' (French) Parish	1706	adjoining St. Thomas'	Berkeley
St. George's Dorchester Parish	1717	upper St. Andrew's	Berkeley
St. Helena's Parish	1712	St. Helena/Port Royal	Granville
St. James Goose Creek Parish	1706	Goose Creek	Berkeley
St. James Santee (French) Parish	1706	James Town	Craven
St. John's Colleton Parish	1734	Edisto and adjacent islands	Colleton
St. John's Parish	1706	Cooper River	Berkeley
St. Luke's Parish	1767	Euhaws	Granville
St. Mark's Parish	1757	Prince Frederick's	Craven
St. Matthew's Parish	1768	Orangeburgh Township	Berkeley
St. Michael's Parish	1751	St. Philip's Charles Town	Berkeley
St. Paul's Parish	1706	Stono and Edisto rivers	Colleton
St. Peter's Parish	1746	Purrysburgh	Granville
St. Philip's Parish	1706	Charles Town	Berkeley
St. Stephen's Parish	1754	upper St. James' Santee	Craven
St. Thomas' (French) Parish	1706	Wando River	Berkeley
Welch Tract (Welch Neck)	1731	Pee Dee River and Jeffry's Creek	Marion District
Williamsburgh Township	1731	Black River	Williamsburgh District

Proprietary Counties

Map	Current County	Proprietary County/ies (1682-1785)
C3	Abbeville	Carteret (Granville)/Colleton
D5	Aiken	Berkeley/Colleton
E6	Allendale	Carteret (Granville)
B2	Anderson	Carteret (Granville)/Colleton
F6	Bamburg	Carteret (Granville)/Colleton
E6	Barnwell	Berkeley/Carteret (Granville)
G8	Beaufort	Carteret (Granville)
H6	Berkeley	Berkeley/Colleton
F4	Calhoun	Berkeley/Colleton
H7	Charleston	Colleton
D1	Cherokee	Craven
E2	Chester	Craven
H2	Chesterfield	Craven
G5	Clarendon	Berkeley/Craven
G7	Colleton	Carteret (Granville)/Colleton
H3	Darlington	Craven
J3	Dillon	Craven
G6	Dorchester	Berkeley/Colleton
D4	Edgefield	Carteret (Granville)/Colleton
F3	Fairfield	Berkeley/Craven
J3	Florence	Craven
J5	Georgetown	Craven
C1	Greenville	Berkeley/Colleton

Map	Current County	Proprietary County/ies (1682-1785)
C3	Greenwood	Colleton
F7	Hampton	Carteret (Granville)
K4	Horry	Craven
F8	Jasper	Carteret (Granville)
G3	Kershaw	Berkeley/Craven
G2	Lancaster	Craven
D2	Laurens	Berkeley/Colleton
G3	Lee	Craven
E4	Lexington	Berkeley/Colleton
J3	Marion	Craven
J2	Marlboro	Craven
C4	McCormick	Carteret (Granville)/Colleton
E3	Newberry	Berkeley/Colleton
A2	Oconee	Carteret (Granville)/Colleton
F5	Orangeburg	Berkeley/Colleton
B1	Pickens	Colleton
F3	Richland	Berkeley
D4	Saluda	Colleton
D1	Spartanburg	Berkeley/Craven
G4	Sumter	Berkeley/Craven
D2	Union	Berkeley
J5	Williamsburg	Craven
E1	York	Craven

South Dakota

LAURA HALL HEUERMANN AND MARSHA HOFFMAN RISING, CG, FUGA, FASG

French explorers are known to have made their way to what is now South Dakota as early as 1743. Creating a topographical transition between the prairies of the Midwest and the Rocky Mountains to the west, South Dakota's eastern glacial drift river region and western Black Hills remained the home of the Arikara and the Sioux until 1825 when tribal conflict drove the Arikara farther west. Sioux remained in the state and still comprise most of South Dakota's Native American population.

The Spanish held dominion over the land for the last part of the eighteenth century, but South Dakota was sold to the United States as part of the Louisiana Purchase in 1803. Early nineteenth-century trappers and traders established headquarters in the area, transporting furs down the Missouri from Fort Pierre, then part of Missouri Territory. It was not until the 1850s that any permanent U.S. settlements began. Land east of the Missouri River fell under the successive jurisdictions of the Michigan, Wisconsin, and Iowa territories before finally settling in Minnesota Territory in 1849. The portion west of the Missouri River became part of the vast, unsettled, northern Nebraska Territory in 1854.

In the winter of 1856–57 the Dakota Land Company from Minnesota received a charter to establish a settlement in Medary, near the town of Brookings. At about the same time, Western Town Company from Iowa received a charter to establish settlements in the area along the Sioux River. A sawmill, store, and houses were built in what is now Sioux Falls.

By 1860 settlements could be found in the southeastern part of the state and along the Missouri, Big Sioux, Vermillion, James, and Red rivers. A bill signed 2 March 1861 by the U.S. Congress created Dakota Territory, then consisting of what would become North and South Dakota, separating it from Nebraska Territory and the recently created state of Minnesota. By the fall of that year, there were eleven post offices in the territory, among them Yankton, Vermillion, and Sioux Falls. Territorial counties were established by the legislature in April 1862: Lincoln, Minnehaha, Brookings, and Deuel. A request to have a military fort for the protection of the settlers led to the creation of Ft. Dakota located in the Sioux Falls area.

During the next two decades, significant changes led to a massive influx of population. The Homestead Act of 1862 encouraged settlers to stake claims. Although economic depression, drought, and grasshoppers plagued expansion, the development of land offices, railroad expansion, and changing crop conditions contributed to the population growth. Gold was discovered in the Black Hills in 1874, a lode that until recently was still the largest in the Western Hemisphere. The discovery pressured western migration into that portion of the state previously closed to settlers by agreement with the Sioux. The state's reservation system began with the Yankton in the southern part of Douglas County in 1858. In 1863 the Winnebago and Santee Sioux were moved from Minnesota to a small reservation near Fort Thompson, which later became the Crow Creek Reservation. The Battle of the Little Big Horn in Montana was chronologically followed by the legal opening of the South Dakota's gold mining region and its adjacent grazing land.

In Minnehaha County, along the Big Sioux River, quartzite was quarried as early as the 1860s, and a good business continued through the 1880s. Many sturdy and attractive public buildings

and residences were built with a number of miners increasing the population. There is some quarrying that continues today with pink quartzite shipped to the east.

With the peak of expansion in 1885, Sioux Falls became an area where people from the east could come for a short period of time and obtain a divorce. Easterners brought a demand for culture with them—operas, plays, concerts, and hotels. Rapidly growing eastern river region settlements and prosperity in the mines created pressure for statehood below the 46th parallel for the southern part of the territory. The U.S. Congress approved the division of the territory creating the states of North Dakota and South Dakota in 1889.

Throughout the push toward statehood, relations between the Sioux and the white settlers remained difficult, climaxing in the warfare at Wounded Knee in 1890. Nearly one-third of the white population at the time was foreign-born, coming primarily from Eastern Europe and Scandinavia.

Life for the pioneer farmers in the Dakota was a hard one, immortalized by the words and experiences of such authors as Laura Ingalls Wilder and Ole Rölvaag. It was not an easy task to develop a home and farm from the raw, pathless prairie. Remote from neighbors, the prairie dweller led a lonely life. Only through perseverance and determination was a home carved out of what had heretofore been wilderness. Today the state's economy remains largely dependent on livestock, food, lumber and wood products, manufacturing, tourism, and service occupations. The Homestake Mine in the Black Hills is no longer in existence. Sioux Falls is the location of a major medical center with an increasing population.

Vital Records

Statewide vital record registration for births, deaths and marriages began in South Dakota in July 1905. Copies of later vital records may be obtained from the State Department of Health, Health Statistics Program, Joe Foss Building, Pierre, SD 57501 <www.state.sd.us/doh/VitalRec/Vital.htm>. The current fee (2004) is $10 for birth and death records; $7 for marriage and divorce records. Some earlier marriage records may be found in the office of the register of deeds of a particular county. Published records of marriages exist for Minnehaha and Pennington Counties. Divorce records were recorded statewide after 1905, but earlier ones may be at the Clerk of the Court in the appropriate county.

Census Records

Federal

Population Schedules
- Indexed—1860, 1870 (both as Dakota Territory), 1890 (fragment), 1900, 1910, 1920, 1930
- Soundex—1880 (Dakota Territory), 1900, 1920

Agriculture Schedules
- 1870, 1880

Mortality Schedules
- 1860, 1870, 1880 (all as Dakota Territory)

Union Veterans Schedules
- 1890

Although the Dakotas fell under Minnesota Territory for the 1850 federal census, the only whites enumerated actually lived in that territory's Pembina County, now North Dakota. Only the schedule for Jefferson Township of Union County remains of the 1890 population census. Microfilmed copies of all federal censuses listed above are available in the South Dakota State Historical Society (see Archives, Libraries, and Societies) and are available from them on interlibrary loan. The 1880 and 1900 Soundexes do not circulate.

The mortality schedules are available on microfilm and also have been indexed by AISI (see page 3). These are available at the South Dakota State Historical Society in Pierre, as well as various other repositories.

The Sioux Falls Public Library, 201 North Main Ave., Sioux Falls, SD 57102, has microfilm copies of the 1860, 1870, and 1880 federal population schedules for the territory, as well as for the state. The 1890 census (as with other states) was destroyed by fire.

School censuses by some counties are in state archives.

Territorial and State

Numerous state-generated censuses for the Dakota Territory and the state of South Dakota were compiled and are available for research at the South Dakota State Historical Society. The Dakota Territory Special Federal 1885 census was taken under federal guidelines right before statehood and is extant for twenty counties in present-day South Dakota: Beadle, Butte, Charles Mix, Edmunds, Fall River, Faulk, Hand, Hanson, Hutchinson, Hyde, Lake, Lincoln, Marshall, McPherson, Moody, Roberts, Sanborn, Spink, Stanley, and Turner. The 1885 census also contains a veterans' census. These listings may be borrowed on interlibrary loan.

State censuses include the 1895 census, available with ledger-style indexes, only for Beadle, Brule, Pratt (now Jones), Presho (now Lyman), Campbell, and Charles Mix counties. The census can be borrowed on microfilm from the South Dakota State Historical Society. Those censuses taken in 1905, 1915, 1925, 1935, and 1945, are also located there, but not on microfilm. Alphabetical card files exist for the 1905 to 1945 censuses. The 1905 census is an especially valuable census for the genealogist since land descriptions are given. This description can then be used to locate federal land records. Additional information in 1905's enumeration gives the length of time the individual was in

South Dakota, and, if the individual was foreign-born, the time of residence in the United States.

Many early censuses of the state's Indian Reservations have been microfilmed and are available at the Family History Library (FHL) in Salt Lake City, as well as the South Dakota State Historical Society, where they are available on interlibrary loan.

Background Sources

The South Dakota State Historical Society published an extensive collection in 41 volumes between 1902 and 1982 of historical material entitled *South Dakota Historical Collections*. An index, published in 1989 is available from the society. Volumes circulate from the state library and a few are still in print and available for sale at the society.

There are many histories of counties and towns found in town or county libraries in the state. The Sioux Valley Genealogical Society (see Archives, Libraries and Societies), for example, has county histories for Minnehaha County as well as histories for Brookings, Brown, Clay, Faulk, Grant, Hamlin, Hand, Hanson, Jerauld, Jones, Lincoln, McCook, Moody, Potter, Turner, and Yankton.

The following provide additional background understanding of South Dakota's history and its people, particularly nineteenth century immigrants:

Dvorak, Joseph A. *Memorial Book: History of the Czechs in the State of South Dakota*. Tabor, S.Dak: Czech Heritage Preservation Society, Inc., 1980. Topics here include church history; Czech history and immigration; and Brule, Trip, Gregory, Charles Mix, Bon Homme, and Yankton county history.

Fanebust, Wayne. *Where the Sioux River Bends*. Sioux Falls: Minnehaha County Historical Society, 1985.

Historical Records Survey. *South Dakota Place Names*. Vermillion, S. Dak.: University of South Dakota, 1940.

Karolevitz, Robert F. *Challenge: The South Dakota Story*. N.p.: Brevet Press, 1975.

Kingsbury, George Washington and George Martin Smith. *History of Dakota Territory and South Dakota: Its History and Its People*. 5 vols. Chicago: S.J. Clarke, 1915. Volumes 4 and 5 contain biographical sketches.

Laubersheimer, Sue. *South Dakota: Changing, Changeless, 1889–1989: A Selected Annotated Bibliography*, N.p.: South Dakota Library Association, 1985. Two supplements consisting of subject index. Pierre: South Dakota Library Association, 1986.

Phillips, George H. *The Postoffices of South Dakota, 1861–1930*. Crete, Nebr.: J-B Publishing, 1975.

Rath, George. *The Black Sea Germans in the Dakotas*. Freeman, S.Dak.: Pine Hill Press, 1977.

Schell, Herbert S. *History of South Dakota*. 3rd. rev. Lincoln, Nebr.: University of Nebraska, 1975. A standard historical account with descriptive maps.

Sittig, Emily Brende and Clara Brende Christenson, trans. *Norwegian Pioneer History of Minnehaha County, 1866–1896*. Freeman, S.Dak.: Pine Hill Press, 1976.

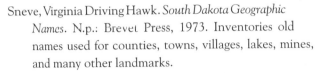

Sneve, Virginia Driving Hawk. *South Dakota Geographic Names*. N.p.: Brevet Press, 1973. Inventories old names used for counties, towns, villages, lakes, mines, and many other landmarks.

Turchen, Van Der West, Lesta, and James D. McLaird. *County and Community: A Bibliography of South Dakota Local Histories*. Mitchell, S.Dak.: the author, 1979.

Watson, Parker. "A Black Hills Bibliography." *South Dakota Historical Collections* 35 (1970): 169-301.

Maps

R.L. Polk and Company, *Northwestern Gazetteer: Minnesota, North and South Dakota and Montana—Gazetteer and Business Directory* (St. Paul: R.L. Polk, 1914) is of great benefit to the Dakota researcher. A good gazetteer containing much local history is *Black Hills Ghost Towns* by Watson Parker and H.K. Lambert (Chicago: Swallow Press, 1974).

A number of county atlases have been filmed and are available on interlibrary loan from the South Dakota State Historical Society. Those accessible to the researcher include the counties of Aurora (1909), Beadle (1906 and 1913), Bon Homme (1912), Brookings (1909), Brown (1905 and 1911), Brule (1911), Campbell (1911), Charles Mix (1906 and 1912), Clark (1929), Clay (1901 and 1924), Codington (1929), Davison (1901 and 1929), Day (1909 and 1929), Deuel (1909), Douglas (1901 and 1910), Edmunds (1905), Faulk (1910), Grant (1910 and 1929), Gregory (1912), Hand (1912), Hanson (1902 and 1910), Hughes (1916), Hutchinson (1910), Hyde (1911), Jerauld (1909), Kingsbury (1909 and 1929), Lake (1911), Lincoln (1910), Lyman (1911), Marshall (1910 and 1924), McCook (1911), McPherson (1911), Miner (1917), Minnehaha (1903), Moody (1909), Potter (1911), Roberts (1910), Sanborn (1912), Spink (1909), Sully (1916), Tripp (1915), Turner (1893 and 1902), Union (1924), Walworth (1941), and Yankton (1910).

Other atlases on microfilm include Andrea's 1884 *Historical Atlas of Dakota* and Peterson's 1904 *Historical Atlas of South Dakota*. The Sanborn fire insurance maps (see page 5) are located at the South Dakota State Historical Society as well.

Land Records

Public-Domain State

The original patents and copies of tract books and township plats are at the Bureau of Land Management (BLM), 222 N. 32nd St., Box 30157, Billings, MT 59107. The United States General Land Office (GLO) unapproved homestead files (1905–20) are housed at the South Dakota State Historical Society as are tract books for land claims (1864–1915). Once granted by the federal government, later land transactions were filed with the county register of deeds.

Probate Records

Wills and intestate proceedings originate at the county in which the deceased lived, usually at the county clerk of the court's office. Some have been transferred to the state archives at the Cultural Heritage Center, cataloged under Unified Judicial System, Circuit Courts, Division of [County name] County (see Court Records below).

Many probate records for Indian agencies have been microfilmed and are available through the FHL. Those that have not will be available through the National Archives (see Special Focus Categories—Native American).

Court Records

The county court had original jurisdiction over all matters of probate, guardianship, and settlement of estate, as well as civil and criminal jurisdiction as may be conferred by law. The circuit courts held some case files, judgments, and depositions related to civil and criminal actions, naturalization records, and juror lists. In November 1972, the state's constitution covering the Judicial Department was amended to create a unified judicial system. All judges then became either circuit court judges or state supreme court judges. This eliminated former county or district courts. Many of the counties simply left their old files with the clerk of the courts in the county. However, the state archives in Pierre has notified all counties that they can transfer their old files to the archives. A few South Dakota counties have turned over some of their court records to the state archives, which also holds criminal dockets for Huron, Beadle County (1919–23); Jones County (1919–39); Mellette County (1912–57); and Minnehaha County (1890–96, 1923–73) with police dockets (1884–1909).

Tax Records

Most tax lists that have survived are housed at the county seat in the auditor's office. A few early tax records have been microfilmed and remain at the South Dakota State Historical Society, including those of "Old Stanley County," comprised of present-day Stanley, Haakon, and Jackson counties. The microfilms for tax records are not always easy to read, but can include county commissions work in selecting juries, docket books, and real and personal property taxes. Others at the archives include Huron; Beadle County (1883–1902); Edmunds (1887–1924); Roberts (1884–1929); Stanley (1891–1930); Union (1870–1901); and delinquent tax lists from Walworth (before 1899).

Cemetery Records

In 1940 the Works Projects Administration (WPA) compiled a "grave registration" that attempted to document the cemeteries of South Dakota. Although incomplete, this survey included either surveys of what cemeteries were available in each county or actual cemetery records. It can be searched at the state historical society and is available through FHL. In 1982 the periodical *South Dakota Genealogical Society Quarterly* began listing the cemeteries in the state and their locations.

As part of the WPA grave registration project, records of burials of Civil War veterans were completed for the following counties: Aurora, Beadle, Bennett, Bon Homme, Brookings, Brule, Butte, Charles Mix, Clay, Codington, Custer, Davison, Douglas, Fall River, Faulk, Gregory, Haakon, Hand, Hanson, Harding, Hughes, Hutchinson, Hyde, Jackson, Jerauld, Jones, Kingsbury, Lake, Lincoln, Lyman, McCook, Meade, Mellette, Miner, Minnehaha, Moody, Pennington, Potter, Sanborn, Shannon, Stanley, Sully, Todd, Tripp, Turner, Union, Washabaugh, and Yankton.

The Sioux Valley Genealogical Society (see Archives, Libraries and Societies) has received a number of grants from the Mary Chilton Chapter of DAR, which have been used to microfilm Minnehaha County cemeteries and those in some neighboring counties. The microfilm, also available through FHL, includes records of funeral homes in the county.

Rapid City Society for Genealogical Research published four volumes of *Some Black Hills Area Cemetery* in an ongoing publication effort begun in 1973. Other genealogical societies have been working diligently to transcribe cemetery records in their areas and publish them in the *South Dakota Genealogical Society Quarterly* or other local genealogical publications.

There is a national cemetery in South Dakota: Black Hills National Cemetery, P.O. Box 640, Sturgis, SD 57785.

Church Records

Most church records remain in private hands. Two helpful publications are *Guide to the Archives of the Episcopal Church in South Dakota*, by Alan Schwartz, archivist, housed at Center for Western Studies, Mikkelsen Library, Augustana College, Sioux

Falls, SD 57102; and *Early Churches and Towns in South Dakota* by Donald D. Parker (Brookings, S.Dak.: the author, ca. 1964). Another publication includes Ralph and Kathleen Tingley, *Mission in Sioux Falls: The First Baptist Church, 1875-1975* (Sioux Falls, S.Dak.: First Baptist Church, 1975).

The Sioux Valley Genealogical Society has been microfilming church and funeral home records in many counties as part of several DAR grants. The society has given a copy of these microfilms to the South Dakota State Historical Society. USGenWeb (see page 16) has a number of church records projects for South Dakota.

Military Records

Microfilmed copies of Union volunteers from the Dakota territories during the Civil War are available from the National Archives and other interlibrary loan resources. They also may be searched at the South Dakota State Historical Society.

A publication that may be useful to the genealogist with early pioneer ancestors is *Memorandum and Official Records Concerning Dakota Militia, Organized in 1862 for the Protection of the Frontier Settlements from the Hostile Sioux Indians*, compiled by R.E. McDowell in connection with Senate Bill No. 5353, Doc. 241, 58th Congress, 2nd session, Washington, DC, 1904.

A roster of soldiers from the First Infantry Regiment, South Dakota Volunteers in the Spanish-American War, has been published in Doane Robinson's *History of South Dakota*, 2 vols. (Chicago: B.F. Bowen & Company, 1904).

South Dakota World War II History Commission records may be used at the archives, and although there are some restrictions, World War II service records from South Dakota may also be researched there.

Some soldiers' discharge papers may be found in the register of deeds office.

The South Dakota State Archives holds a few military records and military benefit records of interest to the genealogist. These include mothers' pension records for Deuel (1913–40), Hughes (1923–40), Kingsbury (1922–40), Lawrence (1918–40), McCook (1917–31), Mellette (1914–40), Minnehaha (1913–40), Union (1922–40), and Walworth (1926–40) counties. These records do have restricted access. They also hold militia lists for Edmunds (1918–19) and McCook (1889–1920).

Periodicals, Newspapers, and Manuscript Collections

Periodicals

Two periodicals with statewide exposure are *South Dakota History*, published by the South Dakota State Historical Society and *South Dakota Genealogical Society Quarterly*, published by that society. Other local societies publish periodicals in their areas.

Newspapers

Approximately 150 weekly and twelve daily South Dakota newspapers (1859–2001) are currently being microfilmed as part of the nearly 1000 titles of South Dakota newspapers located at the state archives. Many can be borrowed by interlibrary loan. No current, reliable published guide exists because the cataloging is continuously updated.

Manuscripts

Manuscript sources include both governmental archival material and personal papers held by repositories. The largest collection in the state for both is at the South Dakota State Historical Society, although the published guide is out-of-date. The following may be of interest to genealogists: records of the State Railroad Division of the Milwaukee Railroad, railroad tract maps, Rapid City flood records, secretary of state papers, teacher certification records, and some state supreme court case files.

A number of school records can be found in the archives at the South Dakota State Historical Society. These consist of teachers' term reports, school censuses, and student records. The records for the specific counties are Aurora (1912–18), Brown (1891–1942), Butte (1918–70), Day (1891–1969), Edmunds (1905–73), Jackson (1918–81), Jones (1916–71), Lyman (1923–69), McCook (1904–11), Perkins (1916–70), Roberts (1944–59), Forestburg District, Sanborn County (1914–81), Spink (few records, 1887–1904), Tripp (1911–73), Turner (1902–69), and Walworth (1906–72). The *Handy Guide to Non-Current South Dakota School Records* (1983) is available from the society.

Other records in the South Dakota archives that should be considered by genealogists include coroners' inquests for Deuel (1889–1952), Edmunds (1887–1912), Hand (1921–69), Hughes (1885–1968), Jones (1922–49), Lawrence (1880–1917), and Minnehaha (1883–1929). The archives also holds insanity records for Deuel (1906–20), Hughes (1881–1956), Lawrence (1879–1976), and Walworth (1891–95) as well as estray records for Edmunds (1897–1912); marks and brands for Union (1865–1900); and records of the Tuberculosis Sanatorium of Deuel (1906–39) and Lawrence (1923–62).

Archives, Libraries, and Societies

South Dakota State Historical Society
Cultural Heritage Center
900 Governors Dr.
Pierre, SD 57501-2294
www.sdhistory.org

The society is administratively responsible for the state's archives and library of printed and microfilm material, which comprise the research collection, as well as the Archaeological Research Center. Its holdings increase annually with many described in various sections of this chapter.

South Dakota Genealogical Society
P.O. Box 1101
Winner, SD 57501-1101
www.rootsweb.com/~sdgenweb/gensoc/sdgensoc.html

In addition to publishing the society's quarterly periodical, the society has a number of affiliated local organizations. The website provides contact information to all those organizations.

The Center for Western Studies
Augustana College
2201 S. Summit Ave., P.O. Box 727
Sioux Falls, SD 57197
www.augie.edu/CWS

This constitutes a fine collection on Native Americans and Scandinavian pioneers in particular.

Sioux Valley Genealogical Society
Old Courthouse Museum
200 W. Sixth St.
Sioux Falls, SD 57104
www.rootsweb.com/~sdsvgs

A good microfilm collection of cemetery and old church records, naturalization records, South Dakota histories, and family records, including a surname file with obituaries and other vital records can be found here.

Special Focus Categories

Naturalization
Naturalization records, including declarations of intent, petitions, and final papers have been deposited in the South Dakota State Historical Society for all counties.

Native American
The account of its native peoples is a bedrock of the culture and fabric of South Dakota history. The three major local history collections in the state for native research are the South Dakota State Historical Society (reservation censuses, school reports, photos, maps, manuscripts); Sinta Gleska College in Rosebud, Rosebud Indian Reservation, South Dakota; and Oglala Lakota College on the Pine Ridge Indian Reservation in Kyle, South Dakota.

Records for several agencies are available on microfilm at both the South Dakota State Historical Society and the FHL.

Among them are Cheyenne River Agency (1886–1951); Crow Creek Agency (1895–1976); Pine Ridge Agency (1874–1932); Rosebud Agency (1886–1942); and Standing Rock Agency (1876–1939). Types of records vary, but many include census and vital statistics. Both the field branches of the National Archives at Kansas City and Denver hold materials generated by the Bureau of Indian Affairs (see page 16).

County Resources

The South Dakota State Historical Society began a project in 1990 to survey the existing records at the county level. In the future, this information will be available at a central location. At present, there are some county records housed at the state archives, but many remain at the local level.

Inventories of county archives were made by the WPA, but were only published for the counties of Bennett, Buffalo, Clark, Faulk, Haakon, Jackson, Mellette, Miner, and Washabaugh. Unpublished materials were deposited at the University of South Dakota in Vermillion.

The register of deeds holds land records, births (except for those adopted), death and marriage records; the clerk of the courts keeps probate records, divorce records, and civil and criminal court cases. Some of the records held by the state archives, such as adoption records, insanity records, and mother's pension records have restricted access. Dates with (?) have not been verified by the state, but are assumed based on the best information presently available. Dates without questions are verified by publications or the county staff.

For some counties on the chart, there are two years listed for "Date Formed." The first is the year the county was created; the second is the year it was fully organized if it differs from the creation year. Under the heading "Parent County/ies," the term "unorganized" means that it was formed from non-county lands, and counties listed with an asterisk (*) are those to which the county was at one time "attached" before it was fully organized.

There were other name changes in counties whose existence was of short duration. For clarification, see Long, *Historical Atlas* (see page 18).

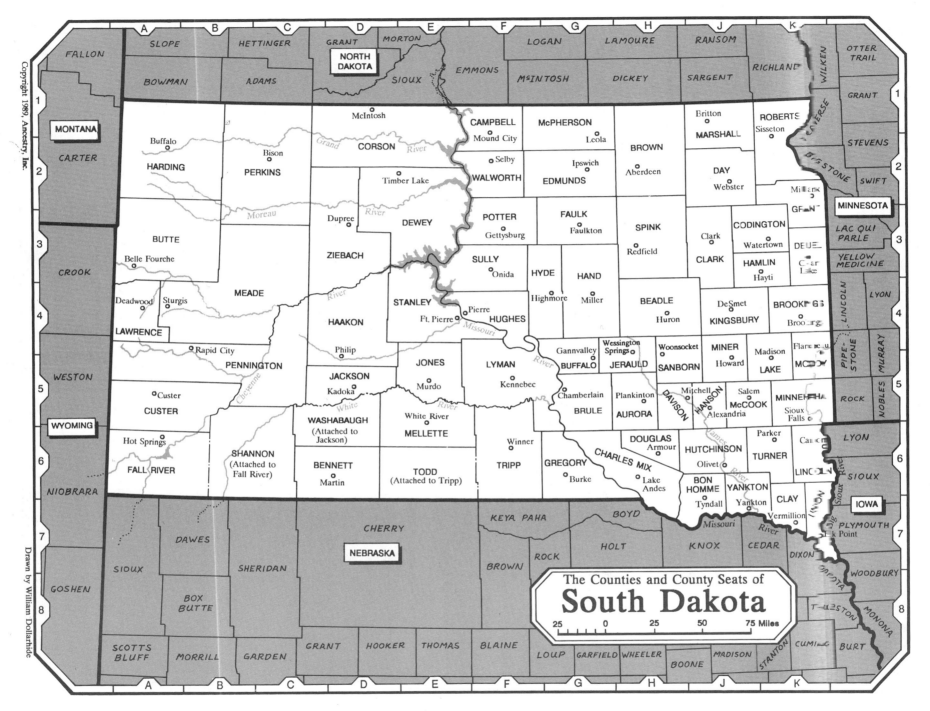

The Counties and County Seats of
South Dakota

SOUTH DAKOTA

Copyright 1989, Ancestry, Inc.

Drawn by William Dollarhide

Map	County Address	Date Formed Parent County/ies	Birth Marriage Death	Land Probate Court
	Armstrong (old)	1873 (abolished, 1879; became part of Hutchinson) Charles Mix/Hutchinson		
	Armstrong (present)	1883 (as Pyatt; renamed, 1895) Cheyenne/Rusk/Stanley *Lawrence		
	In 1952 Armstrong was abolished and became part of Dewey.			
	Ashmore	1873 (abolished 1875)		
H5	Aurora P.O. Box 366 Plankinton 57368	1879 Brule	—— ? ——	1882 1882 1882
	Beadle (old)	1873 (abolished, 1879; became part of Brown)		
H4	Beadle (present) P.O. Box 1358 Huron 57350	1873 (organized 1879) Clark/Spink	—— ? ——	1879? 1882 1882
	The state archives holds probate records, including inventories, appraisements, and wills (1882–1934); and justices' court records (1882–1998).			
D6	Bennett P.O. Box 281 Martin 57551	1909 (1912) Pine Ridge Indian Reservation *Fall River	—— 1912 ——	1907 1912 1912
J7	Bon Homme P.O. Box 6 Tyndall 57066	1862 unorganized	—— 1874	1865 1877 1871
	The state archives holds records (1871–1942).			
	Boreman	1873 (abolished, 1909; became part of Corson) unorganized *Campbell		
	Bramble	1873 (abolished, 1879; became part of Miner) Hanson		
K4	Brookings 314 Sixth Ave. Brookings 57006	1862 (1871) unorganized	—— 1871	1871 ——
	The state archives holds records (1872–1955).			
H2	Brown P.O. Box 1087 Aberdeen 57401	1879 (1880) Beadle (old)/Mills/Stone	—— ? ——	1879? 1879? 1879?
	The state archives holds records (1870–1950).			
	Bruguier	1862 (abolished, 1864; became part of Buffalo and Charles Mix) unorganized *Charles Mix		
G5	Brule 300 S. Courtland Chamberlain 57325	1875 Old Buffalo	—— ? ——	1875? 1875? 1875?
G5	Buffalo P.O. Box 148 Gann Valley 57341	1864 (1871) Bruguier/Charles Mix/ unorganized *Bon Homme	—— 1887	1885 1884 1890
	Parts of the original Buffalo County became counties in North Dakota.			
	Burchard	1873 (abolished, 1879; became part of Beadle and Hand) Hanson		
A3	Butte P.O. Box 237 Belle Fourche 57717	1883 Lawrence/Mandan Harding	—— ? ——	1883? 1883? 1883?
F1	Campbell P.O. Box 146 Mound City 57646	1873 (1884) Buffalo	—— ? ——	1873? 1873? 1873?
H6	Charles Mix P.O. Box 602 Lake Andes 57356	1862 (1879) original	—— ? ——	1875? 1875? 1875?
	Charles Mix was fully organized in 1862, but was dissolved in 1864 and attached to Bon Homme. It was fully reorganized in 1879.			
	Cheyenne	1875 (abolished, 1883; became part of Jackson, Nowlin, Pyatt, and Sterling) Pratt/Rusk/Stanley/unorganized		
	Choteau	1883 (abolished, 1898; became part of Butte and Meade) Martin *Lawrence		
J3	Clark P.O. Box 275 Clark 57225	1873 (1881) Hanson	—— 1883 ——	1881 1882 1885
K7	Clay P.O. Box 377 Vermillion 57069	1862 unorganized	—— ? ——	1862? 1862? 1862?
J3	Codington P.O. Box 1054 Watertown 57201	1877 (1878) Clark/Grant/Gamlin/ unorganized	—— ? ——	1877? 1877? 1877?
	Cole	1862 (named changed to Union)		
D2	Corson P.O. Box 175 McIntosh 57641	1909 Boreman/Dewey/Schnasse unorganized	—— ? ——	1909? 1909? 1909?
	Cragin	1873 (abolished, 1879; became part of Aurora) Hanson		
A5	Custer 420 Mt. Rushmore Road Custer 57730	1875 (1877) unorganized	—— 1891 ——	1875? 1875? 1875?
H5	Davison P.O. Box 927 Mitchell 57301	1873 (1874) Hanson	—— ? ——	1873? 1873? 1873?
	The state archives holds inventory and appraisement books (1915–45); and circuit court journals (1882–1930).			
J2	Day 710 W. First St. Webster 57274	1879 (1882) Greeley/Stone	—— ? ——	1879? 1879? 1879?
	Delano	1875 (abolished, 1898; became part of Meade) unorganized *Lawrence		

Map	County Address	Date Formed Parent County/ies	Birth Marriage Death	Land Probate Court
K3	**Deuel** P.O. Box 125 Clear Lake 57226	1862 (1878) unorganized	—— ? ——	1862? 1862? 1862?

The state archives holds circuit court judgment dockets (1879–1911).

Map	County Address	Date Formed Parent County/ies	Birth Marriage Death	Land Probate Court
E3	**Dewey** P.O. Box 96 Timber Lake 57656	1873 (as Rusk; renamed, 1883) (1910) unorganized	—— ? ——	1883? 1883? 1883?
H6	**Douglas** P.O. Box 36 Armour 57313	1873 (1882) Charles Mix	—— ? ——	1873? 1873? 1873?
G2	**Edmunds** P.O. Box 384 Ipswich 57451	1873 (1883) Buffalo	—— ? ——	1873? 1873? 1873?

The state archives has marriage records (1884–1917); miscellaneous probate records (1893–1958); wills (1884–1919); and circuit court records (1890–1902).

Map	County Address	Date Formed Parent County/ies	Birth Marriage Death	Land Probate Court
	Ewing	1883 (abolished 1890)		
A6	**Fall River** 906 N. River Hot Springs 57747	1883 Custer	—— ? ——	1883? 1883? 1883?

The state archives has records (1891–1915).

Map	County Address	Date Formed Parent County/ies	Birth Marriage Death	Land Probate Court
G3	**Faulk** P.O. Box 357 Faulkton 57438	1873 (1883) Buffalo	—— 1885 ——	1883 1884 1883

The state archives has records of the clerk of the circuit court (1883–1958).

Map	County Address	Date Formed Parent County/ies	Birth Marriage Death	Land Probate Court
	Forsythe	1875 (abolished, 1881; became part of Custer) unorganized		
K2	**Grant** P.O. Box 509 Milbank 57252	1873 (1878) Deuel/Hanson		

Courthouse fire destroyed deed books 17–18 and mortgage books 10a, 18, 26, 28, and 29.

Map	County Address	Date Formed Parent County/ies	Birth Marriage Death	Land Probate Court
	Greeley	1873 (abolished, 1879; became part of Day) Hanson		
G6	**Gregory** P.O. Box 430 Burke 57523	1862 (1898) unorganized "Todd"/Charles Mix	—— ? ——	1862 1862 1862

The state archives holds records (1899–1965).

Map	County Address	Date Formed Parent County/ies	Birth Marriage Death	Land Probate Court
D4	**Haakon** P.O. Box 70 Philip 57567	1914 (1915) Stanley	—— 1915 ——	1893 1915 1915
J3	**Hamlin** P.O. Box 256 Hayti 57241	1873 (1878) Deuel/Hanson	—— ? ——	1873? 1873? 1873?

The state archives holds marriage licenses (1881–1969).

Map	County Address	Date Formed Parent County/ies	Birth Marriage Death	Land Probate Court
G4	**Hand** P.O. Box 122 Miller 57362	1873 (1882) Buffalo	—— ? ——	1873 1873 1873

The state archives holds will records (1891–1974).

Map	County Address	Date Formed Parent County/ies	Birth Marriage Death	Land Probate Court
J5	**Hanson** P.O. Box 127 Alexandria 57311	1871 (1873) Brookings/Buffalo/ Charles Mix/Deuel/ Hutchinson/Jayne/ Minnehaha/unorganized	—— ? ——	1871? 1871? 1871?
A2	**Harding** P.O. Box 534 Buffalo 57720	1881 (1911) unorganized	—— ? ——	1881? 1881? 1881?

The state archives has Territorial Registers of Action (1881–90); probate and circuit court records (1881–1957).

Map	County Address	Date Formed Parent County/ies	Birth Marriage Death	Land Probate Court
F4	**Hughes** P.O. Box 1112 Pierre 57501	1873 (1880) Buffalo	—— ? ——	1873? 1873? 1873?

The state archives has divorce records (1905–34); probate records (1881–1948); district court records (1882–1928); and circuit court records (1881–1957).

Map	County Address	Date Formed Parent County/ies	Birth Marriage Death	Land Probate Court
J6	**Hutchinson** P.O. Box 7 Olivet 57052	1862 (1871) unorganized	—— ? ——	1862? 1862? 1862?
G4	**Hyde** P.O. Box 306 Highmore 57345	1873 (1883) Buffalo	—— ? ——	1873? 1873? 1873?
D5	**Jackson** P.O. Box 128 Kadoka 57543	1883 (1915) Cheyenne/Lugenbell/ White River *Pennington	—— 1915 ——	1901 1915 1915

The state archives holds records (1918–1981).
In 1909 Jackson was abolished and became part of Mellette and Washabaugh. Jackson was re-created from Stanley in 1914, becoming fully organized in 1915.

Map	County Address	Date Formed Parent County/ies	Birth Marriage Death	Land Probate Court
	Jayne	1862 (abolished, 1871; became part of Hanson, Hutchinson, and Turner) Unorganized *Yankton		
H5	**Jerauld** P.O. Box 435 Wessington Springs 57382	1883 Aurora/Buffalo	—— ? ——	1883? 1883? 1883?
E5	**Jones** 310 S. Main Murdo 57559	1916 (1917) Lyman	—— ? ——	1917? 1917? 1917?

The state archives has probate records and circuit court judgments (1917–78).

Map	County Address	Date Formed Parent County/ies	Birth Marriage Death	Land Probate Court
J4	**Kingsbury** P.O. Box 176 De Smet 57231	1873 (1880) Hanson	—— ? ——	1873? 1873? 1873?

The state archives has probate bonds (1882–1964); probate records (1885–1942); and wills (1911–69).

Map	County Address	Date Formed Parent County/ies	Birth Marriage Death	Land Probate Court
K5	**Lake** P.O. Box 447 Madison 57042	1873 Brookings/Hanson/ Minnehaha	—— ? ——	1873? 1873? 1873?
A4	**Lawrence** P.O. Box 626 Deadwood 57732	1875 (1877) unorganized	—— ? ——	1875? 1875? 1875?

The state archives has probate records and wills (1877–1935); guardianship and adoption records (1910–58); marriage records (1879–1956); and circuit court journals (1891–1930).

Map	County Address	Date Formed Parent County/ies	Birth Marriage Death	Land Probate Court
K6	Lincoln 100 E. Fifth St. Canton 57013	1862 (1867) Minnehaha	—— ? ——	1862? 1862? 1862?

The state archives holds probate records (1883–1914).

Map	County Address	Date Formed Parent County/ies	Birth Marriage Death	Land Probate Court
	Lugenbeel	1875 (abolished, 1909; became part of Bennett and Todd) Meyer/Pratt/unorganized		
F5	Lyman P.O. Box 235 Kennebec 57544	1873 (1893) Gregory/unorganized	—— ? ——	1873? 1873? 1873?

The state archives holds records (1904–1968).

Map	County Address	Date Formed Parent County/ies	Birth Marriage Death	Land Probate Court
	Mandan	1875 (abolished, 1887; became part of Lawrence) unorganized		
J1	Marshall P.O. Box 130 Britton 57430	1885 Day	—— ? ——	1885? 1885? 1885?
	Martin	1881 (abolished, 1898; became part of Butte) unorganized *Lawrence		
J5	McCook P.O. Box 504 Salem 57058	1873 (1878) Hanson	—— ? ——	1873? 1873? 1873?

The state archives holds records (1881–1934).

Map	County Address	Date Formed Parent County/ies	Birth Marriage Death	Land Probate Court
G1	McPherson P.O. Box 248 Leola 57456	1873 (1884) Buffalo	—— ? ——	1873? 1873? 1873?
B4	Meade P.O. Box 939 Sturgis 57785	1889 Lawrence	—— ? ——	1889? 1889? 1889?

The state archives holds records (1889–1956).

Map	County Address	Date Formed Parent County/ies	Birth Marriage Death	Land Probate Court
E6	Mellette P.O. Box 257 White River 57579	1909 (1911) Jackson/Meyer/ Washabaugh unorganized	—— 1911 ——	1907 1912 1912

The state archives holds probate cases (1907–1947).

Map	County Address	Date Formed Parent County/ies	Birth Marriage Death	Land Probate Court
	Meyer	1873 (abolished, 1909; became part of Mellette and Todd) unorganized		
J5	Miner P.O. Box 265 Howard 57349	1873 (1880) Hanson	—— 1882 ——	1881 1883 1881
K5	Minnehaha 415 N. Dakota Ave. Sioux Falls 57102	1862 (1868) unorganized *Union	—— ? ——	1862? 1862? 1862?

The state archives holds probate records (1873–1907) and wills (1961–1974).

Map	County Address	Date Formed Parent County/ies	Birth Marriage Death	Land Probate Court
K5	Moody P.O. Box 226 Flandreau 57028	1873 Brookings/Minnehaha	—— ? ——	1873? 1873? 1873?
A5	Pennington P.O. Box 230 Rapid City 57709	1875 (1877) unorganized	—— 1887 ——	1875? 1875? 1875?

Map	County Address	Date Formed Parent County/ies	Birth Marriage Death	Land Probate Court
C2	Perkins P.O. Box 27 Bison 57620	1908 (1909) Butte	—— ? ——	1909? 1909? 1909?
F3	Potter 201 S. Exene Gettysburg 57442	1873 (as Ashmore; renamed, 1875) (1883) Buffalo	—— ? ——	1875? 1875? 1875?
	Pyatt	1883 (renamed Armstrong, 1895) Cheyenne/Rusk/Stanley *Lawrence		
K1	Roberts 411 Second Ave. East Sisseton 57262	1883 Grant/Siseton-Wahpeteon Indian Reserve	—— ? ——	1883? 1883? 1883?

The state archives holds records (1908–1981).

Map	County Address	Date Formed Parent County/ies	Birth Marriage Death	Land Probate Court
	Rusk	1873 (renamed Dewey, 1883) unorganized		
H5	Sanborn P.O. Box 56 Woonsocket 57385	1883 Miner	—— ? ——	1883? 1883? 1883?
	Schnasse	1883 (abolished, 1911; became part of Ziebach) Boreman/unorganized		
B6	Shannon 906 N. River St. Hot Springs 57747	1875 unorganized *Fall River	—— ? ——	1883? 1883? 1883?

Shannon is still attached to Fall River.

Map	County Address	Date Formed Parent County/ies	Birth Marriage Death	Land Probate Court
H3	Spink 210 E. Seventh Ave. Redfield 57469	1873 (1879) Hanson	—— ? ——	1873? 1873? 1873?
E4	Stanley P.O. Box 97 Ft. Pierre 57532	1873 (1890) unorganized	—— ? ——	1873? 1873? 1873?
	Sterling	1883 (abolished, 1911; became part of Ziebach) Cheyenne *Lawrence		
	Stone	1873 (abolished, 1879; became part of Brown and Day) Hanson		
F3	Sully P.O. Box 188 Onida 57564	1873 (1883) Buffalo	—— ? ——	1873? 1873? 1873?
	Todd (old)	1862 (abolished, 1897; became part of Gregory) unorganized		

In 1890 Todd disestablished and attached to Charles Mix.

Map	County Address	Date Formed Parent County/ies	Birth Marriage Death	Land Probate Court
E6	Todd (present) Mission 57555	1909 Meyer/Lugenbeel/Washabaugh unorganized		1909? 1909? 1909?

The state archives has birth register. Todd is still attached to Tripp; see Tripp County for records.

Map	County Address	Date Formed Parent County/ies	Birth Marriage Death	Land Probate Court
F6	Tripp 200 Third St. Winner 57580 *The state archives holds records (1911, 1975).*	1873 (1909) unorganized/Gregory/ Todd (old)	— ? 	1873? 1873? 1873?
K6	Turner P.O. Box 446 Parker 57053	1871 Lincoln/Jayne	— ? —	1871? 1871? 1871?
K7	Union P.O. Box 757 Elk Point 57025 *The state archives has court records including land transactions (1860–1929); marriages (1919–23); wills (1870–1910); probate records (1869–1962); justice dockets (1868–1903); and bonds and court judgment books (1876–1948).*	1862 (as Cole; renamed, 1864) unorganized	— ? —	1862? 1862? 1862?
F2	Walworth P.O. Box 328 Selby 57472 *The state archives holds circuit court judgment records (1884–1932) and school records (1918–1958).*	1873 (1883) Buffalo	— ? —	1873? 1873? 1873?
	Washabaugh Kadoka 57543	1883 Lugenbeel *Custer/*Jackson	— ? —	1883? 1883? 1883?
	Washington	1883 (abolished, 1943; became part of Shannon) Lugenbeel/Shannon *Custer		
	Included land now in Meyer and Pratt.			
	Wetmore	1873 (abolished, 1879; became part of Aurora and Miner) Hanson		
	White River	1875 (abolished, 1898; became part of Jackson) Pratt/unorganized		
J7	Yankton P.O. Box 155 Yankton 57078 *The state archives has probate records (1877–1909); wills (1870–1909); notary records (1877–1909); and judgment books (1898–1907).*	1862 unorganized	— ? —	1862? 1862? 1862?
	Ziebach (old)	1877 (abolished, 1898; became part of Pennington) Pennington		
D3	Ziebach P.O. Box 306 Dupree 57623	1911 Schnasse/Sterling/ Armstrong (Cheyenne River Reservation)	— ? —	1911? 1911? 1911?

Tennessee

WENDY BEBOUT ELLIOTT, Ph.D., FUGA

Tennessee's earliest history includes a rapidly increasing number of Anglo settlements, battles with Native Americans over land rights, constantly violated Native American treaties, and numerous changes in jurisdictions and boundaries. These factors make tracing family history difficult, but knowing the historical background will improve one's chances for success.

European explorers first crossed into present-day eastern Tennessee where Cherokees occupied the region during the late seventeenth and early eighteenth centuries. The area of today's Tennessee and Kentucky served as a hunting ground for many other native groups. Choctaws claimed the area of present-day middle Tennessee, between the eastern and western sections of the Tennessee River. The Chickasaw claimed all of west and some of middle Tennessee as its hunting grounds. Prior to 1714, Shawnee claimed the lower Cumberland region.

The first European claim to the region became part of a huge English grant to Sir Walter Raleigh just prior to the attempted colonization at Roanoke in 1585. The area of present-day Tennessee remained barren of European settlements until the British established Fort Loudon in 1756/57, about thirty miles south of today's Knoxville. At the end of the Seven Years War in 1763, France released its claim to the region, and England drew up its Proclamation Line along the crest of the Appalachian Mountains.

This demarcation line was meant to push natives west and keep settlements east of the line, and to slow the costly confrontations; but in fact its establishment seems only to have stimulated interest in settling farther west. News of the Cumberland Gap through the mountains motivated westward movement during this period. As settlers moved west of the Proclamation Line, battles and treaties increased. None of the treaties stopped the western advancement of American settlers, particularly from North Carolina and Virginia; within a few years new treaties were required to temporarily establish new areas for white frontier families, thus pushing the Cherokee farther west.

In 1769, a few from Virginia and North Carolina settled near the Watauga River. Three years later they formed the Watauga Compact or Association, in an effort to establish self-government. In March 1775, the Watauga Association bought lands along the Watauga, Holston, and New rivers from the Cherokee. That same month, the Transylvania Company, which had purchased over twenty million acres from the Cherokee, began selling land for speculation between the Kentucky and Cumberland rivers.

North Carolina claimed this region, along with portions of what became middle and west Tennessee, based on its colonial charter granting land from sea to sea. Numerous disputes over governance ensued. In 1776 the North Carolina legislature established the Washington District in its western territory (east Tennessee) as part of Rowan County. The next year Washington County, North Carolina, was organized and transferred to Burke County for a few months before becoming an independent county, extending over a large portion of present-day Tennessee. Two years later (1779) settlers—former Wataugans—settled at French Lick, founded Nashborough (Nashville) in middle Tennessee, and organized a government called the Cumberland Compact.

Throughout the Revolutionary War, small groups of hunters and trappers—some with families—trekked across the mountains and through the valleys to establish homes on fertile soil in middle and east Tennessee. Many early settlements became permanent during this period. In April 1783 Davidson County was organized and encompassed the northern half of middle Tennessee. Following the war and a difficult and complicated period of jurisdictional quarrelling, North Carolina ceded its claim to Tennessee to the federal government in 1784, reserving some sections (middle Tennessee) for grants to its Revolutionary soldiers. That same year, settlers in the Watauga Valley, frustrated over proceedings and lack of representation in the North Carolina legislature, formed a new state of Franklin. This new "state" never received formal recognition and lasted only four years but was home to settlers from North Carolina, Virginia, and South Carolina. Congress never resolved the conflicting claims.

Native American resistance to colonization continued despite several treaties, but neither settlers nor natives in the territory accepted the restrictions. In 1790, Congress created the "Territory South of the River Ohio" while conflict over land continued. By 1796 the population of settlers had increased to the required 60,000, and Tennessee became the sixteenth state.

Frontier settlers migrated into Tennessee. Many Scots-Irish traveled through the valleys of Virginia via the Great Wagon Road or Warriors Path; Germans from Pennsylvania and Virginia arrived in the region west of Chattanooga. Others followed Robertson's Road from the Cumberland Gap into middle Tennessee.

During the War of 1812 many men from Tennessee contributed military service to the cause. Others participated in the Indian Wars that followed, resulting in treaties with Native Americans that secured additional lands for the westward-moving Americans. West Tennessee was added to middle and east Tennessee in 1818 after the defeat of and subsequent treaty with the Chickasaw.

The disputed northern boundary between Tennessee and Kentucky was not settled until 1820 when Kentucky accepted the faulty Walker Line, drawn too far north of 36° 30', between the Cumberland Gap and the western Tennessee River. Several sections of the line remained in question until another survey was conducted in 1859. Families who lived in the disputed area did not know in which state they resided; consequently, records are frequently located in both states. Due to changing county boundaries and divisions, Tennessee counties affected include (west to east) Stewart, Montgomery, Robertson, Sumner, Smith, Macon, Clay, Pickett, Jackson, Overton, Fentress, Scott, Morgan, Campbell, and Claiborne.

In 1835 the federal government negotiated a new treaty with representatives of some of the Cherokees; in compliance, the natives left Tennessee and moved farther west. In 1837 and 1838 the federal government and military enforced the removal of the remaining Cherokee and remnants of other tribes in the state, forcing them to move via what became known as the "Trail of Tears" through Missouri and then south into present-day Oklahoma.

Despite strong pro-Union leanings of Tennesseans in the eastern section of the state, the legislature voted to secede in May 1861. As an indication of the anti-secession sentiment, many men from east Tennessee served during the war in the Union army. Most middle and west Tennesseans held opposing sentiments, advocating states' rights and the continuation of slavery to support the plantation economy. During the war, Confederates centered its western defense in the state at Fort Henry on the Tennessee River and Fort Donelson on the Cumberland. Tennessee became an active battleground with over 400 battles fought within its borders.

After several major battles, the Union forces controlled the Tennessee River and the state in 1863. During the conflict, the state's infrastructure took a beating. Tennessee reestablished its government in 1864, abolished slavery within its borders in 1865, and claimed the honor of being the first to be readmitted to the Union in 1866 after ratifying the Thirteenth and Fourteenth Amendments.

Several epidemics swept through the state following the war. Most of the state's railroads were rebuilt during Reconstruction, and the state struggled to regain its importance in agricultural and commercial production.

In the early years of the twentieth century, numerous men labored for the Tennessee Coal and Iron Company owned by a New York bank but bought in 1907 by financier J. P. Morgan. His company, U.S. Steel, was charged with anti-trust action in 1911.

A flood control system began during World War I for the Tennessee River. Work stopped before it was completed, but during the Great Depression, federal funds under the New Deal in 1933 established the Tennessee Valley Authority (TVA), which finished the project to harness the Tennessee River and use its force to generate power for the region. The completion of Wilson Dam, constructed across the state boundary at Muscle Shoals, Alabama, culminated the TVA project. Although this project flooded areas that had been in production for 150 years, TVA generated electricity, controlled flooding, attempted to revitalize the area, and resulted in the creation of new industry and jobs to help end the Great Depression and consequently meet the nation's needs during World War II.

Vital Records

Several early attempts were made to record births and deaths statewide, but these were not effective until 1908 when the first statewide registration began. An older reference for

this information is *Guide to Public Vital Statistics in Tennessee* (Nashville: Tennessee Historical Society Records Survey, 1941).

A 1914 state law required statewide registration of births, marriages, and deaths, but general compliance was incomplete until the late 1920s. Birth records for the last 100 years and deaths, marriages, and divorces for the last fifty years are available from Tennessee Office of Vital Records, 421 Fifth Ave. North, Nashville, TN 37247-0460 <www2.state.tn.us/health/vr>. Records before these cutoff periods are at the Tennessee State Library and Archives (see Archives, Libraries, and Societies), or in the county, as described below.

Beginning in 1881 some counties maintained birth and death records. A few continued for a longer period. These original records are housed in the county courthouses with many microfilm copies at the Tennessee State Library and Archives and the Family History Library (FHL) in Salt Lake City.

Birth records for Nashville from June 1881, Knoxville from July 1881, and Chattanooga from January 1882 are available at the Division of Vital Records in Nashville, although these records are incomplete. Records for Memphis are extant from 1 April 1874 through December 1887 and from 1 November 1898 to 1 January 1914. These are available from the Memphis-Shelby County Health Department, Division of Vital Statistics, 814 Jefferson St., Memphis, TN 38105.

Some deaths were recorded for Nashville as early as July 1874, Knoxville from 1 July 1887, and Chattanooga from 6 March 1872. These are maintained in the Vital Records Office in Nashville. Records for Memphis are extant from 1874 to 1886 and from 1898 to 1 January 1914. Some Memphis death records are extant from 1 May 1848. These can be obtained from the Shelby County Archives and Memphis-Shelby County Health Department (address above).

The Tennessee State Library and Archives maintains a register of the deaths recorded between 1908 and 1912 that does not include parents' names. A partial index to these is available on the TSLA website at <www.state.tn.us/sos/statelib/pubsvs/death.htm> and an index to death notices from Nashville newspapers is at the library.

Marriages were recorded in counties prior to statehood, a few as early as 1778, such as those for Green (1780), Washington (1787), Hawkins (1789), Carter (1790), Jefferson and Knox (1792), and Blount (1795). However, a state law requiring the registration of marriages did not pass until 1815. A subsequent state law in 1838 required marriages to be registered in "well-bound books." Between 1838 and 1919 both marriage licenses and bonds were recorded. In the 1880s marriage records began to include additional information including: names of bride and groom, dates of license and marriage, ages and birthplaces of bride and groom, places of residence at the time of marriage, and groom's occupation. Many county vital records began in that same year.

Most early marriage records for the state have been microfilmed and are available at the Tennessee State Library and Archives. Marriage records are arranged by county (see County Recourses). Some county records are on microfilm and available through interlibrary loan from TSLA. Most are available at the FHL.

An additional source for marriage records are Byron Sistler and Associates' compilations. Their six volumes are divided by geographical section (two each for east, middle, and west) and arranged alphabetically for grooms in one volume and brides in the other. Each entry lists names of couple, date of license and ceremony (when available), and county of record. Edythe Rucker Whitley compiled and published separate marriage records for numerous counties, for example:

Whitley, Edythe Rucker, comp. *Marriages of Blount County, Tennessee, 1795–1859.* Baltimore: Genealogical Publishing Co., 1982.

———. *Marriages of Claiborne County, Tennessee, 1838–1850; and Campbell County, Tennessee, 1838–1853.* Baltimore: Genealogical Publishing Co., 1983.

The Works Project Administration (WPA) copied many early Tennessee marriage records; these are available in some counties, the Tennessee State Library and Archives, the Allen County Public Library (Ft. Wayne, Indiana), and the FHL. These transcripts contain numerous errors; originals should always be checked. The Tennessee State Library and Archives has microfilm copies available on interlibrary loan. An early Tennessee marriage index and an index to marriage notices published by Nashville newspapers are both available at the Tennessee State Library and Archives.

Prior to 1834, divorces could only be granted by an act of the general assembly; therefore, these records are among the legislative papers. The state constitution of 1834 took the power to grant divorces from the legislature and authorized courts to grant them. Divorce records are normally maintained by the respective county's circuit court. Those for the past fifty years are available at the Tennessee Office of Vital Records. Early divorce records are compiled in Gale W. Bamman and Debbie W. Spero, *Tennessee Divorces, 1797–1858* (Nashville: G. Bamman, 1985), which abstracts 750 divorce records statewide.

Census Records

Federal

Population Schedules
- Indexed—1810 (part), 1820 (part), 1830, 1840, 1850, 1860, 1870, 1880, 1900, 1910, 1920, 1930
- Soundex—1880, 1900, 1910, 1920, 1930

Industry and Agriculture Schedules
- 1850, 1860, 1870, 1880

Mortality Schedules
- 1850, 1860, 1880

Slave Schedules
- 1850, 1860

Union Veterans Schedules
- 1890

Federal census records for Tennessee are lost for 1790, 1800, parts of 1810 and 1820, and all of 1890. Some territorial censuses (1791, 1795) were taken, but only statistical data remains. The territorial census, taken in the fall of 1795, validated the population for statehood requirements and showed that the number of residents had more than doubled in four years. One source for pre-territorial enumerations is Lucy Kate McGhee, *Partial Census of 1787 to 1791 of Tennessee as Taken from the North Carolina Land Grants* (Salt Lake City: Genealogical Society of Utah, 1990).

Petitions by settlers help fill the early census void. Many have been published in journals for state historical and genealogical societies, such as Cherel Bolin Henderson, trans., "Petitions to the North Carolina General Assembly from Inhabitants South of the French Broad, 1784–1789," *Tennessee Ancestors: A Tri-Annual Publication of the East Tennessee Historical Society* 17 (December 2001): 208-28. This journal article includes thirteen different petitions (dated from April 1784 to 30 November 1789) and lists hundreds of male residents in the area before a census was taken.

Compilations of early Tennessee tax lists also assist in replacing the lost U.S. censuses. Among these are Byron Sistler and Barbara Sistler, *Index to Early Tennessee Tax Lists* (Evanston, Ill.: Byron Sistler and Assoc., 1977); Pollyanna Creekmore, comp., *Early East Tennessee Taxpayers* (Easley, S.C.: Southern Historical Press, 1980); Mary Barnett Curtis, *Early East Tennessee Tax Lists* (Ft. Worth, Tex.: Arrow Printing Co., 1964); and Richard Carlton Fulcher, comp., *1770–1790 Census of the Cumberland Settlements: Davidson, Sumner, Tennessee Counties (In What Is Now Tennessee)* (Baltimore: Genealogical Publishing Co., 1987).

Only Rutherford County and a portion of Grainger County are available for the 1810 census; the Grainger County 1810 census (about 92 percent of the inhabitants) was published by *Tennessee Ancestors: A Publication of the East Tennessee Historical Society*, vol. 6, no. 2 (August 1990): 90-112.

Twenty-six of Tennessee's counties have federal census records for 1820. These middle and west Tennessee counties are Bedford, Davidson, Dickson, Franklin, Giles, Hardin, Hickman, Humphreys, Jackson, Lawrence, Lincoln, Maury, Montgomery, Overton, Perry, Robertson, Rutherford, Shelby, Smith, Stewart, Sumner, Warren, Wayne, White, Williamson, and Wilson. It is 1830 before a complete list of Tennessee households is available.

The Tennessee State Library and Archives has microfilm copies of all of Tennessee's censuses. In addition to the full indexes on the Internet (see page 3), statewide AISI indexes (see page 3) exist. Some federal population censuses for individual counties have published indexes for 1870, 1880, 1900, and 1910. Abstracted entries of the whole state are published for 1850 and 1860. These are arranged alphabetically and are available from Byron Sistler and Associates, Nashville, Tennessee.

A study of land tenure, slavery, and agricultural economy during the late antebellum period was conducted under the direction of Frank L. Owsley, Professor of History, Vanderbilt University. Data was charted from agricultural census schedules for twenty-two Tennessee counties from the 1850 and 1860 enumerations. These compilations contain a wealth of information, including the amount of improved and unimproved land of each farmer or tenant farmer, types and value of crops produced, value of livestock, value of manufactures, and other related data. Charts were created for the following Tennessee counties: Davidson, DeKalb, Dickson, Dyer, Fayette, Fentress, Franklin, Gibson, Grainger, Greene, Hardin, Hawkins, Haywood, Henry, Johnson, Lincoln, Maury, Montgomery, Robertson, Stewart, Sumner, and Wilson. Entitled "Owsley Charts: Master Charts Compiled from the Unpublished Census, 1850–1860," this compilation was microfilmed and is available at the Tennessee State Library and Archives, Vanderbilt University, and the FHL. Originals of industry and agriculture schedules are at Duke University, Chapel Hill, North Carolina.

The 1870 Mortality Schedules were lost. Others have been published by Byron Sistler and Barbara Sistler: *Tennessee Mortality Schedules, 1850, 1860, 1880* (Nashville, Tenn., 1984). Common (public) schools in Tennessee often kept records that include genealogical data. For instance, *Meigs County, Tennessee, Scholastic Population for 1838* includes information from all eight of its school districts. Each lists the head-of-household and number of children between the ages of six and sixteen in the household.

Some special censuses were taken either at the city or county level. Two of these are *Memphis, Tennessee Census, 1869 (3rd Ward), 1897* (Nashville: Tennessee State Library and Archives) and *Marshall County, Tennessee Agricultural Census, 1857* (Nashville: Tennessee State Library and Archives). Both have been microfilmed and are available at the Tennessee State Library and Archives (TSLA) and FHL.

The only remaining schedule of the federal census for 1890 is the Union Veterans and Widows listing, a special state enumeration taken in 1891. It lists male citizens, twenty-one years and older. The complete listing has been microfilmed and is available at the TSLA. Many of these are included in Sue S. Reed's eight-volume compilation, *Enumeration of Male*

5

5

5TENNESSEE

Inhabitants of Twenty-one Years of Age and Upward, Citizens of Tennessee, January 1, 1891 ... (Houston: the author, 1989).

Background Sources

In the late 1880s, Goodspeed Publishing Company produced eighteen volumes of Tennessee county history, arranged regionally. Many volumes have been reprinted by Southern Historical Press, P.O. Box 738, Easley, SC 29640. Two are *The Goodspeed History of Tennessee: Dyer, Gibson, Lake, Obion and Weakley Counties* (1887; reprint, Easley, S.C.: Southern Historical Press, 1978) and *History of Tennessee: From the Earliest Time to the Present; Together with an Historical and a Biographical Sketch of Maury, Williamson, Rutherford, Wilson, Bedford & Marshall Counties ...* (1886; reprint, Easley, S.C.: Southern Historical Press, 1988).

Other volumes for the following counties are also available: Hamilton, Knox, and Shelby; Fayette and Hardeman; Lawrence, Wayne, Perry, Hickman, and Lewis; Madison; Sumner, Smith, Macon, and Trousdale; Montgomery, Robertson, Humphreys, Stewart, Dickson, Cheatham, and Houston; White, Warren, DeKalb, Coffee, and Cannon.

The WPA, under the New Deal, compiled, transcribed, and organized many valuable records in the state. A guide to these records is *The WPA Guide to Tennessee*, compiled and written by the Federal Writers' Project of the WPA for the state. It was first published in 1939 and was reprinted by the University of Tennessee Press in 1986. Almost every county government now has a website. Many include records or indexes to records held by various county agencies (see County Resources).

Other published sources include the following:

Caldwell, Mary French. *Tennessee, The Dangerous Example: Watauga to 1849.* Nashville: Aurora Publishers, 1974.

Carter, Clarence Edwin, comp. and ed. *The Territorial Papers of the United States: The Territory South of the River Ohio, 1790–1796.* Vol. 4. Washington, D.C.: Government Printing Office, 1953.

Corlew, R. E. *Tennessee: A Short History.* Knoxville: University of Tennessee Press, 1981. This is a condensed version of the standard, larger work, which follows.

Folmsbee, Stanley John, Robert E. Corlew, and Enoch L. Mitchell. *History of Tennessee.* 4 vols. New York: Lewis Historical Publishing Co., 1960. Volume 2 includes a good bibliography, and volumes 3 and 4 contain family history.

Miller, Charles A. *The Official and Political Manual of the State of Tennessee.* 1890. Reprint. Easley, S.C.: Southern Historical Press, 1974. This volume was compiled by the secretary of state in 1890. It includes a chronological table from 1540 through 1888, briefly mentioning factors in Tennessee's history, and the constitutions of 1790, 1834, and 1870.

Schweitzer, George K. *Tennessee Genealogical Research.* Knoxville, Tenn.: the author, 1983. This valuable volume provides historical information as well as listing the most helpful source material. It details library collections and county records with dates.

Smith, Sam B. *Tennessee History: A Bibliography.* Knoxville: University of Tennessee Press, 1974. A comprehensive compilation of works pertaining to the state's history.

Williams, Samuel Cole. *Beginnings of West Tennessee in the Land of the Chickasaws, 1541–1841.* 1930. Reprint. Nashville: Blue and Gray Press, 1971.

——. *History of the Lost State of Franklin.* Johnson City, Tenn.: Watauga Press, 1924. Includes early maps and well-documented history.

Maps

Understanding history and the use of maps and gazetteers are essential for tracing early Tennessee families. The Tennessee State Library and Archives has a fine collection of maps, including early surveyors' maps and civil district maps. Helpful publications include:

Coggins, Allen R. *Place Names of the Smokies* (Louisville, Tenn.: the author). Offers information for east Tennessee towns and sites.

Fullerton, Ralph O. *Place Names of Tennessee.* Bulletin No. 73. Nashville: State of Tennessee, Department of Conservation, Division of Geology, 1974. Arranged alphabetically by counties and, within the counties, alphabetically by place-name. Depicts county outline with geological survey overview.

McBride, Robert M., and Owen Meredith, eds. *Eastin Morris' Tennessee Gazetteer, 1834, Matthew Rhea's Map of the State of Tennessee, 1832.* Nashville: Gazetteer Press, 1971. A valuable guide to Tennessee's early history.

Tennessee maps can be purchased from the State of Tennessee, Department of Conservation, Division of Geology, Nashville, TN 37203. General Highway Maps for Tennessee counties are available from the Tennessee Department of Transportation, Bureau of Planning and Development, Planning Division, Nashville, TN 37219, and from respective counties.

Mountain Press produced a map in 1996 showing the various native tribes in Tennessee and early white settlements and forts. Entitled *Aboriginal Map of Tennessee,* it is available from that press located in Signal Mountain, Tennessee.

The McClung Collection at the East Tennessee Historical Center (see Archives, Libraries, and Societies) includes a set of maps for the state dating from 1777. This series, drawn by

5628

Rene Jordan, depicts the development of east Tennessee over twenty years of county organization and jurisdictional changes (see Manuscripts).

The TSLA holdings include historical and current maps, including the U.S. Geological Survey topographical maps (see page 5). It maintains maps of some Mountain District grants and Ocoee District plat books.

Land Records

State-Land State

Only a small portion of the land granted in Tennessee was free land, and that was granted to those who provided some form of service to North Carolina. Earliest land records, including early grants issued by North Carolina and Tennessee, are microfilmed with a card index available in the Public Services Section of the TSLA. Other holdings include land warrants, survey certificates, and records from county register of deeds offices.

The earliest land grants are now maintained and available on microfilm at the Tennessee State Library and Archives. Official copies of all Tennessee land grants are bound and filed in the archives. All known grants are indexed in the master index, which is included on these microfilm reels. These consist of the following:

- North Carolina grants in Tennessee, 1783–1800, including North Carolina state grants. These land grants are also in the North Carolina State Archives (see North Carolina).
- Tennessee general grants date from 1806 to 1927.
- Grants were issued by district land offices from 1807 through 1838: East Tennessee District grants, from 1807; Hiwassee District grants, from November 1820; Middle Tennessee District, from 1824; West Tennessee District, beginning in 1826; Mountain District, opening in 1828; Ocoee District, starting in 1838. A pamphlet entitled "Land Grants in the Tennessee State Library and Archives" explains the holdings and is available from the repository.

The North Carolina Military Reservation was established in 1783 in the northern section of what was then west Tennessee (present-day middle Tennessee). It encompassed all the area surrounding the loop of the Cumberland River north to the Kentucky/Tennessee state line. A Congressional Reservation was organized on 18 April 1806 in the southwest section of middle Tennessee. The Congressional Reservation's northern border was the North Carolina Military Reservation's southern boundary. The western border for both was that portion of the Tennessee River that flows north. Several published volumes relate to North Carolina Revolutionary service land grants in middle Tennessee.

Land grants for the area south of Walker's Line (in Tennessee) are microfilmed and available through the FHL. Originals are indexed and housed in the Kentucky Land Office, Frankfort. Williard Rouse Jillson's work (see Kentucky) covers these grants. A printed source to North Carolina land grants is Betty G. C. Cartwright and L. J. Gardiner, *North Carolina Land Grants in Tennessee, 1778–1791* (1958; rev. ed., Easley, S.C.: Southern Historical Press, 1981).

The process of obtaining a land grant took three steps. First, the entry includes the name, date, number of acres, and location—usually including the name of a watercourse—and entry number. If improvements had been made, a survey was the second step in the process, conducted within five years after the entry was made. The survey includes great detail about the location and boundaries of the property. It frequently includes a drawing of the plat. The survey usually includes the individual's name, number of acres, entry number, and date. A survey number is also assigned. If the entry was transferred to another individual before the survey was conducted, the entry book details that exchange. The survey includes the names of the "sworn chain carriers" (SCC). The survey could be transferred to another prior to the grant process. The third step was the grant. A person applied for the land grant based on the entry and survey; he also paid a small amount per acre. Each grant has its own number, which differs from the assigned numbers for entries and surveys. It is recorded at both the state and county levels. The TSLA maintains some county land entries and survey abstracts. These are on microfilm; some counties kept the original records.

Beginning with county organization, land records are available from the register of deeds at the respective county courthouse. Land and property records include transfer of real estate or personal property, mortgages, leases, surveys, and entries. The TSLA has microfilmed county deed records that can be ordered by providing name, date, county, and type of record in the request. Some land books contain transcripts of Board of Aid records (a public assistance program during the twentieth century), early wills, and other transactions.

Many publications for county land records are available. An example is Vicky L. Morrow Hutchings' work in abstracting deeds for several Tennessee counties, published by Mountain Press at Signal Mountain, Tennessee.

Probate Records

The county court maintains jurisdiction over probate cases. Wills, administrations, and all other records pertaining to probate are recorded in the respective county clerk's office. If the will or administration was contested, the records of these actions may be filed in the circuit court or chancery court. Shelby and Davidson counties have separate probate courts.

Many early court records and lists of wills were transcribed by the WPA. Copies of these are usually in the county clerk's office and in the Tennessee State Library and Archives. Most records have been microfilmed and are available through the FHL.

Projects to preserve and microfilm probate files, or loose papers, were started in Franklin County in 1979 and in Shelby County in 1981. Microfilm copies are at the TSLA. Other counties are following this fine example of record preservation.

County courts also hear guardianship and minor civil and criminal cases. Court records date from the organization of the county except in cases where records have been destroyed. See Annie W. Burns, *Major Index to Wills and Inventories of Tennessee at the D.A.R. Library*, 6 vols. (Washington, D.C.: n.p., 1962–65), which covers Bedford through Meigs counties alphabetically.

Court orders often are unindexed but contain references to action related to probate, such as dower, year's support, and appointments. Some early wills may be registered in other sources; for instance, in Scott County, Tennessee, wills were not recorded in will books until 1929; prior to that date, wills were recorded in the County Court Minute Books. A few early wills can also be found among deed records. In some counties, separate books were maintained for Estate Settlements and Orphans' Court actions and bonds.

Court Records

Court records for Tennessee can be difficult to use. Indexes are seldom, if ever, complete. Names may be indexed under various letters of the alphabet, but not necessarily by the individual's name. "A" for adoptions or "I" for "in regards to" are examples. Mortgaged estates may be indexed under the name of the bank holding the lien or mortgage, such as "B" for Bank of Commerce. Records may be indexed by other than surname, for example, "C" for commissioners/commission, "J" for jury, and "W" for will. In cases where property is sold by the sheriff, records can be found under "S" for sheriff, who was ordered by the court to sell the property to settle the estate or for back taxes. "S" for state may indicate records in which the state was a party, such as state land grants recorded in court records.

Tennessee court records can be complicated to use because there were various courts in which activities could be recorded. Some larger counties have superior courts of law and equity that hear minor civil and equity cases. Probate records normally were under the jurisdiction of the county court, but if the case was contested, then it could be filed in chancery or circuit court. Chancery courts have jurisdiction over property disputes, and circuit courts oversee criminal cases, divorces, and adoptions. Early courts included courts of common pleas and quarter sessions.

Original court records, including minute and order books, boxes of loose papers, case files, and folders, are maintained by the county. Each source should be thoroughly examined for pertinent entries. Many of these were microfilmed and are available at the TSLA and through the FHL. Marjorie Hood Fischer, comp., *Tennessee Tidbits, 1778–1914*, 4 vols. (vol. 1, Easley, S.C.: Southern Historical Press, 1986; vol. 2, Vista, Calif.: RAM Press, 1988), is a continuing series that contains abstracts of minutes from county courts, circuit courts, and chancery courts. Volume 1 includes abstracts from Blount, Davidson, Dickson, Fayette, Giles, Greene, Hardin, Haywood, Hickman, Humphreys, Lincoln, Putnam, Rutherford, Washington, and Williamson. Volume 2 covers Bedford, Claiborne, Dyer, Fentress, Jackson, Madison, McMinn, Obion, Roane, Robertson, Sevier, Stewart, Washington, and Wilson.

Under the WPA, approximately 1,000 typed volumes of county records were transcribed for most counties in Tennessee. These are microfilmed and available on interlibrary loan from the TSLA. There is a card index inventory to this compilation arranged by county. Court records included in this collection are wills; county, chancery, and circuit court minutes; and estate settlements. Because these WPA transcripts contain numerous transcription and typographical errors, the original records should always be reviewed.

In several counties, the records are dispersed in two or more facilities.

Before 1906 naturalization records are found at the county level. Some compilations are published, such as:

Smith, Mary Sue. *Davidson County, Tennessee Naturalization Records, 1803–1906.* Nashville: Byron Sistler and Associates, 1997.

Tax Records

The 1796 Constitution levied taxes on "every freeman of the age of twenty-one years and upward possessing a freehold in the county wherein he may vote, and being an inhabitant of this State, and every freeman being an inhabitant of any one county in the State six months immediately preceding the day of the election, shall be entitled to vote…"

Many early surviving tax records were published in an effort to replace the missing federal censuses (see Census Records). Original extant tax records are preserved in the respective county courthouse as well as in the TSLA, where a card index exists for tax records in its collection pre-dating 1835, arranged by county, date, and district. Some early original tax lists are available in the McClung Historical Collection at the Lawson McGhee Library (see Archives, Libraries, and Societies), including those for Washington County, 1778 and 1787; Greene County, 1783; Carter and Sullivan counties, 1796; and Grainger County, 1799.

Original tax schedules for most Tennessee counties for 1836 through 1839 are available at the TSLA. In addition, the Indiana State Library, the FHL, and the Allen County Public Library (see Indiana) have microfilmed copies of early Tennessee tax records.

The 1891 tax lists of male inhabitant voters in each county were recently found. Available on microfilm at the TSLA, these nine reels are arranged alphabetically within each district in each county. Tax records from trustees' office in counties are available on microfilm as well.

Cemetery Records

A large collection of transcripts of Tennessee cemetery records has been compiled by members of chapters of the DAR (see page 8). Other compilations of cemetery records are those in the Calvin M. McClung Historical Collection in the Lawson McGhee Library and in the Tennessee Miscellaneous Family and Cemetery Records collection available at the TSLA and through the FHL. The state library and archives has notebooks containing listings of cemetery records.

County genealogical and historical societies and local citizens have collected, compiled, and published numerous volumes of cemetery records. Other notable sources include:

Acklen, Jeannette T., et al. *Tennessee Records.* 2 vols. 1933. Reprint. Baltimore: Genealogical Publishing Co., 1974. Volume 1 contains tombstone inscriptions.

Hunkins, Lillian. *Tombstone Inscriptions and Marriages of Middle Tennessee.* Houston: the author, 1965.

Church Records

Although few histories for Tennessee churches have been published, there are church records for almost every county in the state. Baptist, Presbyterian, and Methodist were the principal religions of early settlers in the state, and documents from these groups make up the largest number of records available. Other representative religions include Lutheran, Church of Christ, Episcopal, Roman Catholic, and Jewish. Most early Tennessee churches only kept minutes and membership records.

Church records could, however, include records of baptism, marriage, burial, membership, or removal, but it is rare to find all or several of these categories maintained by one church. Some Presbyterian churches kept registers with some genealogical information in the session minutes or in a separate register. Each Baptist congregation is usually self-governing, and there is no set procedure for recording data for its members. Methodist ministers were charged with maintenance of permanent records of marriages, baptisms, and dismissals. The Episcopal and Roman Catholic Churches maintain registers that contain genealogical data for all members.

A published guide is Historical Records Survey, *Guide to Church Vital Statistics in Tennessee* (Nashville: War Services Section Service Division, WPA, 1943). Thirty-nine counties compose this historical records survey of Tennessee church records. This reference details records for certain churches, varying from 3 to 349 per county. Beverly West Hathaway, *Genealogy Research Sources in Tennessee* (West Jordan, Utah: Allstates Research Co., 1972), contains a denominationally arranged guide to church records in Tennessee. This data includes dates and places of numerous churches as well as names of organizers.

As with cemetery records, the DAR has collected church records for Tennessee, available at the DAR Library in Washington, D.C., and through the FHL. Many compilations of church records have been compiled and/or published for the state. The TSLA has records of over one hundred churches that pre-date 1900. Byron Sistler and Barbara Sistler compiled an index to these records in *Vital Statistics from 19th Century Tennessee Church Records,* 2 vols. (Nashville: Byron Sistler and Assoc., 1979), which contains births, baptisms, marriages, deaths, and burials from 104 churches and/or church associations in Tennessee.

Individual groups may have published records, for instance: Grime, H. J. *History of Middle Tennessee Baptists: With References to Salem, New Salem, Enon, and Wiseman Associations.* (1902, reprint. Nashville: Byron Sistler and Associates, 2000).

Microfilmed records and manuscripts of several churches in the state are described in the card catalog and published by the Tennessee State Library and Archives' *Guide to the Microfilm Holdings* (see Manuscripts).

The McClung Collection of the Lawson McGhee Library in Knoxville holds microfilm of Methodist, Baptist, and Presbyterian church records. The Burrow Library in Memphis also has Presbyterian church records. The Historical Commission of the Southern Baptist Convention, Disciples of Christ Historical Society, Catholic Diocese of Nashville Archives, and Archives of the Jewish Federation of Nashville and Middle Tennessee, all located in Nashville, hold representative collections. An example is by Steve Phillips, trans., *Buffalo/Grassy Valley Congregation of the Cumberland Presbyterian Church (Humphreys County, Tennessee): General History and Membership Roll, 1840–1884* (Centerville, Tenn.: the author, 2000).

Military Records

Numerous Internet sites are available for Tennessee soldiers (for all ethnic groups) from the Civil War through Vietnam. In addition to sources cited on page 9, another website is <www.tennessee-scv.org> for Confederate soldiers.

Tennessee began granting pensions for military service to resident Confederate veterans in 1891 and to veterans' widows in 1905. The TSLA has the applications and many additional records relating to military and naval service during the War between the States on microfilm. Indexes for Revolutionary War pensioners; muster rolls for soldiers of the War of 1812, Indian wars of 1818 and 1836, Mexican War, Civil War, and Spanish-American War; and service records for Tennesseans who served during the Mexican War and Civil War (both Confederate and Union) are among the archives' collections.

Considerable material exists in the manuscript collection at the state archives. Their Register Number 10 includes an index and list of some holdings for Confederate and Union soldiers. A valuable source is the Confederate and Union veterans' questionnaires sent by the Tennessee Historical Committee. Containing details about military and personal data, these have been published without index in five volumes in Gustavus W. Dyer and John Trotwood Moore, *Tennessee Civil War Questionnaires* (Easley, S.C.: Southern Historical Press, 1985). An unpublished index is available at the state archives.

A card index to the *Confederate Veteran* magazine and a card index to Lindsay, *Military Annals of Tennessee (Confederate),* are maintained in the state archives, as are National Archives indexes for service in the Revolutionary War, War of 1812, Mexican War, and hundreds of monographs concerning the War between the States.

Printed sources abound in the state for military service and pension records. A few are the following:

Allen, Penelope Johnson. *Tennessee Soldiers in the Revolution: A Roster of Soldiers during the Revolutionary War in the Counties of Washington and Sullivan, Taken from the Revolutionary Army Accounts of North Carolina.* 1935. Reprint. Baltimore: Genealogical Publishing Co., 1967.

Armstrong, Zella. *Some Tennessee Heroes of the Revolution.* 3 parts. Chattanooga, Tenn.: n.p., 1933–35.

———. *Twenty-four Hundred Tennessee Pensioners—Revolution, War of 1812.* Chattanooga, Tenn.: n.p., 1937.

———. *Tennessee Soldiers in the War of 1812: Regiments of Col. Allcorn and Col. Allison.* Chattanooga, Tenn.: Tennessee Society U.S. Daughters of 1812, 1947. Taken from the Tennessee State Archives photostats of original records in Washington, D.C.

Brewer, Alberta, and Carson Brewer. *Divided Loyalties: Fort Sanders and the Civil War in East Tennessee.* 1963; Reprint. Knoxville: East Tennessee Historical Society, 2002. This third edition includes new maps, illustrations, and appendixes. Details people who lived and fought and community struggles.

Lindsley, John B. *The Military Annals of Tennessee.* 1886. Reprint. Spartanburg, S.C.: Reprint Co., 1974.

McCown, Mary Hardin, and Inez E. Burns. *Soldiers of the War of 1812 Buried in Tennessee.* Johnson City, Tenn.: Tennessee Society U.S. Daughters of the War of 1812. 1959. Reprint. Johnson City, Tenn.: Overmountain Press, 1977. A standard published source on the subject of Tennessee soldiers.

Mills, Gary. *Civil War Claims in the South: An Index of Civil War Damage Claims Filed before the Southern Claims Commission, 1871–1880.* Laguna Hills, Calif.: Aegean Park Press, 1980.

Sistler, Byron, and Barbara Sistler. *1890 Civil War Veterans Census—Tennessee.* Nashville: Byron Sistler and Assoc., 1978.

Special Presidential Pardons for Confederate Soldiers: A Listing of Former Confederate Soldiers Requesting Pardon from President Andrew Johnson. 2 vols. Signal Mountain, Tenn.: Mountain Press, 1999.

Tennessee Civil War Centennial Commission. *Tennesseans in the Civil War, A Military History of Confederate and Union Units with Available Rosters of Personnel.* 2 vols. 1964–65. Reprint. Nashville: Civil War Centennial Commission, 1981–84.

Tennessee State Library and Archives. *Index to Tennessee Confederate Pension Applications.* Nashville: State Library, 1964.

Wright, Marcus J. *Tennessee in the War, 1861–65. Lists of Military Organizations and Officers from Tennessee in Both the Union and Confederate Armies...* New York, 1908.

Periodicals, Newspapers, and Manuscript Collections

Periodicals

Major periodicals for Tennessee that publish or published source material from most categories include these:

Ansearchin' News (1954-present). A publication of the Tennessee Genealogical Society (see Archives, Libraries, and Societies).

Bulletin (1972-present). A publication of the Watauga Association of Genealogists, P.O. Box 117, Johnson City, TN 37605 <www.rootsweb.com/~tnwag/index.htm>.

East Tennessee Roots. Published by Tennessee Valley Publications, Paula Gammell, ed., 1345 Oak Ridge Turnpike #318, Oak Ridge, TN 37830.

Family Findings (1969-present). A publication of the Midwest Tennessee Genealogical Society, P.O. Box 3343, Jackson, TN 38303.

Pellissippian (1980-present). A publication of the Pellissippian Genealogical and Historical Society, 118 S. Hicks, Clinton, TN 33716.

The River Counties Quarterly (1972-present). Published by Jill Garrett, 610 Terrace, Columbia, TN 38401.

Tennessee Ancestors (1985-present). This publication replaced *Echoes* (1955–84) for the East Tennessee Historical Society (see Archives, Libraries, and Societies).

The Tennessee Historical Quarterly (1942-present). Published by the Tennessee Historical Society.

Newspapers

The TSLA has a large collection of newspapers and an incomplete card index to marriage and death notices published in Nashville newspapers. The Draper Manuscript Collection, housed at the State Historical Society of Wisconsin, includes early Tennessee newspapers (see Wisconsin—Manuscripts). Published compilations of data extracted from Tennessee newspapers include Sherida K. Eddlemon, comp., *Genealogical Abstracts from Tennessee Newspapers, 1791–1808* (Bowie, Md.: Heritage Books, 1988); and Pollyanna Creekmore, *Tennessee Newspaper Extracts and Abstracts: Marriage, Death, and Other Items of Genealogical/Historical Interest.* 2 vols., distributed by East Tennessee Roots, 1345 Oak Ridge Turnpike, #318, Oak Ridge, TN 37830, which includes records from 1816 through 1839.

A guide to Tennessee newspaper collections is:

Tennessee Newspapers: A Cumulative List of Microfilmed Tennessee Newspapers in the Tennessee State Library, 1978 Progress Report. Nashville: Tennessee State Library and Archives, 1978.

Manuscripts

The largest collections of manuscripts pertaining to Tennessee are in the TSLA. Published guides to these collections are available, including *Guide to the Microfilmed Manuscript Holdings of the Tennessee State Library and Archives,* 3d ed. (Nashville: Tennessee State Library, 1983). Acklen's two-volume work (see Cemetery Records) includes references to manuscripts.

In addition to the card indexes cited under land and military records, an interesting index at the state archives is for Tennessee century farms (histories compiled of families whose farms have remained in use by the family for over 100 years).

During the 1930s the WPA collected a series of verbatim transcripts of the records of some Tennessee counties. This includes a considerable number of early county records. The only complete set of abstracts is in the TSLA. Nearly 1,500 volumes are available on ninety-three reels of microfilm.

Archives, Libraries, and Societies

Tennessee State Library and Archives (TSLA)
403 Seventh Ave., North
Nashville, TN 37243-0312
www.state.tn.us/sos/statelib/tslahome.htm

Its holdings include state agency records, executive branch papers, territorial records, records for courts of appeal and state supreme court. Many of the abundant holdings for this repository have already been discussed. As a bicentennial project, the library sponsored an extensive program of microfilming county records, concentrating on the records that were not in the WPA series. Inventories of most Tennessee county records, as well as microfilms of most early county records, are located here. The inventory has been printed and can be purchased from the repository for a nominal fee.

Vertical family files and the genealogical exchange card file are additional sources. The library and archives also maintains territorial and state records as well as county records, providing correspondence service except during the summer months; expect a response time of several weeks. Each request should include name, date of interest or a period of ten years or less, county, and type of record requested. Only one search per request. There is a minimum photocopy charge.

Tennessee Historical Society
War Memorial Building
300 Capital Blvd.
Nashville, TN 37243
www.tennesseehistory.org

Harriet C. Owsley, *Guide to the Processed Manuscripts of the Tennessee Historical Society* (Nashville: Tennessee State Library, 1963), describes and serves as a finding aid to the manuscript section of the archives for the holdings of the Tennessee Historical Society that were processed prior to 1963. The collection is arranged alphabetically, and the entire volume is indexed for ready reference. Information on later accessions to the collection can be found on the TSLA website <www.state. tn.us/sos/statelib/pubsvs/mssguide.htm>.

East Tennessee History Center
600 Market St.
Knoxville, TN 37901
Mailing Address: P.O. Box 1629
Knoxville, TN 37901-1629
www.east-tennessee-history.org

Three distinct entities operate out of this center: The McClung Historical Collection (which is the local history and genealogy department of the Lawson McGhee Library); the Knox County Archives; and the East Tennessee Historical Society.

The McClung Historical Collection <www.korrnet. org/knoxlib/mcclung/htm> contains over 500 manuscript collections, most pertaining to east Tennessee. These holdings must be accessed personally. The Calvin M. McClung Historical Collection maintains a genealogy file that consists of data submitted by various patrons. The staff will try to answer basic genealogical queries from indexed published sources. A self-addressed stamped envelope is necessary.

The collection contains a large body of published works, many of which are rare. Some may no longer be photocopied because of deterioration, but supervised access is allowed. A set of microfilmed records of the surviving service records of Tennessee soldiers for the War of 1812 is found in the collection, which has extensive holdings of the records of the Tennessee WPA and other assorted manuscripts.

The East Tennessee Historical Society <www.korrnet.org/knoxlib/ethc/htm> promotes the development of the library holdings. The East Tennessee Historical Society Museum celebrated a ten-year anniversary in 2003. The permanent and loan collections include decorative arts and furniture from East Tennessee, as well as military items, domestic arts and textiles, photographs, archives, personal items, artifacts, and more.

The Knox County Archives <www.knoxlib.org/departments/ethc/archives/index.php> provides access to the county government records dated from 1792 to present. Among its holdings are marriage records (1792–1974); tax records (1806–1974); court records (1792–1979); chancery court records (1832–); circuit court records (1810–); and Knoxville birth and death records (1881–1911).

Tennessee Genealogical Society
P.O. Box 111249
Memphis, TN 38111-1249
www.rootsweb.com/~tngs

Publishes *Ansearchin' News*. Publication includes materials for the entire state. Articles include abstracted wills, marriage records, probate records, church records, newspaper notices, and more.

University of Tennessee, Knoxville
Special Collections Library
Knoxville, TN 37902
www.lib.utk.edu/spcollect

University of Tennessee, Chattanooga
Lupton Library, Special Collections
615 McCallie Ave.
Chattanooga, TN 37403-2598
www.lib.utc.edu/services/special_collections/index.html

Vanderbilt University
Jean and Alexander Heard Library, Special Collections
419 21st Ave. South
Nashville, TN 37240-0007
www.library.vanderbilt.edu/speccol

Williamson County Public Library
611 W. Main St.
Franklin, TN 37064

This library holds the Whitley collection of marriage and county records from over twenty-two counties, collected by a local genealogist.

Chattanooga-Hamilton County
Bicentennial Library
1001 Broad St.
Chattanooga, TN 37402

University of Memphis
Mississippi Valley Historical Collection
John Willard Brister Library
Memphis, TN 38152
http://exlibris.memphis.edu

Memphis and Shelby County Public Library and Information Center
Genealogical Collection
3030 Poplar Ave.
Memphis, TN 38111-3527
www.memphislibrary.lib.tn.us/history/memphis2.htm

Its collection includes Memphis Archives, Civil War Collection, and Memphis and Shelby County Room among numerous others. The library can only offer limited service to out-of-county correspondents.

Shelby County Archives
150 Washington St.
Memphis, TN 38111
www.rootsweb.com/~tngs/shelbyco.htm

Metro Davidson County Archives
1113 Elm Hill Pike
Nashville, TN 37210

Holdings include chancery court records (1846–1961); circuit court records (1943–55); county clerk papers and records (1783–1971); register of deeds (1785–1951); and various other records. A detailed, itemized description is available upon request from the repository.

An online resource for locating all of Tennessee's active genealogical and historical societies, including website links, can be found through the Genealogical Forum on www.rootsweb.com at <www.genealogyforum.rootsweb.com/gfaol/resource/TN/GS.htm>.

Special Focus Categories

African American

The National Archives (see page 11) and the DAR Library (see page 13) have the original and microfilm slave-owner census schedules for the 1850 and 1860 U.S. censuses. The TSLA has some records of African Americans who served in the Civil War. In addition, websites specific to Tennessee include <www.tulane.edu/amistad> and <www.freedmensbureau.com/tennessee/index.htm>.

Native American

Most records for Native American families from Tennessee are located in Oklahoma. The main repository is the Bureau of Indian Affairs, Department of Interior, Muskogee, OK 74401, although another source is the Oklahoma Historical Society (see Oklahoma—Archive, Libraries, and Societies). A map showing the various native tribes in Tennessee and early white settlements and forts is entitled *Aboriginal Map of Tennessee* (see Maps).

Chickasaw ceded their territory in present-day west Tennessee on 19 October 1818. The Cherokee claimed land in the southeastern section of the state until December 1835, when their final exodus began. Even though all land had been ceded, some Native Americans remained in Tennessee after that date.

Data on Native American endeavors and actions was published in *The American State Papers, Class II, Indian Affairs*. This volume is in the TSLA in closed stacks. A collection of records pertaining to Cherokees (Register Number 11) and the Cherokee Census of 1835 is available to the public. J. J. Hill prepared an index to Emmett Stark's two volumes, *Cherokee Families*. Both are available in the Metro Davidson County Archives in Nashville (see Archives, Libraries, and Societies).

The Eastern Cherokee or Guion Miller Roll is available through the FHL. These records give the names of the Eastern Cherokees who applied for monetary awards in 1905 resulting from a lawsuit against the federal government that the Native Americans won. Approximately 90,000 names appear in these documents. An index is available. Additional sources include:

Armstrong, K. M., and Bob Curry. *Chickasaw Rolls: Annuity Rolls of 1857–1860 and the "1855" Chickasaw District Roll of 1856*. Bowie, Md.: Heritage Books, 1995.

Blankenship, Bob. *Guion Miller Roll "Plus" of Eastern Cherokee, East and West of the Mississippi, "1909."* 2 vols. Cherokee, N.C.: the author, 1992. Includes accepted and rejected lists with Miller and Dawes numbers, plus additional individual information.

Bowen, Jeff. *Cherokee Descendants: An Index to the Guion Miller Applications*. 4 vols. Signal Mountain, Tenn.: Mountain Press, 1996. Each volume is alphabetized separately; application number and family groups are shown.

Edgington, Billy Dubois, and Carol Anne Buswell, eds. *Vital Information from the Guion Miller Roll: Eastern Cherokee Court of Claims, 1906–1909*. Mill Creek, Wash.: Indian Scout Publications, 1998. Extracted from original applications. Gives names, including maiden name, application numbers, address, and some vital information. Includes Creeks and Choctaws, also available in a CD-ROM version.

Hoskins, Shirley. *Cherokee Blood (Tsa-la-gi-yi Gi-gv)*. Chattanooga, Tenn.: n.p., 1983. Gives application number, descendants, birthplace, and birth date.

Jordan, Jerry Wright. *Cherokee by Blood: Records of Eastern Cherokee Ancestry in the U.S. Court of Claims, 1906–1910*. 9 vols. Bowie, Md.: Heritage Books, 1987. Covers applications numbers 1 through 27,800. Each volume is indexed separately. See "Index to the Applications to the Guion Miller Roll of Eastern Cherokees," n.p.: USGen.Net, 2002. See <www.tngenweb.org/cherokee_by_blood/miller.htm>.

County Resources

Tennessee deeds are recorded at the register of deed's office. The county court maintains jurisdiction over the probate and court records, except for Shelby and Davidson counties, where the county court handles probates and circuit court handles civil matters. Dates given are for the first known records in each category at the county seat, but this is not meant to imply that all records are extant from that date. County formation is from information supplied by the TSLA. See the following for further assistance:

Richard Carlton Fulcher, comp., *Guide to County Records and Genealogical Resources in Tennessee*. Baltimore: Genealogical Publishing Co., 1987. This is a county-by-county guide to published WPA typescript and microfilmed records.

Historical Records Survey. *Survey of Tennessee County Court Records, Prior to 1860 in the Second, Third, and Fourth Districts*. Nashville: Historical Records Survey, 1943.

Genealogical facts about counties: <www.state.tn.us/sos/statelib/pubsvs/countypg.htm>

Tennessee County Clerk addresses: <www.tennessee.gov/safety/clerks.html>

Tennessee county records losses: <www.state.tn.us/sos/statelib/pubsvs/lost.htm>

Data for each type of county records noted in the county section is based on microfilmed county records in the online FHL catalog at <www.familysearch.org>. This information includes only dates for county-generated records and the Works Projects Administration's Historical Records Survey. Dates of published or compiled records were not used. For the county clerk's addresses, two sources were used: <www.tennessee.gov/safety/clerks.htm> and <www.genealogy.com/00000271.html>.

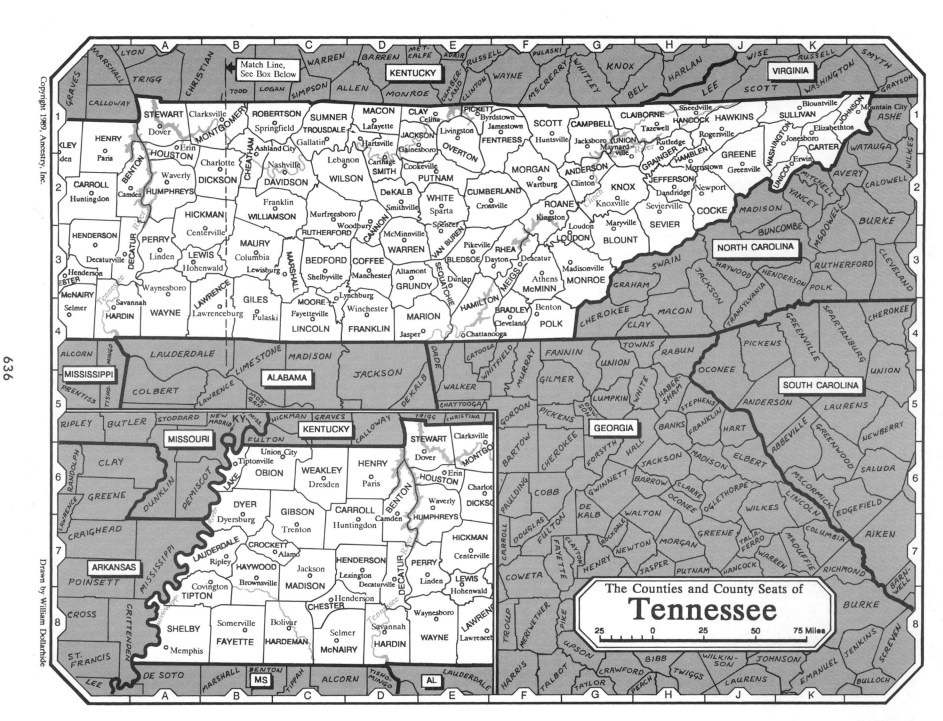

The Counties and County Seats of
Tennessee

25   0   25   50   75 Miles

TENNESSEE

Map	County Address	Date Formed Parent County/ies	Birth Marriage Death	Land Probate Court
G2	Anderson 101 N. Main St. Clinton 37716	1801 Knox/Grainger	1881 1838 1881	1802 1827 1801
C3	Bedford 104 N. Side Sq. Shelbyville 37160	1807 Rutherford/Indian lands	1908 1861 1908	1808 1861 1830
D7,A2	Benton 1 E. Court Sq. Camden 38320	1835 Humphreys/Henry	1881 1838 1881	1820 1836 1836
E3	Bledsoe 116 Main St./P.O. Box 212 Pikeville 37367-0212	1807 Roane/Indian lands	1908 1908 1908	1808 1884 1836
G3	Blount 345 Court St. Maryville 37804	1795 Knox	1881 1795 1881	1794 1795 1795
F4	Bradley 155 N. Ocoee St. P.O. Box 46 Cleveland 37364-0046	1835 Cherokee land	1908 1864 1908	1839 1838 1838
G1	Campbell 195 Kentucky St./P.O. Box 13 Jacksboro 37757-0013	1806 Anderson/Claiborne	1914 1838 1914	1806 1806 1813
D3	Cannon Public Sq. Woodbury 37190	1836 Rutherford/Smith/Warren/ Coffee	1881 1838 1881	1836 1836 1836
A2, D7	Carroll 625 High St./P.O. Box 110 Huntingdon 38344-0110	1821 Chickasaw lands	1908 1838 1908	1820 1822 1821
K1	Carter 801 E. Elk Ave. Elizabethton 37643	1796 Washington	1881 1790 1881	1795 1794 1804
B2	Cheatham 100 Public Sq. Ashland City 37015-1711	1856 Davidson/Dickson/ Montgomery/Robertson	1881 1856 1881	1856 1856 1856
C8	Chester 133 E. Main/P.O. Box 205 Henderson 38340-0205	1879 Hardman/Madison/ Henderson/McNairy	1908 1891 1908	1891 1891 1882
H1	Claiborne 1740 Main St./P.O. Box 34 Tazewell 37879-0034	1801 Grainger/Hawkins	1908 1838 1908	1801 1801 1801
D1	Clay 100 Courthouse Sq./P.O. Box 218 Celina 38551-0218	1870 Jackson/Overton	1908 1871 1908	1871 1871 1871
J2	Cocke 111 Court Ave. Newport 37821	1797 Jefferson	1908 1877 1908	1856 1876 1877
D3	Coffee 300 Hillsboro Blvd. Manchester 37355	1836 Franklin/Warren/Bedford	1881 1853 1881	1836 1833 1836
B7	Crockett 1 S. Bells St. Alamo 30001	1871 Madison/Dyer/ Gibson/Haywood	1909 1873 1909	1870 1873 1871
F2	Cumberland 2 N. Main St. Crossville 38555-9428	1856 Bledsoe/Morgan/White/ Rhea/Fentress/Putnam/Roane	1914 1905 1914	1854 1904 1897
C2	Davidson 700 Seventh Ave. South Nashville 37203	1783 Indian lands	1881 1789 1881	1784 1784 1783
A3, D8	Decatur P.O. Box 488 Decaturville 38329-0488	1845 Perry	1881 1869 1908	1846 1869 1860
D2	DeKalb 1 Public Sq. Smithville 37166	1837 Warren/White/ Jackson/Smith	1914 1848 1914	1838 1838 1837
D6	Dickson 4 Court Sq./P.O. Box 220 Charlotte 37036-0220	1803 Montgomery/Robertson	1859 1817 1908	1804 1800 1804
B6	Dyer 115 Market St./P.O. Box 1360 Dyersburg 38025-1360	1823 Chickasaw lands	1908 1860 1881	1820 1853 1848
B8	Fayette 1 Court Sq./P.O. Box 218 Somerville 38068-0218	1824 Shelby/Hardeman	1914 1838 1914	1821 1836 1824
F1	Fentress 101 Main St./P.O. Box 823 Jamestown 38556-0823	1823 Morgan/Overton/White	1914 1905 1914	1820 1905 1842
D4	Franklin 1 S. Jefferson St. Winchester 37398	1807 Bedford/Warren	1881 1838 1881	1807 1808 1832
C7	Gibson 1 Court Sq./P.O. Box 228 Trenton 38382-0228	1823 Chickasaw lands	1881 1824 1909	1819 1824 1824
B4	Giles 1 Public Sq./P.O. Box 678 Pulaski 38478-0678	1809 Maury	1908 1865 1908	1790 1810 1810
H2	Grainger West Court St., Box 116 Rutledge 37861-0116	1796 Hawkins/Knox	1908 1796 1908	1796 1796 1796
J2	Greene 101 S. Main St. Greeneville 37743	1783 Washington, N.C.	1881 1780 1881	1785 1802 1783
D3	Grundy Hwy 56/P.O. Box 215 Altamont 37301-0215	1844 Franklin/Warren/Coffee/ Marion	1908 1850 1908	1852 1838 1844
H2	Hamblen 511 W. Second N St. Morristown 37814-3964	1870 Grainger/Greene/Jefferson/ Hawkins	1909 1863 1909	1870 1870 1870

TENNESSEE

Map	County Address	Date Formed Parent County/ies	Birth Marriage Death	Land Probate Court
E4	Hamilton, 625 Georgia Ave., P.O. Box 24868, Chattanooga 37422	1819 Cherokee lands	1881 1857 1881	1796 1862 1860
H1	Hancock, Main St./P.O. Box 347, Sneedville 37869-0347	1844 Claiborne/Hawkins	1914 1930 1914	1879 1929 1879
C8	Hardeman, 100 N. Main St., Bolivar 38008-2322	1823 Chickasaw lands	1881 1823 1881	1820 1823 1823
A4, D8	Hardin, 601 Main St., Savannah 38372	1819 Chickasaw lands	1881 1863 1881	1820 1825 1820
J1	Hawkins, 150 Washington St., P.O. Box 790, Rogersville 37857-0790	1785 (as Spencer; renamed, 1786) Sullivan	1914 1820 1914	1787 1786 1810
B8	Haywood, 1 N. Washington St., Brownsville 38012-2557	1823 Chickasaw lands	1881 1859 1908	1793 1826 1808
A3, D7	Henderson, 17 Monroe St./P.O. Box 40, Lexington 38351-0040	1821 Chickasaw lands	1908 1893 1908	1856 1861 1850
A1, D6	Henry, 101 W. Washington St., P.O. Box 24, Paris 38242-0024	1821 Chickasaw lands	1881 1835 1881	1820 1822 1824
A3, E7	Hickman, 101 S. Public Sq., Centerville 37033	1807 Dickson	1914 1868 1914	1808 1846 1844
E6	Houston, 100 Main St./P.O. Box 388, Erin 37061-0388	1871 Dickson/Stewart/Humphreys/Montgomery	1881 1871 1881	1871 1869 1871
A2, E7	Humphreys, 102 Thompson St., Waverly 37185	1809 Stewart	1908 1864 1908	1810 1837 1842
D1	Jackson, 101 E. Hull Ave./P.O. Box 346, Gainesboro 38562-0345	1801 Smith/Indian lands	1881 1870 1881	1817 1839 1839
	James	1871 (abolished; became part of Hamilton, 1919) Hamilton/Bradley		
H2	Jefferson, 204 W. Main St./P.O. Box 710, Dandridge 37725-0710	1792 Greene/Hawkins	1908 1792 1908	1792 1792 1792
K1	Johnson, 222 W. Main St., Mountain City 37683-1612	1836 Carter	1908 1838 1908	1836 1800 1836
G2	Knox, 300 Main St./P.O. Box 1566, Knoxville 37901-1566	1792 Greene/Hawkins	1881 1792 1881	1791 1792 1792
B6	Lake, 116 S. Court St., Tiptonville 38079	1870 Obion	1914 1883 1914	1870 1871 1870
B7	Lauderdale, 100 Court Sq., Ripley 38063	1835 Dyer/Tipton/Haywood	1881 1838 1881	1822 1836 1836
B4, E8	Lawrence, 240 W. Gaines/P.O. Box NBU2, Lawrenceburg 38464	1817 Hickman/Indian lands/Maury	1908 1818 1908	1819 1829 1818
E8	Lewis, 110 N. Park St., Hohenwald 38462	1843 Hickman/Maury/Wayne/Lawrence	1908 1847 1908	1827 1846 1844
C4	Lincoln, 112 Main Ave. South, Fayetteville 37334	1809 Bedford	1881 1834 1881	1810 1809 1810
G3	Loudon, 101 Mulberry St., Loudon 37774	1870 Blount/Monroe/Roane/McMinn	1908 1870 1908	1870 1870 1870
D1	Macon, 104 County Courthouse Public Sq., Lafayette 37083	1842 Smith/Sumner	1908 1901 1925	1901 1901 1843
C8	Madison, 100 E. Main, Jackson 38301	1821 Chickasaw lands	1925 1838 1925	1821 1822 1821
D4	Marion, 1 Courthouse Sq./P.O. Box 789, Jasper 37347-0789	1817 Cherokee lands	1908 1881 1908	1819 1875 1842
C3	Marshall, 207 Marshall Courthouse, Lewisburg 37091	1836 Bedford/Lincoln/Maury	1914 1836 1914	1836 1865 1836
B3	Maury, Public Sq./P.O. Box 769, Columbia 38401-0769	1807 Williamson/Indian lands	1908 1807 1908	1808 1806 1807
F3	McMinn, 6 W. Madison Ave., Athens 37303	1819 Cherokee lands	1908 1838 1908	1820 1819 1819
C8	McNairy, Court Ave., Selmer 38375	1823 Hardin	1881 1861 1925	1823 1857 1855
F3	Meigs, Main St., P.O. Box 218, Decatur 37322-0218	1836 Rhea/Cherokee lands	1909 1838 1909	1835 1836 1836
G3	Monroe, 103 College St., Madisonville 37354	1819 Cherokee lands	1881 1838 1881	1820 1825 1820

County seat was Ooltewah. Records in Chattanooga, Hamilton County.

Map	County Address	Date Formed Parent County/ies	Birth Marriage Death	Land Probate Court
B1, F6	Montgomery 350 Pageant Lane, Ste. 502 Clarksville 37041	1796 Tennessee	1908 1839 1981	1786 1795 1805
C4	Moore 196 Main St./P.O. Box 206 Lynchburg 37352-0206	1871 Bedford/Franklin/ Coffee/Lincoln	1881 1872 1908	1872 1871 1872
F2	Morgan 415 S. Kinston St./P.O. Box 301 Wartburg 37887-0301	1817 Roane/Anderson	1908 1862 1908	1818 1866 1824
B6	Obion 2 Bill Bennett Circle Union City 38261	1823 Chickasaw lands	1881 1824 1881	1820 1833 1824
E1	Overton 317 E. University St. Livingston 38570	1806 Jackson/Indian lands	1914 1867 1914	1792 1870 1815
A3, E7	Perry Main St./P.O. Box 16 Linden 37096-0016	1819/1821 Hickman/Humphreys	1908 1865 1881	1820 1863 1826
E1	Pickett 1 Courthouse Sq./P.O. Box 5 Byrdstown 38549-0005	1879 Fentress/Overton	1934 1934 1934	1934 1934 1934
F4	Polk Hwy 411/P.O. Box 158 Benton 37307-0158	1839 Bradley/McMinn	1908 1894 1908	1894 1873 1840
E2	Putnam 29 N. Washington Ave. Cookeville 38501	1854 White/Jackson/Overton/ Smith/DeKalb	1908 1878 1879	1825 1874 1842
F3	Rhea 1475 Market St. Dayton 37321	1807 Roane	1908 1808 1908	1808 1825 1815
F2	Roane 200 E. Race St./P.O. Box 546 Kingston 37763-0546	1801 Knox/Indian lands	1881 1801 1881	1801 1802 1801
B1	Robertson 101 5th Ave. W. Springfield 37172	1796 Tennessee/Sumner	1908 1829 1908	1796 1796 1796
C2	Rutherford 26 N. Public Sq. Murfreesboro 37130	1803 Davidson/Williamson/Wilson	1881 1804 1881	1804 1804 1804
F1	Scott P.O. Box 69 Huntsville 37756-0069 *Courthouse fire 1946.*	1849 Fentress/Morgan/ Anderson/Campbell	——— 1854 1901	1850 1892 1850
E3	Sequatchie 308 E. Cherry St., Box 248 Dunlap 37327	1857 Hamilton/Marion/Warren	1881 1858 1881	1858 1858 1858
H3	Sevier 125 Court Ave. East Sevierville 37862	1794 Jefferson	1914 1856 1881	1849 1824 1850
A8	Shelby 150 Washington Ave. Memphis 38103	1819 Indian lands, Hardin	1881 1912 1940	1821 1874 1820

Some Shelby County Probate Court records are available at the Shelby County Public Archives—see Archives, Libraries, and Societies. This includes probate minute books, 1867–1900 and loose papers and wills, 1820–1900 for Shelby County. The Probate Court Clerk's Office has wills, 1900–present; minute books, 1900–present; and loose papers, 1900–present.

Map	County Address	Date Formed Parent County/ies	Birth Marriage Death	Land Probate Court
D2	Smith 211 Main St. N. Carthage 37030	1799 Sumner/Indian lands	1881 1838 1881	1801 1805 1799
	Spencer	1785 (renamed Hawkins, 1786) Sullivan		
A1, E6	Stewart 225 Donelson Pkwy, Box 67 Dover 37058-0067	1803 Montgomery	1881 1838 1881	1789 1812 1804
K1	Sullivan 3411 Hwy 126/P.O. Box 530 Blountville 37617-0530	1779 Washington Dist., Va.	1881 1861 1881	1775 1830 1861
C1	Sumner 355 N. Belvedere Gallatin 37066	1786 Davidson	1881 1787 1881	1787 1789 1787
	Tennessee	1788 (abolished; divided into Montgomery and Robertson) Davidson		

County seat was Clarkesville. Records in Robertson County.

Map	County Address	Date Formed Parent County/ies	Birth Marriage Death	Land Probate Court
A8	Tipton 220 Hwy 51 N./P.O. Box 528 Covington 38019-0528	1823 Chickasaw lands	1881 1840 1881	1820 1824 1823
D1	Trousdale 200 E. Main St./P.O. Box 69 Hartsville 37074-0069	1870 Macon/Smith/Wilson/ Sumner	1908 1905 1909	1905 1905 1903
K2	Unicoi 100 Main St./P.O. Box 340 Erwin 37650-0340	1875 Carter/Washington	1908 1876 1908	1876 1876 1875
G2	Union 901 Main St./P.O. Box 395 Maynardville 37807-0395	1850 Anderson/Campbell/Knox/ Claiborne/Grainger	1881 1864 1881	1856 1856 1854
E3	Van Buren Smith St./P.O. Box 126 Spencer 38585-0126	1840 Warren/White/Bledsoe	1908 1840 1908	1840 1840 1840
D3	Warren 201 Locust St./P.O. Box 231 McMinnville 37110-0231	1807 White/Jackson/Smith	1881 1852 1881	1808 1827 1842
K1	Washington 100 Main St./P.O. Box 219 Jonesboro 37659-0219	1777 Act of North Carolina Washington Dist.	1908 1787 1908	1778 1778 1778

TENNESSEE

Map	County Address	Date Formed Parent County/ies	Birth Marriage Death	Land Probate Court
A4, E8	**Wayne** 200 Court Sq./P.O. Box 185 Waynesboro 38485-0185	1817 Hickman/Humphreys	1881 1857 1881	1820 1820 1837

An earlier, but separate, "Wayne County" is included in today's Carter County and part of Johnson County. It was established in 1785 under the state of Franklin but was abolished in 1788.

Map	County Address	Date Formed Parent County/ies	Birth Marriage Death	Land Probate Court
C6	**Weakley** P.O. Box 587 Dresden 38225-0587	1823 Chickasaw lands	1908 1843 1908	1826 1826 1794
E2	**White** 1 E. Bockman Way Sparta 38583	1806 Jackson/Smith	1881 1838 1881	1801 1810 1806

Map	County Address	Date Formed Parent County/ies	Birth Marriage Death	Land Probate Court
B2	**Williamson** 1320 W. Main St./P.O. Box 624 Franklin 37065-0624	1799 Davidson	1881 1800 1881	1799 1800 1800
C2	**Wilson** 228 E. Main St., Box 950 Lebanon 37088-0950	1799 Sumner	1881 1802 1908	1789 1802* 1802

*Wills, 1802.

Texas

WENDY BEBOUT ELLIOTT, Ph.D., FUGA

Native American tribes resided in the area when present-day Texas was settled in 1682 by the Spanish at Isleta, near today's El Paso. Between 1685 and 1700, Franciscan missions and Spanish military outposts (presidios) were established in east Texas at Nacogdoches, Goliad, and San Antonio. In 1718 San Antonio, with its military post and mission, became the administrative headquarters of the region under Spanish jurisdiction. The province of Texas was established in 1727 with vaguely defined boundaries. Groups of colonists supplemented the population of soldiers and priests, particularly in San Antonio and in smaller numbers elsewhere. Early municipalities were organized in Texas under the Spanish and Mexican governments. Between 1731 and 1836 twenty-nine political subdivisions were founded completely or partially in Texas.

As a result of the Louisiana Purchase in 1803, a boundary dispute erupted with Spain over the Louisiana-Texas border. Spain claimed land east to the Red River, while the United States contended its territory expanded west to the Sabine River. A region of neutral ground created in 1806 established a temporary compromise, but because neither country had jurisdiction over this area, it became a haven for outlaws. Beginning about 1809, Quapaw, Osage, and Oto tribes relocated into the region.

Louisiana Catholics were encouraged to emigrate and settle in Texas, and Spanish officials loosened traditional barriers against alien immigration. The Sabine River was accepted as the western boundary of Louisiana in 1819, although border problems continued. The next year Arkansas Territory's Miller County was organized, with land partially inside the Texas border.

Mexico gained its independence from Spain in 1821 and claimed the area of today's Texas. The Mexican government, while insisting that only immigrants of the Roman Catholic faith were desired, did permit American settlers to enter under the auspices of certain grantees (*impresarios*).

When Stephen F. Austin, the first American impresario, inherited his father's grant, he established a colony in Texas under the auspices of the new nation of Mexico. His colonists were among the first Anglo-Americans to settle in present-day Texas. Boundaries remained undefined, and colonists spread from the coast to the old San Antonio road and between the Lavaca and San Jacinto rivers. Austin's colony stimulated others to follow.

Contracts from the Mexican government continued to be issued for settlement through 1832. Large groups from Tennessee and Arkansas migrated into Texas beginning in the 1820s. Others from Pennsylvania, Ohio, and Kentucky followed. The municipality of Refugio was created in 1825, followed by Austin in 1827, Goliad about 1828, and Nacogdoches and Liberty in 1831. Duplication of granted land and undefined boundaries complicated land titles. The number of early municipalities, organized in the eighteenth century under Spanish and Mexican governments, increased in the 1830s. A comparison of names of early and later municipalities reflects the great influx of Americans into present-day Texas during this period.

Families from South Carolina and Georgia migrated overland through Alabama and Mississippi to Texas; others left Alabama and Mississippi for Texas. Some traveled by ship from the port at New Orleans to Galveston and Indianola.

When General Antonio Lopez de Santa Anna led his Mexican troops against American forces, the Battle of the Alamo became the most famous of the battles that took place among the ensuing military conflict. Four days before the decisive victory at San Jacinto, the Republic of Texas was established on 2 March 1836.

By 1836 American citizens residing in the state actively promoted statehood for Texas. To encourage immigration the Republic of Texas offered colonization contracts beginning in 1841. After some boundaries were defined and settled, Congress accepted the Republic of Texas into the Union in 1845 as the twenty-eighth state.

Texas's entry into the union incited the Mexicans and led to the Mexican War, 1846–48, which was fought over and on Texas soil. The Mexican government hoped to retain Texas and other territory in the southwest including California, land both countries claimed. The United States was victorious and made good its claims to the southwest.

To make the area suitable for extending settlements, a number of fortifications were built by the federal government to protect settlers from attacks by Native Americans. Conflict with native groups continued intermittently through the early decades of statehood.

Prior to 1850, over 30,000 Germans had settled in Texas. Sympathies were divided among Texans over the slavery and states' rights issues that preceded the hostilities between the North and the South. Over the objections of Governor Samuel Houston and the German settlers, Texas seceded from the Union and joined the Confederacy, supplying many soldiers to the Confederate army. Texas was readmitted in 1866.

Expansion of cotton and wheat production, livestock, and oil provided great stimuli for growth. In addition to the Germans, several other groups of European immigrants settled in Texas, including Czechs, Poles, Swedes, Norwegians, and Irish. During the Depression, the Post Cereal Company offered inexpensive land in west Texas for those who would contract to grow grain for the company's products. The state has continued to be a destination point for its Mexican neighbors seeking employment in farm and industry.

Vital Records

Between 1873 and 1876, some births were recorded by county district clerks. Many of these were included in *Early Texas Birth Records, 1838–1878* (reprint. Easley, S.C.: Southern Historical Press, 1982) by Alice Duggan Gracy, Jane Duggan Sumner, and Emma Gene S. Gentry. Beginning in 1903 county clerks began to register births and deaths, although compliance was not universal at first. Large cities with vital records offices maintained their own series of birth and death records. Justices of the peace also recorded births.

Mandatory recording of births and deaths began in 1903. Copies of records registered in the counties are maintained at Texas Department of Vital Records, 1100 W. 49th St., Austin, TX (mailing address: P.O. Box 12040, Austin, TX 78711-2040) <www.tdh.state.tx.us/bvs>. Statewide indexes were microfilmed by the Texas State Library (see Archives, Libraries, and Societies), and are available at many genealogical libraries. The birth index (1903–76) is alphabetized by year. The death index is alphabetical within broader periods of time (1903–40, 1940–45, 1946–55, then annually for 1956–73). The Genealogy Section of the Texas State Library provides limited correspondence service by checking indexes for a particular name for a small fee. If a birth or death record is not found at the state level, it is prudent to check the proper municipal or county office. Online indexes for Texas death records (1964–98) can be found at <www.ancestry.com>.

Probated or delayed birth registrations were sometimes submitted to the respective county court for probate matters. These were then forwarded to the State Bureau of Vital Statistics. Microfilm indexes to delayed birth records may have included Texas residents born elsewhere, many of whom were seeking Social Security registration. The bureau ended delayed birth registration in 1959.

Marriage records prior to 1836, if extant, may be in custody of the Roman Catholic Church. Beginning with the date of organization most counties maintain marriage records. These are presently in the jurisdiction of the respective county clerk where the license was issued. Statewide recording of marriages began in January 1966, but certified copies of records are not available through the state office. Marriage records for African Americans were frequently recorded in separate volumes.

Members of the Daughters of the American Revolution (DAR) have compiled many marriage records for Texas. These are available in the DAR Library in Washington, D.C., and on microfilm through the Family History Library (FHL) in Salt Lake City.

Consult the County Resource section in this chapter and the *Guide to Public Vital Statistics Records in Texas* (n.p.: Historical Records Survey, 1941) to determine availability of vital records in municipal and county offices.

Divorce records have been maintained statewide by the Bureau of Vital Statistics since January 1968, but certified copies are not available from this facility. Divorce records are kept under the jurisdiction of the respective clerk of the district court. During the first years of the Republic of Texas, divorces were granted by special acts of Congress, but in 1841 district courts took over this responsibility, with some exceptions. After statehood, district courts had full jurisdiction over divorces.

A sampling of published works containing Texas vital records include:

Dodd, Jordan R. *Texas Marriages: Early to 1850, a Research Tool.* Bountiful, Utah: Precision Indexing, 1990.

Grammer, Norma Rutledge. *Marriage Records of Early Texas, 1824–46.* Fort Worth: Fort Worth Genealogical Society, 1971.

Smith, Bennett L. *Marriage by Bond in Colonial Texas.* Fort Worth: by author, 1972.

Swenson, Helen Smothers. *8800 Texas Marriages, 1824–1850.* Round Rock, Tex.: n.p., 1981.

White, Gifford. *1830 Citizens of Texas: A Genealogy of Anglo-American and Mexican Citizens Taken from Census and Other Records.* Austin, Tex.: Eakin Press, 1999. Includes registers of birth.

Census Records

Federal

Population Schedules
- Indexed—1850, 1860, 1870, 1880, 1890 (partial), 1900, 1910, 1920, 1930
- Soundex—1880, 1900, 1910, 1920

Industry and Agriculture Schedules
- 1850, 1860, 1870, 1880

Mortality Schedules
- 1850, 1860, 1870, 1880

Slave Schedules
- 1850, 1860

Union Veterans Schedules
- 1890

The Texas State Library holds microfilm editions of all extant Texas federal censuses. The 1830 territorial census of Miller County, Arkansas, enumerates an area that is in today's Texas boundaries. Although the 1850, 1860, and part of the 1870 mortality schedules have been published, original mortality schedules are at the Texas State Library and on microfilm. In addition to AISI indexes and online access to census records (see page 3), other published indexes of federal population schedules are available.

Vera Carpenter's *The State of Texas Federal Population Schedules, Seventh Census of the United States, 1850.* 5 vols. (Huntsville, Ark.: Century Enterprises, 1969) is available in a number of large research facilities.

The remaining 1890 population schedules that exist for Texas include Ellis County (Justice Precinct 6, Mountain Peak, and Ovilla Precinct); Hood County (Precinct 5); Rusk County (No. 6 and Justice Precinct No. 7); Trinity County (town of Trinity and Justice Precinct 2); and Kaufman County (Kaufman). Although Greer County in present-day Oklahoma functioned as part of Texas between 1886 and 1896, the 1890 census for this county was enumerated under Oklahoma Territory.

Colonial and Republic

Various censuses were enumerated under Spanish and Mexican governments at times, but these seldom covered all settlements in Texas for any given year. Mission rolls, reports, and statistical reviews were recorded between 1783 and 1796. Some rancho censuses are extant for the years between 1797 and 1826. An 1828 *Padron* lists home, age, occupation, marital status, and religion, as well as family members. This is available at the Texas State Library as part of the records group contained in the Nacogdoches Archives section for 1753 to 1836 on microfilm. Translated mission censuses have been microfilmed and can be reviewed at the Institute of Texas Cultures, University of Texas, San Antonio.

No censuses were taken under the Republic of Texas (1836–45), although tax records provide a substitute census for 1840. See printed sources that follow and Tax Records (below) for examples of such tax records.

Some published census records for this period include:

Connor, Seymour V. *Kentucky Colonization in Texas.* Baltimore: Genealogical Publishing Co., 1983. Includes separate lists of colonists noting name, age, occupation, birthplace, number of children, removal, and county and date of settlement. The first list enumerates those who received land. Others list "colonists who moved away before receiving land," "persons issued county court certificates...probable colonists," "persons issued county court certificates... doubtful colonists," and "persons issued county court certificates who did not receive land." Most dates are between 1844 and 1848.

Mullins, Marion Day. *The First Census of Texas, 1829–1836: To Which Are Added Texas Citizenship Lists, 1821–1845 and Other Early Records of the Republic of Texas.* Washington, D.C.: National Genealogical Society, 1962. Special publication number 22. Lists Texans from lists of citizens and other early records.

Osburn, Mary McMillian, ed. *The Atascosito Census of 1826.* 1963. Reprint from *Texana* 1 (Fall 1963): 299-321. N.p., n.d. A publication for the Liberty County Historical Survey Committee.

Residents of Texas, 1702–1836. 3 vols. San Antonio: University of Texas, Institute of Texas Cultures, 1984.

White, Gifford Elmore, comp. *1830 Citizens of Texas.* Austin, Tex.: Eakin Press, 1983. Taken from records in the U.S. General Land Office (GLO).

——. *The 1840 Census of the Republic of Texas.* Foreword by James M. Day. Austin, Tex.: Pemberton Press, 1966.

——. *1840 Citizens of Texas.* 3 vols. Nacogdoches, Tex.: Ericson Books, 1983–1988.

State

No state censuses were taken for Texas although some counties enumerated children ages six to sixteen years in schools between 1854 and 1855. These usually contain names of parents or guardians and students' names. The archives division of the Texas State Library houses the originals, although name indexes are kept in its Search Room. County lists for those counties beginning with letters "A" through "D" are missing. Mail or phone requests may be made for index entries. Microfilm copies of some are in the FHL. See also Gifford E. White, *Texas Scholastics, 1854–55: Copied from the Originals in the Archives, Texas State Library* (Nacogdoches, Tex.: Ericson Press, 1981).

Background Sources

Regional as well as county histories are available for Texas. John Holmes Jenkins, *Cracker Barrel Chronicles: A Bibliography of Texas Town and County Histories* (Austin, Tex.: Pemberton Press, 1965), is a good bibliographic source for some. Two publications by Tom Munnerlyn add two essential bibliographic sources: *Texas Local History: A Source Book for Available Town and County Local Histories, Local Memoirs and Genealogical Records* (Austin, Tex.: Eakin Press, 1983); and *Texas Counties, a Catalog of In-print and Out-of-print Books, Pamphlets, Maps, Memoirs, etc. Relating to Texas Towns and Counties* (Austin, Tex.: State House Books, 1985).

Biographical articles in published local histories are indexed in the six volumes of *Biographical Gazetteer of Texas: Publication of the Biographical Sketch File of the Texas Collection at Baylor University, an Ongoing Project Supervised by Virginia and William L. Ming* (Austin, Tex.: Morrison Books, 1985–87) with 70,000 entries.

An important collection of manuscript and printed materials relating to Texas is available in the Barker Texas History Center at the University of Texas. A guide, published by the center, *Catalog of the Texas Collection in the Barker Texas History Center of the University of Texas at Austin.* 14 vols. (Boston: G. K. Hall, 1979) describes the collection.

Taylor Publishing Company in Dallas published many county and local histories for Texas. Historical and genealogical societies publish a variety of records including histories of the counties and towns or cities. To obtain a list of available publications, contact the genealogical or historical society in the area in which research is being conducted.

One of the finest volumes of detailed information for genealogists working in Texas records is Imogene Kinard Kennedy

and J. Leon Kennedy, *Genealogical Records in Texas* (Baltimore: Genealogical Publishing Co., 1987). This volume contains historical background, detailed maps, and a county-by-county listing that gives name, pronunciation, parent counties, dates of creation and organization, county seat and zip code, county maps where needed, details of dates available and location of pertinent records, and beginning dates of records available in the county. Some minor errors appear, but as a reference tool, this volume remains valuable.

Other sources include:

Ericson, Carolyn Reeves, and Frances Terry Ingmire. *First Settlers of the Republic of Texas: Headright Land Grants Which Were Reported as Genuine and Legal by the Traveling Commissioners, January, 1840.* Nacogdoches, Tex.: Carolyn R. Ericson, 1982. Taken from records in the Texas State Archives. Counties covered are Austin, Bastrop, Bexar, Brazoria, Colorado, Fannin, Fayette, Fort Bend, Galveston, Goliad, Gonzales, Harris, Harrison, Houston, Jackson, and Jasper.

Ingmire, Frances, and Carolyn R. Ericson. *First Settlers of the Republic of Texas.* Vol. 2. Utica, Ky.: McDowell Publications, 1986. Includes names from the counties of Jefferson, Liberty, Matagorda, Milam, Montgomery, Nacogdoches, Red River, Refugio, Robertson, Sabine, San Augustine, Shelby, Victoria, and Washington.

McLean, Malcolm D., comp. *Papers Concerning Robertson's Colony in Texas.* 13 vols. Arlington, Tex.: University of Arlington Press, 1974–89. This valuable material is published from the collection at the University of Texas at Arlington. Volume 12 contains lists of early colonists.

Williams, Villamae, ed. *Stephen F. Austin's Register of Families.* St. Louis: Ingmire Pub., 1984. Data taken from original documents in the GLO for families who arrived prior to 1845.

Maps

The GLO (see Land Records) houses original plat maps for the state (see <www.glo.state.tx.us/archives/map_description.html>). The Archives Division, Texas State Library, maintains an excellent collection of Texas maps. Original, photocopies, and compiled maps include general state, county survey, road and highway, United States Geological Survey, coastal and nautical, street, town plats, and Birdseye maps with card index to the collection, arranged by date or location. James M. Day's *Maps of Texas, 1527–1900: The Map Collection of the Texas State Archives* (Austin, Tex.: Pemberton Press, 1964) describes maps in the collection acquired prior to 1965. Other printed sources include:

Creuzbaur, Robert J. *DeCordova's Map of the State of Texas.* Compiled from the Records of the General Land Office (GLO) of the State. Houston: n.p., 1849.

Day, James M., et al., comps. *Maps of Texas, 1527–1900: The Map Collection of the Texas State Archives.* Austin, Tex.: Pemberton Press, 1964.

Frantz, Joe Bertram. *Lure of the Land: Texas County Maps and the History of Settlement.* College Station, Tex.: Texas A&M University Press, 1988.

Gamble, W. H. *County Map of the State of Texas: Showing Also Portions of the Adjoining States and Territories.* Philadelphia: n.p., 1879.

Gannett, Henry. *A Gazetteer of Texas.* Washington, D.C.: Government Printing Office, 1904.

Gray, O. W. *Gray's Railroad Map of Texas.* Philadelphia: the author, 1877.

Martin, James C., and Robert S. Martin. *Maps of Texas and the Southwest, 1513–1900.* Albuquerque: University of New Mexico Press, 1984. Brief historical sketches accompany the maps in this atlas.

Pool, William C. *A Historical Atlas of Texas.* Austin, Tex.: Encinco Press, 1975. Maps of the state depict the frontier and various historical periods as well as Indian territories.

Stephens, A. Ray, and William M. Holmes. *Historical Atlas of Texas.* Consultant: Phyllis M. McCaffree. Norman, Okla.: University of Oklahoma Press, 1989.

Tarpley, Fred. *1001 Texas Place Names.* Austin, Tex.: University of Texas Press, 1980.

Texas State Gazetteer and Business Directory. R. L. Polk and Co., 1882–83, 1884–85, 1890–91. These directories provide a means to identifying business owners in Texas towns as well as locating communities that have disappeared.

Webb, Walter Prescott, and Eldon Stephen Branda. *The Handbook of Texas.* 3 vols. Austin, Tex.: Texas State Historical Association, 1952–76.

Wheat, James L. *Postmasters and Post Offices in Texas, 1846–1930.* N.p.: n.p., 1973. Provides most complete list of communities.

Other map collections are housed in the libraries of the University of Texas at Austin and El Paso <http://libraries.uta.edu/SpecColl/mapcoll.html> and Southern Methodist University DeGrolyer Library <www.smu.edu/cul/degolyer/collections.html>.

Land Records

State-Land State

Texas land records were created under various governmental jurisdictions in the course of including Spain, Mexico, and both the Republic and State of Texas. Eleven land districts, each encompassing a number of counties, were established in 1836 under the Republic of Texas, and a central GLO was organized at Austin. The first district office was located near the Red River. The others were at San Augustine, Liberty, Nacogdoches, Matagorda, Washington-on-the Brazos, Cameron, Bastrop, Gonzales, San Antonio, and Victoria. The system of land districts continued when Texas became a state with previous grants being acknowledged. Nearly 150 million acres of state public land in Texas were distributed after 1836.

Texas is not a federal public land state; consequently, there are no federal government original land records. Texas's GLO continues to maintain its own archives and records division, housing all early land grants including those dated in the 1700s and original grants issued by both republic and state governments. Indexes to the *original* land records are maintained at the Stephen F. Austin State Office Bldg., Rm. 800, 1700 N. Congress Ave., Austin, TX 78701-1495 <www.glo.state.tx.us/archives>. Requests for index entries for an individual name with arrival date and county are responded to for a minimum fee. Normal response time about two weeks. Among the various types of original grants were:

Headright grants. Issued to encourage immigration—but not awarded to African Americans or Native Americans—and organized in several classes. Texas issued these grants between 1836 and 1842 to individuals and families who settled in Texas. Class 1 are Spanish or Mexican grants issued to settlers whose arrival was before 2 March 1836. Land allotted was one league and one labor (4,605.5 acres) per family or one-third league (1,476 acres) for unmarried men. Second-class headright grants were given to those who arrived after 2 March 1836 and before 1 October 1837. They received 1,280 acres per family, or half that for unmarried men, with a requirement of three years residence. Third-class headright grants for those who settled from 2 October 1837 to 1 January 1840 were issued for half the acreage allotments but with the same residency requirements as second-class grants. Fourth-class headright grants were issued between 1 January 1840 and 1 January 1842; acreage given was equal to that of third-class headrights. Those awarded equivalent to third-class headrights included colonists in Peters, Mercer, Castro, and Fisher-Miller colonies.

Pre-emption (squatter) grants. Issued between 22 January 1845 and 1854 for no more than 320 acres. Minimum requirement was residence on a particular parcel for three consecutive years after 22 January 1845. After 1854 a limit of 160 acres was established for married men, and half that for single men after 1870. The last pre-emption grant was issued in 1898.

Bounty grants. From 1837 through 1888 Texas issued land in payment for military service to the Republic. The number of acres granted varies as several legislatures modified requirements. Participants in any battle qualified. Later donation lands were awarded to widows and surviving (as of 1881) veterans. Eligibility was limited to one grant. Scrip, a means of awarding or selling

public land, was granted to disabled Confederate veterans or builders of railroads, canals, roads, mills, or factories.

Contracted grants. Both the Republic and State of Texas contracted with various individuals to establish colonies in Texas and receive payment in land. Large grants were made directly to contractors, although individual grants of 640 acres were also given to heads of families and 320 acres to single men.

Miller's work, cited below, gives a complete account of the acquisition and disposition of public land in Texas to 1970. Fraudulent claims and legislation enacted to address these problems are also discussed.

Gillford E. White compiled a series of volumes, *The First Settlers in* [County], *Texas*, copied from originals in the GLO; these often include maps. Most were published by Ingmire Publications, St. Louis, Missouri, between 1981 and 1984. A few were published elsewhere. The state land office has microfilmed copies of federal land sales to individuals up through the 1900s. Only original sales are maintained by state; all other subsequent sales are under county jurisdiction. In addition to the Ingmire and Ericson volumes cited in Background Sources, see:

Abstract of Land Claims: Compiled from the Records of the General Land Office. Galveston: Civilian Book Office, 1852. Arranged alphabetically in districts, lists grants from Spain, Mexico, the Republic of Texas, and the state.

Abstracts of Land Titles of Texas Comprising the Titled, Patented, and Located Lands in the State. 1878. Reprint. San Augustine, Tex.: S. Malone, 1985. County arrangement for the period 1833 to 1877.

An Abstract of the Original Titles of Records in the General Land Office. 1838. Reprint. Austin, Tex.: Pemberton Press, 1964. Details headright grants for 1791 to 1836.

Bascom, Giles. *Abstract of All Original Grants and Locations Comprising Texas Land Titles to August 32, 1945.* 8 vols. *Supplements A, B, C, D, E, F, G, & H.* 8 vols. Austin, Tex.: General Land Office, 1945–80. This set is somewhat difficult to locate. The General Land Offices does sell out-of-print volumes on microfiche. Another publisher reprinted the first volume as *Texas Land Title Abstracts Volume 1-A.* Paris, Tex.: Wright Press, 1984.

———. *History and Disposition of Texas Public Domain.* Austin, Tex.: GLO, 1945.

Bowden, J. J. *Spanish and Mexican Land Grants in the Chihuahuan Acquisition.* Austin, Tex.: University of Texas Press, 1971. Covers the counties of El Paso, Hudspeth, Culberson, Reeves, Jeff Davis, Pecos, Presidio, and Brewer in Texas plus six more in adjacent New Mexico.

Burlage, John, and J. B. Hollingsworth, *Abstract of Valid Land Claims Compiled from the Records of the General Land Office and Court of Claims of the State of Texas.* Austin, Tex.: J. Marshall, 1859.

Ericson, Carolyn Reeves. *Nacogdoches Headrights: A Record of the Disposition of Land in East Texas and in Other Parts of that State, 1838–1848.* New Orleans: Polyanthos, 1977.

Gould, Florence C., and Patricia N. Pando. *Claiming Their Land: Women Homesteaders in Texas.* El Paso: Texas Western Press, 1991.

Miller, Thomas Lloyd. *Bounty and Donation Land Grants of Texas, 1835–1888.* Austin, Tex.: University of Texas Press, 1967.

———. *The Public Lands of Texas 1519–1970.* Norman, Okla.: Oklahoma University Press, 1971. Excellent source describing Texas land records and land history.

———. *Texas Confederate Scrip Grantees, C.S.A.* N.p., 1985.

Purl, Benjamin F. *Republic of Texas Second Class Headrights, March 2, 1836–October 1, 1837.* Houston: A. N. W. Barnes, 1974.

Sadler, Jerry. *History of Texas Land.* Austin, Tex.: GLO, 1964.

Scott, Florence Johnson. *Royal Land Grants North of the Rio Grande, 1777–1821: Early History of Large Grants Made by Spain to Families in Jurisdiction of Reynosa Which Became a Part of Texas after the Treaty of Guadalupe Hidalgo, 1848.* Rio Grande City, Tex.: La Retama Press, 1969. Concerns suits recorded in deed books containing the chain of title and lines of descent and heirship for the counties of Hidalgo, Cameron, Willacy, Kenedy, Brooks, Kleberg, and Nueces. Includes maps.

Taylor, Virginia H. *Spanish Archives of the General Land Office of Texas.* Austin, Tex.: Lone Star Press, 1955.

The Texas Family Land Heritage Registry. 10 vols. Austin, Tex.: Texas Department of Agriculture (1974–   ). These are accounts of farms that have been in agricultural production for a century or more in the same family (not limited to agnate descents) and as such are rich in genealogical detail.

Todd, William N. *Guide to Spanish and Mexican Land Grants in South Texas.* Austin, Tex.: Texas General Land Office, 1988.

White, Gifford E. *Character Certificates in the General Land Office of Texas.* Baltimore: Genealogical Publishing, 1989.

———. *1840 Citizens of Texas.* 3 vols. Austin, Tex.: the author, 1983–88. Volumes 1 and 3 list land grants; volume 2 includes tax rolls and name index to volume 2.

Williams, Villamae. *Stephen F. Austin's Register of Families from the Originals in the General Land Office, Austin, Texas.* Baltimore: Genealogical Publishing, 1989.

Once land was initially granted, all succeeding land transactions fall under the jurisdiction of the county in which the land is located at the time each record is created. County boundaries have changed over time, as have county names. By law, all deeds are indexed by grantor and by grantee. Transcribed deeds from parent counties may be maintained in separate

volumes. County land transactions, including deeds and mortgages, are located at the respective county clerk's office.

Century farm records for those families who worked the same land for 100 years or more are available on microfilm at Department of Agriculture, Century of Agriculture Program, P.O. Box 12847, Austin, TX 78711.

Probate Records

Probate proceedings in Texas are under the jurisdiction of the respective county court clerk except in more largely populated counties where probate courts may fill that function instead. Wills, court orders, letters of administration, inventories, sales, accounts, guardianship, and final accounts are all found in the probate minutes, though they may be filed separately. Probate appeals from either the county or probate court are heard by district courts (see Court Records). Between 1869 and 1876, when the office of county clerk was temporarily abolished, some probate records were filed in District Court Civil Minutes or District Court Minutes.

The Works Progress Administration (WPA) published a series of indexes to probate cases for some of the Texas counties. During the 1980s the set was reprinted as *Index to Probate Cases of Texas* (n.p.) and included the following counties: Atascosa, Bowie, Brazoria, Brazos, Brown, Camp, Chambers, Coleman, Delta, Franklin, Gregg, Guadalupe, Hardin, Hays, Liberty, Marion, Morris, Newton, Nolan, Orange, Robertson, Runnels, Rusk, San Saba, Shelby, Titus, Trinity, Waller, Williamson, and Wood.

The Texas DAR Genealogical Records Committee has compiled wills from various Texas counties as part of its publication series. The Texas State Library and Allen County Public Library (see page 204) have various volumes of the original typescript.

A WPA project generated indexes for probate records for thirty Texas counties. Indexes for an additional eleven of those counties have been combined into a single alphabetical listing with additional counties are being added to these for an online database by a team of high school students working with Rebecca Osborne, Ph.D. See <www.three-legged-willie.org/texas.htm> for an updated listing.

Court Records

Court names and jurisdictions in Texas changed over time. The history of Texas court records with dates and jurisdictions is more thoroughly outlined in the Kennedy and Kennedy, *Genealogical Records in Texas* (see Background Sources). Although English common law is the basis for the court system in Texas, modifications are allowed as dictated by the situation. These were usually changes based upon Spanish law, which proved beneficial to settlers.

From 1836 through 1891 the highest court—the state's supreme court—heard only appellate cases and functioned as a circuit court, holding hearings in Austin, Galveston, and Tyler for three-month sessions, annually. State supreme court records from 1838 to 1940, including litigants' records in appellate civil and criminal cases, are housed in the Archives Division of the Texas State Library.

In 1891 the court of criminal appeals was established to hear criminal cases, thereby reducing the caseload of the state supreme court to hear only appeals of civil disputes. The Supreme Court Record Group, held in the Archives Division of the Texas State Library, contains approximately 4,500 cases. Unfortunately, a large number of files for 1840–53 are lost. Records available include case files, dockets, minute books, and opinions. Published opinions are available for all years except 1844–45. It is best to check the published records available at the archives division covering the periods 1840–44 and 1846–1963 with a direct (plaintiff) and reverse (defendant) card index to the case file numbers for the period 1836 to 1893. For phone or correspondence requests, the archives' staff will check the card index and case file if the case file number is referenced in the card index or can be furnished. Some original records are too fragile to be copied.

The county commissioners court conducts the daily business for each county, among other duties, setting tax rates and county budgets for such categories as schools, roads, and the poor. The county clerk serves as recorder and clerk to the commissioners court and the county court. A large number of records about the daily lives of county residents are kept, as a result, by the county clerk. In counties with less than 8,000 population, one recorder/clerk may serve both county and district courts.

County courts operated from 1836 but were abolished, temporarily, in 1869. Their jurisdiction was transferred to district courts until 1876 when county courts were reinstated. County courts hear most misdemeanor, civil, probate, and guardianship cases, all recorded by the county clerk, along with other instruments such as cattle brands, deeds, and marriage licenses. Naturalization records are found, prior to 1906, in county court records (see Special Focus Categories—Naturalizations).

District courts, one for each county, are the principal trial courts in Texas and serve as the court of appeal in probate matters (from county court) and for the commissioners court. District courts have original jurisdiction for felonies, divorce, land title, name changes, and after 1931, for adoptions. In the 1890s separate divorce minutes appeared. After 1906 the district court continued to handle naturalization matters (see Special Focus Categories—Naturalizations).

Justice of the peace courts, often called "poor man's court," were established in 1845. They handle civil and criminal matters under $200 and issue warrants and writs. In towns of 2,500 or less, these courts act as registrar of vital statistics.

As a result of the destruction of records in the adjutant general's office when it burned in 1855, a court of claims was established from 1856 to 1861 to hear cases against the republic and state for claims of money or land. Approximately two-thirds of the applicants' cases were denied. The old and new "dockets" list applications. Court-approved records relating to nearly 4,500 headright certificates, over 2,000 bounty warrants, more than 650 donation certificates, almost 500 scrip certificates, and rejected claims are deposited in the GLO (see Land Records). Access to county court addresses can be found at Texas Law Organizations Resource Center website <www.txlaw.org/clerks.html>.

Tax Records

Texas tax records constitute one of the most complete sets of available records generated at the county level and maintained by the office of county tax assessor-collector. Tax records through 1980 are filed with the state comptroller of public accounts. These lists may only include approximately sixty percent of eligible males over the age of twenty-one. Persons exempted from taxes included Native Americans and those exempted because of age. Age exemptions varied over time. Years without an older age exemption were 1840 and 1862 to 1870. Between 1841 and 1844, exemptions began at forty-five years; in 1845 and from 1850 to 1861 the upward age was set at fifty years. In 1837, 1848, and 1849 the limit was established as fifty-five, and in 1846 to 1847, and 1871 the upward limit was set at sixty years.

Texas Ad Valorem (poll, personal, and real property) tax records for 1836 through 1976 are available in microfilm at the Texas State Library from the date of respective county organization; these are arranged by county and date and are somewhat alphabetized within each division. Microfilm copies are housed in the Genealogy Section. Tax lists for the various counties from creation to 1901 may be borrowed through interlibrary loan. A record of taxpayers of Houston was enumerated in 1839. Tax records through 1901 through 1947 are readily accessible, but not on interlibrary loan. Those for 1948 through 1976 can be obtained upon request.

Lists for various counties have been published. Some statewide compilations include the following:

Dorman, Beth, and Emily Dorman. *Taxpayers of the Republic of Texas Covering 30 Counties and the District of Panola.* Grand Prairie, Tex.: the authors, 1988.

Mullins, Marion Day. *Republic of Texas: Poll Lists for 1846.* Baltimore: Genealogical Publishing, 1974.

White, Gifford E. *1840 Citizens of Texas.* 3 vols. Austin, Tex.: the author, 1983–1988. Vols. 1 and 3 list land grants; vol. 2 includes tax rolls.

The Texas State Library and Archives website provides catalog access to its holdings in tax records at <www.tsl.state.tx.us/arc/taxrolls.html>. An 1839 tax list for Houston was published in the *Houston Morning Star.* A transcription is available online at <http://ftp.rootsweb.com/pub/usgenweb/tx/harris/taxlists/taxlist.txt>.

Cemetery Records

Many cemetery records have been collected and transcribed. The largest is the numerous volumes compiled by the DAR (see page 8). A two–volume work is available for Peters' Colonists and descendants. The DAR collection, also microfilmed, is available at the Texas State Library and through the FHL.

Some Texas county historical and genealogical societies have published local cemetery and funeral home records. These are normally available for purchase through the respective society. Two references can help determine which cemeteries have been recorded: Kim Parsons, *A Reference to Texas Cemetery Records* (Humble, Tex.: the author, 1988), arranged by county; and Sharry Crofford-Gould, *Texas Cemetery Inscriptions: A Source Index* (San Antonio, Tex.: Limited Editions, 1977).

For general information, see Terry G. Jordan, *Texas Graveyards: A Cultural Legacy* (Austin, Tex.: University of Texas Press, 1984) for a scholarly look at the state's burying practices over time.

A three-volume set of cemetery records by Janet R. Schooley, *The Digger's Index* (Newell, Iowa: Bireline Publishing, 1984–1988, 1998) is an alphabetical listing of old, abandoned, vandalized or still in use cemeteries. It includes various volumes with Texas counties included as follows: Vol. 1. Counties of Tioga, Bradford, Wyoming, Sullivan, Columbia, Luzerne, and Monroe in Pennsylvania; counties of Tioga and Broome in New York—vol. 2. Counties of Bradford, Columbia, Lackawanna, Luzerne, Lycoming, Snyder, Sullivan, Susquehanna, Wayne, and Wyoming in Pennsylvania; Connecticut cemeteries; Sussex County, New Jersey cemetery; Delaware Cemetery in Pike County, Pennsylvania; Harris Cemetery in Caldwell County, Texas; Church cemetery in Delaware County, New York; Lyne Cemetery in Logan County, Kentucky—vol. 3. Counties of Bradford, Columbia, Cumberland, Luzerne, Susquehanna, Tioga, Wyoming, and York; Delaware Cemetery in Washington Township, New Jersey; Presbytery [history] of Luzerne County; Church record (pastors, members, marriages) of Noxen-Stull Church in Wyoming Co.; Membership list of Union Baptist Church, Union Township, Luzerne County.

Two examples of recently released publications include:

Preston, Donald, comp. *Funeral List.* 2 vols. Texarkana: Texarkana USA Genealogical Society, 1995–56. Contains 2,047 burials in the Texarkana area with names listed in alphabetical order.

Vickery, Adele W. *Cemeteries of East Texas*. Weatherford, Tex.: Parker County Genealogical Society, 1999.

Online access to cemetery records includes <www.idreamof. com/cemetery/tx/a_c.html>.

Church Records

During Texas' colonization period, Roman Catholics were the most numerous, but early citizens included those representing other religious faiths such as Baptist, Methodist, Presbyterian, and Christian or Disciples of Christ.

Many Roman Catholic records are in the Catholic Diocese Archives of Texas, N. Congress and W. 16th, Capitol Station P.O. Box 13327, Austin, TX 78711 <www.onr.com/user/cat>. Others are deposited in the various archdiocese archives. The San Antonio archdiocese records begin in 1703.

Two sources for Baptist records in the state are: Baylor University's Texas Collection, Baylor University Library, Box 6396, Waco, TX 76706; and Southwestern Baptist Theological Seminary, A. Webb Roberts Library, Box 22, Fort Worth, TX 76122. A collection of Baptist records maintained outside the state is at Samford University Library, 800 Lakeshore Dr., Birmingham, AL 35229. The collection includes books, church and association minutes, church and association histories, and nineteenth-century Southern Baptist newspapers, many of which are indexed.

Bridwell Theology Library, Southern Methodist University, Dallas, Texas 75275-0476 houses records for Methodists. Austin Presbyterian Theological Seminary Archives, 100 E. 27th St., Austin, TX 78705 <www.austinseminary.edu/library/archive. html> has some history and information.

Military Records

The largest collection of military and related records pertaining to Texans is housed in the Texas State Archives, Adjutant General Record Group. Since 1919 military discharge records are filed at the local county courthouse. An extensive array of military records, too numerous to list here, has been published. The list would include Revolutionary War and War of 1812 veterans who died in Texas, as well as World War I and II veterans.

Earliest Texas military records begin in 1835. Texas War of Independence veterans, or widows or heirs, were eligible for bounty and donation land grants and pensions from the Texas government. Published lists are available of soldiers and sailors of the Republic of Texas, of participants in battles of the Alamo and San Jacinto, and of men in the Texas Rangers, minutemen, and home guard units. Lists of those who served in the Indian Wars have been published. See <www.mindspring.com/~dmaxey>

for a listing organized by H. David Maxey of muster rolls for troops 1835–36.

A large collection of Confederate pension applications is available at the Texas State Library and Archives in Austin. These are arranged in numerical order and are indexed. Both indigent veterans and widows of veterans were allowed pensions. The applications contain some genealogical information. Copies can be obtained through correspondence once the assigned number is known. Confederate scrip was awarded veterans who were permanently disabled or killed, entitling the veteran or his widow to 1,280 acres.

In addition to the National Archives military records (see page 8), other military records are housed in the Texas State Archives and Library; these include Confederate claims (1861–65); Confederate home records (1886–1954); Confederate indigent families list (1863–65); general service records (1836–1902); muster rolls (1836–1917); and payment records (1836–46). Under the Adjutant General Record Group in the state archives are many additional records, including various muster rolls (1836–1911) and service records (1836–1902). Records may be as little as one small piece of paper or as large as a complete file.

The Texas Military Forces Museum at Camp Mabry, 2200 W. 35th St., Austin, TX 78703 <www.kwanah.com/txmilmus> has an extensive library and archives including records of the Texas National Guard.

Among the numerous printed sources that exist for Texan veterans are the following:

Barron, John C., et al. *Republic of Texas Pension Application Abstracts*. Austin, Tex.: Austin Genealogical Society, 1987.

Fay, Mary Smith. *War of 1812 Veterans in Texas*. New Orleans: Polyanthos, 1979. From notes compiled by Mae Wynne McFarland, this is a compilation of names, places, and dates associated with veterans of the War of 1812. Original material is in the library of the Sam Houston State University in Huntsville, arranged alphabetically.

Ingmire, Frances Terry. *Texas Frontiersman, 1839–1860: Minute Men, Militia, Home Guard, Indian Fighter*. St. Louis: the author, 1982. Contains officers index and alphabetically arranged entries taken from military records.

———. *Texas Ranger Service Records, 1830–1846*. St. Louis: Ingmire Publications, 1982. Includes index of officers.

———, comp. *Texas Rangers: Frontier Battalion, Minute Men, Commanding Officers, 1847–1900*. 6 vols. St. Louis: Ingmire Publications, 1982. Each volume separately indexed.

Kinney, John M. *Index to Applications for Texas Confederate Pensions*. Rev. ed. Austin, Tex.: Archives Division, Texas State Library, 1977.

Leiker, James N. *Racial Borders: Black Soldiers along the Rio Grande.* College Station: Texas A&M University Press, 2002.

Manarin, Louis H., ed. *Cumulative Index: The Confederate Veteran Magazine, 1893–1932.* 3 vols. Wilmington, N.C.: Broadfoot Publishing, 1986. Every name index to the *Confederate Veteran.* Includes a comprehensive list of Confederate military organization arranged by local designations.

White, Virgil. *Index to Texas CSA Pension Files.* Waynesboro, Tenn.: National Historical Publishing, 1989.

Periodicals, Newspapers, and Manuscript Collections

Periodicals

Genealogical periodicals are numerous for Texas with some counties having three or more different societies. Some representative titles are:

The Dallas Quarterly. Dallas Genealogical Society, 1955-present.

Footprints. Fort Worth Genealogical Society, 1968-present.

Genealogical Record. Houston Genealogical Forum, 1958-present.

Heart of Texas Records. Formerly Central Texas Genealogical Society Bulletin. Central Texas Genealogical Society, 1958-present.

The Herald. Montgomery County Genealogical and Historical Society, 1978-present.

Nase Dejiny: The Magazine of Czech Genealogy. Hallettsville, Tex.: Old Homestead Publishing Co., 1982-present. Devoted to Czechs who settled in Texas.

Newsletter. German Texas Heritage Society, 1979-present.

Northeast Texas Genealogy and History. Genealogical Society of Northeast Texas, 1965-present.

Oak Leaves. Matagorda County Genealogical Society 1982-present.

Our Heritage. San Antonio Genealogical and Historical Society, 1959-present.

PGST News. Polish Genealogical Society of Texas, 1985-present.

The Roadrunner. Chaparral Genealogical Society, 1974-present.

Stalkin' Kin. San Angelo Genealogical and Historical Society, 1973-present.

Stirpes. Texas State Genealogical Society, 1961-present.

The Thorny Trail. Midland Genealogical Society, 1973-present.

Yellowed Pages. Southeast Texas Genealogical and Historical Society, 1971-present.

Newspapers

The Name Index to Early Texas Newspapers serves as a significant finding tool for names in newspapers between 1830 and 1885. The original card-file index is at the University of Texas Library in Austin, with a forty-three roll set on microfilm and available throughout Texas. The card data includes the name, date, and title as well as other identifying information. Other works include:

Lu, Helen Mason. *Texas Methodist Newspaper Abstracts (17 April 1850–17 Sept. 1881).* 4 vols. Dallas: H. Lu, 1987. Also on microfiche.

Kelsey, Michael. *Genealogical Abstracts from Central Texas Newspapers, 1885–1899.* Temple, Tex.: the author, 1987.

——. *Genealogical Abstracts from the Austin Texas State Gazette 1849–1859.* Temple, Tex.: the author, 1988.

——. *Miscellaneous Texas Newspaper Abstracts, 1856–1870.* Temple, Tex.: the author, 1988.

Swensen, Helen S. *Early Texas News 1831–1848, Abstracts from Early Texas Newspapers.* St. Louis: F. T. Ingmire, 1984.

Manuscripts

Manuscripts containing historical and genealogical data are frequently available in university, historical society, state, and local public libraries throughout the state. Brief examples follow:

Manuscript collections maintained by the Texas State Archives are described in Jean Carefoot, *A Guide to Genealogical Resources in the Texas State Archives* (Austin, Tex.: Texas State Library, Archives Division, 1984), and online at <www.tsl.state.tx.us/arc/index.html>.

The Eugene C. Baker Texas History Center at the University at Austin announced in 1986 the acquisition of the Natchez Trace Collection, an important archive of materials documenting much of the life of the Old South between 1780 and 1900. It measures over 450 linear feet and is a collection of collections, remaining to be cataloged.

See also:

Benavides, Adan. *The Bexar Archives, 1717–1836, A Name Guide.* Austin, Tex.: University of Texas Press, 1989.

Kielman, Chester Valls. *Guide to the Microfilm Edition of the Bexar Archives, 1717–1836.* 3 vols. Austin, Tex.: University of Texas, 1969–71. This work gives a reel-by-reel description of the contents of the 172-reel micropublication.

McLean, Malcolm Dallas. *Papers Concerning Robertson's Colony in Texas.* 19 vols. Arlington, Tex.: University of Texas at Arlington, 1974–1993.

For WPA Life Histories from Texas, see <http://lcweb2.loc.gov/ammem/wpaintro/txcat.html>.

Archives, Libraries, and Societies

Texas State Library and Archives
State Archives and Library Building
1201 Brazos St.
Austin, TX 78711-2927
www.tsl.state.tx.us

Of paramount importance to the genealogical researcher working with Texas records are the holdings of the Texas State Library and Archives.

The website provides a search engine for "genealogy" and "archives and manuscripts" resources in its collections. Holdings of the Texas State Library are divided. Most important for genealogical research are at the Texas State Archives with its Local Records Department, the Records Management Division, and the Information Services Division, which includes a Genealogy Section and a Reference Department.

Many of its extensive holdings have been described in the sections of this chapter (see also Carefoot, *A Guide*, cited under Manuscripts and website <www.tsl.state.tx.us/arc/index.html>).

The Genealogy Section maintains vertical ties that contain notes, clippings, pamphlets, and correspondence on Texas families. These files may be accessed in person, by phone (time limit imposed), or through correspondence.

Because so many records pertaining to Texas are available in microform, much genealogical and historical material is accessible at the following:

Dallas Public Library
1515 Young St.
Dallas, TX 75201
www.dallaslibrary.org

Clayton Library Center for Genealogical Research
5300 Caroline
Houston, TX 77004
www.hpl.lib.tx.us/clayton/

Clayton Library is a unit of the Houston Public Library and, as such, holds one of the largest collections of genealogical materials. The collection, however, does not include newspapers and Texas history. Those are located at the Houston Public Library main library at 500 McKinney, Houston, TX 77002 [www.houstonlibrary.org]

Other libraries with holdings of interest to genealogists include:

Austin History Center
9th and Guadalupe St.
Austin, TX 78701
www.ci.austin.tx.us/library/lbahc.htm

Texas Historical Commission
P.O. Box 12276
Austin, TX 78711-2276
www.thc.state.tx.us

Most other libraries, including public libraries, have valuable material with genealogical information, such as published histories, newspapers, telephone books, city directories, manuscripts, and oral history.

Twenty-five public and university libraries in Texas provide additional storage facilities of local records. These are identified in Heskett's work (see County Resources).

In addition to the Kennedy and Kennedy book (see Background Sources), the following guides to Texas archives and libraries are also valuable:

Keilman, Chester Valls. *Guide to the Microfilm Edition of the Texas Archives.* 3 vols. Austin, Tex.: University of Texas, 1967–71.

——. *The University of Texas Archives, A Guide to the Historical Manuscripts Collections in the University of Texas Library.* Austin, Tex.: University of Texas Press, 1967.

Texas State Library Circulating Genealogy Duplicates List. Austin, Tex.: Texas State Library, 1985. Lists books and materials available on interlibrary loan in Texas and elsewhere.

Special Focus Categories

Immigration
Both New Orleans and Galveston served as ports of entry for those who immigrated and settled in Texas. Some early immigrants entered at New Orleans. The National Archives—Southwest Region in Fort Worth is the regional location for the archives' extensive microfilm collection of immigration lists (see page 12). The FHL has microfilm copies of passenger lists for New Orleans (1820–1921; indexes to 1952); also, the FHL has copies for Galveston (1846–71, 1893, and 1896–1921; with indexes grouped from 1896–1906 and 1906–51). Prior to 1852 there is no separate index to passengers.

Printed sources include the following:

Baca, Leo. *Czech Immigration Passenger Lists.* 3 vols. Hallestville, Tex.: Old Homestead Publishing Co., 1980–83. While not limited to Texas, a great many of the lists do pertain to Texas and are based on records no longer extant in Texas port of arrival records.

Biesele, Rudolph L. *The History of the German Settlements in Texas, 1831–1931.* Austin, Tex.: Von Boeckman-Jones Co., 1931.

Blaha, Albert J. *Passenger Lists for Galveston, 1850–1855.* Houston: the author, 1985. Based on European sources. Galveston and Indianola passenger arrivals are included.

Brown, John Henry. *Indian Wars and Pioneers of Texas.* St. Louis: L. E. Daniels Publishers, 1890.

Brozek, Andrzej, and Henryk Borek. *Pierwsi Slazncy w Ameryce* [First Silesians in America]. Opole, Poland, 1967.

Chabot, Fred Charles. *With the Makers of San Antonio.* San Antonio, Tex.: Ars Graphica, 1937.

Dworaczyk, Edward J. *The First Polish Colonies in America in Texas.* San Antonio, Tex.: Naylor Co., 1936.

Galveston County Genealogical Society. *Ships Passenger Lists, Port of Galveston, Texas, 1846–1871.* Easley, S.C.: Southern Historical Press, 1984. Lists surviving fragments of records.

Geue, Chester, and Ethel H. Geue. *A New Land Beckoned, German Immigration to Texas, 1844–1847.* Waco, Tex.: Texian Press, 1972. These records provide coverage for the period when the Republic of Texas kept no records of immigrants arriving at its ports and complements the fragmentary records for the port of Galveston maintained by the United States.

Geue, Ethel H. *New Homes in a New Land, German Immigration to Texas, 1847–1861.* Waco, Tex.: Texian Press, 1972. These lists are based on records in the Archives of the General Land Office. While there may be some duplication with records maintained by the federal authorities at New Orleans and Galveston, these lists are generally unique.

Haiman, Miecislaus. *The Poles in the Early History of Texas.* Chicago: P.R.C.U. of A. Archives, 1936.

——. *Polish Past in America.* Chicago: P.R.C.U. of A. Archives, 1939.

Hudson, Estelle, and Henry Maresh. *Czech Pioneers of the Southwest.* Dallas: Southwest Press, 1934.

March, Helen, and Timothy March. *Tennesseans in Texas.* Easley, S.C.: Southern Historical Press, 1986.

McManus, J. *Conrad County, Texas: New Braunfels, Texas, German Immigrant Ships, 1845–1846.* St Louis: F. T. Ingmire, 1985.

Przygoda, Jacek. *Texas Pioneers from Poland: A Study in the Ethnic History.* Waco: Texian Press, ca. 1971.

Naturalization

The Republic of Texas had no naturalization requirement. Consequently no records exist before 1846. After statehood and prior to 1906, naturalization records in Texas are found in both the county and district courts in the respective county. The records may be found in county court minutes, county court civil minutes, probate minutes, commissioners court minutes, or in separately maintained volumes. The Act of Congress of 1906 limited naturalization to state courts without original jurisdiction, and Texas county district courts met that requirement. Declarations, affidavits, orders of admission, and other documents are maintained by those courts and the U.S. Federal District Courts.

Native American

The most significant tribes represented in the state include Comanche, Kiowa, Arapaho, Crow, Wichita, Ute, and Creek. Other tribes in Texas include Arkokosa, Attacapa, Caddo, Coahuiltecan, Karankawa, Nacogdoches, Nasoni, Neche, and Tonkawa. Most of those remaining in Texas in 1859 were forcibly removed to Indian Territory. During 1875 the surviving Comanche surrendered to federal forces. The Alabama-Coushatta Indian Reservation remains in the state.

Records for Native Americans in Texas after 1845 are on file in the United States Bureau of Indian Affairs and in Bureau records in the National Archives. Those records in the Texas State Archives pertaining to Native Americans are usually insignificant for genealogical purposes. A better collection is housed by the Oklahoma Historical Society, Indian Archives Division, Historical Bldg., Oklahoma City, OK 73105.

Brown, John Henry. *Indian Wars and Pioneers of Texas.* 1978. Reprint. Easley, S.C.: Southern Historical Press, 1988.

Sowell, Andrew J. *Early Settlers and Indian Fighters of Southwest Texas: Facts Gathered from Survivors of Frontier Days.* New York: Argosy, ca. 1964.

Wilbarger, J. W. *Indian Depredations in Texas.* Austin, Tex.: Eakin Press, 1985.

Republic of Texas Settlers

The Republic of Texas ceased to exist when President Anson Jones handed over the reins of government to the United States of America on 19 February 1846. Descent from one of Austin's Old Three Hundred or other residents of Texas prior to that date has always been a genealogical asset. The following list of publications offers much assistance in investigation of claims to descent:

Jennett, Elizabeth LeNoir. *Biographical Directory of the Texas Conventions and Congresses, 1832–1845.* 1941. Reprint. New York: Antiquarian Press, 1959.

Compiled Index to Elected and Appointed Officials of the Republic of Texas: 1835–1846. Austin, Tex.: State Archives Division, Texas State Library, 1981.

Daughters of the Republic of Texas. *Founders and Patriots of the Republic of Texas, the Lineages of the Members of the Daughters of the Republic of Texas.* 3 vols. Dallas: Huggins Press, 1963–85.

Ericson, Carolyn R. *Nacogdoches: Gateway to Texas, a Biographical Directory, 1773–1849.* 2 vols. Ft. Worth, Tex.: Arrow/Curtis Printing, 1974–87.

Kemp, Louis W. *The Signers of the Texas Declaration of Independence.* Salado, Tex.: Anson Jones Press, 1959.

Morris, Mrs. Harry Joseph. *Citizens of the Republic of Texas.* Dallas: Texas State Genealogical Society, 1977.

Sons of the Republic of Texas. *Lineages of Members.* Microfilm, 37 reels.

African American

Although most histories of Texas refer to African Americans only secondarily, their presence in the state has been long and continuous. In an 1809 census of Nacogdoches there were thirty-three slave owners. Slavery in Texas increased with Anglo-American colonists in the 1820s. Under Mexican jurisdiction, slavery was opposed, and a slave code was instituted in Austin's colony in 1824. Under an 1827 constitution of Coahuila and Texas, babies born of slave mothers were free at birth; a law passed in 1832 limited bondsmen's contracts to ten years. Nevertheless, both laws were frequently overlooked by slave owners in Texas who held and imported slaves. By 1837 slavery was recognized and legalized in Texas.

Many immigrants to antebellum Texas came from southern states, and some brought slaves to Texas. However, less than one-third of the state's population owned slaves during the 1850s. Most free African Americans and slaves lived in rural areas in the eastern half of the state at that time.

Tracing slave ancestors who lived prior to 1865, in most cases, must be accomplished through the records of the slave owners. Owners' wills and estate inventories often list slaves by name—sometimes including an approximate age or other description. Some estate records indicate slave families or state relationships of mother and children. Deeds and bills of sale may also identify slaves showing transfer of ownership. Court records infrequently include mention of slaves and owners. After 1865, records for African Americans are maintained and filed along with others for local and state jurisdictions.

An overview of African Americans in Texas may be obtained through a study of the following:

Barr, Alwyn. *Black Texans: A History of Negroes in Texas, 1528–1921.* Austin, Tex.: Pemberton Press, 1971.

Bugbee, Lester E. "Slavery in Early Texas," *Political Science Quarterly* 13 (1898): 389-412, 648-88.

Campbell, Randolph B. *An Empire for Slavery: The Peculiar Institution in Texas, 1821–1865.* Baton Rouge, La.: Louisiana State University Press, 1989.

Leiker, James N. *Racial Borders: Black Soldiers along the Rio Grande.* College Station: Texas A&M University Press, 2002.

Rice, Lawrence D. *The Negro in Texas, 1874–1900.* Baton Rouge, La.: Louisiana State University Press, 1971.

Smallwood, James M. *Time of Hope, Time of Despair: Black Texans During Reconstruction.* Port Washington, N.Y.: Kennikat Press, 1981.

Woolfork, George Ruble. *The Free Negro in Texas, 1800–1860: A Study in Cultural Compromise.* Published for The Journal of Mexican American History. Ann Arbor, Mich.: University Microfilms International, 1976.

Latino

There were two distinct Spanish colonies in present-day Texas during the early stage of the area's settlement. Although discouraged by Apache and Comanche, the Tejas colony was founded with a mission in 1690; it was located along the Nueces River and then north and east, near present-day Crockett. The other colony was that of Nuevo Santander in the Rio Grande Valley. Twenty-four settlements were established between 1749 and 1755.

Mexican population increased slowly in the state. In the early 1800s the Tejas population was less than 5,000, concentrated near San Antonio, Goliad, and Nacogdoches. In 1835, the population of the Nuevo Santander settlements had increased to 15,000. After statehood Latinos in Texas faced difficulties such as property rights, justice in the American court system, and differences in religion, language, and custom. The 1850 federal census shows that Latinos represented only five percent of the state's population.

During the Civil War, approximately 3,000 Tejanos enlisted in the Confederate Army, but many deserted. Other Tejanos joined the Union Army. The state's constitutional convention of 1868 authorized bounty-land grants for Union service: eight acres for six months service and 320 acres for service of one year or longer. Many Latinos who served for the Union became U.S. citizens during Reconstruction.

During the 1920s there were waves of migration from Mexico into Texas and other southwestern states. In 1960 Latinos numbered 1,448,900 in Texas, the highest concentrations in three counties: Hidalgo, Bexar, and El Paso. In recent history there has been an urban trend, with large numbers leaving rural occupations and moving into cities. Suggested background references include the following:

Barker, Eugene, "Land Speculation as a Cause of the Texas Revolution," *Texas Historical Association Quarterly* (1906): 76-95.

Barrera, Mario. *Race and Class in the Southwest: A Theory of Racial Inequality.* Notre Dame, Ind.: University of Notre Dame Press, 1979.

Briggs, Vernon, Walter Fogel, and Fred Schmidt. *A Statistical Profile of the Spanish-Surname Population of Texas.* Austin, Tex.: University of Texas, Bureau of Business Research, 1964.

Cardenas, Gilberto. "Mexican Migration." Paper presented at Conference on Demographic Study of the Mexican American Population. Austin, Tex.: University of Texas, 17–19 May 1973.

Connell, Earl. *The Mexican Population of Austin, Texas.* San Francisco: R & E Research Association, 1971. Reprint of a thesis, University of Texas, 1925.

Hardman, Max. "The Mexican Immigrant in Texas," *Southwestern Political and Social Science Quarterly* (June 1926): 33-41.

Hufford, Charles. *The Social and Economic Effects of the Mexican Migration into Texas.* San Francisco: R & E Research Association, 1971. Reprint of a thesis, 1929.

Kibbe, Pauline. *Latin Americans in Texas.* Albuquerque: University of New Mexico Press, 1946.

Kielman, Chester V. *Guide to the Microfilm Edition of the Bexar Archives, 1717–1803.* Austin, Tex.: University of Texas Archives Microfilm Division, 1967.

Menefee, Selden. *Mexican Migratory Workers of Southern Texas.* Washington, D.C.: Government Printing Office, 1941.

Moquin, Wayne, and Charles Van Doren, eds. *A Documentary History of the Mexican Americans.* New York: Praeger Publishers, 1971.

Nance, Joseph. *After San Jacinto: The Texas-Mexican Frontier, 1936–1841.* Austin, Tex.: University of Texas Press, 1963.

O'Rourke, Thomas P. *The Franciscan Missions in Texas, 1690–1793.* Washington, D.C.: Catholic University of America, 1927.

Perrigo, Lynn. *Texas and Our Spanish Southwest.* Dallas: Banks Upshaw, 1960.

Rosenbaum, Robert J. *Mexicano Resistance in the Southwest: "The Sacred Right of Self-Preservation."* Austin, Tex.: University of Texas Press, 1981.

Thompson, Jerry. *Vaqueros in Blue and Gray.* Austin, Tex.: Presidial Press, 1976.

Weber, David J. *The Mexican Frontier, 1821–1846: The American Southwest Under Mexico.* Albuquerque: University of New Mexico Press, 1982.

County Resources

In 1972 the legislature established a uniform statewide system for preservation of records in regional historical resources depositories. Under this act, the Local Records Division of the Texas State Library collects and maintains city, county, and local government records; these are available to the public. Michael Heskett, *Texas County Records: A Guide to the Holdings of the Local Records Division of the Texas State Library of County Records on Microfilm* (1978; 2d ed., Austin, Tex.: Texas State Library, 1990), is a valuable guide.

County records, such as land and property records, probate records and wills, marriage records, naturalization papers, and district court minutes, are microfilmed and kept in a depository designated for the county's respective area. Thus there is no one state depository with a complete set of records.

Each of the twenty-six depositories has some original records and manuscripts concerning that particular region. In some instances microfilming of county records has not been done. Inventories of the records available in nearly eighty of the 254 county courthouses have been made. For further information see:

Holley, Edward G., and Donald D. Hendricks. *Resources of Texas Libraries.* Austin, Tex.: Texas State Library, 1968.

Texas State Library. *Inventory of County Records.* Austin, Tex.: Texas State Library, 1973.

Many Texas counties have suffered a loss of records due to courthouse fires, floods, and theft. This is reflected in the earliest dates for record availability.

The first date in the county chart that follows is the creation date. It is sometimes followed by a second date indicating the date of organization, the date from which a researcher can expect to find vital, land, probate, and court records for each county. Some counties were organized twice. Although twenty-seven additional counties were created by the legislature, none were organized. Of these only Buchel, Encinal, and Foley counties had records. Buchel and Foley were incorporated into Brewster County, while Encinal was included in Webb County. As discussed in the appropriate sections above, deeds are located through the county clerk, probates at the county clerk's or the probate clerk's office in larger counties, and court records through the county or district court clerk. Letters should be addressed to the appropriate clerk. Kennedy and Kennedy, *Genealogical Records in Texas* (see Background Sources); Heskett, *Texas County Records...* (cited above); and Texas Law Organizations Resource Center website <www.txlaw.org/clerks.html> are the sources for the following data.

County court addresses cited in the following data were taken from <www.txlaw.org/clerks.html>. This website provides district court clerks' names, addresses, and phone numbers. Erath County is absent.

Data for county formation and record creation were obtained for most counties from the Family History Library Catalog at <www.familysearch.org> and from Kennedy and Kennedy, *Genealogical Sources in Texas.* This information reflects dates of county repository records; other compilations and publications may contain sources with varying dates.

Map	County Address	Date Formed Parent County/ies	Birth Marriage Death	Land Probate Court
N14	Anderson 500 Church St./P.O. Box 1159 Palestine 75001-1159	1846 Houston	1873 1846 1901	1846 1846 1846
F5	Andrews 215 N.W. First St./P.O. Box 328 Andrews 79714-0328	1876 (organized 1910) Young/Bexar	1884 1910 1886	1910 1910 1910
O15	Angelina P.O. Box 908 Lufkin 75902	1846 Nacogdoches	1903 1846 1857	1846 1850 1847
S12	Aransas 301 N. Live Oak Rockport 78382	1871 Refugio	1903 1871 1903	1839 1860 1871
L10	Archer P.O. Box 815 Archer City 76351-0815	1858 (organized 1880) Cooke	1903 1881 1903	1830 1875 1880
B6	Armstrong P.O. Box 309 Claude 79019-0309	1876 (organized 1890) Bexar District	1903 1890 1903	1890 1890 1890
R11	Atascosa 1 Circle Dr. Jourdanton 78026	1856 Bexar	1903 1856 1903	1856 1873 1856
P13	Austin 1 E. Main St. Bellville 77418	1836 (organized 1837) original county; Old Mexican Municipality	1903 1824 1903	1826 1827 1824
C5	Bailey 300 S. First St. Muleshoe 79347	1876 (organized 1919) Young/Bexar	1919 1919 1919	1919 1919 1919
Q10	Bandera P.O. Box 823 Bandera 78003-0823	1856 Bexar/Uvalde	1903 1856 1903	1837 1856 1857
P12	Bastrop P.O. Box 577 Bastrop 78602-0577	1836 (organized 1837) original county; Old Mexican Municipality	1903 1851 1903	1837 1837 1837
L10	Baylor P.O. Box 689 Seymour 76380-0689	1858 (organized 1879) Fannin	1903 1879 1903	1879 1879 1881
S12	Bee 105 W. Corpus Christi St. P.O. Box 666 Beeville 78102-0666	1857 (organized 1858) Live Oak/Goliad/Refugio/ San Patricio/Karnes	1903 1860 1903	1858 1859 1858
O12	Bell 104 S. Main St./P.O. Box 480 Belton 76513-0480	1850 Milam	1903 1850 1903	1850 1800 1852
Q10	Bexar 100 Dolorosa St. San Antonio 78285	1836 (organized 1837) original county; Old Spanish Municipality	1903 1837 1903	1837 1837 1836
P11	Blanco P.O. Box 65 Johnson City 78636-0065	1858 Gillespie/Burnet/Comal/ Hays	1903 1876 1903	1876 1876 1877
E6	Borden P.O. Box 124 Gail 79738-0124	1876 (organized 1891) Bexar District	1903 1891 1903	1891 1891 1891
N12	Bosque P.O. Box 617 Meridian 76665-0617	1854 McLennan/Milam	1903 1860 1903	1854 1855 1856
L15	Bowie P.O. Box 248 Boston 75550 0248	1840 (organized 1841) Red River	1903 1889 1903	1889 1889 1889
R14	Brazoria 111 E. Locust, Ste. 200 Angleton 77515	1836 (organized 1837) original county; Old Mexican Municipality	1903 1829 1903	1837 1837 1837
O13	Brazos 300 S. Texas Ave. P.O. Box 2208 Bryan 77805-2208	1841 (organized 1843) Washington/Robertson	1903 1841 1903	1841 1844 1841
J4	Brewster P.O. Box 119 Alpine 79831-0119	1887 Presidio	1903 1887 1903	1887 1887 1887
C6	Briscoe P.O. Box 375 Silverton 79257-0375	1876 (organized 1892) Bexar/Young	1903 1892 1903	1892 1892 1892
U11	Brooks P.O. Box 427 Falfurrias 78355-0427	1911 (organized 1912) Starr/Hildalgo/Live Oak/ Zapata	1911 1911 1911	1911 1911 1911
N10	Brown 200 S. Broadway Brownwood 76801	1856 (organized 1858) Travis/Comanche	1900 1880 1903	1836 1880 1884
P13	Burleson P.O. Box 57 Caldwell 77836-0057	1846 (organized 1846) Milam/Washington	1903 1846 1903	1841 1848 1880
P11	Burnet 220 S. Pierce St. Burnet 78611	1852 (organized 1854) Bell/Williamson/Travis	1903 1852 1903	1852 1852 1867
Q12	Caldwell P.O. Box 906 Lockhart 78644-0906	1848 Gonzales/Bastrop	1860 1848 1903	1846 1849 1848
S13	Calhoun 211 S. Ann St. Port Lavaca 77979	1846 Jackson/Victoria/ Matagorda	1903 1846 1903	1846 1846 1847
M10	Callahan 400 Market St. Baird 79504	1858 (organized 1877) Travis/Bexar/Bosque	1903 1878 1903	1878 1879 1879
U12	Cameron 974 E. Harrison St./ P.O. Box 2178 Brownsville 78522-2178	1848 Nueces	1903 1848 1930	1848 1848 1849
L15	Camp 126 Church St. Pittsburg 75686	1874 Upshur	1903 1874 1929	1874 1871 1874

TEXAS

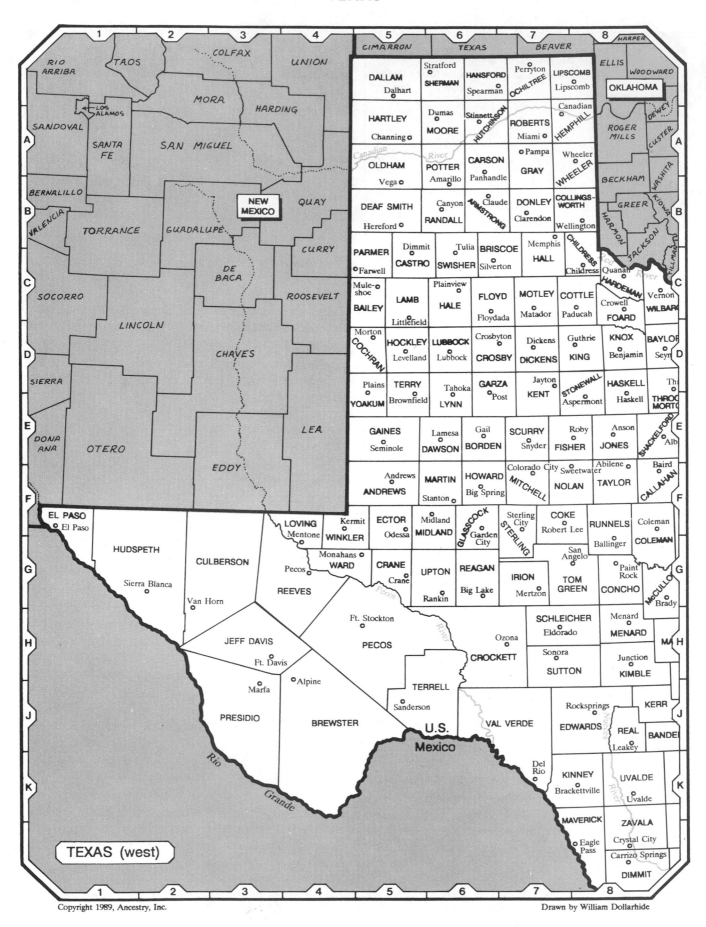

Drawn by William Dollarhide

TEXAS (west)

TEXAS

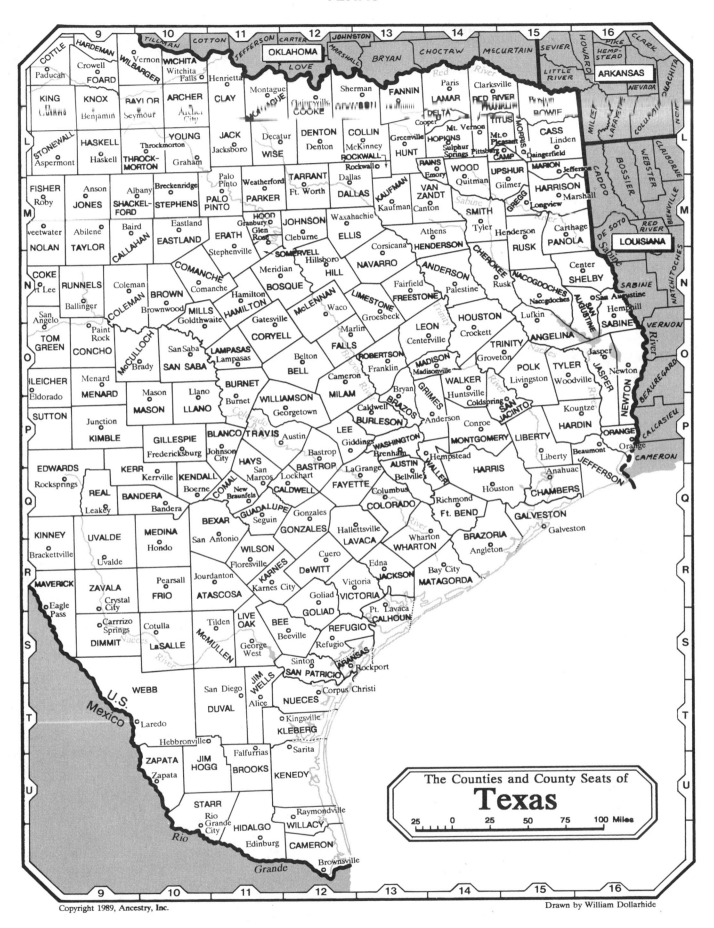

The Counties and County Seats of
Texas

25   0   25   50   75   100 Miles

Drawn by William Dollarhide

TEXAS

Map	County Address	Date Formed Parent County/ies	Birth Marriage Death	Land Probate Court
B6	Carson P.O. Box 487 Panhandle 79068-0487	1876 (organized 1888) Bexar District	1903 1888 1903	1888 1888 1888
L15	Cass P.O. Box 468 Linden 75563-0468	1846 (known as Davis, December 1861–May 1871) Bowie	1870 1847 1903	1844 1846 1846
C5	Castro 100 E. Bedford St. Dimmitt 79027	1876 (organized 1891) Bexar District	1903 1891 1903	1891 1891 1892
Q15	Chambers P.O. Box 728 Anahuac 77514-0728	1858 Liberty/Jefferson	1903 1876 1903	1875 1876 1876
N14	Cherokee P.O. Drawer 420 Rusk 75785-0420	1846 Nacogdoches	1903 1846 1903	1847 1839 1846
C8	Childress 100 Ave. N. N.W./P.O. Box 4 Childress 79201-0004	1876 (organized 1887) Bexar and Young Land Districts	1903 1887 1903	1887 1888 1887
	Cibilo	(see Wilson)		
L11	Clay P.O. Box 548 Henrietta 76365-0548	1857 (organized 1861; disorganized 1862; reorganized 1873) Cooke	1903 1874 1903	1830 1873 1873
D5	Cochran 100 N. Main St. Morton 79346	1876 (organized 1924) Bexar and Young Land Districts	1924 1924 1924	1924 1924 1925
N9	Coke P.O. Box 150 Robert Lee 76945-0150	1889 Tom Green	1903 1890 1903	1891 1891 1891
N9	Coleman P.O. Box 591 Coleman 76834-0591	1858 (organized 1876) Brown/Travis	1903 1876 1903	1876 1876 1876
L13	Collin 210 S. McDonald, Ste. 124 McKinney 75069	1846 Fannin	1903 1846 1903	1846 1846 1846
B8	Collingsworth Courthouse Wellington 79095	1876 (organized 1890) Bexar and Young Land Districts	1903 1890 1903	1890 1890 1891
Q13	Colorado P.O. Box 68 Columbus 78934-0068	1836 (organized 1837) Old Mexican Municipality	1853 1837 1903	1824 1837 1837
Q11	Comal 100 Main Plaza New Braunfels 78130	1846 Bexar/Travis/Gonzales	1903 1846 1903	1847 1846 1846
N10	Comanche Courthouse Comanche 76442	1856 Coryell/Bosque	1903 1856 1903	1856 1856 1858
O9	Concho P.O. Box 98 Paint Rock 76866-0098	1858 (organized 1879) Bexar	1903 1879 1903	1879 1879 1880
L12	Cooke 100 Dixon St. Gainesville 76240	1848 (organized 1849) Fannin	1870 1854 1903	1830 1849 1849
O11	Coryell P.O. Box 237 Gatesville 76528-0237	1854 Bell/McLennan	1867 1854 1884	1854 1854 1856
C8	Cottle P.O. Box 717 Paducah 79248-0717	1876 (organized 1892) Fannin	1903 1892 1903	1892 1892 1892
G5	Crane P.O. Box 578 Crane 79731-0578	1887 (organized 1927) Tom Green	1927 1927 1927	1927 1927 1927
H6	Crockett P.O. Drawer C Ozona 76943	1875 (organized 1891) Bexar	1903 1841 1903	1891 1891 1892
D6	Crosby P.O. Box 218 Crosbyton 79322-0218	1876 (organized 1886) Bexar Land District	1903 1886 1840	1887 1887 1887
G3	Culberson P.O. Box 158 Van Horn 79855-0158	1911 (organized 1912) El Paso	1911 1911 1911	1911 1911 1911
A5	Dallam P.O. Box 1352 Dalhart 79002-1352	1876 (organized 1891) Bexar Land District	1903 1891 1903	1891 1891 1892
M13	Dallas 500 Main St. Dallas 75202	1846 Nacogdoches/ Robertson	1903 1846 1911	1846 1842 1846
	Davis	(see Cass)		
E6	Dawson P.O. Drawer 1268 Lamesa 79331-1268	1858/1876 (organized 1905) Bexar Land District	1905 1905 1905	1905 1905 1905
B5	Deaf Smith 235 E. Third St. Hereford 79045	1876 (organized 1890) Bexar Land District	1903 1890 1903	1890 1890 1890
L14	Delta P.O. Box 455 Cooper 75432-0455	1868 (organized 1870) Lamar/Hopkins	1903 1871 1903	1836 1876 1872
L12	Denton P.O. Box 2187 Denton 76202-2187	1846 Fannin	1903 1875 1903	1854 1876 1877
R12	DeWitt 307 N. Gonzales St. P.O. Box 845 Cuero 77954-0845	1846 Gonzales/Goliad/Victoria	1903 1846 1903	1846 1846 1852

Map	County Address	Date Formed Parent County/ies	Birth Marriage Death	Land Probate Court
D7	Dickens P.O. Box 120 Dickens 79229-0120	1876 (organized 1891) Bexar Land District	1903 1891 1903	1891 1881 1891
K8	Dimmit 103 N. Fifth St. Carrizo Springs 78834	1858 (organized 1880) Bexar/Maverick/Webb/ Uvalde	1903 1881 1903	1880 1881 1881
B7	Donley P.O. Drawer U Clarendon 79226	1881 (organized 1882) Bexar Land District	1903 1882 1903	1882 1882 1882
T11	Duval P.O. Box 248 San Diego 78384-0248	1858 (organized 1876) Nueces/Live Oak/ Hildalgo/Starr	1903 1877 1903	1877 1877 1877
N10	Eastland P.O. Box 110 Eastland 76448-0110	1858 (organized 1873) Bosque/Coryell/Travis	1903 1873 1903	1874 1874 1874
F5	Ector 300 N. Grant/P.O. Box 707 Odessa 79761-0707	1887 (organized 1891) Tom Green	1903 1891 1903	1891 1891 1891
J7	Edwards P.O. Box 184 Rocksprings 78880-0184	1858 (organized 1883) Bexar District	1903 1888 1903	1888 1888 1888
M13	El Paso 500 E. San Antonio Ave. El Paso 79901	1850 (organized 1856; reorganized 1871) Bexar	1903 1866 1903	1856 1866 1861
F1	Ellis 117 W. Franklin/P.O. Box 250 Waxahachie 75165-0250	1849 (organized 1850) Navarro/Robertson	1903 1850 1903	1845 1850 1850
	Encinal	1856 (never organized; abolished 1899—area incorporated into Webb County)		
N11	Erath Stephenville 76401 *Courthouse fire, 1866.*	1856 Bosque/Coryell	1903 1869 1903	1867 1866 1866
O12	Falls P.O. Box 458 Marlin 76661-0458	1850 Milam/Limestone	1903 1854 1903	1850 1851 1851
L13	Fannin 101 W. Sam Rayburn Dr. Bonham 75418	1837 (organized 1838) Red River	1903 1852 1903	1838 1838 1838
Q12	Fayette P.O. Box 59 La Grange 78945-0059	1837 (organized 1838) Colorado/Bastrop	1903 1838 1903	1838 1838 1838
E7	Fisher P.O. Box 368 Roby 79543-0368	1876 (organized 1886) Bexar Land District	1903 1886 1903	1886 1886 1886
C6	Floyd P.O. Box 476 Floydada 79235-0476	1876 (organized 1890) Bexar and Young Land Districts	1903 1890 1890	1890 1890 1890
C8	Foard P.O. Box 539 Crowell 79227-0539	1891 Knox/Hardeman/Cottle/ King	1903 1891 1903	1891 1891 1891
Q14	Fort Bend P.O. Box 520 Richmond 77406-0520	1837 (organized 1838) Austin/Harris/Brazoria	1903 1837 1903	1837 1838 1838
L14	Franklin P.O. Box 68 Mount Vernon 75457-0068	1875 Titus	1903 1875 1903	1841 1875 1875
N13	Freestone P.O. Box 1017 Fairfield 75840-1017	1850 (organized 1851) Limestone	1903 1851 1903	1850 1851 1851
R10	Frio P.O. Box X Pearsall 78061	1858 (organized 1871) Uvalde/Bexar/Atascosa	1903 1871 1903	1871 1873 1873
E5	Gaines Courthouse Seminole 79360	1876 (organized 1905) Bexar Land District	1905 1906 1905	1905 1905 1906
Q15	Galveston P.O. Box 2450 Galveston 77553-2450	1838 Brazoria/Liberty	1903 1838 1903	1838 1838 1839
E6	Garza 300 W. Main/P.O. Box 366 Post 79356-0366	1876 (organized 1907) Bexar Land District	1903 1907 1903	1907 1907 1907
P10	Gillespie 101 W. Main St., Unit 13 Fredericksburg 78624	1848 Bexar/Travis	1840 1850 1903	1850 1850 1849
F6	Glasscock P.O. Box 190 Garden City 79739-0190	1887 (organized 1893) Tom Green	1903 1883 1903	1893 1893 1893
S12	Goliad P.O. Box 5 Goliad 77963-0005	1836 (organized 1837) Old Mexican Municipality	1903 1876 1903	1852 1871 1855
Q12	Gonzales P.O. Box 77 Gonzales 78629-0077	1836 (organized 1837) Old Mexican Municipality	1903 1829 1903	1837 1832 1838
A7	Gray P.O. Box 1902 Pampa 79066-1902	1876 (organized 1902) Bexar Land District	1903 1902 1903	1902 1902 1903
L12	Grayson 100 W. Houston St. Sherman 75090	1846 Fannin	1903 1846 1903	1846 1846 1836
	Greer (now in Oklahoma) Mangum, OK 73554	1860 (organized 1886) Young	1912 1901 1912	1886 1901 1886
M15	Gregg 101 E. Methvin/P.O. Box 3049 Longview 75606-3049	1873 Upshur/Rusk	1873 1873 1903	1873 1873 1873

Map County Address	Date Formed Parent County/ies	Birth Marriage Death	Land Probate Court
P13 Grimes P.O. Box 209 Anderson 77830-0209	1846 Montgomery	1903 1848 1903	1837 1838 1844
Q11 Guadalupe 101 E. Court St./P.O. Box 951 Seguin 78155	1846 Gonzales/Bexar	1903 1846 1903	1846 1846 1846
C6 Hale 500 Broadway, #140 Plainview 79072-8050	1876 (organized 1888) Bexar Land District	1903 1888 1903	1888 1888 1888
C7 Hall 512 Main St. Box 8 Memphis 79245-0008	1876 (organized 1890) Bexar and Young Land Districts	1903 1890 1903	1890 1890 1890
N11 Hamilton Courthouse Hamilton 76531	1842 (organized 1858) Comanche/Bosque/ Lampasas/Coryell	1872 1876 1903	1869 1870 1871
A6 Hansford P.O. Box 397 Spearman 79081-0397	1876 (organized 1889) Bexar and Young Land Districts	1903 1889 1903	1889 1889 1889
C8 Hardeman P.O. Box 30 Quanah 79252-0030	1858 (organized 1884) Fannin	1903 1885 1903	1884 1885 1885
P15 Hardin P.O. Box 38 Kountze 77625-0038	1858 Liberty/Jefferson	1903 1862 1903	1849 1866 1879
Q14 Harris P.O. Box 1525 Houston 77251-1525	1836 (organized 1837) original county	1903 1837 1903	1837 1831 1837
M15 Harrison P.O. Box 1365 Marshall 75671-1365	1839 (organized 1842) Shelby	1869 1838 1849	1839 1838 1840
A5 Hartley P.O. Box 147 Channing 79018-0147	1876 (organized 1891) Bexar and Young Land Districts	1903 1891 1903	1891 1891 1891
L9 Haskell P.O. Box 725 Haskell 79521-0725	1858 (organized 1885) Fannin/Milam	1903 1885 1903	1885 1885 1885
Q11 Hays 137 N. Guadalupe St. San Marcos 78666	1848 Travis	1903 1848 1903	1848 1839 1850
A7 Hemphill P.O. Box 867 Canadian 79014-0867	1876 (organized 1887) Bexar and Young Land Districts	1903 1887 1903	1887 1887 1887
M13 Henderson P.O. Box 632 Athens 75751-0632	1846 Houston/Nacogdoches	1903 1847 1903	1847 1846 1847
U11 Hildalgo P.O. Box 58 Edinburg 78540-0058	1852 Cameron/Starr	1903 1852 1903	1848 1852 1852
N12 Hill P.O. Box 398 Hillsboro 76645-0398	1853 Navarro	1860 1873 1903	1853 1853 1867
D5 Hockley 800 Houston St. Levelland 79336	1874 (organized 1921) Bexar and Young Land Districts	1921 1921 1921	1921 1921 1921
M11 Hood P.O. Box 339 Granbury 76048-0339	1865 Johnson	1903 1875 1913	1875 1875 1875
L14 Hopkins P.O. Box 288 Sulphur Springs 75483-0288	1846 Lamar/Nacogdoches	1903 1846 1903	1846 1846 1846
O14 Houston P.O. Box 370 Crockett 75835-0370	1837 Nacogdoches	1903 1882 1903	1865 1859 1878
F6 Howard P.O. Box 1468 Big Spring 79721-1468	1876 (organized 1882) Bexar and Young Land Districts	1903 1882 1903	1882 1882 1882
G2 Hudspeth P.O. Drawer A Sierra Blanca 79851	1917 El Paso	1917 1917 1917	1917 1917 1917
L13 Hunt P.O. Box 1316 Greenville 75401-1316	1846 Fannin/Nacogdoches	1903 1858 1903	1846 1847 1851
A6 Hutchinson P.O. Box 1186 Stinnett 79038-1186	1876 (organized 1901) Bexar Land District	1903 1901 1903	1901 1901 1901
G7 Irion P.O. Box 736 Mertzon 76941-0736	1889 Tom Green	1903 1889 1903	1889 1889 1889
L11 Jack 100 Main St. Jacksboro 76458	1856 (organized 1857) Cooke	1903 1858 1910	1858 1858 1858
R13 Jackson 115 W. Main St. Edna 77957	1836 (organized 1837) Old Mexican Municipality	1903 1837 1903	1836 1837 1838
O15 Jasper P.O. Box 2070 Jasper 75951-2070	1836 (organized 1837) Old Mexican Municipality	1903 1858 1903	1849 1849 1850
H3 Jeff Davis P.O. Box 398 Fort Davis 79734-0398	1887 Presidio	1903 1931 1931	1887 1887 1887
P15 Jefferson P.O. Box 1151 Beaumont 77704-1151	1836 (organized 1837) Old Mexican Municipality	1903 1837 1903	1836 1838 1844
U11 Jim Hogg P.O. Box 878 Hebbronville 78361-0878	1913 Brooks/Duval	1913 1913 1913	1913 1913 1913

Map	County Address	Date Formed Parent County/ies	Birth Marriage Death	Land Probate Court
T11	Jim Wells P.O. Box 1459 Alice 78331-1459	1911 (organized 1912) Nueces	1911 1911 1911	1911 1911 1911
M12	Johnson P.O. Box 662 Cleburne 76031-0662	1854 Navarro/McLennan/Hill/ Ellis	1860 1854 1885	1854 1854 1852
E8	Jones P.O. Box 552 Anson 79501-0552	1858 (organized 1881) Bexar/Bosque	1903 1881 1903	1881 1881 1881
R12	Karnes 101 N. Panna Maria Ave. Karnes City 78118-2930	1854 Bexar/San Patricio Goliad/Dewitt	1903 1865 1903	1855 1865 1854
M13	Kaufman Courthouse Kaufman 75142	1848 Henderson	1869 1849 1903	1846 1849 1856
Q10	Kendall 204 E. San Antonio St. Boerne 78006	1862 Kerr/Blanco	1903 1867 1903	1862 1862 1862
U12	Kenedy P.O. Box 1519 Sarita 78385-1519	1911 (as Willacy; renamed Kenedy, 1921) Cameron/Hidalgo/Willacy	1911 1860 1911	1832 1860 1911
E7	Kent P.O. Box 9 Jayton 79528-0009	1876 (organized 1892) Bexar and Young Land Districts	1903 1892 1903	1892 1892 1892
J8	Kerr 700 E. Main St. Kerrville 78028-5389	1856 Bexar Land District, no. 2	1903 1856 1903	1840 1856 1856
H8	Kimble 501 Main St. Junction 76849	1858 (organized 1876) Bexar Territory	1903 1884 1903	1884 1884 1884
D8	King P.O. Box 135 Guthrie 79236-0135	1876 (organized 1891) Bexar Land District	1903 1914 1903	1914 1914 1914
K7	Kinney P.O. Drawer 9 Brackettville 78832-0009	1850 (organized 1872) Bexar	1903 1872 1903	1872 1874 1873
T12	Kleberg P.O. Box 1327 Kingsville 78364-1327	1913 Nueces	1913 1913 1913	1913 1913 1914
D8	Knox P.O. Box 196 Benjamin 79505-0196	1858 (organized 1886) Cooke/Bexar/Young	1905 1886 1909	1886 1886 1886
L14	Lamar 119 N. Main St. Paris 75460	1840 (organized 1841) Red River	1903 1841 1903	1838 1841 1863
C5	Lamb P.O. Box 3 Littlefield 79339-0003	1876 (organized 1908) Bexar Land District	1908 1909 1908	1908 1909 1909
O11	Lampasas P.O. Box 347 Lampasas 76550-0347	1856 Travis/Bell	1903 1873 1903	1872 1876 1878
S10	LaSalle P.O. Box 340 Cotulla 78014-0340	1858 (organized 1880) Bexar/Webb	1903 1880 1903	1880 1881 1881
R12	Lavaca P.O. Box 326 Hallettsville 77964-0326	1846 Colorado/Gonzales/ Jackson/Victoria	1903 1847 1903	1846 1846 1847
P12	Lee P.O. Box 419 Giddings 78942-0419	1874 Burleson/Washington/ Bastrop/Fayette	1873 1874 1903	1835 1874 1874
N13	Leon P.O. Box 98 Centerville 75833-0098	1846 Robertson	1903 1885 1903	1836 1846 1846
P15	Liberty 304 Campbell/P.O. Box 369 Liberty 77575-0369	1836 (organized 1837) Old Spanish Municipality	1903 1875 1903	1875 1895 1874
O13	Limestone P.O. Box 350 Groesbeck 76642-0350	1846 Robertson	1903 1873 1903	1873 1874 1870
A8	Lipscomb P.O. Box 70 Lipscomb 79056-0070	1876 (organized 1887) Bexar Land District	1903 1887 1903	1887 1887 1887
S11	Live Oak P.O. Box 280 George West 78022-0280	1856 San Patricio/Nueces	1903 1857 1903	1835 1860 1876
P10	Llano 107 W. Sandstone Llano 78643	1856 Bexar/Gillespie	1903 1880 1903	1875 1881 1882
F4	Loving P.O. Box 194 Mentone 79754-0194	1887 (organized 1893; deorganized 1897; reorganized 1931) Tom Green	1931 1931 1931	1931 1931 1931
D6	Lubbock P.O. Box 10536 Lubbock 79408	1876 (organized 1891) Bexar Land District and Crosby County	1903 1891 1903	1881 1891 1891
E6	Lynn P.O. Box 937 Tahoka 79373-0937	1876 (organized 1903) Bexar Land District	1903 1903 1904	1903 1903 1903
O13	Madison P.O. Box 599 Anderson 77830	1853 (organized 1854) Grimes/Walker/Leon	1903 1874 1903	1835 1873 1873
L15	Marion 102 W. Austin St., Room 206/ P.O. Box F Jefferson 75657	1860 Cass/Titus	1903 1860 1903	1860 1860 1860
F6	Martin P.O. Box 906 Stanton 79782-0906	1876 (organized 1884) Bexar Land District	1903 1885 1903	1885 1885 1885

Map	County Address	Date Formed Parent County/ies	Birth Marriage Death	Land Probate Court
P10	Mason P.O. Box 702 Mason 76856-0702	1858 Gillespie	1903 1877 1903	1877 1877 1877
R13	Matagorda 1700 Seventh St., Rm 202 P.O. Box 69 Bay City 77404-0069	1836 (organized 1837) Old Mexican Municipality	1903 1837 1859	1828 1827 1837
K8	Maverick P.O. Box 4050 Eagle Pass 78853-4050	1856 (organized 1871) Kinney	1903 1871 1903	1871 1871 1871
O10	McCulloch Courthouse Sq. Brady 76825	1856 (organized 1862; reorganized 1876) Bexar	1903 1876 1903	1876 1876 1876
O12	Mclennan P.O. Box 1727 Waco 76703-1727	1850 Milam/Navarro/Limestone	1903 1850 1903	1840 1850 1850
S10	McMullen P.O. Box 235 Tilden 78072-0235	1858 (organized 1862; reorganized 1877) Bexar/Atascosa/Live Oak	1903 1877 1903	1835 1877 1879
R10	Medina 110 16th St. Hondo 78861	1848 Bexar	1903 1848 1903	1848 1848 1849
H8	Menard P.O. Box 1028 Menard 76859-1028	1850 (organized 1866; reorganized 1871) Bexar	1903 1871 1903	1871 1871 1871
F6	Midland P.O. Box 211 Midland 79702-0211	1885 Tom Green	1903 1885 1910	1885 1885 1886
O12	Milam P.O. Box 191 Cameron 76520-0191	1836 (organized 1837) Old Mexican Municipality	1903 1874 1903	1873 1874 1872
	Miller	1820 (in Arkansas Territory; renamed Red River, 1836)		
O10	Mills P.O. Box 646 Goldthwaite 76844-0646	1887 Brown/Lampasas/ Hamilton/Comanche	1903 1887 1903	1887 1887 1887
F7	Mitchell P.O. Box 1166 Colorado City 79512-1166	1876 (organized 1881) Bexar Land District	1903 1881 1903	1881 1881 1881
L11	Montague P.O. Box 77 Montague 76251-0077	1857 (organized 1858) Cooke	1860 1873 1903	1873 1873 1873
P14	Montgomery P.O. Box 959 Conroe 77305-0959	1834 (organized 1837) Washington	1903 1838 1903	1838 1838 1839
A6	Moore 715 S. Dumas Ave. Dumas 79029	1876 (organized 1892) Bexar Land District	1903 1892 1903	1882 1892 1892
L15	Morris 500 Broadnax St. Daingerfield 75638	1875 Titus	1903 1875 1911	1846 1876 1875
D7	Motley P.O. Box 66 Matador 79244-0066	1876 (organized 1891) Bexar Land District	1903 1891 1903	1891 1891 1891
N15	Nacogdoches 101 W. Main St. Nacogdoches 75961	1836 (organized 1837) Old Mexican Municipality	1903 1824 1903	1833 1837 1837
M13	Navarro P.O. Box 423 Corsicana 75151-0423	1846 Robertson	1903 1846 1903	1838 1846 1855
O16	Newton P.O. Box 484 Newton 75966-0484	1846 Jasper	1903 1846 1903	1846 1846 1846
F7	Nolan P.O. Drawer 98 Sweetwater 79556-0098	1876 (organized 1881) Bexar and Young Land Districts	1903 1881 1903	1881 1881 1881
T12	Nueces P.O. Box 2627 Corpus Christi 78403-2627	1846 San Patricio/Bexar	1903 1846 1903	1847 1846 1850
A7	Ochiltree 511 S. Main St. Perryton 79070	1876 (organized 1889) Bexar Land District	1903 1889 1903	1889 1889 1889
A5	Oldham P.O. Box 360 Vega 79092-0360	1876 (organized 1881) Bexar Land District	1903 1881 1903	1881 1881 1881
P16	Orange P.O. Box 1536 Orange 77631-1536	1852 Jefferson	1903 1852 1903	1852 1852 1852
M11	Palo Pinto P.O. Box 219 Palo Pinto 76484-0219	1856 (organized 1857) Bosque/Navarro	1903 1858 1903	1858 1858 1858
M15	Panola 110 W. Sycamore St. Carthage 75633	1846 Harrison/Shelby	1903 1846 1857	1839 1846 1846
M11	Parker P.O. Box 819 Weatherford 76086-0819	1855 (organized 1856) Bosque/Navarro	1903 1874 1903	1874 1874 1874
C5	Parmer P.O. Box 356 Farwell 79325-0356	1876 (organized 1907) Bexar Land District	1903 1907 1907	1907 1907 1907
H5	Pecos 103 W. Callaghan St. Fort Stockton 79735	1871 (organized 1875) Presidio	1903 1875 1903	1875 1875 1875
O15	Polk P.O. Drawer 2119 Livingston 77351-2119	1846 Liberty	1903 1846 1903	1845 1840 1848

Map	County Address	Date Formed Parent County/ies	Birth Marriage Death	Land Probate Court
B6	Potter P.O. Box 9638 Amarillo 79105-9638	1876 (organized 1887) Bexar Land District	1903 1887 1903	1887 1887 1002
J3	Presidio P.O. Box 789 Marfa 79843-0789	1850 (organized 1875) Bexar District	1903 1875 1903	1876 1875 1875
L13	Rains P.O. Box 187 Emory 75440-0187	1870 Wood/Hopkins/Hunt	1903 1879 1903	1870 1880 1880
B6	Randall P.O. Box 660 Canyon 79015-0660	1876 (organized 1889) Bexar Land District	1903 1889 1903	1889 1889 1889
G6	Reagan P.O. Box 100 Big Lake 76932-0100	1903 Tom Green	1903 1903 1903	1903 1903 1903
J8	Real P.O. Box 656 Leakey 78873-0656	1913 Edwards/Kerr/Bandera	1913 1913 1913	1913 1913 1913
L14	Red River 200 N. Walnut St. Clarksville 75426	1836 (organized 1837) Old Mexican Municipality	1903 1846 1903	1837 1838 1840
G4	Reeves P.O. Box 867 Pecos 79772-0867	1883 (organized 1884) Pecos	1903 1884 1903	1884 1884 1885
S12	Refugio P.O. Box 704 Refugio 78377-0704	1836 (organized 1837) Old Mexican Municipality	1903 1851 1903	1839 1840 1841
A7	Roberts P.O. Box 477 Miami 79059-0477	1876 (organized 1889) Bexar Land District	1903 1889 1903	1889 1889 1889
O13	Robertson P.O. Box 1029 Franklin 77856-1029	1837 (organized 1838) Milam	1903 1838 1903	1838 1838 1838
L13	Rockwall 101 E. Rusk St. Rockwall 75087	1873 Kaufman	1903 1875 1903	1873 1875 1875
F8	Runnels P.O. Box 189 Ballinger 76821-0189	1858 (organized 1880) Bexar/Travis	1903 1880 1903	1880 1880 1881
M15	Rusk P.O. Box 758 Henderson 75653-0758	1843 Nacogdoches	1873 1843 1903	1843 1847 1859
N16	Sabine P.O. Drawer 580 Hemphill 75948-0580	1836 (organized 1837) original county	1903 1880 1903	1875 1879 1876
N15	San Augustine 100 W. Columbia St. San Augustine 75972	1836 (organized 1837) Old Mexican Municipality	1903 1837 1903	1833 1837 1837
O14	San Jacinto P.O. Box 669 Coldspring 77331-0669	1869 (reorganized 1870) Polk/Liberty/ Montgomery/Walker	1903 1870 1903	1851 1876 1871
S12	San Patricio 400 W. Sinton, Rm 105/ P.O. Box 578 Sinton 78387-0578	1836 (organized 1837; reorganized 1847) Old Mexican Municipality	1903 1858 1903	1846 1847 1848
O10	San Saba 502 E. Wallace St. San Saba 76877	1856 Bexar	1903 1857 1903	1857 1868 1868
H7	Schleicher P.O. Drawer 580 Eldorado 76936-0580	1887 (organized 1901) Crocket	1903 1901 1903	1901 1901 1901
E7	Scurry 1806 25th St., Ste. 300 Snyder 79549	1876 (organized 1884) Bexar land district	1903 1884 1903	1884 1884 1885
M10	Shackelford P.O. Box 247 Albany 76430-0247	1858 (organized 1874) Bosque	1903 1903 1903	1874 1874 1875
N15	Shelby P.O. Box 592 Center 75935-0592	1836 (organized 1837) Old Mexican Municipality	1903 1882 1903	1838 1881 1882
A6	Sherman P.O. Box 270 Stratford 79084-0270	1876 (organized 1889) Bexar Land District	1903 1889 1903	1889 1889 1889
M14	Smith P.O. Box 1018 Tyler 75710-1018	1846 Nacogdoches	1903 1846 1903	1846 1846 1846
M11	Somervell P.O. Box 1098 Glen Rose 76043-1098	1875 Hood/Johnson	1860 1885 1903	1875 1875 1875
U10	Starr 4th St. and Britton Rio Grande City 78582	1848 Nueces	1903 1858 1903	1848 1848 1848
M10	Stephens 200 W. Walker St. Breckenridge 76424	1858 (as Buchanan; organized 1876) Bosque	1903 1876 1903	1876 1876 1879
F7	Sterling P.O. Box 55 Sterling City 76951-0055	1891 Tom Green	1903 1891 1903	1891 1891 1891
L9	Stonewall P.O. Drawer P Aspermont 79502	1876 (organized 1888) Bexar Land District	1903 1888 1903	1887 1888 1889
H7	Sutton 300 E. Oak St., Ste. 3 Sonora 76950	1887 (organized 1890) Crockett	1903 1890 1903	1890 1890 1891
C6	Swisher Courthouse Tulia 79088	1876 (organized 1890) Bexar and Young Land Districts	1903 1890 1903	1890 1890 1890

Map	County Address	Date Formed Parent County/ies	Birth Marriage Death	Land Probate Court
M12	Tarrant 100 W. Weatherford St. Fort Worth 76196	1849 (organized 1850) Navarro	1903 1876 1903	1850 1856 1876
F8	Taylor 300 Oak St. Abilene 79602	1858 (organized 1878) Bexar/Travis	1903 1878 1903	1878 1878 1879
J6	Terrell P.O. Drawer 410 Sanderson 79848-0410	1905 Pecos	1905 1905 1905	1906 1905 1905
D5	Terry 500 W. Main St., Rm 105 Brownfield 79316	1876 (organized 1904) Bexar Land District	1904 1904 1904	1904 1904 1905
L10	Throckmorton P.O. Box 309 Throckmorton 76483-0309	1858 (organized 1879) Bosque/Fannin	1903 1879 1903	1879 1879 1879
L15	Titus 100 W. First St., Ste. 104 Mt. Pleasant 75455	1846 Bowie/Red River	1870 1895 1903	1846 1895 1895
G7	Tom Green 124 W. Beauregard San Angelo 76903	1874 (organized 1874) Bexar	1903 1875 1903	1875 1875 1875
P11	Travis P.O. Box 1748 Austin 78767-1748	1840 Bastrop	1903 1840 1903	1840 1840 1876
O14	Trinity P.O. Box 456 Groveton 75845-0456	1850 Houston	1903 1876 1857	1873 1876 1887
O15	Tyler 110 Courthouse Woodville 75979	1846 Liberty	1903 1849 1903	1846 1847 1847
M15	Upshur P.O. Box 730 Gilmer 75644-0730	1846 Harrison/Nacogdoches	1903 1846 1903	1846 1846 1846
G6	Upton P.O. Box 465 Rankin 79778-0465	1867 (organized 1910) Tom Green	1910 1910 1910	1910 1910 1910
K8	Uvalde P.O. Box 284 Uvalde 78802-0284	1850 (organized 1856) Bexar	1903 1856 1903	1838 1857 1857
J7	Val Verde P.O. Box 1267 Del Rio 78841-1267	1885 Kinney/Pecos/Crockett	1903 1885 1903	1885 1885 1885
M14	Van Zandt 121 E. Dallas St., Rm 202 Canton 75103	1848 Henderson	1903 1848 1903	1848 1848 1848
R13	Victoria P.O. Box 2410 Victoria 77902-2410	1836 (organized 1837) Old Mexican Municipality	1903 1838 1903	1838 1838 1838
O14	Walker P.O. Box 210 Huntsville 77342-0210	1846 Montgomery	1903 1846 1903	1846 1846 1847
P14	Waller 836 Austin St., #217 Hempstead 77445	1873 Austin/Grimes	1903 1873 1903	1824 1873 1873
G4	Ward 400 S. Allen St. Monahans 79756	1887 (organized 1892) Tom Green	1903 1893 1903	1893 1893 1893
P13	Washington 100 E. Main, Ste. 102 Brenham 77833	1836 (organized 1837) Old Mexican Municipality	1903 1837 1903	1832 1837 1840
T10	Webb P.O. Box 29 Laredo 78042-0029	1848 Bexar/Nueces	1903 1852 1903	1847 1851 1851
R13	Wharton P.O. Box 69 Wharton 77488-0069	1846 Colorado/Jackson/ Matagorda/Brazoria	1903 1847 1903	1837 1846 1847
A8	Wheeler P.O. Box 465 Wheeler 79096-0465	1876 (organized 1879) Bexar and Young Land Districts	1903 1879 1903	1881 1879 1879
L10	Wichita P.O. Box 1679 Wichita Falls 76307-1679	1858 (organized 1882) Cooke and Young Land Districts	1860 1882 1903	1873 1882 1882
L10	Wilbarger 1700 Wilbarger St. Vernon 76384	1858 (organized 1881) Bexar Territory	1903 1882 1903	1881 1882 1886
U12	Willacy 546 W. Hidalgo Ave. Raymondville 78580	1911 (reorganized 1921) Hidalgo/Cameron	1921 1921 1921	1921 1921 1921
P12	Williamson P.O. Box 18 Georgetown 78627-0018	1848 Milam	1873 1848 1903	1848 1848 1848
R11	Wilson P.O. Box 27 Floresville 78114-0027 *Called Ciblio, 1869–1874.*	1860 Bexar/Karnes	1903 1860 1903	1860 1862 1894
F4	Winkler P.O. Box 1007 Kermit 79745-1007	1887 (organized 1910) Tom Green	1910 1910 1910	1911 1910 1910
L11	Wise P.O. Box 359 Decatur 76234-0359	1856 Cooke	1870 1881 1903	1856 1882 1882
M14	Wood P.O. Box 338 Quitman 75783-0338	1850 Van Zandt	1903 1879 1903	1878 1878 1878
E5	Yoakum P.O. Box 309 Plains 79355-0309	1876 (organized 1907) Bexar Land District	1907 1907 1907	1907 1907 1907

TEXAS

Map	County Address	Date Formed Parent County/ies	Birth Marriage Death	Land Probate Court
L10	Young 516 Fourth St., Rm 104 Graham 76450	1856 (organized 1858; reorganized 1874) Jacques/Fannin	1903 1850 1903	1858 1850 1858
U10	Zapata P.O. Box 789 Zapata 78076-0789	1858 Starr Webb	1903 1868 1903	1868 1868 1874
K8	Zavala 200 E. Uvalde St. Crystal City 78839	1858 (organized 1884) Uvalde/Maverick	1903 1884 1903	1838 1885 1885

Utah

PATRICIA LYN SCOTT, CA, AND GARY TOPPING, Ph.D.

Utah's cultural history is considerably enriched by evidence of prehistoric inhabitants dating as far back as 10,000 B.C. When Spaniards, the first Europeans, arrived in the area in the eighteenth century, members of the Gosiute, Southern Paiute, Ute, Shoshone, and Navajo cultures were already here to greet them. Two expeditions led by Juan Maria de Rivera entered southeastern Utah in 1765; eleven years later, in 1776, the Franciscans Dominguez and Escalante reached Utah Lake before turning back to Santa Fe.

Lured by the reports of John C. Fremont, Lansford W. Hastings, and others, emigrants to the Pacific left wheel tracks across Utah during the 1840s. The Bidwell-Bartleson party of 1841 was the first, but the Bryant-Russell, Harlan Young, and Donner-Reed groups added their tracks, followed by the Gold Rushers of the early 1850s. Records of all of these parties are available, mostly in published form.

Utah's first permanent Anglo inhabitants were fur trappers who came west from St. Louis and north from Taos in search of beaver. Osborne Russell's diary records that he wintered in the Weber Valley in 1843 with a party of French-Canadian trappers, and Miles Goodyear started a trading post near present-day Ogden in 1846 to do business with emigrants on the Oregon Trail.

Before Goodyear actually opened his doors, however, he was bought out by Captain James Brown, representing The Church of Jesus Christ of Latter-day Saints, a persecuted religious group that began settling in the Salt Lake Valley in 1847. Since then, the Mormons, as they are popularly known, have written a large share of Utah history, virtually all aspects of which are well documented by their famous and fortunate penchant for record keeping.

Mormonism has a strong communitarian emphasis, which served its adherents well in settling Utah's harsh environment. The resources of the community were pooled through tithing, and Mormon settlement was accomplished by sending settlers out to begin well-planned colonies rather than leaving the settlement of outlying areas to individuals. Mormon colonies included men, women, and children, as well as representatives of every necessary trade and profession: doctors, blacksmiths, carpenters, and especially musicians for the frequent Mormon dances that kept spirits up in the face of daunting material circumstances.

Under the leadership of the sagacious but controversial Brigham Young, Mormon colonies were established during the latter nineteenth century from the Salmon River country of Idaho and the Big Horn Basin of northern Wyoming all through Utah, into northern New Mexico and Arizona, and as far west as Carson City, Nevada, and San Bernardino, California. Hopes for admission of this immense "State of Deseret" to the United States were dashed by the Compromise of 1850, which created a Territory of Utah with dimensions much smaller than Deseret, though larger than the present state of Utah. Fillmore served as the territorial capital from 1851 to 1856, after which Salt Lake City became, and remains, the capital.

Utah's remarkably cosmopolitan population today is a result of two factors: the Mormon missionary program, which drew extraordinary numbers of converts from the Eastern United States, the British Isles, Scandinavia, and the South Pacific; and the development of mines, especially in Carbon, Juab, and

Salt Lake Counties, which brought non-Mormon European immigrants, particularly Slavs, Italians, and Greeks. Railroad construction through Utah and other economic opportunities brought Japanese, Chinese, and blacks to the area. The massive immigration of European converts to Mormonism began soon after the arrival of the first Mormons in Salt Lake Valley. Records of mining and of the experience of non-Mormon and non-Anglo-Saxon Utahns have been preserved and their histories written.

A good deal of nineteenth-century Utah history concerns the relationship between Utah Territory, created out of the Mexican Cession of 1848, and the federal government, who sought to deprive the Mormon hierarchy of political power through its federal governors and judges, regarded as "carpetbaggers" by Utah Mormons. The tension reached a crisis in 1857, when federal troops under Albert Sidney Johnston were dispatched to restore order in Utah. The military presence, first at Camp Floyd west of Utah Lake, then at Fort Douglas east of Salt Lake Valley, provided ongoing friction between the Mormons and the United States.

That friction was exacerbated by the Mormon practice of plural marriage, in which some men took more than one wife. Federal laws against polygamy in the 1880s led to the imprisonment of those found guilty of "cohabitation." Issuance of the "Manifesto" of Mormon President Wilford Woodruff in 1890 called for an end to the practice of plural marriage, and the reward was statehood in 1896.

The "Americanization" of Utah was actually a very complex process in which the abandonment of plural marriage was only one aspect. Perhaps equally important was Utah's emerging demographic diversity and abandonment of the Mormon ideal of self-sufficiency that began with the gold rush of 1849, and was completed by the arrival of the transcontinental railroad in 1869 and the opening of Utah's rich mineral resources—primarily a non-Mormon enterprise—in the 1870s.

The pendulum swing from dissent to conformity achieved its apogee during the early twentieth century, as Utah politics assumed a characteristically conservative quality. During the 1930s, when the Great Depression devastated the state, Utah relied heavily on federal programs. The Works Projects Administration (WPA) and Civilian Conservation Corps (CCC) programs of the New Deal were especially important in Utah's economic recovery. During World War II, Utah's abundant supply of skilled labor led to the establishment of war industries and military bases that have been a prominent part of the state's economy from that time.

Nevertheless, the "Americanization" of Utah did not take place without dissent. The opening of the Uintah Indian Reservation to white settlement in 1905 created a land rush that outraged the Utes and resulted in deep resentment at what they regarded as a betrayal of their interests and cultural integrity. Shortly thereafter, in 1923, the Paiutes of San Juan County

resisted white encroachment in the "Posey War," the most recent major Indian war in the United States. During the 1970s, Utah Governor Scott Matheson assumed leadership of the "Sagebrush Rebellion" to transmit Utah's federally administered lands—a majority of state land—to state control.

While Utah had a theater where plays were performed as early as 1861, during the late-twentieth century Utah cultural life has been enhanced with the emergence of organizations like the Pioneer Theater Company, the Utah Symphony, and Ballet West. The state's major economic resources are tourism, based on the ski industry in the winter and the scenic attractions of the national parks in the southern part of the state in the summer, and the state's abundant and well-educated labor force, which attracts businesses to establish corporate headquarters in the state.

Vital Records

In Utah, the civil registration of births, deaths, and marriages developed slowly, culminating with a statewide system of recording births and deaths beginning in 1905. Certificates for births and deaths from then until the present can be obtained from the Bureau of Vital Statistics and Health Statistics, Utah State Department of Health, 288 North 1460 West, P.O. Box 141012, Salt Lake City, UT 84114-1012 <http://health.utah.gov/vitalrecords/>. According to Utah state law, birth certificates are closed to researchers for one hundred years without the written approval of the subject of the record; death certificates are closed for fifty years. Death certificates older than fifty years are available from the Utah State Archives. (See online reference guides for birth and death reecords at <www.archives.utah.gov/referenc/death.htm> and <www.archives.utah.gov/referenc/birth.htm>.)

In 1860, the Utah legislature empowered (but did not require) Salt Lake City and Ogden to maintain a register of births and deaths within their respective cities, a practice already begun by Salt Lake City in 1847. In 1880 the power to register was extended to all incorporated cities, but not all cities undertook the responsibility, nor were most births registered for areas that did register births. In 1898, the state legislature provided for central county records, requiring county clerks to keep separate birth and death registers.

All surviving early county birth and death registers have been microfilmed and are accessible through the Family History Library (FHL) and the State Archives, both in Salt Lake City. The death registers have been indexed by the Professional Genealogists Chapter, Utah Genealogical Association, *Utah Death Index, 1896–1905,* edited by Judith W. Hansen, vol. 1—excluding Salt Lake County (1995), and vol. 2—Salt Lake

County (1998). The Utah State Archives has a continuing program of indexing the birth registers. Counties that have been completed and are available online as keyword databases are Beaver, Davis, Carbon, Emery, Grand, Iron, Kane, Piute, Rich, Uintah, and Weber. Some of the original books are still at county seats, while others have been transferred to the Utah State Archives (see Archives, Libraries, and Societies). The County Resources section indicates dates of availability by county.

Since marriage was seen as a religious sacrament, the civil registration of marriages was not required in Utah until 1887. The Edmunds-Tucker Act, which outlawed polygamy, required that everyone married in any territory of the United States, "shall be certified by a certificate stating the fact and nature of such a ceremony." In 1889, the territorial legislature accepted the general structure of the act and required the person solemnizing the marriage to return the license and certificate within thirty days of the ceremony.

A few marriage records were created before 1887 and may be found in the county justice of the peace or probate court records. Early marriage records were usually interfiled with other court matters, but others may have been recorded in land records, as is the case with some early Beaver County marriage records. Marriage for the pre-1887 time period may have been performed by an LDS bishop (LDS is an abbreviation for Latter-day Saint) or clergyman of a non-Mormon denomination. See *Marriages in Utah Territory, 1850–1884: from the Deseret News, 1850–1872 and the Elias Smith Journals, 1850–1884*, compiled by Judith W. Hansen and Norman Lundberg (Salt Lake City: Utah Genealogical Association, 1998). From 1889 to the present, a marriage application is completed in order to obtain a license, which is issued by the county clerk. These applications are closed to researchers for seventy-five years without the written approval of the subjects. County issued licenses for some time periods are available on microfilm through the FHL. The Utah State Archives does not generally provide reference services for marriage records; instead, it refers researchers to the appropriate county clerk. The BYU-Idaho Family History Center is extracting early marriage records for many western states as part of their "Western States Historical Marriage Records Index" at <http://abish.byui.edu/specialCollections/fhc/gbsearch.htm>. This online index includes over 64,000 Utah marriages representing many Utah counties. This database can be searched with the name of either bride or groom.

The practice of both open and secret polygamy has certainly had an impact on genealogical research in Utah. For a thorough discussion of marriage practices in the state, see Lyman D. Platt's "The History of Marriage in Utah, 1847–1905," *Genealogical Journal* 12 (Spring 1983): 28-41. For a discussion of the practice of polygamy, see Kathryn M. Daynes *More Wives Than One: Transformation of the Mormon Marriage System, 1840–1910*, (Urbana and Chicago: University of Illinois Press, 2001).

In addition to government-produced vital records, there are a variety of records not recorded in original registers, such as midwives' and physicians' records. Many have been microfilmed and are accessible through the FHL under the heading of Utah, [County], Vital Records. The LDS Church also maintains an extensive array of vital statistics in its own church records. For a comprehensive discussion of various types of records, see Laureen Richardson Jaussi and Gloria Duncan Chaston's *Genealogical Records in Utah* (Salt Lake City: Deseret Book Co., 1974), described in Background Sources below.

Court jurisdiction for divorces in Utah changed back and forth between probate and district courts in the county. By 1877, the district court gained sole jurisdiction. Before statehood, divorce records may be found in either county probate court records, federal (territorial) district courts, or LDS Church records. From 1896 to the present, all divorces are filed through the county's district court and most are held in the clerk of the court's office. Some divorce records have been transferred to the Utah State Archives and a few have been indexed and are available online (e.g., Davis County, 1875–1886). See the Utah State Archives online research guide on "How to Find Utah Divorce Records" at <www.archives.utah.gov/referenc/referen.htm>.

Census Records

Federal

Population Schedules
- Indexed—1850(1), 1860, 1870, 1880, 1900, 1910, 1920, 1930
- Soundex—1880, 1900

Mortality Schedules
- 1850(1), 1860, 1870, 1880

Union Veterans Schedules
- 1890

The 1850 census for Utah Territory was taken in 1851. It has been reproduced alphabetically within each county in Annie Walker Burns, *First Families of Utah, As Taken from the 1850 Census of Utah* (Washington, D.C.: the author, 1949). The index in this volume is to this transcription of the census records and not to the original records. A second index, The Genealogical Society of Utah's *Index to Utah 1851 Census* (Salt Lake City: the author, 1950) refers to the original entry in the federal returns and is indexed by surname. Mortality schedules are available on microfilm through the FHL.

In addition to the AISI (see page 3) indexes for Utah and the online census indexes through subscription databases (see page 17), there is a collapsed index covering the first three federal censuses for the territory:

Kearl, J. R., Clayne L. Pope, and Larry T. Wimmer. *Index to the 1850, 1860, and 1870 Censuses of Utah*. Baltimore: Genealogical Publishing Co., 1981.

Territorial

There are fragments of what could be construed as territorial or state censuses from 1852, 1856, 1872, and 1896 with enumerations derived from tax lists. An example is the 1852 Bishops Reports, listing LDS heads of households in each LDS ward, available on microfilm with an index through FHL.

Of these, only the 1856 list, originally developed in an attempt to apply for statehood, has been indexed and published by AISI and Bryan Lee Dilts in *1856 Utah Census Index* (Salt Lake City: Index Publishing, 1983). The accuracy of the original enumeration has been questioned, however, since it appears to contain names of deceased persons or members of the LDS Church who were not yet in the territory.

Background Sources

The story of the exodus of the Mormons from eastern parts of the United States is not the only aspect of Utah emigration, although it is a large part. Two-thirds of those early immigrants arriving in the Salt Lake Basin in 1847 and thereafter were settlers largely from states north of the Ohio River. Approximately sixty percent were from New York, Pennsylvania, Illinois, and Ohio, with forebears from New England. People from Missouri, Tennessee, and Kentucky comprised the bulk of the remaining U.S.-born emigrants. Foreign-born Mormons originated mostly from the British Isles, with the second largest group coming from the Scandinavian countries. Emigration of other parties and the establishment of mining districts, particularly the Tintic district and mines around Price, Utah, constitute other major settlement groups.

Mormons have written and preserved the history of their ancestors better than most of their contemporaries. The other major settlement groups also have good printed sources regarding their history.

For background reading in Utah history, see:

Alexander, Thomas G. *Utah the Right Place. The Official Centennial History*. Salt Lake City: Gibbs-Smith Publishers, 1995.

Arrington, Leonard J. *Great Basin Kingdom: Economic History of the Latter-day Saints, 1830–1900*. Lincoln, Nebr.: University of Nebraska Press, 1958.

Arrington, Leonard J., and Davis Bitton. *The Mormon Experience: A History of the Latter-day Saints*. New York: Vintage Books, 1980.

Papanikolas, Helen Zeese, ed. *The Peoples of Utah*. Salt Lake City: Utah State Historical Society, 1976. The diversity of population in Utah is covered.

Poll, Richard D., Thomas G. Alexander, Eugene E. Campbell, and David E. Miller, eds. *Utah's History*. Provo, Utah: Brigham Young University, 1978. A collection of chapters written by the editors and others, which covers various aspects of Mormon and non-Mormon Utah history. A bibliographic essay covering Utah's history is included.

Powell, Alan Kent, ed. *Utah History Encyclopedia*. Salt Lake City: University of Utah Press, 1994. Also available online at <www.media.utah.edu/UHE>.

Some unusual, highly informative publications are those by Kate B. Carter: *Heart Throbs of the West* (13 vols., 1939–51); *Treasures of Pioneer History* (6 vols., 1952–57) and *Our Pioneer Heritage* (18 vols., 1959–75), all published in Salt Lake City by the Daughters of Utah Pioneers. Many personal accounts of settlers, as well as invaluable source materials, are included. These publications and other biographical/family history sources are available as part of Ancestry's *LDS Family History Suite 2* (1998).

For genealogical research, Laureen R. Jaussi and Gloria D. Chaston's *Genealogical Records of Utah* (see Vital Records) is an essential guide, detailing church and government-related documents and sources as well as discussing the genealogical uses and limitations of records and sources.

Maps

Division of Community Relations, Department of Transportation, 4501 S. 2700 W., Salt Lake City, UT 84119, provides modern state maps. They may also be ordered online <www.dot.state.ut.us/public/mapinform.htm>. The U.S. Geological Survey maps (see page 5) supplement with additional geographic details. For historical maps, see:

Greer, Deon C., Klaus C. Gurgel, Wayne L. Wahlquist, Howard A. Christy, and Gary B. Peterson. *Atlas of Utah*. Provo, Utah: Brigham Young University Press, 1981.

Miller, David E. *Utah History Atlas*. Salt Lake City, Utah: the author, 1964.

Moffat, Riley Moore. *Printed Maps of Utah to 1900*. Santa Cruz, Calif.: Western Association of Map Libraries, 1981.

The collection of the FHL provides a large group of early maps. See Utah/Maps in the card catalog.

Land Records

Public-Domain State

The arrival of the 1847 emigration of the Mormons marked the first settlement of non-natives in Utah. Following the war

with Mexico, Utah came under United States jurisdiction in 1848, but from March 1849 until it was declared an official U.S. territory in 1850, it was known as part of the Provisional State of Deseret. The Homestead Act did not affect Utah until the first federal district land office was opened in Salt Lake City in 1869. Both Mormon land holding practices and federal distribution of land played important roles in land transactions for the state. Jaussi and Chaston's (1974) and Arrington's publications, described under Background Sources, and Lawrence L. Linford's "Establishing and Maintaining Land Ownership in Utah Prior to 1869," *Utah Historical Quarterly* 42 (1974): 126-43, provide an excellent context for researching Utah's land records. See also Utah State Archives' detailed online research guide "Original Land Titles in Utah Territory" at <www.archives.utah.gov/referenc/land2.htm>.

Before the Homestead Act became effective in the territory, land was distributed by the leaders of the LDS Church in lots that could easily be maintained by a family. With the creation of a Federal Land Office in Salt Lake in 1869, legal titles were granted to land that had been previously held. Since it is a federal land state, division of property was based on a rectangular survey emanating from either the Salt Lake Meridian or a smaller meridian in the Uintah Basin. For Utah there is a master card index for the cash entry files of U.S. lands sold by the Salt Lake Land Office accessible at the National Archives—Rocky Mountain Region or the Bureau of Land Management (BLM) in Washington, D.C. (see page 6).

Although the office was created earlier, the county recorder's deed books did not become the predictable location for land transactions until after 1874. Earlier land records can be found among many classes of documents in the county seat including county court and probate records. But after that date, separate books for land transactions have been continuously kept. All counties will have indexes for their land holdings, usually referred to as grantee and grantor indexes, although they may not encompass all time periods.

Probate Records

Probate functions (testate and intestate proceedings; guardianships for males under age twenty-one and females under age eighteen and those incompetent to handle their legal affairs) were shared by county probate courts and territorial district courts between 1852 and 1896. Records for these are generally at the county seat, though some probate records have been microfilmed and are accessible through the FHL and/or the Utah State Archives. Microfilm coverage varies between counties.

After 1896, jurisdiction for probate matters became the sole responsibility of the District Court that operated for the county. There are now eight judicial districts encompassing twenty-nine counties. To determine exactly which district a county belonged to at a particular time there are two finding aids. One is available at the Utah State Archives and the other is a guide that can be obtained by writing the Utah Judicial Council, Administrative Office of the Courts, 450 S. State St., P.O. Box 140241, Salt Lake City, UT 84114-0241, which has an online directory at <www.utcourts.gov/committees/index.asp>. Since 1 January 1989, all Utah courts were placed under the administration of this office. In trying to determine the county seat that was functioning as the probate court during a particular time period, that office will be the most efficient source.

Currently District 1 includes Box Elder, Cache, and Rich counties; District 2—Davis, Morgan, and Weber; District 3—Salt Lake, Summit, and Tooele; District 4—Juab, Millard, Utah, and Wasatch; District 5—Beaver, Iron, and Washington; District 6—Garfield, Kane, Piute, Sanpete, Sevier, and Wayne; District 7—Carbon, Emery, Grand, and San Juan; and District 8—Daggett, Duchesne, and Uintah.

Court Records

In the first years of settlement, an LDS bishops court system operated within the LDS Church structure, maintaining jurisdiction over criminal and civil cases for those residents in a particular ward of the church. Edwin B. Firmage and Richard C. Mangrum, *Zion in the Courts: A Legal History of The Church of Jesus Christ of Latter-day Saints, 1830–1900* (Urbana: University of Illinois, 1988), expertly covers the time period when church and civil courts overlapped. County courts were created in 1849, overseeing civil and criminal cases involving more than $100 until Utah became a territory in 1851, when the county court was replaced by the county probate court. Justice of the peace courts were established at the same time (1849) for cases involving less than $100 (changed to $300 in 1874) and continue to operate today. When the county probate courts ceased to exist in 1874, civil and criminal matters and probate matters were transferred to the federally operated territorial district court, which had held concurrent jurisdiction with the county probate court since 1852. Concurrent jurisdiction was a result of conflicts between the federal government and local citizens as to who should have legal jurisdiction. For a discussion of court records in Utah, see Jaussi and Chaston (1974), described in Background Sources and James B. Allen, "The Unusual Jurisdiction of County Probate Courts in the Territory of Utah," *Utah Historical Quarterly* 36 (Spring 1968): 132-42. See also an online research guide on court records available from the Utah State Archives at <http://archives.utah.gov/referenc/referen.htm> for a compressed history of court records.

With statehood in 1896, a uniform statewide district court system (see Probate Records) took over civil and criminal

matters as well as probate matters. There are voluminous court records available, but not indexed, on microfilm at the Utah State Archives. Included in their holdings are quite a few miners' courts records, which frequently served the function of a county clerk in registering and transferring claims. Other historical materials on mining camps can be found at the Utah Historical Society (see Archives, Libraries, and Societies).

Since 1999, Utah law permits public access to adoption records over one hundred years old. See the Utah State Archives research guide at <http://archives.utah.gov/referenc/referen.htm>.

Tax Records

Some early tax records have been published as part of a state census (see Census Records), but microfilm copies of manuscript transcripts of crop records, school assessments, and property assessment are available for many counties on microfilm through the Utah State Archives and the FHL.

Cemetery Records

The Utah Cemetery Project attempted to survey all cemeteries in the State of Utah, recording name, location, and ownership information as well as the age of the cemetery and number of burials. Over 286 cemeteries have been inventoried. A computer database contains the names and burial locations of thousands buried in Utah's cemeteries. An online database is available to researchers at <http://history.utah.gov/library/burials.html>.

Good, although by no means complete, sources for cemetery records can be found at the FHL and the Utah State Archives. In the FHL catalog check: Utah/[County]/[Town]/Cemetery listings first, then individual counties. The Utah State Archives has created an online research guide, "Cemetery Records at the Utah State Archives" <http://archives.utah.gov/referenc/referen.htm>. Jaussi and Chaston (see Background Sources) also list a number of sources for death records from funeral homes and cemetery sexton's records in the FHL.

Church Records

The LDS Church is the predominant church in Utah, but other denominations are also represented. Among these is the Catholic Church, whose Cathedral of the Madeleine, was built in 1891. Its archives are maintained by the Catholic Diocese of Salt Lake City, 27 "C" St., Salt Lake City, UT 84103. The Episcopal Diocese of Utah maintains an archive collection at the University of Utah. However, most parish registers remain with the local churches.

Extensive material is available for those with Mormon heritage, whether from Utah or outside of the state. David J.

Whittaker's *Mormon Americana: A Guide to Sources and Collections in the United States* (Provo, Utah: BYU Studies, 1995) serves as an excellent research guide on the LDS Church. The Church Historical Department and the FHL (see Archives, Libraries, and Societies) have extensive collections too numerous to discuss here. For an excellent discussion of the holdings, Jaussi and Chaston's work discussed under Background Sources provides a good overview of what is available and how to locate it both at the FHL and in the Historical Department of the Church.

Military Records

On 19 July 1846, five hundred volunteers of the Mormon Battalion left Council Bluffs, Iowa, heading southwestward at the request of President James K. Polk. They joined other federal troops at Fort Leavenworth, Kansas, and proceeded west to Santa Fe and then to San Diego, California, arriving on 29 January 1847. After a year of duty, the battalion left eighty-one officers and enlisted men in San Diego, while the main group walked north to Sutter's Fort, where half of the contingent remained for a while. Eventually, the entire group was reunited with their fellow Mormons at Salt Lake City.

A Mormon unit of 13,000 troops, known as the Nauvoo Legion, a territorial militia that included both Mormon and non-Mormon military aged males, engaged in military activities from its earliest inception to the end of the Black Hawk War in the late 1860s. The original records for 1849–70 are at the Utah State Archives, along with an extensive collection of other state militia, service, and veterans records including various indexes compiled by the archivists. Many are also available on microfilm through the National Archives (see pages 11-12) and the FHL. An online reference guide "Utah Military Service Records" is at <http://archives.utah.gov/referenc/referen.htm>.

Volunteers from Utah served during the Civil War, and a unit of 500 engaged in the Spanish-American War in 1898; 21,000 soldiers were supplied during World War I, and many more during World War II. Utah servicemen are included in the 1890 special census of the Union veterans and widows of the Civil War, as are those who served elsewhere, but were living in Utah by 1890. Some regular army troops served on the frontier in Utah and remained after discharge to take advantage of mining or commercial ventures.

Printed sources for military history and records include:

Carter, Kate. B. *The Mormon Battalion*. Salt Lake City: Utah Printing, 1956.

Long, E. B. *The Saints and the Union: Utah Territory in the Civil War*. Urbana, Ill.: University of Illinois Press, 1981.

Powell, Alan Kent, ed. *Utah Remembers World War II*. Logan, Utah: Utah State University, 1991.

Prentiss, A. *The History of the Utah Volunteers in the Spanish-American War and in the Philippine Islands*. Salt Lake City, W.F. Ford, 1900.

Ricketts, Norma B. *The Mormon Battalion: U.S. Army of the West, 1846–1847*. Logan: Utah State University, 1996.

Warrum, Noble. *Utah in the World War.* Salt Lake City: Arrow Press, 1924.

For veterans of all wars buried under the jurisdiction of the federal burial program since 1861, write to Cemetery Service, National Cemetery System, Veterans Administration, 810 Vermont Ave., Washington, D.C. 20420. Headstone applications taken from 1879 to 1924 were filed by applicant, state, county, and cemetery.

Periodicals, Newspapers, and Manuscript Collections

Periodicals

Utah Historical Quarterly. Utah Historical Society. Providing good historical context of Utah research, the publication also evaluates source material for genealogical and local history research. The society's *The Utah History Suite Edition 3* (1999), **CD-ROM by Historical Views** contains most issues of the *Quarterly*, plus all 29 centennial county histories.

Genealogical Journal. Utah Genealogical Association. Not restricted to articles on Utah genealogy, the publication is of national interest including methodology and source material from all over the world.

Utah Genealogical and Historical Magazine. Genealogical Society of Utah. Published between 1910 and 1940, its articles were not limited to Utah or Mormon genealogy.

Newspapers

The first newspaper in Utah was the *Deseret News*, which began publication in Salt Lake in 1850. Other nineteenth-century newspapers and their first date of publication include:

Ogden Standard-Examiner, Odgen, 1870.

The Daily Herald, Provo, 1873.

The Salt Lake Tribune, Salt Lake City, 1875.

The Washington County News, St. George, 1896.

Intermountain Catholic, 1899.

Robert P. Holley, Jr., *Utah's Newspapers: Traces of Her Past* (Salt Lake City: University of Utah, 1984), contains a valuable "Checklist of Utah Newspapers" beyond those mentioned here. The university's library holds many obscure Utah newspapers on

microfilm in addition to the major ones. See the Public Pioneer (see Archives, Libraries, and Societies) for information online newspaper indexes.

Both the Utah Historical Society and the Salt Lake City Public Library have extensive subject newspaper clipping files. The most significant clipping file is the LDS Church Historical Department's "Journal History." It is a chronological file beginning in 1830 organized by the event's date of occurrence. Each article has been extensively indexed.

More than 100,000 pages of Utah weekly newspapers are being digitized as part of the ongoing "Utah Digital Newspapers: A Utah Academic Consortium Project." An online searchable database with digital images is available to researchers at <www.lib.utah.edu/digital/unew>.

An Obituary Card Index of those listings found in runs of twelve Salt Lake City newspapers from the beginning of their publication is microfilmed and available through FHL. The earliest newspaper covered is for 1850 with more recent ones running through to 1971.

Manuscripts

The Utah State Historical Society, the Church Historical Department, and each of Utah's major universities maintain large manuscript collections focusing on Utah history and containing material useful to the genealogist. All major Utah repositories maintain skilled reference staffs who are able to answer questions about their holdings and to do limited amounts of research in response to specific questions submitted by telephone or mail.

Archives, Libraries, and Societies

Family History Library
Genealogical Society of Utah
35 N. West Temple
Salt Lake City, UT 84150
www.familysearch.org

Every researcher should know of the Family History Library (FHL), operated under the auspices of The Church of Jesus Christ of Latter-day Saints and situated in Salt Lake City. The collection, owned and maintained by the Genealogical Society of Utah, is of unparalleled importance in the field of family history and is one of the foremost accumulations of records, books, microfilm, microfiche, maps, manuscript, biographies, etc., in the world. For anyone doing genealogical research, a trip to Salt Lake City can be extremely productive since so much is available in one place. If this is not feasible, there are numerous Family History Centers operated by local LDS branch libraries in towns and cities all over the world (see pages 12-13).

UTAH

LDS Church Historical Department
Church Office Building
50 E. North Temple
Salt Lake City, UT 84150

In addition to the Church's library, there is a large church archives department containing many records not at the FHL. Among them are diaries of early Utah settlers and an extensive collection of official church records. For a clear discussion of the department's holdings, see Glenn N. Rowe, "The Historical Department and the LDS Church," in David J. Whittaker, *Mormon Americana: A Guide to Sources and Collections in the United States* (Provo, Utah: BYU Studies, 1995).

Brigham Young University
Harold B. Lee Library
Provo, UT 84601
www.lib.byu.edu/~scm

The university's Special Collections houses rare and unique publications, manuscripts, and archival materials emphasizing Mormon and Western Americana. Its holdings are listed on the library's online catalog at <www.lib.byu.edu.hbll/>."Trail of Hope: Overland Diaries and Letters, 1846–1869" is a significant digital collection of the original writings of forty-nine voyagers on Mormon, California, Oregon, and Montana trails who wrote during their travels <http://overlandtrails.lib.byu.edu/>.

Public Pioneer—Utah State Library
250 N. 1950 W., Ste A
Salt Lake City, UT 84116-7901
http://pioneer.utah.gov/

Public Pioneer is a virtual library created by the Utah State Library Division in cooperation with Utah's libraries. It is one component of the statewide Pioneer Project, which serves Utah's public schools and academic institutions, as well as patrons of public libraries. Public Pioneer offers a portal to carefully selected Internet sites and creates an information center for Utah researchers.

Salt Lake County Archives
2001 S. State St., Ste. 4400
Salt Lake City, UT 84190-1020
www.co.slc.ut.us

The Salt Lake County Archives was established in 1986 as a unit of the Records Management and Archives program. It preserves the historical records of Salt Lake County, provides access to researchers, and ensures that historical evidence and governmental accountability is maintained. Significant holdings include Property Appraisal Cards (1936–87) and Photographs of Historic Buildings of Salt Lake City (1936–75).

Southern Utah University
Sherratt Library–Special Collections
351 W. Center St.

Cedar City, UT 84720
http://archive.li.suu.edu

The Special Collections is a regional history collection of the southwestern Utah area. "SUUper" Search is a full-search tool for information available in manuscript and photographic collections. Many photographs have also been digitized and are available online.

Utah State Archives and Records Service
346 South Rio Grande (after mid-August 2004)
Salt Lake City, UT 84101
Mailing Address:
P.O. Box 141021
Salt Lake City, UT 84114-1021
www.archives.utah.gov

The Utah State Archives permanently preserves and provides access to the records of enduring value created by Utah state, county, and municipal governments. Public records and documents may be used at the Research Room. Various finding aids including online research guides, catalogs, inventories, and indexes assist researchers. There is no fee for reference service; however, photocopying and mailing costs are charged.

In 1999, the state archives initiated a cooperative ongoing program to microfilm historical records in Utah's cities and towns, school districts, and selected county and court records. This microfilm is available at the Utah State Archives and designated regional centers (Utah State University and Southern Utah University). New rolls of microfilm are added weekly.

The state archives and state historical society will share a reading room after December 2004.

Utah State Historical Society
300 Rio Grande
Salt Lake City, UT 84101
http://history.utah.gov/index.html

The society publishes the *Utah History Quarterly and Beehive History* and maintains an extensive, well-managed collection. Because of the focus of the collection at the FHL, the historical society concentrates on printed and state history, as well as maintaining an extensive manuscript collection. Two articles in Utah Genealogical Association's *Newsletter* (4th Quarter, 1988) discuss the usefulness of this collection for genealogists: Max J. Evans' "Genealogy and History" and Standford J. Layton's "Introducing the Utah State Historical Society." The society's website contains "Utah History To Go," an outline course on Utah History that includes bibliographies and suggested readings.

Utah Genealogical Association
Box 1144
Salt Lake City, UT 84110
www.infouga.org

Often confused with the Genealogical Society of Utah, which is a department of the LDS Church, the Utah Genealogical Association publishes the *Genealogical Journal* and a quarterly *Newsletter*, which contains information about new acquisitions in the FHL and articles of local interest. The association meets on a regular basis and is divided into several chapters, each with particular ongoing projects such as indexing birth and death records (see Vital Records).

University of Utah
Special Collections
Marriott Library
Salt Lake City, UT 84112
www.lib.utah.edu/spc/

The Special Collections acquires and makes available books, periodicals, oral histories, photographs, films, and original materials documenting Utah history, Mormon history, Native Americans, and the West. Its holdings are listed on the library's online catalog at <www.lib.utah.edu/information/unis>. Significant collections include the records of local churches (e.g., Episcopal Church Archives) and Sanborn maps. These large-scale maps (1867–1969) were created for fire insurance agents and depict the commercial, industrial, and residential sections of various Utah (and other western states) cities. The Sanborn Digitization Project makes some of these maps available online at <www.lib.utah.edu/digital/Sanborn/browse.html>.

Utah State University
Special Collections and Archives
Merrill Library
Logan, UT 84322
http://library.usu.edu/Specol/

The Special Collections focuses on Mormon history and the Cache Valley (Utah-Idaho) region. Two notable collections include the extensive Leonard J. Arrington Collection and the Cache County Archives (1860–1939). Cache County records include probate court and property tax records. Many of these records have been microfilmed and are also available at the Utah State Archives. The Special Collections website contains a guide for genealogists and family historians.

Special Focus Categories

Naturalization
In general, naturalization records begin with the date the county was organized, and they may be in one of several courts holding concurrent jurisdiction. Naturalizations that were initiated between statehood (1896) and the federal changes in naturalization process (1906) are easier to locate since the district court was the only court in the state where the process

could be started, and each court kept records individually by county in the district court office. Many of these may be found at the Utah State Archives and some are on microfilm at the FHL listed under Utah/[County]/Emigration and Immigration. The Utah State Archives has an excellent online descriptive research guide "Utah Naturalization and Citizenship Records," at <http://archives.utah.gov/referenc/referen.htm>. After 1906, in addition to federal courts, an applicant could apply at the state district court for the county or the state supreme court.

Since a large number of Mormons came to Utah from Europe, the number of naturalizations is rather large for a landlocked state. Passenger lists from those Mormon missions in Scandinavia (1872–94) and Europe (1840–1925) are on microfilm at the FHL. Jaussi and Chaston (1974) describe a full collection of emigration records in their book (see Vital Records).

Native American
The Utah State Historical Society, University of Utah Special Collections, and Southern Utah University Special Collections have extensive collections of materials on native culture and history. See Forest S. Cuch, ed., *A History of Utah's American Indians* (Salt Lake City: Utah State Division of Indian Affairs/Utah State Division of History, 2000). For additional current information, see the Utah Division of Indians Affairs <http://dced.utah.gov/indian/>.

County Resources

The chart that follows is based on information from the Utah State Archives as verified by the *Atlas of Utah* (Provo, Utah: BYU Press, 1981) and John W. van Cott, *Utah Place Names* (Salt Lake City: University of Utah Press, 1990). County recorders maintain those land records of transactions filed in their counties. Many original birth and death records before statewide recording have been transferred to the Utah State Archives. Since this is an on-going process, it is best to contact them first regarding a specific county's records in their holdings. Those county record books before 1905 that have not been transferred are at the county clerk's office.

Courts were divided into districts with different county seats functioning as the seat of record at different times. Some of the original records that are extant for a county may not be in the county seat but may have been transferred to the Utah State Archives (see Probate Records and Court Records). Those at the county seat reside with the county clerk.

The listing of the dates below were verified by the Utah State Archives and checked against the FHL catalog, the State Archives' Series Catalog, the WPA *Guide to Public Vital Statistics of Utah* (Salt Lake City: Utah Historical Records Survey, 1941), and individual county holdings.

UTAH

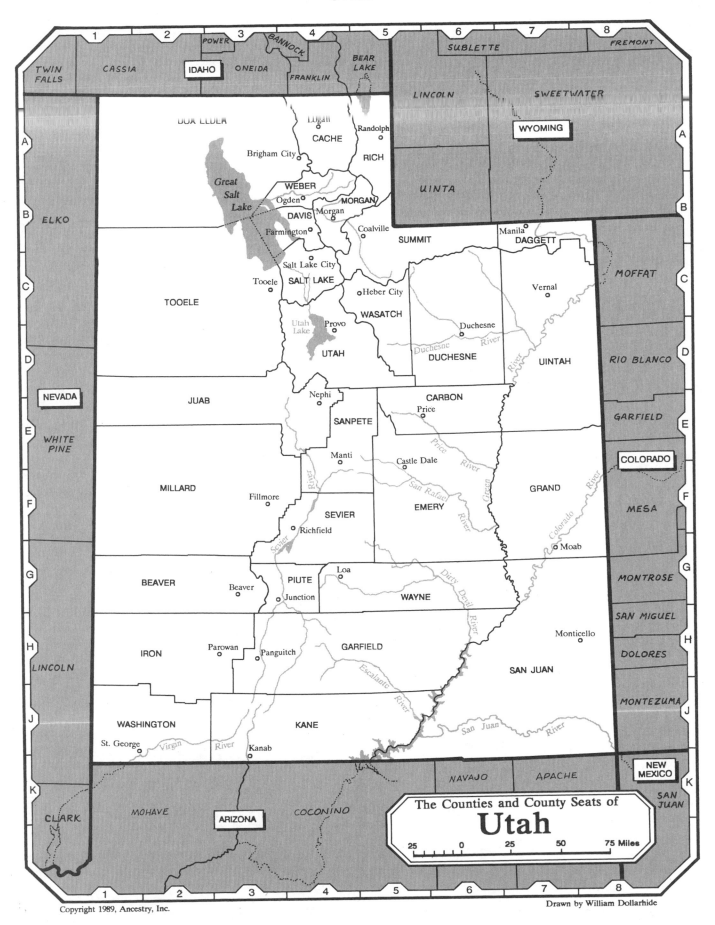

The Counties and County Seats of
Utah

25   0   25   50   75 Miles

Copyright 1989, Ancestry, Inc.

Drawn by William Dollarhide

675

Map	County / Address	Date Formed / Parent County/ies	Birth / Marriage / Death	Land / Probate / Court
G2	Beaver / 105 E. Center / Beaver 84713	1856 / Iron	1898–1905 / 1887 / 1900–05	1867 / 1856 / 1856
A2	Box Elder / 01 S. Main St. / Brigham City 84302	1856 / Green River/Weber	1898–1905 / 1888 / 1898–1905	1856 / 1856 / 1856
A4	Cache / 179 N. Main St. / Logan 84321	1856 / Green River	1898–1905 / 1887 / 1898–1905	1857 / 1860 / 1860
E6	Carbon / 120 E. Main / Price 84501	1894 / Emery	1898–1918 / 1894 / 1898–1905	1894 / 1894 / 1894
	Carson	1854 (became part of Nevada Territory in 1861)		
	Cedar	1856 (abolished 1862; annexed to Utah County)		
B7	Daggett / 95 N. First West / Manila 84046 / *See Uintah County	1917 / Uintah	* / 1918 / *	1918 / 1918 / 1918
B4	Davis / State and Main St. / Farmington 84025	1850 / original	1898–1905 / 1887 / 1898–1905	1870 / 1853 / 1852
	Deseret	1856 (became part of Nevada Territory in 1861)		
C6	Duchesne / 50 E. 100 S. / Duchesne 84021 / *See Uintah County	1914 / Wasatch	* / 1915 / *	1915 / 1915 / 1915
F6	Emery / 95 E. Main / Castle Dale 84513	1880 / Sanpete/Sevier	1898–1905 / 1887 / 1898–1905	1881 / 1887 / 1887
H5	Garfield / 55 S. Main / Panguitch 84759	1882 / Iron/Kane/Washington	1898–1905 / 1887 / ——	1882 / 1883 / 1882
F7	Grand / 125 E. Center / Moab 84532	1890 / Emery/Uintah	1898–1905 / 1890 / 1898–1905	1890 / 1890 / 1890
	Greasewood	1856 (discontinued in 1862; now part of Box Elder)		
	Green River	1852 (annexed to Nebraska Territory in 1861; became part of Wyoming in 1868)		
	Humbolt	1856 (became part of Nevada Territory in 1861)		
H2	Iron / 68 S. 100 E. / Parowan 84761	1850 (as Little Salt Lake) / original	1898–1905 / 1888 / 1898–1905	1851 / 1870 / 1851
E2	Juab / 160 N. Main / Nephi 84648	1852 / original	1898–1905 / 1888 / 1898–1905	1859 / 1859 / 1859
J4	Kane / 76 N. Main / Kanab 84741	1864 / Washington	1900–09 / 1887 / 1900–05	1872 / 1878 / 1878
	Malad	1856 (discontinued in 1862; now a part of Box Elder)		
F2	Millard / 60 S. Main / Fillmore 84631	1852 / Iron	—— / 1887 / ——	1852 / 1852 / 1852
B4	Morgan / 48 W. Young St. / Morgan 84050	1862 / Summit/Weber/Cache	1898–1905 / 1869 / 1898–1905	1869 / 1869 / 1869
G4	Piute / P.O. Box 99 / Junction 84740	1865 / Sevier	1898–1900 / 1872 / ——	1868 / 1869 / 1869
A5	Rich / 20 S. Main / Randolph 84064	1864 / original	1898–1912 / 1888 / 1898–1912	1872 / 1872 / 1872
	Rio Virgin	1869 (became part of Nevada state, 1870)		
	St. Mary's	1856 (became part of Nevada Territory, 1861)		
C4	Salt Lake / 2001 S. State St. / Salt Lake City 84190-1015	1850 / original	1898–1905 / 1887 / 1897–1905	1852 / 1852 / 1851
J7	San Juan / 117 S. Main / Monticello 84535	1880 / Iron/Kane/Piute	1898–1917 / 1888 / 1897–1917	1883 / 1888 / 1898
E4	Sanpete / 160 N. Main / Manti 84642	1850 / original	1898–1905 / 1888 / 1898–1905	1855 / 1852 / 1852
F4	Sevier / 250 N. Main / Richfield 84701	1865 / Sanpete	1898–1905 / 1887 / 1898–1905	1885 / 1865 / 1865
	Shambip	1856 (became part of Tooele County, 1863)		
B5	Summit / 60 N. Main / Coalville 84017	1854 / Green River/Salt Lake	1898–1905 / 1887 / 1898–1905	1862 / 1866 / 1866
C2	Tooele / 47 S. Main / Tooele 84074	1850 / original	1898–1905 / 1887 / 1898–1905	1852 / 1870 / 1859
D7	Uintah / 152 E. 100 N. / Vernal 84078	1880 / Summit/Wasatch/Sanpete	1896–1905 / 1888 / 1896–1905	1880 / 1880 / 1880
D4	Utah / 100 E. Center St. / Provo 84601	1850 / original	1898–1905 / 1887 / 1898–1905	1851 / 1859 / 1852
C5	Wasatch / 25 N. Main / Heber City 84031	1862 / Green River/Davis	1898–1905 / 1887 / 1898–1905	1862 / 1883 / 1862

Map	County Address	Date Formed Parent County/ies	Birth Marriage Death	Land Probate Court
J2	Washington 197 E. Tabernacle St. George 84770	1852 original	1898–1905 1885 1890 1905	1856 1873 1856
G5	Wayne 18 S. Main Loa 84747	1892 Piute	1898–1905 1892 1899–1905	1892 1892 1892
B4	Weber 2549 Washington Blvd. Ogden 84401	1850 original	1898–1905 1887 1898–1905	1850 1852 1852

Vermont

SCOTT ANDREW BARTLEY AND ALICE EICHHOLZ, Ph.D., CD

Vermont had its beginnings in a land controversy. Near the middle of the eighteenth century, both Benning Wentworth, the colonial governor of New Hampshire, and Lt. Governor Cadwallader Colden, representing the colonial government of New York, claimed territory in what is now Vermont. Massachusetts had previously claimed a small part along Vermont's southern border. Each government petitioned the king to validate its boundaries to include the disputed Vermont land. However, the process of petitioning did not stop either New Hampshire or New York from issuing grants for the same land to their own proprietors and the proprietors in turn selling the land to settlers.

Settlers from lower New England and New York began to arrive in "The Grants," as they were called, as early as the 1750s. Life for those settling "The Grants" involved considerable work in clearing rock-laden forests. Previous residents of the land included a few French settlements in the northern part of the state, the remainder of the Native American population in the region after the French and Indian Wars, and some early New England settlers around Fort Dummer on the Connecticut River. By 1760, most of these settlers, with the exception of the remaining Abenaki tribe, had moved back to more populated areas in New England and Canada.

The Vermont land controversy between New York and New Hampshire about the grants was complicated by different types of land ownership practiced by the two colonial governments. Those who received grants from New York were generally from the upper classes and leased their land on a rental basis to others who farmed it for them. New Hampshire grants were generally

given to middle-class farmers and civic leaders, who in turn sold the land outright to those who settled it and farmed it. England settled the controversy in favor of New York in 1764—a decision unpopular with most Vermonters who continued to face the uncertainty as to whether the land they were homesteading was really theirs or belonged to someone else who also thought they had a legitimate claim.

This land controversy, the French and Indian War in the early 1750s and the onset of the American Revolution, kept the number of actual settlers coming into Vermont low. Vermont declared itself independent in 1777, not answerable to England or the governors of New York or New Hampshire. Vermont recognized the land grants made by New Hampshire only and began issuing grants of its own for land previously not claimed. Settlement began in earnest once the Revolution was concluded in 1783. At the same time, Vermont attempted, with a good deal of ambivalence according to some historians, to become part of the union, eventually achieving statehood in 1791.

The availability of open, unsettled land for use by growing families was a central reason for moving northward. Once the more fertile land of central New York and points west became available for settlement, the movement out of Vermont was just as swift as the initial migration to the state.

Initially, after statehood, population soared. Geography played a critical role in the state's settlement. The Green Mountains run north-south through the center of the state, leaving the rivers as the major east-west conduits for travel and dividing the state into mountainous areas and river valleys, flood plains, and rock-laden terrain. Lake Champlain, running along

most of the state's western border provided means of western migration to New York and beyond.

Today's roads generally follow the same migration trails as were cut during the settlement period. Small farms nestled among the valleys and in the Lake Champlain region, and small industries using Vermont's forest resources constituted the major economic life of the state. Merino sheep and Morgan horses have also played their part in the attempt to create a reliable economy.

Following the War of 1812 a series of economic and meteorologic calamities occurred, including the "Year of No Summer" (1816). A major migration of those leaving the state was the result. An influx of new settlers—French-Canadians, Italians, and Irish among them—during the mid-nineteenth century changed, somewhat, the population's ethnic constitution. Vermont contributed more per capita from its treasury and from its population of young men in the Civil War than any other state in the Union. Between the 1860s and the 1970s there was little population growth. In the twentieth century, a devastating flood in the central part of the state in 1927 and the national depression in the 1930s made it difficult for Vermont to recover economically. Tourism became a strong draw in the late twentieth century, with recreational industry and a desire to retreat from urban and suburban living as part of the impetus for new settlement today.

Vital Records

The first settlers of Vermont carried on the early New England tradition of recording events at the town level. The vital records are incomplete before mandatory registration began in 1857, but where they exist before ca. 1820 it is common to find an entire family recorded as a family group. In some cases, although the event was recorded in a particular town, it may have actually occurred in another town or state where the family previously resided. Not all the births were recorded, even for families that did report some. Marriages and deaths in the pre-1857 period were less likely to be recorded.

What was recorded, with some exceptions, has been extracted from the originals in the towns and indexed in a central file held by the Vermont Public Records Division (see Archives, Libraries, and Societies). All events indexed up to the last five years can be seen in person or ordered from the division's new facility at 1078 U.S. Rt. 2, Middlesex, VT (Exit 9 on Interstate 89). The mailing address is General Services Administration, Drawer 33, Montpelier, VT 05633-7601 <www.bgs.state.vt.us/gsc/pubrec/referen/index.html>.

Anyone can search the microfilm at the Public Records Division at no charge, or a search can be requested by mail for a charge of $9.50 per event. This cost includes a certified copy of the microfilmed index card, if found, containing a reference for

locating the original record in the individual town records. The microfilmed card index is broken down into five time periods: 1760–1870; 1871–1908; 1909–41; 1942–54; 1955–1979; and then yearly from 1980 up to, but not including, the most recent five years. The statewide index was created between 1919 and 1920. The state's Vital Records Office (see below) transfers all but the last five years to the Public Records Division. Separate cards for births, marriages (both bride and groom), death, and cemetery records are in the index. Cemetery cards, however, appear only in the 1760–1870 microfilm grouping. The statewide index was created from 1919 to 1920, and in the process, the state surveyed all the cemeteries in Vermont to record deaths before 1857, the year mandatory recording began. Generally, only those gravestones that were still standing in 1919, and mentioned deaths before 1857, were included in the survey and therefore in the index.

Vital records for only the last five years are found at the Vital Records Office, 108 Cherry St., P.O. Box 70, Burlington, VT 05402 <www.healthyvermonters.info/hs/vital/vitalhome.shtml>. All earlier records are at the Public Records Division. Files are open to the public but accessed by a clerk. The cost, either in person or by mail, is $9.50 (in 2004) per event.

No thorough survey has ever been taken to determine whether some towns' early vital records were inadvertently missed in the statewide index. It is known that Holland, Sheffield, Maidstone, and Troy vital records were not included, and some vital records from Burlington in the 1870s seem to be missing entirely.

After 1857, many births were recorded before a child was named. Unnamed infants are listed in reverse chronological order in the front of that surname's listing in the card index. The index is filed in strict alphabetical order. Variants in spellings must be checked thoroughly.

Microfilm copies of the vital records indexes, in the same five time periods described above through 1979 and then in yearly groupings through 1990, are available at the New England Historic Genealogical Society (see page 13) and through the Family History Library (FHL) in Salt Lake City.

The online subscription database at <www.ancestry.com> includes Vermont death index, 1990–2001.

While the state issues a certified copy of the microfilmed index card as its "official" record, the original record is in the town clerk's office, often recorded with other family vital records, may provide additional information helpful in research. Once the index card has been located with the reference for the original record, it is often important to obtain a copy of the event as it appears in its original form. The reference on the index card will indicate where to locate the event in the town's original records. Since a large majority of the town's original records are also on microfilm in the Public Records

Division, microfilm copies of the originals can be researched there. Vermont's town records before 1850 are also on microfilm through the FHL, although the holdings are not as complete as at the Public Records Division.

The Public Records Division has a separate statewide microfilm index for divorce decrees (1861 to 1968); the decree books themselves are also microfilmed and available there. Summary divorce papers (1968–1979) are arranged alphabetically by surname in one group at the division.

Census Records

Federal

Population Schedules
- Indexed—1790 (1791), 1800, 1810, 1820, 1830, 1840, 1850, 1860, 1870, 1880, 1900, 1910, 1920, 1930
- Soundex—1880, 1900, 1920

Industry and Agriculture Schedules
- 1850, 1860, 1870, 1880

Mortality Schedules
- 1850, 1860, 1870, 1880 (all indexed)

Union Veterans Schedules
- 1890 (indexed)

Vermont became a state in 1791 and took the first federal census that year. This census is usually mislabeled as the "1790 census." Families in other states may be listed on that state's 1790 census and again in Vermont's a year later, having migrated in the interim. The Vermont Historical Society (see Archives, Libraries, and Societies) published the full 1800 census, which was reissued in a reprint edition in 1972 by Genealogical Publishing Company. Countywide 1870 census heads-of-household indexes for Windham and Windsor were privately published by Joan M. Morris in separate volumes (1977, 1980). All of Vermont's federal population census records are indexed and available online through subscription databases (see page 17).

The 1810 and 1820 censuses for some Vermont towns include a tally of such things as the number of yards of material made on the premises and the amount of lumber milled. When using the census records, care should be taken to consider alternate spelling, especially for French-Canadians, Italian, and Greek names of new immigrants after 1850.

Original and microfilm copies of the 1850, 1860, 1870, and 1880 population, industry, and agriculture schedules and microfilm of the mortality schedules and microfilm copies of all population schedules are located at Vermont Department of Libraries, State Office Bldg., 109 State St., Montpelier, VT

05609-0601 <http://dol.state.vt.us/> although originals are restricted for general research purposes.

The so-called *1771 Census* by Jay Mack Holbrook (Oxford, Mass.: Holbrook Research, 1982) is not an "official" census. It is a collection of names associated with Vermont in 1771 drawn from several sources in New York, New Hampshire, and Connecticut as well as Vermont. It does include the official New York census for 1771 for Cumberland and Glouster counties (covering land now in Vermont) that was published in Callaghan (see Background Sources). Many of the names listed were granted land but never lived in Vermont. Checking the appearance of the name in the original source should help clarify this.

Background Sources

Bassett, T. D. Seymour, ed. *Vermont: A Bibliography of Its History.* 1981. Reprint. Hanover, N.H.: University Press of New England, 1983. This comprehensive bibliography includes numerous local, state, and town histories, and commemorative publications.

Bartley, Scott Andrew. *Vermont Families in 1791.* vol. 1. Camden, Maine: Picton Press, 1992; vol. 2. St. Albans, Vt.: Genealogical Society of Vermont, 1997. An ongoing series identifying those families enumerated in the first federal census taken for Vermont in 1791 is available through the Genealogical Society of Vermont (see Archives, Libraries, and Societies).

Duffy, John, et al. *The Vermont Encyclopedia.* Hanover, N.H.: University Press of New Hampshire, 2003. Over 1000 entries, contributed by 140 contributors, give the researcher an updated and comprehensive view of life in the Green Mountain State in a range of articles from prehistory to today.

Eichholz, Alice. *Collecting Vermont Ancestors.* 1986. Reprint. Montpelier, Vt.: New Trails! 1993. A genealogical handbook focusing specifically on the availability of the extensive original records in Vermont. A listing of available lot maps for towns (see Maps) is included.

Hemenway, Abby Maria. *Vermont Historical Gazetteer.* 5 vols. Burlington, Vt., and others, 1867–91. Hemenway enlisted the assistance of at least one knowledgeable resident of each town to research and write the histories included in these volumes. Since those people tended to know the individuals about whom they wrote, the information is reasonably good oral history. An index covering all towns except those in Windsor County was published in 1923 by Tuttle Company, in Rutland, Vermont, as Vol. 6 and indicates town as well as volume and page number for person named. A searchable CD-ROM version has been published by New England

Historic Genealogical Society (2003), but is being revised to improve its usefulness.

Jones, Matt Bushnell. *Vermont in the Making.* Cambridge, Mass.: Harvard University Press, 1939. This is probably the most detailed and easy-to-read account of the Vermont land controversy and its role in the Revolution and formation of the United States.

Leppman, John. *Bibliography for Vermont Genealogy.* St. Albans, Vt.: Genealogical Society of Vermont, 2000. As a selective bibliography, it provides a solid reading and reference list for researching Vermont's history and communities, as related to family history.

Melnyk, Marcia D. *Genealogist's Handbook for New England Research.* 4th ed. Boston: New England Historic Genealogical Society, 1999. An essential guide for planning a research trip in Vermont, but because of its date of publication, call ahead to confirm hours, location, and record availability.

O'Callaghan, E. B. *Documentary History of the State of New York.* 4 vols. Albany, N.Y.: Weed, Parson & Co., 1849–51. This work contains much history regarding the land controversy between New York and Vermont. Vol. 4 contains a large number of Vermont-related document transcriptions. Vermonters are included in Holbrook, *1771 Census* (see Census Records).

Sherman, Michael, et al. *Freedom and Unity: A History of Vermont.* Montpelier, Vt.: Vermont Historical Society, 2004. The authors provide a comprehensive view of Vermont with historical, social, economic, political, cultural and demographic perspectives, all in a national context.

Stilwell, Lewis Dayton. *Migration from Vermont.* Montpelier, Vt.: Vermont Historical Society, 1948. This is a superbly documented description, generally using secondary sources, of migration in and emigration from Vermont as it related to social and economic problems encountered by Vermonters through 1860.

Swift, Esther Munroe. *Vermont Place-Names: Footprints of History.* 1977. Reprint. Rockport, Maine: Picton Press, 1996. Swift adeptly portrays the complicated history of Vermont's changing jurisdictions during the land controversy and gives fine descriptive accounts of thousands of place-names in Vermont, including Native American sources and surnames.

Maps

Excellent maps exist for use in solving genealogical problems in Vermont. Because it is still a sparsely settled state, it is possible to retrace many an ancestor's steps, or at least his or her places of residence.

For research and traveling, one superb atlas details town divisions, geographical details, road surface types, routes of transportation, cemeteries and, in older editions, locations of buildings (including those no longer occupied). It is *The Vermont Atlas and Gazetteer* (Freeport, Maine: DeLorme Mapping, 2003), published in updated versions. A smaller alternative publication is *The Vermont Road Atlas and Guide* (Burlington, Vt.: Northern Cartographic, 1985–   ), in its sixth edition includes the names of all roads and geographic features in relief.

For an excellent bibliography of maps, see David A. Cobbs's "Vermont Maps Prior to 1900: An Annotated Carto-bibliography," published as a special double issue of *Vermont History* 39 (Nos. 3 and 4), 1971.

The *Beers Atlas,* detailing the structures and owners in the late nineteenth century in every county, has been reissued in the original county editions by Tuttle Publishing, Box 541, Rutland, VT 05701. Only Bennington, Chittenden, and Windsor maps still remain in print, but the entire series is available at the Vermont Historical Society and other research libraries. Originally published by F. W. Beers between 1869 and 1873, these atlases provide a valuable portrait of communities. The same details exist in a set of maps ten years earlier, but the Wallings Map Series from 1858 is only available for reference in large, wall-sized versions at the Vermont Historical Society and other research libraries.

For solving early genealogical problems in Vermont, the most important maps are the town lotting maps (see Land Records). When each town was granted, the land was divided into lots and numbered. Either the lot's number or the original proprietor are so often used in land descriptions that they are essential for locating a family in relationship to neighbors and the broader community. Lot maps may be found in town offices, the Vermont Historical Society, the Vermont Public Records Division, or other state agencies (see Background Sources—Eichholz's *Collecting Vermont Ancestors,* for location of lot maps).

Land Records

State-Land State

Much land in the state was originally granted by Vermont, New Hampshire, or New York; some were in competing claims. When Vermont declared itself independent in 1777, all land came under its jurisdiction. Consequently, there was no other way to obtain an initial grant of land except through the auspices of the legislature, which first granted the town to a group of individuals called proprietors. The proprietors then met— although not necessarily in the town or even in Vermont—devised a plan for dividing up the land, and drew lots to determine who owned which lots. From then on, that piece of land was identified in

deeds (if the descriptions are detailed enough) as the "original right" of that proprietor.

"Original right" is a term found often in deeds, often delineated as being the first, second, third, fourth, or sometimes fifth division right of the proprietor since not all of a town was divided up at one time. A division usually contained lots of equal acreage. For example, first division lots might be 100 acres, second division lots fifty acres. Some lots were set aside for the ministry, schools, and the governor to use at their discretion, though most of that was later sold in tax sales or leased by the town selectmen.

Occasionally, towns defined "divisions" using a grid of ranges and lots. For example, a first division might include "Lot #5 in 6th range." Once the general plan for numbering the lot—whether by divisions or ranges or a combination—was made, land tended to be sold as portions of the lot such as "south half of Lot #5." Metes and bounds descriptions were added later when land divisions did not fall neatly into portions of the original lot. Such metes and bounds descriptions often indicated names of roads, streams, or neighbors. The town is the primary legal jurisdiction for land records in Vermont. Consequently, original copies of land records are at the town clerk's office (see Town Resources). Each town has separate indexes for the grantees and grantors. Very few women owned land in their own right. They occasionally witnessed deeds but sometimes were asked to release their dower's right. A few land records were recorded by counties and are available at the county courthouse (see County [Probate] Resources), although they are primarily for those towns as noted in the Town Resources that have no formal organization.

With no statewide master index or abstract of land records in the 251 towns, this valuable genealogical information has to be searched out town by town, but it can be done centrally with microfilm copies. Land records for towns whose records were extant in the 1940s had those deed books and indexes microfilmed from inception through 1850. They are available and at the Vermont Public Records Division, and through the FHL. Fortunately, only a few towns had lost their land records in fires or floods by that time. The Vermont Public Records Division is always expanding its microfilm holdings of town records beyond those done in the 1940s, and its collection now includes many town records from 1850 to the present, some of which may also be found in the FHL microfilm collection.

Probate Records

Probate records were filed by probate district and not town or county; however, some counties are divided geographically into two probate districts. For Vermont's fourteen counties (see County [Probate] Resources), there have been twenty probate districts. Two of the districts disbanded—New Haven in 1962, and Bradford in 1994. By percentage, few Vermonters who died in the state have probate records filed. Many people disposed of their holdings to one or more children in land transactions before death.

Probate records are only indexed by district. District offices have indexes filed by decedent only. Microfilm indexes are available at Vermont Public Records Division (see Archives, Libraries, and Societies), New England Historic Genealogical Society (see page 13) and the FHL. Unlike the land records, the Vermont Public Records Division has not extensively continued the microfilming program of probate records. With some exceptions, only the official probate proceedings books were microfilmed to about 1850. Much more information exists in the original probate files that are held in the district itself, along with the probate records after 1850.

A complete probate search involves using all the files that are available in addition to the record books. Insolvent estates are not uncommon.

The only published index currently available is the *Windsor County Probate Index (1778–1899)* by Scott A. Bartley and Marjorie J. Bartley (St. Albans, Vt.: Genealogical Society of Vermont, 2000), which includes both Hartford and Windsor probate districts.

Court Records

Historically, the major purpose of the county system in Vermont was the operation of the county courts, which recorded deeds for unorganized towns, levied county taxes, heard civil and criminal matters, and granted divorces and naturalizations.

Before Vermont became independent (1777), New York and New Hampshire both claimed some county jurisdiction over Vermont land. For this reason, New York and New Hampshire records must be consulted even up to 1791.

Beginning in 1777, each county had one county court that heard both civil and criminal matters. The state supreme court served an appellate function. In 1967 district courts were added, covering territorial units within the counties. District court jurisdiction is not exclusively over criminal cases; it may also hear some civil cases. In 1974, the county courts were renamed superior courts, with countywide jurisdiction over all matters previously entertained by the county courts and not covered by district courts. Beginning in 1990, the superior court functions involving family matters (divorce, child custody, etc.) were transferred to one statewide family court with divisions of that court operating in each of the counties.

The Vermont Public Records Division now has microfilms of county court records for Bennington, Chittenden, and Windsor counties before 1825, with the only index available typed

alphabetically by plaintiff for each book. In early records, debts are the major subject of litigation in the courts. The division is continuing the microfilming of all the county court records and has completed Addison and Washington counties, although no comparable index exists for these. The division houses many of the original early records, sent for preservation by the county courts. Others remain in the county court offices. Check with the division for updated holdings.

Tax Records

Grand lists are the annual assessment for town tax purposes; they were taken every year for every town in Vermont. Many of them are extant, but they are not easy to find. Sometimes they appear as part of the proprietor or town meeting records (which may be in the town records microfilms at Vermont Public Records Division or the FHL) or sometimes in separate books (which might be in town clerks' offices or vaults). The assessment might be for a poll (twenty-one-year-old male or eligible voter—"Freeman" in Vermont), acreage, buildings, cattle, yards of material produced, and clapboards milled. People taxed were not necessarily landowners.

Cemetery Records

Town, church, family, and private cemeteries all exist in Vermont. The cemetery cards in the vital records microfilm of the Vermont Public Records Division constitute the only statewide cemetery index (see Vital Records for limitations). There is a Grand Army of the Republic card index of all veterans' graves through World War II at the Vermont Historical Society Library. Since 1982 there have been a number of projects undertaken to publish some Vermont cemetery records. The Vermont Historical Society has the most extensive collection, but some town offices are known to have good indexes of their own cemeteries.

Burial Grounds of Vermont (Bradford, Vt.: Vermont Old Cemetery Association, 1991), by Arthur L. Hyde and Frances P. Hyde, lists nearly 1,900 cemeteries, indexed by town. Each town entry has a road map with cemetery location and an inventory listing number of graves, condition of cemetery, and whether gravestone inscriptions have been published and where. Joann H. Nichols, Patricia L. Haslam, and Robert M. Murphy's *Index to Known Cemetery Listings in Vermont*, 4th ed. (Montpelier, Vt.: Vermont Historical Society, 1999) provides a list of known published abstracts of Vermont cemeteries whether in journals, separate publications, or in the Daughters of the American Revolution (DAR) collection. Both publications are available from the Vermont Historical Society Bookstore.

Church Records

Church records are under-utilized in Vermont research, but they do contain good sources for genealogical research. Lists of members (sometimes the only place where wives' names are mentioned in any records), baptisms, removals, exclusions, and the intricacies of community life are obvious in many church records. The only easy way to access them is through the Works Projects Administration (WPA) inventory located at the Vermont Public Records Division. The inventory is divided into Protestant Episcopal (published), Congregational, and miscellaneous denominations (only typescript copies), and then by town. The inventory, taken in the 1940s, can be used as a guide for tracking down the whereabouts of many church records that may have been held in private homes of church members, or the town clerk's office, for safe keeping. However, both the Special Collections at University of Vermont's Bailey-Howe Library (see Manuscripts) and the Vermont Historical Society have become repositories for many records if they are not at the local church or in the town clerk's office. In some cases, the records were removed to centralized religious repositories both in and out of state.

During the eighteenth and early nineteenth centuries in Vermont history, tax revenues supported ministers and church buildings for the "majority" church. Those town residents who dissented were eligible to claim a tax exemption with the town, providing supporting evidence for their claim. Abstracts of these "religions certificates," by town, have been published in Alden M. Rollins' *Vermont Religious Certificates* (Rockport, Maine: Picton Press, 2002), although it cannot be considered a complete listing of all such certificates.

Military Records

Original service records for Vermont before 1920 were destroyed in a fire. Printed lists of Vermonters who served in wars from the Revolution through the Desert Storm conflict have been published by the Vermont Adjutant General's Office. If you cannot find a copy of the appropriate volume in a library near you, the Vermont Department of Veterans' Affairs will answer inquiries (mailing address: 120 State St., Montpelier, VT 05620-4401). A few records of Vermont militia for the 1820 to 1830s can be found in some town meeting records.

Muster rolls in the Walter Sheldon papers of the Stevens Collection at the Vermont State Archives (see Archives, Libraries, and Societies) contain information on some who fought in the War of 1812, not only from Vermont.

Periodicals, Newspapers, and Manuscript Collections

Periodicals

Vermont History is published quarterly by the Vermont Historical Society (see Archives, Libraries, and Societies) and has excellent articles on Vermont history, rarely genealogy. It is indexed annually.

Vermont Genealogy (1996– ; formerly *Branches and Twigs*, 1972–95) is published quarterly by the Genealogical Society of Vermont (see Archives, Libraries, and Societies). The *Index to Branches and Twigs, 1972–1995*, edited by Robert M. Murphy (St. Albans, Vt.: Genealogical Society of Vermont, 2000), covers all of the years of its publication under that title.

Rooted in the Green Mountains is a quarterly newsletter focused on Addition and Rutland counties, available from Danielle Roberts, P.O. Box 81, Fair Haven, Vermont 05743.

(See also page 9—Periodicals for *The American Genealogist*; and Massachusetts—Periodicals—*The New England Historical and Genealogical Register.*)

Newspapers

The microfilm collection of all known newspapers covering Vermont since 1781 is at the Vermont Department of Libraries, State Office Building, 109 State St., Montpelier, VT 05609. Under "Newspapers," the card catalog lists the location of publications and all issues available. Some local libraries in the state have extant copies of other newspapers not in the microfilm collection, notable the Swanton Public Library's collection of *Swanton Courier* (1877–1953). Vital records are occasionally included—births rarely. Obituaries are not prominent until well into the twentieth century. A catalog bibliographic listing of available Vermont newspapers can be found at <http://vtnp.uvm.edu>.

Two books offer published access to some of this material:

Bailey, Diana Hebert. *Extracts from "The Repertory," 9 Mar 1826–29 Dec 1831. Published at St. Albans, Franklin County, Vermont.* Bloomington, Minn.: C. Mertz, 1991. Includes marriage and death notices from those issues.

Rising, Marsha Hoffman. *Vermont Newspaper Abstracts, 1783–1816.* Salt Lake City: Ancestry, Inc., 2001. Includes 11,000 references from the *Vermont Gazette, The Vermont Gazette: Epitome of the World, Epitome of the World, The World,* and *The Green-Mountain Farmer.*

An index to the *Burlington Free Press* in typescript form (1848–70) is in the "Vermont Room" at the state library. As a subject index, it is still essential for genealogical research since accidents and deaths, for example, can be located by topic with the names of people involved listed alphabetically.

The University of Vermont Bailey-Howe Library also has a good newspaper collection with copies of the typescript to the index, *Burlington Free Press* (1848–70).

Copies of the *Boston Evening Transcript* genealogy column (See—Massachusetts—Newspapers) for some years are held at the Vermont Historical Society in scrapbook form.

Manuscripts

The Vermont Historical Society Library, Special Collections at the Bailey-Howe Library of the University of Vermont, and the Vermont State Archives (see Archives, Libraries, and Societies) all have excellent, well-cataloged manuscript collections. The Brigham Index at the Vermont Historical Society is a thorough subject and topic index including letters to and from individuals in the collections. Bailey-Howe's collection is thoroughly cataloged and includes church records, an extensive map collection, and business and shipping records for the Lake Champlain region.

Part of Vermont State Archives' collection is every-name indexed for early documents (see Archives, Libraries, and Societies) before ca. 1830. The extensive holdings in the Henry Stevens, Sr., collection (1732–1901) can be accessed through its guide by Eleazer D. Durfee and Gregory Sanford, *A Guide to the Henry Stevens, Sr. Collection at the Vermont State Archives* (Montpelier, Vt.: Vermont State Archives, 1991), available from the archives. In addition, they published an out-of-print booklet entitled "A Guide to Vermont Repositories," indicating the location of many of Vermont's excellent collections of manuscript materials at such places as the Bennington, Shelburne, and Sheldon museums, and local libraries and historical societies. The archives will answer mail and phone inquiries regarding information in this booklet.

A statewide online searchable Catalog of Vermont Archives and Manuscripts can be found at <http://arccat.uvm.edu> updated through the University of Vermont.

Archives, Libraries, and Societies

Vermont Public Records Division
1078 U.S. Rt. 2
Middlesex, VT
Mailing Address: Research & Reference
Drawer 33
Montpelier, VT 05639-7601
www.bgs.state.vt.us/gsc/pubrec/referen/index.html

As the state's official repository for public records, this research facility holds an extensive collection of vital, land,

probate, and court records for all of the state's 251 towns and municipalities described in various section of this chapter. Research in Vermont should start with this centralized group of records before focusing on individual town records.

Vermont Historical Society Library
Vermont History Center
60 Washington St.
Barre, VT 05641-4209
www.vermonthistory.org

Here is the single largest collection of printed Vermont and New England genealogical and historical research material in the state. The microforms room has a growing collection of CD-ROM databases for New England, and online access to federal census records. Their excellent manuscript collection is extensively indexed. Membership is not required to use open stacks and collections. A very limited research service is available, but a list of independent researchers can be supplied.

Vermont State Archives
Redstone Building
26 Terrace St.
Montpelier, VT
Mailing Address:
State Office Bldg.
109 State St.
Montpelier, VT 05609-1101
http://vermont-archives.org/

Officially called the Office of Vermont Secretary of State, State Papers Division, the Vermont State Archives has a large collection of materials regarding all aspects of state (not town) government from the beginning (1777). It is the department of record for all Vermont state government. Petitions, executive papers, confiscations, business patents, lotting plans, and estate sales for state use are all every-name indexed for easy access for the period before 1830. Mail and in-person inquiries are welcome.

While this office is the official archives, it does not hold town records. Rather it technically shares the responsibility with the Vermont Public Records Division, which holds the vital records and microfilm collections of town, land, probate, court, naturalization and some church records (see above).

Vermont Department of Libraries
Reference and Law Division
109 State St.
Montpelier, VT 05609-0601
http://dol.state.vt.us

The library has all federal censuses for Vermont, state and local history collections, and the largest collection of known Vermont newspapers on microfilm. Copies of the newspaper microfilm circulate through interlibrary loan.

Bailey-Howe Library
Special Collections
University of Vermont
Burlington, VT 05101
http://library.uvm.edu/about/specialcollections/index.html

In addition to the church manuscript and newspaper collections, the library has a small collection of printed genealogies and town histories, a fine map collection of the Lake Champlain Region, and an extensive manuscript collection of account books and diaries.

Genealogical Society of Vermont
P.O. Box 1553
St. Albans, VT 05478-1006
www.rootsweb.com/~vtgsv

The society has semi-annual meetings and primarily publishes the journal, *Vermont Genealogy,* and occasional books. Their former library was integrated into the Vermont Historical Society Library collection.

Vermont French-Canadian Genealogical Society
P.O. Box 65128
Burlington, VT 05406-5128
www.vt-fcgs.org

The society meets regularly, maintains a library of records from Quebec, and publishes the journal *Links* and occasional books.

Welsh-American Genealogical Society
60 Norton Ave.
Poultney, VT 05764-1011
www.rootsweb.com/~vtwags

For a list of local historical societies, see <www.vermonthistory.org/links/lhs.htm>.

(See also, Massachusetts—Archives, Libraries and Societies—New England Historic Genealogical Society.)

Special Focus Categories

Immigration
The "Saint Albans Passenger Arrival Records," so called, were maintained by the Immigration and Naturalization Service at St. Albans, Vermont, and span the years 1895 to 1954. This immigration district technically covered the entire U.S. Canadian border and documented people traveling by boat or train to the United States, entering through Canada. The original records, soundexed with three supplements, are at the National Archives and Records Administration in Washington, D.C. A complete set of microfilms is at the National Archives—Northeast Region (see page 11) and at the New England Historic Genealogical Society.

Naturalizations

Naturalizations might have been applied for or obtained through either the county court or U.S. District Courts. The Vermont Public Records Division holds microfilm copies of some naturalizations from 1836 to 1972. Others, notably those filed in Chittenden County, remain at the district probate office. A complete WPA index, which includes Vermont, along with the rest of New England (except Connecticut) for 1790 to 1906, is held at the Boston and Pittsfield facilities of the National Archives—Northeast Region (see page 11) and at the New England Historic Genealogical Society (see page 13).

Native American

Members and descendants of the Abenaki Nation of Missisquoi, St. Francis/Sokoki band in Vermont, are active in genealogical research. Contact the Abenaki Nation of Missisquoi and the Abenaki Tribal Museum and Cultural Center, 100 Grand St., Swanton, VT 05488.

See also:

Calloway, Colin G. *The Western Abenakis of Vermont, 1600–1800: War, Migration, and the Survival of an Indian People.* Norman, Okla.: University of Oklahoma Press, 1990.

Haviland, William A., and Marjory W. Power. *The Original Vermonters: Native Inhabitants, Past and Present.* Burlington: University of Vermont, 1981.

Other Ethnic Groups

A large number of French-Canadians migrated across the border as early as the late eighteenth century and continues today. In addition to a few Quebec census records available at the Vermont Public Records Division, the Vermont French-Canadian Genealogical Society (see Archives, Libraries, and Societies) holds an excellent array of research materials of French-Canadian research. (See also New Hampshire—American-Canadian Genealogical Society; and Massachusetts—New England Historic Genealogical Society).

Migration in the nineteenth century through the turn of this century included Irish, Russians, Italians, Poles, Greeks, and Spanish, as well as numerous other groups, mostly employed in the quarries, iron industry, and manufacturing towns. While no special collections of materials exist for research, the following is an excellent example of what can be found throughout Vermont's research materials:

Beavin, Daniel et al., *Barre, Vermont: An Annotated Bibliography.* Barre, Vt.: Aldrich Public Library, 1979. An itemized list of over 500 documents and groups of materials focusing on the local history of a town heavily influenced by immigration.

County (Probate) Resources

Between 1772 and 1777, four counties existed in what is now Vermont—Albany, Charlotte, Gloucester, and Cumberland. All were politically New York counties even though they encompassed a sizable number of New Hampshire granted towns. Gloucester County court records are extant and have been published. In 1777 two Vermont counties were erected—Bennington, for the west part of the state, and Cumberland for the east. However, the name Cumberland was abandoned in 1781 when four new counties were created—three replacing Cumberland, namely Windham, Windsor, and Orange; Bennington County was subdivided to form Rutland County.

Even though the political division of county has little meaning in Vermont, there are some county land records (see chart), primarily for unorganized towns, and county court records located at the appropriate county office. In addition, county designation is necessary for census research. For nine of Vermont's counties, the probate district follows the county's political boundaries. For six counties—Addison, Bennington, Orange, Rutland, Windham, and Windsor—there are, or have been, two probate districts within the county's boundaries. The divisions for Addison and Orange were dissolved in 1962 and 1994, respectively. The following listing delineates the county address, parent county, and date of formation; what land and other records in addition to those recorded in towns are available that were recorded by entire county; the name and address of the probate district; and the dates probate district records are extant.

Map	County Address Parent County/ies	Land Records	Probate Address	Probate Records
D3	**Addison** 7 Mahady Ct. Middlebury 05753 1785 from Rutland	1774–1926 (county only)	Addison 7 Mahady Ct. Middlebury 05753	See below

Presently includes all the towns in Addison County. The town of Orwell became part of Addison District in 1847 from Fair Haven District. Between 1824 and 1962 the northern part of the county constituted the New Haven District (see below). Those records were filed separately but are now located at Addison County Courthouse as well as an index to them and to all remaining records from Addison after 1852. On 25 February 1852 a fire in the courthouse burned the probate records for Addison district (not New Haven). Only fragments remain for Addison Probate District records before 1852. They are available on microfilm in Montpelier, in chronological order, but are extremely difficult to use.

| | **Addison**
(same) | New Haven | 1824–1962
(same) | |

New Haven District was set off from Addison District in 1824 and then reabsorbed in 1962. Records retained by Addison Probate District.

Map	County Address Parent County/ies	Land Records	Probate Address	Probate Records

H3 Bennington
207 South St.
P.O. Box 45
Bennington 05201
1777 from Albany and Washington counties, New York

Land Records: 1782–1832 (county only)

Probate Address: Bennington, 207 South St., P.O. Box 65, Bennington 05201

Probate Records: 1778–present

Bennington Probate District includes towns in the south part of the county—see Town Resources.

Bennington

Probate Address: Manchester, Rt. 7 Box 446, Manchester 05254

Probate Records: 1778–present

Manchester Probate District includes towns in the north part of the county—see Town Resources.

B6 Caledonia
27 Main St., Box 406
St. Johnsbury 05819
1796 from Orange

Land Records: 1797–1896 (county only)

Probate Address: Caledonia (same)

Probate Records: 1796–present

B3 Chittenden
175 Main St.
P.O. Box 511
Burlington 05402
1791 from Addison

Probate Address: Chittenden, P.O. Box 511, Burlington 05402

Probate Records: 1795–present

Cumberland
Originally a New York county, it went out of existence as a New York entity in 1777 when Vermont became independent. Land that had been in Cumberland and Gloucester counties, New York, then fell under Cumberland County, Vermont, jurisdiction. Cumberland County, Vermont, was abolished in 1781 when Windham, Windsor, and Orange counties were formed.

A7 Essex
Box 426
Guildhall 05905
1796 from Orange

Land Records: 1793–1971 (county only)

Probate Address: Essex, Main St., Island Pond 05846

Probate Records: 1791–present

Probate Office does not have early volumes. They are kept at the county courthouse in Guildhall.

A3 Franklin
17 Church St.
St. Albans 05478
1796 from Chittenden.

Land Records: 1797–1883 (county only)

Probate Address: Franklin, 17 Church St., St. Albans 05478

Probate Records: 1796–present

A2 Grand Isle
P.O. Box 7
North Hero 05474
1801–02 from Chittenden/Franklin.

Probate Address: Grand Isle, P.O. Box 7, North Hero 05474

Probate Records: 1796–present

Jefferson
Formed in 1810; renamed Washington, 1814.

B4 Lamoille
Main St./P.O. Box 102
Hyde Park 05655-0102
1835 from Washington/Orleans/Franklin

Land Records: none

Probate Address: Lamoille, Main St./P.O. Box 102, Hyde Park 05655-0102

Probate Records: 1837–present

D5 Orange
5 Court St./P.O. Box 30
Chelsea 05038
1781 from Cumberland and Gloucester counties, New York; later Cumberland

Land Records: 1771–1952; Tax 1789–1847; Misc. 1770–81 (county only)

Probate Address: Randolph, Now called Orange, 5 Court St./P.O. Box 30, Chelsea 05038

Probate Records: 1792–present

Randolph (now Orange) Probate District covers towns in western part of Orange County. See Town Resources before 1994 and for all towns in Orange County after 1994.

Orange

Probate Address: Bradford

Probate Records: 1781–1994

Probate district covers towns in eastern part of Orange County; Bradford probates absorbed by Orange Probate District (above) 1 June 1994. Court records are now at Vermont Public Records Division.

A5 Orleans
247 Main St.
Newport 05855
1796 from Orange/Chittenden

Land Records: 1799–1849 (county only)

Probate Address: Orleans, 247 Main St., Newport 05855

Probate Records: 1796–present

G3 Rutland
83 Center St.
Rutland 05701
1781 from Bennington

Land Records: 1763–1822 (county only)

Probate Address: Rutland, 83 Center St., Rutland 05701

Probate Records: 1784–present

Rutland Probate District covers towns in eastern part of Rutland County. See Town Resources.

Rutland
83 Center St.
Rutland 05701

Probate Address: Fair Haven, 3 N. Park Place, Fair Haven 05743

Probate Records: 1797–present

Fair Haven Probate District covers towns in western part of Rutland County. See Town Resources.

C4 Washington
39 Main St.
Montpelier 05602
1811 (as Jefferson) from Orange/Chittenden/Addison/Caledonia

Land Records: None

Probate Address: Washington, 10 Elm St. #2, Montpelier 05602

Probate Records: 1811–present

J4 Windham
P.O. Box 36
Newfane 05345
1781 from Cumberland County, Vt.

Land Records: Cumberland County Deeds 1766–74; 1772–77

Probate Address: Marlboro, West River Rd., P.O. Box 523, Brattleboro 05301

Probate Records: 1781–present

Marlboro Probate District covers the towns in southern part of Windham County. See Town Resources.

Windham

Probate Address: Westminster, 39 Square/P.O. Box 47, Bellows Falls 05101

Probate Records: 1781–present

Westminster Probate District covers the towns in northern part of Windham County. See Town Resources.

F4 Windsor
31 The Green/P.O. Box 275
Woodstock 05091
1781–82 from Cumberland County, Vt.

Land Records: 1784–94 (see also Windham County)

Probate Address: Windsor, Rt. 106/P.O. Box 402, North Springfield 05150

Probate Records: 1787–present

Windsor Probate District covers towns in southern part of Windsor County. See Town Resources. First book of guardianships is missing, as are some pages in the recorded probates. Probate files for 1781–1850 were burned.

Windsor
31 The Green/P.O. Box 275
Woodstock 05091

Probate Address: Hartford, Woodstock Green, P.O. Box 275, Woodstock 05091

Probate Records: 1783–present

Hartford Probate District covers towns in northern part of Windsor County. See Town Resources.

VERMONT

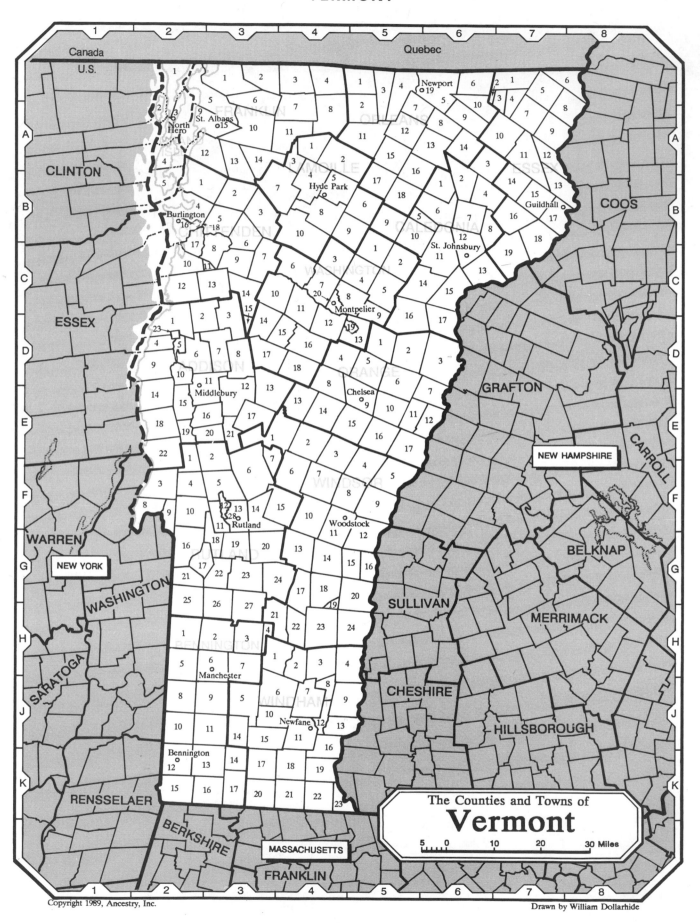

The Counties and Towns of
Vermont

5 0   10   20   30 Miles

Drawn by William Dollarhide

Town Resources

Town records are extremely important in Vermont research. Each town clerk's office holds the original deed, vital, tax, and town meeting records. Included in town or proprietor's meeting records are such valuable sources as lists of freemen (new voters in town), annual election of officers, school records, hog or cattle marks, warnings out to those for whom the town will not assume legal responsibility, militia, and accounts of various town officials. Few of such materials have been published and remain in town records. Notable exceptions are:

Rollins, Alden M. *Vermont Warnings Out, 1779–1817.* Vol. 1, *Northern Vermont.* Camden, Maine: Picton Press, 1995.

_____. *Vermont Warnings Out, 1779–1817.* Vol. 2, *Southern Vermont.* Camden, Maine: Picton Press, 1997.

Many of Vermont's town meeting records have been microfilmed and can be located at either the Public Records Division or through the FHL. Town clerks rarely have time to do more than a cursory search of the deed or vital records indexes; however, each office is open to the public for research purposes.

On the chart below, the town clerk's mailing address (2004 Secretary of State listing at <www.sec.state.vt.us>) is given in the first column. The date that it was granted and the colony that first claimed it are given in the next column. The source here is Swift's *Vermont Place Names* (see Background Sources).

Competing claims as illustrated by Swift are listed underneath. In some cases, competing claims covered more than what is now one town; those are not listed here. For more specific information, see the maps and outlines in Swift. "Other Names" indicates the names used in early town records or the town it was part of before creation. Not all "other names" are given here, only those that are noted specifically by Swift or by the listing at the Public Records Division. The present county, with parent county underneath, is listed in the next column. Since town formation often pre-dates Vermont county formation, the county designation may be helpful in identifying earlier land descriptions and locating towns in census records.

The source for parent county outlines is Steven Farrow's University of Vermont master's thesis, "Vermont Place-Name Changes: Counties, Towns, Gores and the Evolving Map of the State," available at the Vermont State Archives and UVM Bailey-Howe Library (see Archives, Libraries, and Societies). Parent counties will be particularly helpful for census search in Washington and Lamoille County towns since those counties were formed after the 1800 census. Probate district and court district are listed in the last two columns. Use the town address for correspondence with the clerk regarding vital records and land records; use the probate and court addresses in the County (Probate) Resources for those records. See Land and Probate records for microfilm availability. Only a few towns have lost records.

Town Address	Date Formed Claims/Other Names	County Map Parent County	Probate District Court District
Addison 65 VT Rt. 17 W Vergennes 05491	1761 N.H.	Addison (9) Rutland	Addison Addison
Albany 980 Main St. P.O. Box 284 Albany 05820	1782 Vt. Luterloh	Orleans (15) Chittenden	Orleans Orleans
Alburg 1 N. Main St. P.O. Box 346 Alburg 05440	1781 Vt. Allenburg	Grand Isle (1) Franklin	Grand Isle Grand Isle
Andover 953 Weston-Andover Rd. Andover 05143	1761 N.H.	Windsor (22)	Windsor Windsor
Arlington 3828 VT Rt 2A P.O. Box 304 Arlington 05250	1761 N.H.	Bennington (8)	Manchester Bennington
Athens 56 Brookline Athens 05143	1780 Vt.	Windham (8)	Westminster Windham

Town Address	Date Formed Claims/Other Names	County Map Parent County	Probate District Court District
Averill (unorganized)	1762 N.H.	Essex (5) Orange	Essex Essex
Avery's Gore	1791–96 Vt.	Essex (4) Orange	Essex
Bakersfield 15 E. Bakersfield Box 203 Bakersfield 05441	1791 Vt. Knoulton's Gore	Franklin (11) Chittenden	Franklin Franklin
Baltimore 49 Harris Rd. Chester 05143	1793 Vt. part of Cavendish	Windsor (19)	Windsor Windsor
Barnard 115 N. Rd. P.O. Box 274 Barnard 05031	1761 N.H.	Windsor (7)	Hartford Windsor
Barnet P.O. Box 15 Barnet 05821	1763 N.H.	Caledonia (15) Orange	Caledonia Caledonia
Barre City 6 N. Main St. P.O. Box 418 Barre 05641	1894 Vt. Barre Town	Washington (19) Orange	Washington Washington

Town Address	Date Formed Claims/Other Names	County Map Parent County	Probate District Court District
Barre Town 149 Websterville Rd. Box 124 Websterville 05678	1781 Vt. Wildersburgh	Washington (13) Orange	Washington Washington
Barton 34 Main St. P.O. Box 657 Barton 05822	1789 Vt. Providence	Orleans (13) Orange	Orleans Orleans
Belvidere 3996 VT Rt 109 Belvidere Center 05442	1791 Vt.	Lamoille (1) Franklin	Lamoille Lamoille
Bennington 205 South St. Bennington 05201	1749 N.H. N.Y. 1768/ N.Y. 1762 Hoosick/Mapleton	Bennington (12)	Bennington Bennington
Benson P.O. Box 163 Benson 05731	1780 Vt.	Rutland (3) Bennington	Fair Haven Rutland
Berkshire 4454 Watertown Rd. Enosburg 05450	1781 Vt.	Franklin (3) Chittenden	Franklin Franklin
Berlin 108 Shed Rd. Montpelier 05602	1763 N.H.	Washington (12) Orange	Washington Washington
Bethel 134 S. Main St. Box 404 Bethel 05032	1779 Vt.	Windsor (2)	Hartford Windsor
Bloomfield P.O. Box 336 N. Stratford, NH 03590	1762 N.H. Minehead	Essex (9) Orange	Essex Essex
Bolton 3045 Theodore Roosevelt Hwy Waterbury 05676	1763 N.H.	Chittenden (7) Addison	Chittenden Chittenden
Bradford 172 N. Main P.O. Box 339 Bradford 05033	1770 N.Y. Mooretown	Orange (7)	Bradford Orange
Braintree 932 VT Rt. 12A Randolph 05060	1781 Vt.	Orange (13) Rutland	Randolph Orange
Brandon 49 Center St. Brandon 05733	1761 N.H. Neshobe	Rutland (2) Bennington	Rutland Rutland
Brattleboro 230 Main St. Brattleboro 05301	1753 N.H. N.Y. 1766	Windham (19)	Marlboro Windham
Bridgewater 7335 US Rt 4 P.O. Box 14 Bridgewater 05034	1761 N.H.	Windsor (10)	Hartford Windsor
Bridport P.O. Box 27 Bridport 05734	1761 N.H.	Addison (14) Rutland	Addison Addison
Brighton 49 Mill St. Ext. P.O. Box 377 Island Pond 05846	1781 Vt. Random	Essex (10) Orange	Essex Essex
Bristol 1 South St. P.O. Box 247 Bristol 05443	1762 N.H. Pocock	Addison (7) Rutland	Addison Addison
Brookfield 40 Ralph Rd. P.O. Box 463 Brookfield 05036	1781 Vt.	Orange (8) Rutland	Randolph Orange
Brookline P.O. Box 403 Brookline 05345	1794 Vt.	Windham (12)	Westminster Windham
Brownington 509 Dutton Brook Lane Orleans 05860	1790 Vt.	Orleans (8) Orange	Orleans Orleans
Brunswick 994 VT Rt. 102 Guildhall 05905	1761 N.H.	Essex (12) Orange	Essex Essex
Buel's Gore	1780 Vt. Huntington Gore	Chittenden (15) Addison	Chittenden Chittenden
Burke 212 School St. West Burke 05871	1782 Vt.	Caledonia (4) Orange	Caledonia Caledonia
Burlington 149 Church St. Burlington 05401	1763 N.H. incorporated 1864	Chittenden (16) Orange	Chittenden Chittenden
Cabot 3084 Main St. Box 36 Cabot 05647	1780 Vt.	Washington (2) Caledonia/ Orange	Washington Washington
Calais 668 W. County Rd. Calais 05648	1781 Vt. N.Y. 1772 Truro	Washington (4) Caledonia	Washington Washington
Cambridge 55 Main St. P.O. Box 127 Jeffersonville 05464	1781 Vt.	Lamoille (7) Franklin	Lamoille Lamoille

Town Address	Date Formed Claims/Other Names	County Map Parent County	Probate District Court District
Canaan P.O. Box 159 Canaan 05903	1782 Vt. Thirming	Essex (6) Orange	Essex Essex
Castleton 556 Main St. P.O. Box 727 Castleton 05735	1761 N.H.	Rutland (10) Bennington	Fair Haven Rutland
Cavendish 37 High St. P.O. Box 126 Cavendish 05142	1761 N.H. N.Y. 1772	Windsor (18)	Windsor Windsor
Charleston 5063 VT Rt. 105 W. Charleston 05872	1789 Vt. Navy	Orleans (9) Orange	Orleans Orleans
Charlotte 159 Ferry Rd. P.O. Box 119 Charlotte 05445	1762 N.H. Charlotta	Chittenden (12) Addison	Chittenden Chittenden
Chelsea 295 VT Rt 110 P.O. Box 266 Chelsea 05038	1781 Vt. Turnersburgh	Orange (9)	Randolph Orange
Chester 556 Elm St. P.O. Box 370 Chester Depot 05143	1754 N.H. N.Y. 1766 Flamstead	Windsor (23)	Windsor Windsor
Chittenden 337 Holden Rd. P.O. 89 Chittenden 05737	1780 Vt. Philadelphia	Rutland (6) Bennington	Rutland Rutland
Clarendon 279 Middle Rd. P.O. Box 30 Clarendon 05759	1761 N.H.	Rutland (19) Bennington	Rutland Rutland
Colchester 835 Blakely Rd. P.O. Box 55 Colchester 05446	1763 N.H.	Chittenden (4) Addison	Chittenden Chittenden
Concord 374 Main St. P.O. Box 317 Concord 05824	1781 Vt.	Essex (19) Orange	Essex Essex
Cornith 1387 Cookeville Rd. P.O. Box 461 Corinth 05039	1764 N.H. N.Y. 1772	Orange (6)	Bradford Orange
Cornwall 2629 Rt. 30 Middlebury 05753	1761 N.H.	Addison (15) Rutland	Addison Addison
Coventry P.O. Box 104 Coventry 05825	1780 Vt.	Orleans (7) Chittenden	Orleans Orleans
Craftsbury P.O. Box 55 Craftsbury 05826	1781 Vt. Minden	Orleans (17) Chittenden	Orleans Orleans
Danby 130 Brook Rd. P.O. Box 231 Danby 05739	1761 N.H.	Rutland (26) Bennington	Rutland Rutland
Danville P.O. Box 183 Danville 05828	1786 Vt. N.Y. 1770	Caledonia (11) Orange	Caledonia Caledonia
Derby 124 Main St. P.O. Box 25 Derby 05829	1779 Vt.	Orleans (5) Orange	Orleans Orleans
Dorset 112 Mad Tom Rd. Box 0024 East Dorset 05253	1761 N.H.	Bennington (2)	Manchester Bennington
Dover 102 Rt 100 P.O. Box 527 West Dover 05356	1810 Vt. from Wardsboro	Windham (15)	Marlboro Windham
Dummerston 1523 Middle Rd. Putney 05346	1753 N.H.	Windham (16)	Marlboro Windham
Duxbury 3316 Crossett Hill Waterbury 05676	1763 N.H.	Washington (10) Chittenden	Washington Washington
East Haven P.O. Box 10 East Haven 05837	1790 Vt.	Essex (14) Orange	Essex Essex
East Montpelier 40 Kelton Rd. P.O. Box 157 East Montpelier 05651	1848 Vt. from Montpelier	Washington (8) Caledonia	Washington Washington
Eden 71 Old Schoolhouse Rd. Eden Mills 05653	1781 Vt.	Lamoille (2) Orleans	Lamoille Lamoille
Elmore 1175 VT Rt. 12 P.O. Box 123 Lake Elmore 05657	1781 Vt.	Lamoille (9) Washington	Lamoille Lamoille

Town Address	Date Formed Claims/Other Names	County Map Parent County	Probate District Court District
Enosburg 239 Main St. P.O. Box 465 Enosburg Falls 05450	1780 Vt.	Franklin (7) Chittenden	Franklin Franklin
Essex 81 Main St. Essex Jct. 05452	1763 N.H.	Chittenden (5) Addison	Chittenden Chittenden
Fair Haven 3 N. Park Pl. Fair Haven 05743	1779 Vt. N.Y. 1771 Skenesborough	Rutland (9) Bennington	Fair Haven Rutland
Fairfax 67 Hunt St. P.O. Box 27 Fairfax 05454	1763 N.H.	Franklin (13) Chittenden	Franklin Franklin
Fairfield 25 North Rd. P.O. Box 5 Fairfield 05455	1763 N.H. N.Y. 1773 Meath	Franklin (10) Chittenden	Franklin Franklin
Fairlee 75 Town Common Rd. P.O. Box 95 Fairlee 05045	1761 N.H.	Orange (12)	Bradford Orange
Fayston 866 N. Fayston Rd. Moretown 05660	1782 Vt.	Washington (14) Chittenden	Washington Washington
Ferdinand (unorganized)	1761 N.H.	Essex (11) Orange	Essex Essex
Ferrisburgh 6 Little Chicago Rd. P.O. Box 6 Ferrisburgh 05456	1762 N.H.	Addison (1) Rutland	Addison Addison
Fletcher 215 Cambridge Rd. Cambridge 05444	1781 Vt.	Franklin (14) Chittenden	Franklin Franklin
Franklin 5167 Main St. P.O. Box 82 Franklin 05457	1789 Vt. Huntsburgh	Franklin (2) Chittenden	Franklin Franklin
Georgia 47 Town Common Rd. North St. Albans 05478	1763 N.H.	Franklin (12) Chittenden	Franklin Franklin
Glastenbury (unorganized)	1761 N.H. Glossenbury	Bennington (11)	Bennington Bennington
Glover 51 Bean Hill Glover 05839	1783 Vt.	Orleans (16) Orange	Orleans Orleans
Goshen 50 Carlisle Hill Rd. Brandon 05733	1792 Vt.	Addison (21) Rutland	Addison Addison
Grafton 117B Main St. P.O. Box 180 Grafton 05146	1754 N.H. Tomlinson	Windham (3)	Westminster Windham
Granby P.O. Box 56 Granby 05840	1761 N.H.	Essex (15) Orange	Essex Essex
Grand Isle 9 Hyde Rd. P.O. Box 49 Grand Isle 05458	1769 N.Y. Vt. 1779 Two Heros/ Middle Hero	Grand Isle (4) Chittenden	Grand Isle Grand Isle
Granville 4184 VT Rt. P.O. Box 66 Granville 05747	1781 Vt. Kingston	Addison (13) Rutland	Addison Addison
Greensboro 81 Lauredon Ave. P.O. Box 119 Greensboro 05841	1781 Vt.	Orleans (18) Orange	Orleans Orleans
Groton 314 Scott Hwy. Groton 05046	1789 Vt. N.Y. 1772 Penryn	Caledonia (16) Orange	Caledonia Caledonia
Guildhall Rt. 102 P.O. Box 10 Guildhall 05905	1761 N.H.	Essex (17) Orange	Essex Essex
Guilford 236 School Rd. Brattleboro 05301	1754 N.H.	Windham (22)	Marlboro Windham
Halifax P.O. Box 127 West Halifax 05358	1750 N.H.	Windham (21) Windham	Marlboro
Hancock P.O. Box 100 Hancock 05748	1781 Vt.	Addison (17) Rutland	Addison Addison
Hardwick 20 Church St. P.O. Box 523 Hardwick 05843	1781 Vt.	Caledonia (9) Orange	Caledonia Caledonia
Hartford 171 Bridge St. White River Jct. 05001	1761 N.H.	Windsor (9)	Hartford Windsor

Town Address	Date Formed Claims/Other Names	County Map Parent County	Probate District Court District
Hartland 1 Quechee P.O. Box 142 Hartland 05048	1761 N.H. N.Y. 1766 Hereford	Windsor (12)	Hartford Windsor
Highgate 2996 VT Rt. 78 P.O. Box 67 Highgate Center 05459	1762 N.H.	Franklin (1) Chittenden	Franklin Franklin
Hinesburg 10632 Rt. 116 P.O. Box 133 Hinesburg 05461	1763 N.H.	Chittenden (13) Addison	Chittenden Chittenden
Holland 120 School Rd. Holland 05830	1787 Vt.	Orleans (6) Orange	Orleans Orleans
Hubbardton 1831 Monument Hill Rd. Fair Haven 05743	1764 N.H.	Rutland (4) Bennington	Fair Haven Rutland
Huntington 4930 Main Rd. Huntington 05462	1763 N.H. New Huntington	Chittenden (14) Addison	Chittenden Chittenden
Hyde Park P.O. Box 98 Hyde Park 05655	1781 Vt.	Lamoille (5) Orleans	Lamoille Lamoille
Ira 808 Rt. 133 West Rutland 05777	1780 Vt.	Rutland (18) Bennington	Rutland Rutland
Irasburg 161 Rt. 58E P.O. Box 51 Irasburg 05845	1781 Vt.	Orleans (12) Chittenden	Orleans Orleans
Isle La Motte 2272 Main St. P.O. Box 250 Isle La Motte 05463	1779 Vt. N.Y. 1786	Grand Isle (2) Franklin	Grand Isle Grand Isle
Jamaica 17 Pikes Falls P.O. Box 173 Jamaica 05343	1780 Vt.	Windham (6)	Westminster Windham
Jay 1036 VT Rt. 242 Jay 05859	1792 Vt.	Orleans (1) Chittenden	Orleans Orleans
Jericho 67 VT Rt. 15 P.O. Box 67 Jericho 05465	1763 N.H.	Chittenden (6) Addison	Chittenden Chittenden
Johnson 293 Lower Main P.O. Box 383 Johnson 05656	1792 Vt.	Lamoille (4) Franklin	Lamoille Lamoille
Killington 2706 River Rd. P.O. Box 429 Killington 05751	1761 N.H. (renamed Sherburne, 1800; renamed Killington, 1999)	Rutland (15) Bennington	Rutland Rutland
Kirby 346 Town Hall Rd. Lyndonville 05851	1807 Vt.	Caledonia (8) Orange	Caledonia Caledonia
Landgrove P.O. Box 508 Londonderry 05148	1780 Vt. N.Y. 1770	Bennington (4)	Manchester Bennington
Leicester 44 Schoolhouse Rd. Brandon 05733	1761 N.H.	Addison (20) Rutland	Addison Addison
Lemington 2549 River Lemington 05903	1762 N.H. Limington	Essex (8) Orange	Essex Essex
Lewis (unorganized)	1762 N.H.	Essex (7) Orange	Essex Essex
Lincoln 62 Quaker St. Lincoln 05443	1780 Vt. N.Y. 1775	Addison (8) Rutland	Addison Addison
Londonderry 100 Old School St. Box 118 South Londonderry 05155	1780 Vt. N.Y. 1770 Kent	Windham (1)	Westminster Windham
Lowell 2170 VT Rt 100 Lowell 05847	1791 Vt. Kellyvale	Orleans (11) Chittenden	Orleans Orleans
Ludlow 37 Depot St. P.O. Box 307 Ludlow 05149	1761 N.H.	Windsor (17)	Windsor Windsor
Lunenberg 9 W. Main St. P.O. Box 54 Lunenberg 05906	1763 N.H.	Essex (18) Orange	Essex Essex
Lyndon 119 Park Ave. P.O. Box 167 Lyndonville 05851	1780 Vt.	Caledonia (7) Orange	Caledonia Caledonia

Town Address	Date Formed Claims/Other Names	County Map Parent County	Probate District Court District
Maidstone P.O. Box 118 Guildhall 05905	1761 N.H.	Essex (13) Orange	Essex Essex
Manchester 6039 Main St. P.O. Box 830 Manchester Center 05255	1761 N.H. N.Y. 1765	Bennington (6)	Manchester Bennington
Marlboro 510 S. St. Marlboro 05344	1751 N.H.	Windham (18)	Marlboro Windham
Marshfield 122 School St. Rm 1 Marshfield 05658	1782/1790 Vt.	Washington (5) Caledonia	Washington Washington
Mendon 34 US Rt. 4 Mendon 05701	1781 Vt. Medway	Rutland (14) Bennington	Rutland Rutland
Middlebury 94 Main St. Middlebury 05753	1761 N.H.	Addison (11) Rutland	Addison Addison
Middlesex 5 Church St. Middlesex 05602	1763 N.H.	Washington (7) Chittenden	Washington Washington
Middletown Springs 10 Park Ave. P.O. Box 1232 Middletown Springs 05757	1784 Vt.	Rutland (17) Bennington	Rutland Rutland
Milton 43 Bombardier Milton 05468	1763 N.H.	Chittenden (1) Addison	Chittenden Chittenden
Monkton 280 Monkton Ridge North Ferrisburg 05473	1762 N.H.	Addison (2) Rutland	Addison Addison
Montgomery 98 Main St. P.O. Box 356 Montgomery Center 05471	1789 Vt.	Franklin (8) Chittenden	Franklin Franklin
Montpelier 39 Main St. Montpelier 05602	1781 Vt. incorporated 1895	Washington (20) Caledonia	Washington Washington
Moretown P.O. Box 666 Moretown 05660	1763 N.H.	Washington (11) Chittenden	Washington Washington
Morgan P.O. Box 45 Morgan 05853	1780 Vt. Caldersburg	Orleans (10) Orange	Orleans Orleans
Morrisville 18 Lower Main St. P.O. Box 748 Morrisville 05661	1781 Vt.	Lamoille (8) Orleans	Lamoille Lamoille
Mount Holly 50 School St. P.O. Box 248 Mount Holly 05758	1792 Vt.	Rutland (24) Bennington	Rutland Rutland
Mount Tabor 522 Brooklyn Rd. P.O. Box 245 Danby 05739	1761 N.H. Harwich	Rutland (27) Bennington	Rutland Rutland
New Haven 78 North St. New Haven 05472	1761 N.H.	Addison (6) Rutland	Addison Addison
Newark 1336 Newark St. West Burke 05871	1781 Vt.	Caledonia (3) Essex	Caledonia Caledonia
Newbury P.O. Box 126 Newbury 05051	1763 N.H. N.Y. 1772	Orange (3)	Bradford Orange
Newfane P.O. Box 36 Newfane 05345	1753 N.H. N.Y. 1772	Windham (11)	Marlboro Windham
Newport City 222 Main Newport 05855	1917 Vt. Newport Town	Orleans (19) Chittenden	Orleans Orleans
Newport Town P.O. Box 85 Newport Center 05857	1802 Vt. Duncansborough	Orleans (4) Chittenden	Orleans Orleans
North Hero P.O. Box 38 North Hero 05474	1779 Vt. Two Heros	Grand Isle (3) Franklin	Grand Isle Grand Isle
Northfield 51 S. Main Northfield 05663	1781 Vt. N.Y. 1770 Leyden	Washington (16) Orange	Washington Washington
Norton VT Rt. 114 S Norton 05907	1779 Vt.	Essex (1) Orange	Essex Essex
Norwich 300 Main St. P.O. Box 376 Norwich 05055	1761 N.H.	Windsor (5)	Hartford Windsor
Orange P.O. Box 233 East Barre 05649	1781 Vt.	Orange (1)	Randolph Orange

VERMONT

Town Address	Date Formed Claims/Other Names	County Map Parent County	Probate District Court District
Orwell 436 Main St. P.O. Box 32 Orwell 05760	1763 N.H.	Addison (22) Rutland	Addison Addison
Panton P.O. Box 174 Vergennes 05491	1761 N.H.	Addison (4) Rutland	Addison Addison
Pawlet P.O. Box 128 Pawlet 05761	1761 N.H.	Rutland (25) Bennington	Fair Haven Rutland
Peacham P.O. Box 244 Peacham 05862	1763 N.H.	Caledonia (14) Orange	Caledonia Caledonia
Peru P.O. Box 127 Peru 05152	1761 N.H. Brumley	Bennington (3)	Manchester Bennington
Pittsfield P.O.Box 556 Pittsfield 05762	1781 Vt.	Rutland (7) Bennington	Rutland Rutland
Pittsford P.O. Box 10 Pittsford 05763	1761 N.H.	Rutland (5) Bennington	Rutland Rutland
Plainfield 18 High St. P.O. Box 217 Plainfield 05667	1788 Vt. N.Y. 1772 Whitelaw/Savage and Coit Grant	Washington (9) Caledonia	Washington Washington
Plymouth 68 Town Office Rd. Plymouth 05056	1761 N.H. N.Y. 1772 Saltash	Windsor (13)	Windsor Windsor
Pomfret 5188 Pomfret Rd. P.O. Box 64 North Pomfret 05053	1761 N.H.	Windsor (8)	Hartford Windsor
Poultney 9 Main St. Poultney 05764	1761 N.H.	Rutland (16) Bennington	Fair Haven Rutland
Pownal 467 Center St. P.O. Box 411 Pownal 05261	1760 N.H.	Bennington (15)	Bennington Bennington
Proctor 45 Main St. Proctor 05765	1886 Vt. Rutland/Pittsford	Rutland (12) Bennington	Rutland Rutland
Putney P.O. Box 233 Putney 05346	1753 N.H. N.Y. 1776	Windham (13)	Westminster Windham

Town Address	Date Formed Claims/Other Names	County Map Parent County	Probate District Court District
Randolph 7 Summer St [illegible] Randolph 05060	1781 Vt. N.Y. 1770	Orange (14)	Randolph Orange
Reading P.O. Box 72 Reading 05062	1761 N.H. N.Y. 1772	Windsor (14)	Windsor Windsor
Readsboro P.O. Box 187 Readsboro 05350	1764 N.H. N.Y. 1770	Bennington (17)	Bennington Bennington
Richford P.O. Box 236 Richford 05476	1780 Vt.	Franklin (4) Chittenden	Franklin Franklin
Richmond P.O. Box 285 Richmond 05477	1794 Vt.	Chittenden (9) Addison	Chittenden Chittenden
Ripton P.O. Box 10 Ripton 05766	1781 Vt. Riptown	Addison (12) Rutland	Addison Addison
Rochester P.O. Box 238 Rochester 05767	1781 Vt.	Windsor (1)	Hartford Windsor
Rockingham P.O. Box 339 Bellows Falls 05101	1752 N.H.	Windham (4)	Westminster Windham
Roxbury P.O. Box 53 Roxbury 05669	1781 Vt.	Washington (18) Orange	Washington Washington
Royalton 23 Alexander Pl. P.O. Box 680 South Royalton 05068	1769 N.Y.	Windsor (3)	Hartford Windsor
Rupert 187 East St. P.O. Box 140 West Rupert 05776	1761 N.H.	Bennington (1)	Manchester Bennington
Rutland City 1 Strongs Ave. P.O. Box 969 Rutland 05701	1892 Vt. Rutland Town	Rutland (28) Bennington	Rutland Rutland
Rutland Town P.O. Box 225 Center Rutland 05736	1761 N.H.	Rutland (13) Bennington	Rutland Rutland
Ryegate P.O. Box 332 Ryegate 05042	1763 N.H. N.Y. 1775	Caledonia (17) Orange	Caledonia Caledonia

Town Address	Date Formed Claims/Other Names	County Map Parent County	Probate District Court District
St. Albans City 100 N. Main St. Box 867 St. Albans 05478	1902 Vt. St. Albans Town	Franklin (15) Chittenden	Franklin Franklin
St. Albans Town 579 Lake Rd. P.O. Box 37 St. Albans Bay 05481	1763 N.H.	Franklin (9) Chittenden	Franklin Franklin
St. George 1 Barber Rd. St. George 05495	1763 N.H.	Chittenden (11) Addison	Chittenden Chittenden
St. Johnsbury 1187 Main St. St. Johnsbury 05819	1786 Vt.	Caledonia (12) Orange	Caledonia Caledonia
Salisbury P.O. Box 66 Salisbury 05769	1761 N.H.	Addison (16) Rutland	Addison Addison
Sandgate 3266 Sandgate Sandgate 05250	1761 N.H.	Bennington (5)	Manchester Bennington
Searsburg P.O. Box 157 Wilmington 05363	1781 Vt.	Bennington (14)	Bennington Bennington
Shaftsbury 61 Buck Hill Rd. P.O. Box 409 Shaftsbury 056262	1761 N.H.	Bennington (10)	Bennington Bennington
Sharon P.O. Box 250 Sharon 05065	1761 N.H.	Windsor (4)	Hartford Windsor
Sheffield P.O. Box 165 Sheffield 05866	1793 Vt.	Caledonia (1) Orange	Caledonia Caledonia
Shelburne P.O. Box 88 Shelburne 05482	1763 N.H.	Chittenden (10) Addison	Chittenden Chittenden
Sheldon 1640 Main St. P.O. Box 66 Sheldon 05483	1763 N.H. Hungerford N.Y. 1774	Franklin (6) Chittenden	Franklin Franklin
Sherburne	1761 N.H. (renamed Killington, 1999)		
Shoreham 297 Main St. Shoreham 05770	1761 N.H.	Addison (18) Rutland	Addison Addison

Town Address	Date Formed Claims/Other Names	County Map Parent County	Probate District Court District
Shrewsbury 9832 Cold River Rd. Cuttingsville 05738	1761 N.H.	Rutland (20) Bennington	Rutland Rutland
Somerset (unorganized)	1761 N.H.	Windham (14)	Marlboro Windham
South Burlington 575 Dorset St. South Burlington 05403	1864 Vt. incorporated from Burlington, 1971	Chittenden (17) Addison	Chittenden Chittenden
South Hero P.O. Box 175 South Hero 05486	1779 Vt. N.Y. 1769	Grand Isle (5) Chittenden	Grand Isle Grand Isle
Springfield 96 Main St. Springfield 05156	1761 N.H. N.Y. 1772	Windsor (24)	Windsor Windsor
Stamford 986 Main Rd. Stamford 05352	1753 N.H. 1764 N.H. as New Stamford	Bennington (16)	Bennington Bennington
Stannard P.O. Box 94 Greensboro Bend 05842	1798 Vt. Goshen Gore No.1	Caledonia (5) Orange	Caledonia Caledonia
Starksboro P.O. Box 91 Starksboro 05487	1780 Vt.	Addison (3) Rutland	Addison Addison
Stockbridge 1722 Rt. 100 P.O. Box 39 Stockbridge 05772	1761 N.H.	Windsor (6)	Hartford Windsor
Stowe 67 Main St. P.O. Box 248 Stowe 05672	1763 N.H. annexed part of Mansfield, 1839	Lamoille (10) Washington	Lamoille Lamoille
Strafford 227 Justin Morrill Hwy P.O. Box 27 Strafford 05072	1761 N.H.	Orange (16)	Bradford Orange
Stratton 9 W. Jamaica Rd. West Wardsboro 05360	1761 N.H. N.Y. 1775	Windham (5)	Marlboro Windham
Sudbury 36 Blacksmith Sudbury 05733	1763 N.H.	Rutland (1) Bennington	Fair Haven Rutland
Sunderland 181 South Rd. P.O. Box 295 Sunderland 05252	1761 N.H.	Bennington (9)	Manchester Bennington

Town Address	Date Formed Claims/Other Names	County Map Parent County	Probate District Court District
Sutton P.O. Box 106 Sutton 05067	1782 Vt.	Caledonia (2) Orange	Caledonia Caledonia
Swanton P.O. Box 711 Swanton 05488	1763 N.H.	Franklin (5) Chittenden	Franklin Franklin
Thetford 3910 VT Rt. 113 P.O. Box 126 Thetford Center 05075	1761 N.H.	Orange (17)	Bradford Orange
Tinmouth 515 North End Rd. Tinmouth 05773	1761 N.H.	Rutland (22) Bennington	Rutland Rutland
Topsham P.O. Box 69 West Topsham 05086	1763 N.H. N.Y. 1776	Orange (2)	Bradford Orange
Townshend P.O. Box 223 Townshend 05353	1753 N.H.	Windham (7)	Westminster Windham
Troy P.O. Box 80 North Troy 05869	1801 Vt.	Orleans (3) Chittenden	Orleans Orleans
Tunbridge P.O. Box 6 Tunbridge 05077	1761 N.H.	Orange (15)	Randolph Orange
Underhill P.O. Box 32 Underhill Center 05490	1763 N.H.	Chittenden (3) Addison	Chittenden Chittenden
Vergennes City 120 Main St. P.O. Box 35 Vergennes 05491	1788 Vt.	Addison (23) Rutland	Addison Addison
Vernon 567 Governor Hunt Rd. Vernon 05354	1672 Northfield Ma. Hinsdale, N.H. 1753	Windham (23)	Marlboro Windham
Vershire 6894 VT Rt. 113 Vershire 05079	1781 Vt.	Orange (10)	Bradford Orange
Victory 102 Radar Rd. P.O. Box 609 North Concord 05858	1781 Vt.	Essex (16) Orange	Essex Essex
Waitsfield 9 Bridge St. Waitsfield 05673	1782 Vt.	Washington (15) Chittenden	Washington Washington
Walden 12 VT Rt. 215 West Danville 05873	1781 Vt.	Caledonia (10) Orange	Caledonia Caledonia
Wallingford 75 School St., P.O. Box 327 Wallingford 05773	1761 N.H.	Rutland (23) Bennington	Rutland Rutland
Waltham P.O. Box 175 Vergennes 05491	1796 Vt.	Addison (5) Rutland	Addison Addison
Wardsboro P.O. Box 48 Wardsboro 05355	1780 Vt. N.H. 1764	Windham (10)	Marlboro Windham
Warner's Grant	1791 Vt.	Essex (2) Orange	Essex Orange
Warren P.O. Box 337 Warren 05674	1789 Vt.	Washington (17) Addison	Washington Washington
Warren's Gore	1789 Vt.	Essex (3) Orange	Essex Orange
Washington 2895 VT Rt. 110 Washington 05675	1781 Vt. N.Y. 1770 Kingsland	Orange (5)	Randolph Orange
Waterbury 51 S. Main St. Waterbury 05676	1763 N.H.	Washington (6) Chittenden	Washington Washington
Waterford 532 Maple Rd. P.O. Box 56 Lower Waterford 05848	1780 Vt. Littleton	Caledonia (13) Orange	Caledonia Caledonia
Waterville P.O. Box 31 Waterville 05492	1824 Vt.	Lamoille (3) Franklin	Lamoille Lamoille
Weathersfield P.O. Box 550 Ascutney 05030	1761 N.H. N.Y. 1772	Windsor (20)	Windsor Windsor
Wells P.O. Box 585 Wells 05774	1761 N.H.	Rutland (21) Bennington	Fair Haven Rutland
West Fairlee P.O. Box 615 West Fairlee 05083	1797 Vt.	Orange (11)	Bradford Orange
West Haven 2919 Main St. West Haven Center 05743	1792 Vt.	Rutland (8) Bennington	Fair Haven Rutland

Town Address	Date Formed Claims/Other Names	County Map Parent County	Probate District Court District
West Rutland 35 Marble St. West Rutland 05777	1886 Vt. Rutland	Rutland (11) Bennington	Rutland Rutland
West Windsor P.O. Box 6 Brownsville 05037	1848 Vt. from Windsor	Windsor (15)	Windsor Windsor
Westfield 1257 VT Rt. 100 100 Westfield 05874	1780 Vt.	Orleans (2) Chittenden	Orleans Orleans
Westford 1713 VT Rt. 128 Westford 05494	1763 N.H.	Chittenden (2) Addison	Chittenden Chittenden
Westminster P.O. Box 147 Westminster 05158	1752 N.H.	Windham (9)	Westminster Windham
Westmore 54 Hinton Hill Rd. Orleans 05860	1781 Vt. Westford	Orleans (14) Orange	Orleans Orleans
Weston P.O. Box 98 Weston 05161	1799 Vt. from Andover	Windsor (21)	Windsor Windsor
Weybridge 1727 Quaker Village Rd. Middlebury 05753	1761 N.H.	Addison (10) Rutland	Addison Addison
Wheelock 1192 VT Rt. 102 P.O. Box 1328 Lyndonville 05851	1785 Vt. N.Y. 1774 Bamf	Caledonia (6) Orange	Caledonia Caledonia
Whiting 29 S. Main St. Whiting 05778	1763 N.H.	Addison (19) Rutland	Addison Addison
Whitingham 2948 VT Rt. 100 P.O. Box 529 Whitingham 05361	1770 N.Y.	Windham (20)	Marlboro Windham
Williamstown 2470 VT Rt. 14 P.O. Box 646 Williamstown 05679	1781 Vt. N.Y. 1770	Orange (4)	Randolph Orange
Williston 7900 Williston Rd. Williston 05495	1763 N.H.	Chittenden (8) Addison	Chittenden Chittenden
Wilmington 2 E. Main St. P.O. Box 217 Wilmington 05363	1751 N.H. and again in 1763 N.H. as Draper	Windham (17)	Marlboro Windham
Windham 5976 Windham Hill Rd. Windham 05359	1795 Vt.	Windham (2)	Westminster Windham
Windsor 29 Union St. P.O. Box 47 Windsor 05089	1761 N.H. N.Y. 1772	Windsor (16)	Windsor Windsor
Winhall 3 River Rd. Bondville 05340	1761 N.H.	Bennington (7)	Manchester Bennington
Winooski 27 W. Allen St. Winooski 05404	1921 Vt. Colchester	Chittenden (18) Addison	Chittenden Chittenden
Wolcott P.O. Box 100 Wolcott 05680	1781 Vt.	Lamoille (6) Orleans	Lamoille Lamoille
Woodbury P.O. Box 10 Woodbury 05681	1781 Vt.	Washington (1) Caledonia	Washington Washington
Woodford 1391 VT Rt. 9 Woodford 05201	1753 N.H. renewed 1762 N.H.	Bennington (13)	Bennington Bennington
Woodstock 31 The Green Woodstock 05091	1761 N.H. N.Y. 1772	Windsor (11)	Hartford Windsor
Worcester 20 Worcester Village Rd. Drawer 161 Worcester 05682	1763 N.H. Worster	Washington (3) Chittenden	Washington Washington

Virginia

JOHNI CERNY AND GARETH L. MARK

Virginia was established as an economic venture that got off to a very shaky start. In 1584 Queen Elizabeth I of England gave Sir Walter Ralegh (commonly misspelled Raleigh) permission to establish colonies in the New World. Gallantly, Ralegh named the area for the Virgin Queen, but his undersupplied colonies disappeared between one supply ship's arrival and the next.

The second attempt began twenty years later. English entrepreneurs were looking for a financial opportunity that would return their investment on the fabulous scale of the six-year-old British East India Company. The endless lands of the new world appeared to contain such a golden promise.

In 1606 King James I chartered the Virginia Company of London (often called the London Company). In April 1607 the *Susan Constant*, the *Godspeed,* and the *Discovery*, commanded by Capt. Christopher Newport, made landfall at Point Comfort. Sealed orders appointing seven men to the Council were opened, and the Council elected Edward Maria Wingfield president. Under his direction, "gentlemen," craftsmen, and laborers founded the first permanent English settlement on James Isle. Long on expectations but short on experience, they were struck with disaster.

The struggle and hardships that decimated and discouraged the colonists are well known. So few of those who arrived on the first three ships survived that not many Americans living today can trace their ancestry to an original Jamestown settler. The Colony was nearly abandoned in 1610 and might not have survived but for one man—John Rolfe.

In 1612, John Rolfe began experiments in growing and processing tobacco. His export of tobacco to a London merchant

in 1614 began a trade that made Virginia viable economically. Then he married Pocahontas, daughter of the great *werowance*, or sub-chief, Powhatan, which helped assure a few years of peaceful coexistence with the native tribes of Virginia.

The London Company was reorganized under the Great Charter of 1618, and by the end of 1619, several events occurred that had far-reaching impact. Free settlers were granted land, establishing property ownership. The House of Burgesses, America's first representative assembly, was organized, setting an example for representative democracy. A program encouraging emigration of "Maides to make Wives" began in England, ensuring that the population of Virginia would be self-sustaining. Unexpectedly, a Dutch trader from the West Indies arrived in August 1619 with a cargo of African-American colonists who were sold into indentured servitude (slavery did not yet exist in Virginia). This event helped foreshadow slavery and the Civil War.

On Friday, 22 March 1622, disaster struck. The natives, led by Powhatan's successor, Opechancanough, attacked the English settlements, massacred a quarter of the population, and nearly succeeded in driving the English out. However, disaster then struck the natives, for the English established policies that eventually led to the near-total extermination of the Native American people and forceful removal of the survivors to reservations.

In 1624 James I revoked the charter and made Virginia a royal colony, henceforth under the direction—not always peaceable—of crown-appointed governors. Between 1652 and 1660, while Oliver Cromwell was ruling in England, Virginia experimented with what amounted to self-government and was not pleased to relinquish that control again to a royal governor.

The colony had an urgent need of merchants, skilled artisans, woodsmen, and a large labor force to cultivate the tobacco crops. Luring laborers to insect-ridden and swampy regions was a challenge, but this was aided by the English law of primogeniture, which preserved the estates of the landed gentry by transmitting the titles and property intact from eldest son to eldest son. Many younger sons saw Virginia as a prime opportunity. The London Company lured these people to Virginia with land.

The Company agreed to give anyone who paid his way to Virginia fifty acres "for his owne personal adventure." Another fifty acres was offered for each person the adventurer transported "at his owne cost." When Virginia became a royal colony, the headright system continued. Over the next century, thousands of settlers came because of Virginia's headright system.

As the young colony expanded, it experienced growing pains. The difficulty of providing a labor force led to the formal establishment of slavery (1660), disagreements with crown-appointed governors led to Bacon's Rebellion (1676), and a precipitous decline in tobacco prices resulted in the Plant-Cutting Revolt (1682). The end of the century was marked by the removal of the colony's capital to Williamsburg in 1699.

Ironically, the eighteenth century saw both the establishment of the infamous Slave Code of 1705 and the headlong rush toward the American Revolution; each embodied different views of human rights. Even as the slaves' plight grew worse, George Mason penned the Virginia Declaration of Rights. Adopted by the revolutionary convention on 12 June 1776, the Declaration was a model for the United States Bill of Rights.

It is perhaps appropriate that the first president of the United States was a native son of the first permanent English colony in North America. George Washington epitomized the upper-class Virginians of his time: a tobacco farmer, an ardent lover of freedom, and a slaveholder.

The eighteenth century also saw explosive expansion. The Shenandoah Valley and the lands west of the Appalachian Mountains were opened, and settlers poured down the Great Wagon Road from Pennsylvania. In the second half of the century, the Cumberland Gap was discovered and settlers began filling what would become Kentucky and West Virginia. Both were initially part of Virginia; Kentucky became a separate state in 1792, and West Virginia in 1863.

Many of Virginia's records have been lost to fire, war, and time. Jamestown, the original capital, was destroyed three times, and some counties lost records during the Revolutionary War. However, the greatest destruction of Virginia's records occurred during the Civil War. Many courthouses were destroyed, but the most significant loss of records resulted from the burning of Richmond in 1865. Nevertheless, even with the loss of records, research in most Virginia counties remains richly rewarding.

Vital Records

The first laws of Virginia were called the *Lawes Divine, Morall and Martiall,* and were enacted by Sir Thomas Dale in 1610. Dale's Code required colonial Virginia ministers to record all christenings, marriages, and burials in registers, in much the same way those events were recorded in England. Most of the registers compiled in response to the law have not survived. In 1619 ministers were required to present the register to the Secretary of the Colony, and in 1642 the parish clerks were required to submit a monthly list of vital records to the "commander of every monethly court." Few, if any, of the monthly lists were recorded.

The House of Burgesses strengthened the law regarding vital records in March 1660. Act 20, *An Act to record all Marriages, Births and Burials,* decreed, "That every parish shall well, truly and plainly record and sett downe in a booke provided for that purpose, all marriages, deaths and births that shall happen within the precincts of the parish, and in the month of March in every yeare, the person appointed by the parish so to do, shall make true certificate into the clerke of every county to the intent the same may there remaine on record for ever." If the county clerks recorded the certificates, they are unfortunately lost.

Marriage in early Virginia was by publication of banns. In 1631 the House of Burgesses directed that marriage licenses were to be granted by the governor, although couples could have banns read instead and pay less for their marriage. Consent, either written or verbal, was required for anyone under twenty-one and for all servants. Marriages were not to be performed "at any unreasonable tymes but only betweene the howers of eight and twelve in the forenoone."

Marriage bonds were first required as part of the licensing procedure in 1661. The couple wishing a license gave bond to the county clerk that there was no lawful impediment to their marriage; the clerk then issued a license. Every September, the clerk forwarded to the Secretary of the Colony a list of licenses issued. These records were burned in the various fires at Jamestown, Williamsburg, and Richmond.

The existing marriage laws were superseded by an 1853 state law requiring county and independent city clerks to issue marriage licenses and keep marriage registers. Before a license was issued, the parties to be married had to offer the following information: full names, ages, places of birth and residence, proposed marriage date and place, marital status (widowed or single), parents' names, groom's occupation, and minister's name. After the marriage ceremony, the minister returned the information to the clerk, who recorded it in a marriage register. Many counties have the original form on file at the courthouse.

The majority of pre-1853 Virginia marriage records have been published. The Library of Virginia (see Archives, Libraries, and Societies) and the Family History Library (FHL) in Salt Lake

City have the most complete collections of published Virginia marriage records; however, state and genealogical libraries nationwide also have excellent collections. For reference to these, see either John Vogt and T. William Kethley Jr. *Marriage Records in the Virginia State Library. A Researcher's Guide*, 2d ed. (Athens, Ga.: Iberian Publishing Co., 1988), or *Virginia Marriage Records from the Virginia Magazine of History and Biography, The William and Mary Quarterly, and Tyler's Quarterly* (reprint, Baltimore: Genealogical Publishing Co., 2002). A detailed explanation of marriage records is found in Loretto Dennis Szucs and Sandra Hargreaves Luebking, eds., *The Source: A Guidebook of American Genealogy* (Salt Lake City: Ancestry, 1997).

Virginia was one of the first states outside of New England to require its counties to record births and deaths. Registration on the county level began in 1853 and continued until 1896. Many counties abandoned registration during the Civil War, or at best recorded only a small percentage of births and deaths. Except in some independent cities, records were not kept between 1896 and 14 June 1912, when statewide registration of vital statistics began. Early birth records and indexes (1853–96), marriage records (1853–1935), and death records (1853–96) have been microfilmed and are available at the Library of Virginia and the FHL. Additionally, the Library of Virginia has marriage indexes on microfilm (1853–1935). A fully searchable online database for deaths is being developed and will eventually include 1853–96. See <http://eagle.vsla.edu/drip/>. Researchers can access links to birth, marriage, and death records on microfilm <www.lva.lib.va.us/whatwehave/vital/BMDregisters/index.htm>.

Due to limited resources, the Virginia Department of Health will not provide copies of vital records for genealogy purposes. Certificates can be obtained by immediate family members only; thus, aunts, uncles, cousins, in-laws, grandparents, etc., cannot obtain copies of vital records. Immediate family members can obtain a copy of a vital record from the Office of Vital Records, P.O. Box 1000, Richmond, VA 23218-1000, within four to six weeks. Required forms can be downloaded or printed at <www.vdh.state.va.us/vitalrec/vtlapp.asp>. The Virginia Health Department has contracted with the VitalChek Network (see page 1) to assist people in obtaining birth, death, marriage, or divorce certificates within two to five days.

Virginia divorce records from 1 January 1853 to the present are only obtainable from the Division of Vital Records (see address above). Earlier records are filed with the clerk of the circuit court or the Virginia General Assembly.

The Library of Virginia has a large collection of Virginia Bible records that can provide vital records information. See Lyndon H. Hart, *A Guide to Bible Records in the Library of Virginia* (reprint, Richmond, Va.: Library of Virginia, 1999). See also "Using Vital Statistics Records in the Archives" online at <www.lva.lib.va.us/whatwehave/vital/rn2_vitalstats.htm>.

Census Records

Federal

Population Schedules
- Indexed—1810 (part), 1820, 1830, 1840, 1850, 1860, 1870, 1880, 1900, 1910, 1920, 1930
- Soundex—1880, 1900, 1910 (Miracode), 1920, 1930

Industry and Agriculture Schedules
- 1850, 1860, 1870, 1880

Mortality Schedules
- 1850 (indexed), 1860, 1870, 1880

Slave Schedules
- 1850, 1860

Union Veterans Schedules
- 1890

The first federal census was taken in 1790, but neither the first enumeration nor that of 1800 has survived, except for the 1800 censuses of Accomack County (microfilm) and Louisa County (in print). Only part of the 1810 census exists. Virginia Tax lists from 1782 through 1785 (see Tax Records) were used as a substitute for the 1790 census, reportedly lost when the British burned the city of Washington during the War of 1812. Nettie Schreiner-Yantis and Florence Speakman Love, comps., *The 1787 Census of Virginia: An Accounting of the Names of Every White Male Tithable Over 21 Years...*, 3 vols. (Springfield, Va.: Genealogical Books in Print, 1987), is the best substitute available for the 1790 census. Compiled from Virginia's 1787 tax lists, this source offers both more and less information than the original census. The 1790 census listed only heads-of-household but enumerated their families, including women. In contrast, tax commissioners in 1787 were required to list all free males subject to taxation, not just heads-of-household; women were only included if they owned personal property subject to taxation or were widows with sons aged sixteen to twenty-one. In cases where 1787 tax lists have not survived, Schreiner-Yantis and Love substituted other extant records.

Beginning in 1820 and continuing every ten years through 1930 (except for the 1890 census, which was also destroyed by fire), Virginia's federal census records are available on microfilm at the Library of Virginia and through the FHL.

Colonial
Two early censuses of Virginia have survived intact; only statistical abstracts remain of other censuses conducted. The first census is dated 16 February 1624 and is a list of the names of

persons living in Virginia and the names of those who died since April 1623. The colony conducted a second census in January and February 1625. The *Musters of the Inhabitants of Virginia* were taken by household and includes ages, relationships, dates of arrival in Virginia, the name of the ship each person arrived in, and enumerations of weapons, buildings, foodstuffs, and boats. The information included varies from household to household and from plantation (or town) to plantation. Another census was conducted in 1634 but is apparently lost. The best transcription of the 1625 *Musters* is in Virginia F. Meyer and John Frederick Dorman, *Adventurers of Purse and Person, Virginia, 1607–1625*, 3d ed. (Richmond, Va.: Dietz Press, 1987).

Other lists of Virginia inhabitants include militia musters (see Military Records), tithables lists, and quitrent rolls (see Tax Records). These lists cover a single county or precinct rather than the entire colony.

Background Sources

The most important local history resource, and perhaps the single most important Virginia resource, is Earl Gregg Swem, *Virginia Historical Index*, 2 vols. in 4 (1934–36; reprint, Gloucester, Mass.: Peter Smith, 1965). This should be the first resource examined in any Virginia research project.

Virginia's public records are an important source for understanding its settlers in the context of their history. The Virginia Company of London created the colony's first records during its period of governance from 1607 to 1624. Susan Myra Kingsbury transcribed and edited *The Records of the Virginia Company of London*, 4 vols. (Washington, D.C.: Government Printing Office, 1906–35). These volumes include the court book, the company's correspondence and business journals, and miscellaneous material.

The next group of public records are those of colonial Virginia's council and general court, which served both as a court and a legislative body. The Library of Virginia has most of the original records and has published transcriptions of all extant records in H. R. McIlwaine, ed., *Minutes of the Council and General Court of Colonial Virginia*, 2d ed. (Richmond, Va.: Virginia State Library, 1979) and H. R. McIlwaine, ed., *Legislative Journals of the Council of Colonial Virginia*, 2d ed. in 1 vol. (Richmond, Va.: Virginia State Library, 1979). Other records are found in H. R. McIlwaine, Wilmer L. Hall, and Benjamin J. Hillman, eds., *Executive Journals of the Council of Colonial Virginia*, 6 vols. (Richmond, Va.: the Library of Virginia, 1945–78). These volumes include records from 1622 through 1775, although there are many gaps in the early records.

Virginia researchers cannot afford to overlook William Waller Hening, *The Statutes at Large: Being a Collection of all the Laws of Virginia…*, 3 vols. (1819–23; reprint, Charlottesville,

Va.: University Press of Virginia, 1969), which is a transcription of most of the acts of the Virginia General Assembly from 1619 to 1792. Additional acts are found in Waverly K. Winfree, comp., *The Laws of Virginia: Being a Supplement to Hening's "The Statutes at Large," 1700–1750* (Richmond, Va.: Virginia State Library, 1971) and Samuel Shepherd, *The Statutes at Large of Virginia…* (1835; reprint, in 3 vols., New York: A.M.S. Press, 1970), covering 1792 through 1806. Personal names in Hening and Shepherd are indexed by Joseph J. Casey, *Personal Names in Hening's Statutes at Large of Virginia and Shepherd's Continuation* (1896; reprint, Baltimore: Genealogical Publishing Co., 1995). Hening's *Statutes* is fully indexed in Swem.

William P. Palmer, ed., *Calendar of Virginia State Papers and Other Manuscripts*, 11 vols. (Richmond, Va., 1875–93), covers records of land patents, state papers, correspondence, petitions, licenses, and other activities involving the council and general assembly from 1651 to 1869. The *Calendar* is indexed in Swem.

Swem's *Virginia Historical Index* also indexed *The Virginia Magazine of History and Biography* through 1930; *The William and Mary Quarterly*, series 1 and series 2 through 1930; *Tyler's Quarterly* through 1929 (see Periodicals for a discussion of these); *The Lower Norfolk County Virginia Antiquary* (1895–1906); and the *Virginia Historical Register and Literary Advertiser* (1848–53).

The best guide to the records of Virginia's counties and independent cities can be accessed on the website of the Library of Virginia at <www.lva.lib.va.us/whatwehave>. Additionally, there are some helpful guides for the whole state:

Grundset, Eric. *Research in Virginia*. Arlington, Va.: National Genealogical Society, 1998.

Jester, Annie Lash. *Some Peculiarities of Genealogical Research in Virginia: Colonial*. Salt Lake City: Genealogical Society of The Church of Jesus Christ of Latter-day Saints, 1969.

Livingston, Virginia Pope. *Some Peculiarities of Genealogical Research in Virginia: Post Revolutionary*. Salt Lake City: Genealogical Society of The Church of Jesus Christ of Latter-day Saints, 1969.

McGinnis, Carol. *Virginia Genealogy: Sources & Resources*. 1993. Reprint. Baltimore: Genealogical Publishing Co., 1998.

Schweitzer, George K. *Virginia Genealogical Research*. Knoxville, Tenn.: G. K. Schweitzer, 1995.

Wardell, Patrick G. *Timesaving Aid to Virginia-West Virginia Ancestors*. 4 vols. in 1. Athens, Ga.: Iberian Publishing, 1991. More than 300 sources are indexed in this publication.

Maps

The cartographic history of Virginia begins in the early sixteenth century, and maps, atlases, and gazetteers of the area have been

VIRGINIA

produced ever since. Richard W. Stephenson and Marianne M. McKee, *Virginia in Maps: Four Centuries of Settlement, Growth and Development* (Richmond, Va.: the Library of Virginia, 2000) traces the discovery, settlement, expansion, and growths of the commonwealth from the arrival of European explorers to the modern state and contains 187 maps, many in multiple plates, making it an essential tool for all genealogists. Eugene Michael Sanchez-Saavedra, *A Description of the Country: Virginia's Cartographers and Their Maps, 1607–1881* (Richmond, Va.: Virginia State Library, 1975) offers a brief history of Virginia's cartographic trends and early maps. James W. Sames III, comp., *Index of Kentucky and Virginia Maps, 1562 to 1900* (Frankfort, Ky.: Kentucky Historical Society, 1976), indexes the maps on file at the Library of Virginia and the Virginia Historical Society.

The Library of Virginia collection contains more than 40,000 maps and is treated online at <www.lva.lib.va.us/whatwehave/map/index.htm>. The site also links to the Map Collection Index, an electronic card index arranged geographically; *Index to Martin's Gazetteer of Virginia* (1835); and Virginia entries in *Chapin's Gazetteer of the United States* (1844). See also *Using the Map Collection in the Archives of The Library of Virginia* (Research Notes Number 4), which appears at <http://lvaimage.lib.va.us/vtlstif.html>.

The map collection of the Library of Virginia is described in Earl Gregg Swem, comp., *Maps Relating to Virginia in the Virginia State Library and Other Departments of the Commonwealth...* (reprint; Richmond, Va.: Virginia State Library, 1989). This volume also cites maps in other repositories.

The changing boundaries of Virginia's counties are illustrated in Michael F. Doran, *Atlas of County Boundary Changes in Virginia, 1634–1895* (Athens, Ga.: Iberian Publishing Co., 1987). This atlas is a must for Virginia research. See also John S. Hale, *A Historical Atlas of Colonial Virginia* (Staunton, Va.: Old Dominion Publication, 1978).

Maps showing watercourses are necessary for locating land grants and property described in deeds. Maps found in the *County Road Map Atlas: Commonwealth of Virginia* (Richmond, Va.: Department of Transportation, 1987), updated in 1995, can be ordered from the Office of Public Affairs, Cartography Section, 1201 E. Broad St., Richmond, VA 23219. An online order form is available at <http://virginiadot.org/infoservice/resources/Virginia-maps-order-form.pdf>. Detailed topographical maps of Virginia can be found in *Virginia Atlas & Gazetteer*, 4th ed. (Freeport, Maine: DeLorme Mapping Co., 2000).

The list of readily available maps of Virginia is quite long. Some important maps are:

A Map of Virginia and Maryland, 1676. Reprint. Ithaca, N.Y.: Historic Urban Plans, n.d.

Fry, Josue, and Pierre Jefferson. *Carte de la Virginie et Maryland, 1755*. Reprint. Ithaca, N.Y.: Historic Urban Plans, n.d.

McCrary, Ben C. *John Smith's Map of Virginia with a Brief Account of Its History*. Charlottesville, Va.: University Press of Virginia, 1981.

Wright, Louis B. *The John Henry Country Map of Virginia, 1770*. Charlottesville, Va.: University Press of Virginia, 1977.

Identifying no longer used place-names also challenges researchers. Earl Gregg Swem, *Virginia Historical Index* (see Background Sources) includes place-names, and a number of excellent gazetteers and place-name guides are available, including:

Gannett, Henry. *A Gazetteer of Virginia*. U.S. Geological Survey. Washington, D.C.: Government Printing Office, 1904. Reprinted as *A Gazetteer of Virginia and West Virginia*. Baltimore: Genealogical Publishing Co., 1975.

Hall, Virginius Cornick, Jr., ed. "Virginia Post Offices, 1798–1859," *Virginia Magazine of History and Biography* 81 (1973): 49–97.

Hanson, Raus McDill. *Virginia Place Names: Derivations, Historical Uses*. Verona, Va.: McClure Press, 1969.

Hummel, Ray O., Jr., ed. *A List of Places Included in 19th Century Virginia Directories*. 1960. Reprint. Richmond, Va.: Virginia State Library, 1981.

Martin, Joseph. *A New and Comprehensive Gazetteer of Virginia and the District of Columbia*. Charlottesville, Va.: the author, 1835.

Land Records

State-Land State

The original Virginia Charter, granted to the Virginia Company of London in 1606, included provisions for granting land to settlers, called planters, and investors, called adventurers. The revised charter of 1609 specified that planters were to receive fifty acres and adventurers a hundred acres per share, but that all lands were to be held in common for another seven years. About 1614, Sir Thomas Dale began rewarding industrious planters with three-acre plots. John Rolfe's successful experiments with tobacco led many planters to plant their "gardens" with tobacco. Grants of land by the London Company began about 1616; the earliest surviving grant is to Simon Codrington in March 1615/6. The Great Charter of 1618 divided Virginia into four boroughs and set aside land within each borough for public use. The governor and council were given the authority to allot land to individuals within the boroughs. Two copies of each patent were made; one was given to the grantee as proof of title, and the other was retained for company records.

Virginia became a royal colony in 1624. In 1627 Sir George Yeardley determined that, as governor, he had the power to issue patents for settlers who met the old company definition of a

planter. In 1654 the Privy Council finally agreed, and millions of acres were granted to individuals claiming headrights during the seventeenth century.

The headright was the "right" to claim fifty acres for every "head" arriving in the colony; most headrights were claimed by the person who paid the passage. Headrights of indentured servants may have been claimed more than once: by the master of the transporting ship, by the merchant who sold the indenture, by the person who bought the indenture, and/or by the servant. Headrights could be bought and sold; many people who paid their own transportation sold their headrights for money to establish themselves in the colony.

The patenting process required several steps, and most of those steps generated a record. The prospective patentee first petitioned the county court for a "certificate of importation." The certificate, often recorded in county court minute books, was considered proof of the number of headrights claimed. The patentee then carried the certificate of importation to the Secretary of the Colony, who issued a "right" of fifty acres per headright. Once he had a "right," the patentee took it to the county surveyor, who surveyed the chosen land and created a plat. The patentee returned all of these papers to the secretary, who made two copies of the patent. One was signed by the governor, sealed, and delivered to the patentee. The other copy was retained in the secretary's office and was supposed to be recorded.

Once the patent was issued, the patentee had three years to seat and plant the land. "Seating" required payment of the quitrent (see Tax Records), an annual payment to the crown of one shilling for every fifty acres. "Planting" required either cultivating one acre or building a house and keeping livestock. Orphans had three years after their majority to take possession and plant land. Widows could get extensions of the three years by petitioning the county court.

By the end of the seventeenth century, population growth in the colony of Virginia no longer depended on immigration. Native Virginians wanted new land for tobacco, and the crown wanted to expand the colony, so the treasury right was created. Anyone who wanted new land could receive a "right" to fifty acres for a payment of five shillings. After about 1715, most land was patented by treasury right instead of by headright. See also *The Virginia Land Office* (Research Notes Number 20) online at <www.lva.lib.va.us/whatwehave/land/rn20_landoffice.htm>.

Virginia grants and deeds are readily available to researchers, including original patents and land grants from 1619–1921; survey plats from 1779–1878; Northern Neck (the area between the Rappahannock and Potomac Rivers) land grants from 1690–1862; Northern Neck surveys from 1722–1781 and 1786–1874; land warrants from 1779–1926; and miscellaneous land records from 1779–1923. Original land office records are housed at the Library of Virginia. See Daphne S. Gentry, comp., *Virginia Land Office Inventory*, 3d ed., revised and enlarged by John S. Salmon (Richmond, Va.: Virginia State Library and Archives, 1981).

The Library of Virginia has a searchable online index to land patents issued prior to 1779; land grants issued by the Virginia Land Office after 1779; grants issued in the Northern Neck from 1692–1862; and original and recorded Northern Neck surveys (1786–1874). The original Land Office Grants and Patents and the Northern Neck Grants and Surveys have been scanned and appear in chronological order as TIF files. Users must have a Tiff viewer for the images to appear on screen. Instructions on how to obtain a viewer and use the records appear at Tiff Tips <http://lvaimage.lib.va.us/vtlstif.html>.

Many patents have been abstracted and published. They are included in Nell Marion Nugent, *Cavaliers and Pioneers, Abstracts of Virginia Land Patents and Grants*, 3 vols. (1934; reprint, Richmond, Va.: the Library of Virginia, 1992). Vol. 1 covers 1623 to 1666; vol. 2, 1666 to 1695; and vol. 3, 1695 to 1732. The project concluded with Denis Hudgins, ed. *Cavaliers and Pioneers, Abstracts of Virginia Land Patents*, 4 vols. (Richmond, Va.: Virginia Genealogical Society, 1999); vol. 4 covers 1732 to 1741; vol. 5, 1741 to 1749; vol. 6, 1749 to 1763; and vol. 7, 1762 to 1775. The Virginia Genealogical Society published abstracts of the material contained in these two volumes in *The Magazine of Virginia Genealogy*. The Virginia Genealogical Society sponsors a continuation of *Cavaliers and Pioneers*, with abstracts of land patents and grants published regularly in *The Magazine of Virginia Genealogy*. Northern Neck land grants are abstracted and published in Nell Marion Nugent, *Supplement, Northern Neck Grants No. 1, 1690–1692* (Richmond, Va.: Virginia State Library and Archives, 1980), and Gertrude E. Gray, comp., *Virginia Northern Neck Land Grants*, vol. 1, 1694 to 1742 and vol. 2, 1742 to 1775 (Baltimore: Genealogical Publishing Co., 1987, 1988). In addition, Peggy Shomo Joiner, 5008 Dogwood Trail, Portsmouth, VA 23703, has privately published abstracts for Northern Neck warrants and surveys.

When land was sold, the transaction was recorded in county, town, or independent city deed books. Rentals and leases were rarely recorded in deed books, excluding many people from land records. Most deed books are indexed individually, and most Virginia cities and counties have general indexes to grantees and grantors to facilitate research. Copies of deeds can be obtained from county clerks, but most pre-1865 county records in Virginia have been microfilmed and are available at the Library of Virginia and the FHL.

Probate Records

In Virginia, estate records are produced by civil courts on the county level—in the county and circuit courts—except in independent cities where probate matters are the responsibility

of the circuit court. Wills, administrations, guardianships, inventories, appraisals, and settlements are some of the records related to a person's estate or probate record.

The Common Law of England applied in the colony, as did the written laws of England. Two important principles were primogeniture and the right of dower. Primogeniture is the device by which estates, particularly land, were kept whole. Basically, the eldest son, by right of birth, inherited all real estate. The right of dower is an old Common Law principle. Women acquired a dower right in all of their husbands' real estate at marriage. At his death, the widow had the right to a portion of the real estate for the remainder of her natural life; the dower was generally one-third. Widows also had a dower right to their late husbands' personal property; once again, the dower was generally one-third but might be an equal division with all of the surviving children. In 1673 the House of Burgesses confirmed the right of dower. The widow received one-third of her late husband's personal property if there were one or two children; if there were three or more, she inherited equally with the children. She also inherited one-third of her late husband's real estate for life and could not be disinherited.

Probates and administrations could be granted in three different places. English law specified that the Prerogative Court of Canterbury had probate jurisdiction in Virginia; Virginia law required probates and administrations to be granted in the Quarter or General Court; and after 1645, certificates of probate or administration could be granted in the county court. Wills, inventories, and appraisals were supposed to be recorded in both the county and the office of the Secretary of the Colony.

If the probate or administration was granted in England, it has probably been abstracted and published in Peter Wilson Coldham, comp., *American Wills & Administrations in the Prerogative Court of Canterbury, 1610–1857* (Baltimore: Genealogical Publishing Co., 1989). A series of articles in *The Virginia Magazine of History and Biography* was excerpted and reprinted as Lothrop Withington, *Virginia Gleanings in England: Abstracts of 17th and 18th-Century English Wills and Administrations Relating to Virginia and Virginians* (Baltimore: Genealogical Publishing Co., 1980). See also Peter Winston Coldham, *American Wills Proved in London, 1611–1775* (Baltimore: Genealogical Publishing Co., 1992).

The earliest records of probates and administrations are found in Susan Myra Kingsbury, ed., *The Records of the Virginia Company of London* (see Background Sources). Other records of probates and administrations are found in H. R. McIlwaine, ed., *Minutes of the Council and General Court of Colonial Virginia*, 2d ed. (Richmond, Va.: Virginia State Library, 1979).

The greatest source of probate records is the county. Most colonial wills, inventories, and appraisements are indexed in Clayton Torrence, comp., *Virginia Wills and Administrations, 1632–1800* (1930; reprint, Baltimore: Genealogical Publishing Co., 2000). See also Wesley E. Pippenger, comp., *Index of Virginia*

Estate Records, 1800–1865, 3 vols. (Richmond, Va.: Virginia Genealogical Society, 2001–2002); vol. 1 includes all estate-related records for the counties of Arlington (excluding the City of Alexandria), Fairfax, Fauquier, King George, Loudoun, Prince William and Stafford; vol. 2 includes records for the counties of Clarke, Culpeper, Frederick, Greene, Madison, Orange, Page, Rappahannock, Shenandoah, Spotsylvania, and Warren; vol. 3 includes records for the counties of Bland, Buchanan, Carroll, Craig, Dickenson, Floyd, Franklin, Giles, Grayson, Henry, Lee, Montgomery, Patrick, Pulaski, Roanoke, Russell, Scott, Smyth, Tazewell, Washington, Wise, and Wythe.

All aspects of early probate proceedings were generally recorded in will books, including copies of wills, inventories, appraisements, guardianships, appointments, and sales of estate assets. Original will books are available at the county clerk's office or the Library of Virginia; moreover, most surviving will books dated prior to 1904 have been microfilmed and are available at the library and the FHL. A list of holdings for each county of the Library of Virginia is at <www.lva.lib.va.us/whatwehave/local/local_rec/county_city/index.htm>.

Many Virginia counties have "loose papers" or "chancery court records" on file in metal boxes at the clerk's office. These often contain additional information such as affidavits, powers of attorney, letters from individuals living outside the county, and receipts submitted to the court in the process of probating an estate. These records are filed chronologically, have not been filmed, and, in many instances, are in poor condition, but can be searched at the clerk's office.

In addition to printed indexes, many early Virginia will books have been abstracted and published. The Library of Virginia and the FHL have large collections of these works, and many other libraries nationwide have some printed will abstracts. Some indexes to chancery court orders have been microfilmed and can be searched at the Library of Virginia and FHL. Check county holdings online at the website of both libraries.

Court Records

Most courts in America are courts of record, that is, they are required by law to keep a record of their proceedings. Virginia courts are no exception. Understanding Virginia's court system is challenging; taken a step at a time, it can be unraveled. See Suzanne Smith Ray, Lyndon H. Hart III, and J. Christian Kolbe, comps., *A Preliminary Guide to Pre-1904 County Records in the Archives Branch, Virginia State Library and Archives* (Richmond, Va.: Virginia State Library and Archives, 1987) for a more detailed explanation of state courts.

County Court (1619–1902). County courts were the court of record used by most Virginians. In 1904, county courts

ceased to exist, and their functions were taken over by the circuit courts.

County courts were established as the **monthly court** in the Great Charter of 1618. The monthly court was held in different precincts and heard petty civil and criminal cases. It served two primary functions: (1) it relieved the president and council of part of their duties as justices, and (2) it brought justice closer to all Virginians. When the eight original shires were formed in 1634, the monthly court was redesignated the **court of shire,** and by 1642 was called the **county court.** The county court was required to meet at least six times per year.

The justices, first known as commissioners, were appointed by the governor; in 1662 they were called justices of the peace. The court generally included eight to ten justices, with four justices appointed to the **quorum.** One member of the quorum in company with three other justices was sufficient to make up a valid court.

The county court also sat in special terms. These were well-publicized meetings of the court for specific functions. The **orphans' court,** begun in 1642, reviewed annual accounts of orphans' estates and ensured that guardians did not waste the estates or mistreat the orphans. Apprentices could appeal to the orphans' court in cases of mistreatment or failure of masters to live up to their contracts. The **court of claim** was a special session for the county's citizens to present monetary claims against the county before the levy was laid (see Tax Records). Beginning in 1645, the county court also sat as a **court of probate,** granting certificates of probate and administration, ordering inventories and appraisements, and settling estates.

President and Council (1607–19). Until 1619, the president and members of the council heard and decided all civil and criminal cases in Virginia. Unfortunately, no record of their proceedings has survived. When monthly courts were established in 1619, the president and council began to hear appeals of criminal and civil decisions made by those courts.

Quarter Court (1619–61). Starting in 1619, the president and council, and later the governor and council, sat as a quarter court in March, June, September, and December to handle major civil cases, chancery, and appellate matters. When they met in other months, they met as the Council. The quarter court was designated the **general court** in 1661.

General Court (1661–1851). This court had the responsibility of hearing county court appeals, major civil cases, capital crimes, and probate matters until 1851. Two other courts were established during the general court's existence: (1) the high court of chancery, and (2) district courts. The high court of chancery took over appellate functions in county court chancery cases in 1777, and district courts took over appellate functions in county court common law cases in 1789.

The judges of the general court also sat on the district courts. They spent much of their time in the lower court until

1814, when the general court was made the supreme criminal tribunal in Virginia. The general court was abolished by the 1851 state constitution, and its functions were transferred to the state supreme court of appeals.

State Supreme Court of Appeals (1779-present). Since the state supreme court of appeals was created in 1779, it has had final jurisdiction in all civil cases. It has been the state's only court of final appeals since the general court was abolished in 1851.

High Court of Chancery (1777–1802). At its creation in 1777, the high court of chancery assumed jurisdiction over all chancery cases in the state. It was abolished in 1802 and replaced by the superior courts of chancery.

Superior Courts of Chancery (1802–31). Originally, there were three chancery districts, with superior courts of chancery in Staunton, Richmond, and Williamsburg. Additional districts were added including Wythe County, Winchester, and Clarksburg in 1812, and Greenbrier County and Lynchburg in 1814. The Superior Courts of Chancery were abolished in 1831 and replaced by the nearest county's circuit superior court of law and chancery.

District Courts (1789–1808). In 1789 Virginia was divided into eighteen districts, each including several counties. Courts were held twice each year, always in the same location. District courts were replaced by the superior courts of law in 1808.

The eighteen district courts were held at the courthouses in Charlottesville, Fredericksburg, Richmond, Williamsburg, Suffolk, Winchester, Staunton, Dumfries, Petersburg, and possibly others.

Superior Courts of Law (1808–31). Created in 1808, these courts met twice a year in each county and took over the functions of the district courts. They were sometimes called circuit courts because a general court judge rode a circuit throughout his district to hold these courts. These courts were replaced in 1831 by the circuit superior courts of law and chancery.

Circuit Superior Courts of Law and Chancery (1831–51). These courts were organized like the superior courts of law; sessions were held twice a year by a general court judge who rode a circuit. They assumed the functions of the superior courts of law and the superior courts of chancery. The state constitution of 1851 abolished these courts and replaced them with circuit courts.

Circuit Courts (1852-present). Courts were held twice a year in each county, and records were filed with the county. Originally, there were twenty-one judges who rode circuits to hold these courts.

The state constitution of 1902 did not include provisions for continuing county courts, and circuit courts took over their functions. The circuit courts are now the only court of record in Virginia's counties.

Original court records are housed at the Library of Virginia; pre-1865 records are available on microfilm there and at the

FHL. Abstracts of early court records are being printed so rapidly that it is difficult to keep current. While it is always best to rely upon original documents for research, the condition of original court records varies considerably, some are still firmly bound and easy to read, some are faded and crumbling, some are torn or have missing pages, some have been restored, and many have been destroyed or lost. Because of these circumstances, printed transcripts can prove invaluable to researchers who know their limitations and use this resource wisely.

The Library of Virginia and the FHL have most published transcripts, while other libraries have fewer volumes. The best individual collection, published between 1937 and 1949, is Beverly Fleet's thirty-four-volume series of *Virginia Colonial Abstracts* (1937–49; reprinted in 3 vols., Baltimore: Genealogical Publishing Co., 2000). This work brings together a wealth of data from the records of the Tidewater region of Virginia—birth, marriage and death records, tax lists, court orders, militia lists, wills, and deeds. The result of extensive research in county courthouses, municipal and state archives, and private collections, most of the abstracts were based on the earliest records known to exist. The reprinted collection has been rearranged and consolidated in three volumes, each with its own master index.

A similar compilation for the land west of the mountains can be found in Lyman Chalkley, *Chronicles of the Scotch-Irish Settlement in Virginia*, 3 vols. (1912; reprint, Baltimore: Genealogical Publishing Co., 1999). Each volume is indexed separately.

Tax Records

Virginia's tax records are a rich—and largely untapped—resource. During the Colonial period, there were three basic forms of taxation: the quitrent, the parish levy, and the poll tax.

The quitrent was a land tax that had its roots in English manorial society where "the land obligations due the manor, such as plowing and haying the lord's land, were computed to an annual money payment. Upon payment, the obligations were 'quit' for the year." (See Loretto Dennis Szucs and Sandra Hargreaves Luebking, eds., *The Source: A Guidebook of American Genealogy* [Salt Lake City: Ancestry, 1997]). Those living south of the Rappahannock River paid a quitrent to the Crown. An original, incomplete list of landowners for the region in 1704 is in the Public Record Office in London and has been published several times, though not always reliably. Residents of the Northern Neck, between the Rappahannock and Potomac Rivers, paid quitrents to the agents of Lord Fairfax. Many original rent rolls of the Fairfax proprietary are housed at the Huntington Library in San Marino, California. Extant original rent rolls and facsimiles for Virginia are available at the Library

of Virginia. *Using Land Tax Records at the Archives of the Library of Virginia* (Research Notes Number 1) can be accessed online at <www.lva.lib.va.us/whatwehave/tax/index.htm> along with other research notes dealing with taxation in Virginia.

The parish levy was an annual tax paid by all tithables (see below) for support of their ministers, maintenance of the parishes' glebe lands (the parsonage and lands producing income for the parish), and support of the poor of the parish.

Except for a brief period from 1645 to 1648, the poll tax was the main source of revenue for the colony of Virginia. The annual poll tax was computed by dividing the total expenses of the colony and individual counties by the total number of tithables. The result was levied on each tithable.

Tithables were variously defined during the colonial period. The first definition, in 1624, was "every male head above sixteen years of age." All agricultural workers were added in 1629. In 1643 all males and African-American females aged sixteen or over were tithables. Imported male servants of any age were added in 1649.

The definition of "tithable" was rewritten in 1658. Tithables included free males aged sixteen or over, imported African Americans of either sex, imported white male servants, and African Americans servants of either sex; white women employed in agriculture were added in 1662. Complaints from planters with increasing numbers of indentured servants and slaves led to a revision in 1680 that declared Virginia-born male slaves taxable at age twelve and imported male servants taxable at age fourteen; nonwhite women and free males remained taxable at age sixteen.

The laws of Virginia were revised in 1705. From then until 1782, all males and nonwhite females aged sixteen or over were tithables. Wives of free nonwhite males were added in 1723.

While there is no comprehensive list or collection of early tax lists, many fragments have been printed in Virginia genealogical literature. See also *Virginia Tax Records: From the "Virginia Magazine of History and Biography," "The William and Mary College Quarterly," and "Tyler's Quarterly"* (1983; reprint, Baltimore: Genealogical Publishing Co., 2000). Tax lists frequently appear in Virginia periodicals (see Periodicals). Original lists and facsimiles are at the Library of Virginia, and the FHL has microfilmed copies of many lists.

Virginia's tax system changed after the Revolutionary War to include taxing land and personal property in 1782, with further revision in 1787. The bulk of those tax lists prior to 1850 survive and are available on microfilm at the Library of Virginia and the FHL. The 1787 tax lists of Schreiner-Yantis and Love, *The 1787 Census of Virginia* (see Census Records), save researchers considerable time when attempting to pinpoint the origins of a family that had migrated out of Virginia. See also

Using Personal Property Tax Records at the Archives of the Library of Virginia (Research Notes Number 3) online at <www.lva.lib.va.us/whatwehave/tax/index.htm> along with other research notes dealing with taxation in Virginia.

Cemetery Records

The list of published tombstone inscriptions for Virginia, if a comprehensive list existed, would be lengthy. The Daughters of the American Revolution (DAR) has compiled an extensive collection of Virginia tombstone inscriptions. The collection, along with other cemetery record publications, can be found at the Daughters of the American Revolution Library in Washington, D.C., the Library of Virginia, the Virginia Historical Society, and the FHL. See also *The William and Mary Quarterly, The Virginia Magazine of History and Genealogy, Tyler's Quarterly, The Magazine of Virginia Genealogy,* and *The Virginia Genealogist,* since all these periodicals often include cemetery inscriptions in their volumes. Anna M. Hogg and Dennis A. Tosh, *Virginia Cemeteries: A Guide for Resources* (Charlottesville, Va.: University Press of Virginia, 1986), is recommended by the Library of Virginia.

Two websites devoted to publishing tombstone inscriptions from cemeteries throughout the United States have listings from cemeteries in Virginia: Interment.net at <www.interment.net/us/va/> and Find A Grave at <www.findagrave.com> (see page 8).

Church Records

Unlike New England, colonial Virginia left few early church records. The first Virginians were members of the Church of England, or Anglican Church, which became the Episcopal Church in 1786. Early parish registers are incomplete and challenging to use. Parish boundaries changed rapidly and are hard to pinpoint without Charles Francis Cocke's *Parish Lines, Diocese of Virginia* (1967; reprint, Richmond, Va.: Virginia State Library, 1978). This volume begins with a fine introduction to the Church of England's beginnings in the colony. Companion volumes by Cocke include *Parish Lines, Diocese of Southwestern Virginia* (1960; reprint, Richmond, Va.: Virginia State Library, 1980) and *Parish Lines, Diocese of Southern Virginia* (1964; reprint, Richmond, Va.: Virginia State Library, 1979).

Since colonial times, many religious groups have established congregations in Virginia, including Baptist, Catholic, Jewish, Lutheran, Presbyterian, and Quaker or Friends, to name a few. Except for the Quakers, few of these groups kept records containing such genealogical information as birth, marriage, and death dates. A number of church vestry books and registers have been published and are available at the Library of Virginia and the FHL. See Jewell T. Clark and Elizabeth Terry Long, comps.,

A Guide to Church Records in the Archives Branch, Virginia State Library and Archives (Richmond, Va.: Virginia State Library, 1981) for a complete inventory of church records at the Library of Virginia. See also Edith F. Axelson, *A Guide to Episcopal Church Records in Virginia* (Athens, Ga.: Iberian Publishing Co., 1988) for a county-by-county listing of all known records of the denomination.

Several religious denominations have collections of historical, membership, and other congregational records. Contact the organizations below for information about their holdings.

Baptist Church Records
Virginia Baptist Historical Society
Boatright Memorial Library
University of Richmond
P.O. Box 34
Richmond, VA 23173
www.richmond.edu/index.htm

Congregation Beth Ahabah
Museum and Archives Trust
1111 W. Franklin St.
Richmond, VA 23220-3700
www.bethahabah.org/Museum/museum.html

The core collection of the archives includes documents of Beth Shalome and Beth Ahabah congregations of Richmond.

Virginia United Methodist Historical Society
Randolph Macon College
McGraw-Page Library
P.O. Box 5005
Ashland, VA 23005-5505
www.rmc.edu/directory/offices/library/index.asp

Presbyterian Church Records
Union Theological Seminary in Virginia
3401 Brook Rd.
Richmond, VA 23227
www.loc.gov/rr/main/religion/uts.html

Military Records

Colonial Wars. American military history in Virginia began with the establishment of the colonial militia early in the seventeenth century, primarily to fight against attacks from native inhabitants. Service records of Virginia soldiers in the colonial wars (1622–1763) offer more historical than genealogical information and usually provide only the name of the soldier and the unit in which he served. The records consist primarily of rosters, rolls, and lists that survived the wars and several fires and are helpful in placing someone in a particular place at a given time. Most of

these rosters and rolls have been published and can be found in genealogical libraries throughout the nation.

Lloyd Dewitt Bockstruck's *Virginia's Colonial Soldiers* (1988, reprint, Baltimore: Genealogical Publishing Co., 1998) is compiled from county court minutes and orders, bounty-land applications and warrants, records of courts martial, county militia rosters, Hening's *Statutes at Large*, the Draper manuscripts (see Wisconsin—Manuscripts), and manuscripts of the former Public Record Office (now The National Archives) in London. It supplements William A. Crozier, *Virginia Colonial Militia, 1651–1776* (1905; reprint, Baltimore: Genealogical Publishing Co., 2000), and H. J. Eckenrode, *List of the Colonial Soldiers of Virginia* (1917; reprint, Baltimore: Genealogical Publishing Co., 2000).

Another valuable publication is *Virginia Military Records: From the "Virginia Magazine of History and Biography," "The William and Mary Quarterly," and "Tyler's Quarterly"* (1983; reprint, Baltimore: Genealogical Publishing Co., 2000), a reprint of articles published in those periodicals that deal with military records during the colonial and Revolutionary War eras. See also Murtie June Clark, *Colonial Soldiers of the South, 1732–1774* (1983; reprint, Baltimore: Genealogical Publishing Co., 1999).

Revolutionary War. Some of the original service records for the Revolutionary War were destroyed by fire. Those remaining are on file at the National Archives, compiled primarily from rosters and rolls of soldiers serving in Virginia's militia units, with additions from correspondence and field reports of military officers. However, there is no comprehensive list of Virginia veterans of this war. Some published indexes exist, such as John Hastings Gwathmey, *Historical Register of Virginians in the Revolution, Soldiers, Sailors, Marines, 1775–1783* (Richmond, Va.: Dietz Press, 1938). A card index of Virginia soldiers is available only at the National Archives and is not on microfilm.

John Frederick Dorman continues to compile abstracts of files of Virginia soldiers who received pensions or bounty land in *Virginia Revolutionary Pension Applications*, 51 vols. (Washington, D.C., 1958–). The last volume carries the series through the name Harding, Robert. Virgil D. White has compiled abstracts of all Revolutionary War soldiers who applied for pensions or bounty land in *Genealogical Abstracts of Revolutionary War Pension Files*, 4 vols. (Waynesboro, Tenn.: National Historical Publishing, 1990–1992). Vol. 1 covers surnames A-E; vol. 2, F-M; vol. 3, N-Z; vol. 4, Index. Another abstract of information from pension files of soldiers who received pensions from the state of Virginia is *Virginia Revolutionary War Pensions* (1980; reprint, Easley, S.C.: Southern Historical Press, 1982). Virginia Land Office records of Revolutionary War soldiers are found in Louis A. Burgess, comp., *Virginia Soldiers of 1776*, 3 vols. (1927–1929; reprint, Baltimore: Genealogical Publishing Co., 1994). See also *Revolutionary War Virginia State Pensions*, a searchable online database on the Library of Virginia website

at <http://eagle.vsla.edu/rwp/virtua-basic.html>. Document images of this collection are available online.

Bounty-land warrants were issued to Virginia soldiers for their war service. After the war, soldiers who served in the Virginia State Line or Continental Line applied for a warrant and, when approved, received a certificate to be exchanged for a warrant. The land to be issued was located in Kentucky and the Virginia Military District of Ohio. See Gaius Marcus Brumbaugh, *Revolutionary War Records*, vol. 1, *Virginia* (1936; reprint, Baltimore: Genealogical Publishing Co., 1995), for an index of soldiers who received warrants for Ohio. See also Willard Rouse Jillson, *The Kentucky Land Grants: A Systematic Index to All of the Land Grants Recorded in the State Land Office at Frankfort, Kentucky, 1782–1924* (1925; reprint, Baltimore: Genealogical Publishing Co., 1994). In the case of deceased soldiers, their heirs made application. Kentucky land was occupied first, then land was granted in Ohio after 1792.

The Library of Virginia and the FHL have microfilmed copies of applications for Virginia bounty-land warrants. See "Revolutionary War Bounty Warrants and Index" or Hamilton J. Eckenrode, comp., *Virginia Soldiers of the American Revolution*, 2 vols. (1912–13; reprint, Richmond, Va.: State Library and Archives, 1989). Rejected applications are filmed under *Revolutionary War Rejected Claims and Index of Soldiers from Virginia, 1811–51*. See also *Military Land Certificates, 1782–1876*, at the Library of Virginia and the FHL (see also Kentucky and Ohio).

The federal government was not alone in awarding bounty land to citizens and soldiers for services rendered. Nine states (Connecticut, Georgia, Maryland, Massachusetts, New York, North Carolina, Pennsylvania, South Carolina, and Virginia) adopted similar policies but did not create a specific record group to document bounty land grants. Lloyd DeWitt Bockstruck compiled *Revolutionary War Bounty Land Grants* (1996; reprint, Genealogical Publishing Co., 1998) from a variety of manuscript records and printed books. See also Virgil D. White, *Index to Revolutionary War Service Records*, 4 vols. (Waynesboro, Tenn.: National Historical Publishing, 1995), which is an alphabetical index compiled from National Archives Record Series M860. Researchers can use the Library of Virginia website to access *Revolutionary War Bounty Warrants*, a searchable index to the documents used to verify dates and length of service of officers, soldiers, and sailors in a Virginia or Continental unit during the Revolutionary War. The index can be searched at <http://eagle.vsla.edu/rwbw/virtua-basic.html>. Another useful publication is Janice Abercrombie, *Virginia Revolutionary Public Claims* (Athens, Ga.: Iberian Publishing, 1992).

War of 1812. Information included in service records for the War of 1812 is similar to that in the same records of soldiers in the colonial wars and the Revolutionary War. *Soldiers of the War of 1812* (Research Notes Number 19) is a good overview

of records and the soldiers from Virginia who served in the War of 1812 and can be viewed online at <www.lva.lib.va.us/whatwehave/mil/rn19_sold.htm>. The searchable *Index to War of 1812 Muster Rolls and Pay Rolls* can also be accessed on that website at <http://eagle.vsla.edu/war1812>. Only the National Archives has copies of original pension and bounty-land warrant applications for the War of 1812. Researchers can use microfilmed indexes at the National Archives or the FHL. See Stuart Lee Butler, *A Guide to Virginia Militia Units in the War of 1812* (Athens, Ga.: Iberian Publishing Co., 1988), for unit histories and commanding officers, and Virgil D. White, comp., *Index to War of 1812 Pension Files* (Waynesboro, Tenn.: National Historical Publishing Co., 1989).

Civil War. When the Confederate government evacuated Richmond in April 1865, the adjutant and inspector general, Samuel Cooper, took the centralized military personnel records of the Confederate Army to Charlotte, North Carolina. When the Confederate civil authorities left Charlotte after agreeing to an armistice between the armies in North Carolina, President Jefferson Davis instructed Cooper to turn the records over, if necessary, to "the enemy, as essential to the history of the struggle." After the armistice, when Union General Joseph E. Johnston learned that the records were at Charlotte, he turned them over to the Union Commander in North Carolina.

These military personnel records were taken to Washington along with other Confederate records captured by the Union Army and were preserved by the War Department. Between 1878 and 1901, the War Department employed a former Confederate general, Marcus J. Wright, to locate missing Confederate records and borrow them for copying if the possessors did not wish to donate them to the War Department. In 1903 Secretary of War Elihu Root persuaded the governors of most of the southern states to lend to the War Department all Confederate military personnel records still in their possession for copying.

The material gathered became the source for the *Compiled Service Records of Confederate Soldiers Who Served in Organizations from the State of Virginia* (similar records are available for all Confederate and border states). The records are indexed in *Index to Compiled Service Records of Confederated Soldiers Who Served in Organizations from the State of Virginia*. These National Archives microfilm series are available at the Library of Virginia and the FHL. The Library of Virginia has several searchable online databases that every researcher should use, including *Index to Confederate Rosters*, an index to the unofficial rosters of soldiers from Virginia who served in the army of the Confederate States of America during the Civil War. *Index to Confederate Pension Applications* indexes original and amended pension applications filed by resident Virginia Confederate veterans and their widows. The pension applications are available on microfilm at the Library of Virginia and the FHL. The *Confederate Pension Rolls, Veterans and Widows Electronic Card Index* contains information not included in the searchable index. See also *Using Virginia Civil War Records* (Research Notes Number 14). Links to these items appear at <www.lva.lib.va.us/whatwehave/mil/index.htm>.

World War I. Two important collections can be searched for ancestors from Virginia who were eligible to be drafted or who served in World War I. *Draft Registration Cards, 1917–1918* is arranged alphabetically by county or city and then alphabetically. Information on each registration card differs but generally includes full name, date and place of birth, race, citizenship, occupation, personal description, and signature. They can be searched at the FHL or online at <www.ancestry.com>. The Library of Virginia has a collection of World War I History Questionnaires at <www.lva.lib.va.us/whatwehave/mil/index.htm>. Names in the index link directly to images of the questionnaire online.

Periodicals, Newspapers, and Manuscript Collections

Periodicals

Virginia has excellent genealogical and historical periodicals beginning with a trio of early publications: *The William and Mary Quarterly,* 1892-present in three series (Institute of Early American History and Culture); *Tyler's Quarterly Historical and Genealogical Magazine,* 1919–52; and *The Virginia Magazine of History and Biography,* 1893-present (Virginia Historical Society). They are filled with valuable genealogical or historical information about early Virginians. Issues through 1930 (*Tyler's Quarterly* through 1929) are indexed in Swem's *Virginia Historical Index* (cited in Background Sources). Reprints of family history articles in these periodicals appear in an encyclopedic work entitled *Genealogies of Virginia Families* (Baltimore: Genealogical Publishing Co., 1980–82), divided into three series. The first, in five volumes, consists of articles reprinted from *The Virginia Magazine of History and Biography* (reprinted, 2001). The second series of four volumes is composed of articles excerpted from *Tyler's Quarterly* (1981). The last series, derived from the *William and Mary Quarterly* (1985), completes the work in five volumes. Each collection has been published on CD-ROM as part of Family Tree Maker Archives (see page 17).

Other major Virginia periodicals include *The Virginia Genealogist,* 1957-present (independently published, John Frederick Dorman, editor, P.O. Box 5860, Falmouth, VA 22403-5860), a quarterly with source material, genealogies of early Virginia and West Virginia families, and a query section (a cumulative index for volumes 1–20 was produced in 1981), and *The Magazine of Virginia Genealogy* (formerly: *Virginia Genealogical Society Quarterly Bulletin*), 1963-present, the quarterly of the Virginia Genealogical Society.

Newspapers

The most extensive collections of Virginia newspapers are housed at the Library of Virginia and the Virginia Historical Society, as are several indexes to newspaper articles. The Newspapers and Periodicals section of the Library of Virginia website at <www.lva.lib.va.us/whatwehave/news/index.htm> links to a title list of current periodicals and newspapers; African-American newspapers and related databases; eighteenth-century newspapers; newspapers in the Virginia database, and other links. See Lester J. Cappon, *Virginia Newspapers, 1821–1935; A Bibliography with Historical Introduction and Notes* (New York: University of Virginia Institute for Research in the Social Sciences, 1936).

The Virginia Gazette, Virginia's first newspaper, includes personal notices. It is indexed in Lester J. Cappon and Stella F. Duff, *Virginia Gazette Index, 1736–1780*, 2 vols. (Williamsburg, Va.: Institute of Early American History and Culture, 1950).

Manuscripts

The online manuscript catalog of the Library of Virginia includes approximately 20,000 records, with new accessions added daily and cataloging of earlier acquisitions continuing. The types of documents found in the catalog of primary interest to genealogists include Bible, business, cemetery, church, and genealogical notes and charts; military, personal, and family papers; and government records. Search the online catalog at <http://eagle.vsla.edu/bible/virtua-basic.html>. See also any of the guides to manuscript collections produced by the library.

Many repositories in Virginia hold manuscript collections of value to genealogical research. In addition to the sources listed under Manuscripts in the Introduction of this book, several important repositories are listed under Archives, Libraries, and Societies.

An important manuscript collection located outside the state dealing with Virginians is in Wisconsin (see Wisconsin—Manuscripts). The Draper Manuscripts cover a large number of events and people associated with the migration from Virginia to Kentucky, Tennessee, and the Midwest. Microfilm copies of the material are in several research libraries throughout the country and are available through interlibrary loan.

Archives, Libraries, and Societies

The Library of Virginia
800 E. Broad St.
Richmond, VA 23219-8000
www.lva.lib.va.us

The Library of Virginia website provides instant access to information pamphlets and guides at <www.lva.lib.va.us/whatwehave> including a massive online catalog.

Virginia Genealogical Society
5001 W. Broad St., Ste. 115
Richmond, VA 23230-3023
www.vgs.org

The Virginia Genealogical Society publishes *the Magazine of Virginia Genealogy*.

Virginia Historical Society
428 North Blvd.
P.O. Box 7311
Richmond, VA 23221-0311
www.vahistorical.org

The Virginia Historical Society maintains a large collection of Virginiana and publishes *Virginia Magazine of History and Biography*.

Alderman Library
University of Virginia
Charlottesville, VA 22903-4114
www.lib.virginia.edu/alderman
Search the library's website for collection information.

Earl Gregg Swem Library
College of William and Mary
P.O. Box 8794
Williamsburg, VA 23186
www.swem.wm.edu

For reference questions, use the "Ask Earl" feature at <www.swem.wm.edu/Requests/REF/ref.htm>.

Colonial Williamsburg Foundation, Inc.
John D. Rockefeller Jr. Library
P.O. Box 1776
Williamsburg, VA 23187-1776
www.history.org/History/jdrlweb

The John D. Rockefeller Jr. Library at Colonial Williamsburg focuses on the eighteenth century, but the collection covers all periods and aspects of Virginia's history.

Jones Memorial Library
2311 Memorial Ave.
Lynchburg, VA 24501
www.jmlibrary.org

The library has an excellent collection of books and microfilms for Virginia research, including a good collection of family histories and general reference works.

Special Focus Categories

Immigration

The best compilations of immigrants to colonial Virginia have been compiled by Peter Wilson Coldham. *The Complete Book of*

Emigrants, 1607–1660 (1988; reprint, Baltimore: Genealogical Publishing Co., 1998) lists emigrants from England taken from Chancery records, records of the Exchequer, the 1624 and 1625 census of Virginia, records of licenses and examination of persons wishing to "pass beyond the seas." *The Complete Book of Emigrants, 1661–1699* (1990; reprint, Baltimore: Genealogical Publishing Co., 2002) adds 30,000 names to the list of emigrants leaving England for the various colonies. *The Complete Book of Emigrants, 1700–1750* (1992; reprint, Baltimore: Genealogical Publishing Co., 1993), in addition to various English court records, includes entries from Plantation Apprenticeship Bindings, Port Books, and Convict Parson on Condition of Transportation. *The Complete Book of Emigrants, 1751–1776* (Baltimore: Genealogical Publishing Co., 1993) concludes the series and brings the total number of emigrants to approximately 100,000.

Also from Peter Wilson Coldham, *The Bristol Registers of Servants Sent to Foreign Plantations, 1654–1686* (Baltimore: Genealogical Publishing Co., 1988) naming 10,000 servants from the West County, the West Midlands, or Wales, most entries give the servant, the master, and the ship (after 1670); *The Complete Book of Emigrants in Bondage, 1614–1775* (Baltimore: Genealogical Publishing Co., 1988) and *Supplement to the Complete Book of Emigrants in Bondage, 1614–1775* (Baltimore: Genealogical Publishing Co., 1992) list more than 50,000 English men, women, and children sentenced by judicial process to be sent to the American colonies for a variety of crimes; *Emigrants from England to the American Colonies, 1773–1776* (Baltimore: Genealogical Publishing Co., 1988) taken from reports compiled for the Treasury at each port in England and Wales. See also Meyer and Dorman, *Adventurers of Purse and Person* (cited under Census Records), which includes detailed studies of the families of Ancient Planters.

NARA microfilm publication M575, "Copies of Lists of Passengers Arriving at Miscellaneous Ports on the Atlantic and Gulf Coasts and at Ports on the Great Lakes, 1820–1875," includes arrivals at Alexandria, East River, Hampton, Norfolk, Petersburg, Portsmouth, and Richmond.

African American

While county and city estate and property records remain the best sources for identifying slaves and their families, other records, such as lists of free persons of color, marriages, slave lists, apprenticeship bonds, trial dockets, lists of slave owners, church records, family and plantation records, account books, bills of sale, and other miscellaneous records can be found at the Library of Virginia, the University of Virginia, the College of William and Mary, the Institute of Early American History and Culture in Williamsburg, and the Virginia Historical Society.

Keep in mind that not every location in Virginia created or preserved each type of record listed above. In fact, the number of local records attesting to a specific slave is minuscule when compared to those available for people who were not enslaved. See:

Plunket, Michael. *Afro-American Sources in Virginia: A Guide to Manuscripts.* Charlottesville, Va.: University Press of Virginia, 1990.

Byers, Paula K. *African American Genealogical Sourcebook.* New York: Gale Research, 1995.

Heinegg, Paul. *Free African Americans of North Carolina, Virginia, and South Carolina.* 4th ed., Baltimore: Clearfield Publishing, 2001. Contains family histories or genealogies for the majority of "all other free persons" listed in the 1790 and 1800 federal census.

Locate county records pertaining to African Americans available at the Library of Virginia by searching the online catalog <http://eagle.vsla.edu/catalog/virtua-basic.html> using keywords "African American" and the name of the county where an ancestor lived. For a case study approach to using slave records in Virginia, see Johni Cerny, "From Maria to Bill Cosby: A Case Study in Tracing Black Slave Ancestry," *National Genealogical Society Quarterly* 75 (March 1987): 5-14.

County Resources

Most pre-1900 county records have been microfilmed and can be searched at the Library of Virginia and the FHL, although the dates covered by the two collections vary. A list of records available for each county at the Library of Virginia appears at <www.lva.lib.va.us/whatwehave/local/local_rec/county_city/index.htm>. The holdings of the FHL can be searched at <www.familysearch.org>. Most original records remain in the county and independent city courthouses.

Research in the Library of Virginia county collection can be done at a local library as well. The library participates in the American Library Association Interlibrary Loan program and will loan up to five reels of their extensive collection for a period of twenty-eight days. Obtain the microfilm reel number from the Library of Virginia online catalog and ask your local librarian to place the ILL request.

Virginia is the only state with independent cities; they are independent of the county or counties in which they are located geographically. Researchers should treat them as they would a county when constructing a research plan. A list of records for sixteen independent cities is available at the Library of Virginia and can be viewed at <www.lva.lib.va.us/whatwehave/local/local_rec/county_city/index.htm>. Since population determines independent city status in Virginia, twenty-five towns did not incorporate until after 1904. See Lyndon H. Hart III and J. Christian Kolbe, comps., *A Preliminary Guide to Pre-1904 Municipal Records in the Archives Branch, Virginia State Library and*

VIRGINIA

Archives (Richmond, Va.: Virginia State Library, 1983). Many Virginia counties have been absorbed by independent cities. To the extent possible, the records of the county are detailed separately from those of an independent city.

Some counties in Virginia have experienced devastating loss of early records, especially during the Civil War. Researching ancestors from "Burned Record Counties" requires willingness to probe deeply for the few scraps of information that might have survived. The Library of Virginia has a *Burned Record Counties Database* with entries from records mentioning people from a burned county. The Library photocopied these and filed them to form the *Burned Records County Collection*, which can be accessed through the library's manuscript room. See *VA—Notes: Burned County Records* at <www.lva.lib.va.us/whatwehave/local/va22_burnedco.htm> for details about burned county records and a link to the database. Counties with severe record loss include Appomattox, Buchanan, Buckingham, Dinwiddie, Elizabeth City, Gloucester, Hanover, Henrico, James City, King and Queen, Nansemond, New Kent, Prince George, and Warwick. As previously lost records are discovered and new information surfaces from the counties and independent cities, the beginning dates of record categories on the following pages may change.

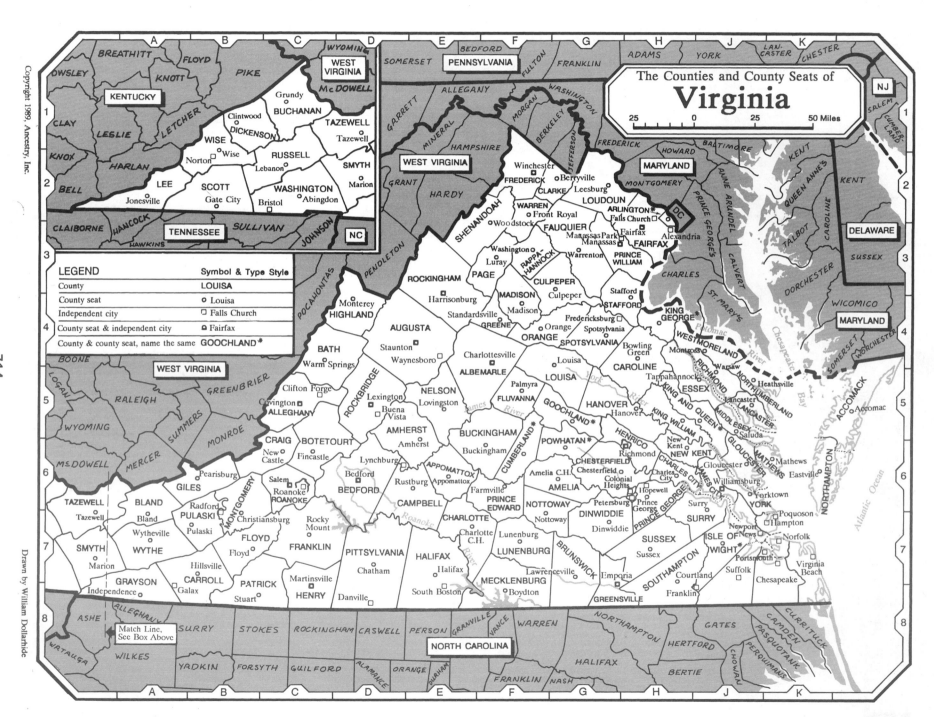

The Counties and County Seats of

Virginia

25   0   25   50 Miles

Drawn by William Dollarhide

714

VIRGINIA

LEGEND

	Symbol & Type Style
County	**LOUISA**
County seat	○ Louisa
Independent city	□ Falls Church
County seat & independent city	⬠ Fairfax
County & county seat, name the same	**GOOCHLAND***

Match Line, See Box Above

VIRGINIA

Map	County Address	Date Formed Parent County/ies	Birth Marriage Death	Land Probate Court
	Accawmack	1634 original		
	Records transferred.			
A5	Accomack P.O. Box 388 Accomack 23301-0388	1663 Northampton	1854 1774 1853	1663 1695 1663
	Temporarily abolished, 1670, restored 1673.			
F4	Albemarle 401 McIntire Rd. Charlottesville 22901-4579	1744 Goochland (part of Louisa added, 1761)	1853 1780 1853	1744 1744 1744
	Alexandria P.O. Box 178 Alexandria 22313-0178	1789 (renamed Arlington, 1920) Fairfax	1853 1801 1853	1669 1778 1772
	Transferred to District of Columbia, 1801; returned to Virginia, 1846.			
C5	Alleghany 9213 Winterberry Ave., Ste. C Covington 24426-6239	1822 Bath/Botetourt/Monroe	—— 1822 ——	1822 1822 1822
G6	Amelia Courthouse P.O. Box A Amelia 23002-0066	1735 Prince George/Brunswick	1853 1735 1853	1734 1734 1734
	Records fragmented.			
E5	Amherst P.O. Box 390 Amherst 24521-0390	1761 Albemarle	—— 1763 ——	1761 1761 1761
E6	Appomattox P.O. Box 863 Appomattox 24522-0863	1845 Buckingham/Campbell/ Prince Edward/Charlotte	—— 1892 ——	1892 1892 1892
	Record loss, 1892.			
H2	Arlington 2100 Clarendon Blvd. Arlington 22201-5445	1789 (as Alexandria; renamed 1920) Alexandria	1853 1801 1853	1669 1778 1772
	Pre-1920 records belong to Alexandria and Fairfax Counties and the District of Columbia.			
E4	Augusta P.O. Box 590 Staunton 24402-0590	1745 Orange	1853 1785 1853	1745 1745 1745
	Authorized in 1738, but the government was not formed until 1745. See also Montgomery County.			
	Barbour	1843 (see West Virginia) Harrison/Lewis/Randolph		
D4	Bath P.O. Box 309 Warm Springs 24484-0309	1791 Augusta/Botetourt/Greenbrier	1853 1791 1853	1791 1791 1791
D6	Bedford 122 E. Main St., Ste. 202 Bedford 24523-2000	1754 Lunenberg	1853 1755 1853	1754 1754 1754
	Berkeley	1772 (see West Virginia) Frederick		
A6	Bland P.O. Box 510 Bland 24315-0510	1861 Giles/Wythe/ Tazewell	1861 1861 1861	1861 1861 1861
	Record loss, 1885.			
	Boone	1847 (see West Virginia) Kanawha/Cabell/Logan		
C6	Botetourt 1 W. Main St., Box 1 Fincastle 24090-0000	1770 Augusta	1853 1770 1853	1770 1770 1770
	Bourbon	1786 (see Kentucky) Fayette		
	Braxton	1836 (see West Virginia) Lewis/Kanawha/Nicholas		
	Brooke	1797 (see West Virginia) Ohio		
G7	Brunswick P.O. Box 399 Lawrenceville 23868-0399	1732 Prince George/Surry/ Isle of Wight	1853 1750 1853	1732 1732 1732
	Authorized in 1720, but the government was not formed until 1732.			
C1	Buchanan P.O. Box 950 Grundy 24614-0950	1858 Tazewell/Russell	—— 1885 ——	1885 1885 1880
	Record losses, 1885, 1977.			
F5	Buckingham P.O. Box 252 Buckingham 23921-0252	1761 Albemarle	1869 1784 1869	1762 1869 1868
	Record loss, 1869.			
	Cabell	1809 (see West Virginia) Kanawha		
	Calhoun	1856 (see West Virginia) Gilmer		
E6	Campbell P.O. Box 100 Rustburg 24588-0100	1782 Bedford	1853 1782 1853	1782 1782 1782
H4	Caroline P.O. Box 447 Bowling Green 22427-0447	1728 Essex/King and Queen/ King William	1864 1787 1865	1728 1732 1665
	Pre-Civil War records fragmented, pre-1728 records from parent counties.			
B7	Carroll 605-1 N. Main St. Hillsville 24343	1842 Grayson	1853 1842 1853	1842 1842 1842
H6	Charles City P.O. Box 128 Charles City 23030-0128	1634 original	1865 1762 1865	1655 1655 1650
	Pre-Civil War records fragmented.			
	Charles River	1634 (renamed York, 1642/43) original		
	Renamed York, 1642/43. Records transferred.			

Map	County Address	Date Formed Parent County/ies	Birth Marriage Death	Land Probate Court
E7	Charlotte P.O. Box 608 Charlotte 23923-0608	1765 Lunenberg	—— 1765 ——	1765 1765 1763
G6	Chesterfield P.O. Box 40 Chesterfield 23832-0040	1749 Henrico	—— 1770 1855	1749 1740 1746
F2	Clarke 102 N. Church St. 2nd Fl. Berryville 22611-1110	1836 Frederick	—— 1836 ——	1836 1836 1836
	Clay	1858 (see West Virginia) Braxton/Nicholas		
C6	Craig P.O. Box 308 New Castle 24127-0308	1851 Botetourt/Giles/ Roanoake/Monroe	1864 1865 1864	1851 1851 1851
G3	Culpeper 302 N. Main St. Culpeper 22701-2622	1749 Orange	1864 1781 1864	1749 1749 1749
F6	Cumberland 1 Courthouse Circle P.O. Box 110 Cumberland 23040-0110 *Records fragmented.*	1749 Goochland	1853 1749 1853	1749 1749 1749
B1	Dickenson P.O. Box 1098 Clintwood 24228-1098	1880 Russell/Wise/Buchanan	1880 1880 1880	1880 1880 1880
G7	Dinwiddie P.O. Drawer 70 Dinwiddie 23841-0070 *Record loss, 1864. Records fragmented.*	1752 Prince George	1865 1850 1865	1755 1704 1789
	Doddridge	1845 (see West Virginia) Harrison/Tyler/Ritchie/Lewis		
	Dunmore *Records transferred.*	1772 (renamed Shenandoah, 1778) Frederick		
	Elizabeth City *Records fragmented. Records transferred to City of Hampton.*	1634 original (merged with City of Hampton, 1952)	—— 1865 ——	1684 1684 1689
H5	Essex P.O. Box 1079 Tappahannock 22560-1079 *Records of Rappahannock County (old) are housed in Essex County.*	1692 [Old] Rappahannock	1853 1804 1853	1692 1692 1692
H3	Fairfax 1200 Government Center Pkwy Fairfax 22035-0066	1742 Prince William	1853 1853 1853	1742 1742 1731
G3	Fauquier 40 Culpeper St. Warrenton 22186-3206	1759 Prince William	1853 1759 1853	1759 1759 1759
	Fayette	1780 (see Kentucky) Kentucky		
	Fayette	1831 (see West Virginia) Logan/Nicholas/Greenbrier/Kanawha		
	Fincastle *Records transferred to Montgomery County.*	1772 (abolished 1777) Botetourt		
B7	Floyd P.O. Box 218 Floyd 24091-0218	1831 Montgomery	1853 1831 1853	1831 1831 1831
F5	Fluvanna P.O. Box 299 Palmyra 22963-0299	1777 Albemarle	1853 1777 1853	1777 1777 1777
C7	Franklin 40 E. Court St. Rocky Mount 24151-1304	1785/6 Bedford/Henry	1853 1785 1853	1786 1785 1786
F2	Frederick 107 North Kent St. Winchester 22601-5039 *Authorized in 1738, but the government was not formed until 1743.*	1743 Orange	1853 1771 1853	1743 1743 1743
B6	Giles 507 Wenonah Ave. Pearisburg 24134-1633	1806 Tazewell/Monroe/Montgomery	1853 1806 1853	1806 1806 1806
	Gilmer	1845 (see West Virginia) Kanawha/Lewis		
J6	Gloucester P.O. Box 329 Gloucester 23061-0329 *Record losses, 1821, 1865. Early records fragmented.*	1651 York	1863 1853 1865	1733 1862 1820
G5	Goochland P.O. Box 10 Goochland 23063-0010	1728 Henrico	1853 1730 1853	1728 1728 1728
	Grant	1866 (see West Virginia) Hardy		
A8	Grayson P.O. Box 217 Independence 24348-0217	1793 Wythe	1853 1793 1853	1793 1793 1793
	Greenbrier	1777 (see West Virginia) Montgomery		
F4	Greene P.O. Box 358 Standardsville 22973-0358 *Pre-Civil War records fragmented.*	1838 Orange	1853 1838 1853	1838 1838 1838
G7	Greensville 1750 Atlantic St. Emporia 23847-6584 *Some records fragmented.*	1781 Brunswick	1853 1781 1853	1781 1781 1781

Map	County Address	Date Formed Parent County/ies	Birth Marriage Death	Land Probate Court
E7	Halifax, 134 S. Main St., Halifax 24558-3215	1752 Lunenburg	1853 1753 1853	1746 1752 1757
	Hampshire	1754 (see West Virginia) Augusta/Frederick		
	Hancock	1848 (see West Virginia) Brooke		
G5	Hanover, P.O. Box 470, Hanover 23069-0470. Record loss, 1865. Records fragmented.	1721 New Kent	1853 1863 1853	1733 1733 1733
	Hardy	1786 (see West Virginia) Hampshire		
	Harrison	1784 (see West Virginia) Monongalia		
H6	Henrico, P.O. Box 27032, Richmond 23273-7032. Pre-Revolutionary War records fragmented.	1634 original	1853 1781 1853	1650 1650 1650
C8	Henry, P.O. Box 7, Collinsville 24078-0007	1777 Pittsylvania	1853 1777 1853	1777 1777 1777
D4	Highland, P.O. Box 130, Monterey 24465-0130. Record loss, 1947.	1847 Pendleton/Bath	1853 1847 1853	1847 1847 1847
	Illinois	1778 Augusta (ceded to the U.S. and became part of Ohio, 1784)		
J7	Isle of Wight, P.O. Box 80, Isle of Wight 23397-0080. Records fragmented.	1637 Warrosquyoake	1853 1771 1853	1636 1636 1746
	Jackson	1831 (see West Virginia) Mason/Wood/Kanawha		
J6	James City, P.O. Box 8784, Williamsburg 23185-8784. Record loss, 1865 (Tax Records, 1768–69, preserved).	1634 original	1865 1865 1864	1854 1865 1865
	Jefferson	1780 (see Kentucky) Kentucky		
	Jefferson	1801 (see West Virginia) Berkeley		
	Kanawha	1789 (see West Virginia) Greenbrier/Montgomery		
	Kentucky	1777 (abolished 1780) Fincastle		
H5	King and Queen, P.O. Box 177, King and Queen 23085-0177. Record losses, 1825, 1865. Records fragmented.	1691 New Kent	1865 1864 1865	1719 1864 1831
H4	King George, 10459 Courthouse Dr. Ste. 200, King George 22485-3866. Records fragmented.	1721 Richmond	1871 1786 1871	1721 1721 1721
H5	King William, P.O. Box 215, King William 23086-2519. Record loss, 1885. Records fragmented.	1701/2 King and Queen	1885 1786 1885	1701 1701 1701
J5	Lancaster, 8311 Mary Ball Rd., Lancaster 22503-2519	1651 York/Northumberland	1853 1701 1853	1652 1651 1652
A2	Lee, P.O. Box 367, Jonesville 24263-0367	1793 Russell	1853 1830 1853	1793 1793 1808
	Lewis	1816 (see West Virginia) Harrison		
	Lincoln	1780 (see Kentucky) Kentucky		
	Lincoln	1867 (see West Virginia) Boone/Cabell/Kanawha/Putnam		
	Logan	1824 (see West Virginia) Giles/Cabell/Tazewell/Kanawha		
G2	Loudoun, 1 Harrison St. SE, Leesburg 20175-3102	1757 Fairfax	1853 1757 1853	1757 1757 1757
G5	Louisa, P.O. Box 160, Louisa 23093-0160	1742 Hanover	1864 1763 1864	1742 1742 1742
	Lower Norfolk. Records are housed in the City of Chesapeake.	1637 New Norfolk (abolished 1691)	—— —— ——	1637 1646 1637
F7	Lunenberg, Courthouse Square, Lunenburg 23952-0000	1745/6 Brunswick	1853 1746 1853	1743 1746 1745
	Madison	1786 (see Kentucky) Lincoln		
F4	Madison, P.O. Box 705, Madison 22727-0705	1793 Culpeper	1853 1793 1853	1792 1793 1793
	Marion	1842 (see West Virginia) Monongalia/Harrison		
	Marshall	1835 (see West Virginia) Ohio		

VIRGINIA

Map	County Address	Date Formed Parent County/ies	Birth Marriage Death	Land Probate Court
	Mason	1789 (see Kentucky) Bourbon		
	Mason	1804 (see West Virginia) Kanawha		
K6	Mathews P.O. Box 839 Mathews 23109-0839 *Record loss, 1865. Records fragmented.*	1791 Gloucester	1865 1827 1865	1817 1795 1795
	McDowell	1858 (see West Virginia) Tazewell		
F7	Mecklenburg P.O. Box 307 Boydton 23917-0307	1764/65 Lunenberg	1853 1765 1853	1765 1764 1764
	Mercer	1786 (see Kentucky) Lincoln		
	Mercer	1837 (see West Virginia) Giles/Tazewell		
J5	Middlesex P.O. Box 428 Saluda 23149-0428	1669 Lancaster	1853 1740 1853	1673 1673 1673
	Monongalia	1776 (see West Virginia) Augusta		
	Monroe	1799 (see West Virginia) Greenbrier		
B6	Montgomery 755 Roanoke St. Ste. 2E Christiansburg 24073-3178 *Includes records of Augusta (1750–72) and Fincastle (1772–76).*	1777 Fincastle	1853 1773 1853	1750 1773 1753
	Morgan	1820 (see West Virginia) Berkeley/Hampshire		
	Nansemond	1642/3 Upper Norfolk	—— 1866 ——	1734 1866 1774
	Incorporated as the City of Nansemond, 1972; merged with the City of Suffolk, 1974. Record loss, 1866. Records transferred to the City of Suffolk.			
	Nelson	1785 (see Kentucky) Jefferson		
E5	Nelson P.O. Box 336 Lovingston 22949-0336	1808 Amherst	1853 1808 1853	1808 1808 1808
H6	New Kent P.O. Box 50 New Kent 23124-0050 *Record losses, 1787, 1865. Records fragmented.*	1654 York	1865 1850 1865	1674 1827 1820
	New Norfolk	1636 (abolished 1637) Elizabeth City (see Lower Norfolk and Upper Norfolk)		
	Nicholas	1818 (see West Virginia) Greenbrier/Kanawha/Randolph		
	Norfolk	1691 Lower Norfolk (merged with the City of Chesapeake, 1963)	1853 1706 1853	1691 1691 1723
	Records transferred to the City of Chesapeake. Records fragmented. Some records may also be in the City of Portsmouth.			
K6	Northampton P.O. Box 66 Heathsville 22473-0066 *Includes records of Accawmack.*	1642/3 Accawmack	1853 1706 1853	1632 1632 1632
J5	Northumberland P.O. Box 129 Heathsville 22473-0129	about 1645 original (formed from Chickacoan Indian District)	—— 1735 ——	1650 1652 1650
	Although not authorized until 1648, Northumberland was in use by about 1645. Record loss, 1710. Records fragmented. Birth and death records, 1650–1810, are in the St. Stephen's Parish records.			
F6	Nottoway P.O. Box 92 Nottoway 23955-0092	1789 Amelia	—— 1784 ——	1789 1789 1789
	Ohio	1776 (see West Virginia) Augusta		
F4	Orange P.O. Box 111 Orange 22960-0800	1734 Spotsylvania	1866 1747 ——	1734 1734 1734
F3	Page 108 S. Court St. Luray 22835-1225	1831 Rockingham/ Shenandoah	1865 1831 1864	1831 1831 1831
B8	Patrick P.O. Box 466 Stuart 24171-0466	1791 Henry	1853 1791 1853	1791 1791 1791
	Pendleton	1788 (see West Virginia) Augusta/Hardy/Rockingham		
D7	Pittsylvania P.O. Box 426 Chatham 24531-0426	1767 Halifax	1853 1767 1853	1737 1767 1765
	Pleasants	1851 (see West Virginia) Wood/Tyler/Ritchie		
	Pocahontas	1821 (see West Virginia) Bath/Pendleton/Randolph		
G6	Powhatan 3834 Old Buckingham Rd. Ste. A Powhatan 23139-7051	1777 Cumberland	1853 1777 1853	1777 1777 1777
	Preston	1818 (see West Virginia) Monongalia		

Map	County Address	Date Formed Parent County/ies	Birth Marriage Death	Land Probate Court
F6	Prince Edward P.O. Box 382 Farmville 23901-0382	1754 Amelia	1853 1754 1853	1754 1754 1754
H6	Prince George P.O. Box 68 Prince George 23875-0068 *Pre-Civil War records fragmented.*	1702 Charles City	1865 1865 1865	1710 1713 1714
G3	Prince William 1 County Court Complex Prince William 22192-9201 *Pre-Civil War records fragmented.*	1731 Stafford/King George	1864 1859 1864	1731 1734 1731
	Princess Anne	1691 Lower Norfolk (merged with the City of Virginia Beach, 1963) *Records transferred to the City of Virginia Beach.*	1853 1724 1853	1691 1691 1691
B7	Pulaski 143 3rd St. NW, Ste. 1 Pulaski 24301-4900 *Marriage bonds, 1844–57, also in Montgomery.*	1839 Montgomery/Wythe	1853 1839 1853	1839 1839 1839
	Putnam	1848 (see West Virginia) Cabell/Kanawha/Mason		
	Raleigh	1850 (see West Virginia) Fayette		
	Randolph	1787 (see West Virginia) Harrison		
	Rappahannock (old)	1656 Lancaster (abolished 1692) *Records transferred to Essex.*	—— —— ——	1656 1656 1665
F3	Rappahannock (present) P.O. Box 519 Washington 22747-0519	1833 Culpeper	1853 1833 1853	1833 1833 1833
J5	Richmond P.O. Box 1000 Warsaw 22572-1000	1692 [Old] Rappahannock	1853 1853	1692 1692
	Ritchie	1843 (see West Virginia) Harrison/Lewis/Wood		
	Roane	1856 (see West Virginia) Gilmer/Kanawha/Jackson		
C6	Roanoake P.O. Box 29800 Salem 24153-0798	1838 Botetourt	1853 1838 1853	1838 1838 1838
D5	Rockbridge 150 S. Main St. Lexington 24450-2359	1778 Augusta/Botetourt	1853 1778 1853	1778 1778 1778
E3	Rockingham P.O. Box 1252 Harrisonburg 22803-1252 *Record loss, 1864.*	1778 Augusta	1862 1778 1862	1778 1778 1778
C2	Russell P.O. Box 1208 Lebanon 24266-1208 *Record loss, 1853.*	1786 Washington	1853 1853 1853	1768 1803 1786
B2	Scott 112 Water St., Ste. 1 Gate City 24251	1814 Lee/Russell/ Washington	1853 1815 1853	1815 1815 1815
E3	Shenandoah 600 N. Main St., Ste. 102 Woodstock 22644-1855 *Includes records of Dunmore (1772–78).*	1778 Dunmore	1853 1772 1853	1772 1772 1772
D2, A7	Smyth 121 Bagley Cir., Ste. 100 Marion 24354-3140 *Some records fragmented.*	1832 Wythe/Washington	1857 1832 1857	1832 1832 1832
H7	Southampton P.O. Box 400 Courtland 23837-0400	1749 Isle of Wight	1853 1750 1853	1749 1749 1749
G4	Spotsylvania P.O. Box 99 Spotsylvania 22553-0099	1721 Essex/King and Queen/ King William	—— 1795 ——	1720 1722 1724
G4	Stafford P.O. Box 339 Stafford 22554-0339 *Pre-Civil War records fragmented.*	1664 Westmoreland	1853 1854 1853	1686 1664 1664
J7	Surry P.O. Box 65 Surry 23883-0065	1652 James City	1853 1768 1853	1645 1652 1645
H7	Sussex P.O. Box 1397 Sussex 23884-0397	1754 Surry	1853 1754 1853	1754 1754 1754
D1, A7	Tazewell 315 School St. Box 2 Tazewell 24651-1398	1800 Wythe/Russell	1853 1800 1853	1800 1800 1800
	Taylor	1844 (see West Virginia) Harrison/Barbour/Marion		
	Tucker	1856 (see West Virginia) Randolph		
	Tyler	1814 (see West Virginia) Ohio		
	Upper Norfolk	1637 New Norfolk *Renamed Nansemond, 1642/43. Records transferred.*		
	Upshur	1851 (see West Virginia) Randolph/Lewis/Barbour		

Map	County Address	Date Formed Parent County/ies	Birth Marriage Death	Land Probate Court
F2	Warren 220 N. Commerce Ave. Ste. 100 Front Royal 22630-4412	1836 Shenandoah/Frederick	1853 1836 1853	1836 1836 1836
	Warrosquyoake Records transferred.	1634 (renamed Isle of Wight, 1637) original		
	Warwick Pre-Civil War records fragmented. Incorporated as City of Warwick, 1952, and merged with the City of Newport News, 1958. Records transferred.	1642/3 (as Warwick River; renamed 1642/43) Warwick River	—— —— ——	1662 1648 1646
	Warwick River	1634 (renamed Warwick, 1642/43) original		
C2	Washington 205 Academy Dr. Abingdon 24210-2635	1777 Fincastle	1853 1782 1853	1778 1777 1777
	Wayne	1842 (see West Virginia) Cabell		
	Webster	1860 (see West Virginia) Braxton/Nicholas/Randolph		
J4	Westmoreland P.O. Box 1000 Montross 22520-1000	1653 Northumberland	1858 1772 1857	1653 1653 1653

Map	County Address	Date Formed Parent County/ies	Birth Marriage Death	Land Probate Court
	Wetzel	1846 (see West Virginia) Tyler		
	Wirt	1848 (see West Virginia) Jackson/Wood		
B2	Wise P.O. Box 570 Wise 24293-0570	1856 Lee/Russell/Scott	1856 1856 1856	1856 1856 1856
	Wood	1798 (see West Virginia) Harrison		
	Woodford	1789 (see Kentucky) Fayette		
	Wyoming	1850 (see West Virginia) Logan		
A7	Wythe 345 S. 4th St. Wytheville 24382-2504	1790 Montgomery	1853 1790 1853	1790 1790 1790
	Yohogania	1776 (ceded to Pennsylvania 1786) Augusta		
J6	York P.O. Box 532 Yorktown 23690-0532 Includes records of Charles River.	1634 (as Charles River; renamed 1642/43) Charles River	1854 1772 1853	1633 1633 1633

City Resources

Map	Independent City / City Hall Address	Established (Parent County/ies) / Town Incorporated / City Incorporated	Birth Marriage Death	Land Probate Court
I13	Alexandria 301 King St. Alexandria 22314	1749 (Fairfax) 1779 1852	— 1870 —	1783 1786 1780
	First named Hunting Creek, then Belhaven. *Declared an independent municipality in 1801.*			
D6	Bedford P.O. Box 807 Bedford 24523-0807	(Bedford) 1839 1969		
	Originally named Liberty; renamed 1890.			
C2	Bristol 497 Cumberland Bristol 24201-4394	1850 (Washington) 1856 1890	— 1890 —	1890 1890 1890
	Originally named Goodson; renamed 1890.			
D5	Buena Vista 2039 Sycamore Ave. Buena Vista 24416-3133	1889 (Rockbridge) 1890 1892	— 1892 —	1892 1892 1892
F4	Charlottesville P.O. Box 911 Charlottesville 22902-0911	1762 (Albemarle) 1801 1888	— — —	1871 — 1888
K7	Chesapeake P.O. Box 15225 Chesapeake 23320	1963 1963		
	Created in 1963 by merger of the City of South Norfolk and Norfolk County.			
C5	Clifton Forge P.O. Box 631 Clifton Forge 24422-0631	1861 (Alleghany) 1884 1906	— 1906 —	1906 1906 1906
	Established as Williamson's Station, renamed 1884.			
H6	Colonial Heights 1507 Blvd. Colonial Heights 23834-3049	1910 (Chesterfield) 1926 1961	— 1961 —	1961 1961 1961
C5	Covington 158 N. Court Ave. Covington 24426	1818 (Alleghany) 1833 1953		
D8	Danville City Courthouse Danville 24543	1793 (Pittsylvania) 1830 1890	1874 1841 —	1841 1857 1859
G8	Emporia Emporia 23847	1887 (Greensville) 1887, 1892 1967		
H3	Fairfax 10455 Armstrong St. Fairfax 22030-3627	1805 (Fairfax) 1874 1961		
	Originally Providence; renamed 1859.			
H2	Falls Church 300 Park Falls Church 22046-3395	1850 (Fairfax) 1875 1948		
J8	Franklin 207 W. 2nd Ave. Franklin 23851-1713	1830–40 (Southampton) 1876 1961		
G4	Fredericksburg P.O. Box 7447 Fredericksburg 22404-07447	1728 (Spotsylvania) 1782 1879	1853 1781 1853	1782 1782 1782
A8	Galax 123 N. Main St. Galax 24333-2907	(Carroll/Grayson) 1906 1954		
	Originally named Bonaparte.			
K7	Hampton 22 Lincoln St. Hampton 23669-3522	1680 (Elizabeth City) 1849, 1852, 1887 1908		
	Extant from 1610. Consolidated with Elizabeth City County, 1952.			
E4	Harrisonburg Rockingham Courthouse Harrisonburg 22801	1780 (Rockingham) 1849 1916	1862 1778 1862	1778 1803 1778
H6	Hopewell 300 N. Main Hopewell 23860-2740	about 1915 (Prince George) 1916	— 1916 —	1916 1916 —
	Founded as Charles City Point, 1613. Renamed Hopewell about 1913. *City Point annexed in 1923.*			
D5	Lexington 300 E. Washington St. Lexington 24450-2720	1778 (Rockbridge) 1874 1965		
D6	Lynchburg P.O. Box 60 Lynchburg 24505-0060	1786 (Campbell) 1805 1852	1853 1805 1853	1805 1805 1787
G3	Manassas 9311 Lee Ave. Manassas 22110-5555	1852 (Prince William) 1874 1975	— — —	— — 1873
G3	Manassas Park 103 Manassas Dr. Manassas Park 22111-2335	1955 (Prince William) 1957 1975		
	Manchester	— 1874		
	Annexed by the City of Richmond, 1910.			
C8	Martinsville P.O. Box 1112 Martinsville 24112-1112	1791 (Henry) 1873 1928	— 1942 —	1942 1942 1942
	Nansemond	1972		
	Created from Nansemond County in 1972, it merged with the City of Suffolk in 1974.			
J7	Newport News 2400 Walsh Ave. Newport News 23607-4301	1880 (Warwick) — 1896	— — —	1866 — 1866
	Extant from 1619. Consolidated with the City of Warwick, 1958.			

Map	Independent City / City Hall Address	Established (Parent County/ies) / Town Incorporated / City Incorporated	Birth Marriage Death	Land Probate Court
K7	Norfolk 100 St. Paul Blvd., Ste. 100 Norfolk 23501-2712 *Some records were destroyed during the Revolutionary War.*	1680 (Norfolk) 1736 1845	1792 1797 1853	1784 1784 1761
B2	Norton P.O. Box 618 Norton 24273-0618 *Originally named Prince's Flats, renamed about 1891.*	about 1787 (Wise) 1894 1954		
H6	Petersburg 7 Courthouse Ave. Petersburg 23803-4459 *Extant by 1645 as Fort Henry; renamed Peter's Point. Pre-1784 records fragmented.*	1748 (Dinwiddie/ Chesterfield/Prince George) 1784 1850	1853 1780 1853	1784 1784 1774
K7	Poquoson 830 Poquoson Ave. Poquoson 23704-1733	1885—88 (York) 1952 1976		
K7	Portsmouth 801 Crawford St. Portsmouth 23704-3822 *Some pre-1858 records may be of Norfolk County.*	1752 (Norfolk) 1836 1858	1853 1782 1853	1776 1755 1743
B6	Radford 319 2nd St. Radford 24141-1512 *Formerly called Lovely Mount, English or Ingle's Ferry, Central Depot, and Central City; renamed 1890.*	1885 (Montgomery) 1887 1892	—— 1892 ——	1892 1892 1892
H6	Richmond 900 E. Broad St. Richmond 23219-1907	1742 (Henrico) 1782 1842	1853 1780 1853	1782 1810 1782
C6	Roanoake 215 Church Ave., S.W. Roanoake 24011-1536 *Originally named Big Lick. Renamed Roanoake in 1882.*	1852 (Roanoake) 1874 1884	1884 1884 ——	1884 1884 1884
C6	Salem P.O. Box 869 Salem 24153-0869	1806 (Roanoake) 1836 1968		
E8	South Boston P.O. Box 417 South Boston 24592-0417 *Originally named Boyd's Ferry.*	1796 (Halifax) 1884 1960		
	South Norfolk *Merged with Norfolk County, 1963, and renamed the City of Chesapeake. Records transferred.*	(Norfolk) 1919 1921		
E4	Staunton P.O. Box 58 Staunton 22401-0058	1761 (Augusta) 1801 1871	1854 1802 1853	1802 1802 1796
J7	Suffolk 441 Market St. Suffolk 23434-5237 *Record loss, 1866. Records fragmented. Merged with the City of Nansemond in 1974.*	1742 (Nansemond) 1808 1910	—— 1866 ——	1866 1734 1774
K7	Virginia Beach Municipal Center County Virginia Beach 23456 *Absorbed Princess Anne County (and its records), 1963.*	(Princess Anne) 1906 1952	—— 1906 ——	1906 1906 1906
	Warwick *Warwick County was incorporated as the City of Warwick in 1952 and merged with the City of Newport News in 1958.*	1952 (Warwick)		
E4	Waynesboro P.O. Box 1028 Waynesboro 22980-1028	1801 (Augusta) 1834 1948	—— 1948 ——	1948 1948 1948
J6	Williamsburg 412 N. Boundary Williamsburg 23185-3656 *Originally Middle Plantation; renamed in 1699 and declared a city in 1722. Record loss, 1865.*	1633 (James City/York) 1722 1884	—— 1854 ——	1865 1858 1865
F2	Winchester 5 N. Kent St. Winchester 22601-5037 *Originally, Opequon; renamed Frederick's Town, and then Winchester in 1852. Early records fragmented.*	1752 (Frederick) 1779 1874	1853 1790 1865	1789 1794 1786

Washington

DWIGHT A. RADFORD

In 1844 a wagon train of settlers arrived in the western district of what was to become Washington. Among them was George W. Bush, a wealthy African American. When he and the wagon train with which he was traveling arrived in Oregon Territory, they were refused settlement south of the Columbia River. Because of his kindness and help to members of the wagon train during their journey, they all decided to stay together and settle north of the Columbia River. This settlement was the start of Tumwater and marked the beginning of serious settlement by Americans north of the Columbia River. Soon afterwards, the California gold rush, beginning in 1849, provided a market for lumber products needed to build the mushrooming San Francisco area. This industry brought settlers and prosperity to the Puget Sound area.

The 1850 U.S. census showed that Oregon Territory north of the Columbia River had more than 1,000 persons; most were Americans from Illinois, Indiana, Iowa, Kentucky, Missouri, Ohio, and Tennessee. A few claims were platted on the site of the present-day city of Seattle in 1850. By 1855, Seattle reported a population of 500.

The reason for the separation of Washington Territory from Oregon was primarily geographic. The settlements around the Puget Sound were a great distance from the territorial capital in Salem, Oregon Territory. Settlers north of the Columbia River felt that because of the sparse population north of the river, the politicians in Salem would neglect their interests. Washington became a territory on 2 March 1853.

The Mullen Road, built from Fort Benton, Montana, to Walla Walla, Washington, was used as a highway for migration to the Columbia River area. It proved to be unsuccessful as a highway for eastern Washington settlement. Most immigrants branched off the Oregon Trail at Hermiston, Oregon, forded the Columbia River, and took up donation land claims where water was available. The rush of population into the "Inland Empire" area started in 1858 with the opening of the country east of the Cascades. In 1860 gold was first discovered in the Clearwater River region. The route to the mines lay up the Columbia River to Walla Walla and then by trail to the mining areas. During the decade of the 1860s, the population of Washington Territory doubled.

The 1880s also saw an increase in population in Washington Territory. One hundred thousand people are estimated to have arrived between 1887 and 1890, most arriving by railroad. Washington was admitted to the Union on 11 November 1889. Washington entered the twentieth century with a population of 518,000.

At the turn of the century, when gold was discovered in Alaska, Seattle was catapulted to the new "jumping-off point" for the rush. By the 1930s, the Works Projects Administration (WPA) brought hydroelectric power as the state pulled out of the Depression. World War II brought growth through defense contracts, but also difficult problems for Japanese-Americans with the creation of relocation centers in the eastern part of the state.

Washington moved past that difficult time in its history with a rapid growth of suburban life following World War II, culminating in the Worlds' Fair in Seattle in 1962. The end of the century brought new jobs in technology and biotechnology,

along with the environmental activism and the challenges to living that come with urban sprawl in the shadow of natural beauty of the landscape.

Vital Records

Prior to 1891, Washington had no legislative provision for the recording of births and deaths. However, some counties and cities did record births and deaths prior to 1891. These records have been microfilmed, and copies are available at the Washington State Archives. Between 1891 and 1907, birth and death registers were kept on the county level. Although not indexed, many birth and death records from 1891 through 1907 have been microfilmed by the Washington State Archives (see Archives, Libraries, and Societies). The mandatory recording of births and deaths on a state level began 1 July 1907, and marriage and divorce records on 1 January 1968.

The filing of marriages with county officials has been required by law since the creation of Washington Territory in 1853. Marriage records such as applications, certificates, and returns usually begin with the date of county formation or shortly thereafter. Prior to 1968, marriages were recorded by the county auditor.

Post-1907 vital records are at the Washington State Department of Health, 112 SE Quince St., P.O. Box 47890, Olympia, WA 98504-7890 <www.doh.wa.gov/>. The Family History Library (FHL), in Salt Lake City, has microfilmed birth indexes (1907–54), birth records (1907–48), delayed birth certificates (1850–1960), index to delayed births (1900–80), death certificate indexes (1907–79), and death certificates (1907–60). The online subscription database at <www.ancestry.com> (see page 17) also has the Washington death index (1940–96) and birth indexes (1907–19).

Divorces were granted beginning in 1854 by the district courts of the territory, and these records were kept from 1854 to 1889 by the clerk of the district court. Washington State Department of Health has divorce records from January 1, 1968. For records before these dates, contact the county clerk where the event occurred.

Census Records

Federal

Population Schedules
- Indexed—1850 (as Oregon Territory), 1860, 1870, 1910, 1920, 1930
- Soundex—1880, 1900, 1920

Industry and Agriculture Schedules
- 1860, 1870, 1880

Mortality Schedules
- 1850, 1860, 1870, 1880

Union Veterans Schedules
- 1890 (indexed)

The 1860 enumeration included what was later to become Idaho Territory and parts of Montana and Wyoming.

Microfilm copies of federal population schedules are available in research repositories in the state, including the National Archives—Pacific Alaska Region (see page 12). The agricultural and industrial censuses are on microfilm at the Washington State Archives.

The Washington GenWeb Project has a searchable index for the state's 1910 census on its website at <www.rootsweb.com/~wagenweb/1910/index.html>. The Washington Secretary of State is indexing Washington's censuses as part of its database "Historical Records Search." This ongoing project includes, among other resources, the state and federal enumerations <www.secstate.wa.gov/history/search.aspx>.

Territorial and State

Several territorial censuses were recorded for Washington; however, all Native Americans were excluded. The schedules, required periodically by the federal government, are available on microfilm through the Washington State Archives or its regional branches (see Archives, Libraries, and Societies). The University of Washington, Suzzalo Library (see Archives, Libraries, and Societies) has a two-volume set of territorial censuses that has been microfilmed and made available through interlibrary loan from the Washington State Library. This particular collection has been marked with an asterisk (*) in the listing below. Many of these are being added to the Historical Records Search on the Washington Secretary of State website at <www.secstate.wa.gov/history/search.aspx>.

State and territorial censuses are available for the following counties and years:

County and Years Available
- **Adams:** 1885, 1887, 1889
- **Asotin:** 1885, 1887, 1889
- **Chehalis:** 1858, 1859*, 1860, 1861*, 1871, 1885
- **Clallam:** 1857, 1860*, 1871, 1883, 1885, 1887
- **Clark:** 1857, 1858*, 1859*, 1860, 1871, 1883, 1885, 1887
- **Columbia:** 1883, 1885, 1887, 1889
- **Cowlitz:** 1859*, 1860*, 1861*, 1871, 1883, 1885, 1887
- **Douglas:** 1885, 1892
- **Franklin:** 1885, 1887
- **Garfield:** 1883, 1885, 1887, 1889, 1892, 1898
- **Island:** 1857, 1859*, 1860, 1871, 1883, 1885, 1887

- **Jefferson:** 1860, 1861*, 1871, 1874, 1877, 1878, 1879, 1880, 1881, 1883, 1885, 1887, 1889, 1891
- **King:** 1856, 1859*, 1860*, 1861*, 1871, 1879, 1880, 1881, 1883, 1885, 1887, 1889, 1892
- **Kitsap:** 1857, 1858*, 1859*, 1860, 1861*, 1871, 1883, 1885, 1887, 1889
- **Kittitas:** 1885, 1887, 1889
- **Klickitat:** 1871, 1883, 1885, 1887, 1889, 1892
- **Lewis:** 1857, 1860*, 1871, 1883, 1885, 1887
- **Lincoln:** 1885, 1887, 1889
- **Mason:** 1857, 1859*, 1861*, 1871, 1879, 1883, 1885, 1887, 1889, 1892
- **Pacific:** 1860, 1883, 1885, 1887
- **Pierce:** 1854, 1857, 1858*, 1859*, 1871, 1878, 1879, 1883, 1885, 1887, 1889, 1892
- **San Juan:** 1885, 1887, 1889
- **Skagit:** 1885, 1887
- **Skamania:** 1860, 1871, 1885, 1887
- **Snohomish:** 1883, 1885, 1887, 1889
- **Spokane:** 1885, 1887
- **Stevens:** 1871, 1878, 1885, 1887, 1892
- **Thurston:** 1871, 1873, 1875, 1877, 1878, 1879, 1880, 1881, 1883, 1885, 1887, 1889, 1892
- **Wahkiakim:** 1857, 1860*, 1885, 1887
- **Walla Walla:** 1860*, 1885, 1887, 1892
- **Whatcom:** 1858*, 1859*, 1860, 1861*, 1871, 1885, 1887, 1889
- **Whitman:** 1883, 1885, 1887, 1889
- **Yakima:** 1871, 1883, 1885, 1887

Background Sources

Andrews, Mildred Tanner. *Washington Women as Path Breakers.* Dubuque: Kendall/Hunt Publishers, 1989. Narrative and archival photographs portray the contributions made by women in Washington.

Brewster, David, and David M. Buerge, eds. *Washingtonians: A Biographical Portrait of the State.* Seattle: Sasquatch Books, 1991. A celebration of the legendary and ordinary men and women who helped shape the first 100 years of Washington's history.

Ficken, Robert E., and Charles P. LeWarne. *Washington: A Centennial History.* Seattle: University of Washington Press, 1988. A colorful and comprehensive account of the beginnings and potential of the state, and of the people who made it what it is today.

LeWarne, Charles P. *Washington State.* Seattle: University of Washington Press, 1986. Intended for high school classroom use.

Pelz, Ruth. *The Washington Story: A History of Our State.* Seattle: Seattle Public Schools, 1993. A general textbook used in the public school systems.

Ruby, Robert H., and John A. Browne. *A Guide to the Indian Tribes of the Pacific Northwest.* Norman, Okla.: University of Oklahoma Press, 1986. In a convenient alphabetical format, it describes the histories and cultures of the various Native American groups.

White, Sid, ed. *Peoples of Washington, Perspectives on Cultural Diversity.* Pullman: Washington State University, 1989. Commemoration and reflection on the rich ethnic legacy Washington has inherited.

Maps

Topographical maps for Washington are available from the United States Geological Survey (USGS). An online list of Washington maps for sale on its website can be found at <www.usgs.gov>.

Major libraries in Washington have been designated by the USGS as map depository libraries. These include Western Washington University at Bellingham <www.wwu.edu/libraries/>; Eastern Washington University at Cheney <www.library.ewu.edu/>; Central Washington University in Ellensburg <www.lib.cwu.edu/>; Washington State Library in Olympia; Washington State University in Pullman <www.wsulibs.wsu.edu/>; University of Washington in Seattle <www.lib.washington.edu/>; Spokane Public Library in Spokane <www.spokanelibrary.org/>; Pacific Lutheran University in Seattle <www.plu.edu/~/libr/>; Tacoma Public Library in Tacoma <http://tpl.lib.wa.us/us/v2/>; University of Puget Sound in Tacoma <http://library.ups.edu/>; and Whitman College in Walla Walla <www.whitman.edu/penrose/>.

Several publications dealing with historical and reference maps of Washington are available to the public. Among these are James R. Scott's *Washington: A Centennial Atlas* (Bellingham: Western Washington University, 1990); James W. Scott and Roland L. DeLorme's *Historical Atlas of Washington* (Norman, Okla.: University of Oklahoma Press, 1988); and Ralph N. Preston's *Early Washington: Overland Stage Routes, Old Military Roads, Indian Battle Grounds, Old Forts, Old Gold Mines* (Corvallis, Ore.: Western Guide Publishers, ca. 1974).

The Washington GenWeb Project has many links to Washington map websites at <www.rootsweb.com/~wagenweb/maps.htm>. The Secretary of State's Historical Records Search offers many historic maps online at <http://secstate.wa.gov/

history/>. The Tacoma Public Library's Northwest Room has "Washington Place Names" on its website at <www.tpl.lib.wa.us/v2/NWRoom/nwroom.htm>.

Land Records

Public-Domain State

Washington was settled through the donation and other land grant acts used by the federal government to attract settlers to sparsely populated regions and to distribute the land fairly to the settlers.

The federal government donated 320 acres of free land to each single man and 640 acres to each married couple who settled in Oregon Territory (including present-day Washington) by 1 December 1850. The terms of the donation stipulated that the settler would homestead for four years. In 1853 the residency was reduced to two years. In 1854 Congress passed another act providing the same donation land grants in Washington Territory.

Donation entry files for Oregon and Washington are on file separately at the National Archives—Pacific Alaska Region in Seattle (see page 12) from 1851 to 1903. A large portion of the donation land claim files have been indexed or abstracted, and these indexes are on file at either the National Archives or the FHL under the title *Abstracts of Washington Donation Land Claims, 1855–1902* (National Archives, 1951). The Seattle Genealogical Society (see Archives, Libraries, and Societies) has indexed and published the Washington Donation Land Records. The major Washington libraries have microfilm copies of the Washington Donation Land Records.

Donation land grants can be of great genealogical value because they provide not only a description of the property, but also the name of the person entering the land, place of residence at the time of notification, citizenship, the date and place of birth, marital status, wife's maiden name (where appropriate), and the place and date of marriage.

Other land entries in Washington were based on either cash payment for the land (cash entries), or on conditions of settlement (homesteads) through land districts. These districts and the dates they opened were as follows: Olympia (1854), Vancouver (1860/1), Walla Walla (1871), Colfax (1876), Yakima (1880), Spokane Falls (1883), North Yakima (1885), Seattle (1887), New Olympia (1890), and Waterville (1890). To be eligible for these entries an individual had to be at least twenty-one years of age or the head of a household (including widows) and a U.S. citizen or having filed intentions to become a citizen. Cash entries could purchase any available tract up to 160 acres. After the National Homestead Act was passed in 1862, anyone meeting the eligibility requirements could purchase up to 160 acres by living on the land for five years, raising crops,

and making improvements. These records were kept by the local General Land Office, which is the modern day Bureau of Land Management (BLM). The land office's records were kept in tract books that recorded land transactions by section and township. These records are now at the Federal Bureau of Land Management, 333 SW 1st Ave., Portland, OR 97204 (mailing address: P.O. Box 2965, Portland, OR 97208) <www.or.blm.gov/>. The BLM website has indexes to the lands that went to patent <www.glorecords.blm.gov/>.

Once land was transferred from the government to private persons, it could be sold again, lost by foreclosure of a mortgage, or distributed through death or divorce. Transactions were recorded by the county auditor in the form of a deed or mortgage and can be obtained by contacting the local county courthouse or regional branch of the Washington State Archives.

Probate Records

In Washington, probate courts had original jurisdiction on matters relating to the probate of wills and administration of estates. These courts were empowered to appoint guardians of minors and insane persons, and to conduct adoption and insanity hearings. The probate courts continued to exist independently until 1891, when its functions were assumed by the state superior court system (see Court Records). Those records generated by the probate courts before 1891 were transferred to the custody of the county clerk. These are collected and deposited at the regional branches of the Washington State Archives.

Court Records

Territorial

The Organic Act of 1853, which created Washington Territory, also established a judicial system. Judicial power was vested in the state supreme court, district court, probate court (see above), and justice court.

Washington Territory was divided into three judicial districts: eastern Washington was assigned to the First Judicial District, southwestern Washington to the second, and northwestern Washington to the third. In 1886 the Fourth Judicial District was created for the central Washington area.

The three District Court Justices (four after 1886) sat as the Supreme Court for Washington Territory. The supreme court heard all appeals from the district court. The supreme court met annually in Olympia at a time set by the Territorial Legislature. Cases from the state supreme court could be appealed to the U.S. Supreme Court.

The district court had original jurisdiction in all cases arising under the U.S. Constitution and the laws of Washington

Territory. This court heard cases in Chancery (Equity) and Admiralty. Admiralty cases related to offenses committed on the seas and disputes relating to maritime matters. The district court heard divorce cases until 1864, when the Territorial Legislature could grant legislative divorces as well. Documents filed with the district court include naturalizations, admission to the bar, and appointments and bonds of officials. The district court had appellate jurisdiction over probate (see Probate Records) and justice courts.

The justice court set up new counties and provided for the establishment of probate and justice courts. The justice court heard petty criminal and civil cases, where less than $100 in debt or damages was involved. Justices of the peace often heard the original complaint in a case and then referred the case to the district court due to lack of jurisdiction.

The Washington State Archives has a collection of 37,000 civil, criminal, and probate cases heard in Washington's Territorial District Courts. Called *Frontier Justice: Abstracts and Indexes to the Records of the Washington Territorial District Courts 1854–1889*, it is indexed by plaintiffs and defendants. Access is through the Washington State Archives or the regional branches (see Archives, Libraries, and Societies). A printed and microfilm version with slightly different title, published in three volumes with four parts, is available at the FHL, however, it is not listed as available for circulation to Family History Centers.

State

The Washington State court system is divided into the supreme court, superior courts, and district courts. The supreme court at Olympia exercises statewide geographic jurisdiction. The state supreme court has final appellate jurisdiction by review of cases from the superior courts. The court determines cases involving constitutional matters, matters of public interest, and those challenging the rule of law.

The twenty-eight supreme courts are the only trial courts of record in the state. They have unlimited jurisdiction. These courts have original jurisdiction over such matters as criminal cases, which includes felonies, misdemeanors, all juvenile matters, and appellate jurisdiction in cases from courts of limited jurisdiction. Superior court cases may be appealed to the state supreme court. Jury trials are available in all cases. Many superior court records are available on microfilm at the Washington State Archives.

Probate records are under the jurisdiction of the superior court, and many are available at the appropriate county courthouses, the state archives, or one of the branch archives.

The sixty-two district courts have limited jurisdiction in criminal cases concurrent with the superior courts regarding all misdemeanors and preliminary hearings for felony cases. Jury trials are available in both civil and criminal cases. Appeals are

to the superior courts. The present district courts are not courts of record, and few archival records are held.

Tax Records

Washington's only tax records are for real and personal property, which were both levied at the county level. The records are held by the county assessors and the county treasurers. In some cases, the Washington State Archives' regional branches have acquired older records. These branches are excellent places to begin searching for county tax records. Not all county tax records have survived. Inheritance tax records are on microfilm at the Washington State Archives from 1901 until the tax was discontinued in 1981.

Cemetery Records

The Washington State Genealogical Society has published statewide inventories of cemeteries in Washington. Several local genealogical societies have published information on tombstones from graveyards in their areas. The USGenWeb (see page 16) has a growing collection of Washington graveyard inscriptions on its website under "Tombstone Transcription Project."

Church Records

Catholic and Protestant faiths were in Washington State from its earliest days. Other American traditions such as Mormonism and the Seventh-day Adventist churches soon followed.

The Presbyterian faith arrived in Oregon Territory in 1838. The collected history for the Presbyterian Church in the United States of America, Synod of Washington, is in *History of the Synod of Washington of the Presbyterian Church in the U.S.A., 1835–1909*, and *Local Presbyterian Church Histories of Washington Associations that Comprise the Olympia Presbyterial, 1890–1972*. A major Presbyterian archive repository is the San Francisco Theological Seminary, 2 Kensington Rd., San Anselmo, CA 94960 <www.sfts.edu/>.

The Methodist Episcopal Church was the first Protestant group to organize a local church east of the Cascades. Methodism arrived in Vancouver in 1848 and in Olympia and Seattle in 1853. The United Methodist Church has a repository of records at the University of Puget Sound, Collins Memorial Library, 1500 North Warner, Tacoma, Washington 98416 <http://library.ups.edu>.

The Roman Catholic Church is one of the oldest denominations in the state and remains today one of its largest. Major Catholic record repositories are at the Diocese of Spokane,

1023 W. Riverside Ave., P.O. Box 1453, Spokane, WA 99201-1453 <www.dioceseofspokane.org>; Archdiocese of Seattle, 910 Marion St., Seattle, WA 98104 <www.seattlearch.org>; and Diocese of Yakima, 5301 Tieton Dr., Yakima, WA 98908 <www.yakimadiocese.org>.

Missionaries from the Utah-based Church of Jesus Christ of Latter-day Saints were sent to the Pacific Northwest as early as 1850. Pockets of Mormons continued to grow although missionary efforts did not begin seriously until the 1880s and 1890s. The church has emerged today as one of the largest denominations in the state. The congregation and mission records have been microfilmed and are deposited at the FHL. Also, missionaries from the Missouri-based Reorganized Church of Jesus Christ of Latter Day Saints (now the Community of Christ) arrived in Washington State in the nineteenth century. The congregation records for this denomination are also on microfilm at the FHL.

Seventh-day Adventists arrived in Washington Territory in the 1860s, with a strong presence in the state today. See the Del E. Webb Memorial Library, Loma Linda University, Loma Linda, CA 92350 <www.llu.edu/llu/library/>.

The Episcopal Church arrived in Washington in 1851 at Cathlamet as a mission outreach from Portland. Its records can be found at the two Episcopal diocese covering the state: The Diocese of Olympia, 1551 Tenth Ave. East, P.O. Box 12126, Seattle, WA 98102 <www.olympia.anglican.org> and the Diocese of Spokane, 245 E. 13th Ave., Spokane, WA 99202-1114 <www.spokane.anglican.org>.

The Lutheran faith arrived in Washington as the result of migration by Scandinavians to the Puget Sound area. The Pacific Lutheran University, Robert A.L. Mortvedt Library, 1010 122nd St. South, Tacoma, WA 98447-0013 <www.plu.edu/~libr/> has many oral histories and historical research papers in their archives concerning the Lutheran faith in western Washington.

Military Records

A series of guides on the Washington State and Territorial Militia entitled *Washington National Guard Pamphlet*, by Virgil F. Field, was published in the 1960s by the Washington State Military Department, Office of the Adjutant General, at Camp Murray in Tacoma. This seven-volume work is an overview history of the Washington National Guard during the territorial period, Indian Wars, Civil War, Philippine Insurrection, World War I, World War II, and the post-World War II era. It is an excellent introduction to the Washington State or Territorial Militia.

The Washington State Archives has early service records for the Indian Wars, which include muster rolls, correspondence and financial records, as well as records of residents of the State Soldiers Home and State Veterans Home to the mid-1930s.

Washington veterans of World War I, World War II, the Korean War, and the Vietnam War could apply for a state bonus. These applications and supporting papers were originally filed with the state auditor and are now deposited at the Washington State Archives. Information listed in these files includes residence of the veteran, occupation, relationships, birthplace, and military information. Also housed in the state archives are National Guard special orders and circular letters as well as National Guard statements of service cards for those guardsmen who participated in World War I and World War II.

The World War I Draft Registration Cards are at the National Archives (see pages 11-12), on microfilm through the FHL, and online at <www.ancestry.com>.

Periodicals, Newspapers, and Manuscript Collections

Periodicals

Periodicals for the state of Washington can be of great genealogical value as they not only contain historical articles but often index cemeteries, church records, and censuses. Otherwise unknown Bible records and letters are additionally included in such periodicals. The Washington State Genealogical Society website has links to societies and their publications statewide. The Washington State Historical Society publishes *Columbia* magazine, which publishes a wide range of articles from a historical perspective. The historical society has an index for the articles published in *Columbia*.

Newspapers

All extant Washington newspapers are on microfilm at the Washington State Library in Olympia. These are available through interlibrary loan. The library's website has a catalog to its holdings that can be accessed by county, and links to current newspapers with some indexes to selected newspapers.

Washington State University has a "Pacific Northwest Clippings Collection" online that consists of articles taken from newspapers from about 1900 to about 1942. Some 10,000 images have been digitized <http://content.wsulibs.wsu.edu/pncc/pncc.htm>.

Manuscripts

Several major historical and genealogical collections are held by repositories throughout the state. The University of Washington has a large holding of manuscript collections that deal with such subjects as Washington politics and government, economic history, forestry, railroads, coal mines and mining, frontier life of Washington Territory, ethnic history, and labor history. These manuscript collections are open to outside use by permission. An

inventory of the manuscript collections has been compiled by name and subject.

The University of Washington's "Northwest Collection" holds material on such regional topics as northwest Native Americans, anthropology, history, and economic and social conditions of the Pacific Northwest. Special collections include diaries of eighteenth- and nineteenth-century explorers of the region and various western states documents. The "Northwest Collection" also includes periodicals, maps, pamphlets, and scrapbooks. Some of these can be obtained through a limited interlibrary loan. A subject index to regional periodicals and newspapers is available.

The Washington State University Library Manuscript Division in Pullman houses a large collection of manuscripts relating to eastern Washington and the Palouse Country, including papers of early business and farming pioneers. The Eastern Washington Historical Society, located in Spokane, has collections relating to eastern Washington and the Inland Empire, including the founding of Spokane and other communities, mining, agriculture, and hydrology. Gonzaga University in Spokane holds records relating to Jesuit missionary activity in the northwest and papers of local pioneers. The Whitman College Library in Walla Walla has papers of local pioneers with an emphasis on missionaries connected with the American Board of Commissioners for Foreign Missions.

Several genealogical collections are available through the FHL. These include family records of pioneers as well as a large collection of compiled family Bibles and a collection entitled "Family Records and Reminiscences of Washington Pioneers prior to 1891," both collections by the Daughters of the American Revolution (DAR).

Archives, Libraries, and Societies

Washington State Archives
520 Union Ave. SE
P.O. Box 40220
Olympia, WA 98504-0220
www.secstate.wa.gov/archives

The central repository receives and catalogs materials for the entire state, and publishes a number of guides to its various collections, the titles of which can be found on its website. Records of a local government nature are collected and preserved in the five regional branch archives, each serving several counties as follows:

Eastern Regional Branch—Washington State Archives
Eastern Washington University
211 Tawanka
Cheney, WA 99004
www.ewu.edu/era/

Covers Adams, Asotin, Columbia, Ferry, Garfield, Lincoln, Oreille Pend, Spokane, Stevens, Walla Walla, and Whitman.

Central Regional Branch—Washington State Archives
Central Washington University, MS-7547
Ellensburg, WA 98926-7547
www.cwu.edu/~archives/

Covers Benton, Chelan, Douglas, Franklin, Grant, Kittitas, Klickitat, Okanogan, and Yakima.

Puget Sound Regional Branch—Washington State Archives
Pritchard-Fleming Bldg.
3000 Landerholm Circle SE, MS-N100
Bellevue, WA 98007-6484

Covers King, Kitsap, and Pierce.

Northwest Regional Branch—Washington State Archives
Western Washington University, MS-9123
Bellingham, WA 98225-9123

Covers Clallam, Island, Jefferson, San Juan, Skagit, Snohomish, and Whatcom.

Southwest Regional Branch—Washington State Archives
1129 Washington St. SE
P.O. Box 40238
Olympia, WA 98504-0238

Covers Clark, Cowlitz, Grays Harbor, Lewis, Mason, Pacific, Skamania, Thurston, and Wahkiakum.

Washington State Library
Point Plaza East
6880 Capitol Blvd.
Tumwater, WA 98501
Mailing Address: P.O. Box 424601
Olympia, WA 98504-2460
www.statelib.wa.gov

Seattle Public Library
1000 Fourth Ave.
Seattle, WA 98104
www.spl.org

Tacoma Public Library
Northwest Room
1102 Tacoma Ave. South
Tacoma, WA 98402
www.tpl.lib.wa.us/v2/

Washington State Historical Society
1911 Pacific Ave.
Tacoma, WA 98402
www.wshs.org/

Washington State Genealogical Society
P.O. Box 1422
Olympia, WA 98507-1422
www.rootsweb.com/~wasgs/

The website has county research guides online.

The Washington GenWeb Project at <www.rootsweb.com/~wagenweb/> has links to the major libraries, archives, and societies. State Library <http://www.secstate.wa.gov/library/libraries/> provides access to catalogs statewide.

Special Focus Categories

Immigration

Immigrants to the state of Washington came through the following ports: Aberdeen, Anacortes, Bellingham, Everett, Friday Harbor, Grey's Harbor, Olympia, Port Angeles, Port Bernard, Port Wells, Princeton, Raymond, Seattle, South Bend, and Tacoma. Points of entry from Canada to Washington were Blaine, Curlew, Marcus, Oroville, and Sumas. These records are filed with the Seattle passenger and ship arrival lists and cover the period from 1890 to 1957. Customs passenger lists of vessels arriving at Port Townsend and Tacoma (1894–1904), passenger lists of vessels arriving at Seattle from Insular Possessions (1908–17), along with the Seattle passengers lists (1890–1957), lists of Chinese passengers arriving at Seattle and Port Townsend (1882–1916), alien certificates issued as "head tax" to immigrants at Vancouver and Victoria B.C. and surrendered at Seattle (1917–24), and crew lists of vessels arriving at Seattle (1903–17) are all at the National Archives—Pacific Alaska Region (see page 12), as well as the FHL.

There is a growing statewide index to naturalizations offered by the secretary of state at <www.secstate.wa.gov/history/search.aspx>.

Native American

The history of Washington's Native American population—Nez Perce, Yakima, and other tribes—is one of conflict with European settlers. However, Washington's native population suffered less from wars with the European settlers than from European diseases. The destruction of the native population was the greatest in the Columbia Valley; within a few years after settlers arrived, the native population of the lower valley was practically wiped out.

Agencies were organized by the U.S. government to administer the affairs of Washington's Native American population. These records include genealogically significant materials such as land ownership, school records, correspondence, ledgers, and tribal council records. They are on file at the National Archives—Pacific Alaska Region, and microfilm copies of selected records are available at the FHL. The agency and the tribes they cover are described below. (For a more detailed explanation of this topic, see Oregon—Native American.)

Colville Agency, Nespellem, Washington (1874–1964), was established in 1872 for the Colville Reservation and later the Spokane and Coeur d'Alene reservations.

Puyallup Agency, Tacoma, Washington (1885–1920), was actually established in 1888 by a merger of the Nisqualli and Skokomish Agency and the Quinault Agency. It was responsible for the Quinaielt, Puyallup, Chehalis, Nisqualli, Squaxin Island, Clallam or Skalallam, and other tribes.

Spokane Agency, Spokane, Washington (1885–1950), was established in 1912 for the Spokane on the Spokane Reservation. The agency was responsible for the Kutenai, Kalispell, Wenatchi, and other tribes.

Taholah Agency, Taholah, Washington (1878–1950), was created in 1914 to administer the affairs of tribes west of the Puget Sound. From 1933 to 1950, the Taholah Agency administrated the affairs of the Chehalis, Hoh, Makah, Nisqualli, Ozette, Quileute, Quinaielt, Shoalwater, Skokomish, and Squaxon Island reservations. This agency includes the Neah Bay Agency.

Tulalip Agency, Tulalip, Washington (1854–1950), administered the Tulalip, Lummi, Port Madison, Swinomish, and Mukleshoot reservations. In 1922 the Puyallup Agency, including the Cushman Indian School, passed under the control of the Tulalip Agency.

Yakima Agency, Toppenish, Washington (1859–1964), Western Washington Agency (1950–64), was established in 1859 and administered the affairs of the Bannock, Nez Perce, Paiute, and Yakima tribes.

Other important Native American sources include school records and special compiled collections. The Chemawa School in Chemawa, Oregon, and the Fort Shaw School in Cascade County, Montana, enrolled students from all parts of the Northwest. The collection entitled "Major James McLaughlin Papers" is an important research tool as is the Pacific Northwest Tribes Missions Collection of the Oregon Province Archives of the Society of Jesus (1853–1960). For additional details about these collections, see Montana—Native American.

George Gibbs' *Indian Tribes of Washington Territory* (Fairfield, Wash.: Ye Galleon Press, 1978) is an excellent firsthand historical account of the tribes and bands of natives in the territory, written in 1855. Another indispensable aid is Charles E. McChesney's *Rolls of Certain Indian Tribes in Washington and Oregon* (Fairfield, Wash.: Ye Galleon Press, 1969). Supervisor McChesney was commissioned by the Department of the Interior in 1906 to proceed to the reservations of Washington and Oregon to confer with Indian Agents and tribe members. Native American genealogical and historical data are found in this book.

Other Ethnic Groups

The pattern of immigration changed throughout western America with the development of the railroad in the 1870s and 1880s. Railroads were advertising all over the United States and Europe that "free" land was available. This brought many immigrants to Washington. By 1920, there were 250,055 foreign-born whites in Washington, the majority of whom came from Canada, Sweden, Norway, England, and Ireland.

A group of Dutch families who had originally settled in the Dakotas came to the Washington coast in 1894. The Dutch who came in the 1890s and 1900s went to Whidbey Island and other parts of the Puget Sound. Lynden (in Whatcom County) became the largest Dutch community in Washington, and other Dutch communities grew in Moxee City, Prosser, and Zillah.

Finns and Italians came to the urban centers of Washington to work as laborers. These two groups quickly merged into the American mainstream.

The Japanese community of Washington was largely employed in truck farming on the coast. The heaviest concentrations were on the outskirts of Seattle and Tacoma. By 1920 only 939 out of 17,387 Japanese residents lived east of the Cascades—mainly working on farms in Yakima County and Spokane.

During World War II, the Japanese minority was singled out and evacuated from the Pacific Coast to relocation centers for the duration of the war. A total of 14,559 Japanese were removed from Washington and sent to Minidoka Center in southern Idaho. About 200 went to Tule Lake Center in northern California. Both areas were suited to truck farming, and many Japanese chose to stay in southern Idaho after the war. The University of Washington Library Archives Manuscript Division has records of Seattle's Buddhist Church from 1938 to 1942, which predates the relocations.

Although African Americans participated in the westward movement in the mid-1800s, it was during World War II that many came to Washington coastal cities to work in the industrial plants. When agricultural workers became scarce during the war, ranchers arranged to bring in groups of Mexicans as transient labor.

The Chinese came to Washington to build the railroads and work in the mining industry, and by 1885 there were 3,000 Chinese in the territory, most of whom were living in the Puget Sound region. Anti-Chinese riots in the territory were set off by the news that a mob in Rock Springs, Wyoming, had driven out 700 Chinese miners on 4 September 1885. This led to violence towards the Chinese community employed in the mines and orchards of Washington. On 3 November 1885, several hundred Chinese were forcibly removed from their homes in Tacoma, and the city's Chinatown was destroyed. As a result, several hundred persons voluntarily left the city for British Columbia or San Francisco.

After the Seattle fire of 1889 many Chinese returned to the city to establish themselves as permanent residents. Chinese organizations, which became part of the community, included the Chinese Benevolent Society, founded in Seattle in 1929; Chinese Baptist Church, founded in Seattle in 1896; Freemason Hall and several Chinese family organizations centered in Seattle.

The Wing Luke Asian Museum, 407 Seventh Ave. South, Seattle, WA 98104 <www.wingluke.org/> has materials relating to the Chinese in the Pacific Northwest and principally the Seattle area. The East Asia Library, at the University of Washington, 322 Gowen Hall, Box 353527, Seattle, WA 98195-3527 <www.lib.washington.edu/east-asia/> has holdings consisting of materials from the Chinese Empire Reform Association, a Chinese-American organization with chapters throughout the western United States.

A large community of Germans from Russia settled in Whitman County, Washington. Before the turn of the twentieth century the center of the immigration was Endicott, and many German immigrants from Russia were farming in the St. John and Colfax area.

In 1887 most of the Endicott colonists identified themselves with the Evangelical Lutheran Synod in Columbus, Ohio. Due to the strict doctrinal interpretation of the Ohio Synod, many colonists changed churches. Seventh-day Adventists came to Endicott in 1893, and by 1912 they had built a church. The Adventists as well as most of the Endicott churches of the period held services in German. By World War II, the German-Russian population in the Endicott area had been almost totally absorbed into the American mainstream. Books detailing the history of this German-Russian colony are Richard Dean Scheurmans' *The Historical Development of Whitman County's German-Russians* (Seattle: University of Washington, 1971), and *The Volga Germans: Pioneers of the Northwest*, also by Richard D. Scheurman and Clifford E. Trafzer (Moscow: University of Idaho, 1980).

Major Scandinavian groups settled in Ballard, Bellingham, Everett, Seattle, Skagit Valley, Stanwood, Stillaguamish Valley, and Tacoma. In Parkland, south of Tacoma, the Pacific Lutheran University was founded and was operated under the Norwegian Lutheran Synod.

County Resources

Although originally held in the county seat, many county land, probate, and court records have been transferred to the state archive's regional branches.

The beginning dates for territorial court and probate records have been taken from the volume *Frontier Justice: Guide to the Court Records of Washington Territory, 1853–1889* (see Court Records—Territorial). For judicial purposes, many

The Counties and County Seats of
Washington

Drawn by William Dollarhide

WASHINGTON

of the counties were attached to other counties. This volume is therefore extremely important as it will direct researchers to the correct county where older records are filed. Other dates were taken from the Washington State Archives Regional Board websites and the Family History Library Catalog.

Updated contact information and websites for Washington's counties can be found at Access Washington at <http://access. wa.gov/home.aspx> and at <.www.mrsc.org/countyprofiles/ profilesmenu.aspx>.

Also consulted were Kathleen Allen O'Connor's "Washington State Genealogical Resource Guide" at the Washington State Genealogical Society website <http://www. rootsweb.com/~wasgs/resguide.htm>, Newton Carl Abbott and Fred E. Carver's "The Evolution of Washington Counties" (Yakima Valley Genealogical Society and Klickitat County Historical Society, 1978), the Washington State Archives— Regional Branch websites and the FHL.

Map	County Address	Date Formed Parent County/ies	Birth Marriage Death	Deeds Probate Court
H5	Adams 210 W. Broadway Av. Ritzville 99169-1060	1883 Whitman	1891 1891 1891	1884 1895 1890
K6	Asotin 135 Second St. Asotin 99402-9532	1883 Garfield	1891 1891 1891	1893 1885 1886
G6	Benton 620 Market St. Prosser 99350-1610	1905 Klickitat/Yakima	1905 1905 1915	1885 1884 1884
	Chehalis	1854 (renamed Grays Harbor, 1915) Thurston		
E3	Chelan 350 Orondo St. Wenatchee 98801-2885	1899 Kittitas/Okanogan	1899 1900 1900	1882 1888 1876
A2	Clallam 223 E. 4th Port Angeles 98362-3015	1854 Jefferson	1895 1878 1891	1859 1862 1889
C7	Clark 1200 Franklin St. P.O. Box 5000 Vancouver 98660-2812	1845 (as Vancouver District; renamed 1849)	1891 1852 1891	1850 1890 1890
J6	Columbia 341 E. Main St. Dayton 99328-1361	1875 Walla Walla	1891 1876 1891	1864 1878 1874
B6	Cowlitz 207 Fourth Ave. N Kelso 98626-4124	1854 Lewis	1891 1854 1891	1854 1860 1872
F3	Douglas 213 S. Rainier Waterville 98858-0516	1883 Lincoln	1891 1887 1891	1884 1887 1888
H2	Ferry 350 E. Delaware Ave. Republic 99166-9747	1899 Stevens	1899 1900 1899	1898 1899 1899
G6	Franklin 1016 N. Fourth Ave. Pasco 99301-3706	1883 Whitman	1891 1890 1891	1880 1884 1874
J6	Garfield P.O. Box 278 Pomeroy 99347-0278	1881 Columbia	1891 1892 1891	1892 1882 1883
G4	Grant 35 C St. NW P.O. Box 37 Ephrata 98823-1685	1909 Douglas	1909 1909 1909	1889 1891 1889
A4	Grays Harbor 100 W. Broadway Montesano 98563-3614	1854 (as Chehalis; renamed 1915) Thurston	1891 1855 1891	1855 1857 1884

Map	County Address	Date Formed Parent County/ies	Birth Marriage Death	Deeds Probate Court
B2	Island 1 NE 7th St. P.O. Box 5000 Coupeville 98239-5000	1853 Thurston	1891 1853 1891	1853 1853 1891
A3	Jefferson 1820 Jefferson St. P.O. Box 1220 Port Townsend 98368-6951	1852 Thurston	1891 1853 1891	1855 1853 1854
D4	King 516 Third Ave. Seattle 98104-2305	1852 Thurston	1891 1866 1891	1853 1854 1864
B3	Kitsap 614 Division St. Port Orchard 98366-4614	1857 (as Slaughter; renamed 1857) King/Jefferson	1891 1860 1891	1857 1861 1888
E4	Kittitas 205 W. Fifth Ave. Ellensburg 98926-2890	1883 Yakima	1872 1882 1882	1882 1884 1884
E7	Klickitat 205 S. Columbus Ave. Goldendale 98620-9279	1859 Walla Walla/Skamania	1882 1867 1891	1863 1882 1880
B5	Lewis 351 NW North St. Chehalis 98532-1926	1845 original	1891 1847 1891	1855 1855 1847
H4	Lincoln 450 Logan St. Davenport 99122	1883 Spokane	1883 1884 1891	1883 1884 1886
B4	Mason I-411 N 5th Shelton 98584-3466	1854 (as Sawamish; renamed 1864) Thurston	1891 1892 1891	1856 1871 1889
G2	Okanogan 123 5th Ave. N., Rm 150 Okanogan 98840-9436	1888 Stevens	1899 1888 1891	1884 1888 1888
A5	Pacific 300 Memorial Ave. South Bend 98586	1851 original	1891 1868 1891	1851 1851 1878
K2	Pend Oreille 625 W. 4th St. Newport 99156-9098	1911 Stevens	—— 1911 1911	1911 1911 1911
C5	Pierce 930 Tacoma Ave. S., Rm 737 Tacoma 98402-2102	1852 Thurston	1891 1853 1891	1858 1855 1855
	Sawamish	1854 (renamed Mason, 1864) Thurston		
B2	San Juan 350 Court St. Friday Harbor 98250-7901	1873 Whatcom	1892 1874 1891	1877 1874 1889
C2	Skagit 700 S. Second St. Mount Vernon 98273-3879	1883 Whatcom	1891 1891 1891	1872 1884 1878
C7	Skamania 240 NW Vancouver St. Stevenson 98648-0790	1854 Clark	1893 1892 1891	1854 1854 1854
D2	Snohomish 3000 Rockefeller Ave. Everett 98201-4046	1861 Island	1881 1867 1891	1862 1866 1876
	Spokane (old)	1859 (abolished; became part of Stevens, 1864) Walla Walla *In 1879 part of this county was set off as present Spokane County.*		
K4	Spokane (present) 1116 W. Broadway Ave. Spokane 99201-2004	1879 Stevens	1882 1880 1889	1879 1880 1878
J2	Stevens 215 S. Oak St. #214 Colville 99114-2862	1863 Walla Walla	1891 1859 1891	1883 1887 1882
B5	Thurston 2000 Lakeridge Dr. S.W. Olympia 98502-6001	1852 original	1891 1877 1891	1852 1853 1852
A6	Wahkiakum 64 Main St. Cathlamet 98612-9508	1854 Lewis	1891 1868 1891	1858 1852 1890
H6	Walla Walla 315 W. Main St. Walla Walla 99362-2864	1854 Clark/Skamania	1883 1862 1884	1859 1859 1860
C1	Whatcom 311 Grand Ave. Bellingham 98225-4048	1854 Island	1891 1854 1891	1854 1872 1883
J5	Whitman 404 N. Main St. Colfax 99111-2031	1871 Stevens	1875 1874 1891	1874 1878 1861
E6	Yakima 128 N. Second St. Yakima 98901-2639	1865 Ferguson	1890 1877 1896	1882 1874 1882

West Virginia

JOHNI CERNY

The part of Virginia that would later became West Virginia was unknown to the adventurers who settled Jamestown in 1607. With the exception of a few scattered frontier outposts and even fewer permanent settlements, the area remained Native American hunting and battlegrounds until well into the 1700s. Virginia's Governor William Berkeley encouraged exploration and trade as early as 1660, but extensive settlement was discouraged by mountain barriers, resistance from original inhabitants, disputed land titles, conflicting English and French claims, and a royal proclamation of 1763 prohibiting settlement beyond the ridge line of the Blue Ridge Mountains. Settlement began in earnest by the 1730s when Morgan Morgan established a settlement in Berkeley County, Virginia.

While eastern tidewater counties of Virginia were settled by English aristocrats and their descendants, pioneers in western Virginia were generally perceived as a ragtag group from Pennsylvania, Maryland, and other parts of Virginia. The 1790 census lists more than 55,000 residents, of whom about 15,000 were of German descent. English immigrants and their descendants settled in Greenbrier, New, Kanawha, and Monongahela valleys, while Scots-Irish settlers made their homes in less accessible areas. West Virginia's mountainous terrain limited agricultural development and reduced the need for slavery. Less than one percent of the population in 1790 was enslaved. After the Civil War, African Americans from southern states moved into West Virginia seeking work in the railroads, mines, and industry.

Vital Records

All but five of West Virginia's counties were formed before 20 June 1863 when Congress officially admitted it as a sovereign state. Those pre-existing counties were governed by the same laws as other Virginia counties, including the requirement to register births and marriages beginning in 1853. When Virginia counties stopped recording birth and deaths in 1896, most West Virginia counties continued registration until 1900 or later in some locations. Statewide registration of births and deaths began 1 January 1917, but most records dated 1917–20 were destroyed by fire.

Microfilmed records dating from 1853 to 1900 can be searched at the Archives and History Library in Charleston (see Archives, Libraries, and Societies), the Library of Virginia (see Virginia) and the Family History Library (FHL) in Salt Lake City. Certified copies of records from 1920 forward can be obtained for a fee from the West Virginia Department of Health and Human Resources, Health Statistics Center, 350 Capitol St., Rm. 350, Charleston, WV 25301-3701 <www.wvdhhr.org/bph/oehp/hsc/vr/birtcert.htm>.

The FHL and the Archives and History Library in Charleston have birth certificates and delayed birth certificates from 1852 to 1930, and death certificates from 1917 to 1973.

Early Virginia law required church officials to record all marriages in registers, but few of those volumes have survived. Ministers were not required to forward a copy of the marriage entry to civil authorities until 1780. That requirement ended in 1853 with a new law requiring county clerks to issue marriage

licenses and keep marriage registers. Before a license could be issued, the parties to be married had to complete a form with the following information: full names, ages, places of birth and residence, proposed marriage date and place, marital status (single or widowed), names of parents, occupation of the groom, and name of the minister.

The FHL has filmed all early county marriage records from those still held by county clerks. The early marriages of some counties have been transcribed and published; they may have found their way into the collections of major genealogical libraries and local libraries in West Virginia. Certified copies of marriage licenses issued from 1 January 1964 can be ordered from the Health Statistics Center (address above). A centralized index dates back to 1921.

County circuit court divorce records can be obtained from the clerk of the Circuit Court in the county where the petition was filed.

Census Records

Federal

Population Schedules

- Indexed—(1810, 1820, 1830, 1840, 1850, 1860 [see Virginia—Census Records]), 1870, 1880, 1900, 1910, 1920, 1930
- Soundex—1880, 1900, 1910 (Miracode), 1920, 1930(partial)

Industry and Agriculture Schedules

- (1850, 1860 [see Virginia—Census Records]), 1870, 1880

Mortality Schedules

- (1850, 1860 [see Virginia—Census Records]), 1870, 1880

Slave Schedules

- (1850, 1860 [see Virginia—Census Records])

Union Veterans Schedules

- 1890

Locate West Virginians prior to 1870 in federal census records of Virginia. Collections of microfilmed census records can be searched at the National Archives and its centers (see page 11); the Archives and History Library in Charleston, West Virginia; West Virginia University in Morgantown; and the FHL. Published abstracts of census records can also be found in the above and at local libraries. All West Virginia federal census records are indexed, with viewable images, and included in online databases (see pages 16-17).

The 1930 Soundex exists for Fayette, Harrison, Kanawha, Logan, McDowell, Mercer, and Raleigh counties.

Background Sources

The following publications are either guides for conducting research in West Virginia or publications including hundreds of biographical sketches about early West Virginia families. Many of those sketches contain ancestral lines and family migration patterns.

Brown, Stuart E., Jr. *Virginia Genealogical Resources.* Detroit: Detroit Society for Genealogical Research, 1980.

Comstock, Jim. *Hardesty's West Virginia Counties.* 8 vols. Richwood, W.Va.: J. Comstock, 1973. Contains biographical sketches of early county residents and their families.

_____. *West Virginia Heritage Encyclopedia.* 25 vols. Richwood, W.Va.: the author, 1976.

_____. *West Virginia Heritage Encyclopedia: Supplemental Series.* 25 vols. Richwood, W.Va.: the author, 1976.

Good, Rebecca H., and Rebecca A. Ebert. *Finding Your People in the Shenandoah Valley of Virginia.* Alexandria, Va.: Hearthside Press, 1988. A guide covering Berkeley, Hampshire, Jefferson, and Morgan counties in now West Virginia and Augusta, Clarke, Frederick, Pay, Rockingham, Shenandoah, and Warren counties in Virginia.

McGinnis, Carol. *West Virginia Genealogy Sources and Resources.* 1988, Reprint. Baltimore: Genealogical Publishing Co., 1998. This recent guide provides a county-by-county breakdown of original source material and a thorough list of microfilms available in the state's repositories (see Archives, Libraries, and Societies).

Rice, Otis K. and Stephen W. Brown. *West Virginia: A History.* 2d ed. Lexington, Ky.: University Press of Kentucky, 1993.

Stewart, Robert Armistead. *Index to Printed Virginia Genealogies..., 1930.* 1930, Reprint. Baltimore: Genealogical Publishing Co., 1997.

Stinson, Helen S. *A Handbook for Genealogical Research in West Virginia.* South Charleston, W.Va.: Kanawha Valley Genealogical Society, 1981.

_____. *Fatalities in West Virginia Coal Mines, 1883–1925.* South Charleston, W.Va.: Stinson, 1985.

Swem, Earl Gregg. *Virginia Historical Index.* 1934–36. Reprint. (2 vols. in 4). Gloucester, Mass.: Peter Smith, 1965.

Wardell, P. G. *Timesaving Aid to Virginia–West Virginia Ancestors: A Genealogical Index of Surnames from Published Sources.* 3 vols. Athens, Ga.: Iberian Publishing Co., 1985.

Williams, John Alexander. *West Virginia: A History.* Reprint. N.p.: W.W. Norton and Co., 1984.

Maps

Maps of early Virginia are crucial when tracing colonial families on the frontier that would later become West Virginia. (See Virginia—Maps for a selected bibliography.) See also Henry Gannett, A *Gazetteer of Virginia and West Virginia*, (1904, reprint, Baltimore: Genealogical Publishing Co., 2002); *Virginia Atlas & Gazetteer*, 2d ed., Yarmouth, Maine: DeLorme Publishing, 2002; and *West Virginia Atlas & Gazetteer*, 2d ed., Yarmouth, Maine: DeLorme Publishing, 2001.

Present-day county road maps can be obtained from West Virginia Department of Highways, Map Sales, 1900 Washington St. East, Charleston, WV 25305. These maps show the location of many cemeteries.

The West Virginia and Regional History Collection (see Archives, Libraries, and Societies) and the FHL have sizable collections of West Virginia maps, including nineteenth-century landownership maps. See Edgar Barr Sims, *Making a State: Formation of West Virginia…*(Charleston, W.Va.: E. B. Sims, 1956).

Land Records

State-Land State

Speculators who formed land companies after 1744 settled much of western Virginia. Companies were awarded 1,000 acres of land for each family they moved into the area. The survey made of each parcel of land was sold to individuals, who then received title to the land in the form of a patent from the secretary of the colony. After 1779, the Virginia Land Office issued the patents. Edgar Barr Sims, *Index to Land Grants in West Virginia* (1952, reprint, Baltimore: Genealogical Publishing Co., 2003), lists the names of grantees by county. See also the supplement to this index, *Making a State: Formation of West Virginia*; and Gertrude E. Gray, *Virginia Northern Neck Land Grants*, 4 vols. (Baltimore: Genealogical Publishing Co., 1987–1993), particularly volume two, which contains abstracts of grants encompassing the area now comprising Hampshire and Berkeley counties in West Virginia.

Some western Virginia lands were redeemed by Bounty Land Warrants issued to Revolutionary War soldiers. Some settled on the land they were granted, but many sold their warrants.

Original surveys, grants, and sales of land in West Virginia can be found at the Office of State Auditor, Capitol Bldg., West Wing 231, Charleston, WV 25305. Other records, on file at the Library of Virginia, appear at <www.lva.lib.va.us/siteindex/index.htm>.

When the person who received a land grant or patent sold that land, the transaction was recorded in deed books in the county where the land was located. Generally, those deed books have been indexed by grantor (seller) and grantee (buyer). Some county clerks have compiled master indexes to all of their deed books. Copies of deed can be obtained from county clerks; however, the deed books for most West Virginia counties have been microfilmed and can be searched at the Archives and History Library in Charleston and the FHL. The West Virginia and Regional History Collection includes the West Virginia Court Record Index (actually a list by county of records filmed at the courthouse), which can be found at <www.libraries.wvu.edu/wvcollection/countycourt/index.htm>.

Probate Records

When West Virginia belonged to the Commonwealth of Virginia, estate records were produced by county and circuit courts. Wills, letters of administration, guardianships, appraisals, and settlements are some of the estate documents recorded by the court. Once a sovereign state, West Virginia continued in the same tradition and heard probate matters in the county courts. Original will books can be searched at the clerk's office in the county where a person died. Microfilmed estate records dated prior to 1968 can be used at the Archives and History Library in Charleston, the West Virginia and Regional History Collection in Morgantown, and the FHL. See Ross B. Johnston, *West Virginia Estate Settlements, 1753–1850* (1969; reprint, Baltimore: Genealogical Publishing Co., 2003) and Clayton Torrence, *Virginia Wills and Administrations, 1632–1800* (1930; reprint, Baltimore: Genealogical Publishing Co., 2000. Both of these publications can be used to identify the counties where a surname appeared.

A number of early Virginia and West Virginia will books have been abstracted and published. The Archives and History Library in Charleston, the West Virginia and Regional History Collection in Morgantown, and the FHL have large collections of these publications.

Court Records

Having been part of Virginia until 1863, West Virginia kept the same court system as its parent state (see Virginia—Court Records). The Historical Records Survey Collection, on film in the West Virginia and Regional History Collection at the West Virginia University Library and the FHL, includes a variety of records: county court records; execution books; fee books; rule books; birth, marriage, and death registers; deed indexes, land taxes, land books, personal property books, justices criminal dockets, and others. Intermingled among court records are naturalizations, emancipations, school commissioner reports, and cattle brands. For a list of records in this collection by

county, see <www.libraries.wvu.edu/wvcollection/countycourt/index.htm>.

Tax Records

Virginia counties, including those counties that now belong to West Virginia, collected taxes from as early as 1624. See the section Virginia—Tax Records for a comprehensive discussion of the laws governing taxes, the types of taxes paid, and where to find early tax lists.

West Virginia has land tax records for all counties covering the years 1782 through 1936, and for some counties through 1959. Those records can be found at the Archives and History Library in Charleston. Most county clerks have duplicate copies in their offices. The Library of Virginia has the personal property tax records from 1782 through 1863, when West Virginia became a separate state.

Cemetery Records

The Historical Records Survey (HRS), created in 1935 as part of the Federal Writers Project by the Works Projects Administration (WPA) in response to massive unemployment during the Great Depression, indexed federal censuses, vital records, military records, and cemetery interments. The HRS compiled the largest collection of West Virginia tombstone inscriptions available today. The collection includes inscriptions prior to 1940 and can be found in the West Virginia and Regional History Collection and on microfilm at the FHL.

The Daughters of the American Revolution (DAR) and others have published volumes of cemetery records and tombstone inscriptions that can be found in local, regional, and genealogical libraries in West Virginia and at the FHL.

Church Records

With the arrival of English and Scots-Irish settlers came West Virginia's early dominant religions. Many families of English origin were Quakers; the Scots-Irish were Presbyterians. Both religions were well established by 1740, and they were followed by Baptists who settled in Berkeley County in 1743 and a Methodist circuit in Berkeley and Jefferson counties in 1778. For a complete discussion of early church records, see Virginia—Church Records.

Since colonial times dozens of religious groups have established congregations in West Virginia including the following: **Baptist**, West Virginia Baptist Historical Society, Rt. 2, Box 304, Ripley, WV 25271 <www.wvbhs.com>; **Methodist**, Methodist Historical Society, West Virginia Wesleyan College,

Annie M. Pfeiffer Library, College Ave., Buckhannon, WV 26201; **Roman Catholic**, Diocese of Wheeling/Charleston, P.O. Box 230, Wheeling, WV 26003; **Episcopal**, Episcopal Diocese of WV, 4032 MacCorkle Ave. SW, Charleston, WV 25309-1510; and **United Brethren**, Historical Library, Church of the Brethren, 1451 Dundee Ave., Elgin, IL 60120 (denominations).

Many religious groups have deposited their records at the West Virginia and Regional History Collection. Church record inventories compiled as part of the Historical Records Survey are available there and at the FHL.

Military Records

West Virginia shares its early military history with Virginia (see Virginia—Military Records). Virgil A. Lewis, the Soldiery of West Virginia (1911, reprint, Baltimore: Genealogical Publishing Co., 2002), has rosters of soldiers from West Virginia who served in the French and Indian War, Indian Wars, Lord Dunmore's War, the Revolutionary War, Whiskey Rebellion of 1794, the War of 1812, Mexican War, and the Civil War. See also:

General

McKinney, Tim. West Virginia Civil War Almanac. Charleston, W.Va.: Pictorial Histories Publishing Co., 1998.

Union

The Roster of Union Soldiers, 1861–1865. Vol. 4. Wilmington, N.C.: Broadfoot Publishing, 1999. Alphabetical listing of Union soldiers in West Virginia. Provides name, regiment, and company.

Confederacy

Berckefeldt, Paul, ed. Index to the Soldiery of West Virginia. Pueblo, Colo.: Pathfinders Books, 1985.

Bockstruck, Lloyd DeWitt. Virginia's Colonial Soldiers. 1988. Reprint. Baltimore: Genealogical Publishing Co., 1998.

Johnson, Ross B. West Virginians in the American Revolution. Baltimore: Genealogical Publishing Co., 1977.

Reddy, Anne Waller. West Virginia Revolutionary Ancestors. 1977. Reprint. Baltimore: Genealogical Publishing Co., 2001. Indexes claims reviewed by the "court of claims" for nonmilitary service.

West Virginia's military divergence came during the Civil War. At the Virginia secession convention in 1861, a majority of the state's western delegates opposed leaving the Union. In later meetings at Wheeling, those delegates declared secession to be an illegal attempt to overthrow the federal government and the Confederate government at Richmond to be void of authority. They voted to restore the Virginia state government and elect

new officers. The governor-elect received federal recognition and governed until Congress admitted West Virginia as the 35th state on 20 June 1863 on the condition that all slaves in its jurisdiction were set free.

As a participant in the Civil War, West Virginia cannot be declared a Union or Confederate state. Like Maryland, Kentucky, Missouri, and other border states, the loyalties of its citizens were divided. Lacking proof of the exact number of soldiers who fought on either side, historians now estimate that at least 10,000 served the Confederacy and approximately 23,000 fought with the Union Army. Consult the standard references for Confederate soldiers (see pages 8-9).

The Archives and History Library, West Virginia and Regional History Collection, and FHL have published military records and indexes in their West Virginia collections.

Periodicals, Newspapers, and Manuscript Collections

Periodicals

Most West Virginia counties have organized genealogical or historical societies, some of which publish excellent quarterly periodicals (see McGinnis under Background Sources). For the pre-statehood period, see the section on Virginia for bibliographical citations of the most valuable and widely used genealogical periodicals and their appropriate indexes.

Newspapers

West Virginia newspaper collections are at the Archives and History Library, and the West Virginia and Regional History Collection. See Barbara Mertin, *Newspapers in the West Virginia University Library* (Morgantown, W.Va.: West Virginia University Library, 1973). Most newspapers have been microfilmed and a large collection is available at the FHL as well.

Manuscripts

The West Virginia and Regional History Collection at West Virginia University in Morgantown includes historical documents dating from the first settlements in the state to the present. A *Guide to Manuscripts and Archives* can be downloaded at <www.libraries.wvu.edu/wvcollection/manuscripts/index.htm>. These three sources can be found in this collection:

Smith-Riffe Collection of New River Genealogy and Local History. This collection pertains to Boone, Fayette, Greenbrier, Mercer, Monroe, Raleigh, and Wyoming counties and is located at the Archives and History Library in Charleston and on microfilm through the FHL.

Elisha B. Iams Collection. This card index of 6,500 entries consists of more than seventy volumes of extracted records from

sixteen counties in southwest Pennsylvania, West Virginia, and Ohio. It can be searched at Citizen's Library, 55 S. College St., Washington, PA 15301.

Willis Guy Tetrick Collection. The Tetrick Collection contains primarily of family group records compiled by family members living in central West Virginia. Some records contain extensive genealogical information, and although others are less complete, they offer excellent clues to follow. While cataloged under Harrison County in the FHL, this collection has information about residents of surrounding counties. The original collection is at the West Virginia and Regional History Collection and also available on microfilm. Since many ancestors mentioned in Tetrick's collection came from counties outside the immediate Harrison County area, it is a good idea to check this source.

Archives, Libraries, and Societies

Archives and History Library
Division of Culture and History
Cultural Center, Capitol Complex
1900 Kanawha Blvd. East
Charleston, WV 25305
www.wvculture.org/history

Publishes *West Virginia History*. The facility consists of the library, archives, and a museum containing materials from 1760 to present.

West Virginia Historical Society
P.O. Box 5220
Charleston, WV 25361
www.wvhistorical.com

The society does not maintain historical or genealogical collections. Write to the Archives and History Library above for information.

West Virginia and Regional History Collection
West Virginia University Library
Colson Hall
Morgantown, WV 26506
www.libraries.wvu.edu/wvcollection

This extensive collection includes the Historical Records Survey for West Virginia on microfilm, the largest collection of West Virginia newspapers, and many unpublished family histories. The *West Virginia Court Record Microfilm Index* (actually a list of microfilmed court records by county) can be accessed at <www.libraries.wvu.edu/wvcollection/countycourt/index.htm>.

West Virginia Genealogical Society, Inc.
P.O. Box 249
Elkview, WV 25071
www.rootsweb.com/~wvgs

Special Focus Categories

African American

As a condition for being granted statehood, residents of the counties that would comprise West Virginia agreed to free all slaves. The Library of Virginia has an impressive collection of African American newspapers published in Virginia between 1865 and the present. See also Virginia—African Americans.

Coal Mining

Woven into West Virginia's history is that of the coal miner. Regarding coal mine accidents, the following may be helpful:

Dillon, Lacy A. *They Died in the Darkness.* Parsons, W.Va.: McClain Printing Co., 1976.

———. *They Died for King Coal.* Winona, Minn.: Apollo Books, 1985.

Stinson, Helen S. *Fatalities in West Virginia Coal Mines, 1883–1925.* N.p.: the author, 1985.

County Resources

All but five of the counties (Grant, Lincoln, Mineral, Mingo, and Summers) that comprise West Virginia were formed between 1754 (Hampshire) and 1860 (Webster). Each county courthouse has the records created by the clerk since its inception. Microfilm copies of the records (nineteenth and early twentieth centuries) can be searched at the Archives and History Library in Charleston, the West Virginia University West Virginia University Library (West Virginia Regional History Collection) in Morgantown, and the FHL.

The chart following this section gives the address of each county courthouse and the years covered by each record source. Some counties will answer mail inquiries, but will charge a fee for the time it takes to perform the search and copy costs. Check <www.naco.org>, the website of the National Association of County Organizations, for additional information.

Land, probate, and vital records are located at the clerk's office at the county seat. Court records, including naturalizations and divorces, are at the circuit court clerk's office at the county seat.

In addition to general sources for all states (see pages 17-18), the following has been used to compile the following chart:

West Virginia County Formations and Boundary Changes. Charleston, W.Va.: Historical Records Survey, 1939.

Sims, Edgar Barr. *Making a State: Formation of West Virginia.* Charleston, W.Va.: the author, 1956.

West Virginia Association of Counties <www.wvcounties.org>. Provides brief overviews and histories of each county.

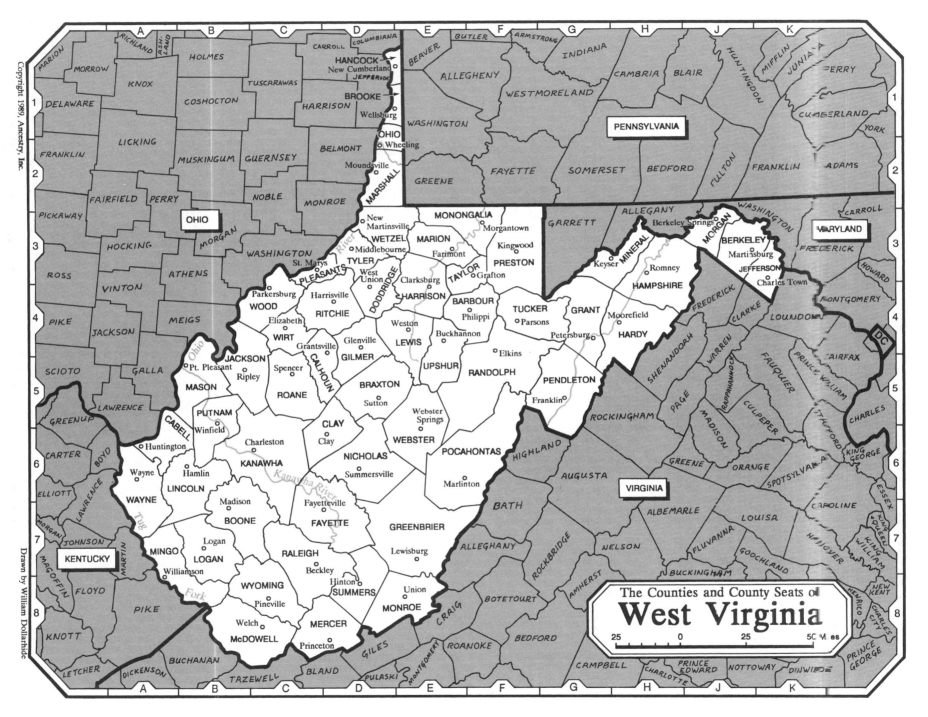

The Counties and County Seats of
West Virginia

741

WEST VIRGINIA

Map	County Address	Date Formed Parent County/ies	Birth Marriage Death	Land Probate Court
F4	Barbour 8 N. Main St. P.O. Box 310 Philippi 26416-1140	1843 Harrison/Lewis/Randolph	1853 1843 1853	1843 1843 1843
J3	Berkeley 126 W. King St. Martinsburg 25401-3210	1772 Frederick, Va.	1865 1781 1865	1772 1772 1772
B7	Boone 206 Court St. Madison 25130-1106	1847 Kanawha/Cabell/Logan	1865 1865 1865	1847 1865 1865
D5	Braxton P.O. Box 486 Sutton 26601-0486	1836 Lewis/Nicholas	1858 1836 1858	1836 1836 1836
E1	Brooke 632 Main St. Wellsburg 26070-1743	1797 Ohio	1853 1797 1853	1797 1797 1797
A6	Cabell 750 Fifth Ave., Ste. 300 Huntington 25701-2019	1809 Kanawha	1853 1809 1853	1808 1809 1809
D5	Calhoun P.O. Box 230 Grantsville 26147-0230	1856 Gilmer	1856 1856 1856	1856 1856 1856
C6	Clay 207 Main St. Clay 25043-0190	1858 Braxton/Nicholas/Kanawha	1858 1858 1858	1858 1858 1858
D3	Doddridge 118 E. Court St., Rm. 102 West Union 26456-1262	1845 Harrison/Tyler/Ritchie/Lewis	1853 1845 1862	1845 1849 1845
D7	Fayette 100 N. Court St. Fayetteville 25840-1200	1831 Logan/Nicholas/ Greenbrier/Kanawha	1866 1831 1831	1831 1832 1831
D4	Gilmer 10 Howard St., Courthouse Glenville 26351-1246	1845 Lewis/Kanawha	1853 1845 1853	1845 1845 1845
G4	Grant 5 Highland Ave. Petersburg 26847-1705	1866 Hardy	1866 1866 1866	1866 1866 1866
E7	Greenbrier P.O. Box 506 Lewisburg 24901-0506	1778 Montgomery, Va./ Botetourt, Va.	1853 1781 1853	1780 1780 1780
H3	Hampshire P.O. Box 806 Romney 26757-0806	1754 Frederick, Va./Augusta, Va.	1865 1824 1865	1757 1756 1736
E1	Hancock P.O. Box 485 New Cumberland 26047-0485	1848 Brooke	1853 1854 1853	1848 1848 1848
H4	Hardy 204 Washington St., Rm 111 Moorefield 26836-1155	1786 Hampshire	1853 1795 1853	1786 1786 1786
E4	Harrison 301 W. Main St. Clarksburg 26301-2909	1784 Monongalia	1853 1784 1853	1786 1788 1784
B5	Jackson P.O. Box 800 Ripley 25271-0800	1831 Mason/Wood/Kanawha	1853 1831 1853	1831 1831 1831
K3	Jefferson 110 E. Washington St. Charles Town 25414-1072	1801 Berkeley	1853 1801 1853	1801 1801 1801
C6	Kanawha 407 Virginia St. East Charleston 25301-2524	1788 Greenbrier/Montgomery	1853 1792 1853	1790 1789 1773
E4	Lewis P.O. Box 466 Weston 26452-0466	1816 Harrison	1853 1816 1853	1817 1816 1817
B6	Lincoln P.O. Box 497 Hamlin 25523-0497	1867–69 Boone/Cabell/Logan/ Kanawha/Wayne	1909 1909 1909	1909 1909 1909
B7	Logan 300 Stratton St. Logan 25601-3924	1824 Giles, Va./Cabell/ Tazewell, Va./Kanawha	1872 1872 1872	1824 1873 1824
E3	Marion 200 Jackson St. Rm. 403 Fairmont 26554-2963	1842 Monongalia/ Harrison	1860 1842 1842	1842 1842 1842
D2	Marshall Drawer B Moundsville 26041-2192	1835 Ohio	1853 1835 1853	1835 1835 1835
B5	Mason 200 Sixth St. Point Pleasant 25550-1131	1804 Kanawha	1853 1806 1853	1803 1805 1805
B8	McDowell 90 Wyoming St., Ste. 111 Welch 24801-2487	1858 Tazewell, Va.	1872 1859 1894	1868 1893 1859
D8	Mercer 1501 W. Main St. Princeton 24740-2600	1837 Giles, Va./Tazewell, Va.	1853 1853 1853	1837 1837 1837
H3	Mineral 150 Armstrong St. Keyser 26726-3500	1866 Hampshire	1866 1866 1866	1866 1866 1866
A7	Mingo P.O. Box 1197 Williamson 25661-1197	1895 Logan	1895 1895 1895	1895 1895 1895
E3	Monongalia 243 High St. Morgantown 26505-5434	1776 District of West Augusta, Va.	1853 1796 1853	1776 (index) 1774 1774

Map	County Address	Date Formed Parent County/ies	Birth Marriage Death	Land Probate Court
E8	Monroe Main St./P.O. Box 350 Union 24983-0350	1799 Greenbrier 1799	1853 1799 1799	1799 1799 1799
J3	Morgan P.O. Box 28 Berkeley Springs 25411-0028	1820 Berkeley/Hampshire 	1865 1820 1865	1820 1820 1820
D6	Nicholas 700 Main St. Summersville 26651-1444	1818 Greenbrier/Kanawha/ Randolph	1853 1817 1853	1818 1820 1818
D2	Ohio 1500 Chapline St. Wheeling 26003-3553	1776 District of West Augusta, Va. 	1853 1793 1853	1778 1776 1777
G5	Pendleton P.O. Box 187 Franklin 26807-0187	1788 Augusta, Va./Hardy/ Rockingham, Va.	1853 1800 1853	1789 1789 1789
C3	Pleasants 301 Court Lane, Ste. 101 Saint Marys 26170-1317	1851 Wood/Tyler/Ritchie 	1853 1853 1853	1851 1852 1851
E6	Pocahontas 900-C Tenth St. Marlinton 24954-1310	1821 Bath, Va./Randolph/ Pendleton	1853 1822 1853	1822 1822 1822
F3	Preston 101 W. Main St. Kingwood 26537-1121	1818 Monongalia 	1868 1869 1868	1818 1869 1881
B5	Putnam 3389 Winfield Rd. Winfield 25213-9370	1848 Kanawha/Cabell/Mason 	1854 1848 1853	1848 1848 1848
C7	Raleigh 215 Main St. Beckley 25801-4612	1850 Fayette 	1853 1850 1853	1850 1850 1850
F5	Randolph P.O. Box 2092 Elkins 26241-2092	1787 Harrison 	1856 1787 1853	1787 1787 1787
D4	Ritchie 115 E. Main St., Rm. 201 Harrisville 26362-1271	1842 Harrison/Lewis/Wood 	1853 1843 1853	1844 1843 1844
C5	Roane P.O. Box 69 Spencer 25276-0069	1856 Kanawha/Calhoun/Jackson 	1856 1856 1856	1856 1856 1856
D8	Summers P.O. Box 97 Hinton 25951-0097	1871 Fayette/Mercer/ Greenbrier/Monroe	1871 1871 1871	1871 1871 1871
E3	Taylor 214 W. Main St. Grafton 26354-1387	1844 Harrison/Barbour/Marion 	1853 1853 1853	1844 1844 1844
F4	Tucker 213 First St. Parsons 26287-1235	1856 Randolph 	1856 1856 1856	1856 1856 1856
D3	Tyler 121 Main St. P.O. Box 66 Middlebourne 26149-0066	1814 Ohio 	1853 1815 1853	1813 1815 1815
E5	Upshur 38 W. Main St. Buckhannon 26201-2259	1851 Randolph/Lewis/Barbour 	1853 1853 1853	1851 1852 1851
A6	Wayne P.O. Box 248 Wayne 25570-0248	1842 Cabell 	1853 1853 1853	1842 1843 1842
E5	Webster 2 Court Sq., Room G-1 Webster Springs 26268-1049	1860 Nicholas/Braxton/Randolph 	1887 1887 1887	1887 1887 1887
D3	Wetzel P.O. Box 156 New Martinsville 26155-0149	1846 Tyler 	1854 1845 (index) 1854	1846 1847 1846
C4	Wirt P.O. Box 53 Elizabeth 26143-0053	1848 Wood/Jackson 	1870 1854 1870	1848 1848 1848
C4	Wood 1 Courthouse Sq. Parkersburg 26101-5399	1798 Harrison 	1853 1800 1853	1798 1800 1798
C8	Wyoming P.O. Box 309 Pineville 24874-0309	1850 Logan 	1853 1855 1853	1850 1850 1850

Wisconsin

DAWN M. KNAUFT AND CAROL L. MAKI

Called the "fairest portion of the Great West," Wisconsin was first observed by Europeans in 1634. Late that summer a young but seasoned voyageur, Jean Nicolet, sent by New France administration in Canada, arrived at Red Banks on the Green Bay of Lake Michigan. He explored the area and returned to Canada to explain to Samuel de Champlain that he had not found the passage to China. In the spring and summer of 1673, Louis Joliet, a cartographer and explorer, Father Jacques Marquette, and five others made a journey that would greatly expand the French knowledge of this territory. The course of their canoes was guided by two Miami-nation guides down the Fox, Wisconsin, and Mississippi rivers. They traversed the Mississippi south to a Quapaw village near the present boundary of Arkansas and Louisiana.

Nicolas Perrot, born in France about 1644, and Toussaint Baudry, one of his partners in a trading company in New France (Canada), visited Green Bay in 1668 by invitation of the Potawatomi they had met in an earlier visit at Chequamegon Bay. Perrot, known as an expert in tribal diplomacy, visited many natives, creating valuable alliances with them. His influence with the Wisconsin tribes continued at least through 1698.

Jesuit Father Claude Allouez opened a mission in 1669 in what is now Brown County. The mission became a major point in the French fur-trading empire until it was closed in 1728. Fort Francis, built on the Fox River in 1717, was rebuilt by the British as Fort Edward Augustus, establishing their presence in the area in 1763. Charles de Langlade and his family arrived at Green Bay in 1765, establishing the first permanent white settlement in Wisconsin.

The Treaty of Paris in 1783 theoretically put Wisconsin under U.S. control, although in reality the British were in command of the area. Four years later Wisconsin was included in the newly organized Northwest Territory and in 1800 was included in Indiana Territory. When Michigan Territory was created in 1805, Wisconsin remained in Indiana Territory. On 3 February 1809, Wisconsin, except for the Door County Peninsula, became part of Illinois Territory. Nine years later Illinois became a state, and Wisconsin was redefined as Michigan Territory. Wisconsin became a territory in 1836 and a state in 1848.

Just two years after statehood, the population of Wisconsin had reached over 300,000. The ratio of American-born to foreign-born was two to one, with immigrants' birthplaces being Canada, England, Switzerland, Germany, Ireland, Wales, the Netherlands, and Norway. Approximately one-fifth of the American-born were Wisconsin-born, and most were children. The migrants came from Ohio, Indiana, Illinois, Michigan, New England, New York, the Mid-Atlantic, and the South. New Yorkers numbered about 68,600 in Wisconsin in 1850 (see Smith in Background Sources).

A few generalizations are important in researching immigrant or migrant Wisconsin ancestors. Most of them traveled directly from their home state or their port of debarkation. Some Germans and some Dutch stayed temporarily in the east for financial reasons, and the Irish often took years to work their way west from the east coast or Canada. Those from New York, Pennsylvania, and New England traditionally made the journey in stages, as indicated by birth records for their children who may be found from the Northeast through Ohio, Indiana, and Illinois.

Vital Records

Wisconsin issued marriage applications as early as the 1820s in some counties, although most jurisdictions began maintaining them with county organization. The state directed the counties, in 1852, to record births and deaths, a mandate generally ignored. In 1878 a similar law received more attention and adherence. A separate volume was kept for recording births that had occurred prior to 1852. The earliest delayed birth record dates to 1746.

Beginning in 1907 the state became responsible for maintaining birth, death, and marriage records. Researchers may apply for records of births, deaths, and marriages at Wisconsin Vital Records, P.O. Box 309, Madison, WI 53701-0309 <www.dhfs.state.wi.us/VitalRecords/>. The website provides updated information about process and costs for obtaining copies. Certified copies are only available to the person on the record or specific relatives of that person, such as parent, spouse, or grandparent. Onsite searching in the state vital records is possible with advance appointments at particular hours and on particular days. Contact the office for complete information on this procedure before traveling to Madison. Some records are not accessible.

Vital records at the county level are held by the register of deeds at each county government center. Indexes and original records may be searched within established guidelines. Photocopies or certificates of county records can be obtained at the same rate schedule as the state's.

Of great value to the genealogist in Wisconsin is the statewide microfiche index to the births, deaths, and marriages recorded in the state prior to October 1907. The Wisconsin Historical Society, all Area Research Centers (see Archives, Libraries, and Societies), and the Family History Library (FHL) in Salt Lake City hold copies of this index that has to be searched in person. The Wisconsin Historical Society Library at Madison has microfilmed copies of the actual records referred to in the index, and each Area Research Center has the microfilmed records for the counties covered by that center. Some records at the county level are not included in the statewide index. Some specific counties are not indexed for specific types of vital events. In the marriage records index, for example, the entries for Racine County are incomplete, and counties following Racine alphabetically are not included. Price County is also missing. However, separate indexes to each of the remaining twenty-one counties are being compiled by volunteers. They are available in print at the Wisconsin Historical Society Library. For those counties without an index, the society also has microfilmed, handwritten registers, arranged chronologically by registration date, and indexed primarily by the first letter of the groom's surname. Despite these limitations, the microfiche index is a tool that should certainly be used in Wisconsin research.

Divorce records are usually found in the county government centers and most often in the civil court records. Post-1907 divorce decrees, although they actually contain very little genealogical information, can be located at the State Bureau of Vital Statistics. From 1836 through 1848, the territorial legislature granted the divorces listed in the *Wisconsin State Genealogical Society Newsletter* (April 1980).

The "Wisconsin Necrology" at the Wisconsin Historical Society is a collection of several thousand selected obituaries of Wisconsin citizens (1890–1945). The obituaries are in scrapbooks that were originally indexed by a card catalog, and are now searchable online at <http://wisconsinhistory.org/wni/>. The scrapbooks have been microfilmed and are available through interlibrary loan.

Other obituary indexes can be located in numerous local libraries and in some Area Research Centers. Some early vital records have been extracted and published in state and county genealogical periodicals.

Census Records

Federal

Population Schedules
- Indexed—1820 and 1830 (as Michigan Territory), 1840, 1850, 1860, 1870, 1880, 1900, 1910, 1920, 1930
- Soundex—1880, 1900, 1920

Industry and Agriculture Schedules
- 1850, 1860, 1870, 1880

Mortality Schedules
- 1850, 1860, 1870, 1880

Union Veterans Schedules
- 1890

All federal census schedules, for all states, are at the Wisconsin Historical Society. The society also has original state copy manuscripts of the 1850, 1860, and 1870 federal census for Wisconsin. Every-name indexes to the state copies of the 1850, 1860, and 1870 censuses, on microfilm, are available through interlibrary loan from that repository. In addition, all the state's federal census records are indexed and available through online database services (see pages 16-17). Some variations between the state and federal copies of the federal population censuses may exist. Mortality schedules are indexed and available through interlibrary loan, except for the 1880, which is not indexed. The 1820 to 1870 censuses for Wisconsin were also indexed by the Works Projects Administration (WPA), listing each individual within the state in a given census year.

Territorial and State

When the territorial government of Wisconsin was established on 20 April 1836, it provided that an enumeration of the inhabitants of the several counties in the territory be taken by the sheriffs and sent to the governor before the election. This first Wisconsin census did not have preprinted forms. The sheriffs wrote the names of heads of white families with the number of persons in each family divided by sex and age in four groups. The sheriff of Crawford County regrouped his constituents who were deaf and dumb, or blind, and included tables of aliens and "slaves and coloured." Some heads of household on this census appear to have unusually large families. It appears, for example, that in Brown County, Daniel Whitney's "family" of forty-nine included his workmen in sawmills, lumber camps, and at the Helena shot-tower.

Wisconsin territorial and state census original schedules, with a few exceptions, are in the State Archives at the Wisconsin Historical Society. Microfilm copies are available in the microforms reading room, through interlibrary loan, and for purchase. They include the following:

1836 (AISI index): Names only head of household, plus numeric listing of household; published in *Wisconsin Historical Collections* 13 (1895): 247-70.

1838 (AISI index): Includes name of master, mistress, steward, overseer, or other principal person; name of head of family and numeric listing of household; extant only for certain counties.

1842 (AISI index): Similar to 1838.

1846: Includes name of head of family; numeric listing of household by sex and color; some counties missing.

1847: Same as 1846; some counties missing.

1855 (AISI index): Similar to 1847, plus number of deaf and dumb, blind, or insane; includes number of individuals in each household of foreign birth; Kewaunee County not included.

1865: Listing same as 1855; schedules apparently were destroyed at an unknown date; only a few schedules survive (Crawford, Dane, Dunn, Green, Jackson, Kewaunee, Ozaukee, Racine and Sheboygan). A printed and bound index by Barry Noonan is available at the Wisconsin Historical Society.

1875: Listing similar to 1855.

1885: Listing similar to 1855, plus some additional information on number of foreign-born persons and a special enumeration of "Soldiers and Sailors of the Late War."

1895: Same as 1885, including veterans' schedules.

1905: Includes name of each individual, relationship to head of household, color or race, sex, age at last birthday, marital status, place of birth, place of birth of parents, occupation, number of months employed, whether home or farm is owned or rented; also includes veterans' enumeration; indexed, by county, on microfilm.

A very complete listing of Wisconsin Territorial and State Censuses is in James P. Danky, *Genealogical Research: An Introduction to the Resources of the State Historical Society of Wisconsin* (Madison, Wis.: State Historical Society of Wisconsin, 1986).

Local census enumerations were taken between 1848 and 1959, ordered for qualification as a municipality by the state. Copies were required to be kept by the county register of deeds and the village or city clerk. Some of these censuses have been found in circuit court files.

Evidence of migration to Wisconsin through the upper Great Lakes may be found in Donna Valley Russell, *Michigan Censuses, 1710–1830, Under the French, British and Americans* (Detroit: Detroit Society for Genealogical Research, 1982). Canadian voyageurs may be found in the same author's *Michigan Voyageurs, From the Notary Book of Samuel Abbott, Mackinac Island, 1807–1817* (Detroit: Detroit Society for Genealogical Research, 1982).

City directories for urban areas may help fill the gaps where census records are nonexistent. The Wisconsin Historical Society has an extensive collection that includes directories for Milwaukee as early as 1846 and several cities for the 1850s. Local libraries, historical societies, and the Area Research Centers network may have directories for their specific locales.

Background Sources

Initial or advanced genealogical research in Wisconsin should include the Wisconsin chapter by James L. Hansen in volume two of *Genealogical Research: Methods and Sources*, edited by Kenn Stryker-Rodda (Washington, D.C.: American Society of Genealogists, 1983).

There is an abundance of county histories for the state of Wisconsin. Some are written for individual counties or several counties together, and others for sections of the state, such as John G. Gregory, *Southwestern Wisconsin: A History of Old Crawford County*, 4 vols. (Chicago: S. J. Clark Pub. Co., 1932). Wisconsin State Genealogical Society (see Archives, Libraries, and Societies) has published every-name indexes to a large number of these county and regional histories. Most, if not all, of the older histories are microfilmed and included in *County Histories of the Old Northwest, Series 1: Wisconsin* (New Haven, Conn.: Research Publications, n.d.). This microfilm is available on interlibrary loan through the Wisconsin Historical Society. The films also include county directories, atlases, plat books, city histories, and biographical compendiums.

For territorial and early state history, the twenty volumes of Lyman Copeland Draper and Reuben Gold Thwaites, eds., *Collections of the State Historical Society of Wisconsin* (Madison, Wis.: the society, n.d.), are outstanding. The scope of the volumes covers every aspect of Wisconsin's creation, from

official documents, census enumerations, and the very earliest baptism and marriage records at Mackinac. Augustin Grignon's "Seventy-two Years' Recollections" (volume 3) and James H. Lockwood's "Early Times and Events in Wisconsin" (volume 2) are personal and detailed accounts of early Wisconsin, including many notations on early settlers. Each volume of the *Collections* is indexed. Volume 21 is an all-volume index. Major research libraries should have the complete set.

Highly recommended is the *History of Wisconsin* series published by the Wisconsin Historical Society between 1973 and 1998 as follows:

Smith, Alice E. *From Exploration to Statehood* (vol. 1).

Current, Richard N. *The Civil War Era, 1848–1873* (vol. 2).

Nesbit, Robert C. *Urbanization and Industrialization, 1873–1893* (vol. 3).

Buenker, John D. *The Progressive Era, 1893–1914* (vol. 4)

Glad, Paul W. *War, a New Era and Depression, 1914–1940* (vol. 5).

Thompson, William F. *Continuity and Change, 1940–1965* (vol. 6).

For a concise one-volume history, see Robert C. Nesbit, *Wisconsin: A History*, 2d ed. (Madison, Wis.: State Historical Society of Wisconsin, University of Wisconsin Press, 1989).

Maps

The Wisconsin Historical Society has microfilm copies of Wisconsin county plat books (ca. 1870–1900), which are accessible through interlibrary loan. Early and later county plat maps are not microfilmed but some can be photocopied on request. State atlases were published for Wisconsin in 1876, 1878, and 1881, and include county maps. They show post offices, schools, churches, and road systems, all valuable information in locating an ancestral family in Wisconsin.

Geraldine Strey's *Land Ownership Maps of Wisconsin, 1836–1960* (Madison, Wis., n.d.) is very important in determining precisely what maps are available at the Wisconsin Historical Society.

Aerial photographs of Wisconsin are in the collection of the Arthur Robinson Map Library, Science Hall, University of Wisconsin, Madison. The first topographical map of Wisconsin, of the Stoughton quadrangle, is dated 1889. Bird's-eye view maps are significant for Wisconsin research, inasmuch as they cover the period from 1867 to the end of World War I. There are over 200 of these maps for Wisconsin towns and villages. Most are listed in Elizabeth Maule, *Bird's Eye View of Wisconsin Communities* (Madison, Wis., 1977), and are also available at the Wisconsin Historical Society. The maps were drawn with great attention to the buildings existing at the time.

The Golda Meir Library at the University of Wisconsin, Milwaukee, holds the map collection of the American Geographical and Statistical Society. The worldwide collection includes thousands of bound books, maps, periodicals and photographs. A unique cataloging program at this repository references maps that appear in books. Queries by mail or phone are answered, most material can be photocopied, and some holdings may be borrowed through interlibrary loan. The library is located at 2311 E. Hartford Ave., Milwaukee, WI; the mailing address is the American Geographical Society Collection, University of Wisconsin, Milwaukee Library, P.O. Box 399, Milwaukee, WI 53201.

Robert E. Gard and L. G. Sorden, *The Romance of Wisconsin Place Names* (1968. Reprint. Minocqua, Wis.: Heartland Press, 1988), has an alphabetical list of towns and cities, the county in which they are located, and a brief history.

The earliest Sanborn map (see page 5) for Wisconsin in the historical society holdings is for 1883. An earlier one exists for LaCrosse in 1879.

Land Records

Public-Domain State

Being a public-domain state, Wisconsin was divided into a grid of 1,554 townships by the General Land Office (GLO) survey crews. The earliest land office was at Mineral Point, opening on 10 November 1834. Land that is presently Grant County, with the exception of mineral land, was available at that time. The local records of the nine GLO district offices are at the Commissioner of Public Lands, P.O. Box 8943, Madison, WI 53708-8943. Many records of the Commissioners of Public Lands are in the State Archives, Wisconsin Historical Society. These include, for example, copies of original federal survey plat books from 1834 to 1858. The State Archives, Wisconsin Historical Society, holds copies of all Wisconsin Local Land Office Tract Books, showing original owners or recipients of most land in Wisconsin. The Bureau of Land Management (BLM) Eastern States Land Office in Alexandria, Virginia (see page 6) <www.glorecords.blm.gov> has patents, copies of tract books, and township plats; an online searchable index and downloadable images of Wisconsin land patents are also available. The National Archives has land-entry case files. See Alexander F. Pratt, "Reminiscences of Wisconsin," in *Collections of the State Historical Society of Wisconsin*, vol. 1, Lyman Copeland Draper, ed. (reprint, Madison, Wis.: State Historical Society of Wisconsin, 1855), 137, regarding claims to associations near Milwaukee in the late 1830s.

Subsequent land transactions after initial ownership are recorded in the county's register of deeds. Most counties have grantor/grantee indexes to their land records. Some are available

on microfilm at the Area Research Centers of the Wisconsin Historical Society and the FHL (see Archives, Libraries, and Societies).

Additional information is available in Paul W. Gates, "Frontier Land Business in Wisconsin," *Wisconsin Magazine of History* 52 (1962): 306-27; and Frederick N. Trowbridge, "Confirming Land Titles in Early Wisconsin," *Wisconsin Magazine of History* 26 (1942): 314-22.

Probate Records

Probate records in Wisconsin include wills, guardianship, administrator or executor bonds, and inventories. These records were usually established with the formation of the county and are the responsibility of the register of probate for the county. The FHL has microfilmed some Wisconsin probate files. Copies of these films and some unfilmed probate records are in the holdings of the appropriate Area Research Centers of the Wisconsin Historical Society.

Court Records

The Northwest Ordinance provided a flexible framework of government that operated in the region until the Wisconsin Territory was formed in 1836. Government control over the area of Wisconsin was, however, minimal during the territorial periods. Civil law at the wilderness outposts of Prairie du Chien and Green Bay was difficult, if not impossible. Travel was dangerous, literate citizens were few and far between, and the upper Mississippi fur-trading frontier seemed somewhat capable of governing itself.

Beginning in the 1820s justices of the peace were appointed. Early records from Green Bay's justices of the peace can be found in the Grignon, Lawe, and Porlier Papers (1712–1884) at the Wisconsin Historical Society.

Lewis Cass, who had been appointed governor of Michigan Territory in 1813, began making county divisions and announcing civil offices in 1818. The justice courts dealt with minor civil cases of $20 or less. County courts covered civil cases not to exceed $1,000 and noncapital criminal cases. The state supreme court, meeting annually in Detroit, had jurisdiction for larger civil cases, appeals from lower courts, and capital criminal cases. In the winter of 1822–23, a separate circuit court was established for the three western counties of Michigan Territory. The new court was, in effect, a supreme court. It was not given a title, however, and was generally called an "additional court." Native Americans accused of crimes were not included in the jurisdiction of the court unless a white person was involved.

When Wisconsin Territory was created in 1836 the judicial system included a supreme court, district courts, probate courts, and justice of the peace courts, which were retained when

statehood was attained in 1848. There were territorial courts in Green Bay, Prairie du Chien, and Mineral Point.

County Government in Wisconsin, vol. 2 (Madison, Wis.: Wisconsin Historical Records Survey, 1942), explains the creation, structure, and function of courts in Wisconsin. Probate and related files can be found in the county courts, while criminal and civil cases are in the circuit courts. Old court records are generally still located in the county's courthouse or may be found at the appropriate Area Research Center of the Wisconsin Historical Society.

Tax Records

The earliest tax records in Wisconsin appear to be for real estate. Brown County has an extant tax roll for 1824. Tax rolls are kept by the county treasurer for each county. Many of these records have been transferred to the appropriate Area Research Centers.

Cemetery Records

Numerous cemeteries have been read and transcribed by local genealogical societies in Wisconsin. The transcriptions are frequently deposited with an Area Research Center, a local library, or the Wisconsin Historical Society. A considerable number have been printed in the *Wisconsin State Genealogical Society Newsletter*. A listing of these can be found on the society's website at <www.wsgs.org>. Some have been privately published.

The Wisconsin State Old Cemetery Society, 6100 W. Mequon Rd., Mequon, WI 53092, publishes a newsletter and maintains an archive of tombstone inscriptions from around the state.

A useful volume is Linda Herrick and Wendy Uncapher, *Cemetery Locations in Wisconsin* (3d ed. Janesville, Wis.: Origins, 2002). It is arranged first by county, then township and section number with a township map for each county.

Church Records

In 1661, Father René Ménard, born in Paris in 1605 and the first Jesuit sent from Canada to Wisconsin, offered the first mass in the state in 1661. Beginning in 1687, the missions became almost nonexistent in Wisconsin because of problems with the natives and the British government in control.

Father Bonduel wrote of Green Bay, "The Catholics of this little French colony lived sometimes ten, twenty, and thirty years without seeing a priest." Marriages and baptisms in the state were often officiated by missionary priests, resulting in large numbers of Catholic records in Wisconsin either being lost or sometimes located in repositories in Quebec Province, Canada. Tracing

Catholic families in Wisconsin could require searching French-Canadian records. Some of the oldest Catholic marriage and baptism records for Wisconsin are in the "Mackinac Register" in *Collections of the State Historical Society of Wisconsin* (see Background Sources).

When the American flag first flew over eastern Wisconsin in 1816, the Catholic religion again took a firm hold among the French settlers in the state. European immigration and American migration brought other religious affiliations, but the heavy German, Irish, and Polish settlement in the state provided for continued numbers in the Roman Catholic denomination.

Missionary clergy for other denominations in the state frequently took their records with them as they traveled from place to place. Therefore, although the search for church records in Wisconsin should begin with the local churches, helpful material may also be found in denominational archives and headquarters.

The most widely represented Protestants in Wisconsin were the Lutherans, the first faithful of that group who came from Germany and Scandinavia. Despite divisions, dissensions, and reorganizations within the Lutherans, they remain a religious force in the upper Midwest.

Smaller numbers of Methodists, Episcopalians, and Congregationalists also settled in Wisconsin. In 1834 the first Baptist Church was established in the state by Brotherton Indians on the east shore of Lake Winnebago.

The Wisconsin Historical Records Survey Project of Madison published the *Directory of Churches and Religious Organizations in Wisconsin* in 1941 and *Guide to Church Vital Statistics Records in Wisconsin* in 1942. In addition the project has numerous publications for specific denominations. Extensive microfilm collections of church records in Wisconsin are available through the FHL. The Wisconsin Historical Society and Area Research Centers also have a variety of church records including microfilm and original records.

Military Records

The Wisconsin Historical Society has very few records of Wisconsin residents involved in military action prior to the Civil War. When beginning a search for a Wisconsin Civil War veteran, researchers would do well to consult the following:

Wisconsin. Adjutant General's Office. *Wisconsin Volunteers, War of the Rebellion, 1861–1865*. Madison, Wis.: Democrat Printing Co., 1914. An alphabetical index (also available on microfiche) to the *Roster of Wisconsin Volunteers, War of the Rebellion, 1861–1865*, 2 vols. (Madison, Wis.: Democrat Printing Co., 1886). This has been digitized and can be browsed at <www.wisconsinhistory.org/roster/search.asp>. Other helpful sources include:

Barker, Brett. *Exploring Civil War Wisconsin: A Survival Guide for Researchers*. Madison, Wis.: Wisconsin Historical Society Press, 2002.

Love, William DeLoss. *Wisconsin in the War of Rebellion: A History of all Regiments and Batteries*. Chicago: Church and Goodman, 1866.

Paul, William G. *Wisconsin's Civil War Archives*. Madison, Wis.: State Historical Society of Wisconsin, 1965.

Quiner, E. B. *The Military History of Wisconsin: A Record of the Civil and Military Patriotism of the State, in the War for the Union*. Chicago: Clarke & Co., 1866.

To re-create the background of a Civil War ancestor in Wisconsin, see Carolyn J. Mattern, *Soldiers When They Go: The Story of Camp Randall, 1861–1865* (Madison, Wis.: State Historical Society of Wisconsin for the Department of History, University of Wisconsin, 1981), and Ethel Alice Hurn, *Wisconsin Women in the War Between the States* (Madison, Wis.: Democrat Printing Co. for the Wisconsin History Commission, 1911).

The Wisconsin Adjutant General's *Regimental Muster and Descriptive Rolls* (known as "Red and Blue Books"), created during and after the Civil War, document the service of Wisconsin soldiers. These records typically show the soldier's name, regiment, company, rank, and date of mustering into service. Many records also include a birthplace, age, residence, occupation, marital status, physical description, muster-out date, and service notes. Copies can be obtained through the Wisconsin Historical Society at <www.wisconsinhistory.org/genealogy/ogrs>. The society's website also provides detailed information on its military record holdings at <www.wisconsinhistory.org/military> some of which are described below.

No pension records, outside of those available through the National Archives (see page 9) exist for Wisconsin. The State Archives of the Wisconsin Historical Society is the repository for other numerous miscellaneous records pertaining to Wisconsin residents and units in the Civil War. These include records of the quartermaster general and various regiments. Of special importance to the genealogist are county draft books, lists of persons eligible for military service, regimental muster rolls, hospital reports, certificates of service, duty rosters, and records of the disposition of personal effects. Not all types of records exist for all regiments. Records are originals, with some indexes, and need to be searched at the archives. Staff assistance is available. The archives has an alphabetical index to soldiers who served in Wisconsin units. A similar index exists for the Spanish American War.

The library of the Wisconsin Historical Society has the World War I Selective Service System Draft Registration Cards (1917–18) and a collection of camp newspapers for both World War I and World War II. The archives has brief service records

compiled by the Adjutant General's office on all Wisconsin World War I military personnel. In addition to the above records, the archives and the library have numerous records, including personal narratives, unit histories, and general histories covering all of the above military conflicts. See Archives, Libraries, and Societies below for contact information. In requests, include full name of veteran, date of birth, approximate date of death, and county or city of residence at time of death, if known.

There are no official records in the archives for veterans of World War II, or the Korean or Vietnam conflicts (except for those serving in the Wisconsin National Guard during the Vietnam conflict).

The Wisconsin Veterans Museum Archives, 30 W. Mifflin St., Madison, WI 53703 <http://museum.dva.state.wi.us> has an invaluable collection of diaries and oral histories created by veterans. Other strengths of the collection include the records of various state veterans' organizations, a file of veteran burials in Wisconsin as well as information on more than 500 veterans' memorials.

Periodicals, Newspapers, and Manuscript Collections

Periodicals

The *Wisconsin Magazine of History,* published in Madison by the Wisconsin Historical Society, is a quarterly publication with historical articles, book reviews, and listings of acquisitions of historical and genealogical material. There are published indexes to this periodical.

The Wisconsin State Genealogical Society *Newsletter,* originally titled *Wisconsin Families* from 1940 to 1941, is available quarterly to members or at subscribing libraries (see Archives, Libraries, and Societies for address). The periodical contains pertinent state activities, queries, and recent publications acquired by the group. The majority of material is the publication of records from Wisconsin counties, including cemetery readings, church records, vital records, newspaper extractions, and other genealogically important items.

Various local and county genealogical and historical societies publish excellent newsletters helpful in research.

Newspapers

Newspaper publishing began in Wisconsin in 1833 with the printing of the *Green Bay Intelligencer.* First issued on 11 December of that year, it contained four twelve-by-eighteen-inch pages, and was printed semi-monthly for $2 a year. A good finding guide to the early papers of that area is Barry C. Noonan, *Index to Green Bay Newspapers, 1833–1840* (Monroe: Wisconsin State Genealogical Society, n.d.). The index includes the name of the newspaper, date, page, column, and brief description of the subject matter.

Included in the outstanding newspaper collection of the Wisconsin Historical Society (second only to the Library of Congress in the United States) are over 1,600 titles of Wisconsin's newspapers, almost three-fourths of all the newspaper issues ever published in the state. James L. Hansen, *Wisconsin Newspapers, 1833–1850: An Analytical Bibliography* (Madison, Wis.: State Historical Society of Wisconsin, 1979), contains information on the very earliest Wisconsin newspapers. An excellent index to this collection, although no longer inclusive, is Donald E. Oehlerts, *Guide to Wisconsin Newspapers, 1833–1957* (Madison, Wis.: State Historical Society of Wisconsin, 1958). This volume lists the papers (organized by county and town), dates of publication, availability for research, and the respective repository. James P. Danky, and Maureen E. Hady, eds., *Newspapers in the State Historical Society of Wisconsin: A Bibliography with Holdings* (New York: Norman Ross Pub., 1993), is a more recent update.

All Wisconsin newspapers held by the Wisconsin Historical Society on microfilm are available through interlibrary loan. The newspaper collection is also useful in the areas of African Americans, ethnic groups, and Native Americans. Specialized bibliographies on some of these collections have been published by the society.

The *Milwaukee Sentinel,* which covered statewide local news, has a two-part index (1837–79, 1880–90). Originals are at the Milwaukee Public Library, 814 W. Wisconsin Ave., Milwaukee, WI 53233, with microfilm copies at the Wisconsin Historical Society.

Manuscripts

Manuscript collections at the Wisconsin Historical Society are extensive. The following are a few representative, important examples:

A manuscript collection with some of the oldest Wisconsin records is the *Grignon, Lawe, and Porlier Papers* (1712–1884). The sixty-five volumes contain the business, personal, and official papers and correspondence of three early Green Bay families that were involved in the fur-trading industry. Included in the papers are allusions to treaties, to annuity payments, and to Native Americans in connection with the fur trade. Related collections can be consulted for early fur trade documentation. An excellent index to all fur trade manuscripts is Bruce M. White, *The Fur Trade in Minnesota: An Introductory Guide to Manuscript Sources* (St. Paul: Minnesota Historical Society, 1977).

Some Pioneer Families of Wisconsin, An Index, 3 vols. (A Bicentennial Project of the Wisconsin State Genealogical Society, Madison, Wisc., 1977, 1987, and 2001) is a collection of indexes of applications for pioneer or century certificates. The indexes include the following, if available: name of ancestor,

birth date and place, death date, name of spouse, county of residence, and name of applicant. The supporting documentation for volumes one and two is deposited in the archives of the Wisconsin Historical Society and is accessible to researchers. Documentation for volume three is available through the Wisconsin State Genealogical Society. Both societies provide photocopies by mail for a fee.

Manuscript collections at this excellent repository are extremely diverse in character and content. Genealogists researching in the state must be diligent and imaginative in using these sources. Many collections not considered genealogical in nature may very well contain valuable information. The society continues to process many important manuscript sources, including several Wisconsin business collections, such as the Island Woolen Company of Baraboo (including payroll books) and the Connor Forest Industries (including records related to the "company towns" of Laona and Wakefield).

The most noted and widely used are the Draper Manuscripts, collected in the nineteenth century by Lyman Copeland Draper. The variety of the collection includes correspondence, interview notes, extracts from newspapers and other published sources, muster rolls, and transcripts of official documents and research notes for the western Carolinas and Virginia, Kentucky, Tennessee, the entire Ohio River valley, and parts of the Mississippi River valley. A mass of genealogical and historical information is available on microfilm (134 reels), which has been deposited in numerous libraries across the nation. Before attempting to use the collection, consult Josephine L. Harper, *Guide to the Draper Manuscripts* (Madison, Wis.: State Historical Society of Wisconsin, 1983).

Archives, Libraries, and Societies

Wisconsin Historical Society
(formerly State Historical Society of Wisconsin)
816 State St.
Madison, WI 53706-1488
www.wisconsinhistory.org

Between its archives and library, nearly one-fifth of the entire Wisconsin Historical Society collection, now containing more than one million items, deals with family or local history, making it one of the largest genealogical collections in the country. It is not, however, limited to Wisconsin history. The library attempts to acquire all U.S. and Canadian historical and genealogical materials. Vital records prior to 1907 are on microfilm for the entire state (see Vital Records). Census holdings include all federal censuses for all states. The society has all federal census indexes for Wisconsin and is acquiring some indexes for other states. There is an extensive collection of passenger lists and one of the nation's largest newspaper collections, national in scope,

but predominantly concerning Wisconsin (see Newspapers, Manuscripts, and Map sections). Books, except for rare editions and pamphlet-size, are on open shelves.

The archives, housed in the Historical Society Building, holds manuscript copies of early state censuses (see Census Records), sets of land, probate, court, and tax records from many Wisconsin counties and municipalities.

For more detail on the society, see James P. Danky, ed., *Genealogical Research: An Introduction to the Resources of the State Historical Society of Wisconsin* (Madison, Wis.: State Historical Society of Wisconsin, 1986) and the society's website. Hours at the library include some evenings, but are also affected by university calendars since the building is on the campus of the University of Wisconsin.

Wisconsin State Genealogical Society
P.O. Box 5106
Madison, WI 53705
www.wsgs.org

The society's mission is to help people discover the excitement of family history; providing leadership to the Wisconsin genealogical community and supporting them through education, communication, advocacy, and development of research materials. It holds two events each year in conjunction with membership meetings. Each event lasts one to two days and features state or national speakers. The quarterly newsletter includes material extracted from original sources. The society also publishes numerous indexes to Wisconsin county histories (see Background Sources). The Wisconsin State Genealogical Society purchased the microfilm copies of the pre-1907 vital indexes and records (see Vital Records), which are held by the Wisconsin Historical Society.

Wisconsin Area Research Center Network

Thirteen area research centers in Wisconsin hold public records transferred by counties, towns, cities, and other local governments and collections of papers and records from private individuals and organizations. The goal of each center is to build comprehensive collections documenting the history of its region. The collections include photographs, newspapers, maps, and family histories. Many of the centers are enhanced by the contributions and volunteer hours of local genealogy groups. Newspaper indexes to vital records, cemetery readings, and original local church records can be located in some of the centers. Centers vary considerably in their collections and, therefore, in their value to genealogists. Archival collections usually located at the Wisconsin Historical Society or at one of the centers may be transferred temporarily within the network to accommodate local researchers (some exceptions apply, particularly for materials heavily used onsite).

All archive and manuscript materials at the centers are cataloged centrally online at <http://arcat.library.wisc.edu/>. Write or call the appropriate center before visiting since hours vary by center, the calendar, staffing, and university schedules. The Wisconsin Historical Society Archives serves Columbia, Dane, and Sauk counties. The other Area Research Centers and the counties they serve are:

History Center and Archives
Northern Great Lakes Center
29270 County Highway G
Ashland, WI 54806-9339
www.wisconsinnorthwoodshistory.org
>Serves Ashland, Bayfield, Forest, Iron, Oneida, Price, Sawyer, Vilas, and Washburn counties.

Special Collections Dept.
William D. McIntyre Library
University of Wisconsin–Eau Claire
Eau Claire, WI 54702-5010
www.uwec.edu/Library/spcoll/arc.html
>Serves Buffalo, Chippewa, Clark, Eau Claire, Rusk, and Taylor counties.

Library-Learning Center
University of Wisconsin–Green Bay
2420 Nicolet Dr.
Green Bay, WI 54311-7001
www.uwgb.edu/library/dept/spc/arc.html
>Serves Brown, Calumet, Door, Florence, Kewaunee, Manitowoc, Marinette, Menominee, Oconto, Outagamie, and Shawano counties.

Eugene W. Murphy Library
University of Wisconsin–La Crosse
1631 Pine St.
La Crosse, WI 54601
http://perth.uwlax.edu/murphylibrary/Departments/archome.html
>Serves Jackson, La Crosse, Monroe, Trempealeau, and Vernon counties.

Milwaukee Urban Archives
Golda Meir Library
University of Wisconsin–Milwaukee
2311 E. Hartford Ave., Rm. W250
Milwaukee, WI 53201
Mailing address:
University of Wisconsin–Milwaukee
Golda Meir Library–Archives
P.O. Box 604
Milwaukee, WI 53201-0604
www.uwm.edu/Library//arch
>Serves Milwaukee, Ozaukee, Sheboygan, Washington, and Waukesha counties.

Forrest R. Polk Library
University of Wisconsin–Oshkosh
800 Algoma Blvd.
Oshkosh, WI 54901
www.uwosh.edu/archives
>Serves Dodge, Fond du Lac, Green Lake, Marquette, and Winnebago counties.

Wyllie Library/Learning Center
University of Wisconsin–Parkside
900 Wood Rd.
Box 2000
Kenosha, WI 53141-2000
http://oldweb.uwp.edu/information.services/library/archives.htm
>Serves Kenosha and Racine counties.

Elton S. Karrmann Library
University of Wisconsin–Platteville
One University Plaza
Platteville, WI 53818
http://vms.www.uwplatt.edu/~swwis
>Serves Crawford, Grant, Green, Iowa, Lafayette, and Richland counties.

Chalmer Davee Library
University of Wisconsin–River Falls
120 E. Cascade Ave.
River Falls, WI 54022
www.uwrf.edu/library/arc
>Serves Burnett, Pierce, Polk, and St. Croix counties.

James H. Albertson Library
University of Wisconsin–Stevens Point
Stevens Point, WI 54481
http://library.uwsp.edu/depts/archives/archives.htm
>Serves Adams, Juneau, Langlade, Lincoln, Marathon, Portage, Waupaca, Waushara, and Wood counties.

Library-Learning Center
University of Wisconsin–Stout
Menomonie, WI 54751
www.uwstout.edu/lib/arc
>Serves Barron, Dunn, and Pepin counties.

Superior Public Library
1530 Tower Ave.
Superior, WI 54880
www.ci.superior.wi.us/library
>Serves Douglas County.

Harold W. Anderson Library
University of Wisconsin–Whitewater
800 W. Main St.
Whitewater WI 53190
http://library.uww.edu/services/archserv.htm
> Serves Jefferson, Rock, and Walworth counties.

Special Focus Categories

Naturalization

Naturalization records for Wisconsin have historically been kept in the county courthouses. However, they are now generally being transferred to the respective Area Research Center. As of 2002, all but three counties have transferred these records. Milwaukee and Waukesha county papers are deposited with the respective county historical society. Menominee County was created in 1961 and has no older records. Its records are at the county courthouse. Some naturalizations for La Crosse and all those applied for in federal courts are at the National Archives—Great Lakes Region (see page 12).

African American

Records indicate, according to Zachary Cooper in *Black Settlers in Rural Wisconsin* (Madison, Wis.: State Historical Society of Wisconsin, 1977), that African Americans were in Wisconsin as early as the 1700s serving as trappers, guides, boatmen, and interpreters to the French voyageurs and fur traders. Southerners from Kentucky, Virginia, and North Carolina who migrated to Wisconsin during the territorial period settled in the lead-mining, southwestern counties of Grant and Iowa, some bringing their slaves. African Americans also came as slaves to military personnel or immigrated as freemen or runaway slaves. In 1840 Wisconsin Territory counted 185 free African Americans and eleven slaves. Ten years later there were 635 free African Americans and no slaves counted.

The numbers from that 1840 census exemplify the state's position on slavery. The first abolitionist society was formed in Racine County in 1840, followed by the publication of the anti-slavery newspaper, *Wisconsin Aegis*, in 1843. African Americans from the South were assisted in the 1850s through the "underground railroad" of Wisconsin to freedom in Canada. In 1857 the legislature passed a "personal liberty law."

The Wisconsin Black Historical Museum, 2620 W. Center St., Milwaukee, WI 53206, is collecting museum artifacts, photographs, papers, and books related to Wisconsin's African-American population, especially from rural areas.

For additional information see:

Clark, James I. "Wisconsin Defies the Fugitive Slave Law: The Case of Sherman M. Booth." *Chronicles of Wisconsin*. Vol. 5. Madison, Wis.: State Historical Society of Wisconsin, 1955.

Danky, James P., ed. *African American Newspapers and Periodicals: A National Bibliography*. Cambridge, Mass.: Harvard University Press, 1998.

Davidson, John Nelson. *Negro Slavery in Wisconsin and the Underground Railroad*. No. 18. Milwaukee, Wis.: Parkman Club Publications, 1897.

Gilson, Norman Shepard. *Papers, 1860–1901*. Wisconsin Historical Society. These papers include muster rolls for the 58th Infantry Regiment of U.S. Colored Troops from Wisconsin, MS 62-2651 at Wisconsin Historical Society.

Native American

When Jean Nicolet landed at the Red Banks of Lake Michigan in 1634, he would have been met by the Winnebago tribe, which lived in large numbers in the Green Bay region. The Native Americans in the seventeenth century included the Sioux, Potawatomi, Sauk, Fox, Mascouten, Miami, Kickapoo, Huron, and Ottawa. In the early nineteenth century, the removal and containment of the natives began its deceptive chronicle. In some cases, land vacated by one tribe was occupied by another, resulting in two treaties on one parcel of land, requiring at times the repurchase of the same land.

There were eleven treaties between 1829 and 1848 with the Native Americans of Wisconsin. The Kickapoo, Winnebago, and Potawatomi migrated to Nebraska, Kansas, Oklahoma, and Mexico after surrendering all their land except for their reservations. The Menominee nation remained in Wisconsin, as did a few Potawatomi and many Chippewa.

In 1984 there were six Chippewa reservations in northern Wisconsin, a group of Potawatomi on federal trust tribal land in Forest County, and a Menominee reservation in Menominee County. The Stockbridge-Munsee reservation is in Shawano County, and the Brotherton tribe has been assimilated into this group. The Oneida reservation lies in Brown and Outagamie counties. The Wisconsin Winnebago, unlike those removed to a reservation in Nebraska, live in tribal settlements and scattered tracts of land across the state. For further information refer to Stewart Rafert, "American-Indian Genealogical Research in the Midwest: Resources and Perspectives," *National Genealogical Society Quarterly* 76 (September 1988): 212-24. This excellent and informative article identifies pertinent local and county level records, extensive federal documentation, and miscellaneous resources.

A search of the county court records could be useful. Many Native Americans tried to sue those settlers who they believed had unjustly acquired their Indian land allotments. Probate files may contain guardianship records. National Archives collections of treaties and annuity rolls are of utmost importance (see pages 11-12).

Also see Philip C. Bantin, *Guide to Catholic Indian Mission and School Records in Midwest Repositories* (Milwaukee, Wis.: Marquette University Libraries, Department of Special Collections and University Archives, 1984); Nancy Oestreich Lurie, *Wisconsin Indians* (Revised. Madison, Wis.: State Historical Society of Wisconsin, 2002); William C. Sturtevant, ed., *Handbook of North American Indians*, vol. 15, "The Northeast" (Washington, D.C.: Smithsonian Institution, 1978–1998) and Patty Loew, *Indian Nations of Wisconsin: Histories of Endurance and Renewal* (Madison, Wis.: Wisconsin Historical Society Press, 2001).

The Wisconsin Historical Society has the largest collection in the United States of Native American newspapers and periodicals. Refer to James P. Danky, *Native American Periodicals and Newspapers, 1828–1982: Bibliography, Publishing Record and Holdings* (Westport, Conn.: Greenwood Press, 1984).

Other Ethnic Groups

French-Canadians were the earliest European immigrants in Wisconsin. They had crossed the border as fur traders and military personnel, settling in Prairie du Chien, Green Bay, and points west, marrying into the native families. Later French-Canadian immigrants came to the state with the lumber industry, and many migrated from previous homes in New York state. There were also numerous Canadian immigrants who were neither of French descent nor from Quebec. Many came from Ontario and the Atlantic provinces.

In 1850 there were over 21,000 Irish living in Wisconsin. The Irish were the largest English-speaking foreign-born group in the state. Their population was spread across the southern counties, with the largest number in Milwaukee County and a sizable number in the lead-mining county of Lafayette. The English also settled in the southern counties, coming to the lead region as early as 1827. Colonies of English settlers were established in Racine, Columbia, and Dane counties. The Scots settled, although not in great numbers, in the southern and eastern sections of the state; the Welsh immigrated to Wisconsin in the 1840s and 1850s. The German influx began in the late 1830s, the first German colony of 800 (possibly an exaggerated number) landing in Milwaukee in 1839. By 1850 first-generation Germans constituted about 12 percent of the state population. The government had actively sought German immigrants, beginning in the 1840s, by distributing leaflets in Germany's coastal areas. Later they established, via an 1852 law, a commissioner of immigration to live in New York and promote Wisconsin's advantages. In 1854 a branch office was established in Quebec, although German immigration through that port was small. However, it was the letters sent from Wisconsin to Germany by the first settlers that actually stimulated the continued immigration to Wisconsin. Many of the letters, telling of good available land and the freedom to prosper, were published in Germany.

Although there were not large numbers of Norwegians in Wisconsin compared to Germans, two-thirds of all Norwegians in the United States in 1850 resided in Wisconsin. Most of the Dutch who had immigrated early to Wisconsin, lived in Sheboygan, Brown, and Milwaukee counties. A few Swiss were in the state as early as 1834 but came in larger numbers in the 1840s. The village of New Glarus in Green County still maintains the Swiss heritage of the original settlers in 1845. Danish immigrants to Wisconsin settled in Winnebago, Racine, and Dane counties prior to 1870. Icelanders settled on Washington Island in Door County in the early 1870s. From 1870 through 1920 there was immigration from Poland to Wisconsin, and by the 1890s Russians made their way to this Midwest state. Finns and Italians arrived after 1900 as did Russian Jews who relocated to Milwaukee in 1910 and 1911.

Sources for ethnic study in Wisconsin include the following centers and publications:

The Vesterheim Genealogical Center, 415 W. Main St., Madison, WI 53703 <www.vesterheim.org/genealogy> is a division of the Norwegian-American Museum of Decorah, Iowa. The collection holds 800 Norwegian local histories, over 4,000 reels of microfilmed church records, 1,800 family histories, immigrant lists, passport records, and more. Some records are available on microfilm on interlibrary loan. The center acts as a clearinghouse for Norwegian-American research.

The Wisconsin Historical Society holds the Rasmus B. Anderson papers (1841–1931), fifty-five boxes of family and personal papers.

The University of Wisconsin Memorial Library at Madison has extensive material on Norwegian local history and United Kingdom research.

The Irish Emigration Library located at the Irish Cultural and Heritage Center, 2133 W. Wisconsin Ave., Milwaukee, WI 53233 <http://my.execpc.com/~igsw/wisconsi.htm> has a small but growing collection of resources. Included are Griffith's Valuation and one of only two copies (the other is located in Dublin) of the microfilm index to sub-denominations (hard-to-find place-names) in the six-inch Maps of Ireland. See also:

Rippley, La Vern J. *The Immigrant Experience in Wisconsin.* Boston: G.K. Hall, 1985.

County Resources

When mailing requests to any Wisconsin county office, use the name of the county and "County Courthouse," with the address listed below. Records at the county level are the responsibility of the following offices: birth, marriage, death, and land—register of deeds; court—clerk of courts; probate—county probate court.

Setting up a county with a fully functional government was usually done in three stages: "establishment," legally

defining a specific area as a county; "organization for county purposes," which involved setting up a governing body or board, land registry office, and fiscal structure; and "organization for judicial purposes," which involved setting up a county court and law enforcement. In some counties the three stages were accomplished more or less simultaneously. In others they were done separately over many years. When a county was established, but not fully organized, it was typically "attached" to another county that was often, but not always, a parent county. Since these levels of organization and questions of attachment affect the creation and location of records, they can be quite important to the researcher.

For example, when Ashland County was attached for judicial purposes to Bayfield County in 1866, the courthouse in Ashland County did not close. The county board still met, land transactions and marriages were still recorded by the register of deeds, and taxes were still collected in and for Ashland County. Only the courts and law enforcement were affected, and for those records between 1866 and 1873, the researcher would have to check in Bayfield County.

The year given in the county charts for "Date Formed" is the year that passage of the law created the county. With that date is the name of the parent county or counties. Additional lines identify the purposes (c-county purposes; j-judicial purposes), the county or counties to which it was attached, and the dates of that attachment.

The date listed for each category of record is usually the earliest registration filed. The earliest date does not indicate that there are numerous records for that year and does not mean that all such events were actually registered. It has been estimated that less than 50 percent of the vital records, for example, were prepared and submitted for permanent filing prior to 1907. Land deeds, probate, and court records generally begin in Wisconsin with the organization of the county. Prior to that date, check the "Parent County." Some counties formed from other counties transcribed their portion of property deeds to be kept with the new county deed records.

Information on county formation and earliest record dates was provided by James L. Hansen, Reference Librarian, Wisconsin Historical Society. Addresses were obtained from the Wisconsin Counties Association website at <www.wicounties.org> or the relevant county's website.

WISCONSIN

The Counties and County Seats of
Wisconsin

25   0   25   50   75 Miles

Drawn by William Dollarhide

Map County Address	Date Formed— Parent County/ies Jurisdictional Purposes	Birth Marriage Death	Land Probate Court
G5 Adams 402 Main/P.O. Box 278 Friendship 53934	1848 Portage (c/j Sauk 1848—53)	1857 1854 1870	1853 1855 1854
C4 Ashland 201 W. Main St. Ashland 54806	1860 La Pointe (j-Bayfield, 1866—73)	1876 1871 1877	1856 1878 1873
Bad Axe	1851 Crawford (renamed Vernon, 1862)		
D2 Barron 330 E. LaSalle Ave. Barron 54812	1859 (as Dallas) Polk (c/j-Polk, 1859—60; Dunn, 1860—68; j-Dunn, 1868—74) renamed Barron, 1869	1877 1868 1877	1870 1880 1874
B3 Bayfield 117 E. Fifth St. Washburn 54891	1845 (as La Pointe) St. Croix (j-Crawford, 1845; St. Croix, 1849—50) renamed Bayfield, 1866	1879 1869 1870	1850 1857 1859
F7 Brown 305 E. Walnut St. Green Bay 54305	1818 unorganized territory	1814 1823 1834	1820 1824 1823
F2 Buffalo 407 S. Second St. Alma 54610	1853 Jackson	1855 1856 1873	1854 1854 1853
C1 Burnett 7410 County Road K Siren 54872	1856 Polk (j-Polk, 1856—59; c/j-Polk, 1859—64; j-Polk, 1866—71)	1853? 1869? 1846?	1866 1868 1870
G7 Calumet 206 Court St. Chilton 53014	1836 Brown (c/j-Brown, 1836—42; j-Brown, 1842—44 Fond du Lac, 1844—50)	1858 1850 1856	1840 1850 1850
E3 Chippewa 711 N. Bridge St. Chippewa Falls 54729	1845 Crawford (c/j-Crawford, 1845—51; La Crosse, 1851—53)	1858 1854 1855	1854 1856 1856
F4 Clark 517 Court St. Neillsville 54456	1853 Jackson (c/j-Jackson, 1853; j-Jackson, 1854—56)	1869 1857 1877	1855 1870 1857
H5 Columbia 400 DeWitt St./P.O. Box 177 Portage 53901	1846 Portage	1860 1849 1877	1826 1847 1851
J3 Crawford 220 North Beaumont Rd. Prairie du Chien 53821	1818 unorganized territory	1858 1816 1876	1820 1819 1824
Dallas	1859 Polk (renamed Barron, 1869)		
J5 Dane 210 Martin Luther King Jr. Blvd. Madison 53703	1836 Crawford/Iowa/ Milwaukee (c/j-Iowa, 1836—39)	1860 1839 1876	1835 1847 1841
H6 Dodge 127 E. Oak St. Juneau 53039	1836 Brown/Milwaukee (c/j-Milwaukee, 1836—40)	1870 1843 1852	1877 1844 1844
E8 Door 421 Nebraska St./P.O. Box 670 Sturgeon Bay 54235	1851 Brown (j Manitowoc, 1851 55; Brown, 1855—60)	1852 1856 1856	1857 1861 1861
D2 Douglas 1313 Belknap St. Superior 54480	1854 La Pointe	1861 1854 1877	1854 1856 1855
E2 Dunn 800 Wilson Ave. Menomonie 54751	1854 Chippewa (j-Chippewa, 1854—56)	1861 1858 1869	1877 1858 1859
F3 Eau Claire 721 Oxford Ave. Eau Claire 54703	1856 Chippewa	1870 1857 1876	1856 1858 1854
C7 Florence 501 Lake Ave. Florence 54121	1882 Marinette/Oconto	1882 1882 1882	1882 1882 1882
H7 Fond du Lac 160 S. Macy St. Fond du Lac 54935	1836 Brown (c/j-Brown, 1836—39; j-Brown, 1839—44)	1852 1844 1854	1836 1839 1844
D6 Forest 200 E. Madison St. Crandon 54520	1885 Langlade	1891 1886 1871	1865 1887 1885
Gates	1901 Chippewa (renamed Rusk, 1905)		
J3 Grant 111 S. Jefferson St. Lancaster 53813	1836 Iowa	1870 1842 1876	1837 1836 1836
K5 Green 1016 Sixteenth Ave. Monroe 53566	1836 Iowa (c/j-Iowa, 1836—38)	1862 1838 1874	1836 1850 1838
H6 Green Lake 492 Hill St. Green Lake 54941	1858 Marquette	1864 1858 1877	1843 1853 1858
J4 Iowa 222 N. Iowa St. Dodgeville 53533	1829 Crawford	1876 1836 1871	1832 1837 1834
B4 Iron 300 Taconite St. Hurley 54534	1893 Ashland	1886 1893 1887	1886 1893 1893
G3 Jackson 307 Main St. Black River Falls 54615	1853 La Crosse	1861 1853 1872	1854 1869 1854
J6 Jefferson 320 S. Main St. Jefferson 53549	1836 Milwaukee (c/j-Milwaukee, 1836—39)	1852 1844 1856	1838 1846 1842
G4 Juneau 220 E. State St. Mauston 53948	1856 Adams	1877 1857 1876	1857 1860 1857

Map	County Address	Date Formed—Parent County/ies Jurisdictional Purposes	Birth Marriage Death	Land Probate Court
K7	Kenosha 1010 56th St. Kenosha 53140	1850 Racine	1876 1850 1876	1838 1850 1852
F8	Kewaunee 613 Dodge St. Kewaunee 54216	1852 Door (j-Manitowoc, 1852–55; Brown, 1855–58)	1861 1859 1872	1856 1859 1858
G3	La Crosse 400 Fourth St. North La Crosse 54601	1851 Crawford	1866 1851 1876	1851 1851 1850
K4	Lafayette 626 Main St./P.O. Box 40 Darlington 53530	1846 Iowa (c/j-Iowa, 1846–47)	1854 1847 1877	1836 1847 1847
E6	Langlade 800 Clermont St. Antigo 54409	1879 (as New) Oconto (c/j-Shawano, 1879–81) renamed Langlade, 1881	1882 1881 1882	1858 1881 1881
	La Pointe	1845 St. Croix (renamed Bayfield, 1866)		
E5	Lincoln 1110 E. Main St. Merrill 54452	1874 Marathon (j-Marathon, 1874–75)	1875 1875 1871	1867 1883 1885
G7	Manitowoc 1010 S. Eighth St. Manitowoc 54220	1836 Brown (c/j-Brown, 1836–38; j-Brown, 1839–48)	1858 1849 1864	1835 1850 1848
E5	Marathon 500 Forest St. Wausau 54403	1850 Portage	1870 1861 1868	1841 1851 1849
D7	Marinette 1926 Hall Ave. Marinette 54143	1879 Oconto	1874 1878 1868	1879 1879 1849
H5	Marquette 77 W. Park St. Montello 53949	1836 Brown (c/j-Brown, 1836–44; j-Fond du Lac, 1844–48)	1864 1848 1876	1836 1860 1849
E6	Menominee P.O. Box 279 Keshena 54135 *In Shawano County, except for Native Americans.	1961 Oconto/Shawano (c/j- Shawano)	1961 1961 1961	1961 1961* 1961
K7	Milwaukee 901 N. Ninth St. Milwaukee 53233	1834 Brown (j-Brown, 1834–35)	1835 1836 1872	1836 1838 1837
G3	Monroe 202 South K St. Sparta 54656	1854 La Crosse	1854 1854 1867	1851 1855 1854
	New	1879 Oconto (renamed Langlade, 1881)		
E7	Oconto 301 Washington St. Oconto 54153	1851 Brown (c/j-Brown, 1851–52; j-Brown, 1852–54, 1855–57)	1876 1859 1872	1838 1857 1857
D5	Oneida 1 Courthouse Sq. Rhinelander 54501	1885 Lincoln (c/j-Lincoln, 1885–86)	1887 1887 1888	1887 1887 1887
F7	Outagamie 410 S. Walnut St. Appleton 54911	1851 Brown/Winnebago (j-Brown, 1851–52)	1856 1852 1869	1851 1853 1852
H7	Ozaukee 121 W. Main St. Port Washington 53074	1853 Washington	1852 1855 1849	1835 1849 1853
F2	Pepin 740 Seventh Ave. W. P.O. Box 39 Durand 54736	1858 Dunn	1863 1858 1857	1855 1856 1858
F1	Pierce 414 W. Main St. Ellsworth 54011	1853 St. Croix	1870 1851 1876	1855 1875 1854
D1	Polk 100 Polk County Plaza Balsam Lake 54810	1853 St. Croix	1867 1855 1865	1853 1855 1859
F5	Portage 1516 Church St. Stevens Point 54481	1836 Brown/Crawford/Iowa/ Milwaukee (c/j-Brown, 1836–41; j-Dane, 1841–44)	1866 1848 1876	1841 1837 1844
D4	Price 126 Cherry St. Phillips 54555	1879 Chippewa/Lincoln (j-Taylor, 1879–82)	1880 1880 1879	1882 1881 1892?
K7	Racine 730 Wisconsin Ave. Racine 53403	1836 Milwaukee	1877 1839 1880	1837 1849 1837
H4	Richland 181 W. Seminary St. Richland Center 53581	1842 Crawford/Sauk (c/j-Iowa, 1842–50)	1875 1850 1876	1850 1839? 1861
K6	Rock 51 S. Main St. Janesville 53545	1836 Milwaukee (c/j-Racine, 1836–39)	1856 1840 1860	1839 1850 1840
D3	Rusk 311 E. Miner Ave. Ladysmith 54848	1901 (as Gates) Chippewa renamed Rusk, 1905	1900 1901 1901	1872 1901 1901
E1	St. Croix 1101 Carmichael Rd. Hudson 54016 Some records. 1840–49 at Washington County Historical Society, Stillwater, Minnesota.	1840 Crawford (j-Crawford, 1843–49)	1858 1852 1876	1849 1849 1850
H4	Sauk 505 Broadway Baraboo 53913	1840 Crawford/Dane/Portage (c/j-Dane, 1840–44)	1864 1844 1876	1844 1847 1844
C3	Sawyer 10610 Main St. P.O. Box 836 Hayward 54843	1883 Ashland/Chippewa (j-Ashland, 1883–85)	1869 1883 1883	1883 1900? 1883

Map	County Address	Date Formed— Parent County/ies Jurisdictional Purposes	Birth Marriage Death	Land Probate Court
F6	Shawano 311 N. Main St. Shawano 54166	1853 Oconto/Waupaca/ Winnebago (j-Outagamie, 1853–59)	1854 1848 1860	1854 1861 1861
H7	Sheboygan 508 New York Ave. Sheboygan 53081	1836 Brown (c/j-Brown, 1836–39; j-Brown, 1839–46)	1848 1852 1854	1835 1860 1851
E4	Taylor 224 S. Second St Medford 54451	1875 Chippewa/Clark/ Lincoln/Marathon	1877 1875 1877	1875 1876 1875
G2	Trempealeau 36245 Main St. Whitehall 54773	1854 Buffalo/Chippewa/ Jackson/La Crosse (j-La Crosse, 1854)	1845 1856 1847	1855 1855 1855
H3	Vernon Courthouse Annex 400 W. Decker Viroqua 54665	1851 (as Bad Axe) Crawford renamed Vernon, 1862	1863 1855 1878	1851 1850 1853
C5	Vilas 330 Court St. Eagle River 54521	1893 Oneida	1889 1893 1889	1893? 1900? 1900?
K7	Walworth 100 W. Walworth Elkhorn 53121	1836 Milwaukee (c/j-Racine, 1836–38)	1872 1839 1872	1839 1839 1840
C2	Washburn 10 Fourth Ave. Shell Lake 54871	1883 Burnett	1883 1883 1883	1883 1883 1878
J7	Washington 432 E. Washington St. West Bend 53095	1836 Brown/Milwaukee (c/j-Milwaukee, 1836–40; j-Milwaukee, 1840–45)	1859 1846 1873	1835 1845 1855
J7	Waukesha 1320 Pewaukee Rd. Waukesha 53188	1846 Milwaukee	1860 1846 1872	1841 1847 1847
F6	Waupaca 811 Harding St. Waupaca 54981	1851 Brown/Winnebago (j-Winnebago, 1851–53)	1858 1852 1848	1851 1860 1853
G5	Waushara 209 S. Saint Marie St. Wautoma 54982	1851 Marquette (j-Marquette, 1851–52)	1859 1852 1876	1852 1854 1868
G6	Winnebago 415 Jackson St. Oshkosh 54901	1840 Brown/Calumet /Fond du Lac/Marquette (c/j-Brown, 1840–42; j-Brown, 1842–44; Fond du Lac, 1844–47)	1876 1848 1863	1837 1838 1848
F4	Wood 400 Market St./P.O. Box 8095 Wisconsin Rapids 54495	1856 Portage	1871 1867 1872	1836 1858 1872?

Wyoming

DWIGHT A. RADFORD

Wyoming Territory was created on 25 July 1868, mostly from Dakota Territory. Forts, fur trading, and the Oregon Trail had been a part of its early history. The coming of the Union Pacific Railroad through Wyoming, from 1867 to 1869, left a string of towns—Cheyenne, Evanston, Green River, Laramie, Rawlins, and Rock Springs—along the railroad line. Much of the business history of present-day Wyoming is connected to the Union Pacific Railroad. The construction of the railroad brought a number of Chinese laborers to Wyoming.

The mining influx during the late 1860s and 1870s brought settlers into Sweetwater country. As mining broadened out to encompass several additional industries, towns such as Atlantic City, Miner's Delight, Red Canyon, South Pass City, and others were formed.

Statehood was achieved 10 July 1890. One-fourth of Wyoming's population at that time was foreign born, originating from England, Germany, Ireland, Scotland, Sweden, Canada, Russia, Denmark, Wales, China, Norway, Italy, Austria, and France.

In January of 1890 two hundred African Americans, mostly from Harrison County, Ohio, were brought to Dana (near Hanna) to work the coal mines, but most did not stay long. A small German-Russian colony from Chicago arrived in the Big Horn Basin in 1896.

Although land opened up for settlement in 1890, very little was filed or patented from 1890 to 1897. In 1909 dry farming was tried in Wyoming, and the enlarged homestead acts brought more dry farmers to the state. Congress changed the homestead residence requirement in 1912 from five years to three years and permitted the homesteaders to absent the property for five months each year. These concessions gave renewed emphasis to dry farming and settlement.

The great era of public land entries in Wyoming was in the twentieth century, with the peak years being 1920–21. But the growth of Wyoming's agricultural industry was severely challenged by years of drought and the Depression. Following World War II, the economy focused on cattle, crude oil, and petroleum, along with industries that support them. Wyoming still remains a sparsely populated state that draws considerable tourism related to year-round recreation.

Vital Records

Wyoming began recording births and deaths in 1909. Very few birth and death records were kept on the county level prior to that time. Most of the early births filed at the state office are delayed birth registrations. When specifics are not known, the officials at the State Department of Health can check the alphabetical index for a desired entry, but an hourly fee will be charged.

Certified copies of birth, marriage, and death certificates for the period after statewide recording are available from the Vital Records Services, Hathaway Bldg., Cheyenne, WY 82002 <http://wdh.state.wy.us/vital_records/>.

Wyoming has been recording marriages and divorces statewide since 1941. Earlier marriages were recorded by the

county clerk in the county where the license was issued. All Wyoming marriage records from 1869 to 1970 are available from the Wyoming State Archives and Historical Department (see Archives, Libraries and Societies) for all Wyoming counties. The Family History Library (FHL) in Salt Lake City has marriage registers on microfilm for many counties. Early divorce records were kept by the clerk of the district court where the divorce took place.

Census Records

Federal

Population Schedules
- Indexed—1850 as Utah Territory; 1860 as Nebraska Territory; 1870; 1910, 1920, 1930.
- Soundex—1880, 1900, 1920

Mortality Schedules
- 1870, 1880 (indexed)

Industrial and Agricultural Schedules
- 1880

Union Veterans Schedules
- 1890 (indexed)

The 1850 U.S. census schedule recorded residents of Fort Bridger in 1851 as part of the Green River Precinct, Weber County, Utah Territory. Green River County was never organized and was discontinued in 1868 when Wyoming Territory was created. Persons residing at Fort Laramie were enumerated as part of the unorganized portion of Nebraska Territory. The census of 1870 was the first federal schedule of Wyoming Territory.

In 1880, Wyoming Territory included seven counties as well as Yellowstone National Park. All counties are extant in the 1880 census. Mammoth Hot Springs of Yellowstone National Park was enumerated with Uinta County. All census years are indexed either through printed indexes or online subscription database services (see page 17).

Territorial

A relatively unknown source is the First Wyoming Territorial Census, which was enumerated soon after formation in 1869. This comprehensive census includes names, lengths of residency, and place of origin. This census is available on microfilm at the Wyoming State Archives and FHL. There are censuses for the city of Cheyenne for 1875 and 1878 that include name, age, sex, birthplace, occupation, and nationality. These are at the state archives.

Background Sources

Bartlett, Ichabod S. *History of Wyoming.* Chicago: S.J. Clark Pub. Co., 1910. This is a three-volume set. Volume one is a history of the state and volumes two and three contain valuable biographies.

Beach, Cora May Brown. *Women of Wyoming.* Casper: S. E. Boyer, 1927. Considering the early equality status of women in Wyoming, this two-volume set of biographies is especially valuable. The photographs of the women in the biographical sketch and the genealogical information are noteworthy.

Beard, Frances Birkhead, ed. *Wyoming from Territorial Days to the Present.* Chicago: American Historical Society, 1935. Three-volume set: volume one is a history and volumes two and three provide valuable biographical sketches, which include church leaders, political figures, ranchers, etc.

Chamblin, Thomas S., ed. *The Historical Encyclopedia of Wyoming.* Cheyenne: Historical Institute, 1970. This work includes biographical sketches of leading citizens and information on places; it also recounts historical and contemporary events.

Erwin, Marie, *Wyoming Blue Book.* Cheyenne: Wyoming State Archives and Historical Department, 1974 reprint. This original three-volume work is currently being updated and republished in four volumes. It should not be overlooked because it is an excellent historical reference for Wyoming.

Hendrickson, Gordon Olaf, ed. *Peopling the High Plains: Wyoming's European Heritage.* Cheyenne: Wyoming State Archives and Historical Department, 1977. This volume examines six of Wyoming's ethnic European groups that contributed to the settlement and development of the state, namely British, German, Italian, Basque, Eastern European miners, and Greeks. It is a welcome contribution to the study of ethnic Wyoming.

Gallagher, John S., and Alan H. Patera. *Wyoming Post Offices: 1850–1980.* Burtonsville, Md.: The Depot, 1980. An excellent genealogical tool for identifying defunct as well as continuous towns throughout Wyoming. The book is divided by county with an accompanying map of each county showing the location of the post offices.

Larson, Taft Alfred. *History of Wyoming.* Lincoln: University of Nebraska Press, 1965. The self-proclaimed purpose of this book is to provide a critical history of Wyoming for adults. It is an excellent history of the territorial and statehood periods of Wyoming. Only minor mention is made of the pre-territorial period.

Murray, Robert A. *Military Posts of Wyoming.* Fort Collins, Colo.: The Old Army Press, 1974. This book provides history,

drawings, and photographs for each of Wyoming's old military posts scattered throughout the state.

Peterson, C. S. *Men of Wyoming*. N.p., Denver, 1915. Contains photographs and biographies for over three hundred men who were residents of Wyoming in 1915.

Rollins, George W. *The Struggle of the Cattlemen, Sheepman, and Settler for Control of Lands in Wyoming: 1867–1910.* Master's thesis, University of Utah, 1951. Outlines the struggles of competing groups on the semi-arid land of Wyoming.

Spiros, Joyce V. Hawley. *Genealogical Guide to Wyoming.* Gallup, N.M.: Verlene Publishing, 1982. No research in Wyoming county sources should begin without examining this book first.

Triggs, J. H. *History of Cheyenne and Northern Wyoming.* Laramie, Wyo.: Powder River Publishers and Booksellers, 1876. This early volume consists of a history of the town of Cheyenne and many portions of Wyoming Territory, including the gold fields of the Black Hills, Powder River, and Big Horn counties.

Urbanek, Mae. *Wyoming Place Names.* 1967. Reprint. Missoula, Mont.: Mountain Press Publishing Co., 1988. A listing of geographic places and town names.

Welch, Charles A. *History of the Big Horn Basin.* Salt Lake City: Deseret News Press, 1940. Details the history of the basin with emphasis on the Mormon colonies in the area. Useful in researching Mormon ancestry.

Wheeler, Denice. *The Feminine Frontier: Wyoming Women…, 1850–1900.* N.p., 1987. The self-proclaimed purpose of this work is to inform readers about the lives and accomplishments of Wyoming's pioneer women. The study is based on local and national historical studies.

Maps

The United States Geological Survey (see page 5) publishes catalogs of topographical maps covering the state of Wyoming: "Wyoming Catalog of Topographic and other Published Maps" and "Wyoming Index to Topographic and other Map Coverage." The catalogs list over-the-counter dealers of U.S. geological maps in Wyoming.

The U.S. Geological Survey has designated certain libraries in Wyoming as map depositories. These include Casper College and Natrona County Public Library in Casper; Wyoming State Library in Cheyenne; Campbell County Public Library in Gillette; University of Wyoming, Coe Library and Geology Library in Laramie; Central Wyoming College in Riverton; Western Wyoming Community College in Rock Springs; and Sheridan College in Sheridan.

The Wyoming State Archives has online historic, detailed maps on its website at <http://wyshs.org/maps.htm>.

Land Records

Public-Domain State

Land records in Wyoming begin as early as 1841, although most county land records begin after 1869. Several land offices were opened in Wyoming, the first having opened at Cheyenne in 1870. As additional land opened up for settlement, other land offices opened at Evanston (1877), Buffalo (1888), Douglas (1890), Lander (1890), and Sundance (1890). Records generated through these offices include cash entries, homestead certificates, canceled homestead entries, timber-culture final certificates, canceled timber-culture entries, desert-land final certificates, canceled desert-land entries, and timber and stone lands.

An inventory of all Bureau of Land Management (BLM) records on file at the National Archives—Rocky Mountain Region (see page 12) can be found in Eileen Bolger, *Preliminary Inventory of the Records of the Bureau of Land Management—Wyoming* (Denver: Federal Archives and Records Center, 1983). BLM records consist of the records of the six land offices and include land patents, rights, and claims. The BLM Wyoming State Office, 5353 Yellowstone Rd., Cheyenne, WY 82003-1828 <www.wy.blm.gov> has records of the grantees of the original land patents. An index to the land that went to patent can be found on the BLM search website at <www.glorecords.blm.gov>.

Most county land records begin after 1869. All county land transactions are available at the Wyoming State Archives from 1869 to 1970, as well as all unpatented homestead records. Later county records can be found in the county's courthouse.

Probate Records

Probate records in Wyoming are kept by the clerk of the district court in each county. During the territorial period, probate records were kept by the territorial probate court and include appraisements, bills of sale, claims against estates, final accounts, guardian bonds, guardian annual reports, inheritance tax records, inventories, letters of testamentary or of administration, oaths and bonds for executors and administrators, petitions, probate journals, and wills. Most county probate records are on file at the Wyoming State Archives.

Court Records

The judicial system in Wyoming was set up in 1868 with a supreme court, which performed the duties of an appellate court. It could hold trials in one of the three judicial districts of the territory. In 1869, women in Wyoming Territory were given the right to vote and, therefore, could become jurists. With statehood the court system developed into three major courts: justice of the peace

courts, district courts, and the state supreme court. The justice of the peace courts are countywide courts with jurisdiction over minor actions and misdemeanors. District courts are countywide courts with jurisdiction over civil cases including criminal cases, divorces, probate matters, and some appeals. The supreme court continues to be the statewide appellate court.

Most Wyoming court records are on file at either the Wyoming State Archives or the local courthouse.

Tax Records

The Wyoming State Archives does not have all of the county tax and assessment records. The county assessor and treasurer use their own discretion as to whether their records are sent to the archives. In order to check the records on file at the Wyoming State Archives, the researcher must know the county (or general area) and the years that the ancestor resided in Wyoming. If tax records are not at the archives, they are likely still at the local courthouses.

Wyoming county tax records may be arranged chronologically and then alphabetically by school district. These records include assessment rolls, inventory, and appraisement of personal and real property for tax purposes. The total amount of tax is then apportioned under the various county and state taxes. Tables list name and address, legal description of the real property, value of real and personal property, amount owed for specific taxes, and date paid.

There are Internal Revenue Assessment Lists for Idaho Territory (1865–66), which will include parts of modern-day Wyoming. These are part of RG 58 at the National Archives and they are on microfilm at the FHL.

Cemetery Records

All Wyoming burials, including pioneer graves, are currently being compiled into a statewide resource. Some are available at the Wyoming State Archives.

Church Records

A guide to church inventories was completed in 1939 by the Works Projects Administration (WPA) and entitled A Directory of Churches and Religious Organizations in the State of Wyoming (Cheyenne, Wyo.: The Historical Records Survey, 1939). This directory listed 470 congregations, institutions, and organizations in Wyoming in the late 1930s. It is not a complete listing for the period, but is useful in locating congregations by county and city.

A few Idaho Mormons settled in Star Valley in the 1870s, and many more arrived in the 1880s. Star Valley has a large Mormon population as a result of this colonization. There were Mormon colonists in the Big Horn Basin by 1895, but the main body of Latter-day Saint settlers came there as an organized group from Utah and Idaho in 1900. All ward/branch and mission records are on microfilm at the FHL.

An inventory of many Presbyterian congregations was undertaken by the WPA in 1936, entitled "Inventory of the Church Archives in Wyoming: Presbyterian Churches." This valuable collection, on file at the Wyoming State Archives, was photocopied and indexed by the Presbyterian Historical Society in Philadelphia, Pennsylvania. This inventory, although very incomplete, is valuable. It consists of nineteen out of the forty-two congregations associated with the Presbyterian Church in the United States and one congregation affiliated with the United Presbyterian Church of North America. These inventories were in the form of questionnaires asking what record sources were available and what years were covered. Histories of each congregation are included in this collection, which has been indexed and microfilmed and is at the FHL.

The Catholic faith came to Wyoming through the migration of many Irish immigrant laborers. The Irish impact on Wyoming Catholicism is reflected in the fact that three out of the first four bishops of the Diocese of Cheyenne were from Ireland. The Diocese of Cheyenne was formed in 1887 and covers the entire state of Wyoming and Yellowstone Park. Requests concerning their record collection should be directed to the Diocese of Cheyenne, 2105 Capitol Ave., Cheyenne, WY 82001. The diocesan cemetery is Olivet Cemetery in Cheyenne.

The Greek Orthodox churches in Cheyenne and Rock Springs were the only two in the state until 1964. Orthodox members from many Eastern European countries became part of the Rock Springs Church.

There are records of Methodists in Wyoming before the area was organized into Wyoming Territory. A church was built in Laramie in 1867 and Cheyenne in 1870. African-American members withdrew from the Cheyenne Church in 1875 to form the African Methodist Episcopal Church. For a detailed history of Methodism in Wyoming, see Doris Whithorn's *Bicentennial Tapestry of the Yellowstone Conference* (Livingston, Mont.: The Livingston Enterprise, 1984).

Wyoming has had a small Jewish community since territorial days, and Cheyenne and Rock Springs both have Jewish communities.

Military Records

Historically, Wyoming was home to several military posts. They played an important role in the history and development of the state, acting as a drawing point for settlers, Native American, and soldiers in an otherwise empty landscape. The Wyoming

State Archives has records for these posts during their period of operations as follows:

Fort Bridger, 1858–90

Fort Casper (Old Platte Bridge), 1865–67

Fort Fetterman, 1867–82

Fort Francis E. Warren (Post on Crow Creek; also known as Fort David A. Russell), 1867–1948

Fort Fred Steele, 1868–86

Fort Laramie, 1849–90

Fort McKinney (Cantonment Reno), 1876–94

Camp O. O. Howard, 1885

Fort Philip Kearney (New Fort Reno), 1866–68

Fort Bridge (Fort Davis, Fort Clay), 1855–59

Pilot Butte, 1885–99

Fort Reno (Fort Connor), 1865–68

Fort Sanders (Fort John Buford), 1866–82

Camp Stambaugh, 1870–78

Fort Washakie (Camp Augur, Camp Brown), 1869–1909

Fort Yellowstone (Camp Sheridan), 1886–1918

For soldiers who served in the Civil War, service records will be found in Nebraska Territory.

The Wyoming State Archives has records of those killed during World War I and the records of National Guardsmen from the state. The WWI Draft Registration Cards for Wyoming (1917–18) are at the National Archives and on microfilm at the FHL. The Wyoming State Archives also has Selective Service Cards (1942–46).

The state archives has military discharge records. Since soldiers were not required to file their discharge records at the county clerk's office, they may not be complete. Most of the discharge records begin in the early twentieth century; in order to check these records the researcher needs to know the county in which the ancestor filed for discharge. Most of the county discharge records are indexed.

The State Adjutant General's Office also has military records. For more information, contact the Adjutant General's Office, 5500 Bishop Blvd., Cheyenne, WY 82002.

Periodicals, Newspapers, and Manuscript Collections

Periodicals

Two periodicals on Wyoming history are valuable to the genealogist. *Bits and Pieces* is a magazine of western history with special interest in Wyoming, the Black Hills area, and surrounding states. It is published monthly from Newcastle, Wyoming, and contains a wide variety of articles. The second periodical is *Annals of Wyoming*, published biannually by the Wyoming State Archives.

Newspapers

The first real newspaper established in Wyoming was the *Cheyenne Leader*, which began in 1867. The first permanent newspaper in Laramie was founded in 1869 and was named the *Laramie Daily Sentinel*.

Lola Homsher has compiled an inventory of all known Wyoming newspapers entitled *Guide to Wyoming Newspapers, 1867–1967* (Cheyenne: Wyoming State Library, 1971). The Wyoming State Archives began collecting and microfilming the state's newspapers in 1953 and maintains the most complete collection in the state.

Manuscripts

The Wyoming State Archives has many collections, as well as county records, that are valuable to the researcher. Other holdings include the "European Heritage Study Collection," which contains administrative records for the Wyoming European Ethnic Project. The collection includes research collected by individual teams on Basque, British, Eastern Europeans, German-speaking Europeans, Greeks, and Italians. It has been subsequently published in *Peopling the High Plains: Wyoming's European Heritage*, described in Other Ethnic Groups (see page 765).

Another widely used collection is the "Carter Collection," which consists of the papers of William Alexander Carter, a settler and post trader at Fort Bridger, Wyoming (1857–81). His business dealings touched every phase of economic development of the Rocky Mountains, Great Basin, Missouri River, and the Pacific. Carter's papers were microfilmed in 1959 from the originals, which are deposited at the Western Americana Division, Yale University Library, New Haven, Connecticut. They consist of twelve rolls of microfilm and include correspondence, forty-five journals, ledgers, cashbooks, and other papers relating to Carter's business activities at Fort Bridger; diaries, genealogy, papers relating to Lot Smith's Company of Utah (Mormon) Militia, and Camps Floyd and Scott (Utah Territory); and legal documents from Carter's term as probate judge of Green River County, Utah.

Archives, Libraries, and Societies

Wyoming State Archives and Historical Department
Barrett Building
2301 Central Ave.
Cheyenne, WY 82002
http://wyoarchives.state.wy.us/

This repository is the prime resource for state and county records. Most county records in Wyoming have been microfilmed and are available at the archives.

Wyoming State Library
2301 Capitol Ave.
Cheyenne, WY 82002-0060
wwwwwsl.state.wy.us

Cheyenne Genealogical Society
Central Ave.
Cheyenne, WY 82001

Fremont County Genealogical Society
1330 W. Park
Riverton, WY 82501

The Wyoming GenWeb Project <www.rootsweb.com/~wygenweb/> has links to local genealogical and historical societies, historical links, and links to newspapers. The Wyoming Librarians Database <www-ws/.state.wy.us/wyld/index.html> provides access to collections in seventy libraries and more than one million titles as well as an online magazine and article database.

Special Focus Categories

Native American

According to the 1900 U.S. census, members of the following tribes were residing in Wyoming: Arapaho, Cheyenne, Cree, Gros Ventre, Menominee, Sioux, Ute, and Ute Southern.

The Wind River Agency was established in 1870 for the Shoshone and Bannock tribes. In 1878 a number of northern Arapaho and a few Cheyenne from the Red Cloud Agency settled on the Wind River Agency. The agency records cover 1873 to 1952 and include letters received and sent, decimal files, school and land records, censuses, and photographs of Indians. These records are available at the National Archives—Rocky Mountain Region in Denver (see page 12) and at the FHL.

Two major school record collections should not be overlooked when researching Native American ancestry in Wyoming. The Fort Shaw School in Cascade County, Montana, and the Chemawa Indian School in Chemawa, Oregon, enrolled students from many states. For more details, see Montana and Oregon—Native American section.

An important collection for Native American history and genealogy is entitled the "Major James McLaughlin Papers." This valuable collection has information on Wyoming's territorial period. For a more detailed discussion of these papers, see Montana—Native American section.

Other Ethnic Groups

In 1976 the Wyoming State Archives conducted a study of six of the major European ethnic groups in the state. This study broke ground in a previously ignored area of Wyoming history. The findings were edited by Gordon Olaf Hendrickson in *Peopling the High Plains: Wyoming's European Heritage* (Cheyenne: Wyoming State Archives and Historical Department, 1977). The six groups represented in this volume are the British, Germans, Italians, Basques, Eastern Europeans, and Greeks.

In 1870 immigrants from the British Isles represented one-fifth of the Wyoming territorial population and over one-half of the foreign-born population. British converts to The Church of Jesus Christ of Latter-day Saints traveled to Salt Lake City through Wyoming. Many of these same converts a few years later colonized the western and north central section of the state.

Soon after the Mormon migration through Wyoming, the Irish came as laborers on the Union Pacific Railroad. Others served as soldiers. Between 1865 and 1874, half of the Regular Army consisted of recruits from foreign countries. Twenty percent were Irish.

British Isles immigrants came to Wyoming as miners, saloon keepers, bankers, and missionaries. Many Irish were Roman Catholic, Scots were Presbyterian, and the English were Episcopalians, Methodists, or Congregationalists. In Wyoming, British companies had considerable land holdings and controlled numerous cattle and horse ranches.

Two groups of Germans came to Wyoming—native Germans and Russian-Germans. These two groups began their migrations westward in the late nineteenth and early twentieth centuries. They usually settled in other states before arriving in Wyoming. In 1870, thirty-one percent of the foreign-born residents of Wyoming Territory were of German origin. The cattle industry and the railroad provided incentive for many Germans to become permanent residents of the state.

In the years 1915 to 1916, a large number of Russian-German people moved into Worland and Lovell, reflecting the beginnings of the sugar beet industry in that part of Wyoming. The largest settlement of Russian-Germans was in Goshen County, where Volga Germans from the Scottsbluff, Nebraska, region settled.

Among the early German immigrants to Wyoming was a group of German Jews. Enough Jewish people came to Wyoming that by 1888 Temple Emmanuel was founded in Cheyenne. Other German Jews were part of Jewish farming communities such as Huntley, Wyoming, founded in 1906. Most of Huntley's Jewish community was from Romania. The community was dissolved in the 1920s.

Wyoming had a visible Italian population at one time. Immigrants came in the late nineteenth and early twentieth centuries, and most worked in Wyoming's mining industry. The bulk of Italian immigration to Wyoming was between 1890 and 1910. By 1910, 7.7 percent of Wyoming's foreign-born population was Italian. The Italian immigrants originated from the northern provinces of Lombardy, Tuscany, and Piedmont.

By 1920 more than sixty percent of Wyoming's Italians lived in Laramie, Sweetwater, and Uinta counties.

The Basque in Wyoming were instrumental in the development of the sheep industry in the state. By 1902 Basque had settled in Buffalo, Johnson County. The founding Basque families in Wyoming were influential in Johnson and Sweetwater counties. Here the Catholic Church helped provide unity between the Spanish and French Basque who settled in the state. Both cultures were united by a common faith and were served by a traveling Basque priest.

Eastern European immigrants to Wyoming came primarily from the Balkans, from what is today Czechoslovakia, Hungary, Poland, and Yugoslavia. Many Eastern Europeans, while still in Europe or upon their arrival in America, learned that jobs were available in Wyoming mines. Many Eastern European Jews first settled in eastern America and then moved to Wyoming. Some who homesteaded near the coal mines in Sheridan County realized considerable profit from their real estate.

The mining communities near Rock Springs, Lander, Riverton, and Sheridan attracted the majority of Eastern Europeans to Wyoming, the largest immigration occurring between 1910 and 1920. Most of the immigrants were either Roman Catholic or Orthodox, and almost every mining community had a Roman Catholic Church, even if it did not have a regular priest. The Orthodox did not always have available churches in the mining communities.

The first permanent Greek residents arrived in Cheyenne near the turn of the twentieth century. Many worked on the railroad as laborers; others moved into business. The Greek Orthodox Church of Saints Constantine and Helen in Cheyenne is the center of the Greek community in the area. Prior to the establishment of this church in 1922, there were two Greek Orthodox Churches in Cheyenne: Holy Trinity, and Saints Constantine and Helen.

Some Greeks came to Wyoming to work in the mines near Hartville-Sunrise and Rock Springs. The Orthodox Church in Rock Springs was founded not only to serve the needs of the Greek community, but also Russian, Serbian, Montenegrin, Slavic, Bulgarian, Romanian, and Dalmatian Orthodox members. Greeks in Casper were ministered to for many years by the priest from the Church of Saints Constantine and Helen in Cheyenne.

From the time of the construction of the Union Pacific Railroad, a number of Chinese laborers had resided in Wyoming. They first appeared in Rock Springs in 1875 to work on the railroad or to work for the railroad's coal contractors. They were disliked and persecuted not only by the white Americans, but by other ethnic groups as well. In 1885 a wave of anti-Chinese violence broke out in Wyoming, which had repercussions throughout the northwestern United States. When white railroad employees went on strike in 1885, the railroad employed a new racially mixed crew of Chinese and white workers. The work force was one-third white and two-thirds Chinese, and the company paid both races the same pay. On 2 September 1885, the coal miners' union massacred twenty-eight Chinese and wounded fifteen. The mobs destroyed Rock Springs' Chinatown and drove several hundred from the city. This event lead to more anti-Chinese violence and murder throughout Washington, Oregon, and Montana. The Chinese returned to Rock Springs under federal troop escort, but they gradually left Wyoming. The Rock Springs massacre has been called the most disgraceful event in Wyoming history. The Wyoming State Archives has many collected articles and old newspaper clippings concerning Wyoming's Chinese community and the 1885 massacre. These should not be overlooked when researching this ethnic group.

County Resources

An important research consideration for Wyoming is that its counties, as they exist today, went through many changes in a relatively short period of time. When organized, it included four counties from Dakota Territory—Albany, Carbon, Carter, and Laramie—and Green County from Utah Territory. When the territory was organized on 19 May 1869, Uinta County was created from the formally unorganized portions of Utah and Idaho. At that time, Carter County was renamed Sweetwater. By 1923, Wyoming had been subdivided into its present twenty-three counties.

In addition to the territorial and homestead land records held by the Wyoming State Archives, the county clerk holds land records filed by county after the date of formation. District clerks are to be addressed for court and probate records, though most will also be found at the Wyoming State Archives. No county birth or death records exist before mandatory statewide recording, but most counties hold marriage records. Some even date before incorporation.

Contact the archives prior to conducting extensive research on the county level to determine which county records have been deposited at the Wyoming State Archives and which are only available on a county level. See also current holdings at <http://wyoarchives.state.wy.us/databases/county/county.htm>.

County addresses in the following charts were taken from the National Association of Counties website at <www.naco.org>. Dates for county records were taken from the Wyoming State Archives website at <http://wyoarchives.state.wy.us>.

WYOMING

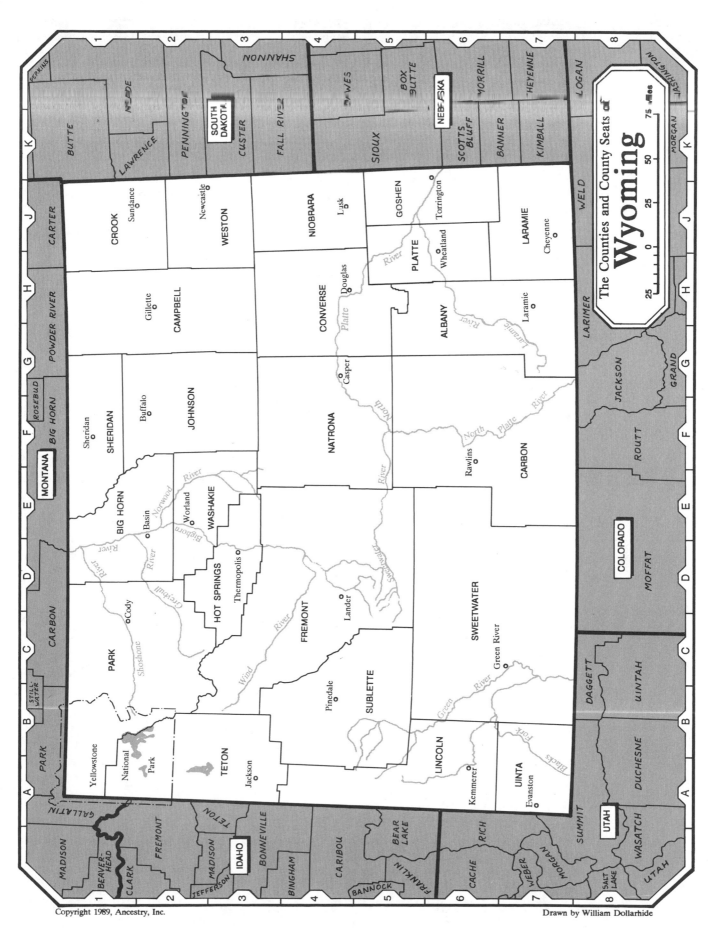

The Counties and County Seats of

Wyoming

Drawn by William Dollarhide

Map	County Address	Date Formed Parent County/ies	Birth Marriage Death	Deeds Probates Court
G6	Albany 525 Grand Ave. Laramie 82070-3836	1868 original (Dakota Territory)	—— 1868 1899	1868 1869 1869
D1	Big Horn 420 W. C St. Basin 82410-0031	created 1890 organized 1897 Fremont/Johnson/Sheridan	—— 1897 ——	1885 1897 1897
H2	Campbell 500 S. Gillette Ave. Ste. 212 Gillette 82716-4239	1911 Crook/Weston	—— 1913 ——	1885 1913 1913
F6	Carbon P.O. Box 6 Rawlins 82301-0006	1868 original (Dakota Territory)	—— 1870 ——	1867 1875 1870
	Carter	1867 (renamed Sweetwater, 1869) Original (Dakota Territory)		
H4	Converse 107 N. 5th St. Ste. 114 Douglas 82633-2448	1888 Albany/Laramie	—— 1888 ——	1882 1889 1888
J1	Crook P.O. Box 37 Sundance 82729-0037	created 1875 organized 1885 Laramie/Albany	—— 1885 ——	1884 1886 1886
D4	Fremont 450 N. Second, Rm. 220 Lander 82520-2360	1884 Sweetwater	—— 1884 ——	1882 1884 1884
J6	Goshen P.O. Box 160 Torrington 82240-0160	created 1911 organized 1913 Laramie	—— 1913 ——	1913 1913 1913
D3	Hot Springs 415 Arapahoe St. Thermopolis 82443-2731	created 1911 organized 1913 Fremont/Big Horn/Park	—— 1913 ——	1893 1912 1911
F2	Johnson 76 N. Main St. Buffalo 82834-1847	created 1875 (as Pease; renamed 1879) organized 1877 Carbon/Sweetwater	—— 1881 ——	1881 1885 1881
J7	Laramie 310 W. 19th St., Ste. 300 Cheyenne 82001-2799	1867 original (Dakota Territory)	—— 1868 ——	1867 1868 1868
A5	Lincoln 925 Sage Ave. Kemmerer 83101-0670	1911 Uinta	—— 1913 ——	1871 1899 1913

Map	County Address	Date Formed Parent County/ies	Birth Marriage Death	Deeds Probates Court
F4	Natrona P.O. Box 863 Casper 82602-0863	created 1888 organized 1890 Carbon	—— 1890 ——	1880 1891 1890
J4	Niobrara 424 S. Elm St. Lusk 82225	created 1911 organized 1913 Converse	—— 1889 ——	1883 1913 1911
C1	Park 1002 Sheridan Ave. Cody 83414-3598	created 1909 organized 1911 Big Horn	—— 1911 ——	1911 1911 1911
	Pease	1875 (renamed Johnson, 1879) Carbon/Sweetwater		
H6	Platte 800 Ninth St./P.O. Box 728 Wheatland 82201-0728	1911 Laramie	—— 1913 ——	1873 1913 1913
F1	Sheridan 224 S. Main St., Ste. B-2 Sheridan 82801-4833	1888 Johnson	—— 1888 ——	1887 1888 1888
B4	Sublette P.O. Box 250 Pinedale 82941-0250	created 1921 organized 1923 Fremont/Lincoln	—— 1923 ——	1922 1923 1923
C6	Sweetwater P.O. Box 730 Green River 82935-0730	1867 (as Carter; renamed 1869) original (Dakota Territory)	—— 1870 ——	1867 1868 1867
A3	Teton P.O. Box 3594 Jackson 83001-3594	created 1921 organized 1922 Lincoln	—— 1922 ——	1902 1923 1922
A7	Uinta 225 Ninth St. Evanston 82930-3415	1869 original (Utah and Idaho Territories)	—— 1872 ——	1861 1861 1872
E3	Washakie P.O. Box 260 Worland 82401-0260	created 1911 organized 1913 Big Horn	—— 1913 ——	1906 1913 1912
J3	Weston 1 W. Main St. Newcastle 82701-2121	1890 Crook	—— 1890 ——	1885 1890 1891

INDEX

N

U

V

W

Y

Z